Kuṇḍalinī.
Haṭha Yoga Pradīpikā

Michael Beloved

**Published in service to Swami Vishnudevananda and Rishi Singh Gherwal, who are both deceased*

Devanagari script: Sanskrit 2003 Font
Transliteration: URW Palladio ITU font
Word-for-Word typeset: Michael Beloved
Proofs Editors: Marcia Beloved, Tobe Terrell
Shiva Art (page 3) Sir Paul Castagna
Illustrations: Author
Correspondence: michaelbelovedbooks@gmail.com
Catalog: michaelbeloved.com

ISBN
9780988401174
LCCN
2014920815

Narrative
Sanskrit Text

ENGLISH
Transliteration / Word-for-Word Meaning
TRANSLATION

Table of Contents

Scheme of Pronunciation....5
Introduction....7
Chapter 1....9
  Physical Body Posture*....9
Chapter 2....150
  Breath-Infusion*....150
Chapter 3....271
  Mystic Arresting Actions*....271
Chapter 4....462
  Linkage to a Divine Environment or Person*....462
Index....604
Index to Translated Verses....645
Selected Sanskrit Words with English Meanings....656
Glossary....683
About the Author....698
Publications....699
Online Resources....706

Scheme of Pronunciation

Consonants

Gutturals:	क	ख	ग	घ	ङ
	ka	kha	ga	gha	ṅa
Palatals:	च	छ	ज	झ	ञ
	ca	cha	ja	jha	ña
Cerebrals:	ट	ठ	ड	ढ	ण
	ṭa	ṭha	ḍa	ḍha	ṇa
Dentals:	त	थ	द	ध	न
	ta	tha	da	dha	na
Labials:	प	फ	ब	भ	म
	pa	pha	ba	bha	ma

Semivowels: **Numbers:**

य	र	ल	व	० १ २ ३ ४ ५ ६ ७ ८ ९
ya	ra	la	va	0 1 2 3 4 5 6 7 8 9

Sibilants: श ष स **Aspirate:** ह
śa ṣa sa ha

Vowels:

अ	आ	इ	ई	उ	ऊ	ऋ	ॠ
a	ā	i	ī	u	ū	ṛ	ṝ
ए	ऐ	ओ	औ	ळ	ॡ	ं	ः
e	ai	o	au	lṛ	lṝ	ṁ	ḥ

Apostrophe ऽ

How to use this book:

Make a casual reading page for page without becoming stressed about the concepts and ideas. Read to become familiar with the language style and presentation. If you read something of particular interest make a mental note and read on to get through the entire book.

Make a second reading pausing at areas of interest, where you feel you can grasp the material. Here and there, you may not follow the meanings but read on nevertheless.

Make a third reading with intent to grasp the concepts and suggestions given.

Finally, make an indepth study of this information.

A note on the diacritical marks and pronounciation:

A name like Krishna is accepted in common English usage. Its English spelling has no diacritical marks.

Sanskrit letters with a ***dot*** *under them, should be pronounced while the tongue touches and is released curling slightly at the top of palate.*

The ***s*** *sound for* ***ś*** *carries an* ***h*** *with it and is said as the* ***sh*** *sound in* ***she****.*

The ***s*** *sound for* ***ṣ*** *carries an* ***h*** *with it and is said as the* ***sh*** *sound in* ***shun****.*

The ***h*** *sound for* ***ḥ*** *carries an echoing sound of the vowel before it, such that* ***oḥ*** *is actually* ***oho*** *and* ***aḥ*** *is actually* ***aha****.*

In many Sanskrit words the ***y*** *sound is said as an* ***i*** *sound, especially when the* ***y*** *sound preceeds an* ***ā****. For instance,* ***prāṇāyāma*** *should be* ***praa-nai-aa-muh****, rather than* ***praa-naa-yaa-muh****.*

The ***a*** *sound is more like* ***uh*** *in English, while the* ***ā*** *sound is like the* ***a*** *sound in* ***far****.*

The ***ṛ*** *sound is like the* ***ri*** *sound in* ***ridge****.*

The ***ph*** *sound is never reduced to an* ***f*** *sound as in English. The* ***p*** *sound is maintained.*

Whenever ***h*** *occurs after a consonant, its integrity is maintained as an air forced sound.*

If the ***h*** *sound occurs after a vowel and a consonant, one should let the consonant remain with the vowel which preceeds it and allow the* ***h*** *sound to carry with the vowel after it, such that Duryodhana is pronounced with the* ***d*** *consonant allied to the* ***o*** *before it and the* ***h*** *sound manages the* ***a*** *after it. Say* ***Dur-yod-ha-na*** *or* ***Dur-yod-han****. Do not say* ***Dur-yo-dha-na****. Separate the* ***d*** *and* ***h*** *sounds to make them distinct. In words where you have no choice and must combine the* ***d*** *and* ***h*** *sound, as in the word* ***dharma****. Make sure that the* ***h*** *sound is heard as an air sound pushed out from the throat. Dharma should never be mistaken for darma. But* ***adharma*** *should be* ***ad-har-ma****.*

The ***c*** *sound is* ***ch****, and the* ***ch*** *sound is* ***ch-h****.*

Introduction

This translation and commentary is a milestone in the history of academically presented yoga techniques. It concerns kundalini yoga for altering the subtle body, and reaching higher planes of existence through meditative access to other visions and dimensions.

I was commissioned with the task of producing literature with details of what advanced yogis, siddhas, do in meditation. This translation and commentary relieved me of much of that responsibility; all by the grace of Swatmarama who wrote the Hatha Yoga Pradipika. Until recently within the past year, I did not take a close look at his Sanskrit text. Since 1973 I looked and looked through numerous translations, particularly the one by Pancham Singh, but these did not give details about kundalini yoga and raja yoga meditation. I was puzzled.

However when I looked directly at the Sanskrit text, I was relieved. Under an inspiration from Rishi Singh Gherwal, Swami Shivananda and Swami Vishnudevananda, who are all deceased, I was tasked to translate and comment on the text, even though I was at the time hoping to never have to translate and comment on Sanskrit literature again. This relieved me of much responsibility for explaining the intricate process of mystic yoga which is required for those who would be siddhas now or hereafter.

After doing the translations and commentary, I was exhausted but from Goddess Ganga, I got some energy to complete the illustrations, glossary and indexes. This is that story:

Breasts Shaped like Mangoes

On August 16, 2014) in meditation after breath infusion, I had an energy surge from the sun-deity. This was a surge of sun energy into the subtler body. Subtle energy from the sun is not the same as the physical heat which the physical body feels from the sun.

In this surge some unresolved issues and things which I carried in my psyche were removed. These were removed not destroyed, so that they were taken out like if one takes a box out of room and relocates it into another building. I do not know where the stuff was relocated but it was removed.

Sometimes there is a mission change for a yogi, where he was assigned one thing and then suddenly that mission is absent from his psyche and some other mission is installed. Like that a yogi may appear to change from time to time because of the content mission of the subtle body.

One might carry energies in one's psyche which belong to others, either to ordinary spirits or to deities even. From time to time these energies might be shuffled or changed either by contact with other ordinary entities or by movements of deities. One may or may not be aware of the movement. It depends on psychic and mystic sensitivity. We have heard of educated people who all of a sudden go crazy and do things which make absolutely no sense. In their case there is some energy shift in the psyche for the worse. We have also heard of criminal people suddenly making a change for the better and remaining on that better course.

There is the story of Saul, a Roman military official, who when he was encountered by the apparition of Jesus Christ, changed permanently for the better and was renamed Paul. He was later canonized as Saint Paul. It happens. In his case because of the divine energy of Jesus Christ, his political nature was gutted out and replaced by a saintly package-energy.

People call such things inspiration but they do not understand how it happens. Some say that it is the Holy Ghost. Otherwise when it is to the contrary, they say it is because of the devil, the Unholy Ghost.

After the energy was changed out, some other energy was infused into my psyche through the sushumna nadi which at the time was like a lit tunnel going downwards from the head. I went down through it. At the bottom there was a flowing river of dark blue-brown water. As soon as I got to the bottom of the sushumna nadi the river converted into a divine woman who was buxom looking. She stood on a place like standing on land. As soon as she touched me, my body converted to that of an infant of about two months old.

Then her top fell off and she nursed me. First one breast, then the next breast, then the first one, then the second one again. Her breasts were shaped like full mangoes; the milk of it was creamy. After she felt that I had sufficient, she threw me into the air. Then I found myself back in an adult astral form out of that place but in another place in the psyche.

I realized that there was a going in and going out of the third eye chakra with a dark blue color of energy, moving out and moving in about the center of the eyebrows.

The goddess was Mother Ganga, the personification of the river Ganges. She is one of Lord Shiva's consorts and is a mother to some of the student yogis.

This happened because on that day, I struggled with one of the illustrations for the Hatha Yoga Pradipika book. I drew an illustration of Lord Shiva, who is the patron deity of the book.

By sucking that milk into my subtle body, I got the energy to finish the book in the months ahead, all by the grace of Goddess Ganga, Lord Shiva and my yoga gurus.

Chapter 1

Physical Body Posture*

Verse 1

श्री–आदि–नाथाय नमो। अस्तु तस्मै

येनोपदिष्टा हठ–योग–विद्या ।

विभ्राजते परोन्नत–राज–योगम्

आरोढुमिच्छरधिरोहिणीव ।। १ ।।

śrī–ādi–nāthāya namo l astu tasmai
yenopadiṣṭā haṭha–yoga–vidyā l
vibhrājate pronnata–rāja–yogam
ārodhumicchoradhirohiṇīva l l 1 l l

śrī – illustrious, ādi – very first, nāthāya – to Lord Shiva, namo – namaḥ – giving honor, astu – let there be, tasmai – to him, yenopadiṣṭā = yena (by which) + upadiṣṭā (taught), haṭha–yoga = kundalini manipulation for subtle body transformation, vidyā – technique, vibhrājate – illuminating, pron – developed, nata = ata = without restriction, rāja–yoga = remaining introverted while externally occupied, ārodhum – to ascend proceed rapidly, icchor = icchoh = desirous, adhirohiṇī – means of ascension, escalator, iva – as if, like

I render honor to the illustrious, first teacher, Lord Adinatha, Shiva, who taught the technique of kundalini manipulation for subtle body transformation. For those who are desirous of rapidly integrating how to remain introverted while externally occupied, it expands and illuminates without restriction. It is like an escalator. (1.1)

Analysis

It is impossible to be successful in yoga practice without taking help from Lord Adinath, Shiva, or from someone who is in the same or a higher category than him.

Recently as I took some instruction from Gautam Buddha, I found myself addressing him as Mahadeva, which is a title for Shiva as the Great Supernatural Being. This was while doing meditation before a sculptured form of Buddha. When I addressed him as Mahadeva, the Buddha deity said, "Which one?"

I considered his question. Then I was inspired to understand that he too was a Mahadeva, a great supernatural being in the system of plural divinities, plural non-conflicting Persons of Godhead.

**The Haṭha Yoga Pradīpikā does not have chapter headings. This title was assigned by the translator on the basis of the verse 20 of this chapter.*

A limited being is not equipped with completion. Awarding one of the limited selves full autonomy is more or less, a grand farce. One has to take assistance from these Mahadevas, either from one or the other; then one can get the energies for success.

Hatha yoga has come to mean asana postures, something which the gymnasts quickly master. However this happened because some advanced yogis who came to the Western countries in the nineteenth and twentieth centuries delivered their posture expertise as hatha yoga.

Originally however the mainstay of hatha yoga was Gorakshnath Mahayogin, who taught kundalini manipulation for subtle body transformation. That is the original hatha yoga which includes asana postures as the basis from which to become proficient in existential transfer to higher planes.

While Patanjali Mahayogin gave eight features for mastership of yoga, Gorakshnath gave six features leaving aside the two preliminary ones given by Patanjali, which are yama moral stipulations and niyama approved behaviors for social refinement which are conducive to yoga attainments.

Asanas as an objective concerns the physical body. This is the least part of the Gorakshnath system. His is focused on the subtle body with emphasis on kundalini manipulation for alterations on the psychic plane.

The author of the Haṭha Yoga Pradipika, Swatmarama Guruji, begins the delivery with honoring Lord Shiva who is reputed as the Master of yogis. This does not mean that every student can actually honor Shiva. Before effectively honoring a supernatural entity, one should have access to that person's psyche. Merely saying, 'God! God!' does not necessarily bring the worshiper within divine range.

Saying *Om Namah Shivaya* does not necessarily cause the chanter to reach Shiva. I took it upon myself to translate and comment on the statements of Swatmarama, but that does not mean that I am inspired and commissioned to explain his work. It is to be verified as to whether my information is useful to serious students of yoga or to myself even.

We should assume that Swatmarama was in touch with Shiva. Whatever he said has the potency of Shiva with potential for spurring student-yogis to liberation.

A question arises as to why bother to do kundalini yoga for subtle body transformation.

What is that for?

What will be gained from it?

How will it feed into material existence and cause the student to benefit even on the material side of life, the place where he or she has a body and is currently focused?

The answer is that rapidly integrating how to remain introverted while being externally occupied, is required in material existence if one is to perform here in the least harmful way. Here we must perform. Here even a lack of performance has consequences and is interpreted by material nature as an act worthy of backlash. Hence any sensible being who wants to have the upper hand will need to remain introvertedly centered while being externally occupied.

It is interesting that in the first verse Guruji Swatmarama attributed Lord Shiva as the person who first taught how to do raja yoga or perform socially without being distracted from the cultivation and maintenance of spirituality.

Why?

In the Bhagavad Gita, there is a claim made by Lord Krishna, stating that he is the only one who perfectly teaches what he termed as his yoga, karma yoga.

Really?

Who then is the original master of the technique?

The answer is given simply in the fact that while Shiva taught it to socially-detached ascetics, Krishna taught it to members of the ruling class who were socially-involved managers of society. He taught it to the second caste in the Vedic sociology, the ksatriya or administrative sector.

Lord Shiva set the example for those ascetics who were exempt from much social responsibility. Lord Krishna set the process for those ascetics who were bogged down with social duties. It is the same system of teaching but with varying emphasis as per the needs of the individual in respect to his or her social obligations.

Persons who have many social duties should carefully study the process explained by Lord Krishna in Bhagavad Gita, while those who have little social affiliation should learn the austerities from Shiva. This however does not mean that the student will be directly taught by Shiva or Krishna.

The first reality we face is that neither Krishna nor Shiva is physically present. Unless we can reach these authorities on a higher plane of existence, their association is off limits to us except by reading their literature. Otherwise our only recourse is to latch on to a yoga-guru who has the link with either or both of these authorities.

Mastery of the social environment in terms of reducing drastic reactions and not laying a foundation for more traumas, is attained through mastery of kundalini yoga for changing the tendencies of the subtle body. That yoga is the way to get the psyche under observation because the kundalini lifeforce is the psychic mechanism which operates the impulsions. At first students are desperate for a method to change some undesirable traits. Once they acquire a method for raising kundalini daily, they begin to see that the first step is inner psyche observation.

It is not why the psyche behaves in a counterproductive way, but rather, how it behaves the way it does. To see its behavior one has to raise the kundalini through the spine into the head. That is the process of haṭha yoga.

Application

To integrate and properly use the information in this book, one has to offer respects to the translator/commentator, to the Sanskrit author Swatmarama Guruji, and to Lord Adinatha, Shiva. We may assume that Swatmarama and Lord Shiva are not physically present except through pictures and sculptured forms which they may use at their convenience. The translator/commentator was present when this book was published in 2014.

Psychic connection with either of these persons is possible and should be cultivated. As for the translator/commentator, if a reader has confidence that the work is not distorted and is not an effort to confiscate and warp the information of Swatmarama Guruji, then that confidence will release the reader from his or her obligation to the author.

I release in this book information which was never released before through the English language. This will be given at minimal cost and without anyone having to bow at my feet or worship me in a formal way. I have no disciples who can create hoops for anyone to jump through to reach this information.

The system of parampara guru lineage in India, stipulated that everything deep be given only confidentially between a guru and his faithful disciple. In this book, I breach that procedure and give confidential process openly.

Why?

The answer is that I have a commission by Deity Shiva to do this. I already opened access to the Bhagavad Gita in three commentaries, with clear explanation of the karma yoga, kriya yoga and brahma yoga processes given by Lord Krishna. Now I will release the ascetic process of raja yoga given out by Lord Shiva. This is as commissioned by them.

Your requirement is to have confidence that I did this in good faith.

Who is Shiva?

He is one in the Vedic pantheon of deities. He is an essential and primal one, along with Brahma and Vishnu. However these terms really apply to a supernatural personality type. This means that there is more than one Brahma, Vishnu or Shiva.

It has come down to us erroneously that somebody is an incarnation of Shiva or Vishnu, as if Shiva and Vishnu are singular personalities. However by a careful study of the Vedic literature, especially of the Puranas written by Krishna Dvaipaiana Vyasa, we come to understand that Shiva is a divine type of being and so is Vishnu. This means that Krishna, the son of Devaki is a Vishnu personality while Bhava is a Shiva personality.

Vedic information gives eleven Shivas or Rudras but these are the primary ones only. There are others. As for the Vishnu divine people, there are many of them, with Krishna being the primary one as the Supreme Personality of Godhead. In this respect we need to accredit two individuals from recent history who clarified this. First it was explained that there were multiple personalities of Godhead. This was told to us by Srila Bhaktisiddhanta Sarasvati, a Vaishnava authority. Then his disciple, Srila Bhaktivedanta Swami, explained it fully.

While in Judaism we were gifted with the understanding of a monotheistic deity, in the Vaishnava doctrine of divinity, we were shown that there were multiple persons in the Godhead but without conflict and with one Supreme Personality as Krishna, as this deity explained in the Bhagavad Gita. The Shiva mentioned here as Adinath is a specific person in the Shiva category of divine beings.

Haṭha yoga or kundalini manipulation for subtle body transformation is a process which uses breath-infusion to charge and relocate the kundalini lifeforce of the subtle body. Raja yoga or remaining introverted while being externally occupied, is a system of practical introspection which must be mastered if a person is to function socially and remained pinned down into spiritual reality. Raja means king. This is the yoga for kings or rulers, so that they can do yoga as an introspective discipline while functioning extrovertly in the execution of duties. Swatmarama will clarify that it is not possible to be introspectively involved without mastering kundalini yoga and conversely one cannot be successful in kundalini yoga without mastering introspective involvement.

Verse 2

प्रणम्य श्री–गुरुं नाथं सवात्मारामेण योगिना ।

केवलं राज–योगाय हठ–विद्योपदिश्यते ।। २ ।।

praṇamya śrī–guruṁ nāthaṁ svātmārāmeṇa yoginā |
kevalaṁ rāja–yogāya haṭha–vidyopadiśyate || 2 ||

praṇamya – giving due honor, śrī – illustrious, guruṁ – guru, spiritual master, nāthaṁ – Nāth, svātmārāmeṇa – by Svātmārāma, yoginā – by Yogi, kevalaṁ – only, alone, raja–yogāya – remaining introverted while externally occupied, haṭha – kundalini manipulation for subtle body transformation, vidyopadiśyate = vidya (technique) + upadiśyate (taught)

Giving due honor to Nath, my illustrious spiritual master, who taught the technique of psychic energy transformation for the sole reason of attaining proficiency in remaining introverted while externally occupied. (1.2)

Analysis

Nāth was a mahasiddha great perfected yogi who instructed the author, Swatmarama. In the tradition and under the authority of Lord Shiva, Nāth taught kundalini yoga and its application to cultural activities which is known as haṭha yoga when it is practiced by ascetics who have few social responsibilities and is called karma yoga when it is used by political administrators who must complete social duties.

The line of authority from Lord Shiva to Nāth Guruji ran through many ascetics. These were yogis with very little social interaction. One may wonder why in the world, a person who has very little social interaction needs to be trained in how to apply kundalini yoga to cultural activities. The reason is that even a little cultural involvement requires the same degree of proficiency as that of those administrators who are bogged down with duties.

Fire is fire. If handled carelessly it will incinerate a tiny hut or a palatial mansion. In either case the same type of precaution is required. However the real issue here is that after the social equations are reduced; there will be the internal struggle with the adjuncts in the psyche. However the real issue here is that once the social equations are reduced, one is faced head-on with the internal power struggle between the adjuncts in the psyche and the core-self, requiring the core-self to bargain for greater autonomy from the kundalini lifeforce.

The kundalini will not yield its authority easily. The core-self will have to confiscate autonomy. Thus even the isolated, community-resistant ascetic will have inner social difficulties with the core-self's affiliate powers which are the sense of identity, the buddhi intellect orb, the kundalini lifeforce, the sensual orbs and the memory chambers.

Application

Respect, honor and love are due to the teacher because of service rendered in giving effective techniques. When one makes the connection with an able kriya master, one is relieved of a tremendous amount of ignorance. This brings happiness to the student. It brings great relief. However that is only the beginning because there are requirements for practice which if not applied, will cause the student to become stagnant.

One may have the greatest guru and still not make advancement, while another student with even a not-so-great guru might excel because of persistent application of techniques.

The effectiveness of kriya training is shown in two ways. The first and very obvious one is how the person manages in the cultural field. The second and covert indication of proficiency is how the person manages within the personal psyche or subtle body in which the core-self is housed. Unfortunately unless one has mystic perception, one cannot accurately grade the covert training. Thus one is apt to misjudge a qualified ascetic by rating his advancement through his overt or physically perceptible activities, his moral conduct.

Verse 3

भ्रान्त्या बहुमत–ध्वान्ते राज–योगमजानताम् ।

हठ–प्रदीपिकां धत्ते स्वात्मारामः कृपाकरः ।। ३ ।

bhrāntyā bahumata–dhvānte rāja–yogamajānatām I
haṭha–pradīpikāṁ dhatte svātmārāmaḥ kṝpākaraḥ I I 3 I

bhrāntyā – by confusion, bahu – diverse, matā – opinions, – dhvānte – in sinking, disintegrating, rāja–yogam – yoga technique for remaining introverted while being externally occupied, ajānatām – people who do not know, haṭha – kundalini manipulation for psychic energy transformation, pradīpikāṁ – crystal clear insight, dhatte – contribute, svātmārāmaḥ – Svātmārāmaḥ, kṝpākaraḥ – merciful

Due to the confusion caused by various opinions, people do not know the yoga technique for remaining introverted while being externally occupied. This merciful Svatmarama contributes crystal clear insight about kundalini manipulation for psychic energy transformation. (1.3)

Analysis

Svatmarama will give the standard process which was taught originally by Lord Adinath, Shiva. The psyche of the human being has not changed over the eons. Thus, the method given long ago is still valid. The kundalini lifeforce is the same as it was in the beginning of time. It will remain unchanged unless the student gets the methods for its reform and alteration from Shiva or his agent.

Alternately one can get it from Krishna or his agent. These two Lords are the ultimate teachers of the yogic technique for remaining introverted while being externally occupied, and even being internally occupied with detachment from the psychic adjuncts. Confusion about methods of becoming transcendental was present in the time of Swatmarama. Some are present today. This text is for clearing the air of invalid processes

Application

Inasmuch as in Sanskrit, Swatmarama gave crystal clear insight about kundalini manipulation for psychic energy transformation, this commentator intends to do the same but in modern English with further clarifications and with any adjustments which I practiced effectively. Swatmarama did not say that a reader has to be his disciple to get the information. The commentator will be just as liberal in divesting the techniques.

Verse 4

हठ–विद्यां हि मत्स्येन्द्र–गोरक्षाद्या विजानते ।

सवात्मारामो।अथवा योगी जानीते तत–प्रसादतः ।। ४ ।।

haṭha–vidyāṁ hi matsyendra–gorakṣādyā vijānate I
svātmārāmo I athavā yogī jānīte tat–prasādataḥ II 4 II

haṭha – kundalini manipulation for subtle body transformation, vidyāṁ – technique, hi – even so, matsyendra – Matsyendra, gorakṣādyā = gorakṣa (Gorakṣa) + adyā – and others, vijānate – they thoroughly know, svātmārāmo = svātmārāmaḥ = Svātmārāma, athavā – or, yogi – yogi, jānīte – learnt, tat – that, prasādataḥ – by a favor

Matsyendra, Goraksha and other siddhas thoroughly know the technique of kundalini manipulation for subtle body transformation. By their favor, Yogi Svatmarama learnt it. (1.4)

Analysis

It is not enough to praise only Lord Adinath, Shiva. If one is in direct contact with Shiva and that is possible, even though it is not likely, that does not mean that appreciation will be due to Shiva only. Direct contact with Shiva does not in any way free a student from obligations to other masters in the lineage. In fact there might be obligations to others outside of the known lineage. There are siddhas from different traditions who might help a student and thus respect, honor, love and service might be due to those teachers.

There is a hitch in the kriya yoga process where any master who developed a certain technique is due for honor by anyone who uses that process even if that master is liberated out of material existence and transited to the divine side of life.

Shiva is the fountainhead of the kriya process. Affection and honor are always due to him but he is not the only contributor. Matsyendranath and Gorakshnath are legendary mahasiddha great perfected yogins, whom all ascetics will take help from in one way or the other, consciously or unconsciously. Gorakshnath is the engineer who designed the haṭha yoga kundalini manipulation for subtle body transformation. This means that one cannot use the system without taking help from him. His guru, Matsyendranath Mahayogin, is fascinating and way beyond our understanding, because he took the information about the mystic arresting actions while he used the body of a fish.

Application

There is this stubborn idea that one should have only one spiritual master and should take instruction from no other. This is propagated by some spiritual teachers who are jealous of every other guru. Some students also have this innate feeling that there should be one spiritual master only. They rile after anyone who has more than one guru. They influence the spiritual master to post as the sat guru or the one-and-only reality-personality on earth. They discredit anyone who opposes this view and discard even sincere disciplines of their guru whom they discover taking help from anyone else.

In the Bhagavad Gita, I searched and searched and searched but could find no supportive statement of Krishna about the reality of having only one Guru. In fact in chapter four of the text Krishna lists several gurus, and in verse 34 of that chapter he listed gurus not guru, even though some masters in the Vaishnava lineage, publicize themselves as the only bonafide guru. Here is the verse from Bhagavad Gita:

tadviddhi praṇipātena
paripraśnena sevayā
upadekṣyanti te jñānaṁ
jñāninastattvadarśinaḥ (4.34)

tad — this; viddhi — know; praṇipātena — by submitting as a student; paripraśnena — by asking questions; sevayā — by serving as requested; upadekṣyanti — they will teach; te — you; jñānaṁ — knowledge; jñāninaḥ — those who know; tattvadarśinaḥ — perceptive reality-conversant sages

This you ought to know. By submitting yourself as a student, by asking questions and by serving as requested, the perceptive reality-conversant teachers will teach you the knowledge. (Bhagavad Gita 4.34)

Jnaninah and tattvadarshinah are plural Sanskrit terms. Krishna never said that there should be only one spiritual master. Still this does not mean that one should not have one high-priority spiritual master and subsidiary ones. There should be one primary teacher from whom one gets the general thrust which is required for one's liberation from material existence. That teacher however may not know all the disciplines one requires; hence the necessity to get techniques from others. Even if the spiritual master knows everything that does not mean that he practices everything then and there when one needs to do it. Hence one will have to go to others who are currently excelling at those disciplines.

Following the trend of Swatmarama, we should offer honor, respect and love to every known and unknown siddha who contributed to the path of spirituality.

Verse 5

श्री–आदिनाथ–मत्स्येन्द्र–शावरानन्द–भैरवाः ।

छौरङ्गी–मीन–गोरक्ष–विरूपाक्ष–बिलेशयाः ।। ५ ।।

śrī–ādinātha–matsyendra–śāvarānanda–bhairavāḥ |
chauraṅghī–mīna–gorakṣa–virūpākṣa–bileśayāḥ || 5 ||

śrī – illustrious, ādinātha – Lord Ādinātha, matsyendra – Matsyendra, śāvarānanda = Śāvara + Ānanda, bhairavāḥ = Bhairava, chaurangī– Chaurangī, mīna– Mīna, gorakṣa – Gorakṣa, virūpākṣa – Virūpākṣa, bileśayāḥ – Bileśaya

The illustrious Lord Adinatha, Matsyendra, Shavara, Ananda, Bhairava, Chaurangi, Mina, Goraksha, Virupaksha, and Bileshaya, (1.5)

Analysis

The legend has it that Guruji Matsyendranath learnt the yoga vidya directly from Lord Shiva. However Matsyendranath was in the body of a fish when he heard Shiva explaining the techniques to Goddess Durga. Apparently the divine lady was inattentive, but in the belly of that fish Matsyendra gave his full interest. Subsequently he became a great siddha yogi.

Guruji Gorakshnath heard the method from Matsyendranath; so we are told. Information about the siddhas is hard to come by because of the passage of time and the confusion regarding which siddha accomplished what kriya practice.

However by the grace of Lord Shiva and with the blessings of many siddhas, Swatmarama gave the techniques in this book. We are under this mercy-energy and are refreshed by it.

Shavara was a hunter who was converted by Lokeshwara, a Buddha of compassion. To impress the hunter with archery skill, Lokeshwara superficially killed one hundred deer. Then he requested that Shavara not eat flesh for one week. Gradually he put down stipulations and the hunter was reformed, and became a siddha.

The path of siddhahood is that of psyche-adjustment perfection. It does not require that one be of moral standing to begin. In fact morality may serve as a discouraging force when a person desires to become a siddha. For siddhahood everything hinges on association with a siddha, on friendly dealings with the teacher, on trust in that person and on following the recommended disciplines.

Killing animals is a basic instinct which is derived from material nature. Either one does the killing oneself or one hides the act by having someone else, a butcher, for example, do it. Material existence is riddled through and through with vicious acts of exploitation by each species.

In time however one should develop a disliking for this requirement of mandatory exploitation. Thus one may stumble upon the idea of another location which has no exploitation. In the Bhagavad Gita, there is a challenge issued by Lord Krishna about migrating to such a place:

tataḥ padaṁ tatparimārgitavyaṁ
yasmingatā na nivartanti bhūyaḥ
tameva cādyaṁ puruṣaṁ prapadye
yataḥ pravṛttiḥ prasṛtā purāṇī(15.4)

tataḥ — then; padaṁ— please; tat— that; parimārgitavyaṁ — to be sought; yasmin — to which; gatā — some; na — not; nivartanti — they return; bhūyaḥ — again; tam — that; eva — indeed; cādyaṁ = ca — and + ādyaṁ — primal; puruṣaṁ — person; prapadye — I take shelter; yataḥ — from whom; pravṛttiḥ — creation; prasṛtā — emerged; purāṇī — in primeval limes

Then that place is to be sought, to which having gone, the spirits do not return to this world again. One should think: I take shelter with that Primal Person, from Whom the creation emerged in primeval times. (Bhagavad Gita 15.4)

nirmānamohā jitasaṅgadoṣā
adhyātmanityā vinivṛttakāmāḥ
dvaṁdvairvimuktāḥ sukhaduḥkha-saṁjñair
gacchantyamūḍhāḥ padamavyayaṁ tat (15.5)

nirmāna — devoid of pride ; mohā — confusion; jita — conquered ; saṅga — attachment ; doṣā — faults; adhyātmanityā = adhyātma — Supreme Spirit + nityā — constantly; vinivṛtta — ceased; kāmāḥ — cravings; dvandvaiḥ — by dualities; vimuktāḥ — freed; sukhaduḥkha — pleasure-pain ; saṁjñaiḥ — known as; gacchanti — they go; amūḍhāḥ — the undeluded souls; padam — place; avyayam — imperishable; tat = tad — that

Those who are devoid of pride and confusion, who have conquered the faults of attachment, who constantly stay with the Supreme Spirit, whose cravings have ceased, who are freed from the dualities known as pleasure and pain, these undeluded souls go to that imperishable place. (Bhagavad Gita 15.5)

na tadbhāsayate sūryo
na śaśāṅko na pāvakaḥ
yadgatvā na nivartante
taddhāma paramaṁ mama (15.6)

na — not; tat — that; bhāsayate — illuminates; sūryo = sūryaḥ — the sun; na — nor; sasaḥko = śaśāṅkaḥ — moon; na — nor; pāvakaḥ — fire; yat — which; gatvā — having gone; na — never; nivartante — they return; tat — that; dhāmā — residence; paramaṁ — supreme; mama — my

The sun does not illuminate that place, nor the moon, nor the fire. Having gone to that location, they never return. That is My supreme residence. (Bhagavad Gita 15.6)

Virupaksha was an exceptional siddha who set very little example for student yogis to follow. He is one of the siddhas whose history is more or less of no use to preliminary students. Still it is good to hear about his activities. There is some reliable information about him in the book *Masters of Mahamudra*. The big event is that Virupaksha took initiation from the sow-faced dakini goddess Vajra Varahi and also from her husband, the deity Hevajra, both of whom are Tibetan Buddhist deities.

He also took initiations from Lord Shiva and goddess Uma (Durga). People sometimes wonder how it is that some of the siddhas took help from the Hindu pantheon of deities and also from Gautam Buddha and his affiliate authorities. Ultimately in the spiritual corpus there is prejudice in selection of teachers.

It is said that Virupaksha drank alcohol and ate pigeon meat, even in the compound of a Buddhist temple. He was kicked out for this but still his siddha condition remained intact. Later he proved that these flawed acts were not what they appeared to be.

Application

*Some legends have it that **Matsyendranath** was a fish in a former life but the Tibetan sources gave it that he was a fisherman living in Bengal. Once while fishing he was* *pulled overboard by a large fish which swallowed him. He remained alive in the belly of the aquatic.*

Once when Lord Shiva instructed goddess Durga, she became inattentive. Matsyendranath, who was in the belly of a giant fish, heard the instruction because the fish was near to where Shiva divulged the techniques of prana subtle energy movements.

Later the fish was caught and when it was slit open, Matsyendranath came out of the stomach to the surprise of the human who dismembered it.

Matsyendranath is also remembered as the spiritual master of Gorakshnath who founded the Nath yogi lineage (sampradaya). Both of them were persons of magic.

In this verse it is assumed that Matsyendranath and Mina (Mee-nuh) is one and the same person but Keith Dowman in his book, Masters of Mahamudra, *explained that Taranath introduced a variation whereby Minapa got the information of Shiva Mahadeva and then had a son named Matsyendranath. After this Minapa the elder instructed Halipa, Malipa and Tibolipa. Matsyendranath the junior instructed Gorakshnath and Chaurangi.*

One should not become confused over these legends. Formerly literature was through aural transmission mostly. In fact the language of Sanskrit is designed for retaining information in a compressed form for aural dissemination with the risk of deliberate or accidental alteration. The validity of Gorakshnath is the literature he left behind in which he admits his guru as Matsyendranath. In Sanskrit, matsya and mina (mee-nuh) are words for fish.

Even though Swatmarama gave this list of siddhas; that does not mean that they are a sequential list of gurus and disciples. These are siddhas who may or may not be related in the order of the names given.

All of the siddhas are special and left valuable contributions in terms of what they did to attain perfection. Each mastered a particular technique which particular students may need to rearrange and redesign the kundalini energy. Regarding Mahasiddha Chaurangi, in a psychic communication Sri Lahiri Mahasaya gave me information about another ancient yogi of that name:

This yogi used a Mongolian body which was hard to curb because of the toughness of the tissue in such forms. However he reeled himself in from its genetic influence and changed the way that body operated, causing the body itself to desire yoga austerities. He used to do postures which only an experienced contortionist could assume. In doing so he caused the tissue of his body to change so that it was conducive to the siddha practices. He would dance, giggle, squiggle, shake, vibrate, twist and turn his body in various postures so as to shake out kundalini from each cell in his body. Sometimes he would be seen shivering for hours on end and people felt that he had muscle spasms and was crippled or diseased.

After he left that body, he instructed many dakini yogini girls who were stuck below the Swargaloka heavenly world and who could not on their own ascend higher. By giving them a buttocks clean-out technique he freed hordes of them. Now however, he is no longer to be found on the material side of existence but his efforts are still there as subtle potency in the astral domains.

I got some hints from Sri Lahiri Baba about how to enter the subtle energy fields left behind by Master Chaurangi. When I entered these astral places my subtle body spontaneously took some of the strange contortions which Master Chaurangi performed. I also got into the discarded form field of one of the dakinis whom he liberated. When I went down into the buttocks of her form to see what Master Chaurangi's kriyas did to it, I first saw some pixels of blood and sex hormones in her buttocks. This was like a blood milk mix with the blood not mixing with the milk. It was like an emulsion. The cells there were like micro-pixels which were colorful and full of lust energy. When these areas were compressed using breath-infusion energy, they would implode into the lumps which were formed and then shatter outwards into micro-micro pixels of translucent light. When this was done over and over, eventually the buttocks of that dakini were full of clear translucent light with all the lust hormone energy and blood being totally absent. The dakini female would then appear as a goddess, having lost all impetus for lust in the astral domains.

Just after I left that astral place where Master Chaurangi's energy was in the astral domain, I passed through a place where I assumed a body from a past life, when I was a warrior somewhere in the Asia. I was in a battle and suddenly another warrior sliced through my buttocks with a sword. It was a clean cut, so that the flesh flayed apart. My body fell to the ground. I could not move. Then I remained there in a pool of blood for some days, as the wound got infected, insects entered it and then after having a high fever I expired from that body. This was a case of a memory slip due to an affiliate experience. This happens spontaneously when a yogi is on higher levels of the subtle body.

Verse 6

मन्थानो भैरवो योगी सिद्धिर्बुद्धश्च कन्थडिः ।

कोरंटकः सुरानन्दः सिद्धपादश्च छर्पटिः ।। ६ ।।

manthāno bhairavo yogī siddhirbuddhaśca kanthaḍiḥ I
koraṁṭakaḥ surānandaḥ siddhapādaśca charpaṭiḥ I I 6 I I

manthāno = manthānaḥ = Manthāna, bhairavo = bhairavaḥ = Bhairava, yogī – yogi, siddhir = siddhiḥ = siddhi, buddhaś = buddhaḥ = Buddha, ca – and, kanthaḍiḥ = Kanthaḍi, koraṁṭakaḥ – Koraṁṭaka, surānandaḥ – Surānanda, siddhapādaś = siddhapādaḥ = Siddhapāda, ca – and, charpaṭiḥ – Charpaṭi

...Manthana, Bhairava, Yogi Siddhir, Buddha, and Kanthadi, Koramtaka, Surananda, Siddhapada, and Charpati, (1.6)

Analysis

Buddha Siddha mentioned above is not Gautam Buddha, who is a Mahasiddha in his own right.

Application

The list of siddhas provided by Swatmarama is not a total call for all siddhas of all times. It is list of some of the most prominent ones whom are under the tutelage of

Lord Shiva. There are many other siddhas. For a siddha, death means translation to higher dimensions. No individual in any life form dies but the material body does perish in the course of time. A siddha's loss of a body is not the same as that of an unenlightened person. A siddha translates to a higher level of the subtle body before death of the physical system. That assures for that perfected yogi or yogini, seamless and easy transition because of not having to make a big shift from physical focus to final astral projection.

While most souls spend their physical lives, focusing on material existence and establishing themselves with a sense of security which is based on physical properties, the siddha expends most of his time shifting to subtle existence and becoming familiar with the security the astral side of life has to offer.

Verse 7

कानेरी पूज्यपादश्च नित्य–नाथो निरञ्जनः ।

कपाली बिन्दुनाथश्च काकछण्डीश्वराह्वयः ।। ७ ।।

kānerī pūjyapādaśca nitya–nātho nirañjanaḥ ।
kapālī bindunāthaśca kākachaṇḍīśvarāhvayaḥ ।। 7 ।।

kānerī – Kānerī, pūjyapādaś = pūjyapādaḥ = Pūjyapāda, ca – and, nitya–nātho = Nitya–nāthaḥ = Nityanātha, nirañjana – Nirañjana, kapālī – Kapālī, bindunāthaś = bindunāthaḥ = Bindunātha, ca – and, kākachaṇḍīśvarāhvayaḥ = Kākachaṇḍīśvara + āhvayaḥ (known as)

...Kaneri, Pujyapada, and Nityanatha, Niranjana, Kapali, Bindunatha, and one known as Kaka Chandishvara, (1.7)

Verse 8

अल्लामः प्रभुदेवश्च घोडा छोली च टिंटिणिः ।

भानुकी नारदेवश्च खण्डः कापालिकस्तथा ।। ८ ।।

allāmaḥ prabhudevaśca goḍā cholī ca ṭiṁṭiṇiḥ ।
bhānukī nāradevaśca khaṇḍaḥ kāpālikastathā ।। 8 ।।

allāmaḥ – Allāmaḥ, prabhudevaś = prabhudevaḥ = Prabhudeva, ca – and, goḍā – Goḍā, cholī – Cholī, ca – and, ṭiṁṭiṇiḥ – Tiṁṭiṇi, bhānukī – Bhānukī, nāradevaś – Nāradeva, ca – and, khaṇḍaḥ – Khaṇḍa, kāpālikas – Kāpālika, tathā – also

...Allamaḥ, Prabhudeva, Goda, Choli, Tindtini, Bhanuki, Naradeva, Khanda and also Kapalika. (1.8)

Verse 9

इत्यादयो महासिद्धा हठ–योग–प्रभावतः ।

खण्डयित्वा काल–दण्डं बरह्माण्डे विचरन्ति ते ।। ९ ।।

ityādayo mahāsiddhā haṭha–yoga–prabhāvataḥ I
khaṇḍayitvā kāla–daṇḍaṁ brahmāṇḍe vicaranti te I I 9 I I

ity = iti = subsequently, ādayo = ādayaḥ = others, mahāsiddhā – great perfected yogis, haṭha–yoga = kundalini manipulation for psychic energy transformation, prabhāvataḥ – splendor, khaṇḍayitvā – having shattered, kāla–daṇḍaṁ = death which is enforced by time, brahmāṇḍe – in the universe, vicaranti – freely transit, te – they

Subsequently, with the splendor from mastery of kundalini manipulation for psychic energy transformation, these great perfected siddha yogis, having shattered death which is enforced by time, freely transit through the universe. (1.9)

Analysis

The term siddha is defined as someone who mastered kundalini manipulation for psychic energy transformation, and who because of shattering death which is enforced by time, has free and easy transit through the universe. The implication is that a siddha perfected yogi can travel here and there into the various dimensions and then select which one he or she would permanently reside.

It is all about environments hereafter. Death means either uncertainty about what happens when the physical body dies or it means certainty about translating to a psychological body when one is deprived of the physical access. To shatter the uncertainty of death, one has to focus on subtle existence while living the physical life but in such a way as to have psychic perception with confidence in subjective viewing and communication. This takes years of practice to master.

The hold of material existence on a particular spirit is due to the access perceptions which are easily afforded to that individual by the physical material nature. If we had no perception of this place, we would not be attached to it. A person who is blind from birth does not go here and there looking for anything but that same person always has this idea about feeling, hearing, tasting and smelling things. Sensual access produces desire for a particular environment.

A blind man is not obsessed by color, and when we tell him of using daylight, he does not become excited. He will not fight with anyone over the red color of a flower. He will however be concerned about the smooth texture of a red rose petal without having any interest in the color of it. Similarly those of us who are psychically blind have no interest in subtle dimensions but we are impulsively attached to what is physical because our sensual access can apprehend objects in the gross environment.

To be a siddha one has to upstage nature's sensual access by developing psychic perception and being more of a subtle body and much less of a physical form. There has to be a transfer of sensual allegiance from the physical to the psychological to such an extent that the physical body seems to be baseless and the psychology energy seems to have a definite form with limbs and senses just as the physical one manifests.

The privilege of a siddha is the ability to consciously transit into or out of subtle dimensions. Curiosity is a hallmark of the individual spirit soul, the particle I-existence. However, for the most part, this prying feature of the soul is a cause for its downfall. Usually it is forced to latch on to what it attempts to pry into, even when the attachment is harmful to itself. Siddhas also pry but they are free from the attachment risks which are imposed on other spirits.

Application

The student yogi has to figure what it means to shatter death which is a manifestation of the power of time. It is time which is the regulator of our lives. It is time which is the medium in which we are permitted to flourish, stagnate or perish. Everything we have in the material world is within the scope of time.

Shattering death does not mean stopping the material body from dying, because it is not possible to perpetuate the material form forever. Shattering death means to step aside willingly when the time factor exhibits its authority and terminates the living condition of the physical form. To do this one has to be familiar with the psychological assets of personality which will survive the physical body.

Due to reliance and focus on the physical system as the person, an individual spirit feels undone when the physical process can no longer be accessed. Then the remaining psychological components seem to be less than the personality even though in fact it is the personality and was that all along.

If one begins the self-conception with add-ons and does not reduce the misconception before death, then one will be undone at death when the add-ons are confiscated by the time factor. To beat this system one should become familiar with the bare self and its surviving psychic adjuncts. One should do so before the physical form dies.

Verse 10

अशेष–ताप–तप्तानां समाश्रय–मठो हठः ।

अशेष–योग–युक्तानामाधार–कमठो हठः ।। १० ।।

aśeṣa–tāpa–taptānāṁ samāśraya–maṭho haṭhaḥ |
aśeṣa–yoga–yuktānāmādhāra–kamaṭho haṭhaḥ || 10 ||

aśeṣa – without exception, definitely, – tāpa – heat, taptānāṁ – of the sun, samāśraya – giving shelter, maṭho = maṭhaḥ = residence, haṭhaḥ – kundalini manipulation for subtle transformation, aśeṣa – definitely, yoga – yoga, yuktānām – of those who are skilled, ādhāra – support, kamaṭho = kamaṭhaḥ – legendary tortoise, haṭhaḥ – kundalini manipulation for subtle transformation

Kundalini manipulation for subtle transformation is like the residence which always gives shelter from the heat of the sun. For the skilled yogi, it is definite and is comparable to the legendary supporting tortoise. (1.10)

Analysis

Kundalini manipulation for subtle transformation became known as kundalini yoga with methods of breath-infusion, energy compression, energy release and kundalini piloting up through the spine of the subtle body into the subtle head. Originally this was termed as hatha yoga by Gorakshnath. Since then however the term hatha yoga, was defined as asana postures which is the elementary part of kundalini yoga.

For this yoga, Gorakshnath listed six aspects which run parallel to the highest of the eight aspects named by Patanjali Mahayogin. Patanjali used a comprehensive list including discouraged and approved social behavior, while Gorakshnath did not take into account the social involvement of the student yogi.

We could declare that kundalini yoga by itself is hatha yoga but kundalini yoga when mixed with social conduct is the ashtanga yoga of Patanjali.

One should practice which one is applicable to one's lifestyle. The ascetic who must be involved socially should use the Patanjali comprehensive system. Those who are socially exempt and who live in relative isolation, should leave aside the social hyphens and stick to kundalini yoga for rapid transcendence.

Application

Kundalini Yoga is definite but we must be clear to explain that it includes pranayama breath-infusion practice as the mainstay for raising kundalini through the spine. It includes meditation which follows the aggressive breath-infusion practice.

Kundalini yoga is so reliable that it is compared to a legendary supporting tortoise upon whose back the entire material existence rests. It is the underlying discipline upon which to build a spiritual practice and cause a definite foothold in your psyche. Until one can come to grips with the psychic adjuncts, there is no hope for modifying one's participation in this existence

Verse 11

हठ–विद्या परं गोप्या योगिना सिद्धिमिच्छता ।

भवेद्वीर्यवती गुप्ता निर्वीर्या तु प्रकाशिता ।। ११ ।।

haṭha–vidyā paraṁ gopyā yoginā siddhimicchatā |
bhavedvīryavatī guptā nirvīryā tu prakāśitā || 11 ||

haṭha – kundalini manipulation for subtle transformation, vidyā – technique, paraṁ – highest, gopyā – by secret, yoginā – by the yogi, siddhim – perfection in practice, icchatā – wishing for, desirous, bhaved = bhavet = become, vīryavatī – is potent, guptā – hiding, nirvīryā – without effect, impotent, tu – but, prakāśitā – by exposing, revealing

The highest technique of kundalini manipulation for subtle transformation is secretive for those who are desirous of success. It becomes potent when concealed, but impotent when revealed. (1.11)

Analysis

The inside scoop, the raw details of the various kriyas, cannot be adopted merely through books or lectures. In this book for instance many of the techniques will be explained but that does not mean that anyone can run away and practice these without consultation of a proficient kriya teacher.

It is not that these techniques are kept under lock and key but there is no point in explaining the details to someone who is not adapted to the practice and who is not trained in the disciplines. Even if it is explained it will remain secretive because unless one has mystic insight one cannot apply the techniques on the psychic plane. Thus one will be out of touch with the essential practice.

The practice becomes more and more potent when the student takes it upon himself or herself to keep the information to himself or herself and does not strive to make disciples. One should not become distracted with disciples but should adhere to the practice as a student of an able ascetic.

If someone wants to learn the techniques, it is best to take that person to the advanced teacher and observe how the guru relates. Otherwise one should not be crazy about making disciples because that will distract one from self-conquest.

If a student speaks about the practice to persons who are not under the discipline of an able guru, the student's progress may be hampered. This will happen because of the movement of dulling, retardative or passionate energy from the psyche of the other person, moving into the subtle body of the student and producing an undesirable effect.

Application

There is a risk that when one gets some techniques of this mystic practice and when these give some results, one will become excited and will proclaim this to one and all, thinking that it is good to introduce part or the entire human race to these valuable disciplines.

However the drain back from human association may wipe out any little progress a student made. Association means a flow of energies in two opposing directions, where it goes from the student to others and then flows from others to the student. Even though kriya practice is powerful, and its results in a student's life are self-evident, still those progressions can be wiped out by materialistic association.

Material nature has a way about it where it does not tolerate interference into the lives of those who are not ready for spiritual evolution. If one gets trigger happy and begins a mission to save the world or to save part of humanity, that endeavor might be regarded as hostile by material nature, with the result that one's spiritual progress will be sabotaged.

One will then become totally disillusioned about the practice, or will develop false confidence and distribute a watered-down compromised teaching, which will in the long run cause one to be ruined.

My advice is that one should adhere to a guru who is proficient in the practice and leave aside one's desire to convert others to the kriya path. Everyone in existence is under the care of the whole scope of reality. Thus one's assistance to manage people's development is not necessary. Most of the desires which one has about introducing mystic techniques to others arise from the mode of passion, which means that these impulsions intend to use this process to form social cliques which will go nowhere.

Flatly stated, one should not make disciples. One should wean oneself from the desire to do so. One should instead develop a disinterest in others and see that they are being cared for by the subtle material nature and by the deities. If God Himself is not concerned, then that is a hint that one should not be aggressive about tilting anyone away from what is natural for that person.

Verse 12

सुराज्ये धार्मिके देशे सुभिक्षे निरुपद्रवे ।

धनुः प्रमाण–पर्यन्तं शिलाग्नि–जल–वर्जिते ।

एकान्ते मठिका–मध्ये सथातव्यं हठ–योगिना ।। १२ ।।

surājye dhārmike deśe subhikṣhe nirupadrave I
dhanuḥ pramāṇa–paryantaṁ śilāghni–jala–varjite I
ekānte maṭhikā–madhye sthātavyaṁ haṭha–yoginā I I 12 I I

surājye – in a prosperous country, dhārmike – in a righteous civilization, deśe – in a suitable place, subhikṣhe – in a place where food is easy to acquire, nirupadrave – in a place which is free from social disruptions, dhanuḥ – perimeter of about the distance an arrow would go when released from a bow, pramāṇa – right perception, peace of mind, paryantaṁ – extensive, śilāgni = śila (stone) + agni (fire), jala – water, varjite – devoid of, ekānte – in one place, maṭhikā – hut, madhye – in the midst, sthātavyaṁ – having settled down, haṭha–yoginā = by the yogi practicing kundalini manipulation for subtle transformation

In a prosperous country, in a righteous civilization, in a suitable place where food is easy to acquire, in a location which is free from social disruption, with a hut on a plot of land, where it is extensive and affords peace of mind, the yogi, practicing kundalini manipulation for subtle transformation, should settle down. (1.12)

Analysis

These are the ideal conditions for a yogi. Ideal as they are most of the modern students will not have this accommodation and cannot arrange for this to occur. We should read this and realize that in the time of Swatmarama; most students could have such surroundings which facilitated the practice.

One other thing is that even if one has these conditions, as some of us do, still this does not guarantee that we will be successful. External conditions which are favorable facilitate practice but do not create the inner impetus to complete the mystic techniques. Even if one does not have a favorable environment, if one is determined and persistent and has the right process, one will be successful. Still, no one should understate the value of a suitable environment.

Application

As a disciple of kundalini manipulation practice, one should understand clearly that one is still under the auspices of providence. This means that one may never be in the

ideal conditions as described by Swatmarama.

What should one do?

One should do the very best one can to improve on the conditions of living but up to a point. If one becomes crazy over atmospheric and social conditions, then this desire may divert one from practice. One may become hung up with endless attempts to improve situations, which might result in partial or total neglect of practice.

The easiest route for a person of little means is to live in the ashram of an able teacher but that may not be as easy as it seems. Some persons who live in the ashram might be envious or insecure. These entities might attack a newcomer or sideline him or her and that might retard the progress which one hopes to gain.

I will discuss the suitable aspects:

prosperous country

The economic situation will affect all residents of a country, either for better or worse. Since a yogi should reduce social participation, he is dependent on the prosperity of fellow citizens. If most people in a country are poor and niggardly, then it may be difficult to procure goods and services which mean that the student might have to spend a greater part of the day for a livelihood.

I have seen members of spiritual communities spend all day walking to solicit funds for the upkeep of the institution. Some groups do this while incorporating spiritual techniques with the hope that this action will save them from the materialistic association and the down time from practice. It is to be seen if their lifestyle will have spiritual worth in the end.

If a student is in an undeveloped country which struggles for finances, that person must be very intelligent and frugal to proceed successfully with the practice. Please keep in mind that in the time of Swatmarama most of the students were of the higher caste, the brahmins. Society was inclined to provide their upkeep. That is in contrast to today where being a brahmin rarely awards one special privileges.

In the developed countries today, there is much prosperity. If one is lucky enough to benefit from it, that is great but a wealthy person runs the risk of becoming absorbed in the capitalistic drive for more and more wealth. Modern economies are corrosive to stationary money. One must invest, reinvest and shift-invest if one is to constantly have access to funds.

The best thing to do if one is serious about this practice, is to reduce desires and become resistant to offers for social participation. It does not matter what human beings think about an ascetic. What counts is the relationship he or she has with material nature. If one can sincerely reduce the desires, then the material energy will itself back away from oneself. This will cause the whole world to leave one aside as it rushes for more and more technology and wealth.

righteous civilization

Rich or poor, if on the average the people of a country are disinclined from righteous conduct; that may be an impediment for the ascetic, since he or she might require protection from criminal elements or militant groups. In so far as one needs a physical body, this is disruptive to practice.

If the physical body is damaged or inconvenienced, that will affect practice because one will have to spend extra time caring for it. Thus if at all possible one should relocate out of a country in which there is widespread criminality or militant policy.

suitable place where food is easy to acquire

The material body requires food for its upkeep. An advanced ascetic may reduce food intake but still there will be a requirement for a basic daily diet. If food is easy to acquire, that is one less concern for the ascetic. It will result in more time for practice. If one has to spend hours scrounging for a meal that will reduce practice.

location which is free from social disruption

Social disruption is a mainstay for materialistic people and for people who thrive on depressed emotional states. One should restrict association with such persons even though one should be friendly and assist others wherever possible. When they are submissive, one should even advise them in how to reduce contact with sources of stress.

Depression is a sinkhole for human emotions. Many of us get accustomed to a diet of depressed energy. An ascetic should keep a distance from people who are habitually depressed; otherwise whatever little progress is made in meditation will be washed out on a daily basis just by spending a few minutes with persons who are emotionally unstable and psychically insecure. It does not matter if such persons are family members or strangers. In fact family members are the worse association in this regard.

hut on a plot of land, where it is extensive and affords peace of mind

If one can have a plot of land, a cabin and extensive forests in the vicinity, then one is lucky. Otherwise if one lives in a modern city, one will have to endure the humbug conditions which are integral to that.

Somehow or the other, a student yogi should settle down with the practice, stick to the routine on a daily basis, keep a log of experiences and become determined to cull out as much time as possible out of every single day which times affords him.

Verse 13

अल्प–द्वारमरन्ध्र–गर्त–विवरं नात्युच्छ–नीछायतं

सम्यग–गोमय–सान्द्र–लिप्तममलं निःशेस–जन्तूज्झितम् ।

बाह्ये मण्डप–वेदि–कूप–रुछिरं पराकार–संवेष्टितं

परोक्तं योग–मठस्य लक्षणमिदं सिद्धैर्हठाभ्यासिभिः ।। १३ ।।

alpa–dvāramarandhra–gharta–vivaraṁ nātyuchcha–nīchāyataṁ
samyagh–ghomaya–sāndra–liptamamalaṁ niḥśesa–jantūjjhitam ।
bāhye maṇḍapa–vedi–kūpa–ruchiraṁ prākāra–saṁveṣṭitaṁ
proktaṁ yoga–maṭhasya lakṣaṇamidaṁ siddhairhaṭhābhyāsibhiḥ ।। 13 ।।

alpa – small, dvāramarandhra – doorway, garta –.hole, vivaraṁ – hollows, nātyuchcha = na (not) + atyuchcha (loud, noisy), nīchāyataṁ – low, samyag – suitable, gomaya – cow dung, sāndra–liptam – plastered, amalaṁ – without dirt, niḥśesa – complete, not lacking, jantūjjhitam = jantūj (jantūḥ –living being,) + jhitam (hitam – facilities), bāhye – on the outside, maṇḍapa–vedi – balcony, kūpa – on posts, – ruchiraṁ – pleasant, prākāra – wall, saṁveṣṭitaṁ – cover, shelter, roof, proktaṁ – were described, yoga–maṭhasya – of the yogi's residence, lakṣaṇam – characteristic, idaṁ – this, siddhair = siddhaih = by perfected yogis, haṭhābhyāsibhiḥ – by those who practice kundalini manipulation for subtle transformation ।। 13 ।।

The room should have a small door, be free from holes and hollows, not noisy, not too low, suitable, well plastered with cow–dung and free from dirt, not lacking living facilities. On its outside there should be a balcony on posts, with pleasantries, with an enclosure wall and a roof. These characteristics of a residence for yogis, was described by adepts of kundalini manipulation for subtle transformation. (1.13)

Analysis

Everything hinges on the facilities provided by providence. Magic or no magic, money or poverty, fate is supreme. If one does not have the ideal conditions one should make do with whatever is available and squeeze out as much time as one can for practice.

In situations where people who have the upper hand are hostile to the practice, one should cease it on the external plane but aggressively pursue it secretly on the introspective level. With materialistic people it is best that they be unaware of one's practice, otherwise the risk is there that they will emit hostile emotional energies which will enter one's psyche and cause mental chaos during meditation.

Application

Do whatever you can do to facilitate practice but do not expect providence to be compliant at all times. Do not be aggravated when it is hostile. Maintain interest in the yoga teacher at all times and in all places. Read books like this work of Swatmarama. Keep the intellectual side of your personality focused on spiritual development.

Verse 14

एवं विधे मठे सथित्वा सर्व– चिन्ता–विवर्जितः ।

गुरूपदिष्ट–मार्गेण योगमेव समभ्यसेत् ।। १४ ।।

evaṁ vidhe maṭhe sthitvā sarva–cintā–vivarjitaḥ I
gurūpadiṣṭa–mārgeṇa yogameva samabhyaset I I 14 I I

evaṁ – thus, vidhe – in that type, maṭhe – in the residence, sthitvā – being seated, sarva – all, cintā – mento-emotional disturbances, vivarjitaḥ – having no, gurūpadiṣṭa – taught by the guru, mārgeṇa – by the process, yogam – yoga, eva – even so, samabhyaset – should proficiently practiceI I 14 I I

Being seated in such a residence, having no mento-emotional disturbances, he should proficiently practice the yoga process taught by the guru. (1.14)

Analysis

Yoga begins in earnest when there are no psychological disturbances. This is the opinion of Patanjali:

yogaḥcittavṛtti nirodhaḥ

atha – now; yogānuśāsanam = yoga – yoga and its practice + ānuśāsanam – explanation

The skill of yoga is demonstrated by the conscious non-operation of the vibrational modes of the mento-emotional energy. (Yoga Sūtras 1.2)

A student can be in the ideal physical circumstances, but if there are psychological hang-ups, there will be no success in practice. Conversely another student may be in an unfavorable environment and due to absence of mento-emotional afflictions, attain success.

Beginners do require a peaceful environment to make progress but that does not mean that such an environment is the essential support. It is a subsidiary aspect. If one goes into a peaceful environment and continues the habit of psychosis, then such an environment will not give the desired effect.

In the Bhagavad Gita, Lord Krishna brought this to our attention:

karmendriyāṇi saṁyamya
ya āste manasā smaran
indriyārthānvimūḍhātmā
mithyācāraḥ sa ucyate

karmendriyāṇi — bodily limbs; saṁyamya — restraining; ya = yaḥ — who; āste — sits; manasā — by the mind; smaran — remembering; indriyārthān — attractive objects; vimūḍhātmā = vimūḍha — deluded + ātmā — self; mithyācāraḥ — deceiver; sa — he; ucyate — it is declared

A person who while restraining his bodily limbs, sits with the mind remembering attractive objects, is a deceiver. So it is declared. (Bhagavad Gita 3.6)

Application

The award of a noise-free, relatively-convenient environment which is free of negative association, serves one purpose for beginner and another for advanced students. Those who are advanced use the facility to practice deep meditation. The beginner uses it to realize the chaos in his trash-filled mind.

Beginners have this idea that the world is the problem, that the environment and other persons are the impediment. When they get the award from providence, where they are in a noise-free relatively-convenient environment, where there is no negative association which they can blame for their psychosis, they realize that the essential problem is an internal one, that the psyche itself must be de-constructed.

When all the lights are out, when the people who irritate me are no longer present, when industrial noises are far far away in the humbug cities, when biting insects are not there, I am forced to face up to my inner chaos.

Why do thoughts and feelings of others reach me even when I am in an isolated place where it is convenient to meditate?

Why am I unable to shut down memories of people and places which divert me from the objective of yoga practice?

Why am I designed as a self-humbug psychological unit?

Verse 15

अत्याहारः प्रयासश्च प्रजल्पो नियमाग्रहः ।

जन–सङ्गश्च लौल्यं च षड्भिर्योगो विनश्यति ।। १५ ।।

atyāhāraḥ prayāsaśca prajalpo niyamāghrahaḥ |
jana–saṅgaśca laulyaṁ ca ṣaḍbhiryogo vinaśyati || 15 ||

atyāhāraḥ = over–eating, prayāsaś = prayāsaḥ – irrational exertion, ca – and, prajalpo = prajalpah = excessive conversation, niyamāghrahaḥ – adhering fanatically to moral stipulations, jana – materialistic people, saṅgaś = saṅgaḥ = association, ca – and, laulyaṁ – being whimsical, ca – and, ṣaḍbhiryogo = ṣaḍbhiḥ (by six) + yogaḥ (yoga), vinaśyati – is ruined

Yoga is ruined by six features, namely, over–eating, irrational exertion, excessive conversation, adhering fanatically to moral stipulations, associating with materialistic people, and being whimsical. (1.15)

Analysis

There are many things which contravene yoga. Hence, the listings given by various yogis vary. Still these listings enable us to get some understanding of the main aspects which stunt a yogi. Each authority stresses certain negative aspects based on the experience of the lineage of teachers and the impediments which the current spiritual master chooses to stress.

Finally, a student should hone in to whatever is the main impediment for him or her. Once the main impediment is tackled successfully, the student hones on in lesser aspects which were hidden and which caused a lack of proficiency. Let me discuss Swatmarama's six negative features:

Over–eating

This has two basic components which are the food matter itself and the impetus which causes over-eating. Any food matter which is excessive for the maintenance of the body must be processed using energy from the psyche. The diversion of such energy is costly for the yogi because it will rob him or her of vital energy which should be used to further yoga, especially the meditation part of the practice.

The impetus for overeating comes from other beings who indulge in diet. A yogi's failure to detect and neutralize such influence is costly. Once the impetus penetrates the psyche; it will force the psyche to complete contrary agendas. This is similar to when a virus enters the body, latches on to good cells, and then forces them to serve its purpose.

To stop overeating one has to curb associations where one becomes distant from persons from whom the impetus for it, originates.

Irrational exertion

There can be no spiritual advancement in kundalini yoga without exertion. There must be impetus to strive and efforts to raise kundalini and reform its behavior. Such impetus should be sensible and not haphazard and irrational. Guidance from more advanced souls is an absolute necessity. If one cannot be under such influence in the physical sense, one should get the association astrally or through psychic sensitivity.

Excessive conversation

For beginners excessive conversation is curbed by not being in the presence of others, by restraining oneself so that one does not see or meet many people. For advanced students it is handled by shutting down the radio-receiver mechanism in the mind which accepts and processes the projected thinking of others.

The mind is a two-way radio which is similar to a modern cellphone. It can be detuned so that it does not absorb every thought which is projected by others.

Adhering fanatically to moral stipulations

Some students come to yoga practice with a pre-coded sense of morality which they feel is necessary as the basis for spiritual life. These persons quickly latch on to the moral stipulations laid down by previous yoga masters like Patanjali. With such principles as weapons, a critical student will emotionally and verbally lacerate any other student or teacher who does not live up to these ideals.

Instead of paying attention to their individual development and honing in their disordered psyches, they make it their duty to track down students and teachers who to their mind contravened the moral principles. In this way their spiritual progress becomes stagnant.

Associating with materialistic people

So long as one has a material body, it may be necessary to associate with materialistic people, hence it is a task to learn how to do that safely. The name of the game is to get ahead, to be on top. Therefore materialistic people have every right to strive for beauty of form, excess in finances, posh surroundings and command over society.

A yogi should not be like that. He should associate with materialistic people as per the dictates of fate. He should do so without absorbing their outlook. Make friends with them whenever providence causes you to be in their association but run away as soon as providence releases you. There is nothing to gain by associating with materialists.

Being whimsical

Some students because of a lack of evolutionary maturity, feel that they should do yoga for the heck of it or just because it is offered for learning. They attend a class or lecture and then decided to sign up for practice with the idea that it might be useful for physical health or stress reduction. These persons totally miss the vital idea in yoga which is that one should strive for liberation from material existence.

Application

To be successful a student should abandon any efforts to clean up the moral behavior of others. One should focus on personal problems which cause the psyche to be resistant to the tenets of yoga. Kundalini yoga concerns what occurs within the psyche of the student; as to the relationship of the core-self and the psychic adjuncts. It has little to do with the psyche of others or with the social operation of material or subtle bodies.

Those who cannot stick to the internal focus and the self-reform methods of higher yoga should leave aside the process and get themselves a larger dose of materialism so that they can acquire the maturity necessary to advance.

Even though many of the spiritual masters list the impediments, some listings do not correspond with the others. That is not an issue because each student has to find the particular aspect which retards advancement and which causes stagnation or resumption of bad traits.

Patanjali Mahayogin gave this listing as the obstacles to yogic progress:

vyādhi styāna saṁśaya pramāda ālasya avirati
bhrāntidarśana alabdhabhūmikatva
anavasthitatvāni cittavikṣepaḥ te antarāyāḥ

vyādhi – disease; styāna – idleness; saṁśaya – doubt; pramāda – inattentiveness; ālasya – lack of energy; avirati – proneness to sensuality; bhrāntidarśana – mistaken views; alabdhabhūmikatva – inability to maintain the progress made, not holding the ground (bhumi); anavasthitatvāni – unsteadiness in the progression; cittavikṣepaḥ – scattered mental and emotional energy; te – these; antarāyāḥ – obstacles.

These obstacles are disease, idleness, doubt, inattentiveness, lack of energy and proneness to sensuality, mistaken views, inability to maintain the progress attained, unsteadiness in progression, scattered mental and emotional energy. (Yoga Sūtras 1.30)

Verse 16

उत्साहात्साहसाद्धैर्यात्तत्त्व–जज्ञानाश्च निश्चयात् ।

जन–सङ्ग–परित्यागात्षड्भिर्योगः प्रसिद्ध्यति ।। १६ ।।

utsāhātsāhasāddhairyāttattva–jñānāśca niścayāt I
jana–saṅga–parityāgātṣaḍbhiryogaḥ prasiddhyati II 16 II

utsāhāt – based on enthusiasm, sāhasād – from being bold, dhairyāt – from being courageous, tattva – essential truth, jñānāś = jñānāḥ = knowledge, ca – and, niścayāt – from determination, jana–saṅga – company of materialistic people, parityāgāt – being detached from, ṣaḍbhir = ṣaḍbhiḥ = of six, yogaḥ – yoga, prasiddhyati – it gives full success

Having enthusiasm, being bold, courageous and having knowledge of essential truth, being determined, being detached from the company of materialistic people; it is by these six attributes that yoga gives full success. (1.16)

Analysis

There are other features for success but these are the ones singled out by Swatmarama.

Having enthusiasm

An applicant for studentship in yoga cannot be successful if he or she does not have enthusiasm. This is because material nature will not sponsor a spiritual practice which will undermine its influence. But this attitude of the psychic material nature has to be used by the aspirant anyway, because he or she must use the passionate force in material nature to generate the enthusiasm.

The student should learn from the teacher how to steal the passionate energy from material nature and use it in the spiritual interest of the core-self. The idea of material nature, and it is an eternal idea, is that the core-self is a power supply and not an actual master or mistress in its own right. Thus even if material nature allows the student to use passion to sponsor the rush for spiritual advancement, material nature will, in the long run, undermine this and use whatever insight the self develops for the purpose of expanding material existence.

One should not arrogantly think that material nature is an unintelligent force. In fact, it is quite sentient. Thus one should not get any smart ideas about commandeering material nature but should stick to the assistance rendered by the great souls who found a way to live and let live with the cosmic power which is within and without our bodies.

The guaranteed way of using the enthusiasm of material nature for spiritual advancement is to get it as a gift from material nature itself. In other words, one has to become a fond son or daughter of material nature. Then it will award one free use of its intelligence. This will allow the yogi or yogini to advance easily either in materialistic or spiritual aspirations. Patanjali Mahayogin recognized the contribution of material nature but he did denigrate it nevertheless. He said this:

varaṇabhedaḥ tu tataḥ kṣetrikavat

nimittaṁ – cause, motive, apparent cause; aprayojakaṁ – not used, not employed, not causing;

prakṛtīnāṁ – of the subtle material energy; varaṇa – impediments, obstacles; bhedaḥ – splitting, removing, disintegrating; tu – but, except; tataḥ – hence; kṣetrikavat – like a farmer.

The motivating force of the subtle material energy is not used except for the disintegration of impediments; hence it is compared to a farmer.

Patanjali asserted that material nature's assistance in the spiritual quest is non-essential. Still, it is required. Beginners must take its favor. Any child can survive on bottled artificial milk but why not take the mother's breast if it is available? Plants will grow even if there is no farmer to tend them but when the farmer is present; the plants usually grow better because of the removal of weeds and the carting of fertile soils.

Being bold

One who is not bold cannot become a successful yogi. One must have the heroic pioneering attitude to be a siddha. It may be that one takes help from a great guru or from a deity, a supernatural being. Who cares?

Do whatever is necessary to be a spiritual hero so that you can get out of this material energy and surface on the divine side of existence. Be bold!

Being courageous

It will take courage to go up against material nature, particularly to try to wrestle from it, control over the adjuncts in the psyche. Material nature will try to scare the student yogi but with help from great souls and from deities like Lord Shiva and/or Lord Krishna, one can get a handle on spiritual advancement and push back the influence of the mundane energy.

Knowledge of essential truth

An ignorant person who lacks spiritual insight cannot become liberated. There might be an argument as to how one will acquire such intuition, as if one may develop it all by oneself or as if it will be awarded by a deity or powerful guru. Irrespective of how it is achieved, it must be acquired. It is not that a student has to become a wise person in this world. That is not it. It is not something like institutionalized education.

The issue here is to develop and use a supernatural body which has within it psychic facilities which penetrate essential truth. In such a body one does not have to generate intelligence nor be educated in the science of this. The body itself perceives the essential truth. Thus if the student is awarded such a body, if the student gets that body accidentally, if the student acquires it by deliberate austerities, the point remains that it is a matter of the type of body and not of an education or generated intelligence.

Being determined

Material nature is quite saturated even on the psychic side of material existence; hence unless a student is determined he or she cannot transcend this existence and reach the divine side. The physical and subtle bodies which we use will always revert back to material nature no matter what. One must be determined to achieve the transcendence. Even if a student is assisted by the greatest person, by Lord Krishna, still if there is no determination old habits will resurface.

How to get such absolute determination?

One must either have it in oneself or one must acquire it by associating with a great soul or deity who awards it or who by association causes one to tap into it. But this bestowal must persist a long time, for long enough for the core-self to become independent of reliance on material nature, even while it is embedded in the mundane energy.

The attraction between the limited self and the subtle material energy has to be terminated in one way or the other but this happens while the self is embedded in material nature. Then a permanent transit to the divine world becomes a possibility.

Being detached from the company of materialistic people

The offer from materialistic souls is privileged placement in one of the environments of the material energy. Once a student decides to forgo the advantages of status, he or she no longer places a high value on such placement. If you do not plan to live in a ghetto, then becoming friends, or patronizing the persons who live there, makes little sense. Hence as soon as a particular self develops a strong desire to transit to the divine world, he or she no longer has to appease materialistic entities.

All the same this does not mean that a yogin becomes hostile to others. Quite to the contrary, the yogi becomes even friendlier because he or she does not want anything from the materialistic souls and wants to give what he or she possesses to those persons for their welfare in consideration of the level of evolution they exhibit.

Application

Patanjali Mahayogin gave a terse instruction:

tatpratiṣedhārtham ekatattva abhyāsaḥ

tat – that; pratiṣedha – removal; ārtham – for the sake of; eka – one; tattva – standard method in pursuit of reality (tattva); abhyāsaḥ – practice.

For the removal of the obstacles, there should be the practice of a standard method used in the pursuit of the reality. (Yoga Sutras 1.32)

A student must be determined to hunt down reality in every time and place, in every relationship and in every nook and cranny of consciousness. When one is absorbed in this way, one can make steady advancement regardless of what providence imposes as fate.

Verse 17

अथ यम–नियमाः

अहिंसा सत्यमस्तेयं बरह्मछर्यं क्षमा धृतिः ।

दयार्जवं मिताहारः शौछं चैव यमा दश ।। १७ ।।

atha yama–niyamāḥ
ahiṁsā satyamasteyaṁ brahmacharyaṁ kṣamā dhṝtiḥ ।
dayārjavaṁ mitāhāraḥ śauchaṁ caiva yamā daśa ।। 17 ।।

atha – regarding, hear now about, yama – restraining behaviors, niyamāḥ – recommended conduct, ahiṁsā – non–violence, satyam – realism, asteyaṁ – non–stealing, brahmacharyaṁ – sexual nonexpressiveness which results in the perception of spirituality, kṣamā – tolerance, dhṝtiḥ – steadiness, dayārjavaṁ = daya (compassion) + arjavam (straightforwardness), mitāhāraḥ – eating the absolute minimum, śauchaṁ – cleanliness, caiva – and so, yamā – restraining behaviors, daśa – ten

Hear now of the restraining behaviors and recommended conducts:

Non–violence, realism, non–stealing, sexual nonexpressiveness which results in the perception of spirituality, tolerance, steadiness, compassion, straightforwardness, eating the absolute minimum, and cleanliness, are the ten restraining behaviors. (1.17)

Analysis

Patanjali Mahayogin listed five restraining behaviors. His opinion was that these should never be violated:

ahiṁsā satya asteya
brahmacarya aparigrahāḥ yamāḥ
jāti deśa kāla samaya anavacchinnāḥ
sārvabhaumāḥ mahāvratam

ahiṁsā – non-violence; satya – realism; asteya – non-stealing; brahmacarya – sexual non-expressiveness which results in the perception of spirituality; aparigrahāḥ – non-possessiveness; yamāḥ – moral restraints.

jāti – status; deśa – location; kāla – time; samaya – condition; anavacchinnāḥ – not restricted by, not adjusted by; sārvabhaumāḥ – relating to all standard stages, being standard; mahāvratam – great commitment.

Non-violence, realism, non-stealing, sexual non-expressiveness which results in the perception of spirituality (brahman) and non-possessiveness are the moral restraints.

Those moral restraints are not to be adjusted by the status, location, time or condition. They, being the great commitment, are related to all stages of yoga. (Yoga Sutras 2.30-31)

To be practical, an ascetic would have to be totally segregated from human society to observe the stipulation of Patanjali to the absolute degree. We do get some insight into the social conditions required for a yogi in the time of Patanjali, when gurus like him facilitated this social conduct. The ascetic who followed the Patanjali system to that degree was totally divorced from social associations except with advanced souls whose social environment supported such extremes.

It would depend on the lifestyle of the student, as to whether he or she could live up to the standard. Failing to do so is not a condemnation provided the yogi knows to what degree he or she departed from the requirements.

Here is Swatmarama's listing of the ten restraining behaviors:

Non–violence

Non-violence became popular in reference to how human beings procure their meals, in terms of not killing animals for dietary necessity. There are many pseudo yogis who feel that since they are vegetarians they qualify as transcendentalists. However the restraining behaviors are not a trend. These are principles of attitude for progression out of the complication of sociology. It is through social energy that we move from body to body in the course of transmigration through similar or dissimilar species of life.

Violence is necessary on the earthly planet because the method of diet is consumption of life forms. There is no way around it even though it can be and should be reduced considerably. If one follows the yoga process, one should not eat flesh foods. In the modern world, there is no necessity to eat flesh because of the organization of agriculture. The human body does not need flesh to survive. It can be nourished just as well eating vegetarian meals.

One should understand that anytime a complex life form is killed, it is a lost investment for material nature; the more complex the form, the bigger the loss. Someone has to compensate for this, particularly the human who does the act of killing. It is best to see the killing of animals as a type of murder of a slightly less degree than the killing of a human being.

A student yogi should do whatever has to be done to decrease resentment in the creation. Resentment is such a potent corrosive energy, that it effects the ascetic's meditation. Therefore one should not kill or assault any other living creature. Of course if one is attacked viciously one should defend one's body but one should not initiate killing just for the sake of eating flesh.

If one derived a body from flesh eating parents, then of course one will have a sensual need for flesh meals but even then one should wean the body from that and adapt it to a vegetarian diet.

Realism

Realism should be practiced after carefully studying books like this text of Swatmarama, as well as other texts like the Bhagavad Gita. It hinges on insight development where one can see beyond the grossness into the subtle reality which supports the physical existence.

Non–stealing

Exploitation is about stealing. Everyone steals from material nature. We do so by necessity and also by superfluous desire. In every respect the only way to reduce this theft is to reduce desire. To grow a plant must steal soil and water. To live an animal must steal the plant which stole the soil and water. To survive a human must eat the plant or animal which are both thieves in their own way. In all respects every life form indulges in theft.

We should reduce desires to a minimum because that is the only way to reduce the exploitative needs.

Sexual non-expressiveness which results in the perception of spirituality

Sexuality is a major form of expression in the human species. It has a large emotional expenditure which causes reduced focus on spiritual achievement. It was always discouraged for students of yoga.

Yogis who are in isolation and who are single should aim for sexual neutrality. Care must be taken on the astral side of existence because otherwise the physical isolation will cause an increase in sexual encounters on the astral side. That would be counterproductive if one's aim is full celibacy.

Celibacy without kundalini yoga to draw up sexual hormones is a farce. If sexual hormones pool in the pubic area, then not being sexually involved has little meaning, because the energy which accumulates will have to be released in one way or the other, either through masturbation, flirtation, fantasy expression or hypocritical morality which are defeatist for those who want to be celibate.

The truth is that material nature created the hormonal system for generation of progeny. If the ascetic has ancestral obligations for begetting bodies and fails to do so, material nature will react in its own way to cause his or her celibate aims to be ineffective. There are also consequential energies from this and from previous physical births as well as complications from previous and current astral involvements. These may carry compulsory sexual liaisons energies. To be realistic a student should consult with an advanced ascetic who has sufficient insight to recommend that which will put one into an advanced state in the long term.

Tolerance

Once a student decides to forgo material existence, tolerance of others comes into play. Unless one wants to be a social liberator which itself is opposed to self-yoga, one should be tolerant of others. Most of all, one should leave aside the access others have to material nature, an access which one should determine as being detrimental to oneself.

A cow which is released from a slaughtering pen should not take it upon itself to alert others of its own kind who are happily walking into the killing area. They have no idea what awaits them but that does not mean that one should alert the conditioned souls about the conditions of existence which they will have to endure because of their ambitions for exploiting these environments.

A student should have confidence that everything in this creation is under the gaze of the Supreme Being, of Krishna. There is no need for an opinion about this. It is really none of our concern if this creation is moth-balled or maintained in the best possible condition. There is absolutely nothing we can do to change the course or destiny of this cosmos. Because we are minute living entities, our significance is conspicuous by its absence.

We have the survival instinct. That drives us to find an eternal position. Yoga practice is designed to reveal that possibility but if we insist on interference, yoga proficiency would never be attained.

Steadiness

The natural way is the one of making haphazard progress which is punctuated by various social involvements where the yogi has to leave aside practice and tend to social problems of relatives and friends. There may be natural or national disruptions caused either by weather or by politicians.

If a yogi is barraged by any of these situations, his or her progress will be sporadic and will never be consummated. The yogi will remain as a mediocre ascetic. Even students of a serious yogi may cause the teacher to become stunted, if such beginners keep harassing the teacher with social problems. It is for this reason that a serious yogi should be alone. Even two yogis practicing together run the risk of associating in a way which would cause the mind to digress to the material level of concerns and the lower astral planes where ordinary people are contacted in dreams.

When a yogi is very close to attaining the siddha status, he or she is at great risk to be pulled away from it by selfish people who are either related or not related physically but whose instinct tells them that their social use of the yogi will be hampered if he secures success.

Compassion

A yogi must be compassionate but without attachment and without a personal mission to help others. This creation already has deities who supervise it. It also has material nature's process which is ongoing and unalterable. Hence a student yogin should not get any hair-brained ideas about becoming a social liberator or a hero of compassion to human beings. There is no need for it.

The concept of being a bodhisattva supernatural being who has the welfare of all living beings in mind, is a lofty view but a yogi may adapt it as a posture of potential concern for others, not as a means to begin a mission of hope for humanity. In fact one should not pose as a bodhisattva unless one is under instructions from Buddha Shakyamuni, Avalokiteshvara or Padmasambhava.

Those who on their own declared themselves as Bodhisattvas without have a commission from Buddha or a similar being, are merely being arrogant, and will ruin themselves and anyone who is unfortunate enough to become a follower.

Even though compassion is a posture of yogi it should not become his or her ultimate aim. Expressing compassion does not in any way empower the yogi to interfere with the layout of material nature and with nature's imposition of hardships and difficulties to others.

Straightforwardness

Straightforwardness is appropriate when a yogi deals with social dependents. It is a welcome attitude for fellow yogis who are advanced enough not to be insecure. With social dependents a yogi should be prompt and exact; otherwise he will be drawn into protracted situations which lubricate family involvement at the expense of spiritual interest.

As nature would have it, the social family misidentifies itself as a spiritual one. The risk is always there that family interchange will lead to a spiritual dead end. Therefore, a yogi cannot afford to mistake the social family as being the spiritual one. This means that spiritual relationships can be mirrored socially but even in that case, there should be no confusion all the same. What is material is material. What is spiritual transcends the mundane world.

The material body always wants to be regarded as a spiritual form. It is not that. It never will be. The ascetic should resist this tendency of the material form. He should use it socially but with full understanding that its sociology is not a spiritual reality

Eating the absolute minimum

Overeating causes distractions in consciousness. These are for the most part subconscious operations which waste much mento-emotional energy. It affects meditation negatively.

Cleanliness

A yogi should be alert to keep the surroundings clean. The physical body should be kept clean and the subtle form as well. Using psychic process, the subtle body should be infused with fresh astral energy through pranayama breath-infusion process.

Application

The ten restraining behaviors are a recommendation for the ease of social relations and even for our interaction with animals and nature at large. If the student yogi does

not learn how to live in this creation with the least possible interaction, then there will never come a time when he or she will be liberated from the influence of material nature.

There is a divine environment but currently it is off-limits to most student yogis. This makes it a difficult objective, because unless one can perceive another state of existence, it is near impossible to aspire for it. The student must take help from superior souls in how to negotiate the social scene, so that the interactions help to terminate these bewildering involvements.

Verse 18

तपः सन्तोष आस्तिक्यं दानमीश्वर–पूजनम् ।

सिद्धान्त–वाक्य–श्रवणं ह्रीमती च तपो हुतम् ।

नियमा दश सम्प्रोक्ता योग–शास्त्र–विशारदैः ।। १८ ।।

tapaḥ santoṣa āstikyaṁ dānamīśvara–pūjanam ।
siddhānta–vākya–śravaṇaṁ hrīmatī ca tapo hutam ।
niyamā daśa samproktā yoga–śāstra–viśāradaiḥ ।। 18 ।।

tapaḥ – deprivation in yoga austerities, santoṣa – contentment, āstikyaṁ – being theistic, dānam – generosity, īśvara–pūjanam – ceremonial worship of the Supreme Lord, siddhānta – technical information about reality, vākya – discourses, śravaṇaṁ – hearing, hrīmatī – modesty, ca – and, tapo = tapaḥ = deprivation as it relates to Vedic religious ceremony, hutam = performance of Vedic religious ceremony with appropriate austerity, niyamā – recommended conduct, daśa – ten, samproktā – being proficient, yoga–śāstra = authoritative yoga books, viśāradaiḥ – by those who are expert

Deprivation in yoga austerities, contentment, being theistic, being generous, doing ceremonial worship of the Supreme Lord, hearing the discourses on the technical information about reality, and being modest, as well as deprivation as it relates to Vedic religious ceremony, performance of such ceremony and proficiency: These are the ten recommended conducts, stated by those who are expert in the authoritative yoga books. (1.18)

Analysis

Deprivation in yoga austerities

Yoga austerities are not fun and games. These disciplines are a serious conduct which should be done to the satisfaction of the proficient yoga-guru. The gist of the austerities recommended for hatha yoga by Gorakshnath Mahayogin is to bring the kundalini lifeforce under subjugation. This force is an unruly intelligence which will not submit itself for direction if it is not forced.

The whole idea of going easy on the kundalini and bringing it to harmony by nice methods is a farce because the kundalini is a most vicious operator which has no regards for the core-self and which sees the core-self as its eternal stooge.

With harsh enemies, harsh methods of confinement are required. That is the conclusion of the conversation about kundalini yoga. Surely, there will always be authorities who advocate a peaceful harmonious gradual method of reforming kundalini but that is not the system recommended by Gorakshnath Mahayogin.

Contentment

Contentment means the checking of the force of desire so that one does not desire anything which is not being served up by providence as a peculiar opportunity for oneself. Desire is endless for everyone. Sri Patanjali said this about it:

jāti deśa kāla vyavahitānām api ānantaryaṁ smṛti saṁskārayoḥ ekarūpatvāt
tāsām anāditvaṁ ca āśiṣaḥ nityatvāt

jāti – status; deśa – location; kāla – time; vyavahitānām – of what is placed apart or separated; api – even, also; ānantaryaṁ – timeful sequence; smṛti – memory; saṁskārayoḥ – of the impressions formed of cultural activities; ekarūpatvāt – due to one form.

tāsām – those; anāditvaṁ – what is without beginning, primeval; ca – and; āśiṣaḥ – hope and desire energies; nityatvāt – what is eternal.

Even though circumstances are separated by status, location and time, still the impressions which form cultural activities and the resulting memories are of one form and operate on a timely sequence.

Those memories and impressions are primeval, without a beginning. Energies of hope and desire are eternal as well. (Yoga Sutras 4.9-10)

So long as an entity is in a certain environment, desires which are in the psyche will keep surfacing. There is no way to stop this. One can however regulate the rate of flow of desires. A student yogi should slow down the rate, so that he or she does not have to fulfill desires at break-neck speed. Those human beings who are addicted to sensation and those who are addicted to excitement become interested in the most rapid rate of desire appearance and manifestation but they do so at their peril.

Desires carry an electric charge which may become so powerful that the entity cannot release itself from the urge. The entity is forced to fulfill the desire no matter what. This is similar to grasping a high-power line. The grasping is easy, the releasing from the grasp is impossible.

Once we realize that desire is eternal, just as Patanjali said, then we can surmise that there is no rush to fulfill anything. Whatever we may desire will be there in the future for eternity. Thus there is no scarcity of desire and fulfilment. Hence a yogi should be cool-headed and just relax without chasing sensations and without craving excitement.

In the normal course of the world, whatever is there will be revealed and experienced in due course. There is no need to push the issue. Sense gratification is so common, as to be without priority. There is no need to rush for it, no need to fight for it, no need to give oneself over for it. It will happen in due course, naturally. Thus one should be content from moment to moment regardless of which desires is facilitated by providence.

Being theistic

There are two related principles which a student yogi must accommodate. These are:

- There are more-evolved beings.
- There are divine beings whose superiority has nothing to do with evolutionary passage.

Those who are more evolved are exponentially advanced over those below them. This means that those below them will never superseded or be equal to them. The divine beings are exponentially superior for a reason other than evolution. Somehow or the other, the student yogi has to appreciate these two categories. There should be no regret if one finds oneself to be an evolutionary being who has a long way to go to reach the siddha status. Among the divine beings there is the special person, Krishna, the Supreme Being. In the Bhagavad Gita, this is how he described the categories:

dvāvimau puruṣau loke
kṣaraścākṣara eva ca
kṣaraḥ sarvāṇi bhūtāni
kūṭastho'kṣara ucyate (15.16)
uttamaḥ puruṣastvanyaḥ
paramātmetyudāhṛtaḥ
yo lokatrayamāviśya
bibhartyavyaya īśvaraḥ (15.17)
yasmātkṣaramatīto'ham
akṣarādapi cottamaḥ

ato'smi loke vede ca
prathitaḥ puruṣottamaḥ (15.18)

dvau — two; imau — these two; puruṣau — two spirits; loke — in the world; kṣaraścākṣara = kṣaraḥ — affected + ca — and + akṣara — unaffected; eva — indeed; ca — and; kṣaraḥ — affected; sarvāṇi — all; bhūtāni — mundane creatures; kūṭastho = kūṭasthaḥ — stable soul ; 'kṣara = akṣara — unaffected; ucyate — is said to be

uttamaḥ — higher: puruṣaḥ — spirit; tu — but; anyaḥ — another; paramātmeti = paramātmā — Supreme Spirit + iti — tims; udāhṛtaḥ — is called; yo = yaḥ — who; lokatrayam — three worlds; āviśya — entering; bibharti — supports; avyaya — eternal; īśvaraḥ — Lord

yasmāt — since; kṣaram — effected; atīto = atītaḥ — beyond; 'ham = aham — I; akṣarāt — than the unaffected spirits; api — even; cottamaḥ = ca — and + uttamaḥ — higher; ato = ataḥ — hence; 'smi = asmi — I am; loke — in the world; vede — in the Veda; ca — and; prathitaḥ — known as; puruṣottamaḥ — Supreme Person

These two types of spirits are in this world, namely the affected ones and the unaffected ones. All mundane creatures are affected. The stable soul is said to be unaffected.

But the highest spirit is in another category. He is called the Supreme Spirit, Who having entered the three worlds as the eternal Lord, supports it.

Since I am beyond the affected spirits and I am even higher than the unaffected ones, I am known in the world and in the Vedas as the Supreme Person. (Bhagavad Gita 15.16-18)

Patanjali gave us the description of the genus of the Supreme Person in these words:

kleśa karma vipāka āśayaiḥ aparāmṛṣṭaḥ
puruṣaviśeṣaḥ Īśvaraḥ
tatra niratiśayaṁ sarvajñabījam
sa eṣaḥ pūrveṣām api guruḥ kālena anavacchedāt

kleśa – affliction, troubles; karma – action; vipāka – developments; āśayaiḥ – by subconscious motivations; aparāmṛṣṭaḥ – unaffected; puruṣa – person; viśeṣaḥ – special; īśvaraḥ – Supreme Lord.

tatra – there, in Him; niratiśayaṁ – unsurpassed; sarvajña – all knowing; bījam – origin.

sa = sah – He; eṣaḥ – this particular person; pūrveṣām – of those before, previous authorities, the ancient teachers; api – even; guruḥ – the spiritual teacher; kālena – by time; anavacchedāt – unconditioned.

The Supreme Lord is that special person who is not affected by troubles, actions, developments or by subconscious motivations.

There, in Him, is found the unsurpassed origin of all knowledge.

He, this particular person being unconditioned by time, is the guru even of the ancient teachers, the previous authorities. (Yoga Sutras 1.24-26)

Being generous

A yogi should be generous as a habit. It is best to surrender property as suggested by providence because otherwise one might make fate one's enemy and then one will have a miserable time in this creation. If a yogi is alone without relatives and people who claim him as their guru then he is free to act. He can be as liberal as desired, as careless as circumstance allows. Otherwise if one is with relatives, one must be prepared for their objections when one is generous to someone other than family members.

Relatives may say,

"Why are you giving that to him? He is not your son."

"Why are you footing her bills, she is not your wife."

"Why are you forsaking your family for other people who have no blood relation with you?"

Thus it is preferred that a yogi should give over his property to relatives, and live incognito, where they have no idea as to whether he is dead or alive. An ascetic who does this and who amasses a following may be recognized by relatives, and then a claim for his mission begins, where the relatives say that it belongs to them and the unrelated disciples say that they deserve it.

Doing ceremonial worship of the Supreme Lord

Ceremonial worship is mandatory for any ascetic who is not isolated. If one lives at home with a family or if one lives in a temple compound, one should not fail to do ceremonial worship of the Supreme Lord. It is a bad idea to allow people to use one's example as an excuse not to worship God.

If in one's practice the ceremonial worship of God is superfluous, then one should be in isolation where one's behavior does not have a negative religious impact on the public. When the ascetic has proficiency in meditation, then external worship or ceremonial procedures are unnecessary if not superfluous. However that does not free the ascetic from the responsibility to instruct and set an example for the public. Hence if the ascetic is not in isolation, he or she must engage in religious ceremonies which are beneficial to one and all.

Hearing the discourses on the technical information about reality

This includes reading books which divulge the information.

Being modest

Modesty is an absolute necessity but this is not sexual modesty.

This is modesty in relation to the ascetic adaptability in skills. As one does more and more yoga and becomes more and more proficient, one will develop a flexibility of intelligence whereby one can expertly apply oneself to just about any situation. Thus if people get to knowing that an ascetic is versatile, they will require his or her services even for the most trivial tasks. If the yogi responds to the needs of many persons, his time for yoga practice will be reduced.

Materialistic people are apt to using a yogi because to their mind their ideas are the priority. Thus an ascetic should keep to himself or herself and not showboat any skill to anyone. One should modestly be a nobody and a very ignorant one indeed. The example for this was Jada Bharat, an ascetic who is mentioned in the Srimad Bhagavatam.

Bharat was born in a brahmin family but he deliberately acted as a stupid nothing just so he would not be enlisted even by religiously oriented materialistic people, even by his family members who were high-class brahmins. This allowed for rapid spiritual integration because of having all the time in the world to practice introspective (inSelf) yoga.

Deprivation as it relates to Vedic religious ceremony

If the ascetic is out in the open, is not in isolation, if he or she has to mix with human society, then religious ceremonies should be attended and the deprivations required should be observed. Strictly speaking such deprivations may or may not coincide with yogic austerities, but regardless the yogi should observe them to encourage non-austere devotees.

There are many requirements for the participants of Vedic religious ceremonies. One may have to fast on certain days. One may have to refrain from sexual intercourse. One may be prohibited from certain food preparations. One may have to eat at times when one does not usually partake of meals. One may have to stay at a temple or shrine for a time. One might have to dress in a certain way in certain colors. One may have to shave the hair from the head. In isolation a yogi is not required to follow such stipulations but if he or she mixes with lay-persons it may be necessary.

Performance of Vedic religious ceremony

Even if one is in isolation one may have to do religious ceremonies as per the recommendation of the yoga-guru. But certainly if one lives in a temple which is frequented by the public, one should set an example and perform religious ceremonies in the most attentive, most efficient way.

While a common devotee may exhibit blind faith in deities, a yogi should be so developed in meditation practice, as to be able to sense the presence of the deity. This will give the ceremony more effectiveness in the lives of the ordinary attendees.

Proficiency

No one should be a student of yoga and not aspire for proficiency. Yoga is not a sit-down process. It is a progressive discipline which is like a journey where the traveler can feel himself or herself progressing day by day, bit by bit, even for the most incremental movement.

Application

A student yogi should be flexible in following the rules and regulations which are given in the recommended yoga books and also what is given by the current yoga-guru. The best situation is to be in isolation, and not even to be at a shrine or ashram which is crowded with people or which specializes in catering to the needs of the public.

If one is so fated as to be involved with the public, then one must be willing to follow stereo-type rules and regulations because that is the system which the lay-people follow for their religious development.

Verse 19

अथ आसनम

हठस्य प्रथमाङ्गत्वादासनं पूर्वमुच्यते ।

कुर्यात्तदासनं सथैर्यमारोग्यं चाङ्ग –लाघवम् ।। १९ ।।

atha āsanam
haṭhasya prathamānggatvādāsanaṁ pūrvamucyate I
kuryāttadāsanaṁ sthairyamāroghyaṁ cānga–lāghavam II 19 II

atha – relating to, āsanam – posture, haṭhasya – of kundalini manipulation process , prathama – first, anggatvād – stage, accessory, āsanaṁ – posture, pūrvam – initial, first, ucyate – is described, kuryāt – do, make, tad = tat = that, āsanaṁ – posture, sthairyam – steady, āroghyaṁ – lacking ill–health, cānga = ca (and) anga (limb), lāghavam – flexibility II 19 II

Now relating to asana postures:

Since that is the first stage of the kundalini manipulation process, it is described initially. Posture causes steadiness, removes ill health and causes flexibility of limbs. (1.19)

Analysis

Depending on the genetic structure of the material body, one may or may not master the asana postures. In the time of Swatmarama, it was normal for the brahmin caste and some of the administrative caste to do asana postures from childhood. The bodies of such persons were habituated to the stretches and did not have pain while assuming difficult positions.

Postures of yoga may promote physical health and psychological relief from stress. The resulting flexibility of limbs causes better circulation of vital fluids which results in less down-time from fatigue. Even so, health of the physical system is not the objective of yoga. Anyone who becomes distracted by using the postures for health and beauty will lose out on the transcendental aim of yoga.

Application

Guruji Gorakshnatha has, in contrast to Sri Patanjali, listed asana postures as the first step in yoga practice. This means that as far as Gorakshnath Mahayogin is concerned, the student should not focus on the disapproved and approved behaviors.

However this means that the path of kundalini manipulation is primarily for people who will live apart from human society. A student who must engage in services to common people will have to give importance to the behaviors.

The material body is a dead weight which hangs from the subtle form. It keeps the subtle body tied down to the material world. In a sense the physical system is like an anchor which hangs down from a ship keeping the vessel from drifting. The asana postures are a way of decreasing the lowering force of the physical form, so that the student can have more awareness of the subtle body. Both physically and psychologically, the physical body feels lighter and lighter as one perfects the asana postures.

Verse 20

वशिष्ठाद्यैश्च मुनिभिर्मत्स्येन्द्राद्यैश्च योगिभिः ।

अङ्गीकृतान्यासनानि कथ्यन्ते कानिछिन्मया ।। २० ।।

vaśiṣṭhādyaiśca munibhirmatsyendrādyaiśca yogibhiḥ |
aṅghīkṛtānyāsanāni kathyante kānichinmayā || 20 ||

vaśiṣṭhādyaiś = vaśiṣṭhādyaiḥ = by Vaśiṣṭha and others, ca – and, munibhir = munibhiḥ = by the yogi philosophers, matsyendrādyaiś = matsyendrādyaiḥ = by Matsyendra and others, ca – and, yogibhiḥ – by the yogis, aṅgīkṛtāny = aṅgīkṛtāni = were adopted, āsanāni – postures, kathyante – were described by, kāni – what, which, chinmayā – with insight by me

The postures which were adopted by the yogis such as Matsyendra and his group, and by other yogi philosophers, as well as by Vashishtha and others will be described with insight by me. (1.20)

Analysis

Vashishtha is a mahayogin of repute but he is of a lineage which denies the existence of a Supreme Person. Their idea is that personality is insignificant and temporary, but energy as a whole is the permanence.

A guru of one of my gurus, the person named Rishi Singh Gherwal, had confidence in Vashishtha and translated the book which is titled Yoga Vashishtha. Rishi titled that book "*Heaven Found.*" This book is currently out of print. In that text, Vashishtha who was the guru of Rama, the son of Dashratha, explained to Rama that the entire world is based on a person's imagination, such that if a person withdrew his imaginative energy or interest there would be no more world.

Once when Rama's father had just died because of shock due to Rama being banished on the request of Rama's stepmother, Rama felt that he had to honor the order for banishment but Vashishtha argued against it explaining that Rama was only tied to the rule because Rama's imagination was invested in that idea and that Rama could change his fortunes in an instant by releasing himself from the imagined obligation. Vashishtha tried to convince Rama about the philosophy of the world being reliant on the imagination of any and everyone but in the Valmiki Ramayana, Rama did not agree to the view and denounced it forcefully.

Both Matsyendranath and Vashishtha are mahayogins of accomplishment. Both believed that asana postures were necessary and useful in yoga practice. Swatmarama stated this to clear the air, so that we can know, that irrespective of being theistic or atheistic, person-reliant or energy-reliant, still asana postures are recommended.

Application

The idea that asana postures are for physical beauty and health is not asserted by Swatmarama. He wrote, describing them with special insight (chinmaya - chit maya). The postures have a psychic counterpart which is of interest when doing kundalini yoga. It is for targeting the subtle body not for the well-being and beauty of the physical form.

Kundalini is a psychic force because it outlives the material bodies which it becomes and inhabits. Kundalini yoga is a psychic discipline which involves use of the physical body.

Verse 21

जानूर्वोरन्तरे सम्यक्कृत्वा पाद–तले उभे ।

ऋजु–कायः समासीनः सवस्तिकं तत्प्रछक्षते ।। २१ ।।

jānūrvorantare samyakkṛtvā pāda–tale ubhe I
ṛju–kāya samāsīnaḥ svastikaṁ tatprachakṣate II 21 II

jānūrvor = jānūrvoḥ = jānu (leg) + ūrvoḥ (of thigh), antare – inside, samyak –

properly, kṝtvā – having inserted, pāda – foot, tale – in sole, ubhe – both, ṝju – erect, kāyaḥ – body, samāsīnaḥ – sitting together with, svastikaṁ – swastika posture, tat – that, prachakṣate – is recognized as

Properly inserting both soles of the feet between the thighs and legs, and sitting with the body erect, that is recognized as the swastika good luck posture. (1.21)

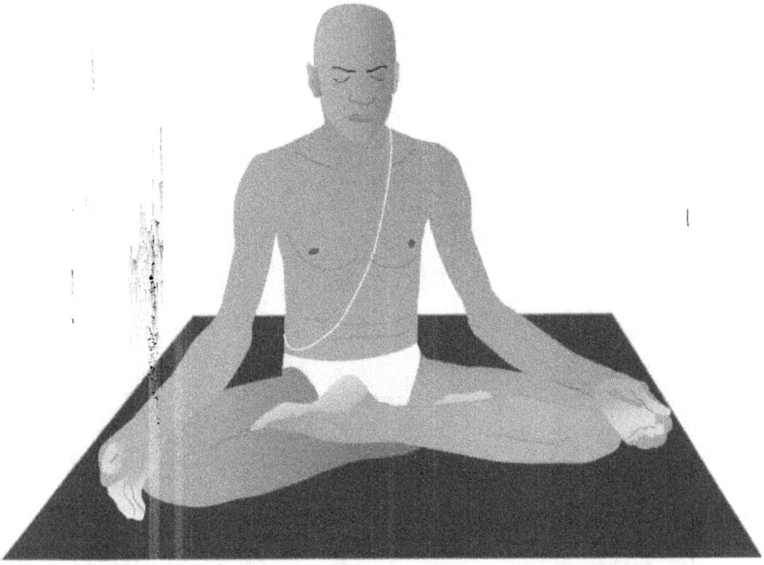

Analysis

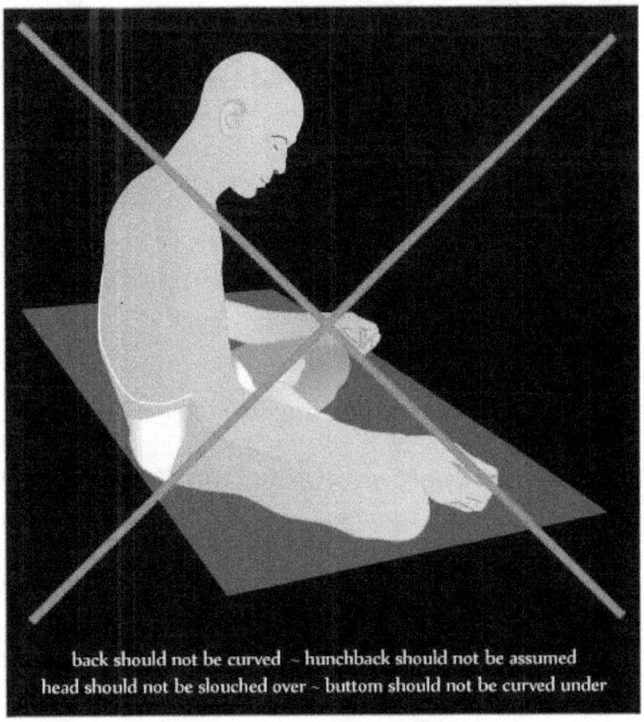

back should not be curved – hunchback should not be assumed
head should not be slouched over – buttom should not be curved under

The swastika good luck posture is a variation of the easy pose which is a simplification of the padmasana lotus posture. Each of these positions has one technicality which is an erect spine with no curvature of the back in the sacral region. The body must be plump on the buttocks so that it does not have a rounded tension in the lower torso. The yogi should not slouch over as in the previous diagram.

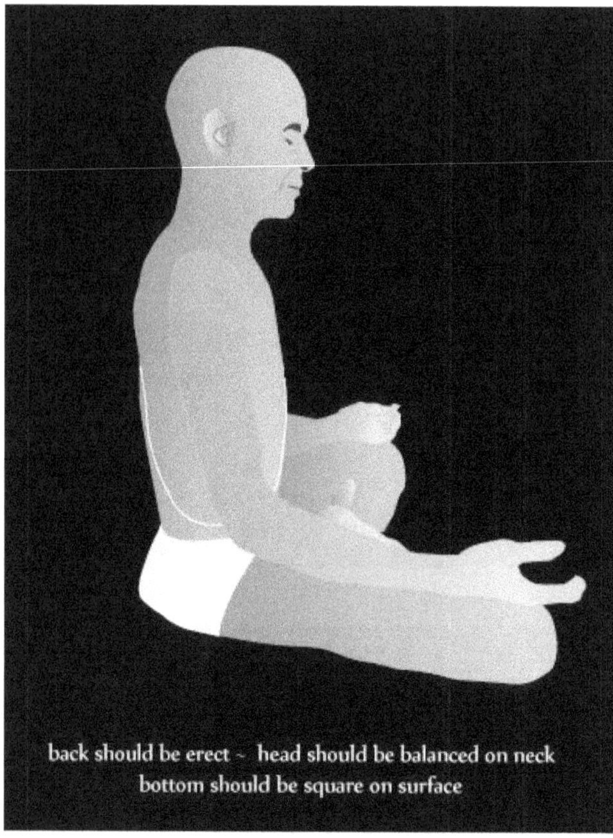

back should be erect - head should be balanced on neck
bottom should be square on surface

This posture, the swastika, is called the auspicious pose or the good luck posture. When a yogi sits in the proper way with the body erect, there is a feeling of being lucky, as if life is easy and convenient.

Application

Teachers may instruct children to do the lotus and its variations and simplifications, like this pose, in a balanced alternation, so that on each day, the first foot is changed from right to left or from left to right accordingly. This will cause the limbs to become balanced over time. Persons, who begin doing yoga after childhood, may discover that a full balance cannot be achieved because the bones were set already with one thigh, leg and foot being more pliable than the other. Some students may begin the fold in of the feet with the right foot, others may use the left foot. Usually one will feel more balanced with a specific foot being folded in first.

The subtle body configuration during this posture is the focus of advanced yogi. Please see these diagrams:

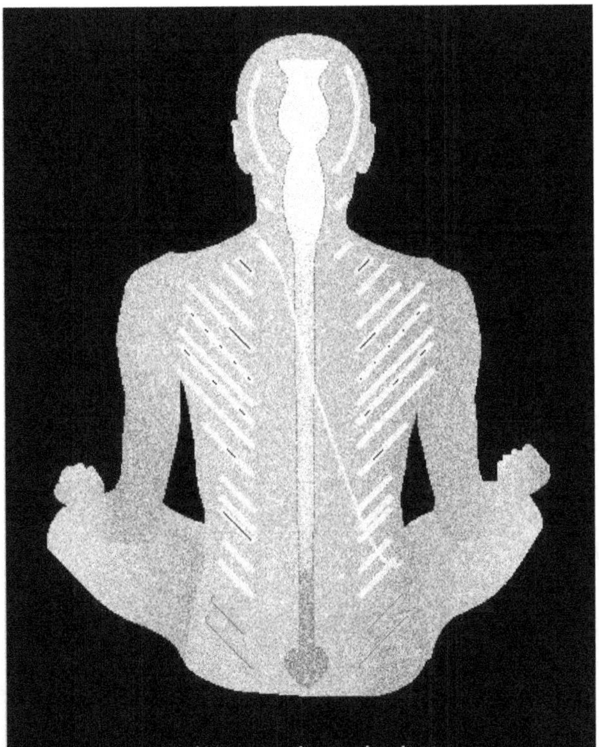

sushumna nadi spinal radiation

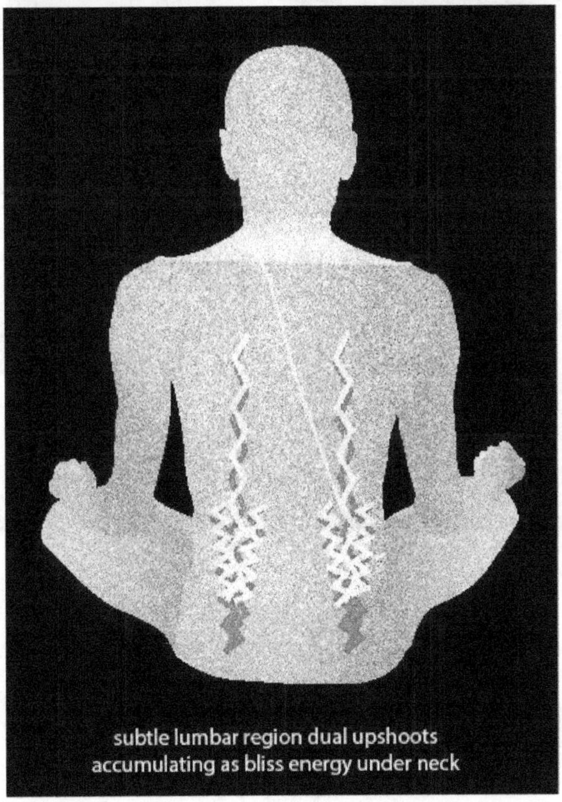

subtle lumbar region dual upshoots
accumulating as bliss energy under neck

Verse 22

सव्ये दक्षिण–गुल्कं तु पृष्ठ–पार्श्वे नियोजयेत् ।

दक्षिणे।अपि तथा सव्यं गोमुखं गोमुखाकृतिः ।। २२ ।।

savye – dakṣiṇa–gulkaṁ tu pṛṣṭha–pārśve niyojayet ।
dakṣiṇe।api tathā savyaṁ gomukhaṁ gomukhākṛtiḥ ।। 22 ।।

savye in the left, dakṣiṇa – right, gulkaṁ – ankle, tu – but, pṛṣṭha – buttock, pārśve – near the side, niyojayet – should position, dakṣiṇe – in the right side, api – also, tathā – thus, savyaṁ – left, gomukhaṁ – cow–face, gomukhākṛtiḥ – resembles the face of a cow

Positioning the right ankle near to the left buttock, and the left ankle by the right buttock, one resembles the face of a cow, in the gomukha cow–face posture. (1.22)

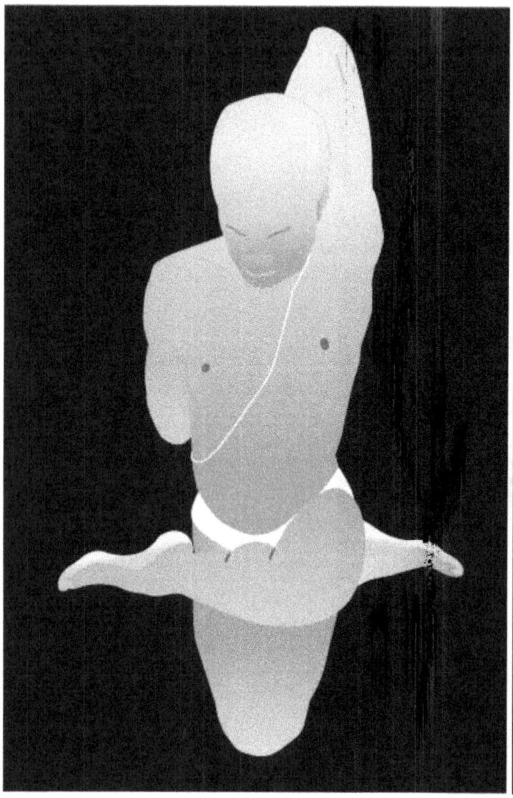
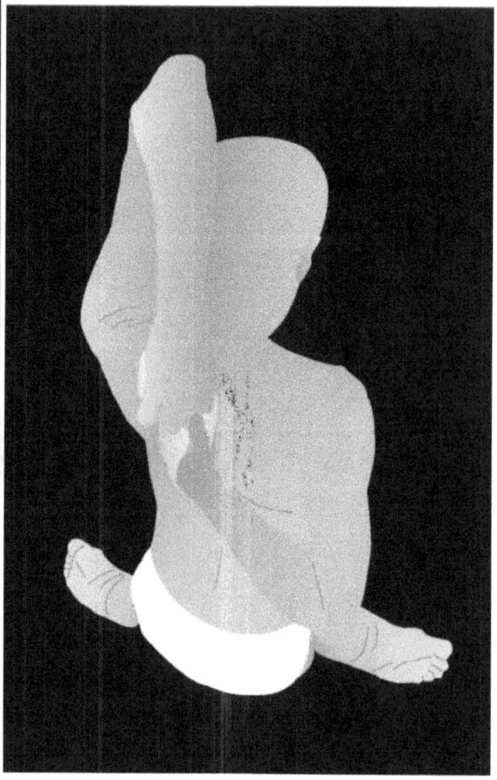

Analysis

This posture is important for understanding how every cell of every part of the body is involved in the spinal column and also in the breasts or chest. Particularly in the female body if one does this posture carefully, one will get some idea of how every cell in the body has to contribute for the production of milk for the infant. When assuming this posture every move should be done with great care and with inner attention.

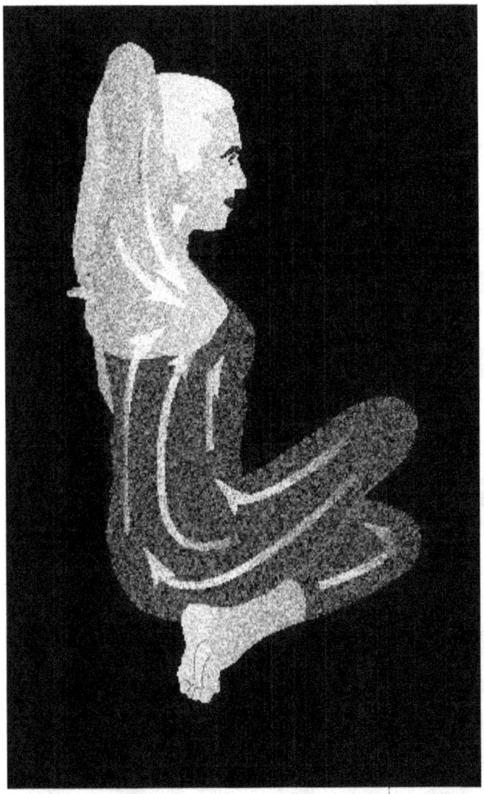

Some postures alone without pranayama are ineffective but if it is done with due care, respect and attention, this cow-face posture is complete all by itself.

Application

As in every posture, there should be balance of each side but if one began yoga after childhood, then that may not be possible, which means that it will always be easier with a specific side as the starting action in a pose. One should do both sides but with the understanding that one side will be easier. This is natural if one began doing postures after childhood.

After the feet are set, one should then set the spine so that it is erect. One should put both hands on the ground to each side of the body and push up the entire spine so that it sits vertically without looping or curving at the lower torso, in the sacral region.

Then one should interlock the hands as shown, doing one side then the other. One should focus within the physical body and within the subtle body simultaneously. One will notice that all the cells utter out some energy which travels to the breast-chest area.

One may meditate in this posture for five, ten or fifteen minutes or more, focusing on the energies which are released from various parts of the body and which immediately go to the breast-chest area like servants who are called by a great ruler.

Verse 23

एकं पादं तथैकस्मिन्विन्यसेदुरुणि सथिरम् ।

इतरस्मिंस्तथा छोरुं वीरासनमितीरितम् ।। २३ ।।

ekaṁ pādaṁ tathaikasminvinyaseduruṇi sthiram I
itarasmiṁstathā chorum vīrāsanamitīritam II 23 II

ekaṁ – one, pādaṁ – foot, tathaikasmin = tatha (as) + ekasmin (one, singly), vinyased = vinyaset = should place by the side, uruṇi – thigh, sthiram – steady, itarasmiṁs = itah (hence, the other) + asmin = (this), tathā – as before, choruṁ – to position, vīrāsanam - hero posture, itīritam – put, position

Placing one foot steadily by the side of its thigh, then the other foot should be positioned likewise near its thigh. This is the virasana hero posture. (1.23)

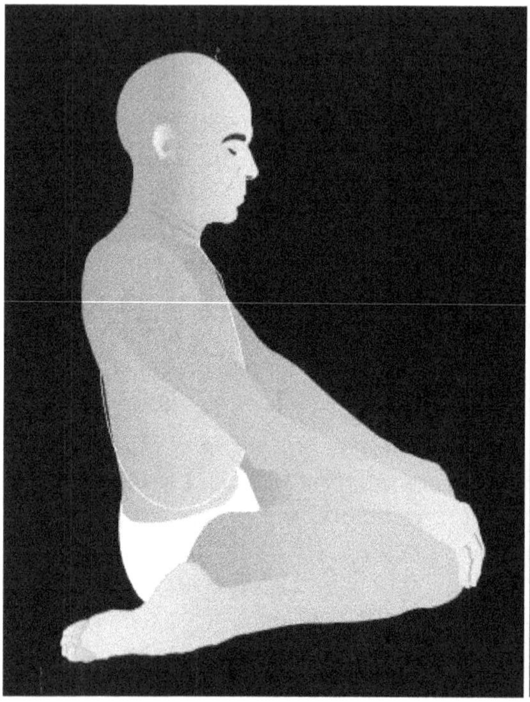

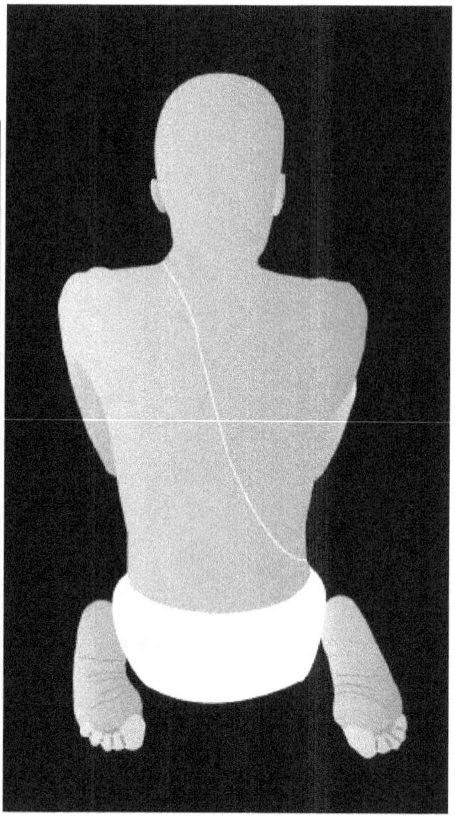

Analysis

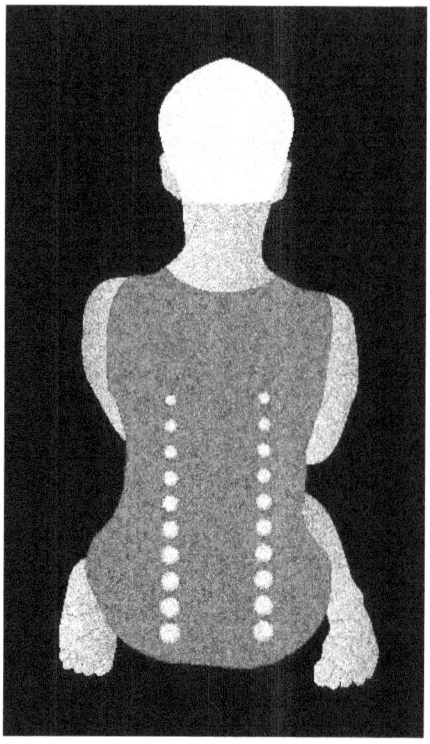

This posture is another one in which pranayama breath-infusion may or may not be done and still there will be benefit if the student focuses internally. Once this posture is assumed, the student should close the eyes and focus on the movement of energy within the psyche.

One feels like a hero when sitting in this pose. The spine should be erect. In fact as soon as one assumes this pose, one should raise the buttocks once or twice and then sit plumb on the ground so that the spine has no kinks, loops or curves. With eyes closed, one will feel energy course up through the body from the pubic-thigh complex of sexually charged energies.

Particularly in female bodies this posture is a master pose for those who desire to pull up and distribute sexual hormone energy.

In this pose one will feel that on either side of the vagina and also on either side of the inner thighs near the vagina, there is a bubbling action of hormone energy flowing about at all times. Depending on the desire to be a female siddha or to be a proficient yogini/dakini, a female can use that posture to create a subtle body which does not have sexual focus in the groin area.

News from the higher dimensions may trickle into this material world. Any sensitive female may tap into this knowledge and get hints about the difference between human female configuration and that of the siddha females in the higher regions of the astral world.

One needs extra-physical news to get a sense of direction about what to do in reconfiguring the kundalini energy to make the subtle body compatible with the higher regions. If this is achieved before passing from the physical form, then surely one would go to a higher zone hereafter.

There are many higher astral regions. Some of these have Buddhist deities. Some have Hindu deities. Some have Christian deities. Some have deities with whom we are not familiar with because they have no dependents in the earth domain at this phase of its history.

In the Buddhist Tushita heavens for instance, there are females and male deities as well as devotees of these divinities. There the female forms are configured without a uterus. There is a vagina but it is very shallow, about one inch deep and there is no passage beyond that like in a human female. In other words there is no access for sexual linkage as we know it.

Sometimes here on earth, we are appalled at nude or near nude females who are on beaches or other places or who come to a public place with very skimpy clothing but in some higher subtle worlds, females may appear without any clothing or with transparent subtle fabric, or with uncovered breasts or without panties even, completely nude.

But that does not mean that they are having sexual intercourse. In many of these places there is no sexual intercourse. There is no thought to it by anyone, because the subtle bodies used there do not have any facility for genital access.

But there are other higher places where there is sexual intercourse in the way we are familiar and also in ways which we have no idea about.

Application

The hero pose is another posture which can be used in meditation either after doing pranayama breath-infusion or without doing that. In that pose one can discover the central passage which is in the center of the trunk of the subtle body. Sexual energy may flow up this passage if one can incline it to do so; otherwise it flows downward as compelled by the gravity of the earth.

Any student, who wants to be urdhvareta or have upward flowing sexual hormones, may use this posture to study how to redesign the subtle body for that.

Verse 24

गुदं निरुध्य गुल्फाभ्यां वयुत्क्रमेण समाहितः ।

कूर्मासनं भवेदेतदिति योग–विदो विदुः ।। २४ ।।

gudaṁ nirudhya gulphābhyāṁ vyutkrameṇa samāhitaḥ I
kūrmāsanaṁ bhavedetaditi yoga–vido viduḥ I I 24 I I

gudaṁ – buttock, nirudhya – by checking, gulphābhyāṁ – ankle, vyutkrameṇa – by conversely, samāhitaḥ – adjusted, kūrmāsanaṁ – tortoise posture, bhaved = bhavet = be, etad = etat = this, iti – thus, yoga–vido = yoga–vidaḥ – those who know yoga proficiently, viduḥ – they declare

By checking one ankle under its buttock, and by adjusting the other conversely, those who know yoga proficiently declare that to be the kūrmāsana tortoise posture. (1.24)

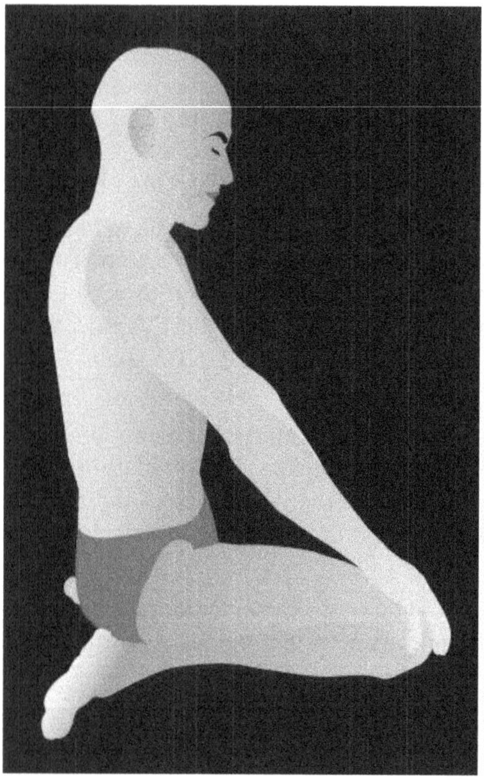

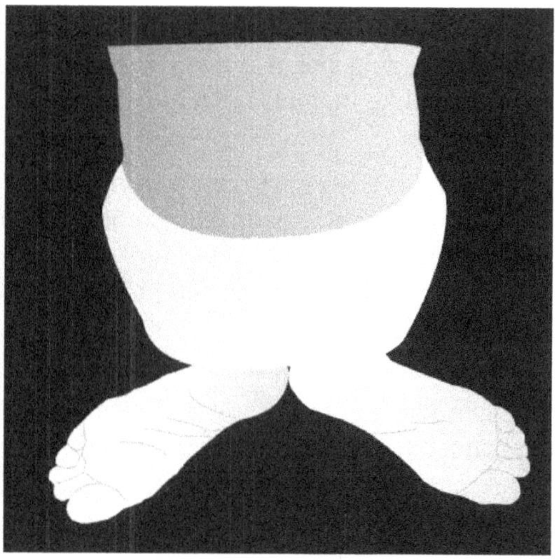

Analysis

There are various groups of yogis who stress different aspects according to the lineage, the dogma and the preference of famous teachers. Some say that asana postures are enough for yoga. Some say that pranayama breath-infusion is it. Others say that postures and breath-infusion should be combined. While yet others say that meditation is all that is needed; with asana and breath-infusion being superfluous. These arguments were there in the past. They are here currently. They will continue into the future.

This particular posture is one of the asanas which gives benefits all by itself without pranayama even though with pranayama it gives even more changes.

Because of the pressure put on the legs, ankles and feet, this posture causes the release of energy from those areas which are usually hidden from the yogi. In this posture, energy released from the legs, ankles and feet will flow upward through the trunk of the subtle body into the neck where it will be slowed to a crawl so that the yogi can observe the neck as a constriction area which stops energy from passing freely from the trunk of the subtle body into its head.

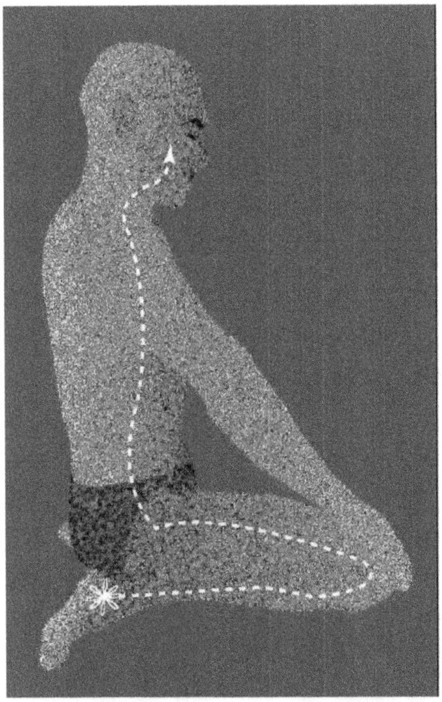

In the astral world, Sri Lahiri Baba who is now long deceased, recently alerted me that the neck as a whole needs to be cleared of heavy astral energy. It should be a sushumna passage instead of being something which contains that passage. Instead of having the central spinal sushumna passage, the yogi should reconfigure the subtle body so that the entire neck is itself the sushumna passage where energy can pass freely from the trunk of the subtle body into the head of the form.

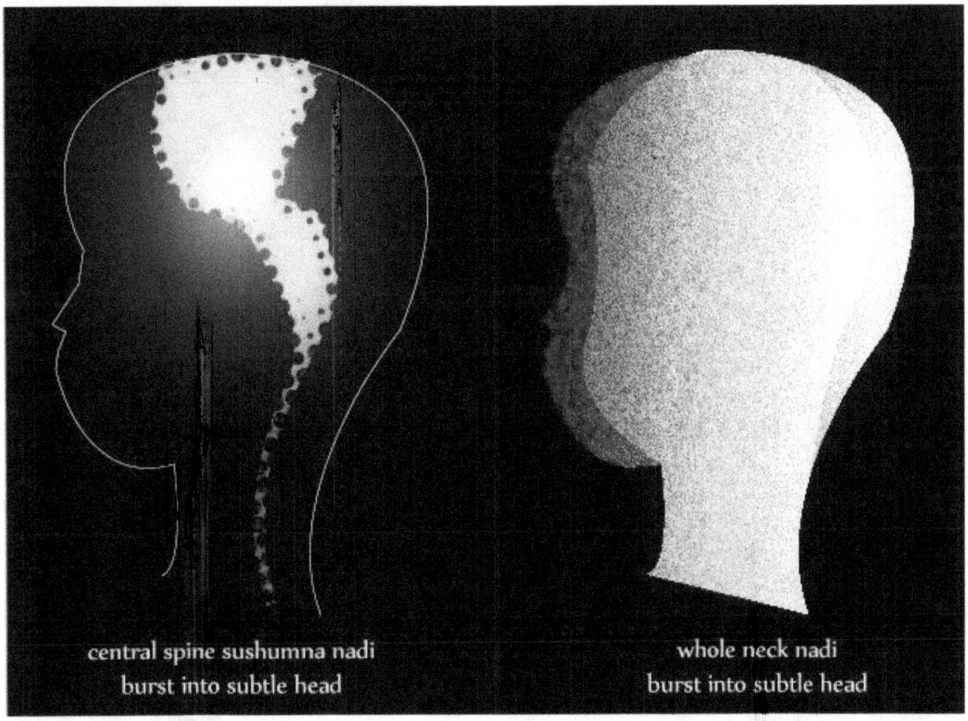

Application

Besides the one described, there are various postures which are called kūrmāsana tortoise pose. My description is the one with sitting on the ankles. For some persons this will be unbearable and so it is not recommended. It is very beneficial for those who have the flexibility which permits sitting like this with ease and with a little tension in the ankle joint. When sitting like this one's feet feel like the back flippers of a turtle.

Verse 25

पद्मासनं तु संस्थाप्य जानूर्वोरन्तरे करौ ।

निवेश्य भूमौ संस्थाप्य वयोमस्थं कुक्कुटासनम् ।। २५ ।।

padmāsanaṁ tu saṁsthāpya jānūrvorantare karau |
niveśya bhūmau saṁsthāpya vyomasthaṁ kukkuṭāsanam || 25 ||

padmāsanaṁ – padmāsana lotus posture, tu – so, saṁsthāpya – assuming, jānūrvor = jānūrvoḥ = jānu (leg) + ūrvoḥ (of thigh), antare – inside, karau – two hands, niveśya - push through, bhūmau – on the earth, saṁsthāpya – placing, vyomasthaṁ – situated in the air, kukkuṭāsanam – kukkuṭāsana rooster posture

Assuming the padmasana lotus posture, pushing the two hands through the leg and thigh, placing the hands on the earth and with the body in the air, that is the kukkutasana rooster posture. (1.25)

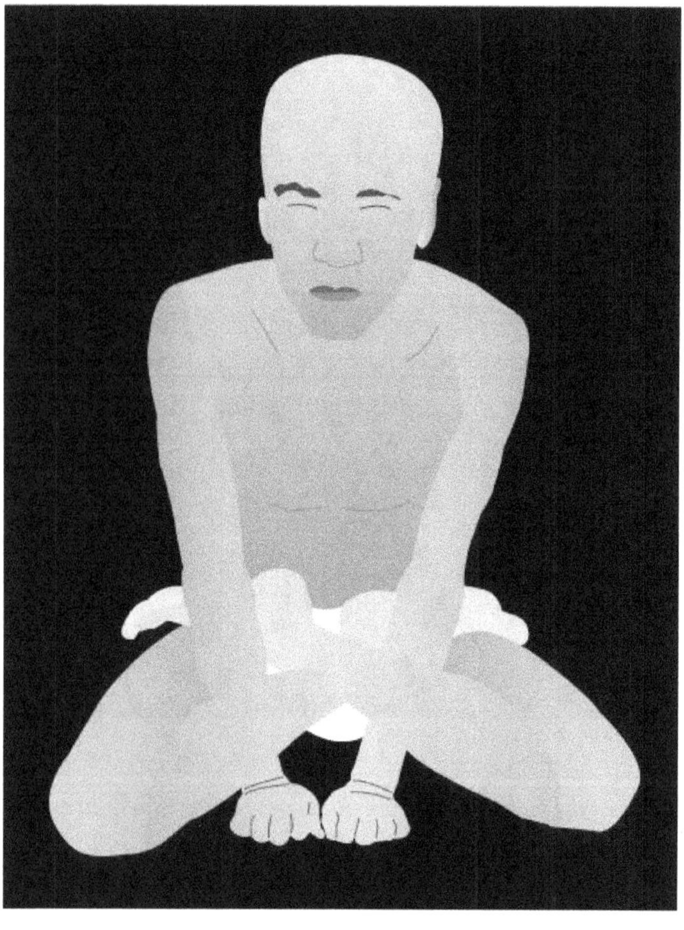

Analysis

Kukkutasana rooster posture is a classic posture for those who have flexible bodies and who have mastered the final forms of many other poses. However, merely doing gymnastics of postures does not in itself denote a yogi unless the person has proficiency on the psychic side of life. It is not what happens physically but what occurs in the subtle body because that body is the one which will survive the current lifetime. That subtle body is the one which has the evolutionary achievements of the person who transmigrated through various species of life and through many bodies even in the same species.

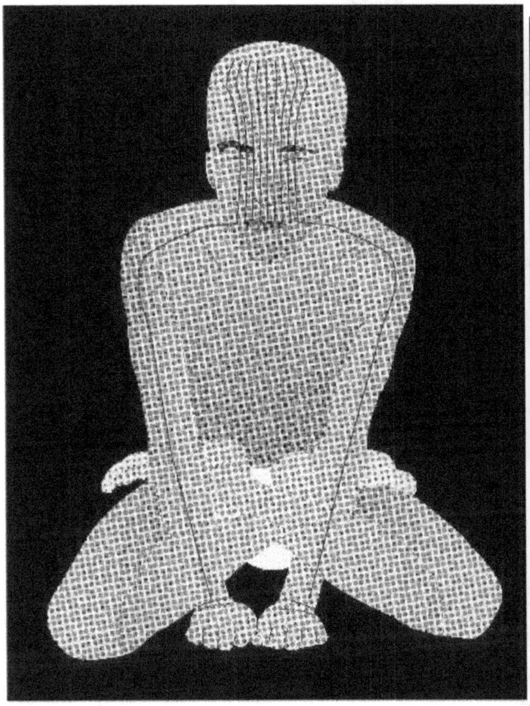
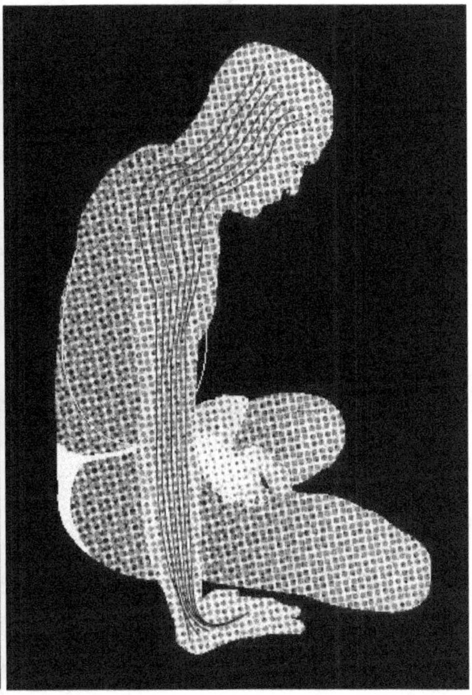

Application

The rooster posture is mastered after perfecting the padmasana lotus posture which is a difficult pose for persons with inflexible limbs. The lotus posture is mastered by persons whose thighs, legs and feet are limber. During the rooster pose the yogi can focus on the hands, forearms and arms which are hard-to-reach areas of the body in terms of changing the energy which inhabits those sections.

This posture illustrated below shows an easy way of doing this posture without having to push the forearms through the crossed legs and thighs which must be assumed for the final form. Assume the lotus or an easy pose. Then with the hands supporting on either side push up the trunk of the body.

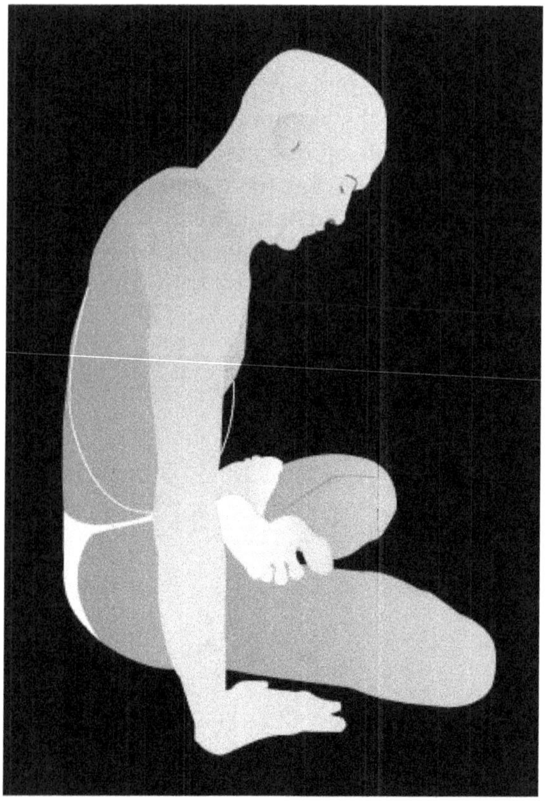

Verse 26

कुक्कुटासन–बन्ध–सथो दोर्भ्यां सम्बद्य कन्धराम् ।
भवेद्कूर्मवदुत्तान एतदुत्तान–कूर्मकम् ।। २६ ।।

kukkuṭāsana–bandha–stho dorbhyāṁ sambadya kandharām I
bhavedkūrmavaduttāna etaduttāna–kūrmakam II 26 II

kukkuṭāsana – kukkuṭāsana rooster posture, bandha–stho = bandha–sthaḥ = firmly held, dorbhyāṁ – forearms, sambadya – joint, kandharām – neck, bhaved = bhavet = should hold, kūrmavad – like a tortoise, uttāna – upturned, etad = etat = this, uttāna–kūrmakam = termed as uttāna–kūrma upturned tortoise posture

With kukkutasana rooster posture firmly held, with forearms pushed through to the joint, hold the neck and be like an upturned tortoise. This is termed uttana–kurma upturned tortoise posture. (1.26)

Analysis

This is another rather difficult posture which cannot be done properly unless padmasana lotus posture is mastered. This pose allows the yogi to realize energies which emanate from the spine and which are connected to the feet, legs and thighs. Here we address the energies in the subtle body, not the physical musculature.

Application

Physical yoga has the subtle body as its objective; otherwise it has no psychic value. Those who do yoga for physical beauty are not yogis in so far as yoga was defined by Patanjali and Guruji Gorakshnath. A person may do the most difficult postures perfectly with a body which is so limber as to win awards in a gymnast contest, and yet that person might have no psychic insight whatsoever. It is better to have a stiff body and much psychic insight than to have a limber body and be blind psychically.

Verse 27

पादाङ्गुष्ठौ तु पाणिभ्यां गृहीत्वा श्रवणावधि ।

धनुराकर्षणं कुर्याद्धनुर-आसनमुच्यते ।। २७ ।।

pādāngguṣṭhau tu pāṇibhyāṁ ghṝhītvā śravaṇāvadhi |
dhanurākarṣaṇaṁ kuryāddhanur–āsanamucyate || 27 ||

pādāngguṣṭhau – big toes, tu – just so, pāṇibhyāṁ – with hands, ghṝhītvā – grasping, śravaṇāv = śravaṇāu = ears, adhi near, dhanur = dhanuḥ = bow, ākarṣaṇaṁ – draw, kuryād = kuryāt = do, dhanur = dhanuh = bow, āsanam – posture, ucyate – is termed

Grasping the big toes with the hands, moving near to the ears as in drawing a bow; this is the dhanurasana bow posture. (1.27)

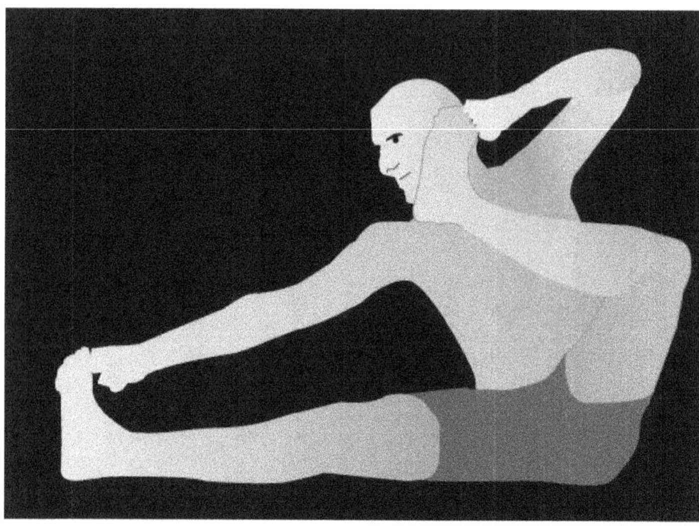

Analysis

The bow pose has much variation. This particular one gives the yogi some insight into the connection between the inner thigh, neck and left or right brain. There is an energy flow which the yogi may realize when doing this posture. This is done without pranayama practice or with controlled deep or suppressed breathing.

Application

A mistake is made doing the asana postures where the students keep their eyes open throughout. This puts one at a disadvantage where one does not focus on the subtle energies which are activated during the posture.

As soon as one assumes a posture, one should close the eyes and become aware of the energy movements which the posture causes.

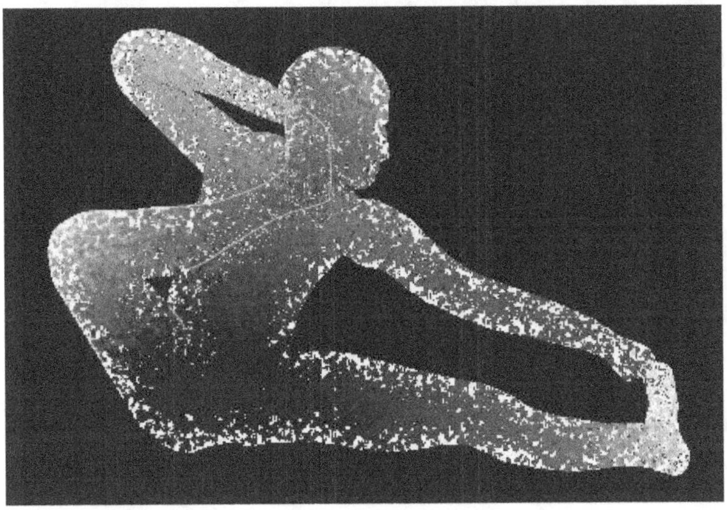

Verse 28

वामोरु–मूलार्पित–दक्ष–पादं

जानोर्बहिर्वेष्टित–वाम–पादम् ।

परगृह्य तिष्ठेत्परिवर्तिताङ्गः

श्री–मत्स्यनाथोदितमासनं सयात् ।। २८ ।।

vāmoru mūlārpita–dakṣa–pādaṁ
jānorbahirveṣṭita–vāma–pādam |
paragṝhya tiṣṭhetparivartitāṅgaḥ
śrī–matysanāthoditamāsanaṁ syāt || 28 ||

vāmoru – left thigh, mūlārpita–placed at the base, dakṣa–pādaṁ = right foot, jānor = jānoḥ = by the knee, bahir = bahiḥ = outside,veṣṭita – enclosed, vāma–pādam = left foot, paragṝhya – grasp around, tiṣṭhet – should situate, parivartitāṅgaḥ = turn–twist about the limb, body, śrī – illustrious, matysanāthoditam – detailed by Matysanath, āsanaṁ – posture, syāt – was

Put the right foot at the base of the left thigh, and the left foot outside the knee. Being situated firmly, grasp around and turn-twist the body. That posture was detailed by the illustrious Matsyanath. (1.28)

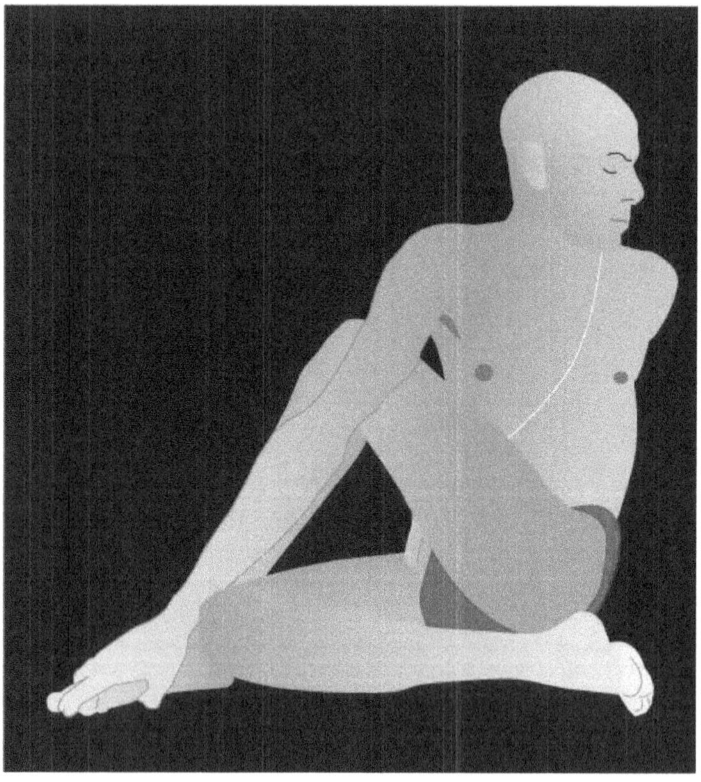

Analysis

The matsyendrasana causes focus on the forearm, arm, ribs and neck and gives insight into the energy distribution of those areas, as well as to their connection. The value of it is the insight for a yogi into how the kundalini energy and the nadis in those areas of the body are distributed.

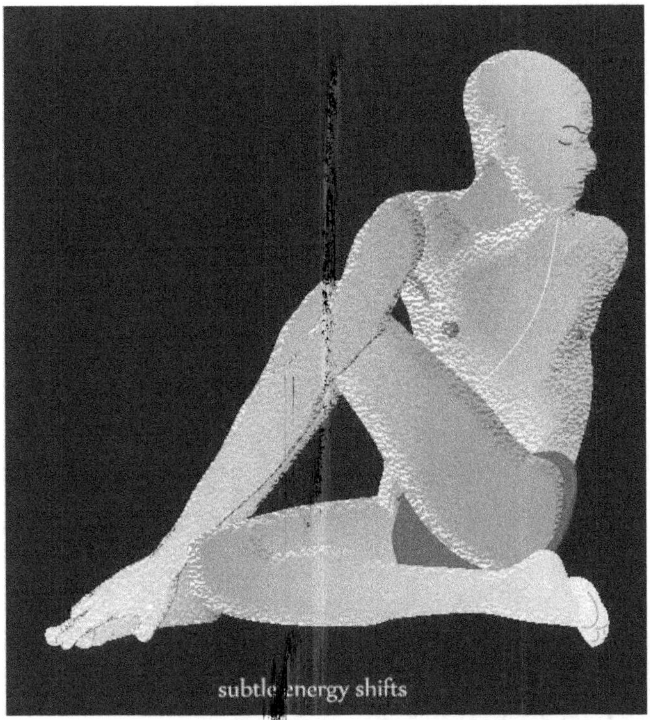

If it is held for at least three minutes, this posture and any of its variations renders knowledge about the individual's psyche. It may be held for longer periods but only by students whose musculature is accustomed to it and who will not strain unduly. Even though this posture involves the upward turning of the spine in a type of retracting corkscrew action, it is more concerned with the torque applied to the rib cage.

Application

In this posture as in the others, the yogi should close the eyelids and study the energy distribution which occurs in the subtle body.

Please see this variation done in the full lotus posture:

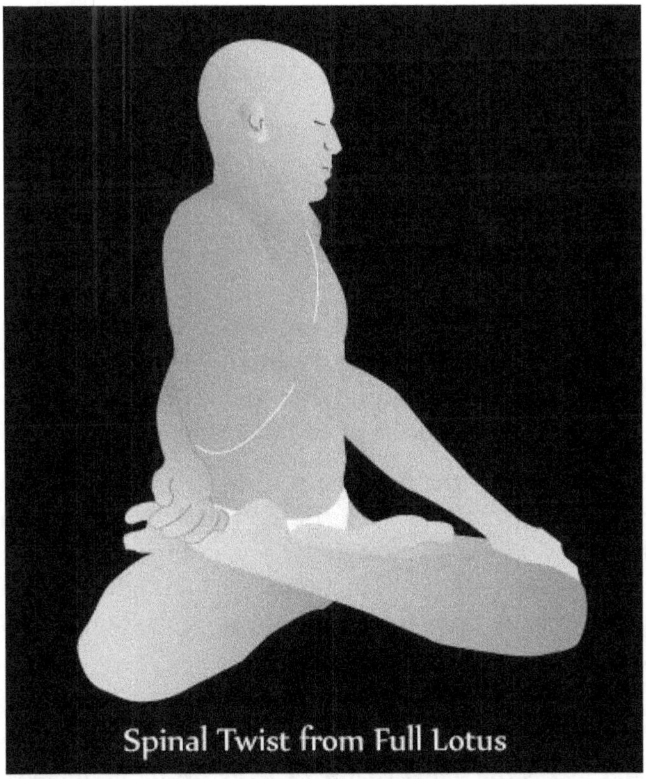

Spinal Twist from Full Lotus

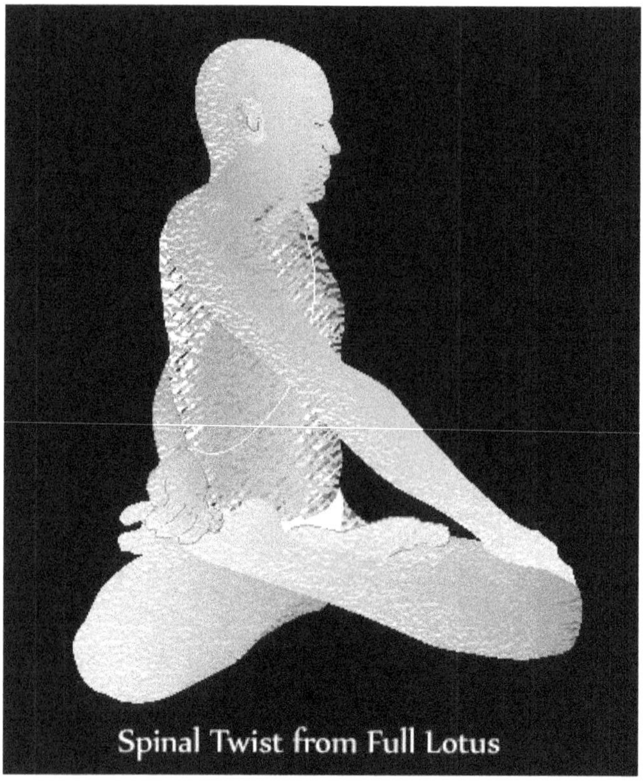

Verse 29

मत्स्येन्द्र–पीठं जठर–परदीप्तिं

प्रचण्ड –रुग्मण्डल–खण्डनास्त्रम् ।

अभ्यासतः कुण्डलिनी–परबोधं

चन्द्र– स्थिरत्त्वं च ददाति पुंसाम् ।। २९ ।।

matsyendra–pīṭhaṁ jaṭhara–paradīptiṁ
pracaṇḍa–rugmaṇḍala–khaṇḍanāstrama
abhyāsataḥ kuṇḍalinī–parabodhaṁ
candra–sthiratvaṁ ca dadāti puṁsām || 29 ||

matsyendra – Matsyendra, pīṭhaṁ – seated posture, jaṭhara – digestive power, paradīptiṁ – inflames, pracaṇḍa – terrible, rugmaṇḍala – range of disease, khaṇḍanāstrama = khaṇḍana (destroying) + astrama (weapon), abhyāsataḥ – practice, kuṇḍalinī – psychic lifeforce, parabodhaṁ – enlightening influence, candra – moon-charged energy, sthiratvaṁ – steadiness, ca – and, dadāti – it makes, puṁsām – humans

Matsyendra seated posture is the weapon which destroys the terrible range of diseases. It influences the digestive power. It activates the enlightening influence of the kundalini psychic lifeforce and makes the moon-charged energy steady in humans. (1.29)

Analysis

The twisting action of this posture involves the stretching and slanting of the rib cage. It tones the vital organs in the chest and abdomen. This may destroy a range of diseases. It will definitely influence digestion.

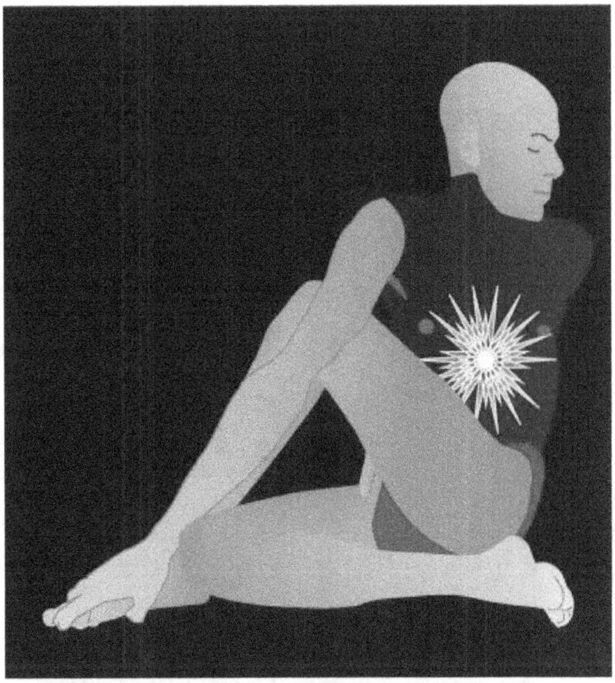

When the spine is twisted upwards during this posture, there is the likelihood that the kundalini lifeforce may be aroused in a dramatic way. If it is not then there will be some slight shift in the energy spread of the kundalini but a student may not be sensitive enough to realize this.

The moon-charged energy is an accumulation. It hangs in the center of the subtle trunk in the area behind the lowest end of the sternum. When this posture is assumed, when it is done correctly, the moon-charge energy is compressed which causes it to sparkle.

If the yogi combines pranayama practice when doing this posture, then he or she can compress the moon-charged energy, resulting in explosions of bundles of subtle force.

Application

A student needs to realize that kundalini yoga concerns the subtle body. In so far as the subtle body is affected by the physical form, physical actions can target the subtle system. However if one does not keep this in mind while practicing, one may focus on the physical side and will never realize an objective of yoga, which is to make a complete transition into the subtle body at the time of death.

Verse 30

प्रसार्य पादौ भुवि दण्ड–रूपौ

दोर्भ्यां पदाग्र–दवितयं गृहीत्वा ।

जानूपरिन्यस्त–ललाट–देशो

वसेदिदं पश्चिमतानमाहुः ।। ३० ।।

prasārya pādau bhuvi daṇḍa–rūpau
dorbhyāṁ padāghra–dvitayaṁ ghṝhītvā I
jānūparinyasta–lalāṭa–deśo
vasedidaṁ paścimatānamāhuḥ I I 30 I I

prasārya – stretching out, pādau – feet, bhuvi – on the ground, daṇḍa–rūpau = both feet like sticks, dorbhyāṁ – forearms, padāghra – feet stretched forward, dvitayaṁ – two, ghṝhītvā – grasping, jānū – thigh, parinyasta – stretched out, lalāṭa – forehead, deśo = deśaḥ = place, vased = vaset = should be placed, idaṁ – this, paścimatānam – paścimatāna fingers–grab–toes–forward–bend posture, āhuḥ – it is identified as

Stretching the feet on the ground like sticks, and grasping the toes of both feet with the hands, with the forehead resting on the thighs, this is identified as pashcimatana fingers-grab-toes forward-bend posture. (1.30)

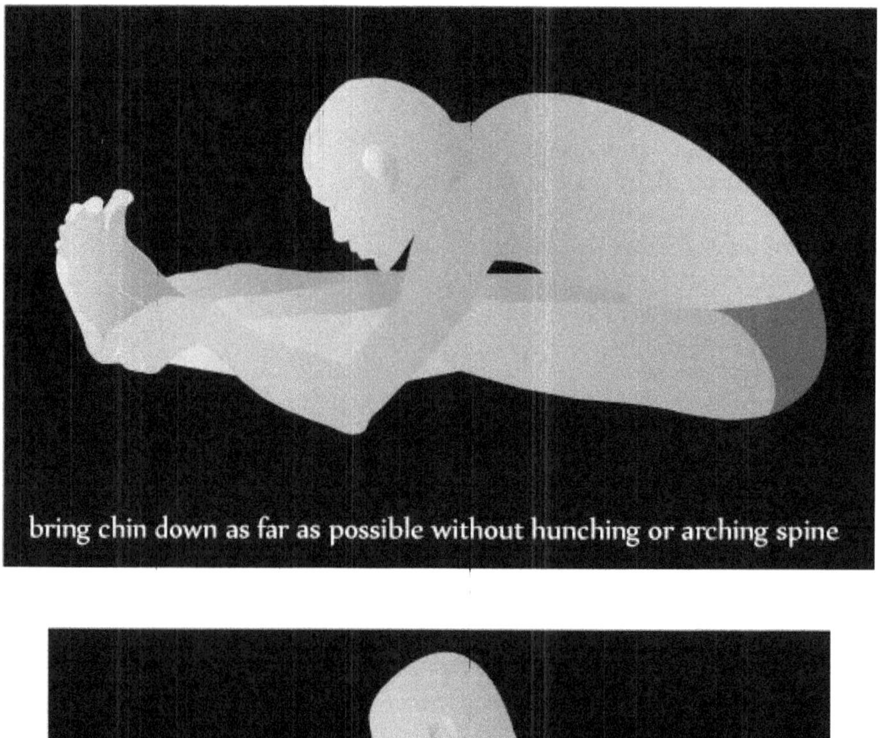

bring chin down as far as possible without hunching or arching spine

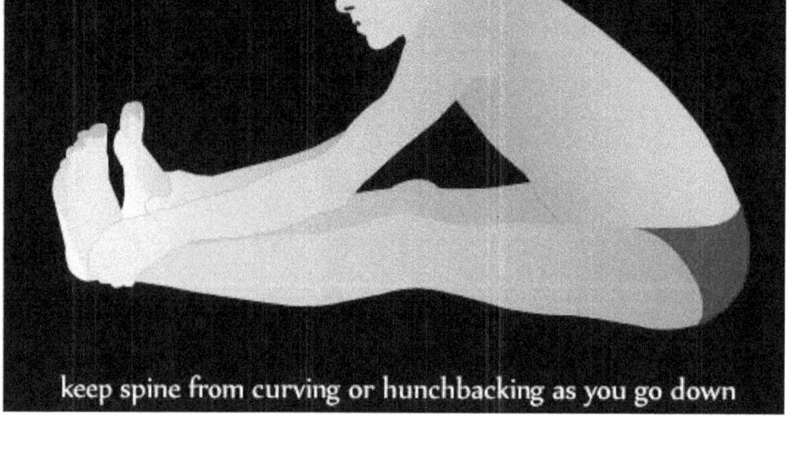

keep spine from curving or hunchbacking as you go down

Analysis

This posture requires that the knees be kept flat down. They should not rise by the pressures of this pose. If there is an inclination for that or if the student feels it cannot be done without the knees rising, the student should hold the shins instead of the toes and keep the knees down.

Energy is released from behind the calves and thighs during this posture. Even though the head should rest on the thighs, that instruction is for those who have supple bodies. Others should not arc or hunch the back so as to get the forehead to rest on the thighs. If for instance one has a pouched belly it would not be possible to bring the forehead to the thighs without hunching the back. But that is the incorrect posture. Thus one should avoid hunching the back and not have the head touch the thighs if the limbs are not supple or if the belly protrudes.

Once the yogi gets into this position, he or she should close the eyes and focus within to detect release of energy from the feet, legs, thighs and lower buttocks where the thigh tendons are connected to the buttocks. This energy will be releasing outwards from the legs and thighs. After the yogi becomes aware of it and recognizes its influence, he should contract the muscles up through the system as if drawing from the feet into the legs and then into the thighs and then into the buttocks and then into the trunk.

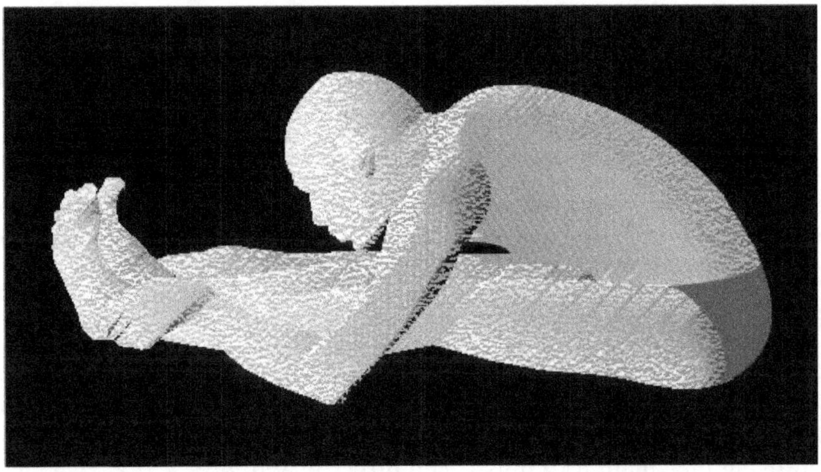

Even though these are physical postures, the focus in kundalini hatha yoga is the subtle body. A yogi should reference all phases of the practice to influence the behavior of the energy in the subtle form.

Application

The feet are the access to independence in fulfillment of desires. They facilitate rapid mobility. In immobile forms, the persons using those bodies are limited in how they can access the creation. For them the exploitive tendency is checked by the availability of materials which are brought to them by various agencies. This limitation is breached in the mobile species which can wander here and there in a jiffy. Misuse of the feet is a necessity in the exploitation business of creature existence. A yogi should study the system and then make changes so that his feet are no longer focused on exploitive pursuits in God's creation.

This posture could give the yogi the impetus to change the mission of the feet, legs and thighs, so that their main interest is to procure experiences which promote spiritual realization.

Verse 31

इति पश्चिमतानमासनाग्र्यं

पवनं पश्चिम–वाहिनं करोति ।

उदयं जठरानलस्य कुर्याद्

उदरे कार्श्यमरोगतां च पुंसाम् ।। ३१ ।।

iti paścimatānamāsanāgryaṁ
pavanaṁ paścima–vāhinaṁ karoti ।
udayaṁ jaṭharānalasya kuryād
udare kārśyamarogatāṁ ca puṁsām ।। 31 ।।

iti – thus, paścimatānamāsana – paścimatāna fingers–grab–toes forward–bend posture, āgryaṁ – foremost, pavanaṁ – lifeforce, paścima – reversal, vāhinaṁ – cause to flow, karoti – it does, udayaṁ – rise, jaṭharānalasya = jaṭhara (digestive power), + analasya (energizes), kuryād = kuryāt = do, udare – in the stomach, kārśyam – causing flatness, arogatāṁ – health, ca – and, puṁsām – people

This pashcimatana fingers-grab-toes forward-bend posture is foremost. It causes a reversal in the flow of lifeforce, energizes the digestive power, flattens the stomach and gives health to people. (1.31)

Analysis

This posture disrupts the lifeforce system because it tugs on the nerves which end at the base chakra, muladhara. Any posture which targets the muladhara chakra will have a similar effect. It is important to use asana postures to attack the base chakra and not be involved in using imagination to do so. The direct way to attack the base chakra is to deal with the nerves at the end of the spinal column. That is a direct way to affect the muladhar chakra which is the base location of the kundalini lifeforce.

Application

Normally the lifeforce is operating on a downward pull operation, based on the earth's gravitational draw on every object in its vicinity. A yogi has a task to reverse this process. However when one does this posture, there will be a reversal where the kundalini lifeforce seems to think of going upward through the spine instead of continuing its occupation of sending commands downwards from the spine into the trunk and limbs of the body.

There is a tilt-up feeling when doing this posture. Those students, who advanced sufficiently, should pull up the released energy into the buttocks and then guide that energy into the base chakra and then up through the center of the spine into the subtle head.

Other benefits which accrue from doing this posture regularly are increased digestive capability with a resulting reduction in belly fat, increased efficiency of the abdomen and draw-up of the abdominal muscles.

Verse 32

धरामवष्टभ्य कर–द्वयेन

तत–कूर्पर–सथापित–नाभि–पार्श्वः ।

उछ्छासनो दण्डवदुत्थितः खे

मायूरमेतत्प्रवदन्ति पीठम् ।। ३२ ।।

dharām avaṣṭabhya kara–dvayena
tat–kūrpara–sthāpita–nābhi–pārśvaḥ I
uchchāsano daṇḍavadutthitaḥ khe
māyūrametatpravadanti pīṭham II 32 II

dharām – earth, avaṣṭabhya – balance on, kara – hand, dvayena – with two, tat – that, kūrpara – elbow, sthāpita – supported, nābhi – navel, pārśvaḥ – limb, uchchāsano = uchchāsanaḥ = elevate, daṇḍavad = daṇḍavat = like a stick, utthitaḥ – elevated, khe – move to, māyūram – peacock, etat – this, pravadanti – (the yogis) term, pīṭham – posture

Balancing on the earth on two hands, with the navel supported on the elbows, the limbs elevated should be stiff like a stick. This, the yogis term, as the mayura peacock posture. (1.32)

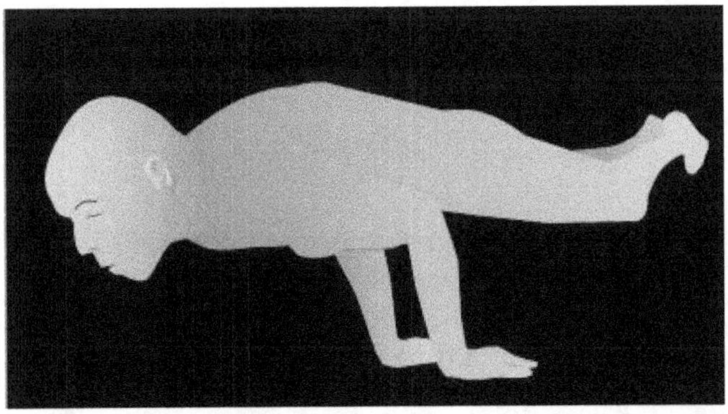

Analysis

The hands, forearms, arms, shoulders, chest and neck are toned in this posture. This is a difficult posture. Students whose use inflexible bodies or whose muscles cannot bear the weight of the body, should do this posture carefully and not push the limit so as to damage any part of the body. In this posture the body can be braced somewhat on the arms and elbows but advanced students need not rely on that support when executing this asana.

Application

In this posture energy is released primarily from the forearms and arms. These are hard-to-reach areas for those who do bhastrika pranayama in kundalini yoga practice. It is important to gradually target and flush out the hard-to-reach zones, so that polluted energy which lingers in those parts of the psyche can be removed in exchange for fresh subtle energy which is brought into the body during breath-infusion practice.

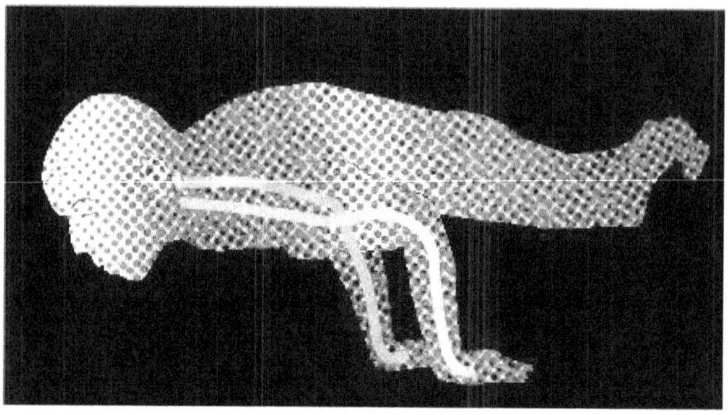

Initially one is told about the kundalini life-force and its arousal up through the spine into the brain but after that is established on a daily practice, one may advance further and infuse fresh energy into the hard-to-reach areas. It is imperative that a yogi realizes that the psyche is more than a spinal column and brain.

Verse 33

हरति सकल–रोगानाशु गुल्मोदरादीन

अभिभवति च दोषानासनं श्री–मयूरम् ।

बहु कदशन–भुक्तं भस्म कुर्यादशेषं

जनयति जठराग्निं जारयेत्काल–कूटम् ।। ३३ ।।

harati sakala–roghānāśu gulmodarādīn
abhibhavati ca doṣānāsanaṁ śrī–mayūram ।
bahu kadaśana–bhuktaṁ bhasma kuryādaśeṣaṁ
janayati jaṭharāgniṁ jārayetkāla–kūṭam ।। 33 ।।

harati – eliminates, sakala – total, roghān – diseases, āśu – rapidly, gulmodar – spleen and abdomen diseases, ādīn – and others, abhibhavati – cures, ca – and, doṣān – upset in psychological and physical physiology, āsanaṁ – posture śrī – illustrious, mayūram – peacock, bahu – much, kadaśana – bad food, bhuktaṁ – ingestion, bhasma – ash, kuryād = kuryāt = does effect, aśeṣaṁ – total, janayati – generate, jaṭharāgniṁ – digestive heat, jārayet – should absorb, kāla–kūṭam – poison drunk by Shiva

The illustrious peacock posture, totally and rapidly, eliminates the spleen and abdomen diseases as well as related ailments and any upset in physical and psychological

physiology. It totally digests much bad food. It increases digestive power and absorbs even the kālakūṭa poison drunk by Shiva. (1.33)

Analysis

The kālakūṭa poison was drunk by Shiva to remove its contamination from the Ocean of Milk. This is related in the legend of the truce between the peace-loving and hostile supernatural beings in their conjoint effort to acquire valuable beings and commodities.

Shiva became known as Nilakantha or Blue-Throat because he drank the kālakūṭa poison but did not allow it to pass below his throat. Its potency caused his neck to be blue.

The illustrious peacock posture may do wonders for the digestive process in a yogi's physical body. Still, a yogi is not primarily concerned with physical aspects. The target is the subtle body for no matter what one achieves in the physical system it is one of short duration. Focus should on the subtle form which outlasts all material forms which a particular self may develop during the manifestation of a cosmos.

Application

Physical benefits are mentioned but there are subtle psychological benefits and emotional reliefs. Any posture any human or animal can take for any reason is a yoga posture, an asana (aa-suh-nuh). Each has advantages and disadvantages. It is left to the yogi to determine which postures to execute for which reason.

Yoga is not a group effort. It is an individual practice under supervision of an advanced teacher. The individual is required to hone his or her practice to determine which postures facilitate the current objectives.

One should become sensitive and adopt postures which cause rapid advancement. It is not stereotyped. The yogi should change postures from time to time, adopting new ones or even discovering postures which he or she was never shown. By all means, a student should feel pressed for time and should approach more advanced yogis on the physical or astral levels so as to be introduced to advanced practice.

Verse 34

उत्तानं शववद्भूमौ शयनं तच्छवासनम् ।

शवासनं श्रान्ति–हरं छित्त–विश्रान्ति–कारकम् ।। ३४ ।।

uttānaṁ śavavadbhūmau śayanaṁ tachchavāsanam I
śavāsanaṁ śrānti–haraṁ chitta–viśrānti–kārakam I I 34 I I

uttānaṁ - lying down, śabavad = śavavat = like a dead body, bhūmau – on the ground, śayanaṁ – resting, tach = tad = that, chavāsanam = śavāsanam = dead man posture, śavāsanaṁ – dead body pose, śrānti – fatigue, haraṁ – eliminates, chitta – mento–emotional energy, viśrānti – restfulness, kārakam – produces

Lying on the ground like a dead body. That is the dead man's posture. It eliminates fatigue and produces restfulness in the mento–emotional energy. (1.34)

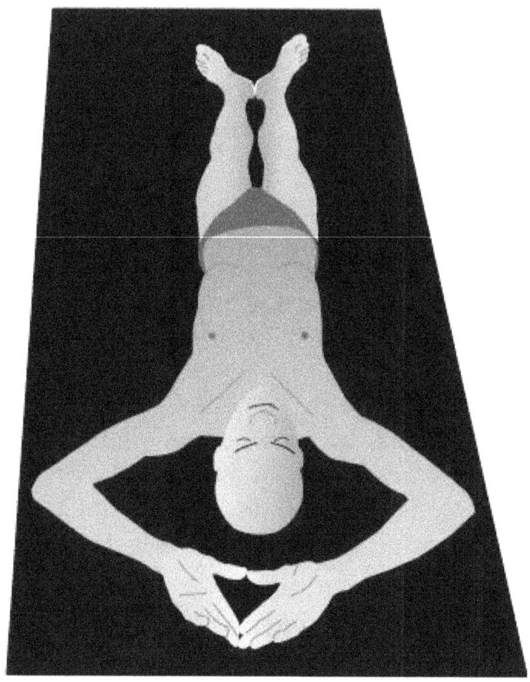

Analysis

Sleep and rest are necessary for a living being. There is no way around it. No one should be fooled by gurus who say that sleep is not a requirement. It may or may not be depending on what part of the psyche we speak of. However the psyche as a whole requires sleep. There is a question of how much sleep, as to the efficiency of sleep but on this level there is no possibility of a total removal of sleep.

A related need is rest, where the self-objectivity is not blanked out but is current and the body is put into a state of relative non-activity. Objectivity has no monopoly on existence. A self may lose objectivity but it will still continue existing.

A living being needs both sleep and rest but that should be done efficiently with the least amount of stupor. On a daily basis, a yogi should take rest, just as nature insists that one sleep within every day's duration. There are many postures in which this rest could be acquired but the shavasana dead body pose is routine for yogis. A variation of it with special benefit for the thighs, legs and feet is legs-feet-up-on-chair posture. This uses gravity to facilitate the energy which is sluggish in the thighs, legs and feet, allowing that used energy to return to the lungs for extraction of polluted gases.

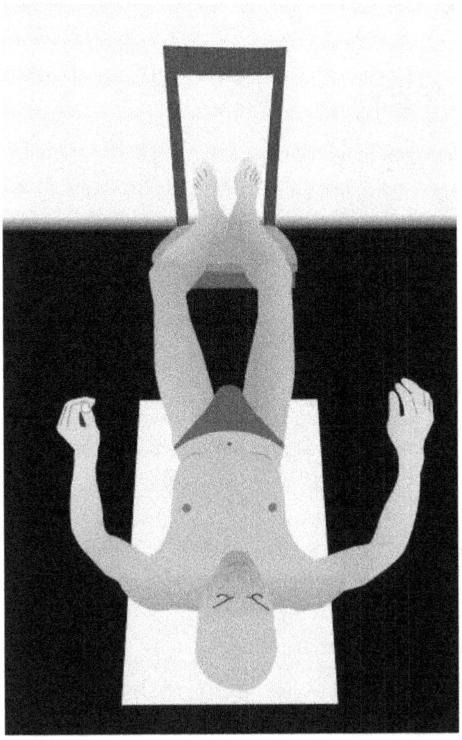

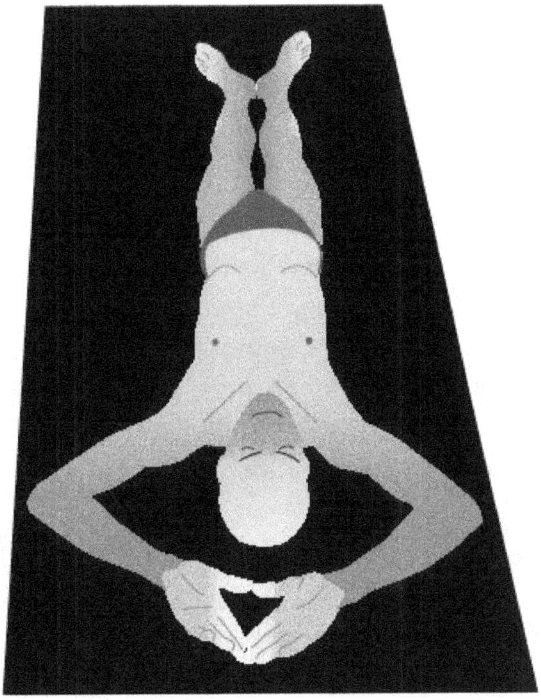

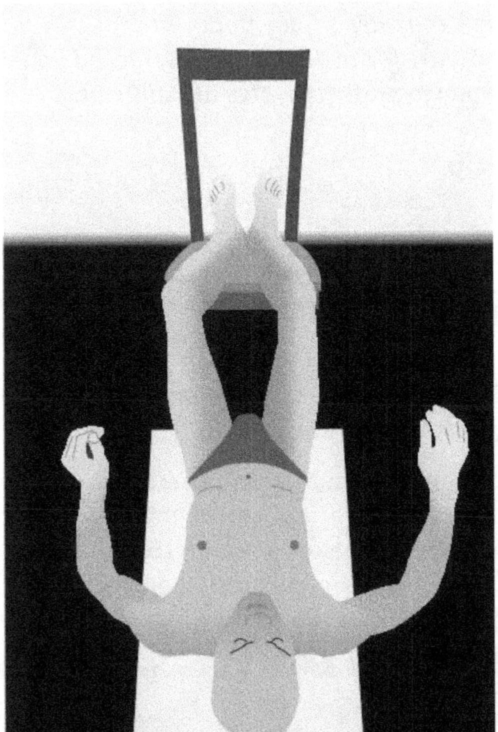

Application

Even if one does not lift a finger, if one remains in a reclined position during the waking hours of one day, still there will be fatigue in the body, because there will be activity in many cells irrespective of immobility.

One measurement of such exhaustion is the percentage of polluted gases in the blood stream. The pranayama breath-infusion practice which will be described in the next chapter, addresses that issue of removal of the exhaust energy from the subtle and gross bodies.

Rest does cause the removal of much pollution but some of it cannot be extracted except through a pulling of the polluted gases for release from the lungs.

Verse 35

चतुरशीत्यासनानि शिवेन कथितानि च ।

तेभ्यश्चतुष्कमादाय सारभूतं बरवीम्यहम् ।। ३५ ।।

caturaśītyāsanāni śivena kathitāni ca
tebhyaścatuṣkamādāya sārabhūtaṁ baravīmyaham || 35 ||

caturaśīty = caturaśīti = eighty–four, āsanāni – postures, śivena – by Shiva, kathitāni – taught, ca – and, tebhyaś = tebhyaḥ = of them, catuṣkam – four, ādāya - extracted, sārabhūtaṁ = best, bravīmy = bravīmi = describe, aham –I

Eighty–four postures were taught by Shiva. Of these, four were selected as the best, which I will describe. (1.35)

Analysis

We may assume that every posture of yoga which is known, every one which is yet to be discovered and every one which was forgotten due to a lack of transmittance through history, is either one or a variation of one of these eighty-four postures.

As legends would have it, Shiva is the master of the yogis. He and Krishna are the ultimate ascetics.

Application

Ideally, the eight-four postures taught by Shiva to Minanatha initially are the way for success of yoga. However students of the modern era may or may not master every one of these poses. It is important to do whatever is easy for the body one has picked up in this current life. Over time one can adapt the body to postures which are difficult.

Verse 36

सिद्धं पद्मं तथा सिंहं भद्रं वेति चतुष्टयम्।

श्रेष्ठं तत्रापि च सुखे तिष्ठेत्सिद्धासने सदा ।। ३६ ।।

siddhaṁ padmaṁ tathā siṁhaṁ bhadraṁ veti catuṣṭayam |
śreṣṭhaṁ tatrāpi ca sukhe tiṣṭhetsiddhāsane sadā || 36 ||

siddhaṁ – siddha perfected yogi pose, padmaṁ – padma lotus pose, tathā – and also, siṁhaṁ = siṁha lion pose, bhadraṁ – bhadra graceful pose, veti – or thus, catuṣṭayam – four, śreṣṭhaṁ – best, tatrāpi – therefore also, ca – and, sukhe – easy, tiṣṭhet – should be adopt, siddhāsane – in the perfected yogi posture, sadā – always

Siddha perfected yogi posture, padma lotus pose, and also lion pose and bhadra graceful pose are the four best postures. One should always adopt the easiest which is the perfected yogi pose. (1.36)

Analysis

These four postures should be studied in details. Beginners should assess as to whether they can adopt these or if over time the body can be trained to assume these.

If the body is resistant one should realize that one may practice easier postures. One should also know that the subtle body is not as constrained as the physical system. In dreams one may be surprised to discover that the subtle body assumes postures which are impossible for the physical one to do safely.

The perfected yogi pose is described as the easiest of those four primary postures but the question is: For whom is it the easiest?

Obviously in the time of Swatmarama, yogis found that to be the easiest but today people of other nations and ethnicities or even people of Indian birth may find what was easy to be impossible even. In the elderly years of a body, it may not do certain postures which were easy for it to assume during youth.

In rare cases a yogi improves postures in an elderly body but usually even a great yogi who practiced classical postures in their final forms, finds that as the body ages, the ability to assume some postures reduces. It all hinges on the type of human body, the environmental circumstances and the persistent will of the yogi to practice.

Application

Sitting cross-legged is the classical way to do meditation practice, because in those poses when the legs lay on each other, the body is locked in a stationary position and the spine may be kept in an erect posture.

Some yogis may sit in these postures for hours without spinal support but unless that is easy for the student, he or she should sit cross-legged but with lower back-supports so that the spine does not collapse.

Verse 37

अथ सिद्धासनम

योनि–सथानकमङ्घ्रि–मूल–घटितं कृत्वा दृढं विन्यसेत्

मेण्ढ्रे पादमथैकमेव हृदये कृत्वा हनुं सुस्थिरम् ।

सथाणुः संयमितेन्द्रियो। अछल–दृशा पश्येद्भ्रुवोरन्तरं

हयेतन्मोक्ष–कपाट–भेद–जनकं सिद्धासनं परोछ्यते ।। ३७ ।।

atha siddhāsanam
yoni–sthānakamaṅghri–mūla–ghaṭitaṁ kṛtvā dṛḍhaṁ vinyaset
meṇḍhre pādamathaikameva hṛdaye kṛtvā hanuṁ susthiram ।
sthāṇuḥ saṁyamitendriyo।achala–dṛśā paśyedbhruvorantaraṁ
hyetanmokṣa–kapāṭa–bheda–janakaṁ siddhāsanaṁ prochyate ।। 37 ।।

atha – now the description, siddhāsanam – siddha perfect yogi posture, yoni – perineum, sthānakam – that position, aṅghri–mūla – heel, ghaṭitaṁ – closely, kṛtvā – having pressed, dṛḍhaṁ – firmly, vinyaset – one should place, meṇḍhre – above the male organ, pādam – foot, athaikam = atha (then) + ekam (one), eva – even so, hṛdaye – in relation to the chest, kṛtvā – having done, hanuṁ – chin, susthiram – very firm, sthāṇuḥ – positioned firmly, saṁyamitendriyo = saṁyamita (complete control) + indriyaḥ (senses), achala – steady, dṛśā – perception interest, paśyed = paśyet = should see, bhruvorantaraṁ – inside between the eyebrows, hyetan = hi (because) + etat (this), mokṣa – liberation from material existence, kapāṭa – door, bheda – split, janakaṁ – produce, siddhāsanaṁ – siddha perfected yogi posture, prochyate – it is known as

Now, for the description of the siddha perfected yogi posture:

Press the heel of the foot firmly against and close to the perineum. Place the other foot above the male organ. Hold the chin firmly above the chest. Completely control the senses. Keep the perception interest inside between the eyebrows. This technique splits open the door to liberation from material existence. It is known as the siddha perfected yogi posture. (1.37)

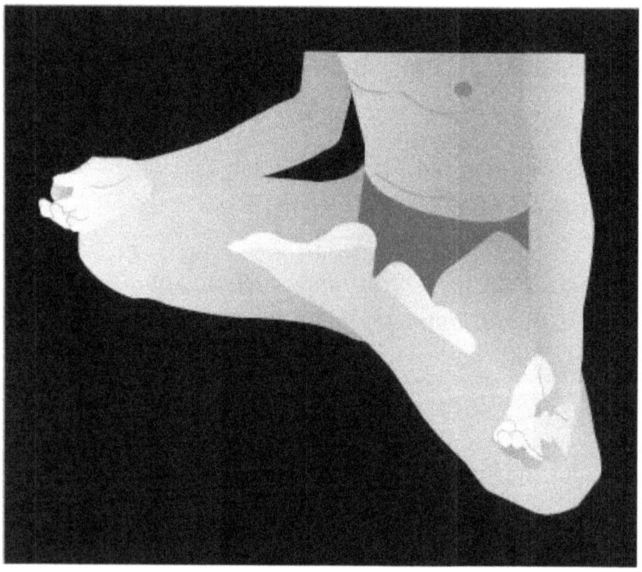

Analysis

This siddha perfected yogi posture is relatively easy to assume. In comparison to the padma lotus posture, the siddha posture is easy and does not entail a painful overlapping of the legs. However even though this posture is easy, a yogi who has not mastered the padma lotus posture cannot derive its full benefit.

This is similar to the use of money by a poverty-stricken man as compared to that for a wealthy individual. Both the poor man and the rich one may buy penny items but the poor man is strained to do so and feels a tension when he does while the rich man experiences ease and feels confident when spending small sums of money.

A yogi who can do the difficult legs-crossing padma lotus posture is at ease in the siddha perfected yogi pose. One who is not proficient is somewhat strained even in the easy siddha perfected yogi pose.

Physically a yogi's limb proportions may be such that he cannot do this posture as stipulated. This is because it depends on the genetic constitution of the body one derived from a particular family, where no matter what one does, one fails to press the heel of the foot firmly against and close to the perineum or one just cannot place the other foot above the male organ.

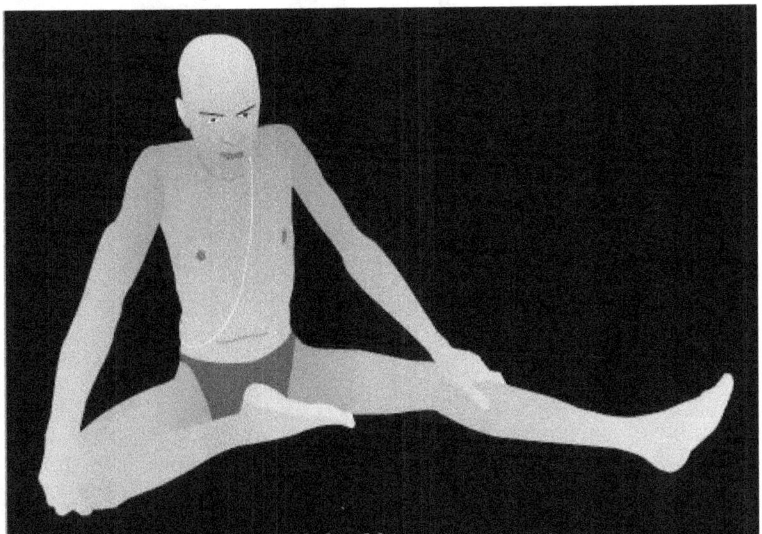

ideally first heel should rest against perineum
males use left hand to move genitals out of the way

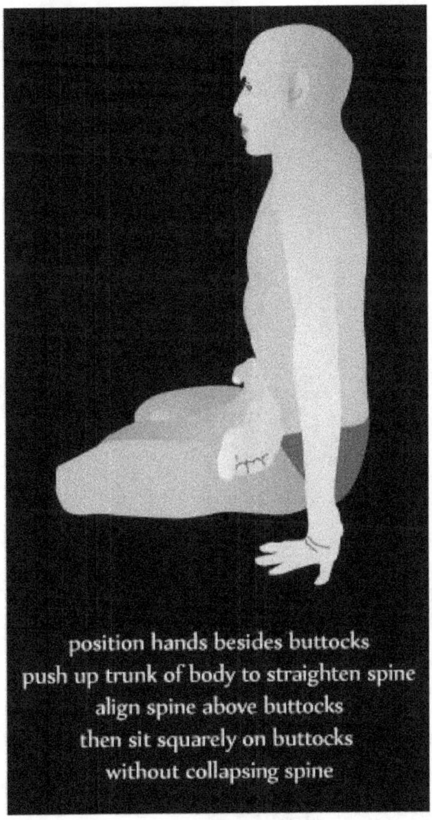

position hands besides buttocks
push up trunk of body to straighten spine
align spine above buttocks
then sit squarely on buttocks
without collapsing spine

The instruction for holding the chin firmly above the chest may be depicted with the head tilted downwards but my view is that the head should not be tilted but the chin should be drawn back tightly against the throat without tilting the head, keeping the head and neck upright.

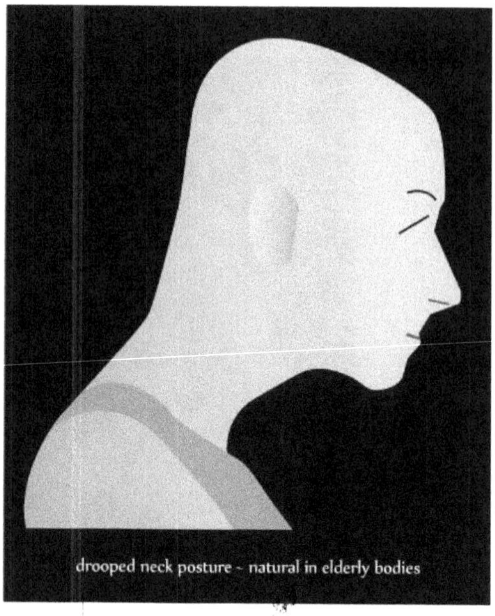

drooped neck posture - natural in elderly bodies

This diagram shows the drooped neck which is natural in elderly bodies. A yogi cannot avoid developing a skeletal situation which is similar to this but he should resist the formation of this by sitting upright during meditation and as well when sitting in chairs. A yogi should notice how people sit carelessly without regard for the upright condition of the spine. Seeing how natural it is to sit with a curved, hunchbacked, acutely-arched or drooped-over spine, he should take precautions to properly support the spine.

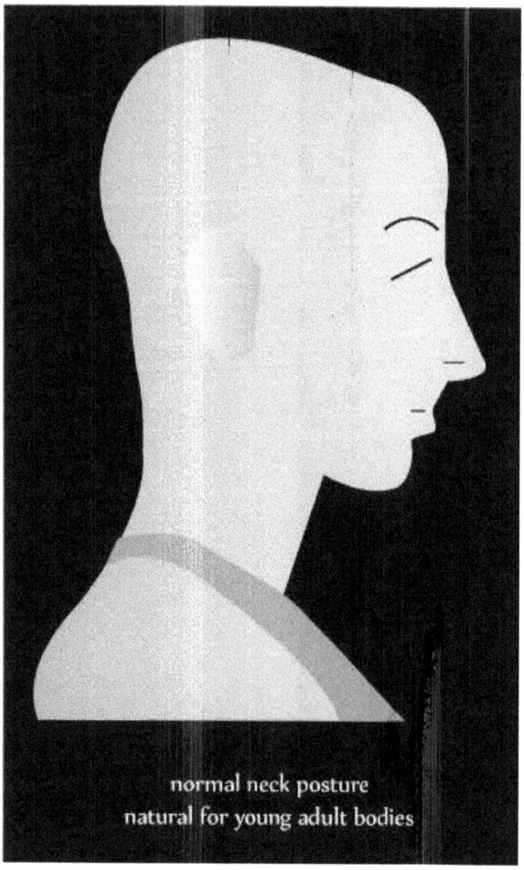

normal neck posture
natural for young adult bodies

In the diagram, the natural shape of the neck for young adult bodies is shown. This condition does not last, because as the body gets older this posture collapses. A yogi should sit and posture the body to slow down its assumption of a drooped condition just after the young adult years. Sooner or later the body, according to its genetic capacity, will become arched but a yogi should make the effort to maintain this young adult condition for as long as nature would permit it.

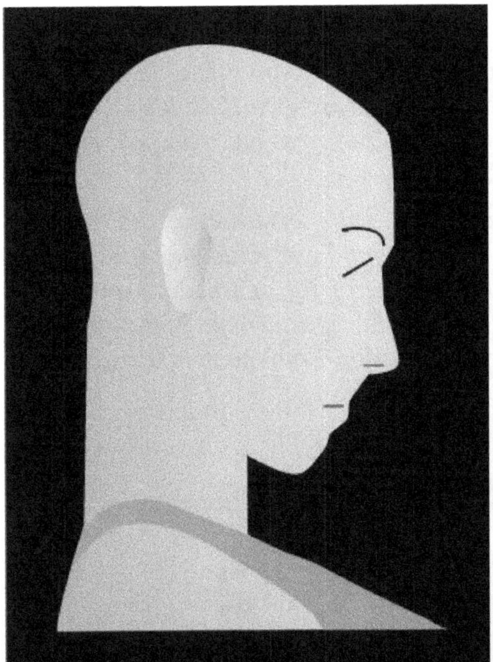

neck lock without chin lock
regulates flow of energy
through sushumna nadi central spinal passage

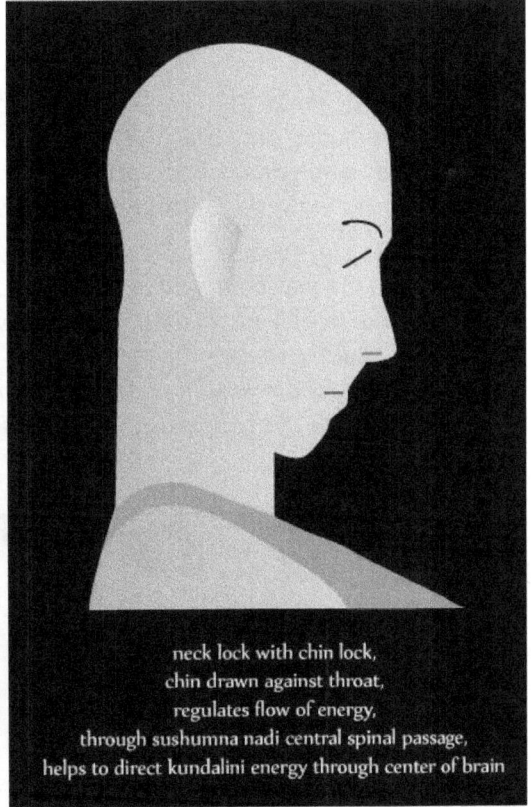

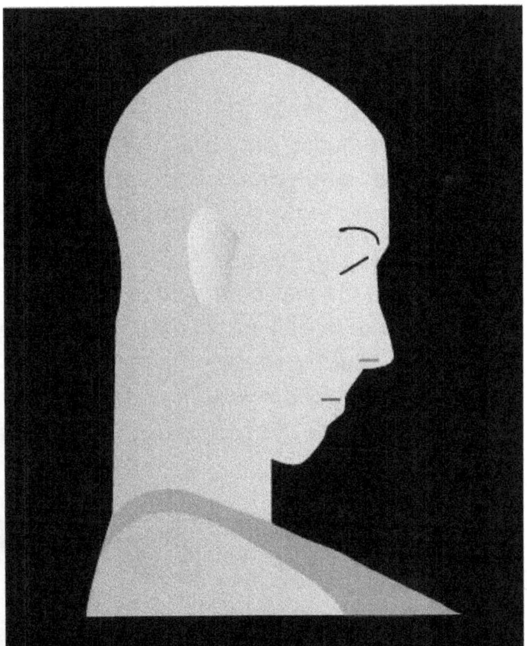

neck lock with chin lock,
chin drawn against throat,
regulates flow of energy,
through sushumna nadi central spinal passage,
helps to direct kundalini energy through center of brain

The left posture illustrates the neck lock. This lock is allied to the chin lock. They are usually applied simultaneously. As the body proceeds to the elderly years, it is more and more unable to assume this lock. Nevertheless a yogi should attempt it even up to the point of a dying old body. This locks helps in keeping the kundalini life force energy funneled through the central sushumna nadi channel in the subtle spine.

In the right posture the neck and chin locks are applied. When students begin doing bhastrika or kapalabhati breath-infusion practice, kundalini is raised. If these two locks are applied the student will have the upper hand. Otherwise kundalini will enter the brain haphazardly. The self will lose its objective control of the body, resulting in the physical form falling to the ground. These two locks when applied efficiently give the core-self the ability to manage kundalini's ascent into the head of the subtle body.

Application

Modern yoga is more about the physique of the physical body than it is about the subtle form. In fact most people doing yoga in the modern setting aim at physical results in the form of healthy body tone. However ancient yoga is more about the subtle body and the tone of the mento-emotional energy.

If one picks up nine out of ten yoga books about postures, one will get a description of the posture with a photo of someone doing the final forms with a description of the physical benefits. But that has little to do with the kind of yoga expounded by Swatmarama.

Yoga does not mean physical asana postures. Yoga includes those postures. Yoga is not indicated by a physically fit body. Physical benefits are superficial and do not necessarily indicate that the psychological aim of yoga is being fulfilled. There are many persons who can do final forms of difficult yoga postures but who have little or no inkling into the psychological gains they should derive.

Once the physical posture is secured, the yogi should shift attention to the essential part, which is the psychological achievement. In this siddha perfected yogi posture, the ascetic should switch his attention to completely control the senses by keeping the perception interest inside the head space behind the spot which is between the eyebrows. This technique splits open the door to liberation from material existence, by providing access to the chit akash sky of spiritual consciousness.

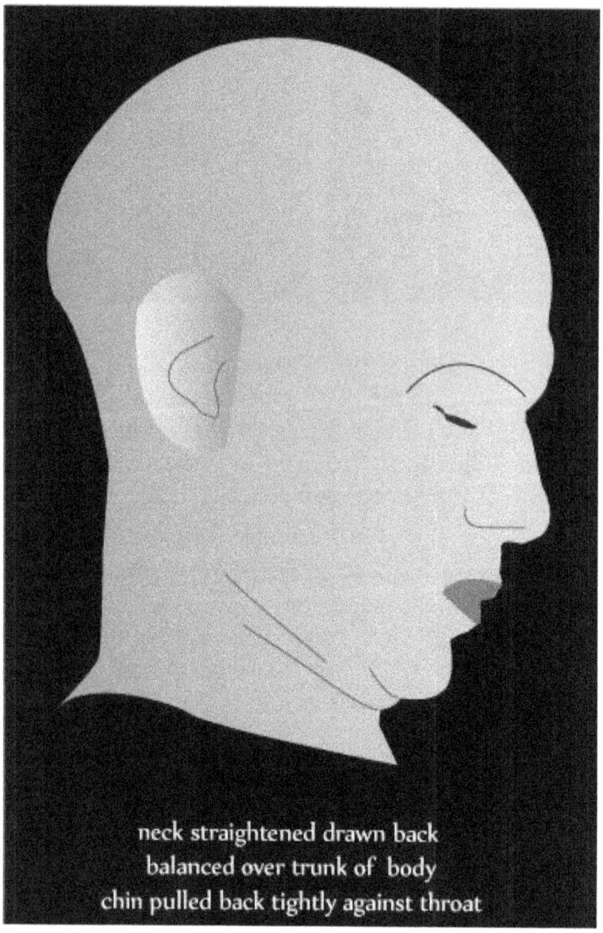

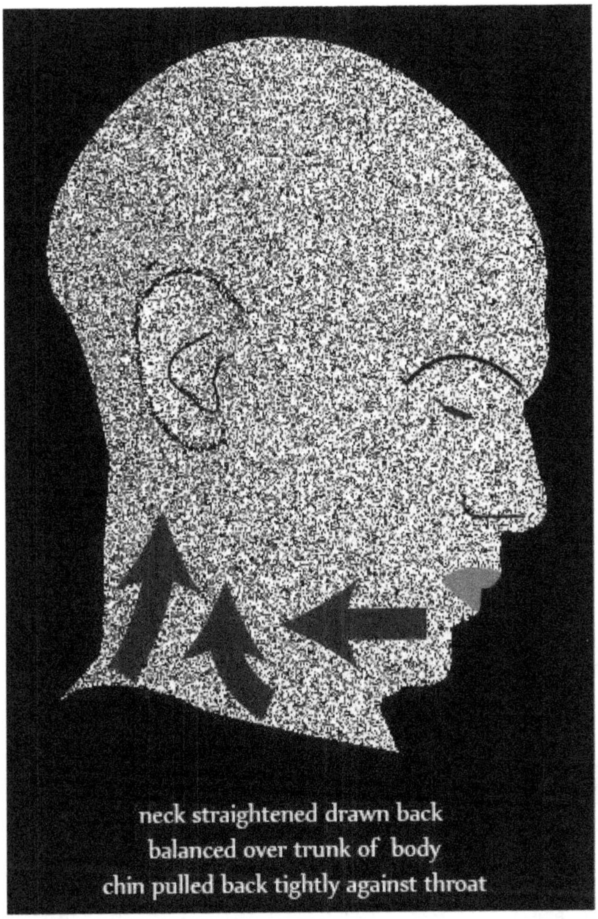

Verse 38

मेण्ढ्रादुपरि विन्यस्य सव्यं गुल्फं तथोपरि ।

गुल्फान्तरं च निक्षिप्य सिद्धासनमिदं भवेत् ।। ३८ ।।

meṇḍhrādupari vinyasya savyaṁ gulphaṁ tathopari ।
gulphāntaraṁ ca nikṣipya siddhāsanamidaṁ bhavet ।। 38 ।।

meṇḍhrād = meṇḍhrāt = regarding the male organ, upari – over, vinyasya – placing, savyaṁ – left, gulphaṁ – ankle, tathopari = tatha (even so) + upari (on top), gulphāntaraṁ = gulpha (ankle) + antaraṁ (other), ca – and, nikṣipya – putting, siddhāsanam – siddha perfected yogi posture, idaṁ – that, bhavet – is called

Placing the left ankle over the male organ, with the other ankle over that, that is also called siddha perfected yogi posture. (1.38)

Analysis

The generative organ is crucial in this practice because the purpose is to rechannel the generative fluids upwards through the body with emphasis upwards through the spine.

Hatha yoga as described in this literature is known today as kundalini yoga. If the generative fluids are not channeled away from the sexual organs, there will be partial success because the energy content in the psyche will be split between reproductive concerns and spiritual interest.

Application

It is more than physical actions. Pressure against the generative organs will not result in the necessary psychic adjustments if there is no control in the subtle body. Students who do these practices with physical expertise but who have no perception of the subtle form, and who cannot cause psychic adjustments, cannot experience the results intended.

Verse 39

एतत्सिद्धासनं प्राहुरन्ये वज्रासनं विदुः ।

मुक्तासनं वदन्त्येके प्राहुर्गुप्तासनं परे ।। ३९ ।।

etatsiddhāsanaṁ prāhuranye vajrāsanaṁ viduḥ I
muktāsanaṁ vadantyeke prāhurguptāsanaṁ pare II 39 II

etat – this, siddhāsanaṁ – siddha perfected yogi posture, prāhur = prāhuḥ = is called, anye – other, vajrāsanaṁ – vajra posture, viduḥ – know, muktāsanaṁ – mukta posture, vadanty = vadanti = they say, eke – these, prāhur = prāhuḥ = is called, guptāsanaṁ – gupta secret posture, pare – others

This is called siddha perfected yogi posture by others. Some know it as vajra diamond posture. Others say it is mukta liberated yogi posture or gupta secret posture. (1.39)

Analysis

There are many lineages. Some are ancient. Some are modern. Some are yet to be created. Each has its special process and queer terminology. Students should be broadminded enough to get to the basics, beyond the terminology and secrecy.

Application

One lineage may be secretive so that one cannot know of the techniques unless one joins the sect and toes the line of their membership requirements.

Another lineage may be open but may have very difficult techniques which even if one knew about them, one could not practice unless one was trained by someone who is proficient in it.

And yet another lineage may have one or two good techniques and much useless process which passes as genuine yoga but which is worthless.

Sometimes a yogi genius invents a new effective process. However there are no new postures in reality because whatever is required was already shown to someone either by Shiva or Krishna. Someone can, however, discover the ancient methods all over again.

Verse 40

यमेष्विव मिताहारमहिंसा नियमेष्विव ।

मुख्यं सर्वासनेष्वेकं सिद्धाः सिद्धासनं विदुः ।। ४० ।।

yameṣviva mitāhāramahiṁsā niyameṣviva I
mukhyaṁ sarvāsaneṣvekaṁ siddhāḥ siddhāsanaṁ viduḥ II 40 II

yameṣv = yameṣu = of the restraining behaviors, iva – as if, as considered, mitāhāram = mita (moderate) + āhāram (consumption), hiṁsā – non–violence, niyameṣv = niyameṣu = of the recommended conduct, iva – as if, mukhyaṁ – primary, sarvāsaneṣv = sarvāsaneṣu = of all, ekaṁ – one, siddhāḥ – subtle body perfected yogis, siddhāsanaṁ – siddha perfected yogi posture, viduḥ – know, according to

As considered, moderate consumption is the key factor of the restraining behaviors. Non–violence is the essential one for recommended conduct. The perfected yogi posture is the primary sitting procedure according to the perfected yogis. (1.40)

Analysis

The **yama restraining behaviors** govern a yogi's consumption of the physical and psychic environments. Consumption is the name of the game in this existence. It is unavoidable and cannot be curtailed completely. It is a matter of regulating the intercourse between the self and the environments.

What is the least amount of any commodity or service which is required?

The material nature is metered. There are costs for consumption. A yogi should integrate this fact, and understand that everything has a flyback. If one takes much; one will reimburse much. This should always be considered.

Whatever one is attracted to the most, what was experienced as being the most pleasurable activity, should be curtailed by an attitude of moderation. If the ascetic does not do this, his spiritual advancement will be sporadic and uncertain due to deficit flyback energies which will be released in the future.

However, an ascetic cannot control all consumption. Some of it will be forced on him and will result in costly mishaps. This occurs because material nature reserves the right to undermine a person's spiritual efforts. In so far as one needs the assistance of material nature to make spiritual advancement, material nature has the right to interfere. This is something one must live with.

The **niyama recommended conducts** are activities which either facilitate yoga or are efficient ways of social intercourse. These are piloted safely if the ascetic has a mood of non-violence towards the creation. One should be friendly with everyone even with animals, insects or vegetation.

In this place, just to survive, there is a pressing need for consumption. Still, one should be friendly to one and all and not press on in a fanatical way for commodities. Reduced consumption is the way to go for friendly dealings with people and environment but with the understanding that people are in lower life forms just the same.

Application

Moderate consumption and a non-violent posture are required for interactions on the social plane in any of these physical or astral existences. Consumption is mandatory. Violence is its corollary. Because consumption must operate, violence as its companion attribute must be enacted. How much can the violence be reduced?

A yogi has the task to be sure that he or she is engaged the least for the smallest possible consumption with its accompanying smallest rate of violence. When this is achieved the yogi can sit to meditate in the perfected-yogi posture, having consumed the least, after exhibiting the minimum violence to other living beings. With that minimal backlog of destructive acts, the yogi makes spiritual advancement.

Verse 41

चतुरशीति–पीठेषु सिद्धमेव सदाभ्यसेत् ।

द्वासप्तति–सहस्राणां नाडीनां मल–शोधनम् ।। ४१ ।।

caturaśīti–pīṭheṣu siddhameva sadābhyaset I
dvāsaptati–sahasrāṇāṁ nāḍīnāṁ mala–śodhanam II 41 II

caturaśīti – of eighty–four, pīṭheṣu – of postures, siddham – perfected yogi pose, eva – even so, sadābhyaset = sadā (always) + abhyaset (should practice), dvāsaptati – in seventy–two, sahasrāṇāṁ – thousand, nāḍīnāṁ – nadi subtle veins and arteries, mala – polluted energy, śodhanam – cleansing

Of the eighty–four (84) postures, the perfected yogi pose should always be practiced, because it results in the cleansing of the polluted energy in the seventy–two thousand (72,000) nadi subtle veins and arteries. (1.41)

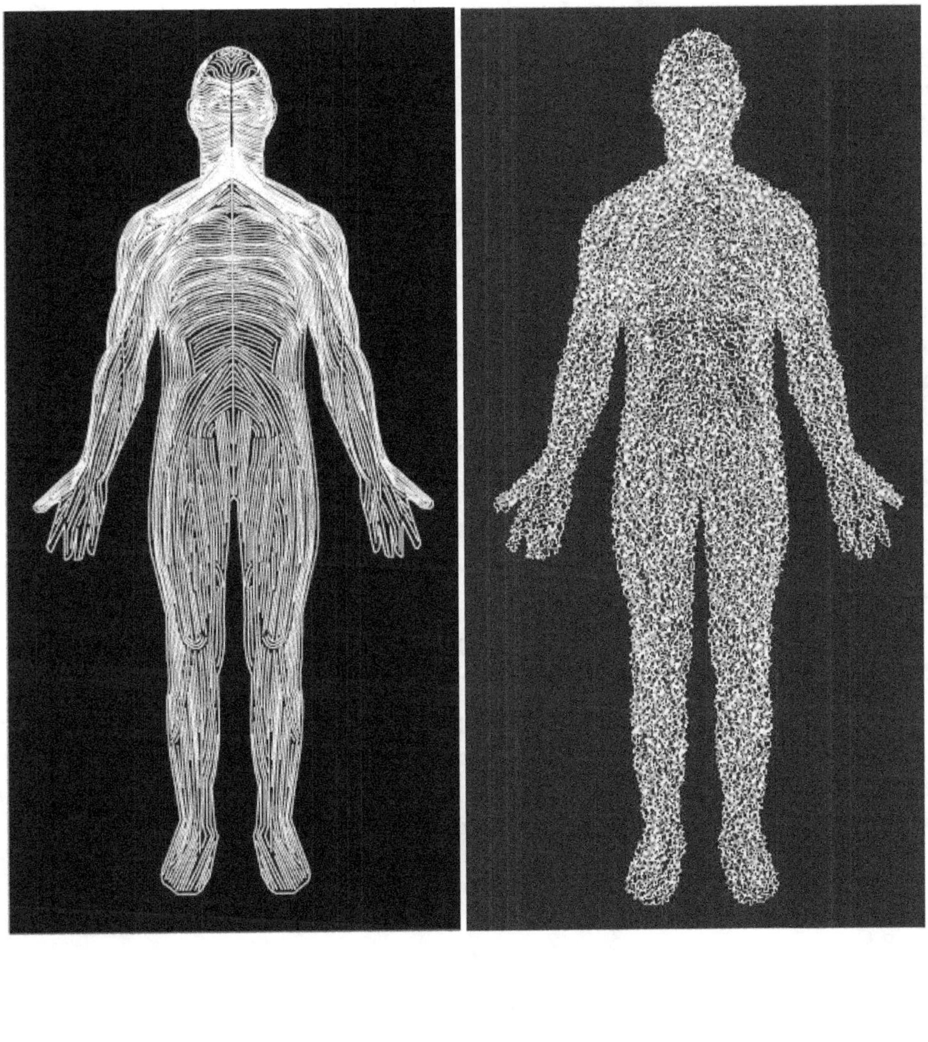

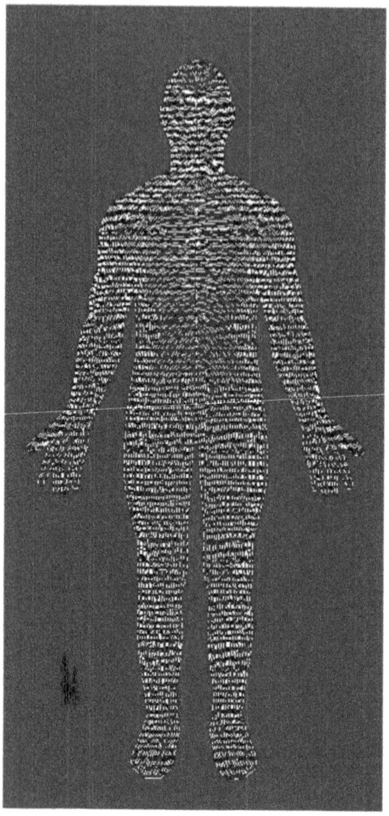

Analysis

The eight-four (84) primary yoga postures are not listed here but it should be known that there are variations of these as well as many other postures.

There is classical yoga with final forms which are ideal but which may not be practical for a specific student. Nevertheless one should do one's best to master whichever poses are easy. Gradually and with patience, one should endeavor to make the body do the ideal forms.

Ultimately it is the subtle body which is the target. That body is the one which must do the classic postures. A student should not regard the physical disciplines of yoga as the final objective.

Application

Asana postures pan out when the subtle body is cleared of polluted and low-grade astral energy. As soon as the subtle body has only clarifying astral force within it, the need for asana postures is lifted. The yogi can then sit to do pranayama breath-infusion and introspective meditation.

When the asana postures are combined with the pranayama breath-infusion, that efficient practice frees the yogi from having to make the pratyahar sensual energy effort a separate endeavor. Successful breath-infusion results in sensual energy withdrawal.

The question remains as to how a physical practice with the asana postures can cause a psychological effect in the form of cleansing the nadi subtle veins and arteries.

The answer is that the physical body is interspaced by the subtle form, which is the existential support of the physical. Hence actions to the physical form may affect the subtle body. Someone who says that he is not the physical body should not forget that his not being the physical form does not mean that he is unaffected by it.

It is more like:

I am not my physical body but I am affected by it.

More precisely, it is:

I am not the physical body but I am not the subtle one either. However, due to the way I am connected to these forms, I am affected by their conditions and behaviors.

Verse 42

आत्म–धयायी मिताहारी यावद्वादश–वत्सरम् ।

सदा सिद्धासनाभ्यासाद्योगी निष्पत्तिमाप्नुयात् ।। ४२ ।।

ātma–dhyāyī mitāhārī yāvaddvādaśa–vatsaram ।
sadā siddhāsanābhyāsādyogī niṣpattimāpnuyāt ।। 42 ।।

ātma – core–self, dhyāyī – spontaneous introspective focus, mitāhārī – with moderate consumption, yāvad = yāvat = until, dvādaśa – twelve, vatsaram – year, sadā – always, siddhāsanābhyāsād – from practicing perfected yogi posture, yogī – yogi, niṣpattim – accomplishment, āpnuyāt – becomes

Through spontaneous introspective focus on the core-self, with moderate consumption, and always practicing the perfected yogi posture for twelve (12) years, the yogi becomes accomplished.

Analysis

During the time of Swatmarama, it took twelve (12) years for proficiency. How much time will it take today without mastering the classical forms and with sloppy application of moderate consumption?

It took a minimum of twelve years just for the attainment of spontaneous introspective focus on the core-self but after mastering moderate consumption and consistently having a non-violent posture even when one's survival was threatened. What was preliminary took much longer and was achieved before reaching the advance stage where the spontaneous introspective core-self focus became the foundational level to begin meditations.

Application

By itself the perfected yogi posture cannot yield perfection in yoga. Gymnasts and others with supple limbs may do final forms. However unless there is proficiency in spontaneous introspective focus on the core-self, their achievement is not yoga.

There is also the requirement of maximum reduction of consumption through the senses and a corresponding reduction in violent behavior. This does not mean violence in the form of assault. It is violence for nutritional and aerobic purposes. For there to be a living material body either as an animal, human or vegetation, there must be violence to some other creatures, even if it is microscopic life forms. Hence the need for maximum reduction of using other life forms to sustain one's life by consuming the least and then doing the least to acquire commodities, food and air.

Verse 43

किमन्यैर्बहुभिः पीठैः सिद्धे सिद्धासने सति ।

प्राणानिले सावधाने बद्धे केवल–कुम्भके ।

उत्पद्यते निरायासात्स्वयमेवोन्मनी कला || ४३ ||

kimanyairbahubhiḥ pīṭhaiḥ siddhe siddhāsane sati
prāṇānile sāvadhāne baddhe kevala–kumbhake |
utpadyate nirāyāsātsvayamevonmanī kalā || 43 ||

kim – what? anyair = anyaiḥ = with others, bahubhiḥ – by many, pīṭhaiḥ – by postures, siddhe – in proficiency, siddhāsane – in the perfected yogi posture, sati – becomes, prāṇānile – in the flow of pranic subtle energy, sāvadhāne – attentively focalized, baddhe – restrained, checked, kevala – aloneness, complete isolation of the core–self, kumbhake – breath retention, utpadyate – arises, nirāyāsāt – effortless, spontaneous, svayam – self, evonmanī = eva (so) + unmanī (thoughtless state of mind during contact with the chit akash sky of consciousness), kalā – increment, short period of time

What about many other postures, when there is proficiency in the perfected yogi pose and the flow of pranic subtle energy becomes attentively focalized and restrained by breath retention during complete isolation of the core–self with thoughtlessness during contact with the chit akash sky of consciousness, occurring spontaneously even for short periods of time?

Analysis

For the advanced yogis, there is no more use for subsidiary postures, or for processes which are preliminary and experimental. That ascetic reached the culmination and knows what is culled out of yoga austerities.

What is the end result?

It is that the flow of pranic subtle energy becomes attentively focalized and restrained by breath-interest suspension during complete isolation of the core–self with thoughtlessness during contact with the chit akash sky of consciousness; even though initially, this happens sporadically and for short periods of time, even for seconds.

Breath-interest suspension in this case does not mean that the ascetic ceases breathing during or after an inhale or exhale. It means that the rhythmic breathing rate slows considerably due to a life-force disinterest in acquiring breath energy. At first this manifests as a drastic reduction in breath-rate.

This does not mean that the core-self lacks interest in breathing. To be clear, one should sort between the kundalini lifeforce psychic mechanism and the core-self. There are two distinct realities with different interests which are sometimes merged into one pursuit or concern. But in this kumblak breath retention, the core-self is not involved in the breath operations, either to promote, disable, or alter that. The lifeforce is involved. The lifeforce itself, which has a running interest in breath, loses that concern and becomes disinterested which causes the breath rhythm to be reduced to almost nil. Simultaneously the core-self maintains its interest in viewing or waiting to view the chit akash sky of consciousness without any interest in breath.

Application

If there is one posture, say for instance the perfected yogi pose mentioned in this verse, in which one can easily reach the culmination of yoga practice, which is to penetrate into the chit akash sky of consciousness, the divine environment, then why should a

yogi assume any other pose?

The ascetic has to begin where he is in terms of the physical posture which he can easily adopt. In time, he may progress to difficult poses. He should learn the breath-infusion methods. He should become proficient in kapala-bhati / bhastrika rapid breathing.

When he can extract all carbon dioxide from the material body, and when he can switch perception over to the subtle form and draw out the negative subtle energy, then he will begin to experience the sensual energy withdrawal which results from that. He can then do breath-infusion with special postures to target hard-to-reach places in the subtle body, places like the thighs, legs, feet, arms, forearms and fingers.

The ascetic must also take shelter in naad sound which is in the subtle body, particularly in the head of that form. When there is sufficient reliance on naad sound resonance, he can come forward in the subtle head. If he is lucky, he may see through into the chit akash sky of consciousness.

At that stage, the siddha perfected yogi posture or a similar pose is used as a mainstay to keep the physical body erect during absorbed states. Some yogis simply recline but that is not recommended unless one uses an elderly body which just cannot sit up due to infirmities.

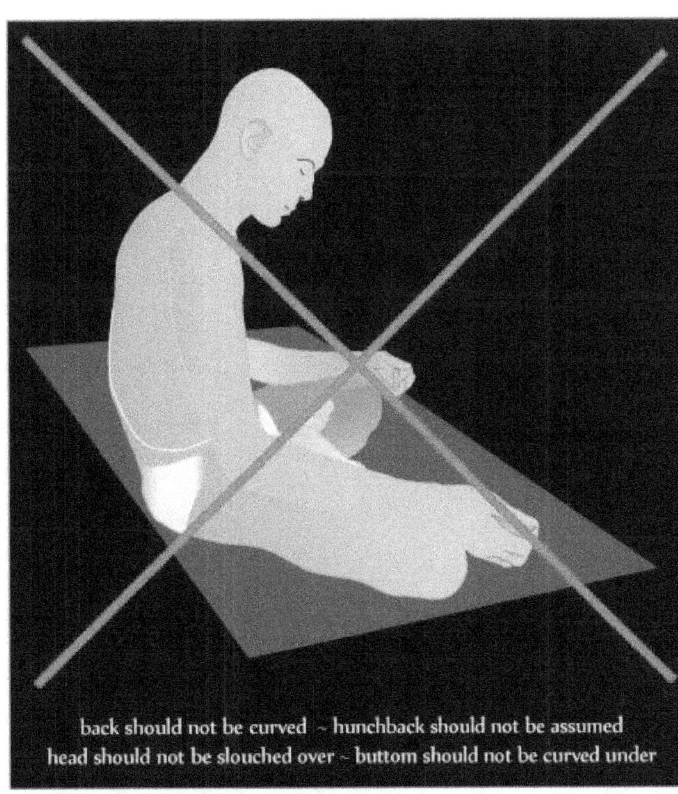

back should not be curved ~ hunchback should not be assumed
head should not be slouched over ~ buttom should not be curved under

Modern people can sit on couches with spine slightly tilted backward from the vertical and the body cushioned in the back and at the sides. This will keep the body from falling forward.

At first the yogi will find that he astral-projects when sitting in these postures. That is the indication that the lifeforce lost its anxieties about releasing the subtle from a non-reclined position. This is a positive development for the yogi, who should persist, struggling to remain conscious in the body with the focus on the naad sound resonance and the advance into the chit akash sky of consciousness.

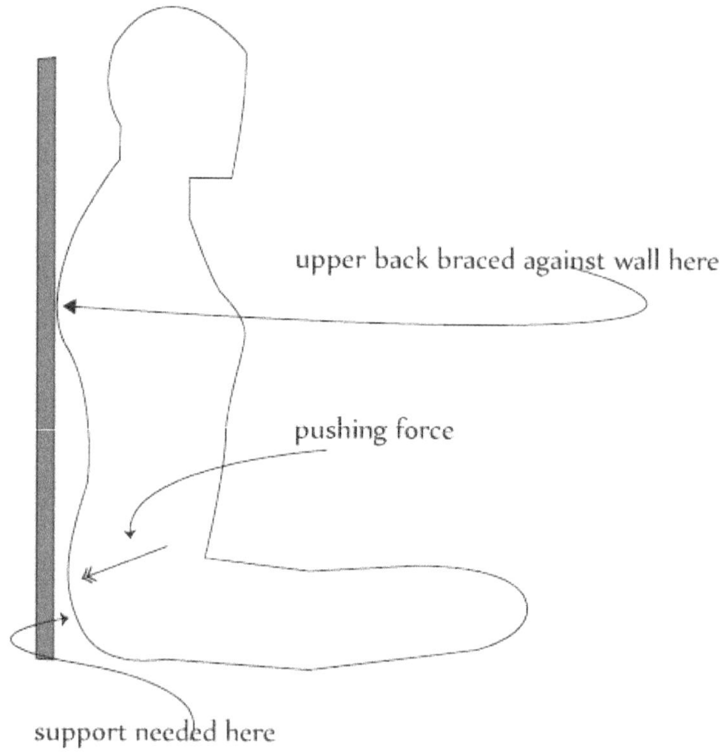
upper back braced against wall here
pushing force
support needed here

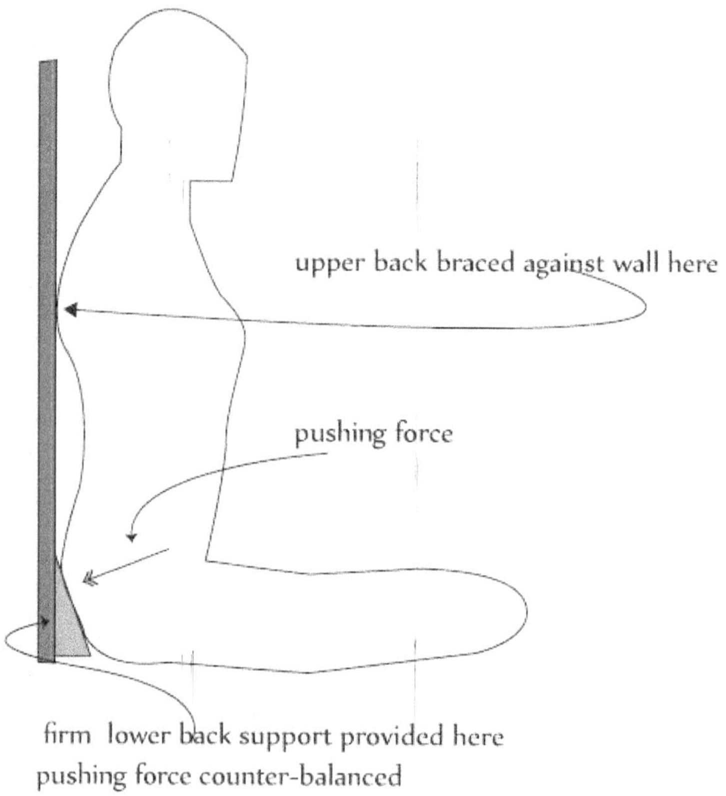
upper back braced against wall here
pushing force
firm lower back support provided here
pushing force counter-balanced

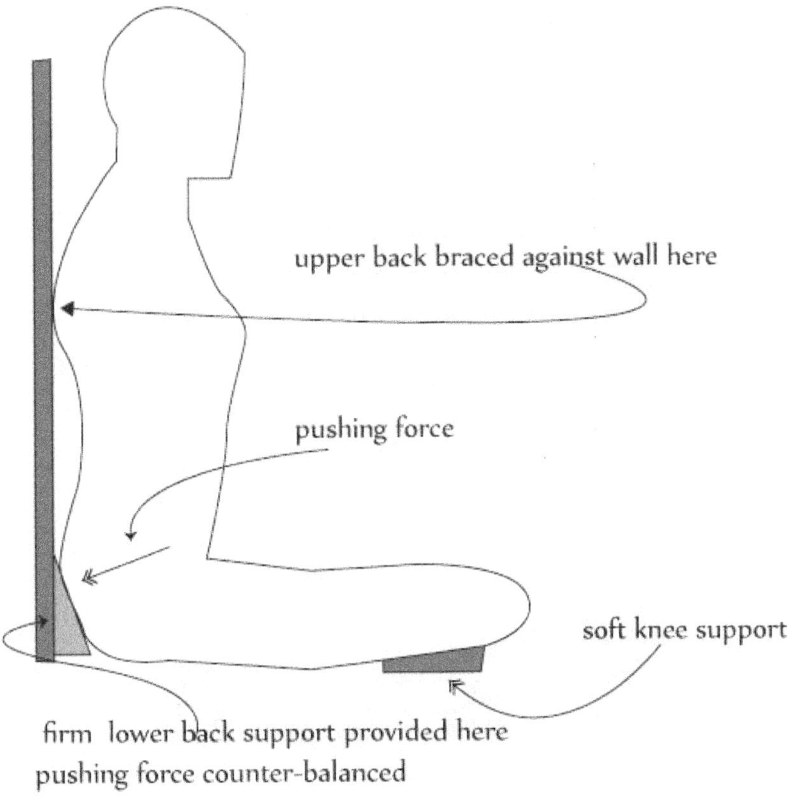
upper back braced against wall here
pushing force
soft knee support
firm lower back support provided here
pushing force counter-balanced

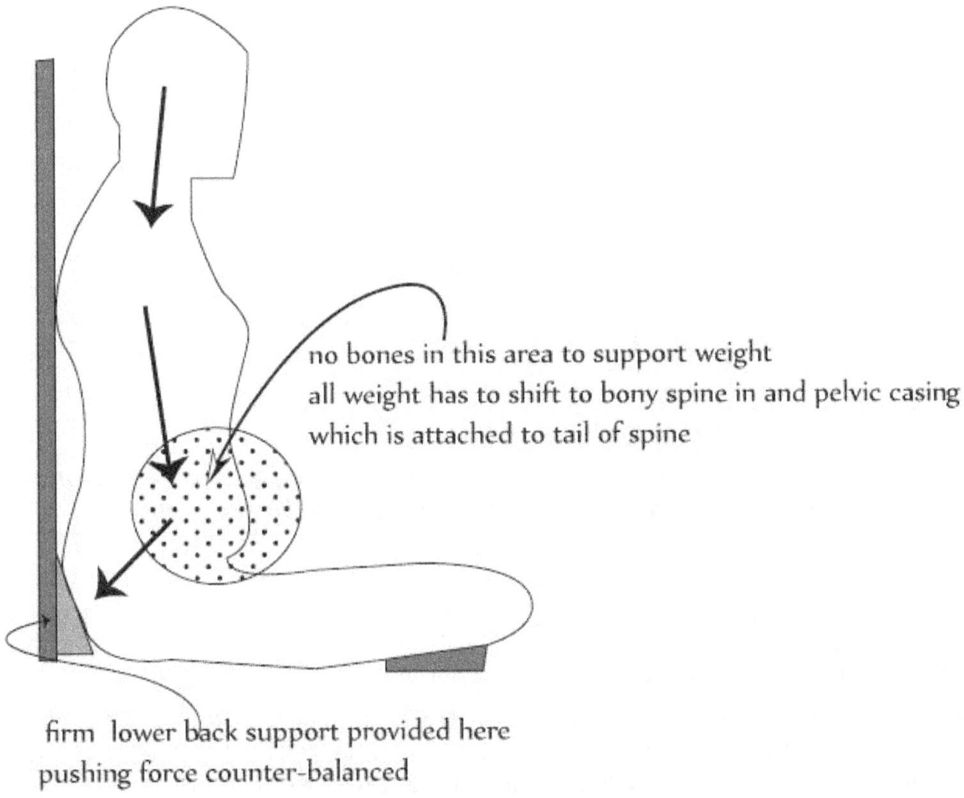
no bones in this area to support weight
all weight has to shift to bony spine in and pelvic casing
which is attached to tail of spine
firm lower back support provided here
pushing force counter-balanced

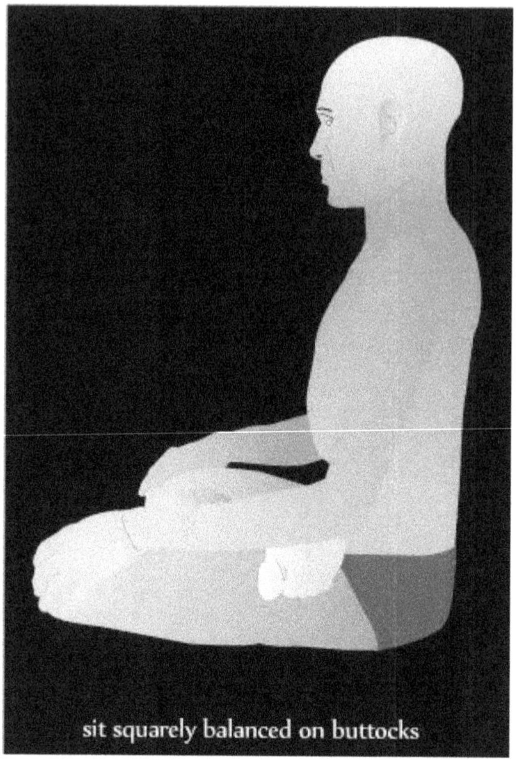

Verse 44

तथैकास्मिन्नेव दृढे सिद्धे सिद्धासने सति ।

बन्ध–तरयमनायासात्स्वयमेवोपजायते ।। ४४ ।।

tathaikāsminneva dṝḍhe siddhe siddhāsane sati I
bandha–trayamanāyāsātsvayamevopajāyate II 44 II

tathaikāsminneva = tathā (even so) + ekāsmin (once) + eva (only), dṝḍhe – in steadiness, siddhe – in proficiency, siddhāsane – in the perfected yogi posture, sati – becomes, bandha – bodily contractions, trayam – three, anāyāsāt – spontaneously, svayam – itself, evopajāyate = eva (so) + upajāyate – is performed

If even once, proficiency and steadiness in the practice of the perfected yogi posture is attained, it causes one to spontaneously perform the three bodily contractions.

Analysis

The perfected yogi posture may cause automatic contractions of the excretion-reproduction, abdomen, and neck areas of the body. These are three classic compressions which restrict and direct subtle energy.

These compressions should be learned from a proficient teacher. There is the uplift of the anal sphincter muscle with urinary and perineum pull-up. There is the navel/lower-abdomen pull-back-and-up. There is the chin pull-back-to-throat compression.

These three are the primary compressions but there are other locks which are applied during the austere practice. These cause compression and redirection of infused breath energy and kundalini aroused force.

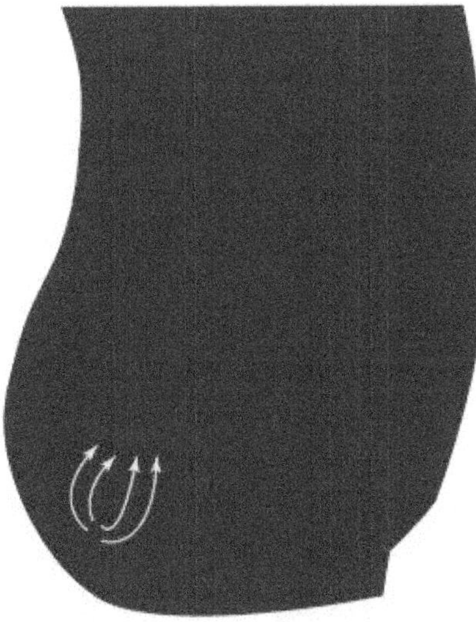

pull-up anal sphincter muscle

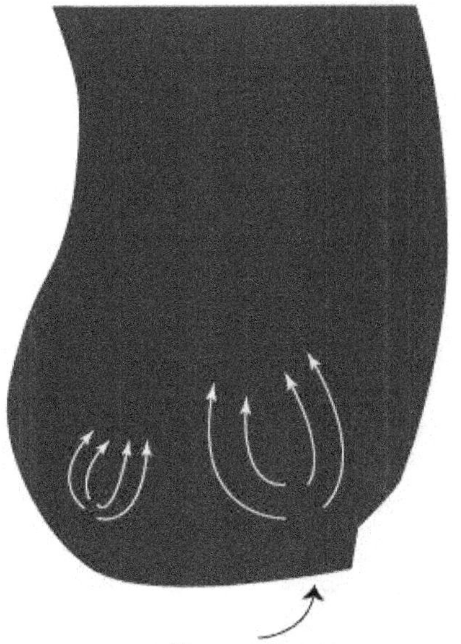

pull-up perineum and urinary muscle

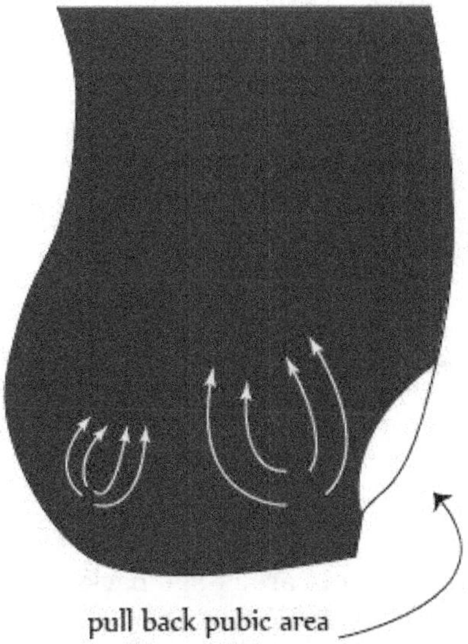

pull back pubic area and lower abdomen

The uplift of the anal sphincter muscle with urinary and perineum pull-up causes the subtle energy to gather in that area and then to be directed upwards through the spine and through the center of the subtle body. It prohibits the energy from its natural route which is through the genitals and rectum. When this is mastered, the yogi conserves vast amounts of energy which used to be funneled downwards into the genitals for charging reproductive fluids. Eventually all energy which was funneled into sexual concerns is conserved and recirculated upwards away from the genitals.

The application of the navel/lower-abdomen pull-back-and-up pressure first forces subtle energy downwards from the navel into the groin area, then it compresses energy behind the navel and in the abdomen, backwards and upwards through the trunk and spine of the subtle body.

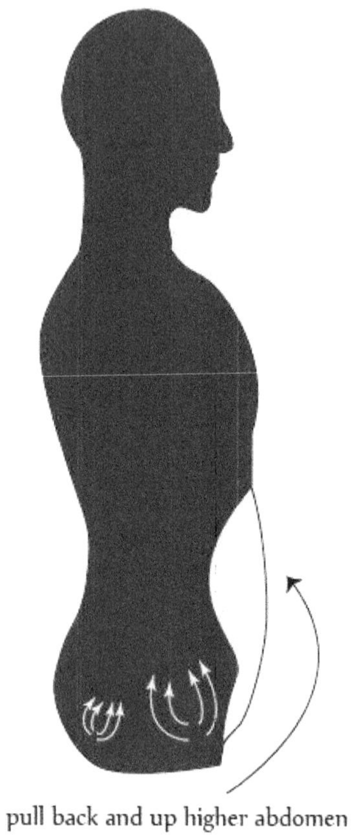
pull back and up higher abdomen

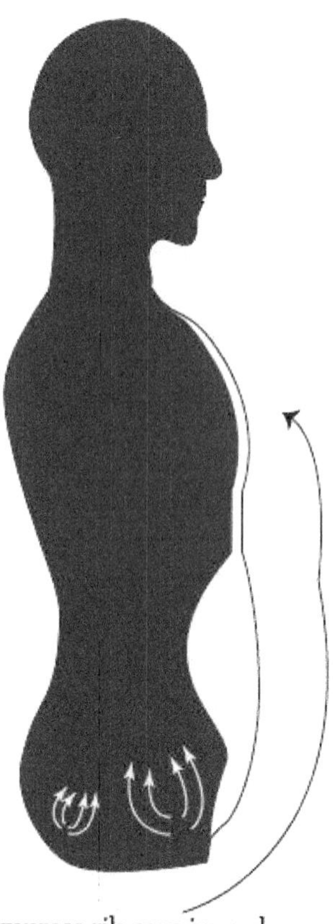
compress rib cage inward

Because the anal sphincter, urinary and perineum areas are compressed inwards and upward, the contraction of the navel/lower-abdomen region causes a backward pressure which forces any energy lingering just above the groin area to go back and up through the subtle body. This captures stray subtle energy making it go upward against the natural flow.

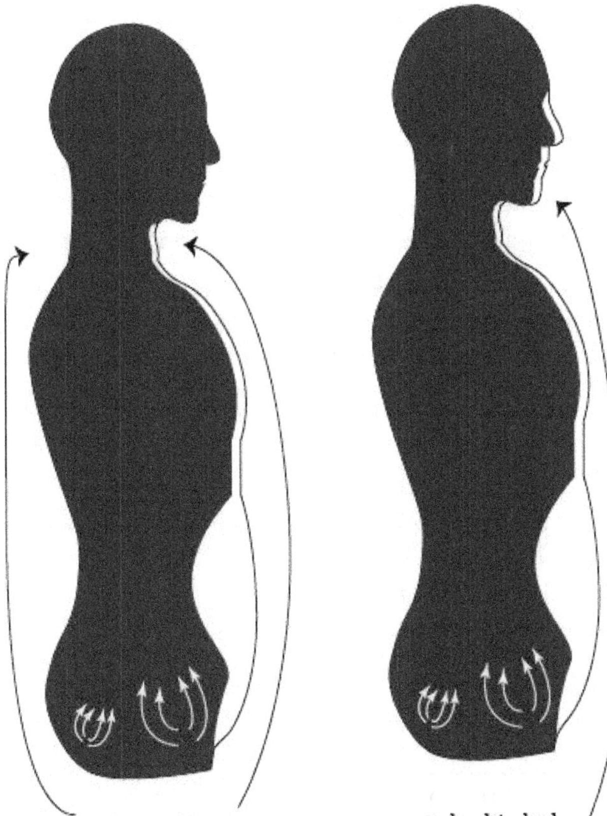
apply neck lock
by firming and straightening
vertebrate in neck
apply chin lock
by drawing chin
tightly against throat

The chin pull-back to throat compression captures the energy which comes up due to the two lower compressions. Under the neck compression, this energy becomes restricted so that it becomes centralized and passes in a disciplined way through the central spinal column in the subtle body, which is known as the sushumna nadi routing.

Application

Each student should, as supervised by an advanced yogi, study his or her psyche to determine the natural routings of the energy. All energy courses which contravene yoga should be manhandled and redirected. This should be done repeatedly until there is a permanent change in the psyche. As long as the system resists the required changes, that is how long the student should redirect and exert counter forces.

Verse 45

नासनं सिद्ध–सदृशं न कुम्भः केवलोपमः ।

न खेचरी–समा मुद्रा न नाद–सदृशो लयः ।। ४५ ।।

nāsanaṁ siddha–sadṝśaṁ na kumbhaḥ kevalopamaḥ |
na khecarī–samā mudrā na nāda–sadṝśo layaḥ || 45 ||

nāsanaṁ = na (not) + āsanaṁ (posture), siddha – perfected yogi posture, sadṝśaṁ – compared, na – not, kumbhaḥ – breath suspension, kevalopamaḥ = kevala (what is spontaneously occuring) + upamah (best), na – not, khecarī – procedure for transiting through kha divine space, samā – like, mudra – physio–psychic application technique, na – not, nāda –naad subtle sound resonance, sadṝśo = sadṝśaḥ = like, layaḥ – dissolution of mundane ideation interest

There is no posture which compares to the perfected yogi pose. The best breath suspension is that which occurs spontaneously. There is no physio–psychic application technique which is like the khecari procedure for transiting through kha divine space. There is no dissolution of mundane ideation interest like absorption in naad subtle sound resonance.

Analysis

These are the classic references used in the time of Swatmarama. For each student however these may not be the best applications because of the stage of meditation and the flexibility of the body in relation to postures.

What for me with an inflexible body is the best posture?

What about you?

What progress can I make in my circumstance and with the genetic attitude of the body I currently use?

Kumblak kevala is the condition of breath where the breath is suspended involuntarily of its own accord without a compulsion from the will power. The yogi does not stop the breath. Instead due to the state of meditation or due to doing a certain pranayama breath-infusion, the psyche goes into a mode where the breath is suspended due to the system not needing fresh air because it has an excess of fresh breath energy. This condition is simultaneous for the physical and subtle bodies.

The breath rhythm may also be reduced or temporarily suspended when there is a deficit of fresh breath energy. This happens when a living body is put under anesthesia. The same may happen to someone who is relaxed or who makes efforts to internalize the attention of the self.

Whatever happens spontaneously which is desirable for attaining deep meditation is a boon for a yogi because he or she would not have to exert any effort to bring that about.

Khecari mudra is described in chapter three of this text:

atha khecarī
kapāla–kuhare jihvā praviṣṭā viparītagā |
bhruvorantargatā dṝṣṭirmudrā bhavati khecarī || 3.32 ||

atha – now will be explained, khecarī – procedure for transiting through kha divine space, kapala – head, kuhare – throat, jihvā – tongue, praviṣṭā – pressing into, viparīta – backward, gā – go, bhruvor – between the eyebrows, antar – internally, gatā – is applied in focus, dṝṣṭir = dṝṣṭiḥ = perception interest, mudrā – mystic–arresting actions, bhavati – is, khecarī – procedure for transiting through kha divine space

> **Now the procedure for transiting through kha divine space will be explained:**
>
> **Press the tongue backwards into the throat and internally focus the perception interest between the eyebrows. This is the mystic arresting action for transiting through kha divine space. (Hatha Yoga Pradipika 3.32)**

This is more than a physical procedure. No one can get the transcendental result of this merely by doing this physically without having the mystic grasp required. This mudra or mystic arresting action is the best process for transiting through kha divine space. With it there must be naad absorption as described.

Naad absorption first quiets the mento-emotional energy which Patanjali Mahayogin instructed should be shut down completely:

yogaḥcittavṛtti nirodhaḥ

atha – now; yogānuśāsanam = yoga – yoga and its practice + ānuśāsanam – explanation

> **The skill of yoga is demonstrated by the conscious non-operation of the vibrational modes of the mento-emotional energy. (Yoga Sutras 1.2)**

Once this is energy silenced there is a lull period in which the yogi gains a footing into the naad sound resonance, which is an incubation place for developing the perception into the chit akash sky of consciousness, the divine environment.

Application

The formula is

- *special posture*
- *spontaneous breath suspension*
- *special physio-psychic application for transiting through kha divine space*
- *dissolution of mundane ideation interest by absorption in naad subtle sound resonance*

*Each aspect must be in place for success. The **special posture** is the one in which the physical body is disciplined so that it demands the least amount of attention from the core-self and the subtle body is released from having to invest interest and concern for the physical system.*

*The **spontaneous breath suspension** occurs with or without a pranayama breath-infusion practice. It is preferred that the yogi do the breath-infusion practice immediately prior to meditation so that the subtle body has an excess of fresh breath energy during the meditation session. However it is possible to have the breath suspension even if the meditator does not do breath-infusion.*

Spontaneous breath suspension is the prelude to deep meditation. Patanjali Mahayogin listed pranayama breath-infusion as the fourth stage of yoga and pratyahar sensual energy internalization as the fifth stage. When the sensual energies are folded in on the core-self, the mental and emotional stimulations slow to a halt. Then deep meditation is experienced because the surface layers of the mind became inoperative.

*The **special physio-psychic application for transiting through kha divine space** is the effort which gives direction to the freed core-self so that it maximizes the opportunity for reaching the divine levels of existence. With this directive energy, the core-self enters into naad absorption:*

*The **dissolution of mundane ideation interest by absorption in naad subtle sound resonance** is vital otherwise the yogi will have to struggle with the part of the mind which is in the frontal part of the subtle head. Such a struggle uses up vital energy which should be applied to do whatever is necessary to elevate the core-self so that it reaches the plane of existence in which it will experience divine perceptions.*

Naad sound resonance is vital as a shelter for the yogi where he can wait it out for the frontal part of the subtle head to cease its ramblings and image-display routines. Remaining in the influence of naad enhances the core-self and incubates it so that it develops divine perceptions rapidly.

Verse 46

अथ पद्मासनम्

वामोरूपरि दक्षिणं च चरणं संस्थाप्य वामं तथा

दक्षोरूपरि पश्छिमेन विधिना धृत्वा कराभ्यां दृढम् ।

अङ्गुष्ठौ हृदये निधाय चिबुक नासाग्रमालोकयेत्

एतद्व्याधि–विनाश–कारि यमिनां पद्मासनं परोछ्यते ।। ४६ ।।

atha padmāsanam
vāmorūpari dakṣiṇaṁ ca caraṇaṁ saṁsthāpya vāmaṁ tathā
dakṣorūpari paśchimena vidhinā dhṛtvā karābhyāṁ dṛḍham ।
aṅguṣṭhau hṛdaye nidhāya cibukaṁ nāsāgramālokayet
etadvyādhi–vināśa–kāri yamināṁ padmāsanaṁ prochyate ।। 46 ।।

atha – now to discuss, padmāsanam – lotus posture, vāmor = vāmoḥ = left, ūpari – over, dakṣiṇaṁ – right, ca – and, caraṇaṁ – foot, saṁsthāpya – well situated, vāmaṁ – left, tathā – and so, dakṣor = dakṣhoḥ = right, ūpari – over, paśchimena – by being behind, vidhinā – by principle, dhṛtvā – having crossed, karābhyāṁ – by the hands, dṛḍham – fixed (firm) ,aṅguṣṭhau – big toes, hṛdaye – in the chest, nidhāya – rest on, cibukaṁ – chin, nāsāgram – at the tip of the nose, ālokayet should focus, etad = etat = this, vyādhi – of diseases, vināśa – elimination, kāri – producing, yamināṁ – those who are existentially self–disciplined, padmāsanaṁ – lotus posture, prochyate – is known

Now, to discuss the padmasana lotus posture:

Properly situate the right foot over the left thigh. Then having crossed the hands in the back, grasp the big toes firmly. Let the chin rest on the chest and maintain steady focus at the tip of the nose. This is known as the lotus posture. It eliminates diseases of those who are existentially self–disciplined.

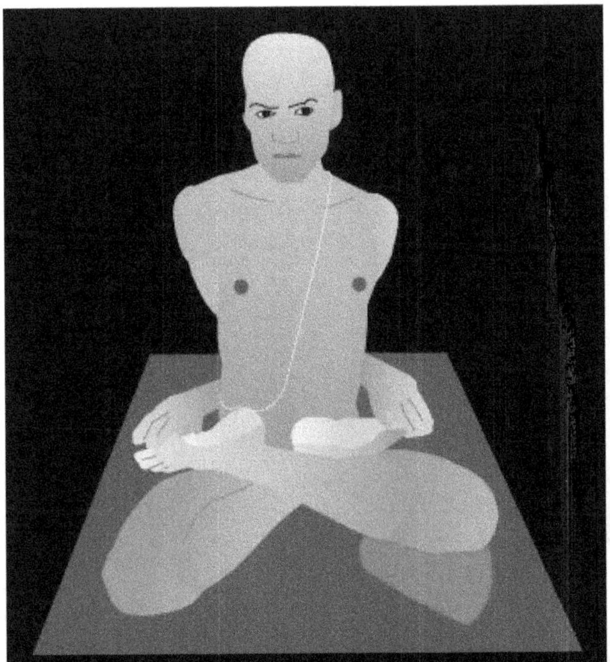

hand-wrapped padmasana lotus posture
with optional cushion under raised knee
nose focus and chin lock not shown

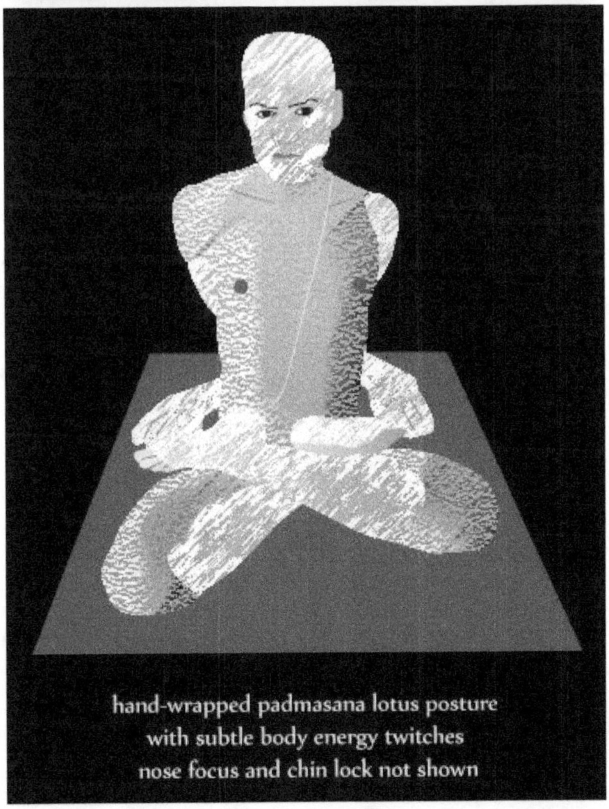

hand-wrapped padmasana lotus posture
with subtle body energy twitches
nose focus and chin lock not shown

Analysis

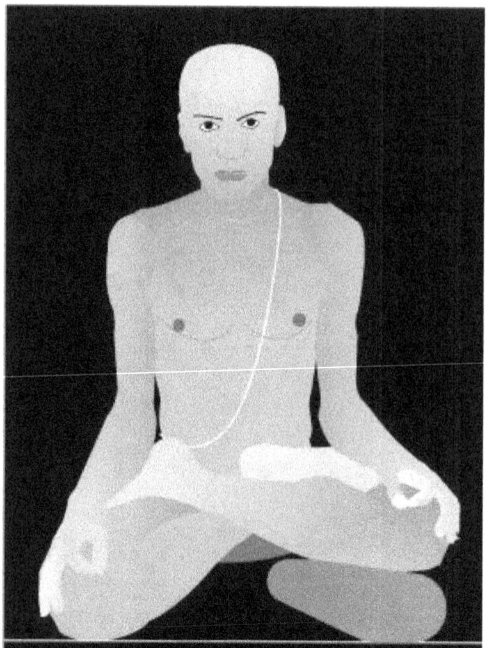

full lotus
with support for raised knee

This is a variation of the lotus posture. It is used by yogis who are advised to do it, for the purpose of bringing the wandering mind under control. Tilting the head forward is not recommended but in this posture it is part of the procedure as otherwise, the mind might wander around if the neck is erect and just the chin is pulled back against the throat.

There are two ways to do this posture. One is with the eyes closed and the focus being applied to the lower tip of the nose. The other is with the eyes open and the focus being applied to the same place. When the eyes are open, there might be felt a strain in the sinuses. When the eyes are close the student may find it difficult to locate the point which is the very tip of the nose.

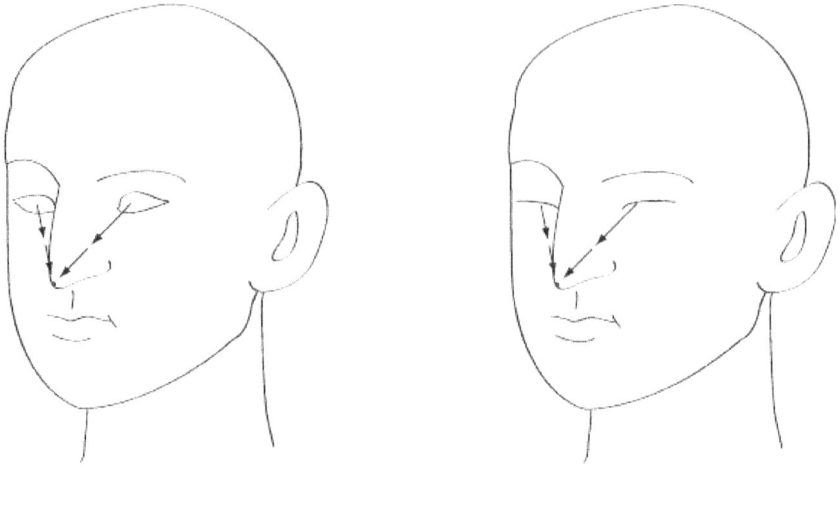

If this posture is done proficiently, it will be impossible to think of anything at the time of its performance. One will naturally begin to hear naad sound resonance.

After doing this posture for a time, if there is a strain in the sinuses or if there arises a headache, one should stop and resume it again on the same or on the following day.

After doing this posture proficiently for a time, and then hearing naad sound resonance blaring in the back of the head, the student should slowly release the core-self from staring at the tip and should retreat backwards into the naad resonance, going as deep into it as one can penetrate.

Application

Yamināṁ *or* ***those who are existentially self-disciplined*** *are the subjects of this declaration about the elimination of diseases through assumption of this posture. Unless one has a strong will and can influence the physical cells away from suicidal needs, it would not be possible to benefit in this way from this posture because the cells will resist the influence and promote undesirable habits.*

Yoga is not a cure for every ailment. Physical health is a byproduct of a proficient yoga practice but it is not the focus of a yogi. In the course of time, in the near future, within one hundred and twenty-five years for the most, the physical system will be dismantled. Then the self will be left with whatever mental and emotional energies survive in cohesion. It is practical to focus on salvaging and reforming the subtle body rather than to focus fanatically on the physical system which will be done within one hundred years.

Crossing the hands in the back and grasping the big toes firmly *causes a pressure which forces the mind to internalize and to focus down into the body while abandoning interest in objects outside of the psyche. The inner concentration of sensing consciousness increases. This inspires the yogi to take note of the components of consciousness and the relationship between the core-self and its mento-emotional adjuncts.*

Some relationships need to be sorted:

What is the relationship between the core-self and the sense of identity?

Is this one and the same energy?

How does the core-self become subjected to thoughts and mental images?

Where does memory derive its power to display itself on the screen of the mind?

What is the screen of the mind?

What should be done to increase the resistance of the core-self so that it is no longer victimized by thought patterns and mental imagery?

Verse 47

उत्तानौ चरणौ कृत्वा ऊरुसंस्थौ प्रयत्नतः।

ऊरुमध्ये तथोत्तानौ पाणी कृत्वा ततो दृशौ॥४७॥

uttānau caraṇau kṛtvā ūrusaṁsthau prayatnataḥ|
ūrumadhye tathottānau pāṇī kṛtvā tato dṛśau||47||

uttānau – soles upward, caraṇau – soles, kṛtvā – having placed, ūru – thigh, saṁsthau – placed on, prayatnataḥ – thoroughly, urumadhye – in the middle of the thighs, tathottānau = tathā (as) + uttānau (palms upward), pāṇī – hands, kṛtvā – having directed, tato = tataḥ = then, dṛśau – eyes, vision energy

With the soles upwards, having placed the feet on the thighs, place the palms of the hands in the middle of the thighs. Then direct the vison energy.

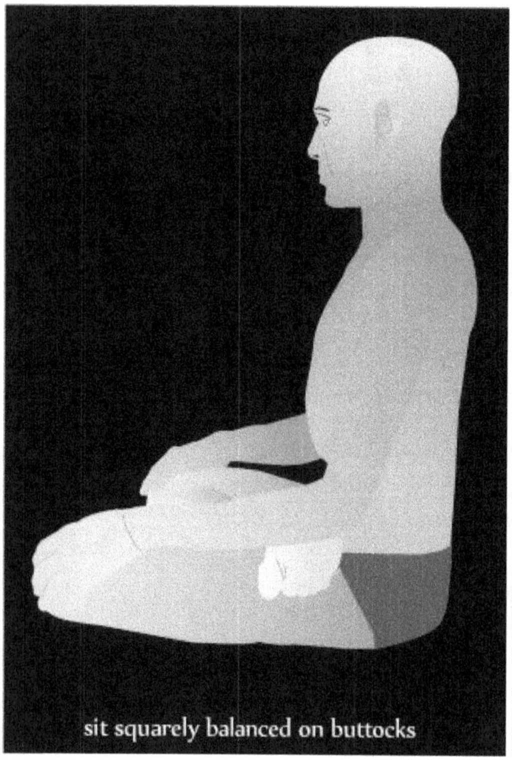

sit squarely balanced on buttocks

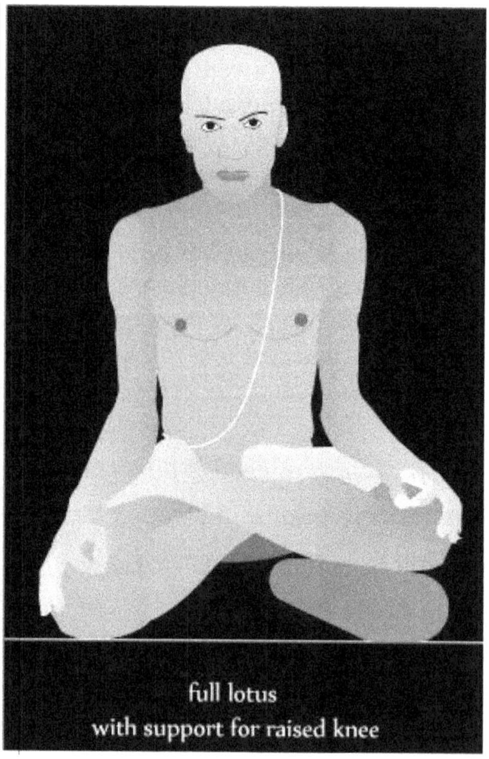

full lotus
with support for raised knee

Analysis

This is a variation of the lotus posture where the yogi assumes this posture easily and then directs the vision energy.

Where does he or she direct that energy?

This depends on the stage of advancement of the yogi and also on the instructions given by the yoga teacher. It varies from person to person depending on the stage of advancement and the lineage involved.

Curbing of the vision energy is an absolute must, because otherwise the yogi will never perceive the chit akash sky of consciousness. In the human form, the vision energy is the chief energy leakage out of the psyche. It is a major cause of lack of psychic perception. The more one uses the vision energy in reference to the material world and the lower astral regions, the more one is blocked from mystic perception, which means one will have less and less faith in supernatural and spiritual realities.

For success in yoga each of the five sensual energies must be shut down, so that their coursing outward from the psyche is curtailed. If this is done for a sufficient time the yogi will develop supernatural perception and could get experience of the divine world.

Application

In the padmasana lotus posture, the neck and head remain erect. The spine may or may not be braced. For persons with a stress-free spine there may be no need for support but it does not hurt to support the lower back and to set the body so that the back is braced and tilted backward slightly from its center of gravity.

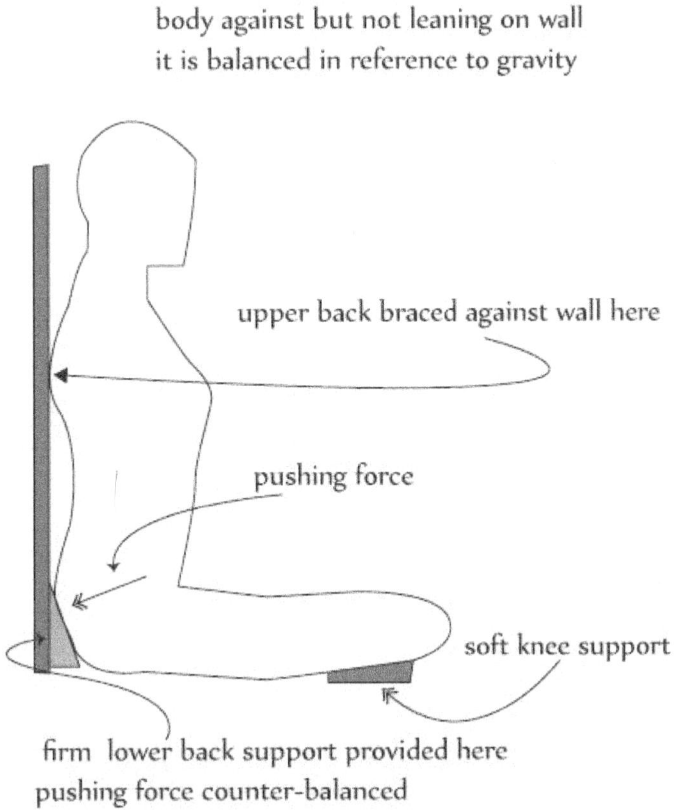

body not against wall - it is centered on lower trunk
due to larger support-cushion, body it floats without contact to wall

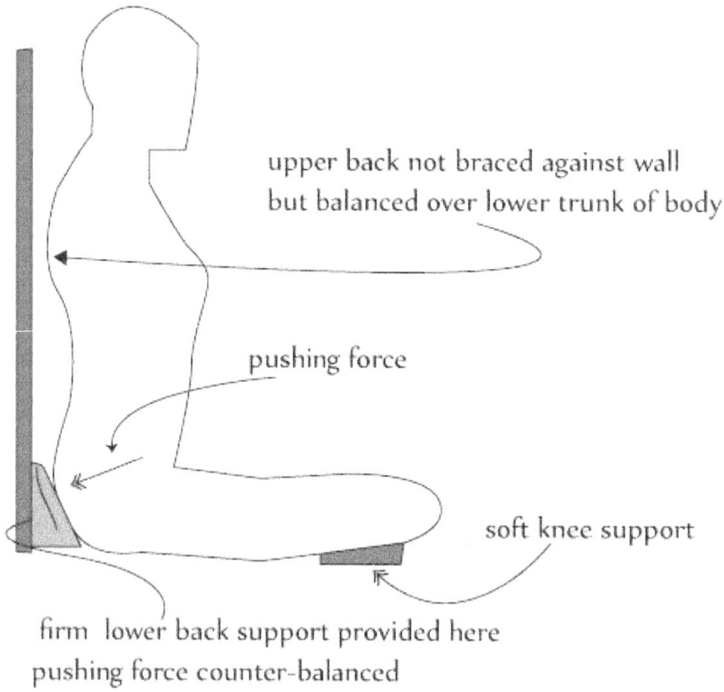

upper back leans to wall

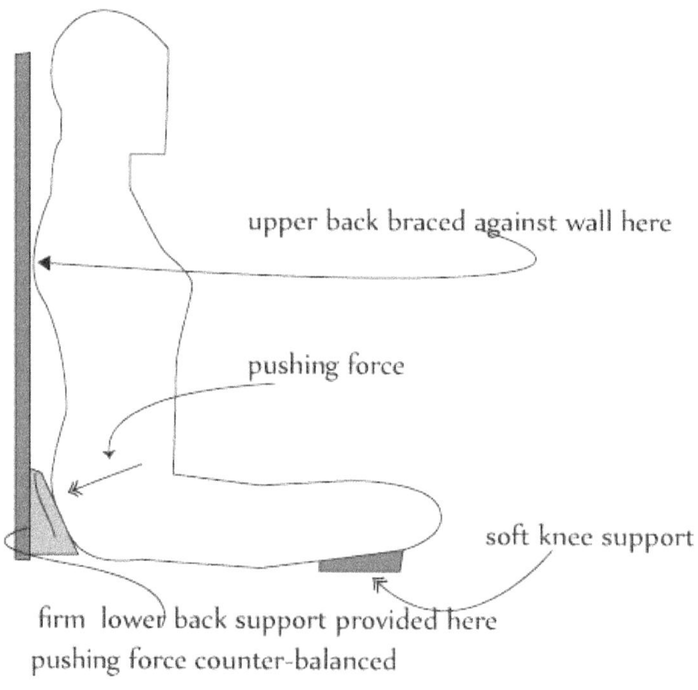

It is very important that the lifeforce be free from anxieties regarding spine collapse and head drooping. If the lifeforce is confident that the spine will not collapse and that the head will not droop, it will release itself from tensions. This will in turn cause easy release of the subtle body from the gross form, even if the subtle one remains interspaced in the gross.

The lifeforce should be relieved of having to procure fresh air. This is not an absolute necessity but it is recommended as pranayama breath-infusion is a section of the yoga process, as its fourth part. We should conclude that ancient yogis found it expedient to do breath-infusion immediately before meditation. They did this for a very solid reason which is that breath-infusion seals the deal for the fifth stage which is pratyahar sensual energy withdrawal.

When I sit to meditate after doing a thorough session of breath-infusion, I find that my sensual energy is already folded inwards. I do not have to endeavor to achieve that.

Sitting to meditate for a minimum of twenty minutes and spending fifteen minutes fighting with the outward sensual push is not efficient. If I do breath-infusion for say half hour, and then I sit to meditate, I find that my sensual energies are folded in and have no interest in anything external to the psyche.

The vision energy is special in this practice, for as soon as one accomplishes sensual energy withdrawal, and one is anchored or absorbed in naad sound resonance, the next step is to express the vision energy towards the front of the subtle head. If when this is expressed the mind resumes its usual trashy thoughts and imaging, then one should abandon the attempt to peer into the sky of consciousness and should resume the naad absorption with no interest in the frontal part of the subtle head. But if when one peers forward, one finds that the mind remains without trashy thoughts and images and that it remains calm or that it has opened to the chit akash sky of consciousness or to a supernatural level of existence which is higher than the lower astral planes, then one should keep peering forward. However one should not assume the usual sensual hunting method, because if one does so, the mind will again shift to a lower plane of consciousness so that it can resume its trashy habits.

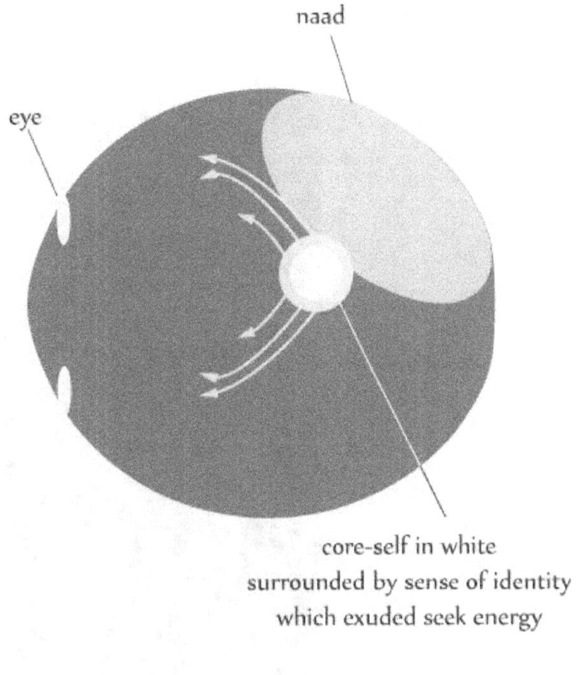

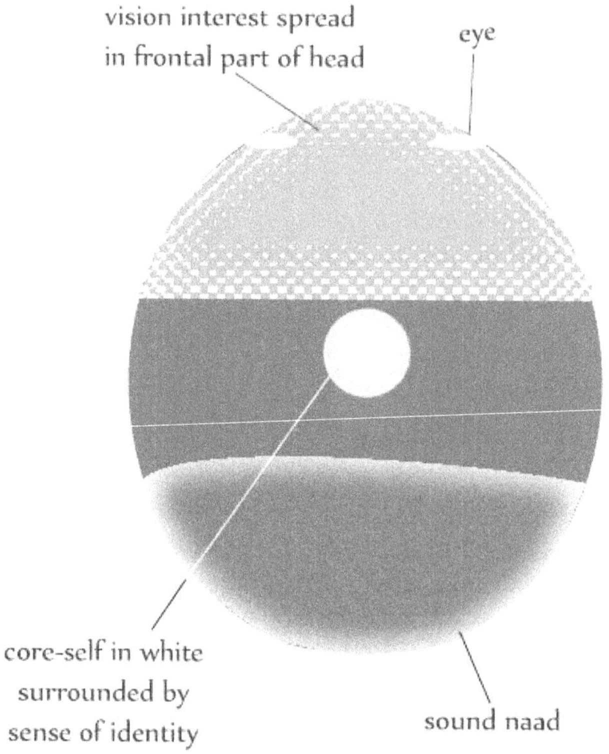
vision interest spread
in frontal part of head
eye
core-self in white
surrounded by
sense of identity
sound naad

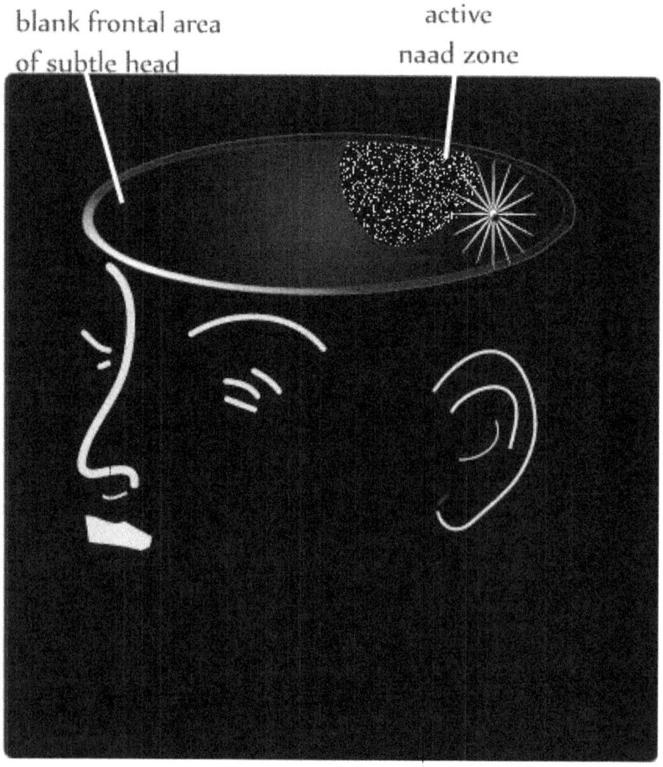
blank frontal area
of subtle head
active
naad zone

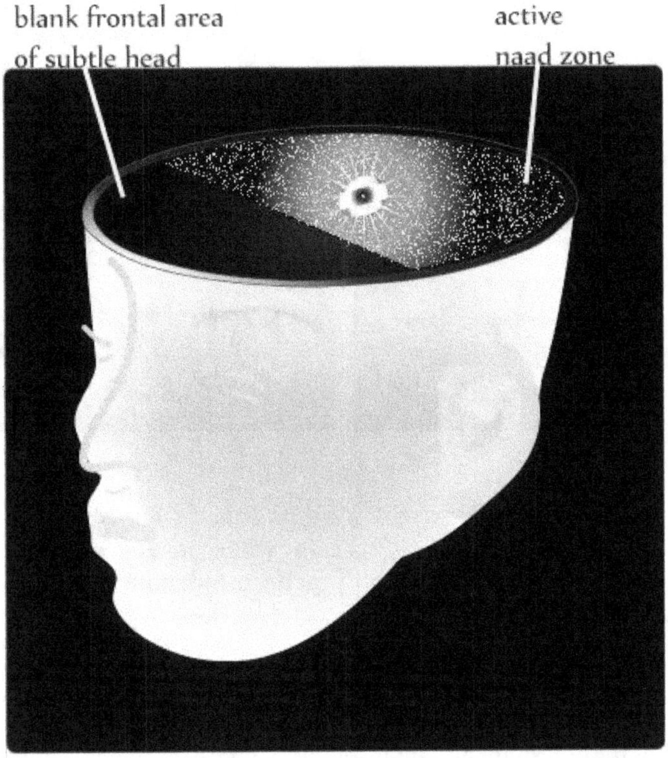

Verse 48

नासाग्रे विन्यसेद्राजद–अन्त–मूले तु जिह्वया ।

उत्तम्भ्य चिबुकं वक्षस्युत्थाप्य पवनं शनैः ।। ४८ ।।

nāsāghre vinyasedrājadanta–mūle tu jihvayā ।
uttambhya cibukaṁ vakṣasyutthāpya pavanaṁ śanaiḥ ।। 48 ।।

nāsāghre – on tip of nose, vinyased = vinyaset = should place, rājadanta – teeth, mūle – on the root, tu – but, jihvayā – tongue, uttambhya – against the chest, cibukaṁ – chin, vakṣasy = vakṣasi = on the chest, utthāpya – raised, pavanaṁ – air-energy in the blood stream, śanaiḥ – gradually

Focusing the attention on the tip of the nose, with the tongue pressed against the root of the teeth, with the chin drawn against the chest; gradually raise the air-energy in the blood stream upwards.

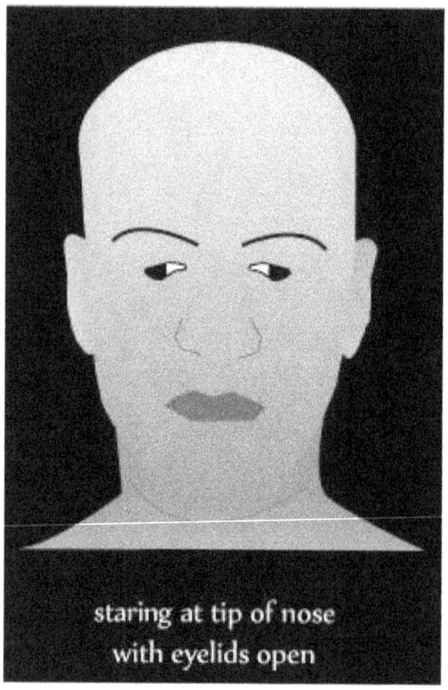

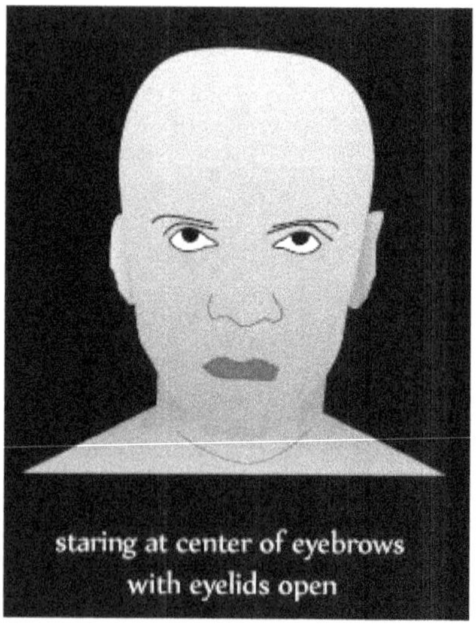

Analysis

This practice is for a yogi whose psyche is responsive to his will. This does not mean wishful thinking or even visualization. This is for when the yogi's energies does what he desires. It usually happens to a yogi who practiced for many years and reformed his psyche into submission to his will power.

The air energy in the blood stream operates as the body requires according to the genetic inclinations of the particular form. This is why a python can remain underwater for over fifteen minutes while a human being cannot do so without special air access. The body of the python has an air-in-blood signature which maintains muscular efficiency even when there is deprivation of fresh air for several minutes. The transit of air from the atmosphere through the lungs and into the cells of the body, as well as the removal of waste air from the cells through the lungs into the atmosphere is conducted according to the design of the species form.

A yogi can work in yoga austerities to make small changes in the attitude of the cells so that over time, these increments would add up to observable adjustments.

Imagination and visualization are not a part of this because visualization even if it is effective for a time will suffer from severe reversals because material nature will disregard it. A yogi has to push for incremental adjustment by using special physio-psychic techniques (kriyas) which adjust the system physically and psychically.

The transit of air through the body is on a conveyor belt system with the heart being the motor for moving the air-laden fluid. The lungs serve as the loading and unloading dock for the fresh and used air. The heart keeps moving the plasma even if the lungs fail to load or unload the fresh or waste gases. If the heart stops then the lung exchange ceases which means that the lungs become disempowered and cannot load or unload due to a lack of movement of the air in and out of the system.

A yogi can increase the quantity of fresh air which is absorbed into the blood stream. He may also increase the amount of polluted gas which is extracted from it. This will result in a surplus of fresh air with a resulting absence of polluted gases. When this happens, if the yogi sits to meditate, the kundalini lifeforce will be disinclined to breathing and may considerably reduce the air transit and blood flow rhythm. This is termed as kevala kumblak or spontaneous breath suspension. This causes the kundalini lifeforce system to lose its anxious attitude, and liberates the mind for deep meditation.

Application

There are two popular techniques used for the tongue but even so there are others which are unknown and which are used by yogis who either discover or are told about them by advanced teachers.

The first popular method is the curling up and back of the tongue where it is pushed into or passes the soft palate. The second method is to push the tip of the tongue against the upper or lower teeth. Usually it is pushed straight towards the lower teeth. The benefits from either of these methods vary from yogi to yogi and even from stage to stage in the case of the same yogi. Initially a yogi may get a certain benefit or no observable result, then at a more advanced stage the same action with the tongue may produce a completely different feature.

I got the technique of curling the tongue back from Yogi Arthur Beverford who was introduced to it by Rishi Singh Gherwal Mahayogin. I used this technique during meditation for many years with varying results depending on the stage of practice and the advancement accomplished.

The technique of pushing the tongue into the front teeth was unknown to me. I discovered that my body did it spontaneously during samadhi trance states.

I would do breath-infusion, sit to meditate, observe that the sensual energies were shut down, become absorbed in naad sound, enter into a high level of consciousness and lose awareness of the physical body. When this higher state would fizz out, I would become aware of the physical body with its head and neck erect or collapsed, with the head dropping forward or to the left or right.

I would then begin the process of repossessing the brain and nervous system. Then when the energy from the core-self would spread through the body, I would find that my tongue was pushed against the lower front teeth and was very stiff in that position. I would instinctively without thinking about it, pull the tongue backwards to relax it into its normal position but then I would feel a stinging sensation because some of the tongue which was squeeze through the small spaces between the teeth, would be pinched when it was pulled back.

After this occurred time and time again, I decided not to pull the tongue back instinctively but to push the tongue forward first, pull it down and then to pull it back slowly. This causes a reduction in the pain felt because of the parts of the tongue which pulled back through the narrow slits between the teeth, not being pinched as much as it was pulled directly back

I found that when the tongue was curled up and pushed back into the soft palate, it would remain stiff in that position, become relaxed there or simply resume its normal position when I came out of samadhi trance states.

However during meditation where there is trance state with awareness of the physical body, I found that a subtle energy flowed through the tongue past the soft palate and on through the back of the neck to the bottom back of the brain. This goes to where the naad sound is heard in the back of the head of the subtle body.

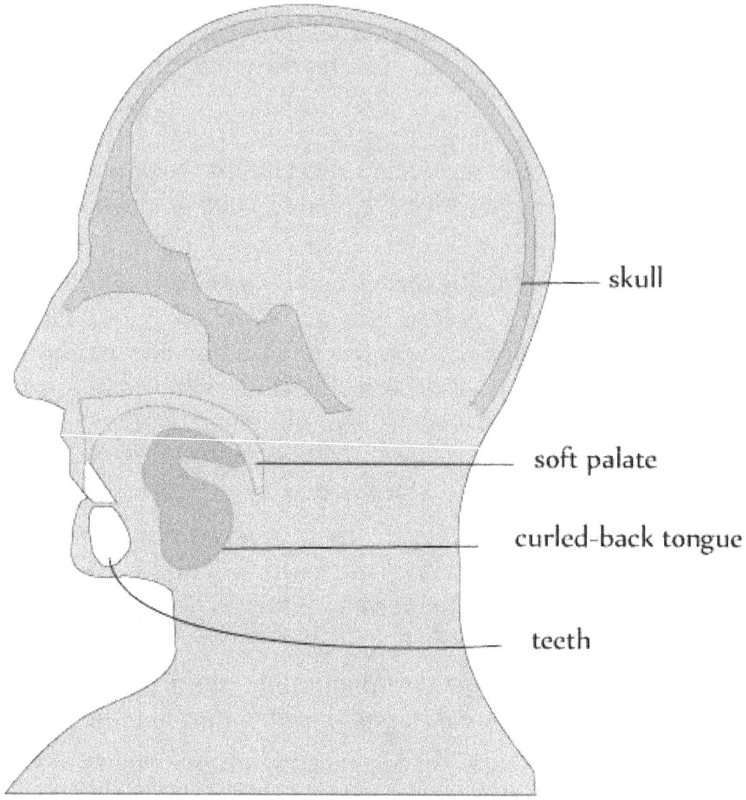
skull
soft palate
curled-back tongue
teeth

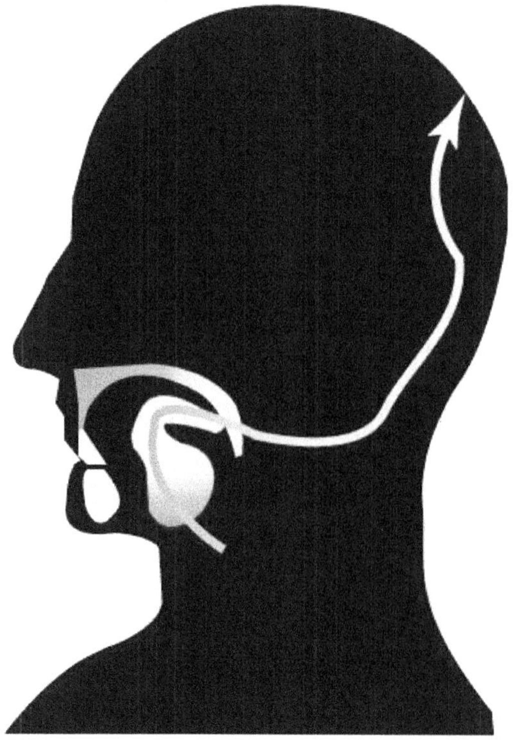

A yogi cannot raise the air-energy in the blood stream upwards merely by imagining that it does so or by visualizing that this will happen. Breath-infusion is the method of doing this because once fresh air is infused into the lungs it is transited through the blood stream by the pumping action of the heart. This is a real action and not an imaginative one which feels good to the mind but which has no real impact to the physical or psychic bodies.

As soon as a yogi does breath-infusion, the heart responds because the brain gives a signal for the heart to accelerate the movement of the infused fresh air through the system, to move the stockpiled air cells away from the lungs for distribution through the body. This is an actual activity as compared to a visualized one.

The drawing of the chin against the throat is the neck lock for constricting and directing energy through the neck in an organized way through the sushumna nadi central spinal passage. This is important for making the infused breath energy to be compressed and to pass into the brain in a way which does not cause headache or dizziness, and which deters the tendency to blackout replacing that with a perceptive objectivity of higher states.

Verse 49

इदं पद्मासनं परोक्तं सर्व–वयाधि–विनाशनम् ।

दुर्लभं येन केनापि धीमता लभ्यते भुवि ।। ४९ ।।

idaṁ padmāsanaṁ proktaṁ sarva–vyādhi–vināśanam |
durlabhaṁ yena kenāpi dhīmatā labhyate bhuvi || 49 ||

idaṁ – this, padmāsanaṁ – lotus posture, proktaṁ – is called, sarva – all, vyādhi – disease, vināśanam – that which destroys, durlabhaṁ – difficult to master, yena – by anyone, kenāpi – also by those, dhīmatā – people with insight consciousness, labhyate – is learnt, bhuvi – in the world

This is practiced while in the padmasana lotus posture. It destroys all disease and is difficult for anyone to master. In this world, it can be learnt by persons with insight consciousness.

Analysis

Yoga without insight consciousness is fake yoga. Still, even a fake process may be beneficial to one and all for physical health and mental balance for counteracting stress and negative anxieties. Yoga is for targeting the subtle body, for achieving the first step in the process of having a material form, which is to secure a foothold in the hereafter before that physical form dies. People with insight consciousness are the ideal students of yoga. They can use whatever physical methods yoga affords to come to the right conclusion about the physical body, which is that it is temporary but it has value and can be used to objectify insight awareness.

The physical form has many flaws. It is ridden with risks but it has that one asset which is that it may be used for realizing the mental and emotional energy which powers it. If this mento-emotional energy can be understood, if it can be segregated from its alliance with the physical, there could be the realization of it here and now. This would bring on confidence in the hereafter by ongoing psychic experiences which are the same as the after-death reality.

With the removal of the insecurity regarding survival of death, the student yogi would then switch interest to discover if there is more than one dimension for transit after death.

If there are multiple hereafter locations, what would be required to access the preferred ones?

Is there a location where there is no perishable condition, where sufficiency is continuous for every type of life form?

Application

The lotus posture and any of its variations, such as the siddha perfected yogi pose, were assumed for long hours of sitting while the subtle body desynchronized from the physical one, even when the subtle body remained interspaced with the physical system.

If one reclines one may also experience the subtle body in segregation from the physical one but it is likely that one will be overcome by stupor and sleep.

The kundalini lifeforce is more apt to cooperate with a yogi if the physical body is upright, especially if it is balanced or propped so that there are no stress points along the spine and no strains because of weight shifts in reference to gravity. Even if one's body cannot assume the lotus posture, one should still respect it as the ideal pose.

Verse 50

कृत्वा सम्पुटितौ करौ दृढतरं बद्ध्वा तु पद्मासनं

गाढं वक्षसि सन्निधाय चिबुकं धयायंश्च तच्चेतसि ।

वारं वारमपानमूर्ध्वमनिलं परोत्सारयन्पूरितं

न्यञ्चन्प्राणमुपैति बोधमतुलं शक्ति–प्रभावान्नरः || ५० ||

kṛtvā samputitau karau dṛḍhataraṁ baddhvātu padmāsanaṁ
gāḍhaṁ vakṣasi sannidhāya cibukaṁ dhyāyaṁśca taccetasi।
vāraṁ vāramapānamūrdhvamanilaṁ protsārayanpūritaṁ
nyañcanprāṇamupaiti bodhamatulaṁ śakti–prabhāvānnaraḥ || 50 ||

kṛtvā – having, samputitau – in cavity (concave area), karau – hands, dṛḍhataraṁ – steadily, baddhvā – being tightly restricted, tu – and, padmāsanaṁ – lotus posture, gāḍhaṁ – firmly, vakṣasi – on the chest, sannidhāya – placing, cibukaṁ – chin, dhyāyaṁś = dhyāyaṁ = spontaneous focus, ca – and. tac = tat = that, cetasi – on the consciousness, vāraṁ vāram = repeatedly, apānam – waste physical and subtle gases, ūrdhvam – upwards, anilaṁ – fresh physical and subtle air, protsārayan – infuse, pūritaṁ – inhaled, nyañcan – going down, prāṇam – fresh air, upaiti – acquires, bodham – spiritual insight, atulaṁ – exceptional, śakti – kundalini psychic lifeforce, prabhāvān = prabhāvāt = illumination, naraḥ – person

Having the hands formed into a concave configuration, and restricting the legs into a tight lotus, keeping the chin pulled against the chest, maintaining spontaneous focus on the consciousness of that self, and repeatedly pulling up the waste physical and subtle gases, infusing and pushing down fresh air, a person acquires exceptional spiritual insight by the illumination of the kundalini psychic lifeforce.

Analysis

The up or down turning of the hands, where the hands rest on or off the body, relates to mudra hand gestures. These should not be done merely in imitation after seeing a proficient yogi in a certain pose. Either one should get instructions from the teacher or one should adopt hand displays as inspired by the energy or level of consciousness one reaches during practice.

When sitting in lotus posture or a variation of it, and meditating, the hands have an effect either to enhance the meditation or to put a damper on it. Much energy radiates through the hands. When the hands touch in one way or the other, energy passes from one side of the body to the other.

In the astral world I was told by Srila Yogeshwarananda that as a general rule, the hands should not touch during meditation, because a current of energy will flow from one hand to the other. This is not an absolute advice; just a general instruction. There are occasions when touching the hands enhances meditation. Therefore the yogi should be flexible and open to be inspired in what to do during a specific session.

Śakti prabhāvān is the **illumination of the kundalini psychic lifeforce**. It pushes the focal consciousness of the meditator to a higher plane from which direct perception of the supernatural and spiritual realities becomes possible.

By pulling up the waste physical and subtle gases and infusing and pushing down fresh air, the subtle body is shifted to a higher plane giving the yogi exceptional spiritual insight.

The kundalini lifeforce is a drag on the spiritual energy of the core-self but if the lifeforce is motivated efficiently, its drag potential decreases with a corresponding surge in the core-self which then conserves more of its energy. If the self shifts its interest away from the mundane reality and the lower astral levels, it would develop supernatural perception.

Application

These practices or kriyas are complicated, whereby the student must master various phases and then use a combination of disciplines on various levels to apply. Consider this:

- *hands form into a concave configuration*
- *legs into a tight lotus*
- *chin pulled against the chest*
- *focus on the consciousness of that self*
- *pulling up the waste physical and subtle gases*
- *infusing and pushing down fresh air*
- *illumination of the kundalini psychic lifeforce*

Each discipline should be mastered before the person sits to meditate. Or it should be mastered just as the person sits to meditate.

Verse 51

पद्मासने सथितो योगी नाडी–द्वारेण पूरितम् ।

मारुतं धारयेद्यस्तु स मुक्तो नात्र संशयः ।। ५१ ।।

padmāsane sthito yogī nāḍī–dvāreṇa pūritam I
mārutaṁ dhārayedyastu sa mukto nātra saṁśayaḥ I I 51 I I

padmāsane – in lotus posture, sthito = sthitaḥ – seated, yogī – yogi, nāḍī – nadi subtle veins and arteries, dvāreṇa – by the orifice, pūritam – infused, mārutaṁ – fresh air, dhārayed = dhārayet = should spontaneously focus, yas = yaḥ = who. tu – but, sa – he, mukto = muktaḥ = is liberated, nātra – not present, saṁśayaḥ – doubt

The yogi who is seated in the lotus posture, who has spontaneous focus due to having infused fresh air into the nadi subtle veins and arteries through the breath openings, is liberated. There is no doubt about this.

Analysis

Pranayama breath-infusion practice is the sure way to accomplish the fifth stage of yoga automatically so that meditation can begin in earnest as soon as the student sits to explore the transits which the psyche is capable of providing.

Astral projection helps in self-realization because through it one gets to understand what it would be like to exist without a physical form. However astral projection is the movement of the subtle body in the subtle world, in that psychic environment.

Psyche meditation, inSelf Yoga™, is different because it is not concerned with the movements of the astral body in the lower astral regions. It researches the transits available from within the psyche, within the astral body without that body moving here or there in the subtle domains. While in astral projection the astral body moves about in the astral world, the way the physical body becomes mobilized on the earth; deep meditation in the subtle body results in mobility through dimensional transfer without the subtle body moving anywhere in the astral domains.

The astral body is not the only transit vehicle for supernatural movements. Rather, within the astral form there are tools of perception and transit accesses through which the yogi can move about in the subtle, super-subtle, causal and divine realms.

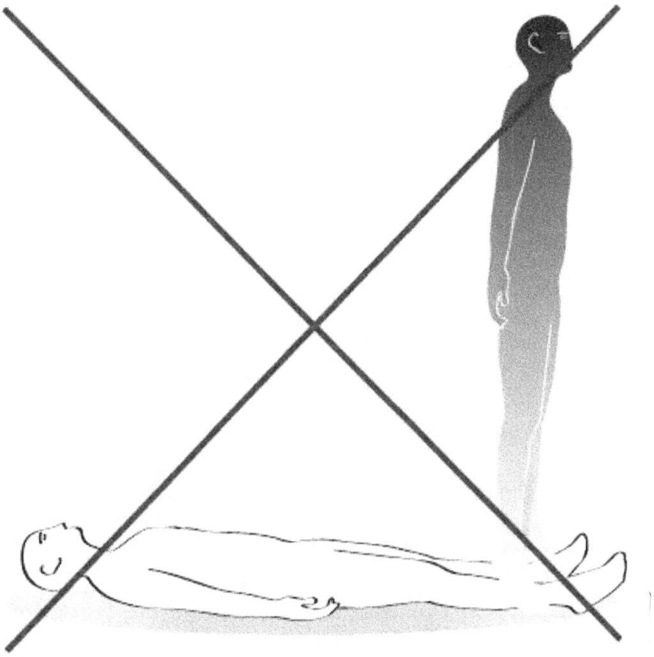

astral projection

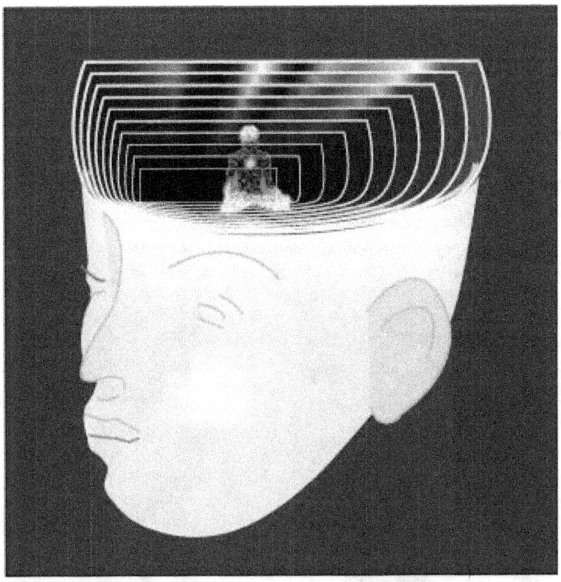

Application

This definition of liberation is based on proficiency in extraction of carbon dioxide and negative subtle energy. This results in changing the nature and perception means of the subtle body so that from within that form, the core-self can perceive into divine environments, the chit akash sky of consciousness.

Access to the divine world cannot be gained by will power actions or by determination or by desire, but it is gained by the subtle body's assumption of a nature which is compatible with that of the divine world.

Any method will do, provided it is effective in changing the energy content of the subtle body, to make that form suitable to the highest level of the psychic material nature. The subtle body will never be a divine form but it can access the divine if it has the highest grade of subtle energy. Then the yogi can use the perception tools in the head of the subtle form to peer into the divine world, a focus through which he or she can gain contact to the spiritual environment.

Verse 52

अथ सिंहासनम

गुल्फौ च वृषणस्याधः सीवन्त्याः पार्श्वयोः क्षिपेत् ।

दक्षिणे सव्य–गुल्फं तु दक्ष–गुल्फं तु सव्यके ।। ५२ ।।

atha siṁhāsanam
gulphau ca vṝṣaṇasyādhaḥ sīvantyāḥ pārśvayoḥ kṣipet ।
dakṣiṇe savya–gulphaṁ tu dakṣa–gulphaṁ tu savyake ।। 52 ।।

atha – regarding, siṁhāsanam – lion posture, gulphau – ankles, ca – and, vṝṣaṇasyādhaḥ = vṝṣaṇasya (of the testes) + adhaḥ (below), sīvantyāḥ – of the perineum, pārśvayoḥ – of both, kṣipet – one should place, dakṣiṇe – in the right, savya – left, gulphaṁ – ankle, tu – and, dakṣa – right, gulphaṁ – ankle, tu – and, savyake – on the left side

Regarding the lion posture:

Place the ankles below the testes at both sides of the perineum, the left one on the right side and the right ankle on the left side.

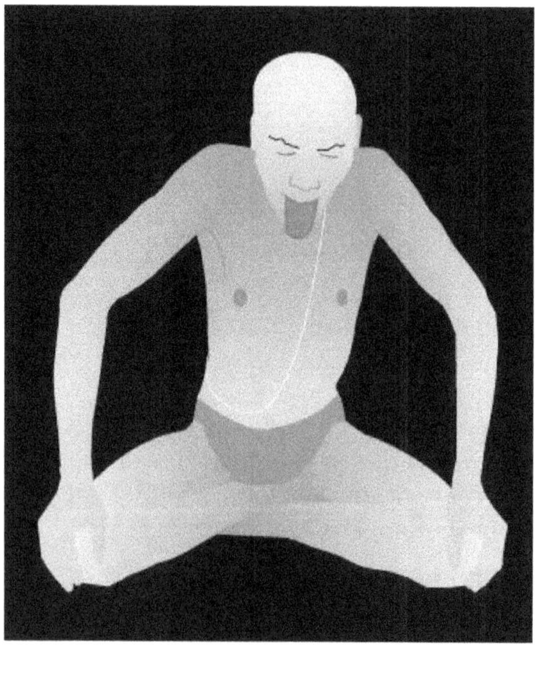

Analysis

Each posture is done in a specific way with specific focus which is developed as the posture is assumed. Hastiness is not part of asana practice. Making a dance of it with graceful movements for display to the public is not a method either.

Ideally, yoga is practiced in isolation under physical or psychic supervision for the benefit of the individual student. It is not for display. It is not for assuming final forms for display. It is not for acquiring the attention of others.

Application

This posture has many variations; some with the ankles crossing each other; some with one foot placed under the buttocks of the same side.

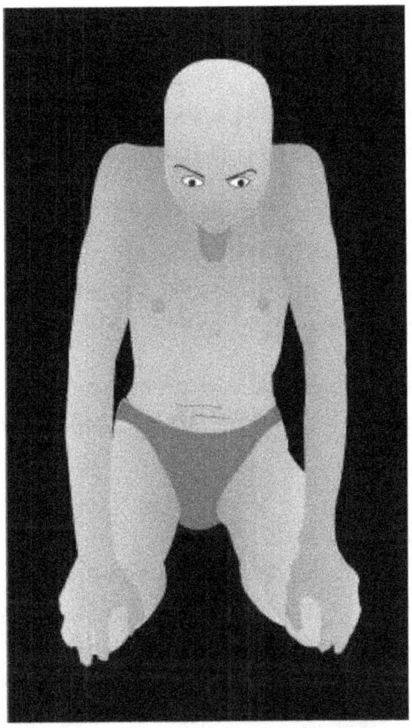

In any posture, the student should gradually assume the pose; then focus internally to sense parts of the psyche which are affected. Whatever is below the neck has corresponding areas in the head of the subtle body. Each asana posture if done properly with the subtle body in mind will cause the student to discover corresponding areas in the brain.

When the ankles are crossed and they are required to endure the weight of the torso and head. This strains the ankles. A pain is emitted except in the case of persons who are extremely supple. This pain should be contacted from within.

The student should be upright on the knees. Then cross the ankles. Then gradually drop the torso with the hands spread for contact with the ground. When the hands are fitted to the ground, the student should close the eyes and focus within downward in the body. The student should then gradually allow the weight of the torso to be transferred through the crossed ankles. Then the student should focus on the pain energy at the ankles and feet and wait at that inner place until there seems to be a corresponding sensitivity in the head.

There are many variations of this posture. Some are done with or without the ankles crossed. Some are done with the thighs close together or spread apart.

Once the pain in the ankles and feet is felt from within with eyes closed, and there is a shift of focus to the subtle head, the student should meditate in the head and feel the corresponding area in the ankles and feet. It is the subtle energy which is targeted for focus. Doing asana postures for antics or to show others one's flexibility contravenes the purpose of yoga.

Verse 53

हस्तौ तु जान्वोः संस्थाप्य स्वाङ्गुलीः सम्प्रसार्य च ।

वयात्त–वक्तो निरीक्षेत नासाग्रं सुसमाहितः ।। ५३ ।।

hastau tu jānvoḥ saṁsthāpya svāṅgulīḥ samprasārya ca ।
vyātta–vakto nirīkṣeta nāsāgraṁ susamāhitaḥ ।। 53 ।।

hastau – hands, tu – now, jānvoḥ – of knees, saṁsthāpya – placing, svāṅgulīḥ = sva (one's) + āṅgulīḥ (fingers), samprasārya – spread apart, ca – and, vyātta – open, vakto = vaktaḥ = mouth, nirīkṣeta – should focus, nāsāgraṁ – tip of the nose, susamāhitaḥ – fully linking the attention to the objective

Place the hands on the knees. Spread the fingers apart. Open the mouth. Focus at the tip of the nose while fully linking the attention to that objective.

Analysis

I wrote it. I will write it again. The purpose of the asana postures is to gain intimate knowledge about the subtle body. Yes, the postures are physical but they are physical in part only because the subtle body is interspaced in the physical during the assumption of the poses. From the pains and strains, from the eases and the good feelings acquired during a pose, one should transfer attention to the subtle body. Then the postures will facilitate higher yoga.

When the focus is applied to the tip of the nose in the lion pose, it is done with the physical eyes. One will feel a strain-energy in the eyes and this will travel backward through the optic nerves to the point where those nerves meet. The student should be aware of this energy convergence.

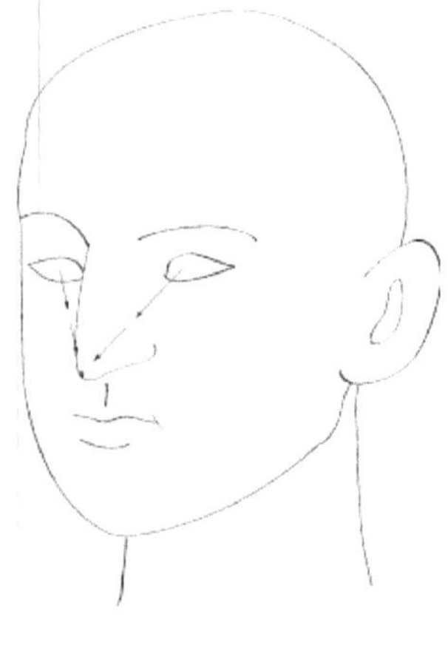

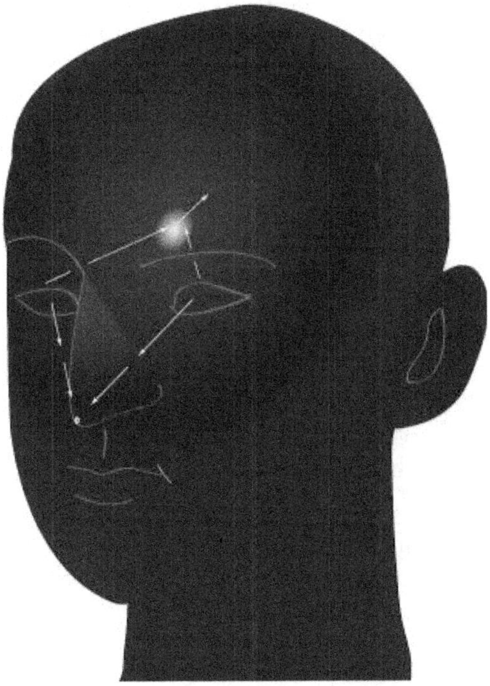

Application

The lion pose is highlighted with the widest opening of the mouth. When a lion yawns it opens its mouth to the fullest. This is also done by the rhinoceros, except that the lion's head stays forward. A rhinoceros usually tilts its head backward when opening its large mouth.

During the opening of the mouth, the tongue is stretched forward the most. It is curled around the bottom lip even to the point of touching or curling around the chin.

Verse 54

सिंहासनं भवेदेतत्पूजितं योगि–पुणगवैः ।

बन्ध–तरितय–सन्धानं कुरुते चासनोत्तमम् ।। ५४ ।।

siṁhāsanaṁ bhavedetatpūjitaṁ yogi–pungavaiḥ I
bandha–tritaya–sandhānaṁ kurute cāsanottamam I I 54 I I

siṁhāsanaṁ – lion pose, bhaved = bhavet = is, etat – this, pūjitaṁ – is worshipped, yogi – yogi, pungavaiḥ - by the greatest , bandha – bodily contraction, tritaya – three, sandhānaṁ – mastership, kurute – facilitates, cāsanottamam = ca (and) + āsana (posture) + uttamam (excellent)

This is the lion pose, which is worshipped by the best of the yogis. This excellent posture facilitates the mastership of the three bodily contractions.

Analysis

The three primary contractions are the chin-to-throat lock, the abdomen up-and-back lock and the anus/reproductive organs pull-up locks. In the lion pose when it is done perfectly, these three locks occur simultaneously without any extraneous effort. In fact, these locks are so natural in this posture that a student may not even notice that they were applied.

The essential action which causes this engagement is the protrusion and curling of the tongue around the lower lip towards the chin. This exercise of the tongue musculature causes the throat and intestinal apparatus to lurch upwards. The result is that the throat is compressed, the abdomen is pulled up, the reproductive system and anus are drawn up.

If the student is attentive within the body, these upsurges may be noticed. The effect on the subtle body may be felt.

Application

The three primary contractions and some other compressions are used to apply pressure and influence to the kundalini psychic lifeforce. This is for elevating the level of consciousness of the subtle body, so that the core-self can access the divine environment.

Even though these contractions are physical, they have simultaneous subtle impact which causes psychic movements. Once the energy from the trunk passes through the neck it enters the brain in a supervised way. It then influences the state of consciousness of the intellect and sensual orbs which are in the head of the subtle form.

There is a reversal in yoga practice which happens because of the kriya special physio-psychic techniques.

How is this done?

Materialistic yogis begin with physical actions in the practice of asana postures. This should evolve into physio-psychic actions which begin with the pranayama breath-infusion. This evolves further into psychological functions which are introduced within the mind when the pratyahar sensual energy procedures are enacted.

Thus for the materialistic students it is a progression from physical to psychological. The truth of the matter is however that there is no such progress because in the first place there must be a psychic reality which supports the physical. Even in physics, it is said that first there was gas and then solid materials evolved from that. But on this planet, we may see the reverse where a solid material when burnt emits gas and then leaves a remnant of dust. Thus from the material view point there was something solid and then gas was created from it. However gas was first. The solid materials were produced thereafter.

When we are in the materialistic frame of mind we perceive the material body as primary, but in fact that form is the effect of the subtle body.

Whatever we do which is physical must have some psychic action that is the basis for it. However the psychic act might be covert or it might even be past, long past, so that it is no longer observable and we are left only with the physical act as evidence.

When one does asana postures, one should close the eyes and search within the psyche for the corresponding psychic impact. Once this is found as a feeling or as an emotion or mental movement, one should hold on to that and release one's interest from the physical aspect. This method will cause the mind to be trained to abandon physical impacts to claim psychic ones.

When doing pranayama breath-infusion one should close the eyes as much as possible. One may even use a blind fold. One should then keep the attention within the confines of the subtle body and keep detailed observation of what takes place on the mental and emotional levels.

The three primary bodily contractions as well as any other major or minor ones are about what happens to the energy in the subtle body. It is not about compressing blood and physical tissue, even though that will occur when these locks are applied.

Verse 55-56

अथ भद्रासनम

गुल्फौ च वृषणस्याधः सीवन्त्याः पार्श्वयोः क्षिपेत् ।

सव्य–गुल्फं तथा सव्ये दक्ष–गुल्फं तु दक्षिणे ।। ५५ ।।

पार्श्व–पादौ च पाणिभ्यां दृढं बद्धा सुनिश्चलम् ।

भद्रासनं भवेदेतत्सर्व–वयाधि–विनाशनम् ।

गोरक्षासनमित्याहुरिदं वै सिद्ध–योगिनः ।। ५६ ।।

atha bhadrāsanam
gulphau ca vṝṣaṇasyādhaḥ sīvantyāḥ pārśvayoḥ kṣipet ।
savya–gulphaṁ tathā savye dakṣa–gulphaṁ tu dakṣiṇe ।। 55 ।।
pārśva–pādau ca pāṇibhyāṁ dṝḍhaṁ baddhvā suniścalam ।
bhadrāsanaṁ bhavedetatsarva–vyādhi–vināśanam ।
gorakṣāsanamityāhuridaṁ vai siddha–yoginaḥ ।। 56 ।।

atha – regarding, bhadrāsanam – grace posture, gulphau – heels, ca – and, vṝṣaṇasyādhaḥ = vṝṣaṇasya (of the testes) + ādhaḥ (below), sīvantyāḥ – perineum, pārśvayoḥ – at both sides, kṣipet – should place, savya – left, gulphaṁ – heel, tathā – thus, savye – on the left, dakṣa – right, gulphaṁ – heel, tu – then, dakṣiṇe – on the right, pārśva – on sides, pādau – thighs, ca – and, pāṇibhyāṁ – by the hands, dṛḍhaṁ – firm, baddhvā – holding, suniścalam = non–moveable, bhadrāsanaṁ – grace posture, bhaved = bhavet = is, etat – this, sarva – all, vyādhi – disease, vināśanam – that which destroys, gorakṣāsanam – Gorakṣa's posture, ity = iti = thus, āhur = āhuḥ = say, idaṁ – this, vai – indeed, siddha – perfected, yoginaḥ – of the yogis

Regarding the bhadra grace pose:

Place the heels on either side of the perineum below the testes, with the left on the left side and the right on the right side. Holding with the hands firmly keep the thighs in a non–moveable position. This bhadra grace pose destroys disease. Perfect yogis say this is the Goraksha posture.

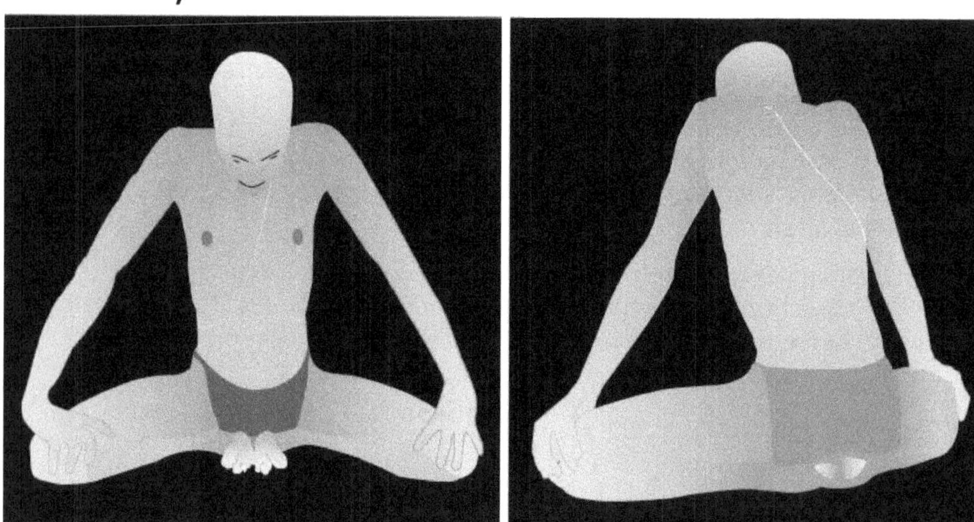

Analysis

A posture was named after a great yogi who either mastered that pose to an absolute degree, and milked its full benefit or was the first yogi to use that pose. It may be inspired into the mind of the yogi by a deity or by a supernatural yogi who is not physically present or it may be graced to the yogi merely because of his astute practice.

Some yogis design new postures to deal with particular flaws in the subtle body, tendencies which contravene yoga and which if not removed bar the ascetic from further progress.

The bhadra grace posture causes release of energies from the feet, heels, ankles, pelvic cage and hip sockets. By it a yogi can make keen observations about the reproduction-excretion machinery in the subtle body. There are physical effects and benefits in this posture but those are not the subject of yoga. Yoga has for its method a progression from physical postures to physio-psychic breath-infusion to psychological pratyahar sensual energy retraction and then to spiritual access into the divine world using the samyama three-component terminal process as explained by Patanjali Mahayogin.

Application

The Goraksha posture is the posture for realizing what happened in the evolutionary progress from quadrupeds to bipeds. In the transition the central loop down the back

of the four legged mammals changed from horizontal to vertical with a corresponding up-lift of the digestive and reproductive biology. The primate forms were the final platform in the process.

When one sits in the bhadra grace pose, one finds it to be unnatural to let the back remain in a careless position. One is inspired to lift the back. This lift action causes a change in attitude of the form.

Each of the asana postures are derived from a particular species form with the benefits which that form afforded. A yogi can track back through numerous transmigrations just by doing the poses in a meditative way.

Verse 57

एवमासन–बन्धेषु योगीन्द्रो विगत–शरमः ।

अभ्यसेन्नाडिका–शुद्धिं मुद्रादि–पवनी–क्रियाम् ।। ५७ ।।

evamāsana–bandheṣu yogīndro vighata–śramaḥ |
abhyasennāḍikā–śuddhiṁ mudrādi–pavanī–kriyām || 57 ||

evam – thus, asana – posture, bandeṣu – physical bodily contraction, yogīndro = yogīndraḥ – yogi who excels all others, vighata – is gone, śramaḥ – fatigue, abhyasen = abhyaset = should practice, nāḍikā – nadi subtle veins and arteries, śuddhiṁ – purification, mudrādi – foremost of the mystic checking practices, pavanī–kriyām – breath-infusion technique

Thus with postures and physical bodily contractions, the yogi who excels all others, should without fatigue, bring into effect the purification of the nadi subtle veins and arteries. He should apply the foremost of the mystic checking practices and the breath-infusion techniques.

Analysis

A yogi must be without fatigue if he wants full success. The continuous reassertion of fatigue in the life of a yogi is a sign of failure. It portends that the yogi is blighted to remain in material existence, to keep transmigrating in temporary bodies.

Can anything be done about such shadows which obscure final progress?

Apart from the efforts of a yogi, there is such a thing as bad luck or good luck. If good luck is there, then the yogi will be successful, otherwise he will surely fail. Nevertheless it is the duty of the yogi to persevere even if the fates are against him. One should not expect to have full cooperation from providence, for fate is independent and is not concerned with twisting the whole existence to indulge one limited individual person-self.

There are two bad lucks, either of which if it confronts a yogi will restrict his advancement and cause a lack of completion in the particular life.

These two are:

- lack of opportunity for isolation
- opportunity for isolation with drastic interruptions

If a yogi does not get isolation, he cannot become liberated. Any yogi who does not get the opportunity for isolation needs to get this idea into his head, that his hope for liberation while using this present life form is nil.

This however is not a cause for discouragement. In fact it is more the reason why the yogi should exert himself for keeping the practice constant and for keeping the hope that sometime in the future there will be good luck.

If an ascetic gets an opportunity for isolation, but if during that time there are drastic interruptions, he should realize that there will not be full liberation while using the current body. For this yogi there will be transcendental experiences. There will be times when there is contact with the divine environment and with deities but it will not be complete at any time.

Drastic interruptions are caused by deities who see it as being fit to stop a yogi from full success. It is a wonder as to why a deity would do anything to curtail the progress of a yogin but that question is beyond the scope of this book.

However I can say this much that there needs be an environment for isolation. As a limited being, a yogi cannot create his or her environment of isolation. The isolation environment must be there somewhere. Hence whosoever owns that place has a right to permit or prevent a yogi from making full use of it. The ascetic should not be distressed because he cannot get an uninterrupted period of time for practice. It is best to work with whatever arrangement one is permitted by fate, making the best use of it.

Even if they are obstructed from time to time, yoga austerities are cumulative. There are digressions when a yogi finds that the progress made during a certain period is erased completely. Then he must begin the process from scratch and forge his way painstakingly again. Still, there is an accumulation of efforts which surfaces as an instinct for understanding what to do to recover progress.

When providence bites into the practice of a yogi, it may bite out a large chunk and leave the yogi to be a laughing stock of critics. Still the ascetic should be confident that he will recover and will again ride the waves to greatness as a spiritual entity.

Application

To remove fatigue certain practices and a conducive lifestyle must be in place. No amount of philosophy, belief, wishful thinking or deliberation can effectively remove fatigue because it is innate in the psyche of all creatures. There is one primary way to reduce fatigue in the physical and subtle bodies. That is by providing fresh air and fresh subtle energy. There must also be a complimentary lifestyle, where the ascetic does not waste energy in futile endeavors, either for social or for self-disciplinary reasons.

The kundalini lifeforce is the mainstay of energy in the physical and subtle bodies. Thus its reform is paramount. This means the practice of kundalini yoga, which is exactly what Swatmarama explained in this text. This book, the Hatha Yoga Pradipika, is a treatise on kundalini yoga using bhastrika pranayama breath-infusion as the main way for removing fatigue. The purification of the nadi subtle veins and arteries occurs by an efficient kundalini practice which consists of arousing the lifeforce which resides at the base of the spine, the muladhara chakra. The main feed energy of the lifeforce is hormone fluids and breath. The yogi should mix reproductive fluids and breath-energy for use by the lifeforce in energizing it sufficiently for it to enter the brain of the physical form and the mind of the subtle body.

Verse 58

आसनं कुम्भकं छित्रं मुद्राख्यं करणं तथा ।
अथ नादानुसन्धानमभ्यासानुक्रमो हठे ।। ५८ ।।

āsanaṁ kumbhakaṁ chitraṁ mudrākhyaṁ karaṇaṁ tathā I
atha nādānusandhānamabhyāsānukramo haṭhe II 58 II

āsanaṁ – posture, kumbhakaṁ – breath-suspension contraction, chitraṁ – range, mudrākhyaṁ – mystic checking practices, karaṇaṁ – technique, tathā – so, atha – as explained, nādānusandhānam = nāda (naad subtle sound vibration) + ānusandhānam (continuous spontaneous inner focus), abhyāsānukramo = abhyāsa (practice) + anukramaḥ (range, syllabus), haṭhe – in kundalini manipulation for subtle body transformation

Postures, the range of breath-suspension contractions, the mystic checking techniques, as well as the continuous spontaneous inner focus on naad subtle sound vibration; these are the syllabus of kundalini manipulation for subtle body transformation.

Analysis

Unknown to many yogis in the modern era, is the fact that this Hatha Yoga Pradipika is the authoritative book about kundalini yoga. The reason for this lack of information is the dearth of knowledge about the contributions of Gorakshnath Mahayogin. He introduced Hatha Yoga not as asana postures but as a six part learning consisting of the six higher stages of the ashtanga yoga system described by Patanjali Mahayogin. Postures are the first of the six stages according to Gorakshnath.

Patanjali defined yoga like this:

yama niyama āsana prāṇāyāma pratyāhāra
dhāraṇā dhyāna samādhayaḥ aṣṭau aṅgāni

yama – moral restraints; niyama – recommended behaviors; āsana – body postures; prāṇāyāma – breath-infusion; pratyāhar – sensual energy withdrawal; dhāraṇā – linking of the attention to higher concentration forces or persons; dhyāna – effortless linkage of the attention to higher concentration forces or persons; samādhayaḥ – continuous effortless linkage of the attention to higher concentration forces or persons; aṣṭau – eight; aṅgāni – parts of a thing.

Moral restraints, recommended behaviors, body posture, breath-infusion, sensual energy withdrawal, linking of the attention to higher concentration forces or persons, effortless linkage of the attention to higher concentration forces or persons, continuous effortless linkage of the attention to higher concentration forces or persons are the eight parts of the yoga system. (Yoga Sutras 2.29)

In contrast, Guruji Gorakshnatha omitted the first two processes of yama moral restraints and niyama recommended behaviors. It all has to do with reform of the kundalini shakti, the psychic lifeforce which impulsively drives the person to act in ways which are counterproductive to spiritual life.

Religion aside, the ascetic must come to terms with the unruly emotional and mental tendencies in the psyche. To achieve this he must master the kundalini shakti lifeforce. There is no better way to achieve this than to force-feed the lifeforce more and more fresh air, so as to disempower it from assuming a spiritually-counterproductive attitude.

With the cooperation of the lifeforce, the yogi can rise to higher planes, experience other realities and develop a transit to a trauma-free divine environment.

Application

The continuous spontaneous inner focus on naad subtle sound vibration is in the syllabus of kundalini manipulation for subtle body transformation. It is instrumental in two achievements:

- *disaffection for the thoughts and images pertaining to the physical world and the lower astral regions*
- *preparation for approaching the chit akash sky of consciousness*

Mere disaffection for thoughts and images pertaining to physical existence and the lower astral planes, is not enough for reaching the chit akash sky of consciousness, but it is the initial qualification. Once the disaffection is established the core-self can squeeze itself away from the frontal part of the subtle head by taking more and more shelter in naad sound resonance. Then over time the psychic mechanism for imagination, memory display and visualization will shut down leaving only a dark void area in the frontal part of the subtle head.

This void space will in time convert into an energy which allows perceptions into the divine world.

A yogi is nurtured by the naad resonance, just as a baby is cared for by its affectionate and dutiful mother. This is required because a yogi, as a person-being, must have a certain amount of affection.

Verse 59

बरह्मछारी मिताहारी तयागी योग–परायणः ।

अब्दादूर्ध्वं भवेद्सिद्धो नात्र कार्या विचारणा ।। ५९ ।।

brahmachārī mitāhārī tyāgī yoga–parāyaṇaḥ |
abdādūrdhvaṁ bhavedsiddho nātra kāryā vicāraṇā || 59 ||

brahmachārī – sexual non – expressiveness which results in the perception of spirituality, mitāhārī – one with sparse diet, tyāgī – one who abandoned the rewards of social contributions, yoga – yoga, parāyaṇaḥ – one who is very sincere, abdād = abdāt = year, ūrdhvaṁ – after, up, bhaved = bhavet = is, siddho = siddhaḥ = perfected yogi. nātra – not present, kāryā – reason, vicāraṇā – to doubt

The person whose lifestyle exhibits sexual non–expressiveness which results in the perception of spirituality, who has sparse diet, who abandoned the rewards of his (her) social contributions, who is very sincere about yoga may become a perfected yogi after one year. There is no reason to doubt this.

Analysis

Sexual non-expression is not something unto itself. It is not an absolute principle in yoga. It has to be honed in by the ascetic so that it results in perception of spirituality. Celibacy for the purpose of status in a religious society or among lay-people is not part of yoga. Celibacy which is a replacement for homosexuality is not part of yoga. Celibacy as a way to cushion one's dislike of the opposite sex is not part of yoga. Celibacy which results in arrogance and pride, because of achieving sexual disaffection, is not part of yoga.

The non-yogic applications of celibacy have their value in their particular spheres but they contravene yoga and are therefore rejected in the path explained by Swatmarama.

Sexual non-expressiveness is a requirement in this yoga process but it becomes offensive when it is done without the support and request of higher beings like yogi-gurus and deities. Even if something is condemned for a yogi, still if a deity requests it or if a great yoga-guru commissions it, it must be done if the yogi wants to maintain his relationship with the authority. I read that Arjun had to kill human beings on the battlefield of Kurukshetra, as requested by Lord Krishna. Killing of human beings is a violation of the non-violent stance which is a mandatory requirement for yogis.

Dogmatic people should stay away from yoga. People who require to be in religious indoctrination should stay away from yoga. Those who want something stereotyped should leave yoga aside. Those who require a system which suits their fancy should remain far away from yoga.

Application

For curbing the kundalini lifeforce the control of used polluted air in the physical and subtle bodies must be brought to fore. Along with this is the control of diet.

Celibacy is a wasted effort if it is not supported by diet control and air infusion. This is because the reproductive fluids will still pool in the groin area irrespective of one's lofty aims. Dormant sexuality either for people who do yoga or for those who know nothing about it, is just what it is, which is not celibacy. There is an ever present danger for those who are not having sexual expression. It is pride and arrogance because of not being involved in a vulgarity.

Social contributions are a difficult thing to give up because it is the means of getting preferred treatment in this world. There is the likelihood that insincere hypocrites will temporarily gave up the benefits of their social contributions only to activate their claims later in this or a future life.

Swatmarama gave one year as a reasonable achievement period for yogis to become perfected but that was in his time. It would be foolhardy to state that this applies today.

On the contrary we cannot estimate how long it would take a modern ascetic because the disciplines are more difficult to perfect, the cultural environment is hostile and our subtle bodies are configured differently in reference to ancient yogis.

Verse 60

सुस्निग्ध–मधुराहारश्चतुर्थांश–विवर्जितः ।

भुज्यते शिव–सम्प्रीत्यै मिताहारः स उच्यते ।। ६० ।।

susnigdha–madhurāhāraścaturthāṁśa–vivarjitaḥ I
bhujyate śiva samprītyai mitāhāraḥ sa ucyate II 60 II

susnigdha – agreeable, easily digestible, madhura – sweet, āhāraś = āhāraḥ = food consumption, caturthāṁśa – one–fourth, vivarjitaḥ – void of, bhujyate – is eaten, śiva –Shiva, samprītyai – thoroughly pleasing, mitāhāraḥ –approved sparse diet, sa – he, ucyate – is declared

Agreeable, easily digestible and sweet food, which is eaten so that one–fourth of the stomach is void of it, and which is eaten for thoroughly pleasing Shiva, is declared as the approved sparse diet.

Analysis

Pleasing Shiva, or alternately Krishna, is the key facet in these practices. Person means a reality which has to relate to persons, especially to persons of higher category. Prancing around in this creation with an atheistic stance may give a human being some satisfaction but it does not erase the person of the person concerned.

As soon as there is a person, there is a need for relationship with other persons, with those who are dependents and those who are seniors. Unless one is the Supreme Being, there will be a need for juniors and seniors because that is the natural requirement. There is no point in arrogantly denying this when it is evident in our psychology.

Student yogis should eat under supervision of an advanced teacher who excelled at the practice. Some teachers know the proper diet because of deep insight even though they did not practice certain techniques. Some know because of getting inspired to teach what they did not practice. There are also fake gurus who do not know but who pretend to be informed or to have practiced. As in any education, the risks are there when learning.

Why is it necessary to please superiors?

The reason is that by nature a person cannot derive all benefits by self-reliance. People need approval even by their dependents what to speak of their spiritual superiors. The concept that no one is a spiritual superior and that we are all equal or that we are all potentially the same, is a good belief for offsetting our existential insecurities. Otherwise it serves no purpose and does not settle the issue of the need for approval, the need for gaining the goodwill of those who are spiritually superior.

The interest in a yogi which is invested by a superior yogi or by deities like Shiva or Krishna is invaluable for securing spiritual advancement. Some stages of advancement are attained by a student because of the interest of a great guru or a deity, and otherwise such progression would not have occurred. It is a fact that some stages are attained because the student felt compelled to do it for the guru or deity, even though the fact is that it was done for the student only.

Some children study and pass exams by request of parents. The children actually think that they do the parents a favor; that the parent benefits from the learning. We know that it is to the contrary where the parents derive little direct consequence.

Both Patanjali and Swatmarama declare a supreme being. Patanjali described attributes of this person and Swatmarama gave Shiva as this person. The indication is that kundalini yoga is for people with a theistic demeanor.

Agreeable, easily digestible and sweet food is vegetarian food produce and dairy products so that one takes milk from the cow but does not eat the animal's body. This was the standard diet for yogis in the time of Swatmarama. Bhagavad Gita also lists these foods as being in the clarifying mode of material nature:

āyuḥsattvabalārogya-
sukhaprītivivardhanāḥ
rasyāḥ snigdhāḥ sthirā hṛdyā
āhārāḥ sāttvikapriyāḥ (17.8)

āyuḥsattvabalārogya = āyuḥ — duration of life + sattva — spiritual well-being + bala — strength + ārogya — health; sukhaprītivivardhanāḥ = sukha —happiness + prīti — satisfaction + vivardhanāḥ — increasing; rasyāḥ — juicy; snigdhāḥ — milky; sthirā — sustaining; hṛdyā — palatable; āhārāḥ — foods; sātvikapriyāḥ — dear to the clear-minded people

Foods which increase the duration of the life, the spiritual well-being, strength, health, happiness and satisfaction, which are juicy, milky, sustaining and palatable, are eatables which are dear to the clear-minded people. (Bhagavad Gita 17.8)

Application

Two factors are important in kundalini yoga practice, which are breath and food. The yogi should increase the percentage of fresh air in the blood stream and extract as much polluted gas as possible.

Food should be vegetarian with or without dairy products. However the time of eating should be coordinated to facilitate the practice of pranayama breath-infusion.

Students should learn about Shiva and Krishna, finding out what these persons did and what can be gained in their association. These are supernatural and spiritual beings with vast powers.

Verse 61

कट्वाम्ल–तीक्ष्ण–लवणोष्ण–हरीत–शाक–

सौवीर–तैल–तिल–सर्षप–मद्य–मत्स्यान ।

आजादि–मांस–दधि–तक्र–कुलत्थकोल–

पिण्याक–हिङ्गु–लशुनाद्यमपथ्यमाहुः ।। ६१ ।।

kaṭvāmla–tīkṣṇa–lavaṇoṣṇa–harīta–śāka–
sauvīra–taila–tila–sarṣapa–madya–matsyān |
ājādi–māṁsa–dadhi–takra–kulatthakola–
piṇyāka–hingu–laśunādyamapathyamāhuḥ || 61 ||

kaṭv = kaṭu = bitter, āmla – sour, tīkṣṇa – pungent, lavaṇoṣṇa = lavaṇa (salty) + uṣhṇa (peppery), harīta – green, śāka – leaves, sauvīra – sour gruel, taila – oil, tila – sesame, sarṣapa – mustard seeds, madya – liquor, matsyān – fish, ājādi – goat and other animals, māṁsa – meat, dadhi – yogurt, takra – buttermilk, kulattha – horse gram beans, kola – jujube, piṇyāka = oil–cake, hingu – asafetida, laśunā – garlic, ādyam – and similar foods, apathyam – unsuitable, āhuḥ – they say

Bitter, sour, pungent, salty, peppery, green leaves, sour gruel, oily foods, sesame, mustard seeds, liquor, fish, goat and other animal meat, yogurt, buttermilk, horse gram beans, jujube, oil–cake, asafetida, garlic and similar condiments, are said to be unsuitable for a yogi.

Analysis

Recently someone brought to my attention that Yogi Bhajan, my spiritual master for bhastrika pranayama practice, always ate foods with garlic and condiments. In fact while I lived in the ashram in Denver, Colorado something in the year of 1972, there was cooking with pungent foods and condiments. I know this for a fact. Yogiji was a Punjabi. It is their cultural heritage to eat such preparations.

However it does not matter if it is my Guruji, myself or anyone else; if there is a violation of yoga procedures, it is a violation. What we do which is counterproductive should not be followed. It is enough to follow what we do which is endorsed in these yoga texts, so that whatever we do which contravenes yoga should be left undone by the new students who aspire for ideal practice.

Yogurt and butter milk are dairy products but they are partially fermented or turned sour either by age or by adding bacteria or another food or acid. Yogis should stick to just milk which turns to yogurt in the gut of the human being through enzyme action.

Currently many persons in India eat yogurt on a daily basis as a balance for pungent and spicy foods. If one does not take the spices then there is no need to counteract their effect by adding acid to milk or culturing yogurt producing bacteria.

Application

For a cross-reference, here is what Krishna said in the Bhagavad Gita about the category of unwanted foods:

kaṭvamlalavaṇātyuṣṇa-
tīkṣṇarūkṣavidāhinaḥ
āhārā rājasasyeṣṭā
duḥkhaśokāmayapradāḥ (17.9)

kaṭvamlalavaṇātyuṣṇa = kaṭv (kaṭu) — pungent + amla — sour + lavaṇa — salt; atyuṣṇa — peppery; tīkṣnarūkṣavidāhinaḥ — tīkṣṇa — acidic + rūkṣa — dry + vidāhinaḥ — overheated; āhārā — foods; rājasasyeṣṭā — rajasasya — of the passionate people + iṣṭā — desired; duḥkhaśokāmayapradāḥ = duḥkha — pain + śoka — misery + āmaya — sickness + pradāḥ — causing

Foods which are pungent, sour, salty, peppery, acidic, dry and overheated, are desired by the passionate people. These foods cause pain, misery and sickness. (Bhagavad Gita 17.9)

yātayāmaṁ gatarasaṁ
pūti paryuṣitaṁ ca yat
ucchiṣṭamapi cāmedhyaṁ
bhojanaṁ tāmasapriyam (17.10)

yātayāmaṁ — stale; gatarasaṁ — tasteless; pūti — rotten; paryuṣitaṁ — left over; ca — and; yat = yad — which; ucchiṣṭam — rejected; api — also; cāmedhyam = ca — and + amedhyaṁ — unfit for religious ceremony; bhojanaṁ — food; tāmasapriyam — cherished by the depressed people

Food which is stale, tasteless, and rotten, which was left over, as well as that which is rejected or unfit for religious ceremony, is cherished by the depressed people. (Bhagavad Gita 17.10)

As far as possible students should avoid the unwanted foods even if a Guruji as great as Harbhajan Singh does not adhere to the rules. This applies to all of yoga practice, where a Guruji or even this commentator does not live up to every standard stipulated.

Learn from a great spiritual master what you can and leave the rest which seems to be in violation to what is ideal.

Verse 62

भोजनमहितं विद्यात्पुनरस्योष्णी–कृतं रूक्षम् ।
अतिलवणमम्ल–युक्तं कदशन–शाकोत्कं वर्ज्यम् ।। ६२ ।।

bhojanamahitaṁ vidyātpunarasyoṣṇī–kṛtaṁ rūkṣam I
atilavaṇamamla–yuktaṁ kadaśana–śākotkaṁ varjyam II 62 II

bhojanam – food, ahitaṁ – what is unfit, vidyāt – should know, punar – again, asyoṣṇī–kṛtaṁ = asya (of this) + uṣṇī–kṛtaṁ (what was heated), rūkṣam – saturated with oil, ati – very, lavaṇam – salty, amla – sour, yuktaṁ – well–prepared, kadaśana – stale, śākotkaṁ = śāka (vegetables) + utkaṁ – too many, varjyam – avoided

One should recognize food which is unfit for human consumption. That which is heated again, which is oil–saturated, which is well prepared but very salty or sour, which is stale or which has too many vegetables, should be avoided.

Analysis

The body of a yogi should not be stressed with spicy, salty, pungent or stale foods. Each type of food has a special effect on the body. A yogi should study the effects and favor for the ones which are conducive to yoga practice, to the elevation of consciousness in a free way.

No narcotic herbs should be used by a yogi, unless these are used in special experiments to judge its influence on consciousness. Mild hallucinogens, stimulants and the like should also be left aside by a yogi. Instead he or she should use the consciousness of the body itself to elevate awareness and bring on insight perception.

An ascetic should develop reliance on what he or she can carry through the portals of death. Whatever helps us now but which we cannot carry beyond the life of the physical body will if we become attached to it, be a source of trauma hereafter. Thus one should not rely on herbal or pharmaceutical stimulants and narcotics.

Always ask yourself if you can take the herb, the chemical or whatever, with you into the hereafter. In fact the details of what exactly you will be allowed to take should be known, so that you can cultivate the allowance and detach yourself from what is forbidden.

When travelling from one country to another, a sane traveler will carry only items which will not be confiscated. Study carefully the mental and emotional facets, to determine which of these will survive death. Cultivate those aspects which will transit intact as or with your personality, leaving all else behind and not giving undue importance to what is useful here and now but which will disappear when one is filtered into the hereafter.

Application

It is my experience that many proficient yogis from India have a bad diet in terms of these statements regarding what to eat and what not to eat for the facilitation of yoga. Why is it that a swami in a respected lineage, would deviate from standards for diet described even in the Bhagavad Gita?

The answer is that material nature is so compelling that even educated Indians who read Bhagavad Gita, even ones who are from brahmin caste families, cannot comply if they were conditioned in childhood and youth to eat and cherish foods which violate the proposals of Krishna.

Such people eat more pepper than a bird and relish foods like onion and garlic which are within the category of prohibited pungent flavors, which condition us to lower tastes and smells.

Material nature is so compelling that even after mastering classic postures in yoga practice, great persons cannot abandon bad dietary habits.

Social influence is also a factor, in that a yogi may find himself in a fix if he goes against the trend. To offset social negativity, he may find it expedient to ignore what Krishna said about diet and follow his family, friends and peers. Such is this life!

As great a person as Paramhansa Yogananda argued about the virtue of eating eggs which were not fertilized by roosters, on the premise that since they were not fertilized they did not have life in them.

Really?

What is an egg, besides the reproductive fluid of a hen?

Is that not life too?

Why do we want to cook and eat the nature-packaged menstrual cycle of a chicken?

Why should there be a defensive argument about that as human diet?

Obviously we are so much under the influence of the senses that we would do anything and defend any habit even ones which make absolutely no sense.

Verse 63-64

वह्नि–स्त्री–पथि–सेवानामादौ वर्जनमाचरेत् ।। ६३ ।।

तथा हि गोरक्ष–वचनम्

वर्जयेद्दुर्जन–परान्तं वह्नि–स्त्री–पथि–सेवनम् ।

परातः–सनानोपवासादि् काय–कलेश–विधिं तथा ।। ६४ ।।

vahni–strī–pathi–sevānāmādau varjanamācaret || 63 ||
tathā hi gorakṣa–vacanam
varjayeddurjana–prāntaṁ vahni–strī–pathi–sevanam |
prātaḥ–snānopavāsādi kāya–kleśa–vidhiṁ tathā || 64 ||

vahni – fire, strī – women, pathi – on roadways, sevānāmādau – travelling about, varjanam – avoidance, ācaret – should practice yoga, tathā – thus, hi – because, gorakṣa – Gorakṣa, vacanam – instruction, varjayed = varjayet = should avoid, durjana – undesirables, prāntaṁ – being confidential, vahni – fire, strī – women, pathi – moving in public places, sevanam – travelling, prātaḥ – early morning, – snānopavāsādi = snāna (bath) + upavāsa (fasting) + ādi (and related restrictions), kaya – body, kleśa – sickness, vidhiṁ – activity, tathā – as well as

Avoiding fire, women and travelling about on roadways, one should practice yoga because the instruction of Goraksha is that one should avoid being confidential with undesirables, fire, women, travelling about, taking bath in the early morning, fasting and related restrictions, and also whatever activity causes sickness in the body.

Analysis

The **prejudice against women** is present all over the Vedic literature. This is the first thing we need to admit. In consideration we should know that in ancient times yoga was mainly a man-thing, a discipline practiced by men mostly. It is only recently, perhaps within the last one hundred and fifty (150) years for the most, that women became included in yoga in a significant way.

In the Western countries particularly, the percentage of women practicing in contrast to men is greater than at any other time in the history of yoga. However it may be asked as to what is yoga today. Is modern yoga the same as the ancient disciplines? It is the same word yoga but is the meaning of the term the same?

We need to understand also that in the time of Swatmarama, boys who were accepted as students of yoga were without sexual needs due to the sexual immaturity of their bodies. When they reached sexual maturity, it was considered as to whether they should be married or should remain single for the rest of their lives.

In the juvenile stage they were considered to be bachelors or brahmacharyas. If they got married they were regarded as householders or grihastas. If they were to remain single for the rest of their lives they were termed as sannyasi, renounced monks with a vow for no sexual indulgence.

To be practical with the Vedic rules for sexual intercourse, men were asked to avoid the association of females. The feeling was that if a male associated freely with females then sexual intercourse would be mandatory because of natural urges. Hence the feeling was that the only way to avoid sexual indulgence was to not be in the proximity of females. This is a bias against females.

Overall the motive for doing higher yoga does not fit well with the psychology of females but it does cater to many males who detest social complication and who feel that material existence may not be worth the while.

There are two aspects to consider in terms of the remark here about avoiding the association of females. These are:

- association with a female which results in a pregnancy
- association with a female or with females which results in increased social responsibilities

If the ascetic has association with a female and this developed into a sexual linkage, and if that develops into a pregnancy, then the ascetic has to calculate that into his lifestyle. In other words he has to adjust his social situation to suit. This may mean a reduction in yoga disciplines since he would have to spend some time responding to the child and its mother. If he fails to service them he will be liable to civil and astral authorities for negligence. This will damage his spiritual practice.

Even if there is no pregnancy, association with a female may result in increased social responsibility. The ascetic may have to get a job or may have to increase the hours of employment. This will bite into the amount of time used for completion of yogic disciplines.

Thus a decision has to be made by the ascetic regarding how much time he will use for austerities and how much he will engage for social duties. There are only so many hours in one day, so many days in one year, so many destined years in the ascetic's lifespan. A certain amount of time is required for the perfection of the yogic disciplines. Should the ascetic risk reducing the time he could devote to practice? Which is the priority? Social means or spiritual practice?

The stipulation about **avoiding fire** has to do with not seeking social comforts. The ascetic was required to maintain the very basic accommodations, and in isolation, without stress on bodily gratification. The Himalayan region is a cold climate. For many months of the year, fire provides heat to counteract the cold temperatures. It gives comfort.

If the ascetic became attached to comfortable circumstances, he was likely to become lax in the austerities which would result in a slackening of interest in the practice. Hence there was a discouragement about being too attached to heat sources.

Fire is useful for cooking. For that matter the food difference in food consumption between man and animal has much to do with man's creation of fire. The animals cannot produce fire as desired. They cannot cook food. An obsession with fire for the purpose of cooking made humans to be superfluous and excessive in diet. This could absorb the time of the ascetic and reduce his interest in the discipline of yoga. Thus fire can be an impediment.

The ascetic is advised to **not be travelling about on roadways**. The reason for this is to limit social involvement. Moving about here and there is a sure way to activate various karmic obligations and to tempt material nature into presenting time-consuming unresolved relationships from previous lives.

A wanted criminal would be a fool to walk boldly in a city. Knowing that posters show his portrait and declare his criminality, he would be foolish to tempt fate by travelling in broad daylight.

An ascetic who is not smart enough to hide from past associations, some of which were maintained in previous existences and which would be enabled again merely by chance meetings, would lose the foothold on yoga austerities as soon as he began to travel about meeting people with whom he had scores to settle in previous existences.

Doing yoga successful is much to do with hiding from people so as to keep past associations in dormancy, lest they be enabled afresh and take over one's life with endless demands for obligations to be met in the social way.

Taking bath in the early morning is necessary for those ascetics who serve as purohitas or ceremonial priests. These pujaris, ritual masters, must cleanse the body early in the morning. Some rise at 2.30am, take bath, saying numerous prayers, prepare sacred articles and sanctified food and do deity worship. However ascetics who do not engage in deity worship and who are not duty bound to do puja ceremonies for lay-people should not be as involved in bodily baths many times per day.

If the ascetic is isolated there is no need to be involved in physical worship of deities. The shift should be made to psychic approaches, which concern the condition of the subtle body. Purification of the subtle body is done through pranayama breath-infusion to remove the negative subtle energies in that form. This is not like in the physical world, where bodily cleanliness hinges on washing the skin of the material form.

Instead of taking bath in the early morning and doing various mantric and article offering rites, the yogi should do pranayama breath-infusion and then sit to meditate to transfer focus to the chit akash divine world sky of consciousness where the divine being resides. The yogi can then worship these personalities in their habitat as contrasted to the pujaris who do so on the material side of existence by approaching pictures, sculptures or yantra symbols.

Fasting has big value for lay people and for ascetics who are socially obligated and must toe the line to set example for the public. However ascetics who are isolated do not have to follow these routines some of which are distractions and counteractions.

If eating rice as a staple should be counteracted by not eating it for one day or a week during a month, then a layperson should fast accordingly. The ascetic however should instead reduce the daily intake of rice or change the diet so that there is no need to fast in relationship to having too much in the body. A well-regulated balanced meal which is taken in moderation deletes the need for fasting. The energy which is involved in fasting could then be used to increase insight perception.

An ascetic should **avoid being confidential with undesirables**. There is an injunction that an ascetic should be friendly to all, even to other species of life, but that does not mean that he should become familiar with everyone. As pressed by fate to meet humans or any other species, the ascetic should be cordial and helpful but all the same he or she should avoid associating with one and all.

There are many undesirable human beings and animals. One should keep a distance from them without being hostile and unfriendly. The main thing is to stop energy from undesirable people from leaking over into one's being. If one fails to do this, there will be numerous diversions and one will never complete the required austerities.

Application

Whatever is undesirable should be avoided. If the student recognizes a danger but is compelled by fate to be subjected to it, then he or she should as soon as possible get away from it.

It is not what we are compelled to do but rather what we do when providence lifts an imposition. Do we run away when we can or do we stay put under negative influences and complain about it?

Let fate be what it is but take every opportunity it affords for escaping from its impositions. The same pressure which forces an ascetic to act in a counterproductive way is the same force which when lifted allows him to escape.

Verse 65

गोधूम–शालि–यव–षाष्टिक–शोभनान्नं

क्षीराज्य–खण्ड–नवनीत–सिता–मधूनि ।

शुण्ठी–पटोल–कफलादिक–पञ्च–शाकं

मुद्गादि–दिव्यमुदकं च यमीन्द्र–पथ्यम् ।। ६५ ।।

godhūma–śāli–yava–ṣāṣṭika–śobhanānnaṁ
kṣīrājya–khaṇḍa–navanīta– sitā –madhūni ।
śuṇṭhī–paṭolaka–phalādika–pañca–śākaṁ
mudghādi–divyamudakaṁ ca yamīndra–pathyam ।। 65 ।।

godhūma – wheat, śāli – rice, yava – barley, ṣāṣṭika – sixty days rice, śobhanānnaṁ – nourishing food, kṣīrājya = kṣīra (milk) + ājya (ghee), khaṇḍa – sugar candy, navanīta – butter, sitā – white sugar, madhūni – honey, śuṇṭhī – dry ginger, paṭolaka – cucumber, phalādika – fruits and related foods, pañca – five, śākaṁ – vegetables, mudghādi – mung and similar foods, divyam – sanctified, udakaṁ – water, ca – and, yamīndra – greatest of the psyche–controlled ascetics, –pathyam – suitable

Wheat, rice, barley, sixty-day rice, nourishing foods, milk, ghee, sugar candy, butter, white sugar, honey, dry ginger, cucumber, fruits and related foods, the five types of vegetables, mung and similar foods, and sanctified water, are considered to be suitable for the greatest of the psyche-controlled ascetics.

Analysis

This list is relevant to the time of Swatmarama. These foods were available to yogis in his vicinity during his time. It depends on location and what is available.

Application

The guideline is to get advice from advanced yogis and be open to being inspired by deities. One should test various foods to see their effect on yoga. Whatever contravenes the process should be adjusted or abandoned. The hard and fast rule is that whatever one eats should assist with practice and should have a positive and encouraging impact on the enthusiasm one needs to complete the austerities.

Verse 66

पुष्टं सुमधुरं सनिग्धं गव्यं धातु– प्रपोषणम् ।

मनोऽभिलषितं योग्यं योगी भोजनमाचरेत् ।। ६६ ।।

puṣṭaṁ sumadhuraṁ snighdhaṁ gavyaṁ dhātu–prapoṣaṇam I
manobhilaṣitaṁ yogyaṁ yogī bhojanamācaret I I 66 I I

puṣṭaṁ – nourishing, sumadhuraṁ – very sweet food, snighdhaṁ – smooth feeling and rich food, gavyaṁ – dairy products, dhātu – body parts, prapoṣaṇam – nourishing food, manobhilaṣitaṁ = manah (feelings) +abhilaṣitaṁ (cherished desire) yogyaṁ yogī – yogi, bhojanam – food, ācaret – should ạccept

Nourishing, very sweet food, smooth feeling and rich food, dairy products, foods which nourish the bodily parts and are feelingly cherished; this is what the yogi should accept.

Analysis

Gifts to a yogi may be detrimental to progress. A yogi should not get in the habit of begging here and there. He should not be in the mood to have people support him merely because he is a religious authority, famous ascetic or good person. If possible a yogi should earn a livelihood by simple means and in a way which does not bite into practice time and cause the yogi to become a money-craving human being.

Gifts are not energy-free. Each gift carries with it an energy which may deter or aid advancement. Some gifts have a dual energy where initially they cause the yogi to be encouraged and then later they sink his progress and put him into a negative mood which ruins the practice.

There are many people who come to a yogi with money or commodities. Some offer with a nice attitude in which there might be delay-destruction energies. Only a naive ascetic feels that every gift is in his interest or that every offering which is given in a good spirit with praise does not contain a delayed-destructive energy.

However this does not mean that a yogi should reject all gifts. Even a yogi should cooperate with fate to a greater degree by accepting even harmful energies from others but the yogi should be aware of the psychic content in these transfers so that he can quarantine or neutralize detrimental ones.

Application

By all means a yogi should cook food. He may have an assistant or wife who makes preparations by the standards which facilitate yoga practice. Some yogis get in the habit of having others take charge of the meals. These others might be a wife or disciple. This is a dangerous habit because usually the assistant develops an arrogant attitude and influences the preparation in such a way as to divert the energy of it so that it adversely affects advancement.

To prevent this, a yogi should be up-and-at-it in the kitchen participating in food preparations. It is not a good thing when a yogi becomes dependent on someone, anyone, even a wife or a devoted disciple.

One simple test serves to determine if the assistant took control of the food preparations. The yogi only needs to go into the kitchen and give advice. Usually the assistant will be annoyed and will argue point for point, claiming that he or she follows what the yogi wanted based on this and that stipulation which the yogi made before. In other words the assistant became independent over the course of time, took charge of the food and infused the food with some other type of energy.

When the yogi tries to reform this, there are hard feelings and resentments. Sometimes the person becomes so offended as to leave the association of the yogi.

Verse 67

युवो वृद्धो। अतिवृद्धो वा वयाधितो दुर्बलो। अपि वा ।

अभ्यासात्सिद्धिमाप्नोति सर्वयोगेष्वतन्द्रितः।। ६७ ।।

yuvo vṛddho | ativṛddho vā vyādhito durbalo | api vā |
abhyāsātsiddhimāpnoti sarva–yogeṣvatandritaḥ || 67 ||

yuvo = yuvaḥ = young, vṛddho = vṛddhaḥ = elderly, ativṛddho = ativṛddhaḥ = very old, vā – or, vyādhito = vyādhitaḥ = sick, durbalo = durbalaḥ = lacking strength, api – also, vā – or, abhyāsāt – from practice, siddhim – proficiency, āpnoti – he achieves, sarva – all aspects, yogeṣv = yogeṣu = of yoga, atandritaḥ – not lazy, energetic

Young, old or too old, sick or lacking strength, one who is energetic, gets proficiency by practicing all aspects of yoga.

Analysis

It does matter when one begins to do yoga as to whether the body is old or young but all the same one should practice even if one has an old or sick body. One should do yoga with moderation when it is difficult to perform.

Yoga involves both physical and psychic actions. Either may be difficult to perform. One may have to do preparatory activities for months or years before one can be proficient but still it does not matter in this regard if one is old or young because one can continue to practice in the hereafter and can resume the practice in the future life as a new human being.

Yoga practice is so important for integrating the evolutionary experience and for spiritual self-reflection that one may begin it even on one's death bed. Because its ultimate target is the subtle body, doing it at the time of death has value. The practice could persists in the afterlife state and continue when one acquires a new body.

Application

An energetic approach is required for yoga. Patanjali Mahayogin mentions the speed with which one progresses in yoga. He wrote:

tīvrasaṁvegānām āsannaḥ

tīvra – very intense; saṁvegānām – regarding those who practice forcibly; āsannaḥ – whatever is very near, what will occur soon.

For those who practice forcefully in a very intense way, the skill of yoga will be achieved very soon. (Yoga Sutras 1.21)

mṛdu madhya adhimātratvāt tataḥ api viśeṣaḥ

mṛdu – slight; madhya – mediocre; adhimātratvāt – from intense; tataḥ – then; api – even; viśeṣaḥ – rating.

Then there are even more ratings, according to intense, mediocre, or slight practice. (Yoga Sutras 1.22)

Verse 68

क्रिया–युक्तस्य सिद्धिः सयादक्रियस्य कथं भवेत् ।
न शास्त्र–पाठ–मात्रेण योग–सिद्धिः प्रजायते ।। ६८ ।।

kriyā–yuktasya siddhiḥ syādakriyasya kathaṁ bhavet |
na śāstra–pāṭha–mātreṇa yoga–siddhiḥ prajāyate || 68 ||

kriya – mystic technique, yuktasya – of those who are proficient, siddhiḥ – perfection, syād = syāt = is, akriyasya – of those who do not practice the mystic techniques, kathaṁ – how, bhavet – should, na – not, śāstra – authoritative book, pāṭha – study, mātreṇa – by merely, yoga–siddhiḥ = perfection in yoga practice, prajāyate – achieve

Perfection is for those who are proficient in the mystic technique. How can one who does not practice become successful? Merely studying authoritative books, one cannot achieve perfection in this practice.

Analysis

Yoga is a mystic process at heart but initially it involves using the physical form. Beings on the astral planes may require a physical body to solidify the practice of yoga but there are astral beings who do yoga using their subtle forms without the need for a physical form. These persons are called siddhas or advanced yogis who do not require physical integration to complete the practice.

Application

Books are useful in so far as they grant insight and award confidence in the process on the basis of what was done by previous ascetics. However one must practice physically and psychically. One should learn how to reform and redirect emotions and mental energy.

As road maps are useful to an educated traveler, books are useful to the enthusiastic yogi. Maps are no replacement for actual travel. Books do not replace actual practice.

Verse 69

न वेष–धारणं सिद्धेः कारणं न च तत–कथा ।

क्रियैव कारणं सिद्धेः सत्यमेतन्न संशयः ।। ६९ ।।

na veṣa–dhāraṇaṁ siddheḥ kāraṇaṁ na ca tat–kathā ।
kriyaiva kāraṇaṁ siddheḥ satyametanna saṁśayaḥ ।। 69 ।।

na – neither, veṣa – clothing, dhāraṇaṁ – wearing, siddheḥ – of perfection, kāraṇaṁ – cause, na – nor, ca – and, tat – that, kathā – discussion, kriyaiva = kriyā (physio–mystic technique) + eva (alone), kāraṇaṁ – cause, siddheḥ – of succcess, satyam – reality, etan = etat = this, na – not, saṁśayaḥ – without a doubt

Neither wearing clothing nor by discussions about that can one attain perfection. Physio–mystic technique alone is the cause of success. Without a doubt that is the reality.

Analysis

One should dress appropriately for religious ceremonies and rituals, for social functions. Appearance is a major part of public displays. Yoga however has other requirements, the first of which is singular practice, isolation under supervision of an advanced yogi.

Religion involves an attempt to communicate with a deity in this physical world. Religion is preferred if it is physically focused either through the use of physical deity forms or by remained pinned down in material existence and assuming that the deity can hear one's physical pleas.

Yoga is different. It is for the ascetic to transit out of the physical into the psychic and super-psychic. Physical appearance is left aside. It is neglected. Astral situation is checked closely.

Application

One cannot transit to a spiritual dimension or to a higher astral dimension by wearing socially-approved clothing. One should wear such garbs appropriately for the occasion, especially for religion-related incidences, but that does not mean anything outside of the physical world's social concerns. Clothing does not affect the inner personality except superficially.

There are many things which we should do socially in this life and yet, we should know that the benefits of such actions are limited to this material existence only and will not give any proceeds elsewhere.

The pride we express and reinforce by grand physical appearances will not translate into spiritual glory. While in the material world I can wear expensive clothing to show importance. If I attempt to do that in the higher astral dimensions, there will be no extravagant attire; only my energy of insecurity will be expressed.

Verse 70

पीठानि कुम्भकाश्छित्रा दिव्यानि करणानि च।

सर्वाण्यपि हठाभ्यासे राजयोगफलावधि॥ ७०॥

pīṭhāni kumbhakāśchitrā divyāni karaṇāni ca |
sarvāṇyapi haṭhābhyāse rāja–yoga–phalāvadhi || 70 ||

pīṭhāni – postures, kumbhakāś = kumbhakāḥ suspension of breathing process, chitrā – types, divyāni – psychic, karaṇāni – causes, means, ca – and, sarvāṇy = sarvāṇi = all, api – also, haṭhābhyāse – in the practice of kundalini manipulation for subtle body transformation, rāja – remaining introverted while externally occupied, yoga – yoga, phalāvadhi = phala (result) + avadhi (until)

Postures, various types of suspension of breathing process and other psychic procedures, should all be done in the practice of kundalini manipulation for subtle body transformation, until the result of remaining introverted while externally occupied, is attained.

Analysis

This is the state of complete pratyahar sensual energy withdrawal, the proficiency of the fifth (5th) stage of yoga. This is the application of that stage of yoga after the yogi mastered it so that it becomes a reflexive instinct in the psyche.

Kundalini yoga is not a simple practice. It is complicated because of the variations in each yogi's psyche and the complicated energies which were amassed through the ages while transmigrating. Kundalini has many unwanted and very stubborn tendencies which do not go away merely by applying effective methods once. The experience is that it takes repeated attempts to gradually erase, reform, or eliminate its behaviors.

Application

Pratyahar sensual energy withdrawal is the fifth (5th) stage of yoga, and yet it persists through the sixth, seventh and eight or final stage. To master it consistently, one should do pranayama breath-infusion which is the fourth (4th) stage. This should be done before each meditation session for the most efficient use of breath intake.

When there is thorough infusion of fresh air into the body with a corresponding extraction of polluted gases, a similar process happens in the subtle form, which results in internalization of the sense organs so that they lose interest in what is outside the psyche and they fold up upon the core-self.

This satisfies the second verse in the Patanjali Yoga Sutras, which states:

yogaḥcittavṛtti nirodhaḥ

yogaḥ – the skill of yoga; cittavṛtti = citta – mento-emotional energy + vṛtti – vibrational mode; nirodhaḥ – cessation, restraint, non-operation.

The skill of yoga is demonstrated by the conscious non-operation of the

vibrational modes of the mento-emotional energy. (Yoga Sutras of Patanjali 1.2)

Patanjali Mahayogin stated this opinion that for yoga to begin there must a shutdown of the outward-going tendency of its senses. To be sure this takes place the yogi should notice that the mento-emotional energies lost their vibrational rattling within the thought/idea illustration screen in the mind.

It is possible for this to happen without doing breath-infusion but it is not likely to be so in the case of most student yogis. One or two exceptional individuals demonstrated such a high degree of will power control over the mind as to cause the shutdown of the mento-emotional vibrations just on command but most others are unable to do this.

However pranayama breath-infusion is the sure way for any person to attain a higher degree of sense control and a shutdown of the mento-emotional drama and sensual pursuits which the mind forcibly enacts within the psyche.

Once the yogi repeatedly did this thorough breath-infusion he will notice its effects and will develop confidence in doing the pranayama practice. This will remove hesitation and doubts, clearing the way for inspirations on how to maximize the process and get a tighter and tighter shut down and fold-inwards of the sensual orbs in the psyche.

With this interiorization will come an attraction to naad sound resonance which will pull the yogi further and further away from the busy-body frontal area of the subtle head.

Naad will help the yogi considerably so that he is no longer distracted within the mind by thoughts and images. These will be absent of their own accord and no meditative energy will be used in shutting these down, in denying them displays or in observing their drama.

Over time when this practice matures, the yogi will notice as stated in this verse that even when socially involved, he remains introverted, even when he is externally occupied.

In the Bhagavad Gita there is a warning about having a false confidence about being advanced in terms of this pratyahar fifth stage of yoga:

yadā saṁharate cāyaṁ
kūrmo'ṅgānīva sarvaśaḥ
indriyāṇīndriyārthebhyas
tasya prajñā pratiṣṭhitā (2.58)

yadā — when; saṁharate — pulls; cāyaṁ = ca — and + ayam — this; kūrmo = kūrmaḥ — tortoise; 'ṅgānīva = aṅgānīva = aṅgāni — limbs + iva — like, compared to; sarvaśaḥ — fully; indriyāṇīndriyārthebhyas = indriyani — senses + indriyarthebhyaḥ — attractive things; tasya — his; prajñā — reality-piercing vision; pratiṣṭhitā — is established

When such a person pulls fully out of moods, he or she may be compared to the tortoise with its limbs retracted. The senses are withdrawn from the attractive things in the case of a person whose reality-piercing vision is established. (Bhagavad Gita 2.58)

viṣayā vinivartante
nirāhārasya dehinaḥ

rasavarjaṁ raso'pyasya
paraṁ dṛṣṭvā nivartate (2.59)

viṣayā = viṣayāḥ — temptations; vinivartante — turn away; nirāhārasya — from(without) indulgence; dehinaḥ — of the embodied soul; rasavarjaṁ = rasa — memory or mental flavor of past indulgences + varjaṁ — except for, besides; raso = rasah — memories (mental flavors); 'pyasya = apyasya = apy (api) — even + asya — of him; paraṁ — higher stage; dṛṣṭvā — having experienced; nivartate — leaves

The temptations themselves turn away from the disciplinary attitude of an ascetic, but the memory of previous indulgences remains with him. When he experiences higher stages, those memories leave him. (Bhagavad Gita 2.59)

This explains the situation that at first when the yogi is successful with pratyahar sensual energy withdrawal, he may be compared to a tortoise with its limbs retracted. The yogi learns how to and actually does retract the sensual orbs in the subtle body. However this only happens in meditation and only in some sessions of meditation, not in all.

For the very advanced yogi, there is the development of reality-piercing vision (prajna), which absorbs his attention and assures that he will not resume the old sensual pursuits which caused the senses to be externally occupied.

But then even so, even though the temptations themselves turn away from the disciplinary attitude of the ascetic, the memory of previous indulgences haunts him. These impressions remain in the psyche as compressed stored potencies which burst out repeatedly whenever there is laxness or social involvement. Gradually over years, and for some of us, over lives, these memories wear away. They fade out due to the induction of new memories from experiences on higher planes of consciousness.

Chapter 2

Breath-Infusion*

Verse 1

अथासने दृधे योगी वशी हित–मिताशनः ।

गुरूपदिष्ट–मार्गेण प्राणायामान्समभ्यसेत् ।। १ ।।

athāsane dṝdhe yogī vaśī hita–mitāśanaḥ I
gurūpadiṣṭa–mārgeṇa prāṇāyāmānsamabhyaset I I 1 I I

athāsane = atha (regarding, once) + āsane (in posture), dṝdhe – in steadiness, yogī – yogi, vaśī – one whose psyche is under control, hita – adequate, mitāśanaḥ = mita(moderate) + aśanaḥ (diet), gurūpadiṣṭa = guru (yoga teacher) + upadiṣṭa (taught by), mārgeṇa – by the method, prāṇāyāmān – breath-infusion technique, samabhyaset – thoroughly practice

Once there is steadiness in posture, the yogi whose psyche is under control, who has a moderate diet, should thoroughly practice the breath-infusion technique by the method taught by the yoga teacher.

Analysis

Patanjali Mahamuni wrote this:

sthira sukham āsanam
prayatna śaithilya ananta samāpattibhyām

sthira – steady; sukham – comfortable; āsanan – bodily posture, prayatna – effort; śaithilya – relaxation; ananta – endless, infinite; samāpattibhyām – meeting, encounter.

The posture should be steady and comfortable. It results in relaxation of effort and meeting with the infinite. (Yoga Sutras of Patanjali 2.46-47)

Moderate diet is required with foods which facilitate the type of consciousness through which one can maintain enthusiasm for practice and can rely more on sober consciousness which is boosted by kundalini upraises.

People who become addicted to marijuana, ayahuasca, cocaine, opium, heroin, morphine, ecstasy, LSD or similar substances or herbs cannot make fit yogis as kundalini yoga is defined in the Hatha Yoga Pradipika. Drugs like marijuana and opium were on the earth for millions of years. They were known to yogis in the time of Swatmarama. Still he did not recommend them; neither did Patanjali and Krishna, both of whom mentioned drugs as a means of altering consciousness.

**The Haṭha Yoga Pradīpikā does not have chapter headings. This title was assigned by the translator on the basis of the verse 1 of this chapter.*

Drugs are a means but if you must use them, then at least know that they are not recommended. As to why, that is not the subject of this book but it will suffice to say that if you are serious about permanent divine world transit hereafter, then know that you must use your psyche and that only to develop that access. To follow the path recommended by Michael Beloved, one has to forego these substances.

One has to realize that if one cannot get high enough without the assistance of herb or drugs, then there is definitely something amiss in the psyche. If I cannot remain on a high level with adjustments in my psyche which are conducted psychologically without any other assistance, then no drug or herb in the world will enable me.

Persons who move from an undeveloped country to a developed one and who do so illegally may be arrested and then deported back to their native land. A deportee usually harbors a desire to return to the developed place. He burns with desire to do so because of having experienced better social conditions.

Similarly, persons who experienced higher states of consciousness or even greater existential happiness through herbs and drugs, harbor such strong desires to return to those states, that they risk arrest and imprisonment by using even illegal substances.

But there is another way of experiencing those states without taking drugs. The method is this kundalini yoga explained by Swatmarama. This is the trouble-free method without reliance on narcotics, hallucinogenic drugs or stimulants.

Application

***Steadiness in posture**, psyche control and moderate diet, are required for success in breath-infusion practice. Steadiness in posture includes inner focus during the assumption of a posture with no spacing-out and mind-wondering outside of the body or into unrelated thinking and imaging.*

***Psyche control** means a grasp on lifestyle so that the student is resistant to non-yogic influences and is separated from social situations which deter progress and cause stagnation.*

***Moderate diet** means the cessation of all food addictions like spices, pungent foods, sugars, oily foods, fermented foods, stale foods, leftovers, vinegars and the like. All foods which have a strong taste and which induce food addictions, overeating and greed should be abandoned by the yogi.*

These aspects take time to master. People who want instant results, who feel that the method should work immediately, are not suited to this practice.

Verse 2

चले वाते चलं चित्तं निश्चले निश्चलं भवेत्।

योगी स्थाणुत्वमाप्नोति ततो वायुं निरोधयेत्॥ २

cale vāte calaṁ cittaṁ niścale niścalaṁ bhavet|
yogī sthāṇutvamāpnoti tato vāyuṁ nirodhayet||2||

cale – irratic, vāte – in comsumption of air, calaṁ – anxious, insecure, cittam =

mento–emotional energy, niścale – in mentally manipulating, niścalaṁ – compressed and distributing, bhavet – is, yogī – yogi, sthāṇutvam – stabalization, āpnoti – attains, tato = tataḥ = then, vāyuṁ – fresh air, nirodhayet – should infuse and channel

When consumption of fresh air is erratic, then the mento–emotional energy is insecure. In comparison, there is stabilization when compressing and distributing while mentally directing the air. Thus the yogi should infuse and channel fresh air.

Analysis

The erratic consumption of air has to do with the healthy or unhealthy condition of the lungs and the purity of the diet. Depending on the type of human body one received from parents, one may or may not have efficient air intake. The attitude of the lifeforce must be studied by the student yogi, not any lifeforce, only his or her individual system, to see its attitude for the percentage of fresh air with which it is comfortable.

If the lifeforce prefers a greater percentage of polluted air, drastic austerities may be performed to reform the system.

Historically human bodies became addicted to tobacco and coffee on a global basis. This is due to two substances which are nicotine and caffeine. Both of these cause increase in toxins in the blood stream. This means that the lifeforce may prefer toxins and will control the lungs for maintaining less fresh air in the system. But this is not conducive to the type of yoga recommended in this book.

Some people become addicted to marijuana and other related substances and then claim that they are not addicted and that they use these drugs by choice. However it does not matter as to the control of the drug or the control of the individual using the drug. That is not the issue. In one sense everything is a drug including potatoes and apples. Therefore that is not the point.

The issue is if the substance drastically increases toxins in the blood stream. Does marijuana use increase or cause a deficit of fresh air in the blood stream?

Application

What we need to understand at least intellectually, is that if we increase the fresh air in the system and extract a greater percentage of polluted gases, the system will become more relaxed. The lifeforce will be less into its survival mode. It will have fewer anxieties and be less grasping of trivial sense objects. This will facilitate meditation and inner psychic research even more.

The air should be taken into the lungs, be absorbed there, be compressed into the blood stream and then be distributed through the body. While this transpires, polluted gases should be extracted from the cells and expelled through the lungs. This will cause a proportionate infusion of fresh air with extraction of stale used gases, resulting in chemical purity in the physical body and astral energy purity in the subtle form.

Verse 3

यावद्वायुः सथितो देहे तावज्जीवनमुच्यते ।

मरणं तस्य निष्क्रान्तिस्ततो वायुं निरोधयेत् ।। ३ ।।

yāvadvāyuḥ sthito dehe tāvajjīvanamucyate |
maraṇaṁ tasya niṣkrāntistato vāyuṁ nirodhayet || 3 ||

yāvad – so long as, vāyuḥ – air, sthito = sthitaḥ = utilized, dehe – in the body, tāvaj = tāvaḥ = so then, jīvanam – living creature, ucyate – is called, maraṇaṁ – death of the physical system, tasya – of this, niṣkrāntis = niṣkrāntiḥ = final out-flow of lifeforce, tato = tataḥ = thus, vāyuṁ – fresh air, nirodhayet – should infuse and channel

As long as air is utilized in the body, that is called a living creature. Death of the physical system occurs when there is the final out-flow of lifeforce. Thus, (to expedite life) one should infuse and channel fresh air.

Analysis

To keep the material body in its healthiest condition, a yogi should infuse and channel fresh air through it on a daily basis, preferably twice per day.

For a person whose body is habituated to a high percentage of polluted gases, a proportionate increase of fresh air, may be upsetting and may contribute to ill-health; but that lifestyle leads in a different direction to the one desired by a yogi.

Some yogis do a breath-infusion process which is the reverse of this recommendation, where they increase the percentage of carbon dioxide in the body and enter trance states as a result. However they go into a blank voidable state of consciousness, a non-objective consciousness or to the subterranean astral regions.

Application

So long as the material body lives, there has got to be a certain amount of fresh air in it. However a yogi should focus on the subtle body and do the needful to keep that body in the best energy configuration possible. Pranayama breath-infusion is the sure way to target the subtle body and cause it not to pattern itself after a failing material form.

As soon as youth is over, the material body begins to fail. The yogi should protect the subtle form from the deteriorating effects which manifest in the life of the physical one. That physical system cannot be saved and will be terminated sooner or later. Realizing this, the yogi should shift his health interest to the subtle form.

In the near future, everyone using a material body will have to leave it and become whatever is left of the psychology on the astral plane. Hence it makes sense to focus on that remnant and supply it with whatever it requires for its upkeep.

If a yogi, or any creature for that matter, does not protect the subtle body from the failing effects of the physical one, then the subtle body will be worn-out and after the death of the physical that subtle form will look like and feel as a worn-out one. This is undesirable. A yogi should maintain the subtle body so that it retains a youthful configuration hereafter.

Verse 4

मलाकलासु नाडीषु मारुतो नैव मध्यगः ।

कथं सयादुन्मनीभावः कार्य–सिद्धिः कथं भवेत् || ४ ||

malākalāsu nāḍīṣu māruto naiva madhyagaḥ I
kathaṁ syādunmanībhāvaḥ kārya–siddhiḥ kathaṁ bhavet I I 4 I I

malākalāsu = mala (pollutants) + ākalāsu (in saturation), nāḍīṣu – in the nadi subtle veins and arteries, māruto = mārutaḥ = subtle air, naiva = not ever, madhya – through the middle channel, gaḥ – pass through, kathaṁ – how? syād = syāt = should happen, unmanī – thoughtless state of mind during contact with the chit akash sky of consciousness, bhāvaḥ – experience, kārya–siddhiḥ = successfully accomplished, kathaṁ – how, bhavet – should

Due to pollutants which are saturated in the nadi subtle veins and arteries, the subtle air in the psyche never passes through the middle channel. How then would the experience of the thoughtless state of mind during contact with the chit akash sky of consciousness be successfully accomplished?

Analysis

It does happen that by chance, a person who does not do pranayama breath-infusion may experience the thoughtless state of mind during contact with the chit akash sky of consciousness. This does happen but quite infrequently and without a definite method of causing it to recur. For a yogi, this haphazard method is unsatisfactory.

If we accept this idea of Swatmarama, it would mean that by chance, sometimes, pollutants which are saturated in the nadi subtle veins and arteries clear away and subtle air passes through the middle channel. But this is not what a yogi wants to achieve. The ascetic wants a definite method which works to clear away the pollutants on a daily basis, if not permanently, to keep the central spinal passage cleared, for continuous access to the chit akash sky of consciousness.

Application

The target is the subtle body. The physical system has little to do with it but the physical so long as it is alive and well, must be used because it is psychically connected to the subtle. The feedback between the physical and subtle makes it necessary to work with both for the upkeep and upgrade of the subtle one.

The physical form was developed from the energy configuration of the subtle body, but all the same, once the physical came into being, it had an effect on the subtle one. This makes it necessary to regulate the behavior of the physical body so that it does not degrade the subtle one. If the human being is not careful in regulating the feedback between the physical and subtle bodies, there is the likelihood that the more enduring subtle form will become degraded, the result of which will be a birth in a lower species in the next life. By all means one should study the relationship between the physical and the subtle and institute disciplines which prohibit the physical from degrading the subtle one.

Even if one fails to further elevate the subtle form, fails to increase its energy upliftment, one should at least keep it on the level it is so that it may develop a human body for itself in the next birth. The subtle body is adaptable to any of the species forms. This adaptability is its risk. Therefore a yogi should always be aware of that and protect it from adapting to the configuration of a lower species.

The danger in taking a lower species birth is that one may completely forget the advantage of human birth and become totally occupied in that lower designation with

the result of losing all ideas about spiritual realization. Once one gets into a lower life form, one's attention will be drawn into the intrigues which that species has to deal with in its evolutionary position. This is the danger. To protect the self from this use of its attention, the human being should make sure that the physical system does not exert a downward spiraling influence on the subtle body.

Verse 5

शुद्धमेति यदा सर्वं नाडी–चक्रं मलाकुलम् ।
तदैव जायते योगी प्राण–संग्रहणे क्षमः ।। ५ ।।

śuddhameti yadā sarvaṁ nāḍī–cakraṁ malākulam |
tadaiva jāyate yogī prāṇa–saṁgrahaṇe kṣamaḥ || 5 ||

śuddham – clearance, eti – accomplished, yadā – when, sarvaṁ – all, nāḍī – nadi subtle arteries and veins, cakraṁ – energy junction vortexes, malākulam = mala (pollutants) + ākulam – (saturated), tadaiva – then only, jāyate – is capable, yogī – yogi, prāṇa – physio-subtle air energy fresh air, saṁgrahaṇe – infusing, compressing, distributing, kṣamaḥ – capable

When clearance of all the energy junction vortexes and their nadi subtle arteries and veins, which are usually saturated with pollutants, is accomplished, then the yogi becomes capable of infusing, compressing and distributing the physio–subtle air energy.

Analysis

An aggressive attitude is required, thus many persons who come to do pranayama yoga go away because this is inconsistent with their process of pacification and natural means of accomplishment. These individuals feel that enlightenment should be achieved by an easy and very natural method which does not have exertion as a process.

Some persons want a method which does not involve breath-infusion and which could be achieved by the exercise of willpower or wishful thinking. Some require a process like prayer and belief. What we need to know is that this system in the Hatha Yoga Pradipika is not for everyone. This is for those who feel the need for radical adjustments in lifestyle and method.

Some pranayama breath-infusion methods do not use aggressive or very forceful means. These can be used for success but the execution requires tremendous patience because it takes a long time to get the subtle body infused by a non-forceful method. Wanting a non-forceful method is one thing. Having the patience to practice is a separate matter.

Application

The student yogi must be determined and must not expect instant results. He must be willing to work for years, if not lives for these achievements. The clearance of the energy junction vortexes and their nadi subtle arteries and veins, happens quickly while doing certain pranayama breath-infusion practice but as soon as the session is over, the system resumes the pollutants.

For permanent clearance the yogi has to work to raise kundalini on a daily basis for

years, while adjusting his lifestyle and greatly restricting his association with human society.

Bhastrika pranayama and alternately kapalabhati breath-infusion are the most efficient and radical ways of achieving the clearance of the nadis and chakras but even these systems must be used for years to cause a permanent clearance of the subtle passages. The reason is that the pollutants are natural and are reinstated time and again by material nature.

This is not a hopeless situation because eventually a yogi will be successful. However the yogi should be realistic and make a decision to work for as many years or lives it would take to make the full achievement.

Verse 6

प्राणायामं ततः कुर्यान्नित्यं सात्त्विकया धिया ।

यथा सुषुम्णा–नाडीस्था मलाः शुद्धिं प्रयान्ति च ।। ६ ।।

prāṇāyāmaṁ tataḥ kuryānnityaṁ sāttvikayā dhiyā ।
yathā suṣumṇā–nāḍīsthā malāḥ śuddhiṁ prayānti ca ।। 6 ।।

prāṇāyāmaṁ – breath-infusion technique, tataḥ – thus, kuryān = kuryāt = should do, nityaṁ – always, sāttvikayā – of the clarifying energy of nature, dhiyā – focalized in the psyche focus, yathā – as, suṣumṇā – sushumna central spinal passage, nāḍī – nadi subtle arteries and veins, sthā – remaining, malāḥ – pollutants, śuddhiṁ – clearance, prayānti – gives, ca – and

Thus one should do breath-infusion technique daily, using the clarifying energy of nature which is focalized in the psyche. This gives clearance of the polluted energies which remain in the sushumna central spinal passage with its accessory nadi subtle arteries and veins.

Analysis

We have to work with what we have including our hope, fear and belief tendencies. There is no point in working with what we imagine we have which we do not actually control. There are things and tendencies in our possession which we have irregular control over. We need to study the accessories and find ways of increasing our autonomy in relation to them.

Nature has a three-way influence giving us clarity, enthusiasm and stupor. Each of these has useful application. Each has its disadvantage in particular situations. The effort at pranayama breath-infusion is for increasing and then making use of the clarifying energy of nature.

The accumulation and subsequent compression, movement and flushing of the fresh air energy results in a cleansing action within the sushumna central spinal passage and its accessory nadi subtle arteries and veins. When the kundalini is struck by the clarifying energy of material nature, it becomes alert and tries to find a passage through and out of the body. By the application of technical locks, it is channeled through the spine into the brain, to express itself through the brow or crown chakra. This causes insight awareness into higher levels.

Application

The initial achievement is to clear all heavy astral energy from within the sushumna central spinal passage. Kundalini is made to move upward by inciting it through infused breath energy which is pulled into the lungs. Once there is enough of this energy in the blood stream, it is directed downward through the groin area by physical and mental pressure. Reaching the groin area, the energy picks up a sexual potency charge. It is hurled across a small gap from the genital region to the stub end of the spinal column which is near the anus.

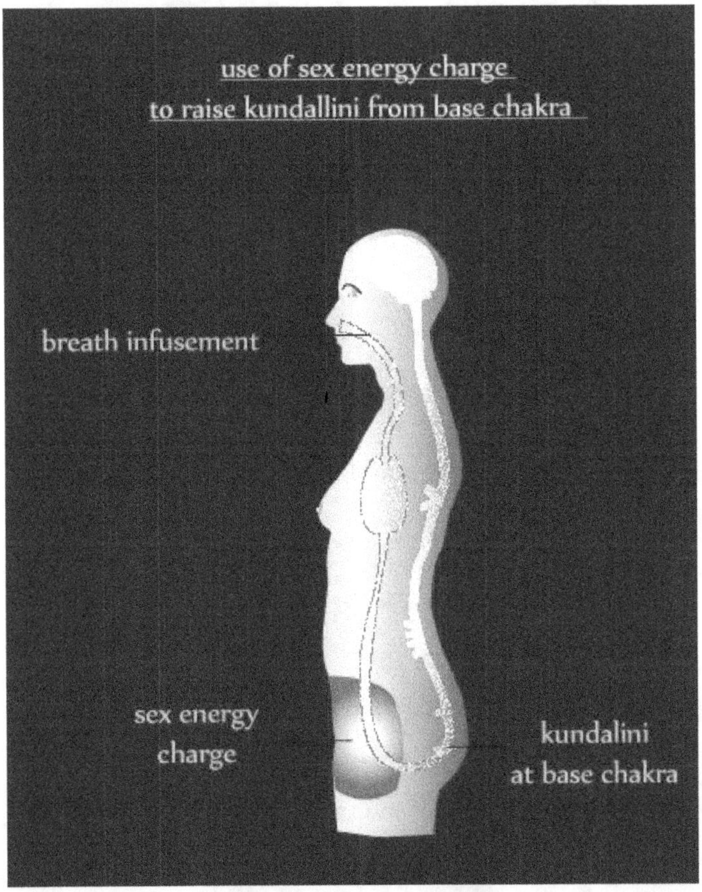

When this charge of energy hits the kundalini lifeforce which is at the base muladhara chakra at the end of the spine, the kundalini attempts to move. Due to the application of specific muscular and mental locks, kundalini finds itself trapped with only one outlet which is up through the spine. However because of the heavy astral energy which is in the spine, kundalini has to exert itself considerably to push against that dark energy.

It does this with the surcharged force which it received when the breath energy jumped into it from the sex organ chakra. Some of the dark energy becomes ignited as it mixes with the sexually charged hormone force. This creates a blast force which explodes up the spine igniting the rest of the energy.

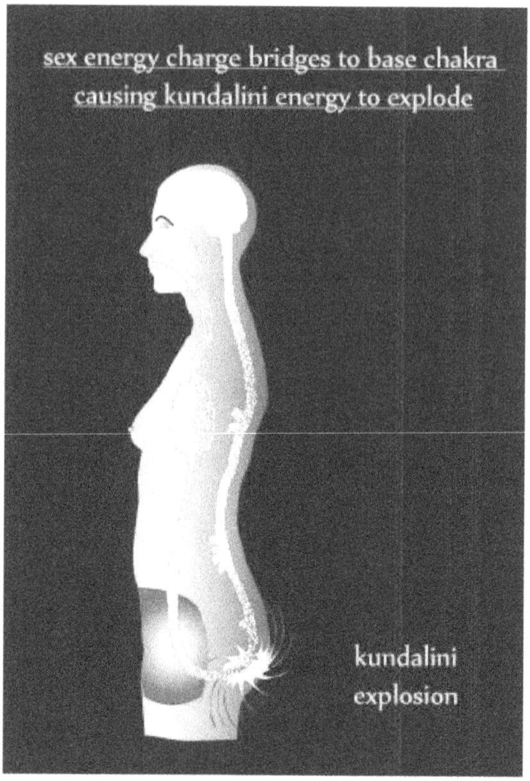

Kundalini shoots through the spine in lightning speed and passes through the neck into the brain.

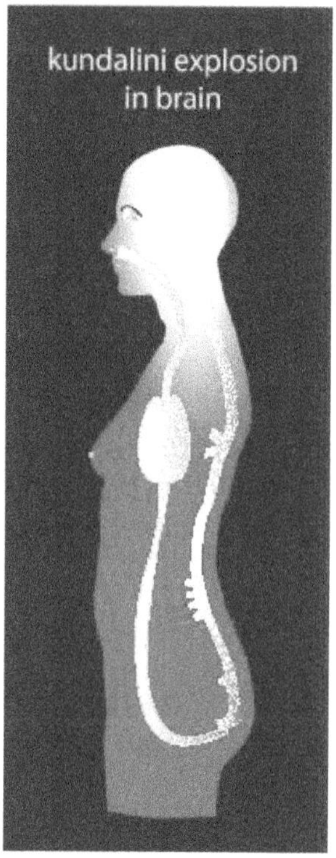

When this occurs the yogi feels a shift in consciousness to a higher plane. Depending on his achievements he may become disoriented and not perceive anything but instead experience total existential black-out. Some yogis feel as if they exist as saturated bliss. Others feel as if they entered a golden light which sheers in all directions. Some perceive divine beings in a divine environment. Some just feel as if existence was suspended for a time.

Verse 7

बद्ध–पद्मासनो योगी प्राणं चन्द्रेण पूरयेत् ।

धारयित्वा यथा–शक्ति भूयः सूर्येण रेचयेत् ।। ७ ।।

baddha–padmāsano yogī prāṇaṁ candreṇa pūrayet I
dhārayitvā yathā–śakti bhūyaḥ sūryeṇa recayet II 7 II

baddha – tight, padmāsano = padmāsanaḥ = lotus posture, yogī – yogi, prāṇaṁ – physio–subtle air energy, candreṇa – by the moon–dominant left side, pūrayet – should inhale, dhārayitvā – by psychically controlling, yathā–śakti = as capable, bhūyaḥ – in turn, sūryeṇa – by sun–dominant right side, recayet – should exhale

In a tight lotus posture, the yogi should inhale the physio–subtle air through the moon dominant left nostril, holding it as he is capable to psychically control its energy, and in turn he should exhale through the sun–dominant right nostril.

Analysis

There is an argument among yogis about which method is the best. It is a worthless argument and yet many yogis get into it and waste valuable time. They create doubts in the minds of beginners as they try to acquire followers with promises of having the best routine.

When it comes right down to it, a student should try whatever method he or she is exposed to by the grace of providence. If a method works continue it. If it does not, then use the effective parts of it. Keep checking with advanced souls for more effective procedures.

If one method, for instance the method described in this verse is tried, and it does not give results, the student should not feel undone and should not think that in every case of every person this method is useless. A method which does not work for one person might produce surprising results in another.

I had experience of teaching methods which worked wonders for one person and for which another person got very little if any advancement. Usually if one person experiences failure with a method, that person will insult the teacher especially if someone else tries the method and gets results from it.

Students should understand that there are many variables from person to person depending on providence which is cast on the basis of current history and previous lifetimes. There is so much variation that it is no wonder that one student fails miserably using a procedure which worked for someone else.

Students should try one method and then another and then another if necessary until a discovery is made that proves to be serviceable. A good method may fail if the student is negatively predisposed to it. A bad method may give flash results if the student is positively attuned to it. So much hinges on attitude and predisposition from past lives. Each person who has the will to do kriya yoga should endeavor with one method after the other in the tireless effort for liberation from material existence.

Application

The air we breathe is physio–subtle which means that it is both physical and psychic. This is why physical breathing may have a psychological effect which is very obvious to the practicing yogi. A student should be confident or should be imparted with confidence through reading books or hearing lectures by yogis who practice pranayama successfully.

Reading books to get confidence is not a waste of time. It is possible to make advancement just by reading books. At least some leaps on spiritual development may be acquired from books. In this book for instance, confidence is granted to anyone who feels a kinship with the writer irrespective of whether he is dead or alive. A reader does not have to meet the writer physically to feel this confidence. It is within the words themselves and can be lifted from the text just by a feeling of kinship with the writer.

Because physical air has a subtle counterpart, any operation in the body with air will have a subtle effect which runs parallel in the subtle body, in the psychology. The idea of the subtle body is not hard to grasp if one can experience oneself objectively in dreams or in conscious astral projections. But even those students who have no psychic expression can study the effects of air intake on the emotions and mentality. This can give one the needed basis for having confidence that by breathing physical air, one can affect the texture of consciousness.

Swatmarama mentioned the assumption of a tight lotus. This is for proficient yogis who practiced for years or who have a body which is supple by genetic composition. If sitting in a tight lotus is painful one would not be successful using it because the mind will be repeatedly drawn to the pain which will disrupt the focus. Those students, who cannot easily sit in lotus posture, should use another pose in which the body is relaxed. Such students should practice difficult postures at another time but not during the meditation session.

Remember that first you do asana postures, then you do pranayama breath-infusion, then you sit to meditate. Do not try to perfect or practice postures when you sit to meditate. Those who do bhastrika or kapalabhati rapid breathing in several postures need not do the poses separately. They do the postures in combination with breath-infusion. Then they sit to meditate.

The breathing procedure given in this verse and in the following one, is the anuloma-viloma alternate procedure. This is a classic method which many successful yogis used in the past and which was serviceable and reliable to grant them access to the chit akash sky of consciousness, the divine atmosphere.

Even though this is the classic method it has certain prerequisites which must be met before one can be successful. One requirement is utmost patience; another is powerful determination. It takes hours of practice and daredevil concentration to complete this method.

The air should not be held to a point of strain. As soon as the body urges for air, one should release the suspension of breath and resume the exhale or inhale accordingly. If this is practiced, there will be an increase in the length of time that the body can tolerate the suspension.

Some students begin this practice with a rate count which is given by a yoga-guru who got that count from his guru or who discovered a practical rate. This however is not recommended by me, even though each teacher has to decide what procedure they prefer.

I feel that initially when using this alternate breathing the student should breathe normally and not maintain a suspension of breath beyond what the body can tolerate. As soon as the body urges for air or for expulsion of air, the student should release the suspension and continue by doing what is to be done next in the sequence. The entire sequence is given in this and in the next verse.

If you have a count for the time of each part of the sequence of this procedure, keep that count in mind and develop yourself to adopt it naturally over a time of doing this practice as described.

The secret of these pranayama practices is the absorption rate of the lungs. Each person has a different rate, so that when I inhale a certain quantity of air, if you inhale the same quantity my lung will absorb a certain percentage of air and your lungs will absorb a different quantity of it.

If your lungs absorb a greater percentage and we have the same average metabolism, then you will be able to maintain breath suspension without strain for a longer period of time. I may over a period of time of practicing cause my lungs to absorb a greater percentage so that my tolerance changes and becomes like your own. Or your absorption rate may keep increasing as mine improves and I may never match your rate even though mine might keep improving.

This means that the ratio of each portion of these breathing techniques will vary from person to person.

The left nostril is considered to be the moon-dominant one. It is influenced more by moon-charged atmospheric energy. The right nostril is sun-dominant. Depending on the moon/sun charge of the atmosphere on a particular day and at a particular time, the yogi may be more sun-charged than moon-charged or vice versa.

A yogi cannot control the weather. He should not make it his concern to worry about the proportion of sun-to-moon charge. The ascetic should make use of the influence of either one or both of these heavenly bodies on a particular day.

Verse 8

प्राणं सूर्येण चाकृष्य पूरयेदुदरं शनैः ।

विधिवत्कुम्भकं कृत्वा पुनश्चन्द्रेण रेचयेत् ।। ८ ।।

prāṇaṁ sūryeṇa cākṝṣya pūrayedudaraṁ śanaiḥ I
vidhivatkumbhakaṁ kṝtvā punaścandreṇa recayet I I 8 I I

prāṇaṁ – physio–subtle air energy, sūryeṇa – by sun–dominant right side, cākṝṣya = ca (and) + ākṝṣya (having drawn), pūrayed = pūrayet = should inhale, udaraṁ – abdomen cavity, śanaiḥ – gradually, vidhivat – by the rules, kumbhakaṁ – breath retention, kṝtvā – having done, punaś = punaḥ = again, candreṇa – by the moon–dominant left side, recayet – should inhale

Drawing the subtle air energy through the sun-dominant right side, gradually filling the abdomen cavity, and then after doing breath retention, he should exhale through the moon-dominant left side.

Analysis

This completes one cycle of the alternate breathing breath-infusion procedure which is designed to systematically extract pollutions from the physical and subtle bodies simultaneously, resulting in rising of kundalini, clearing of heavy astral energy from the subtle body particularly from the sushumna spinal passage.

Swatmarama was particular to include a phrase about gradually filling the abdomen cavity. This practice is not done in a hurry and is not for those who are hasty. This is a long-winded practice which requires acute patience and determination. Each of the actions is done slowly with full concentration. There should be no mental wandering. Each part of the practice is focused. When the abdomen is being filled, the focus should be placed on that filling action. By abdomen is meant when the lungs are being filled to the extent that they cause a distension of the abdomen.

Application

I was introduced to this practice in 1970 in the Philippines on Clark Air Base where Arthur Beverford taught Japanese martial arts. He instructed me in this practice giving me a count rate of 1:4:2 meaning 1 count for inhale, 4 counts for suspension of breathing and 2 counts for exhale.

At first I found it difficult to keep this count. Later in 1974 when I questioned him in Ventura, California, he said to use a count of 2:4:2. He would sit with me on a few occasions and do the practice but since it is an individual and not a shared exercise, his doing it, did not reveal anything about what happened within his psyche.

He did not discuss details about the effects in the subtle body but he said that the main focus should be on the third eye between the brow chakra and that one should track the energy down to the base chakra and up the spine to the third eye.

Beverford learned this from Rishi Singh Gherwal but I sensed that Beverford did not perfect the practice sufficiently to divulge its higher aspects.

Later on my own, I decided to do this practice in a dedicated way but I found that the concentration required was enormous. Here is why. One has to keep track of several aspects simultaneously. These are:

- *referenced counts for inhales, suspension of breathing and exhales*
- *finger movements - closing and opening the nostrils*
- *keeping the spine erect in a sitting posture*

- *keeping the eyes closed and not being distracted by anything aural or keeping the eyes opened but focused on the tip of the nose or between the eyebrows*
- *tracking the inhaled breath down from the nostril through which it is inhaled to the base chakra*
- *holding locks during the suspension of breathing and compressing the energy down at the base chakra*
- *tracing the exhaled energy from the base chakra up to the nostril through which the air is exhaled*
- *tracking the energy during the time that the air is suspended on the completion of the exhale*

This is a tall order for concentrating and tracking simultaneously. I practiced this for weeks in isolation when I lived in Roosevelt, Minnesota around the year of 1976. During some sessions, I made progress in arousing kundalini. In some other sessions, the ida and pingala channels on either side of the sushumna central spinal passage would become electrified. I studied that effect. Then I would relax from this practice and meditate.

Overall I came to the conclusion that unless a yogi was isolated and completely broken off from human relations, he could not be successful using this method. Besides, it requires an enormous amount of concentration which in itself excludes most human beings who cannot sit still for five minutes.

One problem was tension in the spine due to sitting up in lotus posture for more than twenty minutes. Sometimes I would lose count or would lose track of the passage of the energy up or down. Once that happens one has to begin the count all over again. This could take place repeatedly which caused a failure to make a cumulative effect.

A cause for failure of this practice is the manifestation of thoughts and images in the mind, where one's attention is attracted to these distractions and one loses track of the energy distribution and the required count. This happens repeatedly and shows clearly that this practice is not for anyone whose mind is not naturally cleared of images and thoughts.

Would I recommend this procedure?

Yes, but only to persons who are in isolation and who were very determined and capable of vast amounts of concentration.

Verse 9

येन तयजेत्तेन पीत्वा धारयेदतिरोधतः ।

रेचयेच्च ततो।अन्येन शनैरेव न वेगतः ।। ९ ।।

yena tyajettena pītvā dhārayedatirodhataḥ ।
recayecca tato।anyena śanaireva na vegataḥ ।। 9 ।।

yena – by which, tyajet – should exhale, tena – by his, pītvā – having inhaled, dhārayed = dhārayet = should retain with inner focus, atirodhataḥ – to the limit of endurance, recayec = recayet = should exhale, ca – and, tato = tataḥ = then, anyena – by another, śanair = śanaiḥ = gradually, eva na = not so, vegataḥ – rapidly

Having inhaled by the route through which he exhaled, he should, with inner focus, retain to his limit of endurance. Then he should exhale through the other route gradually and not rapidly.

Analysis

This practice is not a group session and yet some teachers sit with groups of students and direct this. The modern situation has made it standard that yoga is not what it was but is something which is suitable to modern tastes and which is adapted for stress-relief and beauty-focus.

The key austerity in alternate breathing is the slow and gradual release of air on the exhale. A student should not misunderstand this and feel that he or she should hold the breath in for as long as possible because if in doing so the lung and blood cells are put to strain, that will result in increase in polluted gases which will not yield the result intended.

When one begins to do this practice, one should not strain the system and should not be concerned with the classical ratio count. The ratios are practiced in the more advanced stages after weeks or years of practice have cause the body to be responsive to fresh air and to have more efficient extraction of stale polluted gases.

This practice is not for group sessions. It should be taught as Beverford instructed me in a one-on-one instruction format. The student must also have a lifestyle which permits that his or her mind be completely devoid of thoughts when doing the practice. That cannot happen with the average human being or with persons who do superficial yoga. One cannot gain proficiency if one is not isolated from human involvement, and if one has many concerns due to a modern lifestyle.

There is really no reason to teach alternate breathing to the people who come for superficial yoga teachings because they cannot do it in the proper way and will develop a flawed sense of confidence which will take them further and further away from yoga as it is defined in the Hatha Yoga Pradipika.

Application

Inner concentration is a must for this practice but not the type which is done by people who engage in a modern lifestyle. We must know that in the time of Swatmarama, only a few persons did these practices. Compared to the modern era those were primitive times and still at that time despite the natural life that people lived without modern amenities, still then only a few people did these practices.

Everyone and anyone were not trained in these methods. It was not divulged to the general public. For instance women were hardly trained in this. There is no history of classic yoga being taught to many women as yoga is taught today in the developed countries. Pretty much all of the names of the siddhas are male beings.

We may question this.

Is it because those ancient cultures were prejudicially patriarchal?

Is it because those teachers felt that women were unfit for yoga?

Irrespective of the reason for the lack of female participation, as to if they were barred or prevented, the fact remains that women were not instructed. The wandering ascetics were males. It is not practical for females to endure such hardships. It is not realistic to ask females to endure sensual curtailment and deprivation.

I can divulge this much, that no one in his right mind, no advanced yogi that is, will encourage women to do yoga austerities as they are described in classical texts like the Hatha Yoga Pradipika. *The austerities involved would be gruesome for women. The time invested would eat up their lives and deprive them of living a fulfilling material existence with family and society.*

Yoga came from tapa which is gruesome austerities. It is said in the Puranas that the deity Brahma, the lord creator of the universe, was afflicted with fear initially because of the violent cosmic storm which he found himself in. He cried out for help and was told by someone to do tapa, yoga austerities.

This creation is here to be exploited or so our senses feel about it. From day one, as soon as I became aware of myself in this creation, it was all about exploitation and consumption for the purpose of extending my presence here. Yoga has little to do with this. It is designed for curtailing exploitation and reducing sensual pursuits. Is this suitable to females?

Buddha did yoga austerities because he wanted out of the trauma-ridden material world. Goddess Durga did austerities because she wanted Shiva to be her husband. These portray the average male and female attitudes. Generally women do yoga for reasons other than finding an exit from traumatic dramas.

Men are pretty much the same, except that some like Buddha become appalled at the quantity of trauma which this creation is capable of enforcing. These few individuals are the ones who may do this yoga.

Verse 10

प्राणं चेदिडया पिबेन्नियमितं भूयो।अन्यथा रेचयेत्

पीत्वा पिङ्गलया समीरणमथो बद्ध्वा तयजेद्वामया ।

सूर्य–चन्द्रमसोरनेन विधिनाभ्यासं सदा तन्वतां

शुद्धा नाडि–गणा भवन्ति यमिनां मास–तरयादूर्ध्वतः ।। १० ।।

prāṇaṁ cediḍayā pibenniyamitaṁ bhūyo|anyathā recayet
pītvā pingalayā samīraṇamatho baddhvā tyajedvāmayā |
sūrya–candramasoranena vidhinābhyāsaṁ sadā tanvatāṁ
śuddhā nāḍi–gaṇā bhavanti yamināṁ māsa–trayādūrdhvataḥ || 10 ||

prāṇaṁ = physio–subtle air energy , ced = cet = if, iḍayā – through the left breath course, piben = pibet = would absorb, niyamitaṁ – what is retained with focus, bhūyo = bhuya = again, anyathā – through the other, recayet – should expel, pītvā – having inhaled, pingalayā – through the right course, samīraṇam – breath, atho =

atha = thus, baddhvā – retaining, tyajed = tyajet = exhale, vāmayā – through the left, sūrya – by sun–dominant right side, candramasor = candramasoḥ = by moon–dominant left side, anena – by this, vidhinābhyāsaṁ = vidhinā (by this method) + abhyāsaṁ (practice), sadā – always, tanvatāṁ – perform, śuddhā – clearance, nāḍi – nadi subtle veins and arteries, gaṇā – groups, bhavanti – become, yamināṁ – those who are existentially self–disciplined, māsa – month, trayād = trayāt = three, ūrdhvataḥ – afterwards

If the physio–subtle air energy is absorbed through the left breath course, it should be retained with focus and then expelled through the other nostril. Then inhaling through the right course, and retaining the breath, it should be exhaled through the left side. By practicing with this method always, clearance of the groups of nadi subtle veins and arteries takes place after three months for those who are existentially self–disciplined.

Analysis

The yaminams, those who are existentially self–disciplined, are those who adhere strictly to the ten yama moral restraints:

atha yama–niyamāḥ
ahiṁsā satyamasteyaṁ brahmacharyaṁ kṣamā dhṛtiḥ |
dayārjavaṁ mitāhāraḥ śauchaṁ caiva yamā daśa || 1.17 ||

atha – regarding, hear now about, yama – restraining behaviors, niyamāḥ – recommended conduct, ahiṁsā – non–violence, satyam – realism, asteyaṁ – non–stealing, brahmacharyaṁ – sexual nonexpressiveness which results in the perception of spirituality, kṣamā – tolerance, dhṛtiḥ – steadiness, dayārjavaṁ = daya (compassion) + arjavam (straightforwardness), mitāhāraḥ – eating the absolute minimum, śauchaṁ – cleanliness, caiva – and so, yamā – restraining behaviors, daśa – ten

Hear now of the restraining behaviors and recommended conducts:

Non–violence, realism, non–stealing, sexual nonexpressiveness which results in the perception of spirituality, tolerance, steadiness, compassion, straightforwardness, eating the absolute minimum, and cleanliness, are the ten restraining behaviors. (Hatha Yoga Pradipika 1.17)

For these persons a period of three months was necessary for complete clearance of the nadi subtle veins and arteries. For others even three lifetimes may not be sufficient. One astral Guru gave me an instruction for a kriya practice which he said would yield the intended result in six months. Even after practicing for six years the result was still not attained.

Why?

There are certain prerequisites which if not secured make it impossible to fulfil these time guarantees. Modern association even with other student yogis infiltrates into one's practice and sabotages success.

Focus is disrupted by these associations making it impossible to consolidate the practice once and for all. It bespeaks only sporadic progress with more ups than downs, where the horizon of final success keeps at a respectable distance from the student.

Some are of the view that anyone can do these practices, irrespective of compliance with the yama moral restraints. That view is flawed. To be realistic we must realize that even though a modern person may practice, he or she will only get haphazard and very irregular results. Even if the mind settles down or appears to do so when the student sits to meditate, the underlying subconscious energy will limit the degree of success the student attains. This is unfortunate. Unless we adhere to the restrictions in full, especially in terms of association, we cannot peel away the impediments and get a right-of-way in the process.

Application

Some people, shallow moralists and yogi-critics, feel that the yama moral restrictions should be enforced on anyone who does yoga-practice and that if any of these are violated; the ascetic is condemned if not lost forever.

But moral restrains in yoga are not the same as moral restrains in religious practice. In religion morality concerns with social relations, one to the other, as human beings living together in a society, where restrictions are in place for the general wellbeing of all and to make it easy to enforce social responsibility and take into account human frailties.

For the purpose of yoga, yama moral restrains have nothing to with anyone but the yogi. It has to do with relationship between the core-self and its adjuncts, which are the sense of identity, the buddhi intellect orb, the sensual energies, the kundalini psychic lifeforce, the subconscious and conscious memories.

What has that got to do with social concerns?

Very little!

This is why for serious yoga; the ascetic must be in isolation, because involvements with society only serve to distract the yogi by causing him to be involved in social morality when the real issue is inSelf or introspective morality.

For a yogi who has the psychic adjuncts under full control, for him or for her, three months of the alternate breathing is what it would take to get full permanent clearance of the groups of nadi subtle veins and arteries.

And what is the purpose of this?

Clearance of negative energy out of the psyche, out of every part of it, results in upward vibrational shifts of the subtle body so that it becomes capable of granting access to the chit akash sky of consciousness.

Verse 11

परातर्मध्यन्दिने सायमर्ध–रात्रे च कुम्भकान ।

शनैरशीति–पर्यन्तं चतुर्वारं समभ्यसेत् ।। ११ ।।

prātarmadhyandine sāyamardha–rātre ca kumbhakān I
śanairaśīti–paryantaṁ caturvāraṁ samabhyaset I I 11 I I

prātar – at sunrise, madhyandine – at noon, sāyam – at sunset, ardha – middle, rātre – in the night, ca – and, kumbhakān – breath retention with energy regulation, śanair = śanaiḥ = gradually, aśīti – eighty, paryantaṁ – up till, catur – catuḥ – four, vāraṁ –

times, samabhyaset – should practice thoroughly

At sunrise, at noon, at sunset, and at midnight, breath retention with energy regulation should be done four times daily until the count of the cycle is eighty.

Analysis

The cycle is numbered by the retentions. The student should begin with as little as he or she can manage and then over time increase the retentions until the count is eighty. Some seasoned yogis say that this means forty counts because there are two retentions in each cycle.

The key aspect is the internal indications which the ascetic feels where he or she maintains concentration without any break in the cycle. As soon as there is a break in concentration the session should begin again. This really means that a modern yogi may not do even one uninterrupted session because modern people, even the yogis and meditators, are unable to maintain pure concentration on any one thing without interruptions of thoughts and images occurring in the mind chamber. It is not what we desire but what our lifestyle enforces.

This does not mean that there should be no attempt by a modern ascetic. It is that the efforts should be made with honesty and with the understanding that one cannot do these practices ideally because of not having the full profile for this behavior.

If perchance some lucky yogi can complete these practices in the ideal way, the count required would hinge on being successful in reaching the chit-akash sky of consciousness or being established in the third eye or crown chakra. As soon as the yogi experiences this in full and is confident that this will not flicker out if he stops the practice, he may discontinue it and silently focus fully into the divine environment.

This is similar to rocket launching, where the payload of fuel must be discharged fully before the rocket can remain floating in space by itself. If the fuel ceases before the rocket reaches outer space, everything will fall back to the earth. The ascetic, if he is anxious and if he ceases the rounds before he is fully transferred to the chit akash sky of consciousness, will find that his access there will be terminated quickly.

It is for this reason that some ancient yogis, did very long periods of alternate breathing, to be sure that their propulsion into the chit akash was so penetrating that they would remain in samadhi continuous effortless linkage into the sky of consciousness for long periods of time, for hours, days or weeks.

Application

This is not an external process. It is one hundred percent introversion with self-honesty and very deep observations. It has nothing to do with the social relations one has in this world. Each yogi must achieve this on his or her own supported by the advice of great yogis who mastered these procedures before.

One should not settle for a pseudo meditation practice, or take kriyas which lead nowhere but which afford a dishonest showing to the public of one being advanced.

Kriya yoga is not a publicity stunt. It is not for giving the ascetic fame or status in the material world. The ancient yogis were forest ascetics mostly not city dwellers with religious institutions providing guest accommodation. They did not have retreats in exotic climates on beaches where leggy women pranced around in bikinis doing classic postures.

There are sufficient stories in the Puranas which describe the poverty of many successful yogis who became known as siddha perfected beings later.

Yoga is not for proving anything to anyone besides the lone ascetic who performs it. He or she proves to himself or herself what the components of the psyche are and how these can be reordered and energized to cause transits to higher dimensions of the astral world and to the divine atmosphere which is beyond what is astral.

Verse 12

कनीयसि भवेद्स्वेद् कम्पो भवति मध्यमे ।

उत्तमे सथानमाप्नोति ततो वायुं निबन्धयेत् ।। १२ ।।

kanīyasi bhavedsveda kampo bhavati madhyame |
uttame sthānamāpnoti tato vāyuṁ nibandhayet || 12 ||

kanīyasi – in the initial stage, bhaved = bhavet = there is, sveda – perspiration, kampo = kampaḥ = trembling, bhavati – it is, madhyame – in the median level, uttame – in the advanced stage, sthānam – steadiness, āpnoti – achieve, tato = tataḥ = hence, vāyuṁ – fresh air, nibandhayet – should retain

In the initial stage there is perspiration. In the median level of practice, there is trembling. In the advanced level steadiness is achieved. Hence the yogi should retain the fresh air.

Analysis

These are the stages of what occurs in terms of physical manifestation, where there is perspiration, trembling and then steadiness where even the material body is traumatized by the practice. At first there is perspiration because the metabolism is forced to change its rate of processing fresh air and polluted gases. Any adjustment in what is normal will produce some type of stress or trauma to the system. When practicing breath-infusion, the yogi wrestles control from the lifeforce which is the psychic function that controls the rate of breathing and heart pulsations.

There is the second stage which is when the body trembles because of suspension of breath. During this stage whatever fresh air was infused into the system is distributed in an organized way because of the yogi's application of special compressions. The compressions cause the infused fresh air to use specific routes, which in turn makes the polluted gases exit through special passages.

In the advanced stage there is steadiness because the yogi's body changes and is receptive to the alternate breathing. It seems then that the body is no longer stressed. It finds the practice to be congenial.

Application

Extraction of carbon dioxide in the physical system and apana subtle air in the astral body is the essential part of any pranayama practice which aims at quelling the unruly mind and reaching the chit akash sky of consciousness.

Infusion of fresh air (mostly oxygen) in the physical system and pranic subtle air in the astral body is the same essential part of the practice. These actions occur automatically one after the other, one into the other during breath-infusion practice.

One should be diligent and do the practice at least twice per day in the early morning before meditation which is before sunrise and in the afternoon just before or at sunset. Swatmarama said it should be done at four times per day. That is ideal.

The infusion of fresh astral energy and extraction of polluted subtle energy result in a higher dimensional content of the subtle body which brings with it the advantage of automatic pratyahar sensual energy withdrawal, making at least the dharana linkage to higher realities beginning with the naad sound resonance, easy to experience with the likelihood of developing naturally into dhyana effortless linkage into higher realities and samadhi continuous effortless linkage into the spiritual sky.

Verse 13

जलेन क्षम–जातेन गात्र–मर्दनमाचरेत् ।

दृढता लघुता चैव तेन गात्रस्य जायते ।। १३ ।।

jalena kṣama jātena gātra–mardanam ācaret I
dṛḍhatā lagutā caiva tena gātrasya jāyate II 13 II

jalena – by the perspiration, kṣama – adequate, jātena – exudes, gātra – body, mardanam – rubbing, ācaret – should do, dṛḍhatā – firmness, lagutā – lightness, caiva – and so, tena – by this, gātrasya – of body, jāyate – produce

The yogi should rub his body with the perspiration produced from adequate practice. By this, firmness and lightness of body are produced.

Analysis

This is not a mere superstition nor is it only a physical occurrence. The perspiration which comes out of the body, as a result of breath-infusion, is special because it exudes as a result of ridding the system of polluted gases and causes a mixture of fresh air energy, hormones and pollution. The pollution is under pressure and is transformed into a pixelated bliss force.

When the perspiration is rubbed into the body, there is a feeling of firmness on the skin along with a coolness which seems to irradiate from the body and then go back into it. The physical body feels as if it can walk on sky and go anywhere, as if it is an infallible form.

Application

On the subtle plane a similar experience is had, where from the pores of the subtle body a whitish yellow creamy subtle substance exudes. The yogi smears this into his subtle body. It acts as a siren-like alert so that angelic women come to the yogi. In a hurry as if travelling at the speed of light, the apsaras and dakini women come to the yogi. They swipe these subtle creams off his body into their hands and rub it over their bodies. From that they derive a pleasure which is just like sexual climax experience.

When the breath-infused energy becomes concentrated, when it is mixed with compressed subtle hormonal energy and with the restricted kundalini, that affects the subtle body so that a nectar-cream exudes from it. This is irresistible to some angelic women.

Even though the yogi may be practicing this yoga on the physical side of existence, the energy from the breath-infusion causes the subtle body to irradiate with flashes of astral light. This attracts some celestial beings who rush to the place where the yogi does the austerities. If the yogi developed psychic perception, he or she will perceive the arrival of the celestial beings. There will be communication with them.

Very advanced yogis who regard these visits as interference and distraction, control the energy in the subtle body so that no flashes of light occur in the astral planes. Their austerities do not attack celestial beings. Patanjali Mahayogin suggested that a yogi should not relate to the celestial beings who might invite him to come to their domains:

sthānyupanimantraṇe saṅgasmayākaraṇaṁ
punaraniṣṭa prasaṅgāt

sthāni – person from the place a yogi would then attain if his material body died; upanimantraṇe – on being invited; saṅga – association; smaya – fascination, wonderment; akaraṇaṁ – non-responsiveness; punaḥ – again; aniṣṭa – unwanted features of existence; prasaṅgāt – due to association, due to endearing friendliness.

On being invited by a person from the place one would attain if the body died, a yogi should be non-responsive, not desiring their association and not being fascinated, otherwise that would cause unwanted features of existence to arise again. (Yoga Sutras of Patanjali 3.52)

This is a strict warning from the teacher that if a yogi should like to be with these celestial beings who are attracted to his austerities or to the effects the austerities have on his subtle body, then he would ruin his chances of going to the divine world as he would be attracted to the heavenly life in the higher astral region with the result of going there for a time, and then again coming down to the ghetto existence in the physical world.

Verse 14

अभ्यास–काले प्रथमे शस्तं क्षीराज्य–भोजनम् ।

ततो।अभ्यासे दृढीभूते न तादृङ–नियम–ग्रहः ।। १४ ।।

abhyāsa–kāle prathame śastaṁ kṣīrājya–bhojanam I
tato l abhyāse dṛḍhībhūte na tādṛn–niyama–grahaḥ I I 14 I I

abhyāsa – practice, kāle – in time, prathame – initially, śastaṁ – mandatory, kṣīra – milk, ājya – ghee, bhojanam – food, tato = tataḥ = then, abhyāse – in practicing, dṛḍhī – consistent, bhūte – in existing, na – not, tādṛn – such, niyama – recommended behavior, grahaḥ – habitual

In this practice, initially food with milk and ghee is mandatory. Then later when the practice is consistent and habitual, that recommendation is not necessary.

Analysis

Initially there has to be some for-sure nutrition for the yogi, otherwise his body will become sick and he will not be able to practice. The student must greatly reduce the quantity of food, the bulk, but with that there needs to be an increase in the nutritious content. This is done by using milk and ghee or conversely some other foods which provide nutrition from small quantities of the preparation.

In the history of yoga, there were successful ascetics who began with sparse diet, committed themselves to the austerity and consistently practiced but later or even while doing so, they developed the habit of over-eating and eating at the wrong times of the day. However students should not take the risk to eat haphazardly or carelessly or to eat for the satisfaction of family and friends who are not yogis.

Even though some of our proficient gurus did breach the rules and were successful nevertheless, we should not attempt to imitate them. There is exception but we should adhere to the recommendations. A student should eat frugally so that the intestinal-colon system is not overtaxed. Too much food bulk of even the right diet may hamper the effectiveness of asana postures and breath-infusion practice.

Initially with the reduction in food quantity, there should be an increase in the nutritional content. This is why milk and ghee are commended. Other foods may be used to achieve the same result.

Application

Once the ascetic's body is adjusted to the sparse but timely yogic diet, he can reduce even the nutritional content of meals.

Why?

Due to the fact that nutrition spurs on the hormone production which in turn boosts the mode of passion, an ascetic has to reduce even the nutritional content of meals. But that should not be done initially, only in the advanced stages when the cells of the body are reformed in their lusty attitude.

Pranayama is the method for lifting the fat and other lust-stimulating productions in the body. These materials are sucked out of the mixed food mass in the stomach and intestines. They are then processed to create hormone concentrations for various usages in the body, with special emphasis on reproduction.

Using pranayama breath-infusion, a yogi can extract these hormonal energies either after they are created or just when the nutrients are extracted from the walls of the intestines and colon. The earlier the better because the longer these substances remain in the body, the more sexually-charged they become.

Once the charge is established, the yogi has no choice but to transmute it by mixing it with fresh air and compressing it using various locks or bandhas. He must also put an emotional and mental squeeze on it to transform its lusty impetus. This is all work for the yogi. Eventually as he gets more of a grip on the situation, he can arrest the nutrients before they are charged naturally. He can direct the energy forthwith and avoid having to deal with the lust charge which is so combative against the aim of the yoga. When this is done successfully, the yogi is regarded as a celibate or brahmachari.

Verse 15

यथा सिंहो गजो वयाघ्रो भवेद्वश्यः शनैः शनैः ।

तथैव सेवितो वायुरन्यथा हन्ति साधकम् ।। १५ ।।

yathā siṁho gajo vyāghro bhavedvaśyaḥ śanaiḥ śanaiḥ |
tathaiva sevito vāyuranyathā hanti sādhakam || 15 ||

yathā – as, siṁho = simhaḥ= lion, gajo = gajaḥ = elephant, vyāghro = vyāghraḥ = tiger, bhaved = bhavet = becomes, vaśyaḥ = submissive, śanaiḥ śanaiḥ = gradually, tathaiva = so even, sevito = savitaḥ = controlled, vāyur = vāyuḥ = air, anyathā – or, hanti – is ruined, sādhakam – the student yogi

As a lion, an elephant, a tiger becomes submissive in time, so even the lifeforce is controlled gradually, or the student yogi is ruined by it.

Analysis

With the lifeforce kundalini psychic mechanism, it is a matter of controlling it ruthlessly or being controlled by it. There is no middle ground with it. If it is in control, it does not allow the core-self any autonomy but the core-self may not realize this. If the core-self is in control the lifeforce indulges in a conspiracy with the sensual energies, the intellect and memory, to wrestle control from the core-self.

In ancient India, the taming of elephants and tigers was a special skill mastered by the warrior caste, the kshatriyas. Swatmarama uses that to give us some idea of the risks involved in trying to control the psyche by taking command of it after subduing the kundalini. However there were instances where a trainer of elephants or tigers was crushed, bit, mauled or eaten by a trained animal.

How is that possible?

It is because the wild nature of the creature went into dormancy and was not eliminated by the training. There were two behaviors present at all times; the old wild habits and the new tamed training. In some cases, even after the training was established, the wild habits entered the conscious observing mind and took control of the psyche just as before.

An honest yogi knows that at any moment any of the previous unwanted behaviors can return. These can impulsively take over the psyche. Idealistic people who are terribly naive and who have just a curiosity about yoga, do sometimes make an effort at a sincere yoga practice, but when they find that the teacher exhibits a questionable behavior, they derive great satisfaction from criticizing him as being deviant and hypocritical.

The fact is however that no matter what a yogi does, no matter how successful he is at reforming the kundalini lifeforce, it will retain its basic tendency underneath the effort. At any moment the reformation could regress.

Dogs are so faithful that sometimes they give their lives for their keepers. Yet sometimes we see that if a master offers a piece of meat to the animal, if the master approaches to take it back, the animal may bear teeth and express terrible aggression being ready to tear apart the master.

The kundalini lifeforce should not be trusted. A yogi should be alert and know for certain that if the lifeforce gets the opportunity, it will shred the yogi and in a moment, delete the progress. This is nothing to be ashamed about. This is not a moral or social issue.

Application

The single enemy of the yogi is the lifeforce mechanism which masquerades under different names and forms. For instance it is mentioned in the Bhagavad Gita as kamarupa, the form of indulgent desire (kama). Here are details about this as described by Lord Krishna:

arjuna uvāca
atha kena prayukto'yaṁ
pāpaṁ carati pūruṣaḥ
anicchannapi vārṣṇeya
balādiva niyojitaḥ (3.36)

Arjuna — Arjuna; uvāca — said; atha — then; kena — by what?; prayukto = prayuktaḥ — forced; 'yaṁ = ayam — this; pāpaṁ — evil; carati — commits; pūruṣaḥ — a person; anicchannapi = anicchan — unwilling + napi (api) — even; vārṣṇeya — family man of the Vṛṣṇis; balād = balāt — from force; iva — as if; niyojitaḥ — compelled

Arjuna said: Then explain, O family man of the Vṛṣṇis, by what is a person forced to commit an evil unwillingly, just as if he were compelled to do so? (3.36)

śrībhagavānuvāca
kāma eṣa krodha eṣa
rajoguṇasamudbhavaḥ
mahāśano mahāpāpmā
viddhyenamiha vairiṇam (3.37)

śri bhagavān — the Blessed Lord; uvāca — said; kāma — craving; eṣa — this; krodha — anger; eṣa — this; rajoguṇasamudbhavaḥ = rajo (rajaḥ) — passion + guṇa — emotion + samudbhavaḥ — source; mahāśano (mahāśanaḥ) = mahā — great + aśana — consuming power; mahāpāpmā = mahā — much + pāpmā — damage; viddhyenam = viddhi — recognize + enam — this; iha — in this case; vairiṇam — enemy

The Blessed Lord said: This force is craving. This power is anger. The passionate emotion is the source. It has a great consuming power and does much damage. Recognize it as the enemy in this case. (3.37)

dhūmenāvriyate vahnir
yathādarśo malena ca
yatholbenāvṛto garbhas
tathā tenedamāvṛtam (3.38)

dhūmenāvriyate = dhūmena — by smoke + āvriyate — is obscured; vahnir = vahniḥ — the sacrificial fire; yathā — similarly; 'darśo = ādarśaḥ — mirror; malena — with dust; ca — and; yatholbenāvṛto = yatholbenāvṛtaḥ = yatho (yatha) — similarly + ulbena — by skin + āvṛtaḥ — is covered; garbhaḥ — embryo; tathā — so; tenedam = tena — by this + idam — this; āvṛtam — is blocked

As the sacrificial fire is obscured by smoke, and similarly as a mirror is shrouded by dust or as an embryo is covered by skin, so a man's insight is blocked by the passionate energy. (3.38)

āvṛtaṁ jñānametena
jñānino nityavairiṇā
kāmarūpeṇa kaunteya
duṣpūreṇānalena ca (3.39)

āvṛtam — is adjusted; jñānam — discernment; etena — by this; jñānino = jñāninaḥ — educated people; nityavairiṇā = nitya — eternal + vairiṇā — by the enemy; kāmarūpeṇa = kāma — yearning for various things + rūpeṇa — by the sense or form of; kaunteya — son of Kuntī; duṣpūreṇānalena = duspūreṇa — is hard to satisfy + analena — by fire; ca — and

The discernment of educated people is adjusted by their eternal enemy which is the sense of yearning for various things. O son of Kuntī, the lusty power, is as hard to satisfy as it is to keep a fire burning. (3.39)

indriyāṇi mano buddhir
asyādhiṣṭhānamucyate
etairvimohayatyeṣa
jñānamāvṛtya dehinam (3.40)

indriyāṇi — the senses; mano = manaḥ — the mind; buddhir = buddhiḥ — the intelligence; asyādhiṣṭhānam = asya — if this + adhiṣṭhānam — warehouse; ucyate — it is authoritatively stated; etair = etaiḥ — with these; vimohayatyeṣa = vimohayaty (vimohayati) — confuses + eṣa — this; jñānam — insight; āvṛtya — is shrouded; dehinam — embodied soul

It is authoritatively stated that the senses, the mind and the intelligence are the combined warehouse of the passionate enemy. By these faculties, the lusty power confuses the embodied soul, shrouding his insight. (3.40)

tasmāttvamindriyāṇyādau
niyamya bharatarṣabha
pāpmānaṁ prajahihyenaṁ
jñānavijñānanāśanam(3.41)

tasmāt — thus; tvam — you; indriyāṇyādau = indriyāṇi — senses + ādau — initially; niyamya — regulating; bharatarṣabha — powerful man of the Bharata family; pāpmānaṁ — degrading power; prajahi — squelch, destroy; hyenaṁ = hy (hi) — certainly + enaṁ — this; jñānavijñānanāśanam = jñāna — knowledge + vijñāna — discernment + nāśanam — ruining

Thus regulating the senses initially, you should, O powerful man of the Bharata family, squelch this degrading power which ruins knowledge and discernment. (3.41)

indriyāṇi parāṇyāhur
indriyebhyaḥ paraṁ manaḥ
manasastu parā buddhir

yo buddheḥ paratastu saḥ (3.42)

indriyāṇi — the senses; parāṇyāhur = parāṇi — are energetic; āhur (āhuḥ) — the ancient psychologists say; indriyebhyaḥ — the senses; paraṁ — more energetic; manaḥ — the mind; manasas — in contrast to the mind; tu — but; parā — more sensitive; buddhir = buddhiḥ — the intelligence; yo = yaḥ — which; buddheḥ — in reference to the intelligence; paratas — most sensitive; tu — but; saḥ — he, the spirit

The ancient psychologists say that the senses are energetic, but in comparison to the senses, the mind is more energetic. In contrast to the mind, the intelligence is even more sensitive. But in reference, the spirit is most elevated. (3.42)

evaṁ buddheḥ paraṁ buddhvā
saṁstabhyātmānamātmanā
jahi śatruṁ mahābāho
kāmarūpaṁ durāsadam (3.43)

evaṁ — thus; buddheḥ — than the intelligence; paraṁ — higher; buddhvā — having understood; saṁstabhyātmānamātmanā = saṁstabhya — keeping together + ātmānam — the personal energies+ ātmanā — by the spirit; jahi — uproot; śatruṁ — enemy; mahābāho — O powerful man; kāmarūpaṁ — form of passionate desire; durāsadam — difficult to grasp

Thus having understood what is higher than intelligence, keeping the personal energies under control of the spirit, uproot, O powerful man, the enemy, the form of passionate desire which is difficult to grasp. (3.43)

Arjuna inquired of Krishna about the psychological force which influences a person to commit an evil unwillingly, just as if he were compelled to do so.

The force is the kundalini lifeforce. The details about what this is and how it covertly operates to manhandle the psyche, are explained by Krishna in those verses.

Krishna gave the mind, senses and intelligence as the storage locations of this kundalini lifeforce, the places in which it hides and through which it distributes influences.

It is left to the yogi to figure how he will overcome this power and keep it suppressed effectively. It is native to this material creation and to the lower astral planes. Hence so long as one is in this vicinity there is the likelihood that one's psyche will be commandeered by it. It should not be underestimated.

Verse 16

प्राणायामेन युक्तेन सर्व–रोग–क्षयो भवेत् ।

अयुक्ताभ्यास–योगेन सर्व–रोग–समुद्गमः ।। १६ ।।

prāṇāyāmena yuktena sarva–roga–kṣayo bhavet I
ayuktābhyāsa–yogena sarva–roga–samudghamaḥ II 16 II

prāṇāyāmena – by breath-infusion process, yuktena – proficiently, sarva – all, roga –

disease, kṣayo = kṣayaḥ = destruction, bhavet – become, ayuktābhyāsa = without proficiency in practice, yogena – by yoga, sarva – all, roga – disease, samudghamaḥ – manifestation

By proficient breath-infusion process, all disease is destroyed but with a non–proficient practice the diseases manifest.

Analysis

The body will be as healthy as it can be if one has a breath-infusion practice but this does not mean that diseases one had prior to the practice will necessarily disappear. The effects of diseases from before may remain because some past actions have an enduring power which even a yogi cannot thwart. However that is not going to stop the ascetic from making advancement.

We need to understand that despite the uphill run through the hurdles of evolution and despite the constant tearing down of our efforts by deep-seated negative tendencies, there is a cumulative effect of practice which will give us the upper hand and allow us to walk out of the swamps of material existence.

Application

What was possible in the time of Swatmarama may not be possible today because of the changed environment. Culturally and environmentally, the situation on earth was altered and irretrievably so. Still, anyone who has a proficient practice of breath-infusion will have more psyche perception about what is taking place within his or her psyche.

Some aspects one can adjust. Some, one will see and know that these cannot be altered. Just the insight into this is an achievement.

The big revelation one gets from breath-infusion practice is that the mission of yoga has to do with the subtle body. The physical form has very little meaning in terms of the lifespan of the astral body.

The subtle body is based on light energy as contrasted to the physical one which is based on solid, liquid and gaseous materials. Our vision energy which is usually funneled through the physical eyes can be directed into the subtle body for perception of subtle frequencies. This is done easily through the breath-infusion practice.

Verse 17

हिक्का श्वासश्च कासश्च शिरः–कर्णाक्षि–वेदनाः ।

भवन्ति विविधाः रोगाः पवनस्य प्रकोपतः ।। १७ ।।

hikkā śvāsaśca kāsaśca śiraḥ–karṇākṣi–vedanāḥ ।
bhavanti vividhāḥ rogāḥ pavanasya prakopataḥ ।। 17 ।।

hikkā – hiccup, śvāsaś = śvāsaḥ = asthma, ca – and, kāsaś = kāsaḥ = cough, ca – and, śiraḥ – head, karṇākṣi = karṇa (ear) + ākṣi (eye), vedanāḥ – pains, bhavanti – manifest, vividhāḥ – various, rogāḥ – disease, pavanasya – of the breath energy, prakopataḥ – pertaining to irregularity

Hiccup, asthma, pains in the head, ears and eyes, these and a variety of diseases manifest by irregularity in the breath energy.

Analysis

These may manifest if pranayama is done improperly or even if it is done properly and there are bacteria and viruses in the air which are breathe into the body.

Students should learn the locks or bandhas particularly the three primary ones which are the anus-perineum pull-up, the abdomen draw-back and the chin pull-to-throat lock. The chin lock is an absolute must because it regulates breath energy which passes from the trunk into the head. If one does not do this lock proficiently, there is the risk of getting headaches, feeling giddy, fainting or become disoriented.

During the years teaching kundalini yoga using the bhastrika or kapalabhati breath-infusion, I corrected many students with the locks. Most persons do not understand how to apply the neck lock unless they are shown physically. Reading books about this lock may not give enough details about it.

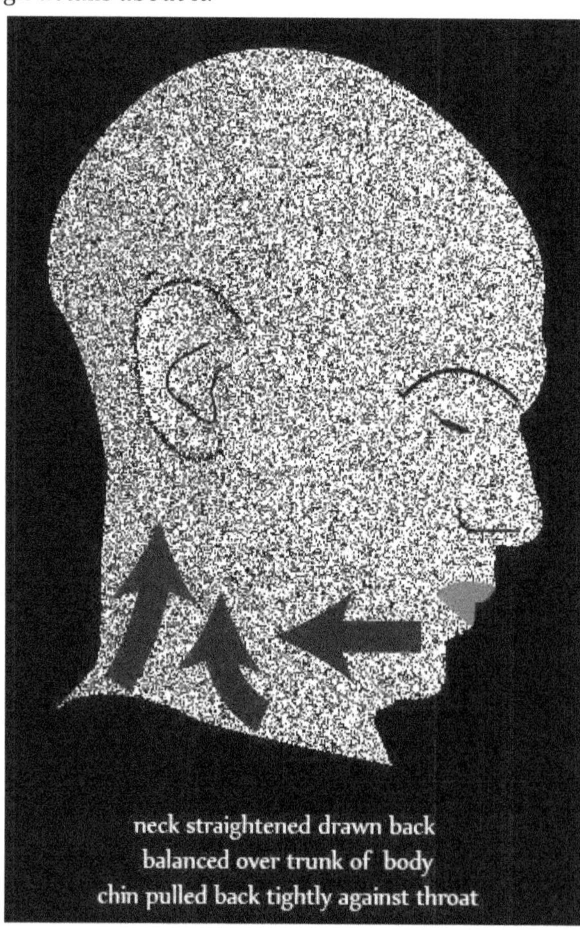

The abdomen draw-back lock is important for compressing the energy which is generated during breath-infusion in the area of the intestines. If this lock is not applied, the energy generated will be diffused around the navel, which will result in increased appetite. More eating will cause an increase in hormone production, which will require more sexual participation to secrete the extra sexual fluids created. This will contravene the yoga objectives.

Application

An ascetic, even one who is proficient, may inadvertently do a posture or breath-infusion method in an unhealthy way. It happens. There might be a pull of a muscle or tendon, a shift of a spinal vertebrate, a lift of an internal organ or ingestion of viral bacteria during breathing. Any of these may cause the health of the body to turn for the worse.

A yogi should not expect that a material body will be defect-free. That is not possible because it is prohibited by the laws of nature. The most we can expect is to keep it in the healthiest condition permitted by its genetic composition and destiny. The summit of destiny for this body is its death. Then all life-functions within it will shut down. Until such time, a yogi should keep the body in the best possible health. If depriving it of luxurious foods are required for that, then so be it.

We saw that many great yogis, develop a distended gut because of succumbing to the social pressures of relatives, religious followers or sincere disciples. That happens. Under social pressure even a great yogi loses control of his eatables and will on occasion eat more than necessary. These are strikes of fate which the ascetic may observe and transcend even though their manifestation is sure to show and people who lack insight are sure to criticize.

Verse 18

युक्तं युक्तं तयजेद्वायुं युक्तं युक्तं च पूरयेत् ।
युक्तं युक्तं च बध्नीयादेवं सिद्धिमवाप्नुयात् ।। १८ ।।

yuktaṁ yuktaṁ tyajedvāyuṁ yuktaṁ yuktaṁ ca pūrayet |
yuktaṁ yuktaṁ ca badhnīyādevaṁ siddhimavāpnuyāt || 18 ||

yuktaṁ – expertise, yuktaṁ – expertise, tyajed = tyajet = should exhale, vāyuṁ – air, yuktaṁ yuktaṁ = very proficient, ca – and, pūrayet – should inhale, yuktaṁ yuktaṁ – very proficient, ca – and, badhnīyād = badhnīyāt = should retain with inner focus, evaṁ – thus, siddhim – success, avāpnuyāt – attains

Air should be exhaled expertly, and should be inhaled proficiently, being retained with inner focus; the yogi will attain success in the process.

Analysis

Pranayama breath-infusion is the way to get the interest focus of the core-self to transfer into the subtle body or psyche. So long as there is a physical body the tendency for focusing down into the material world will be there. This habit will recur, at least until the yogi can fully consolidate the pratyahar sensual energy withdrawal, which in itself is reliant on a firm breath-infusion practice.

Breath is considered to be the bridge between the physical and subtle. It is the way to move the attention and interest of the self from the physical to the astral. It should be stressed to beginners repeatedly that during the pranayama practices, focus should be within the psyche, within the confines of the subtle body.

Application

The interest and attention comes from a subtle source. It chases physical and lower astral phenomena. This should be changed, where this same interest returns to the subtle source and investigates the form and means of that subtle self. Breath-infusion gives an ascetic direct power over the outgoing interest so that it can be focused down into the psyche and it can be turned-about back into the psyche, ceasing its physical and lower astral pursuits.

Verse 19

यदा तु नाडी–शुद्धिः सयात्तथा चिह्नानि बाह्यतः ।

कायस्य कृशता कान्तिस्तदा जायते निश्चितम् ।। १९ ।।

yadā tu nāḍī–śuddhiḥ syāttathā cihnāni bāhyataḥ ।
kāyasya kṛśatā kāntistadā jāyate niścitam ।। 19 ।।

yadā – when, tu – it happens, nāḍī – nadi subtle veins and arteries, śuddhiḥ – purifying clearance, syāt – becomes, tathā – even so, cihnāni – characteristics, bāhyataḥ – external, kāyasya – pertaining to the material body, kṛśatā – thinness, kāntis = kāntiḥ = radiance, tadā – then, jāyate – experiences, niścitam – definitely

When the nadi subtle veins and arteries exhibit a purifying clearance, external features like leanness and radiance show even in the material body, then the yogi definitely experiences success.

Analysis

There are physical showings of the subtle progress of a yogi, and yet the yogi should not be focused on that. He should not allow the admiring public to victimize him with praises because of their noticing changes in his body which are positive and which are due to the austerities.

If possible a yogi should remain in isolation so that his advancement remains a secret. Then he will not have to deal with admiration and acclaim which would eat up time and consume emotional energy. The health of the material body is a mere byproduct of a successful yoga practice. The physical form has limited endurance because no matter how healthy it may become, it will still be subjected to the death as fated.

Application

Some great yogins whose material bodies got radiance did not perceive it. They were so focused on the subtle side of existence, that the condition of the material body was of no concern to them. But then visitors would make remarks about the beauty and glow of their material forms.

There will always be people who want to turn a yogi about so that he refocuses on material existence and uses his insight to improve the status quo. If a yogi yields to

this, he is encouraged to begin a religious organization or yoga institution. Then his life is consumed working for social upliftment under the guise of spiritual elevation.

Verse 20

यथेष्टं धारणं वायोरनलस्य प्रदीपनम् ।

नादाभिव्यक्तिरारोग्यं जायते नाडि–शोधनात् ।। २० ।।

yatheṣṭaṁ dhāraṇaṁ vāyoranalasya pradīpana ।
nādābhivyaktirārogyaṁ jāyate nāḍi–śodhanāt ।। 20 ।।

yatheṣṭaṁ = yatha iṣṭaṁ = as desired, dhāraṇaṁ – deliberate focus on transcendental reality, vāyor = vāyoḥ = infused breath energy, analasya – of digestion, pradīpanam – energizing, nādābhivyaktir = nāda (naad subtle sound) + abhivyaktiḥ (manifestation), ārogharn – without disease, jāyate – experience, nāḍi – nadi subtle veins and arteries, śodhanāt – because of clearing

As desired, the deliberate focus on the infused breath energy, the energization of the digestive process, the manifestation of naad subtle sound, and the absence of disease, occurs as a result of the clearance of the nadi subtle veins and arteries.

Analysis

This means that there will be the absence of new diseases which are not already set into the material body as fated. This does not mean that there will be no disease. It depends on the genetic structure of the body, the consequential fate which is due to the body because of the activities of the family in which it was generated and the misbehavior of the yogi formerly. The main observations about health are in the subtle body, because that is where the nadi subtle veins and arteries are located. They are not in the physical form, even though their counterpart blood tubing is located there.

As one does pranayama breath-infusion more and more, one develops the ability to focus the infused energy and its admixture with hormonal energy and with kundalini psychic lifeforce here or there in the subtle body. This is handy for redesigning subtle configuration so as to convert it into a yoga siddha form.

Breath-infusion is the direct method for controlling the kundalini shakti, as compared to doing so haphazardly by visualization and wishful thinking. The psyche becomes more and more submissive to the self as the breath-infusion practice becomes more and more proficient. That is the benefit in doing pranayama practice.

The energization of the digestive process is one sure way to get physical evidence about breath-infusion. Just by breath-infusion alone the digestive process becomes more efficient, evacuation is more prompt and flushes out with ease from the physical body, while on the subtle side, negative energy is expelled from the subtle body thoroughly.

The manifestation of naad subtle sound is no small achievement. This releases the yogi from reliance on having to physically or mentally say mantra sounds. Naad itself is the free mantra which the yogi can focus on. Its absorption causes the development of insight into the chit akash sky of consciousness.

Application

For clearance of the nadi subtle veins and arteries Swatmarama listed these completions:

- *deliberate focus on the infused breath energy*
- *energization of the digestive process*
- *manifestation of naad subtle sound*
- *absence of disease*

These are centered on the proper breath-infusion technique. The most physical of these aspects is the ***energization of the digestive process****. Though physical it has psychic impact on the subtle body because it releases that form from having to supply excesses of subtle energy to run the intestinal nutrient extraction process. By increasing the percentage of fresh air in the blood stream and decreasing the polluted gases, there is more efficient digestion which results in processing of less bulk of foods. This conserves kundalini energy.*

The ***absence of disease*** *is a result of a tight pranayama practice with asana postures. This occurs as a result of proficiency and is maintained by that practice. However it is really something on the subtle side because the physical body will continue its journey to deterioration and death regardless.*

A yogi who uses an old body seems the same as any other elderly body but the difference is in the subtle form. The energy level of the subtle system of an elderly pranayama yogi is super in comparison to that of another elderly person but unless one has psychic perception one cannot assess this.

Absence of disease really means in the subtle body because the physical form of a pranayama proficient elderly yogi may have disease or may manifest the common symptoms of old age. His breath-infusion keeps the subtle body in tiptop shape just as if it were a youthful astral form, while the same does not hold for elderly persons who do not do breath-infusion.

The ***deliberate focus on the infused breath*** *is mastered step by step over time as the student practices. This usually takes years to master. It entails focusing down into the subtle body during the daily practice sessions. In time doing this, the yogi can keep his attention inside of the psyche throughout the practice session and also during the meditation which follows.*

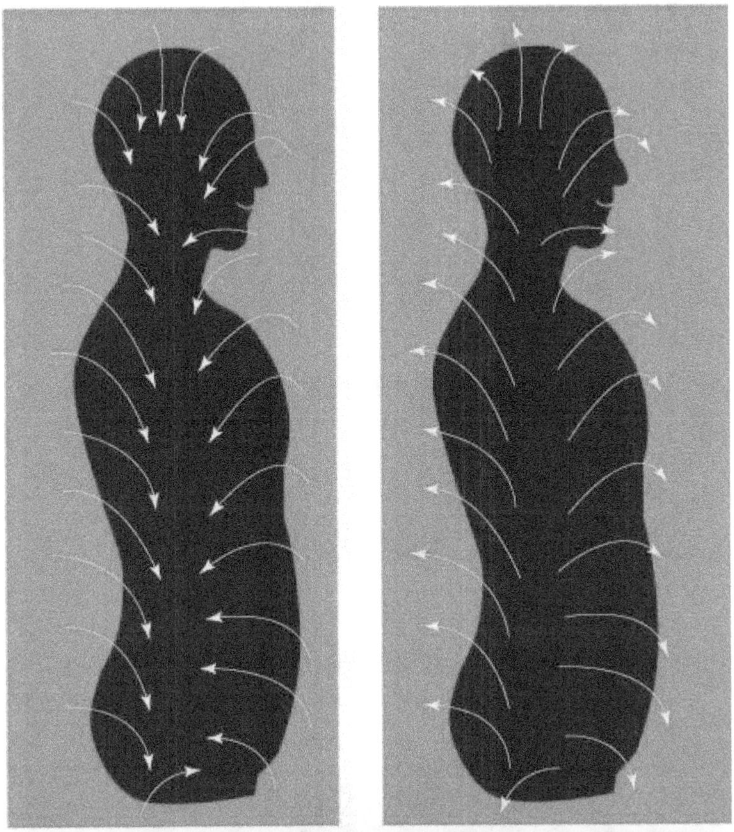

external sensual energy penetrates the subtle body

internal sensual energy departs from the subtle body

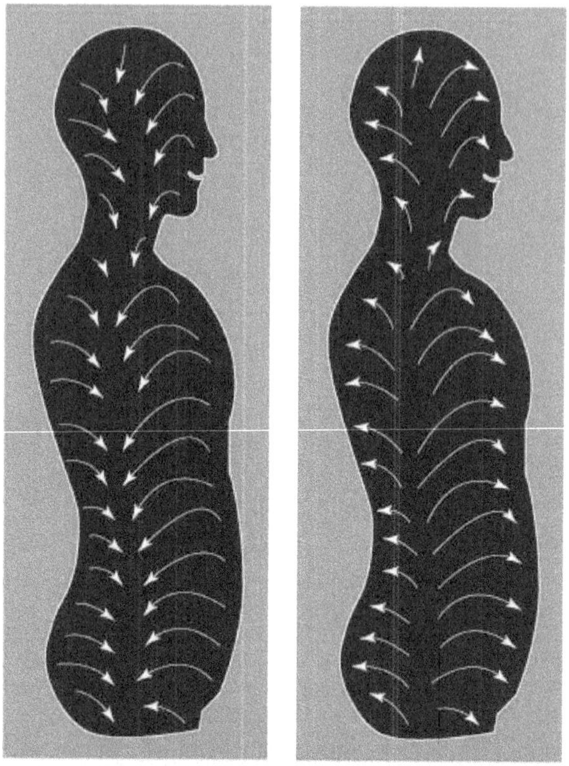

internal sensual energy travels inward in the subtle body

internal sensual energy travels outward but remains restricted within the subtle body

The ***manifestation of naad subtle sound*** *is the culmination of the breath-infusion practice but this is heard as soon as the yogi ceases the breath-infusion when that is noisy. Due to clearance and extraction of subtle energy pollution, the subtle body or psyche becomes full of fresh astral energy, which is an environment which is responsive to naad sound resonance.*

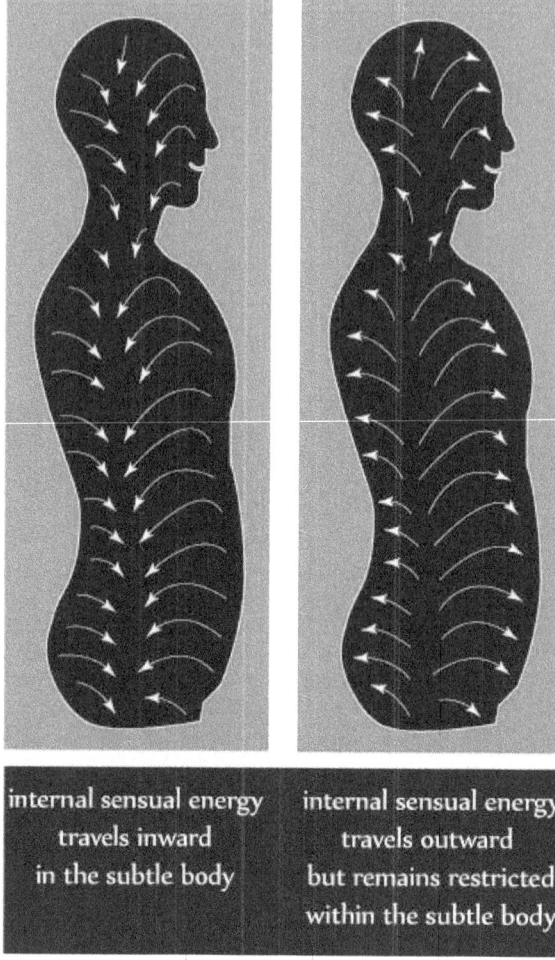

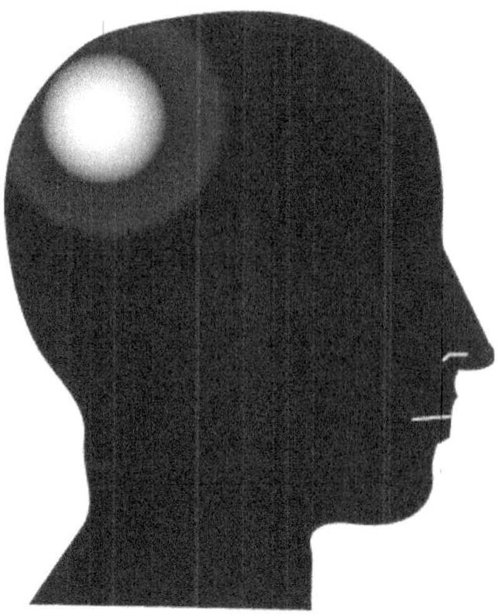

Verse 21

मेद्-शलेष्ह्माधिकः पूर्वं षहट-कर्माणि समाचरेत् ।

अन्यस्तु नाचरेत्तानि दोषणां समभावतः ।। २१ ।।

meda–śleṣhmādhikaḥ pūrvaṁ ṣaṭ–karmāṇi samācaret I
anyastu nācarettāni doṣāṇāṁ samabhāvataḥ II 21 II

meda – fat, śleṣhmādhikaḥ = śleṣma (mucus) + adhikaḥ (excessive), pūrvaṁ – first, ṣaṭ – six, karmāṇi – special actions, samācaret – thoroughly practice, anyas = anyaḥ = another, tu – but, nācaret = na (not) + ācaret (should practice), tāni – those, doṣāṇāṁ – flaws, samabhāvataḥ – totally absent

If there is excessive fat or mucus, one should at first thoroughly practice the six special actions. But those in whom those flaws are totally absent, should not practice that.

Analysis

Two categories are given:

- Those who are healthy without excessive fat or mucus.
- Those in whom such health is totally absent (samabhāvataḥ)

Those in whom these features of ill health are partially present should use any or all of the six special actions which will be mentioned in the next verse.

Application

An effort should be made to cure the ill-health of the body. That is provided the condition is curable. If the body has incurable diseases, a yogi should accept that as being fated. Without depression about its condition, practice should continue as much as can be done in that diseased form. After all, the body is perishable. It will manifest a terminal condition sooner or later. People are sometimes proud to die from natural causes, but a yogi should be detached because death by accident, terrible disease or infirmity, is the same incidence of losing a body.

The importance is on the condition of the subtle form, irrespective of the physical system's acceptable or awful termination.

Verse 22

धौतिर्बस्तिस्तथा नेतिस्त्राटकं नौलिकं तथा ।

कपाल- भातिश्चैतानिषहट-कर्माणि प्रछक्षते ।। २२ ।।

dhautirbastistathā netistrāṭakaṁ naulikaṁ tathā I
kapāla–bhātiścaitāni ṣaṭ–karmāṇi prachakṣate II 22 II

dhautir = dhautiḥ = stomach cleansing action, bastis = bastiḥ = large intestine (colon) cleansing action, tathā – also, netis = netiḥ = nasal–sinus cleansing, trāṭakaṁ – blank staring, naulikaṁ – abdominal muscular action, tathā – so even, kapāla–bhātiś = kapāla–bhātiḥ = intense rapid breathing with stress on exhaling, caitāni = ca (and) + etāni (these), ṣaṭ – six, karmāṇi – purificatory physio–psychic acts, prachakṣate – are considered

Dhauti stomach cleansing action, basti large intestine (colon) cleansing action, neti nasal–sinus cleansing, traatak blank staring, nauli abdominal muscular action, and also kapalabhati intense rapid breathing with stress on exhaling, are considered as the six purificatory physio–psychic acts.

Analysis

These are physio-psychic actions where the physical part is the focus for beginning students and the psychic aspect is the interest of the advanced yogis. These are called shat karmas. Here is the listing:

- dhauti stomach cleansing action
- basti large intestine (colon) cleansing action
- neti nasal–sinus cleansing
- traatak blank staring
- nauli abdominal muscular action
- kapalabhati intense rapid breathing with stress on exhaling

Application

One should practice any or all of these six purificatory cleansing actions as advised by an advanced yogi. These should not be practiced merely because someone said to do it or because one read of it in a book such as this.

The reason is that each of the methods of yoga should be acquired by someone who currently mastered it. The teacher may or may not be taught physically. That does not matter. So long as he has the proficiency he can teach it but that expertise must be there currently.

Each purificatory action will be described in the following verses but that does not mean that one should adopt these. As I said one should learn these from a proficient teacher. This book is a guideline so that one is not misled by anyone who is not proficient but who pretends to be a master of these processes.

I was introduced to the first five methods listed above by Yogi Arthur Beverford on the basis of what he was shown by Rishi Singh Gherwal and also what Rishi wrote in his books. The last method was taught to me by Yogi Harbhajan Singh Sahib.

I found that the first five systems were serviceable up to a point. Then I felt no necessity to continue their practice but the kapalabhati method I continued doing for many years until it evolved into bhastrika pranayama breath-infusion.

Verse 23

कर्म षट्कमिदं गोप्यं घट–शोधन–कारकम् ।

विचित्र–गुण–सन्धाय पूज्यते योगि–पुणगवैः ।। २३ ।।

karma ṣaṭkamidaṁ gopyaṁ ghaṭa–śodhana–kārakam I
vicitra–guṇa–sandhāya pūjyate yogi–pungavaiḥ II 23 II

karma – purificatory physio–psychic acts, ṣaṭkam – six, idaṁ – these, gopyaṁ – confidential, ghaṭa – body, śodhana – purification, kārakam – causing, vicitra – varied, guṇa – natural feature, sandhāya – collective, pūjyate – is sincerely honored, yogi – yogi, pungavaiḥ – by the prominent

These six purificatory physio–psychic acts are confidential. They cause purification of the body, affecting the various natural features collectively. These are sincerely honored by the prominent yogis.

Analysis

Even though the six purificatory techniques are explained in books, still unless one learns it from an advanced yogi, one may not be able to apply them properly. The reason is that there are psychic and mental applications which must be applied with the physical actions. It is not all physical. In some cases a student just cannot get it right unless an advanced yogi enters the student's psyche and makes the application.

Confidential means that there is a psychological application which one must have insight to perceive. Many students just do not have the required insight perception to find all parts of the psyche for these applications; hence the need to take help from a perceptive yogi.

Application

When a yogi uses these applications proficiently, he or she becomes amazed at the effect. Something which could not be achieved by any other means may suddenly click into place permanently through one of the six purificatory processes. Thus yogis sincerely honor these techniques. The fancy is that a student may try to use visualization, mantra chanting and herbal medicines and still not get the result intended. Then when one or a combination of any of the six purificatory procedures is applied, there might be success.

These are not mere physical procedures even though physical application is necessary. These are mental and emotional holds as well. That is why one has to learn these from an advanced ascetic who was successful using these processes.

Verse 24

तत्र धौतिः

चतुरङ्गुलविस्तारं हस्त–पञ्च–दशायतम् ।

गुरूपदिष्ट–मार्गेण सिक्तं वस्त्रं शनैर्ग्रसेत् ।
पुनः प्रत्याहरेच्चैतदुदितं धौति–कर्म तत् ।। २४ ।।

tatra dhautiḥ
catur–aṅgula–vistāraṁ hasta–pañca–daśāyatam ।
gurūpadiṣṭa–mārgeṇa siktaṁ vastraṁ śanairgraset ।
punaḥ pratyāhareccaitaduditaṁ dhauti–karma tat ।। 24 ।।

tatra – Now presented, dhautiḥ – dhauti stomach cleansing action, catur = catuḥ = four, aṅgula – thumb, vistāraṁ – width, hasta – hand, pañca–daśāyatam = pañca–daśa (five and ten, fifteen) + āyatam (length), guru – yoga teacher, ūpadiṣṭa – taught by, mārgeṇa – by the path, siktaṁ – wet, vastraṁ – cloth, śanair = śanaiḥ = gradually, graset – should swallow, punaḥ – again, pratyāharec = pratyāharet = retract, caitad – ca (and) + etat (this), uditaṁ – is acclaimed as, dhauti – dhauti stomach cleansing action, karma – action, tat – that

Now presented is the dhauti stomach muscular cleansing action.

A cloth four thumbs wide and fifteen hands in length should be swallowed gradually as taught by the yoga-guru. This should be extracted in turn. It is acclaimed as dhauti stomach muscular cleansing action.

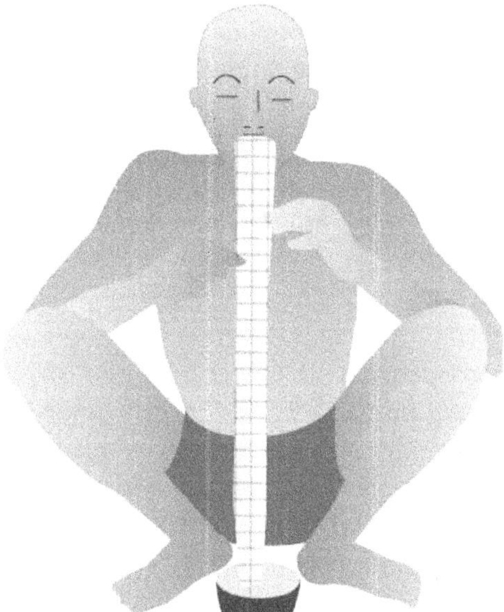

Analysis

Rishi Singh Gherwal instructed Arthur Beverford that the cloth should be of plain cotton, muslin and should be boiled in hot water to clear bacteria. The yogi should ingest it slowly bit by bit.

Application

I tried this procedure after it was explained by Guruji Beverford but I did not find it helpful with meditation or health. This may be because of the stage of advancement when I applied it. The fact that Swatmarama extols it means that it has value even if I

practiced it and could not determine its worth.

From a pure physical perspective this has to do with the esophagus and stomach. The gastric condition of the stomach can be checked by this method because when the fabric is extracted, it may be inspected for enzyme coloring and food material which adheres to it. I found that the psychological advantage was the internalization of the attention, so that I became aware of the cells which lined the stomach.

The subtle part of yoga has much to do with knowing the consciousness of each part of the body. Usually one cannot do this and must rely on medical professionals to go into the body with probes and imaging devices. As a yogi if one can enter the body with insight perception, one can deal with many negative features and treat the psyche psychologically.

Verse 25

कास–शवास–पलीह–कुष्ठं कफरोगाश्च विंशतिः ।

धौति–कर्म–प्रभावेण प्रयान्त्येव न संशयः ।। २५ ।।

kāsa–śvāsa–plīha–kuṣṭhaṁ kapharoghāśca viṁśatiḥ I
dhauti–karma–prabhāveṇa prayāntyeva na saṁśayaḥ II 25 II

kāsa – cough, śvāsa – bronchial disease, plīha – glandular malfunction, kuṣṭhaṁ – skin disease, kapha – sinus, roghāś = roghāḥ = diseases, ca – and, viṁśatiḥ – twenty, dhauti–karma = dhauti stomach cleansing action, prabhāveṇa – by influence of, prayānty = prayānti = diminish, eva – so, na – no, saṁśayaḥ – doubt

Cough, bronchial disease, glandular malfunctions, skin disease and twenty kinds of sinus malfunction diminish by the influence of dhauti stomach cleansing action. There is no doubt about this.

Analysis

In the time of Swatmarama there were no medical institutions with technological devices as we find today. Modern medical research makes the method of this stomach cleansing action to be unnecessary for the most part. Our culture takes help from medical professionals and technology whereby we do not have the patience to use this teaching for the cures mentioned.

However it is informative that previously, advanced yogis recommended these treatments and diagnosed ill health conditions by having students swallow a fabric as described. Health is desirable for yoga practice. Without it the body just does not cooperate. Hence ancient yogis had to know how to bring their bodies into a healthy condition

Application

As defined by Patanjali in the Yoga Sutras, physical health is not the aim of yoga. All the same without physical health, a beginner and even a mediocre student cannot practice successfully. The condition of the physical form affects the subtle body. This will happen until the physical system is permanently disconnected from the subtle body.

Physical health, therefore, is required in achieving the aim of yoga which is to transcend the very physical body and deal with the unruly aspects of the psychology.

Verse 26

अथ बस्तिः

नाभि–दघ्न–जले पायौ नयस्त–नालोत्कटासनः ।

आधाराकुनछनं कुर्यात्क्षालनं बस्ति–कर्म तत् ।। २६ ।।

atha bastiḥ
nābhi–daghna–jale pāyau nyasta–nālotkaṭāsanaḥ I
ādhārākuñchanaṁ kuryātkṣālanaṁ basti–karma tat I I 26 I I

atha – regarding, bastiḥ – basti large intestine (colon) cleansing action, nābhi – navel, daghna – up to, jale – in water, pāyau – in the anus, nyasta – inserted, nālotkaṭāsanaḥ = nāla (tube) + utkaṭāsanaḥ (utkaṭa squatting posture), ādhārākuñchanaṁ = ādhāra (anal sphincter muscle) + ākuñchanaṁ (contraction), kuryāt – should do, kṣālanaṁ – douche using water, basti–karma = basti large intestine (colon) cleansing action, tat – that

Regarding the basti large intestine (colon) cleansing action:

Being up to the navel in water, with a tube inserted into the anus, the yogi, while assuming the utkata squatting posture, should contract the anal sphincter muscle. That douche using water is the basti large intestine (colon) cleansing action.

Analysis

The basti large intestine (colon) cleansing action is important when a yogi will go into samadhi for days or weeks at a time. Then it is hygienic to clear the body of stools prior to assuming the trance state. If the waste matter in the large colon is not removed, it will continue decaying during the prolonged samadhi period, which might cause the body of the yogi to assume a disease or even to die because of bacterial infection.

Application

Currently because of the large scale radio-active, chemical and biological pollution, it is not recommended that a yogi should squat and draw water through the rectum from a river. Radio-active productions, chemical works, sewage discharge and hospital waste which are discharged makes it hazardous to use rivers in this way.

To enter samadhi for many days or weeks continuously requires special preparation and the assistance of knowledgeable yogis who are advanced and can watch the body of the yogi while it is in a trance state. Without that assistance it is hardly likely that a yogi can master the skill of dimensional transit for long periods of time.

Verse 27

गुल्म–पलीहोदरं चापि वात–पित्त–कफोद्भवाः ।

बस्ति–कर्म–प्रभावेण क्षीयन्ते सकलामयाः ।। २७ ।।

gulma–plīhodaraṁ cāpi vāta–pitta–kaphodbhavāḥ I
basti–karma–prabhāveṇa kṣīyante sakalāmayāḥ I I 27 I I

gulma – gland malfunction, plīhodaraṁ = plīha (spleen disease) + udaraṁ (abdomen), cāpi = and so, vāta – air in the intestines, pitta – bile, kaphodbhavāḥ – kapha (sinus problems) + udbhavāḥ (producing), basti–karma = basti large intestine (colon) cleansing action, prabhāveṇa – by means of, kṣīyante – are eliminated, sakalāmayāḥ = sakala (all) + āmayāḥ (diseases)

Gland malfunction, spleen disease, and also abdominal problems, as well as all diseases which develop from air in the intestines, bile imbalance and sinus problems are eliminated by means of the basti large intestine (colon) cleansing action.

Analysis

This was the situation in the time of Swatmarama. Today things are different. Most human beings must use modern medical facilities and their pharmaceutical products. The big difference is the nature of modern diseases which arise on the basis of totally different environmental conditions and which must be cured through modern means which are adapted to these conditions.

Ayur Vedic methods are suited to Ayur Vedic times when most of the population was limited to simpler industrialization. Currently, the ancient cures are mostly irrelevant because of the modern machinery and technological applications where organic chemistry dominates what we smell and eat.

Application

A yogi should not be superstitious or blind-sided by ancient processes but should first consider their application to the modern situation, where new viruses and diseases arise based on modern pollutions and lifestyles.

Yogis who use organic produce, who live apart from the modern means, who are not involved in modern industry, may use the basti large intestine and colon cleansing action successfully. One should test for the intended result but one should not be fanatical, thinking that because it worked previously, it will serve the purpose today.

Verse 28

धात्विन्द्रियान्तः–करण– प्रसादं

दद्याच्च कान्तिं दहन–प्रदीप्तम् ।

अशेष–दोषोपचयं निहन्याद

अभ्यस्यमानं जल–बस्ति–कर्म ।। २८ ।।

dhātvindriyāntaḥ–karaṇa–prasādaṁ
dadyācca kāntiṁ dahana–pradīptam ।
aśeṣa–doṣopacayaṁ nihanyād
abhyasyamānaṁ jala–basti–karma ।। 28 ।।

dhātvindriyāntaḥ = dhātv (dhātu) (basic psychology) + indriya (sensual energy) + antaḥ (internal), karaṇa – psychic organ, prasādaṁ – tranquility, dadyāc = dadyāt = gives, ca – and, kāntiṁ – beauty, dahana – digestive enzymes, pradīptam – effective reactions, aśeṣa – without exception, doṣopacayaṁ = doṣa (diseased condition) + upacayaṁ (excess), nihanyād = nihanyāt = eliminates, abhyasyamānaṁ – practice, jala – water, basti–karma = basti large intestine (colon) cleansing action

The basic psychology, the sensual energy and the internal psychic organ are tranquilized. The condition gives beauty and causes effective reactions of the digestive enzymes. It eliminates diseased conditions without exception. Such is the basti large intestine and colon cleansing action.

Analysis

The psychological effects are those which affect the subtle body. These are the concern of an advanced yogi. The effects which manifest in the physical form are trivial even though these might indicate what takes place in the subtle form.

No matter how one improves the physical system, its repair will become the ridicule of material nature, which will in time bring that form to its end. Even the subtle body will vanish some billion years hence but since its duration is near infinite in comparison, it is worth it for the time being to focus on its repair and upkeep.

Application

When a yogi practiced sufficiently where he or she can enter abstract states (samadhi) for long periods, then it becomes necessary to tightly regulate the diet so that gradually all solid food is terminated and only liquid foods are taken. This serves the purpose for very rapid evacuation. The yogi must consider what will happen to the food in the intestines and the waste in the colon, during prolonged trance states.

With an efficient and energy supplying breath-infusion, the yogi can greatly reduce physical foodstuffs, transferring the energy consumption more to the breath energy. By regulating the time of meals and the quantity of food, he or she can tell when food will be digested and excreted.

In time as the system becomes more and more reliant on breath energy and less reliant on foodstuffs, the yogi can assist the kundalini lifeforce in its evacuation duties.

Before going into samadhi for days at a time, the colon should be cleared of food waste. The basti large intestine (colon) cleansing action is the best way to achieve this.

Srila Yogeshwarananda who instituted this process during the time when he did day-long and week-long samadhis stated that even though one may do the basti large intestine (colon) cleansing action, some food waste might still remain in the system. These will be discovered after the samadhi to be dried out in the colon. These might be so dried as to be like lumps of hard matter.

Formerly yogis would use a marker for the last meal to be taken before entering a samadhi. This would be a meal which usually produced a dyed waste. For instance a yogi might eat a food which is stained by turmeric or by red beets or by spinach so that the food waste is yellow, red or green.

Then the yogi would observe the waste until that colored mass was evacuated. He would do the basti large intestine (colon) cleansing action repeatedly until he was confident that the waste was evacuated.

If he had to eat during this observation, it would only be liquids and not liquids which provide any quantity of solid waste. Milk which produces solid waste, would not be used by the yogi at this time.

Thus during the samadhi, there would be no food in the stomach or small intestines or waste in the large intestines or colon.

Verse 29

अथ नेतिः

सूत्रं वितस्ति–सुस्निग्धं नासानाले प्रवेशयेत् ।

मुखान्निर्गमयेच्चैषा नेतिः सिद्धैर्निगद्यते ।। २९ ।।

atha netiḥ
sūtraṁ vitasti–susnigdhaṁ nāsānāle praveśayet I
mukhānnirgamayeccaiṣā netiḥ siddhairnigadyate II 29 II

atha – regarding, netiḥ – neti nasal–sinus cleansing, sūtraṁ – thread, vitasti – sufficient length, susnigdhaṁ – very soft, nāsānāle – through the nostril, praveśayet – should insert, mukhān = mukhāt = at the mouth, nirgamayec = nirgamayet = should draw out, caiṣā = ca (then) + eṣā (this), netiḥ – neti nasal–sinus cleansing, siddhair = siddhaiḥ = by the perfected yogi, nigadyate – is rated

Regarding neti nasal/sinus cleansing, insert a very soft cord of sufficient length through the nostril, then draw it out through the mouth. This procedure is rated as the nasal and sinus cleansing by the perfected yogis.

Analysis

The physicality of this is indicated but it is the subtle realization which results in the objective. Mere cleaning of the sinus passages will not result in spirituality. These practices caused students of ancient yogis to get firsthand information about the inner construction of the physical body. It attuned their minds to the subtle system because the nerves which were activated in this process invoke subtle feelings which otherwise the student was unaware of. A human being may live a long life with sufficient ignorance of even the physical body. It is a wonder that any of us may perceive what is mental and emotional in great details.

When a very soft cord of sufficient length is inserted through the nostril and then is drawn through the mouth, the student experiences hair raising feelings which rush through the sinus cavity into the brain and neck. With the proper guidance, these feelings can initiate psychic perception of the corresponding parts of the subtle body. Hence this practice is more than an exercise for health of the physical body.

Application

One should do these cleansing actions with inner focus to know the various parts of the physical body and the corresponding subtle layout. Persons who do yoga and whose attention wanders outside the body during postures or cleansing procedures cannot derive the subtle realization from the practice.

Verse 30

कपाल–शोधिनी चैव दिव्य–दृष्टि–प्रदायिनी ।

जत्रूर्ध्व–जात–रोगौघं नेतिराशु निहन्ति च ।। ३० ।।

kapāla–śodhinī caiva divya–dṛṣṭi–pradāyinī |
jatrūrdhva–jāta–rogaughaṁ netirāśu nihanti ca || 30 ||

kapala – skull, śodhinī – clearance, caiva – and so, divya – supernatural, dṛṣṭi – perception, pradāyinī – grants, jatrūrdhva = jatru (collar bone) + ūrdhva (over, up), jāta – appearing, rogaughaṁ = roga (disease) + ogham (various), netir = netiḥ = neti nasal–sinus cleansing, āśu – quickly, nihanti – eliminate, ca – and

Clearance of the skull and supernatural perception are experienced, various diseases which occur above the collar bone are eliminated quickly by the neti nasal–sinus cleansing.

Analysis

Divya–drishti is supernatural perception. Swatmarama now jumps from physical to supernatural. An aim of yoga is supernatural perception. The physical process is the starting point for beginners, who may quickly or slowly advance. Clearance of the skull means removal of heavy astral energy which clouds and shrouds the potential mystic vision of the person concerned.

The neck is a special area which partitions the trunk of the subtle body from its head. The neck should be cleared of all heavy astral energy so that there is free flow through it.

Application

Diseases may pertain to obstructions of subtle energy and compaction of heavy astral force in the subtle body. The neck and lower jaws are compacted with dense astral energy in the average human being. A yogi must work steadily with pranayama breath-infusion and with special holds and releases to extract subtle pollutions. The neck is special in that even if the center of it is cleared, the rest may be blocked with dense astral energy, making that portion impenetrable. The entire neck including what is outside of the spinal center should be blasted out so that it is filled with light and is open for transit of energy in either direction.

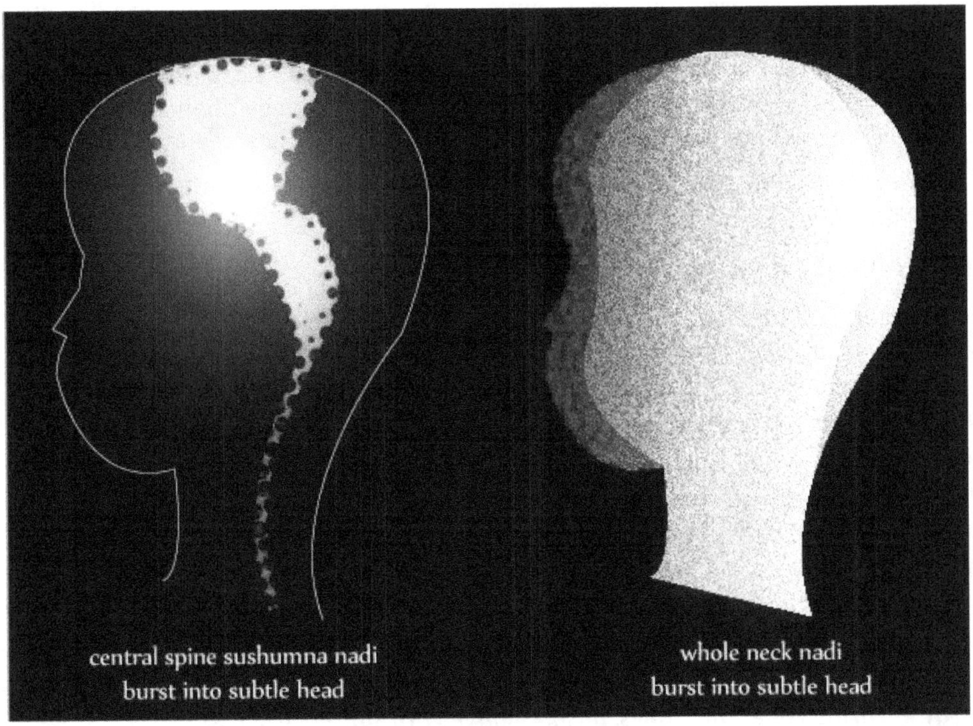

Verse 31

अथ तराटकम

निरीक्षेन्निश्चल–दृशा सूक्ष्मलक्ष्यं समाहितः ।

अश्रु–सम्पात–पर्यन्तमाचार्यैस्त्राटकं समृतम् ।। ३१ ।।

atha trāṭakam
nirīkṣenniścala–dṛśā sūkṣma–lakṣyaṁ samāhitaḥ ।
aśru–sampāta–paryantamāchāryaistrāṭakaṁ smṛtam ।। 31 ।।

atha – regarding, trāṭakam – blank staring, nirīkṣen = nirīkṣet = should look, niścala–dṛśā = without shifting focus, sūkṣma – minute, lakṣyaṁ – mark, samāhitaḥ – meditatively focused, aśru – tears, sampāta – appears, paryantam – until, ācāryais = ācāryaiḥ = by the yoga teachers, trāṭakaṁ – blank staring, smṛtam – is known as

Regarding the traatak blank staring, one should, until tears appear and without shifting focus, look at a minute mark with meditative focus. This is known as blank staring by the yoga teachers.

Analysis

I was introduced to traatak blank staring by Guruji Arthur Beverford, as he was instructed by Rishi Singh Gherwal. At the time I had an interest in seeing auras, and in developing subtle body perception through the two subtle eyes which are usually interspaced into the physical eyeballs.

This practice proved useful in seeing auras even around inanimate objects like stones and trees. Using this method one can develop confidence in psychic perception and in the reality of the subtle body and subtle energy. When using this method one may also see the aura of the earth, the flashing subtle energy around vegetation and the fact that astral life is present in a parallel form which is relative to physical reality.

What is seen easily by persons who take hallucinogenic drugs or herbs, may be seen by using this traatak blank staring method.

Application

Swatmarama mentioned the method of blank staring at a minute mark with meditative focus, until tears appear. There is also the method of blank staring at nothing with no special focus and with the perceptive interest withdrawn or retracted through the eyes of the subtle body into the subtle head.

Either of these methods will result in subtle perception if done for a time. If the eyes burn or if the eyes tear, one should tolerate that. If one cannot then one should slowly close the eyelids, squeeze them together and then open them again and continue the staring. This closing of the eyelids can be done as frequently as necessary, and eventually one will see the auric lights.

The lights may flash or may remain glowing steadily. If the ascetic maintains the stare for a long enough time, the entire environment will appear as being composed of light energy of various hues and tones, flashing alive with subtle energy.

This practice is never a waste of time. An ascetic should develop confidence in having a subtle body and in the fact that there is an astral world which runs parallel to physical existence and which is the basis for physical life.

Verse 32

मोचनं नेत्र–रोगाणां तन्द्रादीनां कपाटकम् ।

यत्नतस्त्राटकं गोप्यं यथा हाटक–पेटकम् ।। ३२ ।।

mocanaṁ netra–rogāṇāṁ tandrādīṇāṁ kapāṭakam |
yatnatastrāṭakaṁ gopyaṁ yathā hāṭaka–peṭakam || 32 ||

mocanaṁ – relief, netra – eye, rogāṇāṁ – diseases, tandrādīṇāṁ = tandra (fatigue) + ādīṇāṁ (and other), kapāṭakam – condition, yatnatas = yatnataḥ = carefully, trāṭakaṁ – blank staring, gopyaṁ – confidential, yathā – as it is, hāṭaka–peṭakam – box of gold

Eye disease, conditions which cause fatigue and similar feelings, are relieved by the practice of traatak blank staring. It is confidential and should be regarded with care like one would a box of gold.

Analysis

Some eyes diseases may be relieved by doing traatak. In addition what it cured in the time of Swatmarama, it may have no effect on today due to the change of the environment and the variation in body types. Fatigue which is based on dulling energies in the brain, either in the physical body or subtle one, may be relieved by it, if the staring results in extraction of that energy or neutralization of it.

Swatmarama compared traatak to a box of gold which would be kept confidentially. Once introduced to this by a yoga-guru, one should not explain this to anyone unless one is given commission to teach others.

Application

Interest in the outward-going senses of the subtle body may be there initially. In the advanced stages, one loses interest in this and graduates to concerns about the components in the psyche and the relationship between these components and the core-self.

The five senses of the physical system are scarcely of interest to any yogi but the five senses of the subtle body are of interest to the neophytes, while for the advanced yogis, those five subtle senses are of little concern.

More important are the psychic organs within the subtle body and the use of these to transit or express insight into other dimensions, especially into the causal level and beyond.

Using the astral body to move about in the subtle world is termed as astral projection which means that the subtle body was displaced from the physical one and moved about on its own without being constrained by the physical. Even though astral projection has value initially, it is of little consequence in the advanced stages, when the yogi ceases interest in its mobility and uses it without displacing it from the physical one.

Verse 33

अथ नौलिः

अमन्दावर्त–वेगेन तुन्दं सव्यापसव्यतः ।

नतांसो भ्रामयेदेषा नौलिः सिद्धैः प्रशस्यते ।। ३३ ।।

atha naulih
amandāvarta–vegena tundaṁ savyāpasavyataḥ |
natāṁso bhrāmayedeṣā nauliḥ siddhaiḥ praśasyate || 33 ||

atha – as for, nauliḥ = nauli abdominal muscular action, amandāvarta = amanda (quickly) + āvarta (turning), vegena – with speed, tundaṁ – abdominal cavity, savyāpasavyataḥ = savya (left) + apasavyataḥ (right), natāṁso = natāṁsaḥ = beginning a circular motion, bhrāmayed = bhrāmayet = should spin, eṣā – this, nauliḥ – nauli abdominal muscular action, siddhaiḥ – by perfected yogis, praśasyate – is known as

As for nauli abdominal muscular action, turning quickly with speed the abdominal cavity to the left and right, the yogi should spin it in a circular motion. This is known as the nauli abdominal muscular action by the perfected yogis.

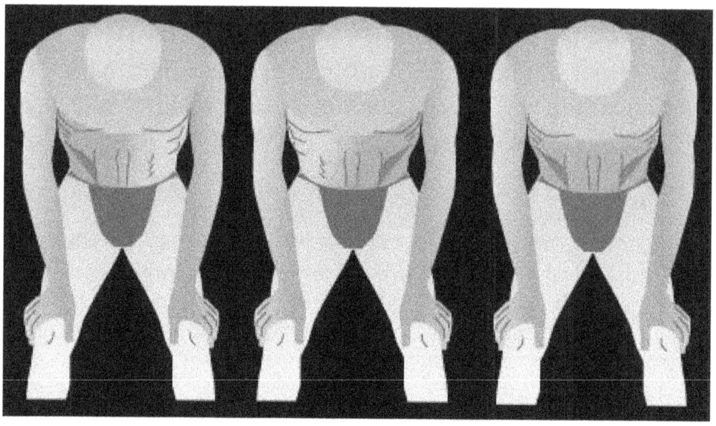

Analysis

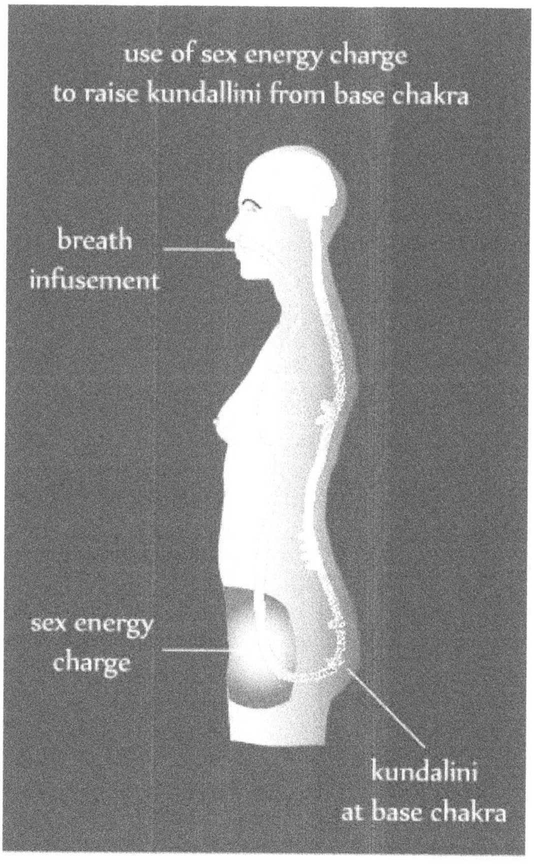

In kundalini yoga, this nauli abdominal muscular action is necessary because food is a main stay of the kundalini psychic lifeforce. Unless eating is adjusted and the digestive and excretory systems are toned, one cannot have full success in kundalini yoga. It is not just a matter of visualization because the kundalini is resistant to will power. This is why we were conditioned by it in the first place. This is why we require disciplines to be free from its dominance.

In a way the management by kundalini is convenient. It frees us from having to maintain the subtle and gross bodies. We can enjoy or suffer according to its decisions without us lifting a finger to help in the maintenance of the two bodies.

The change in this convenience comes about when one can push down the infused breath energy into the sexual hormone energy in the groin. Once there one may increase the push by infusing more fresh air. This causes a cumulative charge at the sex organ chakra which becomes attracted to the kundalini lifeforce at the base chakra.

Repeated actions of charging these energies, causes a gradual but sure change in the attitude of kundalini where it becomes flexible to the will power of a yogi.

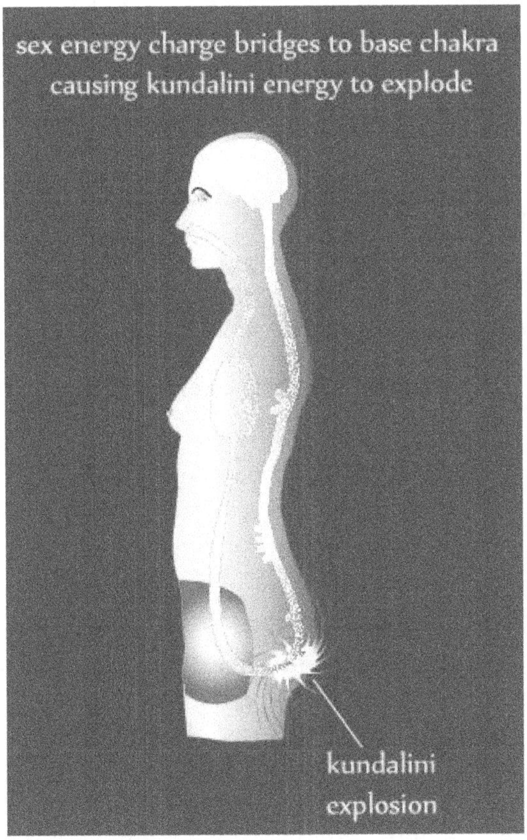

Application

The spinning circular motion of the abdominal cavity is a physical description but it has subtle effect in the astral body. This is a muscular movement which involves the use of the diaphragm and the various tendons and muscles in the cavity and in the outer flesh of the trunk of the body.

There is however a secret circular motion which was explained to me in the astral world by Sri Lahiri Mahasaya. This concerns the circular movement of infused breath energy. It is done in the kapalabhati / bhastrika rapid breathing system, where a yogi infuses energy down into the abdomen and directs the fresh-air saturated cells in the blood stream to travel in a circular motion around the navel. This happens in the physical system to some extent but it is targeted into the subtle body.

To test the effectiveness of this, a yogi should do the infusion in just three or four postures in a session, with repeated emphasis and pushing down the energy in a circular motion and then lifting it out of that upwards. This is done for at least twenty (20) minutes or preferably for about forty (40) minutes.

Then the yogi should be certain that the rest of the psyche is pressurized with fresh air by directing energy to move there as the breathing continues. Thereafter the yogi should meditate and check to be sure that the area around the navel has no heavy astral energy but is transparent as a clear skyline. During the next twenty four hours the yogi should be attentive to evacuation because the evacuation should occur at an earlier time, about at least one to two hours earlier and with much more ease. This is the physical result of doing nauli abdominal breath-infusion action.

Verse 34

मन्दाग्नि–सन्दीपन–पाचनादि–
सन्धापिकानन्दकरी सदैव।
अशेष–दोषामय–शोषणी च
हठ–क्रिया मौलिरियं च नौलिः ॥ ३४ ॥

mandāgni–sandīpana–pācanādi–
sandhāpikānanda–karī sadaiva|
aśeṣa–doṣāmaya–śoṣaṇī ca
haṭha–kriyā mauliriyaṁ ca nauliḥ||34||

mandāgni = manda (slow) + agni (digestive heat), sandīpana – by stimulating (digestive enzymes), pācanādi – good digestion and related bodily functions, sandhāpikānanda = sandhā (link access),+ apika [? api (also) - ka (spiritual space)] + ānanda(bliss), karī – produce, sadaiva – as always, aśeṣa – with no exception, doṣāmaya – consisting of diseases, śoṣaṇī – eliminates, ca – and, haṭha–kriyā = kundalini manipulation for subtle body transformation, maulir = mauliḥ = foundation, iyaṁ – this, ca – and, nauliḥ – nauli abdominal muscular action

It stimulates slow digestive heat, produces good digestion and related bodily functions, as well as giving blissful feelings and access to divine space. With no exception, it always eliminates disease. This nauli abdominal muscular action is the foundation of the kundalini manipulation for subtle body transformation.

Analysis

There is a bundle of energy around the navel. This is carried in the psyche from body to body as the format for new bodies. Seen visually on the psychic plane it is a twisted contorted bunch of tiny tubes which are intertwined.

Liberation cannot occur until this bundle is unraveled. Much of it has to be removed if the psyche is be shorn of its survival tendencies.

A material body, even a healthy youthful one, will soon die if it is not nourished. Whatever pleasure we derive in a body is experienced first of all on the basis of nourishment.

There are many yogis, even successful ones, who never understood the essentiality of nourishment. This is because of focusing on other irritations which are enforced by material nature. Gautam Buddha realized that starving the body would not give him what he wanted which was freedom from trauma. This is because trauma occurs on the emotional plane which may be experienced even if there is no material body with its nutritional needs.

But all the same the nutritional concerns of the material body have basis in the subtle intakes of the astral form. Still, starving the physical or subtle bodies is not the solution.

A yogi has to deal with whatever shocks he puts the bodies through. Any shock forms trauma which the core-self has to compensate for. The secret is to change the needs of the subtle body so that it is no longer reliant on a physio-psychic feeding system. The key to this is the navel. It is at the navel that one begins the life of a particular body in the womb of the mother.

The nauli abdominal muscular action rumps up and eventually unravels the tiny tubes which form the clump of suction ducts at the navel. When breath energy is pressed through the clump, it eventually allows the yogi to gain control and to eliminate the suction mechanism. This awards freedom from rebirth for the individual seeker.

When a disembodied soul looks down acutely to take another body, he or she does so through the navel clump of suction energy which acts as an eye for seeing a birth possibility. In infants this seeing-eye takes the form of the lips which suck the nipple of the mother.

Application

Sometimes by the laws of consequence, I meet a woman who was once my mother. Then my subtle lips take a sucking format because of the subconscious memory of the past life and the familiarity of the woman's subtle form from the past life. This sucking format is sourced in the navel.

If we study the composition of a woman's breast, we will get some idea about the bundle of tubing at the psychic navel which operates to begin feeding in the mother's passage at the start of each embryo.

The nauli abdominal muscular action is more than a physical exercise. When done with fresh air breath-infusion, it may yield the full benefits.

Nauli has come to mean physical pumping of the abdomen but that is preliminary. There should be pumping by moving fresh air-infused blood into the area and polluted air extraction from the area. That is the complete process.

Let us look at some benefits:

- *stimulates slow digestive heat*
- *produces good digestion and related bodily functions*
- *gives blissful feelings*
- *facilitates access to divine space*
- *eliminates disease.*

Slow digestive heat *causes energy overload into the abdominal cavity, which over-taxes the kundalini lifeforce. Any inefficiency in maintaining the body is counterproductive to yoga practice and causes the kundalini to be a dull force with stupor. This does not contribute to enlightenment because the core-self has to provide energy for the kundalini to operate. An inefficient use of the energy means that the core-self will be distracted from its quest for spiritual potential.*

Good digestion *is abdominal region efficiency which causes the conservation of energy so that the kundalini does not have to endeavor as hard to maintain the body.*

This results in increase energy in the astral body with the benefit of more objective psychic perception both in waking and dream states. This gives confidence in the yoga process, which is vital for students to develop resistance to non-yogic influences

***Blissful feelings** are not to be taken lightly, nor should one think that a living entity can live forever without some type of emotional, mental, psychic, supernatural or spiritual happiness. There must be shelter for happiness in some place somewhere. Abandoning happiness on a lower plane of existence will work so long as the yogi finds happiness on a higher level.*

There has got to be happiness. It is merely a matter of the source of it. When a yogi clears away the bunches of pollution at the navel, a bliss energy flows through that area. This provides the needed existential relief.

***Access to divine space** is vital. One can remain in a meditative void or nothingness for a time but sooner or later one needs access to the divine space. If one does not get that, then one returns to a lower environment and must eke out an existence there. Birds fly into space but eventually they are required to alight for resting. A yogi must find a superior environment or he will return to this trauma-ridden place.*

There are two mundane bodies. Both are susceptible to disease. In so far as the nauli abdominal muscular action prevents or cures disease, it is useful to decreasing the inefficiency in either of the bodies. This results in increased psychic perception with a corresponding use of insight.

Verse 35

अथ कपालभातिः

भस्त्रावल्लोह–कारस्य रेच–पूरौ ससम्भ्रमौ ।

कपालभातिर्विख्याता कफ–दोष–विशोषणी ।। ३५ ।।

atha kapālabhātiḥ
bhastrāvalloha–kārasya reca–pūrau sasambhramau ।
kapālabhātirvikhyātā kapha–doṣa–viśoṣaṇī ।। 35 ।।

atha – as for, kapālabhātiḥ – kapālabhāti process which causes light to appear in the head, bhastrā – bellows, val = vat = like, – blacksmith, reca – exhalation, pūrau – and inhalation, sasambhramau – both rapidly, kapālabhātir = kapālabhātiḥ = kapālabhāti process which causes light to appear in the head, vikhyātā – known as, kapha – mucus, doṣa – health problem, viśoṣaṇī – eliminates

As for the kapalabhati process which causes light to appear in the head, it involves breathing with rapid exhalation and inhalation like the bhastra bellows of a blacksmith. This kapalabhati is known for eliminating mucus problems.

Analysis

Kapalabhati means that breath-infusion process which causes light (bhati) to be manifest in the skull or mind (kapāla). It is an aggressive practice which operates the lungs the way a blacksmith (loha-karasya) operates bellows (bhastra) of a smelter. The two terms bhastrika and kapalabhati are sometimes used interchangeably but there is a distinction, where bhastrika is the advanced stage of kapalabhati, with bhastrika having a double focus on the breath rhythm while kapalabhati has only focus on the exhale.

Stated in terms of thrust, kapalabhati has a thrust on the exhale and a reflex inhale which follows rapidly, while bhastrika has thrust on both the inhale and exhale.

My opinion is that there is no sense in a beginner doing bhastrika because it requires double focus merely on the breath rhythm. It is best that a beginner does the kapalabhati until in some months or years that evolves naturally into bhastrika.

This aggressive breath-infusion process forces a fresh air charge into the blood stream which causes the heart to beat faster in its duty of distributing breath energy throughout the body. There is an accumulation of fresh air charge which mixes with the hormone energy. This mixture carries a polarity which attracts it to the kundalini lifeforce. When it strikes that force, the kundalini moves and due to the applied contractions, kundalini moves up through the central spinal passage and enters the head. Its entry causes light to burst out in the subtle body. The light is experienced on a psychic plane.

Application

Beginners should stick with kapalabhati focus-on-the-exhale only process when doing rapid breathing in various postures and continue that for months or years on a daily basis until it evolves naturally in bhastrika. If they do not comply with this, there will be little mystic progress because the inner focus required will be lacking.

It is too much for a beginner to focus on the exhale and inhale and also focus down in the psyche, and keep track of the accumulated fresh air charge and its compression and distribution. Advanced students can keep track of both the exhale and inhale because for them the exhale becomes a mere reflex which does not require special focus. Hence they can keep track of the exhale and these aspects as well:

- *accumulation of fresh air breath energy*
- *extraction of polluted air energy*
- *compression of accumulated fresh air energy*
- *mixing of accumulated fresh air energy with hormonal energy*
- *compressing the mixture inwards upon itself*
- *directing the compressed mixture to appropriate places*
- *forcing the compressed mixture to strike kundalini at muladhara base chakra or elsewhere*
- *keep the aroused kundalini restricted to the sushumna central spinal passage or elsewhere*
- *regulating in minute details kundalini's burst into the head, in the mind chamber or elsewhere*

This is a tall order for any student yogi; hence one should do kapalabhati and let it evolve naturally into bhastrika.

Verse 36

षट्–कर्म–निर्गत–सथौल्य–कफ–दोष–मलादिकः ।

प्राणायामं ततः कुर्यादनायासेन सिद्ध्यति ।। ३६ ।।

ṣaṭ–karma–nirgata–sthaulya–kapha–doṣa–malādikaḥ ।
prāṇāyāmaṁ tataḥ kuryādanāyāsena siddhyati ।। 36 ।।

ṣaṭ – six, karma – purificatory physio–psychic acts, nirgata – disappear, sthaulya – excessive, kapha – mucus, doṣa – disease, malādikaḥ – maladies and related health problems, prāṇāyāmaṁ – breath-infusion, tataḥ – thus, kuryād = kuryāt = should perform, anāyāsena – easily, siddhyati – become proficient

Through the six purificatory physio–psychic acts, excessive mucus, various maladies, related health problems and diseases disappear. Then one should perform breath-infusion and one will gain proficiency easily.

Analysis

This means that the process recommended in this text is compound. One has to be advanced to master this since it involves multiple disciplines. Proficiency is gained easily if one masters the various parts of the procedure and can operate them simultaneously.

Application

Some diseases do disappear through a proficient yoga practice as described but not all. A student should not be in illusion about this. Without health one cannot become proficient in the practice but all the same this does not mean that the material body will never manifest an incurable disease. Certainly a terminal illness will cause the end of the material form.

The focus of this practice is the subtle body. Since the physical one is related to the subtle, some physical actions do benefit the subtle.

Verse 37

प्राणायामैरेव सर्वे प्रशुष्यन्ति मला इति ।

आचार्याणां तु केषाञ्चिदन्यत्कर्म न संमतम् ।। ३७ ।।

prāṇāyāmaireva sarve praśuṣhyanti malā iti ।
ācāryāṇāṁ tu keṣāṁcidanyatkarma na saṁmatam ।। 37 ।।

prāṇāyāmair = prāṇāyāmaiḥ = by breath-infusion, eva – only, sarve – all, praśuṣhyanti – are removed, malā – impurities, iti – thus, ācāryāṇāṁ – authoritative yoga teachers, tu – but, keṣāṁcid = keṣāṁcit = according to some, anyat – other, karma – purificatory physio–psychic acts, na – without, saṁmatam – advocate

Some authoritative yoga teachers advocate that by breath-infusion only, without

performing the purificatory physio–psychic acts, all impurities are removed.

Analysis

Breath-infusion is so reliable of a way of attaining automatic introspection, that even in the time of Swatmarama, some authoritative teachers stated that one does not have to learn the purificatory physio-psychic acts described previously. It was their experience that those were unnecessary as distinct processes.

This is because the purificatory acts may occur spontaneously in the body of a yogi who has a thorough breath-infusion process.

Application

Many modern students either neglect the practice of pranayama or do it superficially. Some feel that it is too forceful and requires too much concentration. However it is a fact that pranayama was listed by Patanjali as the fourth (4th) stage in yoga practice. It is before the psychological practice of pratyahar sensual energy withdrawal. It is my experience that if pranayama is completed expertly, the student gains the advantage of mastery of the next stage as a consequence of pranayama practice.

Pranayama relieves a yogi of the having to use mantras, of having to visualize psychic movements and of having to imagine higher states of consciousness. It is very effective if one has the right method for it.

Verse 38

अथ गज–करणी

उदर–गत–पदार्थमुद्वमन्ति

पवनमपानमुदीर्य कण्ठ–नाले ।

क्रम–परिचय–वश्य–नाडि–छक्रा

गज–करणीति निगद्यते हठज्ञैः ।। ३८ ।।

atha gaja–karaṇī
udara–gata–padārthamudvamanti
pavanamapānamudīrya kaṇṭha–nāle |
krama–paricaya–vaśya–nāḍi–chakrā
gaja–karaṇīti nighadyate haṭhajñaiḥ || 38 ||

atha – regarding, gaja–karaṇī = purificatory action which is like that done by an elephant, udara – stomach, gata – contained, padārtham – items, udvamanti – vomiting, pavanam – air energy, apānam – waste gas, udīrya – by raising, kaṇṭha–nāle = to the throat, krama – sequential process, paricaya – familial, vaśya – controlled, nāḍi – nadi subtle tubes, chakrā – energy gyrating centers, gaja–karaṇīti = gaja–karaṇī (purificatory action which is like that done by an elephant) + iti (thus), nighadyate – is known as, haṭha – kundalini manipulation for psychic energy transformation, jñaiḥ – by those who know

Regarding the purificatory action which is like that done by an elephant, whatever items are contained in the stomach is vomited, and in a sequential process which the yogi is familiar with, the waste air energy is raised to the throat, the nadi subtle tubes and the energy gyrating centers are controlled. This purificatory action is identified as kundalini manipulation for psychic energy transformation by those who know.

Analysis

The vomiting impulse is done by the waste air energy in the muscles and tendons of the throat and abdomen. A yogi may use this impulse to remove food matter from the stomach and also to cause the waste air energy to move upwards so that it can be easily drawn out of the body through the lungs.

In this practice, a yogi may drink a large glass of water and then use two fingers to tickle the throat so as to initiate vomiting. This is done when the stomach is empty. At least that is how I was trained in it by Guruji Arthur Beverford. He said that Rishi Singh Gherwal introduced this for use early in the morning before eating anything when the stomach is empty.

One should get a large glass (tumbler) of warm water. One should mix about half-teaspoon of salt into it. Then one should drink it using large gulps. Immediately after one should be outdoors and should put two fingers into the mouth using them to tickle the throat. This will trigger the vomiting impulse. The salted water will be expelled. If necessary, one should repeat the tickle so as to cause all of the water to be expelled.

This process may cause the eyes to produce tears and the sinuses to burn slightly. The stomach will be refreshed because of the upward surge of its muscles. After this one should do asana and pranayama practice and then meditate.

One should not be surprised to taste bile from the stomach while doing this stomach up-surge procedure. If the mouth feels sour, one should rinse it to remove that taste.

Application

This practice is named after the elephant (gaja) because the elephant uses its trunk as a hand and pushes its trunk into its mouth frequently.

The apana energy in the subtle body is a negative gas, a pollutant. It is useful in the physical form for muscular activity. This energy is represented by carbon dioxide on the physical side of existence. It is used primarily by trees for their inhalation even though it is exhaled as a waste product from mammalian bodies. The kundalini lifeforce hoards a portion of this pollutant for use in various tasks like vomiting, excretion, urination, and muscular movements, including those for sexual intercourse.

Some yogis increase the consumption of this negative pollutant but for the purposes of kriya yoga one needs to decrease it in the physical and subtle bodies. The most efficient and rapid method of doing so is through kapalabhati/bhastrika pranayama breath-infusion.

The increase in pollutants gases in the body has benefits which are not appreciated by an advanced yogi. Examples of such benefits are:

- *increased sex drive*
- *increased athletic stamina*
- *increased competitive zeal*

- *increased desire for animal flesh*
- *increased desire for intoxicants*
- *increased focus down into material existence*
- *steadiness in materialistic thinking*

A kriya yogi should decrease the apana negative gases in the physical and subtle bodies to nil. This should be done by doing pranayama breath-infusion twice per day, working with the body to extract every bit of the negative gases which are lodged in it.

A student should learn how to do this, so that in each and every part of the subtle body, even in the toes and fingers, the negative heavy astral energy is extracted and replaced by fresh astral air.

Purification of the nadi subtle tubes and the energy gyrating centers is caused by extraction of the heavy astral energy which is lodged in them. This is done by a physio-psychic action. It is not achieved by visualization and mantra intonement.

A student should be confident that as the pollutants are extracted physically, it is achieved astrally because the astral body is interspaced into the physical and is directly affected by physical conditions.

Verse 39

ब्रह्मादयो।अपि त्रिदशाः पवनाभ्यास–तत्पराः ।

अभूवन्नन्तक–भयात्तस्मात्पवनमभ्यसेत् ।। ३९ ।।

brahmādayo।api tridaśāḥ pavanābhyāsa–tatparāḥ ।
abhūvannantaka–bhayāttasmātpavanamabhyaset ।। 39 ।।

brahmādayo = brahmā (creator–god Brahmā) + ādayo (ādayāḥ) (and other supernatural rulers), api – specifically, tridaśāḥ – thirty prominent deities, pavanābhyāsa – practice of breath-infusion, tatparāḥ – fully devoted, abhūvan – became, antaka – of death, in the end, bhayāt – due to fear, tasmāt – thus, pavanam – breath-infusion, abhyaset – should practice

Due to the fear of death, creator-god Brahma and other supernatural rulers, specifically the thirty prominent deities, are fully devoted to the practice of breath-infusion. Thus one should practice it.

Analysis

The creator-god Brahma and the other supernatural rulers who are listed in the Vedic pantheon of deities are said to be thirty-three (33) in number of the primary ones. Of these three are most prominent. They are Brahma, Vishnu and Shiva.

These deities are not in the physical dimensions of the creation. They live in supernatural places from which they are not affected by the physical reality which confront us.

These perform yoga austerities from time to time, as was described in the Puranas.

However in their supernatural domains they do not do the austerities, because there is no necessity for it there. The supernatural forms of these deities automatically use only fresh energy and do not generate or retain pollutants.

A student should make the subtle body compatible to a supernatural or divine environment. The first step is to extract from the subtle body whatever is inconsistent with the preferred supernatural environment. Patanjali explained how to do this:

jātyantara pariṇāmaḥ prakṛtyāpūrāt

jātyantara = jāti – category + antara – other, another; pariṇāmaḥ – transformation; prakṛiti – subtle material nature; āpūrāt – due to filling up or saturation.

The transformation from one category to another is by the saturation of the subtle material nature. (Yoga Sutras 4.2)

To create the saturation one has to ingest into the subtle body, energy from the higher dimension. In simple terms to go to heaven, one has to ingest heavenly energy to a saturation point.

Application

Antaka-bhayaat is the trauma which results from fearing the end of one's existence in a particular dimension. It is interesting that as great a yogi as Swatmarama, who codified the technique of kundalini manipulation, made a statement which belittles the thirty primary supernatural rulers of which the three primary ones are included directly and indirectly.

We may say that he did not name Vishnu and Shiva but for sure Brahma was identified.

Any temporary body of anyone has within it the fear of its doom. It does not matter who has the body, whether it is a supernatural being, a spiritual being or me or you. The body itself will have that fear because of the nature of the materials which the body comprises.

To keep a human body in tiptop shape, one should keep it with the least amount of pollutants. It does not matter if one is a divine being or an ordinary spirit. If one has a material form, then it is appropriate to keep it on the highest energy level.

There is no need to do this if one is on a high level, say on the level of Brahma's world, Brahmaloka or Satyaloka. But if one is on the earth place, even if one came from Brahmaloka, one should keep the subtle body in its highest astral condition because by that one would be assured of reentry to the higher place when the link to the physical body is permanently broken.

Verse 40

यावद्बद्धो मरुद्– देहे यावच्चित्तं निराकुलम् ।
यावद्दृष्टिर्भ्रुवोर्मध्ये तावत्काल–भयं कुतः ।। ४० ।।

yāvadbaddho marud–dehe yāvaccittaṁ nirākulam ।
yāvaddṛṣṭirbhruvormadhye tāvatkāla–bhayaṁ kutaḥ ।। 40 ।।

yāvad = yāvat = so long, baddho = baddhaḥ = yogically controlled within, marud = marut = lifeforce, dehe – in the body, yāvac = yāvat = so long, cittaṁ – mento–emotional energy, nirākulam – calm, yāvad = yāvat = so long, dṝṣṭir = dṝṣṭiḥ = perception interest, bhruvor = bhruvoḥ = eyebrows, madhye – between, tāvat – so long, kāla – time approaching with death, bhayaṁ – fear, kutaḥ – why

As long as the lifeforce is yogically controlled in the body, as long as the mento–emotional energy remains pacified therein, as long as the perception interest is pinned between the eyebrows, why would there be fear because of time approaching with death.

Analysis

Death means the dislocation of the kundalini lifeforce. Swatmarama's instructions in this text, has all to do with manipulation of that kundalini energy to gain the upper hand over transits of existence. If kundalini yoga is mastered, the fear of death is neutralized. As soon as the student digresses then this fear will reassert itself. A question arises as to the death dislocation of the lifeforce. How does that take place? Who or what controls that?

If a yogi can master astral projection; if he can get his identity interest transferred to the subtle body; then for him death is no incidence. Many who consciously astral-project cannot transfer the identity interest. As such their astral activities do not in any way cause the removal of physical insecurities. If the identity interest is consistently transferred to the subtle body, then when the physical body dies there will be no radical shift from physical to subtle.

The fear of death is the feeling which one has when the kundalini lifeforce is shifted permanently and fully to the subtle body. During the life of the physical form, the kundalini is anchored in that body at the muladhara base chakra. This provides material security. When at last the kundalini shifts from that place, it fuses into the subtle body in full. This shift is the fear of death. Its potential is always present in a living physical form.

When there is a serious accident, when there are terminal diseases, when there is a threat to one's life, then there may be an attempt by the kundalini to abandon the physical system. Such attempts are interpreted by the emotions as the fear of death. It is always present. A masterful yogi transcends it by shifting the attention-interest over into the subtle body.

Swatmarama listed these conditions as requirements for the removal of the fear of death:

- lifeforce is yogically controlled in the body
- mento–emotional energy remains pacified
- perception interest is pinned between the eyebrows

If the **lifeforce is yogically controlled,** it will not impulsively operate when the situation becomes deathlike. To do this, a yogi must train the lifeforce to move up the spine into the head on impulse of fear. It takes months, years or even lives to train the lifeforce to behave in this way.

When the **mento–emotional energy remains pacified** no matter what, when this is consistent due to breath-infusion which has removed the tendency to hoard polluted astral energy, then the psyche remains in an introverted state and does not become extroverted because of hungrily chasing after sensual pursuits.

When the **perception interest is pinned between the eyebrows** and when this is done due to having made contact with the chit akash sky of consciousness, then the yogi having breached the connection with the material level of consciousness and with the lower astral planes, has no contact with the dimensions in which the fear of death has full expression.

It is not just a matter of focusing between the eyebrows. The focus must be on the chit akash sky of consciousness which the yogi reaches because of the purity of the energy in the subtle body.

Application

Every living being in the material world is under threat of time which ultimately presents itself as death which is the terminal point for a particular life form.

Participation in the history of the world comes about by having a body which is given, maintained and then confiscated by time. Time gave us identity as a newborn, theatrical space as living actors and termination as dead bodies.

People will say that Michael Beloved was born. He endured for a time and wrote yoga books. Then at last he was de-existed. His influence diminished.

Such is the allowance of time. A yogi has no quarrel with time. Whatever allowance it affords, we may use constructively or destructively depending on the influences which prevail over us but which do so under the auspices of time.

Verse 41

विधिवत्प्राण–संयामैर्नाडी–छक्रे विशोधिते ।

सुषुम्णा–वदनं भित्त्वा सुखाद्विशति मारुतः ।। ४१ ।।

vidhivatprāṇa–saṁyāmairnāḍī–chakre viśodhite I
suṣumṇā–vadanaṁ bhittvā sukhādviśati mārutaḥ II 41 II

vidhivat – correctly, prāṇa – vital energy, saṁyāmair = saṁyāmaiḥ = by complete control, nāḍī – nadi subtle veins and arteries, chakre – through the energy gyrating centers, viśodhite – total clearance, suṣumṇā – subtle central spinal passage, vadanaṁ – entry, bhittvā – fissioning, sukhād = sukhāt = easy, viśati – penetrates, mārutaḥ – kundalini lifeforce

By the complete and correct control of the vital energy, with total clearance of the nadi subtle veins and arteries passing through the energy gyrating centers, the kundalini lifeforce easily penetrates through the entry of the subtle central spinal passage.

Analysis

Penetration of kundalini through all parts of the subtle body is not easily achieved. There are natural blockages in the system which are supported by its design and by the influence of physical and psychic material nature. To make the subtle body unresponsive to these influences requires expertise in this kundalini manipulation for subtle body transformation.

Material nature knows what it constructed and for what purpose but its intention is not the same as that of yoga. We need to appreciate material nature for what it is but that does not mean that we should give in totally to its objectives. It all depends on one's evolutionary status. Those who are entertained by nature's constructions have no need for drastic adjustments in the subtle body. In fact when a person is attracted to that, he or she is hardly aware of the subtle form and is mainly interested in the physical creature forms.

Those who are done with the advantages offered by material nature, should make the effort to change the subtle body, or settle for misery from here on out. Patanjali informed us about this:

prakāśa kriyā sthiti śīlaṁ bhūtendriyātmakaṁ
bhogāpavargārthaṁ dṛśyam

prakāśa – clear perception; kriyā – action; sthiti – stability; śīlaṁ – form, disposition; bhūta – mundane elements; indriya – sense organs; ātmakaṁ – self, nature; bhoga – experience; apavarga – liberation; arthaṁ – value or purpose; dṛśyam – what is perceived.

What is perceived is of the nature of the mundane elements and the sense organs and is formed in clear perception, action or stability. Its purpose is to give experience or to allow liberation. (Yoga Sutras 2.18)

kṛtārthaṁ prati naṣṭam api
anaṣṭaṁ tadanya sādhāraṇatvāt

kṛt – fulfilled done; ārthaṁ – purpose; prati – toward; naṣṭam – destroyed, non-existent, non-effective; api – although, but; anaṣṭaṁ – not finished, still existing, effective; tat – that; anya – others; sādhāraṇatvāt – common, normal, universal.

It is not effective for one to whom its purpose is fulfilled, but it has a common effect on the others. (Yoga Sutras 2.22)

Once a person reaches the evolutionary high point which is the human body, then there is a plateau. On that level there are little mounds and gullies but one should not be fooled by them into thinking that one can go higher. There is no higher evolutionary plane besides that of the human species.

After one experienced all there is for that advantage, one should seek out a divine form in a divine environment. To do this one must first upgrade the subtle body. Someone has to upgrade it, either the entity itself or a deity. If a deity graces one with an upgrade, then for sure, one is lucky and need not endeavor for it. But otherwise, one would be foolish to keep struggling with numerous human and animal bodies in an up and down course through a random history.

Application

Total clearance of the nadi subtle tubing and of the energy gyrating centers means that the yogi achieved a yoga siddha body. In such a body the attraction to the material existence and to the lower astral domains is absent. All vulgarity which has to do with creature existence in the material world is non-cognizable.

Just as if one throws a stone up, it will rise for a distance and then fall back to the earth, and just as if one releases a helium balloon it will rise and rise through the sky, so a person with a body which has cleared nadis will go to the higher astral domains. Kundalini yoga as described by Swatmarama is not the only method of achieving this. One can go to a higher place merely by the grace act of a deity. One may go there on the basis of having come from such a place and having exhausted the lowering energy which caused one to appear here.

However if one cannot attract the grace of a deity and if one was not from the higher place to begin with, then one may use the method of kundalini yoga as described.

There is an encouragement about this in the Bhagavad Gita:

uddharedātmanātmānaṁ
nātmānamavasādayet
ātmaiva hyātmano bandhur
ātmaiva ripurātmanaḥ (6.5)

uddhared = uddharet — should elevate; ātmanā — by the self; 'tmānaṁ = ātmānam — the self; nātmānam = na — not + ātmānam — the self; avasādayet — should degrade; ātmaiva = ātmā — self + eva — only; hyātmano = hyātmanaḥ = hy (hi) — indeed + ātmanaḥ — of the self; bandhur = bandhuh — friend; ātmaiva = ātmā — self + eva — as well; ripur = ripuḥ — enemy; ātmanaḥ — of the self

One should elevate his being by himself. One should not degrade the self. Indeed, the person should be the friend of himself. Or he could be the enemy as well. (Bhagavad Gita 6.5)

This advice was given by Krishna, the Supreme Being. If even he says this, then there is no one who can tell us to do otherwise. No one should tell us that we should sit and wait for divine release from this. We should question ourselves as to what we could do in the meantime while we wait for salvation. What is our occupation all the while? If the practice of kundalini yoga could cause release, why are we not applying ourselves to it?

Verse 42

अथ मनोन्मनी

मारुते मध्य– सञ्चारेमनः–सथैर्यं प्रजायते ।

यो मनः–सुस्थिरी–भावः सैवावस्था मनोन्मनी ।। ४२ ।।

atha manonmanī
mārute madhya– sañcāremanaḥ–sthairyaṁ prajāyate |
yo manaḥ–susthirī–bhāvaḥ saivāvasthā manonmanī || 42 ||

atha – regarding, manonmanī – blank thoughtless idealess mental condition, mārute – on the lifeforce, madhya – in the middle, sañcāre – moves, manaḥ – mind, sthairyaṁ – stable, prajāyate – is produced, yo – yaḥ = which, manaḥ – mind, susthirī – complete stability, bhāvaḥ – consciousness, saivāvasthā = sā eva (that condition) + avasthā (state), manonmanī – blank thoughtless idealess mental condition

Regarding the blank thoughtless idealess mental state, when the lifeforce moves in the middle, that produces stability of mind. When the mind has complete stability of consciousness, that condition is the blank thoughtless idealess mental state.

Analysis

The manonmani or unmani blank thoughtless idealess mental state is legendary in the annals of yoga practice. It is a coveted state of consciousness which many yogis strive for year after year but do not attain except momentarily. The secret to understanding this state is to know that it is a neutral position from which to shift from here into the chit akash sky of consciousness, the divine environment.

One cannot move from here into the divine world without passing through the blank thoughtless idealess mental state. There might be a question as to how long one should have to stay there but one will have to be there even if momentarily in the transit. For most ascetics there will be a prolonged engagement with this level of consciousness before transit to the divine world becomes accessible. Patanjali Mahayogin, insisted on the shutdown of mento-emotional energy, which if achieved brings one to this blank thoughtless idealess mental state:

yogaḥcittavṛtti nirodhaḥ

yogaḥ – the skill of yoga; cittavṛtti = citta – mento-emotional energy + vṛtti – vibrational mode; nirodhaḥ – cessation, restraint, non-operation.

The skill of yoga is demonstrated by the conscious non-operation of the vibrational modes of the mento-emotional energy. (Yoga Sutras 1.2)

He gaves a description of this experience:

vyutthāna nirodha saṁskārayoḥ
abhibhava prādurbhāvau nirodhakṣaṇa
cittānvayaḥ nirodhapariṇāmaḥ

vyutthāna – expression; nirodha – suppression; saṁskārayoḥ – of the mento-emotional impressions; abhibhava – disappearance; prādurbhāvau – and manifestation ; nirodha – restraint, cessation; kṣaṇa – momentarily; citta – mento-emotional energy; ānvayaḥ – connection; nirodha – restraint; pariṇāmaḥ – transforming effects.

When the connection with the mento-emotional energy momentarily ceases during the manifestation and disappearance phases when there is expression or suppression of the impressions, that is the restraint of the transforming mento-emotional energy. (Yoga Sutras 3.9)

Application

The value of the blank thoughtless idealess mental state is neither its void condition nor its misconception about oneness; its value is that it is the incubation period in which the yogi may develop supernatural and spiritual senses. It takes time for most ascetics to switch over to divine perception and it is done from that state.

Certainly some yogis get the supernatural perception without having to wait for it in meditation but most will not get it except by remaining in meditation with a blank thoughtless mind.

Some hasty meditators abandon this meditation on the blank thoughtless state and take up other systems of meditation or religion which promise access to the divine environment by instant means.

Verse 43

तत–सिद्धये विधानज्ञाश्चित्रान्कुर्वन्ति कुम्भकान ।

विचित्र कुम्भकाभ्यासाद्विचित्रां सिद्धिमाप्नुयात् ।। ४३ ।।

tat–siddhaye vidhānajñāścitrānkurvanti kumbhakān |
vicitra kumbhakābhyāsādvicitrāṁ siddhimāpnuyāt || 43 ||

tat – that,siddhaye – in gaining proficiency, vidhāna – of the disciplines, jñāś = jñāḥ = knowers, citrān – various, kurvanti – perform, kumbhakān – breath retention with physio–psychic compression, vicitra – various, kumbhakābhyāsād = kumblaka (breath retention with physio–psychic compression) + abhyāsāt (by this practice), vicitrāṁ – various, siddhim – proficiencies, āpnuyāt – attain

For gaining that proficiency in the disciplines, those who are conversant perform various breath retentions with physio–psychic compressions. Due to this practice, various types of proficiencies are attained.

Analysis

There are many breath-infusions described in the Vedic literature. There are some which were not discovered. Regardless, any system is as good as the results which it yields. In addition one should learn the process from someone who used it and got success in the area of asceticism one strives for.

Learning of any mystic practice requires a teacher and self-discovery. The teacher does not have to be physically present. If the student has psychic perception or has a nature which is receptive to inspiration, instructions may be effective even if there is no physical presence.

Because the pollutions of low astral energy are compressed into the subtle body, it takes a certain amount of force and counter-compression to clear the system. This is done by pranayama and by the various muscular and mento-emotional locks.

Application

The practice of yoga is not stereotyped. It varies from student to student. Each ascetic should strive on his or her own under guidance of a great yogin. Much self-discovery must be made. One needs information from books like the Bhagavad Gita and the Yoga Sutras, but one must also practice to verify and directly perceive the realities behind the information.

Due to variations in evolution, differences in body type and unique idiosyncrasies, each student has to take a vastly or slightly different path. A pioneering spirit is required.

Verse 44

अथ कुम्भक–भेदाः

सूर्य–भेदनमुज्जायी सीत्कारी शीतली तथा ।

भस्त्रिका भ्रामरी मूर्च्छा विनीत्यष्ट –कुम्भकाः ।। ४४ ।।

atha kumbhaka–bhedāḥ
sūrya–bhedanamujjāyī sītkārī śītalī tathā |
bhastrikā bhrāmarī mūrcchā plāvinītyaṣṭa–kumbhakāḥ || 44 ||

atha – regarding, kumbhaka – breath suspension with physio–psychic compression, bhedāḥ – applications, sūrya–bhedanam = sūrya–bhedana right nostril infusion, ujjāyī – ujjāyī epiglottis contact infusion, sītkārī – sītkārī hissing breath-infusion, śītalī – śītalī tongue contact infusion, tathā – as well, bhastrikā – bhastrika forceful inhale-exhale infusion, bhrāmarī – bhrāmarī soft humming like a blackbee infusion,mūrcchā – mūrcchā-fainting slow-inhale with long retention infusion, plāvinīty = plāvinī gulp-swallow infusion + iti (thus), aṣṭa – eight, kumbhakāḥ – breath retention with physio–psychic compression

Regarding breath suspension with physio–psychic compression, the applications are eight in number, namely, surya–bheda right nostril infusion, ujjayi epiglottis contact infusion, sitkari hissing breath-infusion, shitali tongue contact infusion, bhastrika forceful inhale-exhale infusion, bhramari soft humming like a blackbee infusion, murccha-fainting slow-inhale with long retention infusion and plavini gulp-swallow infusion.

Analysis

These are the eight standard breath-infusion methods used by yogis in the time of Swatmarama. There are other types which may be used according to the purpose intended. Each method maxes out in particular species of life.

For instance, we see that in cheetahs, the fastest of the large mammals, when they cease a chase, they sit down and do the bhastrika forceful inhale-exhale infusion to recharge their bodies with fresh air, while simultaneously extracting polluted gases from the cell tissues. However they receive no deep insight or sensual energy withdrawal as a result. Thus even if one does any of these practices, one may not get the result intended. Motivation is involved in every activity either to undermine or support it.

During these applications of breath-infusion, there must be breath suspension with physio–psychic compression. This requires special attention, which a human being is capable of.

Application

Physio–psychic compression is for concentrating and directing the infused energy and the mix of that energy with hormone and polluted energy. Breathing on and on in a particular way will not give the result because the attitude of the lungs and the resistance of the cells will buffer the process.

One has to make the lungs and the cells act on the application. The lungs have an attitude to accept only a certain percentage of the fresh air which is made available to

them. The blood cells have their own idea of how much fresh air they should absorb. To change these attitudes, the yogi must compress the air so as to force the lungs and the blood cells to accept a higher or lower percentage of fresh air.

Mostly in the pranayama practices, the yogi wants to increase the percentage of fresh air in the blood stream but in the murccha-fainting slow-inhale with long retention, the intention is to decrease the fresh air percentage and increase the pollutants.

Why would a yogi do this?

The purpose is to find out more about the states of stupor and about life in the subterranean astral world and in lower species of life even that of the vegetation. Some criminal yogis use this method to gain supernatural control over certain astral domains.

Yogis who are curious about their condition in previous lives in lower species, even as vegetation, may practice the stupor pranayama breath-infusion and learn about what they did in past lives in lower species. Such adventures are both embarrassing and amusing. A highly educated and respectable man may on occasion become inebriated from alcohol. When people explain his drunken behavior at a later date, he may not believe it. However if he is shown a film of his activities, he may be amused by it.

Once a living entity becomes a human being, it may be difficult to imagine this same self as a lower creature or even as vegetation which thrives using the pollutants which come out of the human breath discharge and evacuation process. Thus a yogi who is doubtful may use a pranayama method and go back in history to see what sort of creature he or she was in lower species.

Regardless of the application process used for breath-infusion, certain problems remain. These are:

- *receptivity of the lungs to fresh air inhaled*
- *appetite of blood cells for the fresh air*
- *distribution of infused blood cells*
- *willingness of the blood cells to release polluted gases*
- *ability of the lungs to expel polluted gases which are conveyed by the blood cells*
- *compression and transport of blood cells which are charged with fresh air*
- *forcing cells with polluted gas to exchange that content for fresh air or to transit to the lung for the exchange*
- *forcing hormones in the blood stream and in the tissues to mix with fresh air.*
- *compressing the mix of fresh air and hormones*

The ***receptivity of the lungs to fresh air inhaled*** *is reliant on the genetic attitude of the lung cells and on their healthy or unhealthy condition. The genetic attitude can be adjusted to a certain extent by using the habit process where the yogi does extra breathing for a certain amount of time on a daily basis. The system will regress to what it usually does but the yogi can repeatedly do specific breath-infusions to adjust resistant genetic tendencies.*

The health of the lungs may be facilitated by improved diet and by being in a location where lung bacteria do not thrive or are absent.

The ***appetite of blood cells for the fresh air*** *can be adjusted by change in diet, eating foods which cause the blood cells to more easily absorb fresh air. By a daily breath-infusion practice where the compression locks are applied efficiently, a yogi can increase the appetite of the blood cells for fresh air. The greater the percentage of fresh air in the blood stream, the less there will be of pollutants because these are displaced from the body when the quantity of fresh air is increased.*

When the percentage of polluted gases is lowered, it is likely that the mind will be clearer and more settled, less jittery and insecure. This makes for a more productive meditation.

The ***distribution of infused blood cells is*** *neither understood nor completed by beginners. This is because this is an advanced procedure which requires higher mystic insight and supernatural grip on the psyche. However if one practices daily, in time one will derive the perception of how this is achieved.*

If a yogi does breath-infusion for say a session of twelve (12) breaths, there will be an accumulation of fresh air in the blood cells near the alveoli. Thus what should be done next? Should the yogi direct the system in how to distribute this energy or should the system do so involuntarily.

In kundalini yoga, the yogi should direct the distribution. To do so, he should perceive the accumulated energy, apply locks and mentally grip the energy and move it as desired.

After doing a series of breath-infusions, the yogi should stop, apply locks, observe the accumulation energy, observe its location and movement and direct its passage using mental force and the recommended locks (bandhas).

The ***willingness of the blood cells to release polluted gases*** *is based on genetics and diet. Genetics means that the yogi got a body from a family line which produced human forms with a greater or lesser need for polluted gases.*

If the yogi has a body which needs a greater percentage of polluted gases, he will have to work aggressively with breath-infusion to reverse that tendency.

Those who have a body which is more inclined to fresh air, will do less strenuous austerities to achieve the infusion of fresh energy into the psyche.

Asana postures are very useful in the contracting, flexing and relaxing of tissue and bone even. This is required to encourage the cells to relinquish their pollution content. However if the yogi does not do breath-infusion, the released pollutants will re-inhabit the tissues as soon as there is relaxation during postures.

In the asanas, the tissues do release their pollutions but as soon as the body relaxes, the tissues reabsorb the pollutants. If however the yogi does pranayama breath-infusion, the released toxins are hauled out by the blood cells which float in the veins and arteries. These are transported to the lungs where the pollutants are expelled from the body.

Any effective pranayama process will affect the pulsations of the heart, whereby these increase and decrease according to the breathing rate and the compression locks applied.

The ***ability of the lungs to expel polluted gases which are conveyed by the blood cells*** *is based on the health of the lungs, the release-attitude of the blood cells and the breath rhythm used by the yogi. If the lungs have a disease, their release procedure will be inefficient. This will result in less expulsion of pollutants and more retention of the same, which is counterproductive for most yogis.*

The release attitude of the blood cells is based on diet and inherited genetics. A yogi can adjust this by changing diet and having a daily habit of aggressive breath-infusion practice. The breath rhythm used by the yogi varies according to the particular pranayama. Each yogi should be focused in the psyche during practice, so as to gage how well the lungs absorb fresh air and expel pollutants. These observations will eventually cause the yogi to gain more and more mystic control.

The ***compression and transport of blood cells which are charged with fresh air*** *is done efficiently if the lungs are healthy and the cells are cooperative. Initially when a student begins this practice, the cells are uncooperative because they were in the habit of taking fresh air at leisure. Some students cease the practice because of being overwhelmed by the collective depressed attitude of the cells. Some students mention the idea that nothing should be forced; that everything should be achieved naturally.*

After practicing for some time, a student gains an insight into how the lungs absorb fresh air, how they release pollutant gases and how the absorbed fresh air is accumulated near the lungs and then distributed through the system by the pumping action of the heart and the mento-emotional pressure applied in the subtle body.

If there is no efficient compression and transport of fresh air, the pranayama method will have little effect. This will be realized when a student sits to meditate immediately after the breath-infusion session, and finds that the mind is still occupied with trashy ideas and images; that it has not shifted to a higher plane.

The ***forcing of cells with polluted gas to exchange that content for fresh air or to transit to the lungs for the exchange*** *is regulated by the pumping action of the heart, the condition of the veins and arteries and the relationship between the alveoli of the lungs and the blood cells which transit through the body.*

The pumping action of the heart varies according to the breath rhythm which would hinge on the breath-infusion being practiced. If the veins and arteries are clogged with fats and bulges, the transit will be sluggish. This will obstruct distribution of fresh energy transit through the body.

The heart may be in a poor condition which may be due to genetics or ill-health. A yogi may or may not be able to upgrade that organ.

Cells in tissue may be reluctant to exchange their pollution content for fresh air which is transported through the blood stream in mobile cells. These bad attitudes may change if the yogi can psychologically influence the resistant tissues.

Some floating cells may resist transit or proceed voluntarily with transit through the veins and arteries but resist release of pollutants when passing through the alveoli.

The ***forcing of hormones to mix with fresh air*** *is achieved by infusing fresh air into the lungs, compacting that accumulated air, moving it through the body, compressing it using locks (bandhas) causing it to mix with hormone energy, forcing that mixture to strike the kundalini lifeforce at the base chakra, directing the aroused kundalini* *upwards through the sushumna spinal passage into the brain.*

*The **compression of the mix of fresh air and hormones** relates to the efficiency of internal focus. Beginners take some time to get to full internal focus. This is because they are habitually attracted to what is external to the physical body and what is created as thoughts and images by the mind. However, in time students develop a liking for introspection. They harbor an interest in the abstract events which take place on the psychic level. This gives power over the energy where the self can direct the charge of compressed subtle force to arouse spinal or cellular kundalini.*

Verse 45

पूरकान्ते तु कर्तव्यो बन्धो जालन्धराभिधः ।

कुम्भकान्ते रेचकादौ कर्तव्यस्तूड्डियानकः ।। ४५ ।।

pūrakānte tu kartavyo bandho jālandharābhidhaḥ I
kumbhakānte recakādau kartavyastūḍḍiyānakaḥ II 45 II

pūrakānte = pūraka (inhalation) + ante (at the end), tu – but, kartavyo = kartavyaḥ = is done, bandho = bandhaḥ = physio–psychic compression, jālandharābhidhaḥ = jālandhara (chin to throat compression) + abhidhaḥ is known as, kumbhakānte = kumbhaka (breath retention after inhalation and compression) + ante (in the end), recakādau = recaka (exhalation) + ādau (beginning), kartavyas – is done, tūḍḍiyānakaḥ = tu (then) + uḍḍiyānakaḥ = abdomen uplift compression

At the end of inhalation, chin-to-throat physio–psychic compression should be performed. Then at the end of breath retention after inhalation and compression and at the beginning of exhalation, uddiyana abdomen uplift compression should be applied.

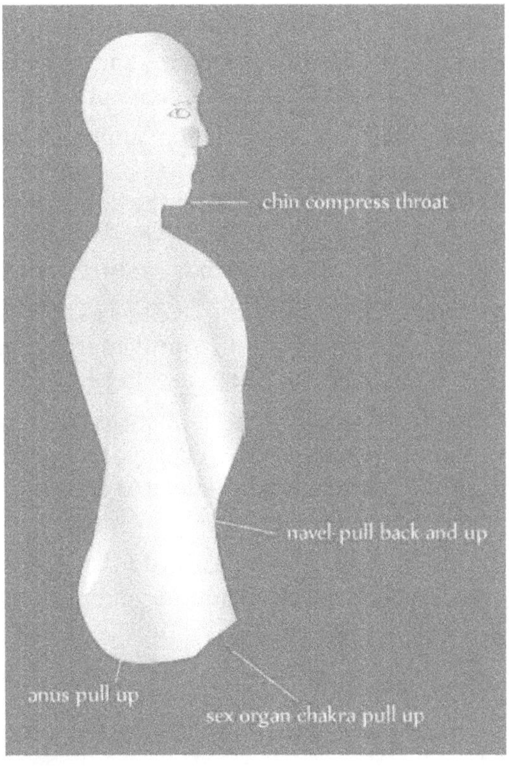

Analysis

This is for kundalini arousal on the basis of pushing down infused breath energy to force it to mix with polluted energy at the navel and then mix with hormone energy in the lower trunk, and then thrust it into the kundalini at the muladhara base chakra.

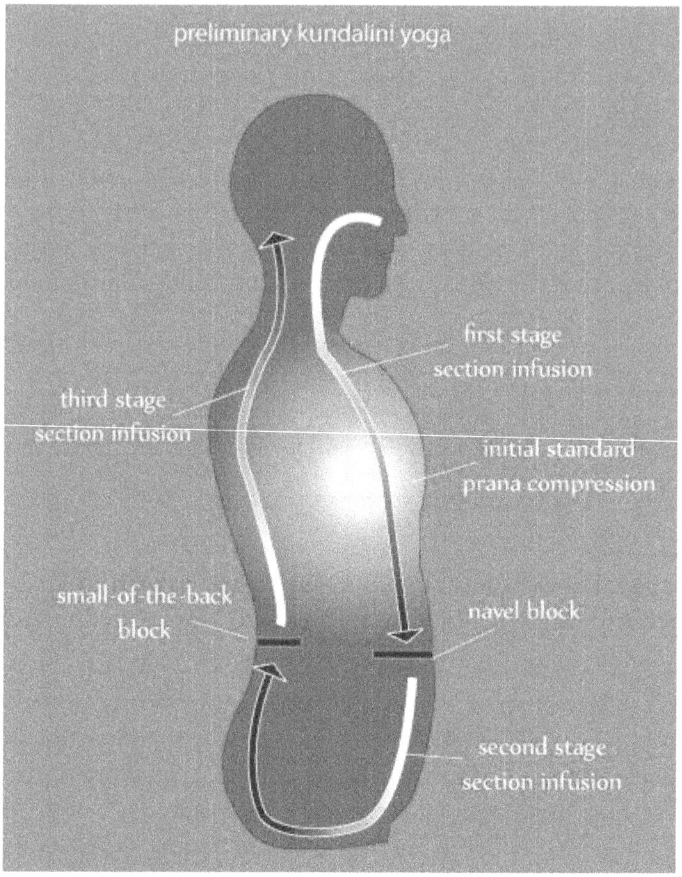

There are other kundalini arousal practices but this one is preliminary. This is the classic process. In kapalabhati/bhastrika breath-infusion a different procedure is used but with the same objective in the previous paragraph.

When doing anuloma-viloma alternate breathing, one should immediately after an inhale apply the chin-to-throat physio–psychic compression. If one fails to do this it is likely that the energy will not be compressed downwards but will come up and become diffused in the neck. This will discourage the accumulation of a charge and disempower the yogi for raising the kundalini lifeforce through the sushumna central spinal column.

As soon as the chin-to-throat physio–psychic compression is applied after an inhale, the energy of the inhale is discouraged from going upwards and diffusing in its own way. It feels trapped and develops an interest in descending.

A yogi can perceive these abstract feelings of the energy and take advantage of the situation, by pushing the energy down mentally as soon as it is develops the slightest desire to go downward. Failure to do this, results in more inefficiency so that even if the yogi practices for days, weeks or years, he or she will not get the result intended.

In this procedure one has to do this sequence with full internal focus, not perceiving outside colors, forms or sounds and not being enthralled by thoughts and images.

The sequence is:

- inhalation
- chin-to-throat physio–psychic compression

- breath retention
- exhalation with simultaneous uḍḍiyāna abdomen-uplift compression applied

Application

When doing kapalabhati/bhastrika breath-infusion, the sequence is different. In most postures during this rapid breathing, a series of very aggressive and rapid inhales and exhales are done.

How many?

That depends on the absorption rate of the student. As soon as the student feels that the lungs are no longer absorbing the breathing stops and the student applies concentration to locate and distribute the infused energy.

Here is the sequence for kapalabhati/bhastrika breath-infusion:

- many rapid inhales and exhales
- suspension of breathing after an inhale but before an exhale (and rarely is this done on an exhale before an inhale, but it is done)
- chin-to-throat physio–psychic compression
- anal sphincter muscle up-pull
- perineum up-pull
- lower abdomen up-pull
- exhalation with simultaneous uḍḍiyāna abdomen-uplift compression applied, with other locks relaxed or applied, depending on the posture and the state of the energy in reference to kundalini

Verse 46

अधस्तात्कुञ्चनेनाशु कण्ठ–सङ्कोचने कृते ।

मध्ये पश्चिम–तानेन सयात्प्राणो बरह्म–नाडिगः ।। ४६ ।।

adhastātkuñcanenāśu kaṇṭha–saṅkocane kṝte ।
madhye paścima–tānena syātprāṇo brahma–nāḍigaḥ ।। 46 ।।

adhastāt – underneath, kuñcanenāśu = kuñcanena (by contraction/compression with psychic focus) + āśu (promptly), kaṇṭha – throat, saṅkocane – in synchronization, kṝte – is done, madhye – in the center, paścima – pulling up, tānena = ta (it) + anena (by this), syāt – was, prāṇo = prāṇaḥ = vital energy, brahma–nāḍi = central spinal subtle spirit-access passage through to brahmarandra, gaḥ – flow

By promptly contracting and compressing from underneath, while applying psychic focus to the throat and doing so with synchronization with pulling up the center of the body, the vital energy flows through the central spinal subtle spirit-access passage and pierces through to brahmarandra.

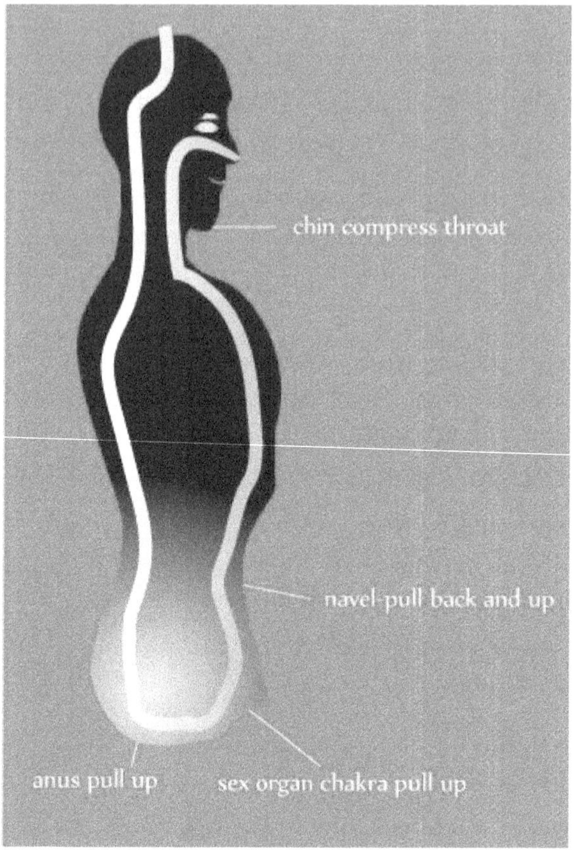

Analysis

There is simultaneous downward and upward compression. There is also a side inwards pressure which is applied in the advanced stage. This is to force the compressed energy to strike kundalini at the base chakra.

In addition to the throat lock, a psychic focus must be applied. Standing guard at the throat but in the spine itself is essential because the kundalini may become aroused suddenly with the result that the physical body will fall to the ground if the yogi was inattentive or did not know what to do with the event.

The center of the body must be pulled up. This causes the reproductive energy to be compressed. That energy becomes concentrated and bunches in the lower abdomen.

It is squeezed there and is then directed to the kundalini. If sufficient energy strikes the kundalini will move but if the chin lock and the other locks are applied, the yogi will have control in the strike.

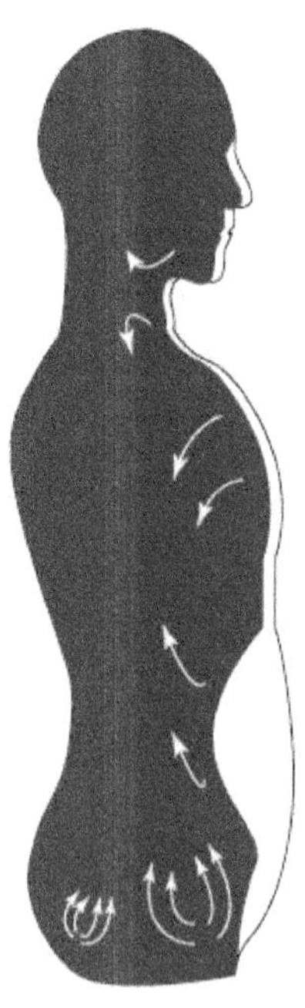

lock pressure (bandhas)

Application

The sushumna nadi central spinal passage is a spirit access elevator which allows the core-self to move up and down through the energy gyrating centers, the chakras. If this passage is blocked, or if it is clouded by heavy astral energy, the spirit cannot transit as desired.

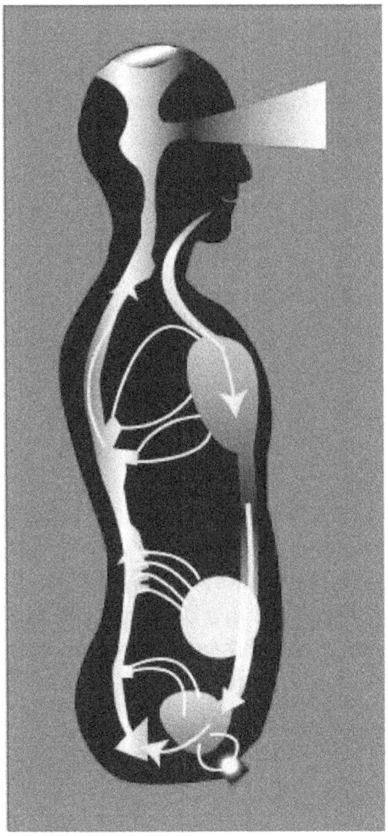

It is required that the student blast this passage out using the aroused kundalini which was stuck into activation by breath-infused energy which was mixed with hormonal force.

The top of the elevator is the brahmarandra exit at the top of the subtle head. The lowest access is the muladhara base chakra. Between in an ascending transit, there is the sex chakra, the navel chakra, the heart-lung complex chakra, the throat chakra and the third eye chakra. Besides these there are minor chakras which are attended to by a yogi from time to time. Each of the vital organs has its own chakra. The sex organs have a chakra which is a multiplex system.

The passage used by the kundalini at the time of death of the physical form is indicative of where the person-self will go in the astral world hereafter. If for instance the kundalini is trapped at the bottom chakra and cannot passage upwards in the sushumna nadi central passage, it will leave through the muladhara chakra exit, which is a microscopic hole at the base of the subtle spine.

Leaving from such a place would cause the person-self to adopt the lowest astral profile which results in existence in the subterranean astral domains.

Rebirth in a physical dimension from such a place will be in an animal body or even in a species lower than that, or in a family of humans who have a lifestyle which is as basic as that of the animals.

A thorough sex pleasure occupation could cause a brilliant light at the sex chakra on the spinal column and displayed or invisible energy arousal at the sex organ chakra at the time of death, with the result that the person-self leaves the body through the sex orifice in the subtle body.

This would cause the adoption of an astral profile of a lust-being with a human or animal form which is ever-occupied hereafter with sexual pleasure. From there one might return into physical existence as a creature that is over-occupied with sexual indulgence due to genetic disposition of the new body one adopted from animal parents. Or one may return into a family of people who are obsessed with sexual indulgence as the means of livelihood.

Departure from the body through the navel orifice would cause a person-self to be profiled for endless eating with focus on nothing else. This would result in being in an astral domain where the bodies are eating and excreting endlessly, or eating and not excreting but getting bigger and bigger with every bite. From there one would come back into physical existence as tiny worm which bores into creature bodies or vegetables, or even as a human being who is obsessed with eating either as an obese form or as a slim form which excretes frequently.

Departure from the lung-heart complex chakra would cause the person-self to find itself in an astral dimension of kind people who are inter-related emotionally and who are healthy because of nourishing astral energy in that dimensional environment. These would be people who are not sexually focused but who have sex relation potential as a non-primary means of association.

A person-self taking a physical birth from such a location would become a child in a family of well-to-do parents where the child would be sheltered emotionally and would have sufficiency.

Departure from the throat chakra would cause a person to be with people who are eloquent and who even in the astral existence cultivate educational aspects with interest in the arts and science. Taking an embryo after being in such a dimension the person-self would be in an environment of educated people and would have the advantages of aristocracy.

Departure from the third eye chakra would put a person-self among the siddha perfected yogis, or among people with tremendous psychic sensitivity. Such persons usually see the celestial angels and their lords who oversee the destiny of lower beings. These person-selves who leave the body finally through the third eye chakra may not take another material body because of having subtle forms which assume permanent compatibility with the heavenly world in the higher astral regions.

Departure from the brahmarandra chakra would put a person-self with the highest of the siddha perfected yogis, and with the supervisory angelic lords or even with the Supreme Lord, or in the energy of the divine world which is beyond the highest astral regions.

It is hardly likely that such a person-self would again take another physical body, even though it might happen at the request of a deity.

Verse 47

आपानमूर्ध्वमुत्थाप्य प्राणं कण्ठादधो नयेत् ।

योगी जरा–विमुक्तः संषोडशाब्द–वया भवेत् ।। ४७ ।।

āpānamūrdhvamutthāpya prāṇaṁ kaṇṭhādadho nayet I
yogī jarā–vimuktaḥ saṁṣoḍaśābda–vayā bhavet I I 47 I I

apanam – polluted waste gases, ūrdhvamutthāpya – pulling up, prāṇaṁ – fresh air intake, kaṇṭhādadho = kaṇṭhāt (from the throat) + adhaḥ (downwards), nayet – should channel, yogī – yogi, jarā – from old age, vimuktaḥ – liberated from, saṁṣoḍaśābda – sixteen years old, vayā = youthfulness, bhavet – should feel

By pulling up the polluted waste gases and by channeling fresh air intake down through the throat, the yogis, liberated from the effects of old age, feel as if the body was sixteen years of age.

Analysis

A question arises as to which body feels as if it is sixteen years of age.

Is it the material body?

Is it the subtle one?

Is it both bodies simultaneously?

The removal of polluted waste gases and the infusion of fresh air into any material body aids in the upkeep of the form. In the subtle body a similar effect is experienced and since the subtle form will outlive the physical one, it makes sense to focus on that long-term body and not be obsessed about the physical one which must perish regardless of the healthy or unhealthy habits it is subjected to.

All material forms, those with bad diet, and those with good diet, will die. All subtle bodies, those with bad psychological energy and those with degraded subtle content, will persist. Hence it makes sense to focus on the upkeep of the subtle, even at the expense of the physical. It so happens that the upkeep of the subtle body usually benefits the physical one anyway.

When a yogi does breath-infusion proficiently, the subtle body feels as if it were a sixteen year old healthy youthful form even if the physical one appears to be old and diseased.

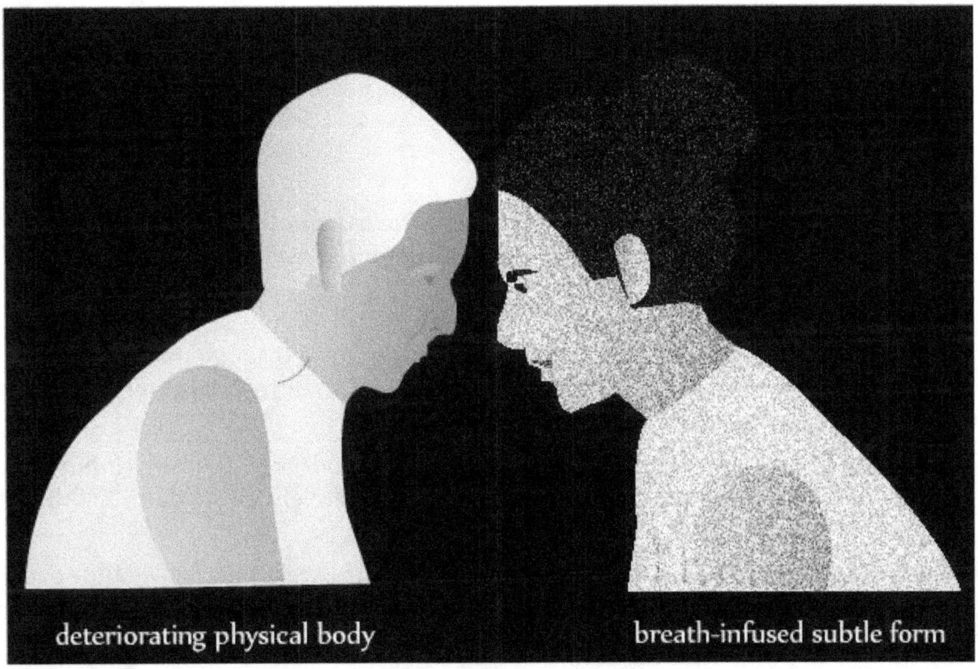

Application

For the purpose of kundalini yoga, this interest in maintaining youthfulness of a body has to do with the subtle form. The yogi does breath-infusion to protect the subtle body from becoming degraded by its affiliation with the physical one which was developed for it in the mother's uterus.

The subtle body is the basis for the development of millions of physical forms over the course of a particular universe, and yet, even though it is so primary and important, it can deteriorate when a physical body deteriorates. It can regenerate when a physical body is born.

A yogi, as a psychic engineer, acts to stop the subtle body from patterning itself after the physical system. There is a limit to what a yogi can do in this regard but the limit does not mean that he or she should do nothing.

Verse 48

अथ सूर्य–भेदनम

आसने सुखदे योगी बद्ध्वा चैवासनं ततः ।

दक्ष–नाड्या समाकृष्य बहिःस्थं पवनं शनैः ।। ४८ ।।

atha sūrya–bhedanam
āsane sukhade yogī baddhvā caivāsanaṁ tataḥ I
dakṣa–nāḍyā samākṝṣya bahiḥsthaṁ pavanaṁ śanaiḥ II 48 II

atha – now to explain, sūrya –right nostril, bhedanam – infusion, āsane – in the posture, sukhade – in comfort, yogī – yogi, baddhvā – firmly situated, caivāsanaṁ = caiva (and so) + āsanaṁ – posture, tataḥ – then, dakṣa – right side, nāḍyā – nadi subtle passage, samākṝṣya – drawn together, compressed, focalized, bahiḥsthaṁ – outside, pavanaṁ – fresh air, śanaiḥ – gradually

Now to explain the right nostril infusion:

In a comfortable posture, the yogi being firmly situated should gradually draw in and focalize fresh air from outside the body into it through the right nadi subtle passage.

Analysis

The right side is more powerful for two reasons: It is infused through the largest lung. It is sustained by the sun planet. The left lung is smaller than the right one. The sun is more powerful than the moon.

When the right nostril remains open, it is understood that the sun influence is predominant. So long as the air above our heads is relatively clear, there will be sun dominance on planet earth.

If there is a saturation of the sun dominant right side, the excess energy will flow over to the moon dominant left portion. When both sides are saturated, the psyche will experience quiescence. This is ideal for meditation.

Application

A yogi would deliberately inhale but would be focused on the subtle effects. The air would be pulled down to the muladhara chakra. Its minor or major effect on kundalini would be observed. Then the yogi could continue the practice making minute or drastic adjustments as advised by the teacher.

Verse 49

आकेशादानखाग्राच्च निरोधावधि कुम्भयेत् ।

ततः शनैः सव्य–नाड्या रेचयेत्पवनं शनैः ।। ४९ ।।

ākeśādānakhāgrācca nirodhāvadhi kumbhayet I
tataḥ śanaiḥ savya–nāḍyā recayetpavanaṁ śanaiḥ I I 49 I I

ākeśād = ā (from) + keśāt (hair), ānakhāgrāc = ā (to) + nakha (nail) + āgrāt (tip), ca – and, nirodhāvadhi = nirodha (checking thoroughly) + avadhi (until), kumbhayet – should retain breath with physio–psychic compression, tataḥ – then, śanaiḥ – gradually, savya – through the left, nāḍyā – nadi subtle passage, recayet – should exhale, pavanaṁ – air, śanaiḥ – gradually

Feeling the energy from the hair to the tips of the nails, checking it thoroughly, one should retain breath with physio–psychic compression, and then gradually one should exhale through the left nadi subtle passage.

Analysis

This practice requires great concentration. The strain of it is patience and mental quietude. A person with a jumpy mind, who is hasty, cannot do this practice properly. Right now, unless we are isolated from others and can disconnect ourselves from social concerns our social conditions do not permit us to do these practices.

The energy in every part of the body must be sensed and checked, even from the tips of the nails and from the very end of the hairs. This means that no feelings should be out of reach or should be externally focused. When the breath is restrained after the inhale through the right nostril, the yogi should apply the physio-psychic compressions so as to compress the combination of the inhale air, the pollutant air which adheres to it and the hormone energy which is attracted to it.

The exhale through the left nostril is done gradually and with great care without anxiety and without a rush to exhale. This means that one should not retain the air beyond one's capacity because that will make it necessary to exhale quickly which would ruin the practice.

In the slow exhale the yogi must check closely to see how the system releases pollutants and how these are compacted for transport to the lungs. He must also check to see what percentage of this polluted air is released from the lung cells and what part of it is retained by them.

Application

A complete investigation into the formation, components and operation of the subtle body is made through pranayama breath-infusion. This is necessary so that the yogi can see how much he can alter. The subtle body is the root of the transmigrations through mundane life forms. It is imperative to understand how the person-self is conducted through the evolutionary cycle by this subtle form.

Verse 50

कपाल–शोधनं वात–दोष–घ्नं कृमि–दोष–हृत् ।

पुनः पुनरिदं कार्यं सूर्य–भेदनमुत्तमम् ।। ५० ।।

kapāla–śodhanaṁ vāta–doṣa–ghnaṁ kṛmi–doṣa–hṛt I
punaḥ punaridaṁ kāryaṁ sūrya–bhedanamuttamam II 50 II

kapala – head, śodhanaṁ – clearance, vāta – wind, doṣa – discomfort, ghnaṁ – destroys, kṛmi – intestinal worm, doṣa – malfunctions, hṛt – eliminates, punaḥ punar= punaḥ punaḥ = repeatedly, idaṁ – this idaṁ, kāryaṁ – is practiced, sūrya = sun–dominant right channel, bhedanam – infusion, uttamam – foremost technique

It results in the clearance of the head, the removal of discomfort caused by bodily air and the elimination of malfunctions caused by intestinal worms. This foremost technique for infusion of the sun–dominant right channel should be practiced repeatedly.

Analysis

In the time of Swatmarama, yogis got these results from the practice of right nostril infusion. At the time the intestinal worms even were affected by the increase in sun energy in the body.

This increase through the right channel will eventually fill the right side of the nadi system. Then the excess will flow over into the left side, the moon dominant channel. When the yogi fills the left side through this overflow, he will realize it and will keep the practice for a time to be sure that all pollutants are extracted.

Application

In the subtle body, this inflow of sun energy into the right channel causes an electric feeling on the right side of the sushumna nadi central channel. This affects that central nadi causing it to have a dual polarity. After the right side is filled with charge, the energy will leap over to the left. If when this happens the yogi continues to infuse energy, the left side will eventually fill up by the overflow which enters it.

This will cause the left channel to hold a corresponding charge. There will be a clash of this energy which will result in arousal of kundalini lifeforce. The yogi should keep the kundalini in the central passage while checking to see if the force on each side achieves equal charge.

By application of the chin lock, the energy will be restricted within the trunk of the subtle body and will enter the head only as allowed by the lock. If the lock is inefficient the result will be that kundalini will enter into the head in a haphazard way which is not controlled by the yogi. If the lock is efficient, kundalini will go into the subtle head in an orderly way with the yogi objectively experiencing transit of consciousness to higher levels.

Verse 51

अथ उज्जायी

मुखं संयम्य नाडीभ्यामाकृष्य पवनं शनैः ।

यथा लगति कण्ठात्तु हृदयावधि स–स्वनम् ।। ५१ ।।

atha ujjāyī
mukhaṁ saṁyamya nāḍībhyāmākṛṣya pavanaṁ śanaiḥ |
yathā lagati kaṇṭhāttu hṛdayāvadhi sa–svanam || 51 ||

atha – now is explained, ujjāyī – ujjāyī epiglottis contact procedure, mukhaṁ – mouth, saṁyamya – closing, nāḍībhyām – through the two subtle passages, ākṛṣya – drawing in, pavanaṁ – air, śanaiḥ – gradually, yathā – just as, lagati – saturates, kaṇṭhāt – from the throat, tu – but, hṛdayāvadhi = hṛdaya (chest region) + avadhi (down to), sa–svanam = with a sound

Now is explained the ujjāyī epiglottis contact procedure:

Closing the mouth, gradually drawing air in through the two subtle passages, it saturates from the throat to the chest region, while making a sound.

Analysis

In this infusion the breath is pulled downwards just after it enters the nostrils. This causes the air to rub against the epiglottis. It produced a sound from that friction. This practice and all others are best done with eyes closed so that full inner concentration can be applied.

A student is required to make minute observations about what transpired in the subtle body as a result. The cavity of the lungs is filled by this breath but the student should be focused down through the chest of the subtle body.

Application

This breath-infusion has a sound which is similar to when a boa constrictor breathes while swallowing large prey. At the time the snake breathes through a protruding tube and makes a dragging sound on the inhale. If the prey is very large, the snake's throat is stretched to the limit. The reptile swallows the animal bit by bit while breathing with a labored tone.

The observation which the yogi should make with this ujjāyī epiglottis contact infusion is how the lungs are filled in regular breathing, how they absorb the air which enters, how that is infused into the cells which flow in the blood stream, how pollutants are excreted by those cells and how the lungs discharge the said toxins.

Verse 52

पूर्ववत्कुम्भयेत्प्राणं रेचयेदिडया तथा ।
शलेष्म–दोष–हरं कण्ठे देहानल–विवर्धनम् ।। ५२ ।।

pūrvavatkumbhayetprāṇaṁ recayediḍayā tathā I
śleṣma–doṣa–haraṁ kaṇṭhe dehānala–vivardhanam II 52 II

pūrvavat = as before, kumbhayet – breath retention with physio–psychic compression, prāṇaṁ – infused breath energy, recayed = recayet = exhale, iḍayā – through the left subtle channel, tathā – as, śleṣma – mucus, doṣa – malfunction, haraṁ – eliminates, kaṇṭhe – in the throat, dehānala = deha anala = digestive functionality, vivardhanam – increases

Just as before, there should be breath retention with physio–psychic compression of the infused breath energy, then there should be exhalation through the left subtle channel. This eliminates mucus problems in the throat and increases digestive functionality.

Analysis

In the ujjayi epiglottis contact procedure, after inhaling through both nostrils and dragging the inhaled breath over the epiglottis, the yogi should apply the locks and suspend breathing. Then before there is any discomfort, he should exhale through the left subtle channel. If done with concentration and with inner focus having the eyes closed even, the yogi will experience a shift of the balanced energy to the left subtle channel. There will be a resistance energy which will spring from the center of the body but the yogi should note and ignore it.

Application

Normal relaxed or involuntary breathing causes energy to reach down to the navel. The energy is then distributed but with acceptance of pollutants.

Very deep breathing, done with effort and focus, where the air reaches down to the bottom of the lungs, results in energy penetrating through the groin area. This infusion also becomes mixed with pollutants but it carries a charge from the hormonal energy which it touches.

When a yogi habitually gets the air to go to the very bottom of the lungs, he gains some grasp on the muladhara chakra where the kundalini normally resides.

Some yogis press down the infused breath energy so that it flows past the navel, penetrates the groin region and then bridges to muladhara base chakra. If this happens, the pollutants which are fused into the breath energy as it courses through these areas, meets with kundalini and may, if kundalini is aroused sufficiently, ascend the spine into the brain.

This may cause a black-out or white-out where the person-self loses objective awareness for a short period of time.

If possible a yogi should extract the pollutants through the lungs by pulling them up from the bottom of the subtle trunk. But otherwise the pollutants may mix with infused

fresh air and then move into the head and out of the body when kundalini rises through the spine after being jolted by the mixed energy.

Verse 53

नाडी–जलोदराधातु–गत–दोष–विनाशनम् ।

गच्छता तिष्ठता कार्यमुज्जाय्याख्यं तु कुम्भकम् ।। ५३ ।।

nāḍī–jalodarādhātu–gata–doṣa–vināśanam ।
gacchatā tiṣṭhatā kāryamujjāyyākhyaṁ tu kumbhakam ।। 53 ।।

nāḍī – nadi subtle veins and arteries, jalodarā – body swelling (dropsy, edema), dhātu – body cell structure, gata – related to, doṣa – malfunction, vināśanam – elimination, gacchatā – walking, tiṣṭhatā – sitting or lying, kāryam – performing, ujjāyy – ujjāyi epiglottis contact infusion, ākhyaṁ – known as, tu – but, kumbhakam – breath retention with physio–psychic compression

For the elimination of malfunctions relating to the nadi subtle veins and arteries, bodily swelling (dropsy, edema), and cell structure malformations (anemia), either while walking, sitting or lying, one should do the breath retention with physio–psychic compression which is known as ujjayi epiglottis contact infusion.

Analysis

This would have to be done with full concentration and with some expertise in yoga meditation as it is defined throughout this book. A superficial application of this instruction will not result in the benefits mentioned.

There is also the factor of our changed environment, where the causes of body swelling and cell structure malformation may be different to that in the time of Swatmarama, which means that other remedies would be suitable and not the one used by the ancient yogis. A student must know that these procedures required hours of practice for completion.

Application

The defects listed are:

- *malfunctions relating to the nadi subtle veins and arteries*
- *bodily swelling*
- *cell structure malformations*

The ***malfunctions relating to the nadi subtle veins and arteries*** *is a subtle body problem which may or may not have a physical coordinate. To cure this using the ujjayi epiglottis contact infusion, the yogi must use a tremendous amount of concentration while doing the practice. He must continue the practice for hours up to the point of full infusion of the sun-dominant right side, the overflow of that energy into the moon-dominant left side and the checking for balance between the two, where their percentages converse to fill the whole psyche. This yogi must have developed acute mystic perception prior to doing this exercise because that is the only way he can* *tally these references.*

If there is a physical coordinate where the disease manifests in the physical body, with malfunctions in the veins and arteries in that body, the yogi must also make dietary and lifestyle adjustments to facilitate the cure.

Bodily swelling, *dropsy or edema may require complicated diagnostics. A yogi using the ujjayi epiglottis contact infusion for cure would have to work for hours or might be required to do this for weeks, months or even years. Nowadays it is best to take medical treatment and to realize that the modern methods were not available in the time of Swatmarama.*

The highlight of the ancient medical process is that a yogi had to solve out diseases before he could proficiently meditate. Ancient ascetics were willing to do this. A student had to cure himself using methods which were recommended by advanced yogis who were expert in Ayur Veda.

Cell structure malformation *is known today as anemia. Its diagnostics is complicated. We are also subjected to machine radiation in the modern environment. Formerly a yogi used mystic perception to deal with cell structure malformation but the machine influence was not present for the ancient yogis.*

If it is just a matter of location, diet and lifestyle change, then the ujjayi epiglottis contact infusion may serve the purpose; otherwise doing it will not produce cure. If someone's body was subjected to massive doses of radiation, the solution would be the death of the physical form, because then the subtle one could breach away and cure itself overtime in the astral environments. No amount of pranayama would cure a physical body which absorbed lethal doses of radiation.

Verse 54

अथ सीत्कारी

सीत्कां कुर्यात्तथा वक्त्रे घ्राणेनैव विजृम्भिकाम् ।

एवमभ्यास–योगेन काम–देवो द्वितीयकः ।। ५४ ।।

atha sītkārī
sītkāṁ kuryāttathā vaktre ghrāṇenaiva vijṝmbhikām |
evamabhyāsa–yogena kāma–devo dvitīyakaḥ || 54 ||

atha – now will be described, sītkārī – sītkārī hissing breath-infusion, sītkāṁ – seet sound, kuryāt – should be done, tathā – as, vaktre – through the teeth, ghrāṇenaiva = ghrāṇena (through the nose) + eva (even so), vijṝmbhikām – sucking air in, evam – thus, abhyāsa – practice, yogena – by yoga, kāma–devo = kāma–devaḥ = deity who inspires love, dvitīyakaḥ – second

Now the sitkari hissing breath-infusion technique will be described:

It is done by making the seet sound while sucking air through the teeth and then exhaling through the nose. By this yoga practice the yogi becomes a second deity for inspiring love.

Analysis

This procedure is with the lips tightly hugging the teeth, with the lips kept apart, with the teeth exposed, and the tongue touching the palate. During the inhale, the air is drawn through the spaces between the teeth. This makes a hiss sound which is like saying seet. After the inhale, breathing is suspended while the locks are applied to the neck, anus, perineum and abdomen. For the exhale the air is passaged through the nostrils.

Because of the position of the tongue and due to the focus on drawing air through the teeth, the infused energy rises into the brain. The ascetic finds that he is located in the mind cavity with the buddhi intellect organ. Due to this the body straightens so that the spine is vertical and balanced.

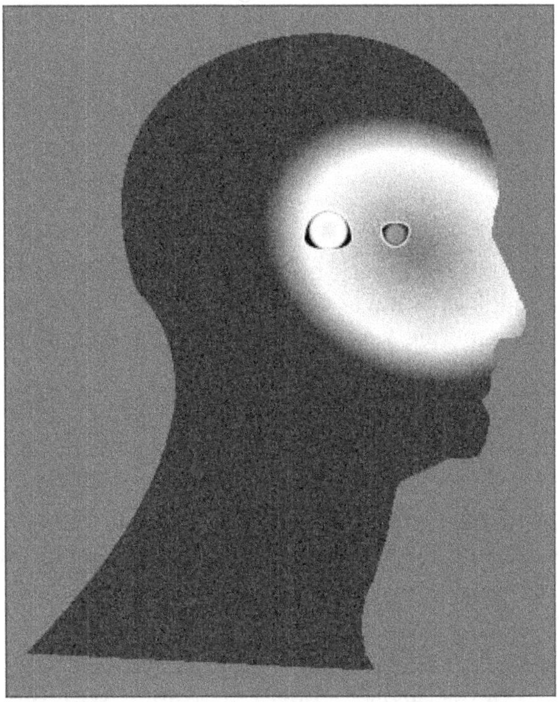

This, if done proficiently, gives a sense of security where a person feels as if he or she was the god of love. The material world is the bastion of spiritual insecurity. Every creature in this existence clambers for a foothold in love. What could be a more secured position than being the distributor of affection? A yogi does not become the deity of love but when this breath-infusion is mastered, one gets the feeling as if one were that entity. For the time being, this suspends the insecurities.

Application

Each student should study this thesis of Swatmarama. Cull out procedures for spiritual advancement. Test various methods as inspired or advised.

Do not be superstitious. Have an open mind so that you can judge the effects to determine what assists you and what does not.

Verse 55

योगिनी चक्र–संमान्यः सृष्टि–संहार–कारकः ।

न क्षुधा न तृषा निद्रा नैवालस्यं प्रजायते ।। ५५ ।।

yoginī cakra–saṁmānyaḥ sṛṣṭi–saṁhāra–kārakaḥ I
na kṣudhā na tṛṣā nidrā naivālasyaṁ prajāyate I I 55 I I

yoginī – of yoginis, cakra – associate group, saṁmānyaḥ – completely fascinated by, sṛṣṭi – creation, saṁhāra – dissolution, kārakaḥ – cosmic engineer, na – not, kṣudhā – hunger, na – nor, tṛṣā – thirst, nidrā – sleep, naivālasyaṁ = na (nor) + eva (even) + ālasyaṁ (procrastination), prajāyate – manifest

The associate group of yoginis, (female ascetics), are completely fascinated by that yogi, who is like the cosmic engineer of creation and dissolution. No hunger, thirst, sleep or even procrastination manifest in him.

Analysis

The associate group of yoginis is a special set of angelic females who are expert in assuming yoga postures and in practicing advanced meditation techniques which are taught to them by the siddhas. Some of these womem take physical bodies from time to time. Usually they do this to follow a fallen yogi or to be with an advanced yogi who is commissioned to take a material body.

Here on earth and in the celestial world as well, males are the leading ascetics because the austerities are not suited to female bodies. It appears to be a prejudice but it is actually a restriction which occurs because of the bodily configuration of female forms.

A yogi who becomes existentially stabilized and who flushes out of his psyche, its insecurities by any which means, becomes a focus of attention for the yoginis. However, any such yogi runs the risk of losing the foothold in higher yoga.

As a man may be a distraction for a woman, so a woman may divert a man. If a yogi is not careful, if he does not adhere to his spiritual masters, he is likely to become absorbed in the desires of the angelic woman or women, with the result that his yoga practice may stagnate.

Desire is the enemy of yoga. Hence if an ascetic gets to fulfilling desires for pleasing anyone, even to please himself, there is the likelihood that the enthusiasm for yoga may be transferred to desires which will diminish the practice.

Application

When a yogi has a pranayama proficiency which results in a lack of hunger, thirst, sleep or procrastination, that ascetic is just like a supernatural controller, a demigod. However if he is not careful, he runs the risk of becoming degraded. This could happen by virtue of desire energies which might creep into his psyche and commandeer it.

If an ascetic is destined to be responsible for a group of angelic women, then no one or nothing may stop the imposition of that. Still, if he is not careful, the same providence which facilitated that will ruin him. No one should play with fate. No one should trust that fate has one's interest as its primary concern. Each of us is a utility of fate but we can become useless to it as well.

An ascetic must comply with fate or face dire consequences. All the same, one should be alert to jump out of the way when fate runs contrary.

By yoga practice one may become like a god of love but all the same, fate may reverse that and put one in dire straits. No sane person should rely on fate to maintain the fortune which it awards him. Any of us may ride a wave of success and have utmost fulfillment of desire but we should not be foolhardy to think that fate will not terminate facilities and take us into a valley of sorrows.

One should respect fate and look for its cues so that one knows when to abandon its fortunes at its command.

Verse 56

भवेत्सत्त्वं च देहस्य सर्वोपद्रव–वर्जितः ।

अनेन विधिना सत्यं योगीन्द्रो भूमि–मण्डले ।। ५६ ।।

bhavetsattvaṁ ca dehasya sarvopadrava–varjitaḥ I
anena vidhinā satyaṁ yogīndro bhūmi–maṇḍale II 56 II

bhavet – becomes, sattvaṁ – clarifying energy of subtle material nature, ca – and, dehasya – of the body, sarvopadrava = sarva (all) + upadrava (contamination), varjitaḥ – devoid of, anena – by this, vidhinā – process, satyaṁ – really happen, yogīndro = yogīndraḥ = lord of yogis, bhūmi – earth, maṇḍale – on the entire

The clarifying energy of subtle material nature, which is in his body, becomes devoid of contamination. By this process, it really happens that he becomes a lord of the yogis on the entire earth.

Analysis

A lord of yogis is a yogi who mastered the disciplines and became a siddha perfected being, even while using a material body. Some masterful yogis achieve the lordly status in the afterlife because they were protected by their gurus who make it easy for them not to take another material body and to continue making progress using a subtle form only.

Some masterful yogis take a body to teach yoga or to become a leader of religiously inclined human beings. These are lords of yogis as well but with a different mission for catering righteous lifestyle to the public. That is not yoga, but it helps human society to maintain itself in demarcation to the animal kingdom.

When the clarifying energy of subtle material nature is cleared of the two lowering influences, the yogi finds that his insight is not prejudiced for ruining spiritual perception. There are related verses in the Bhagavad Gita:

śrībhagavānuvāca
kāma eṣa krodha eṣa
rajoguṇasamudbhavaḥ

mahāśano mahāpāpmā
viddhyenamiha vairiṇam (3.37)

śri bhagavān — the Blessed Lord; uvāca — said; kāma — craving; eṣa — this; krodha — anger; eṣa — this; rajoguṇasamudbhavaḥ = rajo (rajaḥ) — passion + guṇa — emotion + samudbhavaḥ — source; mahāśano (mahāśanaḥ) = mahā — great + aśana — consuming power; mahāpāpmā = mahā — much + pāpmā — damage; viddhyenam = viddhi — recognize + enam — this; iha — in this case; vairiṇam — enemy

The Blessed Lord said: This force is craving. This power is anger. The passionate emotion is the source. It has a great consuming power and does much damage. Recognize it as the enemy in this case. (Bhagavad Gita 3.37)

dhūmenāvriyate vahnir
yathādarśo malena ca
yatholbenāvṛto garbhas
tathā tenedamāvṛtam (3.38)

dhūmenāvriyate = dhūmena — by smoke + āvriyate — is obscured; vahnir = vahniḥ — the sacrificial fire; yathā — similarly; 'darśo = ādarśaḥ — mirror; malena — with dust; ca — and; yatholbenāvṛto = yatholbenāvṛtaḥ = yatho (yatha) — similarly + ulbena — by skin + āvṛtaḥ — is covered; garbhaḥ — embryo; tathā — so; tenedam = tena — by this + idam — this; āvṛtam — is blocked

As the sacrificial fire is obscured by smoke, and similarly as a mirror is shrouded by dust or as an embryo is covered by skin, so a man's insight is blocked by the passionate energy. (Bhagavad Gita 3.38)

A man is not God but still a man has some insight. Whatever that is, however accurate it is, there needs to be clarity to exploit it; otherwise we are bound to remain less than what we could be.

So long as we are in the material world, using a psyche which is made of subtle material nature, we will have to make do with this energy. However, we do not have to remain under the lowest energy type. We should develop the highest possible insight.

Application

The clearance of the clarifying energy takes place over a period of years. It does not happen overnight. It is a fact that a yogi has momentary glimpses of the divine world but it is not ongoing except for those ascetics who practice long and hard and whose advancement was sustained. Any yogi who is socially involved has little hope of full clarity and permanent clearance of lower energies. For such a yogi, he may become elevated during the daily meditation sessions but invariably his psyche will dip down into a lower plane as its routine medium.

Verse 57

अथ शीतली

जिह्वया वायुमाकृष्य पूर्ववत्कुम्भ-साधनम् ।

शनकैर्घ्राण–रन्ध्राभ्यां रेचयेत्पवनं सुधीः ।। ५७ ।।

atha śītalī
jihvayā vāyumākṝṣya pūrvavatkumbha–sādhanam ।
śanakairghrāṇa–randhrābhyāṁ recayetpavanaṁ sudhīḥ ।। 57 ।।

atha – now it will be explained, śītalī – the śītalī tongue contact infusion, jihvayā – through the (u–shaped curled) tongue, vāyum – fresh air, ākṝṣya – draw in, pūrva – before, vat – like, kumbha – suspension of breathing with compression of accumulated breath energy, sādhanam – spiritual self–disciplinary practice, śanakair – gradually, ghrāṇa–randhrābhyāṁ = through the nostrils, recayet – should exhale, pavanaṁ – fresh air, sudhīḥ – very perceptive person

Now the shitali tongue contact infusion will be explained:

Draw in fresh air through the (u–shaped curled) tongue. Do suspension of breathing with compression of accumulated breath energy as before. The very perceptive yogi should gradually exhale through the nostrils.

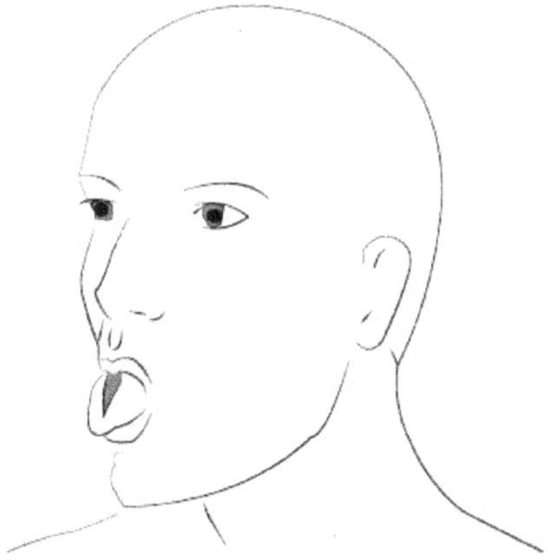

Analysis

The shitali tongue contact infusion should be done with full concentration as every other yoga technique. The target should be the subtle body and the psychic effects. This procedure makes the yogi aware of the lower back of the brain and the passage to the back top of the head where naad sound is heard.

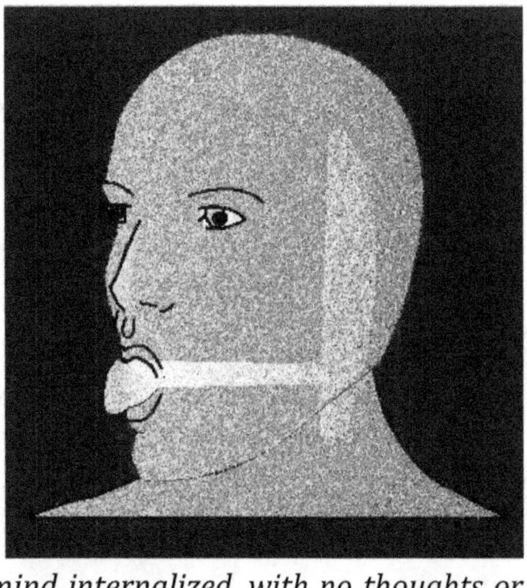

The tongue is curled up and protrudes through the lips slightly in this practice. These are singular exercises and not group session events as some people have publicized.

Application

One should do this with closed eyes, with the mind internalized, with no thoughts or images to distract the attention. Since it cools the tongue, the air should be pulled in

slowly and steadily. As the air is inhaled the yogi should place the attention at the back of the head where the air seems to reach the end of a psychic passage.

When this is done correctly, the student will know because it will seem as if one should cease inhaling and yet, it will be that one can continue on and on for a long time. Then after a spell, there will be a silence and the inhale will cease. At that time one should shut down all interest in the inhale, close the mouth and apply the chin lock, the anus lock, the perineum lock and the abdomen uplift lock. Then one should wait until the system begins to call for a release.

As soon as the release impulse is felt one should exhale very slowly through the nostrils without jerking, abruptness or anxiety. If there is anxiety one should note it and when one does the next sequence one should not suspend the breathing for such a long time but should release for exhale as soon as there is the slightest call for release.

This is a powerful practice for training the mind to appreciate the naad sound resonance and for finding secret passages in the back of the head of the subtle body. A yogi should do this practice privately in isolation without anyone knowing about it except the yoga teacher and serious aspirants. This is done best in a dark quiet place with full ventilation. If one does not have a dark place, one may use a blindfold to keep light from affecting the eyelids. It should be done using a posture which is easy so that no attention is given to the physical body during the session.

Verse 58

गुल्म–पलीहादिकान्रोगान्ज्वरं पित्तं क्षुधां तृषाम् ।

विषाणि शीतली नाम कुम्भिकेयं निहन्ति हि ।। ५८ ।।

gulma–plīhādikānrogānjvaraṁ pittaṁ kṣudhāṁ tṛṣām |
viṣāṇi śītalī nāma kumbhikeyaṁ nihanti hi || 58 ||

gulma – gland malfunction, plīhādikān = spleen and other specific disorders, rogān – diseases, jvaraṁ – fever, pittaṁ – bile, kṣudhāṁ – hunger, tṛṣām –thirst, viṣāṇi – poisons, śītalī – the śītalī tongue contact infusion, nāma – that which is called, kumbhikeyaṁ = kumblikā (breath retention after inhalation and compression) + iyam (this), nihanti – attacks (removes), hi – certainly

Gland malfunction, spleen and other specific disorders, diseases, fever, bile upsets, hunger, thirst and poisons are removed by this retention practice which is known as shitali tongue contact infusion.

Analysis

In the time of Swatmarama, this tongue contact infusion was used as part of the Ayur Veda system of healing where some ascetics with ailments were cured by using this procedure. However that is not the primary purpose. For yoga practice one requires healthy physical and subtle bodies. Both systems should be in order but in any case, eventually the physical system will fail. Thus the real drive is for the subtle body to be in tiptop shape.

Undoubtedly pranayama breath-infusion is the prime method for keeping the subtle body surcharged with the best type of psychic energy for its upkeep.

Application

Let us look at the list of disorders which this practice cured in the time of Swatmarama:

- *Gland malfunction*
- *spleen and other specific disorders*
- *disease*
- *fever*
- *bile upset*
- *hunger*
- *thirst and poison removal*

This is amazing but we must take into consideration that the lifestyle was different. There were other events of the culture which are unknown to us today. It is not that the shitali tongue contact infusion alone was the cure. It was supported and subsidized by other processes which are not mentioned.

Since some aspects are absent today, we cannot expect the pranayamas to work in the same way on the physical system. There is no need to lose faith in yoga because these procedures do not yield these benefits currently.

Verse 59

अथ भस्त्रिका

ऊर्वोरुपरि संस्थाप्य शुभे पाद–तले उभे ।

पद्मासनं भवेदेतत्सर्व–पाप–प्रणाशनम् ।। ५९ ।।

atha bhastrikā
ūrvorupari saṁsthāpya śubhe pāda–tale ubhe ।
padmāsanaṁ bhavedetatsarva–pāpa–praṇāśanam ।। 59 ।।

atha – now this will be explained, bhastrika – bhastrika rapid breath-infusion, ūrvor = ūrvoḥ = of the thighs, upari – on top, saṁsthāpya – in position, śubhe – beautiful, pāda – of feet, tale – in soles, ubhe – of two, padmāsanaṁ – lotus posture, bhaved = bhavet = assume, etat – this, sarva – all, papa – faults, praṇāśanam – termination

Now the bhastrika rapid breath-infusion will be explained:

By positioning the two beautiful soles of the feet on top of the thighs, the lotus posture is assumed. This is the termination of all faults.

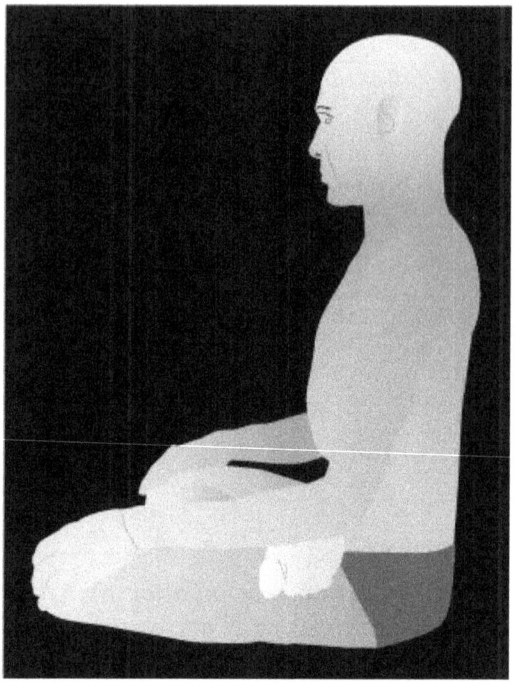

Analysis

Bhastrika rapid breath-infusion is scary for most students. It has a reputation as being the most advanced of the breathing methods. Many teachers are afraid of it. They will neither practice nor recommend it. Their only advice is to stay away from it.

In my experience, bhastrika rapid breath-infusion is the sure way to do pranayama practice. It is definite and gives instant perception of psychic energy. It shifts the mind from lower modes and makes the shifty thought-image display to disappear from the gaze of the meditator. I recommend it.

One should be trained in it by someone who mastered it. The mastery of the locks is vital in the practice of this rapid breath-infusion process. Bhastrika should not be practiced as a beginning process. It is a graduation from the kapalabhati rapid breath-infusion method. My advice is that the student should do kapalabhati until that evolves on its own into bhastrika.

Application

Kapalabhati is rapid breathing with stress on the exhale so that the inhale occurs impulsively without any stress or concentration of the student. The focus should be on the exhale. Bhastrika is focused on the exhale and inhale, but if my advice is followed and the student does kapalabhati until it evolves into bhastrika, there will be focus on the inhale with automatic push on the exhale during bhastrika because by the time one evolves into bhastrika the system would be accustomed to the forceful exhale which would become a reflex and would require little if any attention.

If a student does bhastrika before mastering kapalabhati where kapalabhati was not developed into a reflex, then the practice will be spoilt because there will be too much focus on the breathing action and too little focus on the internal compression and distribution of energy. One must also keep track of the kundalini during the session. This requires much attention. Therefore one should not do bhastrika outright but only as a graduate development of kapalabhati. Please heed this advice.

Verse 60

सम्यक्पद्मासनं बद्धा समग्रीवोदरः सुधीः ।

मुखं संयम्य यत्नेन प्राणं घ्राणेन रेचयेत् ।। ६० ।।

samyakpadmāsanaṁ baddhvā sama–grīvodaraḥ sudhīḥ ।
mukhaṁ saṁyamya yatnena prāṇaṁ grāṇena recayet ।। 60 ।।

samyak – proficiently, padmāsanaṁ – lotus posture, baddhvā – assuming, sama – with alignment, grīvodaraḥ = grīva (neck) + udaraḥ (abdomen), sudhīḥ – competent perceptive yogi, mukhaṁ – mouth, saṁyamya – closing, yatnena – with force, prāṇaṁ – air, grāṇena – through the nose, recayet – should exhale

Proficiently holding the lotus posture with the neck and abdomen in alignment, the competent perceptive yogi should, after closing the mouth, forcefully exhale through the nose.

Analysis

Swatmarama shows us that in his time, this procedure was matched with the ultimate asana posture which is the lotus pose. This is classic. Yogis using the lotus with bhastrika were at the end of the line as adepts.

Let us consider the progression from asana to pranayama which Patanjali lists as the third (3rd) and fourth (4th) stages of yoga. Initially asana postures are a physical process. However if the poses are done correctly under expert guidance the student soon realizes that the physical is only applied to target the psychological body. When electricity flashes in the sky it is called lightning. When it flashes through a wire it is termed as electricity. When there is only a subtle body and no physical system is developed for it, it is called a ghost or astral being. When the subtle body has a physical casing it is called a living creature, animal or human being.

Initially asana postures are a physical process. Everything about it seems to be physical motion. Yet it is actually meant to target and make the student become aware of the subtle form. If I hold an electric cable, I will receive no shock or indication of it as a live wire. If however the plastic jacket is removed, I will instantly get the understanding of the power flowing through the wire. While doing the asana postures, if one is attentive introspectively, one will become aware of the subtle body.

Students who mistake asana postures for being a physical process are either dense in consciousness or are misled by teachers who never progressed beyond the physical.

One should do the asana postures but with the right supervision so that one can come to understand that a subtle body is interspaced in the physical system. This subtle body may mimic the physical one just as the physical one may sometimes repeat the actions of the subtle system. As the physical body does follow the will and desire of the self, so the subtle body may follow the impulsive actions of the physical one. The inter-relation between the physical and subtle systems should be realized. In fact the asana postures are designed for making one come to this understanding though introspective insight which is applied while doing the postures.

Once the student gets some insight into the subtle body, he is ready to be taught the breath-infusion system. With the introspective hint of a subtle body, the student can do the breath-infusion in a psychologically meaningful way. If one learns pranayama as a physical process only, then it means one was introduced to it by an incompetent teacher. However that is not necessarily the fault of the teacher. He may have leant it from a master who was not properly trained.

Pranayama is for the psychological development of yoga while asana postures are for the physical development which graduates into the psychological. This is the system.

Application

The standard teaching in the time of Swatmarama was to teach each stage of yoga, one by one in a gradual progression which took years. In fact Rishi Singh Gherwal indicated to Arthur Beverford that for asana, it took twelve years for mastery and for pranayama breath-infusion it took about the same.

If we take this opinion seriously, that would mean that for each stage of the eight stages of yoga, it would take a total of 8 X 12 or nine-six (96) years. This would be impractical today. If I began yoga practice in childhood, I would require a lifespan of at least 6 + 96 years or one hundred and two (102) years to complete the practice.

To be practical, a student should aim for developing a subtle body which is resistant to rebirth, which has lost the tendency to be attracted to physical history. If the subtle body can be reconfigured in that way, it would not matter when the physical body died because the yogi could continue the practice without birth interruption in the hereafter.

The problem with taking another material body is that it is risky since the parents may not be yogis, the society may be politically unstable and so many other factors may be disruptive, so that when the yogi comes out again physically as someone's son or daughter, there is a circumstance of birth in which yoga practice is conspicuous by its absence.

The ideal achievement is to become liberated before leaving the physical form but since that is not likely; a student should aspire for a subtle body which can continue the practice to perfection in the astral world hereafter without having to take another material form.

To accelerate the process some yogis developed a practice of consolidating the asana, pranayama and pratyahar practice. Patanjali, the author of the Yoga Sutras, explained the consolidation of the dharana, dhyana and samadhi superior stages of yoga into one practice which he termed as samyama or the complete restraint.

This means that yoga can be reduced to three processes where the first two stages are considered as one practice. The third, fourth and fifth stages are considered as another practice. The last three stages are considered to be yet another practice.

As itemized this would be:

Righteous Behavior = *yama + niyama*

Kundalini Yoga	=	*asana + pranayama + pratyahar*
inSelf Yoga™ Meditation	=	*dharana + dhyana + samadhi*

Let us review Patanjali's syllabus for yoga:

yama niyama āsana prāṇāyāma pratyāhāra
dhāraṇā dhyāna samādhayaḥ aṣṭau aṅgāni

yama – moral restraints; niyama – recommended behaviors; āsana – body postures; prāṇāyāma – breath infusion; pratyāhar – sensual energy withdrawal; dhāraṇā – linking of the attention to higher concentration forces or persons; dhyāna – effortless linkage of the attention to higher concentration forces or persons; samādhayaḥ – continuous effortless linkage of the attention to higher concentration forces or persons; aṣṭau – eight; aṅgāni – parts of a thing.

Moral restraints, recommended behaviors, body posture, breath-infusion, sensual energy withdrawal, linking of the attention to higher concentration forces or persons, effortless linkage of the attention to higher concentration forces or persons, continuous effortless linkage of the attention to higher concentration forces or persons are the eight parts of the yoga system. (Yoga Sutras 2.29)

*For beginners, the **righteous behaviors** consist of approvals and disapprovals for particular social actions. Students should study these and fine-tune their lifestyles accordingly. For advanced students these righteous behaviors have nothing to do with social action but relates only to the relationship between the core-self and its psychic adjuncts. A student must repeatedly go back and repair the behaviors just to facilitate the higher stages of yoga.*

*The endeavor for **kundalini yoga** consists of asana postures and pranayama breath-infusion to remove all pollution-influences from the subtle body and to ingest into it fresh subtle energy from the clarifying energy of material nature. If this is done proficiently it progresses on its own to the achievement of pratyahar sensual energy withdrawal. In practical terms this means that if I complete the asana and pranayama practice proficiently, when I sit to meditate immediately, I will find that my mind assumes the sensual energy withdrawal so that I would not be required to practice that. I can begin the meditation at the sixth stage of yoga which is dharana.*

If I am lucky this will progress naturally into dhyana which will evolve into samadhi. If I am unlucky or if my kundalini yoga practice was not that proficient, I would be in a partial completion of pratyahar sensual withdrawal and could make the endeavor to complete that and go further.

***inSelf Yoga™ Meditation** begins after achieving pratyahar sensual energy withdrawal. If the student sits to meditate without doing an efficient pranayama practice, it is likely that there will be a struggle in the mind. The core-self will be drawn into a conflict with the buddhi intellect orb which will try to resume its behavior of entertaining and controlling the core-self by exposing it to thoughts and images.*

Many meditators spend their entire session fighting with the intellect, pleading with it to stop its thought-image display sequences. Of course most of them do this to no avail because the energy in the psyche effortlessly and sequentially generates the images.

Modern yogis, who fail to appreciate pranayama breath-infusion, will continue doing pratyahar to a complete or incomplete stage but that is not meditation. According to Patanjali meditation is samyama which is the complete restraint of the mento-emotional energy. It begins with dharana which is deliberate focus on higher realities without having to stop the mind from thinking and imaging in relation to the physical and lower astral worlds.

Your best bet is to learn an efficient pranayama method. Use it before meditation so that the mind assumes a complete pratyahar sensual energy withdrawal when you sit to meditate. This will accelerate the process and will put you in touch with Patanjali's syllabus. Any pranayama breath-infusion method which does not result in pratyahar sensual energy withdrawal is useless for this objective. To test a method, sit to meditate without doing it and note carefully the behavior of the mind. Then practice the method and sit to meditate and note if there is a difference in the behavior of the mind. If there is no noticeable reduction or shut down of thinking and imaging the process is worthless. Bear in mind that you must be doing the process correctly to make a fair assessment.

It is not a good idea to bombast a process. We experienced that sometimes one person gets success with a process and some other person just cannot extract the benefit from it. One should not be arrogant. If one goes to a teacher and is supervised in the practice, and still does not get the result intended, one should go away quietly and find some other teacher and method. There is no need to criticize any teacher or process. Yoga is not for publicity. It is not for criticizing and venting resentments for teachers and methods. It is for individual practice and advancement by paying attention to the self and its struggle with the psychic adjuncts.

Verse 61

यथा लगति हृत–कण्ठे कपालावधि सस्वनम् ।

वेगेन पूरयेच्चापि हृत–पद्मावधि मारुतम् ।। ६१ ।।

yathā lagati hṝt kaṇṭhe kapālāvadhi sasvanam |
vegena pūrayeccāpi hṝt–padmāvadhi mārutam || 61 ||

yathā – as, lagati = thrusting, hṝt = hṝt = chest, kaṇṭhe – in the throat, kapālāvadhi = kapāla (head) + avadhi (up to), sasvanam – loud sound, vegena – with rapidity, pūrayec = pūrayet – should inhale, cāpi – and also, hṝt – chest, padmāvadhi = padma (lotus) + avadhi (up to), mārutam – fresh air

Thrusting the air into the chest, throat and head while making a loud sound with the rapid breathing, the yogi should inhale the fresh air into the lotus chest region.

Analysis

Bhastrika breath-infusion is mainly a process of aggressively thrusting air into the lungs, compressing it into the blood stream, pushing it down around the pubic loop so that the mix of fresh air, polluted air and hormonal energy develops an electric charge which fuses into the kundalini lifeforce at the muladhara base chakra. This is the rapid very definite way of arousing kundalini on a daily basis.

When the fresh air is absorbed by the lungs, and more air is ingested, the newly ingested air compresses the air which was absorbed before it. This forces the air to move into the blood stream where it accumulates near to the lungs. Sensing the increase in air in the blood stream, the central nervous system gives instructions for the heart to distribute the infused air. The yogi keeps on pulling in more and more air, until he feels that the lungs are no longer absorbing it. Then he suspends breathing on an inhale and compresses the trunk of the body by applying the chin lock, anus lock, perineum and abdomen lifts. While doing these physical compressions, he mentally forces down the compressed energy so that it passes through the navel region and goes into the groin.

This mental pushing is related to the emotional content of the compressed energy. This is a composite of physical, mental and emotional energy. The yogi uses the mental energy which is responsive to his will power and with that he crunches the emotional energy downward. Since the physical locks were already applied, this seals the compression on the physical, mental and emotional planes.

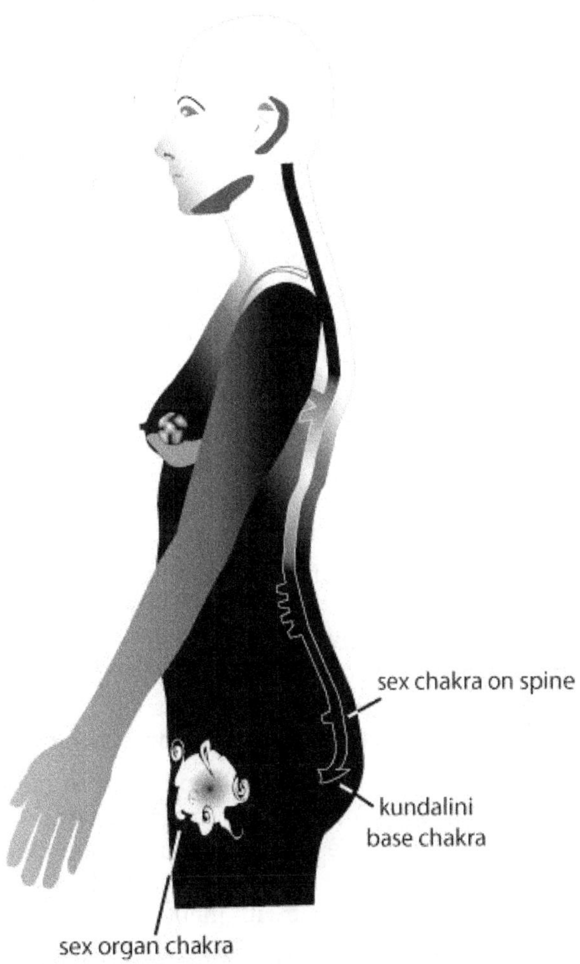

In the groin the air energy mixes with sex hormones. An electric charge develops which the yogi grasps and directs emotionally. He pushes it into the muladhara base chakra at the end of the spine.

When this mixed charged energy strikes the base chakra, it arouses the kundalini psychic life-force but due to the locks, this force finds that the only direction in which it can go is up through the central spinal column.

There are three components of the mixed energy which leaps across from the sex organ complex to the muladhara chakra. Please note that the sex organ chakra is not the sex chakra on the spine. The sex organ chakra is located at the genital region of the body. The three components of mixed energy are:

- fresh physical air / fresh subtle air

- polluted physical air / polluted subtle air
- gross hormones /subtle hormones

There is physical energy but our interest is the subtle body.

Fresh subtle air (prana) is ingested with each breath. This is compacted into the subtle lungs and goes into the subtle energy stream. It is transported through the nadi subtle channels.

Polluted subtle air (apana) is in the system. Some of it is expelled through the subtle lungs but some remains fused in the subtle body. When the fresh subtle energy enters the blood stream, it makes contact with some of the polluted energy. It mixes with this to form a semi-pure condition. This mix moves down under the pressure of more and more infusion and locks.

Subtle hormone (reta/rajas) is in the system as a matter of course. Its primary concern is to set the stage for generating new baby forms. However it produces pleasure and infatuation when it is agitated. We become attached to pleasure. This energy is the main absorber of nutrients which enter the body. It serves to slow down the liberation quest of the core-self. To counteract the negative influence of this hormonal force, a yogi has to mix it with the fresh and polluted subtle energy and hurl the mixture into the kundalini lifeforce.

As sailors on ship harpoon a powerful whale and cause the creature to dive into the deep, so a yogi hurls the mixed charged force into the kundalini at the base chakra. This causes it to be aroused. At first the kundalini tries to escape by going downwards through a microscopic hole at the base chakra but since the yogi applied the anus lock, the kundalini finds that it cannot do so. It then tries to go through the sex chakra on the central spine but since the yogi applied the perineum lock, kundalini finds that exit to be blocked.

If it still has enough moving impetus, it will try to go through the navel chakra but since the yogi applied the abdomen lock, kundalini realizes that exit to be blocked. It then tries to go upwards. If it has enough impetus, it tries to go through the neck in a haphazard way so that it can spray itself through the head randomly but since the yogi applied the chin lock, it is forced to go through the central spinal passage only.

If it still has impetus, it finds that it enters the head in an organized way but as soon as it does so, it tries to spread haphazardly but since the yogi was vigilant and had developed the mind lock, where the third eye is focused on and the energy in the head is centralized on the core-self, the kundalini finds that it has to be routed from the sushumna central passage to the sense of identity which surrounds the core-self and then to the third eye chakra and the brahmarandra crown chakra.

In some students kundalini will endeavor to burst out through the heart/lung chakra and through the throat chakra. To prevent it from exiting through those subtle orifices the chest lock and the chin lock should be applied. The chest lock is a shoulder pull-down action with tensing of the intercostal muscles. The chin lock is the pulling back of the chin against the throat with mental focus of a spiked energy going upwards.

Students who are compassion-saturated may have difficulty applying the chest lock but it can be accomplished by knowing that the burst of kundalini into the head would include the compassionate energies but at a higher octave where it would be more insightful because of the enlightenment energy on the higher plane.

Application

Rapid breath-infusion using forceful exhales or forceful inhales or forceful dual exhales and inhales is the express method of breath-infusion. It requires a higher percentage of concentration, more efficient application of locks and tight directive force over the energy, to make it conform to the desire of the yogi.

What is this desire?

Curbing the kundalini lifeforce so that the psyche is not forced to obey its counterproductive survival impulsions.

The plan of the kundalini is this:

- *acquire a material body*
- *exploit the environment*
- *reproduce other material bodies*
- *acquire another material body from one of the reproduced forms*

Such a plan though practical in terms of material nature's inability to produce eternal forms, makes no sense ultimately because it is a circular go-nowhere plan.

Since kundalini survives in the interim phase between losing a body and acquiring a new one, it should investigate the possibility of remaining in the interim state perpetually. However kundalini is incapable of making this consideration. Therefore the core-self should act to restrict the influence of kundalini since it is incapable of being selective.

Verse 62

पुनर्विरेचयेत्तद्वत्पूरयेच्च पुनः पुनः ।
यथैव लोहकारेण भस्त्रा वेगेन चाल्यते।। ६२ ।।

punarvirecayettadvatpūrayecca punaḥ punaḥ I
yathaiva lohakāreṇa bhastrā vegena cālyate II 62 II

punar = punaḥ = again, virecayet – should exhale, tadvat – like, pūrayec = pūrayet = should inhale, ca – and, punaḥ punaḥ = repeatedly, yathaiva = yathā eva = as, lohakāreṇa – by the blacksmith, bhastrā – bellows, vegena – rapidly, cālyate – is pumped

Again, it should be exhaled and inhaled repeatedly as before, just as bellows are pumped rapidly by the blacksmith.

Analysis

Some yogis do a sequence of rapid inhales and exhales for a particular number of times or they time it and breathe for a certain number of minutes. Each student should make a decision on what to do and should be flexible if inspired to do it in a different way. When all is said and done, you should ask yourself if you got the desired result.

What is this desired effect?

It is that after doing breath-infusion one should sit to meditate immediately after and during the meditation one should notice that one achieved the pratyahar sensual energy withdrawal as a byproduct of the pranayama practice.

I advise the following:

Do as many breaths as it takes for the lungs to become non-absorbent. Cease breathing on an inhale. Apply the locks efficiently. Check in the psyche to see where the energy moved and accumulated.

How many breaths would it take for the lungs to become non-absorbent?

That depends on the absorbency rate of the lungs. In one student the lungs may become non-absorbent in ten breaths while in someone else it might in forty breaths.

As soon as the lung becomes non-absorbent, it makes no sense to continue breathing because the lungs will simply reject the air, which will be going in and out needlessly.

Absorbing the air is one factor which should be supported by efficient prompt distribution of the infused energy. As soon as the student suspends breathing on an inhale, he or she should focus on distribution of the accumulated energy. As soon as this energy is diffused away from the lungs and is absorbed by cells and tissues, the lungs will become absorbent again. Then a session of rapid breaths should begin again, followed by suspension and distribution.

The student should continue this repeatedly until he or she is confident that the entire psyche is saturated with the fresh energy which displaced the polluted air which was expelled through the lungs. This is physical and emotional as well. This moved blood through the physical system. It relocated emotions in the subtle body.

Application

A student should remember the purpose of the pranayama breath-infusion. The asana postures can vary during a session to target particular areas of the physical and subtle bodies. Each student should be vigilant and develop the practice with the aim of getting the entire subtle body cleared of pollution.

At first it is necessary to focus on arousing the kundalini into the subtle head. Once that becomes consistent the student should target hard-to-reach areas, extracting pollutions and infusing fresh air as the displacement. Eventually even the toes and fingers should be trained to release polluted air in exchange for fresh energy.

Verse 63

तथैव स्व–श्रीर–सथं चालयेत्पवनं धिया ।

यदा श्रमो भवेद्देहे तदा सूर्येण पूरयेत् ।। ६३ ।।

tathaiva sva–śarīra–sthaṁ cālayetpavanaṁ dhiyā ।
yadā śramo bhaveddehe tadā sūryeṇa pūrayet ।। 63 ।।

tathaiva = tathā eva = similarly, sva – own, śarīra – material body, sthaṁ – situated, cālayet – should infuse, pavanaṁ – vital air, dhiyā – with focused attention, yadā – when, śramo = śramaḥ = fatigue, bhaved = bhavet = is experienced, dehe – in the physical body, tadā – then, sūryeṇa – by sun–dominant right side, pūrayet – should inhale

Similarly, with focused attention, the vital air in one's material body should be infused. When fatigue is experienced, one should inhale into the physical body through the sun–dominant right side.

Analysis

If one does bhastrika on and on without checking for the absorption rate of the lungs, there will come a time when one feels fatigued. When this happens, then one should inhale through the sun-dominant right side and then suspend breathing while applying the chin lock, the anus lock, the perineum lock, the abdomen retraction lock and the shoulder/intercostal muscles lock. As soon as this is achieved which should be seconds after that last inhale, one should compresses everything downwards mentally and emotionally, arresting the mento-emotional energy and compressing it inwards upon itself. One should not allow the energy to escape but should keep compressing it inwards on itself until it implodes.

If the student does this inefficiently, the energy will escape the mental grip and will travel in one direction or the other. If it does so the student should begin the rapid breath-infusion again but with the eyes closed and the infused energy going into the moving mass of compressed force. This will give the student the ability to emotionally capture the energy and direct it.

Application

The procedure given in this verse is not for beginners but everyone should note this so that when one reaches a more proficient state, one can adopt this. In this system of rapid breath-infusion, the adept lost interest in arousing kundalini. But this is long after effectively raising kundalini on a daily basis. Those who successfully raise kundalini daily, and who tamed it to a degree; those whose sushumna central passage remains free of dense astral force, should shift to this advanced practice.

Here there is concern with infusing the vital air on the spot wherever it may be in the psyche. This is for targeting the cell kundalini, which is a micro-energy which each cell has as its personal lifeforce. The ascetic infuses air into the subtle body. The air goes out on a march like soldiers who are instructed to comb through every inch of the countryside. As soon as the infused energy senses vital energy in even the smallest of cells, it latches on to that energy and causes a small charge then and there. This continues on and on, until every cell in every part of the psyche is affected and yields a small accumulated charge.

Honestly speaking, in this current body, I was introduced to this procedure by Sri Lahiri Mahasaya in the astral world, where he wanted me to practice it so as to see what its effects would be on the psyche of a modern human being. This is a wonderful practice because it frees the ascetic from relying on the traditional kundalini which is housed at the base chakra. Such freedom is impeccable. Its value in the life of a yogi cannot be estimated.

Verse 64

यथोदरं भवेत्पूर्णमनिलेन तथा लघु ।

धारयेन्नासिकां मध्या–तर्जनीभ्यां विना दृढम् ।। ६४ ।।

yathodaraṁ bhavetpūrṇamanilena tathā laghu I
dhārayennāsikāṁ madhyā–tarjanībhyāṁ vinā dṛḍham II 64 II

yathodaraṁ = yathā (as) + udaram (abdomen, lungs), bhavet – should be, pūrṇam – entirely filled, anilena – with air, tathā – so, laghu – quickly, dhārayen = dhārayet = should close while focusing internally, nāsikāṁ – nostrils, madhyā–tarjanībhyāṁ = middle and index fingers, vinā – without, dṛḍham – firmly

According to the routine, the entire lungs should be rapidly filled with air. Without using the middle and index fingers, one should firmly close the nostrils while focusing internally.

Analysis

Normal breathing which occurs involuntarily does not include the bottom of the lungs. Even labored breathing which is due to fatigue does not include the entire lung. Rapid breathing after running does not include the bottom of the lung. In this practice however after doing rapid breath-infusion, the student on the last inhale, should deliberately draw air in until the entire lung is expanded with air. The student should attentively pull air down to the bottom of the lung. He or she should keep pulling the air until the entire lung space is filled. This will cause the abdomen to be extended.

While focusing internally, one should close the nostrils using the thumb and third fingers.

Application

As soon as a set of rapid breaths are suspended the student should inhale or exhale and then apply the locks. Thereafter there should be the checking to see how the energy accumulated, where it is located and what would be the best way to deal with it.

Should it be compressed further?

Should it be compressed into itself to make it smaller and more potent?

Should more air be compressed into it to intensify it and cause it to implode?

Should it be moved from its location to some other part of the psyche?

Should it be pushed into the kundalini lifeforce at the muladhara base chakra?

Verse 65

विधिवत्कुम्भकं कृत्वा रेचयेदिडयानिलम्।

वात–पित्त–शलेष्म–हरं श्रीराग्नि–विवर्धनम् ।। ६५ ।।

vidhivatkumbhakaṁ kṛtvā recayediḍayānilam I
vāta–pitta–śleṣma–haraṁ śarīrāgni–vivardhanam II 65 II

vidhivat – consistently, kumbhakaṁ – breath retention with physio–psychic compression and internal focus on energy distribution, kṝtvā – did, recayed = recayet = should exhale, iḍayā – through the left subtle channel, anilam – air, vāta – cellular air, pitta – bile, śleṣma – mucus, haraṁ – elimination, śarīrāgni = śarīra (physical body) + agni (digestive heat), vivardhanam – increase

Consistently doing breath retention with physio–psychic compression and internal focus on energy distribution, he should exhale through the left subtle channel. That causes elimination of irregular cellular air, bile and mucus. It produces an increase of digestive heat.

Analysis

As soon as the energy is distributed, the yogi should exhale or inhale and continue the practice. If the yogi stopped with an inhale and then compressed the system with the locks, then when the accumulated air is distributed, the yogi should exhale and begin a session of rapid breath-infusion again.

If the yogi stopped on an exhale and applied the compression locks, then as soon as the accumulated air is distributed, the yogi should inhale and begin a session of rapid breathing again or he may inhale while keeping the compression locks, and then exhale, then inhale again, then exhale, then suspend breathing by tightly applying the locks. Soon after when the yogi senses that every bit of the infused air is distributed, he should relax the breathing and sit to meditate, or continue the rapid breathing as intended.

Application

There are many hard-to-reach places in the psyche. For instance, there is the area behind the knee. There is the knee cap. There are the toes and fingers. There is the area on either side of the neck. There is the lower jaw. There are the buttocks. How can a yogi be sure to reach these areas for an energy exchange, so that the heavy astral energy is replaced by fresh subtle force?

At some point one has to understand that even if there is light in the head of the subtle body, if the rest of that form has heavy astral energy, this will cause one to be drawn to a lower astral domain hereafter. The entire subtle form should be upgraded, not just the head of it.

Suppose a brilliant scientist is crippled in every part below the neck, with his brain in working order, is that satisfactory? The entire system should be in working order with all parts functioning to their capacity. Health should pervade. A yogi must use the entire subtle body not just the head of it. In the hereafter, if one does not instantly assume a divine body at death of the physical form, one will resume the astral form with every defect within it. Thus it makes sense to consider the whole subtle body when doing yoga kriyas.

Sri Lahiri Baba asked me to stress this point to the kriya students. They should not neglect the subtle body below the neck. The light should shine evenly throughout the psyche. Pranayama breath-infusion is a sure way of achieving this.

Verse 66

कुण्डली बोधकं क्षिप्रं पवनं सुखदं हितम् ।

बरह्म–नाडी–मुखे संस्थ–कफाद्य–अर्गल–नाशनम् ।। ६६ ।।

kuṇḍalī bodhakaṁ kṣipraṁ pavanaṁ sukhadaṁ hitam I
brahma–nāḍī–mukhe saṁstha–kaphādy–argala–nāśanam I I 66 I I

kuṇḍalī – kuṇḍalinī, bodhakaṁ – perceptively arouses, kṣipraṁ – quickly, pavanaṁ – air infusion, sukhadaṁ –that which yields happiness, hitam – beneficial, brahma–nāḍī = center of the sushumna nadi central spinal passage, mukhe – at the opening, saṁstha – lying, kaphādy = kapha (mucus) + ādi (and the like), argali – psychic pollution, nāśanam – removal

Quickly, the kundalini is perceptively aroused by the air infusion, which yields happiness and is beneficial. It causes the removal of mucus and the psychic pollution which is at the opening of the central sushumna nadi central spinal passage.

Analysis

Breath-infusion gives this minimum benefit which is encouraging to the student yogi. If one is sincere and practices consistently day after day, it can do much more in time. The method of clearing the sushumna nadi of heavy astral energy is to do breath-infusion and pilot the infused energy to the kundalini psychic lifeforce at muladhara base chakra. When kundalini is sufficiently motivated by the infused energy, it moves up the spine in a jiffy. As it transits it ignites the heavy astral energy, forming a subtle fire which clears the sushumna passage by burning away the heavy astral force.

One practice session is not enough. One has to practice daily for years before the sushumna central spinal passage remains open permanently. Some students achieve this in a few years; some may take decades. Each has to work with his or her psyche and do the needful austerities to achieve sushumna nadi permanent clearance. There must also be lifestyle changes because it is the social habits and the internal disarray of the psychic adjuncts which causes the clouding or complete blockage of the sushumna central passage.

Once the ascetic cleared the sushumna, a larger task becomes evident which is that all of the subtle body below the neck should be full of light astral energy. No part of the subtle body should have heavy astral force.

Application

Some people are hopeful that kundalini will rise of its own accord or that it may rise because of an accident where the spine or brain is affected and results in a blatant kundalini experience. Some others think that by prayer or meditation kundalini may be aroused. Others think that if they visualize the kundalini will be aroused. Some feel that by taking drugs the kundalini will be aroused. Some say that by chanting special mantras the kundalini will be aroused. Some feel that by dancing the kundalini will be aroused. Some think that by making love the kundalini will be aroused. Some feel that by getting massages the kundalini will be aroused. Some feel that by listening or playing music the kundalini will be aroused. Some feel that by eating a certain diet the kundalini will be aroused. Some feel that by doing strenuous exercises or by lifting heavy objects the kundalini will be aroused. Some feel that by reclining or sleeping the kundalini will be aroused.

However for the purpose of kundalini yoga, pranayama breath-infusion is the sure way to raise kundalini on a daily basis. Kundalini may be aroused by breath-infusion; then controlled by compressions and mento-emotional guidance within the psyche.

The first consideration is that the kundalini is aroused when the body becomes awake after sleep. The second realization is that for sexual expression the kundalini must be aroused. Sex pleasure is a mixture of reproductive hormones, breath energy and kundalini. This same mixture is manipulated for kundalini's arousal in yoga practice, except that the breath energy is highly charged with fresh air and is compressed in the system when it is mixed with the hormone energy.

In sex experience the kundalini is attracted to the sex organ chakra where the reproductive hormones are mixed with the breath energy in the blood stream. Then the kundalini moves from the muladhara base chakra to the sex organ chakra (not the sex chakra on the spine).

In kundalini yoga experience, the mix of hormone energy with the infused fresh air breath energy becomes attracted to kundalini. It goes to the kundalini at the base chakra. It leaves the sex organ chakra and goes to the base chakra where it strikes kundalini, which then moves up the spine.

The difference is that instead of being expressed through the genitals as in sex experience, in kundalini yoga, the kundalini is expressed through the spine into the brain. It has a bliss aspect all the same. It has a transcendental pleasure experience in it.

Verse 67

सम्यग्गात्रसमुद्भूतग्रन्थित्रयविभेदकम्।

विशेषेणैव कर्तव्यं भस्त्राख्यं कुम्भकं त्विदम्॥६७॥

samyaggātra–samudbhūta–granthi–traya–vibhedakam ।
viśeṣeṇaiva kartavyaṁ bhastrākhyaṁ kumbhakaṁ tvidam ।। 67 ।।

samyag = samyak = proficiently, gātra – in the body, samudbhūta – that is, granthi – congestion of subtle energy, traya – three, vibhedakam – it penetrates, viśeṣeṇaiva = viśeṣeṇa eva = specifically, kartavyaṁ, having done, bhastrākhyaṁ – known as bhastrika breath-infusion, kumbhakaṁ – breath retention with physio–psychic compression and internal focus on energy distribution, tv = tu = but, idam – this

When done proficiently, it specifically penetrates the three congestions of subtle energy. It is known as bhastrika breath-infusion or breath-retention with physio–psychic compression and internal focus on energy distribution.

Analysis

Congestions of subtle energy are littered in every part of the subtle body, but the three primary ones are the brahma granthi at the muladhara base chakra, the vishnu granthi at the lung-heart chakra plexus on the spine and the rudra granthi at the third eye between the eyebrows. These are penetrated by doing bhastrika breath-infusion because that method is forceful enough to blast away, ignite and consume the pollutions.

Depending on the strength of the charge, a yogi may open the base chakra congestion alone. But if the charge is more powerful, it will proceed up the spine and open the lung-heart chakra plexus. If it is still more powerful, it will continue and blast away the dense astral energy at the third eye brow chakra.

When struck by the infused breath energy, kundalini will make an effort to move. This is comparable to a sleeping man who is kicked by someone. Depending on the force of the kick, the man may awaken partially or fully. If it is a slight kick, the man might turn to one side and continue sleeping without ever awakening. If however it is a very forceful kick, then he might awaken, stand up and try to defend himself.

Kundalini will nudge slightly if it is a small charge of breath-infused energy. If the charge is sufficient, kundalini will become fully aroused and will make an effort to move. If the yogi applied the chin lock, anus lock, perineum and abdomen locks, then kundalini will be forced to go up the spine but it might ascend only as far as the sex chakra. Then it will immediately subside back to the base chakra without going a step further.

To make it proceed further, the yogi has to push a strong charge behind it so that it feels that it has no choice but to move up because of the force of the charge which pushes it. Provided the charge is really powerful, kundalini will be discouraged from descending and will ascend. As it rises it will clear away any dense astral energy, any pollutants, until it passed through the neck and enters the head of the subtle body, where it will break out and try to escape from the grip of the yogi.

Students, who are not proficient with the mind lock, will lose track of kundalini once it passes through the neck into the head. This means that they will lose control of the material body when this happens.

The mind lock is the practice of focusing on the brow chakra, the third eye and also practicing core-self centering in meditation for some years. This gives the yogi the ability to lock down the kundalini and guide it when it enters the head in an aroused condition.

Those who are not proficient at the mind lock will experience a space-out, a stun-out, a black-out, a grey-out, a white-out or a gold-out* when kundalini rises into the head. If the physical body was standing when this happened, it may fall to the ground. If it was sitting it may slump over. This may last from a few seconds to say about twenty (20) seconds for the most. Then the person will resume consciousness on this material side of existence with or without memory of the incidence.

> * *The experience of a **space-out** occurs when kundalini ascends through the spine, fizzes out at the top of the neck and just sprinkles a little of its energy into the brain. This results in a spaced out feeling as if the person lost control of their objective observing posture in the mind. The person may see a little bit of diffused light or have no sight but feel as if he or she was in a large spacious chamber. The person loses grip on memories and has no concept of identity or persona. There is a conversion from being a social unit to be just a space which has no focus. This will last for a few moments or for longer and then the person gradually comes to his or her senses and resumes the normal personality but with a feeling of having temporarily lost the self in the process.*

If the physical body was standing when this happened, it will usually fall to the ground. If it sat it may lean to one side or crumple over. Then when the person resumes objectivity, he or she will realize the changed posture.

The experience of a **stun-out** *occurs when kundalini ascends through the spine and burst into the brain into white-gold light, and remains there at the top of the neck in the lower head for some moments or minutes and then quickly descends back to its base at the muladhara end-of-spine chakra. When this happens the physical body may not fall to the ground but may remain in one position or will keep moving into an intended position in slow motion. The yogi will feel as if he was stunned where there is no sensual perception, and he just existed with stationary awareness of being just there.*

The experience of a **black-out** *occurs when kundalini ascends through the spine while carrying heavy astral energy which it picked up as it ascended the central spinal passage. It may then burst into the brain into total psychic darkness, giving the person absolutely no insight consciousness. It may hit the buddhi intellect orb which it will surround in psychic darkness with the result that the person will lose objective consciousness. The person's physical body will fall to the ground or loop over or tilt to the side. This may last for moments, or for a few minutes, and then the person will resume objectivity with the understanding that time stood still and his existence was suspended for the time.*

The experience of a **grey-out** *occurs when kundalini ascends through the spine while carrying clouds of heavy astral energy which was interspaced with light astral force. As soon as this energy is released into the brain, it will surround the buddhi intellect orb and cause it to be uncertain and to lack clarity. The person will feel as if he is neither here nor there, as if he is conscious and unconscious at the same time. He will be riddled with uncertainty as to there being any type of objective existence. If the body was standing when this occurred, it will immediately fall to the ground.*

The experience of a **white-out** *occurs when kundalini ascends through the spine while carrying medium weight astral energy which it picked up as it ascended the central spinal passage. It may then burst into the brain into a white energy cloud which is opaque and which does not allow any objective perception, giving the person slight insight consciousness. It may hit the buddhi intellect orb which it will surround in an astral cloud of energy with the result that the person will retain some degree of objective consciousness but not enough for clarity. The person's physical body may fall to the ground or fold over or tilt to the side. This may last for moments or for a few minutes. Then the person will resume objectivity with the understanding that time stood still and his existence was suspended for the time.*

The experience of a **gold-out** *occurs when kundalini ascends through the spine while carrying light-weight astral energy which it produced by a rapid burning explosion through the spine. It will then burst into the brain into a gold or white-gold energy which is transparent and which gives insight consciousness. It will hit the buddhi intellect orb which it will* *penetrate with the result that the person will retain some degree of objective consciousness with partial or full clarity. The person's physical body may fall to the ground or loop over or tilt to the side. This may last for moments or for a few minutes and then the person will resume objectivity with the understanding that time stood still and his existence was reinforced or revealed on the spiritual plane. The gold-out has a spiritual bliss aspect to it which is lust free and transcendental.*

Application

In the average human being the base chakra has dense astral energy which is crusted around the kundalini. This cluster of energy is called the brahma granthi dense pollution. It serves the purpose to generate a heat at the base chakra which is used to run evacuation and final escape from a material body. Kundalini is similar to radioactive material in a natural alloy of mineral rock in the earth. The radioactive material may not be seen but it can be felt through its heating effects in the mineral.

At the time of death of the body, all body heat comes to an end but it does so gradually. At the base chakra the heat remains for a time and then when this heat is extinguished it is understood that the body is dead. Once the kundalini leaves the base chakra for good, no amount of medical assistance or sympathy can enliven the body.

The crusted dense energy at the muladhara base chakra is counterproductive for the yogi but that condition is useful for those who are hopeful for material existence. Using breath-infusion practice, a yogi may accumulate a charge of fresh air energy which is mixed with hormone force. This mixture develops a high charge and becomes polarized so that it is attracted to the kundalini. When it fuses into the kundalini that energy becomes aroused and moves in whatever direction it finds to be easy.

The shift of the accumulated charge into fusion with the kundalini causes a small explosion of energy which burns all or some of the crusted dense energy which was around the kundalini. The blast force of this explosion caused the kundalini to go upward through the sushumna nadi but it may go elsewhere if the yogi did not apply the chin lock, anus lock, perineum lock and abdomen lock.

When kundalini surges upwards it does so at the speed of light. It may or may not penetrate the rudra granthi dense astral energy at the lung-heart chakra complex. If it is not powerful enough to penetrate that, it will subside and return to the base chakra henceforth.

If kundalini penetrates the lung-heart chakra complex and is pushed by a strong enough charge, it will penetrate the neck and enter the head. Once it enters the head, it becomes uncontrollable except for advanced students who apply the mind lock.

In the spine, physical locks help to keep kundalini confined in the sushumna nadi central channel, but in the head, there is no such physical conduit for compression and restricting kundalini. In the head the only means of control is through psychological channeling. This is why most students lose control of the body when and if kundalini enters the head. Mastery of the mind lock is required but that is a complex practice which takes some months if not years to master.

Verse 68

अथ भ्रामरी

वेगाद्घोषं पूरकं भृङ्ग–नादं

भृङ्गी–नादं रेचकं मन्द–मन्दम् ।

योगीन्द्राणमेवमभ्यास–योगा–

च्चित्ते जाता काचिदानन्द –लीला ।। ६८ ।।

atha bhrāmarī
vegādgoṣaṁ pūrakaṁ bhṝnga–nādaṁ
bhṝngī–nādaṁ recakaṁ manda–mandam ।
yogīndrāṇamevamabhyāsa–yogāc
citte jātā kācidānanda–līlā ।। 68 ।।

atha – now to be described, bhrāmarī – bee, vegād = vegāt = with rapidity, goṣaṁ – sound, pūrakaṁ – inhalation, bhṝnga – drone bee, nādaṁ – sound, bhṝngī – female black bee, nādaṁ – subtle sound, recakaṁ – exhalation, manda–mandam = slowly, yogīndrāṇam = king of the yogis, evam – thus, abhyāsa – practice, yogāc = yogāt = due to yoga, citte – in the mento–emotional energy, jātā – manifests, kācid = kācit = any, ānanda – transcendental happiness, līlā – spontaneously happening

Now to be described is the bee-like sound infusion:

With rapid inhalation there is the sound like a drone bee, with exhalation slowly there is the sound like a female bee. Thus due to this yoga practice, the king of the yogis experiences transcendental happiness and spontaneous supernatural happenings in the mento–emotional energy.

Analysis

The bee-like sound infusion is done with a widened nostril strong-pull inhale which is done rapidly and which is pulled with great force until the lungs are filled with fresh air. As the yogi draws this breath which sounds like the vibration of a flying drone bee, his nostrils will widen. There will be a drag force through the sinuses and esophagus. The yogi should close his eyes and focus within to feel as if there is one large lung chamber with the sides of it feeling as compacted tissue and the middle of it having a passage where the air flutters down into a blank chamber.

As the air enters, it will take more and more air, which will seek to disappear in a blank chamber underneath. There will be a lifting of the chest. There will be a pressure from underneath as if the blank chamber filled and became a hard ball which presses upwards and lifts the chest to its maximum rise. Then the inhale will stop.

The yogi should apply the chin lock, anus lock, perineum lock, and abdomen lock. Then he should focus internally to compress everything and check the distribution of that infused breath.

When the system distributed the energy the yogi should begin the exhale which should be done slowly in contrast to the rapid forceful inhale. During the exhale the yogi will feel a passage where the air flows up in a constant stream from the blank area below. Even though there are two lungs the yogi will feel one passage in the central chest. He should not allow the air to come out rapidly or forcefully. It should come out at the slowest rate and very gently. While the air is exhaled in this way, a yogi should note what happens to the energy which is wrapped around the chest area.

Application

This bee-like sound infusion produces a balanced charge of the breath energy which then mixes with hormone energy and strikes kundalini in a mild way. At first kundalini does not become excited enough to leave muladhara base chakra. However if this practice is continued for a time, the charge gradually accumulates into a powerful enough motivator for kundalini which moves up the spine gracefully and not as rapidly as it would when doing the kapalabhati-bhastrika rapid infusion.

Kundalini will rise slowly like the surface of a pot of milk which rises gradually because it is on a small fire which is not enough to cause the milk to boil rapidly. While in rapid infusion, kundalini is struck suddenly and moves rapidly at the speed of light, in the bee-like sounding infusion, kundalini rises gradually over time with one doing the practice for an hour or more. It slowly goes up but only if there is no slackening of the practice. The yogi must do one round after the other without interval and with full concentration. If there is slackening then kundalini will fall down partially or fall all the way to muladhara chakra. The yogi will either abandon the session or begin it again. Patience is the key to this pranayama.

Verse 69

अथ मूर्च्छा

पूरकान्ते गाढतरं बद्ध्वा जालन्धरं शनैः ।

रेचयेन्मूर्च्छनाख्येयं मनो–मूर्च्छा सुख–प्रदा ।। ६९ ।।

atha mūrcchā
pūrakānte gāḍhataraṁ baddhvā jālandharaṁ śanaiḥ ।
recayenmūrcchākhyeyaṁ mano–mūrcchā sukha–pradā ।। 69 ।।

atha – now to describe, mūrcchā – mūrcchā technique, pūrakānte = pūraka (inhalation) + ante (at the end), gāḍhataraṁ – more compression, baddhvā – adopting, jālandharaṁ – tightly pulling the lower jaw back against the throat, śanaiḥ – gradually, recayen = recayet = should exhale, mūrcchākhyeyaṁ = mūrcchā (mūrcchā technique) + ākhyā (is termed) + iyaṁ (this), mano = manaḥ = mind, mūrcchā – lapse in objectivity while transiting to other dimensions, sukha = happiness, pradā – yields

Now, to describe the murccha fainting slow-inhale with long retention infusion:

At the end of inhalation, while adopting more compression and tightly pulling the lower jaw back against the throat, the yogi should exhale gradually. This is termed the murccha fainting slow-inhale with long retention infusion which yields happiness and causes lapses of objectivity while transiting to other dimensions.

Analysis

This is the special pranayama for exploring the edges of unconsciousness, both the introductory and concluding edges. The introductory one is when a person's observer awareness begins to lose grasp on objective consciousness and then loses it altogether. The concluding edge is when from not being aware; a person gradually or rapidly becomes objectively aware.

The development of these states is studied by some yogis who want to master unconsciousness. Some sorcerers who desire this have criminal intentions. They want to exert psychological control over other selves.

It may be necessary for a yogi to study the transit from objective awareness to unconsciousness or the one from unconsciousness to objective awareness. We endure these states daily before and after the sleeping phase of the body, and yet we are very unfamiliar with it because psychic nature is so designed that it confiscates our objectivity so that we cannot make the observations. By practicing the murccha fainting slow-inhale with long retention a yogi can retain a residual self-awareness which is so small that it can bypass the unconscious phase and observe what happens on the threshold of unconsciousness both when approaching or when disengaging from it.

Application

When doing this murccha fainting procedure, a yogi can test his limit of endurance to find out what would happen when the universe crashes on the subtle plane, when all beings are vanquished by the sleep of Brahma, the local creator-god.

Verse 70

अथ पलाविनी

अन्तः प्रवर्तितोदार–मारुतापूरितोदरः ।

पयस्यगाधे।अपि सुखात्प्लवते पद्म–पत्रवत् ।। ७० ।।

atha plāvinī
antaḥ pravartitodāra–mārutāpūritodaraḥ ।
payasyagādhe।api sukhātplavate padma–patravat ।। 70 ।।

atha – now to discuss, plāvinī – flotation technique, antaḥ – inside the body, pravartitodāra = pravartita (introduce) + udāra (ample), mārutāpūritodaraḥ = māruta (air) + āpūrita (full) + udaraḥ (abdomen), payasy = payasyi = water, agādhe – in deep, api – also, sukhāt – easy, plavate – floats, padma – lotus plant, patravat – like a leaf

Now to discuss the floatation technique:

Putting an ample amount of air filling inside the body, and making the abdomen filled as well, one can, in deep water, float easily like a lotus leaf.

Analysis

This practice was used by yogis who wanted to float across rivers or streams and also by yogis who wanted to submerge their bodies in rivers for a time and then float up at their will. Some human bodies are capable of holding more air in the lungs than other human forms. Some can take air easily into the stomach. Such air is not absorbed by the body, as would air which is ingested into the lungs. The air in the stomach would provide floatation effects for the body of the yogi.

Application

These practices form part of kriya yoga only in so far as they are serviceable and not when they are used for display to the public or to fascinate others. Some yogis used to float across streams at their convenience but usually they did this when no one was there to witness it. A yogi who displays special abilities may get a backlash in the form of censure or in the form of having to satisfy the needs of others, who ask the yogi to use the skill on their behalf, thus distracting him from the objective of yoga.

Verse 71

प्राणायामस्त्रिधा परोक्तो रेच–पूरक–कुम्भकैः ।

सहितः केवलश्चेति कुम्भको द्विविधो मतः ।। ७१ ।।

prāṇāyāmastridhā prokto reca–pūraka–kumbhakaiḥ |
sahitaḥ kevalaśceti kumbhako dvividho mataḥ || 71 ||

prāṇāyāmas – breath-infusion, tridhā – three kinds, prokto = proktaḥ = said, reca – exhalation, pūraka – inhalation, kumbhakaiḥ – breathing suspension with physio–psychic compression and internal focus on energy distribution, sahitaḥ – willful, kevalaś = kevalaḥ = spontaneous, ceti – and thus, kumbhako = kumbhakaḥ = breath cessation with physio–psychic compression and internal focus on energy distribution, dvividho = dvividhaḥ = two types, mataḥ – categorized as

There are said to be three kinds of pranayama breath-infusion actions, namely exhalation, inhalation and breathing suspension with physio–psychic compression and internal focus on energy distribution. There is willful and spontaneous breath cessation, which are the only two types categorized.

Analysis

Breath-infusion is a tri-part system of exhalation, inhalation and breath suspension but the suspension may be applied after an inhale or exhale. The suspension period is the time for checking the distribution of the inhaled energy. If there is a series of rapid inhales followed by exhales, there will be an accumulation of breath-energy in the blood stream. The body will be in anxiety about the distribution of this accumulated force, so that as soon as the yogi suspends the breathing, the body will take steps to scatter the accumulated energy here and there in the physical and subtle bodies.

When there is suspension after an inhale, there is maximum compression from the lungs into the blood stream. When there is suspension during an inhale that has the maximum compression from the blood stream into the lungs. Yogis study these effects to determine the advantage in each.

Application

Willful suspension of breath occurs when the yogi deliberately wills the lungs to cease the breathing rhythm. This is unnatural but it is done by the yogi as he practices as inspired or advised. For many years, a student may engage in this willful suspension during breath-infusion practice. If done with the proper guidance, the student will make progress. A time will come when he or she finds that the body engages in a spontaneous suspension. This is the independent type which is treasured by yogis.

The independent suspension occurs when the lifeforce feels that it has sufficient energy. It loses its sense of anxiety and relaxes or it focuses on distributing excess breath energy which was infused into the psyche.

When doing bhastrika/kapalabhati breath-infusion if there is a surcharge of breath-energy, then when the student suspends the breathing either after an inhale or exhale, he or she will find that the system loses its anxiety about procuring air. It will have no concern with breathing out polluted gases. It will instead be absorbed in distributing the accumulated energy which was compressed into the blood stream. This is a form of independent suspension. A yogi should take note of it.

Eventually during meditation, a yogi will find that the breathing becomes suspended or its frequency is drastically reduced. This results in partial or total absence of thoughts and images during meditation.

Verse 72

यावत्केवल–सिद्धिः सयात्सहितं तावदभ्यसेत ।

रेचकं पूरकं मुक्त्वा सुखं यद्वायु–धारणम् ।। ७२ ।।

yāvatkevala–siddhiḥ syātsahitaṁ tāvadabhyaset |
recakaṁ pūrakaṁ muktvā sukhaṁ yadvāyu–dhāraṇam || 72 ||

yāvat = until, kevala – spontaneous, siddhiḥ – perfectional skill, syāt – there is, sahitaṁ – dependent, tāvad = tāvat = so as, abhyaset – should practice, recakaṁ – exhalation, pūrakaṁ – inhalation, muktvā – being freed from, sukhaṁ – easy, yad – that, vāyu – lifeforce, dhāraṇam – mental and emotional focus

Until there is the perfection of the spontaneous breath suspension, one should continue with the willful type. Being freed from having to inhale and exhale, the yogi will easily maintain mental and emotional focus on the lifeforce.

Analysis

It is the life-force which is freed of the task of breathing not the core-self. Breathing occurs for the most part involuntarily with very little willpower contribution. On occasion but not frequently we engage in willful breathing but that is not the mainstay.

When the lifeforce is relieved of its breathing duties, the core-self gets an ease because it does not lose as much energy for bodily maintenance. The core-self can observe the lifeforce in details if that force ceases the survival operations. When the kundalini lifeforce is engaged in exploiting the environment, its movements are bewildering to the core-self which fails to fathom its activities.

Slowing down the lifeforce, reducing its duties, results in insight consciousness, so that the core-self can understand its part in the maintenance of the psyche.

Application

Freedom from having to inhale and exhale is a benefit mainly of the lifeforce not of the core-self but the self must commit to a practice which will allow the lifeforce this advantage. The method is breath-infusion.

If the polluted gases are extracted from the subtle body, and if there is an excess of fresh astral energy stored in the psyche, then the spontaneous suspension of breathing will occur.

Pranayama breath-infusion is worthwhile if its proficiency results in the accomplishment of sensual energy withdrawal, where the senses are no longer interested in pursuing the physical objects or their memory impressions.

Verse 73

प्राणायामो।अयमित्युक्तः स वै केवल–कुम्भकः ।
कुम्भके केवले सिद्धे रेच–पूरक–वर्जिते ।। ७३ ।।

prāṇāyāmo।ayamityuktaḥ sa vai kevala–kumbhakaḥ ।
kumbhake kevale siddhe reca–pūraka–varjite ।। 73 ।।

prāṇāyāmo = prāṇāyāmaḥ = breath-infusion practice, ayam – this, ity = iti = thus, uktaḥ – said, sa – that, vai – certainly, kevala – spontaneous, kumbhakaḥ – breathing suspension, kumbhake – in breathing suspension, kevale – in spontaneity, siddhe – with spontaneous skill, reca – exhalation, pūraka – inhalation, varjite – without

Here is what was said about this breath-infusion practice: Spontaneous breath suspension is when the suspension of the breathing rhythm occurs as a spontaneous skill, without the person exhaling or inhaling.

Analysis

The spontaneous breath suspension happens involuntarily either as a result of doing a proficient breath-infusion practice or otherwise. One does not have to be doing breath-infusion for it to occur. However if one does the infusion, then it is more likely to occur, especially if one extracts the greater percentage of polluted gases from the body, and in turn infuses fresh astral energy into the form just before the meditation session.

Application

The sign of a proficient pranayama breath-infusion session is the achievement of the pratyahar sensual energy withdrawal fifth stage of yoga. If when the yogi sits to meditate immediately after breath-infusion, he finds that the senses internalized of their own accord without any effort on his part, then he knows that the breath-infusion session was somewhat thorough.

In time, the regular daily completion of a full pranayama session results in the establishment of spontaneous breath suspension during meditation. The advantage of

this is that the probability of reaching the chit akash sky of consciousness increases for that yogi.

Verse 74

न तस्य दुर्लभं किञ्चित्त्रिषु लोकेषु विद्यते ।

शक्तः केवल–कुम्भेन यथेष्टं वायु–धारणात् ।। ७४ ।।

na tasya durlabhaṁ kiṁcittriṣu lokeṣu vidyate ।
śaktaḥ kevala–kumbhena yatheṣṭaṁ vāyu–dhāraṇāt ।। 74 ।।

na – not, tasya – of his, durlabhaṁ – difficult, kiṁcit – anything, triṣu – in three, lokeṣu – perception environments, vidyate – there is, śaktaḥ – able to do, kevala – independent, kumbhena – by breath suspension with physio–psychic compression and internal focus on energy distribution, yatheṣṭaṁ = yatha (as) + iṣṭaṁ (desired), vāyu – lifeforce, dhāraṇāt – from mental and emotional focus

For someone who masters the spontaneous breath suspension with physio–psychic compression and internal focus on energy distribution by the method of mental and emotional focus on the lifeforce, nothing desired is difficult to achieve in the three perception environments.

Analysis

In the subtle and gross material world, the transition from one place to another is open or restricted according to the condition of the kundalini psychic lifeforce of the individual self. The power exhibited by each species is based on the status of the kundalini lifeforce. Much depends on its configuration and energization.

For physical transit, a physical body is required. For astral transit, a subtle body is needed. For internal-dimensional transit, inner upgrade of the energy in the subtle body is required.

The three perception environments are the objective, subconscious and unconscious planes. These are means of perception, rather than objects of perception. Kriya yoga concerns the means of perception more than it does the objects of perception. No matter what the object of perception is, if one does not secure the proper means of perception, the object will remain unknown.

When the core-self is linked to an objective means, then if that means is clarified, there will be clear views. If the self is linked to a subconscious means of perception, then it will be burdened with the task of moving that information into the objective means of perception. If otherwise the self is linked to the unconscious plane, then no matter what the object is, the self will not perceive it.

Application

We usually take the lifeforce for granted, except for when we are subjected to acute traumas like sexual pleasure climax and a painful wound in the body. In all respects the experiences we endure in the material body and also in the astral existence are rated through the kundalini psychic lifeforce and not directly by the core-self.

Kundalini yoga switches the relationship between the kundalini and the self so that instead of the self being focused on the pursuits of the kundalini; it becomes focused on the kundalini itself. Instead of being directed by the kundalini to perceive this or that subtle or gross object, the self becomes perceptive of the kundalini.

Grasping the kundalini for this examination is not easy. It is done through breath-infusion primarily. Since kundalini is a psychic phenomenon which has physical power, yoga achieves the control of it by physical and emotional means. These begin with the yama restraints, niyama approved behaviors and asana postures.

Postures give physical gripping of the kundalini by sensing, tensing and relaxing the tissues of the body. That is completed by pranayama breath-infusion which allows for emotional confinement of subtle energy through locks and internal mental focus. Over time this ability is retained even when the exercises are not being done by the yogi.

Verse 75

राज–योग–पदं चापि लभते नात्र संशयः ।

कुम्भकात्कुण्डली–बोधः कुण्डली–बोधतो भवेत् ।

अनर्गला सुषुम्णा च हठ– सिद्धिश्च जायते ।। ७५ ।।

rāja–yoga–padaṁ cāpi labhate nātra saṁśayaḥ I
kumbhakātkuṇḍalī–bodhaḥ kuṇḍalī–bodhato bhavet I
anargalā suṣumṇā ca haṭha–siddhiśca jāyate I I 75 I I

rāja–yoga–padaṁ = the accomplishment of remaining introverted while being externally occupied, cāpi – and also, labhate – obtain, nātra = not here, saṁśayaḥ – certainly, kumbhakāt – due to breath suspension with physio–psychic compression and internal focus on energy distribution, kuṇḍalī – kuṇḍalinī lifeforce, bodhaḥ – intellect psychic organ, kuṇḍalī – kuṇḍalinī lifeforce, bodhato = bodhataḥ = highest perceptive state of intellect psychic organ, bhavet – becomes, anargalā – without dense energy, suṣumṇā – sushumna central spinal passage, ca – and, haṭha – kundalini manipulation for psychic energy transformation, siddhiś = siddhiḥ = perfectional skill, ca – and, jāyate – manifesting

Without a doubt, that yogi achieves the accomplishment of remaining introverted while being externally occupied. Due to breath suspension with physio–psychic compression and internal focus on energy distribution, the kundalini lifeforce strikes the intellect psychic organ and through that infusement the highest perceptive state of the intellect psychic organ is experienced, the sushumna central spinal passage is cleared of dense energy and the kundalini manipulation for psychic energy transformation becomes a perfectional skill.

Analysis

Modern yogis become more and more disinclined from breath-infusion, or they do it superficially without the proper preparation and application. Its benefits however are legendary. It is more than a physical process, more than a routine practice, because it gives the accomplishment of the fifth (5th) stage of yoga which is pratyahar sensual energy withdrawal.

A proficient pranayama session before meditation gives the yogi a free and easy condition of introverted senses when he sits to meditate. This is not an ordinary achievement because otherwise the yogi will have to spend time quieting the mind and may fail to do so because of the lower energization level of the psyche.

The extra achievement of remaining introverted while being externally occupied is listed in this verse, as a bonus for any proficient pranayama yogi. This means that the yogi will be a master of karma yoga, the yoga application to cultural activities, so that necessary or imposed worldly association may superficially and not meaningfully impact the yogi.

Application

The very important buddhi intellect organ is mentioned directly for the first time by Swatmarama. This radiant organ in the head of the subtle body is the target of the kundalini psychic lifeforce. In sex experience this organ is pulled down into the region of the genitals and is subjected to powerful discharges of physio-psychic energy which are interpreted emotionally as sexual pleasure or ecstasy.

An advanced yogi is perceptively situated to rate it as an electric sensation but others view it as ecstatic pleasure. Being fascinated by it, being addicted and craving it, many persons, even yogis and yoginis cannot forget it and do not develop the need to forego it.

The bodhato intellect psychic organ is also known as buddhi. In the Bhagavad Gita in chapter two an application of yoga for controlling it is described. It is inclusive of kundalini yoga because the mere control of this radiant organ which is the head of the subtle body cannot be achieved by visualization and determination.

In sexual intercourse, the buddhi intellect organ is dragged down from the head of the subtle body into the lower groin area, pulled there by the attractive force of the kundalini. In kundalini yoga the kundalini is taken into the head of the subtle body to meet the buddhi organ.

In both experiences the two principles meet but in different locations and with different degrees of control of the core-self.

Verse 76

हठं विना राजयोगो राज–योगं विना हठः ।

न सिध्यति ततो युग्ममानिष्पत्तेः समभ्यसेत् ।। ७६ ।।

haṭhaṁ vinā rājayogo rāja–yogaṁ vinā haṭhaḥ ।
na sidhyati tato yugmamāniṣpatteḥ samabhyaset ।। 76 ।।

haṭhaṁ – kundalini manipulation for psychic energy transformation, vinā – without, rājayogo = rājayogaḥ = mystic process of remaining introverted while being externally occupied, rāja–yogaṁ = mystic process of remaining introverted while being externally occupied, vinā – without, haṭhaḥ – kundalini manipulation for psychic energy transformation, na – not, sidhyati – he is proficient in, tato = tataḥ = thus, yugmam – both, ā – until, niṣpatteḥ – highest accomplishment, samabhyaset – proficiently practiced

There is no proficiency in kundalini manipulation for psychic energy transformation without perfecting the mystic process of remaining introverted while being externally occupied. And remaining introverted while being externally occupied cannot be perfected without kundalini manipulation for psychic energy transformation. Thus the yogi should proficiently practice both processes until the highest accomplishment is attained.

Analysis

This means that valid raja yoga cannot take place without mastery of kundalini yoga. The converses hold true just the same. This declaration of Swatmarama makes most modern teachings of raja yoga and kundalini yoga to be farces.

The reason is simple. For remaining introverted while being externally occupied, or for being an expert in the application of karma yoga, one has to have the kundalini under control, after effectively reforming it. All the same for reform of the kundalini, for its total subjugation, one has to get the lifestyle under control. Lifestyle control is achieved by mastery of karma yoga.

What is karma yoga?

It is the application of the detachment and insight gained by yoga practice applied to social involvement, so that the yogi is impacted the least by mandatory duties in the social field, and can serve in it without having to give up the practice or be reduced in the insight gained in high-end meditation (samyama).

Application

What is the advice of Swatmarama Guruji?

It is this:

Practice both processes proficiently until the highest accomplishment is attained. That might take more than one month, more than one year or even more than one life. The yogi must be determined and patient to achieve this. Whatever impurities one has in the psyche, which cannot be removed overnight, which will take months, years or lives of disciplines to remove, should be patiently treated by effective methods which are learnt, discovered, or inspired.

Verse 77

कुम्भक–प्राण–रोधान्ते कुर्याच्चित्तं निराश्रयम् ।

एवमभ्यास–योगेन राज–योग–पदं व्रजेत्।। ७७ ।।

kumbhaka–prāṇa–rodhānte kuryāccittaṁ nirāśrayam ।
evamabhyāsa–yogena rāja–yoga–padaṁ vrajet ।। 77 ।।

kumbhaka – breath retention with physio–psychic compression and internal focus on energy distribution, prāṇa – vital energy, rodhānte = rodha (checking action) + ante (in the end), kuryāc = kuryāt = should make, cittaṁ – mento–emotional energy, nirāśrayam – non–reliant, evam – thus, abhyāsa – practice, yogena – by yoga, rāja–yoga–padaṁ = the accomplishment of remaining introverted while being externally occupied, vrajet – he achieves

At the end of the checking action of breath retention with physio–psychic compression and internal focus on energy distribution, the mento–emotional energy should be in a state of non–reliance. By this yoga practice, the yogi achieves the attainment of remaining introverted while being externally occupied.

Analysis

In meditation after thorough breath-infusion, the mento-emotional energy should be in a state of non-reliance on incidences from material existence and from the lower astral planes. Usually in meditation when it is done without first doing a thorough breath-infusion, the mind maintains its reliance on mundane incidences. It terrorizes the yogi because it effortlessly and continually displays a string of references to mundane affairs.

Patanjali Mahayogin gave the alert that for yoga to begin in earnest there must be a shutdown of the mento-emotional flickering in the mind. If one thinks that if one sits to meditate and observes thoughts in a detached mood or ignores such thoughts that one is meditating, then it means that one does not accept Patanjali's definition for meditation.

Everything done to bring thoughts and images to an end in the mind is preliminary to meditation and is not meditation or samyama as Patanjali defined it.

Breath-infusion is the sure way to develop an incident-free state of mind before meditation practice begins; otherwise one may experience that off and on, sporadically and at the whim of the mind, instead of definitely as is achieved by a thorough breath-infusion.

What is breath-infusion?

It is any method which causes the greater percentage of polluted gases to be extracted from the physical body, and which displaces those pollutions with fresh air. The actual target is the subtle body because as one does this physically, it is done on the subtle level simultaneously. The result is that the mind relinquishes reliance on incidences from material existence. The focus is lifted from the level where such reliance is the mind's mainstay.

Application

By repeatedly doing breath-infusion before meditation on the average at least twice per day, the yogi, gradually, over time, experiences that the states reached in meditation begin to carry over even during regular social activity. He notices that his mind no longer latches on to the mundane incidences which before was its main diet for the construction of memories. Now the mind diverts from the social incidences and does not retain a strong imprint of those affairs.

This frees the yogi from having a psyche which is bogged down with heavy subtle energy in the form of retained memories imprinted on the conscious and subconscious

levels of mind.

Verse 78

वपुः कृशत्वं वदने प्रसन्नता
नाद–सफुटत्वं नयने सुनिर्मले ।
अरोगता बिन्दु–जयो। अग्नि–दीपनं
नाडी–विशुद्धिर्हठ–सिद्धि–लक्षणम् ।। ७८ ।।

vapuḥ kṝśatvaṁ vadane prasannatā
nāda–sphuṭatvaṁ nayane sunirmale |
arogatā bindu–jayo|agni–dīpanaṁ
nāḍī–viśuddhirhaṭha–siddhi–lakṣaṇam || 78 ||

vapuḥ – physical body, kṝśatvaṁ – elegance, vadane – demeanor, prasannatā – cheerfulness, nāda – naad subtle sound resonance, sphuṭatvaṁ – manifestation, nayane –in the eyes, sunirmale – absence of flaws, arogatā – without disease, bindu – reproductive energy, jayo = jayaḥ = subjugation, agni – digestive heat, dīpanaṁ – trigger effect, nāḍī – nadi subtle veins and arteries, viśuddhir = viśuddhiḥ = clearance of dense energy, haṭha – kundalini manipulation for psychic energy transformation, siddhi – perfection, lakṣaṇam – indication

Elegance of body, cheerfulness in demeanor, manifestation of naad subtle sound resonance, with a total absence of flaws in the eyes, with no disease, with subjugation of the reproductive energy, with triggering effect of the digestive heat, with clearance of dense energy in the nadi subtle veins and arteries, one has the indication of perfection in the kundalini manipulation for psychic energy transformation.

Analysis

This is itemized:

- elegance of body
- cheerfulness in demeanor
- manifestation of naad subtle sound resonance
- total absence of flaws in the eyes
- no disease
- subjugation of the reproductive energy
- triggering effect of the digestive heat
- clearance of dense energy in the nadi subtle veins and arteries

Elegance of body is produced by pranayama practice in combination with the proper diet and a lifestyle which is free from social stress. This applies to both the physical and subtle bodies but more to the subtle one because the physical system must by law of nature develop disease. The last foothold of the physical body is its condition just before its death. Since death is inevitable it is futile to work for the salvation of the physical form. A yogi should shift interest to the subtle form and work for its elegant upkeep.

Cheerfulness in demeanor develops because of losing the foothold in the struggle for existence, being responsive to the dictates of providence and feeling that one does not have to survive physically. There should be no regrets about the uncertainty of mundane existence. A yogi should master astral projection to know factually what he will be after death. This will give direct confidence which validates scriptures and authorities.

The manifestation of naad subtle sound resonance is necessary. This is a vital part of meditation practice. It gives the yogi the foothold he needs to escape from the demands of the thought-image producing mechanism in the mind. This mechanism is the buddhi intellect orb which is an analytical psychic technology which every spirit is tagged with and must reform to become liberated.

There is one thing that the Supreme Being will not do for anyone, which is to reform that person's buddhi intellect organ. The Supreme Lord will instruct anyone in how to achieve that but the entity must himself or herself get that done.

The method?

Whatever works for the individual student is suitable. Even though it was indicated in one verse, naad sound was not mentioned in details in the Bhagavad Gita. However in the instructions to Uddhava concerning jnana yoga it was explained in some details. It should not be neglected by any serious yogi because it frees the ascetic from the need for chanting mantras either audibly or mentally. Naad is the supreme shelter. It cushions and cares deeply for the yogi. A very personal relationship is developed between naad resonance and the ascetic.

The total absence of flaws in the eyes comes about by a steady pranayama practice in combination with asana postures and the proper diet. The target of this is the subtle body. The physical eyes will deteriorate as a matter of necessity but the development of the subtle body will continue so long as the ascetic practices.

No disease occurs by a rigid pranayama practice with asana postures and proper diet but this applies to the subtle body. The gross form will develop disease over time. It will perish sooner or later.

The **subjugation of the reproductive energy** is done by raising kundalini where the reproductive hormones are trained to go to the kundalini at the base chakra rather than attract the kundalini to the sex organ chakra. It is absolutely necessary for the ascetic to train his energy in this way, or he will not be liberated from material existence ever. One cannot go to the siddhaloka heavenly places where great yogins reside if one does not reform the attitude of the reproductive energy.

The **triggering effect of the digestive heat** happens by asana posture and breath-infusion efficiency.

The clearance of dense energy in the nadi subtle veins and arteries is another necessary achievement for the yogi because unless this is done, even if the yogin sees light in the head of the subtle body, he will be dragged down to lower planes which are in the vibratory range of the dense energy which is somewhere else in the psyche. The entire subtle body must be upgraded not just the head of it.

Application

The illustrious guru, Swatmarama, gave us a revealing explanation of yoga practice and its benefits in the first two chapters of this very revealing (pradipika) Hatha Yoga manual. We are obligated to him!

Chapter 3

Mystic Arresting Actions*

Verse 1

स–शैल–वन–धात्रीणां यथाधारो।अहि–नायकः ।

सर्वेषां योग–तन्त्राणां तथाधारो हि कुण्डली ।। १ ।।

sa–śaila–vana–dhātrīṇāṁ yathādhāro।ahi–nāyakaḥ ।
sarveṣāṁ yoga–tantrāṇāṁ tathādhāro hi kuṇḍalī ।। 1 ।।

sa – with, śaila – mountain, vana – forsest, dhātrīṇāṁ – of the earth, yathādhāro = yathā (as) + ādhāraḥ (supportive base), ahi – serpent, nāyakaḥ – king, sarveṣāṁ – of all, yoga – yoga, tantrāṇāṁ – of mystic proficiency practice, tathādhāro = tathā (as) + ādhāraḥ (foundation), hi – certainly, kuṇḍalī – kuṇḍalinī lifeforce

As the king of the serpents is the supportive base of the earth with its mountains and forests, so the mystic proficiency practice of yoga has the kundalini lifeforce as its foundation.

Analysis

As the Indian Mythology would have it the earth is supported on the back of a tortoise (kurma) or by the head of the king of snakes (Ananta / Ahi–nayakaḥ). In comparison an individual's material existence is supported by the kundalini lifeforce. This psychic mechanism is so vital, that if it is removed from the physical body, even if the spirit core-self remains interspaced in the body, the body will deteriorate and could not be operated by that individual soul.

The return of the subtle body or astral form into the physical whenever the physical system sleeps, is operated not by the spirit-person but by the kundalini lifeforce. When there is an astral projection, if there is danger to the physical or to the separated subtle form, the kundalini lifeforce will yank the subtle body back into the physical one, thus causing the person to become objectively aware in the physical dimension.

Tantra has various meanings but in this *Hatha Yoga Pradipika,* it is the mystic proficient practice of yoga as described herein. This includes the range of human experience as that relates to the progression or suppression of spiritual insight.

**The Haṭha Yoga Pradīpikā does not have chapter headings. This title was assigned by the translator on the basis of the verse 5 of this chapter.*

Application

This is admittance by Swatmarama, that as far as he is concerned the mystic proficiency practice of yoga cannot be achieved without mastery in kundalini yoga. If the yogi fails to reform the behavior of the kundalini lifeforce, if it is left to its own devices, if the spiritual discipline does not budge it, the practice is flawed and will not give the intended results.

Verse 2

सुप्ता गुरु–प्रसादेन यदा जागर्ति कुण्डली ।

तदा सर्वाणि पद्मानि भिद्यन्ते ग्रन्थयो ।अपि च ।। २ ।।

suptā guru–prasādena yadā jāgarti kuṇḍalī I
tadā sarvāṇi padmāni bhidyante granthayo I api ca II 2 II

suptā – sleeping, guru – teacher, prasādena – by special favor of, yadā – when, jāgarti – aroused, kuṇḍalī – kuṇḍalinī lifeforce, tadā – then, sarvāṇi – all, padmāni = lotus–shaped energy vortexes, bhidyante – are penetrated, granthayo = granthayaḥ = energy congestion location, api – also, ca – and

When by special favor of the teacher, the sleeping kundalini lifeforce is aroused, then every lotus shaped energy vortex and all energy congestion locations are penetrated.

Analysis

For some reason, if one is to raise kundalini on a daily basis, one has to get the special favor of an able spiritual master, a proficient yogi. Methods are there for doing this but unless one gets an up-to-date process from a physical or astral guru, one cannot succeed. The reason is that control of the kundalini, its reform, is a process which the kundalini itself is resistant to. Hence it will not provide the core-self with information about its control. No energy or person knowingly contributes to its downfall.

The kundalini has an instinct of its own. It has intelligence. If it senses that the person wants to control it, it will not cooperate or it will cooperate superficially while retaining autonomy. Because the lifeforce bare-handedly created the material body in the womb of the mother, it has autonomy even though that power is not in the spiritual interest of the self.

There is an alliance between the kundalini and the core-self but that is for the convenience of the kundalini. If the core-self wants to change this so that the alliance serves its spiritual interest, it will have to wrestle control from the kundalini. This will happen as a power struggle between the core-self and its psychic adjuncts. Every psychic facility besides the kundalini serves the behest of the core-self when that self contributes energy to fulfil the desire of the kundalini; otherwise the adjuncts resist the influence of the self. Usually they resist the self effectively, leaving the self to ponder its helplessness.

Application

If the subtle body is not upgraded by the displacement of its lower astral energies and

by infusion of fresh higher astral force, there cannot be liberation for the individual soul. Sure, the soul/core-self is neither its physical or subtle body, but that does not mean that it is not affected by these. Death of a physical form is an easy feat, something which we are familiar with. Death of the subtle body is beyond the scope of the limited entity. Some very special and powerful yogis destroyed their subtle bodies and retreated to the causal level where one may exist without having to transmigrate physically and dimension-hop astrally but usually a yogi cannot do this. It is beyond scope.

Hence there is a need to upgrade the subtle body, so that higher insight is the norm for the yogi. His subtle body should have higher sensual facilities which can perceive supernatural environments.

Verse 3

प्राणस्य शून्य–पदवी तदा राजपथायते ।

तदा चित्तं निरालम्बं तदा कालस्य वञ्छनम् ।। ३ ।।

prāṇasya śūnya–padavī tadā rājapathāyate ।
tadā cittam nirālambaṁ tadā kālasya vañchanam ।। 3 ।।

prāṇasya – of the breath–derived energy, śūnya – idealess imageless mental content, padavī – passage, tadā – then, rājapathāyate – main access, tadā – then, cittam = mento–emotional content, nirālambaṁ – free of conventional impressions, tadā – then, kālasya – of death which is imposed by time, vañchanam = side–stepping

Then the idealess imageless mental content of the breath–derived energy serves as the main access, causing the mento–emotional content to be free of conventional impressions, and death which is imposed by time, is avoided.

Analysis

Once the subtle body is upgraded with a higher type of astral energy and with pollutions extracted from the form, it automatically assumes the idealess imageless mental content, which is suitable for higher meditation.

The conventional impressions occur because of the status of the subtle body and not due to habits. For there to be habits there must first be a form in which to cultivate those behaviors. A human being cannot become intoxicated with liquor, if the fluid is not available. The tendency for such intoxication will have no fulfilment if liquor is not produced. Hence, if a man was not in an environment where liquor was supplied, his inebriation would be nil.

In this yoga process, a scientific study of nature is required. Then one can come to the proper conclusion to realize that habits are based on access to particular environments. I may or may not have a tendency but if there is no environment, the tendency cannot manifest.

Someone said that he will not do this or that he will not do that. This determination is reliant on will power but unfortunately will power of a limited being is not absolute. It is best to be in an environment which supports desired habits but which is devoid of the unwanted facilities. If the subtle body is upgraded where it will not manifest what is unwanted and it will only display what is desirable, that would achieve the objective.

Application

I wrote this before and I may write it again: Proficiency in the pranayama breath-infusion fourth stage of yoga results in the free achievement of the pratyahar sensual energy withdrawal fifth stage of yoga.

If the yogi does proficient breath-infusion, just before sitting to meditate, he will find that his sensual energies are internalized and the conventional impressions, which are usually being displayed in the mind, are conspicuous by their absence.

This means that the yogi can meditate as desired instead of struggling with the conventional mind content which has thoughts and images having to do with the material world and its social outlays.

Death is enforced by the time factor, irrespective of whether it is a welcome event or not. In addition once a body is dead, the person who used it cannot revive the form. Someone may desire death and it may come as wished. Another person may commit suicide when frustrated. All the same none of these persons can revive the dead body.

By transferring interest into the upgraded subtle form, a yogi can transcend death which has jurisdiction over the material body and over the un-upgraded subtle body. An un-upgraded subtle body will survive death of the physical form, but that subtle body will be affected by the loss of the physical one which will result in subtle energy de-energization. A yogi avoids the effects of death by constantly surcharging the subtle body through pranayama breath-infusion and by the meditation which follows immediately after the infusion practice.

Verse 4

सुषुम्णा शून्य–पदवी बरह्म–रन्ध्रः महापथः ।

श्मशानं शाम्भवी मध्य– मार्गश्चेत्येक–वाचकाः ।। ४ ।।

suṣumṇā śūnya–padavī brahma–randhraḥ mahāpathaḥ |
śmaśānaṁ śāmbhavī madhya mārghaścetyeka–vācakāḥ || 4 ||

suṣumṇā – subtle central spinal passage, śūnya – idealess imageless mental content, padavī –content, brahma–randhraḥ = mystic opening at the top of the subtle head, mahāpathaḥ – great transit, śmaśānaṁ – cremation area, śāmbhavī – visual focus between the eyebrows, madhya–mārghaś = madhya–mārghaḥ = central passage, cetyeka = ca (and) + iti (thus) + eka (one), vācakāḥ – nomenclature

The sushumna subtle central spinal passage, the idealess imageless mental content, the brahmarandra mystic opening at the top of the subtle head, the great transit, the cremation area, the shambhavi visual focus between the eyebrows, and the central passage are one subject.

Analysis

These are one subject because the proficient completion of one causes the automatic accomplishment of the others. This is the listing:

- subtle central spinal passage
- idealess imageless mental content
- mystic opening at the top of the subtle head
- great transit
- cremation area
- visual focus between the eyebrows
- central passage

If the **subtle central spinal passage** is cleared of dense astral energy and of polluted astral charges, the influence of the bright and effulgent kundalini will spread through the spinal column, through the neck into the brain, where it will result in insight awareness.

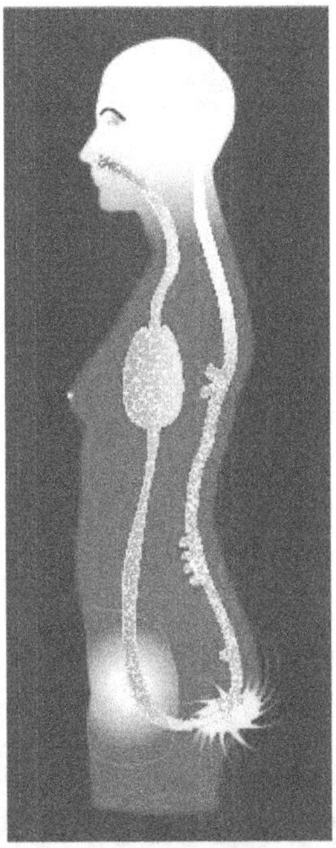

If for any reason, one experiences the **idealess imageless mental content,** the conventional thoughts and images would have ceased, resulting in a higher level of consciousness which is compatible with a higher plane.

The **mystic opening at the top of the subtle head** signals the completion of a full kundalini arousal into the head of the subtle body. This produces a gold-out in consciousness with accompanying vision insights into higher dimensions or into the spiritual world, the divine environment. By this method, the yogi reaches the brahman plane of existence where the sat, chit and ananda features of spiritual reality are realized as secure existence, awareness of being and blissful consciousness.

The **great transit** is done totally from the internal plane. It has nothing to do with moving the astral body in the subtle world. It is an internal elevator for transiting to higher dimensions, especially to the chit akash sky of consciousness.

The **cremation area** is the summary development of a yogi who became liberated while using a material body. The Sanskrit term for this is jivanmukta which means that the yogi is liberated before the death of his physical form. Cremation is the burning of the physical body but in this usage it is the termination of the cause of taking rebirth for the yogi. It means that his subtle body is so transformed that its supportive basis for rebirth was eliminated from it.

The **visual focus between the eyebrows** is the traditional recommendation for doing kriya yoga. It was mentioned by Krishna in the Bhagavad Gita which proves that it is an ancient method. This feature of practice is successful only when the yogi can penetrate out of this environment into the chit akash sky of consciousness.

The **central passage** is not the sushumna central spinal passage listed before. It is the central passage in the head of the subtle body. This passage connects the naad sound resonance in the back of the subtle head, to the core-self which is in the existential center of the head, to the buddhi intellect organ which is in the frontal part of the subtle head and then to the third eye chakra and the brahmarandra crown chakra. These are the transits points for an advanced yogi who does not focus on moving the subtle body but on the internal dimension-shifts within the subtle form.

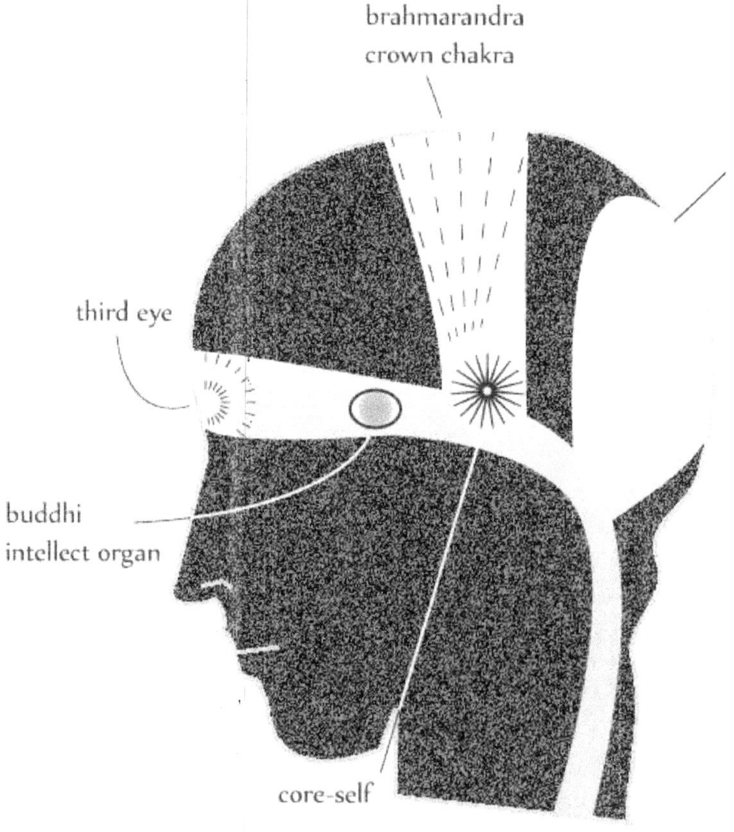

Application

There are many recommendations and processes given by various teachers and discovered by students. These gave practical results in terms of transiting to higher dimensions. Each of the methods has a particular stressed austerity. One should try one method after the other, until one practices a system which gives the desired effect.

Verse 5

तस्मात्सर्व–प्रयत्नेन प्रबोधयितुमीश्वरीम् ।

बरह्म– द्वार–मुखे सुप्तां मुद्राभ्यासं समाचरेत् ।। ५ ।।

tasmātsarva–prayatnena prabodhayitumīśvarīm I
brahma–dvāra–mukhe suptāṁ mudrābhyāsaṁ samācaret || 5 ||

tasmāt – thus, sarva – all, prayatnena – with effort. prabodhayitum – to infuse with the highest consciousness–energy, īśvarīm – goddess, brahma–dvāra = door to spiritual consciousness, mukhe – at the entrance, suptāṁ – sleeping, mudrābhyāsaṁ – the practice of mystic–arresting actions, samācaret – should thoroughly practice

Thus with all efforts to infuse the highest consciousness–energy into the sleeping goddess who is at the entrance to the passage to spiritual consciousness, the yogi should thoroughly practice the mystic–arresting actions.

Analysis

The sleeping goddess kundalini is honored in every creature by the living condition of the form. A spiritual self may be present. An intellect may be present. Some senses may be present. Memory may be present. But unless the kundalini lifeforce is operative within a body, that body is known as a dead form. This is why the kundalini is appraised as a sleeping goddess.

To direct her, the yogi must master certain mystic arresting actions (mudras). With these he may energetically infuse, confine and direct this powerful life energy. Otherwise he will be controlled by it, and will for better or worse, have to underwrite its schemes.

Application

The kundalini enlivening energy resides primarily at the muladhara base chakra, at the entrance to the sushumna nadi central spinal passage, at the very bottom of the passage. From there it operates the maintenance of the material body and the routing of the astral from in and out of synchronization with physicality.

Using mystic-arresting actions, a yogi can infuse kundalini, hold it in position, infuse it more until it is fully aroused, where the yogi may apply locks to keep kundalini from expressing itself in the traditional way of eating, sleeping, mating and defending.

Apart from eating, sleeping, mating and defending, there should be considerations about transiting out of this survival world. However, kundalini has no sincere interest in that. It is up to the core-self to procure the kundalini in a way which supports achieving that transit.

Verse 6-7

महामुद्रा महाबन्धो महावेधश्च खेचरी।

उड्डीयानं मूलबन्धश्च बन्धो जालन्धराभिधः ॥ ६ ॥

करणी विपरीताख्या वज्रोली शक्ति–चालनम् ।

इदं हि मुद्रा–दशकं जरा–मरण–नाशनम् ।। ७ ।।

mahāmudrā mahābandho mahāvedhaśca khecarī|
uḍḍīyānaṁ mūlabandhaśca bandho jālandharābhidhaḥ||6||
karaṇī viparītākhyā vajrolī śakti–cālanam |
idaṁ hi mudrā–daśakaṁ jarā–maraṇa–nāśanam || 7 ||

mahāmudrā – great mystic compression direction control, mahābandho = mahābandhaḥ = great sealing containment control, mahāvedhaś = mahāvedhaḥ = great centralized upper flow, ca –and, khecari – blocking the air pathway with the tongue, uḍḍīyānaṁ – drawing the abdomen cavity up under the rib cage and back towards the spine, mūlabandhaś = mūlabandhaḥ = uplifting the anal sphincter muscles, ca – and, bandho = bandhaḥ = physio–psychic compression, jālandharābhidhaḥ = jālandhara (compressing the lower jaw against thethroat) + abhidhaḥ (known as)
karaṇī viparītākhyā = karaṇī viparīta (upturning the body to use gravity to reverse the flow of bodily fluids) + ākhyā (called), vajrolī – urinary and sexual muscle upward–contraction, śakti – breath-infused mento–emotional energy, cālanam – compressing and relocating, idaṁ – this list of techniques, hi – indeed, mudra – foremost of the mystic checking practices , daśakaṁ – ten, jarā – old age, maraṇa – death, nāśanam – eliminates

The mahamudra great mystic compression direction control, the mahabandha great sealing containment control, the mahavedha great centralized upper flow, khecari blocking the air pathway with the curled-back tongue, uddhiyana drawing the abdomen cavity up under the rib cage and back towards the spine, mulabandha uplifting the anal sphincter muscles, doing what is known as jalandhara compressing the lower jaw against the throat,

...karani viparita upturning the body to use gravity to reverse the flow of bodily fluids, doing vajroli urinary and sexual muscle upward–contraction, doing shakti–calanam compressing and relocating breath-infused mento–emotional energy; this is the list of ten of the foremost mystic checking practices which eliminate old age and death.

Analysis

These are listed:

- mahamudra great mystic compression direction control
- mahabandha great sealing containment control
- mahavedha great centralized upper flow
- khecari blocking the air pathway with the curled-back tongue
- uddhiyana drawing the abdomen cavity up under the rib cage and back towards

the spine

- mulabandha uplifting of the anal sphincter muscles
- jalandhara compressing the lower jaw against the throat
- karani viparita upturning the body to use gravity to reverse the flow of bodily fluids
- vajroli urinary and sexual muscle upward–contraction
- shakti–calanam compressing and relocating breath-infused mento–emotional energy

The **mahamudra great mystic compression direction control** is a conjoint compression where the perineum or cervix is lifted-contracted. The tongue is curled up and pushed back to the soft palate. The hands are used to close the eyelids and press on the outer ear to block the entry of external sounds.

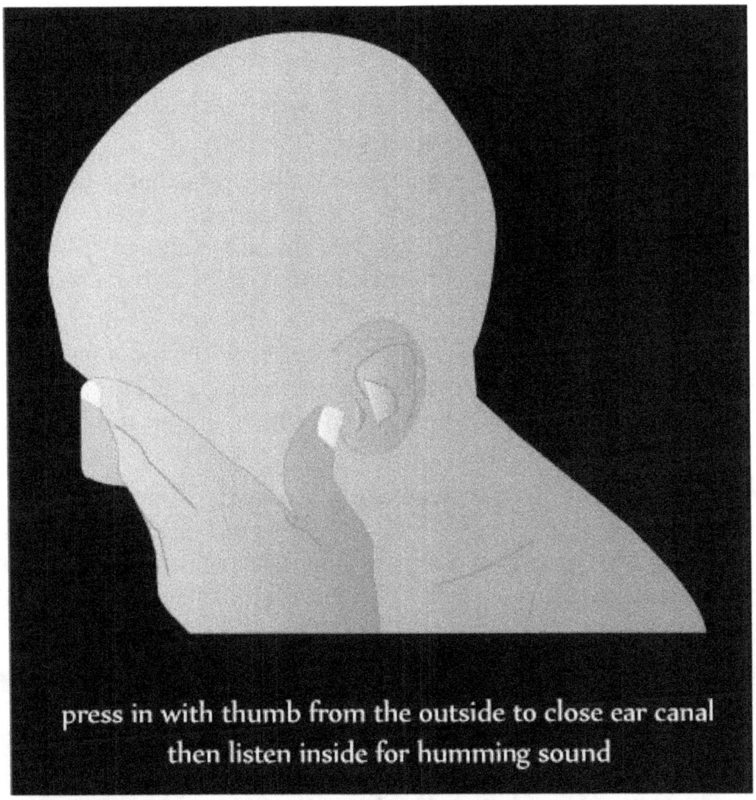
press in with thumb from the outside to close ear canal
then listen inside for humming sound

This is done while the yogi is in special postures like the lotus and other classical poses. The main objective of this is to meditate and reach the chit akash sky of consciousness from within the psyche from within the head of the subtle body without moving the astral body to any subtle location.

The **mahabandha great sealing containment control** is a conjoint practice which is developed in the psyche of a yogi, so that when there is breath-infusion, this lock takes place as a reflex and keeps the infused energy and the kundalini in a desired concentration. This is a combination of various locks applied as soon as there is suspension of breathing either after an inhale or exhale.

This lock is used with various sealing focuses. It depends on the particular asana and breath-infusion being practiced. It hinges as well on what the yogi does emotionally to pursue and direct the infused energy and the aroused kundalini.

Beginners should use this conjoint lock to push the infused energy down into the pubic area. Once it is located and kept there, the yogi should push it around the pubic loop and cause it to be attracted to the muladhara base chakra where kundalini resides. Again once kundalini is aroused, this great sealing containment lock should be applied firmly to cause kundalini to go up the spine through the neck into the brain.

This lock consisted of the following in combination as one conjoint mystic checking action:

- breath suspension after breath-infusion
- chin-to-throat lock
- anus lock
- sex lock
- navel lock

The main purpose of this conjoint compression is to restrict kundalini's movement so that it cannot wander through the psyche in a random way.

The **mahavedha great centralized upper flow** is for serious hatha yogis who are done with material existence and who become determined to shatter the power of the kundalini lifeforce. As a snake is caught by its tail and is slapped to the ground to its death, so the yogi captures the kundalini shakti and wiggles it to cause it lose its power over the psyche.

This practice is done in many postures but particularly in the lotus posture with a tight neck lock and with compression of the abdomen so that it pulls up under the rib cage; the hands are used to lift the body while they release it so that the buttocks strike the ground.

The **khecari blocking the air pathway with the curled-back tongue** is a special technique for controlling the passage of air after the yogi infused the subtle body and wants to temporarily take control of the breathing rhythm. This procedure is legendary. Many modern students get the idea that they can master this method, even though it is not intended for beginners.

To use this practice, one must be proficient in breath-infusion to such an extent that the breath rhythm of the body ceases operation on its own impulse due to having an excess of fresh air in the body. Gasping for breath occurs because of a deficit of fresh air. Similarly an excess of it may cause suspension of breathing. When a yogi did so much breath-infusion in a practice session, that there is an excess of fresh air, the brain gives a signal for the suspension of breathing. Then the yogi may apply this khecari blocking the air pathway with the curled-back tongue procedure to make sure that the system does not begin the rhythmic breathing prematurely. The advantage of this is that the mind remains in the voidal state with no thoughts or ideas. The yogi is free to focus into the chit akash divine places.

There is one other factor which should be given consideration, which is the genetic composition of the body the yogi uses. If one has a body with a relatively short tongue, it may not reach back to the soft palate and into the throat sufficiently to do this practice.

Formerly student yogis under supervision of teachers, used to cut the frenum over a period of weeks or months, so as to allow the tongue to reach down into the air passage and block it completely. However it depends on the type of body the yogi has. Some bodies have proportionately short tongues which cannot reach unless they are cut considerably.

Sri Lahiri Mahasaya did not like the cutting action and did not think that it was necessary or that a student would advance by doing just that. I am of the same opinion. As stated above the key issue is to infuse the body with so much fresh air, that there is excess of it. The system will then suspend the breathing rhythm for a time.

The **uddhiyana drawing the abdomen cavity up under the rib cage and back towards the spine** is a routine practice which all pranayama yogis are required to master. This should become a reflex of the yogi. When doing pranayama breath-infusion this lock is applied automatically and efficiently to stop the infused energy from being distributed carelessly through the navel region and also to stop it from increasing the appetite. Initially when students do this practice, it causes the appetite to increase. The student finds himself eating more food than usually. Over time however, this changes. The student finds that it curtails appetite by causing very efficient digestion of whatever foods are processed through the intestines.

This practice begins with the student attempting to pull up the lower abdomen. When the yogi becomes proficient in this, he pulls up and back simultaneously and controls his diet and time of eating to facilitate this lock during the breath-infusion practice. Ultimately he has to target the energy which is secured in the intestines/colon mass. This energy must be compressed inwards on itself but at first the student should compact it and push it down so that it goes around the pubic loop, mixes with the sex hormone energy and is fused into the kundalini at the muladhara base chakra. If there is enough charge of energy the kundalini will respond by moving in whatever direction it finds to be easy. It is preferred that it should move through the sushumna central spinal passage so that it could go into the head of the subtle body causing higher insight.

The **mulabandha uplift of the anal sphincter muscles** is for closing the lowest exit of the kundalini lifeforce, so that the subtle body does not go to the subterranean astral region either during the lifetime of the body or hereafter.

The core-self will follow the trend of the kundalini after death of the physical form. This is what usually happens. The fact that the core-self is greater than the kundalini lifeforce does not diminish in any way the power of the lifeforce over the self. Being greater than, may not mean that one has the upper hand; or that one can seize control.

Usually at the time of death, the kundalini leaves the physical body through a lower entrance. It is best if the kundalini would leave through the skull but it is more likely that it will leave through the anus, the genitals, the navel or the mouth. When the kundalini makes a final exit from the physical form, the rest of the subtle body leaves with it. This includes the core-self which is the highest component of psychic consciousness.

It is a task for a yogi to train the kundalini to go up through the sushumna central spinal passage into the brain because the kundalini prefers to remain at the muladhara base chakra and to make its exit from there or from some other lower access. When one first begins to apply this base chakra upward contraction, one might feel a heat there. This heat is also felt when the body is just about to die, where the last heated part of the body may be the anal region. One should pull up the anus. This application is also called ashvini mudra which means the inward contracting action of a horse's (ashva) arse.

A yogi will feel as if heat oozes out of the anus. This feeling is checked when the contraction is applied. The kundalini energy, when it is aroused in kundalini yoga practice, in breath-infusion, will pour out of the base chakra downwards. To stop it from dissipating in that way, one should apply this lock.

The **jalandhara compressing the lower jaw against the throat lock** is the compression which regulates how kundalini passes upward through the neck. This action is vital in causing kundalini to remain in the sushumna nadi passage when it passes through the neck. It gives the yogi control over how kundalini will transit once it enters the brain. If kundalini enters the brain without this regulation, it is likely that the person may get a headache, may black-out, may become unconscious or may even get seizures. Yogis who teach kundalini yoga should master this lock to such proficiency that it is done automatically by their bodies as soon as kundalini is aroused. They should carefully supervise students whom they teach, so as to not subject such students to headaches, black-outs or seizures.

When doing this lock the neck should remain in an upright position so that the head is not tilted forward. the chin should be pulled back so that the lower jaw clamps horizontally against the throat. There is a reverse neck lock which is when the head is tilted all the way up and back with the chin coming up as far as it will rotate upward. This reverse compression is rarely used but it has some application when doing breath-infusion.

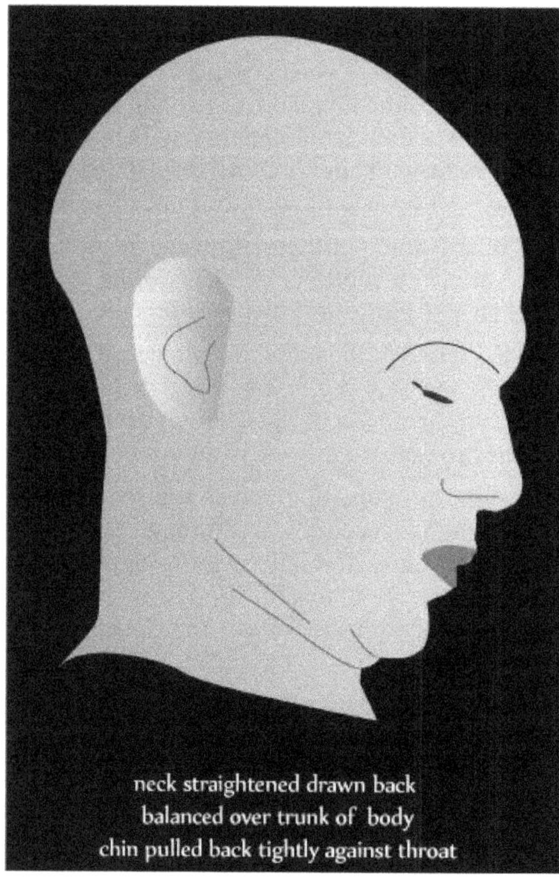

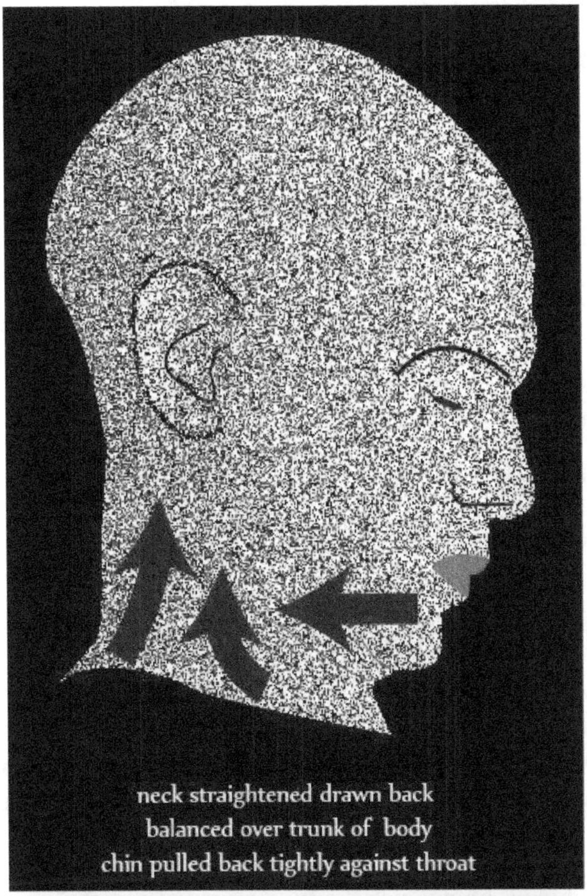
neck straightened drawn back
balanced over trunk of body
chin pulled back tightly against throat

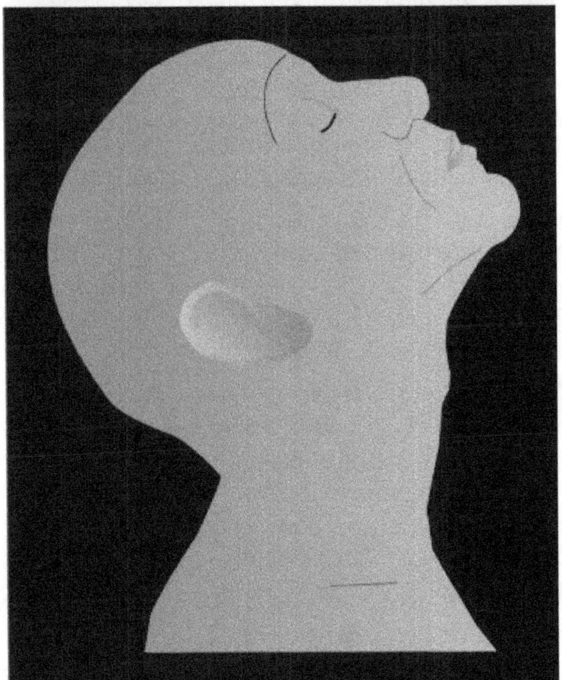

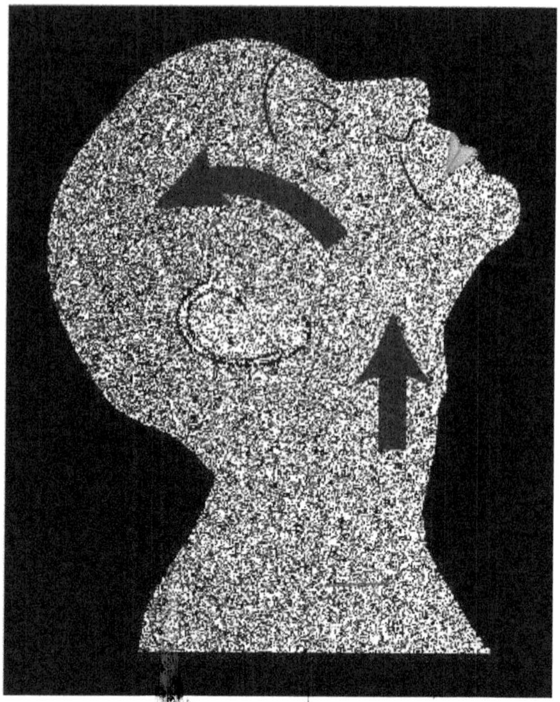

Those who do not master this compression of the lower jaw against the throat should not do rapid breathing infusion practice.

The **karani viparita upturning the body to use gravity to reverse the flow of bodily fluids** is practiced by yogis who feel the need to reverse the influence of the gravity of the earth. This power of the earth keeps the living entity earth-bound so that the astral body remains with heavy subtle energy which makes it time-constrained and causes it to retain a rebirth tendency which is antagonistic to the objectives of yoga.

Merely doing headstands and various postures which cause the reverse flow of fluids in the veins and arteries, will not necessary cause a change in the rebirth-intention of the subtle body. One has to do more than that. One has to change the tendency of the lifeforce by force-feeding it a higher type of subtle energy. Patanjali stated that for translation to a higher domain, the yogi has to saturate his subtle body with the energy from that higher locale.

The **vajroli urinary and sexual muscle upward-contraction** is designed to change the reproductive hormone system which is a chief cause for discouragement of yoga practice. It diverts vital energy away from sexual liaisons which are devoid of spiritual interest. This practice is called amaroli when done by females.

In males, the syringe squirt of sexual hormone is designed for a downward outlet, which is focused through the bottom front part of the body. Nature's idea is that a life begins in the father's body as a sperm particle. On the physical side this is manufactured in the testes. It is then transported through the penis with the hope that it would be lodged into the uterus during sexual penetration of the body of the would-be mother. In the uterine passage, the sperm adheres to an egg. Thus an embryo body develops.

The squirting action of the male reproductive energy is run by the kundalini lifeforce and by the muscular coordination in the sexual tubing of the male. This causes the kundalini to become addicted to sexual expression with no view towards lust-free spiritual bliss experience.

A yogi has a task to change this lust-reinforced bliss addiction of the kundalini. It is counterproductive for higher yoga but it is a stubborn and persistent nature-urge with a memorable fulfillment. It discourages the development of spiritual bliss experience which should occur primarily in the head of the subtle form. So long as the kundalini is habituated to arching across to the genitals and experiencing sexual ecstasy there, the possibility of kundalini permanently ascending the spine into the brain is nil. So long as the reproductive energy is under the influence of the earth's gravity, it is hardly likely that it will go upwards to make the yogi into an urdhvareta siddha, or a perfected yogi with upward-flowing semen.

The vajroli and the amaroli disciplines are for reversing the influence of gravity so that as soon as they are formed the reproductive fluids flow upwards.

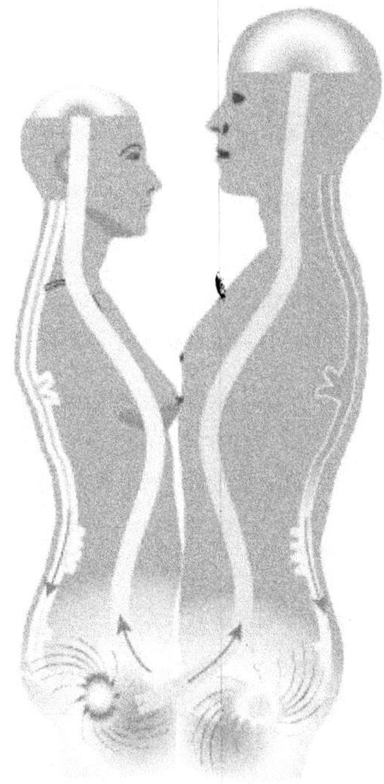

The **shakti-calanam compressing and relocating breath-infused mento-emotional energy** is the secret technique of not using kundalini to move the infused energy but infusing the breath energy into the cells of the body and having each cell activate its mini-kundalini. Usually, according to the posture assumed by the yogi, this happens in bunches in various parts of the subtle body.

When the infused breath energy accumulates sufficiently it is experienced as compacted bliss energy which the yogi compresses in on itself and infuses more energy into, until the charge become concentrated and implodes. The energy then shatters into bliss pixels and attempts to go here or there wherever it can in the psyche, but the yogi controls this because of having developed the ability to command the emotional force.

Application

These mystic checking practices eliminate old age and death by causing the interest-energy of the yogi to transfer to the subtle body which is a durable form. It is as durable as the duration of the universe. It hinges on the life of the sun. When the sun is destroyed, that may be the end of the astral body which we currently use in dreams. Physical habitats vary from time to time, according to the construction of such domains by material nature. The subtle body takes advantage of any opportunities to develop for itself a physical form.

However, even though the kundalini is accommodating of physical existence, a yogi is resistant to it. There is a necessity to use this yoga to curb the kundalini and to disincline it from physical manifestation.

The subtle body, although it is durable, is affected by the elderliness and death of the physical forms which were developed for it. A yogi can learn how to make the subtle body be least affected by the deterioration and death of a physical system.

Verse 8

आदिनाथोदितं दिव्यमष्टैश्वर्य-प्रदायकम् ।
वल्लभं सर्व-सिद्धानां दुर्लभं मरुतामपि ।। ८ ।।

ādināthoditaṁ divyamaṣṭaiśvarya–pradāyakam |
vallabhaṁ sarva–siddhānāṁ durlabhaṁ marutāmapi || 8 ||

ādināthoditaṁ = ādinātha (Lord Shiva) + uditaṁ(explained), divyam – divine, aṣṭa – eight, iśvarya – supernatural powers which are natural for God, pradāyakam yields, vallabhaṁ – endearing, sarva – all, siddhānāṁ – perfected beings, durlabhaṁ – difficult to acquire, marutām – air regulator deities who regulate subtle breath energy, api – even

This was explained by Lord Shiva. It yields the eight supernatural powers which are natural for God, and which are endearing by all the perfected beings but which are difficult to attain even by the air regulator deities who regulate subtle breath energy.

Analysis

The mystic checking practices are magical. If a yogi attains proficiency in their practice he would derive from them the eight supernatural powers which are natural for Ishwar, the Supreme Person.

One should not misunderstand this however. It means that due to changes in the composition of the subtle body, the yogi experiences the eight supernatural powers as natural functions.

These powers were listed by Lord Krishna:

aṇimā mahimā mūrter
laghimā prāptir indriyaiḥ |
prākāmyaṁ śruta-dṛṣṭeṣu
śakti-preraṇam īśitā ||

animā — becoming atomic; mahimā — becoming cosmic; mūrter = mūrteḥ — pertaining to form of the yogi; laghimā — technique of weightlessness; prāptir = prāptiḥ — acquiring or experiencing; indriyaiḥ — through sense organs; prākāmyam — enjoying almost anything desired; śruta-

dṛṣṭeṣu = śruta — of what is heard of only + dṛṣṭeṣu — what can be seen normally; śakti-preraṇam — the ability to manipulate mundane potency; īśitā — power of ruling others.

Becoming atomic, becoming cosmic, pertains to a form of the yogi, as well as being weightless, acquiring or experiencing through the sense organs of others, enjoying what was heard of and what was seen normally, manipulating mundane potency, ruling over others, (Uddhava Gita 10.4)

guṇeṣv asaṅgo vaśitā
yat-kāmas tad avasyati |
etā me siddhayaḥ saumya
aṣṭāv autpattikā matāḥ ||

guṇeṣv = guṇeṣu — to the mundane influence; asaṅgo = asaṅgaḥ — non-attachment; vaśitā — technique of controlling one's nature; yat — what; kāmas = kāmaḥ — desire; tad = tat — that; avasyati — can obtain; etāḥ — these; me — my; siddhayaḥ — mystic skills; saumya — dear friend; aṣṭāv = aṣṭau — eight; autpattikā = autpattikāḥ — natural; matāḥ — considered.

...non-attachment to mundane influences, which results in the technique of controlling one's nature, and obtaining what is desired; these my dear friend, are considered to be the eight natural skills. (Uddhava Gita 10.5)

Application

The Marutas are supernatural beings who regulate the appreciation and resentment energies which exude from human society. They collect these psychic charges and hurl them back to humanity in the form of favorable or unfavorable wind motion. Even these demigods, or devatas as they are termed in Hinduism, strive for the eight supernatural powers which are natural for the Supreme Being. However a yogi, who becomes proficient in the mystic checking practices, develops those mystic skills to the degree which is appropriate to his sense control and capacity for responsibility.

No yogi becomes God or becomes Lord Krishna or Lord Shiva. A yogi could gain potential spiritual glory in terms of what he is as a living entity and what his responsibilities are in relation to the spiritual authorities.

Verse 9

गोपनीयं प्रयत्नेन यथा रत्न–करण्डकम् ।

कस्यचिन्नैव वक्तव्यं कुल–सत्री–सुरतं यथा ।। ९ ।।

gopanīyaṁ prayatnena yathā ratna–karaṇḍakam |
kasyacinnaiva vaktavyaṁ kula–strī–surataṁ yathā || 9 ||

gopanīyaṁ – confidential process, prayatnena – in all respects, yathā – just as, ratna – diamonds, karaṇḍakam – jewelbox, kasyacin = kasyacid = anyone, naiva = not even, vaktavyaṁ – discussed, kula – family, strī – woman, urataṁ – love motions, yathā – just so

Just as one keeps diamonds in a jewelbox, this is a confidential process in all respects. It should not be discussed just as one would regard the love motions of a woman of the family.

Analysis

It is not that one should astutely hide kundalini yoga practice. All the same it should not be publicly displayed. It is an individual and very personal practice which requires inner concentration. Anything which serves to distract the yogi while practicing is counterproductive.

If a respectable woman becomes pregnant and is seen in public, people will draw conclusions. However that does not mean that a family member should invite anyone for a demonstration of what she did to become impregnated. One who does yoga should be discreet about it, because really it is not public matter. It is not the concern of others besides the student and the teacher.

As one keeps diamonds in a jewel box, as the love motions of a respectable woman are never seen in public, so a yogi should not exhibit this practice. And yet people will realize it just as they come to know of an aristocratic woman's sexual behavior by her visible pregnancy.

Application

As one progresses in yoga, it becomes necessary to teach others but one should get cues from the yoga-guru on how to do this. Not every person who shows interest in yoga should be taught it. A student should never get this idea of being a teacher because that will cause too much involvement with learners which will result in less and less inner focus.

It is best to avoid demonstrating yoga. The session should be done in private either alone, with the yoga-guru or with other serious students. Influence from others may cause a yogi to cease practicing. Therefore one should not expose oneself unless one has the approval of the teacher.

Verse 10

अथ महा–मुद्रा

पाद्–मूलेन वामेन योनिं सम्पीड्य दक्षिणाम् ।

प्रसारितं पदं कृत्वा कराभ्यां धारयेद्दृढम् ।। १० ।।

atha mahā–mudrā
pāda–mūlena vāmena yoniṁ sampīḍya dakṣiṇām ।
prasāritaṁ padaṁ kṛtvā karābhyāṁ dhārayeddṛḍham ।। 10 ।।

atha – now to discuss, mahā–mudrā – great mystic compression direction control, pāda–mūlena = by the heel, vāmena – by the left, yoniṁ – location where the female vaginal passage is or could be, sampīḍya – pressing, dakṣiṇām – right, prasāritaṁ – stretched, padaṁ – foot, kṛtvā – did, karābhyāṁ – with both hands, dhārayed = dhārayet = should hold, dṛḍham firmly

Now to discuss, the mahamudra great mystic compression direction control:

Pressing the left heel into the location where the female vaginal entrance is or could be, the yogi should stretch out the right leg, while holding that foot firmly with both hands.

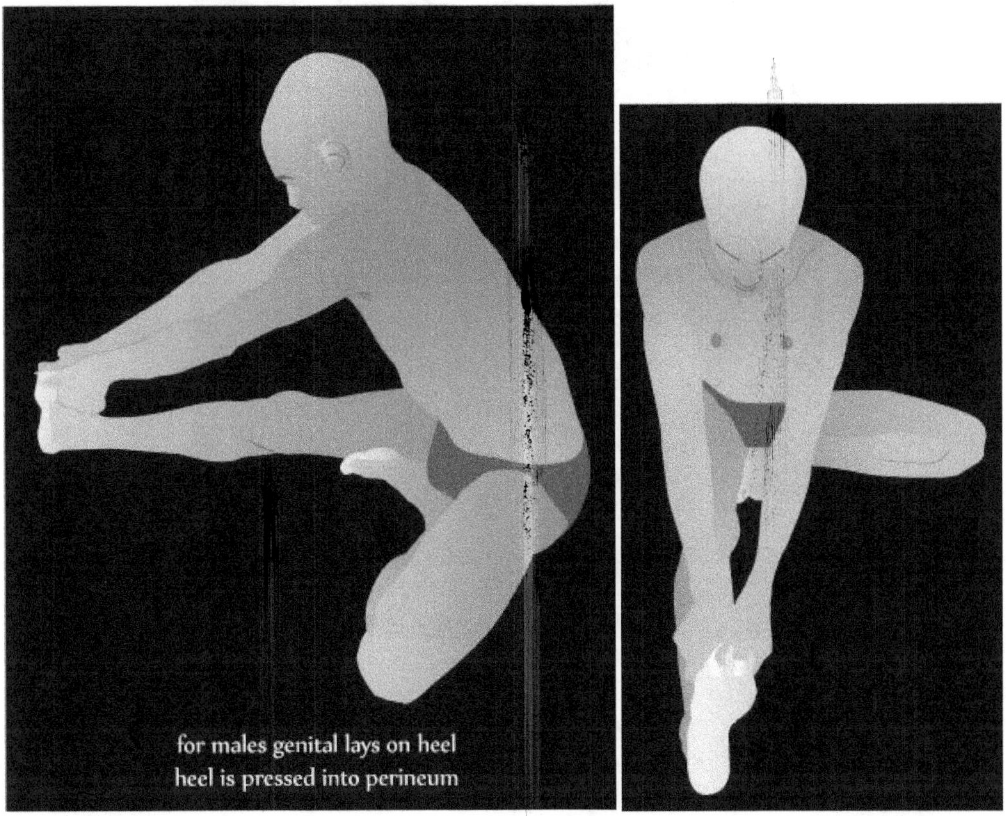
for males genital lays on heel
heel is pressed into perineum

Analysis

To realize this posture, the yogi must close the eyelids and concentrate to see where the energy is focalized as this posture is assumed. It is centralized and it pulls from the perineum in males and cervix in females. Males should use the left hand to lift the genitals when placing the left foot firmly against the perineum. Because of physiology, females have no concern to lift the genitals.

The tongue should be curled up and back until it touches the soft palate. The mind should be kept inside the psyche. It should not be allowed to contemplate thoughts and images. The neck lock should be firmly applied with the chin pulled back against the throat. The back should not be curved. There should be no adoption of a hunched back. The spine should be kept vertical. Energy will be released from the perineum, spine and rib cage. It should be arrested by inner focus.

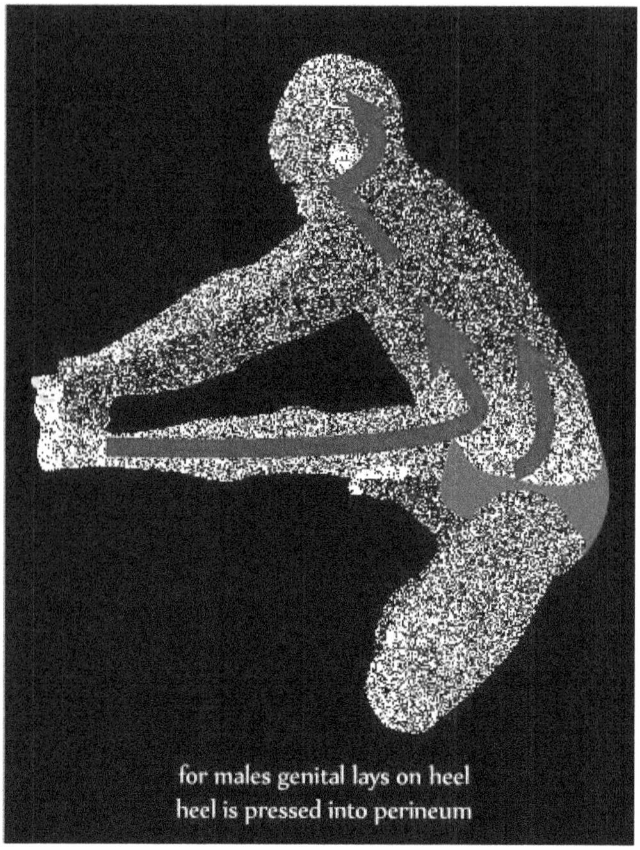
for males genital lays on heel
heel is pressed into perineum

Application

This first action when assuming the mahamudra great mystic compression direction control, is completed not just by assuming the posture but after many years of practice of asana postures and pranayama breath-infusion with inner concentration where the emotional energy in the body has complied with the will of the yogi for its reform.

As soon as the proficient yogi does this posture, the emotional energy and its hormonal assistant power, becomes aligned with the upward pulling force of the yogi. All energy near the sushumna central passage becomes aligned in a slanted upward-going direction. Then all energy which is near the middle of the trunk of the subtle body becomes aligned as well in a slanted upward-going direction through the center of the trunk of the subtle body. These two energy flows pass through the neck and go to the place where the tongue is curled up and pushed into the soft palate.

At this time the yogi hears the naad sound at the back top of the head. The emotional energy follows the core-self to be under the influence of the naad resonance.

Verse 11-12

कण्ठे बन्धं समारोप्य धारयेद्वायुमूर्ध्वतः ।

यथा दण्ड–हतः सर्पो दण्डाकारः प्रजायते ।। ११ ।।

ऋज्वीभूता तथा शक्तिः कुण्डली सहसा भवेत् ।

तदा सा मरणावस्था जायते द्विपुटाश्रया ।। १२ ।।

kaṇṭhe bandhaṁ samāropya dhārayedvāyumūrdhvataḥ |
yathā daṇḍa–hataḥ sarpo daṇḍākāraḥ prajāyate || 11 ||
ṝjvībhūtā tathā śaktiḥ kuṇḍalī sahasā bhavet |
tadā sā maraṇāvasthā jāyate dvipuṭāśrayā || 12 ||

kaṇṭhe – by the throat, bandhaṁ – physio–psychic compression, samāropya – restricting, dhārayed = dhārayed = hold, vāyum – lifeforce, ūrdhvataḥ – upward, yathā – as, daṇḍa – stick, hataḥ – struck, sarpo = sarpaḥ = serpent, daṇḍākāraḥ = daṇḍa (stick) + ākāraḥ (adopts), prajāyate – becomes, ṝjvībhūtā – becomes straight, tathā – so, śaktiḥ – potency, kuṇḍalī – kuṇḍalinī psychic lifeforce, sahasā – once, bhavet – become, tadā – then, sā – that, maraṇāvasthā = maraṇa (death) + āvasthā (existential state), jāyate – occurs, dvi – two, puṭāśrayā = puṭa (channels) + āśrayā (relating)

By holding the throat under restriction in the physio–psychic compression, the lifeforce is channeled upwards. As a serpent when struck by a stick, adopts the form of a stick, so the kundalini psychic lifeforce potency becomes straightened. Then it assumes an existential state as if dead in relation to the two channels.

Analysis

This is not as easy as it is presented in this verse, because students have to be proficient in asana postures and breath-infusion for this verse to hold true in their situation. Otherwise one may do this posture for years and never experience what Swatmarama so knowledgeably described.

Before one can strike a serpent one has to acquire a stick. One must also have the courage to approach the animal. One has to see the animal. One must get near to the animal. One must hit the creature and not miss it. It is easier to approach a serpent than it is to perceive the kundalini lifeforce at muladhara base chakra.

Since we have natural perception in the physical world, we can easily see serpents but can we see the kundalini? What perception is required for that? How can we develop that insight?

Application

First one must learn how to accumulate a psychic charge of energy using infused breath and hormonal force. Once this is done, one has to direct that charge of energy to the kundalini psychic lifeforce. If the energy is sufficient it will arouse kundalini.

Some yogis who are proficient can raise kundalini without first accumulating a psychic charge but these persons do this because of years of proficiency raising kundalini using breath-infusion and special asana postures. There are persons who say that their kundalinis are awakened even though they have never done asana postures or breath-infusion practice but most of these teachers are fakes. Rarely is an individual able to command kundalini to become aroused even though there are exceptions in every case of anything which is unusual for human beings to achieve.

Some teachers introduced a system of dance, or a system of touching disciples, or one of looking into the eyes of disciples, or one of making disciples chant special mantras. These are all to be tested by the students because no matter how one feels under the influence of a teacher, if one does not develop transcendental insight and if one does not experience changes in the life style which are conducive to more control of the psyche, the method is inadequate. The student should be honest enough to realize this.

My recommendation is consistent practice of the ashtanga yoga system. Following the system of Patanjali Mahayogin, one should do asana postures and breath-infusion, either separately or conjointly, to infuse the required energy into the psyche and to cause it to mix with the hormonal energy in the body. This combination should then be driven around the pubic loop into the muladhara chakra, where it will strike and arouse the sleeping goddess kundalini, which will then move up through the sushumna nadi spinal passage if the locks are properly applied.

Merely holding the throat under restriction in the physio–psychic compression, will not cause the lifeforce to be channeled upwards. One must first stimulate the kundalini lifeforce and cause it to move through the spine into the throat. We know of a natural and very simple way to arouse the kundalini. That is the common method of having sexual pleasure experience. By fondling the genitals one can easily cause the hormonal charge to be generated to such an extent, that the kundalini leaps across from the muladhara base chakra to the sex organ chakra. Then there is a massive arousal of kundalini which terminates in a sexual pleasure experience.

Taking a cue from this we can understand that by various asana postures and breath-infusion techniques a person can, on the spur of the moment, arouse the kundalini just as he or she can do so by stimulating the sexual organs either through self stimulation or with the help of a partner. One can experience sexual pleasure by seeing erotic images, sculptures or films which through vision can cause kundalini to be aroused.

For the purpose of the yoga described in this book, the method is asana postures and breath-infusion for raising kundalini. As a snake which is struck by a stick straightens out, the coiled suppressed kundalini at the base chakra becomes aroused, moves and stretches itself out as it is infused by the conjoint breath and hormonal energy. It shoots through the spine with a white, white-yellow, yellow, yellow-orange, orange, orange-red, red, red-brown or brown color or with a gradient of these hues.

When kundalini does this it displays non-attachment, a lack of interest, in the two channels of ida left side, and pingala right side, which are on either side of the spinal column. The yogi is then focalized into the spine and brain, with no interest in the rest of the body.

Verse 13

ततः शनैः शनैरेव रेचयेन्नैव वेगतः ।

महा–मुद्रां च तेनैव वदन्ति विबुधोत्तमाः ।। १३ ।।

tataḥ śanaiḥ śanaireva recayennaiva vegataḥ |
mahā–mudrāṁ ca tenaiva vadanti vibudhottamāḥ || 13 ||

tataḥ – then, śanaiḥ śanair = śanaiḥ śanaiḥ = gradually, eva – even, recayen = recayet = should exhale, naiva – not even, vegataḥ – forcefully, mahā–mudrāṁ = great mystic compression direction control, ca – and, tenaiva = tena (due to this) + eva (even), vadanti – explains, vibudhottamāḥ – best of those with the spiritualized intellect

Then it should be exhaled gradually, not forcefully. The mahamudra great mystic compression direction control was explained by the best of those with the spiritualized intellect.

Analysis

The posture used is pressing the left heel into the location where the female vaginal entrance is or could be, stretching the right leg out, while holding that foot firmly with both hands. There are two breath sequences used when doing this posture. One is for non-proficient students. The other for the advanced yogis who already blasted out sushumna nadi to such an extent that it no longer harbors any heavy astral force.

For the non-proficient students kapalabhati/bhastrika rapid breath-infusion is done in other postures and then in this posture as a final position. As soon as a sequence of rapid breaths is completed and the student is satisfied that the system is saturated with the infused energy, he should stop on an inhale and apply the locks fittingly. He should be focused within the psyche with no attention diffusing extrovertly through the senses. Then, squeezing and compressing the accumulated charge of energy, he should begin a slow and very gradual exhale, while compressing the locks tightly as the breath is exhaled slowly.

For an advanced yogi, he may assume this posture then take a full inhale, apply the compressions, check to be sure there is no extrovert tendency and that the mind is not engaged in its convention of thoughts and images. He should begin the long and gradual exhale while remaining focused, compressing in on the system and drawing the kundalini up through the spine into the brain.

Application

The spiritualized intellect is what differentiates an advanced yogi from others. It is not a concept. It is not an intellectual feat. It is not detailed knowledge of the Vedic literature. It is not charismatic power. It is the upgraded buddhi intellect psychic organ which is in the subtle body.

Through the practice of pranayama breath-infusion, a yogi can upgrade the intellect by first reconfiguring it so that it ceases its conventional operations of assisting the kundalini lifeforce in the struggle for existence. The intellect is not our understanding even though it funds that analytical task. It is an organ in the head of the subtle body. It is one of the components of consciousness. By adhering to Patanjali's request for ceasing the cittavritti mento-emotional operations, by mastering the disciplines which Lord Krishna expounded as buddhi yoga in chapter two of the Bhagavad Gita, a yogi upgrades the intellect so that it gives supernatural perception and loses its conventional addictions.

Verse 14

इयं खलु महामुद्रा महा–सिद्धैः प्रदर्शिता ।

महा– क्लेशादयो दोषाः क्षीयन्ते मरणादयः ।

महा–मुद्रां च तेनैव वदन्ति विबुधोत्तमाः ।। १४ ।।

iyaṁ khalu mahāmudrā mahā–siddhaiḥ pradarśitā I
mahā–kleśādayo doṣāḥ kṣīyante maraṇādayaḥ I
mahā–mudrāṁ ca tenaiva vadanti vibudhottamāḥ || 14 ||

iyaṁ – this, khalu – indeed, mahāmudrā – great mystic compression direction control, mahā–siddhaiḥ – greatest among the perfected yogis, pradarśitā – shown, mahā – prominent, kleśādayo = kleśādayaḥ = kleśa (emotional trauma) + ādayaḥ (related states), doṣāḥ – flaws, kṣīyante – eliminated, maraṇādayaḥ = maraṇa (death) + ādayaḥ (what relates to it), mahā–mudrāṁ – great mystic compression direction control, ca – and, tenaiva = tena (due to this) + eva (even), vadanti – speak, vibudhottamāḥ – best of those with the spiritualized intellect

Indeed, this mahamudra great mystic compression direction control is shown by the greatest among the perfected yogis. Emotional trauma and related states, flaws, death and what relates to it, are eliminated by this great mystic compression direction control. The best of those with the spiritualized intellects speak of it.

Analysis

This mahamudra great mystic compression direction control is the way to change the configuration of the subtle body. It is the method for squeezing the heavy astral energy in the subtle body and for mixing that with fresh astral force for purification and clearance of the subtle body. It is the way to capture and direct hidden energies which keep the subtle body time-bound and reincarnation-oriented.

There are various parts to this great mystic compression procedure. A student should patiently learn each, practice daily, for years if necessary, and then reach the proficiency where the conjoint locks become spontaneous, and kundalini behaves in a subordinate way.

Application

Emotional trauma, flaws and death become trivial to a yogi who masters the great mystic compression procedure. This is because traumatic states, flaws in behavior and the constant threat of death along with its allied uncertainties are no longer in the focal consciousness of an advanced yogi. This material world has a potential trauma-content. A yogi cannot alter that. One liberated yogi or even one million ascetics cannot in any way alter the trauma potency of the material world. What we can do is side-step it by de-tuning from the trauma environments.

Yogis, if they have any sense at all, will transit out of this dimension and not attempt what is foolish, which is to try to upset this determined Death Valley. Gautam Buddha gave an important hint about disengaging from everything that concerns trauma.

Verse 15

चन्द्राङ्गे तु समभ्यस्य सूर्याङ्गे पुनरभ्यसेत् ।

यावत–तुल्या भवेत्सङ्ख्या ततो मुद्रां विसर्जयेत् ।। १५ ।।

candrāṅge tu samabhyasya sūryāṅge punarabhyaset I
yāvat–tulyā bhavetsaṅkhyā tato mudrāṁ visarjayet II 15 II

candrāṅge – in the moon–dominant left side, tu – but, samabhyasya – of thorough practice, sūryāṅge – in sun–dominant right side, punar = punaḥ = repeat, abhyaset – should practice, yāvat – until, tulyā – as is, bhavet – be, saṅkhyā – accounting, tato = tataḥ = then, mudrāṁ – of mystic–arresting actions, visarjayet – should release

After thoroughly practicing on the moon–dominant left side, the yogi should repeat the practice on the sun–dominant right side. When the accounting is even, he should release the mystic–arresting actions.

Analysis

In the time of Swatmarama, the alternate breathing procedure was current. It can be used today provided the yogi is isolated, has completely split off from social circumstances, is patient, has very tightly regulated diet, and is supervised by a physically or astrally present yogi who used the process and was successful with it.

The alternative is to use the kapalabhati/bhastrika rapid breathing method which I practiced and was successful with.

What is the difference?

In the final analysis there is no difference provided the subtle body is fully infused with fresh astral energy and all of its pollutants are removed. There are two experiences to observe which are the saturation of the subtle body with fresh astral energy while the subtle body retains pollutants and its saturation with fresh energy after it discharged the pollutants.

Beginners will achieve the saturation with pollutants while the advanced students should strive for the saturation with the extraction of pollutants.

In either case there will be a point at which the student feels that the system is saturated and can take in no more compressed air. It is for this reason that this is an individual practice and not a group session. The teacher should deal with students one on one to teach according to the level of advancement.

When pressured by insecure emotionally-needy students, teachers are induced to teach in a class format with many students but this type of influence ruins yoga for one and all. Students do this to their instructor because the students need to mix with others and want to make the yoga class an opportunity to get attention and create trivial talk. A teacher should effectively resist this and even neglect students whose influence results in the group teaching format.

If the student is in the neophyte state, the saturation will occur with pollutants because the cells of the body will not release their stockpile of pollutants. The student will be unable to influence the body to do so. However in time, after practicing for months or years, this will change if the student gets superior guidance.

Advanced students learn how to extract the pollutants and to command the cells to release their pollutant stockpiles. Some mental force is required to upset the emotional resistance of the cells.

Application

The application of the alternate breathing procedure is done with even counts for each side, either with one side then another repetitively or with a series of breaths for one side, and then an equivalent series of the other side. However this does not always produce a balance. In some instances according to how the sun, or moon, charged the atmosphere, the student may have to do more of a count on one side and less on another. If for instance there is sun dominance, then say about 16 breaths in succession on the right side may require say about 20 or more counts on the left side. This is because the right side will be open and have easy access while the left will be blocked and will take in less energy for each pull of breath and will require many more pulls to produce the required balance.

In doing kapalabhati/bhastrika rapid breathing the yogi does not have to regard this, because an excess of energy which comes into the open side will flow over automatically into the blocked area.

However regardless of the method used, the student should be attentive to know which side needs to be tended to strike the balance and surcharge the entire subtle body.

As soon as it is saturated, and the yogi extracted the pollutants, he should cease the practice and sit to meditate. He should then observe the impact of the infusion to see if the mind abandoned the level where it indulges in the conventional thoughts and images. He should also check to see his relationship with the naad sound and his access or lack of access to the chit akash sky of consciousness.

Verse 16

न हि पथ्यमपथ्यं वा रसाः सर्वे।अपि नीरसाः ।

अपि भुक्तं विषं घोरं पीयूषमपि जीर्यति ।। १६ ।।

na hi pathyamapathyaṁ vā rasāḥ sarve|api nīrasāḥ |
api bhuktaṁ viṣaṁ ghoraṁ pīyūṣamapi jīryati || 16 ||

na – not, hi – because, pathyam – supportive, apathyaṁ – damaging, vā – or, rasāḥ – flavor, sarve – all, api – even, nīrasāḥ – without flavor, api – also, bhuktaṁ – what is consume, viṣaṁ – poison, ghoraṁ – deadly, pīyūṣam – nectar, api – even, jīryati – digests

Nothing is supportive or damaging. Due to this process, the yogi can digests anything with or without flavor. Even a deadly poison is consumed as if it were nectar.

Analysis

When breath-infusion is done to the full proficiency, many miraculous things happen in the life of yogi but since he is isolated and is not under observation of the public, he alone, his yoga-guru and some other advanced yogi may come to know of it.

The reason for supernatural occurrence is the reconfiguration of the subtle body, so that it operates on higher planes and also functions on the material level. Due to all-round detachment even the cells of his physical body exhibit strange behaviors.

Application

For such a yogi, the action/reaction cyclic way of dealings is terminated but that continues for others. It appears to the world that the yogi too is within the confines of ordinary standards, even though he is beyond their limit.

It is not in the interest of such an advanced soul to explain his immunity from problematic complications of destiny. Instead when things happen which go contrary in the life of the yogi, things which people find reason to criticize, the yogi should allow them to relish those occurrences while they revile the yogi. All in all what is in this world is in this world and will remain here. There is no reason for a yogi to object to critics.

Verse 17

क्षय–कुष्ठ–गुदावर्त–गुल्माजीर्ण–पुरोगमाः ।

तस्य दोषाः क्षयं यान्ति महामुद्रां तु यो।अभ्यसेत् ।। १७ ।।

kṣaya–kuṣṭha–gudāvarta–gulmājīrṇa–purogamāḥ ।
tasya doṣāḥ kṣayaṁ yānti mahāmudrāṁ tu yo।abhyaset ।। 17 ।।

kṣaya – consumption, kuṣṭha – leprosy, gudāvarta – chronic constipation, gulmājīrṇa = gulma (abdominal disorders) + ajīrṇa (indigestion), purogamāḥ – irregularities, tasya – of this, doṣāḥ – bodily imbalances, kṣayaṁ – health problems, yānti – they disappear, mahāmudrāṁ – great mystic–arresting actions, tu – but, yo = yaḥ = one who, abhyaset – practices

Consumption, leprosy, chronic constipation, abdominal disorders related to indigestion and other irregularities; those imbalances and health problems disappear for one who practices the great mystic–arresting actions.

Analysis

A diseased body can be problematic for any yogi. It is only the very advanced yogis who can keep practicing on an internal plane while the material body is bogged down by sickness. Some reputed teachers are affected but they learn what to say to present the idea that they are immune to whatever material nature can throw at them.

The truth is that one does best in yoga with a healthy body. In fact if one can leave the body at death and do so from a relatively healthy old body, that is the best way to leave a material body. However a yogi cannot expect to be serviced by providence because the material body which one uses has to suffer and enjoy through circumstances for which that body was destined. Some opportunities are presented by fate because the body was designed to serve ancestors not oneself.

Misfortune that is due to the ancestors may victimize the body. Good luck which is due to them may also assail it. The ugly question arises often in the life of a yogi, as to who owns the form.

Does the father own the body, because after all the body began as a sperm particle, a little aquatic creature, in the father's form?

Does the mother own the body? It is in her body that the aquatic form changed into becoming a full-fledged air-breathing creature.

Does the midwife or doctor own the body?

Does the school teacher own the body?

Does the government which registers the body's birth, own it?

Does the religious official own the body?

Since the ancestors contributed to its formation, do they own the body?

Application

By all means, a yogi should keep his body as healthy as possible. He should strip away from his lifestyle all counterproductive behaviors which aggravate health flaws in the body or which in the long range cause the body to suffer. One should not allow any sense to commandeer the body where that sense gets its fulfilment at the cost of the health of the body. A yogi should apply discipline to the components of consciousness for the progress of yoga.

Verse 18

कथितेयं महामुद्रा महा–सिद्धि–करा नृणाम् ।
गोपनीया प्रयत्नेन न देया यस्य कस्यचित् ।। १८ ।।

kathiteyaṁ mahāmudrā mahā–siddhi–karā nṝṇām |
gopanīyā prayatnena na deyā yasya kasyacit || 18 ||

kathiteyaṁ = kathitā (said) + iyaṁ (this), mahāmudrā – great mystic–arresting action, mahā – great, siddhi – supernatural skills, karā – action, nṝṇām – from human beings, gopanīyā – highly confidential, prayatnena – with special effort, na – not, deyā – reveal, yasya – whosoever, kasyacit – anyone

This great mystic arresting action is said to yield great supernatural skill for the human beings. With special effort, keep it confidential. Do not reveal it to anyone no matter whom it may be.

Analysis

Any supernatural power that a yogi develops deliberately or undeliberately should not be revealed to others. A yoga-guru will know if a student develops such powers but others may not detect it unless it is demonstrated.

It is a fact however, that even the most materialistic and spiritually-blind person may intuitively know that a yogi has supernatural powers. But unless a yogi displays feats, he will not have to worry about demands for its usage.

As soon as one displays a supernatural power one become responsible for its exploitation by others. This is why it is not sensible to display the perfectional skills.

The purpose for development of mystic perfection skills in the life of a yogi, is the investment of that ability to make further advancement. Unless one gets supernatural perception one cannot advance into the higher states of yoga practice. A yogi should use the skills to further the practice not to impress others.

Say for example that a yogi can read the mind of others accurately. This skill can be used to avoid unfavorable circumstances. That will help the yogi by conserving time for more practice. But if the yogi tells others that he can read minds and if he gives a convincing demonstration, he will find that these persons will demand of him that he reveals to them the ideas of persons whom they dislike or suspect. This will cause the yogi to leave aside his spiritual life and become servile to non-yogis.

Application

As soon as a student realizes that a mystic perfectional skill was developed, he should consult with the yoga-guru to find the method of using it constructively to advance the practice. The best student is the one who instinctively tries to increase access to the higher astral planes and the chit akash sky of consciousness. Such a disciple will have no interest in demonstrating miracles to ordinary people.

A yogi should have an attitude of non-interference in the lives of others. He should do this with respect to providence and material nature, which operates the dynamic of the relationships between worldly people. If the yogi unduly interferes with the plan of material nature, even for better, that yogi will find that his spiritual progress is impeded.

Verse 19

अथ महा–बन्धः

पार्ष्णिं वामस्य पादस्य योनि–सथाने नियोजयेत् ।

वामोरूपरि संस्थाप्य दक्षिणं चरणं तथा ।। १९ ।।

atha mahā–bandhaḥ
pārṣṇiṁ vāmasya pādasya yoni–sthāne niyojayet I
vāmorūpari saṁsthāpya dakṣiṇaṁ caraṇaṁ tathā II 19 II

atha – now it is described, mahā–bandhaḥ = great sealing containment control, pārṣṇiṁ – heel, vāmasya – of the left, pādasya – of the foot, yoni – perineum, –sthāne – in the location, niyojayet – place, vāmorūpari = vāma (left) + ūru (thigh) + upari (over), saṁsthāpya – placing, dakṣiṇaṁ – right, caraṇaṁ – foot, tathā – so

The mahabandha great sealing containment control is now described:

The heel of the left foot should be placed at the location of the perineum. Then place the right foot over the left thigh.

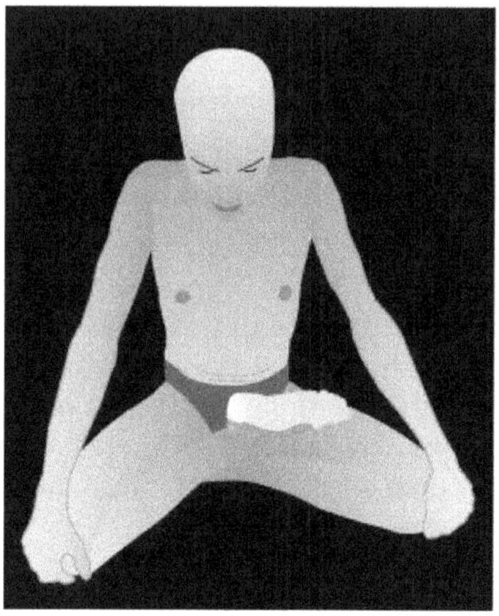

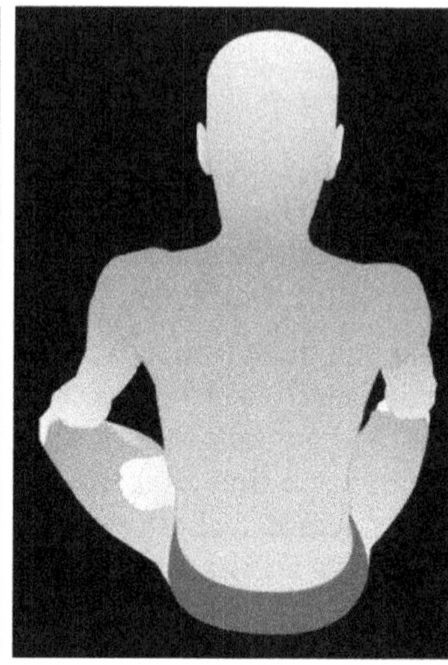

Analysis

Because of the varying proportions of the limbs of a material body, everyone cannot do this posture properly. When some persons attempt this pose, they will discover that the heel does not reach or that it over-reaches the perineum area and is not centered on it.

However in either case, it can be practiced. When this posture is assumed, as soon as the yogi completes these actions he should focus on the perineum area and should feel an energy rising from there and bubbling through the center of the subtle body.

Application

This posture targets the kanda bulb which is centralized in the pubic area of the subtle body. This psychic container holds sexual energy. A yogi should infuse fresh breath energy into this sexual potency and then either hurl it at the kundalini life-force or pull it up through the center of the trunk of the subtle body, through the neck into the subtle head.

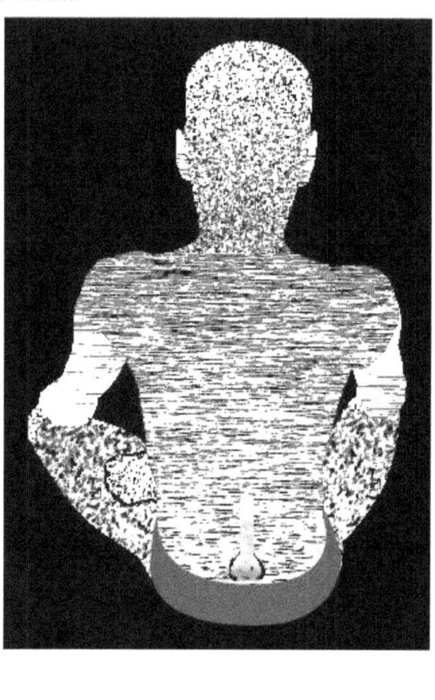

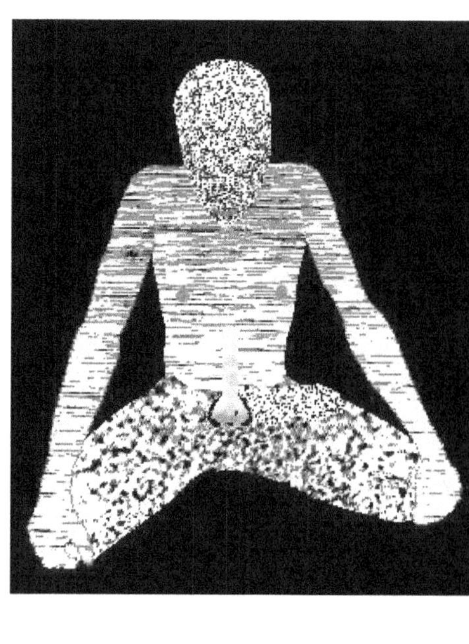

Verse 20

पूरयित्वा ततो वायुं हृदये चिबुकं दृढम् ।

निष्पीड्य वायुमाकुञ्च्य मनो–मध्ये नियोजयेत् ।। २० ।।

pūrayitvā tato vāyuṁ hṝdaye cibukam dṝḍham ।
niṣpīḍya vāyumākuñcya mano–madhye niyojayet ।। 20 ।।

pūrayitvā – inhaling, tato = tataḥ = then, vāyuṁ – fresh air, hṝdaye – on the chest, cibukam – chin, dṝḍham – firmly, niṣpīḍya – press, vāyum – fresh air, ākuñcya – compress, mano = manaḥ = mind energy, madhye – in the middle, niyojayet – should focus consciousness

Then inhaling fresh air, press the chin firmly onto the chest, compress the inhaled air, while focusing consciousness in the middle of the mind.

Analysis

This practice is done with the head tilted down partially or fully or with the neck erect and the head square on without tilting. If the head it tilted forward then there is the likelihood that the focus will be in the lower part of the back of the head, where the neck meets the head.

As stated, the focus should be in the middle of mind (mano-madhye) which is the default location of the core-self, the primary inhabitant of the psyche.

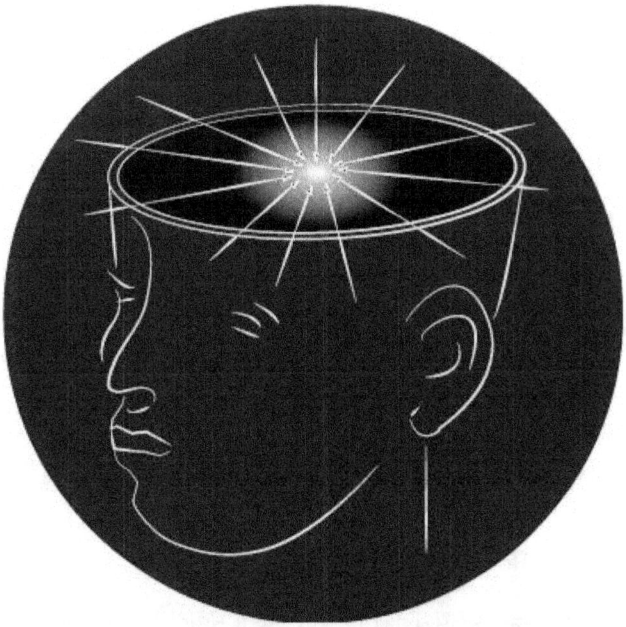

Some yogis feel that unless the head is tilted down it will not be possible to press the chin firmly onto the chest. However this can be achieved with the head erect on the neck by pulling the chin straight back against the throat and holding it there.

Application

When this posture is assumed, as soon as the chin is pulled against the throat and held there with the inhaled air under compression from the chin, anus, perineum and abdomen locks, the yogi will feel a downward pressure on either side of the spinal column. This will cause an upward rise of energy through the center of the spine, which will cause the kundalini to be inclined to travelling upwards for entry into the brain. The yogi should look down that central channel to observe the scene.

Verse 21

धारयित्वा यथा–शक्ति रेचयेदनिलं शनैः ।

सव्याङ्गे तु समभ्यस्य दक्षाङ्गे पुनरभ्यसेत् ।। २१ ।।

dhārayitvā yathā–śakti recayedanilaṁ śanaiḥ I
savyānge tu samabhyasya dakṣānge punarabhyaset II 21 II

dhārayitvā – compressing the air energy while focusing on it internally, yathā – according to, śakti – power potential, recayed = recayet = should exhale, anilaṁ – air, śanaiḥ – gradually, savyānge – on the left side, tu – also, samabhyasya – having practiced, dakṣānge – on the right side, punar – again, abhyaset – should practice

Compressing the air energy while focusing on it internally, according to one's power potential, he should exhale gradually. Having practiced on the left side, he should practice on the right side.

Analysis

Switching from one side to the next causes a polarity charge to accumulate. This arouses the kundalini lifeforce. Students should not expect instant results. One may have to practice for twenty (20) minutes or more before one feels the charged energy jumping from the right to left side at the bottom of the spine. If one does kapalabhati/bhastrika rapid breathing prior to doing this exercise, one may feel the arcing of the energy immediately. Kundalini will be aroused in the nick of time.

Application

The objective is to arouse kundalini by creating a polarity arcing between the left and right side of the spinal column. The locks are required to concentrate the charged force and to guide kundalini once it is aroused.

Verse 22

मतमत्र तु केषाञ्चित्कण्ठबन्धं –बन्धं विवर्जयेत् ।

राज–दन्त–सथ–जिह्वाया बन्धः शास्तो भवेदिति ।। २२ ।।

matamatra tu keṣāṁcitkaṇṭha–bandhaṁ vivarjayet I
rāja–danta–stha–jihvāyā bandhaḥ śasto bhavediti II 22 II

matam – opinion, atra – here, in this practice, tu – but, keṣāṁcit – some, kaṇṭha – throat, bandhaṁ – physio–psychic compression, vivarjayet – not practiced, rāja–danta = front teeth, stha – placed against, jihvāyā – tongue, bandhaḥ – physio–psychic compression, śasto = śastaḥ = recommended, bhaved = bhavet = is, become, iti – thus

Some have the opinion, that in this practice the physio–psychic compression of the throat should not be done. Instead the physio–psychic compression of the tongue against the front teeth is recommended.

Analysis

Different teachers according to their pioneering methods and according to how they were instructed by teachers, give variant ways of doing these mystic arresting actions.

What should a student do?

Which teacher is valid?

It hinges of whom one is fated to be instructed by. Some teachers gave methods which they are confident of but which they were only partially successful with. Others are such that unless they successfully use a method they will not divulge it. A student must work with fate and get from a teacher whatever worthy method he may divulge. Ultimately it rests with the student to judge what benefit is derived from a particular practice.

Application

In my practice, I used the chin lock when doing the kapalabhati/bhastrika breath-infusion technique. When I sit to meditate, I relax the locks and focus internally. I am not attentive to muscular locks during meditation. Initially however some years ago when I first began to apply the locks, I found it necessary to put them into place during meditation. The anus lock was useful at that time because I would be aware of a leaking of kundalini energy in the form of physical and subtle heat going downwards through the base chakra.

In the advanced stage even when the anus lock is relaxed, this does not occur. Hence there is no necessity to do it while meditating but it should be done during breath-infusion to secure the compressions which will drive kundalini up through the spine.

I never practiced the physio–psychic compress of the tongue against the front teeth but I used to find that in some meditation sessions, after a while, the tongue would itself move into this position. During samadhis, I find that on occasion the tongue is pushed against the lower front teeth, and forced so hard against it, that when it is pulled back, there is a pinching sensation as some of the tongue was squeezed through the spaces between the teeth.

This was discovered after coming out of the samadhi. I learnt to push the tongue forward and then pull it down slightly before pulling it back so as to decrease the pinching sensation which is felt when retracting the tongue

As for the upper front teeth I rarely find the tongue pushed into that, but once or twice it happened. I have yet to discover why the lifeforce pushed the tongue into the lower or upper front teeth in this way.

Verse 23

अयं तु सर्व–नाडीनामूर्ध्वं गति–निरोधकः ।

अयं खलु महा–बन्धो महा–सिद्धि–प्रदायकः ।। २३ ।।

ayaṁ tu sarva–nāḍīnāmūrdhvaṁ gati–nirodhakaḥ |
ayaṁ khalu mahā–bandho mahā–siddhi–pradāyakaḥ || 23 ||

ayaṁ – this, tu – for certain, sarva – all, nāḍīnām – nadi subtle veins and arteries, ūrdhvaṁ – upward, gati – passage, nirodhakaḥ – restraint, ayaṁ – this, khalu – indeed, mahā–bandho = mahā–bandhaḥ = great sealing containment control, mahā – great, siddhi – mystic perfectional skills, pradāyakaḥ – yields

For certain, this restrains the upward flow of all nadi subtle veins and arteries. Indeed, this mahabandha great sealing containment control results in the accomplishment of great mystic perfectional skills.

Analysis

This practice requires years of service with patience and isolation to complete. It is doubtful if many modern students will accomplish this. For one thing we lack the isolation required and our attention span even during meditation is haphazard.

Application

Failure in meditation practice, results from the inability to honor the second verse of the Yoga Sutras of Patanjali:

yogaḥcittavṛtti nirodhaḥ

yogaḥ – the skill of yoga; cittavṛtti = citta – mento-emotional energy + vṛtti – vibrational mode; nirodhaḥ – cessation, restraint, non-operation.

The skill of yoga is demonstrated by the conscious non-operation of the vibrational modes of the mento-emotional energy. (Yoga Sutras of Patanjali 1.2)

Unless this is achieved, yoga practice will be a failure no matter how much one dedicates to some process or discipline. The missing ingredient is thorough breath-infusion. That is what causes the subtle body to abandon its conventional operations of flashing thoughts and images.

A mental or emotional means of phasing out the flash of thoughts and images is praiseworthy but it is unreliable. Pranayama breath-infusion is the surety.

Verse 24

काल–पाश–महा–बन्ध– विमोचन–विचक्षणः ।

तरिवेणी–सङ्गमं धत्ते केदारं प् प्रापयेन्मनः ।। २४ ।।

kāla–pāśa–mahā–bandha–vimocana–vicakṣaṇaḥ |
triveṇī–saṅgamaṁ dhatte kedāraṁ prāpayenmanaḥ || 24 ||

kāla – death, pāśa – noose, mahā–bandha = great sealing containment control, vimocana – being freed from, vicakṣaṇaḥ – proficient, triveṇī – three primary nadi subtle passages, saṅgamaṁ – fussion, dhatte – gives, kedāraṁ – level of Shiva, prāpayen = prāpayet = conveys, manaḥ – mind

The mahabandha great sealing containment control is the proficient way for being freed from the noose of death. It causes the fusion of the three primary nadi subtle passages and conveys the mind to the level of Shiva.

Analysis

Freedom from the uncertainty of death comes about by redesigning the kundalini lifeforce. It is that psychic mechanism which engineers passage out of the body at death. It routes itself into the father's sexual fluids at the beginning of the next life.

A spirit cannot transmigrate from one dead form to a living physical one without being allied to a lifeforce psychic mechanism. The spirit cannot directly create, inhabit and leave a physical body. It does so through its alliance with the lifeforce.

First a student must dedicate himself to studying the lifeforce. To achieve this he has to develop psychic perception. That requires isolation and meditation. If after being isolated and meditating, the student finds that he fails to develop psychic perception, he should check with an advanced yogi to get a method which serves the objective.

Application

The fusion of the three primary nadi subtle passages conveys the mind to the level of Shiva, where the chit akash sky of consciousness is available. Such perception of the divine world is the relief from all traumatic horrors.

Verse 25

रूप–लावण्य–सम्पन्ना यथा स्त्री पुरुषं विना ।

महा–मुद्रा–महा–बन्धौ निष्फलौ वेध–वर्जितौ ।। २५ ।।

rūpa–lāvaṇya–sampannā yathā strī puruṣaṁ vinā |
mahā–mudrā–mahā–bandhau niṣphalau vedha–varjitau || 25 ||

rūpa – sexually–appealing, lāvaṇya – feminine charm, sampannā – endowed, yathā – as, strī – woman, puruṣaṁ – male, vinā – without, mahā–mudrā = great mystic compression direction control, mahā–bandhau = and the great sealing containment control, niṣphalau – are without consequence, vedha – centralized upper flow, varjitau – without

As being endowed with a sexually–appealing form and feminine charm has no reference in a woman if she does not have a male companion, so the mahamudra great mystic compression direction control and the mahabandha great sealing containment control are without consequence without the application

of the mahavedha centralized upper flow.

Analysis

Some aspects, even in the fullness of their displays, do not qualify as finished. Some yogis can do the mahamudra great mystic compression direction control and the mahabandha great sealing containment control fittingly and yet because they cannot apply it to the mahavedha centralized upper flow they have not completed the practice.

Some of these become global authorities even. This is because there is rampant ignorance about the components of consciousness and naturally most human beings feel that their consciousness is or should be one reality with no differentiated parts.

As sexual appeal and feminine form are complementary to masculine handsomeness and male physique, so locks and containment of energy finds its utility in the centralized upper flow of kundalini through the sushumna nadi central passage.

No matter the achievement of the yogi, a blocked sushumna highlights the failure to come to terms with the kundalini psychic lifeforce. It signifies that after leaving the body at its death, the yogi will loop back into a material form either as a human or as something less.

Application

Advanced yoga is a complicated discipline which cannot be simplified, except through learning each part step by step under superior guidance of a yogi who was successful with the methods and techniques used. The teacher does not have to be physical. He can be astrally responsive and directive in the life of a student.

Those who say that one must have a physical sat guru express an untruth which is serviceable to insecure people who want to form an exclusive institution where newcomers cower in awe of the teacher and have high expectation based on the sensational reports of excited disciples who had, or who imagined, fantastic experiences when they were touched, seen or handled in some way by the guru.

The fact remains that a guru may be astrally present and from the astral domains, he can influence someone just as powerfully as he could if he were physically here. Everything hinges on the result attained in the life of the student. Even in the case of the physical sat guru, if the result of his influence is short-lived, if it is a spell of excitement, then if there is no permanent development for the student, it is invalid. The same applies to astral or supernatural contact with a spiritual authority.

Verse 26

अथ महा–वेधः

महा–बन्ध–सथितो योगी कृत्वा पूरकमेक–धीः ।

वायूनां गतिमावृत्य निभृतं कण्ठ–मुद्रया ।। २६ ।।

atha mahā–vedhaḥ
mahā–bandha–sthito yogī kṛtvā pūrakameka–dhīḥ ।
vāyūnāṁ gatimāvṛtya nibhṛtaṁ kaṇṭha–mudrayā ।। 26 ।।

atha – now it is described, mahā–vedhaḥ = great centralized upper flow, mahā–bandha = great sealing containment control, sthito = sthitaḥ = sitting, yogī – yogi, kṛtvā – having done, pūrakam – inhalation, eka–dhīḥ = one focal awareness, vāyūnāṁ – of air, gatim – flow, āvṛtya – restraining, nibhṛtaṁ – immoveable, kaṇṭha–mudrayā = compression of the throat

Now the mahavedha great centralized upper flow is described:

Sitting while applying the mahabandha great sealing containment control, the yogi having inhaled should have one focal awareness. While being immovable and applying compression to the throat, the flow of the air should be restrained.

Analysis

When doing breath-infusion practice, if there is no focus down into the psyche, the practice is deviant and will not give the results described by Swatmarama.

Hatha Yoga is a forceful process. It is the means of reconfiguring the kundalini lifeforce which is the natural caretaker of the physical and subtle forms. This lifeforce cannot be deprived of its autonomy without a forceful method. It has a strong instinct for control. Even though it yields power to the core-self on occasion it has no intention of fully relinquishing control at any time.

Application

As soon as the yogi secures the accumulated fresh air energy charge, he should focus more closely within to hold that energy and direct it to the kundalini lifeforce at muladhara chakra. This effort is amply rewarded if kundalini moves up the spine into the brain because that gives more supernatural insight.

Verse 27

सम–हस्त–युगो भूमौ स्फिचौ सन्ताडयेच्छनैः ।

पुट–द्वयमतिक्रम्य वायुः सफुरति मध्यगः ।। २७ ।।

sama–hasta–yugo bhūmau sphicau santāḍayecchanaiḥ ।
puṭa–dvayamatikramya vāyuḥ sphurati madhyagaḥ ।। 27 ।।

sama – similar, hasta – hands, yugo = yugaḥ = two, bhūmau – on the ground, sphicau – buttocks, santāḍayec = santāḍayet = struck with force, chanaiḥ = śanaiḥ = gently, puṭa – buttocks, dvayam – two, atikramya – passing over, vāyuḥ – air, sphurati – quivers, madhyagaḥ – goes through the middle

Putting the hands in a similar way on the ground, the yogi should strike the buttocks gently but with force. The air passing through the two passages quivers and goes through the middle.

Analysis

There are many quivering, shaking, stretching, relaxing, quirky and jerky movements which are used in kundalini yoga. Some of these are explained and demonstrated by the advanced teacher. Some are discovered by the student.

Why is this done?

When the fresh air is infused into the body, it is forced to mix with the hormone energy.

Why is it forced?

The reason is that it will mix on its own only to a certain degree and only with the conventional impetus provided to it by the kundalini which operates for survival and reproduction of material forms. Since yoga concerns the upgrading of the subtle body, the natural impetus should be changed or the yogi will never be successful and will try again and again life after life and not succeed in effectively resisting the need for rebirth.

Gautam Buddha spoke of this as being the last birth. For that to happen something drastic must be done to the kundalini lifeforce so that it is no longer under the conventional process. The routine of the kundalini is to develop a physical body, reproduce other physical forms, transmigrate from the old physical body to one of the reproduced ones and then come out as the child of a mother somewhere in the material world.

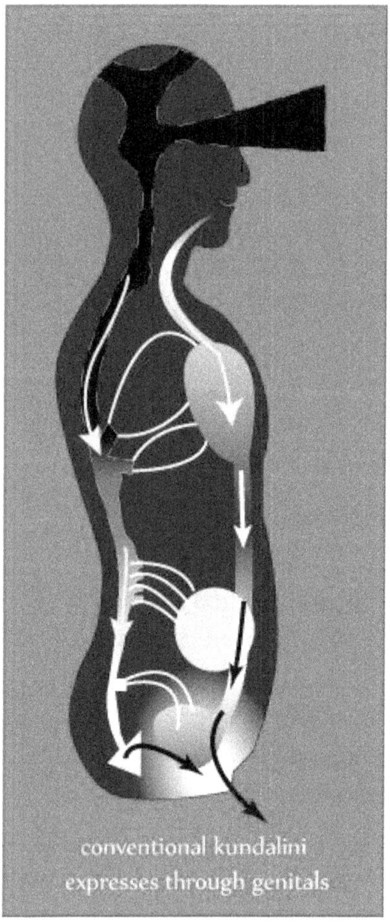

conventional kundalini
expresses through genitals

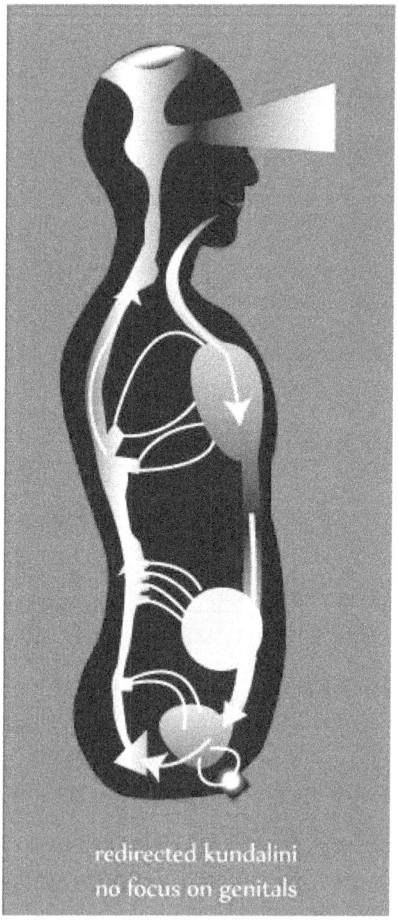

redirected kundalini
no focus on genitals

When the fresh air is mixed with the hormone energy, that mixture is fused into the kundalini at the muladhara base chakra. This action causes the kundalini to become active when the locks are applied, it is forced to go through the spine upwards into the head of the subtle body. Conventionally, for reproduction to secure future bodies, kundalini likes to express its arousal through the genitals. For the purpose of yoga this expression has to be redirected up the spine into the brain.

Sometimes some of the infused fresh air with hormonal energy remains in a certain part of the subtle body and does not target the kundalini at the muladhara chakra. To get this energy to move here or there, a yogi may compress it in on itself until it implodes in the subtle body. He may quiver, shake, stretch, relax, quirk or jerk part or all of the body to cause the energy to move or to break up, to pixelate, so that he can direct it to a targeted area of the subtle form.

This is the way a yogi shatters the supremacy of the kundalini by taking control of its energy-feed system and directing it for liberating the subtle form from the need for physical existence.

Application

A yogi must be willing to do whatever is necessary to reform the kundalini lifeforce. Once it is brought under subjugation, there will be more territory to cover in the form of dealing with the individual cells of the material body and the corresponding parts of the subtle form.

Infusion of fresh air into hormone energy and the fusion of that into the kundalini is just the beginning of the quest to control the psyche. The yogi must also teach the cells of the body how to yield their micro-kundalinis for use in the head of the subtle body. These cells are coded to contribute their essence to sexual indulgence for the purpose of creating new forms which resemble those of the parent body. A yogi has to upset this plan and train the cells to yield their micro-kundalinis into the brain of the subtle body and not into the genitals which is the natural depository.

Even though we interpret sexual intercourse as a primary pleasure source, that is incidental to nature's motive which is reproduction of life forms. As soon as we can overcome this pleasure need, we may develop the insight to rate the value of nature's intention.

Then we can decide on a preference. Should we continue taking advantage of the reproduction plan? Or should we forego sexual pleasure? Do we want sexual intercourse and the pleasure it affords along with more and more opportunities for taking material bodies whenever nature provides environments which support these? Or do we want to be in a place which does not have these pleasures and their necessary traumas?

Verse 28

सोम–सूर्याग्नि–सम्बन्धो जायते चामृताय वै ।

मृतावस्था समुत्पन्ना ततो वायुं विरेचयेत् ।। २८ ।।

soma–sūryāgni–sambandho jāyate cāmṛtāya vai ।
mṛtāvasthā samutpannā tato vāyuṁ virecayet ।। 28 ।।

soma – moon–dominant left channel, sūryāgni = sūrya (sun–dominant right channel) + agni (fiery breath energy), sambandho = sambandhaḥ = infused composition, jāyate – produce, cāmṛtāya = ca (and) + amṛtāya (immortality), vai – indeed, mṛtāvasthā – death–like state, samutpannā – emerges, tato = tataḥ = then, vāyuṁ – air, virecayet – should exhale

The infused composition of the moon–dominant left channel, the sun–dominant right channel and the fiery breath energy, is produced, resulting in immortality. When a death–like state is experienced, then the yogi should exhale the air.

Analysis

The fiery breath energy is the infused air which scatters out and then becomes collectively distributed in the form of bricks of compacted subtle force. This feels like a multicolored granite brick which has many small fragments in its composition. It feels like ice-fire, sparkling with a bliss aspect. A yogi should notice it but should not be enamored, the way humans adore sexual pleasure.

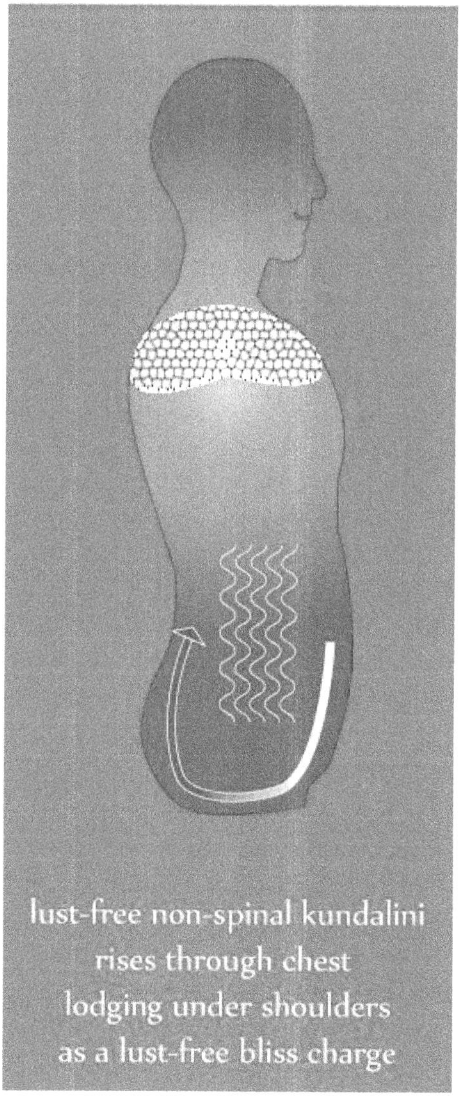
lust-free non-spinal kundalini
rises through chest
lodging under shoulders
as a lust-free bliss charge

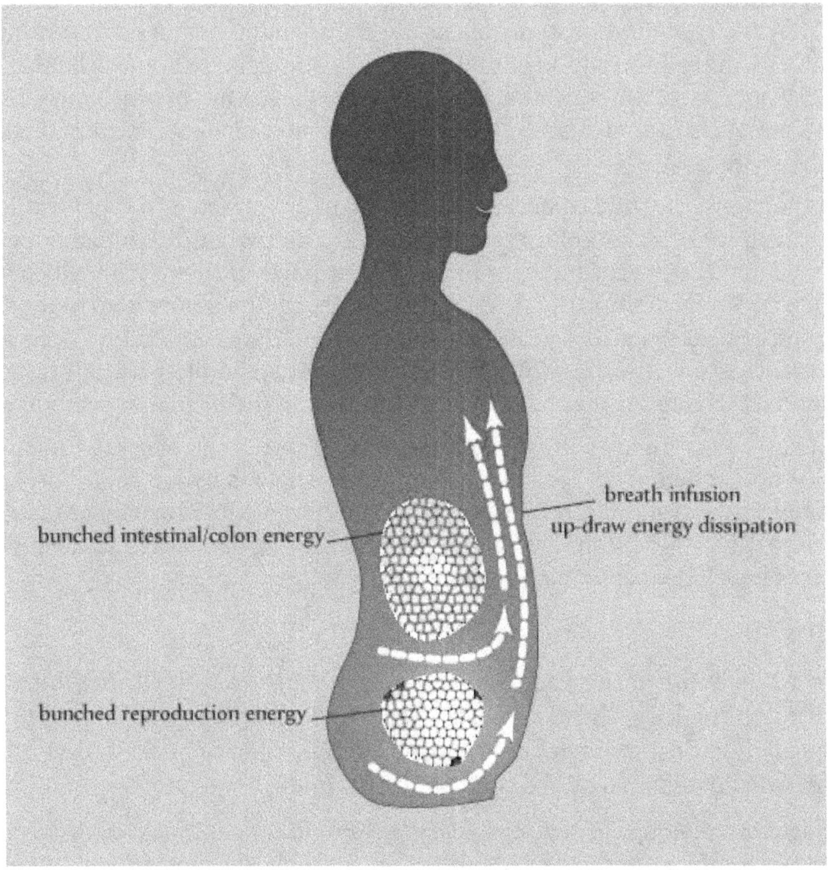

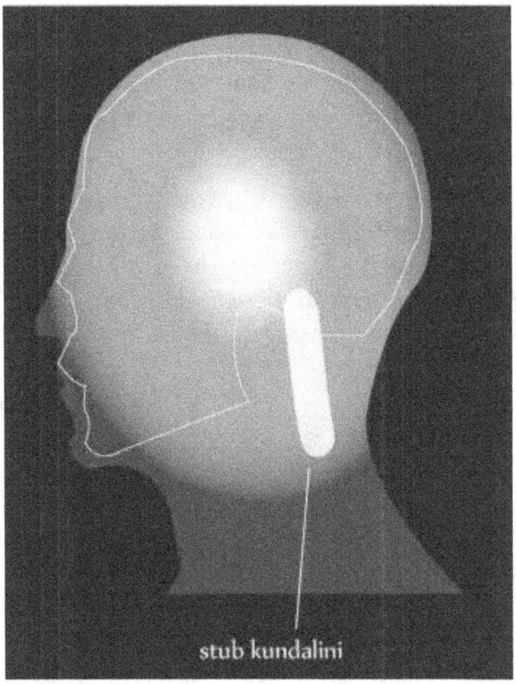

Just as when having sexual intercourse a human looses objectivity and is conveyed helter skelter by the pleasure, so a student may become lost in the bliss yields of this kundalini yoga practice, but that is not desirable. One should keep the observational powers in the fore so that one can report to the yoga-guru to get advice on how to proceed.

The dear Swami Vishnudevananda, who provided some of the impetus for this translation and commentary, translated that **the union of the moon, sun and fire (ida, pingala and sushumna) surely leads to immortality**. This is the traditional view. But there is another aspect which is when the kundalini adheres to the base of the brain as stub kundalini.

In that configuration there is no spinal kundalini in the sushumna nadi channel. This happens after the student repeatedly blasts out the sushumna nadi on a daily basis, once if not twice or more per day. Eventually because the central spinal channel remains cleared of heavy astral energy, the kundalini can no longer remain anchored at the muladhara base chakra. It floats up and remains at the back bottom of the brain, hanging there precariously.

When this happens, the infused breath energy is hardly attracted to the muladhara base chakra because there is no polarity energy there. Then when the infusion occurs, the student finds that the energy bunches up in various parts of the psyche which are hard-to-reach normally. By continually infusing the air, these areas bunch up more and more and are compressed inwards by the locks. Then the energy implodes. Then again the student compresses it inward with more infusion, until it implodes and explodes itself and becomes distributed throughout the psyche, even in the head of the subtle body.

At this stage a death-like state is experienced as the yogi becomes aware of the enhanced subtle body only. It feels like a bliss form which is hyper-energetic, as if it has no affiliate physical system. After a time, this state fizzes out. Then the yogi exhales. He continues the infusion or stops, sits and meditates, taking advantage of the higher level of awareness which the subtle body attained.

Application

When the air is exhaled, the yogi should make a decision to continue infusing or to desist and meditate. It depends on several factors, the primary one being as to whether the psyche is fully saturated with fresh air and if the polluted energy from all parts of it is fully extracted and released outside the subtle body.

If the pollutants are not fully removed, the yogi should target the relevant areas where this energy is combined into the cells. He should gradually infuse fresh air into these areas, causing the pollutants to be displaced. Some pollutants will be extracted directly through the lungs where it will be released in exhaled breath but some of it will combine with the incoming fresh air, and then will move through the system in that combination. By compressing more fresh air into these accumulations of energy, a heat is generated in them. This will be compressed more and more by the yogi until it implodes and explodes.

At first when the yogi suspends breathing after charging the system, he should observe the distribution of the accumulated energy. According to how it is configured, he should direct it here or there as adviced previously by the yoga-guru. When the distribution is completed, the yogi should exhale, then begin another breathing sequence or resume normal breathing while sitting to meditate.

Verse 29

महा–वेधो।अयमभ्यासान्महा–सिद्धि–प्रदायकः ।

वली–पलित–वेप–घ्नः सेव्यते साधकोत्तमैः ।। २९ ।।

mahā–vedho।ayamabhyāsānmahā–siddhi–pradāyakaḥ ।
valī–palita–vepa–ghnaḥ sevyate sādhakottamaiḥ ।। 29 ।।

mahā–vedho = mahā–vedhaḥ = great centralized upper flow, ayam – this, abhyāsān = abhyāsāt = from the practice, mahā – great, siddhi – mystic perfectional skills, pradāyakaḥ – yields, valī – wrinkles, palita – grey hair, vepa – old age, ghnaḥ – is eliminated, sevyate – practiced, sādhakottamaiḥ – by the best of the adept yogis

From this practice of the great centralized upper flow which yields great mystic perfectional skills; wrinkles, grey hair and old age are eliminated. Thus it is practiced by the best of the adept yogis.

Analysis

This should be understood as a development in the subtle body but it may occur for a time in the material form as well. The mystic perfectional skills are sensual advantages of the upgraded subtle body. These capacities may or may not surface in the physical form. Even if he makes advancement and appears to be without fault, a yogi who is focused on physical existence is fallen. One who is focused into the subtle body for its upgrade is elevated even if he appears to be flawed.

Associating with materialistic people, using their standards for behavior as the reference is detrimental to spiritual progress. A yogi should be detached from people who desire status for him in the material world. If one comes under the influence of materialistic souls, even the ones who pose as spiritualists, one will lose the footing in spiritual progress and will find the self to be thinking of itself as a material body.

Application

A yogi should use every means to protect the subtle body from deterioration. It does not matter what happens to the physical form. Ultimately it will be confiscated within one hundred and twenty-five years. It is foolish to live in such a way as to upgrade the physical body at the expense of the subtle one.

Suppose one lives in such a way that the physical body is not properly maintained but the subtle one is.

Is that preferred?

Suppose the physical body is improved by using drugs and cosmetics.

Is the subtle one enhanced or degraded by this?

What is sensible for worldly people may be contrary for a yogi.

Verse 30

एतत्त्रयं महा–गुह्यं जरा–मृत्यु–विनाशनम् ।
वह्नि–वृद्धि–करं चैव ह्यणिमादि–गुण–प्रदम् ।। ३० ।।

etattrayaṁ mahā–guhyaṁ jarā–mṛtyu–vināśanam ।
vahni–vṛddhi–karaṁ caiva hyaṇimādi–guṇa–pradam ।। 30 ।।

etat – this, trayaṁ – triple procedure, mahā – great, guhyaṁ – secret, jarā – old age, mṛtyu – death, vināśanam – eliminates, vahni – fire, vṛddhi–karaṁ = increases, caiva – and so, hy = hi = because, aṇimādi = aṇimā (becoming minute) + ādi (and other mystic perfectional skills), guṇa – characteristic, pradam – causes the development

This triple procedure is the great secret, which eliminates old age and death, increases appetite and causes the development of the characteristics of becoming minute as well as the other mystic perfectional skills.

Analysis

The development of the mystic perfectional skills is the indication of the success in upgrading the subtle body. This guarantees a promotion to a higher dimension or even to the divine world. The yogi should not display the mystic skills but should use them to accelerate progression and to better communicate with astral yoga-gurus and deities of the higher realms.

Experience of past lives give the yogi a lift where he can assess his position in the material world in relationship to what experiences he endured in many past lives as this or that child of numerous entities who served as parents.

Application

What causes increase of appetite in the beginning stages of yoga, causes an efficient digestion and a decrease in quantity of food required in the advanced stages. If possible, if there is a preference afforded by fate, a yogi should use rich protein foods in small quantity rather than eat low protein foods in large amounts.

The smaller the quantity of food the better but it must have sufficient protein and other content for the sustenance of the material body. Insufficient food may make a yogi famous as a person of sparse diet. By it he might get acclaim as a great ascetic but in the long term this will cause him to become a glutton, as the sensual orifices will harbor greed which will in time became so overpowering that in this life or the next, it will force the yogi to over-indulge to his ruin.

The senses are one reality and the core-self is another. The core-self, once it takes control of the psyche away from the kundalini lifeforce, should be sure to supply the senses with due quota of satisfaction. This means no overindulgence but it also means adequate gratification. The senses might be compared to children, who should eat a balanced diet but who should not be allowed to satisfy mere greed.

A yogi should not confuse the needs of the core-self and that of the senses and the kundalini. It is a bad idea to say that the core-self does not need to fulfill the senses and the kundalini because in practice, the self should sponsor a legitimate quantity of those needs.

I was once in a spiritual society where there was this belief that a human being only required five hours of sleep for the most in twenty-four hours. They said that actually the self has no sleep need. These ideas are hype. These statements mean absolutely nothing in the face of reality, which is that the lifeforce needs what it needs, irrespective of the status of the core-self.

Since it is in an alliance, not a unity, with the kundalini, the core-self has to tend to the needs of the kundalini. If it fails to do that, it will be victimized by time and circumstance and will be forced to over-indulge the psyche.

Buddha is usually acclaimed for his declaration of Middle Way of austerities and gratification but before him there was a teaching given to Arjuna by Krishna:

nātyaśnatastu yogo'sti
na caikāntamanaśnataḥ
na cātisvapnaśīlasya
jāgrato naiva cārjuna (6.16)

nātyaśnatas = na — not + atyaśnatas — of too much eating; tu — but; yogo = yogaḥ — yoga; 'sti = asti — it is; na — not; caikāntam = ca — and + ekāntam — solely; anaśnataḥ — of not eating at all; na — not; cātisvapnaśīlasya = ca — and + atisvapna - too much sleeping + śīlasya — of habit; jāgrato = jāgrataḥ — of staying awake; naiva = na — nor + eva — indeed; cārjuna = ca — and + arjuna — Arjuna

But Arjuna, yoga practice does not consist of eating too much. And it is neither the practice of not eating at all, or the habit of sleeping too much nor staying awake either. (Bhagavad Gita 6.16)

yuktāhāravihārasya
yuktaceṣṭasya karmasu
yuktasvapnāvabodhasya
yogo bhavati duḥkhahā (6.17)

yuktāhāravihārasya = yukta — regulated + āhāra — eating + vihārasya — of leisure; yuktaceṣṭasya = yukta — disciplined + ceṣṭasya — of endeavor; karmasu — in duties; yuktasvapnāvabodhasya = yukta — disciplined + svapna - sleep + avabodhasya — of waking; yogo = yogah — yoga practice; bhavati — is; duḥkhahā — distress-removing

For a person who is regulated in eating and in leisure, who is disciplined in the endeavor of duties, who is moderate in sleeping and waking, for him, the yoga practice is a distress-remover. (Bhagavad Gita 6.17)

Verse 31

अष्टधा क्रियते चैव यामे यामे दिने दिने ।

पुण्य–संभार–सन्धाय पापौघ–भिदुरं सदा ।

सम्यक्शिक्षावतामेवं स्वल्पं प्रथम–साधनम् ।। ३१ ।।

aṣṭadhā kriyate caiva yāme yāme dine dine I
puṇya–saṁbhāra–sandhāya pāpaugha–bhiduraṁ sadā I
samyak–śikṣāvatāmevaṁ svalpaṁ prathama–sādhanam II 31 II

aṣṭadhā – eight, kriyate – is done, caiva – and so, yāme yāme = every three hours, dine dine = day by day, puṇya – meritorious actions, saṁbhāra – quantity, sandhāya – increases, pāpaugha = pāpa (fault) + ogha (various), bhiduraṁ – reduces, sadā – always, samyak – exactly, śikṣāvatām – instruction, evaṁ – thus, svalpaṁ – little by little, prathama – beginning, sādhanam – disciplined regular practice

This should be done in eight ways, every three hours and daily. It always increases the quantity of meritorious actions and reduces the faulty social performance. Thus little by little, exactly as instructed, one should begin the disciplined regular practice.

Analysis

This was the routine for isolated ascetics in the time of Swatmarama. We can do this today if we have the time and are at a place where this is easy to schedule.

Faulty social performance is rapidly decreased if this practice is done frequently because the yogi will not be involved with others physically. He can tone psychic associations by first realizing their influences and then working to curtail that.

With the resulting purification, the yogi would eliminate the need to converse with people who have no interest in yoga and whose influence causes stagnation in progress or regression to a mundane lifestyle.

Application

Sincere yoga practice is disturbing to materialistic entities. If one does the practice in their vicinity, it might cause them to become hostile or to create circumstances for disrupting the practice. If one spends many hours doing asana postures and breath-infusion, or doing meditation and if that becomes known to those who cannot appreciate yoga, there will be for the ascetic an unfavorable backlash in the form of negative energy which would enter his mind and pollute it.

Verse 32

अथ खेचरी

कपाल–कुहरे जिह्वा प्रविष्टा विपरीतगा ।

भ्रुवोरन्तर्गता दृष्टिर्मुद्रा भवति खेचरी ।। ३२ ।।

atha khecarī
kapāla–kuhare jihvā praviṣṭā viparītagā |
bhruvorantargatā dṛṣṭirmudrā bhavati khecarī || 32 ||

atha – now will be explained, khecarī – procedure for transiting through kha divine space, kapala – head, kuhare – throat, jihvā – tongue, praviṣṭā – pressing into, viparīta – backward, gā – go, bhruvor – between the eyebrows, antar – internally, gatā – is applied in focus, dṛṣṭir = dṛṣṭiḥ = perception interest, mudrā – mystic–arresting actions, bhavati – is, khecarī – procedure for transiting through kha divine space

Now the procedure for khecari transiting through kha divine space will be explained:

Press the tongue backwards into the throat and internally focus the perception interest between the eyebrows. This is the mystic arresting action for transiting through kha divine space.

Analysis

This procedure produces the results intended for very advanced yogis who meet certain preliminary requirements. He must be connected to a siddha. He must have fulfilled the requirement for a mind which is free from the conventional mento-emotional operations.

When the tongue is pressed backward into the throat and there is internal focus of the perception interest between the eyebrows, if the yogi is in a confidential relationship with the naad sound resonance and if the frontal part of the subtle head is devoid of conventional thoughts and images, there is the likelihood that the yogi will transit into the kha divine space which is the environment of the spiritual world.

The transit happens spontaneously. It is not created by the yogi. It does not occur by his request. On this side of existence, his only actions set up the preparatory conditions, which are compatible with the spontaneous opening of a passage from the kha divine space into his psyche.

Application

When the tongue is pressed backwards into the throat, the yogi finds that his interest is switched to the naad sound at the back of the subtle head. There will be a passage between the contact point of the soft palate and the sound resonance location. After securing a relationship with naad sound whereby it surrounds the core-self and shields it, the yogi checks to see if his interest energy is shut down. If it is he will open it and check to see what is in the frontal part of the subtle head. If the interest energy is open he will peer into the frontal part.

The interest energy is the sense of identity (ahankara) which surrounds the core-self spherically. It serves as an access from the core-self to the adjuncts, the chief of which are the buddhi intellect organ and the third-eye/brahmarandra chakra complex.

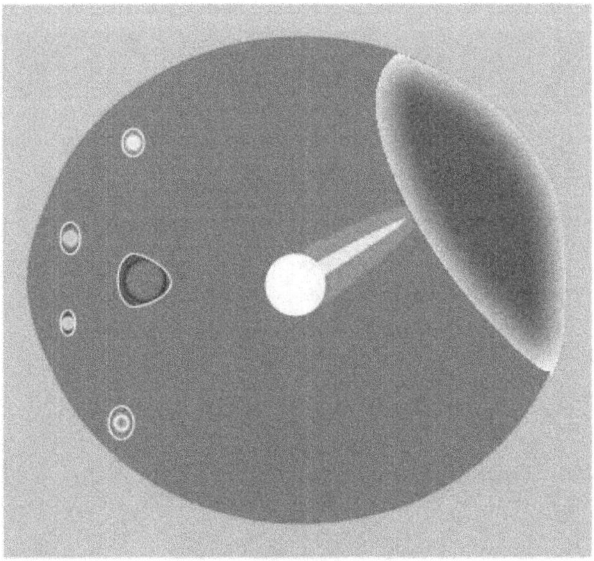

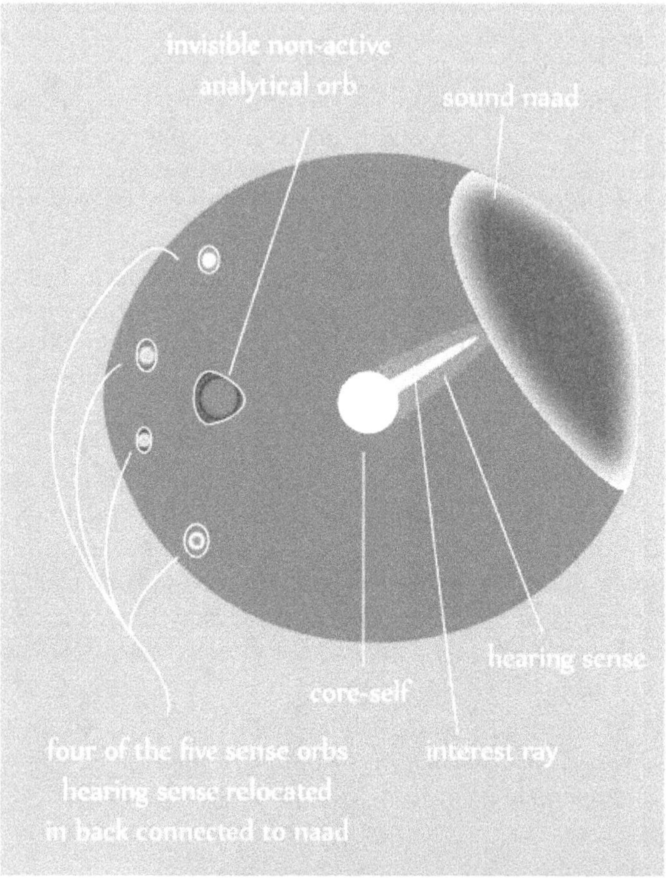

Attainment of a blank frontal part of the subtle head with naad sound being predominant in the back part of the subtle head is produced by a thorough breath-infusion practice, but some very advanced yogis can sit to meditate and experience this condition even if they have not done breath-infusion.

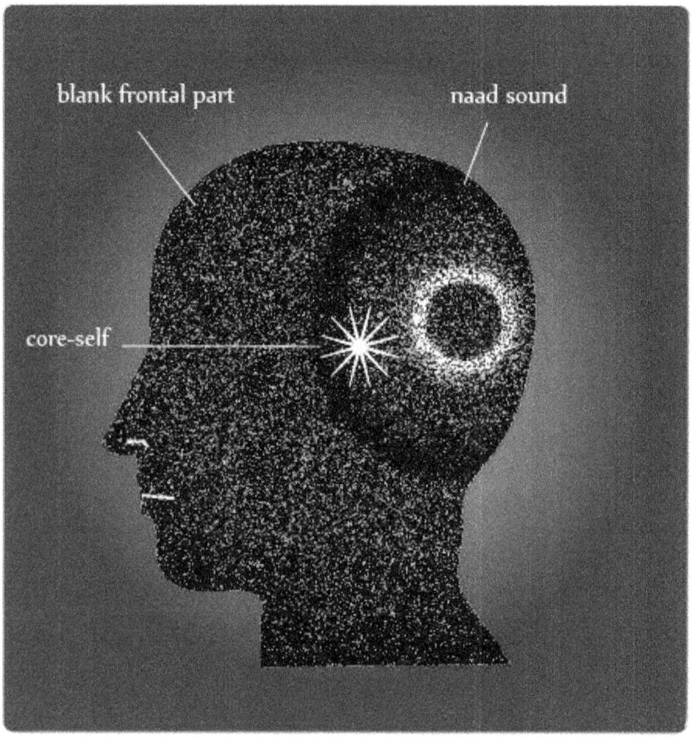

Verse 33

छेदन–चालन–दोहैः कलां क्रमेणाथ वर्धयेत्तावत् ।
सा यावद्भ्रू–मध्यं सपृशति तदा खेचरी–सिद्धिः ।। ३३ ।।

chedana–cālana–dohaiḥ kalāṁ krameṇātha vardhayettāvat I
sā yāvadbhrū–madhyaṁ spṝśati tadā khecarī–siddhiḥ II 33 II

chedana – cutting, cālana – pulling, dohaiḥ – by milking (pressing to the tip), kalāṁ – tongue, krameṇātha = krameṇa (by degrees) + atha (over time), vardhayet – should be stretched, tāvat – so long, sā – that, yāvad = yāvat = until, bhrū–madhyaṁ = between eyebrows, spṝśati – touches, tadā – then, khecarī – procedure for transiting through kha divine space, siddhiḥ – mystic perfection

Cutting, pulling and milking by degrees over time, the tongue should be stretched until it touches the space between the eyebrows, then the mystic perfectional procedure for transiting through kha divine space is accomplished.

Analysis

This is an extreme procedure done by certain isolated yogis in ancient times. These yogis were completely done with human social dealings except for affiliation with yoga teachers. They aimed for the siddhaloka heavenly place or Brahmaloka or the spiritual world proper. Some persons with ulterior motives for control of the world, for supernatural powers over others, also did these procedures.

There is no guarantee that by cutting, pulling and milking the tongue, one will achieve transit into the kha divine space. The reason is that one must have permission from a deity to enter the divine territories. Even if one does this procedure one may not be permitted to find the spiritual sky. Locating the spiritual sky is not just a matter of searching in the astral and supernatural spaces for an entry point. One must have an opening from the divine world into the dimension one resides in on this side. If there is no opening from the other side, one will never penetrate because the nature of the subtle material energy is that it does not provide the access.

Divine places are deity-regulated. They are based on deity vibrations and relations. Nothing which is incompatible with a deity can gain access in the deity's domain in the spiritual territories.

Even great sorcerers like Hiranyakashipu were unable to reach even the Brahmaloka heaven of the local creator-god. Instead the deity sensed the desire of Hiranyakashipu for an interview and came into the place where Hiranyakashipu's austerities were registered.

There cannot be incongruences in the kingdoms of God. Nothing can occur in God's kingdom which is incompatible with the deity. In this world we find that many contrary things occur. We heard legends from scriptures about disobedience of persons in relation to the will of God. But that is not so in the divine world of the Supreme Personality. The allowance for disharmony is restricted to the subtle and physical material worlds.

Application

I do not recall using the cutting, pulling and milking of the tongue procedure in many past lives of doing yoga austerities but it was a procedure used by some yogis over the centuries. Recently Sri Lahiri Mahasaya chastised disciples who used that method. He never recommended it.

It is a valid procedure. It is especially useful for yogis who want to control the duration of samadhi continuous effortless focus into the supernatural and divine existences.

There are two masterful ways of doing samadhi trance states. One is to let it occur by itself for its own duration. The other is to regulate the duration or have someone regulate it by bringing one back to the material body on a predetermined schedule.

Those who want to control the samadhi duration can do so by using the tongue to block the esophagus channel where the air passes to go into the lungs.

If the samadhi trance state occurs by itself and is left to itself, it will cease according to the breath energy which is deposited into the body before one entered the state. For instance in the case of bears which hibernate, they enter into a stupor samadhi (jada samadhi). When the temperature is elevated they are aroused and resume activities. That is a nature-controlled samadhi which begins when the temperature is depressed climatically.

A yogi can induce samadhi easily by doing a thorough breath-infusion session. Many modern yogis who are fake ascetics do not know that the induction of samadhi is done by pranayama-infusion. They have no confidence in this and do not get the hint as to why pranayama is the fourth stage of yoga and pratyahar sensual energy withdrawal is the fifth stage just before the sequential development of samyama which culminates into samadhi trances.

Samadhi begins with the internalization and termination of sensual interest where the energy which courses out of the psyche remains within it without any urge to sense anything outside of the psyche of the yogi.

Sri Lahiri Baba did not explain his objections to cutting, pulling and milking the tongue to me. However I surmised the reason. It is unnecessary in kriya yoga because the focus there is the subtle body. In the subtle body the tongue can be stretched in any way necessary without it having to be cut, pulled or milked.

This means that these accomplishments can be achieved if the disciple has full confidence in the subtle body and has switched his interest into that form, leaving aside the importance of the physical system and not trying to use it to reach the subtle.

However the fact remains that some ancient yogis used the physical actions and achieved the desired accomplishments.

Verse 34

सनुही–पत्र–निभं शस्त्रं सुतीक्ष्णं सनिग्ध–निर्मलम् ।

समादाय ततस्तेन रोम–मात्रं समुच्छिनेत्।। ३४ ।।

snuhī–patra–nibhaṁ śastraṁ sutīkṣṇaṁ snighdha–nirmalam |
samādāya tatastena roma–mātraṁ samucchinet || 34 ||

snuhī – milkhedge, patra – leaf, nibhaṁ – similar, śastraṁ – knife, sutīkṣṇaṁ – very sharp, snighdha – smooth, nirmalam – stainless, samādāya – taking, tatas – then, tena – with that, roma – hair, mātraṁ – measure, samucchinet – should cut

Taking a knife which is very sharp, which is smooth and stainless, which is similar to the milkhedge leaf, cut the tongue a hair's diameter.

Analysis

If one does this procedure which was used by ancient yogis, one should know that it may not give the intended results. This is because if there is no mystic accompanying action, merely cutting the frenum will give a physical result only. Some yogis used a sharp grass leaf or razor grass instead of a knife. Other yogis achieved this patiently over a period of years by pushing out the tongue and stretching it using fingers daily during their asana/pranayama practice. And there are some yogis whose tongues are designed to do this even without cutting because of the genetic structure of their bodies.

Application

Whatever one does to the body for the sake of yoga, should be done with the subtle body as the ultimate target. If one acts with the physical system and gets no benefit in the subtle body which furthers the objective of yoga, then the action has no value or worse, it may cause the practice to be retarded.

The benefit in the subtle body does not have to come immediately. In fact some physical actions in yoga result in subtle benefits long after those acts are committed. This is why one needs to consult with a yogi who was successful, so that one can have the confidence that the actions will pay off in the long range.

A yogi should always be on guard for material actions which are productive physically but which bring no astral showing or which even retard the spiritual progress.

Verse 35

ततः सैन्धव–पथ्याभ्यां चूर्णिताभ्यां प्रघर्षयेत् ।

पुनः सप्त–दिने प्राप्ते रोम–मात्रं समुच्छिनेत् ।। ३५ ।।

tataḥ saindhava–pathyābhyāṁ cūrṇitābhyāṁ pragharṣayet |
punaḥ sapta–dine prāpte roma–mātraṁ samucchinet || 35 ||

tataḥ – then, saindhava – rock salt, pathyābhyāṁ – turmeric, cūrṇitābhyāṁ – powdered, pragharṣayet – should rub, punaḥ – again, sapta – seven, dine – in days, prāpte – after, roma–mātraṁ = a hair's width, samucchinet – should cut

Then the yogi should rub rock salt and powdered turmeric. Again after seven days, he should cut a hair's width.

Analysis

This is hygienic. At this time with sophisticated and very exacting safe surgery, one may even engage a licensed physician to do this. But again the cutting of the frenum does not guarantee the astral application of this procedure.

Suppose I use myself as a tester. Suppose I do this and then I cannot get myself into samadhi. Then what? Suppose some delicate nerve is cut which causes my tongue to operate improperly. How will that be rectified?

Application

Swatmarama gave the advice about this being done over a long time, just a hair's width per week. This would allow the student to assess if it is a harmless procedure.

Verse 36

एवं क्रमेण षण्मासं नित्यं युक्तः समाचरेत् ।

षण्मासाद्रसना–मूल– सिरा –बन्धः प्रणश्यति ।। ३६ ।।

evaṁ krameṇa ṣaṇ–māsaṁ nityaṁ yuktaḥ samācaret ।
ṣaṇmāsādrasanā–mūla–sirā–bandhaḥ praṇaśyati ।। 36 ।।

evaṁ – thus, krameṇa – methodically, ṣaṇ = ṣaṭ = six, māsaṁ – month, nityaṁ – regularly, yuktaḥ samācaret – should practice, ṣaṇ = ṣaṭ = six, māsād = māsāṭ = from months, rasanā – of the tongue, mūla – root, sirā–bandhaḥ = frenum, praṇaśyati – cut

Methodically, the yogi should regularly practice this for six months. At six months, the root of the tongue, the frenum, will be cut.

Analysis

Six by four would give approximately twenty-four hair's width cuttings. That should be sufficient for releasing the tongue so that it would go up into the back of the nasal cavity and also down through the esophagus. But again if there is no mystic accomplishment to supplement this, it would be a wasted action with the yogi not making progress and nor having additional insight.

Application

One lesson to be learned from this is that yoga is progressive. Much of it is incremental rather than drastic. It may take not just months but years to master certain disciplines, especially the psychological ones, especially when dealing with the kundalini shakti which has stubborn and very persistent yogically-detrimental traits.

A yogi can raise kundalini on a daily basis, once or twice or even thrice per day and still after years, it will subside back down into the base chakra and will not remain shining through the sushumna central route into the brain.

A yogi should be persistent. He should be so determined to have the stamina to endeavor daily for years, or lives even, for the required success.

Verse 37

कलां पराङ्मुखी कृत्वा तरिपथे परियोजयेत् ।

सा भवेत्खेछरी मुद्रा वयोम–चक्रं तदुच्यते ।। ३७ ।।

kalāṁ parāṅmukhī kṛtvā tripathe pariyojayet I
sā bhavetkhecarī mudrā vyoma–cakraṁ taducyate II 37 II

kalāṁ – tongue, parāṅmukhīṁ – turn up and backward, kṛtvā – having done, tripathe – three conduits, pariyojayet – should press into, sā – that, bhavet – is, khecarī – procedure for transiting through kha divine space, mudrā – mystic checking practices, vyoma – spiritual sky, cakraṁ – circular energy formation, tad = tat = which, ucyate – is known as

Having turned up and pushed back the tongue, it should be pressed into the three conduits. That is the mystic checking procedure for transiting through kha divine space. It is known as the way for experiencing the circular energy formation of the spiritual sky.

Analysis

The ultimate purpose of yoga is to transit out of the material cosmos into the divine cosmos but this requires certain prerequisites. One by one, in a particular order, the student must learn and practice the methods. When one system becomes proficient, that is invested in a more advanced one in a sequence.

From within the psyche, from within the subtle body, within the head of that form, the yogi discovers an opening in the mind atmosphere where access is given to the spiritual sky. This usually takes the form of a circular opening (chakra).

A step by step purification is required, which is:

- interioriation of the sensual interest (pratyahar)
- focus into the spiritual environment (dharana)
- spontaneous focus into the spiritual environment (dhyana)
- continuous spontaneous focus into the spiritual environment (samadhi)

Questions arise in this regard about the methods of achieving these prerequisites. How should one **interiorize the sensual interest (pratyahar)?**

The method of doing this is not the issue. Whatever method works is sufficient. The query is this:

What is the result of interiorization of the sensual interest?

The answer is that the conventional mind content will be conspicuous by its absence. When the yogi meditates after achieving the interiorization of sensual interest, the usual thoughts and images will not occur in the mind. At the mental place where these ideas usually flourish, there will be nothing. The pressure for sensual pursuits will be absent. This text recommends the pranayama breath-infusion as the means of achieving this but that is not the only way. If someone can achieve this without doing breath-infusion then that is satisfactory.

For most students the **focus into the spiritual environment (dharana)** occurs sporadically, if it happens at all. This is because one cannot force open the mundane cosmos to find the divine world. A big realization for meditators is that from this side of existence, one can do nothing to cause the divine world to reveal itself. One can make oneself compatible to a revelation of the divine world but that is the most one can do.

If that is the case, then how can a yogi do the dharana focus into the spiritual environment practice? The answer is that he has to use the naad sound resonance as the focus. When that becomes steady and consistent in meditation there is the likelihood that a passage from the divine world to this side of existence will occur. When that happens, the yogi can focus into the divine world, even though he will still be located on this side.

The **spontaneous focus into the spiritual environment (dhyana)** occurs sporadically in meditation. It is not controlled by the yogi; the opportunity comes and goes haphazardly. At least that is the way it seems from this side of existence. When this happens for split seconds or moments, a yogi may be frustrated by it.

In the advanced stages however, a yogi may experience long sessions of this spontaneous focus. This is because of stability in listening to naad, conquest over the kundalini shakti and complete silencing of the sensual energies. In the mind space, in the head of the subtle body, the conventional display of thoughts and images do not occur during these meditations and not because of the will power of the yogi, but rather due to the high level of mental energy which saturated the mind chamber.

The **continuous spontaneous focus into the spiritual environment (samadhi)** is achieved by yogis who consistently achieved the spontaneous focus into the spiritual environment (dhyana). This happens as a matter of course, as a development out of the spontaneous focus. Patanjali Mahayogin grouped the three higher states of yoga together as the samyama sequential meditation.

Application

The shutdown of the three conduits of the ida left side, the sushumna central channel and the pingala right side causes a complete silence in the mind space in the head of the subtle body. This facilitates listening to the naad resonance which is the vibratory level of the contact between the material and spiritual realities.

When the yogi is situated on this side of existence with that shut down of the energies, and with loving attunement to the resonance of naad sound, he is fit for access to the chit akash sky of consciousness which is termed as the vyoma in this verse.

Verse 38

रसनामूर्ध्वगां कृत्वा क्षणार्धमपि तिष्ठति ।
विषैर्विमुच्यते योगी वयाधि–मृत्यु–जरादिभिः ।। ३८ ।।

rasanāmūrdhvagāṁ kṛtvā kṣaṇārdhamapi tiṣṭhati I
viṣairvimucyate yogī vyādhi–mṛtyu–jarādibhiḥ II 38 II

rasanām – tongue, ūrdhva – up and backward, gāṁ – push, kṛtvā – having done, kṣaṇārdham = twenty four minutes (half–hour), api – also, tiṣṭhati – stays, viṣair =

viṣaiḥ = with poison, vimucyate – is freed, yogī – yogi, vyādhi – disease, mṛtyu – death, jarādibhiḥ – old age and such infirmities

The yogi, who sits, while pushing the tongue up and back for half–hour, is relieved of poisons, disease, death, old age and related infirmities.

Analysis

This is the result derived by yogis in the time of Swatmarama. We are not doing the complete practice. We are in a cultural medium which is not supportive of the lifestyle of ancient yogis. Thus it is to be seen if any of us can get this result currently

Application

Pushing the tongue up and back for half hour is a feat for any yogi but it must be done with all the other features in place as described. The practice should be a daily one which lasts for months if necessary. Yoga in the time of Swatmarama was a lifetime commitment. It will not serve the purpose if it is fad or side feature.

Verse 39

न रोगो मरणं तन्द्रा न निद्रा न क्षुधा तृषा ।

न च मूर्च्छा भवेत्तस्य यो मुद्रां वेत्ति खेचरीम् ।। ३९ ।।

na rogo maraṇaṁ tandrā na nidrā na kṣudhā tṛṣā ।
na ca mūrcchā bhavettasya yo mudrāṁ vetti khecarīm ।। 39 ।।

na – not, rogo = rogaḥ = disease, maraṇaṁ – death, tandrā – fatigue, na – not, nidrā – sleep, na – not, kṣudhā – hunger, tṛṣā – thirst, na – not, ca – and, mūrcchā – stunned condition, bhavet – there is, tasya – of him, yo = yaḥ = who, mudrāṁ – mystic checking practices, vetti – is proficient, khecarīm – procedure for transiting through kha divine space

There is no disease, death, fatigue, sleep, hunger, thirst nor stunned condition for him who is proficient in the mystic checking procedure for transiting through kha divine space.

Analysis

This is true from the perspective of the yogi being transferred to the subtle body, where his interest is lifted completely from the physical form, which lost significance to his consciousness.

Disease, death, fatigue, sleep, hunger, thirst or a stunned condition is related to the material body more than it is to the subtle form. **Disease** affects both bodies but usually humans are focused on physical aspects without any idea of how that transfers or is coordinated with the subtle body. **Death** completes its application to the physical body. It may affect the subtle one by shock or temporary decrease in vitality.

Fatigue affects both the physical and subtle systems, with the physical one being the focus for those who have little or no subtle register. **Sleep** affects both bodies, but those who are materially focused or who are not conscious of the subtle form on a regular basis, feel that sleep is a physical aspect for the most part. The subtle body does sleep. It can do so when it is interspaced in the physical form or otherwise, when it is displaced from it in astral projections.

Hunger and **thirst** affect both bodies. The subtle body can exist without eating but only if it is upgraded. It can exist on sheer energy, like on moon beams or sunbeams or any other form of light or radio wave energy. When the subtle body is degraded to having the need for a physical form, it has a hunger-thirst need which is fulfilled by ingestion of subtle foodstuffs.

The first step in the upgrade of the subtle body is the infusion of fresh subtle energy. This is done by doing pranayama breath-infusion. Since physical air has a subtle counterpart, the infusion into the physical system achieves subtle air infusion simultaneously. The proportionate increase in fresh subtle air will over time cause the reduction in the need for mouth eating.

The **stunned condition** may affect both the physical and subtle systems. However, if one masters the yoga process one can delete the stunned capacity of the subtle body by removing the potential of it. This is achieved by curbing the kundalini shakti.

Application

This yoga process concerns a shift in interest from physical to subtle. At first the student thinks that it is a shift from the physical body to the subtle body in terms of lucid dreaming and astral projection experiences with the subtle body moving about in the astral world as it is displaced from the physical body.

This initial stage is a misunderstanding of what kriya yoga practice is. Yet, it is a vital development for those persons who are materialistic and who cannot perceive themselves as anything besides a material body.

When the student gets it into his head, that the material body will be junked shortly within one hundred and twenty-five years for the most, he thinks that it is important to transfer his interest into the subtle form because that body may exist for at least until the sun explodes causing the complete reconfiguration of our local planetary system as we know it.

When the student gets a grip on dreams, on astral projection, he loses the fear of the death, because he is assured by direct experience that when the material body is done for, the subtle one will continue existing willy nilly, come what may, in some form, in some subtle place, in a physically-abstract way.

This same subtle body, he comes to understand, will again develop for itself another physical form by its irresistible attraction to sexual intercourse. Under the circumstance he will conclude that there is no need to fear the death of the physical body. Its elimination cannot in any way completely erase all the emotional and mental aspects of the person-self, the character which was known as the physical form.

However this is still not kriya yoga, even though it should be rated as elementary mysticism.

Verse 40

पीड्यते न स रोगेण लिप्यते न च कर्मणा ।

बाध्यते न स कालेन यो मुद्रां वेत्ति खेचरीम् ।। ४० ।।

pīḍyate na sa rogeṇa lipyate na ca karmaṇā I
bādhyate na sa kālena yo mudrāṁ vetti khecarīm II 40 II

pīḍyate – traumatized, na – not, sa – he, rogeṇa – by disease, lipyate – polluted, na – not, ca – and, karmaṇā – social activity, bādhyate – limited, na – not, sa – he, kālena – by death, yo = yaḥ = who, mudrāṁ – mystic checking practices, vetti – is proficient, khecarīm – procedure for transiting through kha divine space

Due to being proficient in the mystic checking procedure for transiting through kha divine space, the yogi is not traumatized by disease, nor polluted by social activity, nor limited by death.

Analysis

This happens because of a definite shift of attention to the subtle where the yogi's mind is permanently unhinged from the material social scene. Some do not understand how a yogi can do this. They disbelieve the possibility especially in the case of yogis who remain partially or fully socially involved. There is a yoga specialty called karma yoga, which was taught by Krishna to Arjuna. That is the method of remaining involved in the world and still remaining detached from it simultaneously. In this text, Swatmarama listed it as raja yoga or remaining introverted while being externally occupied.

The term jivan mukti which means that someone became fully liberated while using a material body, would have no meaning if it was not possible for a yogi to shift his attention to the subtle side of existence even while living in the physical situation. One should have confidence that this can happen, even though one may harbor doubts about suspect yogis.

Disease, social involvement and death may not affect the shift of attention of a yogi, which means that as soon as providence releases the yogi from a material body and from a lower astral plane, he would immediately be translated over to a higher dimension while the lower astral level, or physical plane where he lived before, would continue existing just as before.

What is here that is good or bad, remains here. A yogi's absence or presence here does nothing to remove or support the potential energy. An advanced yogi understands and appreciates his dispensability in the material world. He does not think that he is essential or that he must be here for this energy to resolve old issues and generate new concerns. The yogi is free to leave this place as soon as fate would permit an exit.

A yogi, once he goes to a higher dimension, does not miss the traumas and relational agreements which are formulated in this world. This place becomes something that is long forgotten, something which has a non-register in his elevated consciousness.

Application

If he is not careful, a yogi's progress will be torn apart by critics who dislike him for

real or imagined grievances. The yogi should push on with yoga practice, no matter what, and should realize that the resentment energy of this material world is ongoing. It is relentless in its pursuits of victims. Hence if someone dislikes a yogi, even if that person is mistaken, even if the yogi is not at fault really, still the yogi should know that it is natural for people to express due or undue prejudices because those energies are part and parcel of the material creation and impose themselves on entities who have little or no mental and emotional control.

A yogi should see the big picture which is that the material energy expresses its urges through the living entities. It uses them as pawns in a game of polarity which surfaces in the mind and emotion as liking and disliking. Material nature is camouflaged. It appears to be other than itself. It appears as the persons who act under its influence. A yogi should see this and overlook attacks by others who are induced to bicker and criticize needlessly.

Verse 41

चित्तं चरति खे यस्माज्जिह्वा चरति खे गता ।

तेनैषा खेचरी नाम मुद्रा सिद्धैर्निरूपिता ।। ४१ ।।

cittam carati khe yasmājjihvā carati khe gatā |
tenaiṣā khecarī nāma mudrā siddhairnirūpitā || 41 ||

cittam – mento–emotional energy, carati – shifts, khe – in divine space, yasmāj = yasmāt = due to the fact, jihvā – tongue, carati – shifts, khe – in the divine space, gatā – gone, went, tenaiṣā = tena (by this) + eṣā (this), khecarī – procedure for transiting through kha divine space, nāma – name, mudrā – mystic checking practices, siddhair = siddhaiḥ = by the perfected yogis, nirūpitā – was designed

Due to the fact that by this, the mento–emotional energy and the tongue shifts into the divine space, the perfected yogis designed this mystic checking procedure for transiting through kha divine space.

Analysis

In the subtle body, on the mystic side of existence, when this kriya is done proficiently, the tongue's placement into the soft palate at the back of the mouth, causes all energy below the neck to be funneled in a concentrated form into the tongue and into the contact point between the tongue and the soft palate. This energy reaches such a concentration that it converts into a tiny white light and pierces through to the back of the head. This is the place of the kha divine space which the tongue shifts into.

Correspondingly at the front part of the subtle head, the mento-emotional energy which is usually sponsoring conventional thoughts and images, is absent. A new type of energy, the divine sky, the chit akash, is there.

Application

The siddha perfected yogis whose faces are partially turned in the direction of the earth planet, are always figuring methods of liberation which are suitable for student yogis on earth. Many siddhas being fully involved with their own efforts at complete

transit to the divine atmosphere have no concern with the earthling yogis and yet on occasion their methods do inspire the mind of a student on earth.

Some siddhas are assigned as lineage teachers. They remain in the astral world in a place where they are within restricted reach of earth-yogis. These direct advanced students who share the techniques with their students in turn.

This mystic checking procedure for transiting through kha divine space is still current but some preliminary requirements are necessary for its success. A student must have a connection with one of these siddhas or with an advanced student of a siddha. With that assistance the process is revealed. Students must also take help from Krishna by studying his Bhagavad Gita discourse. It is also necessary to learn the Yoga Sutras of Patanjali.

Verse 42

खेचर्या मुद्रितं येन विवरं लम्बिकोर्ध्वतः ।

न तस्य क्षरते बिन्दुः कामिन्या आश्लेषितस्य च ।। ४२ ।।

khecaryā mudritaṁ yena vivaraṁ lambikordhvataḥ I
na tasya kṣarate binduḥ kāminyā āśleṣhitasya ca I I 42 I I

khecaryā – procedure for transiting through kha divine space, mudritaṁ – compressed, yena – by this, vivaraṁ – cavity, lambikordhvataḥ = lambika (soft palate) + ūrdhvataḥ (above), na – not, tasya – his, kṣarate – flow, binduḥ – semen, kāminyā – a seductive woman, āśleṣhitasya – embraced, ca – and

By compressing the cavity above the soft palate with the procedure for transiting through kha divine space, the semen would not flow even when the yogi is embraced by a seductive woman.

Analysis

This happens not just by doing the tongue curl-up-and-back procedure but also by disabling the reproductive switch. The first step in doing this is to cause the kundalini lifeforce to be uplifted from the sushumna nadi central passage. It has to be relocated into the head. So long as kundalini is lodged at muladhara base chakra, it will always resume a conventional behavior anytime effective pressure for its reorientation is relaxed. This means that whenever the yogi is not doing the asana postures and breath-infusion, the kundalini will resume its location at the muladhara base chakra. It will reestablish its evolutionay habits.

Even after years of practice, many students are stymied by this repeated resumption of kundalini. They do not know how to make kundalini abandon its lair at muladhara chakra. Thus they have a dead-end accomplishment which is to raise kundalini on a daily basis and take whatever benefit they can accrue from this action over time.

The only way to change this is to relocate kundalini into the head of the subtle body. However when that is done, the system will still retain the tendency for reproduction. The yogi must systematically attack this function in the body. Srila Yogeshwarananda gave the hint about using the genitals only for urination, ignoring its reproductive capacity.

Some interested parties say that it is a sexual problem but that is a misunderstanding which occurs because of the natural misinterpretation of reproduction as a sexual drive. Nature's idea is for reproduction not sexuality but it uses sexual polarity to sponsor the reproduction of some life forms. In some others, for instance in some vegetation, we see that one may cut a limb from a plant and cause the plant to reproduce through the cut stalk. However if we cut a limb from human body, it will not produce another human being. For reproduction, sexual polarity is necessary in many higher life forms. Hence, to suit its purpose nature develops and promotes gender.

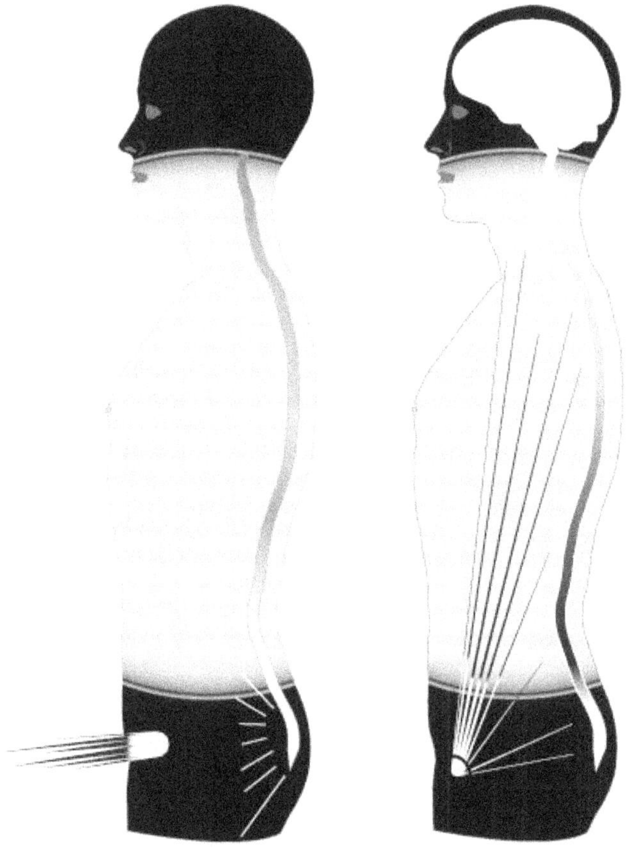

reproductive switch externalized

reproductive switch internalized

We normally confuse gender with sexuality. Many people run away with the idea that if we get rid of sexuality our problems will be solved. However as long as the reproductive operations are in place, nature will repeatedly contrast the genders.

At the root of the issue is not sex or even reproduction, it is nutrition. Reproduction's main sponsor is nutrition. If we interfere with that we can undermine the reproduction tendency.

Sexual orientation is not the problem. Sexual indulgence even is not the issue. These aspects are operative only if they are inspired by nutrition. Hence if the yogi gets the diet under control and if he can lift every bit of the hormonal energy before it is charged by the sex organ chakra, there would be no downward flow of semen.

That is easier said than done because these bodies were designed by nature with a genetic system for sponsoring the downward flow of bodily fluids. Only a few yogis may physically achieve the up-flow in full because the amount of progress which is required to achieve that cannot be amassed in the life time of the average ascetic.

Instead of becoming occupied with the physical up-flow it is best to aim for control in the subtle body and especially control of interest in sexual pleasure consumption. Ultimately, this body belongs to material nature not to the core-self. At some point the self should understand that no matter what, it cannot absolutely possess the body. It cannot permanently change material nature. It will not substantially override nature's planned activities which were transpiring for billions of years.

When a yogi realizes this, he extracts his interest from material affairs. He lets the body do what it must do and focuses on the isolation of the core-self from its adjuncts. This is called kevala or kaivalya in Sanskrit. It means aloneness or oneness with one being a core-self in isolation from the influences of the psychic adjuncts in its psyche. It does not mean mergence but rather transcendental segregation.

Application

To make us understand the extent of control required, Swatmarama wrote of a yogi being embraced by a kamini attractive woman. Usually when a male is embraced by an attractive female, there is sexual arousal in the body of the male. By reproductive design the male system has a pump which emits semen in a downward spouting flow. If a male is in the proximity of an attractive female it is likely that this reproductive apparatus will be activated with the result being that the male's genitals will emit semen.

Those yogis who transit through kha divine space find that their evolutionary habits become altered if not deactivated altogether. The body no longer responds to the conventional stimuli.

Verse 43

चलितोऽपि यदा बिन्दुः सम्प्राप्तो योनि–मण्डलम् ।

वरजत्यूर्ध्वं हृतः शक्त्या निबद्धो योनि–मुद्रया ।। ४३ ।।

calito'pi yadā binduḥ samprāpto yoni–maṇḍalam |
vrajatyūrdhvaṁ hṛtaḥ śaktyā nibaddho yoni–mudrayā || 43 ||

calito = calitaḥ = moves, 'pi – api, even, yadā – when, binduḥ = semen, samprāpto = samprāptaḥ = reaches, yoni–maṇḍalam = vagino–uterine chakra, vrajaty = vrajati = draw, ūrdhvaṁ – upward, hṛtaḥ – took, śaktyā – by forcibly, nibaddho = nibaddhaḥ = arrested, yoni – vaginal parallel in yogi's body, mudrayā – by the mystic checking practice

Even when the semen reaches the vagino-uterine chakra, the yogi can draw it upward by forcibly arresting it using the mystic checking procedure

for the vaginal parallel retraction.

Analysis

This procedure may be physical only. It may be psychic only. It may be done in the self-tantric practice when there is no partner and the yogi performs mystic arresting actions using his body as having male and female composites.

The vagino-uterine chakra is the sex organ chakra of a female. It is not the same as the sex chakra on the spinal column. This corresponds with the penis-testes chakra of the males which is not the same as the sex chakra on the spine. The difference between these two chakras, of the sex organ chakra and the sex chakra, is that the sex organ chakra is creative and expressive, while the sex chakra is directive.

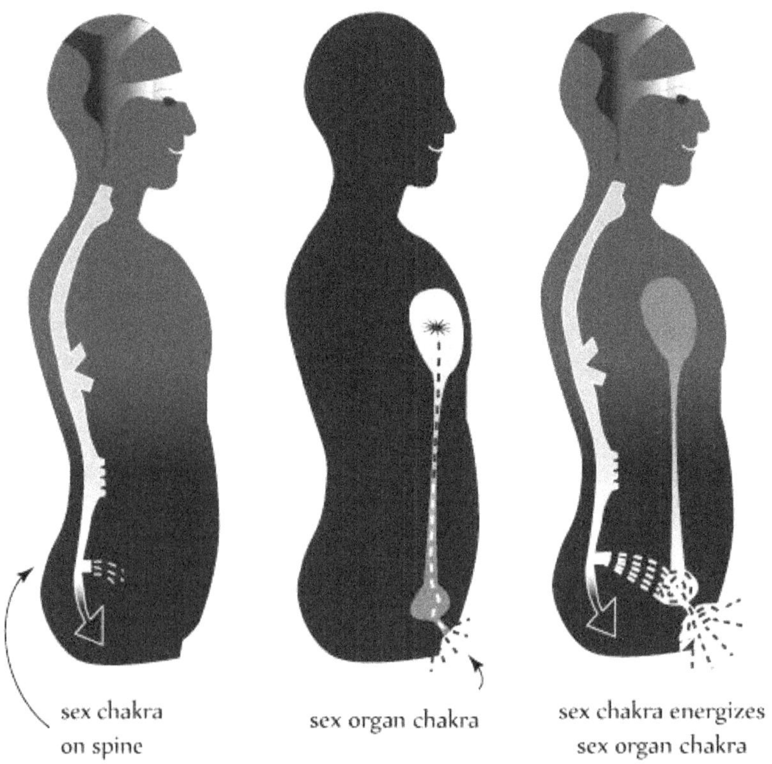

The sex chakra directs the genitals and the reproductive organ from a distance by the use of electric signals while the sex organ chakras take those directives and operate their functions.

There are two distinct parts to the sex organ chakra which are the reproductive area and the expressive area. In males the reproductive area is the testes while the expressive area is the penis. In females the reproductive area is the ovary-uterine combination while the expressive area is the vaginal passage.

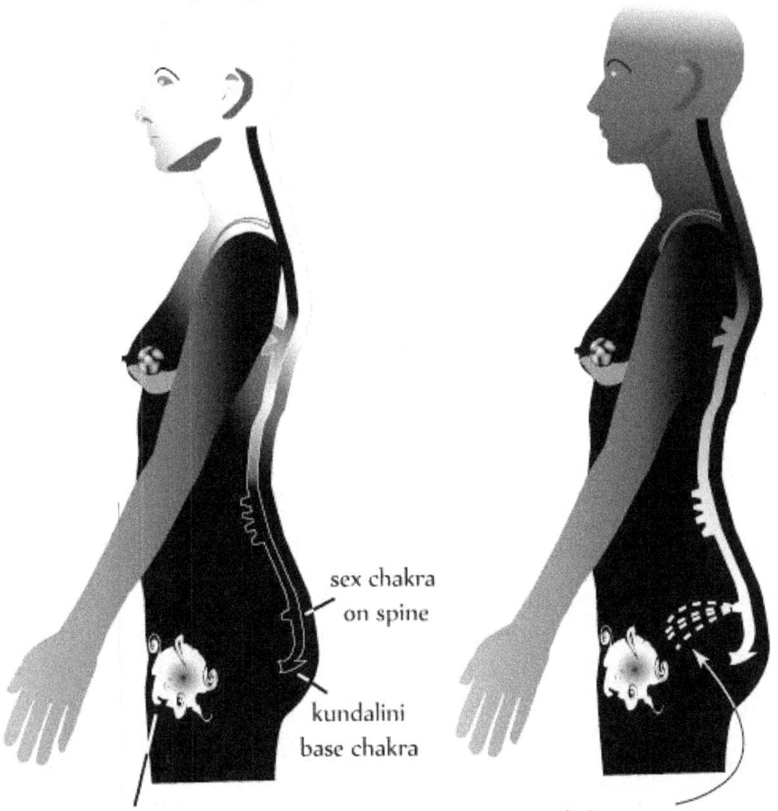

By convention, the male system is designed for emitting sexual fluids not for absorbing fluids. The female format is for absorption and emittance. Females have the dual system because their bodies serve to carry a fetus and it must also secrete fluids primarily for creating eggs which are the first feeding facilities for the sperm particles which carry the kundalini system for the developing embryo.

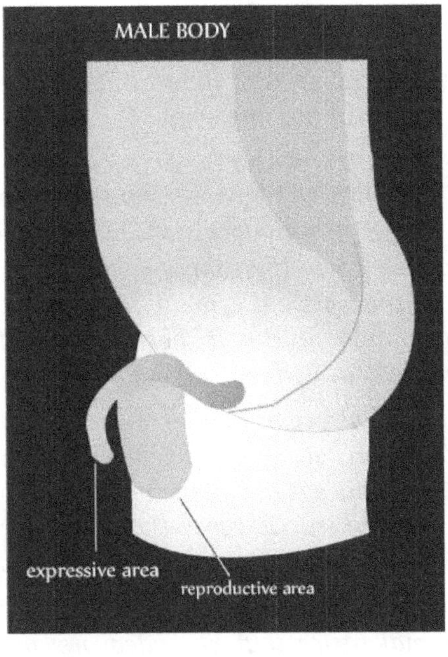

Males are equipped for very limited development of sperm. Their sexual secretions concern fluids for sperm survival and easy passage of sperm through their tubing. Females in contrast have secretions for development of eggs, passage of the same and lubrication of the vaginal passage for easy transit of the male organ through the vagina.

By convention, the female sexual organ has a psychic sucking action just as we see that infants have a mouth sucking action which draws milk from a woman's breast. Without being told, a newborn infant will begin sucking even in the absence of its mother's breast.

Both in the physical and subtle bodies, there is a sucking action in the female vagina for extracting the semen from the male organ. To compliment this and to make nature's intentions very clear, there is a pumping action in the male sexual apparatus which squirts fluids into the woman vagina or into the entrance of her uterus.

Thus from at least a psychic view point, there is a fluid expression in the male which is complimented by a suction extraction in the female. This is for accelerating the delivery of the sexual fluids from the male body into the female one. It makes clear nature's intention because it is an involuntary operation.

Just as an infant, without being told and even in the absence of breasts, will begin the sucking action with its mouth, so a male body might emit semen and a female body might have a suction feeling even if the persons involved never experienced sexual intercourse.

Human beings do learn to exploit these feelings which they interpret as sexual pleasure but irrespective, the system is basically an involuntary operation of nature.

Application

The practice of males retracting their semen begins with the sex lock which is the contraction and up-draw of the pubio-coccyx muscle. There are two muscles involved. One is used for stopping urination where the tube which descends from the bladder is contracted. The other is for checking the squirt impulse for semen. This squirt impulse is involuntary and is difficult to control. Even if it is controlled, still it may operate regardless of the willpower application to stop it. This is because this is a primal instinct in material nature which was not designed for will power application. It may take weeks or years of practice to begin to control the downward flow of semen. It is a hard feat for a yogi.

Formerly due to cultural cooperation, a yogi could easily control this but due to the predominance of sexual gratification in modern times, it is near impossible to come to grips with this impulse. Regardless, a yogi should aspire for this because the attempt even if it fails in this current body would create a providential opportunity in the future life or in the astral world hereafter for completion of this austerity.

Initially students cannot differentiate between the urinary lock and the sex lock. This is because nature linked the two contractions. After some practice however students who focus internally can sort the two areas and isolate one from the other. Over time the yogi gains mastery and can stop semen from flowing down the tubing, even during intercourse with a voluptuous female. It is not that a yogi should seek out a companion. That is the not the attitude of a genuine yogi. But if there is a fated relationship then the yogi could observe how much his body can apply these locks.

Formerly there was support for these practices in the culture of human society. That assistance contributed to the success of the few yogis who became proficient. Now that the culture is mostly antagonistic to celibacy, that assistance is not forthcoming and so it is hardly likely that a yogi can master these techniques. However that does not matter provided the yogi sincerely endeavors and stays in association with the siddhas.

A yogi does not have to be successful with every technique and in fact he will not be if certain supports are absent. He should however make sure that he endeavors and satisfies his yoga-gurus by implementing the practices which are inspired by them. The opinion of people besides the yoga-gurus and the deities is totally irrelevant.

Verse 44

ऊर्ध्व–जिह्वः सथिरो भूत्वा सोमपानं करोति यः ।
मासार्धेन न सन्देहो मृत्युं जयति योगवित् ।। ४४ ।।

ūrdhva–jihvaḥ sthiro bhūtvā somapānaṁ karoti yaḥ I
māsārdhena na sandeho mṝtyuṁ jayati yogavit II 44 II

ūrdhva – upward, jihvaḥ – tongue, sthiro = sthiraḥ = steady, bhūtvā – become, somapānaṁ – subtle liquid which trickles from above the palate, karoti – does, drinks, yaḥ – who, māsārdhena – by half of a month, na – no, sandeho = sandehaḥ = doubt, mṝtyuṁ – death, jayati – transcend, yogavit – a proficient yogi

With the tongue upward, with it becoming steady in that position, drinking the subtle liquid which trickles down from above the palate, there is no doubt, that a proficient yogi will transcend death in half of a month.

Analysis

What was achieved in half a month during the time of Swatmarama may take half a lifetime in the modern era. Unless a yogi achieved the urdhvareta upward flowing of semen status, he cannot get these experiences; and he must achieve that on a consistent basis for some time. He must be in the right social environment.

Yogis used to be in isolation, away from the haunts of human beings. This requirement still holds for full success but some teachers issue a pretense as if it does not matter what the social environment imposes. Social assistance with yoga practice is a big issue. The analogy that a yogi is like a lotus leaf which always resists the water which falls on it, is valuable when we consider that the plant is supported by the soil under the water from which it extracts chemicals to manufacture its resistant leaf tissue. A yogi must also draw a certain amount of support from society. If he is without that, his accomplishment will be limited.

The subtle liquid which trickles down from above the palate is the same liquid which is used in sexual experience to give heightened feelings to the genitals. The yogi manipulates the subtle body so that this liquid does not go down into the reproductive glands but instead goes up through the neck into the brain.

With his interest retracted from the sensual focus in a material body, the yogi becomes detached from death and its effects due to not having a focus in the planes of consciousness where death has a register. The influence of death continues unabated but since the yogi moved his concern from the realms which death affects, he become immune to its spell.

Application

We do not have a similar social environment to that of the ancient yogis who were successful in just half a month. Yet, we should do our best and aspire so that we may

continue this practice to proficiency in the astral domains hereafter. If a yogi fails to complete the practice there, it will be necessary for him to take another embryo, whereby he would begin this history of birth, growth of a body, reformatory yoga practice to change the non-yogic tendencies of that body, attainment of advanced yoga, and finally, full success.

Taking another body is risky due to the fact that the parental environment may have retardative influences which make it impossible for the yogi to finish the practice successfully during the lifetime of that form. Despite these uncertainties, a yogi should persist until providence gives him the perfect opportunity.

Verse 45

नित्यं सोम–कला–पूर्णं श्रीरं यस्य योगिनः ।

तक्षकेणापि दष्टस्य विषं तस्य न सर्पति ।। ४५ ।।

nityaṁ soma–kalā–pūrṇaṁ śarīraṁ yasya yoginaḥ I
takṣakeṇāpi daṣṭasya viṣaṁ tasya na sarpati I I 45 I I

nityaṁ – always, soma – the subtle liquid which trickles down from above the palate, kalā – nectarine, pūrṇaṁ – full, śarīraṁ – body, yasya – whose, yoginaḥ – yogi, takṣakeṇāpi = takṣakeṇa (Takshak poisonous serpent) + api (also), daṣṭasya – stung by, viṣaṁ – venom, tasya – him, na – not, sarpati – spread

If the yogi whose body is full of the subtle liquid which trickles down from above the palate is stung by the Takshak poisonous serpent, its venom would not spread through his body.

Analysis

The Takshak poisonous serpent fatally bit King Parikshit. Even though the king was a pious ruler, even though he was forgiven by the brahmin whom he insulted, even though his grandfather was Arjuna, the famous warrior-yogi of the Bhagavad Gita, even though he was amply protected by mantras and incantations of qualified Vedic priests, even though he isolated himself on a snake-inaccessible platform and even though he repented, still nothing could stop the fate which empowered the poisonous snake.

With this in mind, Swatmarama swore that when the yogi's body is saturated with the subtle liquid which trickles down from above the palate, even the infallible killing power of Takshak would be thwarted.

To understand this perspective, we could reconsider sexual experience, where during that pleasure we feel the whole body contributing special feelings to the genitals.

Why are the genitals the focal region?

Why does every other part of the body contribute a minute or significant quantity of bliss energy to the climax of the experience?

If the cells contribute their bliss content into the head of the subtle body and if that contribution collects there and then drips to the upturned tongue, redistribution to the cells may cause a change in their genetic disposition, making it impossible for even venom to affect the body.

Application

The cellular bliss energy is burnt out in the body through basic sensual activities especially through sexual intercourse. These utilities are conventional, being created, maintained and utilized by material nature in its survival-of-the-species plan. Yoga directs the student in changing the configuration so that the bliss energy is collected and distributed in a different way which facilitates spiritual consciousness and unplugs the psyche's interest from the material and lower astral regions.

Kundalini hatha yoga is the way to do this by mystic actions rather than by visualization and hope aspirations.

The course is:

- *Infuse fresh air into the lungs of the physical body.*
- *Cause that air to go down against the energy which is at the navel.*
- *Infuse more fresh air into the lungs.*
- *Push that air and the previous mix of fresh air and navel energy downwards to the pubic floor.*
- *Infuse more fresh air, forcing it down to the mix accumulated before.*
- *Infuse more fresh air.*
- *Push it through the groin area to muladhara base chakra.*
- *Infuse more fresh air.*
- *Press that into muladhara chakra.*
- *Apply the neck, anus, perineum, and abdomen locks.*
- *Infuse more fresh air.*
- *Sense the energy which swiftly moves through the spine into the head.*

Do this practice for weeks, months or years until you are familiar with it and mastered the energy which comes into the head, so that there is no space-out, stun-out, black-out, grey-out, white-out or gold-out of consciousness where you lose control of the material body.

Once you master this, do the following:

- *Do breath-infusion but instead of pushing the air down towards the navel, pull the hormonal energy up from the navel.*
- *This is a subtle exercise which means that you must pay attention within the psyche and not be distracted or you will not sense what is required. Wear a blindfold to increase and confine visual concentration within the psyche.*
- *Keep doing breath-infusion and pull up the hormonal energy from in the trunk of the body through the neck of the form.*
- *Do not worry about arousing the kundalini through the sushumna central passage.*

- *After some breath sessions infusing the hormonal energy, when you feel that the lungs are saturated and will absorb no more air, stop at the end of an inhale. Apply the neck, anus, perineum and abdomen locks.*
- *Wiggle the body this way and that way according to how you are inspired by the infused energy and the release of bliss force. This release of bliss force may be so slight, so negligible, that it may hardly be observed if you are not very attentive within the psyche. In some experiences it will be sensational and obvious.*
- *Keep infusing fresh air, then applying locks; then check for the distribution of the bliss energy through the psyche.*
- *Continue infusing until you are certain that every part of the psyche is infused. Use various postures as you are inspired to extract pollutants which hide here and there in the subtle body.*

This process will give you the ability to move the bliss energy into the head of the subtle body so that the configuration or conventional movement of it is upwards into the brain as contrasted to the normal behavior which is that the bliss force is accumulated in the genital region of the body.

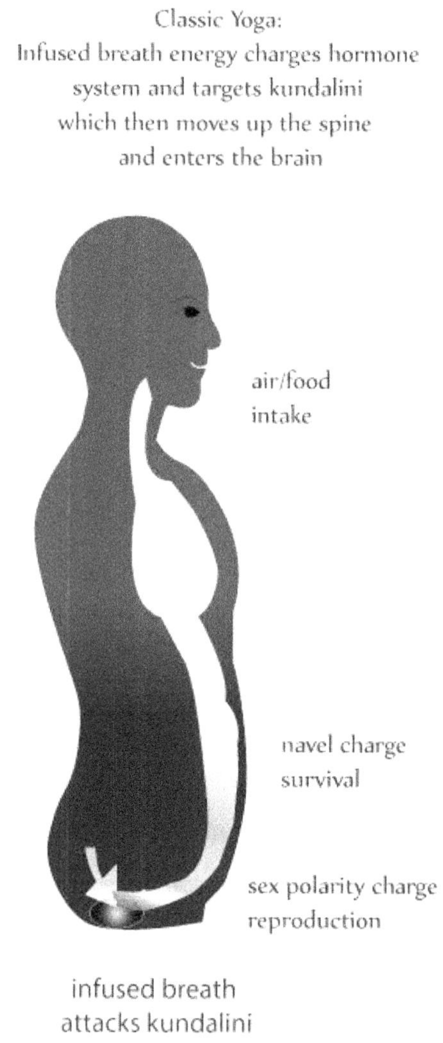
Classic Yoga:
Infused breath energy charges hormone system and targets kundalini which then moves up the spine and enters the brain
air/food intake
navel charge survival
sex polarity charge reproduction
infused breath attacks kundalini

Reverse gravity method:
air/food energy never reaches kundalini.
It is pulled up by breath infusion pulling
force and is then distributed without being surcharged
for survival and reproduction.
Kundalini is deprived of its main food source.

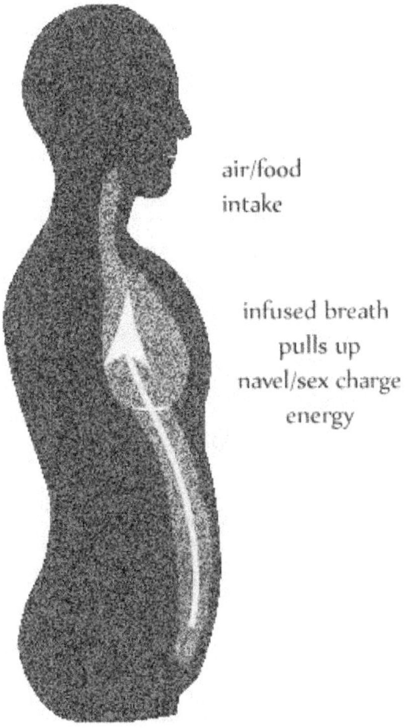

Verse 46

इन्धनानि यथा वह्निस्तैल– वर्त्तिं च दीपकः ।
तथा सोम–कला–पूर्णं देही देहं न मुञ्चति ।। ४६ ।।

indhanāni yathā vahnistaila–varttiṁ ca dīpakaḥ ।
tathā soma–kalā–pūrṇaṁ dehī dehaṁ na muñchati ।। 46 ।।

indhanāni – fuels, yathā – as, vahnis = vahniḥ = fire, taila–varttiṁ = oil lamp, ca – and, dīpakaḥ – wick, tathā – so, soma – moon, kalā – nectar, pūrṇaṁ – full, dehī – psychological inhabitant of the body, dehaṁ – physical body, na – not, muñcati – abandon

As the fire is not extinguished if there are fuels, as the oil lamp does not cease illuminating so long as there is a wick, so the psychological inhabitant of the body does not abandon it, so long as it is filled with moon nectar.

Analysis

The dehi (day-hee) psychological inhabitant of the body, the core-self, cannot leave the body until there is a complete shutdown of generating nectar. Each healthy cell in the body produces this nectar which in the physical form is hormonal energy. This is generated by instruction from the kundalini lifeforce. Normally, the core-self neither generates it or distributes it but the self is leashed to the lifeforce and must comply with the movements of that power.

By and by, over time, a yogi gains control of the distribution of this hormonal energy. Then at last he directs its generation as well. This happens after months or years of proficient practice, after he wrestled control of the system from the kundalini, after it was displaced from the muladhara base chakra into the brain of the subtle body.

As nature would have it the nectar energy or bliss force is focused into the genital region in an adult body but a yogi's task is to relocate it into the brain. When it is focused into the genital region it is considered to be sun nectar, a heated substance. When they are sexually aroused, people say that they are hot. When the nectar is focused in the head region of the body, it is cool and is regarded as a moon energy.

There is no transit of feelings in a body if the hormone energy is not generated. This is irrespective of where that energy normally accumulates; if it does so in the genitals or in the head. This hormonal energy is the electric conduit for voluntary and involuntary commands to operate the body.

Initially this is all done by the kundalini lifeforce but through hatha yoga kundalini practice, a yogi gains control of this system and the core-self operates it with very little help from the kundalini. That is how the self becomes the actual lord of the psyche. As nature would have it, the self poses as master of the body, even though it is in fact a peon in the system. But through this yoga, that lordship of the core-self can become a reality.

Application

The problem with dying is that the lifeforce will follow the nectar energy which is left in the body when it is near its death. Wherever there is life in the body when it is near its death, there will be heat at that place in the body or there might be a special cooling sensation which is unusual except for bodies which die from hypothermia in very cold locations.

Heat is the sign of life in a body but at death it is the sign of where the lifeforce will be at the last moment before exiting the body. As nature would have it, the hormonal energy is mostly focalized in the genitals. From there it is distributed in a stingy way to other parts of the form. This distribution is done with reproduction being the foremost consideration of the lifeforce.

Whichever part of the body aids the most in sexual intercourse is given the largest supply of hormonal energy by the lifeforce. This is its selfish operation. Even in people who have no sexual intercourse, even in people who feel that they are morally-inclined, even they are configured for the most distribution of hormonal energy for sexual intercourse. They may not use the energy because they may not indulge in sex pleasure but that in no way contradicts that the sex organs are the most prominent storage area.

Even if there is no war where the explosions occur, every army has an ammunition dump. Some armies use their ammunition constantly and resupply their stocks. Other armies remained penned up in barracks but their dumps remain stocked with the explosives nevertheless. They restock old ammo as they defuse old bombs.

When celibacy means storage of sexual energy, it is not celibacy even though it suits the requirement for morality. Yoga is not morality and strictly speaking it has no concern with that. Unfortunately for yoga and for them, many moralists who come from many lives of using morality to maintain the status quo, begin the practice of yoga and bring into the yogic association their corrupt opinions about the value of morality, even though in yoga it has no prominence.

Yama moral restraints and niyama approved behaviors have nothing to do with social interaction or conventional morality, but beginners usually feel that it is related to that. They pride themselves in their application of the yoga practice in so far as it can be applied to social standing.

At the time of death, the lifeforce will follow its customs. It will not be concerned with moral standing. If its main focus was the genitals, then irrespective of what the person believed in, that is where it will go. If for instance my focal storage of hormones was the genitals, I will go there at the time of death on the basis of the lifeforce attraction to that, irrespective of my religious or moral belief or performance.

It is not what I believe or how I religiously conduct myself but what the lifeforce actual does behind the scenes. Hence if somehow I can master this kundalini yoga system described by Swatmarama, the lifeforce will travel into the head at the time of death, and I as the core-self will leave the body from that perspective, which is great as far as my wanting to go where the siddhas are located in the astral domains.

Morality has all the value for the social dealings in this world and for my investing in privileged social status in future lives but beyond that it is near to being worthless. This is not because it has no application and value. In fact it has worth even to Krishna as he explained in the Bhagavad Gita. The reason why morality is worthless in the final analysis is that the kundalini lifeforce runs the show, not the core-self. The kundalini does not give a hoot about morality except to use it at its convenience in the struggle for existence in the survival game. The core-self's obsession with morality is its last ditch effort to make a showing of itself as being the lord of its psyche even though the kundalini is really the master of this game.

Verse 47

गोमांसं भक्षयेन्नित्यं पिबेदमर-वारुणीम् ।

कुलीनं तमहं मन्य इतरे कुल–घातकाः ।। ४७ ।।

gomāṁsaṁ bhakṣayennityaṁ pibedamara–vāruṇīm |
kulīnaṁ tamahaṁ manya itare kula–ghātakāḥ || 47 ||

go – cow, māṁsaṁ – flesh, bhakṣayen = bhakṣayet – would swallow, nityaṁ – always, pibed = pibet = drink, amara – deathless, vāruṇīm – liquor, kulīnaṁ – good family, tam – him, ahaṁ – I, manya – consider, itare – others, kula – clan, ghātakāḥ –

degraders

Those who always swallow cow flesh and drink the deathless liquor; I consider to be of good families. Others are degraders of the clan.

Analysis

Swatmarama gave a questionable statement which may cause doubt in the minds of readers. For yogis, cow flesh is taboo and so is liquor. Both substances are prohibited in the yama moral restraints. In fact any kind of flesh of any animal is negative for a yogi. Any type of liquor or intoxicant is prevented. Thus why did Swatmarama appraise swallowing cow flesh and drinking deathless liquor?

This has to do with the technique of curling up and pushing back the tongue into the soft palate. This has a feeling which is similar to what the mouth enjoys while a carnivorous human being eats cow flesh. The nectar which drops from above feels as if it is deathless liquor. The yogi becomes habituated to this. Just as some humans become preoccupied eating flesh and drinking liquor, the yogi spends hours of meditation doing this.

normal human being
with nutrition/reproduction focus
kundalini used this energy for sexual pleasure
and other types of exploitive pursuits

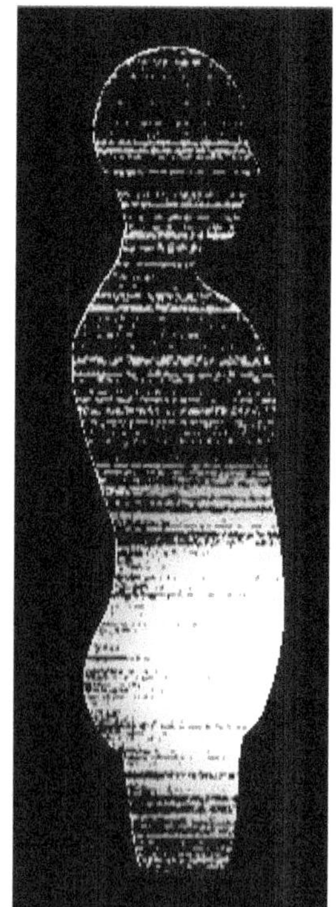

Application

Until a yogi reaches the level of advancement where the nectar in the body accumulates in the brain and not in the genitals, regardless of his sexual participation, he is considered to be neophyte and has not attained success in practice. His fate is uncertain as to what will be his lot hereafter and in the next life which he must take because there is nothing to stop him from going through the rebirth cycle.

To stop rebirth or even to be choosy as to where one might take the next body, one has to remove the reproductive urge from the subtle body. This is done by tearing kundalini away from muladhara chakra and relocating the hormone reservoir into the head of the subtle body.

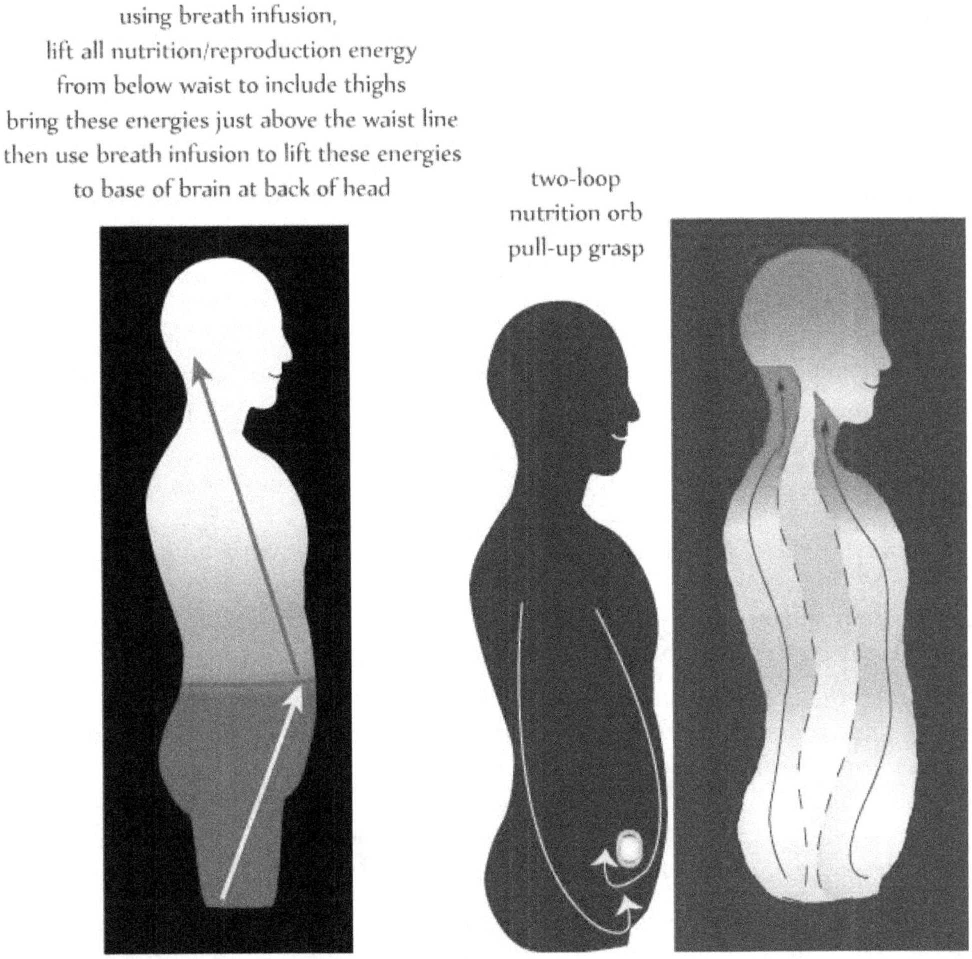
using breath infusion,
lift all nutrition/reproduction energy
from below waist to include thighs
bring these energies just above the waist line
then use breath infusion to lift these energies
to base of brain at back of head
two-loop
nutrition orb
pull-up grasp

If the genitals can be described as the sexual brain of the body, then that reproductive intelligence must be relocated into the head of the subtle form for changing the method of material nature which is to automatically re-route a disembodied psyche back to developing an embryo.

Verse 48

गो–शब्देनोदिता जिह्वा तत्प्रवेशो हि तालुनि ।

गो–मांस–भक्षणं तत्तु महा–पातक–नाशनम् ।। ४८ ।।

gośabdenoditā jihvā tatpraveśo hi tāluni |
gomāṁsabhakṣaṇaṁ tattu mahāpātakanāśanama || 48 ||

go – cow, śabdenoditā = śabdena (by word) + uditā (as used), jihvā – tongue, tat – that, praveśo = praveśaḥ = insertion, hi – because, tāluni – into the palate, go – cow, māṁsa – flesh, bhakṣaṇaṁ – eating, tat – that, tu – indeed, mahā – great, pātaka – faults, nāśanam – means of elimination

In this usage, the word cow means tongue. Its insertion into the palate is termed eating cow flesh. Indeed it causes the means of elimination of great faults.

Analysis

Eating impulse is the root cause of hormone accumulation in the first place. This accumulation results in craving, some type of craving, somewhere in the body involving one or more senses. The manager of this is the kundalini lifeforce which harnesses and employs the senses in a go-and-get syndrome.

Once an edible gets into the mouth, the eating impulse operates to provide touching and tasting satisfactions. It is of two varieties essentially, which are touching the form and tasting the chemicals in the substance. The kundalini derives satisfaction from this.

When the tongue is inserted into the soft palate, the touching and tasting sensations get satisfaction and the psyche is relieved of the need for eating.

Application

A yogi must realize sooner or later that the sensual urges cannot be eliminated altogether. The senses of one level can be removed by exiting from that plane of existence or a person might fold a sense into itself and shut it down for the time being. Ultimately there is no way to completely destroy the senses.

Practical methods for suspending sensual operations must be found by the student or he may be introduced to serviceable techniques by the yoga-guru. By all means the student must be realistic for there to be success.

When the senses are retracted upon themselves and when the kundalini lifeforce is fully aroused and is lifted into the head of the subtle body, something happens where the tasting sense is pulled up into the location where the tongue is attached to the base of the mouth. This entire faculty of eating is then shrunk into its essential form and is directed into the cavity in the back of the head. If seen it looks like a white flame about one-quarter inch across and about seven inches high.

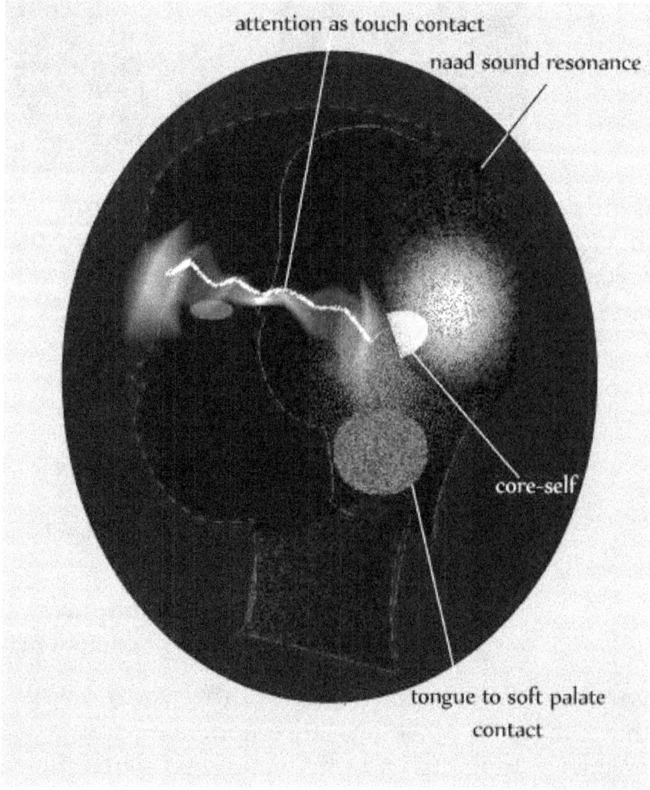

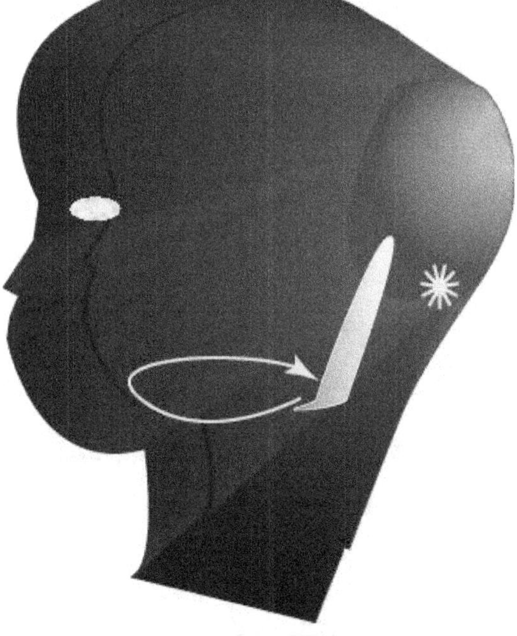

Verse 49

जिह्वा–प्रवेश–सम्भूत–वह्निनोत्पादितः खलु ।

चन्द्रात्स्रवति यः सारः सा सयादमर–वारुणी ।। ४९ ।।

jihvā–praveśa–sambhūta–vahninotpāditaḥ khalu |
candrātsravati yaḥ sāraḥ sā syādamara–vāruṇī || 49 ||

jihvā – tongue, praveśa – insertion, sambhūta – manifests, vahninotpāditaḥ = vahninā (by fire) + utpāditaḥ (is produced), khalu – indeed, candrāt – from the moon-like cool nectar, sravati – flows, yaḥ – which, sāraḥ – essence, sā – that, syād = syāt = is, amara – deathless, vāruṇī – liquor

Indeed, it is produced by the fire which manifests from the insertion of the tongue. The deathless liquor is the essence which flows from the moon-like cool nectar.

Analysis

When the nutrition sense is pulled up, retracted fully under the tongue, and when the tongue is pushed into the soft palate with the kundalini lifeforce being in the head as its primary residence, then the hormone energy accumulates in the head.

This is a cooling force as compared to the heating energy of the hormones in the sex organ chakra. For a time, the nutrition energy absorbs the nectar force but later when the yogi retreats into the naad sound resonance, this process of consumption ceases.

Application

In kundalini yoga when one uses the sex hormones with the infused breath energy to

arouse the kundalini, one finds that a bliss-energy is produced which is like sunshine and which has a slight heating effect. But when kundalini is drawn up into the brain permanently, after it abandons its muladhara base chakra, and when the nutrition energy becomes upward bound instead of gravity controlled, the hormones accumulate in the head of the subtle body but with a cooling energy that is similar to that of the moon. This is a bliss force as well but it feels more like a mint-camphor cooling bliss sensation.

Verse 50

चुम्बन्ती यदि लम्बिकाग्रमनिशं जिह्वा–रस–सयन्दिनी

स– सक्षारा कटुकाम्ल–दुग्ध–सदृशी मध्वाज्य–तुल्या तथा ।

वयाधीनां हरणं जरान्त–करणं शस्त्रागमोदीरणं

तस्य स्यादमरत्वमष्ट –गुणितं सिद्धाङ्गनाकर्षणम् ।। ५० ।।

cumbantī yadi lambikāgramaniśaṁ jihvā–rasa–syandinī
sakṣārā kaṭukāmla–dughdha–sadṝśī madhvājya–tulyā tathā |
vyādhīnāṁ haraṇaṁ jarānta–karaṇaṁ śastrāgamodīraṇaṁ
tasya syādamaratvamaṣṭa–guṇitaṁ siddhānganākarṣaṇam || 50 ||

cumbantī – touches, yadi – if, lambikāgram = lambikā (palate) + agram (above), aniśaṁ – constantly, jihvā – tongue, rasa – flavor, syandinī – flows, sakṣārā – salty, kaṭukāmla = kaṭuka (pungent) + amla (sour), dughdha – milk, sadṝśī – like, madhv = madhu = honey, ājya – ghee, tulyā – like, tathā – so, vyādhīnāṁ – diseases, haraṇaṁ – eliminator, jarāntakaraṇaṁ = what causes the end of old age, śastrāgamodīraṇaṁ = śastra (weapon) + agama (attack) + udīraṇaṁ (prevention), tasya – his, syād = syād = is, amaratvam – immortality, aṣṭa – eight, guṇitaṁ – supernatural skills, siddhānganākarṣaṇam = siddhā (perfected yoginis) + anginā (women) + ākarṣaṇam (attract)

If the tongue constantly touches the palate; the flavor flows, having salty, pungent and sour taste, as well as flavors like milk, honey or ghee. It causes the elimination of disease, the end of old age, prevention of attack by weapons, immortality, the eight supernatural skills and attraction of the perfected yogini women.

Analysis

There are many side effects to the pushing of the tongue into the soft palate at the back of the mouth. Some, Swatmarama listed as follows:

- taste of salty, pungent and sour flavors
- taste of milk, honey or ghee
- elimination of disease
- end of old age
- prevention of attack by weapons
- immortality

- eight supernatural skills
- attraction of the perfected yogini women

A **taste of salty, pungent and sour flavors** occurs on occasion when the yogi pushes the tongue back into the soft palate. This should be observed but a yogi should not become attached to this. He should not hanker for these tastes nor seek them out. As when travelling one passes scenic surroundings, so the yogi should observe this and continue the progression.

The realization to extract from this is that in the psyche, there is a blueprint for every recognizable taste. This means that whatever salty, pungent or sour flavor one recognizes is done based on a registry of flavors which is lodged in the nutrition sense which is a light in the subtle body. There is no need to pursue such flavors because their formats outside the subtle body are recognized only because of a matching taste aspect within it.

The **taste of milk, honey or ghee** comes from actual molecules within the body which create such liquids in the form. Milk for instance is created in the breasts of women as part of the reproductive fluids. Ghee is milk fat. Honey is created in the hormone producing glands of the body. These liquids are tasted when the tongue is pushed into the soft palate. They are not imaginations of the yogi.

When these tastes are experienced, a yogi can evaluate them and check their addiction potential. He can decide to forgo cravings for these liquids and to get satisfaction from their tastes when doing the tongue-into-soft-palate procedure.

The **elimination of disease** is possible by control of tasting. It may be said that the body begins at its birth. However it may be argued that the body begins as a viable sperm particle in the body of the father. Then it may be posited that the body began as the body of the father. Then it may be said that the body began with a departed ancestor. Since the trail of the origin of the body cannot be determined in full at this stage of the creation, it should be concluded that elimination of disease cannot be attained.

In the meantime, a yogi can gain as much control as possible. By doing so he may not aggravate what is fated as mandatory diseases for the body. By meditating deeply on the nutrition urge while pushing the tongue into the soft palate, a yogi can know to what extent he may protect the body from disease. He may also perceive which diseases cannot be prevented from accessing the body.

The **end of old age** is perceived by a yogi who is proficient in the tongue-push-into-soft-palate procedure because old age is based on the genetic deterioration of the physical body which is directly related to nutrition. The gradual deterioration of the body from the peak of its youth is a special study for yogis who want to research how it grows to its maximum potential and then recedes away from that rapidly.

In conclusion a yogi understands that no matter the diet whether it be nutritious or poisonous, the body will deteriorate. This is because of preset parameters from before the beginning of the universe, factors which no one can adjust at this stage.

When all is said and done, a physical being will be left with what survives in the hereafter as his remnant psychology. Therefore a yogi switches interest to that and abandons concerns about saving the material form.

The **prevention of attack by weapons** is studied by a yogi because the material body has this uncertainty factor and the ever-ready potential for wounds. Perceiving the violence potential in the material world, the yogi smiles because he understands that there is no way to decrease mandatory incidences. A certain amount of trauma will be played out.

Many pseudo yogis who had criminal intent pressured supernatural beings to award immunity from bodily harm; but the supernaturals explained that due to the nature of the world, no one can give anyone else absolute physical protection

A yogi can act to reduce provocations. He may also sidestep some resentment even though some are sure to impact him. The one way to avoid this is to migrate out of the material level and the lower astral regions. The zone of escape is the chit akash sky of consciousness which is accessed from within the psyche of a yogi.

Immortality pertains to the subtle body in a comparative way and to the core-self in an absolute manner. A yogi gets insight into the comparative longevity of the subtle body. There are legends about yogis who used physical bodies for hundreds and even thousands of years but there is no instance of a physical body lasting forever. The subtle body may be here for the duration of the universe, at least until the sun is demolished. In reference to the disease-ridden short-duration physique, the subtle body is relatively immortal. It is the subtle body which is used as the basis for transmigrating from one physical form to another. The core-self cannot transmigrate unless it is housed in a subtle form.

In reference to the subtle body, the core-self is infinite. This self will persist even the destruction of the universe. How it will exist at that time is in question.

Realizing that the physical form is the least durable utility, a yogi shifts interest from it. He transfers the concerns first to the subtle body; for this he develops astral projection. Later his interest is transferred to the inside of the subtle body. Within it there are orifices and transit gateways to higher dimensions. The yogi checks these in the hope of finding a divine place.

The eight supernatural skills were listed by Krishna in the Uddhava Gita (10.4-5), the eleventh canto of the Srimad Bhagavatam. I translated these as follows:

- becoming atomic
- becoming cosmic
- being weightless
- acquiring or experiencing through the sense organs of others
- manipulating mundane potency
- ruling over others
- non-attachment to mundane influences, which results in the technique of controlling one's nature
- obtaining what is desired

The **attraction of the perfected yogini women** happens naturally at a certain stage of advancement when the yogi's subtle body is enhanced and changed into a frequency which is perceived by celestial women who are masterful yoginis but who are not yet paired with a perfected yogi. In the siddha loka astral places, they wait for suitable companions.

Yogis are usually advised to avoid the angelic women because pairing with one may mean a delay of thousands or millions of years before going into the divine atmosphere. Some encounters however are fated and cannot be avoided.

Application

Supernatural events will occur to anyone who does yoga sincerely. There will be development of supernormal powers; some consistently; some sporadically. Certain experiences will be onetime events. Other incidences will occur now and again, while yet others will occur with regularity.

There should be a general progression which a student may observe when he follows instructions of the yoga-guru. Now and again things will happen which concern other aspects of yogic progress.

Verse 51

मूर्ध्नः षोडशपत्रपद्मगलितं प्राणादवाप्तं हठा
दूर्ध्वास्यो रसनां नियम्य विवरे शक्तिं परां चिन्तयन्।
उत्कल्लोल–कला–जलं च विमलं धारामयं यः पिबेन्
निर्व्याधिः स मृणाल–कोमल–वपुर्योगी चिरं जीवति ।। ५१ ।।

mūrdhnaḥ ṣoḍaśapatrapadmagalitaṁ prāṇādavāptaṁ haṭhād
ūrdhvāsyo rasanāṁ niyamya vivare śaktiṁ parāṁ cintayan।
utkallola–kalā–jalaṁ ca vimalaṁ dhārāmayaṁ yaḥ piben
nirvyādhiḥ sa mṛṇāla–komala–vapuryogī ciraṁ jīvati ।। 51 ।।

mūrdhnaḥ – from the head, ṣoḍaśa – sixteen, patra – petals, padma – lotus throat chakra, galitaṁ – oozes, prāṇād = prāṇāt = from breath-infusion, avāptaṁ – is due, haṭhād = haṭhāt = due to kundalini manipulation for psychic energy transformation, ūrdhvāsyo = ūrdhva(upward) + āsyaḥ (mouth), rasanāṁ – tongue, niyamya – restricted, vivare – in the cavity, śaktiṁ – kundalini, parāṁ – primal, cintayan – mentally and emotionally focused, utkallola – flooding, kalā–jalaṁ = bliss–yeilding subtle fluid, ca – and, vimalaṁ – flawless, dhārāmayaṁ – spontaneous stream of emotion, yaḥ – who, piben = pibet = drinks, nirvyādhiḥ – without disease, sa – that, mṛṇāla – fiber of lotus, komala – delicate, vapur = vapus = body, yogī – yogi, ciraṁ – extended period, jīvati – lives

Due to breath-infusion and kundalini manipulation for psyche energy transformation, it oozes from the head into the sixteen petaled lotus throat chakra, when the tongue is channeled upward and back into the cavity, subsequently the primal kundalini becomes mentally and emotionally focused. The yogi drinks the flood of bliss-yielding fluid, which is flawless and which causes him to be without disease, to be delicate like the fiber of a lotus stalk and to live for an extended period of time.

Analysis

The sixteen-petaled lotus chakra is the throat chakra. It is involved in a downward operation where it lowers energy into the trunk of the subtle body. Conventionally it has no interest in eating hormone nectar. Its function as designed is to provide foods from which nectar is extracted for consumption by the reproductive organs.

Nature is hell-bent for reproducing because that is the method of survival by hopping from an old form or even from a damaged new one to some other life form which is capable of sponsoring a new body. Thus once a form appears in an environment, it strives to survive because it may be eaten by another form which needs nutrients for the same reason. Once survival is assured, the entity thinks about prolonging its existence but it is faced with the inevitability of deterioration and death. It develops new bodies in its form and releases those one by one as they are capable of surviving on their own.

Once these child forms come out, the parent entity tends them just as if they were itself. The parent, selfishly but subconsciously, desires to use such forms in the future to resume existence as the child as such progeny. This is the story of reincarnation. It is carried out instinctively by the kundalini psychic lifeforce.

Because a yogi foregoes material existence, he can afford to upset the system of reincarnation. He can sidestep the natural process of looping around and coming back into the world as the child of his progeny. Hence the yogi can upset the system by changing the mission of the throat chakra. Instead of providing nutrients for reproduction, the throat chakra may provide nutrients for self-realization in terms of increased clarity and insight in the head of the subtle body.

Application

The two practices, namely, breath-infusion and kundalini manipulation for psyche energy transformation, gives the yogi the upper hand so that he can keep the physical body in its maximum health potential. This is not for making it live eternality. This is for using the body while keeping it in its most healthy condition. Whatever diseases or ill fortune is due for the body, will assail it by the laws of nature which are greater than anyone's wish or desire.

A student should not be concerned to nullify nature's impositions but should make the best use of the body even when it is afflicted. A yogi should not waste valuable time and energy counteracting what nature will surely impose. It is best to switch the interest to the subtle body, to refine it in relation to subtle operations which could upset nature's system in the long run.

Verse 52

यत्प्रालेयं प्रहित– सुषिरं मेरु–मूर्धान्तर–सथं

तस्मिंस्तत्त्वं प्रवदति सुधीस्तन–मुखं निम्नगानाम् ।

चन्द्रात्सारः स्रवति वपुषस्तेन मृत्युर्नराणां

तद्बध्नीयात्सुकरणमधो नान्यथा काय–सिद्धिः ।। ५२ ।।

yatprāleyaṁ prahita–suṣiraṁ meru–mūrdhāntara–sthaṁ
tasmiṁstattvaṁ pravadati sudhīstan–mukhaṁ nimnagānām ।

candrātsāraḥ sravati vapuṣastena mṛtyurnarāṇāṁ
tadbadhnīyātsukaraṇamadho nānyathā kāya–siddhiḥ || 52 ||

yat = which, prāleyaṁ – subtle secretions, prahita – are deposited, suṣiraṁ – cavity, meru – sushumna central channel, mūrdhāntara = mūrdha (peak) + antara (middle), sthaṁ – situated, located, tasmiṁs = tasmin = in that, tattvaṁ – insight, pravadati – declares, sudhīs = sudhīḥ = wise yogi, tan = tat = this, mukhaṁ – topmost, nimnagānām – nadi subtle channel, candrāt – from the moon-like cool nectar, sāraḥ – subtle hormone, sravati – flows, vapuṣas = vapuṣaḥ = of the body, tena – by this, mṛtyur = mṛtyuḥ = death, narāṇāṁ – men, tad = tat = that, badhnīyāt – should assume, sukaraṇam – excellent practice, adho = adhaḥ = hence declared, nānyathā = not otherwise, kaya – body, siddhiḥ – perfection

Subtle secretions are deposited in the cavity, which is located in the middle of the peak of Meru sushumna central channel. From that insight, the wise yogi declares that as the topmost nadi subtle channel. From the moon-like cool nectar the subtle hormone which causes the death of men flows through the body. Hence assume that excellent practice, otherwise bodily perfection will not be attained.

hormone tradition

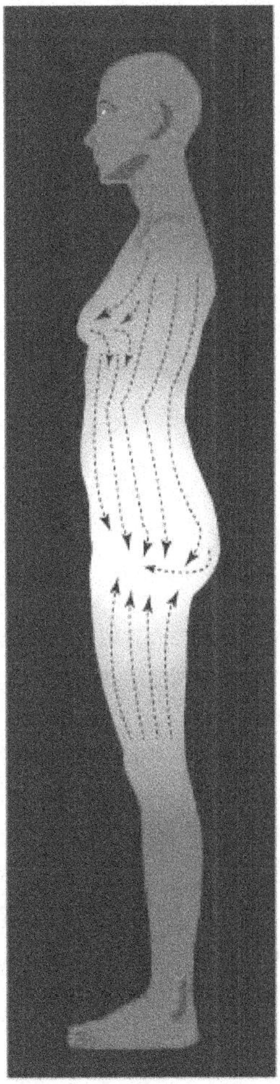

downward movement from neck to groin
upward movement from knee to groin
pubic area centralization

Analysis

This verse gives the secret of how to end the glory of sexual pleasure. The question arises as to why anyone would desire that. If there is no reproduction, life as we know it will come to an end. Since sexual pleasure is an integral part of reproduction, it follows that to secure the reproductive capacity of these bodies, we are required to be sexually involved.

Swatmarama proposes that the yogi should put an end to the downward flow of the moon-like cool nectar subtle hormone which passes through the neck and becomes scattered everywhere in the subtle body. His proposal is that unless one terminates this downward movement, perfection of the subtle body cannot be attained.

There are two important observations which a yogi should make in this regard: which are travel of bliss energy from the cells of the body to the genitals, and travel of the nutrients to the reproductive organs. Some of the energy travels downward, and some upward, with the reproductive organs being the deposit area. Everything from the navel upwards travels downwards. Everything below the groin travels upwards.

Energy in the thighs, legs and feet travel upwards, making deposits in the groin area. Energy from the neck down to the navel travels downwards.

During sexual pleasure experience, the genitals command the attention of the rest of the psyche and demand deposits of bliss energy from each cell in every part of the body. As all roads in a city will eventually lead to the city hall; all hormonal energy generated anywhere in the body, travels to the rotunda of the sexual organ chakra. Once there, the energy is either stored or is used immediately for sexual expression.

Swatmarama proposed a new configuration where every part below the neck contributes energy to the head of the subtle body. In turn the head will send that energy down but it will dissipate above the neck at the place where the tongue is pushed into the soft palate. Instead of genital nectar, there will be brain nectar. That is another way to phrase this.

non-sex centralization

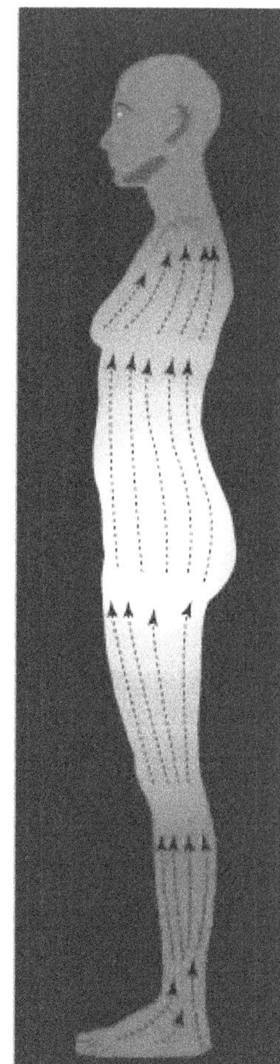

upward movement
from feet to legs
to thighs to lower trunk
to chest to neck

Application

Nature assisted us by introducing the sexual pleasure yield of the body. We recognize that capacity. Swatmarama introduced the moon-like cool-nectar which is experienced in the head of the subtle body and which may spread from there to other parts. Since we became habituated to the sex pleasure yield, which is a bliss force in its own right, we may transfer our interest into the head of the subtle body and experience a lust-free bliss energy there. This will be accompanied by spiritual insight which is a major benefit which the sex pleasure yield does not afford.

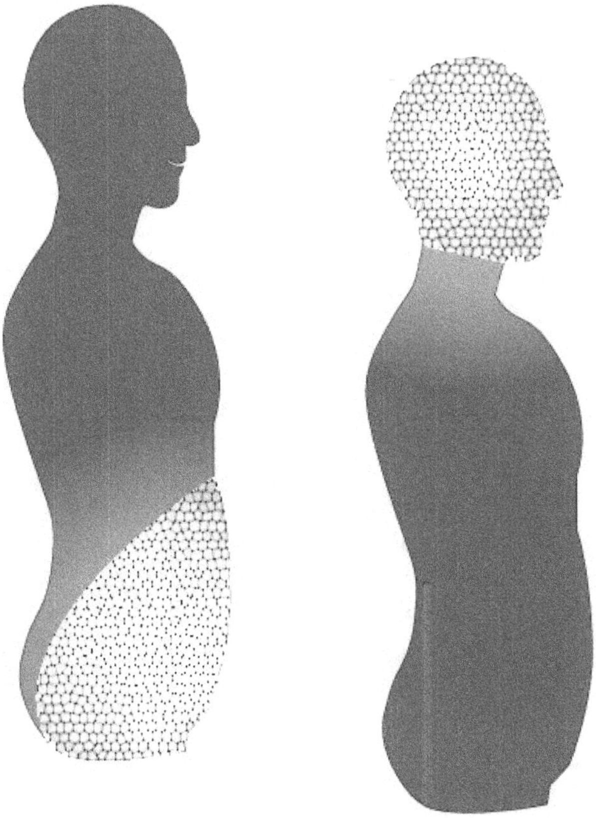

Verse 53

सुषिरं ज्ञान–जनकं पञ्च– स्त्रोतः–समन्वितम् ।

तिष्ठते खेचरी मुद्रा तस्मिन्शून्ये निरञ्जने ।। ५३ ।।

suṣiraṁ jñāna–janakaṁ pañca–srotaḥ–samanvitam |
tiṣṭhate khecarī mudrā tasminśūnye nirañjane || 53 ||

suṣiraṁ – cavity, jñāna – techniques, janakaṁ – production, pañca – five, srotaḥ – subtle channel, samanvitam – is connected, tiṣṭhate – is established, khecarī – procedure for transiting through kha divine space, mudrā = mystic–arresting actions, tasmin – in that, śūnye – in a blank state, nirañjane – spotless, pure

That cavity is the producer of techniques. It is connected to the five subtle channels. In that blank spotless state, the khecari mystic–arresting procedure for transiting through kha divine space, is established.

Analysis

Swatmarama did not name the five nadis but we can assume that three of them are the ida left channel, the sushumna middle channel the pingala right channel.

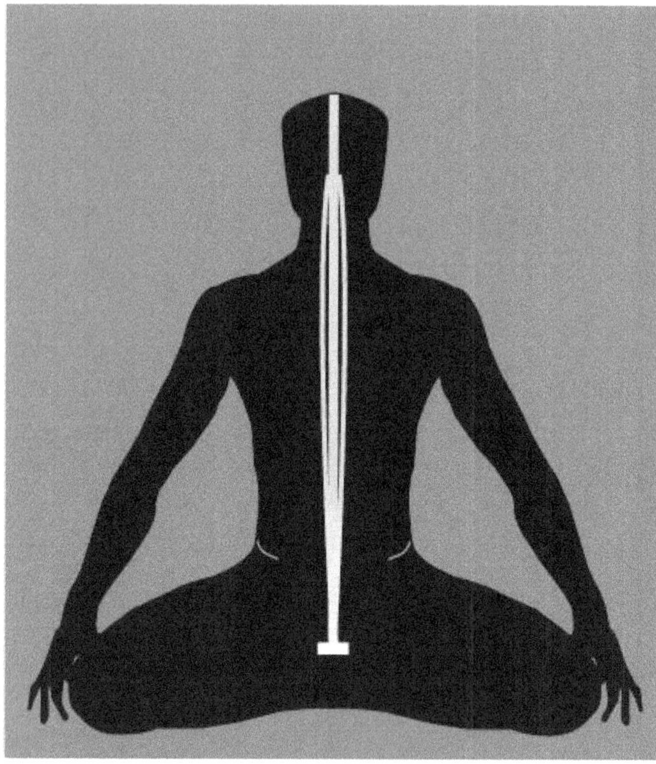

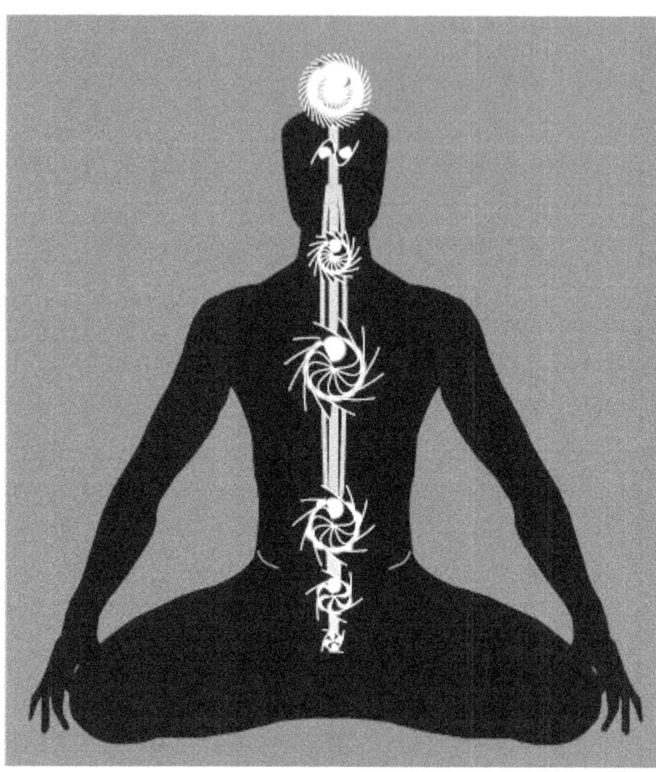

The two other nadis which converge at the place where the tongue is pushed into the soft palate, may be discovered by the student who practices.

A blank spotless space is the result of a thorough breath-infusion session, provided that the student extracted all or most pollutants from the cells and blood stream.

Application

It is in the blank thoughtless space that the transit access appears. The yogi uses this to peer into the chit akash sky of consciousness. Later when the austerities are complete, the student leaves for the spiritual world through that access.

Verse 54

एकं सृष्टिमयं बीजमेका मुद्रा च खेचरी ।

एको देवो निरालम्ब एकावस्था मनोन्मनी ।। ५४ ।।

ekaṁ sṝṣṭimayaṁ bījamekā mudrā ca khecarī I
eko devo nirālamba ekāvasthā manonmanī II 54 II

ekaṁ – one, sṝṣṭimayaṁ – magic creation, bījam – origin, ekā – one, mudrā – mystic checking practice, ca – and, khecarī – procedure for transiting through kha divine space, eko = ekaḥ = one, devo = devaḥ = predominating deity, nirālamba – without support, ekāvasthā – singular state, manonmanī – blank thoughtless idealess mental condition

There is one origin of this magical creation. There is one mystic checking practice which is the procedure for transiting through kha divine space. There is one predominating deity who is without support. There is a singular state which is the blank thoughtless idealess mental condition.

Analysis

This creation is one cosmic something which originated from one magical instance which burst out from a causal origin. Because it is one system, it has no dual feature but within its oneness there is varied expression. It will not be possible for any limited being to reenact that one magical instance but we can surmise that eventually this will fizz out and simmer down to nothingness.

Swatmarama listed the khecari procedure for transiting through kha divine space as the one mystic checking practice which is the culmination of all mystic techniques which are used in the subtle body below the neck. When all those kriyas are mastered and have outlived their usefulness, when they evolved until they are done with, then one can perfect that last mystic checking practice.

Swatmarama is not an atheist. Like Patanjali he attests to the supreme deity, eka-deva, the one God. Swatmarama offered both an impersonal (bija) and a personal (deva) ultimate source.

He gave the singular approved mental state for a yogi which is the blank thoughtless idealess mental condition. This is thoroughly consistent with Patanjali's declaration about yoga as being the conscious non-operation of the vibrational modes of the mento-emotional energy:

yogaḥcittavṛtti nirodhaḥ

yogaḥ – the skill of yoga; cittavṛtti = citta – mento-emotional energy + vṛtti – vibrational mode; nirodhaḥ – cessation, restraint, non-operation.

The skill of yoga is demonstrated by the conscious non-operation of the vibrational modes of the mento-emotional energy.

Application

Yoga is not an atheistic system. It includes theism or the belief in a Supreme Person. Both Patanjali and Swatmarama attest to this. Krishna, who declared himself as that Supreme Somebody, explained details of yoga both to Arjuna and to Uddhava in the Bhagavad Gita (Mahabharata) and the Uddhava Gita (Srimad Bhagavatam). On a close inspection the yoga explained in the Bhagavad Gita is the same yoga explained by Patanjali in his Yoga Sutras. But Krishna explained its application to cultural activities as the special teaching called karma yoga.

This does not mean that a person has to be a theist to study yoga. In fact in the Upanishads, Ramayana, Mahabharata and Puranas, there are many stories of persons who mastered aspects of yoga and who were outright atheists.

However to study this Hatha Yoga Pradipika with an attitude of submission to the writer, I suggest that readers have an open mind about what he termed as the One God, eka deva.

Verse 55

अथ उड्डीयान–बन्धः

बद्धो येन सुषुम्नायां प्राणस्तूड्डीयते यतः ।

तस्मादुड्डीयनाख्यो।अयं योगिभिः समुदाहृतः ।। ५५ ।।

atha uḍḍīyāna–bandhaḥ
baddho yena suṣumṇāyāṁ prāṇastūḍḍīyate yataḥ ।
tasmāduḍḍīyanākhyo।ayaṁ yogibhiḥ samudāhṝtaḥ ।। 55 ।।

atha – now it is explained, uḍḍīyāna – drawing the abdomen cavity up under the rib cage and back towards the spine, bandhaḥ = physio–psychic compression, baddho = baddho = is confined, yena – by which, suṣumṇāyāṁ – in sushumna central spinal passage, prāṇas = breath–infused energy, tūḍḍīyate = tu (but) + uḍḍīyate (rises), yataḥ – then, tasmād = tasmāt = therefore, uḍḍīyanākhyo = uḍḍīyanākhyaḥ = uḍḍīyana (flying upwards procedure) + ākhyaḥ(is called), ayaṁ – this, yogibhiḥ – by yogis, samudāhṝtaḥ – known

Now the technique of drawing the uddhiyana abdomen up-and-under the rib cage and back towards the spine with physio–psychic compression is explained:

It is the technique by which the breath-infused energy, being confined, rises through the sushumna central spinal passage. It is called the uddhiyana flying-upward procedure.

This is how it is known by the yogis.

Analysis

The uddhiyana flying-upward procedure is vital for two reasons:

- curbing and redesigning the navel/intestines front chakra
- restricting kundalini from expressing itself through the navel chakra on the spinal column

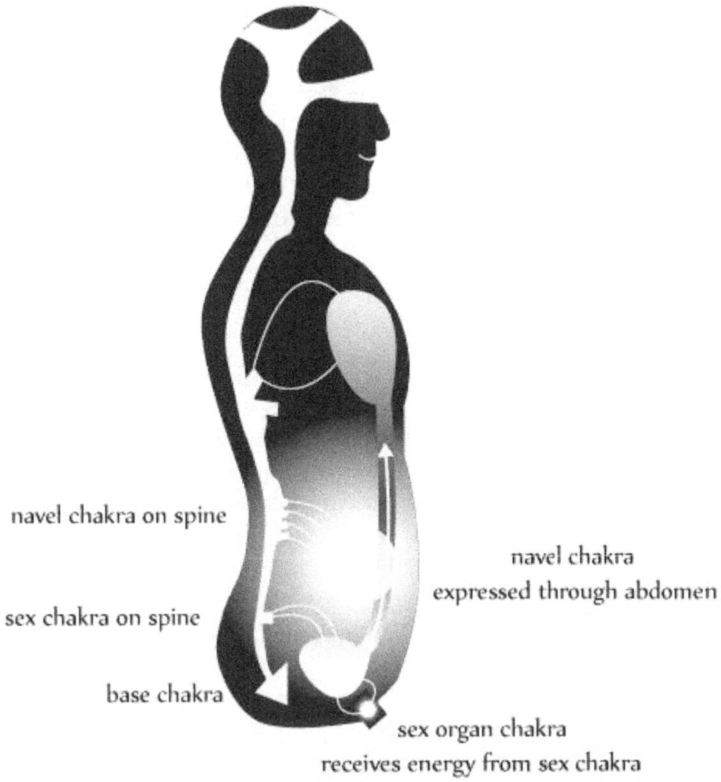

A yogi cannot effectively raise kundalini unless these two aspects are accomplished. The navel/intestines front chakra must be purified. Its knotted complexity must be released and unwound. If the yogi fails to do this he will not be able to tackle the reproduction/sex-pleasure facilities which are below the navel. If the reproduction center is not reformed, there will be no success in reforming the kundalini.

If the yogi can rectify the navel/intestines front chakra, and can subdue the reproduction/sex-pleasure chakra complex, then he will arouse kundalini. However its arousal may not include its control. Striking a snake or presenting it with fire, will certainly cause it to move but it may not go in the direction intended unless it is forced to do so.

With the application of the navel lock so that the navel chakra on the spine cannot express itself through the navel/intestines front chakra, kundalini will be forced to go straight up through sushumna nadi when it comes to the navel chakra on the spine. If it is allowed to diffuse itself through the navel/intestines front chakra, that will cause the yogi to have increased appetite, where he will eat more than necessary and generate more sex hormones resulting in increased need for sexual indulgence. This in turn will ruin yoga.

A yogi whose appetite increases because the aroused kundalini expresses itself through the navel chakra will have to procure a sex partner. Because of the increased production of sexual hormones he will become inclined to sexual indulgence with the result of added responsibility in the form of children generated, plus the emotional interplay with a spouse. If for one reason or the other, children are not produced, there will still be complexities because the missing children will be present in the form of departed ancestors of himself and his partner. These departed souls having entered his mind will make demands. Their energy will operate his thinking and emotions, which will in turn ruin yoga.

Sometimes a yogi who already has a partner adopts another partner. Then the previous partner becomes annoyed and harasses the yogi. The ancestors of that previous partner sense the ancestors of the new partner. They inspire the first partner to object vehemently. This creates an emotional interplay which is unfavorable and which ruins the practice of all those involved. Thus it is vital to keep the navel chakra under control so that there is no leakage of energy to it which causes an increase in appetite.

Increase in appetite directly implies increase in sex hormone production, which in turn means increase in sexual needs, which means operation of the reproductive urges, which means generation of progeny, which means increased responsibility and ancestral management. Such is the life.

There are many disembodied souls who think that a yogi should be their father. Any of these entities may exert an influence to cause a yogi to have an increased appetite. Once that happens, the yogi's body will become inhabited by those disembodied beings. Others in his proximity on the physical level may object to such influence because the whole material world is funded by prejudices and family lineage struggles for power. One ancestral line is against another and does not want the other to benefit. This is played out on the physical level by objections of family members when a yogi takes another spouse. People object but their objection is not for themselves only, it represents the disapproval of a whole clan of family members on one side. Since they feel they own the body of the yogi, his indication that he might generate progeny for another family is the threat to their sense of security. Therefore the yogi will find that he is blighted with their disapproval. That is a hard card to be served but it is the reality of social dealings. A yogi should therefore carefully control his food intake. It is best that a yogi cook his own food because otherwise he will more than likely come under the control of one group of ancestors who will force him to serve them only and to leave aside everyone else in the universe.

Application

Control of the navel/intestines front chakra is of utmost importance. It is a hard system to control, so much so that we find that some great yogis lose their grip on it. If we take pictures of great yogis from say about 200 or so years in the past, most of them might begin in their youths with a body which is slim and trim. Then overtime despite their doing the postures and breath-infusion practice, their abdomens become distended.

As great a person as our dear father-guru, Swami Shivananda, left his last body in a stomach-distended condition. Even another of our gurus, Swami Vishnudevananda, who instructed the composition of this book and inspired some of its content, left his last body with an abdomen which was greatly extended. Swamiji authored one of the first comprehensive books of asanas postures, an all-time yoga classic.

Thus we must ask ourselves as to why these Swamis could not control the navel chakra. Why were they overeating? They were not householder gurus (rishis). They were single celibate monks (swamis) and still they could not control the food intake. Subsequently, their abdomens bloated considerably, being stretched beyond capacity night after night.

This does not mean that these Swamis were not siddhas or potential siddhas, because they were exceptional ascetics, but it does mean that we cannot underestimate the power of the navel chakra to draw energy from the kundalini to sponsor food greed.

It may be posited in a Swami's defense that the food greed was in the genetic attitude of the body they derived in the particular life. This is a valid argument but it also illustrates the same power of the navel chakra to cheat the system of yoga by taking extra energy from the kundalini to fund increased appetite.

Even in Swamis who will not become householders at least physically, the navel chakra and the ancestors who control it, express influence and produce a showing in the form of distended stomach for physically-celibate monks.

It begs the question as to whether these ancestors lived in the body of these monks even though the monks did not abandon their vows for physical isolation from sexual access.

Verse 56

उड्डीनं कुरुते यस्मादविश्रान्तं महा–खगः ।

उड्डीयानं तदेव स्यात्तत्र बन्धो।अभिधीयते ।। ५६ ।।

uḍḍīnaṁ kurute yasmādaviśrāntaṁ mahā–khagaḥ ।
uḍḍīyānaṁ tadeva syāttatra bandho।abhidhīyate ।। 56 ।।

uḍḍīnaṁ kurute = will energetically fly up, yasmād = yasmāt = due to that, aviśrāntaṁ – constantly, mahā–khagaḥ = kundalini, the great bird, uḍḍīyānaṁ = flying–upward procedure, tad = tat = that, eva – also, syāt – is, tatra – there, bandho = bandhaḥ = physio–psychic compression, abhidhīyate – is known as

Due to that procedure, kundalini, the great bird, constantly and energetically flies up. That physio–psychic compression is known as the flying-upward procedure.

Analysis

No matter how much a bird flies upwards, it always descends to rest its feet on something solid. A bird is not perpetually airborne. The kundalini which is compared to a great bird has a similar aspect where even if the yogi infuses it with activity-energy on a daily basis, its ascent up through the spine into the brain, is followed by its descent back to the muladhara base chakra.

Students sometimes ask:

How long will I have to do this?

When will kundalini remain in the brain and not descend to the base chakra?

The answer is that permanent buoyancy of kundalini so that it remains in the head of the subtle body, varies from person to person according to the evolutionary status and the intensity of practice.

It is not how long it will take to achieve that but rather how much of a priority this practice is to the student. Some students may achieve it in weeks; some in months; some in years; some in lifetimes of practice.

Application

If the breath is infused sufficiently into the blood stream, if the locks are efficiently applied, the kundalini will be aroused. It will fly through the central spine into the brain. However, soon after when the charge of breath energy is reduced, kundalini will return to the muladhara base chakra. The pressure of the abdomen flying-upward procedure will keep kundalini flying upwards in the head of the subtle body for as long as the breath-hormone energy charge is maintained. When that fizzes out, then even if one applies the flying-upward procedure, kundalini will float back down either slowly or rapidly, just as a bird which loses buoyancy will glide to the earth.

If however the yogi adjusted his lifestyle over time, and if he removed the reproductive hormone storage tendency of the body, the kundalini would no longer be interested in descending and will remain lodged at the lower back of the subtle head. This is called stub kundalini.

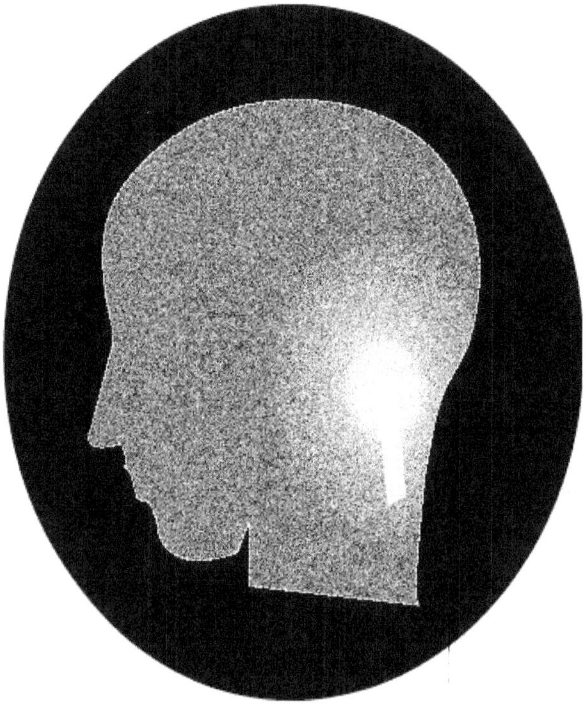

Kundalini remains attached to muladhara base chakra because of two tendencies. One

is mere survival. The other is tactical survival in the form of reproductive capability which is an investment in future survival. Immediate survival is for making the body survive in its immediate circumstance. Tactical survival is to invest in new body opportunities. One concerns the present. The other is to gain a grip on the future.

So long as kundalini has the survival and tactical survival tendencies, it will always return to muladhara chakra no matter what the yogi achieves.

Stated more precisely even if a yogi has lofty experiences in meditation, he will resume another embryo after the death of the physical form. Even if he transits to a higher dimension after death, he will still return to take another physical body.

For full resistance to reincarnating in gross forms, the yogi has to remove the survival and tactical tendencies but that is easier said than done.

For one thing, these tendencies are permanently a part of material nature, which means that they cannot be erased altogether. No yogi can change the nature of nature. However, a yogi can delete his interest in nature. That is what he can surely do.

By withdrawing interest in nature's concerns while being satisfied for material nature to remain as it is, the yogi can get kundalini to fly up into the brain permanently, abandoning its lair at muladhara base chakra.

Verse 57

उदरे पश्चिमं तानं नाभेरूर्ध्वं च कारयेत् ।

उड्डीयानो ह्यसौ बन्धो मृत्यु–मातङ्ग–केसरी ।। ५७ ।।

udare paścimaṁ tānaṁ nābherūrdhvaṁ ca kārayet I
uḍḍīyāno hyasau bandho mṛtyu–mātaṅga–kesarī II 57 II

udare – in the abdomen, paścimaṁ – behind, tānaṁ – retract, nābher = nābheḥ = to the navel, ūrdhvaṁ – upward, ca – and, kārayet – should do, uḍḍīyāno = uḍḍīyānaḥ = flying–upward procedure, hy = hi = indeed, asau – that, bandho = bandhaḥ = physio–psychic compression, mṛtyu – death, mātaṅga – elephant, kesarī – lion

The yogi should continually retract the abdomen back and the navel up. Indeed, that flying upward procedure is the physio–psychic compression which is the lion for killing the elephant of death.

Analysis

The uddhiyana retraction of the abdomen backwards and the navel upwards is a pressure message to kundalini not to descend to its default residence which is the muladhara base chakra. However if there is not enough of an energy charge pushing kundalini through the spine, it will descend even if that lock is applied. In the rough this means that if the yogi did not infuse fresh air energy through the groin area, and if that combination of energy was not compressed and guided through the sushumna nadi central channel, kundalini will not remain floating high in the head of the subtle body.

Swatmarama expertly compared the navel-abdomen lock with a lion. Due to its large size and great height the elephant is an inconvenience to a lion. Unless the lion can maneuver into a special position it cannot bring down the elephant. The navel-abdomen lock needs special accessory actions to cause its completion. The chief of these supports is a high charge of the fresh air and reproductive hormone energy.

Application

Kundalini may be compared to an elephant because it is a huge reality to contend with. It controls death because it operates the life mechanism of the material body and the dimensional shifting of the astral form. Death of a physical body really means the permanent disconnection of the kundalini lifeforce from that form.

The core-self should gain control of the movement of the subtle body in and out of the astral dimensions. It should also gain some input into the rebirth possibilities. The core-self should wrestle control of the psyche from the kundalini. As a lion may successfully challenge the largest of the land mammals, the elephant, so by using the navel-abdomen lock in conjunction with other techniques the yogi may eventually cause the kundalini to remain floating in the head of the subtle form.

Verse 58

उड्डीयानं तु सहजं गुरुणा कथितं सदा ।

अभ्यसेत्सततं यस्तु वृद्धो।अपि तरुणायते ।। ५८ ।।

uḍḍīyānaṁ tu sahajaṁ guruṇā kathitaṁ sadā |
abhyasetsatataṁ yastu vṛddho|api taruṇāyate || 58 ||

uḍḍīyānaṁ – flying–upward procedure, tu – but, sahajaṁ – easy, guruṇā – by the proficient teacher, kathitaṁ – taught, sadā – when, abhyaset – should practice, satataṁ – always, yas – who, tu – but, vṛddho = vṛddhaḥ = elderly body, api – too, taruṇāyate – become sprite and youthful

The flying-upward procedure is easy to learn when taught by a proficient teacher. Indeed, if they practice regularly, the elderly too, become sprite and youthful.

Analysis

Swatmarama encourages even elderly persons to do flying-upward procedure. By regulating their intake of food nutrients, it will help them to be more selective in birth opportunities. That is the minimum benefit from the practice. At first it will increase the appetite and make for a more rapid transit of food mass through the intestines and colon. That would do wonders for the health of the elderly.

Application

There are other technical muscular contractions when doing the uddhiyana navel-abdomen pull-up procedure. In the advanced stages there is a shoulder push-down lock which seals the navel-abdomen lock. These can be learned from a teacher who progressed in the practice. An instructor is necessary but he does not have to be physically present. The guru can be on the astral planes, where the psychically-sensitive disciple can consult or absorb practice-influence.

A student would be inspired by the practice itself but that is not sufficient. It must be supplemented by advisories of physically or astrally present advanced teachers.

Verse 59

नाभेरूर्ध्वमधश्चापि तानं कुर्यात्प्रयत्नतः ।

षण्मासमभ्यसेन्मृत्युं जयत्येव न संशयः ।। ५९ ।।

nābherūrdhvamadhaścāpi tānaṁ kuryātprayatnataḥ ।
ṣaṇmāsamabhyasenmṝtyuṁ jayatyeva na saṁśayaḥ ।। 59 ।।

nābher = nābheḥ = navel, ūrdhvam – above, adhaś = adhaḥ = below, cāpi – and so, tānaṁ – retract, kuryāt – should perform, prayatnataḥ – with effort, ṣaṇ – six, māsam – month, abhyasen = abhyaset = practice, mṝtyuṁ – death, jayaty – jayati – supersedes, eva – even so, na – no, saṁśayaḥ – doubt

The areas above and below the navel should with effort be retracted. There is no doubt, that a yogi who practices this for six months supersedes death.

Analysis

This six month practice was current in the time of Swatmarama. Today it would take more time according to the intensity of practice and the genetic resistance of the physical body.

No limited being can remove all genetic traits of its body. Some only can be adjusted. Still, a yogi should make the effort. When there is sufficient effect in the physical system, the yogi should transfer his interest into the subtle form and continue the techniques there.

Ultimately the material body will perish. Whatever are the effects of practice, may feed over into the subtle form, as the continuing result.

Application

The retraction of the areas above and below the navel, when done to completion, upsets the reproductive system of nature. A complete shutdown of that system, would free the subtle body from its need to develop and use material forms. The subtle body develops and uses such forms and when those physical systems become nonresponsive, the subtle body finds itself to be without those gross forms. It then develops and uses another gross form. This goes on and on and on, and is described as a circular existence transit or as samsara.

What would it be if the subtle body no longer developed and used physical forms?

Where would it go after the physical body died?

How would it live in that place?

How would it procure satisfactions?

Verse 60

सर्वेषामेव बन्धानां उत्तमो ह्युड्डीयानकः ।

उड्डियाने दृढे बन्धे मुक्तिः सवाभाविकी भवेत् ।। ६० ।।

sarveṣāmeva bandhānāṁ uttamo hyuḍḍīyānakaḥ I
uḍḍiyāne dṛḍhe bandhe muktiḥ svābhāvikī bhavet II 60 II

sarveṣām – all, eva – even so, bandhānāṁ – physio–psychic compression, uttamo = uttamaḥ = best, hy = hi = indeed, uḍḍīyānakaḥ – flying–upward procedure, uḍḍiyāne – in retracting the abdomen cavity up under the rib cage and back towards the spine, dṛḍhe – tightly, bandhe = in physio–psychic compression, muktiḥ – liberation, svābhāvikī – inherent, bhavet – is

Of the physio–psychic compression techniques, the flying-upward of the abdomen procedure is the best. Liberation is inherent in a tightly held compression of the abdominal cavity which is retracted back and upward to the spine.

Analysis

Since it regulates the nutrition system of the physical body, and the corresponding system in the subtle form, the flying-upward of the abdomen procedure is rated as the most useful physio–psychic compression technique. When all is said and done, the physical body is just as good as its nutritional intake. Shut down nutrition and the body will die shortly. When a yogi takes proficient command of the nutrition system and re-orients its operation, he can apply that proficiency to become liberated from the need for having material forms

Application

Mastery of yoga takes time. It requires careful consideration. All hastiness of the student will have to be abandoned and a serious long-termed approach be put into place. One must get help from an advanced soul who is present physically or astrally.

Verse 61

अथ मूल–बन्धः

पार्ष्णिभागेन सम्पीड्य योनिमाकुनछयेद्गुदम् ।

अपानमूर्ध्वमाकृष्य मूल–बन्धो।अभिधीयते ।। ६१ ।।

atha mūla–bandhaḥ
pārṣṇi bhāgena sampīḍya yonimākuñchayedgudam I
apānamūrdhvamākṛṣya mūla–bandho I abhidhīyate II 61 II

atha – now to be explained, mūla – anus–coccyx complex, bandhaḥ = physio–psychic compression, pārṣṇi – heel, bhāgena – region, sampīḍya – compressing, yonim – vaginal passage, ākuñchayed = ākuñchayet = should contract, gudam – rectum, apanam – negatively charged breath energy, ūrdhvam – upward, ākṝṣya – upward coursed, mūla = anus–coccyx, bandho = bandhaḥ = physio–psychic compression, abhidhīyate – called

Now the mulabandha physio-psychic compression of the anus-coccyx complex is explained:

Pressing the heel against the vaginal or potential vaginal passage, the yogi should contract the rectum. This causes the negatively charged breath energy to course upward. It is called the mulabandha anus-coccyx physio-psychic compression.

Analysis

This anus-coccyx physio-psychic compression is vital for reining in the kundalini because it is most attached to the two lowest chakras and their operative expressions in the physical and subtle bodies. Survival is the objective of the kundalini psychic lifeforce but it realizes that it cannot do that on the material plane without transmigrating to new life forms. Kundalini is like a frog. It is a hopping mechanism, where when it becomes established in one life form, it develops the access to jump to a new form as soon as the old form perishes.

Nutrition is important in this scheme of transmigration but the kundalini arranged that to be operated automatically by the force of gravity which is global on any material planet. As soon as kundalini acquires a new form, it settles into the new environment by protecting itself from being eaten by any other creature. Once it secures itself, it plans how it can migrate to a species which will give it the advantages it estimates it would require to be on top of the food chain.

To jump in this way, it has to transmigrate. To transmigrate it must have an emotional connection through which it may transit away from a dying body to a parent form which will create an embryo for it. This concerns the two lowest chakras with the lowest one, the muladhara base-center, controlling survival, and with the svadhishthana sex chakra controlling reproduction.

To upset the plan of kundalini, the yogi must bring these chakras under control. He must change their design so that the interest in survival of material bodies is removed from the psyche.

Application

Even though this text was primarily meant for male ascetics, Swatmarama cited a location of female anatomy for this posture. He mentioned that the heel should be pressed against the vaginal or potential vaginal passage. This identifies this place in a unique way because the male anatomy does not have such an obvious opening at that location.

The meatus or fleshy part of the male organ enters the body at this location. A male can locate it easily by discovering the focal spot of sexual excitement during sexual climax experience. To assume this pose the male should raise the penis and scrotum and gently but firmly place the heel at the place where the penis enters the body where it passes through the two bones which occur at that place.

In conjunction with this sex lock, the anus lock should be contracted upwards into the body. That seals both entrances which discourages kundalini from going downward

through the base of the spine or leaving in an angular way through the genitals which is a passage it is all too familiar with and all too ready to access.

Verse 62

अधो–गतिमपानं वा ऊर्ध्वगं कुरुते बलात् ।

आकुञ्चनेन तं पराहुर्मूल–बन्धं हि योगिनः ।। ६२ ।।

adho–gatimapānaṁ vā ūrdhvagaṁ kurute balāt I
ākuñcanena taṁ prāhurmūla–bandhaṁ hi yoginaḥ II 62 II

adho = adha = downward, gatim – coursing, apānaṁ – negatively charge breath energy, vā – indeed, ūrdhvagaṁ – going upward, kurute – should go, balāt – due to being forced, ākuñcanena – by contraction, taṁ – that, prāhur = prāhuḥ = said, mūla = anus–coccyx complex, bandhaṁ = physio–psychic compression, hi – indeed, yoginaḥ – yogis

The downward coursing negatively charged breath energy should go upwards by forceful contraction. The yogis call that procedure the anus-coccyx physio-psychic compression.

Analysis

The two lowest chakras use negatively charged breath energy, polluted air, for much of their operations. For the force of evacuation, the polluted gas is useful. For sponsoring libido or sexual drive, it is valuable. The thrusting action of the male body when penetrating the female requires assistance from the pollutants. The voluptuous movements of females during intercourse also use pollutants. The discharge of unused eggs during the menstrual cycle of females requires the use of the pollutants.

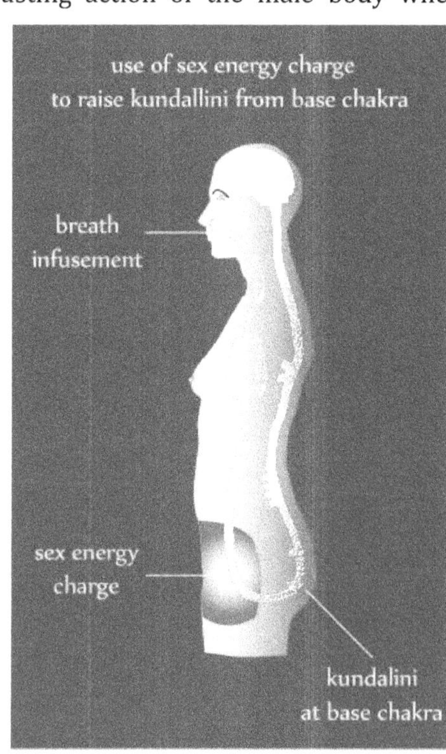

When doing kundalini yoga, the pollutants are also used but in a constructive way which is supportive of the aims of yoga, which in that case is to get the kundalini to leave the base chakra and go into the brain. For this to take place, the fresh air which is infused is mixed with the pollutant gases and with hormonal energy which has some pollutants as part of its composite. Some pollutants are extracted from the body with each exhale during breath-infusion. However, some pollutants remain resistant to the infused air. This resistant gas is driven down from the lungs through the navel region and then into the groin area. It is forced through the groin area and sent to the muladhara chakra where it strikes kundalini just before the infused

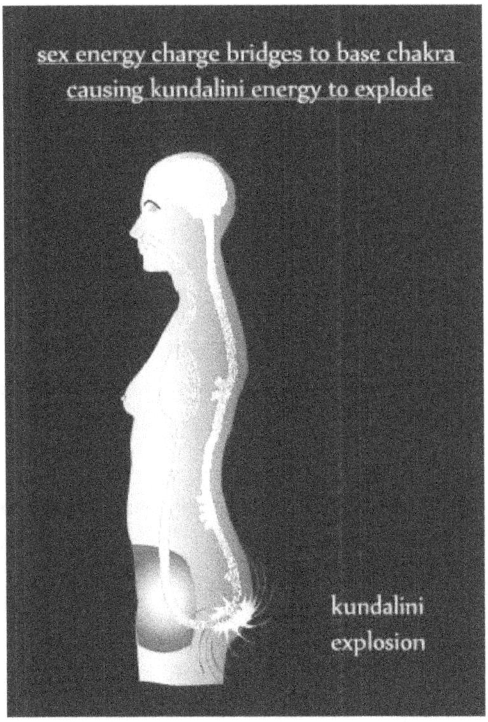

energy hits the kundalini as well. This causes a small explosion at the muladhara chakra which motivates the kundalini to move up through the spine. As it moves it pushes pollutants through the sushumna central passage into the head.

Some students find that they enter into a black-out of consciousness when kundalini enters the head. This is because of polluted gases which enter the head because of being pushed through the neck by a sluggish kundalini which when it is just about to enter the head, subsides back down to muladhara chakra after having pushed polluted gases into the head. The effect of those pollutants is experienced as a black out by some students.

A yogi must be fearless when doing kundalini yoga but he must also have direction from an advanced teacher. Nobody is afraid of sexual indulgence which is the natural way to raise the kundalini to the second chakra for pleasure extraction. Thus why should anyone be afraid of raising kundalini into the brain? However one should seek advice from a great yogin.

Application

Swatmarama instructed that the downward coursing negatively charged breath energy should go upwards by forceful contraction but he did not give every details. This means that one should learn this from an advanced teacher who recently did this and knows the application for our culture and situation.

Some negatively charged breath energy is extracted through the lungs when doing breath-infusion but all of it will not leave the body in this way. Some will leave by being forced out when the kundalini moves through the sushumna nadi central channel in the spine of the subtle body. If a pipe has corrosion and pollutants, those substances may be blasted out by a clean forceful jet of water. Similarly the kundalini if it acquires a sufficient charge can expel the heavy astral energy from the sushumna passage.

However some of the pollutants which are in cells in the body, will combine with the incoming fresh air. The yogi should compress this inwards on itself and keep compressing more and more fresh air into it, until it implodes in the subtle body.

I listed three means of extraction of the pollutants:

- *removal in exhales through the lungs*
- *forceful blasting out of the sushumna central passage*
- *compression inwards of the pollutants which combine with fresh astral energy*

Verse 63

गुदं पार्ष्ण्या तु सम्पीड्य वायुमाकुञ्चयेद्बलात् ।
वारं वारं यथा चोर्ध्वं समायाति समीरणः ।। ६३ ।।

gudaṁ pārṣṇyā tu sampīḍya vāyumākuñcayedbalāt |
vāraṁ vāraṁ yathā cordhvaṁ samāyāti samīraṇaḥ || 63 ||

gudaṁ – rectum, pārṣṇyā – with the heel, tu – indeed, sampīḍya – pressing, compressing, vāyum – infused air, ākuñcayed = ākuñcayet = should contract, balāt – due to force, vāraṁ vāraṁ = repeatedly, yathā – accordingly, cordhvaṁ = ca (and) + urdhvam (upward), samāyāti – goes, samīraṇaḥ – breath energy

Indeed, by pressing the rectum with the heel, the infused air should be forcibly contracted. Doing this repeatedly the breath energy will go upward.

Analysis

This will not happen if the yogi has no psychic control of the infused breath energy. It is not just a physical process. Even though it built the physical body, kundalini is essentially psychic. Physical actions alone cannot lead to its subjugation. A student can press the rectum with the heel for as long as the body will live and that alone will not cause the kundalini to yield its authority or to submit itself for achieving the objectives of yoga.

When the kundalini is boxed into a psychic corner by the core-self and when it has no way to circumvent the interest of the self, then one will be successful in reforming its behavior.

Application

In this verse a key technique is divulged. The infused air itself should be compressed. It should be compressed in on itself. Then there should be more infused air forced into it; then that should be compressed. This should continue until there is an implosion or flash of light in the subtle body.

The yogi must be attentive within the psyche which means that if possible one should use a blindfold to keep the attention and interest within the subtle body. There should be a directional force as the locks are applied. The infused energy by itself or in combination with hormone energy or in combination with the kundalini, should be compressed and directed as advised by the advanced teacher.

Verse 64

प्राणापानौ नाद–बिन्दू मूल–बन्धेन चैकताम् ।
गत्वा योगस्य संसिद्धिं यच्छतो नात्र संशयः ।। ६४ ।।

prāṇāpānau nāda–bindū mūla–bandhena caikatām |
gatvā yogasya saṁsiddhiṁ yacchato nātra saṁśayaḥ || 64 ||

prāṇāpānau – positively and negatively charged subtle force, nāda – naad supernatural sound resonance, bindū – causal node sources, mūla = anus–coccyx complex, bandhena = physio–psychic compression, caikatām = ca (and) + ekatām (one, unity), gatvā – gives way, causes, yogasya – of yoga, saṁsiddhiṁ – full perfection, yacchato = yacchataḥ = yields, nātra = not here, saṁśayaḥ – doubt

When positively and negatively charged subtle forces, as well as the naad supernatural sound resonance and the causal node sources are united by the application of the physio-psychic compression of the anus-coccyx complex, then that yields full perfection of yoga. Of this there is no doubt.

Analysis

This verse is the summary explanation of the kundalini yoga process. This is the syllabus:

- compression and direction of positively and negatively charged subtle forces
- focus in naad supernatural sound resonance
- recognition and focus into causal node sources
- application of the physio-psychic compression of the anus-coccyx complex

The **compression and direction of positively and negatively charged subtle forces** causes changes in the attitude of all cell structures below the neck. These cells must be reformed so that they become cooperative with the objectives of yoga.

The **focus in naad supernatural sound resonance** is a must for advanced yogis in terms of being granted access to the chit akash sky of consciousness, the divine environment. The yogi must be in the influence of naad sound resonance when he sits to meditate.

The **recognition and focus into causal node sources** must happen before the yogi can penetrate through to the chit akash sky of consciousness. Between the highest astral regions and the spiritual world is the causal zone. A yogi transits through it to reach the divine places.

The **application of the physio-psychic compression of the anus-coccyx complex** must be achieved because otherwise the kundalini will retain its survival instincts and will undermine all progress made through the austerities. A yogi must disable the survival capacity of the individual kundalini which he is allied to.

Application

The destruction of the survival and tactical survival tendencies of the kundalini is no small achievement for a yogi. Even though the muladhara base chakra and the svadhishthana sex chakra are the two lowest energy gyrating centers and are the furthest ones on the spine when measured from the brain, still these chakras actually run the show in the psyche.

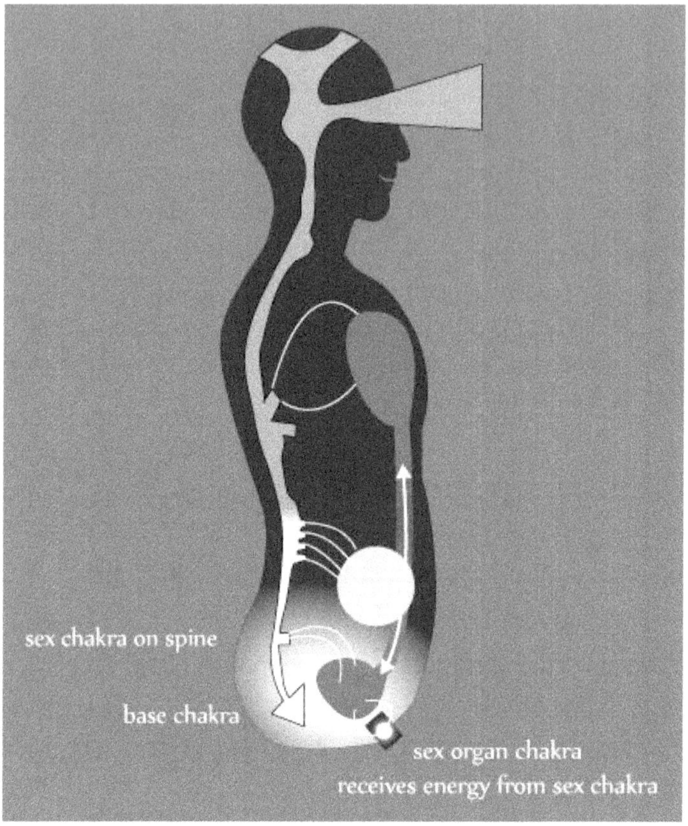

Swatmarama proposed that if the two lowest chakras are subdued completely, the student will attain the unity of the positive and negative subtle forces with naad sound resonance and causal nodes. This is something that requires detailed study and definite application.

Verse 65

अपान– प्राणयोरैक्यं क्षयो मूत्र–पुरीषयोः ।

युवा भवति वृद्धो।अपि सततं मूल–बन्धनात् ।। ६५ ।।

apāna–prāṇayoraikyaṁ kṣayo mūtra–purīṣayoḥ I
yuvā bhavati vṝddho I api satataṁ mūla–bandhanāt II 65 II

apāna–prāṇayor = apāna–prāṇayoḥ = of the positively and negatively charged subtle forces, aikyaṁ – combination, kṣayo = kṣayaḥ = decrease, mūtra–purīṣayoḥ = urine and feces, yuvā – youth, bhavati – becomes, vṝddho = vṝddhaḥ = elderly human, api – also, satataṁ – constantly, mūla–bandhanāt = due to physio–psychic compression of the anus–coccyx complex

By the combination of the positively and negatively charged subtle forces, the urine and feces decrease. The elderly ones become youthful by constantly applying the physio-psychic compression of the anus-coccyx complex.

Analysis

Inevitably anyone who learns breath-infusion practice will experience an increase in appetite and diet. This might be counterproductive initially because it may increase hormone production in the body which will in turn induce increased sexual interest. However as the student progresses, this will change and he will gain efficiency in the physio-psychic compression of the anus-coccyx complex. This will cause a reduction in food intake which will be due to more efficient extraction of nutrients. The result will be a decrease in hormone production with no excessive sexual demands.

There are ancestral obligations; which means that an ascetic may be compelled to provide bodies for his ancestors. Thus a certain amount of mandatory sexual activity may be required. There may also be right conjugal obligation which may be related or not related to ancestral needs.

Efficiency in the physio-psychic compression of the anus-coccyx complex is a boon for a yogi who uses an elderly body because it targets the subtle form and keeps that body in tip top shape on the astral planes. This is not observed by people who have no psychic perception. However, through intuition, even they may suspect that despite an aged body, the yogi is psychologically healthy.

Application

The lesson is that even if the body is aged, the yogi should continue breath-infusion and keep a progressive course so that there is more and more advancement even in old age. Srila Yogeshwarananda requested of this writer that he continue the practice of asana postures and pranayama breath-infusion for as long as the body would allow it. The guru thinks that a yogi should not retire from practice. A yogi should not pretend that he is so advanced that he no longer has to do postures and breath-infusion. There is everything to be gained by a yogi who continues the practice for as long as the body is capable of it. For one thing it sets the example for others and personally it assures that the subtle body of the yogi will be kept in the best possible condition.

Verse 66

अपान ऊर्ध्वगे जाते प्रयाते वह्नि–मण्डलम् ।

तदानल–शिखा दीर्घा जायते वायुनाहता ।। ६६ ।।

apāna ūrdhvage jāte prayāte vahni–maṇḍalam I
tadānala–śikhā dīrghā jāyate vāyunāhatā I I 66 I I

apāna – negatively charged subtle force, ūrdhvage jāte = directed upward, prayāte – it moves, vahni – fiery force, maṇḍalam – digestive chakra complex, tad = tat = that, ānala – energized region, śikhā – spike, flame, dīrghā – long, jāyate – becomes, vāyun – infused fresh air, āhatā – infused into

When, as directed, the negatively charged subtle force moves upward into the fiery digestive chakra complex, that energized region becomes long and spikey, as the infused fresh air is fused into it.

Analysis

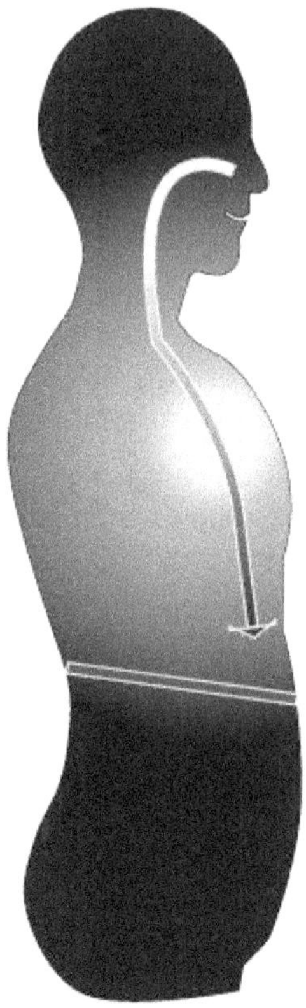

resistant abdomen/intestines complex of energies

This is experienced early on in kapalabhati/bhastrika breath-infusion practice, where the fresh air moved down from the lungs and is confronted by pollutant energy which blocks its downward passage. The student pushes down mentally against the resistance but physically he pulls up the abdomen/intestines complex of energy. This causes an exchange of electrostatic charge between the infused fresh air and the polluted gases which were in the body. This exchange is experienced as a warming of the gut region.

The student should repeatedly infuse fresh air and push it down, challenging the polluted air which blocks the passage and prevents the fresh air from being distributed. Eventually after weeks, months or years of practice, the digestion-reproduction complex becomes sorted so that the infused fresh air passes through those regions easily and without generating the heat which used to occur there because of the friction produced by the blockage.

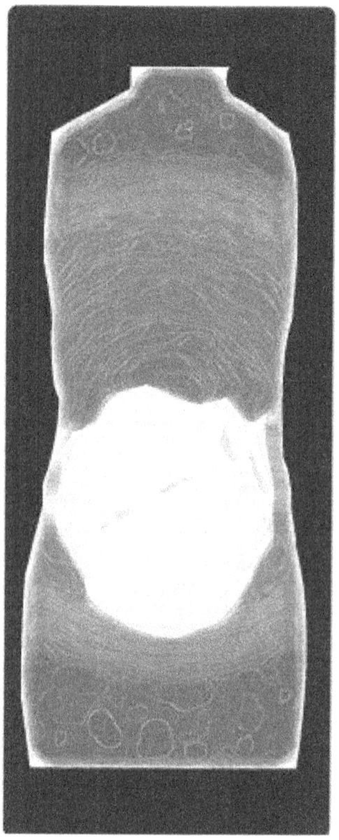

The long spikey energized region occurs somewhere between the navel and the groin. The yogi should force that energy through the groin area where it will pick up an extra electrostatic charge. Then it should be sent to the muladhara chakra where it will attach itself to the kundalini, which in turn will react by moving up through the spine into the brain.

This change of direction of travel of kundalini is vital for attaining higher yoga proficiency. So long as kundalini is eager to go from muladhara chakra to the sex chakra only, a yogi will be stymied taking one body after another haphazardly as dictated by sex attraction. The yogi's task is to train kundalini to ascend through the spine, but it will not be receptive to the training if the yogi is unable to get the electrostatic charge in the genitals to spike across to the muladhara base chakra.

As nature would have it, the natural way is for kundalini to be attracted to the pleasure expression in the genitals but a yogi must alter this system so that the sexual potency goes to meet kundalini, rather than have the kundalini travel to that potency.

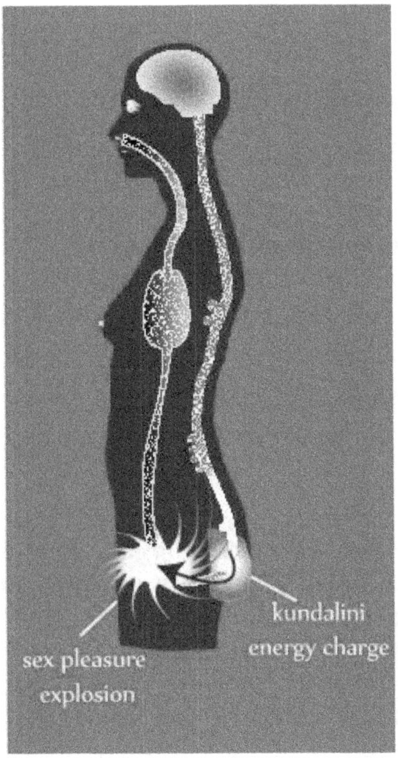

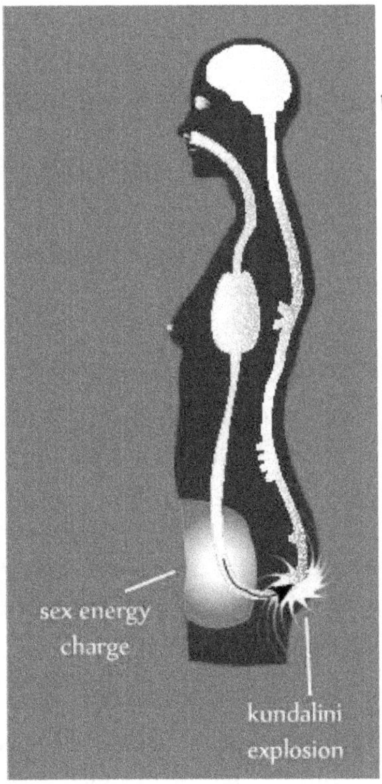

Application

The fiery digestive chakra complex is a spread energy which dominates the area which is lower than the rib cage but higher than the groin area. Below it is the sex organ complex but in females these areas have a common sharing where the ovaries are involved in their reproductive creations. When a yogi reforms the digestive chakra complex, the spread of its influence is reduced. His gut area becomes toned. Instead of having a large abdomen, he has a smaller one which does not require as much food, which has prompt digestion and excretion. That energized region becomes long and spikey. It allows the infused energy to pass freely so that there is no burning sensation during breath-infusion practice.

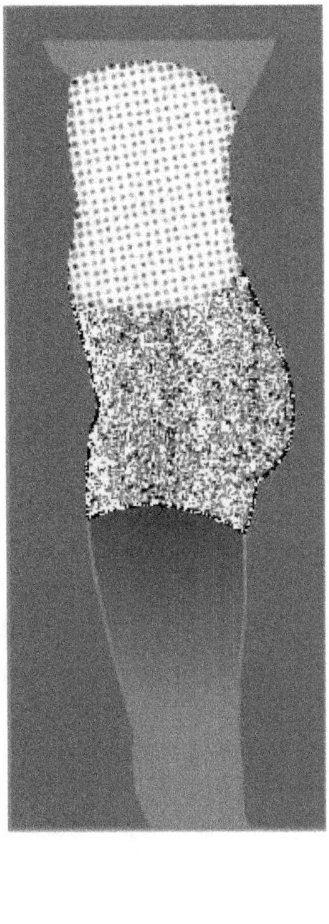

Verse 67

ततो यातो वह्न्य–अपानौ प्राणमुष्ण–स्वरूपकम् ।

तेनात्यन्त–प्रदीप्तस्तु जवलनो देहजस्तथा ।। ६७ ।।

tato yāto vahny–apānau prāṇamuṣṇa–svarūpakam |
tenātyanta–pradīptastu jvalano dehajastathā || 67 ||

tato = tataḥ = hence, yāto = yātaḥ = fused into, vahny = vahni = digestive/hormone energy, apānau – negatively charged subtle force, prāṇam – positively charged subtle force, uṣṇa – hot, svarūpakam – inherent nature, tenātyanta = tena (by this) + atyanta (greatly), pradīptas = illuminated, tu – but, jvalano = jvalanaḥ = blazing energy, deha – body, jas – produced in, tathā – as

Hence when the digestive/hormone energy is fused into the negatively charged subtle force, the positively charged energy becomes heated which is its inherent nature. By this a blazing energy which is generated in the body, is illuminated greatly.

Analysis

This is another verse in which the process is summarized. Elementary kundalini yoga takes years to master. This is because of the complexity of the energies which one has to manipulate to achieve it.

We have air in the body but most of it is polluted waste gases. The body uses these waste materials and even hoards much of it. There are hormones in the body, the primary one being the reproductive fluids. These are stored in sexual indulgence which as far as nature is concerned is for reproducing bodies. To us however the reproductive fluids are there to yield sexual pleasure.

As nature would have it there need be no change in the configuration of the body. It could continue living with the gas pollutants and hormone fluids. But for yoga, this natural system is off. Hatha Yoga means an effort to change this by kundalini manipulation for subtle body transformation.

The hormone energy is stored at numerous places in the body, in particular glands. It is also stored in incremental amounts in cells and in spaces between cells. When the body requires the use of these liquids, they are transported and mixed with pollutant gasses. A yogi learns how to mix these energies for causing the kundalini to ascent through the central spine.

By ingesting fresh air faster than the lungs and heart can distribute it, the yogi causes an accumulation of compressed air in the blood stream. This travels through the body and confronts both the hormone energy and the polluted gases.

By applying locks and mental focus, the yogi compresses the fresh air energy into the hormone-pollutants mixture which results in an electrostatic charge. This charge is increased and then it is compressed in on itself. From that comes a flash of light which illuminates the subtle form.

Application

The observations are made in the subtle body. Light is seen in that form by the yogi who is internalized during practice. Some perception is purely subjective, making it difficult for the yogi to verbalize. A yogi develops different types of psychic and supernatural perception during the breath-infusion practice and in the meditation which is done immediately after.

These perceptions do not involve the two eyes of the subtle body. These are:

- *direct core-self perception*
- *sense of identity perception*
- *buddhi intellect orb perception*
- *third eye brow chakra perception*
- *brahmarandra crown chakra perception*
- *prana-vision*
- *kundalini burst vision*
- *cell micro-kundalini vision*

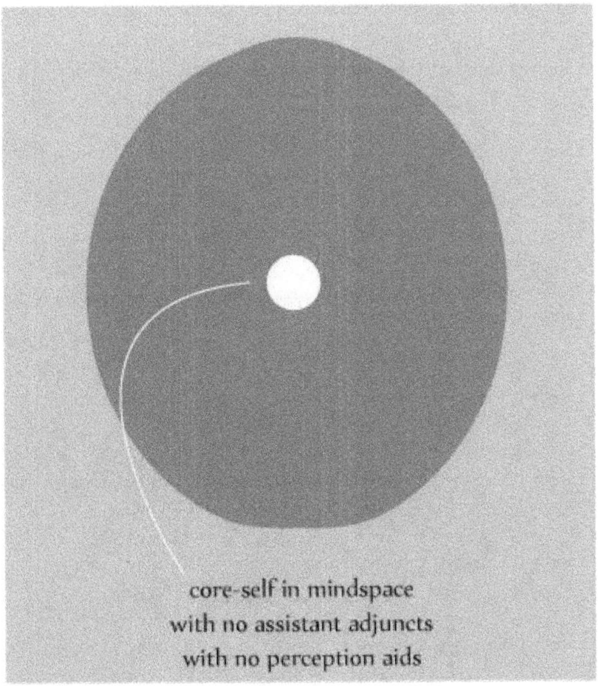

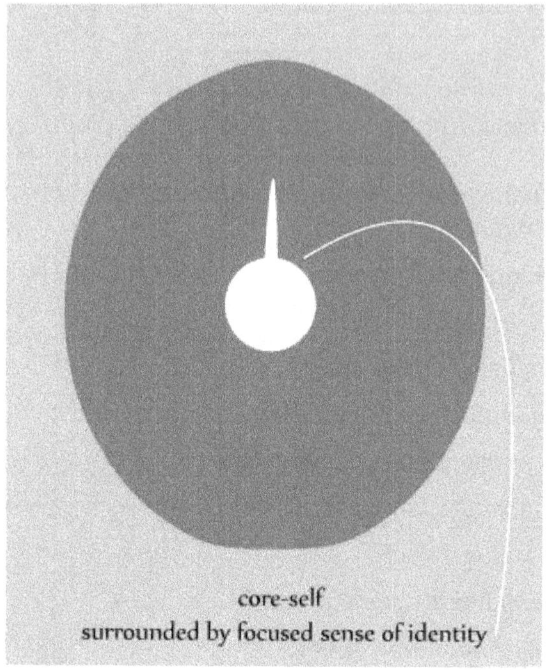
core-self
surrounded by focused sense of identity

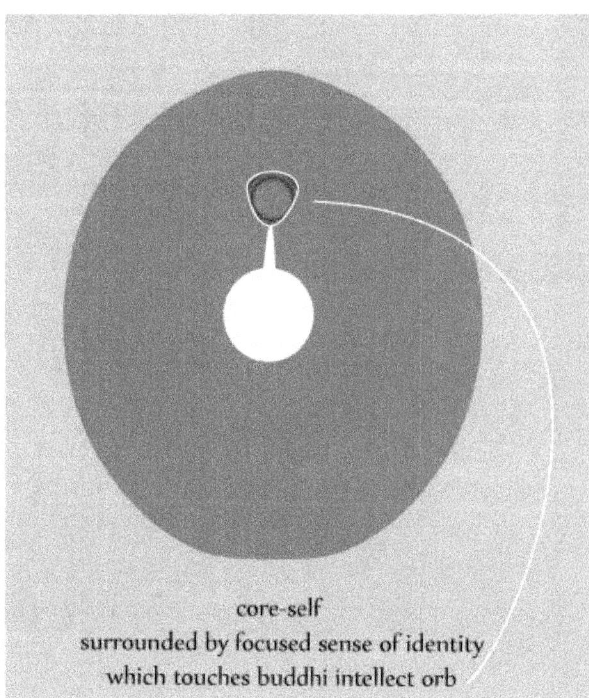
core-self
surrounded by focused sense of identity
which touches buddhi intellect orb

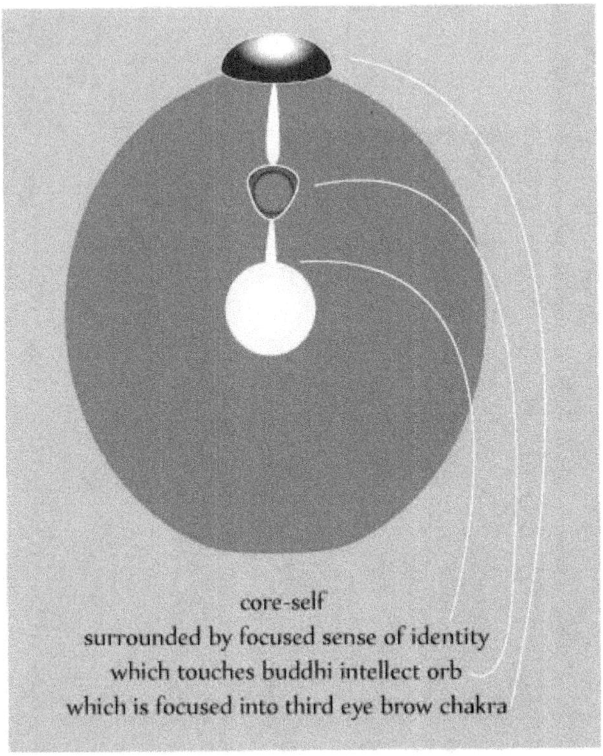
core-self
surrounded by focused sense of identity
which touches buddhi intellect orb
which is focused into third eye brow chakra

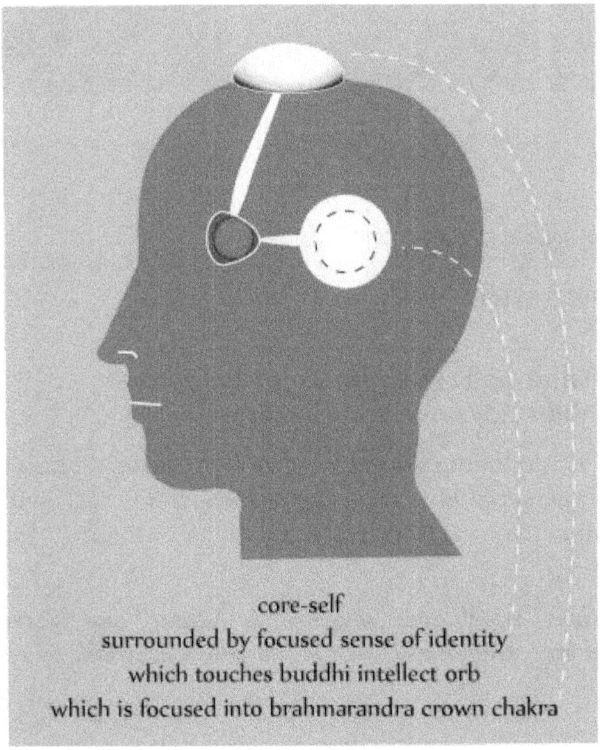
core-self
surrounded by focused sense of identity
which touches buddhi intellect orb
which is focused into brahmarandra crown chakra

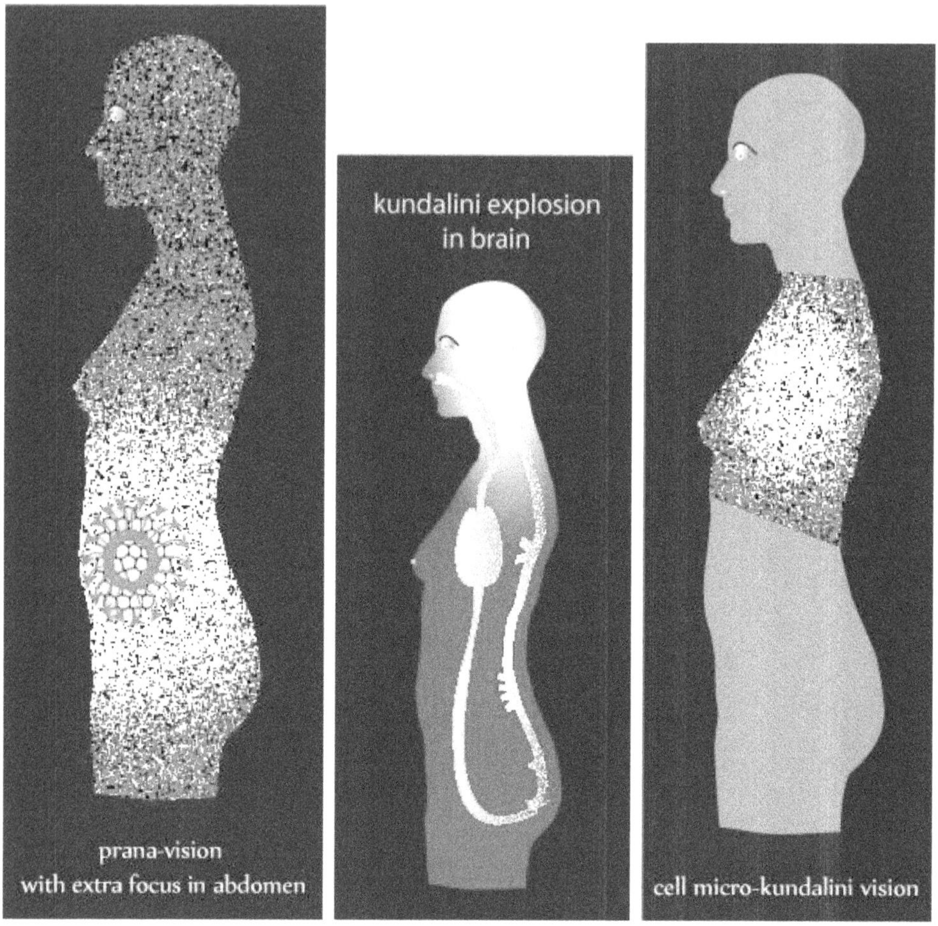

Verse 68

तेन कुण्डलिनी सुप्ता सन्तप्ता सम्प्रबुध्यते ।

दण्डाहता भुजङ्गीव निश्वस्य ऋजुतां वरजेत् ।। ६८ ।।

tena kuṇḍalinī suptā santaptā samprabudhyate |
daṇḍāhatā bhujaṅgīva niśvasya ṛjutāṁ vrajet || 68 ||

tena – by this, kuṇḍalinī – kundalini lifeforce, suptā – sleeping, santaptā – very infused, samprabudhyate – perceptively aroused, daṇḍāhatā = struck with a stick, bhujaṅgīva = bhujaṅgi (snake) + iva (similarly), niśvasya – hissing, ṛjutāṁ – is subdued, vrajet = straighten

By this, the kundalini lifeforce which was sleeping, is infused and is perceptively aroused. It hisses, is subdued and straightens like a snake which is struck by a stick.

Analysis

There are many persons who say that kundalini should not be aroused by a yoga process. Their opinion is that it is dangerous and may lead to insanity, schizophrenia, seizures, brain damage or nervous disorder.

Anything is possible in the material world. There is danger at every step. Even if one does not practice kundalini yoga one is still under threat by nature to come to misfortune.

The deliberate arousal of kundalini should be done under supervision of a person who practiced for years and is proficient in it. He or she should be able to demonstrate the practice to any perspective student. The student can then evaluate and make a decision either way.

Application

When kundalini is pierced by the infused breath energy, which is mixed with hormonal force, it hisses and attempts to move. If the force is weak, it will not move but will be like a sleeping serpent which was touched by a feather.

If the force had a large charge of electrostatic energy, kundalini will move. At first it will go in the direction it instinctively desires to but if the student applied locks, kundalini will be restrained and will not be able to take its usual route.

The locks cause it to move in a restricted way through the center of the spine, the sushumna nadi channel. If the charge was large but not so large, kundalini will ascend as far as the charge pushed it but it will descend as soon as the charge fizzes out. It could descend back to the base chakra after reaching the second, third, fourth or fifth chakra or it may go further entering the head of the subtle body.

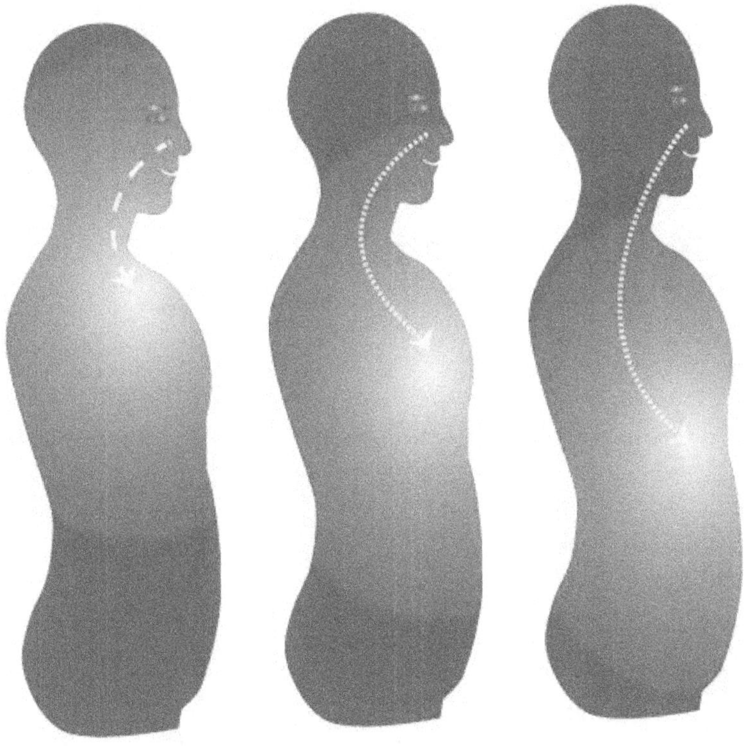

breath energy to top of lungs | breath energy to middle of lungs | breath-energy to bottom of lungs

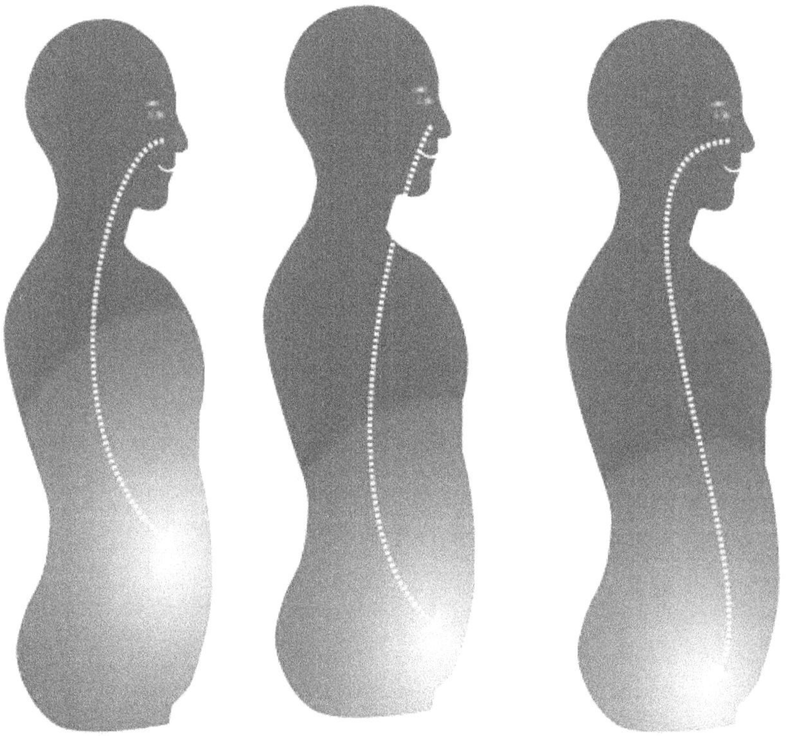

breath-energy to navel zone

breath-energy mix with nutrients

breath-energy with nutrients mix with hormones

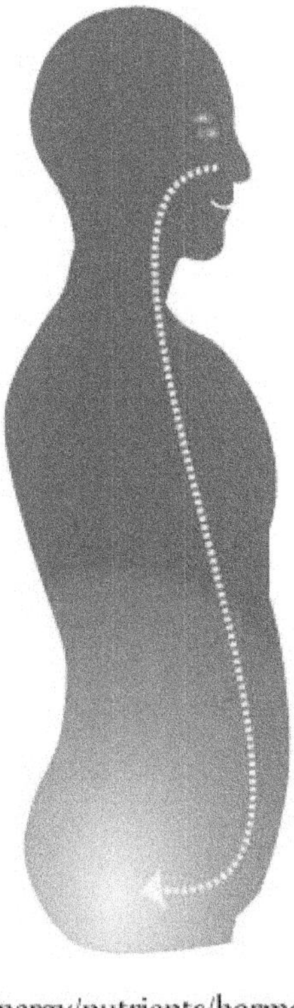

breath-energy/nutrients/hormone mix
shifting to muladhara base chakra

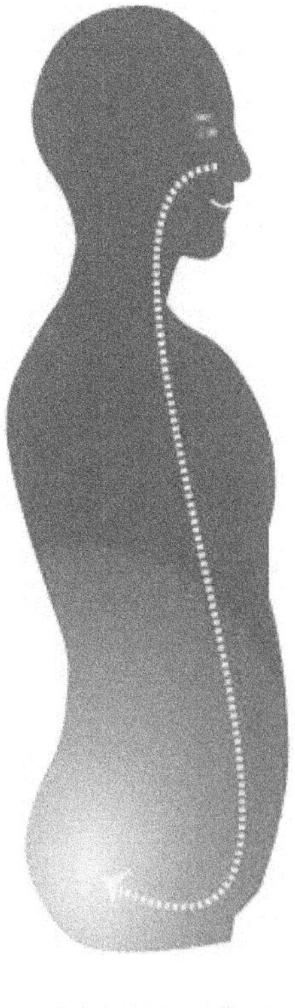

breath-energy/nutrients/hormone mix
fuse to base chakra

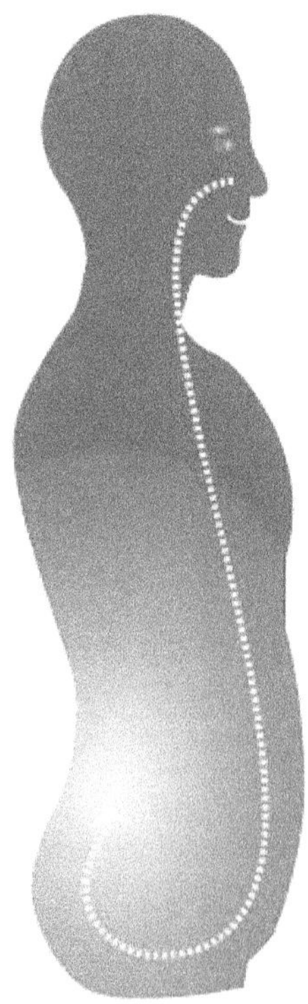

breath-charged kundalini
climbs to sex chakra on spine

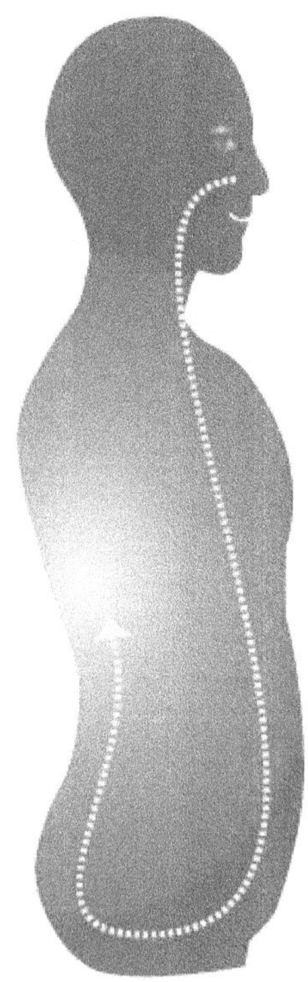

breath-charged kundalini
climbs to navel chakra on spine

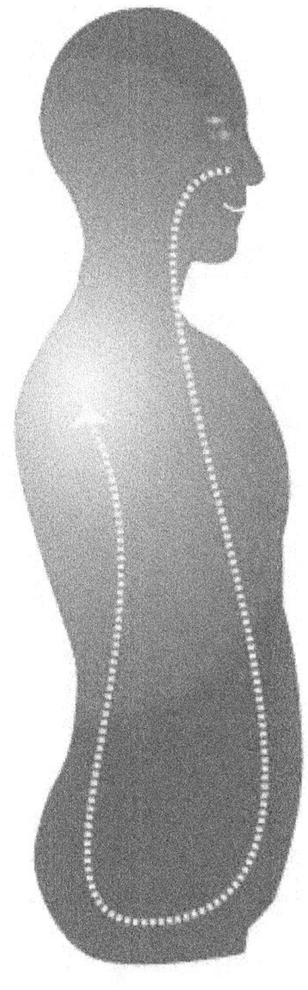

breath-charged kundalini
climbs to lung-heart chakra complex

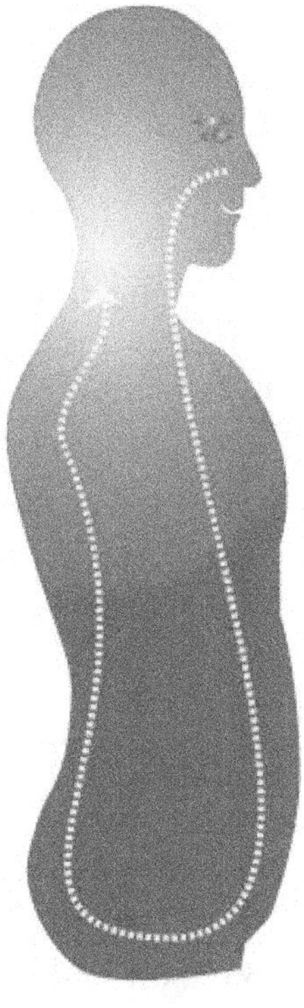

breath-charged kundalini
climbs to throat chakra complex

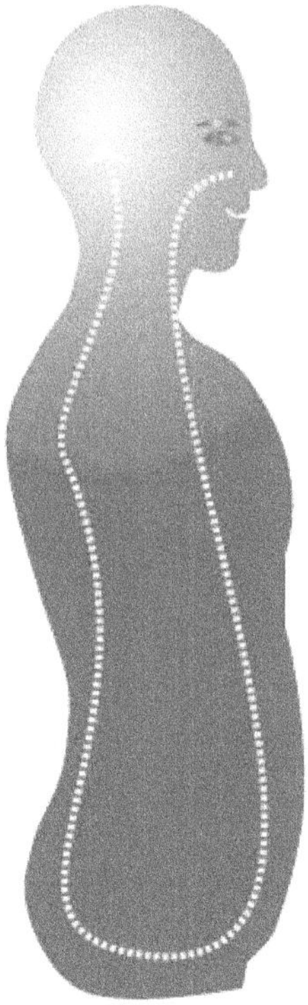

breath-charged kundalini
climbs into brain

Verse 69

बिलं प्रविष्टेव ततो बरह्म–नाड्यं तरं वरजेत् ।

तस्मान्नित्यं मूल–बन्धः कर्तव्यो योगिभिः सदा ।। ६९ ।।

bilaṁ praviṣṭeva tato brahma–nāḍyaṁ taraṁ vrajet ।
tasmānnityaṁ mūla–bandhaḥ kartavyo yogibhiḥ sadā ।। 69 ।।

bilaṁ – hole, praviṣṭeva = praviṣṭā (enters) + iva (as if), tato = tataḥ = then, brahma–nāḍyaṁ = microscopic central channel, taraṁ vrajet = transits, tasmān = tasmāt = thus, nityaṁ – always, mūla = anus–coccyx complex, bandhaḥ = physio–psychic compression, kartavyo = kartavyaḥ = be performed, yogibhiḥ – by the yogis, sadā – consistently

The physio-psychic compression of the anus-coccyx complex should be practiced by the yogis always. Kundalini enters the brahma nadi microscopic central channel, just as a serpent enters its hole. Therefore, the yogi should consistently practice this anus-coccyx physio-psychic compression.

Analysis

The brahma nadi microscopic central channel runs through the central sushumna spinal passage. It has a tiny hole at its bottom end in muladhara chakra. This is closed by effective application of ashwini mudra, which is the anus lock. Brahma-nadi runs through the central spine, through the neck. When it enters the head it disappears. It runs to the brahma randra crown chakra but due to the radiance at that center, the brahma-nadi becomes imperceptible.

When kundalini punches through the neck and enters the head, it becomes bewildered. It sways and looks around in an attempt to get its bearings. It then instinctively strikes out for the buddhi intellect orb. If it hits that orb when the buddhi least expects, the physical body may fall to the ground because the core-self will be jarred loose from its objective awareness of the physical system.

The core-self will then experience a gold-out or white-out, where it loses objectivity, loses contact with routine time and has self-perception only in reference to sheer gold or white light, which is a type of superconsciousness.

Application

After sufficient practice, which varies from student to student, there will come a time when the microscopic escape hole at the lower end of the brahma-nadi channel remains permanently sealed, so that kundalini makes no attempt to leave through it. When this happens, the yogi is assured that he will not go to the subterranean astral domains when his physical body dies.

When kundalini becomes habituated to going upwards into the brain, and when further, it anchors itself in the head of the subtle body and that becomes its default location, the yogi no longer has to be concerned about taking haphazard rebirth.

Verse 70

अथ जलन्धर–बन्धः

कण्ठमाकुञ्च्य हृदये सथापयेच्छिबुकं दृढम् ।

बन्धो जालन्धराख्यो।अयं जरा–मृत्यु–विनाशकः ।। ७० ।।

atha jalandhara–bandhaḥ
kaṇṭhamākuñcya hṛdaye sthāpayeccibukaṁ dṛḍham |
bandho jālandharākhyo|ayaṁ jarā–mṛtyu–vināśakaḥ || 70 ||

atha – now it will be explained, jalandhara – liquid-arresting, bandhaḥ = physio–psychic compression, kaṇṭham – throat, ākuñcya – contracting, hṛdaye – against the chest, sthāpayec = sthāpayet = should place, cibukaṁ – chin, dṛḍham – firmly, bandho = bandhaḥ = physio–psychic compression, jālandharākhyo = jālandhara (liquid-arresting) + ākhyaḥ (called), ayaṁ – this, jarā – old age, mṛtyu – death, vināśakaḥ – destroys the effects

Now the liquid-arresting physio-psychic throat compression will be explained:

Contract the throat while placing the chin firmly drawn to the chest. This is called the liquid arresting physio-psychic throat compression. It destroys the

effects of old age and death.

Analysis

Contracting the throat while placing the chin firmly drawn to the chest causes the liquid energy mix of kundalini and breath-infused energy to vaporize just before this energy squirts through the neck into the head of the subtle body. This chin lock is also known as the neck lock. It consists of drawing the chin firmly towards the throat. There is a reverse version of this lock where the head is tilted back as far as possible with the chin pointing up to the sky. There is also a variation of the chin lock which is done with the head slightly or gravely tilted forward.

If the head is tilted forward, it is likely that the kundalini will burst out of the body through the back top part of the neck. That is not recommended. To make kundalini travel from the neck into the head, it is best to keep the neck and head erect and without tilting the head forward, draw the chin back towards the throat.

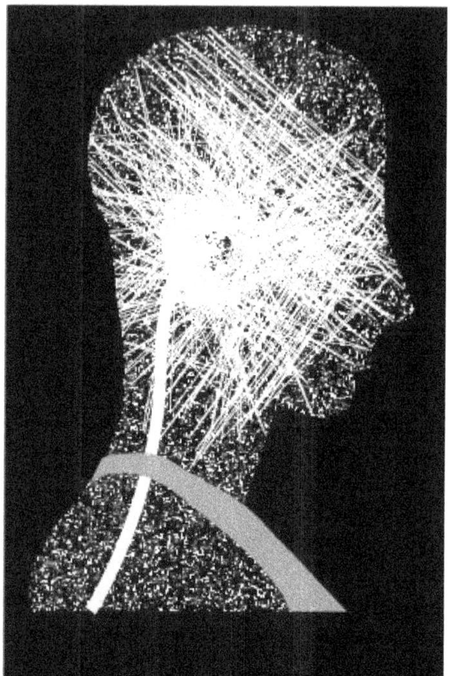

normal neck posture
natural for young adult bodies
kundalini scatters randomly
due to lack of chin lock

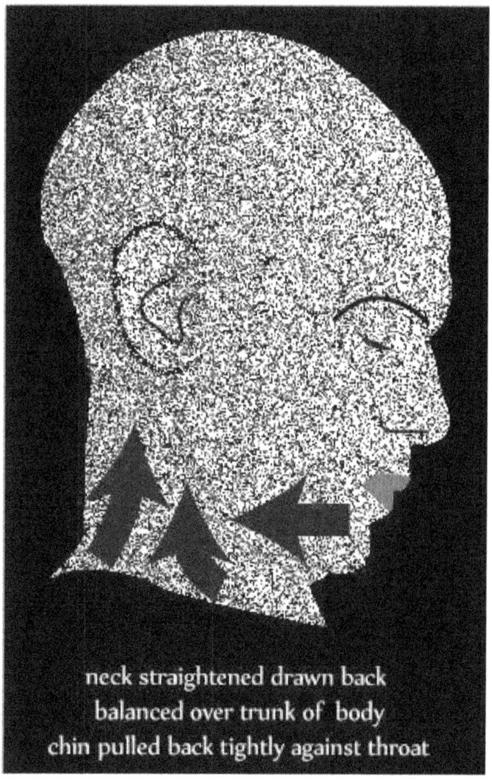

neck straightened drawn back
balanced over trunk of body
chin pulled back tightly against throat

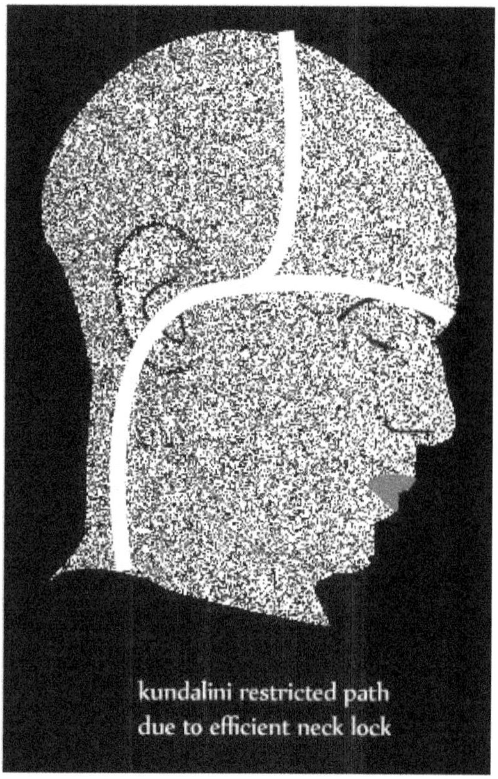

kundalini restricted path
due to efficient neck lock

This throat compression is part of the stop-eating command which a yogi has to enforce in the psyche if he wants to become freed from the need for rebirth in physical life forms. This lock compresses the nutrition orb which is in the throat.

Application

If a yogi can compress all breath and hormone energy, if he can force that compression around the pubic loop to the muladhara base chakra, if he can penetrate kundalini there and circumstantially cause it to go up the central sushumna passage, if he can make it reach the neck, if the neck lock is expertly applied, then for him old age and death are small wonders. This is because of dis-orienting the kundalini from its downward course.

Left to itself, kundalini will take a downward route at the time of death, exiting through the muladhara base chakra or leaving the body under the auspices of the reproductive equipment. A yogi is tasked with the mission of changing that route so that before the death of the physical body, kundalini becomes habituated to the upward course.

Verse 71

बध्नाति हि सिराजालमधो–गामि नभो–जलम् ।

ततो जालन्धरो बन्धः कण्ठ–दुःखौघ–नाशनः ।। ७१ ।।

badhnāti hi sirājālam – adho–gāmi nabho–jalam I
tato jālandharo bandhaḥ kaṇṭha–duḥkhaugha–nāśanaḥ II 71 II

badhnāti – it compresses, hi – indeed, sirājālam – network of nadi subtle tubes, adho–gāmi = descending, nabho = nabhaḥ = heaven, jalam – nectar, tato = tataḥ = hence, jālandharo = jalandharaḥ = liquid arresting, bandhaḥ = physio–psychic compression, kaṇṭha – throat, duḥkhaugha = duḥkha (suffering) + ogha (various), nāśanaḥ – removes

It compresses the network of nadi subtle tubes through which the nectar of heaven falls. Hence the liquid-arresting physio–psychic compression removes various types of suffering of the throat.

Analysis

The financial outlay for reproduction is the largest most expensive one in the body but it is financed by the kundalini lifeforce because of the necessity for survival and the tactical procedure of reserving rights in any progeny which the kundalini reproduces. Most of the energy from nutrients is trucked away from the intestines to the reproduction faculty or to its accessory agencies which are wherever there is fat storage in the body. Some such places are the cheeks, neck, abdomen, groin, breasts, hips, buttocks, and thighs. If somehow a yogi can change this system; if he can cause the energy culled out from the intestines to be routed into the brain, then the moon-like cooling influence will be felt and the sun-like lust-yielding process in the genitals would be reduced considerably.

It may be considered that the more pleasure the better, or that the more food consumed, the more hormones will be available to the reproductive glands. But actually this is an oversight because an increase in food consumption which will result in increased hormone for reproduction implies responsibility for the progeny produced.

If there is no progeny then the matter becomes more complicated because nature may keep tally of the consumption and levy penalties to the individual at a later date. Excess hormone is a self-inflicting injury, because nature will call to account the usage. It is best for the glands to manufacture as little hormone as possible. The promise of pleasure is there but the expense of it is unfavorable.

A yogi should eat in such way that a minimum of hormone energy is produced. This quantity would be routed up through the trunk of the body into the neck for transit into the brain, from where it should fall down to the tongue which is curled back and up into the soft palate. In such a state the yogi can make intimate contact with naad sound vibration, which would serve the purpose to replace his interest in the genitals.

Application

The sufferings of the throat are due to what is ingested by the mouth and nostrils. Sensible control of intakes means reduction of pollutions even on the physical end. But this yoga concerns the subtle body. The dripping of the nectar from in the head relates totally to the subtle body. The physical actions are performed because the subtle system is interspaced in the physical and operate when the physical is put into motion.

Verse 72

जालन्धरे कृते बन्धे कण्ठ– सङ्कोच–लक्षणे ।

न पीयूषं पतत्यग्नौ न च वायुः प्रकुप्यति ।। ७२ ।।

jālandhare kṛte bandhe kaṇṭha–saṅkoca–lakṣaṇe |
na pīyūṣaṁ patatyagnau na ca vāyuḥ prakupyati || 72 ||

jālandhare – in liquid arresting, kṛte – doing, bandhe = in physio–psychic compression, kaṇṭha – throat, saṅkoca – contraction, lakṣaṇe – characterized, na – no, pīyūṣaṁ – nectar, pataty = patati = falls, agnau – into fiery energy, na – no, ca – and, vāyuḥ – infused air, prakupyati – is scattered

In the liquid arresting physio–psychic compression, the characteristics of a throat contraction are that the nectar does not fall into the fiery energy and the infused air is not scattered.

Analysis

The convention is that whatever enters the mouth and nostrils takes a downward path through the intestines and through the blood vessels which course elsewhere in the body. The main direction is downhill because gravity dictates that whatever is not supported should fall towards the center of the earth.

Food nutrients and breath energy combine to make hormones, which are primarily used in the reproductive glands. In the groin and navel regions heat is generated. It consumes the hormonal energy. A yogi redesigns this system so that the nutrients and hormones go upward. Then there is a cooling effect in the head of the subtle body and the heat effect of the genitals is no longer prominent.

Instead of pleasure in the genitals, the system expresses pleasure in the head. Instead of pleasure focalized in the sex organs, it becomes focused in the head and in other parts of the psyche.

Application

As nature would have it, the air which is infused involuntarily is scattered haphazardly around the body. This is systematic in its own way. The evidence of this is that the body operates for some years before it becomes non-functional. However for the purpose of yoga, this system is tampered with.

A yogi infuses air and sends that air to particular parts of the body. At first the objective is to combine this air with the hormonal energy and thrust that mixture force into the kundalini lifeforce so that the energy would be inclined to move away from muladhara base chakra.

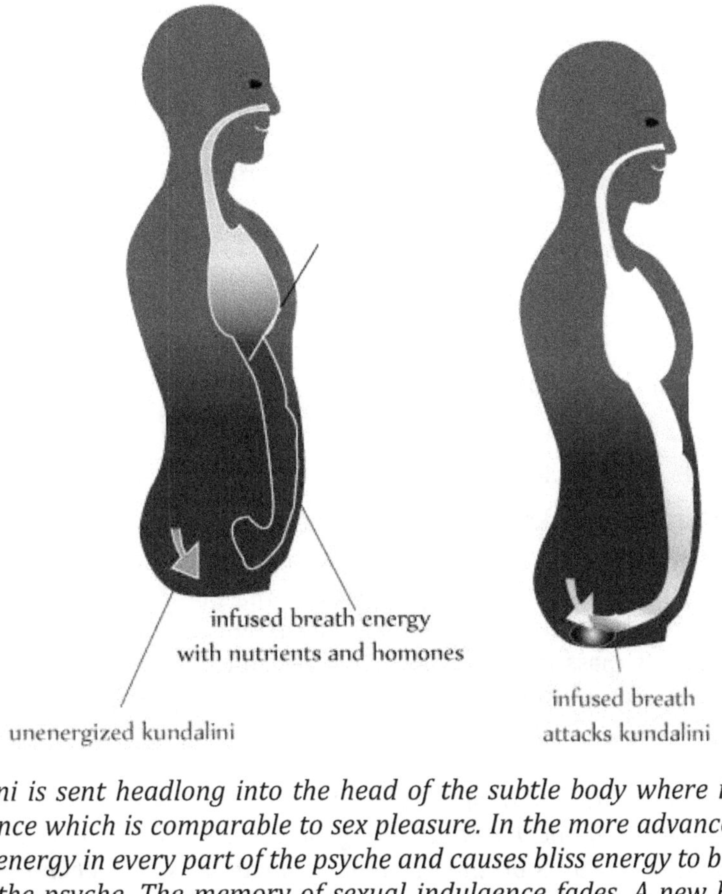

The kundalini is sent headlong into the head of the subtle body where it provides a bliss experience which is comparable to sex pleasure. In the more advanced stage, the yogi infuses energy in every part of the psyche and causes bliss energy to be manifested throughout the psyche. The memory of sexual indulgence fades. A new habit of bliss saturation in all parts of the psyche prevails.

Verse 73

कण्ठ–सङ्कोचनेनैव द्वे नाड्यौ सतम्भयेद्दृढम् ।
मध्य–चक्रमिदं ज्ञेयं षोडशाधार–बन्धनम् ।। ७३ ।।

kaṇṭha– saṅkocanenaiva dve nāḍyau stambhayeddṛḍham ।
madhya–cakramidaṁ jñeyaṁ ṣoḍaśādhāra–bandhanam ।। 73 ।।

kaṇṭha – throat, saṅkocanenaiva = saṅkocanena (by contracting) + eva (only), dve – two, nāḍyau – two nadi subtle channels, stambhayed = stambhayet = supressed, dṛḍham – firmly, madhya – central, cakram – energy gryating center, idaṁ – this, jñeyaṁ – known, ṣoḍaśādhāra = ṣoḍaśa (sixteen) + ādhāra (vital support), bandhanam = physio–psychic compression

By contracting the throat, the two nadi subtle channels are firmly suppressed. This chakra is known as the central energy gyrating center. Here is the location for physio–psychic compression of the sixteen vital supports.

Analysis

There are seven major chakras. These begin with the lowest, the muladhara chakra, which is at the base of the spine. It is the default location of the kundalini psychic mechanism. Here is a list of these major energy gyrating centers in their descending order:

- sahasrara crown of head chakra
- ajna center of eyebrows chakra
- vishuddhi throat chakra
- anahata lung-heart complex chakra
- manipura navel chakra
- svadhishthana sex chakra
- muladhara base chakra

The vishuddhi throat chakra is said to have sixteen petals or spreads of energy which correspond to vital supports in various parts of the body. This chakra governs the communication between the trunk and head of the body. Even though it is not in the center of the body's mass it is rated as being centralized between the trunk and the head. It negotiates the relationship between the head and the rest of the body.

Application

A yogi must clear the dense astral energy from the sushumna central passage but he must also clear the entire neck so that energy passes freely in both directions through the neck. At first the focus is on the sushumna central passage. When that cylinder is permanently cleared the yogi turns his attention to the area around it, the flesh part of the neck.

Clearance of the sushumna central passage is beneficial but it is not the clearance of the whole psyche. For that one must clear the entire neck so that it becomes a sushumna central passage that is so clear that there be nothing in it to obstruct the passage of energy into and out of the head.

Verse 74

मूल–सथानं समाकुञ्च्य उड्डियानं तु कारयेत् ।

इडां च पिङ्गलां बद्धा वाहयेत्पश्चिमे पथि ।। ७४ ।।

mūla–sthānaṁ samākuñcya uḍḍiyānaṁ tu kārayet
iḍāṁ ca pingalāṁ baddhvā vāhayetpaścime pathi || 74 ||

mūla = anus–perineum, sthānaṁ – region, samākuñcya – contract completely, uḍḍiyānaṁ – drawing the abdomen up under the rib cage and back towards the spine, tu – but, kārayet – should perform, iḍāṁ – left spinal nadi passage, ca – and, pingalāṁ – right spinal nadi passage, baddhvā – by suppressing, vāhayet – should flow, paścime – in the rear, pathi – passage

Completely contract the anus–perineum region, and perform the drawing up of the abdomen up under the rib cage and back towards the spine. By suppressing on the left and right spinal passages, the yogi should restrict the flow through the passage in the rear.

Analysis

Center front, center center, left and right sides must be retracted towards the spine with the anus-perineum region tightly contracted upward. This lets the kundalini know that it has no outlet and must abide by the desire for it to ascend the sushumna central passage.

The degree of efficiency of these locks varies from student to student but as anyone practices, there should be increased proficiency. The diet and the time of eating should be regulated to aid this practice. Even the lifestyle should be adjusted.

Much of this is in the subtle body in terms of tracking the infused breath energy as it is compressed, directed and made to fold in on itself. When compressed sufficiently, it will implode and explode in one direction or the other. The locks give control of the diffusion of the compressed energy. The locks are designed to give the yogi the upper hand over the movement of the kundalini psychic lifeforce.

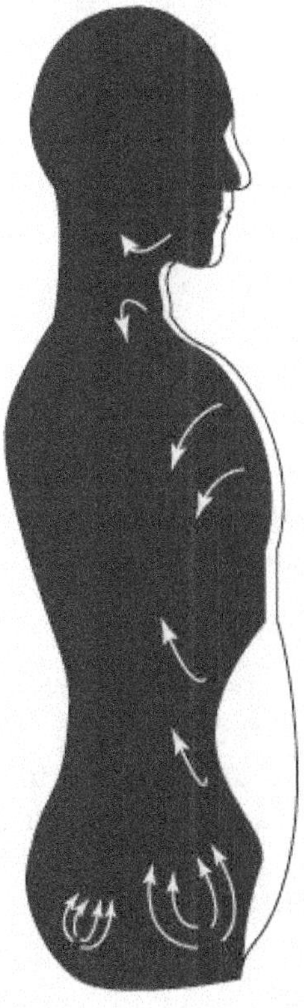

lock pressure (bandhas)

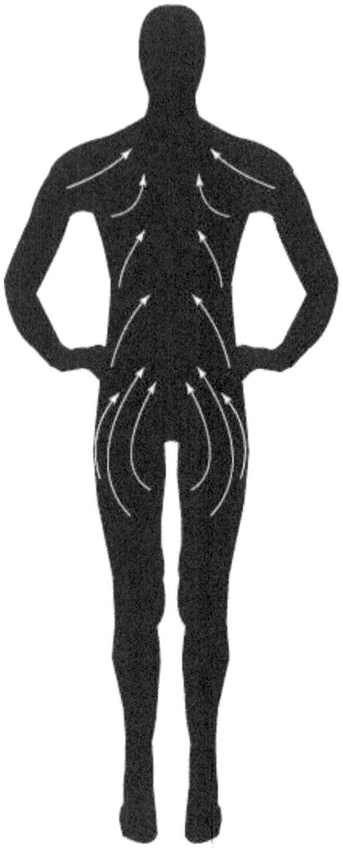

upward pressure from each side

Application

Energy is scattered through the human body in a haphazard way which is serviceable to the struggle of existence. The yogi wants to get out of the survival game but it is not just a matter of wishful thinking, nor that of hoping that a deity will arrange transit.

The deity already came and went. He is Krishna. His instructions for the escape are in the Bhagavad Gita. Our part is the application of his teachings.

Verse 75

अनेनैव विधानेन प्रयाति पवनो लयम् ।

ततो न जायते मृत्युर्जरा–रोगादिकं तथा ।। ७५ ।।

anenaiva vidhānena prayāti pavano layam I
tato na jāyate mṛtyurjarā–rogādikaṁ tathā I I 75 I I

anenaiva = anena (by this) + eva (so), vidhānena – by technique, prayāti – is quiescent, pavano = pavanaḥ = psyche–energy, layam = absence of mento–emotional trauma, tato = tataḥ = then, na – no, jāyate – is applicable, mṛtyur = mṛtyuḥ = death, jarā – old age, rogādikaṁ – disease and related trauma, tathā – even so

By this technique, the psyche–energy becomes quiescent with the absence of mento–emotional trauma. Then death, old age, disease and related trauma are not applicable.

Analysis

When the core-self shifts away from the trauma-ridden planes of existence, it is no longer traumatized by the disease, infirmity and death of the physical body. However to achieve this one has to change the configuration of the kundalini lifeforce. A human being can say whatever comes to mind. He may boost faith in what is not to be. In the final analysis; the kundalini will do what its tendencies dictate. Hence the necessity to reconfigure it.

The yoga practice with asana postures and breath-infusion techniques, causes the psychic energy to become quiescent and the mento-emotional trauma to disappear. It provides a condition for access to the divine atmosphere.

Application

Death, old age, disease and related trauma continue for the material body of the yogi. It continues for the yogi just as it does for others. However because the yogi's interest in existence shifted to the divine atmosphere, the fluctuations in material existence have no feedback to the core-self of the yogi.

People without psychic perception cannot understand how a yogi sidesteps the unwanted features. They see the yogi's body in the same dilemma as their own. They assume that the yogi is not transcendent. They miss the investigation as to the investment of his spiritual interest through the sense of identity.

Has the yogi shut down the sense of identity so that it does not express interest through the intellect and sensual energy?

How can we tell if the yogi's innate interest is completely retracted while material nature as his physical body, continues impulsive activities?

Verse 76

बन्ध–तरयमिदं श्रेष्ठं महा–सिद्धैश्च सेवितम् ।

सर्वेषां हठ–तन्त्राणां साधनं योगिनो विदुः ।। ७६ ।।

bandha–trayamidaṁ śreṣṭhaṁ mahā–siddhaiśca sevitam I
sarveṣāṁ haṭha–tantrāṇāṁ sādhanaṁ yogino viduḥ II 76 II

bandha = physio–psychic compression ,trayam – three, idaṁ – this, śreṣṭhaṁ – best, mahā – great, siddhaiś = siddhaiḥ = perfected yogis, ca – and, sevitam – serviced, sarveṣāṁ – all, haṭha – kundalini manipulation for psychic energy transformation, tantrāṇāṁ – mystic proficiency practice, sādhanaṁ – procedure, yogino = yoginaḥ = yogis, viduḥ – know

These three physio–psychic compressions are the best. They were serviced by the great perfected yogis. Of all mystic proficiency practices for kundalini manipulation and psychic energy transformation, the yogis know this as the procedure.

Analysis

The human body in each case has a limited and very specific layout with very few variations in general. These methods used by ancient yogis can be serviceable today.

Application

To become liberated, a student has to cease speculation and try methods which are proven to give results. After trying a method, the student should be honest enough to know if there is promise in it. There should be no pride in using any practice. Every method should be honestly accessed for its actual worth.

Methods used by ancient yogis may or may not be effective today. We must be sure that we have the complete discipline because parts of a discipline may be insufficient. One should consult with an advanced teacher who practiced the method. If one gets a method from a book, one has to carefully test it to be sure that it is effective.

Verse 77

यत्किञ्चित्स्रवते चन्द्रादमृतं दिव्य–रूपिणः ।

तत्सर्वं ग्रसते सूर्यस्तेन पिण्डो जरायुतः ।। ७७ ।।

yatkiñcitsravate candrādamṝtaṁ divya–rūpiṇaḥ – form,
tatsarvaṁ grasate sūryastena piṇḍo jarāyutaḥ || 77 ||

yatkiñcit = whatever, sravate – flowing, candrād = candrāt = from the moon–like energy, amṝtaṁ – nectar, divya – divine, rūpiṇaḥ – form, tat – that, sarvaṁ – all, grasate – consume, sūryas – sun–like energy, tena –by this, piṇḍo = piṇḍaḥ = body, jarāyutaḥ = being with old age

Whatever flows from the moon–like energy is like nectar and gives divine form. When that is consumed by the sun–like energy, the body develops old age.

Analysis

This is a coded message which when deciphered reads that sexual pleasure is the cause of old age, while conservation of sexual energy and its transport into the head of the subtle body is the cause of immortality.

Application

This has little to do with physical or even subtle celibacy. It concerns a change in the configuration of the subtle body, irrespective of what happens in the physical world to the physical system.

When the sexual hormones are consumed by the sun-like lusty energy in the reproductive system, that causes old age in the physical body and lowering of vibration in the astral form. It has little to do with whether the person has sexual intercourse or not. People, who have no sexual intercourse, may still have their hormonal energies be consumed by the sun-like lusty energy. It is just that their rate of consumption is much less that those who are indulgent.

Those who have the hormonal energy come into the head of the subtle body and whose core-self's interest is lifted from the physical and sensual enjoying utilities, are not bogged down by the body's activities.

Verse 78

अथ विपरीत–करणी मुद्रा

तत्रास्ति करणं दिव्यं सूर्यस्य मुख–वञ्चनम् ।

गुरूपदेशतो ज्ञेयं न तु शास्त्रार्थ–कोटिभिः ।। ७८ ।।

atha viparīta–karaṇī mudrā
tatrāsti karaṇaṁ divyaṁ sūryasya mukha–vañcanam |
gurūpadeśato jñeyaṁ na tu śāstrārtha–koṭibhiḥ || 78 ||

atha – now it is explained, viparīta – flow inversion, karaṇī – procedure, mudra – mystic checking practices, tatrāsti = tatra (there) + asti (is), karaṇaṁ – procedure, divyaṁ – mystic, sūryasya – of the sun, mukha – from the opening, vañcanam – illusion, trick, gurūpadeśato = guru (proficient yoga teacher) + upadeśataḥ (instructions), jñeyaṁ – is learnt, na – not, tu – but, śāstrārtha = śāstra (scripture) + artha (statements), koṭibhiḥ – millions

Now the viparita flow inversion mystic checking practice is explained:

There is a mystic procedure which tricks the opening of the sun. It is learnt from the instructions of a yoga teacher but not from millions of scriptural statements.

Analysis

To some extent yoga is secretive but it is not a matter of hiding the information. A technique can be described openly but the application requires mystic expertise. The flow inversion mystic checking practice does involve upturning the physical body to reverse the flows which gravity usually commands, but mere physical movements do not yeild the result intended.

Scriptural statements with detailed descriptions may be followed to a tee but that in no way guarantees the psychic actions which are complementary for success.

Application

Yogis who are masters of mystic perception may act with the subtle body and not reflect those actions in the physical form, which means that observers will have no idea how those yogis make progress.

Someone may think that a yogi is all washed-up, done-for as far as spiritual progress is concerned, but if the yogi kept doing the austerities on the subtle plane, he may achieve success. It is not what the physical body does but what the subtle body adheres to in its own way.

Ultimately it is no one's concerns as to whether a yogi lives up to social expectations or not. Spiritual progress does not concern the physical body. Status of that body does not translate over to the supernatural environment. Hence it is important that every student tend to his or her progress and not censure other yogis.

Verse 79

ऊर्ध्व–नाभेरधस्तालोरूर्ध्वं भानुरधः शशी ।

करणी विपरीताख्या गुरु–वाक्येन लभ्यते ।। ७९ ।।

ūrdhva–nābheradhastālorūrdhvaṁ bhānuradhaḥ śaśī ।
karaṇī viparītākhyā guru–vākyena labhyate ।। 79 ।।

ūrdhva – above, nābher = nābheḥ = navel, adhas – below, tālor = tāloḥ = palate, ūrdhvaṁ – over, bhānur = bhānuḥ = heating sun feature, adhaḥ – below, śaśī – cooling moon feature, karaṇī – procedure, viparītākhyā = viparita (flow inversion) + ākhyā (named), guru – proficient yoga teacher, vākyena – by instruction, labhyate – is obtained

Above is the navel and below is the palate. The heating and cooling feature reversed respectively. This flow inversion procedure is acquired through the instructions of a proficient yoga teacher.

Analysis

As nature would have it everything that enters the mouth moves downward. Even most of the breath energy moves downward. Thus the most powerful force in the body is the heating feature in the abdominal/groin region. The most hormone production is in the reproductive center of the body. It is a heating feature called the sun plexus in the body. Psychically, it has extensive power, beginning with the stomach under the neck and ending at the genital/excretion complex of energies.

Way above in the head there is the cooling feature which is minor because the main features of the kundalini are devoted to survival primarily. Use of the brain for thinking and sensing is subservient to survival as far as the kundalini is concerned.

The yogi's task is to upset this natural way of nature, to make the psychic organs in the brain the foremost features and to sublimate the survival/reproduction complex. This is easier said than done, because the psychic functions in the brain are addicted to sexual pleasure which the kundalini linked to reproduction. Unless this addiction can be broken there is no hope for the yogi to take possession of the psyche.

It is not sexual indulgence which is the problem. It is rather the interest in it. When all is said and done, even if one remains non-sexual for a million years, one will resume sexual behavior as soon as one has a form which facilitates it. But if the interest in it is removed, then one will not be focused into it even if one has a form which must have it.

Yogis should understand these matters clearly and not superficially make a show of sexual resistance merely because of using a life form which is devoid of libido. Some sexual interest which is based on spiritual reality cannot be removed. A yogi must also research in his own psyche to discover this. But he must clearly tally the accounts so that the kundalini's sexual adventures are not mistaken as spiritual pastimes.

Application

Doing head stand postures and other practices with the body flipped upside down, with the feet in the air and the head on the ground, do supply health to certain glands and to the feet, legs and thighs but these physical postures do not necessarily give the psychic results described by Swatmarama. The flip must occur even when the body is erect in its normal configuration with the head above and feet below and with gravity exerting its downward influence.

Verse 80

नित्यमभ्यास–युक्तस्य जठराग्नि– विवर्धिनी ।

आहारो बहुलस्तस्य सम्पाद्यः साधकस्य च ।। ८० ।।

nityamabhyāsa–yuktasya jaṭharāgni–vivardhinī |
āhāro bahulastasya sampādyaḥ sādhakasya ca || 80 ||

nityam – constant, abhyāsa – practice, yuktasya – of proficiency, jaṭharāgni – gastric heat, vivardhinī – increases, āhāro = āhāraḥ = food, bahulas – ample, tasya – his, sampādyaḥ – to accomplish, sādhakasya – of the student, ca – and

The constant proficient practice of this increases the gastric heat. To accomplish this, the food of the student-yogi should be ample.

Analysis

Some exercises have a negative aspect and must be compensated by certain specific actions. This is why one should learn a practice from a yogi who mastered it, and knows the ups and downs and can advise one accordingly.

Doing the headstands and other postures, which cause gravity to pull everything to the head of the body, will cause certain aspects which are negative, like increasing of gastric heat which will produce increased need for food because otherwise the increased production and secretion of digestives enzymes and bile, may burn holes in the stomach lining or intestinal walls.

If one does these practices and does not know about these upsets, one may get negative reactions and may be unable to trace that to the practices which one will continue doing in ignorance to one's detriment.

Application

To compensate for the increase in gastric heat the yogi should increase protein quantity, either by increasing the food mass or by increasing the quality of protein using a more protein-concentrated food. Gravity will exert its influence. It will not let up. Thus if one works against it one must have a way to compensate for depriving it of exerting itself in the way nature intended.

Verse 81

अल्पाहारो यदि भवेदग्निर्दहति तत–क्षणात् ।

अधः–शिराश्छोर्ध्वे–पादः क्षणं सयात्प्रथमे दिने ।। ८१ ।।

alpāhāro yadi bhavedagnirdahati tat–kṣaṇāt |
adhaḥ–śirāśchordhva–pādaḥ kṣaṇaṁ syātprathame dine || 81 ||

alpāhāro = alpa (insufficient) + āhāraḥ (food), yadi – if, bhaved = bhavet = there is, agnir = agniḥ = digestive heat, dahati – chemically burns, tat – that, kṣaṇāt – from the moment, adhaḥ – down, śirāś = śirāḥ = head, chordhva = ca (and) + ūrdhva (above, up), pādaḥ – feet, kṣaṇaṁ – moment, syāt – is, prathame – on the first, dine – on a day

If the food is insufficient even for a moment, the digestive heat will chemically burn. On the first day, for a moment, he should stand with his head down and feet up.

Analysis

These are precautions which cover the liability of someone reading Swatmarama's information and using it without the proper guidance and with an eagerness to progress even though the person does not have the evolutionary background which would sponsor that development.

Yoga is for those souls who reached the top of evolutional passage through the various life forms, even through human opportunity. It is not just a matter of having a human body, because one may have one and may not be evolved sufficiently to do yoga.

As in climbing trees the supportive branch becomes thinner and thinner as one ascends, so in the practice of yoga, it gets more and more hairy scary as one advances. This means that just as in tree climbing only a lightweight human can go to the top, in yoga only those who lost their evolutionary requirements can do the advanced procedures. Others, even if they are shown these in details, cannot activate them until the evolutionary needs are considerably reduced.

A human being, who has much to experience in the mundane evolutionary cycle, is so heavy with that energy that he or she cannot make the full use of the yoga disciplines, just as a heavy-weight human being cannot go to the very top of a tree.

Application

Little by little with the right instructor, a student can progress in yoga but this does not mean that one can become a great yogin if one has not matured through the evolutionary process of material nature. What may happen is that if one develops an interest even before one matured, then by doing yoga, one will learn how to more efficiently integrate the evolutionary drives. One should be patient; realizing that one cannot do the advanced processes until one experienced certain aspects in the evolutionary cycle.

It is okay to stay in touch with yoga and yogis as one moves through the evolutionary course but there is no way that one will bypass what is necessary learning in the process. This is why it is important to have connection with a siddha if one does yoga. One simply cannot figure it out by oneself because one must also calculate one's relation with material nature and know how to negotiate that efficiently.

Verse 82

क्षणाच्च किञ्चिदधिकमभ्यसेच्च दिने दिने ।

वलितं पलितं चैव षण्मासोर्ध्वं न दृश्यते ।

याम–मात्रं तु यो नित्यमभ्यसेत्स तु कालजित् ।। ८२ ।।

kṣaṇācca kiṅcidadhikamabhyasecca dine dine |
valitaṁ palitaṁ caiva ṣaṇmāsordhvaṁ na dṝśyate |
yāma–mātraṁ tu yo nityamabhyasetsa tu kālajit || 82 ||

kṣaṇāc = kṣaṇāt = from the time, ca – and, kiṅcid = kiṅcit = something, adhikam – more, abhyasec = abhyaset = should practice, ca – and, dine dine = day by day, daily, valitaṁ – wrinkle, palitaṁ – grey hair, caiva = and even so, ṣaṇ – six, māsordhvaṁ = māsa (month) + ūrdhvaṁ – after, na – not, dṝśyate – are experienced, yāma – three hours, mātraṁ – merely, tu – indeed, yo = yaḥ = who, nityam – daily, abhyaset – practice, sa – he, tu – indeed, kālajit – one who supersede death

He should increase the practice daily. Wrinkles and grey hair are not experienced after six months. He, who practices daily for three hours, supersedes death.

Analysis

Imagine practicing a posture like the headstand for three hours daily for six months. What is the possibility of a modern yogi doing that. Even if he does that will he get the intended result? Will he have the expert supervision indicated by Swatmarama? The reconfiguration of genetic behavior for removing wrinkles and grey hairs, occurred in the era when Swatmarama authored the Sanskrit of this book. This may not happen today.

Application

We recommend that students appreciate these statements about ancient yogis, and not expect to get the same results, except in the subtle body.

The deterioration by age of the physical form feeds over into the subtle body. A yogi should make every effort to check the languishing of the subtle body. To do this the main tool is pranayama breath-infusion. That combined with asanas prevents the physical system from pulling down the subtle body.

Verse 83

अथ वज्रोली

स्वेच्छया वर्तमानो।अपि योगोक्तैर्नियमैर्विना ।

वज्रोलीं यो विजानाति स योगी सिद्धि–भाजनम् ।। ८३ ।।

atha vajrolī
svecchayā vartamāno| api yogoktairniyamairvinā |
vajrolīṁ yo vijānāti sa yogī siddhi–bhājanam || 83 ||

atha – now it is described, vajroli – upward muscular redirection of male sexual emission, svecchayā = sva icchayā = whimsically as desired wish, vartamāno = vartamānaḥ = acting, api – also, yogoktair = yoga (yoga) + uktaiḥ (established), niyamair = niyamaiḥ = by recommended behaviors, vinā – without, vajrolīṁ – upward muscular redirection of male sexual emission, yo = yaḥ = who, vijānāti – qualifies, sa – he, yogī – yogi, siddhi – mystic perfectional skill, bhājanam – deserving person

Now the vajroli upward muscular redirection of male sexual emission is described:

Even if the yogi acts whimsically as desired, without respect to the established recommended behaviors for yoga practice, if he practices the vajroli upward muscular redirection of male sexual emission, he qualifies as a person deserving of mystic perfectional skills.

Analysis

Vajroli upward muscular redirection of male sexual emission is legendary. It is abhorred by moralists the world over, who feel that yogis use this to justify sexual indulgence with tantric partners. The truth behind this issue is that there was a time in India, when this practice was used and abused by the ksatriya warrior caste. These were ruling class families in which kings and princes married multiple spouses and had concubines and servant-girls to sexually service.

The Hatha Yoga Pradipika was designed primarily for use by brahmin ascetics not by the second caste, the warriors. However because many kings and princes had sexual access to multiple females, there arose the necessity to control their sexual organs so that they could indulge in more sexual intercourse than the human body would normally afford.

The male human body is not designed to service many females on a daily basis. It produces only so much sexual hormones and maintains erection for only so long. However by using herbs, physical processes and high-protein oily foods, males increased sexual stamina and found that their bodies performed satisfactorily for the sexual challenges.

This has nothing to do with yoga, but some of the kings and princes did get advice from yogis about Ayur Vedic methods, asana postures and breath regulations which helped them to increase or prolong sexual stamina. In the Kama Sutra many classic yoga postures are used in sexual intercourse. This caused a misunderstanding where people felt that in tantric practice, those poses were adapted from the yoga techniques. However the real source of varied sexual postures is the evolutionary designs for sexual indulgence which nature displays in various species of life. Specific creature forms become sexually linked for transmission of male sexual fluids into a female body in a particular format or body pose. These are the origins of the postures in the Kama Sutra. It has little to do with yoga asana. It is adapted directly from the genetic code which stipulates which species should engage in which bodily linkage for reproduction.

The sum total evolutionary experience in all its aspects, of which sexual dalliance is just a small part, is in the human being because the human form is the pinnacle of evolution and contains the contents of all other species which the form evolved from.

Vajroli upward muscular redirection of male sexual emission is more than a physical process. It has some important psychological supports. If these are absent, then the physical practice will not yield mystic controlling results.

Lifting male sexual emission without deleting the male sexual expression tendency is meaningless on the psychological level. The males are bogged down in this existence by the sexual expression tendency. Even if the semen is retracted as described, still if the expression need continues, the lift would be superficial only. It may occur on the physical plane but it will not affect the subtle level.

Application

Swatmarama excused yogis who master this technique on the physical and psychological levels and who act whimsically as desired, without respect to the established recommended behaviors. This is because such persons are not under the jurisdiction of moral conduct in terms of traditional dealings. Because these yogis have to be concerned only with the moral conduct between their core-selves and the psychic adjuncts in their individual psyche, what they do is of no concern to others and does not fall under the jurisdiction of dharma righteous behavior in so far as that is interpreted in a linear way.

An advanced yogi makes use of providential circumstances to quickly bleach consequential equations which are hurled at him by fate. That requires radical actions which may seem to contravene morality but which in fact honor reality in a complex way which requires deep insight to fathom.

Traditional morality concerns one life only. It has to do with behavior within the format of the present body and its relations but a yogi cannot be restricted to that. He may maneuver situations which involve other past lives and even other existences in other dimensions.

People sometimes get this idea that a yogi is their utility or is their family member and should conform to the plan for family elevation in the material world. However that is not the mission of an ascetic.

Verse 84

तत्र वस्तु–दवयं वक्ष्ये दुर्लभं यस्य कस्यचित् ।

क्षीरं चैकं दवितीयं तु नारी च वश–वर्तिनी ।। ८४ ।।

tatra vastu–dvayaṁ vakṣye durlabhaṁ yasya kasyacit I
kṣīraṁ caikaṁ dvitīyaṁ tu nārī ca vaśa–vartinī II 84 II

tatra – in this respect, vastu – thing, dvayaṁ – two, vakṣye – I will mention, durlabhaṁ – difficult to acquire, yasya – of which, kasyacit – whoever, kṣīraṁ – milk, caikaṁ = ca (and) + ekam (one), dvitīyaṁ – second, tu – indeed, nārī – woman, ca – and, vaśa–vartinī = vaśa (cooperative) + vartinī (practicing yogini)

In this respect, I will mention two things which are difficult to acquire. Milk is the first, and indeed, a cooperative practicing yogini woman is the second.

Analysis

Milk is relatively easy to obtain in contrast to a cooperative practicing yogini. For the practice of vajroli some nutritious foods are required, either milk or its equivalent. Isolated yogis in the time of Swatmarama could not easily obtain milk because they lived away from human farm communities. A yogi did not keep domestic animals. To get milk he relied on donations from farmers who were willing to supply his daily upkeep.

The real difficulty however is for a yogi to find a cooperative practicing yogini who matched his psyche and who by good luck was at a stage of advancement where this practice of sexual intercourse would be beneficial to yoga practice.

To handle this issue efficiently, some yogis find help on the astral planes where they are many dakinis and other angelic females who are suitable for assisting a yogi in this practice. Of course only very advanced yogis can use such methods because it requires well-developed and very keen psychic perception.

If a yogi can meet celestial women who can participate beneficially in this practice, then he would need neither milk nor a yogini with a material body. Therefore the difficulty would not be there for him, and he would avoid criticism of people who do not have the insight to understand these practices but who would ridicule and harass a yogi so as to bring him in line with their moral views.

Everything hinges on fate however. A yogi cannot all of a sudden produce a yogini on the physical plane. Such a person would have to have already taken birth, raised by parents and have done some yoga practice. Thus fate plays a great part in whether a yogi will have a physical companion or be without one. In all respects however it hinges on subtle existence because in the end of the physical body, only the subtle one will be available to the yogi.

Application

It is preferred that a yogi should do self-tantric. This means that he uses his body to do all practices which usually require a woman companion. However, a yogi should observe the movements of fate and work accordingly because there are responsibilities which are hurled in the path of a yogi which he should deal with.

In some cases, a yogi meets a willing yogini whom he must liberate or whom he must train for attaining the liberated state. He may have responsibility for that person from past lives, or from subtle existence. He should recognize the situation and with the help of the deities and the yoga-gurus, he should manage it accordingly.

Self tantric is a secret which only the siddhas can teach a student. Most siddhas are in the astral world. Only a few have material bodies. Those with material bodies are difficult to discover because of their antisocial methods which cause people to turn away from them and to think that they are not qualified to teach anything.

If one is lucky enough to meet a proficient self trantic in a physical body, then by his instruction one can learn how to use one's body and complete the sexual experiences which are necessary for liberation.

Self tantric begins with the insight of knowing that the material body which one uses, and the subtle form as well, began as a female form and then it had some adjustments which expressed its male potential. Hence since the root-energy of the body is female, is from the Goddess Durga, the woman of primal nature, one can discover everything there is to know about females by reverting to the initial format of these forms.

A yogi who does self tantric is not recognized by the public because his practice is mystic. Non-yogis and mystically-blind people cannot see his subtle activities. Thus even if people suspect that he is involved in supernatural activity, since they have no gross evidence he warrants no disapproval.

Verse 85

मेहनेन शनैः सम्यगूर्ध्वाकुनछनमभ्यसेत् ।

पुरुषो।अप्यथवा नारी वज्रोली–सिद्धिमाप्नुयात् ।। ८५ ।।

mehanena śanaiḥ samyagūrdhvākuñchanamabhyaset |
puruṣo|apyathavā nārī vajrolī–siddhimāpnuyāt || 85 ||

mehanena – while in sexual intercourse, śanaiḥ – gradually, samyag – thoroughly, ūrdhvākuñchanam = ūrdhva (upward) + ākuñchanam (contraction), abhyaset – should practice, puruṣo = puruṣaḥ = male human, apy = api = regardless, athavā – or, nārī – woman, vajroli – upward muscular redirection of male sexual emission, siddhim – yogic perfectional skill, āpnuyāt – would get

While in sexual intercourse, if one gradually but thoroughly practices contracting upward, regardless of whether one is a male or female, one would get the yogic perfectional skill which results from upward muscular redirection of male sexual emission.

Analysis

Swatmarama declared that even females can master the upward muscular redirection of sexual emission. In fact a yogini who is involved with a yogi who practices vajroli retraction of semen, more than likely will be required to master the practice in her body. It varies from person to person. There is no set rule that says that every ascetic must do this. Some may bypass this practice and become liberated while others must complete it. To find out one should consult with a yoga-siddha guru.

According to how one is spiritually-related to the deity and to the yoga-guru, that is how it will be determined if one has to complete this or that process before qualifying for liberation. Most of it is a matter of the responsibilities which one will be tagged with as one advances.

Sometimes in the astral regions hereafter, a student who approaches a siddha guru, is asked about the condition of a certain female yogi. Then the student is told that he cannot advance a step further unless he elevates or trains that person. This is bad news because it would mean that the yogi has to take another material body or several other material forms, to be placed providentially on the path of that other person so as to get that person trained in yoga. This is why a yogi should break off from social morality and adhere instead to the yoga-gurus so that he can learn of the requirements for his actual elevation hereafter instead of working to suit the needs of materially-conditioned entities who are phony moralists whose primary concern is to secure for themselves an approved moral rating life after life on the earth plane and who would do anything to force a yogi to comply with non-spiritual traditions which pass on the earth as genuine religious principles.

Application

Any yoga practice which involves sexual intercourse or the promise of it, even if it is mere flirtation without completed sexual acts, is dangerous for yogi. This is why the state of celibacy under the Sanskrit term of brahmacharya, was always praised in the Vedic culture. Monks who are lifelong bachelors are honored because of their non-familiarity with carnal activity.

But this does not mean that every ascetic can become liberated without having sexual indulgence. In specific cases it might be necessary. As great a celibate monk as Sri Adi-Shankaracharya was circumstantially compelled to have sexual experience to complete the mission for which he took a human body. He did not use his physical form to acquire the skill but he took the body of another person and practiced sexual indulgence to get the required insight.

People think that a yogi who is sexually involved is no better than anyone else and should be dishonored. This is because most human beings when involved in sexual pleasure lose their objectivity and become incapable of insight during the experience. Thus people feel that a yogi is no better.

Nevertheless a student should do whatever is required as suggested by fate and as advised by the competent yoga-guru. It does not matter what critics say because they, like everyone else, will have to leave their bodies shortly. No amount of morality can save a person's physical body. Morality does not remove life's uncertainties. Therefore despite its usefulness in helping to maintain human society, morality is not the cure for our existential woes.

Verse 86

यत्नतः शस्त–नालेन फूत्कारं वज्र–कन्दरे ।

शनैः शनैः प्रकुर्वीत वायु–सञ्चार–कारणात् ।। ८६ ।।

yatnataḥ śasta–nālena phūtkāraṁ vajra–kandare |
śanaiḥ śanaiḥ prakurvīta vāyu–sañcāra–kāraṇāt || 86 ||

yatnataḥ – carefully, śasta–nālena = by a tube, phūtkāraṁ = hissing sound, vajra–kandare = in the uro–genital channel, śanaiḥ śanaiḥ = gradually, prakurvīta – should do, vāyu – air, sañcāra – flow, kāraṇāt – from the cause

Carefully using a pipe, because of the flow of the air there will be a hissing sound in the uro–genital channel.

Analysis

This is an ancient procedure for inserting a hollow grass straw or some other tubing into the penis. Once this was inserted the yogi would operate the abdomen lift to create a suction system into the bladder. This would begin with the muscles of the bladder contracting and relaxing so that the movement of air would be heard as a hissing sound in and out of the tubing.

Over time the yogi would draw up a liquid like water and then a more viscous liquid like honey. Then he would be ready to draw up semen which was released into a woman's passage. The target however is the subtle body. If the yogi achieved this muscular control and did not retract the interest in sexual expression, then the practice could not be recognized as being part of yoga.

Application

There is a dip point just prior to sexual climax. The yogi is supposed to go to that place and then turn back, or turn his face, his expectations, away from that, so that he deprives himself of the climax. For this he requires the cooperation of a dakini. Other women cannot assist in this because their psyches are not equipped with the sexual understanding for this practice.

Each woman is endowed with particular aspects which another woman may lack. This is also true for males. It is not cause for alarm or for invoking insecurity. This creation is varied with some aspects missing here and some missing there.

Apart from inserting the tubing as described by Swatmarama, the other aspect, the subtle one, must be mastered, otherwise this practice would be a mere physical achievement with no siddha status attained.

A yogi should not pursue a female companion to practice this. One should only do this if this is required for one in the course of liberation.

Here is the gist of this:

Have regular sexual intercourse without using a yoga technique but carefully observe the way that material nature engineered the experience. Notice specifically how the energies are crescendoed until there is a climax. Then notice how after the climax the energy is flattened like when the pressure in an artesian well is lowered. At that time the water pours out of the ground without gushing upwards. This must be repeatedly observed for some time, before the student gains the required objectivity.

A yogi must be sure that the female he is engaged with, is destined to be with him in this sexual practice, because otherwise he would incur a bad reaction for engaging another woman in this way. Some women should not be linked in this way, which means that a yogi should not engage this practice with any and every woman, even with a legitimate partner, even with a wife. The woman must be destined to do this practice with the yogi because otherwise it may have a harmful effect in the woman's life which will cause bad reactions to come to the yogi.

Taking out a marriage license from the government or going through a religious ceremony with a woman where she becomes one's wife, does not give one the right to link her body in this way. A yogi must be aware of this and heed this advice or he will incur unfavorable reactions for involving a woman, when she is not supposed to be in it. A yogi should also not accept a woman for this practice, merely because the woman requested to be a tantric partner. Permission from a woman to do this will not protect the yogi from a bad reaction, if the said woman does not have a liability-free destiny for this. One should be sensitive to the deities and to the yoga-gurus to know which woman is the correct reaction-free partner.

If a yogi does not have a physical partner and feels the need to do this, then he should understand that in the astral world, there is such a partner. Hence there is no need to be frustrated about this because such a person can be found easily in the astral domains. This is a subtle body attainment for the most part. Doing it in a physical body is not essential.

I remember some years ago, a woman approached me with a twinkle in her eye. She requested that I be her tantric partner. She inquired about the tantric process and someone told her to ask me about it. She felt that I might be an expert. She was eager to enjoy tantric sexual practices. Seeing the twinkle in her eye, I graciously declined. A yogi should not feel obligated to have sexual intercourse with a woman merely because she is eager to experience sexual pleasure while assuming tantric sexual poses and using Ayur Vedic ointments and oils. One should not waste time merely doing this or that upon request of others. One should stick to the system of learning and practice given by the trustworthy yoga-guru. If sexual indulgence is part of that, then so be it. Otherwise one should carefully side-step anything including sexual expression.

The yogi should observe the dip point, the very last dip point before the climax of sexual experience. He must note this over and over, until he can recognize this without fail. This may take repeated intercourses and climaxes to understand. It depends on the sensitivity of the yogi. An ascetic who is very sensitive might only require one sexual experience to mark this dip, while another ascetic who is not so intuitive might have to spend his entire life just to get the perception of the dip point. After knowing for sure where the very last dip point before the firing of climax is, the yogi should have intercourse and reach that dip point over time, while noticing all other dip points which lead up to the very last one. He should then cease all movements during the intercourse just before that last dip point and apply the sex lock. For this the cooperation of a female is required because if the female moves her body then the whole practice is ruined because the final dip point will be lost and there will be a climax in the body of the male yogi.

At soon as the last dip point is reached, the yogi should cease all movement, remain penetrated in the woman's passage but with no movement from either partner. The yogi should then apply the sex lock and internally stop the energy from being transported.

This has to be mastered before a yogi can do the sexual expression and retraction procedure of vajroli.

Verse 87

नारी–भगे पतद्बिन्दुमभ्यासेनोर्ध्वमाहरेत्।

चलितं च निजं बिन्दुमूर्ध्वमाकृष्य रक्षयेत् ।। ८७ ।।

nārī–bhage patad–bindumabhyāsenordhvamāharet ।
calitaṁ ca nijaṁ bindumūrdhvamākṛṣya rakṣayet ।। 87 ।।

nārī – woman, bhage – in vagina, patad – falling, bindum – reproduction hormone concentrate, abhyāsenordhvam = abhyāsena (by practice) + ūrdhvam (upward), āharet – should be drawn, calitaṁ – falling, ca – and, nijaṁ – one's own, bindum – reproduction hormone concentrate, ūrdhvam – upward, ākṛṣya – by pulling, rakṣayet – should be preserved

The reproduction hormone concentrate which is falling into the woman's vagina should be drawn upward. By pulling upward one's reproduction hormone concentrate it would be preserved.

Analysis

When Swami Vishnudevananda asked me to do a translation and commentary on Swatmarama's book there was already an edition published for him. In the astral world in the presence of Swami Shivananda, Vishnudevananda handed me his book and then turned away. Some of the verses, for instance this verse, were not translated by him and that was in order because in his last body he was a lifelong bachelor, a traditional Swami. Such a person having no carnal knowledge in the present body is not qualified to comment on sexual union between males and females.

Sri Adi Shankaracharya explained conjugal love and sexual affairs in the debate with Mandana Mishra but he did so after experiencing sexual intercourse while using the body of another person. His physical form, true to the Swami vows was never involved in carnal affairs. It may be challenged however that his subtle body certainly was and hence he technically violated the vows.

However the reason why Vishnudevananda asked me to comment on this, is the fact that I have no Swami vow to uphold. I do have carnal knowledge in my current body and can give practical commentary.

Application

The practice mentioned in this verse is when the yogi is in sexual contact with a yogini woman and can observe in minute details every aspect of the energy and note the rate of flow of the emotions and pleasure force. There is no release or giving up of the energy in this practice. Even if there is a sexual climax, there is no release within that. A membrane of control remains around the energy which is released. The yogi then retracts this energy because it was never totally released in the first place.

This may be understood by conceiving of a plastic sack of water which is lowered into a stream. Even though the water is in the stream, yet the water is not released to mix with the stream's content. Thus when the sack is lifted out of the stream, the water in it, remains intact.

On the other hand, if the sack is lowered into the stream and if it hits a sharp object, the object will puncture the sack and the water in it will be released never to be retrieved again.

Because there is no release, the pleasure potency of a mix of energies of the male and female is not experienced. However the yogi can see the pleasure of the female as he looks through his contained sexual energy which is not released. He can see the fluctuations in that energy in response to the woman's feelings.

Think of a fish swimming in a plastic sack of water which is lowered into a stream. If the plastic sack is transparent and if the water in it is also transparent, the fish would see objects in the stream. Similarly a yogi can see through his sexual energy by

pranavision. He can know and experience directly in that way without the release and mix of his energy with the female. This is a celibate practice even though it involves sexual penetration by the yogi. It is celibate because for the yogi there is no release of sexual expression into the psyche of the female partner.

We can get some insight into this by studying the operation of a generator, where a magnet is rotated and influences electrons in a wire to produce a current. The magnet does not enter the wire and still it influences electrons and produces a current. The male energy can be contained and still cause effective emotions in the female system. This can be perceived by the male through pranavision which is developed by doing pranayama breath-infusion practice.

Verse 88

एवं संरक्षयेद्बिन्दुं मृत्युंजयति योगवित् ।
मरणं बिन्दु–पातेन जीवनं बिन्दु–धारणात् ।। ८८ ।।

evaṁ saṁrakṣayedbinduṁ mṛtyu jayati yogavit I
maraṇaṁ bindu–pātena jīvanaṁ bindu–dhāraṇāt II 88 II

evaṁ – thus, saṁrakṣayed = saṁrakṣayet = fully contain, binduṁ – reproduction hormone concentrate, mṛtyu – death, jayati – supersedes, yogavit – master of yoga techniques, maraṇaṁ – death, bindu – concentrate, pātena – by ejaculating, jīvanaṁ – life, bindu – reproduction hormone concentrate, dhāraṇāt – focal containment

Thus by fully containing the reproduction hormone concentrate, the master of yoga techniques supersedes death, which comes by ejaculating the concentrate. But by focal containment of the concentrate, one promotes life.

Analysis

Death of the physical system must happen no matter how celibate or semen-retentive an ascetic or anyone else may be. It is the effects of retention on the subtle body that has value ultimately. Hence those persons who are physically celibate and who do not transfer this accomplishment into some spiritual realization and perception in the subtle body are gaining only the social status for their current material body, and the habit of sexual resistance to be carried over into the next material form which the subtle body creates for itself.

The containment of subtle reproduction hormone concentrate has value for an ascetic who would soon attain the siddha status, because he would not have to reinvest in the struggle for existence of material bodies by taking another embryo which would require a deposit for ancestors due to owing favors to the dearly departed who helped to generate for him a new body.

Application

It is the going-outside-of-the-psyche for pleasure, by mixing of energies, which causes the ascetic to take material bodies haphazardly. This extrovert behavior is curbed by retention of sexual fluids if that retention is done under the guidance of great yogis and the deity. Those who retain semen and who do not have such guidance, become great moralists in the material world. This greatness causes them to become charismatic which in turn causes them to become sexually in demand because of having a status which is attractive to others. This in turn forces them to become sexually excited for divesting the parental social interest which they developed.

Such people become great politicians or social liberators. Eventually they amass much reproductive energy and are forced into wanton sexual behavior with many others. Thus what began as sexual fluid retention converts in widespread promiscuous behavior.

A short-sighted person, a person with no insight into the ways of material nature, cannot figure his or her future. The very same thing he or she works for in one life might be denied him or her in the next existence. Thus it is important to take guidance from a siddha and from the deity. It is best to assume that one knows nothing, that one has limited perception, and to seek out a great siddha or deity and get valid information.

Verse 89

सुगन्धो योगिनो देहे जायते बिन्दु–धारणात् ।

यावद्बिन्दुः सथिरो देहे तावत्काल–भयं कुतः ।। ८९ ।।

sugandho yogino dehe jāyate bindu–dhāraṇāt ।
yāvadbinduḥ sthiro dehe tāvatkāla–bhayaṁ kutaḥ ।। 89 ।।

sugandho = sugandhaḥ = pleasing fragrance, yogino = yoginaḥ = of the yogi, dehe – in the body, jāyate – supersede, bindu – reproduction hormone concentrate, dhāraṇāt – from focal containment, yāvad – so long, binduḥ – reproduction hormone concentrate, sthiro = sthiraḥ = maintained consistently, dehe – in the body,tāvat – until, kāla – death, bhayaṁ – fear, kutaḥ – where

Due to the focal containment of the reproduction hormone concentrate, the body of the yogi emits a pleasing fragrance. So long as the concentrate is maintained consistently in the body, there is no fear of death.

Analysis

Concentration of the reproduction hormone concentrate because of not having sexual expression where the energy is not redistributed though the subtle body and ignited by being mixed with infused breath energy, results in a misconception which is harmful to a yogi. One becomes a moral idiot if one is unable to mix the conserved sexual energy with infused air and distribute it evenly through the subtle body.

Those who do not conserve the energy and who are using sexual pleasure as a mainstay of enjoyment, have no conservation problems. But their usage of the sexual hormone concentrate causes a lack of vitality and a poor energy supply to the intellect. That also contravenes yoga.

Application

Every sexual intercourse a human being engages in carries that person one step closer to death. However avoiding sexual intercourse, not engaging in it, does not protect one from death either. This is why it may be better to engage and have a result of social responsibility for infants. From the infants one may get a new embryo after one's old material body is finished.

Verse 90

चित्तायत्तं नृणां शुक्रं शुक्रायत्तं च जीवितम् ।
तस्माच्छुक्रं मनश्चैव रक्षणीयं प्रयत्नतः ।। ९० ।।

cittāyattaṁ nṝṇāṁ śukraṁ śukrāyattaṁ ca jīvitam I
tasmācchukraṁ manaścaiva rakṣaṇīyaṁ prayatnataḥ II 90 II

cittāyattaṁ = citta (mento–emotional energy) + āyattaṁ (dependency), nṝṇāṁ – of men, śukraṁ – semen, śukrāyattaṁ = śukra (semen) + āyattaṁ (dependency), ca – and, jīvitam – life, tasmāc = tasmāt = therefore, chukraṁ = śukraṁ = semen, manaś = manas = mind, caiva – and also, rakṣaṇīyaṁ – conserve, prayatnataḥ – with great effort

A male's semen directly relies on his mento–emotional energy, while his life depends on his semen. Therefore conserve semen and the mind and do so with great effort.

Analysis

The material body is designed in such a way that its health and upkeep is reliant on its use of the semen it generates. Just as the body produces enzymes from the food it eats and uses the said enzymes to aid in digestion of the next meal, so the semen which is generated is used for the body's upkeep.

As bees eat some of the nectar which they acquire and store some for future use, so the body uses some of the hormones which it generates and stores some for generation of progeny. Along with this is a pleasure potency which is there for sensual satisfaction. In sexual performance, each sense becomes involved seeking its pleasure. It is a complex array of expression and reception, but it is ruinous if one does not manage it properly.

Since sexual pleasure is so powerful, so attractive, the likelihood is that it will not be managed. That will lead to ruination. All the same, avoidance of sexual expression and reception has its downside as well because sexual energy has a covert aspect which is more dangerous than a sleeping cobra. Dormancy of sexual desire is not celibacy but people with little insight regard it as so.

Application

There is a connection between bodily consciousness and semen. Bodily awareness is in part powered by hormone energy. Bodily consciousness is a composite energy, a mix of various fuels. A shortage or reduction in supply means an adjustment for better or worse in the perceptive aspect of consciousness.

A person who is starved may hallucinate whereby the perception shifts to a subtle plane which does not tally with the physical reality before the person. Similarly, disembodied entities on the astral planes may begin seeing physical reality and may mistake that for astral terrain.

Too much hormonal energy causes excitement and enthusiasm while too little causes depression and lethargy. But we find that someone may conserve sexual fluids and still be depressed, while another person may consume the sexual energy and be elated nevertheless.

In the astral world, Swami Shivananda once showed me how the sexual hormone energy supports the sober consciousness of a human body. It is similar to a wick system in a kerosene lamp. If the kerosene is too low in the reservoir, it will not feed up naturally through the wick. Thus there will be a dry wick which cannot sustain a flame. As soon as the kerosene is at the proper height in the reservoir it feeds up through the wick continuously and the lamp shines without interruption.

In the human body, there is a flow of sexual hormonal energy which is used to sponsor bodily awareness. If this energy is not used whimsically, the awareness of the body will be sober and even. That is provided the person does nothing which is counterproductive.

It does not matter if one does sexual expression for good or bad purposes. In either case it will have a negative effect, just as when a person removes kerosene from the reservoir of a lamp, the flame eventually sputters out, irrespective of whether he used the fuel in useful or useless way. Those who use sex whimsically will suffer for it and so will those who use it constructively such as to please their lawfully married spouses or to generate children. Material nature is based on mathematics not morality.

Verse 91

ऋतुमत्या रजो।अप्येवं निजं बिन्दुं च रक्षयेत् ।
मेढ्रेणाकर्षयेदूर्ध्वं सम्यगभ्यास–योग–वित् ।। ९१ ।।

ṛtumatyā rajo apyevaṁ nijaṁ binduṁ ca rakṣayet ।
meḍhreṇākarṣayedūrdhvaṁ samyagabhyāsa–yoga–vit ।। 91 ।।

ṛtumatyā – menstruation, rajo = rajaḥ = female reproductive fluid, apy = api = also, evaṁ – thus, nijaṁ – his own, binduṁ – reproduction hormone concentrate, ca – and, rakṣayet – should conserve, meḍhreṇākarṣayed = meḍhreṇa (through the penis) + ākarṣayed (ākarṣayet) (should extract), ūrdhvaṁ – upward, samyag = samyak = efficiently, abhyāsa – technique, yoga–vit = master of yoga

He should conserve his own reproduction hormone concentrate and even the female reproductive fluid of one who is menstruating. The master of this yoga technique should efficiently extract upward (the reproductive fluids) through the penis.

Analysis

The technicality is that the subtle body should be brought out of expression, even if the material body remains in it. The material body is a misleading form. Its security will be trashed sooner rather than later, while the subtle body may last for the duration of the universe. Transmigration is done by the subtle body, with material forms being developed on the basis in part of the condition of the subtle form. Hence an intelligent person, who can shift interest from the physical plane, will invest in the welfare of the subtle body.

In the years of teaching yoga and writing explanations in numerous books, I found that most students just do not understand the value of the subtle form. A student may follow my explanations but when it comes to living as if the physical body has little meaning, he cannot adhere to that. Invariably the students are disinclined to shift from the physical. They cling to a physical aspect and defend it no matter what, while grasping at what they can from the yogic texts to justify their materialistic demeanor.

The reason for this is that it is all too natural to be a physical being. The physical is convincing, while the subtle is abstract and vague. Students go half way into yoga, then criticize the process, then badger the teacher, then explain the failure to succeed and then retreat to the materialistic view point all the while pretending that they are in defense of spirituality.

Containment of hormone energy is the key with limit to the amount of nutrients taken into the body. If there is no need for a material body, then why is there need to contribute to reproduction of material life forms? Material nature will continue its reproductive thrust irrespective of a yogi's participation. Even the yogi's body is part of material nature and must to an extent comply with nature's objectives.

Application

Sexual intercourse makes sense only in terms of mixing of sexual energies of the parties involved. Masturbation is different because it does not involve the mixing from one psyche with another. In the human species, nature has its sexual objective as reproduction. The evidence for this is the fertility capability of human forms in terms of sperm and ovum. Sperm is the motivating kundalini. Ovum is the body producing agency. Both are required for an embryo to be created.

If we forget about sexual pleasure for a moment, we can see that from nature's view, sexual indulgence is all about reproduction. If the yogi has no intentions of taking a new body, and if he can enforce that by changing the configuration of the subtle body, then as far as nature is concerned, he does not have to participate in reproduction. Hence what is the need for mixing of his sperm with a female's ovum?

Can a yogi extract himself from the reproduction equation in the material world?

This is the question.

Verse 92

अथ सहजोलिः

सहजोलिश्चामरोलिर्वज्रोल्या भेद् एकतः ।

जले सुभस्म निक्षिप्य दग्ध–गोमय–सम्भवम् ।। ९२ ।।

atha sahajoliḥ
sahajoliścāmarolirvajrolyā bheda ekataḥ |

jale subhasma nikṣipya daghdha–gomaya–sambhavam || 92 ||

atha – now it is explained, sahajoliḥ – upward muscular redirection of female sexual emission, sahajoliś = sahajoliḥ = upward muscular redirection of female sexual emission, cāmarolir = ca (and) + amarolir (amaroliḥ) (self–urine consumption), vajrolyā – by upward muscular redirection of male sexual emission, bheda – distinct, two, ekataḥ – one, equivalent, jale – in water, subhasma – selected ashes, nikṣipya – put, daghdha – burnt, gomaya – cowdung, sambhavam – produced from

Now the sahajoli upward muscular redirection of female sexual emission is explained:

That sahajoli female extraction and amaroli self–urine consumption are distinct processes which are the equivalent of the vajroli upward muscular redirection of male sexual emission. Selected ash, which is produced from burnt cow dung, should be put in water.

Analysis

Sahajoli female sexually-expressed fluids and amaroli self-urine consumption are distinct processes for attaining the same vajroli upward muscular redirection of sexual emission, except that when females retract sexual fluids it is called sahajoli and when anyone drinks his or her urine, it is called amaroli.

Let us recall that this concerns the elimination of sex desire as we know it in physical bodies which as far as nature is concerned is required for reproduction, while for our sake, it is for sexual pleasure and for autonomy over any infants produced.

Drinking of your urine is not recommended by this commentator. I do not think that anyone should do this, unless advised by a yogi who did this, got the results intended and who takes the responsibility for the student. One should not recommend this to others, if one has not done this and got the desired results.

Modern students are not using the foods and do not have the cultural environment which Swatmarama lived in. We should take that into consideration. Our urine has many other pollutants which if taken back into the body via the stomach might do damage to the kidneys which will again attempt to filter the compounds out. If the chemicals in urine are put back into the body, that would be a major concentration of these liquids, which might harm the kidneys, liver, brain and other organs. Persons who have kidney malfunction where the chemicals which compose urine become concentrated in their bodies suffer from organ and tissue damage, especially from brain cell deterioration. This is well documented.

Within the context of the usage mentioned by Swatmarama, this has to do with control of sexual energies.

What type of control?

That of retraction of sexual fluids, even of fluids which passed through the penis tubing and entered the passage of a female, and even for a female to extract her sexual fluids which were expressed in her vaginal track.

If a teacher recommends this, we should inquire into if he attained this by drinking urine. Did he find that his sexual fluid no longer descended even when he was embraced by a much desired voluptuous woman, even with his instrument inserted erect in the woman's passage. If he cannot give us a honest answer to the positive, then there is no sense in doing this, unless we want to experiment on ourselves to see if we can derive the result.

Application

The ash process is part of Vedic ritual activities which cannot be grafted into other cultures. People who were born in the Vedic ritualistic environment may have a certain sentiment to ashes and to Lord Shiva which would give a high value to the ash which accumulates in sacred ceremonies. Others may use these procedures but without the psychic connection of the Vedic culture.

If one uses either the sahajoli female extraction or the amaroli self–urine consumption or the vajroli male extraction, one should desist if one does not get the result intended which is to self contain and de-express sexual energy.

Verse 93

वज्रोली–मैथुनादूर्ध्वं स्त्री–पुंसोः स्वाङ्ग–लेपनम् ।

आसीनयोः सुखेनैव मुक्त–व्यापारयोः क्षणात् ।। ९३ ।।

vajrolī–maithunādūrdhvaṁ strī–puṁsoḥ svāṅga–lepanam |
āsīnayoḥ sukhenaiva mukta–vyāpārayoḥ kṣaṇāt || 93 ||

vajroli – upward muscular redirection of sexual emission, maithunād = maithunāt = during sexual intercourse, ūrdhvaṁ – upright, strī – woman, puṁsoḥ – man, svāṅga – own organs, lepanam – smearing, āsīnayoḥ – sitting, sukhenaiva = sukhena (with happiness) + eva (even), mukti – released from, vyāpārayoḥ – embrace, kṣaṇāt – from the moment

After sexual intercourse in the upright position, during which there was the application of vajroli upward muscular redirection of sexual emission, the woman and man should smear their organs, sitting happily even from the moment they released their embrace.

Analysis

The upright position means in a posture which is similar to the padmasana lotus posture. Usually this is done with the female's legs wrapped around the male. There are other variations. The reason for this posture is that it allows the yogi and yogini to focus on the energy and to control the kundalini in the sushumna central passage. This book concerns the technique of kundalini manipulation for subtle body transformation. It does not concern sexual intercourse or exploitation of sexual pleasure in a human body. In so far as sexual energy is involved with kundalini manipulation for subtle body transformation, this book features that.

The smearing of the organs with ashes, in this case sacred ashes, which was used in a Vedic ritual ceremony before the intercourse, is done to complete the ceremony. In such a ceremony the partners ask permission of Lord Shiva and Goddess Durga to have the intercourse and to gain the required realization which would facilitate their progress towards spiritual enlightenment. Both partners recall the deities before, during and after the activity.

No human being has a right to have sexual intercourse autonomously. Every sexual act of every creature in the material world is a parody of the sexual interplay between Lord

Shiva and the Goddess. Sexual polarity is their monopoly. We borrowed gender identity from them. A yogi and yogini realizes this and consults with the deity before having these sexual acts.

The yogi does not become Shiva. The yogini does not become the Goddess. What happens is that the deities themselves in so far as their energy is partitioned into the body of the partners, take the opportunity to have these yogically-controlled sexual acts.

Application

Sexual intercourse as described in this verse is at the tail end of a very advanced kriya practice, a tantric process. It cannot be done by persons who have not mastered the kundalini psychic lifeforce.

Both partners must have upgraded their sexual apparatus by ridding the organs of lower deities. First one has to see the deities. Secondly one has to get a method from an advanced tantric guru of how to upgrade the organs so that lower deities voluntarily exit and higher deities take their seats in the organs.

Merely drinking urine or contracting the urinary and sexual muscles to extract or pull up sexual fluids is not sufficient for completing this practice.

A person, who is proficient in kundalini to the extent that the kundalini has jumped into the base of the brain and uses that location as its default residence, may, if he or she is persistent, develop the psychic perception to see the deity who possesses each chakra.

There may be sexual acts which must be performed for pleading with lower deities to leave the organs. This is like when someone who is a tenant has to be reimbursed for being evicted from a residence at an earlier date than was agreed in a contract.

Telling a lower deity to leave the sexual organs is a complete waste of time, because they do not respond to verbal commands and to desires for an upgrade. To speak to them one has to change the habits of the psyche so that these supernatural beings find it inconvenient to reside in the organs. They can always go elsewhere but why should they if they are comfortable where they are.

Verse 94

सहजोलिरियं परोक्ता श्रद्धेया योगिभिः सदा ।

अयं शुभकरो योगो भोग–युक्तो।अपि मुक्तिदः ।। ९४ ।।

sahajoliriyaṁ proktā śraddheyā yogibhiḥ sadā ।
ayaṁ śubhakaro yogo bhoga–yukto।api muktidaḥ ।। 94 ।।

sahajolir = sahajoliḥ = upward muscular redirection of female sexual emission, iyaṁ – this, proktā – titled, śraddheyā – reliable, yogibhiḥ – by yogis, sadā – always, ayaṁ – this, śubhakaro = śubhakaraḥ = auspicious, yogo = yogaḥ = yoga, bhoga – enjoyment, yukto = yukta = mixed, api – also, muktidaḥ – what gives liberation

This is titled as the sahajoli upward muscular redirection of female sexual emission.

It is always reliable for the yogis. This auspicious yoga even when mixed with enjoyment gives liberation.

Analysis

Bhoga is what is consumed. Usually whatever is consumed is supposed to be enjoyed. However in the case of an advanced yogi who mastered this process, there is no question of enjoyment. A person cannot make minute observations which result in spiritual progress through enjoying anything.

There is the question as well as to what part of the psyche enjoys. Can one part of the psyche enjoy while the rest of the psyche is observant and does not participate in the consumption? Ordinarily we find that this is not possible but it is for an advanced soul. That is why this practice is auspicious (shubhakara) and not degrading (ashubhakara) for the advanced yogi. But all the same it would be degrading for those students who are not equipped with the required skills for mastery.

Application

Enjoyment is not linear where there is a being who is one whole homogenous reality to enjoy anything. Enjoyment is carried out in each case disproportionately in reference to the psychic adjuncts which are involved. For instance in the case of color, the ear cannot enjoy it to the same degree as the eyes. In the case of sound, the eyes cannot enjoy that to the same degree as the ears. In the case of a colorful bird which makes a harmonious sound, the eyes and ears may both be enjoying to the same degree or in a lopsided manner with one sense enjoying more than the other.

In the case of emotions, the intellect may not get as much out of it as the kundalini psychic life-force. In the case of rational thought, the kundalini may not be fulfilled as much as the intellect. This means that enjoyment is not linear.

An advanced yogi can sort the various psychic adjuncts. He can observe their respective acquisitions. And yet, people do not understand how that could be.

Enjoyment or no enjoyment, if a yogi can sort the components of consciousness and measure their respective indulgence and remain detached even from their frenzied feeding on different fulfillments, then he is destined for liberation shortly.

Verse 95

अयं योगः पुण्यवतां धीराणां तत्त्व–दर्शिनाम् ।

निर्मत्सराणां वै सिध्येन्न तु मत्सर–शालिनाम् ।। ९५ ।।

ayaṁ yogaḥ puṇyavatāṁ dhīrāṇāṁ tattva–darśinām |
nirmatsarāṇāṁ vai sidhyenna tu matsara–śālinām || 95 ||

ayaṁ – this, yogaḥ – yoga, puṇyavatāṁ – pious entities, dhīrāṇāṁ – devoted entities, tattva–darśinām = reality–perceptive personalities, nirmatsarāṇāṁ = kind–hearted, vai – indeed, sidhyen = sidhyet = succeeds, na – not, tu – but, matsara – selfish, śālinām = those who are well–to–do

Indeed this yoga succeeds for those who are pious, devoted, reality-perceptive and kind-

hearted, but not for those well-to-do persons who are selfish.

Analysis

One has to be both pious and reality-perceptive. Piety alone is insufficient because its application will be short sighted if one does not have a reality-perceptive psyche. A person may be well-to-do and by all indications be pious, devoted and kind-hearted, but if he or she lacks insight into reality's networks, the actions will be lacking in the consideration of the past and future lives. Seeing only in the immediate time and place, and feeling that is relevant for all time, causes a person to make decisions which will prove to be self-destructive. This is because the main guiding principle would be the kundalini lifeforce in its survival mode.

The ascetic must work on the kundalini until it stops directing the psyche. It is not a bad deal for the kundalini to control the life of the material body. There are benefits in that but these do not serve the purpose of yoga which is to give power to the core-self and to have the kundalini be subordinate to the self's interest.

Since the self requires no survival support, the kundalini needs to be reoriented to a new mission which is completely different to its obsession with making physical forms for the subtle body. People who are not self realized but who become familiar with yogic parlance, sometimes take it upon themselves to advise a great yogin. Their opinions are worthless in terms of the objectives of yoga but they feel that they speak in the best interest of a genuine ascetic.

Application

The convenience of having the kundalini lifeforce operate the body is that the core-self has to do nothing but lay back and enjoy whatever happens. However it does that at its own expense because it has to provide psychological power to sponsor the lifeforce. This power is extracted from the core-self because it is a perpetual energy generator which can produce energy forever and ever.

With the kundalini in charge, the self can relax and simply enjoy, except that the kundalini miscalculates on occasion and then the self is taxed to compensate for the mistakes. The self interprets these compensations as afflictions or emotionally painful experiences.

If the core-self makes an attempt to take control of the psyche it is faced with a dilemma where it finds that it is not skilled in the operations and if it takes control, the kundalini may effectively oppose its instructions. The realization is that if the core-self relaxes, then it is liable for whatever mistake the kundalini makes but it benefits from whatever correct decision it commits. But then if the self wants to control everything, it has to exert itself and gain an understanding of how to operate the psyche in the struggle for existence.

This is why a fool cannot be liberated because he would have to manage the intelligent operations which the kundalini used to operate with its instinctive perspective. Learning how to manage a psyche is not an easy education for the core-self and this is why most entities are simply not interested in advanced yoga practice.

Verse 96

अथ अमरोली

पित्तोल्बणत्वात्प्रथमाम्बु–धारां

विहाय निःसारतयान्त्यधाराम् ।

निषेव्यते शीतल–मध्य–धारा

कापालिके खण्डमते। अमरोली ।। ९६ ।।

atha amarolī
pittolbaṇatvātpratham āmbu–dhārāṁ
vihāya niḥsāratayāntya dhārām |
niṣevyate śītala–madhya–dhārā
kāpālike khaṇḍamate|amarolī || 96 ||

atha – now it is explained, amaroli – self–urine consumption, pittol – bile, baṇatvāt – saturated with, pratham – first, āmbu – urine, dhārāṁ – flow of urine, vihāya – leave aside, niḥsāratayāntya = niḥsāratayā (rejected) + antya (last part), dhārām – flow of urine, niṣevyate – drink, śītala – cool, madhya = mid–portion, dhārā – flow of urine, kāpālike – in Kapalika Yoga Sect, khaṇḍamate– in the procedure of, amarolī – self–urine consumption

Now the amaroli self-urine consumption is explained:

Leave aside the first part of the flow which is saturated with bile, and the last part which is rejected. Drink the mid–portion which is cool. That is the procedure of the Kapalika Yoga Sect.

Analysis

The Kapalika Yoga Sect was and still is an extreme sect. Those yogis would do anything and everything to attain their objectives. They are not necessarily consistent with every aspect of the ashtanga system defined by Patanjali.

Application

Because the heavier part of the liquid settles to the bottom of the bladder the first flow of urine is denser than the rest. The advice is to leave that aside, use the middle portion and discard the last flow.

Since I do not use this procedure, I cannot vouch for it but we should have faith because Swatmarama listed it as valid for containing and retracting sexual energy.

Verse 97

अमरीं यः पिबेन्नित्यं नस्यं कुर्वन्दिने दिने ।

वज्रोलीमभ्यसेत्सम्यक्सामरोलीति कथ्यते ।। ९७ ।।

amarīṁ yaḥ pibennityaṁ nasyaṁ kurvandine dine |
vajrolīmabhyasetsamyaksāmarolīti kathyate || 97 ||

amarīṁ – mid portion of the flow of urine, yaḥ – who, piben = pibet = drink, nityaṁ – daily, nasyaṁ – snuff, kurvan – doing, dine dine = daily, vajrolīm – upward muscular redirection of male sexual emission, abhyaset – should practice, samyak – precisely, sāmarolīti = sa (that) + amaroli (self–urine consumption) + iti (thus), kathyate – is attributed

One who drinks the mid portion of the flow of urine daily, snuffs it daily, and practices the vajroli upward muscular redirection of male sexual emission, is attributed as being precise in the practice of amaroli self–urine consumption.

Analysis

Swatmarama repeatedly tagged the amaroli self–urine consumption to the vajroli upward muscular redirection of male sexual emission. The amaroli practice is not listed by itself but only as a companion practice of the sexual energy retraction action. Smelling of the urine is mentioned.

Application

The indication in this verse is that the smell and ingestion of one's urine, may assist in the effort to retract expressed sexual energy. When a yogi becomes determined to be without sexual access, then on occasion he might be circumstantially induced or forced to abandon his plan. At the time the yogi will either struggle against the flow of fate or voluntarily agree to live with it. Either way, he will continue existing and will have to consider how to get himself back on track.

He may use radical methods of curbing the sexual energy expression. One such method is to drink one's urine as described by the Kapalika yogis. This drinking and smelling of it, may cause the hormone production of the reproductive glands to change in orientation. If we study the animals, we find that male dogs will smell and lick the urine and vaginal secretion of female canines but we hardly ever see the reverse where the females lick and smell the male organs.

If a female dog is in heat, is in her fertile season, a male dog upon smelling her secretions, will attempt to mount to discharge semen. The Kapalikas discovered methods of reducing sexual expression by drinking and smelling their urine.

Verse 98

अभ्यासान्निःसृतां चान्द्रीं विभूत्या सह मिश्रयेत् ।

धारयेदुत्तमाङ्गेषु दिव्यदृष्टिः प्रजायते ।। ९८ ।।

abhyāsānniḥsṛtāṁ cāndrīṁ vibhūtyā saha miśrayet |
dhārayeduttamāngeṣu divya–dṛṣṭiḥ prajāyate || 98 ||

abhyāsān = abhyāsāt = practice, niḥsṛtāṁ – diffused, released. cāndrīṁ – subtle liquid, vibhūtyā – sanctified cowdung ashes, saha – with, miśrayet – mix, dhārayed

= dhārayet = smear, uttamāngeṣu = uttama (best) + āngeṣu (parts), divya – supernatural, dṝṣṭiḥ – perception, prajāyate – occurs

The subtle liquid diffused in this practice should be mixed with sanctified cow dung ashes. The smearing of it on the best parts of the body gives supernatural perception.

Analysis

Fluids discharged during sexual intercourse are warm liquids. The candrim liquid mentioned here is a cool moon-influenced bliss yielding liquid. It is not a physical substance. It is psychic. The sanctified cow dung ash is both physical and psychic. The yogi should mix the bliss-yielding liquid with the psychic ashes and smear that on the best parts of the body. This is a subtle body activity.

Application

This concerns the subtle body. It is not a physical practice in total. The physical part of it occurs because the subtle system is interspaced in the gross body. Ultimately it is the subtle body which will persist, while the physical one will perish. The yogi is concerned with the supernatural not the natural world.

Verse 99

पुंसो बिन्दुं समाकुञ्च्य सम्यगभ्यास–पाटवात् ।

यदि नारी रजो रक्षेद्वज्रोल्या सापि योगिनी ।। ९९ ।।

puṁso binduṁ samākuñcya samyagabhyāsa–pāṭavāt I
yadi nārī rajo rakṣedvajrolyā sāpi yoginī I I 99 I I

puṁso – man, binduṁ – male reproduction hormone concentrate, samākuñcya – full extraction, samyag – proper, abhyāsa – practice, pāṭavāt – proficiency, yadi – if, nārī – woman, rajo = rajaḥ = female reproduction hormone concentrate, rakṣed = rakṣet = should converse, vajrolyā – by upward muscular redirection of sexual emission, sāpi = sa (he) + api (also), yoginī – yogini

Fully extracting the male reproduction hormone concentrate, if a woman also conserves her reproductive concentrate by the upward muscular redirection of sexual emission, she is a yogini.

Analysis

To be clear, Swatmarama defines what he termed as a yogini, where the female ascetic has to master the retraction of reproductive concentrate by the vajroli upward muscular redirection of sexual emission for containment and dissolution of the bliss energy up through the trunk of the subtle body into the head.

Expression through the genitals must be totally reversed. Females have the special task of being motivated to do this, because over all the material creation is more partial to females. It seems to accommodate them more than it does males. Females have to find a self-convincing reason for abandoning the reproductive bliss force, or wanting to retract it.

Application

The vajroli upward muscular redirection of male sexual emission is for males but females may also use it as described and for the same purpose which is to contain, retract and reabsorb sexual hormones into the psyche. A question arises as to why express sexually in a sexual intercourse between opposite genders if one intends to retract the expression. The answer is that this is part of a reformative action to get the conventional method of reproduction expression by sexual means reduced and then totally curtailed, so that the ascetic can develop a subtle body which is compatible to the siddhaloka or satyaloka places.

Obviously some women are interested in this transit. Thus the method is open to them if they can complete the austerities.

Verse 100

तस्याः किञ्चिद्रजो नाशं न गच्छति न संशयः ।

तस्याः शरीरे नादश्च बिन्दुतामेव गच्छति ॥ १०० ॥

tasyāḥ kiñcidrajo nāśaṁ na gacchati na saṁśayaḥ |
tasyāḥ śarīre nādaśca bindutāmeva gacchati || 100 ||

tasyāḥ – her, kiñcid = kiñcit = some, rajo = rajaḥ = female reproduction hormone concentrate, nāśaṁ – lost, na – not, gacchati – secrete, na – none, saṁśayaḥ – doubt, tasyā– her, śarīre – in the body, nādaś = nādaḥ – naad subtle resonance, ca – and, bindu – subtle hormone concentrate, tām – her, eva – only, gacchati – fuses with

None of her female reproduction hormone concentrate is lost. Undoubtedly, none is secreted. In her body naad subtle resonance fuses with her subtle hormone concentrate.

Analysis

The conservation result intended is mentioned in this verse as being a full retention of the female reproduction hormone concentrate. The Sanskrit raja is unambiguous. From a psychological level this means no expression with intent for any type of reception or penetration. The value is to get the subtle body to adopt a similar configuration as the spiritual forms in the divine world. This is stated here indirectly by linking to naad subtle sound resonance.

Naad resonance is in the head of the subtle body, in the back part of it. That is its default location. It is also in the sushumna nadi spinal passage when that subtle passage is cleared of all dense astral energy. However if a male or female ascetic terminates the sexual expression and penetration tendencies in the psyche, then the reproduction hormone concentrate would float up as a matter of course, disregarding gravity and it will link itself to the naad sound resonance in the subtle head. This would cause the trunk of the subtle body to develop a vibration which is compatible to living in the siddhaloka places.

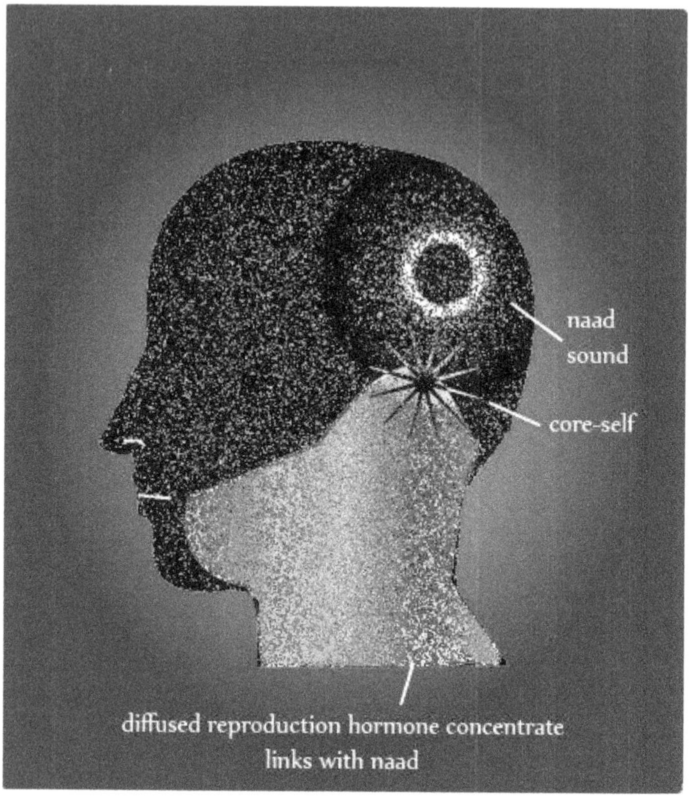

Application

Where does the ascetic want to live after leaving the current physical body?

That is the question!

Depending on where one wants to transit into, one should qualify oneself for such residence. The first thing is to know where you desire to relocate. The next thing is to study the tendencies of the people who are native to that other place or dimension. The final aspect is to change the energy in the subtle body so that it is compatible with persons in that other place.

Verse 101

स बिन्दुस्तद्रजश्चैव एकीभूय स्वदेहगौ ।

वज्रोल्य–अभ्यास–योगेन सर्व–सिद्धिं प्रयच्छतः।। १०१ ।।

sa bindustadrajaścaiva ekībhūya svadehagau I
vajroly–abhyāsa–yogena sarva–siddhiṁ prayacchataḥ II 101 II

sa – that, bindus = binduḥ = subtle male hormone concentrate, tad = tat = that, rajaś = rajaḥ = female reproduction hormone concentrate, caiva – and also, ekībhūya – in combination, svadehagau – own body, vajroly = vajroli = vajroli urinary and sexual muscle upward–contraction, abhyāsa – practice, yogena – with yoga, sarva – all, siddhiṁ – perfection, prayacchataḥ – gives

The subtle male hormone concentrate and the female reproductive concentrate combined in one's body by the vajroli urinary and sexual muscle upward-contraction yoga practice, gives perfection.

Analysis

This technique is for male yogis who have their austerities cut out for them because of having to liberate themselves as well as females with whom they have to engage with sexually.

This is not for every ascetic. It is not for experimentation. This is only for ascetics who are restricted because of having responsibility for females who cannot get out of this creation unless they work their way through sexual experience under superior guidance of a male who can service them sexually in a way which in the long run would result in their liberation from the physical existence and from the lower astral realms.

Because of an overproduction of female reproductive concentrate, the yogi must find a way to contain the excess and then over time compress it so that it becomes even more concentrated but is in less quantity. Then the yogi has to extract its bliss aspect and train the female in how to do this. This may require years of training and also a completion in training in the astral world hereafter.

One who is assigned such a destiny is in a way unfortunate because the likelihood of success with this is very slim. Most of the yogis, who are fated like this, do not become liberated. They get stuck in the material world for millions of years or they move to an astral domain and remain there for eons without moving up to the siddhaloka or satyaloka places. Such is the technicality of that practice.

Application

In his English translation, Swami Vishnudevananda tactfully did not translate these sexually explicit verses. That was good for him because he was using a body which was not familiar with carnal knowledge and he took a vow of celibacy as a Swami. He met me astrally and in the presence of Swami Shivananda asked that I should comment on this book. After translating these sexually descriptive verses, I understood why he did not translate them and why he later assigned the task to me.

All in all these practices are legendary. Only a few yogis were successful using them. I know a little about it, so I wrote this translation and commentary but not to advocate tantric sexual activities, only to give the information so that everyone can know the risks and dangers involved.

What is fated is fated. Those who are unfortunate and who have to liberate females on their way out of the material world need to get help from great yoga-gurus and from deities. Without that assistance they are doomed to failure because of the technicalities.

Material nature has no intention of liberating any of the entities who are in its proximity. It never had such intentions. It does not have such intentions now. It will not have any such intentions in the future. This means that the weight of getting freed from material existence is borne on the back of the entity who desires liberation.

Freeing oneself is a task that in most cases is greater than the individual can complete. What then can be said about freeing others? The whole scope of it is risky. At any point in the life of a yogi, if he makes a mistake he can sink down terrible in some lower life form and remain transmigrating in that species for millions of years. This place is so dangerous. If rescuing oneself is an almost impossible task, how can we rate having to rescue others?

Male and female psychologies are completely different, as if they were totally different species. Material nature is a favorite of most females. Hence the task of freeing any female is momentous. If Goddess Durga was inattentive to Lord Shiva when he explained kriya yoga, then how can any other person in this creation expect success liberating any female? Thus these instructions should be left where they are. One should try to free oneself and pray that fate spares one the task of helping others. If such prayers are not fulfilled, then one should consider oneself to be a doomed yogi.

Verse 102

रक्षेदाकुञ्चनादूर्ध्वं या रजः सा हि योगिनी ।

अतीतानागतं वेत्ति खेचरी च भवेद्ध्रुवम् ।। १०२ ।।

rakṣedākuñcanādūrdhvaṁ yā rajaḥ sā hi yoginī I
atītānāgataṁ vetti khecarī ca bhaveddhruvam II 102 II

rakṣed = rakṣet = conserve, ākuñcanād = ākuñcanāt = through extraction, ūrdhvaṁ – up, over, yā – who, rajaḥ – female reproduction hormone concentrate, sā – she, hi – indeed, yoginī – yogini, atītānāgataṁ = atīta (past) + anāgataṁ (future), vetti – know, khecarī – one who transits through kha divine space, ca – and, bhaved = bhavet = can, dhruvam – definitely

She who conserves her reproduction hormone concentrate through extraction is indeed, a yogini. She knows the past and future and definitely transits through kha divine space.

Analysis

The yogini Chitralekha was such a person but there were very few others. The reason is that there is a symbiosis between material nature and the female humans which makes it near impossible for a female to desire liberation ardently. In the history of yoga, there were few successful yoginis, One was Shabari, who was a disciple of Matanga Rishi. She lived in the time of Lord Rama. Her history is in the Valmiki Ramayana and is given in a totally misleading way in the Ramacharita Manas. Another such person was Vak, the daughter of Brahma who was tutored by Vashishtha Muni.

Supernatural controllers like Mother Ganges are within this category as well, even though from time to time, she releases her reproduction hormone concentrate. Such a personality being a goddess eternally can become involved on a lower level for a time and then miraculously leave aside that plane at will. However other females cannot do this.

The kha divine spice is the spiritual world, the divine atmosphere. Going there is a tall order for any yogi or yogini. One has to have good luck, be very proficient to attain that and there must be the grace-pull of a deity.

Application

A female can do self-tantric and contain her sexual expression or reception and the potential of it. In each case of every male or female it may not be necessary to assist or elevate anyone else. Only certain ascetics must work with others sexually to complete the austerities required for liberation. One should not assume that one must be sexually involved to be liberated. The history of yoga is that most ascetics are freed alone without companions.

Verse 103

देह–सिद्धिं च लभते वज्रोल्य–अभ्यास–योगतः ।

अयं पुण्य–करो योगो भोगे भुक्ते।अपि मुक्तिदः ।। १०३ ।।

deha–siddhiṁ ca labhate vajroly–abhyāsa–yogataḥ |
ayaṁ puṇya–karo yogo bhoge bhukte|api muktidaḥ || 103 ||

deha – body, siddhiṁ – perfection, ca – and, labhate – obtain, vajroly = vajroli = upward muscular redirection of male sexual emission, abhyāsa – practice, yogataḥ – specific process in yoga, ayaṁ – this, puṇya – pious, karo = karaḥ = results, yogo = yogaḥ = yoga, bhoge – in enjoyment, bhukte – pleasure, api – also, muktidaḥ – what gives liberation

One attains bodily perfection from the specific yogic process of vajroli upward muscular redirection of male sexual emission. This yoga process yields meritorious results and liberation even though pleasure is enjoyed.

Analysis

Even though there is pleasure expressed during this type of sexual intercourse with a female, it does not mean that the yogi enjoys in the way people normally do. It is offensive to feel that because a yogi has sexual intercourse, he enjoys it just as anyone else and hence conclude that he is fallen or that he was degraded thereby.

If one cannot retain one's confidence in a sexually-involved yogi, the best way to handle that is to go away from him, and take instruction elsewhere without forming any adverse opinion. That is the safe procedure because if the yogi is not fallen or is not degraded really, then one would have hurt one's progress by having those contrary opinions.

Students who cannot sort the various components of consciousness cannot understand how a yogi can be involved in a pleasurable activity and not be overtaken by it all the same.

How is that possible?

They think that no one can be involved in sexual pleasure and not be bogged down by it. However, if a yogi can sort the components of consciousness and can quarantine the interest of each psychic adjunct, isolating pleasures and restricting them to certain features, are easy feats for him.

Application

Some people feel that when a yogi becomes sexually involved with a female, the morality of the issue should be considered. They feel that a yogi should be a compliant agent in human society, following all social regulations. If he fails to do that they feel that he is a bad example, is fallen and is disruptive to righteous conduct.

It is for this reason that yogis are supposed to be in isolation and to be outside of society. But circumstances may force a yogi to be in society despite these considerations. Then a yogi will have to yield to what is fated for him.

It is best to leave the judgment to God and not try to make pronouncements on a yogi about his immoral activities, because unless one has insight consciousness which can penetrate past and future lives and also consider the applications in this life, one cannot possibly know what is right or wrong in the life of a yogi.

Verse 104

अथ शक्ति–चालनम्

कुटिलाङ्गी कुण्डलिनी भुजङ्गी शक्तिरीश्वरी ।

कुण्डल्यरुन्धती चैते शब्दाः पर्याय–वाचकाः ।। १०४ ।।

atha śakti–cālanam
kuṭilāṅgī kuṇḍalinī bhujaṅgī śaktirīśvarī ।
kuṇḍalyarundhatī caite śabdāḥ paryāya–vācakāḥ ।। 104 ।।

atha – now to be described, śakti – subtle creative energy, cālanam – mobility, kuṭilāṅgī = all–penetrating energy, kuṇḍalinī – kundalini lifeforce which stays in the fire pit, bhujaṅgī – bhujaṅgī female serpent, śaktir = śaktiḥ = intelligence personified, īśvarī – supreme lady, kuṇḍaly = kundali = coiled potency, arundhatī – conjugal loyalty personified, caite = ca (and) + ete (these), śabdāḥ – term, paryāya – synonym, vācakāḥ – words

Now the shakti mobile and subtle creative energy is described:

It is known as all–penetrating energy, kundalini lifeforce which stays in the fire pit, female serpent, emotional intelligence personified, supreme lady, coiled potency, conjugal loyalty personified. These are synonyms of the same potency.

Analysis

The shakti mobile and subtle creative energy is popular as the kundalini psychic lifeforce. It is described thus:

- all–penetrating energy
- kundalini lifeforce which stays in the fire pit
- female serpent
- emotional intelligence personified
- supreme lady

- coiled potency
- conjugal loyalty personified

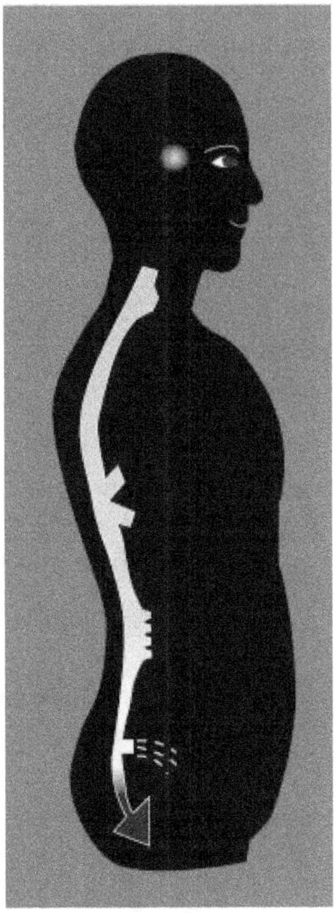

As the **all-penetrating energy**, the kundalini has energy distributed in every part of the physical and subtle bodies. It does this in varying degrees of penetration and quality. Every cell of the body has its own kundalini which is part of the collective energy of the psyche.

The **kundalini lifeforce, which stays in the fire pit**, refers to the psychic energizing system, which is a heat generating psychic mechanism, which funds the operation of intelligence in material elements. It carries its own fire pit or container which in the human body is the muladhara base chakra. It accepts breath energy and food nutrients as fuel for its fire. Both energy sources have subtle counterparts which the kundalini feeds on in addition to their physical substances.

Kundalini acts as bhujangi, a **female serpent**. It wiggles like a snake. When aroused by breath energy, it hisses like a serpent. It stands on its tail as some serpents attempt to do when full of anxiety. It attacks various parts of the body according to how it is infused with breath and food energy.

Kundalini is literally the **emotional intelligence personified**. It is devoid of rationality but it makes up for this by its developed instincts. It complements the buddhi intellect orb which is the psychic technology for rationality. Together they make decisions for the formulation, use and protection of the physical form.

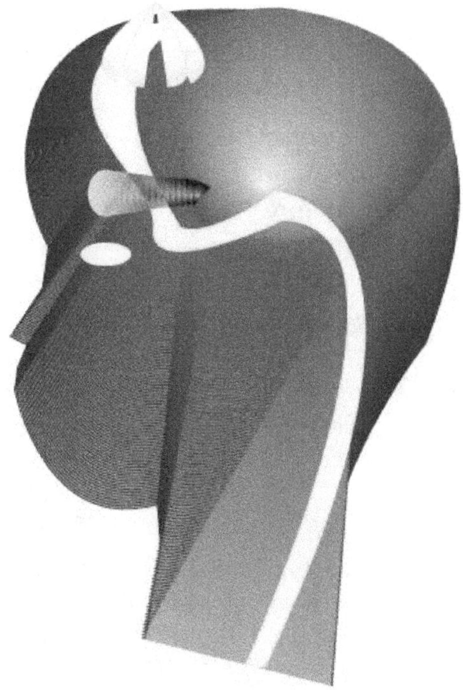

Kundalini is addressed as the **supreme lady** in the body. It is in fact the manager of the material body. It supervises the development of the embryo. Kundalini proudly regards itself as the fitting compliment to the core-self which is the only spiritual accessory among the adjuncts in the body. When kundalini ascends through the sushumna central passage and enters the brain it strikes the buddhi intellect orb, and stands its ground as the perfect complement to the core-self. The intellect orb is usually baffled when kundalini enters the brain and confronts it.

Kundalini is **coiled potency**. It has the complete compliment of motivation which a particular core-self would require in the material creation. In a jiffy it can adapt to any species of life. It is compressed power with a spring-like ability. It can move as rapidly as the speed of light.

Kundalini is rated as **conjugal loyalty personified**. It is compared to the chaste celestial lady Arundhati, whose fame is impeccable and who is the ultimate in feminine loyalty and modesty. Even though the individual kundalini likes to socialize, it remains with a particular core-self for billions of years for the duration of the cosmos.

Application

Breath-infusion practice which is the fourth of the eight disciplines of yoga is the one which causes the complete mastership of the kundalini lifeforce. The reason is that kundalini lives on breath energy for the most part. Air for breath may be extracted directly from the atmosphere or it may, as in the case of aquatics, be extracted from water but it must be supplied to the kundalini if mammalian life is to continue in a material body.

The core-self may be present. A sense of identity may be felt. The intellect may be there. If there is no breath energy which is suitable to the kundalini, it will permanently vacate the life form and move into a dimension which is suitable to it.

For that matter death of a physical body occurs when the kundalini can no longer access breath energy through that body. Then kundalini slips away into a dimension in which it can exist with access to psychic breath-energy. Mastery of kundalini is gained rapidly by mastery of pranayama breath-infusion.

Verse 105

उद्घाटयेत्कपाटं तु यथा कुञ्चिकया हठात् ।
कुण्डलिन्या तथा योगी मोक्षद्वारं विभेदयेत् ।। १०५ ।।

udghāṭayet kapāṭaṁ tu yathā kuñcikayā haṭhāt I
kuṇḍalinyā tathā yogī mokṣadvāraṁ vibhedayet II 105 II

udghāṭayet – open, kapāṭaṁ – door, tu – but, yathā – as, kuñcikayā – by a key, haṭhāt – from kundalini manipulation for psychic energy transformation, kuṇḍalinyā – by kundalini lifeforce, tathā – so, yogī – yogi, mokṣadvāraṁ = entry to liberation, vibhedayet – opens

As a door is opened by a key, so a yogi opens the door to liberation by kundalini manipulation for psychic energy transformation.

Analysis

Pranayama breath-infusion was stressed for ancient yogis. There are many stories in the Puranas about the breath-infusion austerities of ancient yogis, both those who are righteous and those who were criminally motivated. It is essential as the definite way to reach the chit akash sky of consciousness, the kha divine atmosphere.

Recently due to the hastiness of this era, people became disinclined from breath-infusion. There was also the influence of Western religions. These systems rely on song, scriptural reading and prayer as their main access to the higher dimensions. However pranayama is the sure route because it gives the core-self the power to manipulate the kundalini for psychic energy transformation. It places the power to change in the hands of the student. He does not have to sit and wait for divine grace. He can approach the Supreme by transiting through many dimensions to get nearer to the divine world.

Application

There are only two methods of getting into a divine environment. Both are controlled by presiding deities. The first and easiest method is to be transferred into the divine world by a mercy act of the deity. The second and effortful method is to make oneself eligible for a transfer grace-act of the deity. One can either wait for the easy method to manifest or make the effort.

Verse 106

येन मार्गेण गन्तव्यं बरह्म–सथानं निरामयम् ।

मुखेनाच्छाद्य तद्वारं प्रसुप्ता परमेश्वरी ।। १०६ ।।

yena mārgeṇa gantavyaṁ brahma–sthānaṁ nirāmayam I
mukhenācchādya tadvāraṁ prasuptā parameśvarī II 106 II

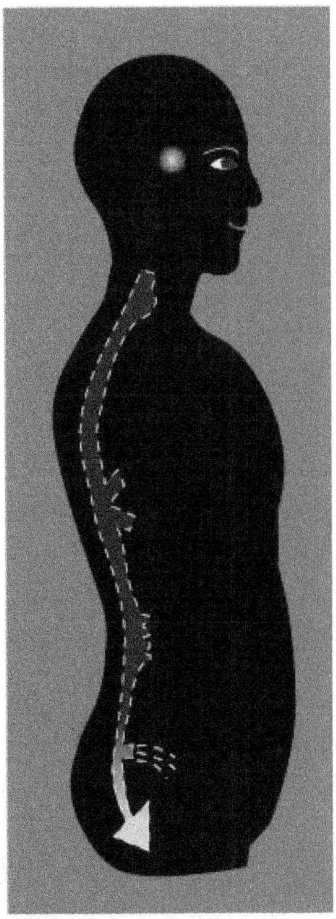

yena – by which, mārgeṇa – by transit, gantavyaṁ – going, brahma – exclusive spiritual existence, sthānaṁ – location, nirāmayam – free of trauma, mukhenācchādya = mukhenāt (by the entrance) + chādya (cover), tad = tat = that, vāraṁ – passage, prasuptā – sleep, parameśvarī – supreme goddess kundalini

The supreme goddess kundalini sleeps while covering the opening to the entrance, by which one can transit to the trauma-free location of exclusive spiritual existence.

Analysis

The conventional relationship between the kundalini and the core--self is that of the kundalini sleeping silently in the muladhara chakra with everything above it in darkness. Kundalini keeps a dim light at the base chakra and lights up other features of the psyche as it sees fit.

When it is ready to digest food, it gives heat energy to the stomach-intestinal complex. When it desires to excrete food waste, it gives energy for evacuation to the colon-rectum complex. When it is inclined to beget, it creates a large energy charge in the sex organs. When it feels the need to get conclusions, it gives psychic power to the intellect. When it desires to sleep or to deprive the core-self of the services of the material body, it induces stupor.

In the Bhagavad Gita there are two verses which give us a summary understanding of the essential functions which are operated independently by the kundalini:

naiva kiṁcitkaromīti
yukto manyeta tattvavit
paśyañśṛṇvanspṛśañjighrann
aśnangacchansvapañśvasan (5.8)
pralapanvisṛjangṛhṇann
unmiṣannimiṣannapi
indriyāṇīndriyārtheṣu
vartanta iti dhārayan (5.9)

naiva = na — not + eva — indeed; kiṁcit— anything; karomīti = karomi — initiate + iti — thus; yukto = yuktaḥ — proficient in yoga; manyeta — he thinks; tattvavit — knower of reality; paśyan — seeing + śṛṇvan — hearing; spṛśan — touching + jighran — smelling; aśnan — eating; gacchan — walking; svapan — sleeping + śvasan — breathing

pralapan — talking; visṛjan — evacuating; gṛhṇan — holding; unmiṣan — opening the eyelids; nimiṣan — closing the eyelids; api — also; indriyāṇīndriyārtheṣu = indriyāṇi — senses + indriyārtheṣu — in the attractive objects; vartanta — interlock; iti — thus; dhārayan — considers

"I do not initiate anything." Being proficient in yoga, this is what the knower of reality thinks. While seeing, hearing, touching, smelling, eating, walking, sleeping and breathing,

...while talking, evacuating, holding, opening and closing the eyelids, he considers, "The senses are interlocked with the attractive objects." (Bhagavad Gita 5.8-9)

This means that as directed by the kundalini, the senses get interlocked with the attractive objects. The core-self has little to do with it, except that it is forced to provide energy for these operations. Kundalini generates its own energy but it also pilfers energy from the core-self.

Eventually the core-self realizes that it does not initiate anything. However this realization does not immediately free it from having to contribute energy to the operations supervised by the kundalini. The self has to gradually gain control of the kundalini. This is done most efficiently through breath-infusion followed by meditation, a practice which modern humans are disinclined to practice. Modern people want to meditate but they feel it is not necessary to do breath-infusion prior. This is a serious oversight.

Application

Kundalini as it is naturally inclined is not interested in giving control to the core-self. It runs the show of acquiring, maintaining and exiting from material creature forms. It has no intentions of giving control of this nomadic life to the core-self. It hides the entrance to the sushumna central passage because if energy flows freely through that space, the core-self will be freed from mundane dominance. So long as the kundalini can keep pushing various aspects of mundane existence before the core-self, that self cannot use higher perception and cannot have experience of higher dimensions. This results in the core-self having to take cues from the kundalini which will continually show the way to take material bodies, maintain them, transit from them, and acquire new bodies in a circular motion.

As a servant of a great woman is afraid to offend her, so the core-self is scared of kundalini and would do anything to support its schemes. This situation should not continue in the yogis, however. They should rock the boat of this arrangement, create disarray for kundalini, upset it as much as they can, take its power away and run the show themselves.

The core-self should transit to the trauma-free location of exclusive spiritual existence. It should do whatever it would take to make that transfer even if it has to get help from the kundalini, which it must. But since the kundalini will not voluntarily help the self, because it is afraid that such a plan would eliminate it, the self should force the kundalini to render assistance.

Verse 107

कन्दोर्ध्वे कुण्डली शक्तिः सुप्ता मोक्षाय योगिनाम् ।

बन्धनाय च मूढानां यस्तां वेत्ति स योगवित् ।। १०७ ।।

kandordhve kuṇḍalī śaktiḥ suptā mokṣāya yoginām |
bandhanāya ca mūḍhānāṁ yastāṁ vetti sa yogavit || 107 ||

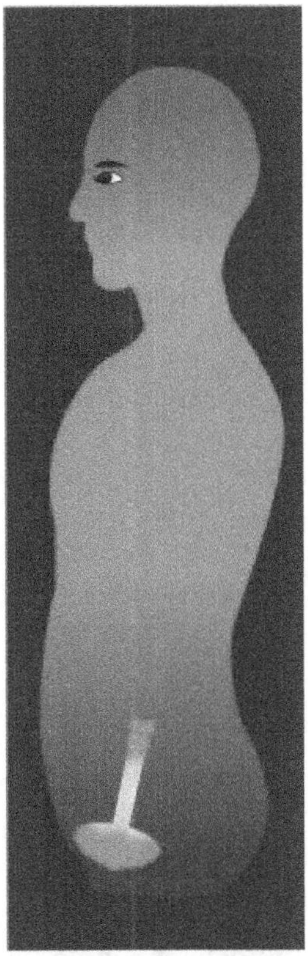

kandordhve = kanda (bulb) + ūrdhve (on), kuṇḍalī – kundalini lifeforce, śaktiḥ – energy potency, suptā – sleep, mokṣāya – liberating, yoginām – of yogis, bandhanāya = give restrictions, ca – and, mūḍhānāṁ – foolish people, yas = yaḥ = who, tāṁ – her, vetti – know, sa – he, yogavit – proficient yogi

The kundalini lifeforce energy potency sleeps on the bulb. It gives liberation to yogis and restriction to foolish ones. The proficient yogi knows kundalini.

Analysis

When the physical body rests, kundalini repairs it. With the core-self decommissioned from the body but with the self's energies still being utilized, and with the subtle form displaced out of the physical one, the kundalini completes routine maintenance.

After the repairs are done, kundalini instructs that nutrients be distributed to various cells. These nutrients are slowly transported to various parts of the body. A small quantity is used by each cell but most of it is held in storage just outside a cell or in a special pocket in a cell.

Kundalini tallies this to calculate the total energy reserve stored in the trunk of the body. This tally system as seen on the psychic plane takes the form of kanda bulb which is located in the central trunk of the body.

Application

In advanced yoga practice, a yogi, gradually over a long time, slowly but surely, strips the kundalini of its autonomy. This is not easy to accomplish because the yogi must take up many tasks which the kundalini did all by itself.

As a great king may never have put on his shirt, pants and shoes and may have no idea how to do that, so the core-self may be ignorant of how to maintain the inside of the subtle body. Servants of the king know the chores of dressing the monarch. If the king dismisses them and does not know how to do their services, he will be lost because of ignorance.

Many people come to learn kundalini yoga but when they are confronted with having to assume tasks which kundalini does, they become discouraged. It is possible to take control from kundalini and if it were not, there would be no hope of liberation for any living entity. However it requires patience and consistent practice.

Kundalini runs a bliss energy taxation system where it takes pleasure in return for the services it performs in maintaining the psyche. A yogi should change this system so that the excess energy of the cells is used in the head of the subtle body and not in the sexual facilities of it.

Verse 108

कुण्डली कुटिलाकारा सर्पवत्परिकीर्तिता ।

सा शक्तिश्चालिता येन स मुक्तो नात्र संशयः ।। १०८ ।।

kuṇḍalī kuṭilākārā sarpavatparikīrtitā ।
sā śaktiścālitā yena sa mukto nātra saṁśayaḥ ।। 108 ।।

kuṇḍalī – kundalini lifeforce, kuṭilākārā – , coiled shape, sarpavat – like a serpent, parikīrtitā – fittingly describe, sā – she, śaktiś = śaktiḥ = energy potency, cālitā – moved, yena – by which, sa – he, that, mukto = muktaḥ = liberation, nātra – not here, saṁśayaḥ – doubt

Kundalini lifeforce was fittingly described as a coiled shape which is like a serpent. He who moves that energy potency is no doubt liberated.

Analysis

In the reptilian forms, like those of alligators, the kundalini is extended much further down, so that muladhara chakra has a wider distribution through a tail. Four footed well-developed animals like tigers also have that extension in the form of tail. In the human species the tail is absent and muladhara chakra ends a short distance from the sex organ chakra but with nerves which extend downwards through the thigh, legs and feet.

Kundalini's whole length extends through the spine, through the neck, into the head with enough length to peek out through the brow or crown chakras but it cannot maintain itself in that stretched feature. Its natural shape is from muladhara chakra to halfway between the navel and heart-lung complex chakra. This is why it is said to have three and one half coils.

The first and most powerful coil is at the base chakra. The second and most excitement-driven coil is at the sex chakras. The third and most invigorating coil is at the third chakra. The remaining half coil is a conduit which communicates the heart-lung complex with the navel complex.

While for most human beings it is sufficient for kundalini to remain in three and one-half coils, for a yogi that is unsatisfactory. The yogi reconfigures the kundalini by forcing it to straighten out. It does not do so willing and even when it is motivated to straighten, it desires to go wherever it will. A yogi applies the locks which barricade it and causes it to go through the sushumna nadi central spinal passage into the brain. Once it enters the brain it hesitates for an instant and if the yogi does not have sufficient energy pushing it, it subsidizes again into the three and one half coils. If there is sufficient energy under it, it will try to go in any which direction once it enters the head of the subtle body, but the yogi defines where it will go by applying the mind lock.

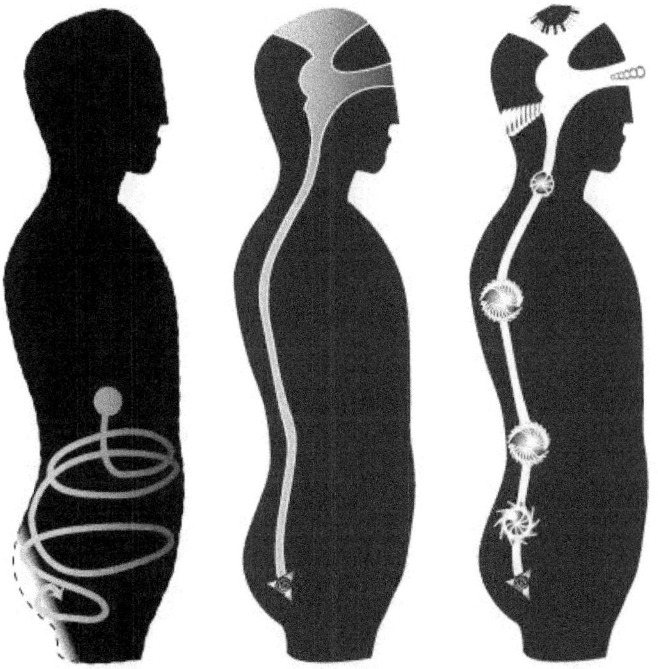

Application

Just moving the kundalini up through the spine does not qualify a yogi as a liberated entity but it does mean that he is no longer a regular in the mundane evolutionary cycle. Once a yogi habitually raises kundalini on a daily basis, he is on his way to becoming a siddha perfected being who has stepped away from the mundane evolutionally cycle.

Initially the subtle body is upgraded by taking help and suggestions from material nature. At first the subtle body is a spatial form which is spherical without limbs or even senses.

Those who have just come into the material creation from the brahman effluence spiritual existence become involved in the development of material bodies. They also have subtle bodies but those subtle forms are physical-body-dependent psychic mechanisms. Over time, over billions of years, over millions of eons, these entities get suggestion from material nature, as to the possibility of how to better differentiate themselves from other living entities who transmigrate through the life forms side by side with them.

Eventually after becoming many life forms of varied species, they find themselves in the species of a leading predator, a creature whose form has the tools and weapons necessary to dominate the environment.

After spending millions of years as the top predator, they get the idea that there might be another type of evolution somewhere somehow. This idea is brought into the material world by divine beings like Krishna and Shiva. Taking assistance from these deities and their agents, such souls get transferred into the siddha loka environment where they can upgrade their subtle bodies and move to a divine situation in the chit akash sky of consciousness.

Verse 109

गङ्गा–यमुनयोर्मध्ये बाल–रण्डां तपस्विनीम् ।

बलात्कारेण गृह्णीयात्तद्विष्णोः परमं पदम् ।। १०९ ।।

gaṅgā–yamunayormadhye bāla–raṇḍāṁ tapasvinīm I
balāt kāreṇa gṛhṇīyāttadviṣṇoḥ paramaṁ padam II 109 II

gaṅgā – Ganges–like subtle channel, yamunayor = yamunayoḥ = Yamuna–like subtle channel, madhye = in–between, bāla–raṇḍāṁ = young widow, tapasvinīm – ascetic widow, balāt – from strength, kāreṇa – by work, gṛhṇīyāt – arrested, tad = that, viṣṇoḥ – of God Vishnu, paramaṁ – supreme, padam – residence

The young widow ascetic who is between the Ganges-like and Yamuna-like subtle channels should be arrested with great force for access to the supreme residence of God Vishnu.

Analysis

Control of kundalini, willy-nilly, by any which means, is necessary for a living entity to get transferred from the material world to the divine environment where Vishnu's supreme residence is located. Vishnu or the Supreme Lord, Krishna, has residences both in the material and spiritual atmospheres. His homes in the material situation are places of relative significance when compared to the superlative divine locations. In the Bhagavad Gita the suggestion for migration to that place is given in these verses:

tataḥ padaṁ tatparimārgitavyaṁ
yasmingatā na nivartanti bhūyaḥ
tameva cādyaṁ puruṣaṁ prapadye
yataḥ pravṛttiḥ prasṛtā purāṇī(15.4)

tataḥ — then; padaṁ— please; tat— that; parimārgitavyaṁ — to be sought; yasmin — to which;

gatā — some; na — not; nivartanti — they return; bhūyaḥ — again; tam — that; eva — indeed; cādyaṁ = ca — and + ādyaṁ — primal; puruṣaṁ — person; prapadye — I take shelter; yataḥ — from whom; pravṛttiḥ — creation; prasṛtā — emerged; purāṇī — in primeval limes

Then that place is to be sought, to which having gone, the spirits do not return to this world again. One should think: I take shelter with that Primal Person, from Whom the creation emerged in primeval times. (Bhagavad Gita 15.4)

nirmānamohā jitasaṅgadoṣā
adhyātmanityā vinivṛttakāmāḥ
dvaṁdvairvimuktāḥ sukhaduḥkha-saṁjñair
gacchantyamūḍhāḥ padamavyayaṁ tat (15.5)

nirmāna — devoid of pride ; mohā — confusion; jita — conquered ; saṅga — attachment ; doṣā — faults; adhyātmanityā = adhyātma — Supreme Spirit + nityā — constantly; vinivṛtta — ceased; kāmāḥ — cravings; dvandvaiḥ — by dualities; vimuktāḥ — freed; sukhaduḥkha — pleasure-pain ; saṁjñaiḥ — known as; gacchanti — they go; amūḍhāḥ — the undeluded souls; padam — place; avyayam — imperishable; tat = tad — that

Those who are devoid of pride and confusion, who have conquered the faults of attachment, who constantly stay with the Supreme Spirit, whose cravings have ceased, who are freed from the dualities known as pleasure and pain, these undeluded souls go to that imperishable place. (Bhagavad Gita 15.5)

na tadbhāsayate sūryo
na śaśāṅko na pāvakaḥ
yadgatvā na nivartante
taddhāma paramaṁ mama (15.6)

na — not; tat — that; bhāsayate — illuminates; sūryo = sūryaḥ — the sun; na — nor; sasaḥko = śaśāṅkaḥ — moon; na — nor; pāvakaḥ — fire; yat — which; gatvā — having gone; na — never; nivartante — they return; tat — that; dhāmā — residence; paramaṁ — supreme; mama — my

The sun does not illuminate that place, nor the moon, nor the fire. Having gone to that location, they never return. That is My supreme residence. (Bhagavad Gita 15.6)

When all there is to see in this material world is seen, when all there is to sense is checked, when all advantage over others is exploited, then someone tries to locate someone and something else. This is concisely explained in this Bhagavad Gita verse:

bahūnāṁ janmanāmante
jñānavānmāṁ prapadyate
vāsudevaḥ sarvamiti
sa mahātmā sudurlabhaḥ (7.19)

bahūnām — of many; janmanām — of births; ante — at the end; jñānavān — the informed devotee; mām — Me; prapadyate — surrenders to; vāsudevaḥ — son of Vasudeva; sarvam — everything; iti — thus; sa = saḥ — he; mahātmā — great soul; sudurlabhaḥ — hard to locate

At the end of many births, the informed devotee surrenders to Me,

thinking that the son of Vasudeva is essential to everything. Such a great soul is hard to locate. (Bhagavad Gita 7.19)

Application

It is precise that Swatmarama described kundalini as a female in two instances, now as a young widow and before as a supreme goddess. She is a young widow because she lives alone at the muladhara base chakra doing domestic chores moment after moment. It is said that she never sleeps. She is ever concerned with protecting the material body. When that body is done, she becomes occupied with one thing which is to procure an embryo.

She is a widow because her husband the core-self is located in the head of the subtle form, far away from her. She finds that she cannot permanently move into the subtle head to live with her husband. Normally her way of becoming sexually unified with him is to forcibly bring him down to the sex organ chakra during sexual climax experience, otherwise she remains separated from her spouse and only communicates with him using his messenger which is the buddhi intellect orb which resides close to her spouse in the subtle head.

A yogi should arrest this young widow, kundalini. He should cause her to straighten her body through the sushumna central passage. He should infuse her with enough energy that she is forced to ascend to the brahmarandra crown chakra. This will provide for the core-self a passage to Vishnu's supreme residence.

Verse 110

इडा भगवती गङ्गा पिङ्गला यमुना नदी ।

इडा–पिङ्गलयोर्मध्ये बालरण्डा च कुण्डली ।। ११० ।।

iḍā bhagavatī gaṅgā pingalā yamunā nadī ।
iḍā–piṅgalayormadhye bālaraṇḍā ca kuṇḍalī ।। 110 ।।

iḍā – left spinal nadi subtle channel, bhagavatī – goddess, gaṅgā = Ganges–like channel, pingalā – right spinal nadi subtle channel, yamunā = Yamunā–like, nadī – nadi subtle veins and arteries, iḍā – left spinal nadi subtle channel, piṅgalayor = piṅgalayoḥ = of right spinal nadi subtle channel, madhye – between, bālaraṇḍā – young widow, ca – and, kuṇḍalī – kundalini lifeforce

The left spinal nadi subtle channel is analogous to Goddess Ganges and the right spinal nadi subtle channel to Goddess Yamunā. In between the left and right is the kundalini lifeforce which is like a young widow.

Analysis

With the conjugal excitement over, with nothing to look forward to but death, a young widow remains stable. Between the right and left spinal nadi subtle channels, there lies the kundalini in the sushumna nadi central passage. It balances itself between the two charges of energy. If one is greater than the other, it shifts accordingly. If they are both equal, it remains smack center.

If the energy below it has thrusting power and it is confined on either side, it gushes upwards becoming elevated. It ascends with delight and enters the brain with blissful rapture.

Application

Goddesses Ganges and Yamuna are emblems of fertility, supplying both female and male beings with reproductive power. Supported by these celestial ladies on either side, the supreme goddess Kundalini moves upwards and enters the brain where it is met by the psychic adjuncts which reside in the head of the subtle body.

Verse 111

पुच्छे प्रगृह्य भुजङ्गीं सुप्तामुद्बोधयेच्च ताम् ।

निद्रां विहाय सा शक्तिरूर्ध्वमुत्तिष्ठते हठात् ।। १११ ।।

pucche praghṝhya bhujaṅgīṁ suptāmudbodhayecca tām |
nidrāṁ vihāya sā śaktirūrdhvamuttiṣṭhate haṭhāt || 111 ||

pucche – tail, praghṝhya – grasping, bhujaṅgīṁ – she–serpent, suptām – slumber, udbodhayec = udbodhayet = should be aroused, ca – and, tām – her, nidrāṁ – sleep, vihāya– abandons, sā – her, śaktir = śaktiḥ = emotional intelligence personified, ūrdhvam – up, uttiṣṭhate – ascends, haṭhāt – due to kundalini manipulation for subtle body transformation

Grasping the tail of the sleeping she-serpent, the yogi should arouse her. Due to kundalini manipulation for subtle body transformation, the emotional intelligence personified abandons her sleep and ascends upward.

Analysis

The process of kundalini yoga begins with the understanding that kundalini should be aroused by infusing energy into the muladhara base chakra. This is so because otherwise, kundalini might be aroused from another center and then have to go in two directions. If it is aroused from the base chakra and if the locks are applied, then it will have only one direction for travel. It will ascend in the order in which the energy gyrating centers were arranged, one above the other, according to the evolutionary lay out in material nature.

An important reason for this is that the sexual energy is the base energy in the frontal part of the trunk of the body. The groin area and the genitals are located there. Since gravity causes the hormone energy to accumulate at the bottom of the trunk of the body, this pool of energy has to be dealt with efficiently. Thus in doing breath-infusion, that compressed fresh air is pushed down the front of the body where eventually it floods into the groin area where it mixes with the reproductive hormones. This mixture is potent and explosive.

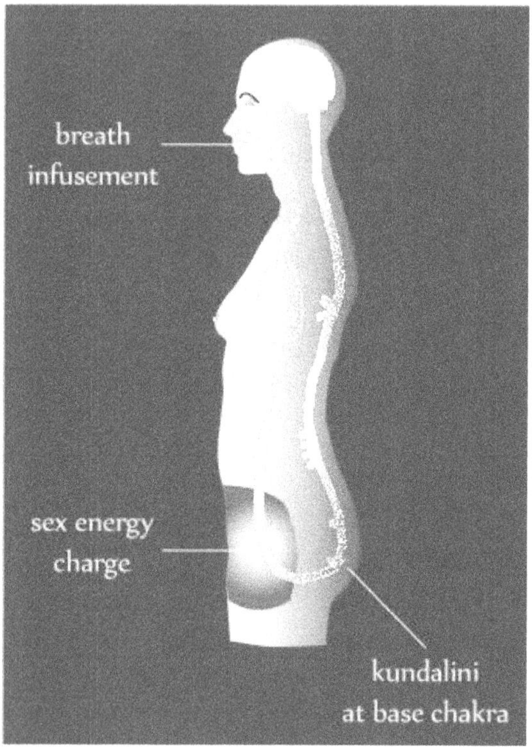

The yogi should compress this energy in on itself and then force it across a gap into the muladhara base chakra. This causes the kundalini to become alarmed. It tries to move. If the charge is sufficient it will move. The yogi should apply the locks so that when kundalini moves its only option is to go upwards through the sushumna nadi central spinal passage. If there is enough energy in the charge, kundalini will forge its way through the entire central passage. It will enter the brain as soon as it bores through the neck. It will clear the passage by pushing any dense astral energy out of the passage.

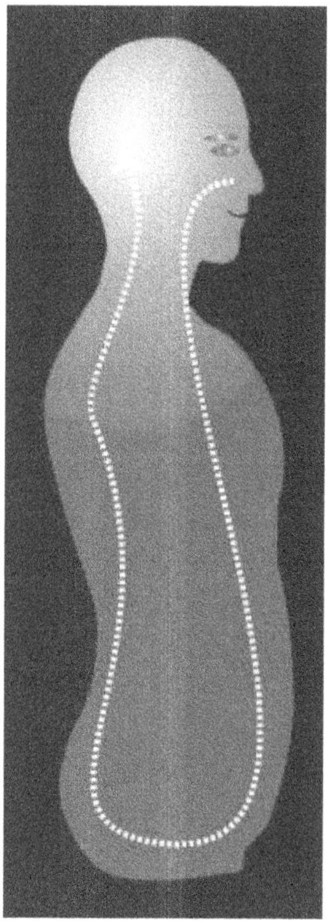

Application

A yogi should arouse the sleeping kundalini twice per day and cause it to course through the entire sushumna nadi central passage. This daily action will in time cause the passage to remain open continuously, which will result in psychic insight during meditation and during routine awareness.

If the passage is cleared of dense astral energy and if it remains cleared, then the kundalini, even if it is still lodged at the muladhara base chakra, will shine its light through the tunnel into the brain. This will secure insight awareness even when the yogi is not in a meditative state.

Eventually this practice will be such that the kundalini no longer considers the muladhara base chakra to be its default location. It will jump up to the base of the brain, right above the neck and hang there as stub kundalini. Any yogi who achieved this is considered to be a jivanmukta or a person who is liberated even while using a material body.

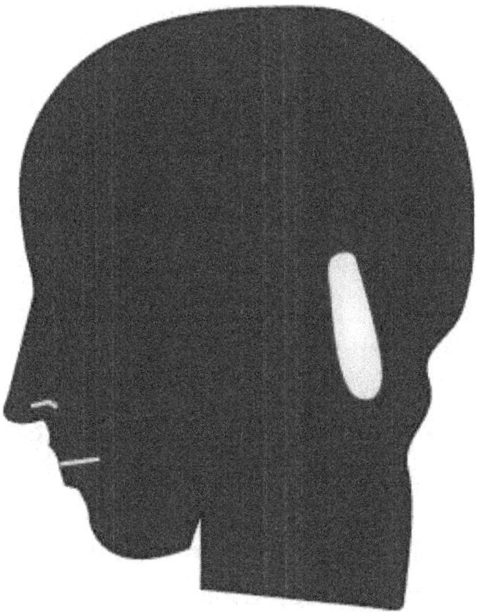

This is however not necessarily so. It can be that this happened and the ascetic is not fully liberated. But what is factual is that if this yogi passes from the body, he will meet the siddhas and will continue the practice in the world hereafter in an astral dimension where great yogis practice to complete their spiritual quest.

Verse 112

अवस्थिता चैव फणावती सा

प्रातश्च सयं प्रहरार्ध–मात्रम् ।

प्रपूर्य सूर्यात्परिधान–युक्त्या

प्रगृह्य नित्यं परिचालनीया।। ११२ ।।

avasthitā caiva phaṇāvatī sā
prātaśca sayaṁ praharārdha–mātram |
prapūrya sūryātparidhāna–yuktyā
praghṝhya nityaṁ paricālanīyā || 112 ||

avasthitā – situated, caiva = and so, phaṇāvatī – supernatural serpent, sā – she, prātaś = prātaḥ = morning, ca – and, sayaṁ – evening, praharārdha – half of three hours (90 minutes), mātram – period, prapūrya – filled, sūryāt – from the sun-dominant right side, paridhāna – compression, yuktyā – thoroughly, praghṝhya – arrested, nityaṁ – always, paricālanīyā – motivate to move

This supernatural she-serpent being self-situated, should be arrested and motivated to move in the morning and evening for a period of ninety minutes, by filling the sun-dominant right side, while thoroughly compressing the infused breath energy.

Analysis

The arrest of kundalini happens by first infusing it and then by immediately keeping it confined by certain locks. A yogi must repeatedly do the breath-infusion and meditate immediately after he filled the subtle body with the infused energy which is mixed with any hormone energy which accumulated in the psyche.

Swatmarama gave a period of ninety minutes for practice but that means proficient application. Students who do the practice sloppily will not get the intended results except occasionally. Still, they should not be despondent but should continue the practice regularly and develop confidence over time, as they feel the increase in efficiency and expertise.

The sun is more predominant on this planet than the moon. For that matter the moon takes energy from the sun and then reconditions it, just as female anatomy may accept male sperm in its uterus, then develop and birth it. The body will take both sun and moon-charged fresh air but the sun charged air is predominant.

Application

Kundalini has this self-centered attitude where it resists control by the core-self. Kundalini as emotional intelligence feels that it knows everything even though it has to rely on assistance from the senses, memory and intellect. Kundalini also feels that it energizes the body even though in fact it steals energy from the core-self to stimulate its natural forces. Over all the kundalini is arrogant. The core-self needs to realize this.

The social life of a yogi is the relationship between the core-self and its adjuncts. The self-centered attitude of the kundalini has to be broken because it results in unnecessary liabilities which the core-self has to account for.

Swatmarama indicated, rightfully, that a yogi should grab the kundalini by its tail and straighten it so that it ceases its coil power which is dedicated to survival in the struggle for existence. The core-self is an everlasting spiritual principle and should not be engaged in a struggle for existence just for struggling sake.

Verse 113

ऊर्ध्वं वितस्ति–मात्रं तु विस्तारं चतुरङ्गुलम्।

मृदुलं धवलं परोक्तं वेष्टिताम्बर–लक्षणम्।। ११३ ।।

ūrdhvaṁ vitasti–mātraṁ tu vistāraṁ caturaṅgulam |
mṛdulaṁ dhavalaṁ proktaṁ veṣṭitāmbara–lakṣaṇam || 113 ||

ūrdhvaṁ – up, vitasti – 12 fingers, mātraṁ – interval, tu – indeed, vistāraṁ – width, catur = catuḥ = four, aṅgulam – fingers, mṛdulaṁ – soft, dhavalaṁ – dazzling white, proktaṁ – appears, veṣṭitāmbara – folded cloth, lakṣaṇam – characteristic of, looks like

The bulb is twelve fingers above being four fingers wide. It is soft and dazzling white. It looks like a folded cloth.

Analysis

At the bottom of the trunk of the subtle body there is a kanda bulb which serves as a reservoir for much of the stored hormone energy. This energy is contained in that bulb and is not allowed to pass to the thighs, legs and feet. It is collected there for reproducing other bodies, a service which is necessary if the kundalini is to reproduce sexually and use the progeny in the future to provide for it a new life form.

Swatmarama gave a width of about two inches. This bulb may expand or contract according to the lifestyle of the person. It is about 6 inches high. It may shrink or become elongated. Its color is listed as being dazzling white but it may be white-yellow, gold, orange or light-blue. A yogi should use breath-infusion to vaporize the hormone energy in this bulb, pulling that vaporized force up through the trunk of the subtle body into the head.

Convention dictates that this bulb should have tubing running downward from it, through which it drains hormone energy into the genitals for sexual expression. A yogi has a task to change the design of the subtle body so that this bulb disappears and does not serve the evolutionary purpose intended which is to beget progeny for the selfish purpose of using such progeny to acquire an embryo.

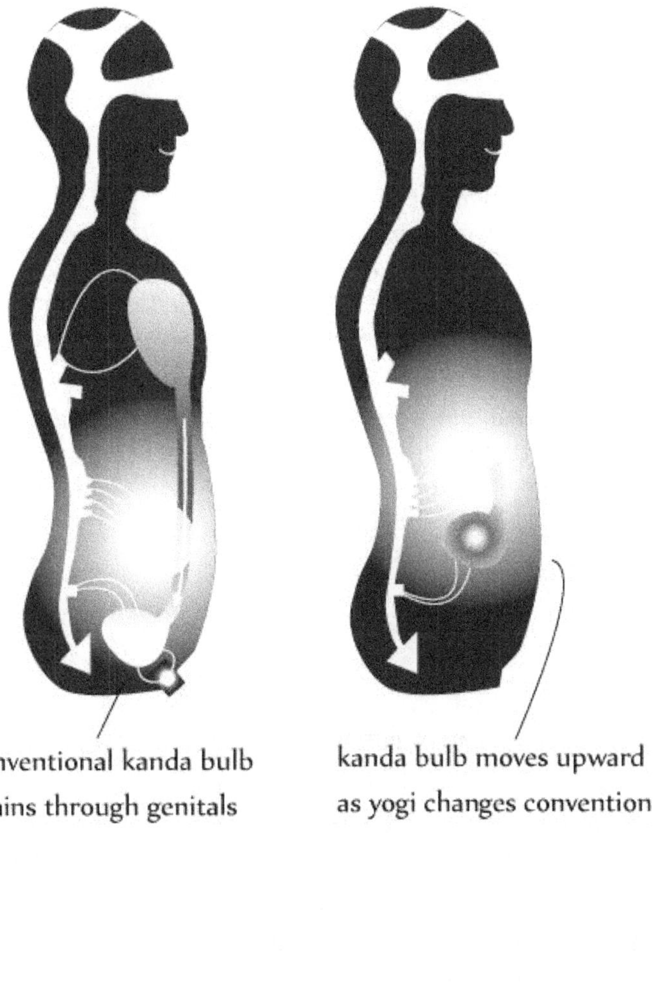
conventional kanda bulb
drains through genitals
kanda bulb moves upward
as yogi changes convention

kanda jumped up and out of sex zone

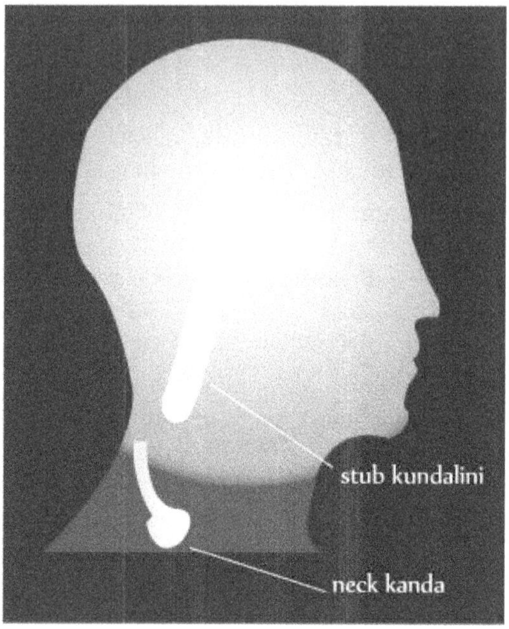

kanda is present in neck
with no sex kanda anywhere else
stub kundalini replaced spinal kundalini

Application

Ultimately the kanda bulb which is full of sexual essence will have to be dissolved out of existence. That is if the yogi wants to become a siddha. The kundalini created this bulb for the purpose of generating and storing sexual fluids which sponsor physical body reproduction. Once a yogi is done with the experiences afforded in a human body, and once he is not interested in any other mundane species, he may consider changing the subtle form so that it is not physically reliant.

It is not a matter of desire in not wanting any other physical body. It is not a matter of determination in saying to oneself that one's will power will be set not to take another embryo. It is the reality of the existence of the kanda bulb and the elimination of that psychic accessory in the subtle form. It is a psychic anatomical redesign.

Verse 114

सति वज्रासने पादौ कराभ्यां धारयेद्दृढम् ।

गुल्फ–देश–समीपे च कन्दं तत्र प्रपीडयेत् ।। ११४ ।।

sati vajrāsane pādau karābhyāṁ dhārayeddṝḍham ।
gulpha–deśa–samīpe ca kandaṁ tatra prapīḍayet ।। 114 ।।

sati – positioned, vajrāsane – vajra diamond posture, pādau – feet, karābhyāṁ – with hands, dhārayed = dhārayet = should hold, dṝḍham – firmly, gulpha – ankle, deśa – position, samīpe – near, ca – and, kandaṁ – bulb, tatra – there, prapīḍayet – should be compressed

With the feet positioned in vajra diamond posture, being held firmly by the hands, the bulb will be near the ankles where it should be compressed.

Analysis

The kanda bulb is not a physical gland. It is in the subtle body and does not have an exact physical counterpart. There can be contraction of the perineum and other parts of the physical system but these though related are not the kanda bulb.

The compression is done using pranayama breath-infusion energy to fuse into the kanda, penetrate its reserve of subtle hormones and press inwards on it spherically. This results in a fire and ice situation, where the energy folds in on itself continually until it implodes in the subtle body. It is then compressed in on itself further. Then it is fused through the muladhara base chakra, where it strikes kundalini, causing it to move through the spine into the subtle head.

Application

There are several variations of the vajra posture, each giving the yogi specific insight into the formation and compression of the kanda bulb which is in the subtle body. The subtle body is coded to reserve subtle sexual hormonal energy for sexual enjoyment and for reproducing physical forms. The subtle body does not biologically reproduce forms because there is no necessity for that in the astral dimension. However the subtle form has a tendency for reproducing physical bodies. This tendency surfaces as a psychic bulb which is called a kanda in Sanskrit.

A yogi must at first take the energy from this psychic bulb, invest it in the kundalini at the muladhara base chakra, and cause the kundalini to go through the spine into the head. In a more advanced stage, a yogi learns how to use breath-infusion to directly mist out the hormone energy in the kanda, so that there is no need to send it downwards at a slant to the muladhara base chakra. The energy of it can be transferred directly into the head of the subtle form without it going downwards at a slant to the base chakra. A yogi must eventually absorb the contents of the bulb and the bulb itself, so that no energy accumulates in the lower central trunk of the subtle form.

Verse 115

वज्रासने सथितो योगी चालयित्वा च कुण्डलीम् ।

कुर्यादनन्तरं भस्त्रां कुण्डलीमाशु बोधयेत् ।। ११५ ।।

vajrāsane sthito yogī cālayitvā ca kuṇḍalīm I
kuryādanantaraṁ bhastrāṁ kuṇḍalīmāśu bodhayet II 115 II

vajrāsane – vajra diamond posture, sthito = sthitaḥ = sitting, yogī – yogi, cālayitvā – motivate to move, ca – and, kuṇḍalīm – kundalini lifeforce, kuryād = kuryāt = should do, anantaraṁ – continuous, bhastrāṁ – rapid breath-infusion, kuṇḍalīm – kundalini lifeforce, āśu – quickly, bodhayet – should arouse

Sitting in vajra diamond posture and motivating the kundalini lifeforce to move, the yogi should continuously do bhastrika rapid breath-infusion to arouse the kundalini lifeforce quickly.

Analysis

Kapalabhati/bhastrika rapid breath-infusion is the superior and very prompt method of infusing the gross and subtle bodies. A yogi should not sit and wait for kundalini to arise by accident. He should do breath-infusion.

Some students are fearful of doing bhastrika. They feel it will give them a swinging head or make them faint or make them lose consciousness. To alleviate these fears, the student should find a qualified teacher. Have him or her demonstrate the practice and then decide if one desires to use it. The teacher should demonstrate. If the student is satisfied, the student should practice with the teacher on a daily basis if possible and for a period of at least six months.

Application

Kapalabhati/bhastrika rapid breathing requires effort for sure but the benefits make it worth the while. It gives the advantage of pratyahar sensual energy withdrawal as an automatic benefit, provided the yogi sits to meditate immediately after.

Fears about breath-infusion as being hyperventilation, which may cause giddiness, accelerated heart rhythm, and chest pains, need not be considered if one can learn from a proficient yogi. One should learn the anus, perineum, abdomen and chin-to-neck locks. These control the compressed air and the response of the kundalini when it is aroused.

Verse 116

भानोराकुञ्चनं कुर्यात्कुण्डलीं चालयेत्ततः।

मृत्यु-वक्र-गतस्यापि तस्य मृत्यु-भयं कुतः ।। ११६ ।।

bhānorākuñcanaṁ kuryātkuṇḍalīṁ cālayettataḥ।
mṛtyu–vaktra–gatasyāpi tasya mṛtyu–bhayaṁ kutaḥ ।। 116 ।।

bhānor = bhānoḥ = sunlike nutrition compact (orb), ākuñcanaṁ – contract, kuryāt – do, kuṇḍalīṁ – kundalini lifeforce, cālayet – motivate to move, tataḥ – thence, mṛtyu – death, vaktra – mouth, gatasy = gatasi = goes into, āpi – also, tasya – his, mṛtyu – death, bhayaṁ – fear, kutaḥ – wherefrom

Contract the sunlike nutrition compact (orb), to motivate kundalini to move. Even if he goes into the mouth of death, there is no fear of death for one who does this.

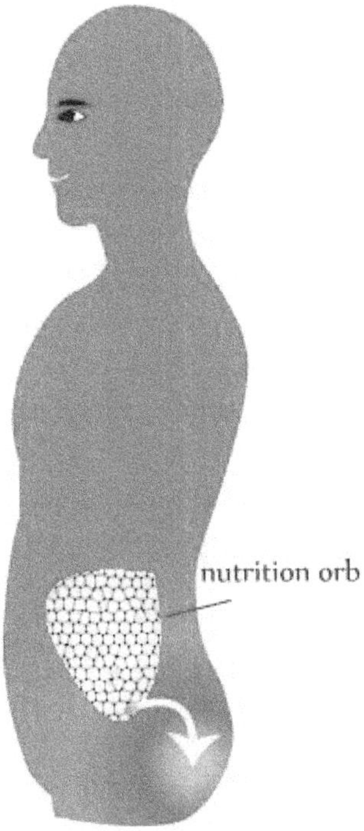

Analysis

The sunlike nutrition compact (orb) has for its mission immediate and long-ranged survival of material bodies. It sponsors survival of the body but it is concerned that when the threat to the body is finally served, it will have to continue in another body. Hence its intuition tells it to generate another body which may be used as a utility to develop its new physical form.

How does this work?

Once the kundalini lifeforce gets a sperm form in the body of the father, it motivates him to transfer it into the body of the mother, where it develops into an embryo. When it is well developed and can survive on its own with some support, this embryo is evicted from the mother or from her proxy.

Once the new form is secured, the lifeforce again feels a threat of death. It acts to ward off that insecurity but it senses that in time, the threat will be served in a way which is unalterable. It therefore makes a hormonal investment for the creation of other bodies in its form. These other bodies hold the promise for it to derive another body when the threat is finally served. It therefore begets other bodies with the motive of using those forms in the future to generate for itself another form when again, the threat of death is finally served.

Application

People who have a little understanding about yoga feel that the key issue is celibacy, the conservation of sexual fluids. A whole institution, the sannyasi order, was developed in India around this concept of sexual fluid conservation. From it came some very important words which are brahmacharya, sannyasi and swami. Each of these is a technical term. The brahmachari is the bachelor student. He has no wife and no access to sexual conduct. The sannyasi is the bachelor teacher who was either a bachelor student or a householder student but who took a vow to be a bachelor for the rest of the life of the physical body. The swami is the sannyasi who is a recognized teacher.

Because of one simple fact which is their bachelorhood, their lack of sexual facility, persons who have these titles are highly respected in the Vedic culture.

However after discussing some sexual concerns in the yoga process, Swatmarama graciously took us to the nutrition compact, the essential issue which transcends even sexual restraints. Sexual indulgence for all it is, for the bother that it was to many ancient yogis, for the distraction it is for many ascetics, cannot function if there is no nutritional support.

It was said by Napoleon Bonaparte that an army marches on its stomach. Indeed we can borrow this from him and apply it fittingly to yoga practice. For sexual expression, one has to take help from the abdomen.

Verse 117

मुहूर्त–द्वय–पर्यन्तं निर्भयं चालनादसौ।
ऊर्ध्वमाकृष्यते किञ्चित्सुषुम्नायां समुद्गता ।। ११७ ।।

muhūrta–dvaya–paryantaṁ nirbhayaṁ cālanādasau ।
ūrdhvamākṝṣyate kiñcitsuṣumnāyāṁ samudgatā ।। 117 ।।

muhūrta – forty-eight minutes, dvaya – two, (muhūrta–dvaya = two periods of forty-eight minutes each), paryantaṁ – extended time, period, nirbhayaṁ – without fear, cālanād = cālanāt = cause to move, asau – this, ūrdhvam – up, ākṝṣyate – exctract, kiñcit – some, suṣumnāyāṁ – sushumna central spinal passage, samudgatā – comes through

By causing this to move for ninety minutes, it is extracted somewhat and comes through the sushumna central spinal passage.

Analysis

If the yogi uses kapalabhati/bhastrika rapid breathing, kundalini can be aroused in the nick of time as soon as a charge of fresh air energy is pushed down past the navel region. However this arousal will be short-lived. For sustained arousal one has to do the practice for some time, for at least half the time mentioned by Swatmarama, for about forty-five minutes.

During that time kundalini will repeatedly rise through the spine and subside, then rises through the spine and then subside again and again, until the sushumna nadi central channel remains free of heavy astral energy. This means that when the yogi sits to meditate, regardless of whether kundalini remains in the head of the subtle body or not, its energy will freely and continuously radiate through the central channel.

If the yogi uses another breath-infusion method, another pranayama, it may require a longer period to get kundalini aroused. He will have to continue that practice to force kundalini to remain in the aroused configuration so that it can eliminate all heavy astral energy which is in the central channel.

Application

A yogi must have a daily fail-safe procedure which works to raise kundalini. Initially kundalini will not remain in the aroused condition. It will consume the infused energy but when that energy no longer has the force to motivate it, kundalini will descend the sushumna central spinal passage to sleep in its lair which is the muladhara base chakra.

A student must find a way to make kundalini stay awake when it returns to muladhara chakra. This requires certain lifestyle changes and stict adherence to the yoga-guru. The one indispensable part of this practice is to use pranayama breath-infusion to raise kundalini on a daily basis, preferable twice per day.

Verse 118

तेन कुण्डलिनी तस्याः सुषुम्नाया मुखं धरुवम् ।

जहाति तस्मात्प्राणो।अयं सुषुम्नां वरजति स्वतः ।। ११८ ।।

tena kuṇḍalinī tasyāḥ suṣumnāyā mukhaṁ dhruvam I
jahāti tasmātprāṇo I ayaṁ suṣumnāṁ vrajati svataḥ II 118 II

tena – by this, kuṇḍalinī – kundalini lifeforce, tasyāḥ – hers, suṣumnāyā – sushumna central spinal passage, mukhaṁ – opening, dhruvam – definite, jahāti – leaves, tasmāt – therefore, prāṇo = prāṇaḥ = subtle breath energy, ayaṁ – this, suṣumnāṁ – sushumna central spinal passage, vrajati – goes into, svataḥ – itself

By this, the kundalini lifeforce definitely leaves the mouth of the sushumna central spinal passage. Then subtle breath energy goes into the passage by itself.

Analysis

For student yogis, even raising kundalini once in a definite way, using pranayama breath-infusion, is an accomplishment. Then the method must be tried repeatedly to see if it can be relied on. An unreliable method will not do for this practice. The yogi must find a system he can use twice per day and raise kundalini without fail. If this happens then over time, the sushumna central passage will remain open, will be free of dense astral energy, allowing infused force to travel through it continuously and allowing the kundalini itself to remain awake in a sober state radiating its glory.

Application

The free flow of energy through the sushumna central passage is required in the advanced stages of kundalini yoga practice. Eventually, having lost interest in the struggle for existence, the kundalini will jump into the base of the brain and remain there as stub kundalini. It can resume its default home which is the muladhara base chakra. Therefore a yogi must continue the practice to make sure that kundalini does not again reinstate its survival interests. There is no need for the subtle body to survive through a physical form. It is not necessary. The yogi should relieve himself of physical existence permanently. He can then focus on the subtle world and be informed of the divine atmosphere which is beyond.

Verse 119

तस्मात्सञ्चालयेन्नित्यं सुख–सुप्तामरुन्धतीम् ।

तस्याः सञ्चालनेनैव योगी रोगैः प्रमुच्यते ।। ११९ ।।

tasmātsañcālayennityaṁ sukha–suptāmarundhatīm I
tasyāḥ sañcālanenaiva yogī roghaiḥ pramucyate || 119 ||

tasmāt – therefore, sañcālayen = sañcālayet = should be motivated, nityaṁ – constantly, sukha – comfortably, suptām – sleeping, arundhatīm – conjugal loyalty personified , tasyāḥ – her, sañcālanenaiva = sañcālanena (by the impetus) + eva (also), yogī – yogi, roghaiḥ – of diseases, pramucyate – eliminates

Therefore, this comfortably sleeping conjugal loyalty personified, the kundalini, should always be motivated. By such impetus, the yogi eliminates diseases.

Analysis

It is a full time self-service to always keep kundalini alert and aroused and coming up into the brain, rather than remaining drowsy and lusty in its lair, the muladhara chakra, from where it can easily reach for sexual pleasure in its perpetual quest for creating material bodies in the game of survival.

Besides the diseases which afflict the material body, which kundalini itself is responsible for and which kundalini strives day and night to eliminate, there is the one psychological disease which is chronic to the subtle form. That is the need for physical existence. If a yogi can irradiate that tendency, his problems with physical existence would terminate.

The devas, devatas, or supernatural controllers, have subtle bodies which do not have the need for physical forms. Even though they interact with us, direct and control us, still they are personally exempt from physical existence. Their subtle forms do not have the recurring need to be interspaced into physical bodies.

It does not matter what I desire, or what my philosophical view is, if my subtle body has the tendency for using physical forms, I will again take another material body, regardless of whether I desire to do so or not. The urgency is to eliminate this need in the subtle form.

Application

There are two ways of executing this existence. The first and most common method is the natural way which requires little or no impetus on the part of the core-self. That is the system where kundalini runs the show and provides entertainment for the core-self. It does this however at the core-self's expense with the self not realizing that to be the fact. Kundalini pilfers energy from the self and treats the self as a fuel supply but the self does not realize how it is used because it is entertained through mental and emotional displays.

The second and least common method is the unnatural process which requires much impetus on the part of the core-self. That is the technique of kundalini manipulation for subtle body transformation described herein by Swatmarama. The problem with this method is that the core-self will no longer be entertained. It will have to become a worker in its own interest. It will have to struggle to gain control of the psyche from the kundalini lifeforce, which is unwilling to give up autonomy over the physical and subtle bodies.

Instead of having kundalini pilfer energy from the core-self, in this unnatural system, the core-self will provide the kundalini with energy as the core-self deems to be necessary. It will control how the kundalini uses that energy. It will cease the indulgent attitude and abandon the convenience of having the kundalini provide entertainments for it in the form of mental and emotional gratifications.

Verse 120

येन सञ्चालिता शक्तिः स योगी सिद्धि भाजनम् ।

किमत्र बहुनोक्तेन कालं जयति लीलया ।। १२० ।।

yena sañcālitā śaktiḥ sa yogī siddhi–bhājanam |
kimatra bahunoktena kālaṁ jayati līlayā

yena – by which, sañcālitā – motivated, śaktiḥ – subtle creative energy, sa – he, yogī – yogi, siddhi – success, bhājanam – entitlement, kim –what? atra – here in this matter, bahunoktena = bahuna (more) + uktena (by saying), kālaṁ – time advancing as death, jayati – supersedes, līlayā – playfulness

That yogi, who motivates the subtle creative energy, kundalini, is entitled to success. In this matter, what more should be said? He playfully supersedes time which advances as death.

Analysis

The escape from time is committed by anyone who can slip out of the dimension in which that time reigns supreme. Remaining in a dimension and hoping to supersede its time rate is vain. If one cannot escape, the best situation to cope with time, is to work with it if you are situated in a position to do so.

Time has the scope of its dimension which means that one cannot supersede it unless one is identical to it. If at any time one is not identical to the whole scope of it, that means that one is not the deity of that cosmic medium, which means that one is a limited being under its scope.

Application

The yogi does not conquer or change time, nor does he stop the advance of time in the form of death. Time and time as death continues on its mission to terminate both the body of the yogi and the universes in which that body resides.

The yogi supersedes time and death by being granted access to a dimension in which

this time has no jurisdiction. However, leaving one dimension where one type of time rules does not mean that one will not enter into other realms where another type of time is in control.

Verse 121

ब्रह्मचर्य–रतस्यैव नित्यं हित–मिताशिनः ।
मण्डलाद्दृश्यते सिद्धिः कुण्डल्य–अभ्यास–योगिनः ।। १२१ ।।

brahmacarya–ratasyaiva nityaṁ hita–mitāśinaḥ I
maṇḍalāddṛśyate siddhiḥ kuṇḍaly–abhyāsa–yoginaḥ II 121 II

brahmacharya = sexual non–expressiveness, ratasyaiva = ratasya (of delight) + eva (specifically), nityaṁ – always, hita – ample, interest, mitāśinaḥ – one with a sparse diet, maṇḍalād = maṇḍalāt = from circle, period of forty days, dṛśyate – observing, siddhiḥ – success, kuṇḍaly = kuṇḍali = kundalini lifeforce, abhyāsa – disciplinary practice, yoginaḥ – of yogis

Specifically taking delight in sexual non–expressiveness, always having a sparse but ample diet, there is success after observing this practice of kundalini yoga for forty days.

Analysis

This was the situation in the time of Swatmarama. Today it is a bit different. A yogi may gain success now after weeks, months, years or even lives of practice. It depends on the condition of the subtle body and the amount of effort it would require to reconfigure it.

Sexual non-expressiveness usually causes a person to become depressed. We observed that when a person is deprived of sexual pleasure, he or she enters into a depressed state and becomes reluctant to do yoga or does it with a motivation to find a replacement for sexual excitement. Since yoga practice may not provide that, he or she leaves aside the practice in a sour mood and condemns the teacher.

Sexuality is a lubricant which makes it easy for people to take responsibility for their social burdens. Hence if they are deprived of sex pleasure, one has hell to pay to get them to serve in a congenial mood.

For success the yogi must be different where he or she takes delight in sexual non-expressiveness, where he or she becomes jovial when sexual indulgence is not available or is discouraged. A yogin should not begrudge ordinary people or ascetics who have access to sexual pleasure but should be happy for not being involved in the very taxing and demanding needs of sexual intercourse.

A sparse and simple diet is related to the reduction in sexual expressiveness. If one continues with a sumptuous diet while one has a reduction in sexual expressiveness, one will become perverted because the diet will produce sexual hormones which in turn will twist the form this way and that way to express the reproductive energy. Many sincere yogis and monks, who plan to be celibate bachelors, are found to be deviant to their vows because of having a sumptuous diet.

Application

By studying this verse and seeing the forty day period of such a rapid change in the attitude of the physical and subtle bodies, we can get some idea of what was possible for ascetics in the time of the Swatmarama.

Is this possible today?

If it is not possible, then what can we achieve now and in how much time?

Verse 122

कुण्डलीं चालयित्वा तु भस्त्रां कुर्याद्विशेषतः।

एवमभ्यस्यतो नित्यं यमिनो यमभीः कुतः॥१२२॥

kuṇḍalīṁ cālayitvā tu bhastrāṁ kuryādviśeṣataḥ।
evamabhyasyato nityaṁ yamino yamabhīḥ kutaḥ।।122।।

kuṇḍalīṁ – kundalini lifeforce, cālayitvā – causing to move, tu – indeed, bhastrāṁ – rapid breath-infusion, kuryād = kuryāt = should do, viśeṣataḥ – specifically, evam – thus, abhyasyato = abhyasyataḥ = practice, nityaṁ – always, yamino = yaminaḥ = disciplinary authority, yamabhīḥ = of Yama, the deity who supervises the criminally–liable departed souls, kutaḥ – why

In particular, the yogi should do rapid breath-infusion, thereby causing kundalini lifeforce to move. Constantly doing this practice, why would the yogi be worried about the disciplinary authority of Yama, the deity who supervises the criminally–liable departed souls?

Analysis

Yama has authority in certain dimensions. If a yogi can slip out of the realms which Yama supervises, the consequential acts from this or past lives will have no bearing on the yogi.

Is this unfair?

Some people feel that a yogi should not be exempt from moral laws. They resent the idea of a yogi ever escaping. They feel that he should be under the thumb of providence just as everyone else.

However the point is that anyone who can slip out of a dimension can escape from the laws which govern those places. However we must be sure that what we conceive of as mandatory morality is actually that and is not a ruling concocted by our mento-emotional energy for its twisted psychological satisfaction. After all it is reasonable to assume that the providence of this place will not cater to the needs of any limited entity in its jurisdiction. When it seems that fate suits the actor, that may well be a misunderstanding. In a jiffy, the same fate may turn against the same actor and oppose his or her ideas.

Application

Even if a yogi does not complete this practice proficiently before the time of death, still whatever the yogi masters will go to his credit. The likelihood is there that without having to take another material body, he may complete it in the astral world hereafter.

In a case where a yogi fails to complete this practice before death, and if his subtle body has to develop another material form, that failed yogi will still be better off for having done some practice in the previous life. This is because in the subtle form, the tendency for practice will carry over to the next physical body and will induce its resumption at some stage in the life of the new form.

Verse 123

द्वा–सप्तति–सहस्राणां नाडीनां मल–शोधने ।

कुतः प्रक्षालनोपायःकुण्डल्य–अभ्यसनादृते ।। १२३ ।।

dvā–saptati–sahasrāṇāṁ nāḍīnāṁ mala–śodhane |
kutaḥ prakṣālanopāyaḥ kuṇḍaly–abhyasanādṛte || 123 ||

dvā – two, saptati – seventy, sahasrāṇāṁ – thousand, nāḍīnāṁ – nadi subtle channels, mala – flaws, śodhane – in purifying, kutaḥ – what other, prakṣālanopāyaḥ = prakṣālana (cleansing) + upāyaḥ (method), kuṇḍaly – kundalini lifeforce, abhyasa – practice, nādṛte = na (no) + ādṛte (careful, earnest)

For clearing the seventy-two thousand (72,000) nadi subtle channels, in fact, there is no other method besides the practice of kundalini lifeforce arousal.

Analysis

This is a take-it-or-leave-it statement by the writer of the Hatha Yoga Pradipika. Traditionally there are considered to be seventy-two thousand (72,000) nadi subtle channels. Most of these are tiny microscopic subtle tubes. The largest of these is the sushumna nadi central spinal passage.

Application

Initially the student is only concerned with the sushumna nadi central passage but in time he is introduced to the reality that the entire subtle body must be cleared of all dense astral energy. This means that a student will have to work even harder to completely reconfigure the entire subtle form.

Verse 124

इयं तु मध्यमा नाडी दृढाभ्यासेन योगिनाम् ।

आसन–प्राण–संयाम–मुद्राभिः सरला भवेत् ।। १२४ ।।

iyaṁ tu madhyamā nāḍī dṛḍhābhyāsena yogināṁ I
āsana–prāṇa–saṁyāma–mudrābhiḥ saralā bhavet I I 124 I I

iyaṁ – this, tu – indeed, madhyamā – middle, nāḍī – nadi subtle channels, dṛḍhābhyāsena = dṛḍha (firmly) + ābhyāsena (by practice), yogināṁ – of yogis, āsana– yoga posture, prāṇa – breath-infusion, saṁyāma – linking focus meditation, mudrābhiḥ – by mystic–arresting actions, saralā – straight, bhavet – become

By consistent practice of the yogis, the middle nadi subtle channel is straightened using yoga postures, breath-infusion, linking focus meditation and mystic–arresting actions.

Analysis

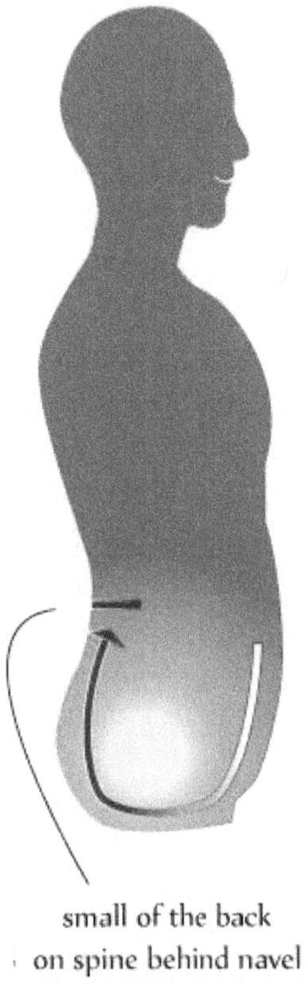

There is at least one kink and many areas where dense astral energy lingers in the middle nadi subtle channel. The kink(s) must be straightened so that the energy from the aroused kundalini can pass freely through the central spine into the head. The only way to achieve this is to raise kundalini on a daily basis, preferably twice per day. Each student has a different time requirement for achieving this, all depending on the intensity of practice, the past life record of achievements, the submissiveness to the yoga-guru, the degree of isolation from non-yogis and the evolutionary pressures which one has to overcome.

The major kink along the sushumna spinal passage is at the small of the back. This is the location where if a person arches the physical body backwards, there will be a place where the spine is pivot-angled the most. At this location any bliss energy which enters the spine is kept from passing through the spine into the brain. A yogi has to remove this kink in the spine.

Some students have other kinks which the yoga-guru may reveal or which they might discover as they practice. There are also areas where dense astral energy lingers. These energies form blockages which stop kundalini from routing itself from muladhara base chakra through the spine. To remove the kink(s) and the heavy astral force a yogi must infuse breath energy into the body and push it down so that it mixes with the reproductive hormone influence. Then this combined force should be fused into the kundalini at muladhara base chakra. This will cause kundalini to be aroused and if the locks are applied, it will move through the spine straightening the kink(s) and blasting out the dark astral energy through the neck into the brain in a bliss energy explosion.

Application

Here the requirements are itemized:

- *consistent supervised yoga practice*
- *use of yoga postures to straighten the middle nadi subtle channel*

- *breath-infusion*
- *linking focus meditation*
- *mystic–arresting actions*

*There must be **consistent supervised yoga practice** which is checked frequently by a yoga-guru. That guru does not have to be physically present. He can be astrally aware of the student's performance. In addition one can have more than one yoga-guru. Each will check on his area of expertise according to the austerities which he mastered previously.*

*It will be necessary to **use various yoga postures to straighten the middle nadi subtle channel**. Each student has a different body which might have different impediments in the form of resistant genetic traits and past life abnormalities which transferred into the new physical body because the subtle body retained flaws from the last material form it inhabited.*

People who insist on doing group sessions and who feel lonely when doing this practice alone, cannot be successful, because it requires full internal attentiveness to master this process, and to come to terms with the kundalini lifeforce.

***Breath-infusion** is necessary but one student may use one type of pranayama or one rate of doing it, as compared to another. Either way one has to infuse fresh air into the system and then push that down so that it mixes with the reproductive hormones. The mixture of these should be thrust into the kundalini at the base chakra. That is how the kundalini will be aroused.*

*A **linking focus meditation** should be learnt from the yoga-guru, but a student should also study the Bhagavad Gita and the Yoga Sutras to get some idea of the standard process and to take help from Lord Krishna and Patanjali Mahamuni.*

*The **mystic–arresting actions** which were described in this chapter should be mastered. One has to learn these from a yoga-guru either by meeting him in the physical or astral existence.*

Verse 125

अभ्यासे तु विनिद्राणां मनो धृत्वा समाधिना ।

रुद्राणी वा परा मुद्रा भद्रां सिद्धिं प्रयच्छति ।। १२५ ।।

abhyāse tu vinidrāṇāṁ mano dhṛtvā samādhinā |
rudrāṇī vā parā mudrā bhadrāṁ siddhiṁ prayacchati || 125 ||

abhyāse – during practice, tu – but, vinidrāṇāṁ – sleepless, mano = mana = mind, dhṛtvā – stabilizing, samādhinā – by continuous linkage to a higher environment or person, rudrāṇī = śāmbhavī arresting visual focus between the eyebrows, vā – or, parā – other, mudrā – mystic–arresting actions, bhadrāṁ – auspicious, siddhiṁ – mystic skill, prayacchati – acquire

Being sleepless during practice, having stabilized the mind by continuous linkage to a higher environment or person, the yogi acquires auspicious mystic skills by arresting the

visual focus between the eyebrows or by other mystic arresting actions.

Analysis

To remove sleep energy during practice, a yogi should do pranayama breath-infusion just before meditating. Sleep is described by Patanjali as being one of the cittavritti mento-emotional processes which a yogi must eliminate to complete meditation (samyama). The psychic adjunct which regulates sleep is the kundalini lifeforce. By doing breath-infusion thoroughly prior to meditation, there is the likelihood that one will not be affected by the sleep energy.

Telling oneself that one will not sleep and that one should stay awake during meditation, saying that one's body should only require so many hours of sleep, will not stop the subtle body from entering the sleep mode. To affect that one has to provide the kundalini with its required quota of energy. One must also have a lifestyle which does not abuse the kundalini.

The mind becomes stabilized when the mento-emotional energy is quieted, when it is free from ideas and images, when its applications have ceased for the time being. Then the yogi can meditate in earnest and reach the divine atmosphere.

There may be a lull period just before access to the chit akash sky of consciousness comes into focus. A yogi should patiently wait in this gap and should not be hasty. Access opens from the other side to this side, from the divine world to the highest level of the material world. A yogi cannot open access from this side. He can wait for access and be ready to utilize it once it is available.

Application

The arrest of the visual focus between the eyebrows has become like a prostitute which every man uses for his sexual satisfaction, and which as a result degrades the status of the woman involved. Due to certain kriya masters who popularized this method, it became more or less useless and does not give the intended result. It causes dishonesty where students pretend that they utilize the brow chakra even though they do not.

First of all, a person could stare between the eyebrows until the end of the time. That may not result in anything but peeking into mental darkness. Some persons may see circular lights when doing this. Some may see a tiny twinkling star for an instant. Some may find that a window in time opens and they peer in another environment. Much can happen when placing the mental focus between the eyebrows.

There is a chakra there, the brow chakra, the third eye or ajna chakra as it is called. However unless the student can stop the conventional images and ideas from flashing in the mind, staring at the third eye will not give the intended result.

Verse 126

राज–योगं विना पृथ्वी राज–योगं विना निशा ।

राज–योगं विना मुद्रा विचित्रापि न शोभते ।। १२६ ।।

rāja–yogaṁ vinā pṛthvī rāja–yogaṁ vinā niśā |
rāja–yogaṁ vinā mudrā vicitrāpi na śobhate || 126 ||

rāja–yogaṁ = mystic process of remaining introverted while being externally occupied, vinā – without, pṛthvī – earth, rāja–yogaṁ = remaining introverted while being externally occupied, vinā – without, niśā – night, rāja–yogaṁ = remaining introverted while being externally occupied, vinā – without, mudrā – mystic arresting actions, vicitrāpi = vicitra (various) + api (also), na – not, śobhate – appealing

Without the mystic process of remaining introverted while being externally occupied, the earth, the night and the mystic arresting actions are not appealing.

Analysis

The earth and its objects are visible in daylight. These serve as a bother to the non-yogi because their usages cause complex consequential equations to develop. These equations are later served to the entities as convenient and inconvenient fate.

The night puts a damper on the visibility of the earth and its objects. It is when sleep is induced, when the physical system rests and the astral bodies separate and become busy. Who is conscious during sleep? Who can consciously direct the separated astral form?

The mystic arresting actions have little value if they are not effective on the subtle level. Yoga is more than gymnastics. It is for reconfiguring the subtle form.

Unless a yogi can remain introverted while he is externally occupied, he will not be able to use the earth, the night and the mystic arresting actions to thwart the materialistic tendencies of his subtle body.

Application

Mastery of remaining introverted while being externally occupied, is a must for yogis. If one cannot do this, then one cannot be liberated. We may argue about methods of achieving this but the mastery must be there if one is to be liberated.

It is called raja yoga because raja means king. It was the yoga of kings, which in the Bhagavad Gita, is termed as karma yoga, which Krishna said that he reestablished through teaching Arjuna. It was the method of applying the psychological insight one develops in yoga to one's cultural participation.

Without it the cultural life proves to be spiritually counterproductive. Arjuna once saw a contradiction in the instructions of Krishna, where he felt that Krishna told him to be renounced on one hand and to be involved on the other. He said to Krishna:

arjuna uvāca
jyāyasī cetkarmaṇaste
matā buddhirjanārdana
tatkiṁ karmaṇi ghore māṁ
niyojayasi keśava (3.1)

arjuna — Arjuna; uvāca — contested; jyāyasī — is better; cet = ced — if; karmaṇaḥ — than physical action; te — your; matā — idea; buddhirjanārdana = buddhiḥ — mental action + janārdana — motivator of men; tatkiṁ = tat (tad) — them + kiṁ — why; karmaṇi — in action;

ghore — in horrible; māṁ — me; niyojayasi — you urge; keśava — handsome-haired one

Arjuna contested: O motivator of men, if it is Your idea that the mental approach is better than the physically-active one, then why do You urge me to commit horrible action, O handsome-haired One? (Bhagavad Gita 3.1)

vyāmiśreṇaiva vākyena
buddhiṁ mohayasīva me
tadekaṁ vada niścitya
yena śreyo'hamāpnuyām (3.2)

vyāmiśreṇaiva = vyāmiśreṇa — with this two-way + iva — like this; vākyena — with a proposal; buddhiṁ — intelligence; mohayasīva = mohayasi — you baffle + iva — like this; me — of me; tad — this; ekaṁ — one; vada — tell; niścitya — surely; yena — by which; śreyo = śreyaḥ — the best; 'ham = aham — I; āpnuyām — I should get

You baffle my intelligence with this two-way proposal. Mention one priority, by which I would surely get the best result. (Bhagavad Gita 3.2)

Lord Krishna replied:

na karmaṇāmanārambhān
naiṣkarmyaṁ puruṣo'śnute
na ca saṁnyasanādeva
siddhiṁ samadhigacchati (3.4)

na — not; karmaṇām — concerning cultural activity; anārambhān — not being involved; naiṣkarmyaṁ — freedom from cultural activity; puruṣo = puruṣaḥ — a person; 'śnute = aśnute — attains; na — not; ca — and; saṁnyasanādeva = saṁnyasanād (saṁnyasanāt) — from renunciation + eva — alone; siddhiṁ — spiritual perfection; samadhigacchati — achieves

A man does not attain freedom from cultural activity merely by not being involved in social affairs. And not by renunciation alone, does he achieve spiritual perfection. (Bhagavad Gita 3.4)

One has to use the insight gained through renunciation to guide one's behavior in the cultural area. That is karma yoga or raja yoga. It was attributed as part of the education of Vedic kings, especially of the rulers of Mithila, the Janaks. They mastered yoga in their youth and then used the insight gained to guide them through the social challenges.

Verse 127

मारुतस्य विधिं सर्वं मनो–युक्तं समभ्यसेत् ।
इतरत्र न कर्तव्या मनो–वृत्तिर्मनीषिणा।। १२७ ।।

mārutasya vidhiṁ sarvaṁ mano–yuktaṁ samabhyaset I
itaratra na kartavyā mano–vṛttirmanīṣiṇā II 127 II

mārutasya – relating breath energy, vidhiṁ – techniques, sarvaṁ – all, mano–yuktaṁ = yogically controlled mind, samabhyaset – thoroughly practice, itaratra – elsewhere, na – not, kartavyā – perform, mano–vṝttir = mano–vṝttiḥ = mento–emotional energy of the mind, manīṣiṇā – by a wise yogi

All techniques relating to breath-energy should be thoroughly practiced with a yogically controlled mind. The mento-emotional energy of a wise yogi should not wander elsewhere.

Analysis

Pranayama breath-infusion is an individual practice which is done under supervision of an advanced yogi who mastered the technique. It is inappropriate for a teacher to give methods which he did not practice but which are in books or were given by his guru. The teacher must have practiced recently and should know the extent of the practice at this time of history with the condition of bodies we currently have.

Pranayama should not be done whimsically. It is not a group session practice. Some proficient teachers for efficiency sake and to get the word out and teach group sessions. For instance, one of my teachers, Yogi Harbhajan Singh, taught large numbers of students. Sometimes he taught hundreds at one time in a group class. However that is exceptional and ultimately each student should hone in on his psyche and do the needful for integrated and very attentive advancement.

Application

Over time when doing practice, one should be focused inside the psyche. If need be one should use a blind fold. Some ancient yogis meditated in dark caves far away from the haunts of humans. They did this because one makes advancement more rapidly in isolation.

Verse 128

इति मुद्रा दश प्रोक्ता आदिनाथेन शम्भुना ।

एकैका तासु यमिनां महा–सिद्धि–प्रदायिनी ।। १२८ ।।

iti mudrā daśa proktā ādināthena śambhunā |
ekaikā tāsu yamināṁ mahā–siddhi–pradāyinī || 128 ||

iti mudrā – mystic arresting actions, daśa – ten, proktā – mentioned, ādi – very first, nāthena – by lord, śambhunā – by Shiva Shambhu, ekaikā – each one, tāsu – of these, yamināṁ – those who are existentially self–disciplined, mahā – great, siddhi – mystic skills, pradāyinī – confers

There are ten mystic arresting actions, which were mentioned by the very first Lord, Shiva Shambhu. Each one confers great mystic skills on those who are existentially self-disciplined.

Analysis

Unless one is existentially self-disciplined one cannot get the blessings of Shiva Shambhu. Without that one is doomed to failure and is accursed in this creation which is existentially reliant on the energy of Shiva's wife, the Goddess Durga.

There is more to this practice besides the practice itself. The lords of the practice need be taken into account. If one uses a technique and does not get the grace energy which accompanies it, one will be ruined. There will be no success in the process even though one may feel an advantage which will eventually lead to ruin.

One must adhere to a yoga-guru and to a deity. The yoga-guru may not be physically present but he must exist somewhere in the astral or spiritual domains. The blessing of the deity, of Shiva, is an absolute necessity.

A question may arise as to which deity.

That is not the issue. The situation is one of attitude. This system and also the Patanjali ashtanga yoga is not for atheists. It was not designed like that. There are systems for atheists but these are not so. One needs to have an open attitude to the deity. One does not have to know the deity but one should have an open attitude to whosoever that deity is. In this text Shiva was mentioned from the very start but when we read the Yoga Sutras of Patanjali, the characteristics are mentioned without naming the deity. Here we have the reverse, where the name is given but not the characteristics.

Application

The mystic skills are necessary tools for further advancement. Those who say that the mystic skills should not be used are naive because it is not possible to advance in high-end yoga practice without using mystic skills.

What you need to know is that you should get directions from the yoga-guru and the deity in how to use the mystic powers. If you do not use them you will be condemned. If you misuse them you will suffer for it. For advancement they must be used.

Verse 129

उपदेशं हि मुद्राणां यो दत्ते साम्प्रदायिकम् ।

स एव श्री–गुरुः सवामी साक्षादीश्वर एव सः ।। १२९ ।।

upadeśaṁ hi mudrāṇāṁ yo datte sāmpradāyikam I
sa eva śrī–guruḥ svāmī sākṣādīśvara eva saḥ II 129 II

upadeśaṁ – teaching, hi – because, mudrāṇāṁ – mystic arresting actions, yo = yaḥ = who, datte – imparts, sāmpradāyikam – lineage of teachers, sa – he, eva – only, śrī – illustrious, guruḥ – proficient yoga teacher, svāmī – worthy master, sākṣād = regarded as the same or the equivalent of, īśvara – Supreme Lord, eva – only, saḥ – he

He who is in the lineage of teachers, and who imparts the teachings of the mystic arresting actions, is the illustrious proficient yoga teacher, the worthy master, who is regarded as being the same or the equivalent of the Supreme Lord.

Analysis

The Supreme Lord is Krishna but Shiva is also considered as such. This is not contradictory. We need not bog ourselves down trying to understand multiple deities. It is not necessary to get into arguments about it. It should not be subjected to logic. There are some things which one should accept and continue the practice, making progress.

I was commissioned to write this translation and commentary by Rishi Singh Gherwal, Swami Vishnudevananda, and Swami Shivananda. These persons are deceased. This means that my authority is astral. In addition I had to tune into the remnant astral energy which was left behind by the original author, Swatmarama Guruji.

How then am I positioned in the lineage of teachers?

I should be considered to be empowered by Swatmarama to translate and give revelatory remarks about this technique of kundalini manipulation for subtle body transformation. In so far as a person makes advancement from this information, I may be regarded as being empowered by the Supreme Lord, by Krishna, as well as the Supreme Lord, by Shiva.

Application

The lineage of teachers, the sampradaya, is not always physical. It is not always linear where it makes sense on the material plane of existence in terms of one body taking physical initiation from a senior. A student should be perceptive enough to sense when a person is empowered even if that person has no physical connection to display. Spiritual information may come without being routed through a physical lineage.

Verse 130

तस्य वाक्य–परो भूत्वा मुद्राभ्यासे समाहितः ।

अणिमादि–गुणैः सार्धं लभते काल–वञ्चनम्।। १३० ।।

tasya vākya–paro bhūtvā mudrābhyāse samāhitaḥ I
aṇimādi–guṇaiḥ sārdhaṁ labhate kāla–vañcanam II 130 II

tasya – his, vākya – words, paro = paraḥ = superior, bhūtvā – believing, mudrābhyāse = mudra (mystic arresting actions) + abhyāse (in practice), samāhitaḥ – focusing, aṇimādi – becoming infinitesimal and related supernatural skills, guṇaiḥ – with natural abilities, sārdhaṁ – in combination, labhate – gets, kāla – death which is enforced by time, vañcanam – cheating

By focusing on the practice of mystic arresting actions, believing his superior words, one gets the mystic perfectional skills like being infinitesimal and being capable of cheating time which enforces death.

Analysis

One cannot make advancement without applying mystic perfections. But certainly one cannot get into the high-end of yoga without superior guidance in how to use the mystic perfections so that they do not cause one to perform criminal actions and self-defeating motions. It is simply impossible for a yogi on this planet to be successful without the superior guidance of both Shiva and Krishna.

Application

Krishna left the Bhagavad Gita instruction, as well as his complete discourse to Uddhava and the Anu Gita which concludes the Bhagavad Gita. There is also the Yoga Sutras of Patanjali. If a yogi fails to use their information, then we may conclude that he is doomed to failure.

Chapter 4

Linkage to a Divine Environment or Person*

Verse 1

नमः शिवाय गुरवे नाद–बिन्दु–कलात्मने ।

निरञ्जन–पदं याति नित्यं तत्र परायणः ।। १ ।।

namaḥ śivāya gurave nāda–bindu–kalātmane I
nirañjana–padaṁ yāti nityaṁ tatra parāyaṇaḥ II 1 II

namaḥ – honor, śivāya – to Shiva, gurave – to the proficient yoga teacher, nāda – naad supernatural sound resonance, bindu – causal node source, kalātmane = kalā (atom–like) + ātmane (self), nirañjana – flawless, padaṁ – existential environment, yāti – achieves, nityaṁ – eternal, tatra – there, parāyaṇaḥ – one who is devoted

I honor Shiva, the proficient yoga teacher, the naad supernatural sound resonance, the causal node source, the self who is atomic. One who is devoted to him achieves the flawless existential environment, the eternal abode.

Analysis

Shiva is identified like this:

- proficient yoga teacher
- naad supernatural sound resonance
- causal node source
- self who is atomic

Shiva is the ultimate **proficient yoga teacher**. He continuously practices yoga during the creation. His instructions are practical in so far as he does it himself. This does not mean that another yogi can do every technique Shiva demonstrates but it is fair to everyone that he practices and advises as a teacher who is active.

One of the criticisms that is leveled at Shiva is that he always does austerities. There are stories in the Puranas about the other supernatural controllers being impatient with Shiva because of his preoccupation with yoga.

Can we benefit from this?

~ Yes and No ~

**The Haṭha Yoga Pradīpikā does not have chapter headings. This title was assigned by the translator on the basis of the verse 2 of this chapter.*

We may benefit indirectly but it is hardly likely that we will benefit directly by becoming his immediate disciples. We may learn from someone, who learnt from someone, who learnt from someone who learnt from Shiva, but it is not likely that we will learn directly from him. In fact that is not necessary. We need to learn from someone who recently became proficient in the techniques we currently require.

Shiva is the **naad supernatural sound resonance**. This is interesting because the naad resonance which a yogi hears in the subtle head is the sound of the continuous contact between the spiritual and subtle material atmospheres. According to the Srimad Bhagavatam, Shiva is in a category as a Personality of Godhead but existentially, he is somewhere between the Paramatma Vishnus and the atma limited entities.

Shiva is regarded as the Paramatma and so are the Vishnus. It is important to know that the Shivas and Vishnus are a category of spiritual person, meaning that there are plural entities, plural Godhead. If someone says that Vishnu is the Supreme Person, then we may query as to which Vishnu. If someone says that Shiva is the Supreme Person, we may inquire similarly.

If the Vishnus are Personalities of Godhead, if the Shivas too are regarded as such, then which is the Supreme Personality of Godhead? How are we to process information about plural Godhead? To escape this controversy, we could become Jews or Christians where the matter is simplified with no plurality in the Godhead.

Shiva is the **causal node source,** the point of origin of the universe. Ultimately we may conceive that everything will retrogress into the being of Shiva. Then sometime in the remote future, everything will again emerge from him. When these things retrogress, their termination does not in any way affect other manifestations which Shiva maintains. The end of this is not the end of everything. This is an isolated expression with termination and re-emergent energies within it.

Shiva is the **self who is atomic**, who enters into everything, who has cosmic and microscopic access. Shiva is God.

Application

To achieve the flawless existential environment, the eternal abode, one must have a subtle body which is very similar to and is near compatible to a spiritual body. It is not just a matter of faith in Shiva. There are millions of people in India, and now worldwide, there are thousands of people, who have full confidence in Shiva. That faith alone will not provide access to the eternal abode. The quality of the faith must be taken into consideration as well as the basis upon which the faith was derived. Patanjali Maharshi alerted us to an important qualification for transiting to the divine world:

jātyantara pariṇāmaḥ prakṛtyāpūrāt

jātyantara = jāti – category + antara – other, another; pariṇāmaḥ – transformation; prakṛiti – subtle material nature; āpūrāt – due to filling up or saturation.

The transformation from one category to another is by the saturation of the subtle material nature.

This means that for going to even a higher astral region, the yogi must first do something to change the energy in the subtle body. It must be saturated with the energy of the desired location.

The subtle body will not become a spiritual one at any stage, no more than the physical system will become subtle. However, before he can assume a spiritual form, a yogi must bring the subtle body to a condition which is similar to that of a spiritual one.

Being devoted to Shiva is not a matter of doing fasts as described in the Shiva Purana for Ratri ritual season. One cannot be devoted to Shiva if one is not a yogi with intentions to abandon materialistic living just as Shiva did. One cannot be devoted to Shiva if one wants boons from Shiva. Swatmarama, the writer of the Hatha Yoga Pradipika, is an example of a devotee of Shiva.

Verse 2

अथेदानीं प्रवक्ष्यामि समाधिक्रममुत्तमम् ।
मृत्युघ्नं च सुखोपायं बरह्मानन्द–करं परम् ।। २ ।।

athedānīṁ pravakṣyāmi samādhikramamuttamam I
mṛtyughnaṁ ca sukhopāyaṁ brahmānanda–karaṁ param II 2 II

athedānīṁ = atha (now is explained) + idānīṁ (at this time), pravakṣyāmi – I explain, samadhi – continuous linkage to a higher environment or person, kramam – procedure, uttamam – best, mṛtyu – death, ghnaṁ – destroyer, ca – and, sukhopāyaṁ = sukha (happiness) + upāyaṁ (conveyor), brahmānanda – feelings of exclusive spiritual bliss, karaṁ – producer, param – supreme cause

At this time, I will explain the best procedure for continuous linkage to a higher environment or person. It is the destroyer of death, the conveyor of happiness, the producer of feelings of exclusive spiritual bliss. It gives contact with the supreme cause.

Analysis

The best procedure for continuous linkage to a higher environment or person must serve as:

- the destroyer of death
- the conveyor of happiness
- the producer of feelings of exclusive spiritual happiness
- giving contact with the supreme cause

We need a procedure which serves as **the destroyer of death**, in the sense of giving us access to a death-free environment. There should be no concern in the student for ridding this world of death. The student should be mature enough, and confident enough of a transcendental zone, that death which is prevalent here is positively acknowledged by the student because he located a viable alternative through gaining access to the divine world.

The procedure should put the student in a position to be in contact with **the conveyor of happiness** which is a medium in the divine world. This will be interpreted by the subtle body as the absence of its sense of insecurity.

The procedure should put the student in a position whereby in meditation, he crosses over to the other side, the divine world, where he experiences **feelings of exclusive spiritual happiness.**

The procedure should **give contact with the supreme cause,** the source of the physical and psychic material world.

Application

Samadhi is the final objective of the yoga process which Patanjali gave as eight processes with the three highest stages as one sequential event, samyama. Roughly speaking the Sanskrit term samyama as used by Patanjali is the equivalent of meditation as used in English language.

The four higher states of yoga concern psychological adjustments. These begin with pratyahar sensual energy withdrawal from concerns outside the subtle body. Before meditating the yogi is expected to withdraw all sensual interest so that his power of pursuit has no application outside the subtle form. He must withdraw concern from the physical existence which is outside and inside the physical body, as well as from the subtle existence which is outside of his subtle form. He must maintain interest inside the subtle form because that is how he will transit to the divine world if he ever qualifies to do so or if he is ever graced to do so even momentarily.

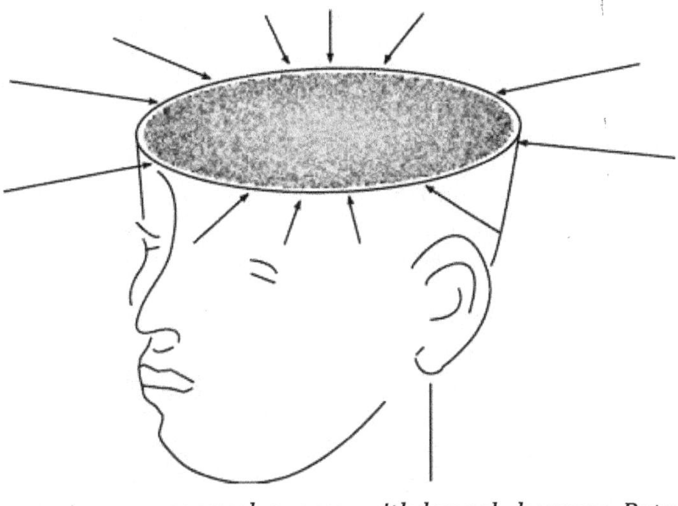

Meditation does not mean sensual energy withdrawal, because Patanjali indicated meditation as samyama which is the three highest states of yoga, as one sequential event. However for novices, meditation is sensual energy withdrawal. This is because their minds are resistant to the three higher aspects. When a novice sits to meditate, he will do sensual energy withdrawal and will not progress beyond that until he can proficiently command the senses to cease their external pursuits.

Once the subtle energies cease coursing out of the psyche, once they have the habit of looking inwards, the yogi must stabilize the self in that internally-focused sensuality. When this stabilization occurs, the student can begin meditation by doing the first stage of samyama which is dharana or deliberate linkage to a higher concentration force or person. To link to anything, one must first perceive whatever or whoever that higher principle is. When this practice of deliberate linkage is steady the student will realize that from time to time, the linkage is effortless. When that effortless linkage occurs frequently, the yogi will discover that it is continuous.

Verse 3-4

राज–योगः समाधि श्च उन्मनी च मनोन्मनी ।

अमरत्वं लयस्तत्त्वं शून्याशून्यं परं पदम् ।। ३ ।।

अमनस्कं तथाद्वैतं निरालम्बं निरञ्जनम् ।

जीवन्मुक्तिश्च सहजा तुर्या चेत्येक–वाचकाः ।। ४ ।।

rāja–yogaḥ samādhiśca unmanī ca manonmanī I
amaratvaṁ layastattvaṁ śūnyāśūnyaṁ paraṁ padam II 3 II
amanaskaṁ tathādvaitaṁ nirālambaṁ nirañjanam I
jīvanmuktiśca sahajā turyā cetyeka–vācakāḥ II 4 II

rāja–yogaḥ = mystic process of remaining introverted while being externally occupied, samādhiś = samādhiḥ = continuous linkage to a higher environment or person, ca – and, unmanī – void of mental content, ca – and, manonmanī – blank thoughtless idealess mental condition, amaratvaṁ – existentially like a god, layas – variety dissolution, tattvaṁ – primal cause, śūnyāśūnyaṁ = subjective reality/objective reality, paraṁ padam = supreme residence, amanaskaṁ – without mental dominance, tathādvaitaṁ = tathā (as) + advaitam (one reality without diversification), nirālambaṁ – independent of everything else, nirañjanam – flawless, jīvanmuktiś = jīvanmuktiḥ = liberated while using a material body, ca – and, sahajā – original, turyā – fourth state, cetyeka = ca (and) + iti (thus) + eka (one), vācakāḥ – discussion

Mystic process of remaining introverted while being externally occupied, continuous linkage to a higher environment or person, being void of mental content, having a blank thoughtless idealess mental condition, existing like a god, experiencing a variety dissolution, perceiving a primal cause, experiencing subjective reality and then experiencing objective reality, entering the supreme residence, being without mental dominance, experiencing just one reality without diversification, feeling independent of everything else, experiencing a flawless condition, being liberated while using a material body, experiencing originality, and experiencing the fourth state; these are one and the same discussion.

Analysis

There are several valid perspectives or approaches for reaching the ultimate objective of yoga which is relocation to a divine environment. Any system is valid if it yields the intended result. Swatmarama listed these:

- mystic process of remaining introverted while being externally occupied
- continuous linkage to a higher environment or person
- being void of mental content

- having a blank thoughtless idealess mental condition
- existing like a god
- experiencing a variety dissolution
- perceiving a primal cause
- experiencing subjective reality and then experiencing objective reality
- entering the supreme residence
- being without mental dominance
- experiencing just one reality without diversification
- feeling independent of everything else
- experiencing a flawless condition
- being liberated while using a material body
- experiencing originality
- experiencing the fourth state

A person who is proficient in the **mystic process of remaining introverted while being externally occupied,** is free from being tagged for his good or bad acts because of disconnection of his sense of identity from the properties of material nature. Whatever happens be it good or bad, constructive or destructive, occurs within the confines of the physical and psychic material nature. The entity has value in terms of his investment of attention. As much as he can slacken the interest, as much as he can subtract himself from the operations, he will only be tagged in proportion to his acquirement attitude.

One, who has a **continuous linkage to a higher environment or person,** has the experience which foreshadows the insecurities of material existence and also of the flimsy subtle reality which shifts radically and which is known as the astral world. A yogi only requires one such experience in a lifetime. That is such a special occurrence that just one incidence is sufficient to balance out the uncertainty principles which haunts material existence.

Any definite process which will cause the mind of the yogi to be **void of mental content**, of the conventional thoughts and images, may be regarded as valid as a precursor to meditation. Patanjali said that yoga begins when the mento-emotional energy is silent. So long as the yogi has ideas and images flashing in the mind, he cannot link to a divine person or environment.

The state of being void of mental content is different to having a **blank thoughtless idealess mental condition.** When the mind is void of mental content, the yogi feels as if the mental content is missing, as if it should be there but it is not. When he has a blank thoughtless idealess mental condition, he does not feel as if the mental content is missing but rather that something is there which is healthy and life-giving but which is there in a blank mental space.

One who **exists like a god** is either using a subtle body which does not require a gross accompanying form or using a spiritual body which is imperishable in the absolute sense. Even though it is not eternal, the subtle body is termed as imperishable in reference to the physical form. Thus anyone who uses such a body and who lives in the celestial world using a form which is made of light energy is regarded as deathless. A physical being also has a subtle body but it has the need for physical forms and is considered to be fallible or subjected to energy alternation according to the status of having a physical system or not having one.

A divine being who has or does not have a subtle body, and who has or does not have a material body but who is aware of the spiritual body is regarded as being God or a god. To which ever level a living entity is focalized, that place serves as the base for its existence. Hence there is no limit to the glory of someone who can remain focalized on divine format.

One, who **experiences variety dissolution** here and now, has insight into the end of what is perishable, and of the perpetual observer status of the living entity. Knowing the contrast between what will be dissolved and what will persist, that person is disconnected from the property of uncertainty, which is an eternal feature of what must be dissolved.

One who **perceives a primal cause** gets the confidence about substrata and is able to go into deep meditation to research origins. This person leaves all fears behind and ventures to his or her root existence. A yogi can dive into his origin to locate what existed before he became aware as an entity. One may also research into the origin of the material and psychic phenomena.

A yogi, who distinctly **experiences subjective reality and then experiences objective reality,** is a master of insight perception. Convention has it that first one should master objective reality. This is because from the birth of one's body, the struggle for existence begins with awareness of the surroundings. However this survival concern is extrovert and does not allow the ability to assess the perception equipment.

A yogi gets the hint from a yoga-guru either from a lecture, from literature or from being inspired that the crisis concerns calibrating the perception equipment. Objectivity is qualified on the accuracy of the perception equipment which is observed through subjectivity. First one must master the subjective situation of the self. Then one can tackle what is objective to it.

Anyone who can **enter the supreme residence** should be regarded as God or as a god. However it is not easy to verify this. There are many yogis and other types of spiritualists who claim to enter the supreme residence but this cannot be verify without using the senses of a divine body. Swatmarama stated this for the record. This cannot be checked except by those who are focalized into the spiritual body.

Every living entity has spiritual presence because every entity is spiritual in essence. However the majority of entities in this world are focalized in mundane reality. They are anchored in the material world. Their spiritual focus is all but absorbed by the psychic and physical material nature. Only those entities who are anchored to the spiritual side of existence can have relevant information about the supreme residence.

It is necessary that a yogi **be without mental dominance**. There are psychic adjuncts which accompany the core-self through its travel in the subtle and gross material creations. The adjuncts should be roped in by a yogi. From the view point of energy consumption, the core-self foots the bill for the expenditures even though it may not compose the reactions to nature's schemes. Anyone who pays a bill should have a majority influence in the service which is provided. Unfortunately the convention of material nature is that the core-self should foot the bill and only be a spectator.

A student should learn from the yoga teacher of methods of changing that conventional format of material nature. This means that the adjuncts must be controlled by the core-self so that they do not have the freedom to make decisions for which the core-self is liable.

Mental dominance comes from two angles, the emotional basis and the rational sector. Both of these are erosive to the hope of control by the core-self. The emotional basis is sourced in the kundalini psychic lifeforce while the rationality is the design of the buddhi intellect psychic mechanism. A yogi must find methods of restricting and ordering these adjuncts.

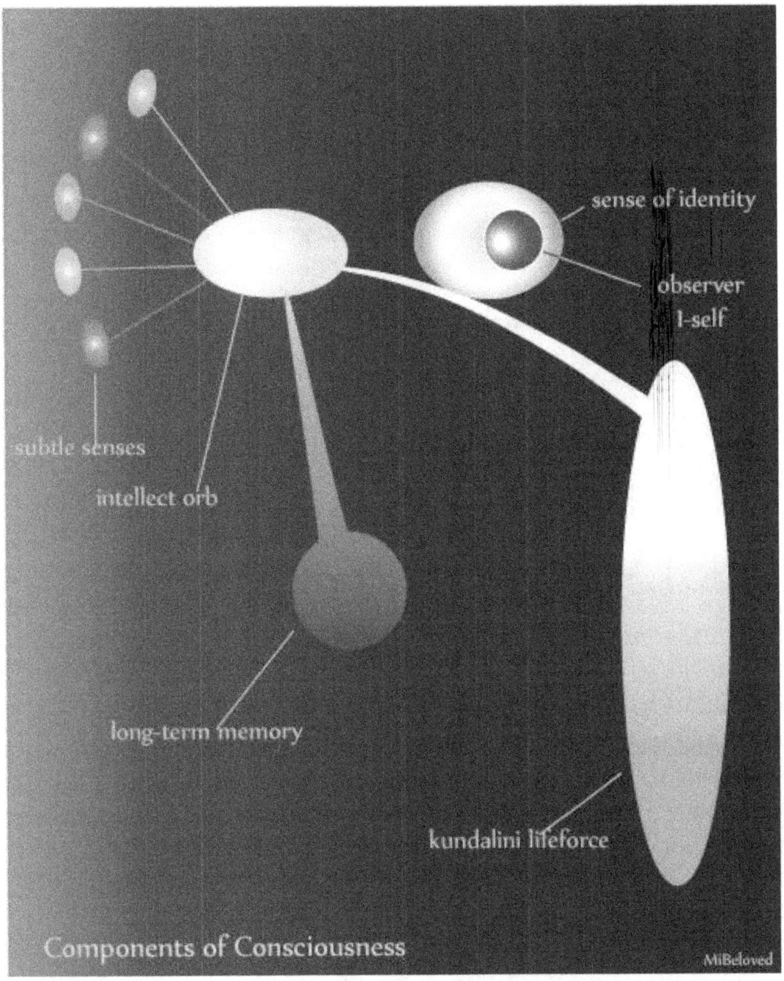

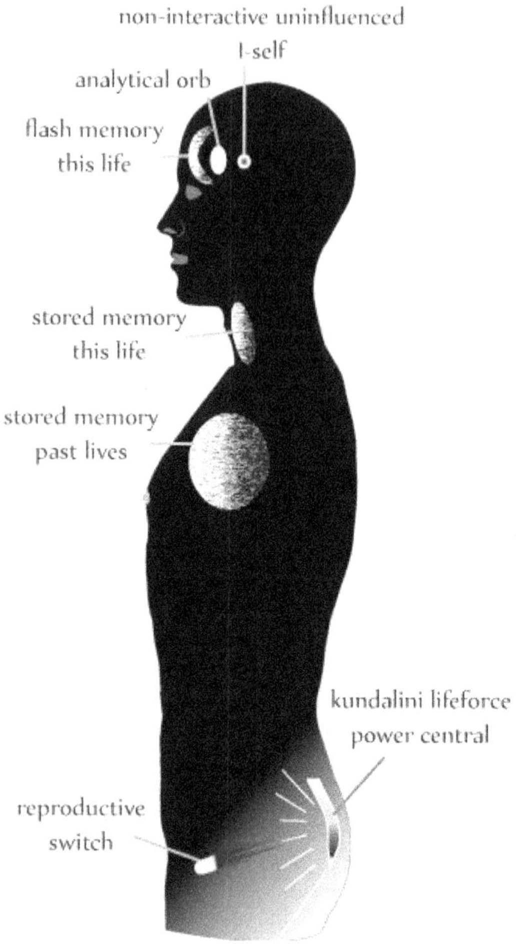

A yogi is required to get into position to **experience just one reality without diversification.** This system of material nature is a closed-unit as one cosmic mechanism. Within it there is and always will be diversification, even though when this is dissolved out its variation will be unsupported. The absence of diversification is not evidence of the lack of it. We experience grossly that a calm breeze and a relatively still ocean gives the impression of stability but we know that this energy will sooner or later manifest itself violently. It is one system but with varied possibilities. We must accept that. Both realities must be comprehended and accepted by a yogi, that of oneness and diversification.

A yogi should **feel independent of everything else,** but with the understanding that circumstantially there is reliance in all directions. This is the magic of existence where an aspect is independent and dependent simultaneously. Because of singleness or individuality, each spirit is an independent reality but it is surrounded by trillions of similar realities, sub-realities and super-realities.

A yogi should have the **experience of a flawless condition** of the core-self. This happens in deep meditation after a full introspective closure of the senses to the external physical and astral dimensions. From within the psyche, a yogi should part out the core-self from its psychic adjuncts like the sense of identity, the buddhi intellect orb, the kundalini lifeforce, the sensual energies and, the memories

Patanjali instructed that the self should part itself off from its psychic equipment for as long as it would take to become distinct from that and experience itself as something which is not influenced by the equipment. For purifying the adjuncts, he recommended their deactivation and gradual activation under full control of the core-self. This can only be done in trance consciousness. Hence the necessity to practice pranayama, for getting the cooperation of the kundalini lifeforce which is the adjunct that serves as the mechanic of the psyche.

A yogi should qualify as **being liberated while using a material body.** Failure to achieve this, means that the yogi will have to take another material form. There were exceptions but they are few and far between. Usually if a yogi does not qualify for liberation before leaving the material body, he will have to take another physical form and strive again for the achievement.

If one is not liberated and one is lucky, then one will be protected from having to take rebirth even though one's subtle body will feel the need to do so. This is achieved if one gets the shelter under a siddha in the astral world hereafter and if one remains under the influence of that person without being contacted by entities who have an interest in one's rebirth. Such interests are usually cultural relationships only, with only superficial spiritual concerns, if any.

If a yogi is not liberated and he has to permanently leave his material body, then he should seek out a siddha in the astral world hereafter. Once he makes contact with that person, he should hide from all vibrations which come from other entities who are socially sympathetic. Family members and even fellow yogis are dangerous to a yogi who does not want to take rebirth, because even the slightest contact with such persons could cause a yogi to find himself as an embryo of some physical woman on this or some other earth planet. In fact, one might even find the self to be an embryo of an animal or an insect even.

The influence of a siddha hereafter can suspend the force of the rebirth tendency of a student's subtle body. During the suspension that student can develop such a strong interest in everything other than physical existence, that the rebirth tendency would eventually be washed out of the psyche completely. But if the student yogi yields to social pressure from relatives and beginner yogis, his psyche will move away from the siddha. He will find himself in the association of people who are bound for physical rebirth. He will then develop an embryo and come out in the world as someone's baby.

Yoga is a complex course of activity which includes **experiencing originality.** Because this creation was developing for billions of years, nearly everything we encounter lacks originality. Thus a yogi has to enter into trance states to find origins and their covert sources.

There is this three dimensional physical world and there are its corresponding astral dimensions. These are lumped together as one reality with the astral under-basis as the direct cause of gross matter. Beyond these there is the **fourth state** which a yogi is required to experience. Escape to the fourth state, the divine world, is the culmination of yoga practice. It is what the yogi strives for. From within the psyche access is granted to that fourth state but it is opened from the other side of existence. The yogi cannot force a passage from this physical and psychic material nature but he can shift to the highest energy level in his psyche. That will make it likely that someone in the divine atmosphere will open a portal for the yogi.

At first the yogi is allowed to peer into the divine world only but as this peering becomes more and more regular, he is allowed, at last, the entry!

Application

There are many yoga teachers; some proficient, some not. There are many sects; some valid, some not. There are many definitions of yoga; some useful, some not. All in all it is a matter of reaching the fourth dimension which is known as the chit akash sky of consciousness. The akash is the astral atmosphere which is made up of psychic energy. Science terms it as radio and light frequency. Chit akash is not this place. Chit akash was termed by Siddha Swami Muktananda as the sky of consciousness. It is the divine atmosphere, a place in which chit or consciousness abounds in every nook and cranny. This is in contrast to the akash astral places where consciousness radiates unevenly.

To reach the astral world, one has to use the astral body which is currently interspaced in the physical form. In those dimensions, the astral body can move about just as in the physical world, the physical body becomes active. To reach the chit akash, one has to use the adjuncts in the subtle body and access the sky of consciousness from within the astral form without going outside of it into the astral dimensions.

Verse 5

सलिले सैन्धवं यद्वत्साम्यं भजति योगतः ।

तथात्म–मनसोरैक्यं समाधिरभिधीयते ।। ५ ।।

salile saindhavaṁ yadvatsāmyaṁ bhajati yogataḥ I
tathātma–manasoraikyaṁ samādhirabhidhīyate II 5 II

salile – in water, saindhavaṁ – salt, yadvat – just as, sāmyaṁ – identification with, bhajati – assume, yogataḥ connection, tathātma = tathā (so) + ātma (spiritual self), manasor = manasoḥ = mind, aikyaṁ – unity, samādhir = samādhiḥ = continuous linkage, abhidhīyate – is called

Just as salt in water assumes the same identification in connection with the liquid, so when the spiritual self and the mind are in a unity, it is called samadhi continuous linkage.

Analysis

The first stage of samadhi, the most common way to get an understanding of what samadhi is, may be explained by the salt in water analogy. However a student should not prostitute or ride this analogy all the way to being imaginary and non-practical.

If the self links with the mind and if the mind is the lower principle, then that is a samadhi from higher to lower for the self but one of lower to higher for the mind. However Patanjali objects that there can be an observation by the mind. He contests the idea that the mind is an observer. Here is the statement:

cittāntaradṛśye buddhibuddheḥ
atiprasaṅgaḥ smṛtisaṅkaraḥ ca

cittāntara – dṛśye = citta – mento-emotional energy + antara – another person + dṛśye – in the perception of; buddhi-buddher = buddhi – the intellect organ + buddheḥ – of the intellect organ; atiprasaṅgaḥ – absurd argument, unwarranted stretching of a rule or argument; smṛti – memory; saṅkaraḥ – confusion; ca – and.

In the perception of mento-emotional energy by another such energy, there would be an intellect perceiving another intellect independently. That would cause absurdity and confusion of memory. (Yoga Sutras 4.21)

Patanjali says that one mind, or one mento-emotional energy, cannot perceive another mind independently without there being a spiritual self, involved. The intellect cannot function on its own to make observation, nor can the kundalini psychic lifeforce.

The unification of the core-self and the mind is the most basic form of samadhi continuous linkage to anything. Nature arranged this connection. The yogi only needs to objectively observe it in the privacy of his mind

When salt is dissolved in water, the salt can be repossessed through dehydration but when the self becomes subjective in reference to its mind, that self has difficulty sorting what is itself and what is the mind. The process of yoga is the method for extracting the core-self from the mind.

Application

To understand what samadhi is, the student should study his mind. There is a temporary unification between the core-self and the mind. This is arranged by the grace of nature. The self should cease involvements in the mind and study how it is connected with the psychic adjuncts and how it lives in the existential space called the mind.

Verse 6

यदा संक्षीयते प्राणो मानसं च प्रलीयते ।

तदा समरसत्वं च समाधिरभिधीयते ।। ६ ।।

yadā saṁkṣīyate prāṇo mānasaṁ ca pralīyate |
tadā samarasatvaṁ ca samādhirabhidhīyate || 6 ||

yadā – when, saṁkṣīyate – is diffused, prāṇo = prāṇaḥ = subtle breath energy, mānasaṁ – mind's natural interest, ca – and, pralīyate – dissolved, tadā – then, samarasatvaṁ – being similar, ca – and, samādhir = samādhiḥ = continuous linkage, abhidhīyate – is called

When the subtle breath energy is diffused and the mind's natural interest is dissolved, then the two being similar, it is called a samadhi continuous linkage.

Analysis

This is another example of samadhi. This is another application. Samadhi is to be applied. It is not one state. It is a condition of fusion of two states or aspects where either is saturated into the other, where homogenization took place.

Application

By doing pranayama a yogi causes an accumulation of breath energy. This is then compressed. Then even more breath energy is ingested. This in turn is compressed. The procedure is repeated until the yogi is satisfied that he removed the stale air and other gaseous pollutants in the body. Once this is done, the yogi should apply the locks and check to see how the energy is distributed to various parts of the psyche.

When the breath is distributed through the system, the yogi will notice that the mind was affected in that its image-display mechanism ceases for the time being. He will conclude that an effective pranayama practice causes the mind to be dissolved so that it normal configuration disappears. It either becomes weak in power or it ceases altogether.

When the breath energy is infused into the subtle body, and when the stale polluted gases, are removed, The yogi finds that the mind dissolves. It loses its directive authority. It does not overwhelm the core-self.

Verse 7

तत–समं च द्वयोरैक्यं जीवात्म–परमात्मनोः ।

प्रनष्ट–सर्व–सङ्कल्पः समाधिः सो।अभिधीयते ।। ७ ।।

tat–samaṁ ca dvayoraikyaṁ jīvātma–paramātmanoḥ |
pranaṣṭa sarva saṅkalpaḥ samādhiḥ so|abhidhīyate || 7 ||

tat – that, samaṁ – similarity, ca – and, dvayor = dvayoḥ – two, aikyaṁ – unity, jivatma – limited individual spirt, paramātmanoḥ – of the supreme spirit, pranaṣṭa– ceased, sarva – all, saṅkalpaḥ = mento–emotional intentions, samādhiḥ – continuous linkage to a divinity, so = saḥ = he, abhidhīyate – is called

That similarity between the two: the limited individual spirit and the supreme spirit, their unity when all mento–emotional intentions cease, is called a samadhi continuous linkage.

Analysis

This is the third explanation of samadhi, the third application of continuous linkage. Samadhi is the intercommunication between two principles, one could be higher or lower but there must be an observer in one of the aspects. If both have non-observer status then it is not samadhi linkage.

Let us review the previous examples:

- salt in water
- subtle breath energy diffusing the mind's natural interest

The first example is an analogy. It is a purely physical example citing two physical substances, salt and water. The second is also analogy. It is psychological citing subtle breath energy and the mind's natural interest which is thought and image creation. The definition of samadhi as the term is used by Swatmarama is honed in these two examples. We should not be confused, nor be involved in side-roading his meanings. He illustrated this using contextual applications.

In this verse a third application of samadhi is given, using two aspects:

- limited individual spirit
- supreme spirit

This is a practical example because both aspects are observers. For samadhi we require two aspects but at least one must be an observer. If both aspects are non-observers as in salt and water, then it is an analogy only and is not an example.

If Swatmarama was an atheist, or an agnostic, he would not have cited the Paramatma Supreme Spirit. If he thought that individuality was an illusion, he would not have cited the jivatma which specifies a particular individual entity.

Application

Patanjali Mahayogin requested of yogis that to begin the practice, they should first shutdown the mento-emotional gyrations of the mind. Swatmarama stated that the unity of the limited individual spirit and the Supreme Spirit manifests when the motivations (sankalpa) of the mento-emotional energy ceases. He also stated that the similarity between the two becomes manifest.

One other way of stating this is that merely by closing the motivations of the mento-emotional energy, the self can achieve a status which is similar to that of the Supreme Soul.

Strangely there is an explanation by Lord Krishna which tells the story of how the self became isolated from the Supreme Person:

mamaivāṁśo jīvaloke
jīvabhūtaḥ sanātanaḥ
manaḥṣaṣṭhānīndriyāṇi
prakṛtisthāni karṣati (15.7)

mamaivāṁśaḥ = mama — my + eva — indeed + aṁśaḥ — partner; jīvaloke = jīva — individualized conditioned being + loke — in the world; jīvabhūtaḥ individual soul; sanātanaḥ — eternal; manaḥ — mind; ṣaṣṭhānindriyāṇi = saṣṭhāni — sixth + indriyāṇi — sense, detection device; prakṛtisthāni — mundane; karṣati — draws

My partner is in this world of individualized conditioned beings. He is an eternal individual soul but he draws to himself the mundane senses of which the mind is the sixth detection device. (Bhagavad Gita 15.7)

Verse 8

राज–योगस्य माहात्म्यं को वा जानाति तत्त्वतः ।

ज्ञायं मुक्तिः सथितिः सिद्धिर्गुरु–वाक्येन लभ्यते ।। ८ ।।

rāja–yogasya māhātmyaṁ ko vā jānāti tattvataḥ I
jñānaṁ muktiḥ sthitiḥ siddhirguru–vākyena labhyate II 8 II

rāja–yogasya = yoga achievement of remaining introverted while externally occupied, māhātmyaṁ – magnificence, ko = kaḥ = who, vā – or, jānāti – know, tattvataḥ – essential cause, jñānaṁ – philosophy, muktiḥ – liberation, sthitiḥ – condition, siddhir = siddhiḥ = perfectional skill, guru – proficient yoga teacher, vākyena – through instruction, labhyate – understood

Or who can know the magnificence of the yoga achievement of remaining introverted while being externally occupied? The essential cause, the philosophy, liberation, condition and the perfectional skill is understood through the instructions of the proficient yoga teacher.

Analysis

Somewhere in the picture, there must be a proficient yoga teacher. This person may not be physically present but he must be somewhere in some existence, and within reach of the student. He can expand our insight into these aspects:

- essential cause
- philosophy
- liberation
- condition
- perfectional skill

The **essential cause** is one in terms of the Absolute; otherwise there are many origins which fold into other origins, all the way to the Primal Creative Cause. The yoga-guru explains this to encourage the student to investigate in trance states. As soon as a yogi sees the essential causes, the value of the gross manifestation decreases for him.

There should be in the student's mind a **philosophy** which clarifies the actions within material nature. This prevents the student from impractical ideas and useless ponderings about the paradoxes of nature. The recommended philosophy is the Samkhya doctrine of Kapila, the son of Devahuti and Kardama.

Liberation is an absolute must for a yogi. It is what he works for day and night through performance of austerities. It cannot be achieved without the blessings of Shiva or Krishna

The **condition** of any substance or aspect should be intuited by the yogi but only if it will enhance or upset his progress. Whatever is in this creation which is neutral to the yogi should be left uninvestigated. There should be no undue exploration or interference by a yogi into this material nature. To learn how to figure conditions one needs to get hints from the advanced entity.

Perfectional skill is a must because one cannot safely negotiate this creation without mystic perception. Nature is both physical and psychic with the psychic as the under-basis. One must develop mystic powers to successfully transit through this.

Application

Raja Yoga is defined this way and that way, with most commentators listing it as mental command over meditative states. Exactly what that means hardly a soul knows. Teachers usually cannot give a clear cut definition because they are confused by the abstraction of meditation and do not have the required clarity.

Raja Yoga was derived from karma yoga when karma yoga meant yoga + karma or yoga + cultural activities. Usually yoga has little to do with cultural activities and therefore when it is applied to that, it is termed as karma yoga.

This was initially taught to the warrior caste which was instructed by brahmin rishis during and after the period of the Upanishads. Lord Krishna briefed Arjuna about the origins of raja yoga in this statement:

karmaṇaiva hi saṁsiddhim
āsthitā janakādayaḥ
lokasaṁgrahamevāpi
saṁpaśyankartumarhasi (3.20)

karmaṇaiva = karmaṇa — by cultural activities + eva — alone; hi — indeed; saṁsiddhim — perfection; āsthitā — attained; janakādayaḥ = janaka — Janaka + ādayaḥ — beginning with; loka — world + saṁgraham — maintenance + eva — only + api — only; saṁpaśyan — seeing mentally; kartum — to act; arhasi — you should

Beginning with Janaka, perfection was attained by cultural activities alone. Seeing the necessity for world maintenance, you should act. (Bhagavad Gita 3.20)

This means that those who were in the warrior caste learnt yoga and used its insight to guide their judgment in cultural activities. When yoga is used in social activities; that is termed as karma yoga. The state of mind of a political person, who maintains the insight of yoga, while proceeding with duty, is raja yoga. It means that the person remains introverted while being externally occupied.

Normally one has to release oneself from the insight of yoga to function efficiently in ordinary social activities. However if one has learnt karma yoga, one can remain with yogic insight and function precisely and in a spiritually beneficial way in the social activities.

As great a person as Arjuna did not think it was possible to focus on the objectives of yoga and also perform culturally. He questioned the proposal for doing this:

arjuna uvāca
jyāyasī cetkarmaṇaste
matā buddhirjanārdana
tatkiṁ karmaṇi ghore māṁ
niyojayasi keśava (3.1)

arjuna — Arjuna; uvāca — contested; jyāyasī — is better; cet = ced — if; karmaṇaḥ — than physical action; te — your; matā — idea; buddhirjanārdana = buddhiḥ — mental action + janārdana — motivator of men; tatkiṁ = tat (tad) — them + kiṁ — why; karmaṇi — in action; ghore — in horrible; māṁ — me; niyojayasi — you urge; keśava — handsome-haired one

Arjuna contested: O motivator of men, if it is Your idea that the mental approach is better than the physically-active one, then why do You urge me to commit horrible action, O handsome-haired One? (Bhagavad Gita 3.1)

vyāmiśreṇaiva vākyena
buddhiṁ mohayasīva me
tadekaṁ vada niścitya
yena śreyo'hamāpnuyām (3.2)

vyāmiśreṇaiva = vyāmiśreṇa — with this two-way + iva — like this; vākyena — with a proposal; buddhiṁ — intelligence; mohayasīva = mohayasi — you baffle + iva — like this; me — of me; tad — this; ekaṁ — one; vada — tell; niścitya — surely; yena — by which; śreyo = śreyaḥ — the best; 'ham = aham — I; āpnuyām — I should get

You baffle my intelligence with this two-way proposal. Mention one priority, by which I would surely get the best result. (Bhagavad Gita 3.2)

It is possible to do yoga and serve in the cultural area just as well. In fact one can serve in a more efficient and spiritually harmless way if one uses yogic insight to steer the self through the morass of cultural activity. But Arjuna had doubts about the ability to do that.

Krishna convinced Arjuna in this way:

na karmaṇāmanārambhān
naiṣkarmyaṁ puruṣo'śnute
na ca saṁnyasanādeva
siddhiṁ samadhigacchati (3.4)

na — not; karmaṇām — concerning cultural activity; anārambhān — not being involved; naiṣkarmyaṁ — freedom from cultural activity; puruṣo = puruṣaḥ — a person; 'śnute = aśnute — attains; na — not; ca — and; saṁnyasanādeva = saṁnyasanād (saṁnyasanāt) — from renunciation + eva — alone; siddhiṁ — spiritual perfection; samadhigacchati — achieves

A man does not attain freedom from cultural activity merely by not being involved in social affairs. And not by renunciation alone, does he achieve spiritual perfection. (Bhagavad Gita 3.4)

This means that yoga alone will not necessarily cause a person to achieve spiritual perfection. It all depends on the demands upon his life by providence. If he is fated to be culturally involved, then detachment would be offensive to providence which will serve to be his undoing.

All the same, being socially involved and not having the insight to make spiritually-beneficial decisions will not help the actor either. That will merely complicate the situations further. One should learn yoga and apply it to the cultural situations one is providentially assigned.

Verse 9

दुर्लभो विषय-तयागो दुर्लभं तत्त्व-दर्शनम् ।

दुर्लभा सहजावस्था सद्-गुरोः करुणां विना ।। ९ ।।

durlabho viṣaya–tyāgo durlabhaṁ tattva–darśanam I
durlabhā sahajāvasthā sad–guroḥ karuṇāṁ vinā I I 9 I I

durlabho = durlabhaḥ = difficult to acquire, viṣaya – desired sense objects, tyāgo = tyāgaḥ indifference, durlabhaṁ – difficult to acquire, tattva – essential causes, darśanam – direct perceptional insight, durlabhā – difficult to acquire, sahajāvasthā = sahaja (original) + avasthā (condition), sad = sat = reality perceptive, guroḥ – proficient yoga teacher, karuṇāṁ – special attention, vinā – without

The indifference to desired sense objects is difficult to acquire, and so is attainment of direct perceptional insight into the essential causes. Without special attention of the reality perceptive proficient yoga teacher, it is difficult to realize the original condition.

Analysis

The most frequent desired sense object is sexual expression and reception. Everything having to do with eating for enjoyment's sake, terminates in sexual containment which once it accumulates must be expressed. Even vision terminates in colors and shapes which ultimately are internalized through channels of sexual expression and reception. Indifference to this is difficult to acquire because the psychic material nature sponsors sex expression. If there is no assistance from material nature, the core-self must struggle all by itself against a formidable counter-power.

The attainment of direct perceptional insight into the essential causes is difficult to achieve because the conventional senses are not interested in the origins. They cannot perceive the origins anyway but they have a resistance which is lodged in the psyche, and which makes the yogi's mind reluctant to develop transcendental insight.

As it stands now, according to where we are existentially located, it is difficult if not impossible to realize the original condition. There is no telling how long we were transmigrating in this universe. There is no telling about the indefinite potential for reincarnation. Since our normal existence has no long range memory, we can assume that in the future we will become awake somewhere somehow, like people who went into a coma but who awaken with no memory of their previous identity.

Without help from superior souls, it is doubtful if we could ever make contact with the original condition and if we do, that does not mean that we can remain embedded in it. A tree's realization that it came from a seed, does not give the tree the power to convert itself into that primal state.

Application

It is repeated over and over that unless one has a Satguru, one cannot become liberated, one cannot have access to the chit akash sky of consciousness. This instruction may be contested but only on the basis of not requiring a physical guru. The guru does not have to be physically present but the disciple has to be psychically aware.

There are exceptions to just about every rule. For instance Gautam Buddha was an exception because he attained his transcendental objective without taking instruction from a Satguru. However his uniqueness is rare and should not be cited. He even said that there will not be another person like him for thousands of years.

If a seeker does not have keen psychic perception, it means that his opportunity is limited to having a physical Satguru. The authority must himself have penetrated from here to the spiritual universe. He must know the way from here to there. I said previously that it never opens from this side to the other side. Rather it always opens from the other side to this side. Hence the spiritual master gives the disciple methods of making a soft spot on this side. Then it is likely that there will be a pierce-through from the other side.

Verse 10

विविधैरासनैः कुभैर् विचित्रैः करणैरपि ।

प्रबुद्धायां महा–शक्तौ प्राणः शून्ये प्रलीयते ।। १० ।।

vividhairāsanaiḥ kubhair vicitraiḥ karaṇairapi I
prabuddhāyāṁ mahā–śaktau prāṇaḥ śūnye pralīyate II 10 II

vividhair – with various, āsanaiḥ – with postures, kubhair = kubhaiḥ = with body compression and breath energy distribution, vicitraiḥ – with different, karaṇair =

karaṇaiḥ = by performing, cause, api – also, prabuddhāyāṁ – perceptively aroused, mahā – great, śaktau – subtle creative energy, prāṇaḥ – infused kundalini lifeforce, śūnye – in the mental state devoid of impressions, pralīyate – is absorbed

By performing various postures, different body compressions and breath energy distributions, when the great subtle creative energy is perceptively aroused, then the infused kundalini lifeforce becomes absorbed in the mental state which is devoid of impressions.

Analysis

This is the summary of everything required to create a soft spot on the inner membrane of the psyche so that energy from the divine world can punch through the partition between here and there. A yogi cannot pierce through from this side but he can create a soft spot which would increase the likelihood of an opening being bored through from the divine side. There is only one aspect lacking which is absorption of naad sound resonance. It is lacking here because naad sound is not the result of the effort of the yogi. Naad sound is a free contribution. Everything else which is mentioned in this verse occurs by some effort on the part of the student:

- performing various postures
- different body compressions
- breath energy distributions
- great subtle creative energy is perceptively aroused
- infused kundalini lifeforce becomes absorbed in the mental state which is devoid of impressions

By **performing various postures,** the yogi can target various areas of the psyche to remove used pollutions which linger in hard-to-reach places. The further an area is from the chakra which maintains it, the more likely it is to hoard pollutions. A yogi is required to extract all polluted astral energy from the subtle form. Different postures give different accesses to particular areas.

Those who think that postures are unnatural or that postures are simply a waste of time, should find another way of removing the pollution. They can use will power, mantra sacred sounds, visualization, massage or any other process, provided they get the results intended.

The **different body compressions** are required for concentrating and directing infused energy. The pressures are applied, physically and/or psychically. Willpower may be ineffective at certain stages but physical application may in time cause willpower control. Once the infused breath energy is concentrated, it can be directed to selected parts of the psyche. Under compression, it may also be mixed with subtle hormone energy.

For targeting kundalini and for causing cells to yield their incremental bliss force, the **breath energy distributions** must be mastered by the yogi. Once the yogi infuses fresh air into the system, the lungs will gradually decrease absorption of the air. Then the yogi should apply the locks and focus within to manage the energy distribution. Once the accumulated fresh air moves away from the lungs, the yogi may again do a session of breaths to infuse more air. This is done repeatedly until he is satisfied that all parts of the psyche are fresh air saturated.

The yogi must act in a way, must adjust his lifestyle, so that the **great subtle creative energy is perceptively aroused**. Initially, and this is a great achievement even, the yogi does this by doing breath-infusion in daily practice sessions to create a fresh air energy charge which fuses into the hormonal energy which is in the pubic area. This conjoint force targets the lazy kundalini which resides at the muladhara base chakra. When struck by the air-hormonal force, kundalini moves and because the locks restrict it and blocks it passages, it moves in the only available access which is the sushumna nadi central spinal passage. But this is just the beginning.

For as long as the yogi takes to get this to be a permanent condition with the kundalini always having a clear passage through the central spinal passage, that is as long as the yogi will not realize that the great subtle creative energy is more than the kundalini, that it is in every part of the body, with each cell having a micro-kundalini. A yogi has to act in such a way and adjust the lifestyle so that these cellular micro-kundalinis are perpetually aroused.

A yogi must know what to do in the psyche to cause the **infused kundalini lifeforce to be absorbed in the mental state which is devoid of impressions.** This should not be a hit-and-miss process but something that he can do on a daily basis, preferably twice per day, to bring the mind into a state which is devoid of the conventional thoughts and ideas. The recommended method is pranayama, preferable kapalabhati/bhastrika breath-infusion.

Application

If a yogi does not consistently, on a daily basis, utilize an effective method which causes him to reach the mental state which is devoid of conventional impressions, it is to be understood that his yoga practice will result in failure. The argument about methods, or lineage, falls apart because it does not matter what process one used or what lineage of great teachers one is initiated into or is identified with, if one does not have the blank mind during meditation where the conventional images cease of their own accord or where they are just absent due to the level of the mind content; then it should be admitted that one is not doing kriya yoga and one's practice will result in failure to reach the chit akash.

Verse 11

उत्पन्न–शक्ति–बोधस्य तयक्त–निःशेष–कर्मणः ।

योगिनः सहजावस्था सवयमेव प्रजायते ।। ११ ।।

utpanna–śakti–bodhasya tyakta–niḥśeṣa–karmaṇaḥ |
yoginaḥ sahajāvasthā svayameva prajāyate || 11 ||

utpanna – move up, śakti – subtle creative energy, bodhasya – of spiritual insight, tyakta – abandon, niḥśeṣa – all, karmaṇaḥ – cultural activity, yoginaḥ – of yogis, sahajāvasthā = sahaja (original) + avasthā (condition), svayam – self, eva – also, prajāyate – attains

Once the subtle creative energy moves up with spiritual insight, and all cultural activity is renounced, the yogi, by himself, attains the original existential condition.

Analysis

The original existential condition is the status of the core-self just before it was fused with the psychic adjuncts, especially with the sense of identity. In the primeval condition, there was no material world, either the physical or psychic aspect of it. The self should go to that location, to see what it was when it was all by itself, when it was alone (kaivalyam).

- What was its condition?
- What was its interest?
- What was its involvement?
- Who or what were its relations?
- Can it permanently return to that state?
- How was it shifted into this situation?
- By whom or what was its existence ordered to be here?

Application

For attaining the original existential condition two requirements were listed:

- *subtle creative energy moves up with spiritual insight*
- *cultural activity is renounced*

The ***subtle creative energy moves up with spiritual insight*** *when the kundalini psychic lifeforce is infused with a high grade of subtle energy. Kundalini moves or is aroused but it may do so without spiritual insight. For instance we are familiar with kundalini moving in a pleasurable way during sexual climax experience but few of us consider that to be rendering of spiritual insight. Even though most of the adults in the world are involved on sexual climax experience, we do not experience that most of them express spiritual insight or have a lifestyle which reflects that.*

The ***cultural activity is renounced*** *by the yogi because its involvements are ongoing and it inefficiently consumes time and energy. However we should not conclude that renunciation of cultural activity means that there will be no such activity. There may be. Even so, a yogi will not have a genuine interest in it, even though superficially he may display a concern for it. One essential trick for yogis is to act as if they are concerned even though in fact, they do not give a damn about anything concerning cultural elevation.*

A yogi should not participate like a hungry lion, which chases a deer, kills it violently and then discovers that it has no appetite to eat it. For the lion it is a real chase and there is genuine enthusiasm but for the yogi, none of it has substantiality. Yet, the yogi has to play the game of nature because this is nature's domain and there is nothing to gain by always resisting it. With nature, a yogi should give a little and take a little but always keeping the attention on the yoga objective no matter what.

Verse 12

सुषुम्णा–वाहिनि प्राणे शून्ये विशति मानसे ।

तदा सर्वाणि कर्माणि निर्मूलयति योगवित् ।। १२ ।।

suṣumṇā–vāhini prāṇe śūnye viśati mānase ।
tadā sarvāṇi karmāṇi nirmūlayati yogavit ।। 12 ।।

suṣumṇā – sushumna central spinal passage, vāhini – flushes through, prāṇe – infused breath energy, śūnye – idealess imageless mental content, viśati – enters, mānase – mind, tadā – then, sarvāṇi – all, karmāṇi – cultural activities, nirmūlayati – without grip, yogavit – skilled yogi

When the infused breath energy flushes through the sushumna central spinal passage and the mind enters the idealess imageless mental content, then all cultural activities have no grip on the skilled yogi.

Analysis

A good or bad act which a yogi committed while transmigrating in the present body or in a previous form, cannot adhere to him when he enters the idealess imageless mental content. Breach of moral principles and observation of the same become irrelevant for the yogi while he is in the idealess imageless mental content. This gives the yogi some firsthand idea of what it will be like when he permanently escapes from the conventional existence in the material world.

People sometime balk that a yogi committed a criminal act, and therefore should be held responsible for it, and should be punished sufficiently. Others who favor a yogi say that he committed many virtuous acts and should live on to enjoy the rewards which are due. However an advanced yogi has no connection to pious or impious activities. He relinquishes both reactions to material nature which is the founder, organizer and regulator. Lord Krishna stated it in this way:

yogayukto viśuddhātmā
vijitātmā jitendriyaḥ
sarvabhūtātmabhūtātmā
kurvannapi na lipyate (5.7)

yogayukto = yogayuktaḥ — one proficient in yoga; viśuddhātmā — one of purified self; vijitātmā — one who is self-controlled; jitendriyaḥ — one who has conquered his senses; sarvabhūtātmabhūtātmā = sarva — all + bhūta — being + ātma — self + bhūta — being + ātmā — self (sarvabhūtātmabhūtātmā - one who feels related to all beings); kurvan — acting; api — even; na — not; lipyate — is implicated

A person who is proficient in yoga, whose soul is purified, who is self-controlled, who has conquered his senses, whose self feels related to all beings, is not implicated when acting. (Bhagavad Gita 5.7)

naiva kiṁcitkaromīti
yukto manyeta tattvavit

paśyañśṛṇvanspṛśañjighrann
aśnangacchansvapañśvasan (5.8)

naiva = na — not + eva — indeed; kiṁcit— anything; karomīti = karomi — initiate + iti — thus; yukto = yuktaḥ — proficient in yoga; manyeta — he thinks; tattvavit — knower of reality; paśyan — seeing + śṛṇvan — hearing; spṛśan — touching + jighran — smelling; aśnan — eating; gacchan — walking; svapan — sleeping + śvasan — breathing

"I do not initiate anything." Being proficient in yoga, this is what the knower of reality thinks. While seeing, hearing, touching, smelling, eating, walking, sleeping and breathing, (Bhagavad Gita 5.8)

pralapanvisṛjangṛhṇann
unmiṣannimiṣannapi
indriyāṇīndriyārtheṣu
vartanta iti dhārayan (5.9)

pralapan — talking; visṛjan — evacuating; gṛhṇan — holding; unmiṣan — opening the eyelids; nimiṣan — closing the eyelids; api — also; indriyāṇīndriyārtheṣu = indriyāṇi — senses + indriyārtheṣu — in the attractive objects; vartanta — interlock; iti — thus; dhārayan — considers

...while talking, evacuating, holding, opening and closing the eyelids, he considers, "The senses are interlocked with the attractive objects." (Bhagavad Gita 5.9)

Application

Pranayama breath-infusion practice is so effective and so necessary for this practice, that only a foolish yogi will refuse to learn and practice it. If the subtle body jumps in frequency and goes to a higher plane, it no longer has to respond to its destiny on a lower level. However as soon as it returns to the lower level, it will have to tend to any providence which is current there. The destiny of each plane of consciousness does not necessarily overlap to other levels. A higher plane may not respond in any way to a lower level. Thus if a yogi goes to a higher plane, his karmic destiny will be left on the lower level and will be serviced there by material nature, which may distribute it to others. This will be resulted in some person getting good luck and some other person getting bad luck, so that the yogi's criminal activities will latch on to someone else, while his pious acts may cling to the same or some other person.

Verse 13

अमराय नमस्तुभ्यं सो।अपि कालस्त्वया जितः ।

पतितं वदने यस्य जगद् एतच् चराचरम् ।। १३ ।।

amarāya namastubhyaṁ so।api kālastvayā jitaḥ ।
patitaṁ vadane yasya jagad etac carācaram ।। 13 ।।

amarāya – to the deathless person, namastubhyaṁ – I offer due regards, so = saḥ = he, api – even so, kālas – time approaching as death, tvayā – by you, jitaḥ – conquered, patitaṁ – fallen, vadane – in the mouth, yasya – whom, jagad – world, etac = etat = this, carācaram – mobile and immobile creatures

I offer due regards to the deathless person. Even time approaching as death, in whose mouth, the mobile and immobile creatures of the world are fallen, was conquered by you.

Analysis

Any yogi who has regularly accessed the idealess imageless mental content, is worthy of veneration. Such a person should be regarded as being deathless, meaning that he accessed the deathless region, the chit akash sky of consciousness. More important than honoring such a yogi, is being his submissive student. Those who honor him are likely to inherit his pious karma; while his critics may attract the reactions to his criminal acts. His submissive students are likely to get his method of liberation.

Application

99.99% of the creatures in the material world are doomed to failure. This is because they have little or no spiritual footing. They are pawns of evolution, which itself will spur them on until they get the hint that there may be another existence in which mortality does not play a part. This hint comes from the divine beings who enter the material world and share their understanding of transcendence. It is the presence of these strange aliens, which causes material nature to give a hint of the existence of something besides the material world and its nothingness source-energy.

Anyone who masters this yogic process should be honored as a person who slipped away from the jurisdiction of time, as a prisoner who somehow or the other escaped.

Verse 14

चित्ते समत्वमापन्ने वायौ वरजति मध्यमे ।

तदामरोली वज्रोली सहजोली प्रजायते ।। १४ ।।

citte samatvamāpanne vāyau vrajati madhyame |
tadāmarolī vajrolī sahajolī prajāyate || 14 ||

citte = in the mento–emotional energy, samatvam – equanimity, āpanne – felt, experienced, vāyau – and the lifeforce, vrajati – goes through, madhyame – in the middle channel, tadāmarolī = tadā (then) + amarolī (self–urine consumption), vajrolī – urinary and sexual muscle upward–contraction, sahajolī – upward muscular redirection of female sexual emission, prajāyate – achieve

When the mento–emotional energy is felt as equanimity and the lifeforce goes through the middle channel, then amaroli self–urine consumption, vajroli urinary and sexual muscle upward-contraction, and also sahajoli upward muscular redirection of female sexual emission is achieved.

Analysis

The two requirements are:

- mento-emotional energy is felt as equanimity
- lifeforce goes through the middle channel

The **mento-emotional energy is felt as equanimity** when the kundalini lifeforce abandons its natural residence which is the muladhara base chakra. Kundalini has to be aroused sufficiently to be relocated into the head of the subtle body with the sushumna central passage cleared of all dense astral energy.

There are several causes for the **lifeforce going through the middle channel**. The most reliable one is pranayama breath-infusion, where the compressed breath energy mixes with hormonal force and penetrates into the lazy kundalini, arousing it and causing it to course upwards through the center of the spine.

Application

Swatmarama gave an important piece of information in this verse, that by doing pranayama proficiently, a yogi may not have to do the amaroli, vajroli or sahajoli processes. Why? Because that is the efficiency and thoroughness of a complete kapalabhati/bhastrika breath-infusion process. If one sticks sincerely to the breath-infusion practice, it will in time cause one to achieve much without actually doing everything that may be required if one tries to complete these practices without the pranayama efficiency.

The three practices which may be waivered are:

- *amaroli self-urine consumption*
- *vajroli urinary and sexual muscle upward-contraction*
- *sahajoli upward muscular redirection of female sexual emission*

*The **amaroli self-urine consumption** is not recommended for brahmins, especially those brahmins who do deity worship and chant mantras from the Vedas. There are strict rules for such brahmins as for instance about the use of the right or left hand, with the right hand being used for sacred services and the left being used for profane actions.*

Undue handling of the genitals is not permitted for brahmins unless they are initiated into tantric process and have permission of a powerful yoga-guru or a deity like Shiva Bhairava or Kali Mata.

This writer does not recommend urine consumption because he is not in a lineage which permits it and so far he received no instruction from a yoga-guru or deity to use it. Personally he has no interest in it and does not find it to be necessary. But all the same he is not on a crusade to stop others from using it or from approaching a yoga-guru who recommends it.

*The **vajroli urinary and sexual muscle upward-contraction** is for males, for yogins. It should be practiced as part of the breath-infusion process because when the breath energy is compressed into the blood stream, the energy should be restricted from spreading through the genitals. To achieve this one has to apply this lock. If the genitals are not isolated out of the infused energy, then it will hardly be possible to develop a high enough charge of mixed energy for attacking kundalini at muladhara* *base chakra.*

As far as using those locks during sexual intercourse with a woman, yogis who are involved with females and who feel that they can benefit from this practice, may do it with the understanding that it involves some risk. If one does not have the supervision of a great yogi who mastered this, then one must realize that this may cause one to lose one's footing in the practice. The student must decide for himself how far he should proceed with this.

We find that in yoga, on occasion, a student has to make mistakes and then correct himself. In some cases a practice proves to be merely a waste of time or it may cause digression. In either case, as soon as the student realizes, he should adjust himself and progress further.

*The **sahajoli upward muscular redirection of female sexual emission** is a special practice for females, for yoginis. The problem with this practice is that the female has to have a certain type of body as well as a certain type of destiny to meet a qualified yogin. It is under the direction of a great yogin that a female may succeed using this practice. Irrespective, as with males, this practice has to be used with breath-infusion to restrict the compressed energy from spreading through the genitals. It is also required to draw out sexual potency from the sex organ chakra and offer it into the lazy kundalini for arousing kundalini through the central spine into the brain.*

I recommend the upward muscular redirection of male or female sexual apparatus while doing breath-infusion, so as to compress and direct the infused energy and hormones into the base chakra for arousing kundalini up the spine. This practice does not include a partner but is done by the yogi or yogini alone.

Verse 15

ज्ञायं कुतो मनसि सम्भवतीह तावत्

प्राणो।अपि जीवति मनो म्रियते न यावत् ।

पराणो मनो द्वयमिदं विलयं नयेद्यो

मोक्ष्हं स गच्छति नरो न कथंचिद् अन्यः ।। १५ ।।

jñānaṁ kuto manasi sambhavatīha tāvat
prāṇo|api jīvati mano mriyate na yāvat |
prāṇo mano dvayamidaṁ vilayaṁ nayedyo
mokṣaṁ sa gacchati naro na kathaṁcidanyaḥ || 15 ||

jñānaṁ – insight consciousness, kuto = kutaḥ = how, manasi – mind, sambhavatīha = sambhavati (integrate) + īha (here), tāvat – so long as, prāṇo = prāṇaḥ = lifeforce, api – also, jīvati – pursues mundane existence, mano = manaḥ = mind, mriyate = phased–out, na – not, yāvat – until, prāṇo = prāṇaḥ = lifeforce, mano = manaḥ = mind, dvayam – both, idaṁ – this, vilayaṁ – disappearance, nayed = nayet = obtain, yo = yaḥ = who, mokṣaṁ – liberation, sa – he, gacchati – goes, naro = naraḥ = man, na – not, kathaṁ – how, cid = cit = perceives, anyaḥ – other person

How could there be insight consciousness integrated into the mind, so long as the lifeforce is pursuing mundane existence and the mind was not phased-out? Whoever causes the disappearance of both faculties of the lifeforce and mind, that person perceives liberation not others.

Analysis

Insight consciousness remains conspicuous by its absence in those persons who are dominated by the instincts of the kundalini lifeforce. One has to shake off the influence of the kundalini by arousing and sending it in a hurry up through the spine into the brain. If it is not aroused sufficiently by the breath and hormone energy in the body, it will not do this. Kundalini is dormant power. It can become aroused without doing the yoga process but it is disinclined from doing so. This is why yoga is necessary.

Application

Eventually a yogi must shed the lifeforce completely. This happens just before the yogi attains the siddha status. In the meantime the best practice is the one which results in kundalini remaining aroused with the sushumna nadi central spinal passage cleared of dense astral force.

Verse 16

जज्ञात्वा सुषुम्णासद् –भेदं कृत्वा वायुं च मध्यगम् ।

सथित्वा सदैव सुस्थाने ब्रह्म–रन्ध्रे निरोधयेत् ।। १६ ।।

jñātvā suṣumṇāsad–bhedaṁ kṛtvā vāyuṁ ca madhyagam |
sthitvā sadaiva susthāne brahma–randhre nirodhayet || 16 ||

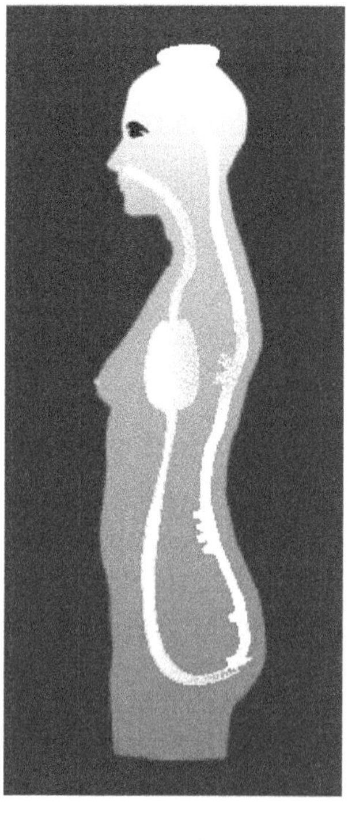

jñātvā – knowing the technique, suṣumṇāsad – subtle central spinal passage, bhedaṁ – piercing through, kṛtvā – making, vāyuṁ – infused air, ca – and, madhyagam – middle course, sthitvā – being situated, sadaiva – always, susthāne – suitable place, brahma–randhre = in the central top of the skull, nirodhayet – should direct

Knowing the technique of piercing the subtle central spinal passage, making the infused air flow through the middle course, always living in a suitable place, the yogi should direct the lifeforce to the central top of the skull.

Analysis

This is the basic kundalini yoga procedure. If one cannot do this on a daily basis, preferably twice per day, it means that one does not have an effective practice and should consult with a yoga-guru who mastered this procedure.

Application

Preferably, a yogi should live in a place where he is not prohibited from doing kundalini yoga. The place should not have hesitation or discouragement energies otherwise his practice will be stalled or will cease completely. No yogi should have the attitude that he can do anything anywhere. It does matter where one is located. Books like the Uddhava Gita, Bhagavad Gita and the Yoga Sutras of Patanjali gave advisories about selecting the place for practice.

A yogi should downplay his importance to humanity and become a humble nobody, so as to find time to practice. A great yogin by the name of Jada Bharata retreated from privileges just to find time to complete austerities.

Verse 17

सूर्य–चन्द्रमसौ धत्तः कालं रात्रिन्दिवात्मकम् ।

भोक्त्री सुषुम्ना कालस्य गुह्यमेतदुदाहृतम् ।। १७ ।।

sūrya–candramasau dhattaḥ kālaṁ rātrindivātmakam
bhoktrī suṣumnā kālasya guhyametadudāhṛtam || 17 ||

sūrya – sun, candramasau – and moon, dhattaḥ – is presented, kālaṁ – time, rātrindivātmakam = rātrin (night) + diva (day) + ātmakam assumes the form, bhoktrī – consumer, suṣumnā – subtle central spinal passage, kālasya – of time, guhyam – secret, etad = etat = this, udāhṛtam – declared

Time assuming the form of day and night, is presented by the sun and moon. The subtle central spinal passage is the consumer of time. This is a secret.

Analysis

The timeless dimensions are in the chit akash sky of consciousness, the divine world. For as long as a yogi is granted access to these places, that is how long he is exempt from the time-occupied zones of the psychic material nature. A genuine taste for timelessness, develops after one peers into a divine atmosphere.

Application

One may imagine infinity and what timelessness may be as an experience, but until one transits into or is allowed peering-access into the divine world, one cannot understand timelessness and cannot long for it, in fact. One single contact with the chit akash sky of consciousness or with a divine being residing in that world, is sufficient to create in the yogi the impetus and longing to be transferred to the divine places.

Verse 18

द्वा–सप्तति–सहस्राणि नाडी–दवाराणि पञ्जरे ।

सुषुम्णा शाम्भवी शक्तिः शेषास् त्व् एव निरर्थकाः ।। १८ ।।

dvā–saptati–sahasrāṇi nāḍī–dvārāṇi pañjare |
suṣumṇā śāmbhavī śaktiḥ śeṣāstveva nirarthakāḥ || 18 ||

dvā – two, saptati – seventy, sahasrāṇi – thousand, nāḍī – nadi subtle veins and arteries, dvārāṇi – entrances, pañjare – in the psyche (body), suṣumṇā – subtle central spinal passage, śāmbhavī – visual focus between the eyebrows, śaktiḥ – subtle creative energy, śeṣās – the others remaining, tv = tu = but, eva – even so, nirarthakāḥ – without value

In the psyche, there are seventy-two thousand (72,000) nadi subtle veins and arteries. When compared to the sushumna nadi subtle central spinal passage where the subtle creative energy originates causing visual focus between the eyebrows, the other nadis are without value.

Analysis

The sushumna nadi central spinal passage is the essential and most important of the subtle passages through which astral energy courses in the subtle form. A student has it as a task to keep this passage cleared of dense energy, to keep the kundalini in it aroused and expressing itself freely upwards through the neck into the brain.

Application

When the kundalini comes into the brain, it seeks out a passage. At first it hesitates for a split second. Then it looks this way and that way to find something to be attracted to. Usually it tries to go through the back of the head but when it makes the effort to do so, it finds that it is turned to the front of the brain because of the strong pull of the buddhi intellect orb. To reach this organ it has to pass the core-self and sense of identity.

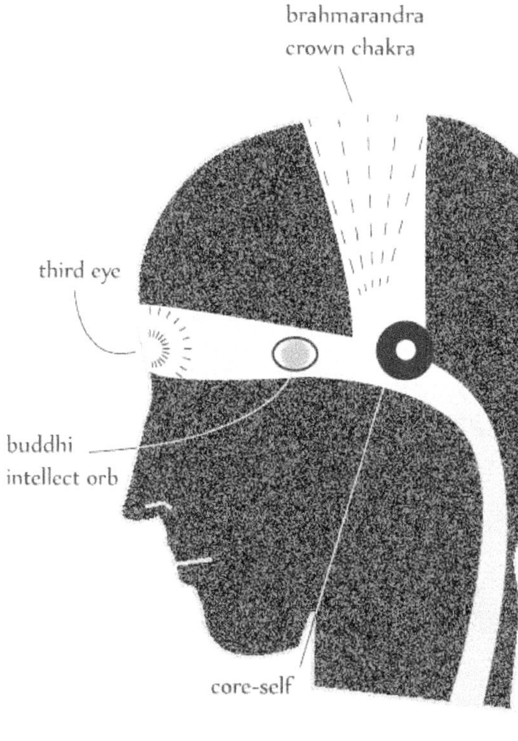

Just before deciding what to do next, the kundalini will usually find itself sinking down through the sushumna nadi central passage; the only way it will not do this is if it has a higher charge of breath-infused energy under it, pushing it. If that charge fizzes out soon after kundalini passes through the neck, kundalini will be lowered back down to muladhara base chakra.

If there is enough infused energy to buoy it up and push it further, kundalini will try to reach the buddhi intellect orb and it will be pulled so that it passes through the edge of the sense of identity before it reaches the intellect orb. If after reaching the orb it still has a charge of energy pushing it, it will either go upward to the brahmarandra crown chakra or to the third-eye brow chakra.

Verse 19

वायुः परिचितो यस्मादग्निना सह कुण्डलीम् ।

बोधयित्वा सुषुम्नायां प्रविशेदनिरोधतः ।। १९ ।।

vāyuḥ paricito yasmādagninā saha kuṇḍalīm I
bodhayitvā suṣumṇāyāṁ praviśedanirodhataḥ II 19 II

vāyuḥ – infused breath energy, paricito = paricitaḥ = directed, yasmād = yasmāt = so that, agninā – by internal heat, saha – with, kuṇḍalīm – kundalini lifeforce, bodhayitvā – insight perception consciousness, suṣumṇāyāṁ – subtle central spinal passage, praviśed = praviśet = should enter, anirodhataḥ – spontaneously

Being directed, having internal heat and fused with kundalini, with insight perception consciousness, the infused breath energy enters the subtle central spinal passage spontaneously.

Analysis

The list of events which affect the infused breath energy is:

- being directed
- having internal heat
- fused with kundalini
- insight perception consciousness

Being directed by the yogi, the infused breath energy reaches certain locations in a compressed form. Then it either scatters or becomes concentrated and forms a pixeled brick-like mass of dense astral energy. Doing breath-infusion haphazardly, not paying attention internally to the accumulated energy, not knowing how to direct it, would result in failure of the practice.

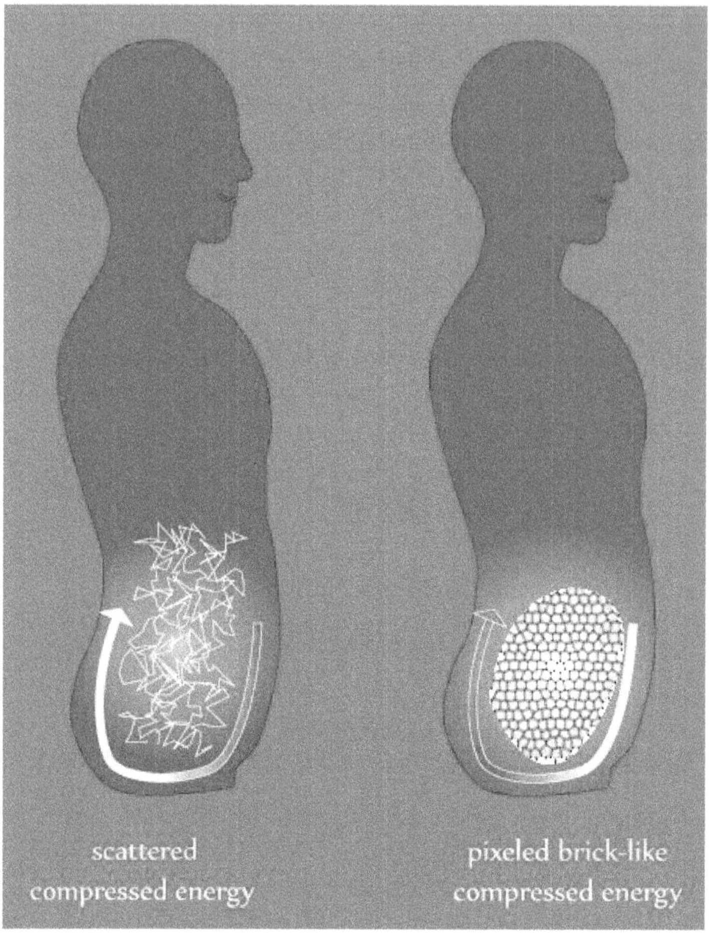

The infused breath energy **acquires internal heat** when it is compressed into the lungs. After it accumulates there on the other side of the alveoli, it buffers against the used air in the blood stream. This conflict causes heat. As the energy is pushed down past the navel, more heat is generated. And as the energy mixes with the reproduction hormones even more heat is generated.

However in the advanced stage, this heating process does not take place because there is no buffering of the fresh air which is infused against the polluted air in the blood stream. Due to repeatedly clearing the system, the fresh air passes without resistance. Instead of heating energy, a cooling energy predominates.

After being directed and being heated, the infused breath-energy **fuses with kundalini**. It does this after it descends through the navel region and groin area. It arcs across to muladhara base chakra where it attaches itself to the kundalini. This causes the kundalini to twist and turn either with some discomfort or with extreme happiness.

Being unified with kundalini, the infused breath energy acquires **insight perception consciousness**, which is a type of emotional intelligence or high-end intuition. With this the kundalini no longer relates to its usual physical body interest. It moves up through the spine into the brain trying to find transcendental objects. By neglecting its conventional concerns, the physical body is left to fend for itself. Thus we see that in some students the physical form falls to the floor. This is because the kundalini lost interest in it and developed a curiosity about what is supernatural or transcendental. If when this happens the core-self does not manage the physical body, it will collapse until the kundalini is no longer aroused and regains the conventional concerns.

Application

Kundalini must be directed by the yogi. One must learn from an advanced teacher how to do this. A lazy happy-go-lucky person cannot change the conventions of the kundalini. One has to be very directive to manage it. Mere will power is insufficient for its control. The higher the level that the subtle body is synchronized to, the more likely one is to control the kundalini.

Verse 20

सुषुम्णा–वाहिनि प्राणे सिद्ध्यत्येव मनोन्मनी ।

अन्यथा त्व् इतराभ्यासाः प्रयासायैव योगिनाम् ।। २० ।।

suṣumṇā–vāhini prāṇe siddhyatyeva manonmanī ।
anyathā tv itarābhyāsāḥ prayāsāyaiva yogināṁ ।। 20 ।।

suṣumṇā – subtle central spinal passage, vāhini – flushes through, prāṇe – in subtle breath energy energy, siddhyaty = siddhayati = is fully accomplished, eva – even so, manonmanī – blank thoughtless idealess mental condition, anyathā – other, tv = tu = but, itarābhyāsāḥ = itara (other) + abhyāsāḥ (practice), prayāsāyaiva = prayāsāya (strenuous) + eva (only), yogināṁ – for the yogi

When subtle breath energy flushes through the subtle central spinal passage, the blank thoughtless idealess mental condition is fully accomplished. But regarding other practices, those are strenuous only for the yogi.

Analysis

Swatmarama shows his preference by sarcastically mentioning other methods as being a strain only. The preferred method for attaining the blank thoughtless idealess mental condition is that the yogi should do a thorough breath-infusion before sitting to meditate.

Application

There are other practices, some Vedic and some otherwise, of which the teacher attests to the validity. However Swatmarama explained that when the subtle breath energy flushes the subtle central passage, the blank thoughtless idealess mental condition is fully accomplished. This means that when the subtle central spinal passage is completely flushed of dense astral force, the mind will assume a blank state. If kundalini's entry through the subtle channel only removes some dense energy, there will not be a blank state but rather a partially blank one.

Alternately if someone has not done breath-infusion and has used another method which resulted in the blank thoughtless idealess mental condition, we can assume that his sushumna central spinal passage was cleared for the duration of the thoughtless condition.

Verse 21

पवनो बध्यते येन मनस्तेनैव बध्यते ।

मनश् च बध्यते येन पवनस्तेन बध्यते ।। २१ ।।

pavano badhyate yena manastenaiva badhyate I
manas ca badhyate yena pavanastena badhyate II 21 II

pavano = pavanaḥ = infused breath energy, badhyate – forcefully compressed and directed, yena – by whom, manas – mind, tenaiva = tena (by which) + eva (only), badhyate – forcefully compressed and directed, manaś = manas = mind, ca – and, badhyate – forcefully compressed and directed, yena – by whom, pavanas – infused breath energy, tena – by which, badhyate – forcefully compressed and directed

Whosoever forcefully compresses and directs the infused breath energy, in turn, causes the mind to be likewise controlled. Conversely, if the mind is compressed and directed, the infused breath energy is controlled.

Analysis

The relationship between the infused breath energy and the mind's blank or thought-ridden condition is direct. One can forcefully compress and direct the infused breath energy, which will result in a thought free blank mental condition, or one may compress and direct the mind and that will in turn cause any breath energy to be efficiently channeled.

The control of infused breath energy causes mind control, and the contrary is applicable as well. Gautam Buddha successfully used the method of compressing and directing the mind (manas ca badhyate).

Application

The recommendation by Patanjali and Swatmarama is the pranayama breath-infusion. If however one can use another system which gives the result, there is no objection.

Verse 22

हेतु–दवयं तु चित्तस्य वासना च समीरणः ।

तयोर् विनष्ट एकस्मिन्तौ द्वावपि विनश्यतः ।। २२ ।।

hetu–dvayaṁ tu cittasya vāsanā ca samīraṇaḥ
tayor vinaṣṭa ekasmintau dvāvapi vinaśyataḥ

hetu – cause, dvayaṁ – two, tu – in fact, cittasya – of the mento–emotional energy, vāsanā – desire energy, ca – and, samīraṇaḥ – lifeforce energy, tayor – tayoḥ – of these, vinaṣṭa – elimination, ekasmin – one, tau – both, dvāv = dvāu = two, api – also, vinaśyataḥ – elimination

There are two causes of the stimulation of the mento-emotional energy, namely, desire and lifeforce energy. Of these the elimination of one is the elimination of both.

Analysis

The mento-emotional energy changes in condition either by desire or lifeforce energy. Of the two, desire is the easiest, except that the mento-emotional energy may be unresponsive to it. Desire is a sophisticated technology but it is unreliable. Lifeforce manipulation through breath-infusion is more primitive but it is definitely responsive. Kundalini is a primitive instinct used in all life-forms. Because of its primeval construction, it requires a mechanical rather than psychological motivation.

Application

Many persons feel that by desire alone they can bring the mento-emotional energy to order. Provided it works, this feeling is fine. For definite results and for changing deep within, the pranayama breath-infusion for influencing the lifeforce, is recommended.

Verse 23

मनो यत्र विलीयेत पवनस्तत्र लीयते ।

पवनो लीयते यत्र मनस्तत्र विलीयते ।। २३ ।।

mano yatra vilīyeta pavanastatra līyate I
pavano līyate yatra manastatra vilīyate II 23 II

mano = manaḥ = mind, yatra – whenever, vilīyeta – becomes quiescent, pavanas – lifeforce, tatra – there, līyate – is stilled, pavano = pavanaḥ = lifeforce, līyate – is stilled, yatra – when, manas – mind, tatra – there, vilīyate – becomes quiescent

Whenever the mind becomes quiescent, the lifeforce is stilled. Conversely when the lifeforce is stilled, the mind becomes quiescent.

Analysis

The condition of mind is a direct indication about the status of the lifeforce. Conversely the behavior of the lifeforce gives the clue about the state of mind.

Application

If the mind and lifeforce were one and the same aspect, this statement would be meaningless. Swatmarama felt that the mind was not the lifeforce. The mind is the head part of the subtle body, while the kundalini is resides in the subtle spinal passage of that same body. During the life of the physical form the kundalini resides more on the physical side than on the subtle side. It may be admitted that even though it is a psychic force the kundalini is obsessed with physical perception. Because the mind is affected by the condition of the kundalini, it is imperative that the kundalini be upgraded for improving the mind content.

Verse 24

दुग्धाम्बुवत्संमिलितावुभौ तौ

तुल्य–क्रियौ मानस–मारुतौ हि ।

यतो मरुत्तत्र मनः–प्रवृत्तिर

यतो मनस्तत्र मरुत–प्रवृत्तिः ।। २४ ।।

dughdhāmbuvatsaṁmilitāvubhau tau
tulya–kriyau mānasa–mārutau hi I
yato maruttatra manaḥ–pravṝttir
yato manastatra marut–pravṝttiḥ II 24 II

dughdhāmbuvat = dughdha (milk) + āmbuvat (like water), saṁmilitāv = saṁmilitāu = fused, ubhau – two, tau – both, tulya – equal, kriyau – both activities, mānasa – with the mind, mārutau – with breath–infused kundalini energy, hi – indeed, yato = yataḥ = where, marut – breath–infused kundalini energy, tatra – there, manaḥ – mind, pravṝttir – movement, yato = yataḥ = where, since, manas – mind, tatra – there, marut = breath–infused kundalini energy, pravṝttiḥ – movement

Like milk and water, both the mind and the breath-infused kundalini energy are reflected in each other's activities. Wherever there is breath-infused kundalini energy there is the movement of the mind, and wherever the mind is there is movement of the breath-infused kundalini energy.

Analysis

With milk and water, if they are put together, there is some give and take, depending on the percentage of each liquid in the mix. This is an apt analogy because the condition of the breath-infused kundalini energy directly affects the condition of mind, and conversely the mind affects the kundalini.

What happens if the kundalini is not breath-infused, if the person does not do pranayama?

In that case the same equation applies because the kundalini is always breath-infused. Pranayama is merely a way of increasing the extent to which the kundalini is fresh air breath-infused.

Application

A student should study how breath-infusion affects the kundalini and the mind. It is not a matter of having confidence in a process of pranayama. It is not a belief method. It is not based on the power to visualize changes in the psyche. One should make a test by learning pranayama from an advanced teacher, then doing it for the specified time, then sitting to meditate and testing to see what effect it has on the mind.

One should meditate without doing pranayama. Then meditate immediately after doing it. Then compare to see if there is a difference. There is no superstition in this process. It should be tested. If there are no results or if the result goes to the negative, one should cease the practice.

Verse 25

तत्रैक–नाशादपरस्य नाश

एक–प्रवृत्तेरप्र–प्रवृत्तिः ।

अध्वस्तयोश् चेन्द्रिय–वर्ग–वृत्तिः

प्रध्वस् तयोर् मोक्ष–पदस्य सिद्धिः ।। २५ ।।

tatraika–nāśādaparasya nāśa
eka–pravṝtterapara–pravṝttiḥ |
adhvastayoś cendriya–varga–vṝttiḥ
pradhvas tayor mokṣa–padasya siddhiḥ || 25 ||

tatraika = there in relation to one, nāśād = nāśāt = from suspension, aparasya – of the other, nāśa – suspension, eka – one, pravṝtter = pravṝtteḥ = movement, apara – other, pravṝttiḥ – movement, adhvas – flow, tayoś = tayoḥ = two, cendriya = ca (and) + indriya (senses), varga – category, vṝttiḥ – function, pradhvas – cessation, tayor – of their, mokṣa – liberation, padasya – of the situation, siddhiḥ – success

In relation, the suspension of one is the suspension of the other. The movement of one is the movement of the other. When they flow the senses get involved in their functions. When they are in cessation, success with the situation of liberation is attained.

Analysis

This is the suspension which results from the full arousal of kundalini. There is also a suspension which comes from the full sleeping of kundalini which results in stupor or jada samadhi, fusion into full-blown lack of awareness.

Application

Sri Patanjali Maharshi alerted all yogis that the flow of the mento-emotional energy causes the senses to be involved in their functions. That is converse to yoga. It is a description of the senses which are oriented to material nature. When those senses are put out of commission, and when the person is wide awake, then another group of senses is experienced. Those are the supernatural and spiritual perceptive means.

Verse 26

रसस्य मनसश् चैव चञ्चलत्वं स्वभावतः ।

रसो बद्धो मनो बद्धं किं न सिद्ध्यति भूतले ।। २६ ।।

rasasya manasaś caiva cañcalatvaṁ svabhāvataḥ |
raso baddho mano baddhaṁ kiṁ na siddhyati bhūtale || 26 ||

rasasya – of quicksilver, manasaś – mind, caiva – and also, cañcalatvaṁ – shifty, svabhāvataḥ – what is inherent, raso = rasaḥ = mercury, baddho = baddhaḥ = what is compressed and channeled, mano = manaḥ = mind, baddhaṁ – what is compressed and channeled, kiṁ – what, na – not, siddhyati – accomplishes, bhūtale – in the world

Inherently, quicksilver and the mind are shifty. In this world, what cannot be accomplished when these are compressed and channeled?

Analysis

Quicksilver is much like the mind. It glitters. We are attracted to it. It moves quickly. We have problems trapping, confining and making it do our bid. As scientists took centuries to understand the atomic composition of mercury, so it takes quite some time to understand the components of consciousness and the situation of the mind.

Application

When the mind is isolated, observed and regulated, the yogi can find a way to transcend the reality of material nature. He will not change this nature ever but he does not have to remain in its jurisdiction either.

Verse 27

मूर्च्छितो हरते व्याधीन् मृतो जीवयति स्वयम् ।

बद्धः खेचरतां धत्ते रसो वायुश् च पार्वति ॥२७॥

mūrcchito harate vyādhīn mṛto jīvayati svayam I
baddhaḥ khecaratāṁ dhatte raso vāyuś ca pārvati I I27

mūrcchito = mūrcchitaḥ = disabled, harate – controlled, vyādhīn – piercing, mṛto = mṛtaḥ = death, jīvayati – lives, svayam – itself, baddhaḥ – what is compressed and channeled, khecaratāṁ – procedure for transiting through kha divine space, dhatte – gives, raso = rasaḥ = quicksilver, vāyuś = vāyuḥ = breath energy, ca – and, pārvati – Parvati

It is controlled when disabled. It gives life when there is death. When it is compressed and channeled, it causes transit through kha divine space. Quicksilver and breath energy gives that, O Parvati.

Analysis

The disabling of breath energy is not a competitive method where the ascetic suspends breathing during, before, or after an in-breath or out-breath. It is not kumblak or exhaling and suspending breath movement for as long as one can bear. Neither is it rechak or inhaling and suspending breath movement.

It is a spontaneous behavior which the psyche assumes because it has an excess of fresh air and has an absence of polluted gases. The student should do pranayama breath-infusion for as long as is required to achieve this excess of fresh air and lack of pollution. Then the psyche will have no anxiety for breath because of having a full charge of fresh air with no exhaustion in the form of polluted gases. Whatever pranayama should be done to achieve this, should be performed, for as long as is required to flush out the polluted gasses and compress in the fresh air energy.

Application

This instruction was originally given to Parvati, Shiva's consort. The Lord explained this to her as she was his first student.

Verse 28

मनः सथैर्यं सथिरो वायुस्ततो बिन्दुः सथिरो भवेत् ।

बिन्दु– स्थैर्यात्सदा सत्त्वं पिण्ड– स्थैर्यं प्रजायते ।। २८ ।।

manaḥ sthairyaṁ sthiro vāyustato binduḥ sthiro bhavet I
bindu–sthairyātsadā sattvaṁ piṇḍa–sthairyaṁ prajāyate II 28 II

manaḥ – mind, sthairyaṁ – stabilized, sthiro = sthiraḥ = steady, vāyus – breath energy, tato = tataḥ = hence, binduḥ – reproduction hormone concentrate, sthiro = sthiraḥ = steady, bhavet – is, becomes, bindu – reproduction hormone concentrate, sthairyāt – due to stability, sadā – regular, sattvaṁ – charifying influence, piṇḍa – subtle body, sthairyaṁ – stability, prajāyate – produces

When the mind is stabilized and the breath energy is steady, then the reproduction hormone concentrate also becomes stabilized. From the stability of the reproduction hormone concentrate, there arises stability of the subtle body and regular clarifying influence.

Analysis

The reproductive hormone concentrate is a troublesome energy for the yogi. It can be harnessed so that it reinforces the spiritual practice but that requires a certain amount of effort. Some yogis because of their past life affiliation with that energy must strive for days, weeks, months, years or even lives, to reel this energy in. Its main compulsion is expression. The yogi has to curtail its expression regularly and then over time, he will notice that its extrovert tendency reduces considerably. This is a personal energy which means that each yogi must struggle with it himself or herself.

While one yogi can substantially curtail his reproductive energy in a jiffy, another one might struggle for years or lives to attain the same degree of control. Each student should tackle the problem in a personal way. When this energy is stabilized, there arises stability of the subtle body and regular clarifying influence so that the yogi becomes exempt from most of the sexual approaches which otherwise would manifest as his or her destiny.

Application

In cases where there are mandatory sexual expressions, which are forced into the life of a yogi by the time factor, by unavoidable destiny, the yogi, if he made enough effort to curtail sexual expression, will be inspired with the technique for not becoming bogged down by the involvements. But in any case, sexual expression was always noted as a bane of yoga, and a reason for the disintegration of advancement. As one should never trust a viper, a yogi should never feel safe with sexual expression.

Verse 29

इन्द्रियाणां मनो नाथो मनोनाथस्तु मारुतः ।
मारुतस्य लयो नाथः स लयो नादमाश्रितः ।। २९ ।।

indriyāṇāṁ mano nātho manonāthastu mārutaḥ I
mārutasya layo nāthaḥ sa layo nādamāśritaḥ I I 29 I I

indriyāṇāṁ – senses, mano = manaḥ = mind, nātho = nāthaḥ = manager, manonāthas – controller of the mind, tu – indeed, mārutaḥ – breath–infused energy, mārutasya – of the breath–infused energy, layo = layaḥ = blank thoughtless idealess mental condition, nāthaḥ – master, sa – that, layo = layaḥ = blank thoughtless idealess mental condition, nādam – naad supernatural sound resonance, āśritaḥ – is reliant on

The mind is the manager of the senses but indeed, the breath–infused energy is the controller of the mind. The mind is mastered by the blank thoughtless idealess mental condition, which is reliant on the naad supernatural sound resonance.

Analysis

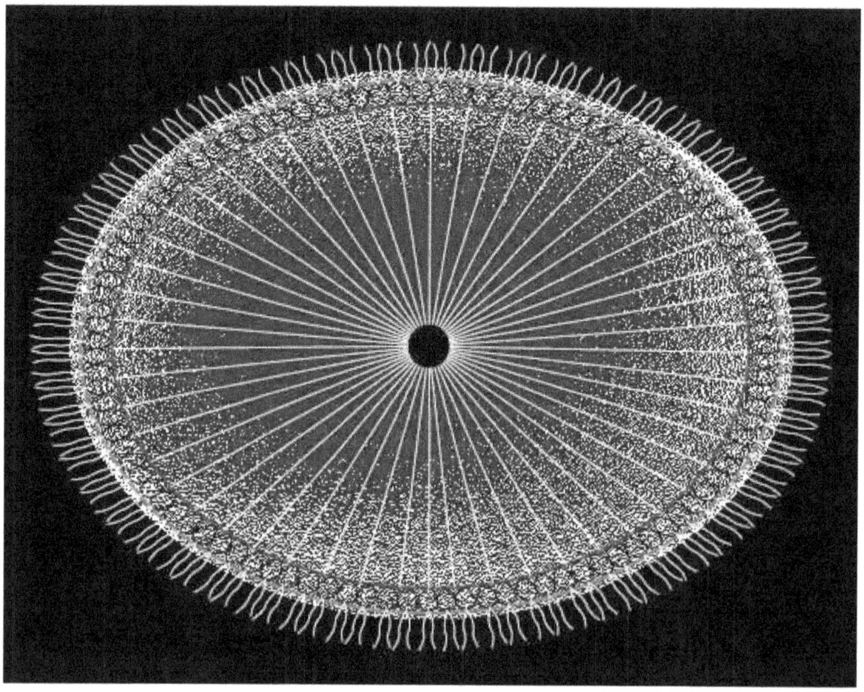

The senses operate on the surface membrane of the mind. The mind itself is primarily in the head of the subtle body, with the sensual orbs on that surface facing forward. At first when a limited self becomes aware in the psychic material nature, that self has a spherical configuration with a sensing membrane as its only sense. At that time its singular sense organ which is its psychic membrane serves to distinguish it from and give it information about everything else. In that stage proximity is its only fear and so the sense of touch becomes predominant. Within its psyche, it is all about feeling but that converts into the tactile sense at the edge of its membrane which is a spherical psychic skin. According to the environment it finds itself in, according to the neighborhood, the psyche develops particular senses in particular order according to its survival needs.

In this verse, the term mind has a dual meaning as the buddhi intellect orb and as the mental environment in the head of the subtle body. It is important to know which meaning is used. Clarity is important in kundalini yoga. The subtle head as a whole may be considered as a sensing device, as the mind. The contents of the subtle head may also be considered to be the mind. The buddhi intellect orb which does the analytical calculations may also be considered as the mind.

When the mind is the manager of the senses, it may be the buddhi intellect orb or it may be the general collective of the subtle head which has several components acting rapidly in unison as the mind. The screen of a computer monitor shows the user many things which are formed on the screen from various inputs from within the machine. The computer is regarded as one item even though it is a composite of devices.

The buddhi intellect orb manages the senses but it is not the only monitor of the sensual activities. There is also sensual energy which comes from the trunk of the subtle body which takes control of the senses and directs their pursuits.

Breath-infused energy sets the tone or mood of the mind. The mind accepts breath-infused energy as its fuel for operations. The quality of this infused energy directly causes the mind to operate in a certain way. The energy in the psyche is always breath-infused. It is a question of what quality of air or gas is it infused with.

Application

The blank thoughtless idealess mental condition is the compliment to the naad sound resonance. In ideal meditation conditions, one side of the mind will have the blank thoughtless idealess mental condition. On the other side there will be the naad sound resonance. The core-self should establish itself in the naad resonance, where it should silently wait for the blank condition to open to the chit akash sky of consciousness.

Some yogis gave the center of the eyebrows, the third eye, as the place at which the chit akash opens. However, it can open from anywhere in the blank thoughtless idealess mental condition. It may open from up above, from the right, left, center top or bottom. This is why it is important not to put a sharp focus on the center of the eyebrows when doing this practice of being in naad sound resonance and looking ahead in the subtle body. Pressure from this side, desire from this side will not open the chit akash sky of consciousness. Therefore the yogi should simply wait patiently for the event to happen of its own accord.

Verse 30

सो।अयमेवास्तु मोक्षाख्यो मास्तु वापि मतान्तरे ।

मनः–प्राण–लये कश्चिद् आनन्दः सम्प्रवर्तते ।। ३० ।।

so ayamevāstu mokṣākhyo māstu vāpi matāntare |
manaḥ–prāṇa–laye kaścid ānandaḥ sampravartate || 30 ||

so = saḥ = that, ayam – this, evāstu = eva (so) + astu (is), mokṣākhyo = mokṣākhyaḥ = called liberation, māstu = mā (not) + astu (is), vāpi = or as well, matāntare – in a different opinion, manaḥ – mind, prāṇa – subtle breath energy, laye – in the blank thoughtless idealess mental condition, kaścid – anyone, ānandaḥ – spiritual pleasure, sampravartate – is experienced

That specific blank thoughtless idealess mental condition is called liberation or those who are of a different opinion say it is not so. For anyone, the blank thoughtless idealess mental condition which is the result of infused subtle breath energy's influence in the mind, is experienced, as spiritual pleasure.

Analysis

It does not matter what the critics say. These procedures do not have to fit the description of perfection or near-perfection for every group of yogis or ascetics. If this process seems to be the thing for you, use it. Check it to see if it gives the results intended. If it does not, then find another process.

When the blank thoughtless idealess mental condition happens as a result of infused subtle breath energy's influence in the mind, it yields spiritual pleasure but a bliss-energy without the lusty flavor. In sexual climax experience, there is bliss energy with lust excitement and responses in it, but when the infused breath energy attacks kundalini at muladhara base chakra, arousing it, its transit through the central spine into the brain, causes kundalini to consume the lust aspect. Thus when kundalini enters the head it has a lust-free content.

Application

The blank thoughtless idealess mental condition is called liberation. It takes a long time for a student to accomplish this. It is a protracted struggle to get the mind to abandon its conventional mental displays and emotional influences. When at last the yogi accomplishes a natural mental condition which is blank and thoughtless, he rightly and proudly declares success. It is not the full success but it is the stage before chit akash transit. It facilitates immersion in naad sound resonance and makes the yogi become more and more compatible with the divine environment.

Patanjali declared that the blank thoughtless idealess mental condition is the precursor for yoga. If the yogi does not begin meditation there or on a level which is higher, he is not doing meditation. He may be preparing for meditation.

Verse 31

प्रनष्टश्वासनिश्वासः प्रध्वस्तविषयग्रहः ।
निश्चेष्टो निर्विकारश्च लयो जयति योगिनाम् ॥ ३१ ॥

pranaṣṭa–śvāsa–niśvāsaḥ pradhvasta viṣaya–grahaḥ |
niśceṣṭo nirvikāraś ca layo jayati yoginām ||31||

pranaṣṭa – suspension, śvāsa–niśvāsaḥ = respiration, pradhvasta – cessation, viṣaya – sense objects, grahaḥ – grasping, niśceṣṭo = niśceṣṭaḥ = motionless, nirvikāraś – without changes, ca – and, layo = layaḥ = blank thoughtless idealess mental condition, jayati – achieves, yogināṃ – yogi

With the suspension of respiration and the cessation of the tendency of grasping the sense objects, when the mind is motionless and without changes, the yogi achieves the blank thoughtless idealess mental condition.

Analysis

The specific blank thoughtless idealess mental condition, which serves the purpose for this yoga discipline, is qualified on these conditions:

- suspension of respiration
- cessation of the tendency of grasping the sense objects
- mind is motionless and without changes

The method for **suspension of respiration** is to infuse fresh air into the blood stream and to do so until the polluted gases are displaced by fresh energy. It is not a matter of how long a person can suspend breathing. The measure is how much of the polluted gases he can extract, and how much fresh air he infuses into the body. The suspension occurs when the body finds that it has to make no effort to procure fresh air, because it is so saturated that it spontaneously ceases the effort to acquire it.

The **cessation of the tendency of grasping the sense objects** becomes manifest when the yogi has completed the extraction of his interest energy from the frontal part of the subtle head, and has replaced that pursuit with interest in the components of the consciousness. This is the completion of the pratyahar sensual energy withdrawal fifth stage of yoga. It is assisted by completion of the pranayama breath infusing fourth stage of yoga, because in that stage one upgrades the energy in the subtle body, which causes the mind to lose interest in conventional ideas.

The condition where the **mind is motionless and without changes** occurs when the content energy in the mind changes, where the conventional operations are no longer supported and no longer can occur because of having no supportive energy which may invoke memories and create fantasies.

Application

Some yogis use the method of forcing the mind to abandon its conventions of ideation and imaging. They use brute willpower in the effort to command the mind to cease thinking and remembering operations. However, so long as the lifestyle is counterproductive to the interest of yoga, the mind will have the power to resist the willpower.

Verse 32

उच्छिन्नसर्वसङ्कल्पो निःशेषाशेषचेष्टितः ।

स्वावगम्यो लयः कोऽपि जायते वागगोचरः ॥३२॥

ucchinna sarva–saṅkalpo niḥśeṣāśeṣa ceṣṭitaḥ I
svāvagamyo layaḥ ko'pi jāyate vāg–agocaraḥ II32II

ucchinna – are absent, sarva – all, saṅkalpo = saṅkalpaḥ = intentions, niḥśeṣāśeṣa – totally absent, ceṣṭitaḥ – enthusiams, svāvagamyo = sva (self) + avagamyaḥ (intuition), layaḥ = blank thoughtless idealess mental condition, ko'pi = kaḥ (who) + api (also), jāyate – achieve, vāg = vāk = speech, agocaraḥ – inconceivable

When all intentions are absent and the enthusiasms are totally absent, then the self-intuition, which is inconceivable and indescribable, occurs in a blank thoughtless idealess mental condition.

Analysis

Unless the conventional intentions and enthusiasms are booted out, the yogi cannot use the self-intuition. This means that he cannot reach the divine environment. He will be bogged down by the psychic and/or physical material nature. The mistake in this endeavor is to think that the intentions and enthusiasm can be booted out of the mind when the mind remains on the conventional level of consciousness which a person is endowed with freely by material nature.

It is not possible to remove the conventions in the mind while the mind is on the lower planes of consciousness because these demeanors are native to such levels. A yogi can suppress and he can put into dormancy the conventions but he cannot eliminate them on the lower planes. The way to get rid of these conventions is to depart from the lower levels. The yogi should leave those planes intact and migrate to a higher one where naturally the conventions are conspicuous by their absence.

I have many stubborn students who simply refuse to accept this truth and who insist on cleaning up the conventional levels of the mind. They are failures. As long as they cannot hear what I am saying and will not put my advice into practice, they will remain as blighted yogis.

Application

Yogis who buy into the idea that one can reach the divine world by doing physical deity worship without meditating deeply to make contact with the deity in the divine world, cannot be successful in this practice. Those who feel that the blank thoughtless idealess mental condition is against personal worship of God or against Krishna Consciousness cannot be successful either. A yogi must nurture the blank thoughtless idealess mental condition for some time, at least until his mind is totally weaned away from its thought and image producing tendency, even its tendency to create images of valid deities like Krishna through visualization in the mind.

Reaching a voidal blank state of mind in meditation is a spiritual achievement. It is not a way of avoiding the Personality of Godhead in the spiritual world. For that matter one cannot develop access to a spiritual body with spiritual senses unless one uses the voidal blank state of mind to wean the self away from the conventional imagining features of the mind. A yogi devotee must agree to put down everything which is visualized on this side of existence, even images of the Deity created in the mind. When this is achieved then it becomes possible to use spiritual senses in a spiritual body to see the Deity in his spiritual features in a totally spiritual environment.

Verse 33

यत्र दृष्टिर्लयस्तत्र भूतेन्द्रिय–सनातनी ।

सा शक्तिर्जीव–भूतानां द्वे अलक्ष्ये लयं गते ।। ३३ ।।

yatra dṝṣṭirlayastatra bhūtendriya–sanātanī I
sā śaktirjīva–bhūtānāṁ dve alakṣye layaṁ gate II 33 II

yatra – where, dṝṣṭir = dṝṣṭiḥ = insight perception, layas – blank thoughtless idealess mental condition, tatra – there, bhūtendriya – sensual material nature, sanātanī – eternal, sā – that, śaktir = śaktiḥ = subtle energy, jiva – individual, bhūtānāṁ – living beings, dve – two, alakṣye – uncharacteristic, layaṁ – blank thoughtless idealess mental condition, gate – is absorbed

Where there is insight perception, there is the blank thoughtless idealess mental condition. Then that subtle energy which is in the individual living beings, is absorbed in the blank thoughtless idealess mental condition, without characteristics.

Analysis

Insight perception occurs from the neutrality of the mind which is experienced as its blank thoughtless idealess mental condition. From that location, the mind becomes open to transcendental dimensions. This allows the core-self which is trapped in the psyche to escape to higher dimensions of the astral existence, to the causal plane, and to the chit akash divine sky of consciousness.

Application

A yogi should not be afraid of the blank thoughtless idealess mental condition. It occurs when the mind is void of conventionally manufactured ideas and images, even religiously-oriented compositions which are based on valid scriptural references. There is a time for putting aside the mental and emotional constructions which are based on this side of existence.

There is a blank place between here in the material existence and there in the divine world; a yogi should not be afraid to go into that blankness. He should patiently wait in it, for being granted access to the divine world.

There are two blank states, one inferior which is derived from a struggle with the mind, and one superior that comes as a result of first upgrading the mind through breath-infusion in removing polluted psychic energy from the subtle form.

A yogi should use the superior method but those who do not know pranayama procedures may struggle with mind until it relaxes and loses interest in ideation and imaging. The superior method using breath-infusion is encouraging because it has a mild bliss aspect to it which encourages the yogi to wait. It also affords the yogi contact with the naad sound.

Verse 34

लयो लय इति प्राहुः कीदृशं लय–लक्षणम् ।

अपुनर–वासनोत्थानाल्लयो विषय–विस्मृतिः ।। ३४ ।।

layo laya iti prāhuḥ kīdṛśaṁ laya–lakṣaṇam |
apunar–vāsanotthānāllayo viṣaya–vismṛtiḥ || 34 ||

layo = layaḥ = blank thoughtless idealess mental condition, laya – blank thoughtless idealess mental condition, iti – thus, prāhuḥ – they say, kīdṛśaṁ – what kind, laya – blank thoughtless idealess mental condition, lakṣaṇam – characteristic, apunar – not again, vāsanotthānāl = due to upheaval of desires, layo = layaḥ = blank thoughtless idealess mental condition, viṣaya – sense objects, vismṛtiḥ – non–recollection

They stress thoughtlessness, but what are its characteristics? It is the non–recollection of the sense objects due to there being no more upheaval of desires.

Analysis

Even though it is near impossible for any human being, even the ascetic and pseudo ascetics to attain it, thoughtlessness is stressed by many sects. There is a global scam where spiritual sects advertise thoughtlessness as a condition which their process can yield. Honesty is hard to come by in spiritual circles, especially in the ones which have a commercial or popularity interest. They will advocate anything to increase the membership. What, however, is the real situation of mind control? What is the possibility of making the mind thoughtless?

Application

The condition of thoughtlessness as Swatmarama intended has two components:

- *non–recollection of the sense objects*
- *no upheaval of desires*

First there must be ***no upheaval of desires.*** *How should the mind be brought into a condition where there is no manifestation of current, past or potential desires having to do with whatever was encountered in the physical world? If there is upheaval of desires, there will be recollection of sense objects. The secret is to bring the mind into a desire-less stage where no images and ideas are manifesting.*

If there is no upheaval of desires, there will be ***no recollection of sense objects*** *which relate to those desires. The mind will remain neutral. It will not be depressed or elated. It will not have boredom or enthusiasm. It will not hanker or lament. It will have sober awareness with some slight bliss aspect.*

Verse 35

वेद–शास्त्र–पुराणानि सामान्य–गणिका इव ।

एकैव शाम्भवी मुद्रा गुप्ता कुल–वधूरिव ।। ३५ ।।

veda–śāstra–purāṇāni sāmānya–gaṇikā iva |
ekaiva śāmbhavī mudrā guptā kula–vadhūriva || 35 ||

veda – Vedas, śāstra – Vedic scriptures, purāṇāni – ancient, sāmānya – common, gaṇikā – prostitute, iva – like, ekaiva = as one, śāmbhavī – visual focus between the eyebrows, mudrā = mystic–arresting actions, guptā – secluded, kula–vadhūr = kula–vadhūḥ = aristocratic lady, iva – comparable

The Vedas and ancient Vedic scriptures are like common prostitutes, while the mystic–arresting action of shambhavi visual focus between the eyebrows is the one technique which is comparable to a secluded aristocratic lady.

Analysis

The Vedas have value and so do the ancient Vedic scriptures which developed from the history of the people who produced and adhered to the Vedas, and yet when compared to transcendental experience which comes from using the mystic-arresting action of visual focus between the eyebrows, those scriptures lose their primacy.

In the Bhagavad Gita, Lord Krishna made this statement:

na hi jñānena sadṛśaṁ
pavitramiha vidyate
tatsvayaṁ yogasaṁsiddhaḥ
kālenātmani vindati (4.38)

na — nothing; hi — indeed; jñānena — with direct experience; sadṛśaṁ — compared with; pavitram — purifier; iha — in this world; vidyate — is relevant; tat — that realization; svayaṁ — himself; yogasaṁsiddhaḥ = yoga — yoga practice + saṁsiddhaḥ— perfected; kālenātmani = kālena — in time + ātmani — in the self; vindati — he locate

Nothing, indeed, can be compared with direct experience. No other purifier is as relevant in this world. That man who himself is perfected in yoga practice, will in time, locate the realization in himself. (Bhagavad Gita 4.38)

Application

The Vedas and its corollaries may be compared to the common prostitute, because everybody and anybody may approach those texts or listen to lectures based on those scriptures, and develop some hope for salvation. In practice however, the Vedas were always the exclusive property of caste brahmins, most of whom kept it under lock and key and only doled out a little of it at a time to selected audiences.

Still, no matter how the Vedas were a monopoly of families who were versed in Sanskrit recitation and Vedic rituals, that cannot be compared with the yoga techniques which are practiced individually and not collectively in religious ceremonies.

As an aristocratic lady remains secluded and is known only to one man, so the yogic process is only for the individual student who privately practices under tight supervision of the yoga-guru.

Verse 36

अथ शाम्भवी

अन्तर्लक्ष्यं बहिर्दृष्टिर्निमेषोन्मेषवर्जिता ।

एषा सा शाम्भवी मुद्रा वेदशास्त्रेषु गोपिता ॥ ३६ ॥

atha śāmbhavī
antarlakṣyaṁ bahirdṛṣṭirnimeṣonmeṣa–varjitā I
eṣā sā śāmbhavī mudrā veda–śāstreṣu gopitā I I36I I

atha – now to describe, śāmbhavī – visual focus between the eyebrows, antar – internal, lakṣyaṁ – focus, bahir = bahiḥ = external, dṛṣṭir = dṛṣṭiḥ = gaze, nimeṣonmeṣa – blinking of eyelashes, varjitā – without, eṣā – this, sā – that, śāmbhavī – visual focus between the eyebrows, mudrā – mystic–arresting actions, veda – Veda, śāstreṣu – with scriptures, gopitā – concealed

Now is described the shambhavi visual focus between the eyebrows:

Its focus is internal. Its gaze is external but without blinking of eyelashes. This is the visual focus arresting-action, which is concealed in the Vedic scriptures.

Analysis

This is an internal mystic practice but it has external format with the gaze of the eyes. A dissimilar practice is used by mystics for gazing at auras but that procedure though having the same physical format does not contain the same internal focus.

In this practice there is no vision of what is seen outside of the psyche or subtle body of the yogi. The two physical and two subtle eyes are not used in this practice. The yogi lets his vision energy protrude out of the subtle eyeballs but without any interest in their ray-like protrusion. This means that no vision of anything subtle is seen by the yogi, because unless the interest energy travels through the vision energy there can be no perception of the objects the rays touch.

When doing this practice, the yogi becomes aware of the meeting point of the optic energy and then with further withdrawal of the interest energy, he discovers the protrusion point of the interest energy as it comes out of the sense of identity, which is representative of the core-self. This diagram may give insight:

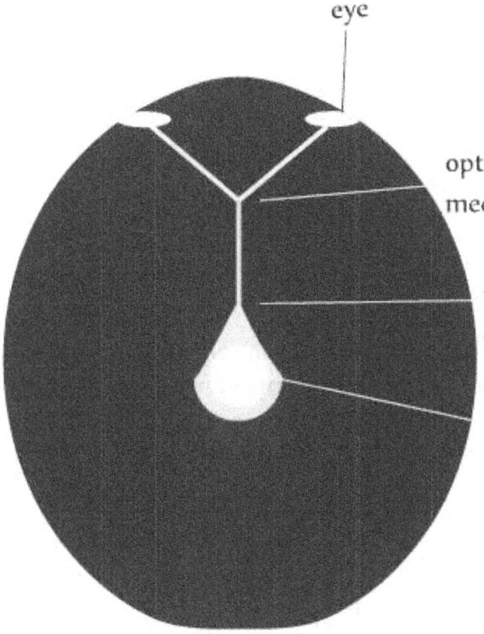

Application

The shambhavi visual focus between the eyebrows is an internal practice but with the visual focus energy rushing outwards in the beginning and with it losing its blast current as the practice develops. This may be compared to blast thrust of a rocket booster, which initially squirts out fuel. After a time, the fuel is spent and everything goes quiet.

This practice begins with the eyes blaring open and with intention to keep the eyelids wide apart. This causes a burning sensation in the eyes. The yogi should tolerate this but if he is unable to, he may close the eyes, pulling the eyelids together tightly, and then open the eyes and allow them to blare again.

As soon as the eyes are blared, the yogi should retract his interest energy from the optic energy which courses outward through the eyes. He should retract that energy and hold it inside of the psyche so that none of it goes outwards with the optic energy. He should continue extracting the interest energy until he retracts it into the sense of identity which surrounds the core-self.

The yogi should hold that interest energy in the sense of identity and not allow it to be fused into the optic energy. This will cause realization of the buddhi intellect orb. It will cause an opening into the chit akash divine sky of consciousness.

In the dissimilar practice, a mystic sees the auras of objects, which are the subtle body or the energy body of objects. In this yogic shambhavi mudra, the yogi does not see the auras and has no concern with that.

Verse 37

अन्तर् लक्ष्यविलीनचित्तपवनो योगी यदा वर्तते

दृष्ट्या निश्चलतारया बहिर् अधः पश्यन्न् अपश्यन्न् अपि ।

मुद्रेयं खलु शाम्भवी भवति सा लब्धा प्रसादाद् गुरोः

शून्याशून्यविलक्षणं स्फुरति तत् तत्त्वं पदं शाम्भवम् ॥३७॥

antar lakṣya–vilīna–citta–pavano yogī yadā vartate
dṛṣṭyā niścala–tārayā bahir adhaḥ paśyann apaśyann api ǀ
mudreyaṁ khalu śāmbhavī bhavati sā labdhā prasādād guroḥ
śūnyāśūnya–vilakṣaṇaṁ sphurati tat tattvaṁ padaṁ śāmbhavam ǀǀ37ǀǀ

antar – interior, lakṣya – focus, vilīna – phased, citta = mento–emotional energy, pavano = pavana = infused breath energy, yogī – yogi, yadā – when, vartate – assumes a state, dṛṣṭyā – perception, niścala – immovable, tārayā – conceal, bahir = bahiḥ = exterior, adhaḥ – below, paśyann = paśyan = vision, apaśyann = apaśyan = lack of vision, api – also, mudreyaṁ – practice of mystic–arresting actions, khalu – indeed, śāmbhavī – visual focus between the eyebrows, bhavati – is, sā – that, labdhā – obtain, prasādād – special favor, guroḥ – of empowered yoga teacher, śūnyāśūnya = idealess imageless and idea–saturated image–prone mental content, vilakṣaṇaṁ – insight perception, sphurati – manifest, tat – that, tattvaṁ – primal cause, padaṁ – position, śāmbhavam – state of Shambhu Shiva

When the yogi phased the mind and infused breath energy into the interior focus, with the perception being immovable, while there is no vision of anything outside or below. It is the shambhavi practice of arresting the visual focus between the eyebrows. It is achieved by the special favor of an empowered yoga teacher. Its insight perception has idealess, imageless, idea–saturated or image–prone content. It is the primal cause and positions the yogi in the state of Shambhu Shiva.

Analysis

To be in a state which is similar to the natural state of Lord Shiva, the yogi meets these requirements:

- phase the mind
- infuse breath energy into the interior focus
- have immovable perception
- have no vision of anything outside or below
- master shambhavi practice of arresting the visual focus between the eyebrows
- achieve the special favor of an empowered yoga teacher.

To **phase the mind** the yogi must undermine the conventional mental intentions and purposes. This is accomplished by being alerted by an advanced teacher and by reading books like Bhagavad Gita and Yoga Sutras. If the mind is not undermined, the student will be unable to overcome its resistance and will continue to be a novice.

To **infuse breath energy into the interior focus,** the yogi must practice pranayama breath-infusion to the extent that during each session of practice, he extracts toxic gases from the body and infuses fresh air into it. While doing this he must be focused within the psyche so that none of his attention comes outside of the confines of the body during the practice. Except for the brahmarandra crown chakra and the ajna chakra third eye perception, the yogi should not allow the energy to leak out of the psyche. This means that he must master the various locks which keep the infused energy and the kundalini contained for compression and implosion within the subtle body.

To **have immovable perception,** the yogi must achieve the shutdown of the conventional operations of the mind. He must be situated confidentially and devotedly in the naad resonance.

To **have no vision of anything outside or below,** the yogi must be divorced from all conventional emotions. This is a positional or locational situation, where the yogi is at the core-self in the existential center of the subtle head with naad sound resonance to his back, with no distracting energy coming up from underneath, from the kundalini psychic lifeforce, with no enthrallment from the front, from the buddhi intellect orb, with no attacks from the memory, and with no interest of the senses in finding their objects outside of the body.

To **master shambhavi practice of arresting the visual focus between the eyebrows,** the yogi must be intimately connected to the naad sound resonance and would have mastered the pranayama breath-infusion practice so that it yielded for him the completion of the pratyahar sensual energy withdrawal fifth stage of yoga.

To **achieve the special favor of an empowered yoga teacher,** the yogi must have completed many austerities which are described in this thesis of Swatmarama and should have applied the principles and methods suggested by Lord Krishna in the Bhagavad Gita and Patanjali Mahamuni in the Yoga Sutras.

Application

This insight perception has idealess, imageless, idea-saturated or image-prone content but it is all of a supernatural or spiritual essence and not a physical or astral content. There is a shift first into the idealess imageless state of mind and then after hearing naad sound resonance, the yogi either remains in naad with no other objective perception, or remains in naad, and experiences vision into the chit akash sky of consciousness where there is an environment with persons using their bare core-selves as spiritual bodies.

Verse 38

श्रीशाम्भव्याश् च खेचर्या अवस्थाधामभेदतः ।

भवेच् चित्तलयानन्दः शून्ये चित्सुखरूपिणि ॥ ३८॥

śrī–śāmbhavyāś ca khecaryā avasthā–dhāma–bhedataḥ |
bhavec citta–layānandaḥ śūnye cit–sukha–rūpiṇi ||38||

śrī – choice, śāmbhavyāś = śāmbhavyāḥ = visual focus between the eyebrows, ca – and, khecaryā – procedure for transiting through kha divine space, avasthā – state, dhāma – zone, bhedataḥ – different, bhavec = bhavet = become, citta – mento-emotional energy, layānandaḥ = laya (absence of mento-emotional trauma) + ānandaḥ (bliss), śūnye – idealess imageless mental content, cit – spiritual objective awareness, sukha – happiness, rūpiṇi – spiritual form

The two choice states of visual focus between the eyebrows and transiting through kha divine space are different because of the zones where they occur. They cause the mento-emotional energy to be devoid of trauma while having spiritual bliss. In the idealess imageless mental content there occurs spiritual objective awareness with happiness in the spiritual form.

Analysis

Visual focus between the eyebrows as mentioned in this verse pertains only to stable visual focus from a position in the naad sound resonance. The core-self has to be in naad sound resonance and in a confidential relationship with naad. Then it may peer forward and if it is lucky maintain a visual focus between the eyebrows. This focus may have a pin-point light as a target or just nothing but mental space as target. In this practice the yogi remains on this side of the existential divine, in the psychic material world and peers through an opening into the transcendental atmosphere.

Transiting through kha divine space is special because the yogi leaves this side of existence and crosses into the transcendental atmosphere. Then he returns to this plane of existence with clear recall of what took place. In this experience, the yogi finds that at first his psyche or subtle body is flooded with a special type of supernatural energy. This surrounds the core-self. Then that self is conveyed into the spiritual sky. But again as if miraculously, the yogi discovers himself existing on this side of existence but with clear memory of what took place.

In either experience, the mento-emotional energy of the yogi is upgraded supernaturally, such that the new insert of energy is devoid of trauma and has spiritual bliss as its texture.

Application

Bliss is the texture of the spiritual body but there is also insight awareness. Spiritual happiness is there but ignorance is replaced by spiritual objective awareness, so that the yogi has supernatural perception. This is a special type of happiness which is different to conventional joy.

Verse 39

तारे जयोतिषि संयोज्य किञ्चिदुन्नमयेद्भ्रुवौ ।

पूर्व–योगं मनो युञ्जन्नुन्मनी–कारकः क्षणात् ।। ३९ ।।

tāre jyotiṣi saṁyojya kiñcidunnamayedbhruvau ।
pūrva–yogaṁ mano yuñjann unmanī–kārakaḥ kṣaṇāt

tāre – radiant, jyotiṣi – spiritual light, saṁyojya – linking focus, kiñcid = kiñcit = a little, unnamayed = unnamayet = should raise, bhruvau – visual focus between the eyebrows, pūrva – as before, yogaṁ – yogic state, mano = manaḥ = mind, yuñjann =

yuñjan = practicing, unmani – devoid of ordinary mental content, kārakaḥ – producer, kṣaṇāt – instantly

Applying the linking focus on the radiant spiritual light and raising the visual focus to between the eyebrows, with the mind in the yogic state as mentioned before, this will instantaneously produce a state devoid of ordinary mental content.

Analysis

First the radiant spiritual light must appear in the psyche of the yogi. It usually appears in the frontal part of the subtle head within the peripheral vision. If the light does not appear, the yogi cannot force it to do so by focus or by any other means. He can however set himself into a position which is favorable for its appearance. The most frequent means is to remain embedded in naad sound resonance while the frontal part of the subtle head remains devoid (unmani) of ordinary mental content.

Once the light appears, the yogi may raise the visual focus to between the eyebrows but that is only if that focus was lower. In the case of raising it, that should be done very gently without jarring willpower movements, because these might put the core-self into a lower plane of existence with the result that the light will disappear. The light is always in its own dimension and does not hop from level to level. The self is the shifter, but it will seem that the light disappeared.

Application

The procedure is:

- *Do pranayama breath-infusion until the subtle body is saturated with fresh pranic energy and the stale polluted pranic energy is extracted.*
- *Sit to meditate immediately after completing breath-infusion, so as to take advantage of the upgrade of energy in the subtle body.*
- *When you first begin to meditate, discover a state devoid of ordinary mental content. If the mind is not mentally silent, it means that the breath-infusion was insufficient. Cease the meditation. Do another breath-infusion session; then sit to meditate.*
- *As soon as you sit to meditate and find that the ordinary mental content is absent and that there is stillness of mind with no imaging and thinking, pull the core-self back into the naad sound resonance.*
- *Adhere to naad while waiting for appearance of radiant spiritual light.*
- *Apply the linking focus on the radiant spiritual light but do so without haste, without a grabbing attitude, calmly and patiently.*
- *If the visual focus was lowered or if it was shut down complete, gradually raise it between the eyebrows or to where the radiant spiritual light appeared.*

Verse 40

केचिदागम–जालेन केचिन्निगम–सङ्कुलैः ।

केचित्तर्केण मुह्यन्ति नैव जानन्ति तारकम् ।। ४० ।।

kecidāgama–jālena kecinnigama–saṅkulaiḥ |
kecittarkeṇa muhyanti naiva jānanti tārakam || 40 ||

kecid = kecit = some, āgama – scriptures, jālena – in the lure, kecin = kecit = some, nigama – ritual worship, saṅkulaiḥ – with confusion, kecit – some, tarkeṇa – with logic, muhyanti – they are mistaken, naiva = not ever, jānanti – they know, tārakam – crossing beyond material existence

Some are involved in the lure of the scripture. Some are confused by ritual worship. Some use logic. They are mistaken and do not know the way of crossing beyond material existence.

Analysis

Scripture, ritual worship and logic have their time and place. These could help a yogi considerably. These are not however a replacement for practice of yoga along the lines given by Swatmarama. Scripture alone is not sufficient because even though it gives one faith, it is not the actual practice. Ritual worship is a way of approaching deities using sanctified material objects. That method may or may not facilitate the grace of a deity. But again that grace must be translated into actual yoga practice. It does not replace the practice. The inspiration one gets from a deity should motivate practice, not discourage one from it. Logic and philosophy provides a framework of reason to support rituals and austerities but by itself logic stunts the mind and gives a false sense of confidence.

Application

In the bid for liberation, there are suggestions which we get from the psychic material nature. These are very convincing but they are useless in terms of actually becoming freed from the material energy. At some point, a living being decides to leave aside nature's suggestion and to adhere to the genuine yoga-guru who progressed beyond nature. The student loses interest in the lure of scripture, ritual worship and logic. He decides to honestly practice to gain the objective of departure from being within the range of material nature.

Verse 41

अर्धोन्मीलित–लोचनः सथिर–मना नासाग्र–दत्तेक्षणश

चन्द्रार्कावपि लीनतामुपनयन्निस्पन्द–भावेन यः ।

जयोती–रूपमशेष–बीजमखिलं देदीप्यमानं परं

तत्त्वं तत–पदमेति वस्तु परमं वाच्यं किमत्राधिकम् ।। ४१ ।।

ardhonmīlita–locanaḥ sthira–manā nāsāgra–dattekṣaṇaś
candrārkāvapi līnatāmupanayannispanda–bhāvena yaḥ |
jyotī–rūpamaśeṣa–bījamakhilaṁ dedīpyamānaṁ paraṁ
tattvaṁ tat–padameti vastu paramaṁ vācyaṁ kimatrādhikam || 41 ||

ardhonmīlita = ardha (half–closed) + unmīlita (open), locanaḥ – eye, sthira – steady, manā – mind, nāsāgra – tip of the nose, datte – focused, kṣaṇaś = kṣaṇaḥ = moment, candrārkāv = candra (moon dominant left channel) + ārkāu (and sun dominant right channel), api – also, līnatām – dissolved, upanayan – focusing, nispanda – motionless, bhāvena – with being, yaḥ – who, jyotī – light, rūpam – form, aśeṣa – without remainder, bījam – source, akhilaṁ – whole, dedīpyamānaṁ – blazing, paraṁ – supreme, tattvaṁ – essential origin, tat – that, padam – foundation, eti – approach, vastu – object, paramaṁ – supermost, vācyaṁ – what is said, kim – what, atrādhikam = atra (here) + adhikam (more)

With half-closed eyes, steady mind, being focused at the tip of the nose, with the sun-dominant right channel and moon-dominant left side focused and dissolved motionlessly, he perceives light and endless form, the source, the whole reality, blazing, supreme, the essential origin, the approach to the foundation, the supermost object. What more can be said of this?

Analysis

For perception of supernatural and spiritual reality, there must be:

- half-closed eyes
- steady mind, focused at the tip of the nose
- sun-dominant right channel and moon-dominant left side focused and dissolved motionlessly

Half-closed eyes is a method used by some yogis but fully closed eyelids could be effective as well. Half-closed eyes should be used when the yogi is in surroundings which do not have light penetrating, so that there is no difference between closing the eyelids and opening them, so that when the eyelids are open, due to the dense physical darkness there is only the mind sky to view.

Some yogis in the lineage from Lahiri Mahasaya show pictures of him with half closed eyes but that practice should be done in a cave where no daylight penetrates. It is an isolated practice and is not done to be photographed or displayed, even though a proficient yogi may for training purposes demonstrate it to others.

The gist of this practice has nothing to do with the closing or opening of the eyelids really. It has to do with retracting the interest energy which courses through the senses, particularly through the visual sense. That energy has to be retracted so that it does not penetrate outside the subtle body. Once the yogi is stabilized in this retraction which is the pratyahar sensual energy fifth stage of yoga, he should withdraw the interest energy into the core-self so that his interest is no longer invested into the buddhi intellect orb, or the kundalini, or the sensual energy or the memory chambers.

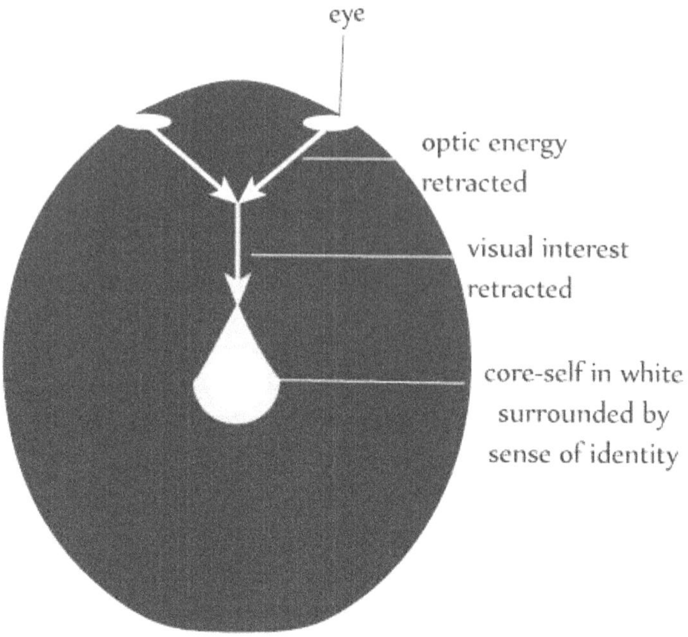

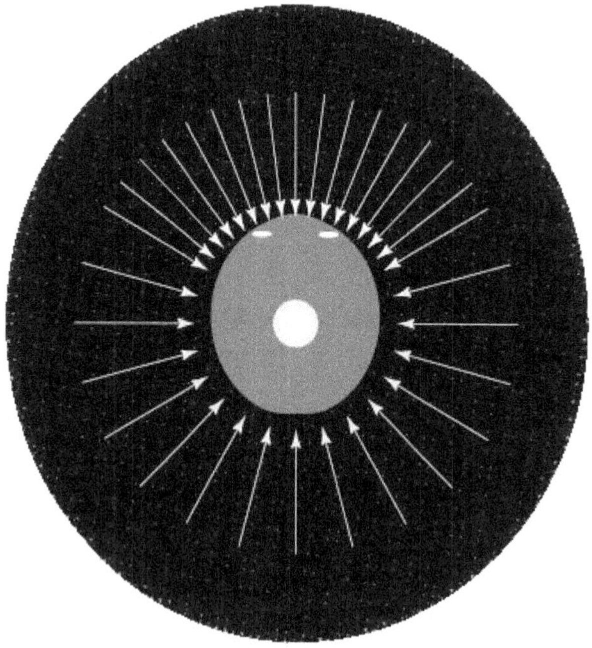

all sensual energy which pours out of the psyche
is retracted
through the outer edge layer of the psyche

The eyes are mentioned because the vision sense is predominant in the human species, where a greater percentage of sensual energy is divested through the visual apparatus. Thus, if he does this practice where light strikes his head, the yogi may even blindfold the eyes with a dark cloth.

A **steady mind** is necessary. Patanjali alerted that the cittavritti mental operations should be shut down before yoga can begin in earnest. If the mind has ideas and images, it will flicker as it presents suggestions. This behavior cancels meditation.

The **focus at the tip of the nose** is said to be at the top of the nose which is between the eyes but some yogis say that it is at the lower point of the nose. Others recommend the center of the incline of the nose. This practice is for quelling the interest of the buddhi intellect orb so that it remains centralized in the energy which is in the frontal part of the subtle head.

An alternate method is to retract the interest of the self from the optic channels and then through the buddhi intellect orb, and then through the sense of identity into the core-self. This method, which I explored recently, gives the result just as well.

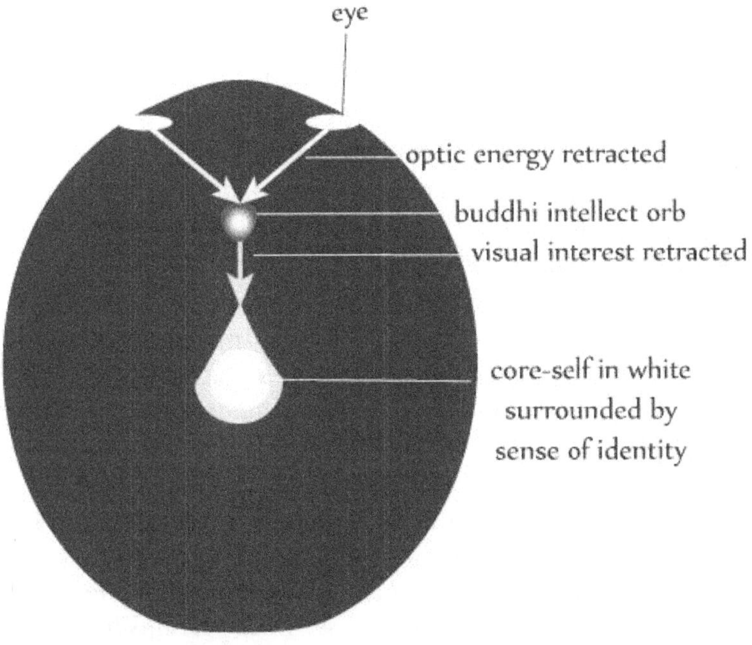

The **sun-dominant right channel and moon-dominant left side are focused and dissolved motionlessly** when the sushumna nadi central passage is brushed through by the kundalini psychic lifeforce which was infused with fresh breath energy. Mastery of kundalini yoga is required to achieve this.

Application

The results intended are perception of these supernatural and spiritual aspects:

- *light*
- *endless form*
- *the source*
- *the whole reality, blazing, supreme*

- *the essential origin*
- *the approach to the foundation*
- *the supermost object*

***Light** is perceived when the yogi achieved the simmering down of the mind so that its conventional operations cease without the yogi making any effort to terminate mental activity. The yogi does not cause the light to appear. The trick is to learn from which state of mind the light is likely to appear and then assume that. The most reliable method is to be absorbed in naad sound resonance and to wait in the darkness of the mind for the light to manifest.*

Once the light appears if the yogi rushes after it or tries to focus too sharply on it, the light will disappear either by fading rapidly in the distance or by falling to the side or downwards. Sometimes the light appears from overhead. Then when the yogi tries to look up to view it, it recedes from him backwards and upwards, so that he cannot perceive it.

Instead of seeing the actual light, a yogi may see the glowing radiance which the light produces. The yogi should peer at this glow and wait for the approach of the source. Sometimes the yogi actually sees the brilliant and blinding radiance of a vast cosmic light. This is so bright as to be blinding to the yogi who may try to cover his vision because of the tremendous power fusing out of that source.

*The perception of **endless form** occurs in some meditations, where the yogi sees supernatural beings in various dimensions. Rarely is a yogi able to see divine beings but that does happen though infrequently. A yogi may also see super-subtle astral forms which are interspaced in each other crossing various dimensions.*

*It happens that a yogi may perceive **the source** of particular realities or the source of everything within the brahmanda or cosmos he is in. Markandeya Yogi got that experience which is mentioned in the Markandeya Samasya part of the Mahabharata. Perception of the source may be personal or impersonal, according to how the yogi is graced by providence.*

*It is rare for a yogi to perceive **the whole reality, blazing and supreme**. Usually a yogi sees only a portion, and only that part which relates to his individual situation. A yogi cannot command that he should see the whole reality. He may however get the grace of a yoga-guru or a deity so that he can see what pertains to his connection to a deity, to a pre-lord and to an environment where he has existential rights.*

*Some yogis perceive **the essential origin** in deep meditations but only after years of practice. They must clear the psyche of heavy astral energy and of noise vibration energies, so that it is quieted sufficiently to detect very abstract energy.*

*A yogi can perceive **the approach to the foundation** but not the foundation itself. There is a statement in the Bhagavad Gita which mentions this:*

śrībhagavānuvāca
ūrdhvamūlamadhaḥśākham
aśvatthaṁ prāhuravyayam
chandāṁsi yasya parṇāni
yastaṁ veda sa vedavit (15.1)

śrī bhagavān — The Blessed Lord; uvāca — said; ūrdhvamūtam = urdhva —upward + mūlam — root; adhaḥśākham = adhaḥ — below + śākham — branch; aśvatthaṁ — ashvattha tree; prāhuḥ — the yogī sages say; avyayam — imperishable; chandāṁsi -Vedic hymns; yasya — or what which; parṇāni — leaves; yaḥ — who; taṁ — this; veda — knows; sa = saḥ— he; vedavit — knower of the Vedas

The Blessed Lord said: The yogi sages say that there is an imperishable Ashvattha tree which has a root going upwards and a trunk downwards, the leaves of which are the Vedic hymns. He who knows this is a knower of the Vedas. (Bhagavad Gita 15.1)

adhaścordhvaṁ prasṛtāstasya śākhā
guṇapravṛddhā viṣayapravālāḥ
adhaśca mūlānyanusaṁtatāni
karmānubandhīni manuṣyaloke (15.2)

Adhaścordhvaṁ = adhaḥ — downward + ca — and + urdhvam — upward; prasṛtāh — widely spreading; tasya — of it; śākhā — branches; guṇa — mundane influence; pravrddhā — nourished; viṣayapravālāḥ = viṣaya — attractive objects + pravālāḥ — sprouts; adhaśca = adhaḥ — below + ca — and; mūlāni — roots;— stretched out; karmānubandhīni = karmā — action + anubandhīni — promoting; manuṣyaloke = manuṣya — of human being + loke — in the world

Branches spread from it, upwards and downwards. It is nourished by the mundane influences and the attractive objects are its sprouts. The roots are spread below, promoting action in the world of human beings. (Bhagavad Gita 15.2)

na rūpamasyeha tathopalabhyate
nānto na cādirna ca saṁpratiṣṭhā
aśvatthamenaṁ suvirūḍhamūlam
asaṅgaśastreṇa dṛḍhena chittvā(15.3)

na — not; rūpam — form; asyeha - asya — of it + iha — in this dimension; tathopalabhyate = tathā — thus + upalabhyate — it is perceived; nānto = nāntah = na — not + antaḥ — end; na — nor; cādiḥ = ca — and + ādiḥ — end; na — nor; ca — and; saṁpratiṣṭhā — foundation; aśvatthaṁ — ashvattha tree; enam — this; suvirūḍhamūtam = suvirūḍha — well-developed + mūlam — root; asaṅgaśastreṇa = asaṅga — non-attachment + śastreṇa — with the axe; dṛḍhena — with the strong; chittvā — cutting down

Its form is not perceived in this dimension, nor its end, nor beginning nor foundation. With the strong ax of non-attachment, cut down this Ashvattha tree with its well-developed roots. (Bhagavad Gita 15.3)

From this side of existence, a person cannot get into the foundation even though one can approach it and get as far as one is able to maintain objectivity in the subjective abstract environment of the subtle material nature. In retrogressing like this, a yogi reaches a zone in which his objectivity simply disappears. Beyond that place his investigations cannot register.

But there is another type of foundation which is the person-source research Krishna said this about that objective:

jñeyaṁ yattatpravakṣyāmi
yajjñātvāmṛtamaśnute
anādimatparaṁ brahma
na sattannāsaducyate (13.13)

jṇeyaṁ — to be known, the desired subject; yat — which; tat — that; pravakṣyāmi — I will explain; yat — which; jñātvā — knowing; 'mṛtam = amṛtam — eternal life; aśnute — he gets in touch with; anādimat — beginningless; paraṁ — supreme; brahma — reality; na - not; sat — substantial; tat — this; nāsat = na — not + asat — non-substantial; ucyate — is said

I will explain that which is to be experienced, knowing which one gets in touch with eternal life. The beginningless Supreme Reality is said to be neither substantial nor insubstantial. (Bhagavad Gita 13.13)

sarvataḥpāṇipādaṁ tat
sarvatokṣiśiromukham
sarvataḥśrutimalloke
sarvamāvṛtya tiṣṭhati (13.14)

sarvataḥ — everywhere; pāṇi — hand; pādaṁ — foot; tat = tad — this; sarvato = sarvataḥ — everywhere; 'kṣiśiromukham= akṣiśiromukham= akṣi— eye + śiraḥ — head + mukham — face; sarvasaḥśrutimat - sarvasaḥ — everywhere + śrutimat — having hearing ability; loke — in the world; sarvam — all; āvṛtya — ranging over; tiṣṭhati — stands

Everywhere is Its hands and feet, everywhere Its eyes, head and face, everywhere is Its hearing ability in this world; It stands, ranging over all. (Bhagavad Gita 13.14)

sarvendriyaguṇābhāsaṁ
sarvendriyavivarjitam
asaktaṁ sarvabhṛccaiva
nirguṇaṁ guṇabhoktṛ ca (13.15)

sarvendriyaguṇābhāsaṁ = sarva —all + indriyaḥ — sensual + guṇa — mood + ābhāsaṁ — appearance; sarvendriyavivarjitam = sarva — all + indriya — sensuousness + vivarjitam — freedom from; asaktaṁ — unattached; sarvabhṛt — maintaining everything; caiva = ca — and + eva — indeed; nirguṇaṁ — free from the influence of material nature; guṇabhoktṛ — experiencer of the modes of material nature; ca — and

It has the appearance of having all sensual moods, and It is freed from sensuousness. Though unattached, It maintains everything. Though free from the influence of material nature, It is the experiencer of that influence nevertheless. (Bhagavad Gita 13.15)

bahirantaśca bhūtānām
acaraṁ carameva ca
sūkṣmatvāttadavijñeyaṁ
dūrasthaṁ cāntike ca tat (13.16)

bahiḥ — outside; antaḥ — inside; ca — and; bhūtānām — of the beings; acaraṁ — non-moving; caram — moving; eva — indeed; ca — and; sūkṣmatvāt — from subtlety; tat — this; avijñeyaṁ — not to be comprehended; dūrasthaṁ — situated far off; cāntike = ca — and + antike — in the location; ca — and; tat = tad — this

It is outside and inside the moving and non-moving beings. Because of Its subtlety, this beginningless Supreme Reality is not comprehended. This Reality is situated far away and it is in the location as well. (Bhagavad Gita 13.16)

avibhaktaṁ ca bhūteṣu
vibhaktamiva ca sthitam
bhūtabhartṛ ca tajjñeyaṁ
grasiṣṇu prabhaviṣṇu ca (13.17)

avibhaktam — undivided: ca — and; bhūteṣu — among the beings: vibhaktam — divided; iva — as if; ca — and; sthitam — remaining; bhūtabhartṛ = bhūta — being + bhartṛ — sustainer; ca — and; tat — this; jñeyaṁ — to be known; grasiṣṇu — absorber; prabhaviṣṇu — producer; ca — and

It is undivided among the beings, but It appears as if It is divided in each. It is the sustainer of the beings and this should be known. It is the absorber and producer. (Bhagavad Gita 13.17)

jyotiṣāmapi tajjyotis
tamasaḥ paramucyate
jñānaṁ jñeyaṁ jñānagamyaṁ
hṛdi sarvasya viṣṭhitam (13.18)

jyotiṣām — of luminaries; api — also; tat = tad — this; jyotiḥ — light; tamasaḥ — of gross or subtle darkness; param-beyond; ucyate — declared to be; jñānaṁ — information; jñeyaṁ — education; jñānagamyaṁ = jñāna — education + gamyam — goal; hṛdi — in the psychological core; sarvasya — of all; viṣṭhitam — situated

This is declared as the light of the luminaries, but It is beyond gross or subtle darkness. It is the information, the education and the goal of education. It is situated in the psychological core of all beings. (Bhagavad Gita 13.18)

*For a person being, the **supermost object** is the divine body of Shiva or Krishna. Fortunate is that yogi who is graced to view either of their transcendental forms directly.*

Verse 42

दिवा न पूजयेल्लिङ्गं रात्रौ चैव न पूजयेत् ।

सर्वदा पूजयेल्लिङ्गं दिवारात्रि–निरोधतः ।। ४२ ।।

divā na pūjayellingaṁ rātrau caiva na pūjayet ।
sarvadā pūjayellingaṁ divārātri–nirodhataḥ ।। 42 ।।

divā – day influence, na – not, pūjayel = pūjayet = worship, focus, lingaṁ – erect kundalini, rātrau – at night energy, caiva = and so, na – not, pūjayet – worship, focus, sarvadā – always, pūjayel = pūjayet = worship, focus, lingaṁ – erect kundalini, divārātri = day influence and night energy, nirodhataḥ – compressing and directing

One should not focus on the erect kundalini during the day influence or the night energy, but focus on it always after compressing and directing both influences.

Analysis

This is a cryptic, having a veiled meaning. The Sanskrit word **lingam** is used in no other verse, and thus to extract the meaning one has to consider the context. The most common meaning of linga is male generative organ. Usually it pertains to that of Shiva, who is worshiped as the Shiva Linga formations in Vedic ritual ceremonies.

I translated linga as the erect kundalini because of the context of the verses before and after this one. We focus on the erect kundalini as a matter of course, as compelled by the spread of energy of the lifeforce. Early in the morning, we awaken when kundalini becomes erect in the sushumna nadi passage and energizes the brain circuits. At night we sleep when kundalini descends down the passage and shuts down power to the chakras.

A yogi must break this control of material nature where it dictates to the core-self what it should do and when it should perform. This is done though breath-infusion where the kundalini is aroused and influenced to act in a way which supports the progress of yoga.

Application

Both the day and night influences which are expressed by kundalini are the natural way for operation of these material bodies, even the lower life forms. A yogi must redesign the system so that it serves the interest of yoga, which is to migrate to a spiritual environment. In the material world, there is an environment but it is based on temporary manifestation and a whole lot of undesirable trauma. The ascetic should reconfigure the operation of the kundalini for supporting the objective of yoga.

Verse 43

अथ खेचरी

सव्य–दक्षिण–नाडी–सथो मध्ये चरति मारुतः ।

तिष्ठते खेचरी मुद्रा तस्मिन्स्थाने न संशयः ।। ४३ ।।

atha khecarī
savya–dakṣiṇa–nāḍī–stho madhye carati mārutaḥ ।
tiṣṭhate khecarī mudrā tasminsthāne na saṁśayaḥ ।। 43 ।।

atha – now is described, khecari – procedure for transiting through kha divine space, savya – left, dakṣiṇa – right, nāḍī – subtle nadi channel, stho = sthaḥ = stationary, madhye – in the middle, carati – flowing through, mārutaḥ – air–infused breath energy, tiṣṭhate – accomplished, khecarī – procedure for transiting through kha divine space, mudrā = practice of mystic–arresting actions, tasmin – this, sthāne – in condition, na – no, saṁśayaḥ – doubt

Now the procedure for transiting through kha divine space is described:

When the air–infused breath energy is stationary in the left and right subtle nadi channels and it flows in the central channel, then transiting through kha divine space is accomplished. Of this there is no doubt.

Analysis

When the kundalini is involved in servicing the survival, reproductive and exploitive tendencies of the lower subtle and material bodies, it does not disinterestedly flush through sushumna central spinal passage to reach the brain. Instead it stops to service each of the spinal chakras, and it gets so stalled, so bogged down, that it never reaches into the brain except to send a trickle of energy through the neck.

A yogi must train the kundalini to lose interest in the various chakras, and to be primarily concerned with rapidly passing up through the central channel through the neck and reaching the brain with a full charge of energy, instead of in a spent-out tired condition. Its obsession with the svadhishthana sex chakra must be eliminated. Its reliance on the manipura digestion chakra must be broken. Its hypnotic attitude in the anahata third lung-heart chakra complex must be shattered and its selfish concerns with the vishuddha throat chakra must be rooted out.

The compelling influence of kundalini is broken once the interest of the core-self is extracted from it. Then it does not matter if the yogi continues doing materialistic activities. Because his interest is lifted, the actions are hollow. They carry no repercussions which will dampen spiritual progress. A yogi has no concern with material nature, or in setting it for a higher status through ethnicity or morality. A yogi is interested in exiting from it.

Application

Transiting through kha divine space is a tall order for any ascetic. It is not an easy achievement. It does not occur when a yogi has a sloppy practice or a method which was not proven by ancient yogis. It does not occur based on visualization. One cannot visualize oneself into the divine atmosphere because the psychic equipment used for such mental creations is inoperative and non-existent in the divine places.

Verse 44

इडा–पिङ्गलयोर्मध्ये शून्यं चैवानिलं ग्रसेत् ।

तिष्ठते खेचरी मुद्रा तत्र सत्यं पुनः पुनः ।। ४४ ।।

iḍā–pingalayormadhye śūnyaṁ caivānilaṁ graset ।
tiṣṭhate khecarī mudrā tatra satyaṁ punaḥ punaḥ ।। 44 ।।

iḍā–pingalayor = iḍā–pingalayoḥ = left and right channels, madhye – in center, śūnyaṁ – idealess imageless mental content, caivānilaṁ = caiva (and so) + ānilaṁ (fresh air), graset – should move, tiṣṭhate – permanent basis, khecarī – procedure for transiting through kha divine space, mudrā – mystic arresting action, tatra – there, satyaṁ – reality, punaḥ punaḥ – continuously

When fresh air is conveyed through the center between the left and right channels, the idealess imageless mental content is experienced. Then on a permanent basis, the khecari mystic arresting action for transiting through kha divine space would be a continuous reality.

Analysis

Pranayama breath-infusion is given in this verse as the anila fresh air infusion which results in kundalini getting sufficient energy to rapidly transit through the center between the right and left channels. Just as when a horse is excited, it runs on a track and does not stop to eat the grass which is under its hoofs, so the kundalini rapidly ascends the central channel without showing any concern for the chakras on the spinal column.

If the yogi can cause kundalini to be infused continuously, it will consistently lose interest in the lower five chakras. This will result in a reduction or termination of conventional thoughts and images occurring in the head of the subtle body, which will be experienced as a blank non-troublesome mental atmosphere in meditation.

Application

The mystic arresting action for transiting through kha divine space is adherence to naad sound resonance after assuring that the subtle body is filled with fresh subtle energy and all heavy astral force is extracted from it. Once this is achieved by whatever method, the yogi should patiently wait for the supernatural or spiritual environment to become available.

Verse 45

सूर्याचन्द्रमसोर्मध्ये निरालम्बान्तरे पुनः ।
संस्थिता वयोम– चक्रे या सा मुद्रा नाम खेचरी ।। ४५ ।।

sūryācandramasormadhye nirālambāntare punaḥ I
saṁsthitā vyoma–cakre yā sā mudrā nāma khecarī I I 45 I I

sūryā = sun–dominant right channel, candramasor = candramasoḥ = moon–dominant left channel, madhye – in between, nirālambāntare = nirālamba (self–supporting) + āntare (existential space), punaḥ – again, saṁsthitā – performed, vyoma – spiritual sky, cakre – in circular pattern, yā – who, sā – that, mudrā – practice of mystic–arresting actions, nāma – is called, khecarī – procedure for transiting through kha divine space

The supportless existential space is located between the sun–dominant right channel and the moon–dominant left channel. It is called the practice of mystic-arresting actions for khecari transiting through kha divine space.

Analysis

The support-less existential space is the sushumna central passage but only when it is completely cleared of heavy astral energy. In that condition kundalini has no affiliation with any spinal chakra, hence it floats up into the head of the subtle form. Thus it is said to be support-less. It rises into the head of the subtle body. Eventually it abandons the muladhara base chakra. It makes its home in the head of the subtle body where it adheres to the bottom-back of the brain.

Application

The sun–dominant right channel and the moon–dominant left channel tug the kundalini or the kundalini's energy here or there. This causes haphazard actions, which support the creature survival premise in the material world. When the yogi permanently excavates kundalini and lifts it out of the sushumna nadi mineshaft, he becomes relatively free from the survival impulses.

Verse 46

सोमाद्यत्रोदिता धारा साक्षात्सा शिव–वल्लभा ।

पूरयेदतुलां दिव्यां सुषुम्नां पश्चिमे मुखे ।। ४६ ।।

somādyatroditā dhārā sākṣātsā śiva–vallabhā I
pūrayedatulāṁ divyāṁ suṣumnāṁ paścime mukhe I I 46 I I

somād = somāt = from negatively–charged moon energy, yatroditā = yatra (where) + uditā (expressed, experienced), dhārā – stream, sākṣāt – directly, sā – that, he, śiva – Shiva, vallabhā – sweetheart, pūrayed = pūrayet = compress, atulāṁ – incomparable, divyāṁ – divine, suṣumnāṁ – subtle central spinal passage, paścime – behind, mukhe – in the mouth

The stream which flows from the moon source energy is directly Shiva's sweetheart. The sushumna subtle central spinal passage which is incomparable and divine should be compressed from the behind the mouth.

Analysis

There are many people who become yogis for the purpose of getting yoga under their thumbs, so that they can dictate what a yogi can and cannot do for liberation. Actually yoga controls the yogi and dictates his preferences. God Shiva has wives with Durga the Goddess, being the primary one and yet Shiva has no wife except his psyche. Shiva is rated as the Supreme Tantric and yet Shiva is the Supreme Self-Tantric, who makes love to no one but Himself.

Secretly, Shiva enjoys his sweetheart, the stream of moon bliss energy which flows from above and which brings tremendous spiritual pleasure when it makes contact behind the subtle mouth. Instead of meeting his consort outside the subtle body by sexual penetration and reception, Shiva meets her in his subtle body unseen to everybody.

Application

A student-yogi should be attached to three factors only. These are the yoga-guru, the yoga process itself and the deity indicated by the yoga-guru or experienced directly by the student.

Of these three, two are outright personal. One seems to be impersonal. However, on a close examination we find that the impersonal one is actually very personal because

the yoga process means handling the psyche of the yogi, his components of consciousness. That is extremely personal. Whatever is in the psyche which is not worthy of the dearest love and affection by the core-self should be adjusted for conformity.

Verse 47

पुरस्ताच्चैव पूर्येत निश्चिता खेचरी भवेत् ।

अभ्यस्ता खेचरी मुद्राप्युन्मनी सम्प्रजायते ।। ४७ ।।

purastāccaiva pūryeta niścitā khecarī bhavet ।
abhyastā khecarī mudrāpyunmanī samprajāyate ।। 47 ।।

purastāc = purastāt = from the front, caiva = as well, pūryeta – compression, niścitā – definite, khecarī – procedure for transiting through kha divine space, bhavet – is, abhyastā – practiced, khecarī – procedure for transiting through kha divine space, mudrāpyunmanī = mudra (mystic–arresting actions) +api (also) + unmanī (void of mental content), samprajāyate – experienced

It can be done from the front as well, definitely, and then it is a khecari procedure for transiting through kha divine space. By practice, this discipline causes the void mental content to be experienced.

Analysis

Kundalini arrest and movement into the head of the subtle body can be done using the conventional sushumna nadi central passage, as well as any other route which leads upward through the trunk of the subtle body. There is front kundalini, left side kundalini, right side kundalini, smack-center of the subtle trunk kundalini, middle left side kundalini, middle right side kundalini, inside the body near the sushumna nadi kundalini and many other routes which are investigated by qualified ascetics.

There is also cell kundalini which is different to the massive kundalini which governs the psyche. Cell kundalini can be bunched or grouped so that a part of the body, a gland, a set of cells, a tendon or a portion of the body operates together to produce a collective kundalini, which could be compressed inwards on itself, and then directed by the yogi into the subtle head or be directed to burst out where it is to light-burn heavy astral energy from various hard-to-reach places in the psyche. These actions assure that all of the subtle body is upgraded just as the head of it is using the conventional sushumna nadi central passage route.

Application

The secret is the void mental content and causing that on demand by a yogic foolproof very reliable method. Ancient yogis used pranayama breath-infusion. Some used infusion and inaudible mantras called ajapa. Whatever the method if the result is acquired, the yogi is likely to experience vision into or transit into the kha divine space.

Verse 48

भ्रुवोर्मध्ये शिव- स्थानं मनस्तत्र विलीयते ।

ज्ञातव्यं तत-पदं तुर्यं तत्र कालो न विद्यते ।। ४८ ।।

bhruvormadhye śiva–sthānaṁ manastatra vilīyate |
jñātavyaṁ tat–padaṁ turyaṁ tatra kālo na vidyate || 48 ||

bhruvormadhye = in between the eyebrows, śiva –Shiva, sthānaṁ – position, manas – mind, tatra – there, vilīyate = fused–focused, jñātavyaṁ – what is known, tat – that, padaṁ – situation, turyaṁ – fourth state, tatra – there, kālo = kālaḥ = time approaching as death, na – no, vidyate – exists

Shiva's position is between the eyebrows. There the mind is fused-focused. That situation is known as the fourth state. Time approaching as death does not exist there.

Analysis

The fourth state is the divine world, a place in which there is no perishable or temporary manifestion and no energy-draining trauma. There everything is pre-reinforced and perpetual, with no survival needs, and no exploitive habits. Shiva and alternately Krishna is the Deity of those places. In the Bhagavad Gita, a brief description is given:

avyaktādvyaktayaḥ sarvāḥ
prabhavantyaharāgame
rātryāgame pralīyante
tatraivāvyaktasaṁjñake (8.18)

avyaktād = avyaktāt — from the invisible world; vyaktayaḥ — the visible world; sarvāḥ — all; prabhavanty = prabhavanti — they are produced; aharāgame — at the beginning of Brahma's day; rātryāgame — at the beginning of Brahma's night; pralīyante — they are reverted back; tatraivāvyaktasaṁjñake = tatra — at the time + eva — indeed + avyakta — invisible world + saṁjñake — is understood as

When the day of Creator Brahma begins, all this visible world is produced from the invisible world. When his night comes, the manifested energies are reverted back into the invisible world. (8.18)

bhūtagrāmaḥ sa evāyaṁ
bhūtvā bhūtvā pralīyate
rātryāgame'vaśaḥ pārtha
prabhavatyaharāgame (8.19)

bhūtagrāmaḥ — multitude of beings; sa = saḥ — this; evāyam = eva — indeed + ayam — this; bhūtvā bhūtvā — repeatedly manifesting; pralīyate — is shifted out of visibility; rātryāgame — at the arrival of Brahma's night; 'vaśaḥ = avaśaḥ — happening naturally; pārtha — O son of Pṛthā; prabhavaty = prabhavati — it comes into existence; aharāgame — on the onset of Brahma's day

O son of Pritha, this multitude of beings which is repeatedly manifested, is naturally shifted out of visibility at the arrival of each of Brahma's nights.

It again comes into existence at the onset of Brahma's day. (8.19)

parastasmāttu bhāvo'nyo
'vyakto'vyaktātsanātanaḥ
yaḥ sa sarveṣu bhūteṣu
naśyatsu na vinaśyati (8.20)

paraḥ — high; tasmāt — than this; tu — but; bhāvo = bhāvaḥ — existence; 'nyo = anyaḥ — another; 'vyakto = avyaktaḥ — invisible; 'vyaktāt = avyaktāt — than the unmanifest state of the dissolvable creation; sanātanaḥ — primeval; yaḥ = which; sa = saḥ — it; sarveṣu — in all; bhūteṣu — in creation; naśyatsu — in the disintegration; na — not; vinaśyati — is disintegrated

But higher than this, there is another invisible existence, which is higher than the primeval unmanifested states of this dissolvable creation. When all these creatures are disintegrated, that is not affected. (8.20)

avyakto'kṣara ityuktas
tamāhuḥ paramāṁ gatim
yaṁ prāpya na nivartante
taddhāma paramaṁ mama (8.21)

avyakto = avyaktaḥ — invisible world; 'kṣara = akṣara — unalterable; ity = iti — thus; uktaḥ — is declared; tam — it; āhuḥ — authorities say; paramām — supreme; gatim — objective; yam — which; prāpya — attaining; na — not; nivartante — return here; tad — that; dhāma — residence; paramam — supreme; mama — My

That invisible world is unalterable, so it is declared. The authorities say that it is the supreme objective. Attaining that, they do not return here. That place is My supreme residence. (8.21)

Application

Both Shiva and Krishna appear in the material world but they simultaneously maintain parallel realities in the divine world. Krishna's self-assessment was explained in the Bhagavad Gita:

ajo'pi sannavyayātmā
bhūtānāmīśvaro'pi san
prakṛtiṁ svāmadhiṣṭhāya
saṁbhavāmyātmamāyayā (4.6)

ajo = ajaḥ — birthless; 'pi = api — even though; sann = san — being; avyayātmā = avyaya — imperishable + ātmā — person; bhūtānām — of the creatures; īśvaro = īśvaraḥ — Lord; 'pi = api — even; san — being; prakṛtiṁ — material energies; svām — my own; adhiṣṭhāya — controlling; saṁbhavāmyātmamāyayā = sambhavāmy (saṁbhavāmi) — I become visible + ātma — self + māyayā — by supernatural power

Even though I am birthless and My person is imperishable, and even though I am the Lord of the creatures, by controlling My material energies, I become visible by My supernatural power. (4.6)

Verse 49

अभ्यसेत्खेछरीं तावद्यावत्स्याद्योग–निद्रितः ।

सम्प्राप्त–योग–निद्रस्य कालो नास्ति कदाचन ।। ४९ ।।

abhyasetkhecarīṁ tāvadyāvatsyādyoga–nidritaḥ I
samprāpta yoga–nidrasya kālo nāsti kadācana II 49 II

abhyaset – should practice, khecarīṁ – procedure for transiting through kha divine space, tāvadyāvat – until, syād = syāt = is, yoga – yoga, nidritaḥ – state of blissfull, restfull suspended animation, samprāpta – transited to, yoga – yoga, nidrasya – of blissfull, restful suspended animation, kālo = kālaḥ = time approaching as death, nāsti = is not, kadācana – any time

The khecari procedure for transiting through kha divine space should be practiced until there is the yogic state of blissful, restfull, suspended animation. Being transited to that, the yogi is never intimidated by time which approaches as death.

Analysis

A yogi must experience the transit time after time using a goof proof method that works every time when the yogi practices. That is the only sure way to assure that he will actually transit after his physical form dies. A onetime experience, a once-in-a-while event of this nature, does not guarantee that he will transit. It must be repeatedly and consistently done using a reliable mystic process.

Application

Contact with the kha divine space results in a blissful, restful suspended animation which is much desired by a yogi who experienced it. There are many sources of addiction in the material world, but none are as powerful as the experience of energy from the divine world. Once a yogi experiences that he spends his life, in fact lives, trying to reconnect with it and to eventually transit permanently over to that side of reality.

Verse 50

निरालम्बं मनः कृत्वा न किंचिदपि चिन्तयेत् ।

स–बाह्याभ्यन्तरं वयोम्नि घटवत्तिष्ठति धरुवम् ।। ५० ।।

nirālambaṁ manaḥ kṛtvā na kiṁcidapi cintayet I
sa–bāhyābhyantaraṁ vyomni ghaṭavattiṣṭhati dhruvam II 50 II

nirālambaṁ – free of conventional impressions, manaḥ – mind, kṛtvā – having done, na – not, kiṁcid = kiṁcit = anything, api – also, cintayet – considering, sa – that, bāhyābhyantaraṁ = external and internal, vyomni – in space, ghaṭavat – like a jug, tiṣṭhati – sit, dhruvam – fixed

Having freed the mind of conventional impressions, and considering absolutely nothing, the yogi should sit as fixed as a jug which is externally and internally surrounded by space.

Analysis

This is a description of how a yogi waits for access to the divine world. The opportunity may be visual only or it may be a transit where he is relocated there for a limited period of time and is then reinstated into his physical body with the memory of the transcendence.

Application

The ascetic must practice regularly so that over time, there is a permanent partition between the core-self and the mind's conventional impressions, some of which it must keep so long as there is a physical body and lower levels of the astral form.

The analogy of the jug applies. As a yogi sits in his psyche in meditation, there is an opening which has access either to the psychic material world or the spiritual atmosphere. If the yogi has access to the spiritual world, the energy from that place may leak over into the psyche, causing him to experience himself as a spiritual body. This is in contrast to the regular experience in meditation, where the ascetic knows himself as a core-self in a subtle form which is interspaced in a physical body. In a spiritual body, the core-self is the body. That self is not encased magically in a subtle form which in turn may or may not be interspaced in a physical one.

Verse 51

बाह्य–वायुर्यथा लीनस्तथा मध्यो न संशयः ।

सव–सथाने सथिरतामेति पवनो मनसा सह ।। ५१ ।।

bāhya–vāyuryathā līnastathā madhyo na saṁśayaḥ ।
sva–sthāne sthiratāmeti pavano manasā saha ।। 51 ।।

bāhya – external, vāyur = vāyuḥ = breath, yathā – as, līnas – becomes unwanted, tathā – so, madhyo = madhyaḥ = middle energy, na – no, saṁśayaḥ – doubt, sva–sthāne = psyche–situated, sthira – stabalized, tām – that, eti – flows, pavano = pavanaḥ = infused breath energy, manasā – mind, saha – with

As the external breath becomes unwanted, and so also the middle energy stops moving, then without a doubt the infused breath-energy flow is stabilized and is psyche-situated within the mind.

Analysis

For the most part, this hinges on a proficient breath-infusion practice. This can happen without such practice, but rarely so, except for a few exceptional individuals like Gautam Buddha for instance or like Sri Ramana Maharshi in recent times. Usually meditators do not attain this without using pranayama practice.

The external breath becomes unwanted when there is an excess of fresh subtle energy infused into the subtle body and when there is efficient abstraction of polluted astral energy from the form. The middle energy stops moving when it cleared the sushumna central passage and when also the rest of the psyche is infused with a saturation of fresh astral energy. If only the head and spine of the subtle body are cleared of pollution, there will be a tension between the rest of the subtle body and the head/spine of it, which will cause an energy flow due to the polarity difference. Hence it is important to clear the entire subtle form of heavy astral energy and infuse into it fresh energy by breath-infusion.

Application

The ascetic has to bring the psyche into a quiescence based on infusing into it the highest grade of subtle energy. This results in a lack of flow of energy between the physical world and the psyche of the yogi. The sensual interplay between the two ceases for the time being. The senses display no interest in the physical world and seem to be non-existent.

Verse 52

एवमभ्यस्यतस्तस्य वायु–मार्गे दिवानिशम् ।

अभ्यासाज्जीर्यते वायुर्मनस्तत्रैव लीयते ।। ५२ ।।

evamabhyasyatastasya vāyu–mārge divāniśam I
abhyāsājjīryate vāyurmanastatraiva līyate II 52 II

evam – thus, abhyasyatas – practice, tasya – of this, vāyu – air, mārge – in the course, divāniśam = day and night, abhyāsāj = abhyāsāt = due to practice, jīryate – increase, vāyur = vāyuḥ = air, manas – mind, tatraiva = there also, līyate – be quiescent

Thus practicing, bringing the air to course night and day, and increasing the process, causes the mind to be quiescent.

Analysis

This is the repeated stressing by Swatmarama of the practice of pranayama breath-infusion. Is there any other process?

That is not the question.

If someone has another process which is effective, which is reliable, then he should use that method. The author cites pranayama because he was successful using it.

Application

Because it has this deep-seated need to participate in the mundane evolutionary cycle, kundalini cannot be reoriented in a jiffy. Even if the yogi was very near to liberation in the previous birth, still kundalini will have this idea that it should resume its evolutionary behaviors. While the embryo is in the mother's uterus, kundalini will reinstall the survival tendencies just as if the person did no yoga before. The yogi will have to work again to reorient it and to cause it to abandon its natural means.

The way out of this is to train the subtle body not to need a physical form. If a yogi can achieve that, he would not find himself as a human embryo or as some other type of

physical creature again. The exception is a siddha who is instructed by a yoga-guru or deity to take a physical body for one reason or the other. But such a person does not have to worry about the behavior of kundalini because he will be rescued by the authority who instructed him to take the physical form.

It is more important to strive for the subtle body's resistance to rebirth, than it is to strive for full liberation. It is hardly likely that one will get the full liberation before death of the physical form. At least if one strives for subtle body resistance to rebirth, if one attains that, one can remain in the astral world and attain liberation there. But if one strives for liberation and neglects to develop the resistance in the subtle form, one will be compelled to assume another material body.

Verse 53

अमृतैः पलावयेद्देहमापाद्–तल–मस्तकम् ।

सिध्यत्येव महा–कायो महा–बल–पराक्रमः ।। ५३ ।।

amṝtaiḥ plāvayeddehamāpāda–tala–mastakam |
siddhyatyeva mahā–kāyo mahā–bala–parākramaḥ || 53 ||

amṝtaiḥ – subtle pleasure energy, plāvayed = plāvayed = saturating, deham – body, āpāda – from the foot, tala – lower part, mastakam – head, siddhyaty = siddhyati = achieves, eva – so, mahā–kāyo = mahā–kāyaḥ = superfit body, mahā–bala = great strength, parākramaḥ = tremendous energy

Saturating the body with the subtle pleasure energy from the head to the foot, one achieves a superfit form, great strength and tremendous energy.

Analysis

The amrita pleasure energy is a bliss force which is felt in the heavenly world. As on earth we experience certain types of intoxication by taking liquors, stimulants and narcotics, so in the heavenly world, the celestial people experience a certain bliss feeling in their celestial forms when they take a beverage called amrita. A yogi gets this experience even while using the material body. It is attained easily by doing the kundalini yoga practice described in this book by Swatmarama Guruji.

At first this experience comes from arousing kundalini where it goes through the sushumna central passage into the brain. In a more advanced state it is experienced in various parts of the subtle body, not just in the spine and head of it. The process one uses has to saturate the entire subtle body with the subtle pleasure energy.

Application

The superfit form with great strength and tremendous energy is the subtle form. It is not the material body. In this practice, the material body is not the focus even though it is involved. Great strength of the subtle body means that it resists degrading astral energies which otherwise would cause it to appear in hellish or subterranean astral places.

Verse 54

शक्ति–मध्ये मनः कृत्वा शक्तिं मानस–मध्यगाम् ।

मनसा मन आलोक्य धारयेत्परमं पदम् ।। ५४ ।।

śakti–madhye manaḥ kṝtvā śaktiṁ mānasa–madhyagām |
manasā mana ālokya dhārayetparamaṁ padam || 54 ||

śakti–madhye = into kundalini subtle creative energy, manaḥ – mental focus, kṝtvā – fusing, śaktiṁ – subtle creative energy, mānasa – into mental focus, madhyagām – fusing into, manasā – into mental focus, mana = manaḥ = mental focus, ālokya – perceiving, dhārayet – focus to link, paramaṁ – supreme, padam – situation

Fusing the mental focus into the kundalini subtle creative energy, and doing the converse by perceiving what is mental focus using the kundalini, the yogi should intently link to the supreme situation.

Analysis

The mental focus and the kundalini in this usage are two different aspects of the individual psyche. The Sanskrit word manas is generally translated as mind; the word shakti as female energy. In this usage the word manas means mental focus in the head of the subtle body and not mind as the entire psyche or astral form.

Besides its head, the subtle body has a trunk and limbs. In the average human, the kundalini is in the spinal column of the subtle body but for the yogi, depending on his stage of advancement it may be in the spine or head of the subtle form. In this verse the mental focus psychic apparatus (the intellect) is fused with the aroused kundalini, and conversely the kundalini is fused into the mental focus. The yogi must research this while making detailed observations.

Application

This verse can be understood by those yogis who master kundalini yoga and who repeatedly on a daily basis can arouse kundalini by a reliable method. The term manas in this verse really means the term buddhi which is the analytical orb in the subtle body. It is an organ of the subtle body which does all analysis and reasoning. It is not the mind but it is the main functioning tool used in the mind. It is therefore addressed as being the mind in some usages of the word manas. Even in the Bhagavad Gita, Lord Krishna used the term manas to mean either the mind chamber or head of the subtle body and the buddhi intellect orb which is a psychic organ in the mind chamber.

If possible a yogi should study the movement of the buddhi intellect during sexual climax experience but only if that is his providence. One should not pursue sexual relationship just to experience this but if one has access to sexual intercourse and can study how the buddhi intellect orb moves down from the head into the trunk of the subtle body to merge or fuse itself into the kundalini lifeforce which is fused into the sex organ chakra, then one could get firsthand experience about the reverse principle of the intellect fusing into the kundalini.

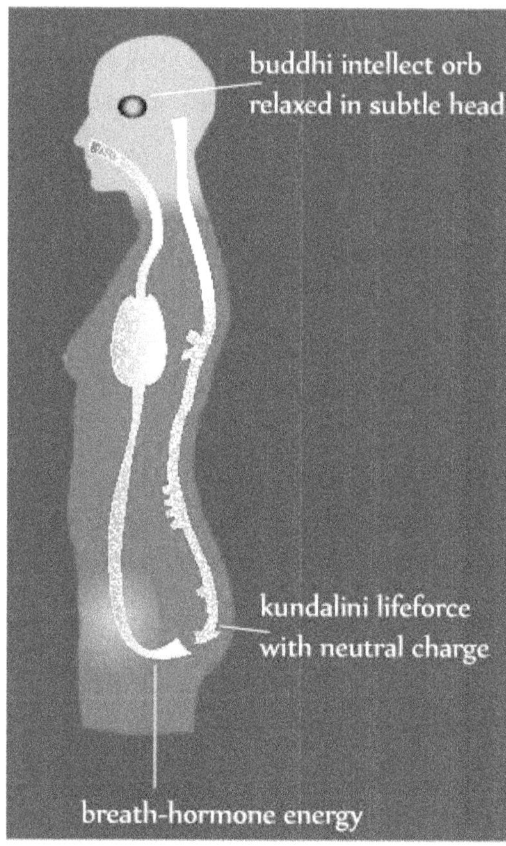

Kundalini lifeforce and breath-hormone energy
remain isolated from each other

sexual climax experience

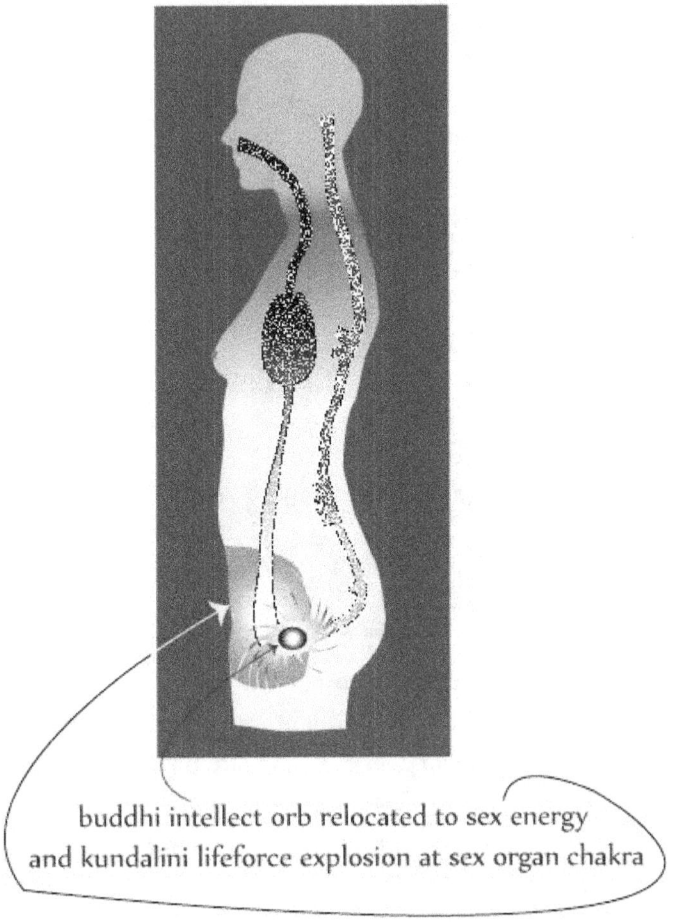
buddhi intellect orb relocated to sex energy
and kundalini lifeforce explosion at sex organ chakra

kundalini lifeforce jumps across to sexual energy charge
which is mixed with breath-hormone energy
buddhi intellect orb is forced to relocate at genitals

kundalini lifeforce
explosion in subtle head
buddhi intellect orb is affected

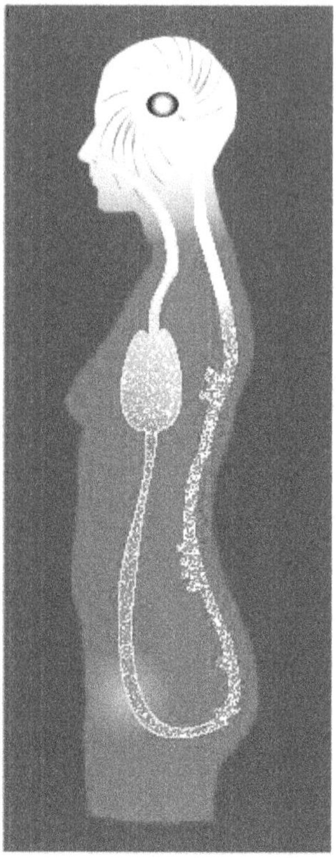

breath-hormone energy
arches over to kundalini lifeforce power central
causing kundalini energy to ascend into the brain
where it explodes into bliss awareness

Everyone should not aspire for this because it could cause loss of spiritual advancement. It requires a certain type of destiny for one to do this safely, otherwise one will lose the spiritual footing and leave the path of yoga altogether.

During sexual intercourse experience, at the beginning of it, the intellect remains in its default position which is in the head of the subtle body, somewhere between the core-self and the center of the eyebrows. However as the charge of energy increases, the resistance of the intellect decreases inversely, so that as the power of the sexual pleasure in the genitals increases, the intellect loses its resistance energy. At a certain point, the intellect loses every bit of resistance. It is forced by an irresistible pulling force from the kundalini to fuse itself into the kundalini. This fusion continues until there is a sexual climax experience or until there is frustration.

Even though for the average human being sexual pleasure is bewildering where all objectivity is lost, for the advanced yogi it is not so. Critics usually ridicule a yogi who indulges in sexual intercourse. They do this on two bases. One is that a yogi is supposed to be celibate. The other is that a yogi is supposed to be a leading moralist. If a yogi is found to be indulging in sexual intercourse people form the opinion that he is no longer celibate and that he is immoral. They have no idea about the research work a yogi must do with the sexual climax experience.

Some yogis do this work on the astral plane far from perceptive abilities of critics. In that way these yogis maintain their status as celibates and moralists. The critical human gives such astrally indulgent yogis a pass as being reliable religious leaders.

If a yogi cannot observe the movement of the buddhi intellect orb down into the body during sexual climax experience, it is hardly likely that he will note it at any other time, including while doing kundalini yoga. The reason for this is that it is more obvious to note this during sexual experience than it is otherwise. If one cannot observe what is obvious how will one see what is subtle?

- *The first observation to be made when doing kundalini yoga is how the kundalini lifeforce leaves the muladhara base chakra and goes through the spine into the head. A yogi must note this over and over on a daily basis using a reliable method of kundalini arousal.*
- *The next observation is how kundalini stalls for a bit, even for a moment, as soon as it burst through the neck into the head of the subtle body. There is a momentary stall but in some experiences the stall lasts for more than a moment and can be astutely observed.*
- *The next observation is how kundalini looks in either direction to the back and to the front of the subtle head before it makes a decision about which direction it will take.*
- *The next observation is that it goes in the direction of the buddhi intellect orb usually. That is its main attraction. It will on occasion go to the back of the head and try to burst through or punch a hole for an exit out of the subtle head, but this rarely happens, especially if the yogi applied the chin lock effectively.*
- *The next observation is what it does to the buddhi organ. Kundalini has a big influence on the buddhi organ even when kundalini is at the base muladhara chakra. The buddhi organ is prejudiced to the kundalini, so much so that the organ will make decisions and execute them even if the core-self disagrees, but provided those suggestions came from the kundalini lifeforce.*
- *The next observation is how the core-self loses control of the physical body once the kundalini effectively fuses into the buddhi intellect orb. The yogi has a task to study why this happens. He must also study how to stop this from occurring, where he can maintain objectivity even when the analytical orb is hit by the fully aroused kundalini.*

Observing what happens when the kundalini rises into the subtle head and fuses into buddhi intellect orb, is a difficult feat but it is easy compared to observing what happens when the buddhi organ moves out of the head during a kundalini arousal and goes down into the trunk or limbs of the subtle body to fuse into kundalini. This is why the observation can be made first in sexual intercourse experience and then the yogi may, if he can transfer some of the insight, comprehend what happens when kundalini goes down into the subtle trunk, leaving its default position in the subtle head.

Verse 55

ख–मध्ये कुरु चात्मानमात्म–मध्ये च खं कुरु ।

सर्वं च ख–मयं कृत्वा न किंचिदपि चिन्तयेत् ।। ५५ ।।

kha–madhye kuru cātmānamātma–madhye ca khaṁ kuru I
sarvaṁ ca kha–mayaṁ kṛtvā na kiṁcidapi cintayet II 55 II

kha–madhye = in kha divine space, kuru – situating, cātmānamātma = ca (and) + ātmānam (into the core–self) + ātma (core–self), madhye – into, ca – and, khaṁ – divine sace, kuru – locating, sarvaṁ – all, ca – and, kha–mayaṁ = divine environment, kṛtvā – having located, na – not, kiṁcid = kiṁcit = anything, api – also, cintayet – should contemplate

Situating the core-self in kha divine space and doing the converse, having located all interest into the kha divine environment, the yogi should contemplate nothing else.

Analysis

This verse described in brief the objective of kriya yoga, the system of realization which was taught by Sri Lahiri Baba. Fortunately for me, he clarified many meanings for some verses which I was not competent to discuss. Having psychic perception where one can take instructions from departed yogis is the gateway to success in the practice. If one is restricted to only physical access to yogis, then one is truly limited.

Application

The first task in this skill is to learn how to situate the core-self in the kha divine space. This is not easy to attain because the truth is that by itself, the self cannot situate itself there. The reason is simple. The self is limited. It is not responsible for its appearance in the psychic material environment. The question of how the core-self got inside the material nature was still not answered satisfactorily by the students.

Regardless of the answer given, regardless of how logical that answer is, we should consider that if the core-self did not deliberately place itself in the medium of material nature, it cannot declare truthfully that it can remove itself from this environment.

It is not possible to bore oneself through to the divine environment from in the material nature. What is to be achieved is to be in a position where an access will be provided by another source other than the self. The self's work is to find an existential location in which such access has the maximum probability of occurring.

The second task is to cause the core-self to be saturated with energy from the chit akash sky of consciousness. This is also a difficult attainment because the chit akash is a complete environment with no need for embedding itself into limited psyches. The yogi has to learn from a yoga-guru a method of drawing the chit akash energy into the psyche.

Verse 56

अन्तः शून्यो बहिः शून्यः शून्यः कुम्भ इवाम्बरे ।

अन्तः पूर्णो बहिः पूर्णः पूर्णः कुम्भ इवार्णवे ।। ५६ ।।

antaḥ śūnyo bahiḥ śūnyaḥ śūnyaḥ kumbha ivāmbare I
antaḥ pūrṇo bahiḥ pūrṇaḥ pūrṇaḥ kumbha ivārṇave II 56 II

antaḥ – interior, śūnyo = śūnyaḥ = idealess imageless mental content, bahiḥ – external, śūnyaḥ – idealess imageless mental content, śūnyaḥ – idealess imageless mental content, kumbha – jar, ivāmbare – like in the sky, antaḥ – interior, pūrṇo = pūrṇaḥ = full, bahiḥ – outside, pūrṇaḥ – full, pūrṇaḥ – full, kumbha – jar, ivārṇave – like in the ocean

On both the interior and exterior of the psyche, there should be the idealess imageless mental content, which is like a jar in the sky. It should be full inside and full outside like a jar in the ocean.

Analysis

This is a description of the advanced level of psyche saturation, when the spiritual environment is inside and outside the psyche of the yogi. In other words, at this stage the yogi translated to the divine environment in full.

Application

When a yogi got the mind in a blank condition, where of its own accord, it does not generate conventional thoughts and images, and when the yogi is embedded in naad sound, then he sets the condition which is suitable for getting access into the kha divine sky. He is concerned with peering into the divine sky.

Later he wants to enter into that environment. He finds that does not happen. He consults with a yoga-guru who advises him to hold steady in meditation and reach the chit akash on a daily basis.

After some years of practice with a resulting stability of focus into the chit akash, the yogi feels that the divine energy is partially surrounding him but there is still some of material nature which commands his attention and which claims him as its very own.

At some point in the practice, the yogi is alerted by a yoga-guru that the psyche which was used in the psychic material nature is non-existent in the divine world. It does not exist there. If he is to transit, he must leave aside the subtle body. In the spiritual world, the core-self will have to be its own psyche all by itself, without the psychic adjuncts.

Verse 57

बाह्य–चिन्ता न कर्तव्या तथैवान्तर–चिन्तनम् ।
सर्व–चिन्तां परित्यज्य न किंचिदपि चिन्तयेत् ।। ५७ ।।

**bāhya–cintā na kartavyā tathaivāntara–cintanam ।
sarva–cintāṁ parityajya na kiṁcidapi cintayet ।। 57 ।।**

bāhya – outside, cintā = mento–emotional energy, na – not, kartavyā – should be involved, tathaivāntara = tathā (as) + eva (also) + antara (inside), cintanam – mento–emotional energy, sarva – all, cintāṁ – ideation tendencies, parityajya – abandoning, na – not, kiṁcid = kiṁcit = anything, api – also, cintayet – should consider

The yogi should not be involved with the outside or the inside mento–emotional energy. He should abandon all ideation tendencies and should consider none of it.

Analysis

The abandonment of the outside of the mento-emotional energy is the first accomplishment of a yogi. This is done in the practice of the pratyahar sensual energy fifth stage of yoga. For some students it is a great struggle because of the momentum extrovert force of the sensual energies which pour out of the psyche in the pursuits of sense objects. People who were introverted before becoming students of yoga, have an easier time surmounting the sensual energy withdrawal stage but even they meet a challenge when they understand that this is just the beginning of the war which must be fought against the unruly adjuncts.

The completion of detachment from the external sense objects is aptly described by Lord Krishna in this verse:

*yadā saṁharate cāyaṁ
kūrmo'ṅgānīva sarvaśaḥ
indriyāṇīndriyārthebhyas
tasya prajñā pratiṣṭhitā (2.58)*

yadā — when; saṁharate — pulls; cāyaṁ = ca — and + ayam — this; kūrmo = kūrmaḥ — tortoise; 'ṅgānīva = aṅgānīva = aṅgāni — limbs + iva — like, compared to; sarvaśaḥ — fully; indriyāṇīndriyārthebhyas = indriyani — senses + indriyartheblyaḥ — attractive things; tasya — his; prajñā — reality-piercing vision; pratiṣṭhitā — is established

When such a person pulls fully out of moods, he or she may be compared to the tortoise with its limbs retracted. The senses are withdrawn from the attractive things in the case of a person whose reality-piercing vision is established. (Bhagavad Gita 2.58)

However this accomplishment does nothing to upset the inner quest for the sense objects. Initially the ascetic thinks that the problem is the presence of external objects but when the senses are retracted there is a discovery that the need for sensual quest remains. This was described by Krishna:

viṣayā vinivartante
nirāhārasya dehinaḥ
rasavarjaṁ raso'pyasya
paraṁ dṛṣṭvā nivartate (2.59)

viṣayā = viṣayāḥ — temptations; vinivartante — turn away; nirāhārasya — from(without) indulgence; dehinaḥ — of the embodied soul; rasavarjaṁ = rasa — memory or mental flavor of past indulgences + varjaṁ — except for, besides; raso = rasah — memories (mental flavors); 'pyasya = apyasya = apy (api) — even + asya — of him; paraṁ — higher stage; dṛṣṭvā — having experienced; nivartate — leaves

The temptations themselves turn away from the disciplinary attitude of an ascetic, but the memory of previous indulgences remain with him. When he experiences higher stages, those memories leave him. (Bhagavad Gita 2.59)

yatato hyapi kaunteya
puruṣasya vipaścitaḥ
indriyāṇi pramāthīni
haranti prasabhaṁ manaḥ (2.60)

yatato = yatataḥ — concerning an aspiring seeker; hyapi = hi — indeed + api — also; kaunteya — son of Kuntī; puruṣasya — of the person; vipaścitaḥ — of the discerning educated; indriyāṇi — the senses; pramāthīni — tormenting; haranti — seize, adjust; prasabhaṁ — impulsively, by impulse; manaḥ — mentally

Concerning an aspiring seeker, O son of Kuntī, concerning a discerned educated person, the senses do torment him. By impulses, the senses do adjust his mentality. (Bhagavad Gita 2.60)

This means that even though the external temptation will back away from the ascetic because of the pressure he places on material nature, still internally the senses will readjust him so that he must again pursue the rejected objects. This is when the ascetic realizes that a redesign of the psyche is necessary. This is when he will travel to the ends of the earth to meet a kriya master.

Application

The mento-emotional energy of the individual is housed in a subtle membrane. This is called a subtle body. It is similar to the physical form which has organs, tissues and bones housed in a skin. At first sensual energy withdrawal means stopping the pursuit of objects which are outside of the membrane. On the completion of that practice, when the sense objects are no longer as attractive and the yogi is detached from cravings, he realizes that those objects were not the impediment.

The handicap, which was the need for the said objects, was inside the membrane, inside the subtle body. To terminate the urges, the yogi has to eliminate the ideation tendencies and their supportive psychic apparatus. This requires kriya yoga which is the psychological disciplinary practice for the psyche. In the Bhagavad Gita, it is termed as buddhi yoga:

dūreṇa hyavaraṁ karma
buddhiyogāddhanaṁjaya

buddhau śaraṇamanviccha
kṛpaṇāḥ phalahetavaḥ (2.49)

dūreṇa — by far; hyavaraṁ = hi — surely + avaraṁ — inferior + karma — cultural action; buddhiyogād = buddhiyogāt — intellectual discipline through yoga; dhanaṁjaya — victor of wealthy countries; buddhau — mystic insight; śaraṇam — location of confidence; anviccha — put; kṛpaṇāḥ — low and pathetic; phalahetavaḥ — people motivated for a result

Surely, cultural action is by far inferior to intellectual discipline through yoga (buddhiyoga). O victor of wealthy countries. One should take shelter in mystic insight, for how pathetic are those who are motivated by the promise of results. (2.49)

The intellect is involved analyzing and supporting the sensual quests. A yogi must study the intellect's alliances. One such ally of the intellect is the memory which operates with rapid speed and which presents to the intellect supportive information which is based on past incidences. A yogi has to shut down the automatic link between the memory and the buddhi intellect orb otherwise his struggle to end the conventional thinking and imaging will be perpetually frustrated.

Verse 58

सङ्कल्प–मात्र–कलनैव जगत्समग्रं

सङ्कल्प–मात्र–कलनैव मनो–विलासः ।

सङ्कल्प–मात्र–मतिमुत्सृज निर्विकल्पम्

आश्रित्य निश्चयमवाप्नुहि राम शान्तिम् ।। ५८ ।।

saṅkalpa–mātra–kalanaiva jagatsamagraṁ
saṅkalpa–mātra–kalanaiva mano–vilāsaḥ ।
saṅkalpa–mātra–matimutsṝja nirvikalpam
āśritya niścayamavāpnuhi rāma śāntim ।। 58 ।।

saṅkalpa – mental conjecture, mātra – essential compostion, kalanaiva = kalana (cause) + eva (also), jagat – world, samagraṁ– aggregate energies, saṅkalpa – mental conjecture, mātra – essential compostion, kalanaiva = kalana (cause) + eva (also), mano = manaḥ = mind, vilāsaḥ – fanciful idea, saṅkalpa – mental conjecture, mātra – essential compostion, matim – thought, utsṝja – suspend, nirvikalpam – idealess transcendental consciousnes, āśritya – rely on, niścayam – eternally consistent reality, avāpnuhi – attain, rāma – Rama, śāntim – psychological peace

The aggregate energies, which are this world, are essentially composed of mental conjecture. It is the same for the fanciful ideas of the mind. One should suspend thoughts and their essential composition for the idealess transcendental consciousness. Rely on the eternally existent reality and attain psychological peace, O Rama.

Analysis

This is from the *Yoga Vashishtha* which is attributed to Valmiki Muni the author of the Valmiki Ramayana. It is the philosophy of Advaita Vedanta but it was an instruction which Vashishtha Rishi pressed on Rama, the son of Dashratha. Later Rama rejected the doctrine when an elder of the government used it as an argument to convince Rama not to honor his stepmother's request for banishment.

In so far as this philosophy explains the relationship between the influence of the mind and the behavior of the psyche, it is valid. But in so far as it depicts the limited self as being absolute, it is misleading and should be rejected.

Swatmarama was not an atheist and still he quoted from this text which denies the supremacy of a deity. He did so because this particular declaration is valid. It is said that one can take gold even from a cesspool. One can use a truthful aphorism even from a literature which presents a distorted view.

Application

The aggregate energies, which are this world, are essentially composed of mental conjecture, but it is a question of whose ideas. Obviously it is not formed on the basis of the ideas of the limited individual self but of the Supreme Being as Rama, Shiva or Krishna. However on a small scale the same can be applied for the fanciful ideas in the mind of the limited person-self. Therefore one should suspend thoughts and their essential composition for the idealess transcendental consciousness. We should, if possible rely on the eternally-existent reality and thus attain psychological peace.

Verse 59

कर्पूरमनले यद्वत्सैन्धवं सलिले यथा ।

तथा सन्धीयमानं च मनस्तत्त्वे विलीयते ।। ५९ ।।

karpūramanale yadvatsaindhavaṁ salile yathā I
tathā sandhīyamānaṁ ca manastattve vilīyate I I 59 I I

karpūram – camphor, anale – in fire, yadvat – as, saindhavaṁ – salt, salile – in water, yathā – as, tathā – so, sandhīyamānaṁ – united, ca – and, manas – mind, tattve – in causal energy, vilīyate – assume the nature

As for camphor in fire, salt in water, so the mind when united into causal energy assumes the causal nature.

Analysis

The nature of the mind is to adopt the coloration of the medium to which it is connected to. The mind has prejudices and preferences which run contrary to the aims of yoga. Hence the mind must be redirected even against its native tendencies. Camphor helplessly melts when it makes contact with fire but all the same the problem is to cause the association. The yogi has a task to link his mind to the causal energy.

Application

When a student first makes contact with the causal plane or with a level below that which is a source-point for a physical or lower astral reality, he may not realize that plane of consciousness and may still be referring back to normal phenomena with an idea that nothing happened. This is due to the abstractness of the causal plane or source-point. To break this ignorance a yogi should repeatedly do the meditations, and have faith that over time, sensual perception of the higher level will develop and become objectified.

Verse 60

ज्ञेयं सर्वं प्रतीतं च ज्ञायं च मन उच्यते ।

ज्ञायं ज्ञेयं समं नष्टं नान्यः पन्था द्वितीयकः ।। ६० ।।

jñeyaṁ sarvaṁ pratītaṁ ca jñānaṁ ca mana ucyate I
jñānaṁ jñeyaṁ samaṁ naṣṭaṁ nānyaḥ panthā dvitīyakaḥ II 60 II

jñeyaṁ – what is known, sarvaṁ – all, pratītaṁ – wisdom, ca – and, jñānaṁ – knowledge, ca – and, mana – mind, ucyate – concerns, jñānaṁ – knowledge, jñeyaṁ – what is known, samaṁ – equal, naṣṭaṁ – disappeared, nānyaḥ = na (non) + anyah (other), panthā – process of transcendence, dvitīyakaḥ – second

All that can be known, wisdom itself and theory, concerns the mind; when knowledge and what is to be known disappears then there is no other process of transcendence.

Analysis

This happens when the yogi reached the causal plane where everything existing in the physical and psychic material nature is sourced. Seeing and feeling the essential basis (tattva) of what was manifested in the physical and psychic material nature, the yogi is satisfied to know that this is all there is. It is the foundation, the root, the primal cause.

The yogi dives into the causal plane to become familiar with the feel of it, to ingest its energy so as to satisfy the craving for its manifestation as subtle and gross reality. Some yogis go into the causal plane and remain there for millions of years. They become absorbed in its energy so that when they again come out of it, they feel no acute attraction to any manifestation which was sourced from it.

Application

Failure to reach the causal plane is caused by immaturity of some students who want to be successful in yoga but who are not evolved sufficiently through the mundane evolutionary cycle, to actually abandon gross gratification. When a living entity is first manifested in the material creation, it is awarded a content psyche which has certain urges embedded in it. These must be fulfilled to a greater degree before the entity can be liberated.

Verse 61

मनो–दृश्यमिदं सर्वं यत्किंचित्स–चराचरम् ।

मनसो ह्युन्मनी–भावाद्वैतं नैवोलभ्यते ।। ६१ ।।

mano–dṝśyamidaṁ sarvaṁ yatkiṁcitsa–carācaram |
manaso hyunmanī–bhāvāddvaitaṁ naivolabhyate || 61 ||

mano = manaḥ = mind, dṝśyam – means of perception, idaṁ – this, sarvaṁ – all, yat – which, kiṁcit – something, sa – that, carācaram – mobile and immobile life forms, manaso = manasaḥ = mind, hy = hi = because, unmani – void of mundane content, bhāvād = bhāvāt = from a state, dvaitaṁ – conflicting states, naivo = na (not) + eva (so), labhyate – exists

The mind is the means of perception of all this, which is the mobile and immobile life forms. Thus when the mind is devoid of mundane content, there are no conflicting states.

Analysis

The relational faculty is the subtle body which is a complex perception machine. It has many components which include the core-self which is the spiritual object within it. The relationship with the material world can be diced by restricting the subtle body's involvement with gross and/or psychic material phenomena. When the mind is devoid of mundane content, the mundane history continues unabated but it is terminated for the time being for that particular yogi.

Application

A yogi must spend hours meditating in a neutral state where there is neither attraction nor repulsion from the sense objects; where those objects, their names and values, just do not arise. This gives the yogi a neutral basis to enjoy. When he gets used to this he abandons memories of previous excitements and progresses to the chit akash sky of consciousness.

Verse 62

ज्ञेय–वस्तु–परित्यागाद्विलयं याति मानसम् ।

मनसो विलये जाते कैवल्यमवशिष्यतेते ।। ६२ ।।

jñeya–vastu–parityāgādvilayaṁ yāti mānasam |
manaso vilaye jāte kaivalyamavaśiṣyate || 62 ||

jñeya – what is known, vastu – object, parityāgād = parityāgāt = due to complete abandonment, vilayaṁ – dissolution, yāti –shifts into, mānasam – mind, manaso – manasaḥ = mind, vilaye – dissolved, jāte – usually, kaivalyam – isolated core–self, avaśiṣyate – without remainder

Due to complete abandonment of what can be researched and of objects, the mind shifts into a state of dissolution. When the mind is dissolved the isolated core–self alone remains.

Analysis

The full dissolution of the inner psyche, of its component influences, causes the disappearance of the kundalini lifeforce and the buddhi intellect orb. With these two predominators out of the picture, the core-self is free at last and can experience itself by itself rather than know itself as something which was always under those influences.

It is a question of how to achieve this.

Can this become a reality by willpower command over the mind, as Gautam Buddha did?

Does the student have to use special methods of the ashtanga yoga process?

Application

In the Yoga Sutras, Patanjali explained what it is like to achieve this state:

prasaṁkhyāne api akusīdasya sarvathā
vivekakhyāteḥ dharmameghaḥ samādhiḥ

prasaṁkhyāna – in the abstract meditation; api – even so; akusīdasya – of one who has no interest or sees no gain in material nature; sarvathā – in all ways; vivekakhyāteḥ – with super discrimination; dharmameghaḥ = dharma – nature's way of acting for beneficial results + meghaḥ – mento-emotional clouds of energy; samādhi – continuous effortless linkage of the attention to higher reality.

For one who sees no gains in material nature, even while perceiving it in abstract meditation, one has the super discrimination. One attains the continuous effortless linkage of the attention to higher reality which is described as knowing the mento-emotional clouds of energy which compel a person to perform according to nature's way of acting for beneficial results. (Yoga Sutras 4.29)

tataḥ kleśa karma nivṛttiḥ

tataḥ – subsequently; kleśa – afflictions; karma – cultural activities; nivṛttiḥ – stoppage of the operation of the mento-emotional energy.

Subsequently there is stoppage of the operation of the mento-emotional energy in terms of generation of cultural activities and their resulting afflictions. (Yoga Sutras 4.30)

Verse 63

एवं नाना–विधोपायाः सम्यक्स्वानुभवान्विताः ।
समाधि–मार्गाः कथिताः पूर्वाचार्यैर्महात्मभिः ।। ६३ ।।

evaṁ nānā–vidhopāyāḥ samyaksvānubhavānvitāḥ ।
samādhi–mārgāḥ kathitāḥ pūrvācāryairmahātmabhiḥ ।। 63 ।।

evaṁ – thus, nana – various, vidhopāyāḥ – process, samyak – precise, svānubhavānvitāḥ – by personal insight, samadhi – continuous effortless linkage to a higher environment or person, mārgāḥ – techniques, kathitāḥ – they taught, pūrvācāryair = pūrvācāryaiḥ = by ancient yoga teachers, mahātmabhiḥ – by the great souls

Thus various processes were developed through precise personal insight, which rendered techniques of continuous effortless linkage to a higher environment or person

as taught by the great–souled ancient teachers.

Analysis

Various ancient yogis were successful with various methods which they imparted to their disciples. There must be personal insight in each of the students by whatever process used. It should not be a collective farce which thrives on numbers of followers and conjoint confidence which boosts self-esteem but which gives no access to the higher environments and super-persons.

Application

Personal insight is everything in the yoga process. It was summarized by Lord Krishna:

na hi jñānena sadṛśaṁ
pavitramiha vidyate
tatsvayaṁ yogasaṁsiddhaḥ
kālenātmani vindati (4.38)

na — nothing; hi — indeed; jñānena — with direct experience; sadṛśaṁ — compared with; pavitram — purifier; iha — in this world; vidyate — is relevant; tat — that realization; svayaṁ — himself; yogasaṁsiddhaḥ = yoga — yoga practice + saṁsiddhaḥ— perfected; kālenātmani = kālena — in time + ātmani — in the self; vindati — he locate

Nothing, indeed, can be compared with direct experience. No other purifier is as relevant in this world. That man who himself is perfected in yoga practice, will in time, locate the realization in himself. (Bhagavad Gita 4.38)

Verse 64

सुषुम्णायै कुण्डलिन्यै सुधायै चन्द्र–जन्मने ।
मनोन्मन्यै नमस्तुभ्यं महा–शक्त्यै चिद्–आत्मने ।। ६४ ।।

suṣumṇāyai kuṇḍalinyai sudhāyai candra–janmane I
manonmanyai namastubhyaṁ mahā–śaktyai cid–ātmane II 64 II

suṣumṇāyai – O subtle central spinal passage, kuṇḍalinyai – O kundalini lifeforce, sudhāyai – ambrosia, candra–janmane = what is produced from the moon, manonmanyai – O blank thoughtless idealess mental condition, namastubhyaṁ – I give reverential honor, mahā–śaktyai = great intelligent energy personified, cid–ātmane = insightful self consciousness

O subtle central spinal passage, O kundalini lifeforce, O ambrosia which is produced from the moon, O blank thoughtless idealess mental condition, I give reverential honor to you, great intelligent energy and insightful self-consciousness personified.

Analysis

This explains the complexity of the liberation which is described in the Hatha Yoga Pradipika. Let us partition it out:

- subtle central spinal passage
- kundalini lifeforce
- ambrosia, which is produced from the moon
- blank thoughtless idealess mental condition
- great intelligent energy
- insightful self-consciousness personified

By hook or crook, any which way, the **subtle central spinal passage** should be cleared of heavy astral energy which is laden with urges from the mundane evolutionary process of the psychic material nature. There is no argument about methods, even though Swatmarama made recommendations in the text. The issue is accomplishment.

The **kundalini lifeforce** must be reformed, changed, so that it no longer runs the show in the psyche, so that it serves the purpose of yoga which is for the core-self to transit to the divine world as soon as possible. Kundalini must be driven out of its lair which is the muladhara base chakra. The yogi must drive it out day after day, persistently, until it no longer desires to stay there and of its own accord permanently relocates into the brain.

The **ambrosia, which is produced from the moon,** is the nectar energy which is produced in the head of the subtle body as compared to the bliss energy which is produced in the reproductive organs. The moon energy is cool. The sun energy is heated.

The **blank thoughtless idealess mental condition** is a must. There is no access to the chit akash sky of consciousness without first being in this state. It is the transit access to the divine world. It is void of the conventional ideation and imaging energy which usually saturates the mind space.

The **great intelligent energy** is the fully aroused, fully cooperative kundalini lifeforce. If left to its own device, this same energy causes utter degradation of the spiritual self.

The **insightful self-consciousness personified** is the core-self when it is free from the influence of the adjuncts but after it evolved through mundane life forms and summarily dismissed in itself the need for those experiences but simultaneously gained a connection with Shiva, Krishna and their divine locales.

Application

In this verse, the great mantra for this process was divulged freely by Swatmarama Mahayogin. Why did he write it down if it is a confidential mantra which cannot be used unless it is shared by an accomplished yoga-guru?

The reason is simple:

No one can use this mantra effectively if that person is not at an advanced level and does not have a serviceable connection with the yoga-guru who is connected with Shiva and Krishna; and was not expressly bestowed with this prayer.

Here in English is the pronunciation:

su-shum-naa-yai kun-da-lin-yai
sud-haa-yai chan-dra jan-ma-ne
ma-non-man-yai na-mas-tubh-yam
ma-haa shak-tya chid at-ma-ne

*(The syllable **ne** is pronounced as **nay** just as **ay** is said in the word **day**.)*

One should not chant this mantra unless one gets permission from an accomplished teacher of kundalini yoga, as well as be shown how to connect to the deity of that teacher. If the teacher is atheistic or advocates that there is no supreme being, that there is no Shiva in control, that there is no Krishna in control, then one should not receive this mantra from him because he would be inconsistent with the teaching of Swatmarama Guruji.

Verse 65

अशक्य–तत्त्व–बोधानां मूढानामपि संमतम् ।

प्रोक्तं गोरक्ष–नाथेन नादोपासनमुच्यते ।। ६५ ।।

aśakya–tattva–bodhānāṁ mūḍhānāmapi saṁmatam I
proktaṁ gorakṣa–nāthena nādopāsanamucyate II 65 II

aśakya – not capable, tattva – reality, bodhānāṁ – integral insight, mūḍhānām = by those who are dull–witted, api – even, saṁmatam – appreciated, proktaṁ – explained, gorakṣa–nāthena = by Gorakshnath, nādopāsanam = nāda (naad supernatural sound resonance) + upāsanam (practice), ucyate – will describe

Those who are incapable of integral insight into reality, who are dull–witted, even they are appreciative of the practice of naad supernatural sound resonance which I will describe as explained by Gorakshnath.

Analysis

Even non-yogis, even pseudo-yogis, even Neanderthal humans whom have somehow acquired a modern human body, may appreciate the practice of hearing naad supernatural sound resonance. They will not access the chit akash sky of consciousness from it, but they will benefit in terms of relieving the stress of survival. They may be inspired with easier lifestyle, entailing less violence in the struggle for existence.

Application

Gorakshnath Mahayogin, one of the siddhas, introduced the importance of naad sound resonance. He wiped out the fantasy about using mantras. He stressed the natural mantra which is naad. Some are of the opinion that naad is not that important and that the use of mantras is more essential and is the Vedic way. Some people feel that listening to a sound in your head cannot possibly give one access to the divine world.

However the key point about Gorakshnath's process is that when chanting mantras, the yogi has to chant the sound and endeavor to listen to it or he has to chant it and focus on letting the intonation saturate his psyche. The effort to do that is conserved and can be used for chit akash focus if the yogi uses naad which is intoned into his psyche causelessly. The yogi makes no effort to chant naad but can instead hear it using full attention rather than attention which is split into chanting and then focused hearing. The method of Gorakshnath facilitates the dharana-dhyana-samadhi samyama process which is the high end of meditation practice.

Verse 66

श्री–आदिनाथेन स–पाद–कोटि–

लय–प्रकाराः कथिता जयन्ति ।

नादानुसन्धानकमेकमेव

मन्यामहे मुख्यतमं लयानाम् ।। ६६ ।।

śrī–ādināthena sa–pāda–koṭi
laya–prakārāḥ kathitā jayanti I
nādānusandhānakamekameva
manyāmahe mukhyatamaṁ layānām II 66 II

śrī – illustrious, ādināthena – by Lord Adinath, Shiva, sa–pāda = one and one–fourth, koṭi – ten million, (sa–pāda–koṭi = twelve and one half million), laya – absence of mento–emotional trauma, prakārāḥ – types, kathitā – described, jayanti – effective, nādānusandhānakam = nāda (naad supernatural sound) + anusandhānakam (spiritual focus into resonance), ekam – one, eva – only, manyāmahe – I think, mukhyatamaṁ – most important, layānām = absence of mento–emotional trauma

The illustrious Lord Adinath, Shiva, described twelve and one–half million types of absences of mento–emotional trauma, which are effective. The only special one is the spiritual focus into the naad supernatural sound resonance. I think it is the most important one for attaining absence of mento–emotional trauma.

Analysis

Forget mantras!

Get with naad supernatural sound resonance. It is the quickest launch pad into the chit akash sky of consciousness.

Application

Patanjali established the rule that for meditation, one must first have the absence of the mento-emotional traumas in the mind. But a momentary achievement of this either by effective effort or occurring spontaneously is not sufficient for access into the kha divine space. The ascetic must find a method where the mind remains without its conventional thoughts and images for some time. Patanjali hinted this:

vyutthāna nirodha saṁskārayoḥ
abhibhava prādurbhāvau nirodhakṣaṇa
cittānvayaḥ nirodhapariṇāmaḥ

vyutthāna – expression; nirodha – suppression; saṁskārayoḥ – of the mento-emotional impressions; abhibhava – disappearance; prādurbhāvau – and manifestation ; nirodha – restraint, cessation; kṣaṇa – momentarily; citta – mento-emotional energy; ānvayaḥ – connection; nirodha – restraint; pariṇāmaḥ – transforming effects.

When the connection with the mento-emotional energy momentarily ceases during the manifestation and disappearance phases when there is expression or

suppression of the impressions, that is the restraint of the transforming mento-emotional energy. (Yoga Sutras 3.9)

tasya praśāntavāhita saṁskārāt

tasya – of this; praśānta – spiritual peace; vāhita – flow; saṁskārāt – from the impressions derived.

Concerning this practice of restraint, the impressions derived, cause a flow of spiritual peace. (Yoga Sutras 3.10)

sarvārthatā ekāgratayoḥ kṣaya udayau
cittasya samādhipariṇāmaḥ

sarvārthatā – varying objective; ekāgratayoḥ – of the one aspect before the attention; kṣaya – decrease; udayau – and increase; cittasya – of the mento-emotional energy; samādhi – the continuous effortless linkage of the attention to the higher concentration force, object or person; pariṇāmaḥ – transforming effects, change.

The decrease of varying objectives in the mento-emotional energy and the increase of the one aspect within it are the changes noticed in the practice of continuous effortless linking of the attention to higher concentration forces, objects or persons. (Yoga Sutras 3.11)

tataḥ punaḥśānta uditau tulya pratyayau
cittasya ekāgratāpariṇāmaḥ

tataḥ – then; punaḥ – again; santoditau = śānta – tranquilized, settled, subsided + uditau – and agitated, emerging; tulya – similar; pratyayaḥu – conviction or belief as mental content, instinctive interest; cittasya – of the mento-emotional energy; ekāgratā – of what is in front of one aspect before the attention; pariṇāmaḥ – transforming effects, change.

Then again, when the mind's content is the same as it was when it is subsiding and when it is emerging, that is the transformation called "having one aspect in front of or before the attention." (Yoga Sutras 3.12)

Verse 67

मुक्तासने सथितो योगी मुद्रां सन्धाय शाम्भवीम् ।

श्रृणुयाद्दक्षिणे कर्णे नादमन्तास्थमेकधीः ।। ६७ ।।

muktāsane sthito yogī mudrāṁ sandhāya śāmbhavīm I
śṝṇuyāddakṣiṇe karṇe nādamantāsthamekadhīḥ II 67 II

muktāsane – in the liberation posture, sthito = sthitaḥ = sitting, yogī – yogi, mudrāṁ – mystic–arresting actions, sandhāya – combining, śāmbhavīm – Shambhavi visual focus between the eyebrows, śṝṇuyād = śṝṇuyāt = due to hearing, dakṣiṇe – in the right, karṇe – in the ear, nādam – naad supernatural sound resonance, antāstham – inside positioned, ekadhīḥ – one focusing interest

Sitting and combining the liberation posture with the mystic arresting action of the Shambhavi visual focus between the eyebrows, the yogi, should with one focusing

interest in the right ear, hear naad supernatural sound resonance.

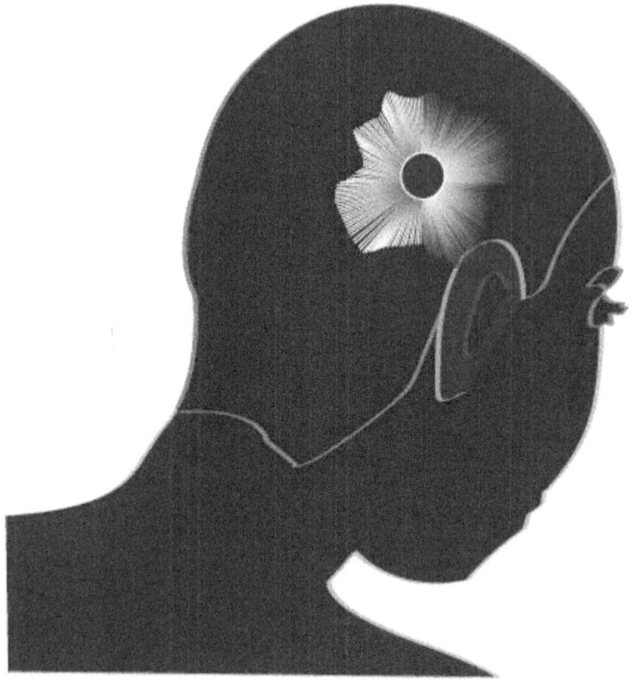

Analysis

Naad is reported to be in the zone of the right ear. However some ascetics hear naad on the left side. Others hear it at the back of the head; others in other places either in the head, neck, spine or trunk of the subtle body. No matter where naad is contacted, the yogi should enter into it.

Application

Muktasana is a variation of the easy pose. It should be used when doing the visual focus between the eyebrows but with naad sound resonance as the background focus.

Sri Lahiri Mahasaya, instructed me in doing this practice in this order:

- *sit in liberation posture*
- *express focusing interest in the right ear to hear naad supernatural sound resonance*
- *combine the mystic arresting action of the visual focus between the eyebrows with naad absorption.*

There is one small detail to be added which is that after focusing on naad sound resonance, the yogi should apply khecari mudra in its simplest form which is to push the tongue up and back to the soft palate. Then the yogi should do the focus between the eyebrows but Sri Lahiri instructed that the focus should be done at first with the touching sense and should be applied visually only when a light appears or if the third eye opens or if bliss energy becomes manifest.

शरवण–पुट–नयन–युगल
घ्राण–मुखानां निरोधनं कार्यम् ।
शुद्ध–सुषुम्णा–सरणौ
सफुटममलः श्रूयते नादः ।। ६८ ।।

śravaṇa–puṭa–nayana–yugala
ghrāṇa–mukhānāṁ nirodhanaṁ kāryam ।
śuddha–suṣumṇā–saraṇau
sphuṭamamalaḥ śrūyate nādaḥ ।। 68 ।।

śravaṇa – hearing sense, puṭa–nayana = eye , yugala – pair, ghrāṇa – smelling sense, mukhānāṁ – mouth, nirodhanaṁ – externally withdrawn and internally focused, kāryam – do, śuddha – cleared, suṣumṇā – subtle central spinal passage, saraṇau – flowing, coursing, sphuṭam – causal vibrations, amalaḥ – distinct, śrūyate – is heard, nādaḥ – naad supernatural sound resonance

Externally withdrawing the hearing sense, pair of eyes, smelling sense and mouth; then the distinct naad supernatural sound resonance is heard in the cleared subtle central spinal passage through which causal vibrations flow.

Analysis

This is a double checking procedure so that the yogi makes certain that there is no leakage of sensual energy going outside of the psyche. This check is unnecessary for those yogis who did a thorough breath-infusion. It is for those advanced yogis, who even without breath-infusion, can order the shutdown of all extrovert sensual tendencies.

Application

When all the senses are shut down and they have no covert or obvious interest in pursuing anything outside of the psyche, then the yogi should check to be sure that no sensual energy leaks through the hearing sense, the visual sense, the smelling sense or the tasting concern. Naad sound will intensify and increase in frequency if the sensual interests are effectively retracted. It will be heard then not only in the head of the subtle body but in the cleared subtle central spinal passage, the sushumna nadi. This can only happen if that passage is cleared of all dense astral energy. That is why it is necessary to do a thorough session of breath-infusion immediately prior to this practice.

Sushumna nadi should be blasted out by the breath-infused kundalini. That is the method of clearing the central passage of dense astral energy.

Verse 69

आरम्भश्च घटश्चैव तथा परिचयो।अपि च ।
निष्पत्तिः सर्व–योगेषु स्यादवस्था–चतुष्टयम् ।। ६९ ।।

ārambhaśca ghaṭaścaiva tathā paricayo|api ca |
niṣpattiḥ sarva–yogeṣu syādavasthā–catuṣṭayam || 69 ||

ārambhaś = ārambhaḥ = preliminary, ca – and, ghaṭaś = ghaṭaḥ = containment, caiva = and so, tathā – so, paricayo = paricayaḥ = integration, api – also, ca – and, niṣpattiḥ – full proficiency, sarva–yogeṣu = of all yoga methods, syād = syāt = is, avasthā – conditions, catuṣṭayam – four

The preliminary, containment, integration and full proficiency are the four conditions of all the yogic processes.

Analysis

At the **preliminary stage** most students stumble around trying to figure the correct procedure. This is the most frustrating level. Some students remain here for the entire lifetime of practice, while others only stay here for the shortest possible period. Students who mastered the practice in past lives, will advance rapidly and may become objects of resentment and envy.

The **containment stage** is the effort to make the method a habit. Because of resistance the psyche may exclude the method such that even though there is regular practice, its effects do not penetrate deeply. Students who have difficulty at this stage usually approach the yoga teacher stating that despite their efforts, the old lifestyle which they intend to change or eliminate, still remains and causes them to act counterproductively.

The **integration stage** is when the student is so habituated to the practice, that there is no turning back. The student's psyche has a positive attitude to the method. He is urged on by this. He is encouraged tremendously.

The **full proficiency** is when the student mastered the practice, where it becomes a reflex and where he can consolidate the progress and proceed to even higher techniques.

Application

A student needs a philosophical basis for doing kundalini yoga. This skill of thinking and reasoning in a way that is supportive of the practice, comes from reading Bhagavad Gita, the Yoga Sutras and similar texts.

Verse 70

अथ आरम्भावस्था

बरह्म–ग्रन्थेर्भवेद्भेदो हयानन्दः शून्य–सम्भवः ।

विच्चित्रः क्वणको देहे।अनाहतः श्रूयते धवनिः ।। ७० ।।

atha ārambhāvasthā
brahma–grantherbhavedbhedo hyānandaḥ śūnya–sambhavaḥ |
vicitraḥ kvaṇako dehe|anāhataḥ śrūyate dhvaniḥ || 70 ||

atha – now to be described, ārambhāvasthā – preliminary stage, brahma–granther = brahma–grantheḥ = energy congestion of brahma, bhaved = bhavet = is, bhedo =

bhedaḥ = shattered, hy = hi = because, ānandaḥ – blissful feelings, śūnya – idealess imageless mental content, sambhavaḥ – experience, produce, vicitraḥ – various, kvaṇako = kvanakaḥ = here–there, dehe – in the body, anāhataḥ – spontaneous sounds, śrūyate – heard, dhvaniḥ – musical tones

Now the preliminary stage is described:

When the energy congestion called brahma is shattered, the yogi experiences blissful feelings in the idealess imageless mental content, and various musical tones are spontaneously heard here and there in the body.

Analysis

The energy congestion called brahma is located at the muladhara base chakra, the default residence of the kundalini lifeforce. Students get experience of this location when doing kundalini yoga. The kundalini moves from the muladhara base chakra as it is urged by the infused breath energy. If there is enough of that energy, kundalini will move through the spine into the neck and will then burst into the head of the subtle body. It will head for the buddhi intellect orb and after attacking this psychic organ, it will go upwards to the brahma randra crown chakra in the head of the subtle body. This causes the energy congestion at the base to be shattered. This will result in a black-out, white-out or gold-out but the student may not hear naad sound resonance or any musical tones as stated by Swatmarama.

It is important to know that whatever Swatmarama Guruji wrote is ideal. These requirements and incidences are valid for those who have the proficiency. Beginners may have totally different experiences. Swatmarama gave these subtle occurrences:

- blissful feelings in the idealess imageless mental content
- various musical tones which are spontaneously heard

That will happen in this condition:

- energy congestion called brahma is shattered

He calls this the preliminary stage. However for most beginners, this is the advanced level. For shattering of the base chakra brahma energy congestion, a yogi must have a sufficient breath-infusion thrusted or targeted into the kundalini at the muladhara base chakra, whereby kundalini moves with such an impetus that it cannot stop itself along the ascent through the sushumna nadi central spinal passage. In addition once it gets through the passage and bores through the neck, it should have enough energy to propel it all the way to the buddhi intellect orb and then to go through the crown chakra. This is not an easy achievement. To do this daily in kundalini yoga practice, the yogi must have the right pranayama breath-infusion method and must have mastered the anus, perineum, abdomen, chest, and chin locks. All of these must be applied because otherwise kundalini will likely leak energy through the spinal chakras and the charge of infused breath energy will fizz out, resulting in kundalini ascending partially up the spine and then subsiding back down to muladhara base chakra without going into the head.

In event that the yogi succeeds in bringing kundalini through the neck, then still the kundalini may look around in the head of the subtle body, move a little in the direction of the buddhi intellect orb, and then return down to muladhara base chakra without penetrating the crown chakra. If that happens the student may experience a stun-out, black-out or white-out.

If fortunately kundalini has enough charge to pierce the buddhi intellect orb and to turn upwards and penetrate the crown chakra then the student will experience a gold-out.

Application

The following resultant states of consciousness caused by the aroused kundalini are discussed below:

- *space-out*
- *stun-out*
- *black-out*
- *grey-out*
- *white-out*
- *gold-out*

The experience of a ***space-out*** *occurs when kundalini ascends through the spine, fizzes out at the top of the neck and just sprinkles a little of its energy into the brain. This results in a spaced out feeling as if the person lost control of their objective observing posture in the mind. The person may see a little bit of diffused light or have no sight but feel as if he or she was in a large spacious chamber. The person loses grip on memories and has no concept of identity or persona. There is a conversion from being a social unit to be just a space which has no focus. This will last for a few moments or for longer and then the person gradually comes to his or her senses and resumes the normal personality but with a feeling of having temporarily lost the self in the process.*

If the physical body was standing when this happened, it will usually fall to the ground. If it sat it may lean to one side or crumple over. Then when the person resumes objectivity, he or she will realize the changed posture.

The experience of a ***stun-out*** *occurs when kundalini ascends through the spine and bursts into the brain into white-gold light, and remains there at the top of the neck in the lower head for some moments or minutes and then quickly descends back to its base at the muladhara end-of-spine chakra. When this happens the physical body may not fall to the ground but may remain in one position or will keep moving into an intended position in slow motion. The yogi will feel as if he was stunned where there is no sensual perception, and he just existed with stationary awareness of being just there.*

The experience of a ***black-out*** *occurs when kundalini ascends through the spine while carrying heavy astral energy which it picked up as it ascended the central spinal passage. It may then burst into the brain into total psychic darkness, giving the person absolutely no insight consciousness. It may hit the buddhi intellect orb which it will surround in psychic darkness with the result that the person will lose objective consciousness. The person's physical body will fall to the ground or loop over or tilt to the side. This may last for moments, or for a few minutes, and then the person will resume objectivity with the understanding that time stood still and his existence was suspended for the time.*

The experience of a ***grey-out*** *occurs when kundalini ascends through the spine while carrying clouds of heavy astral energy which was interspaced with light astral force. As soon as this energy is released into the brain, it will surround the buddhi intellect* *orb and cause it to be uncertain and to lack clarity. The person will feel as if he is neither here nor there, as if he is consciousness and unconscious at the same time. He will be riddled with uncertainty as to there being any type of objective existence. If the body was standing when this occurred, it will immediately fall to the ground.*

The experience of a ***white-out*** *occurs when kundalini ascends through the spine while carrying medium weight astral energy which it picked up as it ascended the central spinal passage. It may then burst into the brain into a white energy cloud which is opaque and which does not allow any objective perception, giving the person slight insight consciousness. It may hit the buddhi intellect orb which it will surround in an astral cloud of energy with the result that the person will retain some degree of objective consciousness but not enough for clarity. The person's physical body may fall to the ground or fold over or tilt to the side. This may last for moments or for a few minutes. Then the person will resume objectivity with the understanding that time stood still and his existence was suspended for the time.*

The experience of a ***gold-out*** *occurs when kundalini ascends through the spine while carrying light-weight astral energy which it produced by a rapid thorough burning explosion in the spine. It will then burst into the brain into a gold or white-gold energy which is transparent and which gives insight consciousness. It will hit the buddhi intellect orb which it will penetrate with the result that the person will retain some degree of objective consciousness with partial or full clarity. The person's physical body may fall to the ground or loop over or tilt to the side. This may last for moments or for a few minutes and then the person will resume objectivity with the understanding that time stood still and his existence was reinforced or revealed on the spiritual plane. The gold-out has a spiritual bliss aspect to it which is lust free and transcendental.*

The ***energy congestion called brahma*** *which is the dark heavy astral energy at the muladhara base chakra is like a dark brown crystal brick. It is compacted with energy from the negative psychic end of material nature. By infusing breath and hormone energy into it with sufficient force, the brick explodes and then implodes upon its fragments. It becomes shattered into micro-crystals, which the yogi compresses inwards upon itself. This in turn explodes and moves up the sushumna central passage into the head of the subtle body where it immediately attacks the buddhi intellect orb and brilliantly flashes through the brahma randra crown chakra at the top of the subtle head.*

Verse 71

दिव्य–देहश्च तेजस्वी दिव्य–गन्धस्त्वरोगवान् ।
सम्पूर्ण–हृदयः शून्य आरम्भे योगवान्भवेत् ।। ७१ ।।

divya–dehaśca tejasvī divya–gandhastvarogavān ।
sampūrṇa–hṛdayaḥ śūnya ārambhe yogavānbhavet ।। 71 ।।

divya – divine, dehaś = dehaḥ = body, ca – and, tejasvī – radiant, divya – divine, gandhas – odor, tv = tu = but, arogavān – healthy, sampūrṇa – complete, hṛdayaḥ –

core existence, śūnya – idealess imageless mental content, ārambhe – in the preliminary, yogavān – proficient yogi, bhavet – become

The divine body, radiant, with a divine odor, healthy, with the complete core existence, having an idealess and imageless content: That is the preliminary proficiency of the yogi.

Analysis

When a yogi has a clean kundalini, it is understood that he attained the siddha level and can use a divine body which is radiant, with a divine odor, healthy, with the complete core-existence of the individual spiritual self, having an idealess imageless content, with such clarity as to bypass all conventional perceptions which to others have so much meaning.

Application

The destruction of the muladhara base chakra is the hallmark for a yogi that his creature existence stint is over. The basis for his quest in the mundane evolutionary cycle, being destroyed, he no longer has any reason to be in the material world, even though he is fated to still use a physical body. Such a yogi may sometimes appear to be an aimless purposeless wanderer, who is regarded as a wasted nuisance in human society. Others, who are elevated in this way, serve humanity responsibly and beneficially but with expert pretense because they know material existence to be a total washout.

Verse 72

अथ घटावस्था

द्वितीयायां घटीकृत्य वायुर्भवति मध्यगः ।

दृढासनो भवेद्योगी जञानी देव–समस्तदा ।। ७२ ।।

atha ghaṭāvasthā
dvitīyāyāṁ ghaṭīkṛtya vāyurbhavati madhyagaḥ |
dṛḍhāsano bhavedyogī jñānī deva–samastadā || 72 ||

atha – now to be described, ghaṭāvasthā – containment condition, dvitīyāyāṁ – second progression, ghaṭīkṛtya = doing the containment condition, vāyur = vāyuḥ = infused breath energy, bhavati – becomes, madhyagaḥ – flow through the middle channel, dṛḍhāsano = dṛḍhāsanaḥ = firm and steady, bhaved = bhavet = is, yogī – yogi, jñānī – perceptive person, deva–samas = same as a supernatural ruler, tadā – then

Now the containment condition is described:

In this second progression, having contained the energy, the infused breath flows through the middle channel. The yogi becomes firm and steady and is perceptive, being equivalent to a supernatural ruler.

Analysis

The **containment** condition is the one attained by yogis who are able to arouse kundalini all the way through the spine into the brain on a daily basis, so that eventually the sushumna central passage remains free of heavy astral energy and the kundalini at muladhara chakra remains in an aroused condition shining like a mini sun. Because of full time kundalini arousal even during the most mundane of activities, this yogi is regarded as being similar to the deva supernatural rulers who live in the celestial world exerting vast influences.

Application

Such a yogi sees the supernatural rulers, the siddhas, and the deities who abound in the subtle material world. He converses with them during dreams and during waking consciousness, in the daytime or at night. He can get whatever spiritual information he needs to further his practice. He may be in abject poverty or he may be wealthy. It does not matter because he leans on spiritual security and is inattentive to mundane luxury. He is careless in regards to his destiny because he relinquished control of his actions to inscrutable fate and no longer challenges its flexibility. As a man who is condemned to die does not care if he eats or drinks, if he is happy or unhappy, if he is sick or well, if he is offered the best or the worse, so this yogi is unconcerned with his destiny.

Verse 73

विष्णु–ग्रन्थेस्ततो भेदात्परमानन्द– सूचकः ।

अतिशून्ये विमर्दश्च भेरी–शब्दस्तदा भवेत् ।। ७३ ।।

viṣṇu–granthestato bhedātparamānanda–sūcakaḥ I
atiśūnye vimardaśca bherī–śabdastadā bhavet II 73 II

viṣṇu–granthes (grantheḥ) = energy congestion of Vishnu anahata lung-heart chakra complex, tato = tataḥ = then, bhedāt – due to piercing, paramānanda – most sublime pleasure, sūcakaḥ – indicated, atiśūnye – state beyond the idealess imageless mental content, vimardaś = vimardaḥ = tumultous, ca – and, bherī = kettledrum, śabdas – sound, tadā – then, bhavet – developed into

Then the energy congestion of Vishnu anahata lung-heart chakra complex is pierced, which is indicated by the most sublime pleasure. Then in the state beyond the idealess imageless mental content, the tumultuous kettledrum sound is manifested.

Analysis

This is the bursting of the anahata lung-heart chakra complex. This complex is subservient to the reproductive energy of the body and thus it has no independence. It is lust-infested. Even though kundalini may pass through the sushumna central spinal passage in a hurry and with high-grade astral energy, still it may pierce though this chakra without purifying the spread of this chakra's energy. People sometimes wonder why a person who did kundalini yoga for some years remains with lusty habits and is baffled repeatedly by sex attraction. The reason has more to do with this chakra than it does with the sex chakra on the spine or the sex organ chakras in the genitals.

This chakra in its polluted form sponsors various types of compassion and magnanimity. It misleads just about everybody.

When the yogi can make the infused breath energy, and the kundalini, target this chakra complex, imploding its energy on itself repeatedly, then eventually this area becomes cleared of medium dense astral energy. Its lust and social compassion aspects are obliterated, freeing the entity from complications of destiny which before were so attractive.

When this chakra is cleared of astral energy, it becomes idealess and imageless and does not emit plans for the future. It has no concerns about the social life in the material or lower astral worlds. Then the yogi hears the naad sound resonance as a tumultuous kettledrum sound in the zone of this chakra.

Application

There are various types of bliss of various degrees of mixed energy. Material nature made it easy for us to identify the lust bliss through sexual climax experience. That is a combination energy in which it is difficult to sort the lust flavor from the neutral bliss. As soon as the student can identify the neutral bliss aspect, he can make rapid advancement in the course of becoming a siddha.

More or less, being a siddha means forgetting about sexual climax experience, forgetting about the lust bliss aspect and not becoming morose because of not having access to that. There are many persons who pose as celibate ascetics. Surprisingly, there are even females who do this. However, not having sexual experience does not mean that one is not morose over not having access to lust-bliss.

When a yogi is satisfied with the neutral bliss energy, he can walk freely with the siddhas. If the lust energy is in the psyche, it limits his access to them. When it is not expressed for pleasure purposes, it converts into a morose mood-energy. Thus sexual abstinence has that as its undesirable side effect. A yogi has to filter this energy, removing its lust aspect.

Verse 74

अथ परिछयावस्था

तृतीयायां तु विज्ञेयो विहायो मर्दल–धवनिः ।

महा–शून्यं तदा याति सर्व–सिद्धि–समाश्रयम् ।। ७४ ।।

atha parichayāvasthā
tṛtīyāyāṁ tu vijñeyo vihāyo mardala–dhvaniḥ ।
mahā–śūnyaṁ tadā yāti sarva–siddhi–samāśrayam ।। 74 ।।

atha – now to be described, parichayāvasthā – integration condition, tṛtīyāyāṁ – third progression, tu – but, vijñeyo = vijñeyaḥ = what is known, vihāyaḥ = vihāyo = psychological sky, mardala – drum, dhvaniḥ – sound, mahā–śūnyaṁ = great idealess imageless mental content, tadā – then, yāti – goes, sarva – all, siddhi – mystic perfection skills, samāśrayam – complete source

Now the integration condition is described:

In this third progression, the sound of a drum is known to manifest in the psychological sky. Then the infused energy goes into the great idealess imageless mental content, which is the total source of all mystic perfectional skills.

Analysis

This is the migration of the focal consciousness of the yogi into the chit akash sky of consciousness, which is titled as the kha divine space by Swatmarama. Based on the nomenclature of the Bhagavad Gita, this place is called dhama paramam or the place where the infallible personalities reside. It is called Vishnu Loka. It is called Shiva Loka. It is called Vaikuntha. It is called the brahman effulgence. It is called the spiritual world. It is termed the divine world.

Application

The access to the divine atmosphere is an inside transit. It does not concern using the subtle body to move about in the astral domain. The astral body is good up to the causal plane where it vanishes into nothing, and where the core-self is left with only its sense of identity. Beyond the causal plane there is the brahman spiritual effulgence and beyond that there are the divine living environments.

At first, a yogi gets vibrational access to the divine place. This involves using the spiritual sense of touch. Then he gets a visual clue in the form of light or glow light. If he can maintain focus on this light, then it develops into sound access which is more than the basic naad sound resonance. It has more variety of spiritual sounds in direct contrast to the naad supernatural resonance.

The divine mystic perfection skills were listed to Uddhava by Lord Krishna in this way:

śrī-bhagavān uvāca
siddhayo 'ṣṭādaśa proktā
dhāraṇā yoga-pāra-gaiḥ
tāsām aṣṭau mat-pradhānā
daśaiva guṇa-hetavaḥ (10.3)

śrī-bhagavān – the blessed lord; uvāca — said; siddhayo = siddhayaḥ — mystic skills; 'ṣṭādaśa = aṣṭādaśa — eight and ten, eighteen; proktā — state; dhāraṇā — the linking of the attention to various concentration forces; yoga — yoga; pāra-gaiḥ — one whose interest has progressed the farthest; tāsām — of them; aṣṭau — eight; mat-pradhānā = mat-pradhānāḥ — prominent in me; daśaiva = daśa — ten + eva — indeed; guṇa – influences of material nature; hetavaḥ — causes.

Those who progressed the farthest in yoga, state that there are eighteen mystic skills, and eighteen types linkage of the attention to eighteen types of concentration forces. Eight of these are prominent in Me, the remaining ten are caused by a particular influence of material nature. (Uddhava Gita 10.3)

aṇimā mahimā mūrter
laghimā prāptir indriyaiḥ

prākāmyaṁ śruta-dṛṣṭeṣu
śakti-preraṇam īśitā (10.4)

animā — becoming atomic; mahimā — becoming cosmic; mūrter = mūrteḥ — pertaining to form of the yogi; laghimā — technique of weightlessness; prāptir = prāptiḥ — acquiring or experiencing; indriyaiḥ — through sense organs; prākāmyam — enjoying almost anything desired; śruta-dṛṣṭeṣu = śruta — of what is heard of only + dṛṣṭeṣu — what can be seen normally; śakti-preraṇam — the ability to manipulate mundane potency; īśitā — power of ruling others.

Becoming atomic, becoming cosmic, pertains to a form of the yogi, as well as being weightless, acquiring or experiencing through the sense organs of others, enjoying what was heard of and what was seen normally, manipulating mundane potency, ruling over others, (Uddhava Gita 10.4)

guṇeṣv asaṅgo vaśitā
yat-kāmas tad avasyati
etā me siddhayaḥ saumya
aṣṭāv autpattikā matāḥ (10.5)

guṇeṣv = guṇeṣu — to the mundane influence; asaṅgo = asaṅgaḥ — non-attachment; vaśitā — technique of controlling one's nature; yat — what; kāmas = kāmaḥ — desire; tad = tat — that; avasyati — can obtain; etāḥ — these; me — my; siddhayaḥ — mystic skills; saumya — dear friend; aṣṭāv = aṣṭau — eight; autpattikā = autpattikāḥ — natural; matāḥ — considered.

...non-attachment to mundane influences, which results in the technique of controlling one's nature, and obtaining what is desired; these my dear friend, are considered to be the eight natural skills. (Uddhava Gita 10.5)

anūrmimattvaṁ dehe 'smin
dūra-śravaṇa-darśanam
mano-javaḥ kāma-rūpaṁ
para-kāya-praveśanam (10.6)

anūrmimattvam = anūrmi – not wavering, not fluctuating, not being affected + mattvam — my-ness, possessiveness, the sense of identification; dehe – in the boby; 'smin = asmin — this; dūra — afar, at a distance; śravana — hearing; darśanam — seeing; mano = manaḥ - mind; javaḥ — speed; kāma – desire; rūpam — form; para – other; kāya — body; praveśanam — entering.

Being unaffected by the sense of self identification with the body, hearing from a distance, seeing from a distance, moving at the speed of the mind, assuming any desired form, entering anyone's body, (Uddhava Gita 10.6)

svacchanda-mṛtyur devānāṁ
saha-krīḍānudarśanam
yathā-saṅkalpa-saṁsiddhir
ājñāpratihatā gatiḥ (10.7)

svacchanda-mṛtyur = svacchanda — own desire + mṛtyur (mṛtyuh) — death, dying; devānām — of the supernatural rulers; saha — with; krīḍānudarśanam = krida — sports + anudarśanam — participating; yathā — as; saṅkalpa — motive; saṁsiddhir = saṁsiddhiḥ — perfect fulfilment; ājñāpratihatā = ajna — command + apratihatā — unopposed; gatih — course.

...dying as desired, participating in the sports of the supernatural rulers, perfect fulfillment of one's motive, and to command circumstances from an unopposed course anywhere, (Uddhava Gita 10.7)

tri-kāla-jñatvam advandvaṁ
para-cittādy-abhijñatā
agny-arkāmbu-viṣādīnāṁ
pratiṣṭambho 'parājayaḥ (10.8)

tri – three phases; kāla – time factor; jñatvam — know, knowing, knowledge of; advandvam — not being affected by the dualities of heat and cold, happiness and distress; para — of others; cittādy = citta — mental and emotional energy + ādy (ādi) — and related privacies; abhijñata — knowing; agny (agni) — fire; arkāmbu = arka — sun + ambu — water; viṣādīnām = visa — poison + ādīnām — and other dangers; pratiṣṭambho = pratiṣṭambhah — counteracting; 'parājayaḥ = aparājayaḥ = aparā – not others + jayah - being conquered.

...knowing the three phases of the time factor, not being affected by heat and cold, happiness and distress, knowing the mental and emotional energy and other related privacies of others, counteracting the influence of fire, sun, water, poison and other dangers, not being conquered by others: (Uddhava Gita 10.8)

Verse 75

चित्तानन्दं तदा जित्वा सहजानन्द–सम्भवः ।

दोष–दुःख–जरा–वयाधि–क्षुधा –निद्रा–विवर्जितः ।। ७५ ।।

cittānandaṁ tadā jitvā sahajānanda–sambhavaḥ I
doṣa–duḥkha–jarā–vyādhi–kṣudhā–nidrā–vivarjitaḥ II 75 II

cittānandaṁ = pleasures of the mento–emotional energy, tadā – then, jitvā – becoming objective to, sahajānanda – spontaneous spiritual feelings, sambhavaḥ – production, doṣa – flaws, duḥkha – trauma, jarā – old age, vyādhi – disease, kṣudhā – hunger, nidrā – sleep, vivarjitaḥ – lacking

Becoming objective to the pleasures of the mento–emotional energy, spontaneous spiritual feelings which lack flaws, trauma, old age, disease, hunger and sleep, become manifest.

Analysis

There are two types of mento-emotional energy. One type is on this side of the spiritual divide which is manufactured using the modes of material nature. The other type, the absolute, is on the other side in the spiritual world. It is created from the spiritual energy without any tinge of material nature. A yogi must become objective to the pleasures of the mento-emotional energy which was derived from the modes of material nature. The problem with this energy is that it has an infinite variety of displays which confounds the person.

There are two types of entities who are moving about in the material creation. Lord

Krishna listed these as follows:

dvāvimau puruṣau loke
kṣaraścākṣara eva ca
kṣaraḥ sarvāṇi bhūtāni
kūṭastho'kṣara ucyate (15.16)

dvau — two; imau — these two; puruṣau — two spirits; loke — in the world; kṣaraścākṣara = kṣaraḥ — affected + ca — and + akṣara — unaffected; eva — indeed; ca — and; kṣaraḥ — affected; sarvāṇi — all; bhūtāni — mundane creatures; kūṭastho = kūṭasthaḥ — stable soul ; 'kṣara = akṣara — unaffected; ucyate — is said to be

These two types of spirits are in this world, namely the affected ones and the unaffected ones. All mundane creatures are affected. The stable soul is said to be unaffected. (Bhagavad Gita 15.16)

The unaffected spirits are the ones who are objective to the pleasures of the mento-emotional energy. This does not mean that they do not experience such pleasures. They do because so long as a core-self uses a subtle body, there will be such experiences. But the effect of the experience is different in the case of the unaffected spirit as compared to the affected one. Those who are affected center their lives on the fluctuations in the mento-emotional energy which was derived from material nature; while the unaffected spirits because of a causeless contact with the divine side of existence are subconsciously de-focused from the mundane side. These unaffected spirits appear to be the same as the affected ones but there is a difference even though it is not evident to limited sense perception.

Application

To sort between spiritual emotion and emotion which is based on the energy of material nature, one has to check to see if the emotion has a content which lack flaws, trauma, old age, disease, hunger and sleep. Doing this is not easy because it requires supernatural perception. Thus the confusion as to who is who in the material world will continue indefinitely.

Verse 76

अथ निष्पत्त्य-अवस्था

रुद्र- ग्रन्थिं यदा भित्त्वा शर्व-पीठ-गतो।अनिलः ।

निष्पत्तौ वैणवः शब्दः क्वणद्-वीणा- क्वणो भवेत् ।। ७६ ।।

atha niṣpatty–avasthā
rudra–granthiṁ yadā bhittvā śarva–pīṭha–gato।anilaḥ ।
niṣpattau vaiṇavaḥ śabdaḥ kvaṇad–vīṇā–kvaṇo bhavet ।। 76 ।।

atha – now to be described, niṣpatty–avasthā = full proficiency condition, rudra–granthiṁ = energy congestion of Rudra third-eye chakra, yadā – when, bhittvā – penetrate, śarva –Shiva, pīṭha – location, gato = gataḥ = goes into, anilaḥ – infused breath energy, niṣpattau – full proficiency, vaiṇavaḥ – flute, śabdaḥ – sound, kvaṇad

= here–there, vīṇā – vina stringed instrument, kvaṇo = kvaṇaḥ = here–there, bhavet – manifest

Now the full proficiency condition is described:

When the energy congestion known as Rudra third-eye chakra is penetrated, the infused breath energy goes into the location of Shiva. Then the full proficiency becomes evident by the sound of a flute here and there, as well as that of a vina stringed instrument.

Analysis

The Rudra congestion is at the ajna chakra, a place which becomes blocked with a complex array of dense subtle energies. It becomes contaminated with materialistic objectives and their related reinforcements and memories. To remove this blockage the yogi must infuse breath energy into the kundalini lifeforce, cause it to move into the brain with enthusiasm and then have it penetrate through the dense subtle energy which is between the eyebrows and which is in the inside of the subtle forehead.

There must also be a reduction of the allied negative influences which assail a yogi so that during meditation he can focus on naad and is not induced forcibly to invoke and develop materialistic memories. A yogi must curb his associations so that he is not influenced by people who have no interest or a badly-motivated interest or even a subconscious interest which contravenes progress.

Application

When the brow chakra is cleared of dense astral energy, the yogi reaches the chit akash easily. He hears melodious sounds which come from the chit akash sky of consciousness.

Verse 77

एकीभूतं तदा चित्तं राज–योगाभिधानकम् ।

सृष्टि–संहार–कर्तासौ योगीश्वर–समो भवेत् ।। ७७ ।।

ekībhūtaṁ tadā cittam rāja–yogābhidhānakam I
sṛṣṭi–saṁhāra–kartāsau yogīśvara–samo bhavet || 77 ||

ekībhūtaṁ – one causal medium, tadā – then, cittam – mento–emotional energy, rāja–yogābhidhānakam = rāja–yoga (mystic process of remaining introverted while being externally occupied) + abhidhānakam (sound), sṛṣṭi – creation, saṁhāra – destruction, kartāsau – master of both, yogīśvara– Lord of yogis, samo = sama = same as, like, bhavet – becomes

Then the mento-emotional energy as one causal medium is the condition of remaining introverted even while being externally occupied. As a master of both creation and destruction, the yogi becomes like the Lord of yogis.

Analysis

Patanjali described this development in this way:

vyutthāna nirodha saṁskārayoḥ
abhibhava prādurbhāvau nirodhakṣaṇa
cittānvayaḥ nirodhapariṇāmaḥ

vyutthāna – expression; nirodha – suppression; saṁskārayoḥ – of the mento-emotional impressions; abhibhava – disappearance; prādurbhāvau – and manifestation ; nirodha – restraint, cessation; kṣaṇa – momentarily; citta – mento-emotional energy; ānvayaḥ – connection; nirodha – restraint; pariṇāmaḥ – transforming effects.

When the connection with the mento-emotional energy momentarily ceases during the manifestation and disappearance phases when there is expression or suppression of the impressions, that is the restraint of the transforming mento-emotional energy. (Yoga Sutras 3.9)

tasya praśāntavāhita saṁskārāt

tasya – of this; praśānta – spiritual peace; vāhita – flow; saṁskārāt – from the impressions derived.

Concerning this practice of restraint, the impressions derived cause a flow of spiritual peace. (Yoga Sutras 3.10)

sarvārthatā ekāgratayoḥ kṣaya udayau
cittasya samādhipariṇāmaḥ

sarvārthatā – varying objective; ekāgratayoḥ – of the one aspect before the attention; kṣaya – decrease; udayau – and increase; cittasya – of the mento-emotional energy; samādhi – the continuous effortless linkage of the attention to the higher concentration force, object or person; pariṇāmaḥ – transforming effects, change.

The decrease of varying objectives in the mento-emotional energy and the increase of the one aspect within it are the changes noticed in the practice of continuous effortless linking of the attention to higher concentration forces, objects or persons. (Yoga Sutras 3.11)

tataḥ punaḥśānta uditau tulya pratyayau
cittasya ekāgratāpariṇāmaḥ

tataḥ – then; punaḥ – again; santoditau = śānta – tranquilized, settled, subsided + uditau – and agitated, emerging; tulya – similar; pratyayaḥu – conviction or belief as mental content, instinctive interest; cittasya – of the mento-emotional energy; ekāgratā – of what is in front of one aspect before the attention; pariṇāmaḥ – transforming effects, change.

Then again, when the mind's content is the same as it was when it is subsiding and when it is emerging, that is the transformation called "having one aspect in front of or before the attention". (Yoga Sutras 3.12)

Application

Literally speaking, in the aspect of freedom from worrying about transition, the yogi, once he changes the mento-emotional energy so that its texture is that of one causal medium, becomes like a god on earth. He is free to roam hither and thither anywhere in the material or astral creations because his mental and emotional basis is not the survival of kundalini psychic lifeforce mechanism.

Because of immunity from the shifty mental and emotional states, some other ascetics regard him as being the equivalent of the Lord of yogis. The ascetic takes note of their adoration and appraisal but does not let go of his submission to the yoga-gurus and deities. He does not allow people to encourage him to pose as Shiva or Krishna but rather instructs others how to properly approach the deities.

Verse 78

अस्तु वा मास्तु वा मुक्तिरत्रैवाखण्डितं सुखम् ।

लयोद्भवमिदं सौख्यं राज–योगादवाप्यते ।। ७८ ।।

astu vā māstu vā muktiratraivākhaṇḍitaṁ sukham I
layodbhavamidaṁ saukhyaṁ rāja–yogādavāpyate I I 78 I I

astu – let it be, vā – or, māstu = not to be, vā – or, muktir = muktiḥ = liberation from material exisence, atraivākhaṇḍitaṁ = atra (here and now) + eva (also) + akhaṇḍitaṁ (infinite), sukham – pleasure, layodbhavam = focus into spiritual existence, idaṁ – this, saukhyaṁ – happiness, rāja–yogād = rāja–yogāt = due to the mystic process of remaining introverted while being externally occupied, avāpyate – achieved

Let there be or let there not be liberation from material existence! Regardless, infinite pleasure is the result of this here and now. This focus into the spiritual existence and its happiness is achieved by means of the mystic process of remaining introverted while being externally occupied.

Analysis

This statement is made by Swatmarama because of his insight about the ways and means of existence for a limited being. Even a successful yogin, if he is a limited entity, cannot guarantee for himself liberation from material existence. Any such transit is regulated by deities. All statements about a limited being having absolute access must be underlined with permission of a deity.

Since the yogi cannot control if he will transit from the material world, his powers are limited to preparing himself for the transit. He should achieve what is practical and within his reach, which is to remain introverted while being externally occupied. To be precise, he must be a master of raja yoga. The raja yogi does well if he remains in the material world because of a lack of transit to the divine situation, and if he does get the access, he is qualified by his practice for the transfer.

Application

Infinite pleasure is the request of a person-self. This request cannot be fulfilled in the physical or psychic material world. To get this, the self has to either connect to the divine atmosphere or completely relocate into it. This relocation is only possible by action of the deity. To be practical, a yogi should dictate to himself what is required which is access from this material side of existence. That is done through portals which open from the divine side into the psyche of the yogi.

The subtle body, the astral form, even in its highest vibration cannot transit across the existential divide between the material world and the spiritual territories, but in the subtle body there is a way to either enter into the spiritual places or to peer into them.

That is done through the yoga explained in this Hatha Yoga Pradipika. With the permission of the deity, of Shiva or Krishna, a yogi may transit across but if the deity does not have that plan, then the yogi may learn how to peer into the spiritual places while remaining on this side of existence.

Verse 79

राज–योगमजानन्तः केवलं हठ–कर्मिणः ।

एतानभ्यासिनो मन्ये प्रयास–फल–वर्जितान् ।। ७९ ।।

rāja–yogamajānantaḥ kevalaṁ haṭha–karmiṇaḥ I
etānabhyāsino manye prayāsa–phala–varjitān II 79 II

rāja–yogam = mystic process of remaining introverted while being externally occupied, ajānantaḥ – those who do not know, kevalaṁ – only, haṭha–karmiṇaḥ = practicioners of kundalini manipulation for psychic energy transformation, etān – these, abhyāsino = abhyāsinaḥ = practicioners, manye – I think, prayāsa – exertion, phala – result, varjitān – lacking without

Those who do not know the raja yoga mystic process of remaining introverted while being externally occupied, and who practice only kundalini manipulation for psychic energy transformation, will exert themselves, without getting the desired result.

Analysis

A limited being cannot expect to be completely exempt from participating in the social construction of the world. So long as one is in manifestation on this side of existence, one will have to participate, willy nilly, in a meaningful or trivial way as dictated by providence. Thus a yogi has no choice but to learn raja yoga process of remaining introverted while being externally occupied.

Who knows how long a yogi will have to remain on this side of the existential divide?

For a million more years?

For a million more creations of material worlds?

Only the deity can tell, because only the deity can release the yogi and cause permanent transit to the other side.

Application

One must learn kundalini manipulation for psychic energy transformation. When that is mastered one should learn raja yoga process of remaining introverted while being externally occupied. In the words of the Bhagavad Gita, this means that one should master yoga and then learn from Krishna how to do karma yoga, which is the application of yoga expertise to social activities.

This karma yoga is not the same as seva religious activities and donation to religious causes. It is not the practice of devotion to Krishna or to any other deity. Karma yoga in this usage is yoga + karma, or in plain English, the mastery of ashtanga yoga applied to cultural activities in the material world.

It was the specialty of yogi-kings who learnt the yoga process from yoga rishis and then learnt how to apply their psychological detachment while presiding politically over a kingdom. It was taught to Arjuna by Krishna on the Battlefield of Kurukshetra in a political circumstance.

Verse 80

उन्मन्य–अवाप्तये शीघ्रं भ्रू–धयानं मम संमतम् ।

राज–योग–पदं प्राप्तुं सुखोपायो।अल्प– चेतसाम् ।

सद्यः प्रत्यय–सन्धायी जायते नादजो लयः ।। ८० ।।

unmany–avāptaye śīghraṁ bhrū–dhyānaṁ mama saṁmatam |
rāja–yoga–padaṁ prāptuṁ sukhopāyo|alpa–cetasām |
sadyaḥ pratyaya–sandhāyī jāyate nādajo layaḥ || 80 ||

unmany = unmani = void of mental content, avāptaye – attain, śīghraṁ – quickly, bhrū – between the eyebrows, dhyānaṁ – effortless focus, mama – my, saṁmatam – definite opinion, rāja–yoga–padaṁ = accomplishment of remaining introverted while externally occupied, prāptuṁ – to obtain, sukhopāyo = sukhopāyaḥ = easy mastery, alpa – small, cetasām – intellect, sadyaḥ – rapidly, pratyaya – perception, sandhāyī – spiritually fused, jāyate – achieves, nādajo = nādajaḥ = produced by naad supernatural sound resonance, layaḥ – focused absorption

For achieving the void mental content, my advice is the effortless focus between the eyebrows. For those with a small intellect, that method is easy for mastery of remaining introverted while externally occupied. The focused absorption produced from listening to naad supernatural sound resonance rapidly gives spiritually fused perception.

Analysis

Focus between the eyebrows may or may not cause the assumption of the void mental content which is necessary as a prerequisite of these practices. The reason is that the focus must be done in a particular way. One may require guidance unless one is lucky to discover the right method initially. A person can spend months, years even, meditating between the eyebrows and still not achieve the void mental content.

Why?

Because focusing between the eyebrows with the conventional mental attitude will cause an increase in thoughts and images to arise in the mind space.

Swatmarama advised that a person should do the effortless focus between the eyebrows to achieve the void mental condition but he is not physically present to give the details, other than what he wrote in this text. He stated here that even a person with a small intellect could use the method. This means even a person who has not mastered the Samkhya philosophical doctrine and who did not have exposure to mystic education which was available in the time of Swatmarama. For a human being today, that is perplexing.

Application

The last sentence is the instruction for modern yogis. One should focus on naad supernatural sound resonance. That will over time give spiritually fused perception. If one adheres to naad resonance, one will abandon the frontal part of the subtle head, which will result in the mind's abandonment of its conventional contents. However, this practice should be done for a long time, especially for a yogi who did not do pranayama breath-infusion before each meditation. The value of breath-infusion is that if done proficiently, it causes the mind to assume total introversion so that the yogi does not have to endeavor for that separately.

Verse 81

नादानुसन्धान–समाधि–भाजां

योगीश्वराणां हृदि वर्धमानम् ।

आनन्दमेकं वचसामगम्यं

जानाति तं श्री–गुरुनाथ एकः ।। ८१ ।।

nādānusandhāna–samādhi–bhājāṁ
yogīśvarāṇāṁ hṛdi vardhamānam |
ānandamekaṁ vacasāmagamyaṁ
jānāti taṁ śrī–gurunātha ekaḥ || 81 ||

nādānusandhāna = nādānusandhāna = nāda (naad supernatural sound) + anusandhāna (spiritual focus into resonance), samadhi – continuous linkage to a higher environment or person, bhājāṁ – acclaim, yogīśvarāṇāṁ – of the Lords of yoga, hṛdi – heart, existential cores, vardhamānam – fullness, ānandam – spiritual happiness, ekaṁ – one, vacasām – description, agamyaṁ – beyond, jānāti – knows, taṁ – him, śrī – illustrious, gurunātha – master of the guru lineage, ekaḥ – only

Spiritual focus into naad supernatural sound resonance, for those who are acclaimed for continuous linkage to a higher environment or person, who are lords of yoga with fullness in their existential cores, having particular spiritual happiness which is beyond description, are known by the master of the guru lineage only.

Analysis

The Gurunath is the master of the guru lineage. He may or may not have a material body but there is always a person in this category on the astral planes. He is usually based in the siddhaloka dimension-place. Such a person is the direct representative of Shiva and Krishna. In a rare appearance either Shiva or Krishna functions as this Gurunath but usually it is someone else, a divine being or a limited person who mastered the disciplines and has direct insight into the ways and means of enlightenment.

Swatmarama made no claims as a Gurunath, but I conclude from his literature that he is in the category. My dedication and submission is due to him! When a limited being masters the science of yoga sufficiently, he may be selected to be a Gurunath. He will then get permanent residence in the siddha loka place. He will assume permanence there and will replace the previous Gurunath as requested by him.

Application

The master of the guru lineage has four aspects:

- *spiritual focus into naad supernatural sound resonance*
- *continuous linkage to a higher environment or person*
- *lord of yoga with fullness in the existential core*
- *having particular spiritual happiness which is beyond description*

The ***spiritual focus into naad supernatural sound resonance*** *is an essential requirement because it frees the yogi from having to chant mantras. It effortlessly links the yogi to the chit akash sky of consciousness and without a force-the-door-open attitude.*

The ***continuous linkage to a higher environment or person*** *is done with or without effort during meditation after the mento-emotional energy was shut down, where it no longer has interest in anything outside of the psyche. It consist of the three higher stages of yoga, which Patanjali Mahayogin listed under one heading as* ***samyama*** *or the sequential progression from dharana to dhyana to samadhi.*

Dharana *is when with effort, the yogi links his interest to something higher. It could be an environment, a light, a dimension, a person, a deity or yoga-guru. This meditation requires that the yogi should continue applying himself to the linkage. As soon as he relaxes his hold either voluntarily or involuntarily, he is released from the transcendental object and must endeavor again to reconnect with it.*

Dhyana *is when the yogi is linked spontaneously, where he finds that he is linked to the desired transcendental place or person and he made no effort to do so, and no effort is required to maintain the linkage. In some meditations when the yogi makes the effort, he may find that this develops into a spontaneous connection, so that when he relaxes, he is still linked as if something holds the attention on the desired transcendental object.*

Samadhi *is when the linkage occurs spontaneously and for a long time.*

A lineage guru (Gurunath) must be a ***lord of yoga with fullness in the existential core****. He must have thoroughly practiced many yoga systems to know their specific applications. His information and advisories must be practical, tailored to the individual student.*

A lineage guru must ***have particular spiritual happiness which is beyond description.*** *He should not rely on the material energy to provide sensual satisfaction. He should not be starved of transcendental happiness. He should be joyful to the core with a happiness which comes from being in contact with the persons and place in the chitakash.*

Verse 82

कर्णौ पिधाय हस्ताभ्यां यः शृणोति ध्वनिं मुनिः ।

तत्र चित्तं सथिरीकुर्याद्यावत्स्थिर–पदं व्रजेत् ।। ८२ ।।

karṇau pidhāya hastābhyāṁ yaḥ śṛṇoti dhvaniṁ muniḥ ।
tatra cittam sthirīkuryādyāvatsthira–padaṁ vrajet ।। 82 ।।

karṇau – ears, pidhāya – covering, hastābhyāṁ – with fingers, yaḥ – which, śṛṇoti – hears, dhvaniṁ – sound, muniḥ – yogi philosopher, tatra – there, cittam – mento–emotional energy, sthirī – is steadily focused, kuryād = kuryāt = should do, yāvat – until, sthira–padaṁ – existential steady position, vrajet – becomes

The sound which the yogi hears when covering the ears with the fingers, should be a steady focus for the mento–emotional energy, until he becomes existentially steady.

Analysis

This sound is more than naad sound resonance. This is a combination vibration of which naad is part of the composite. However, when the yogi releases the fingers from the ears and listens, it detunes into naad sound resonance, which is the actual focus of this practice. Students who cannot hear naad sound may tune into it by using this method of blocking the ears with fingers and listening intently for a time, then releasing the ears and listening to the residual sound, then blocking the ears again, then releasing repeatedly. This will orient the mind to the naad sound.

The same technique may be used to become familiar with the third eye chakra. The student may use the fingers to apply a slight inward pressure on the tightly closed eyelids. After a time doing this, and staring smack center, the student will see random lights, pattern lights, or orderly geometrically shaped lights. The student should focus in the middle of this display and hold the fingers tightly on the eyelids. After a time the fingers should be released. The student should keep staring in the center. In this practice a ringed circular shape or a bunched irregular shape or a doughnut shape will appear with bright or dull colors. These are energy configurations of the third eye chakra.

Application

The naad sound resonance should be exactly as stated by Swatmarama. It should be a steady focus for the mento–emotional energy. The student should use it for weeks or years, until he becomes existentially steady. It is an anchor which the yogi should use to escape from the conventional displays in the mind. It is the escape from mental and emotional instability.

Verse 83

अभ्यस्यमानो नादो।अयं बाह्यमावृणुते ध्वनिं ।

पक्षाद्विक्षेपमखिलं जित्वा योगी सुखी भवेत् ।। ८३ ।।

abhyasyamāno nādo।ayaṁ bāhyamāvṝṇute dhvanim ।
pakṣādvikṣepamakhilaṁ jitvā yogī sukhī bhavet ।। 83 ।।

abhyasyamāno = abhyasyamānaḥ = practicing, nādo = nāda = naad supernatural sound resonance, ayaṁ – this, bāhyam – external, āvṝṇute – not heard, dhvanim – sound, pakṣād = pakṣāt = two weeks, vikṣepam – distractions, akhilaṁ – every, jitvā – transcends, yogī – yogi, sukhī – happy, bhavet – becomes

Practicing this naad supernatural sound resonance causes the external sounds not to be heard. The yogi becomes happy, after transcending every distraction in the space of two weeks.

Analysis

For those who are naturally attuned to naad, and who are expert at locating it, even external sounds do not prevent them from locating and tuning into naad. Others however need to be in a relatively quiet place or near a large body of water before they can hear it.

The time of two weeks was current for yogis in the time of Swatmarama. It may take longer for students today. Some find naad to be a dull tone. Some may find it to be boring. Due to the prevalence of technology, modern students hear many electronically produced sounds. Their minds became scarred with the same. This might cause naad sound to be undesirable initially.

Naad is very pleasant to advanced yogis. It is personal and full of loving feelings. It even gives shelter to a yogi just as a beloved would a lover, a friend would a friend, a parent would a child, and a teacher would a student.

Application

Two important benefits one gets from naad are:

- *relief from having to chant a mantra*
- *relief from loneliness in a void mind content*

The energy and attention used to chant a mantra and the effort made to hear the same is conserved if one simply listens to naad which resonates of its own accord and which is pleasant for a yogi who is not addicted to manmade musical sounds. Naad also provides comfort and association during the time which a yogi will have to wait in meditation before the chit akash sky of consciousness is accessed.

Verse 84

श्रूयते प्रथमाभ्यासे नादो नाना–विधो महान् ।

ततो।अभ्यासे वर्धमाने श्रूयते सूक्ष्म – सूक्ष्मकः ।। ८४ ।।

śrūyate prathamābhyāse nādo nānā–vidho mahān ।
tato।abhyāse vardhamāne śrūyate sūkṣma–sūkṣmakaḥ ।। 84 ।।

śrūyate – heard, pratham – initially, ābhyāse – in the practice, nādo = nādaḥ = naad supernatural sound resonance, nānā – variety, vidho – demanding, mahān – very, tato = tataḥ = then, abhyāse – practice, vardhamāne – increases, śrūyate – heard, sūkṣma – subtle, sūkṣmakaḥ – subtler

Initially when heard, the naad supernatural sound resonance has variety and is very demanding. When the practice increases it is heard to be subtle and subtler.

Analysis

At a certain stage of hearing naad it seems to be very demanding. In fact while listening to naad during meditation, one may find that it jumps to higher or lower frequencies. It may appear to discard the listener or compel the listener to hear more intently. It may have nodes where it seems to be sourced. It may have textures which cause it to be detected by the tactile sense, by feelings.

Application

Naad sound may also distance itself from the yogi. This happens when the yogi has a lapse in practice, or even if the practice continues but the yogi is circumstantially forced to adjust his lifestyle to a stage which is counter-productive to quality meditation. Then the yogi will find that naad is indifferent to him or seems to reject him, just as one may be spurned by a lover if one does not live up to expectations. As soon as the yogi resumes a yogically-productive life style, naad will change its attitude and reinstate the cozy relationship as before.

Verse 85

आदौ जलधि–जीमूत–भेरी–झर्झर–सम्भवाः ।

मध्ये मर्दल–शङ्खोत्था घण्टा–काहलजास्तथा ।। ८५ ।।

ādau jaladhi–jīmūta–bherī–jharjhara–sambhavāḥ I
madhye mardala–śaṅkhotthā ghaṇṭā–kāhalajāstathā I I 85 I I

ādau – in the beginning, jaladhi – ocean, jīmūta – cloud, bherī – kettledrum, jharjhara – drum, sambhavāḥ – what is produced, madhye – in the median stage, mardala – drum, śaṅkhotthā – sound out of a conch, ghaṇṭā – bell, kāhalajās – horn, tathā – as

In the beginning sounds like the ocean, the clouds, a kettledrum and a jharjhara drum are produced. In the median stage, it is like a mardala drum, a conch, a bell and a horn.

Analysis

Various tones, ranges and types of sounds are produced in naad sound resonance, all for the pleasure and productive association of the yogin.

Application

Naad has a vibrational aspect which engages the sense of feeling and anchors the yogi until the chit akash sky of consciousness is accessed. It may be a long or short wait for the yogi to gain such access and until it is provided he should remain absorbed in naad.

Verse 86

अन्ते तु किङ्किणी-वंश-वीणा- भ्रमर-निःस्वनाः ।

इति नानाविधा नादाः श्रूयन्ते देह-मध्यगाः ।। ८६ ।।

ante tu kinkiṇī–vaṁśa–vīṇā–bhramara–niḥsvanāḥ I
iti nānāvidhā nādāḥ śrūyante deha–madhyagāḥ I I 86 I I

ante – in the end, tu – however, kinkiṇī – anklebell, vaṁśa – flute, vīṇā – vina stringed instrument, bhramara – bee, niḥsvanāḥ – non–physical sounds, iti – thus, nānāvidhā – various types, nādāḥ – naad supernatural sound resonance, śrūyante – are heard, deha – body, madhyagāḥ – coursing through the middle

In the end, those non–physical sounds are like that of anklebells, the flute, the vina stringed instrument and the bee. Then various types of naad supernatural sound resonance are heard coursing through the middle of the body.

Analysis

There is naad sound vibration in every part of this creation, in every dimension, varying in frequency according to the subtle plane of the listener. The common place for hearing naad is in the head of the subtle body. It is usually heard in the back part of the head and on the right side but some yogis hear it on the left, bottom, top, middle or front of the head. Some say that it is all-pervasive.

Naad may also be heard in any other part of the body but for those who do breath-infusion practice it is likely to be heard as described in this verse, in the middle of the trunk of the body.

Krishna mentioned naad sound to Uddhava in this way:

hṛdy avicchinam oṁkāraṁ
ghaṇṭā-nādaṁ bisorṇa-vat
prāṇenodīrya tatrātha
punaḥ saṁveśayet svaram (9.34)

hṛdy = hṛdi — in the heart chakra; avicchinnam — continuous without breakage; oṁkāram — Om sound; ghaṇṭā — bell; nādam — sound; bisorṇa-vat = bisa – fibre + ūrna – lotus + vat — like; prāṇenodīrya = prāṇena — by the vitalizing energy + udīrya — raising; tatrātha = tatra — there + atha — thus; punaḥ — again; saṁveśayet — one should blend with; svaram — of musical notes, tones.

In the heart chakra, the Om sound which is like the continuous peal of a bell, resonates continually, like a fibre in a lotus stalk. Raising it by using the vitalizing energy, one should blend that sound with the musical tones. (Uddhava Gita 9.34)

Application

Naad is heard deeply and sincerely when the yogi ceases interest in material sound vibration. Then his attention shifts to the subtle level and also to the supernatural range which is between the subtle and the spiritual planes of existence. Absorption in naad sound is definitely an indication that the yogi is becoming eligible to transit to the divine atmosphere.

Verse 87

महति श्रूयमाणे। अपि मेघ–भेर्य–आदिके धवनौ ।

तत्र सूक्ष्मात्सूक्ष्मतरं नादमेव परामृशेत् ।। ८७ ।।

mahati śrūyamāṇe।api megha–bhery–ādike dhvanau ।
tatra sūkṣmātsūkṣmataraṁ nādameva parāmṛśet ।। 87 ।।

mahati – loud, śrūyamāṇe – hearing, api – though, megha – cloud, bhery = bheri = kettledrum, ādike – initially, dhvanau – sounds, tatra – there, sūkṣmāt – from subtle, sūkṣmataraṁ = from super–subtle, nādam – naad supernatural sound resonance, eva – so, parāmṛśet – should sensitively be absorbed

Though hearing loud sounds like the sound of clouds and kettledrums initially, one should sensitively be absorbed in the subtle and super–subtle supernatural resonance.

Analysis

At first a student is all too anxious to hear naad as loud as possible because the subtle resonance is hardly audible to beginners. They prefer its louder tones. It is easier for students to stay focused on a loud resonance. However, for the advanced students a super-subtle supernatural resonance is preferred because that is closer to the chit akash sky of consciousness which is the objective of this yoga practice.

Application

A student yogi should be realistic which means that if one is not advanced, one should lean towards the loud tones otherwise if the sound is too subtle, one may not hear it or one may hear it and then discover that one lost contact for a long period during meditation and was regrettably shifted to the conventional mental level viewing trivial thoughts and images.

Verse 88

घनमुत्सृज्य वा सूक्ष्मे सूक्ष्ममुत्सृज्य वा घने ।

रममाणमपि क्षिप्तं मनो नान्यत्र चालयेत् ।। ८८ ।।

ghanamutsṛjya vā sūkṣhme sūkṣmamutsṛjya vā ghane ।
ramamāṇamapi kṣiptaṁ mano nānyatra cālayet ।। 88 ।।

ghanam – what is prominent, utsṛjya – leaving aside, vā – or, sūkṣme – in the subtle, sūkṣmam – subtle, utsṛjya – abandoning, vā – or, ghane – in what is prominent, ramamāṇam – enjoying, api – also, kṣiptaṁ – distraction, mano = manaḥ = mind, nānyatra = nowhere, cālayet – should wander

Leaving aside the prominent sounds, adopting the subtle type, abandoning the subtle, adopting the prominent type and enjoying this, the mind should not wander to any distraction anywhere.

Analysis

Without being distracted, the yogi should remain emerged in naad sound, going through its tones and frequencies from its prominent obvious sounds to the subtler ones. The mind should have such a liking for naad, and should enjoy and relish it to such an extent that conventional music causes the mind to turn to naad for relief.

Application

There is a period of meditation where naad is itself the objective. When this is well developed, naad is used as an anchor point for the core-self as it waits for access to the divine atmosphere.

A yogi must dig deep into naad, become emerged into it, into its sound, into its vibratory energy. He should locate its node(s) and get as close as possible. He should note naad's blaring tones and its very subtle almost non-existence emittances. The yogi should do this and should not be distracted. However there will be distractions. A yogi must research to know why he was distracted. He should find methods of reducing the diversions to nil. The methods should be foolproof.

Verse 89

यत्र कुत्रापि वा नादे लगति प्रथमं मनः ।

तत्रैव सुस्थिरीभूय तेन सार्धं विलीयते ।। ८९ ।।

yatra kutrāpi vā nāde lagati prathamaṁ manaḥ |
tatraiva susthirībhūya tena sārdhaṁ vilīyate || 89 ||

yatra – where, kutrāpi = where as well, vā – or, nāde – in naad supernatural sound resonance, lagati – enters, prathamaṁ – first, manaḥ – mind, tatraiva = there as well, susthirī – complete stability, bhūya – being, tena – by this, sārdhaṁ – join equally, vilīyate – completely enter into

At first, wherever the mind enters into the naad supernatural sound resonance, it becomes stable being completely absorbed and joined into that.

Analysis

Naad sound resonance may be homogenous or variant. For a yogi who sincerely and repeatedly adhered to naad, wherever the mind enters it, the meditation becomes stabilized.

Application

A yogi has everything to gain by becoming deeply absorbed in naad. That will eventually take him to the chit akash sky of consciousness.

Verse 90

मकरन्दं पिबन्भृङ्गी गन्धं नापेक्षते यथा ।

नादासक्तं तथा चित्तं विषयान्नहि काङ्क्षते ।। ९० ।।

makarandaṁ pibanbhṝngī gandhaṁ nāpekṣate yathā I
nādāsaktaṁ tathā cittam viṣayānnahi kāṅkṣate I I 90 I I

makarandaṁ – flower nectar, piban – drink, bhṝngī – bee, gandhaṁ – odor, nāpekṣate = having no interest, yathā – as, nādāsaktaṁ = absorbed in naad supernatural sound resonance, tathā – so, cittam = mento–emotional energy, viṣayān – sense objects, nahi – surely not, kāṅkṣate – desire

As a bee while drinking flower nectar loses interest in the odor of the flower, so when the mento–emotional energy is absorbed in naad supernatural sound resonance, it surely does not desire the sense objects.

Analysis

Naad absorption provides permanent relief from the pursuit of sense objects and related memories. By convention the mind is continually obsessed with external objects and/or the memories of the same. When a yogi ceased such indulgence and spent time focusing on naad resonance, he gets the result of freedom from hankering for the objects.

When flying, a bee may smell the fragrance of a flower. This puts the bee on the alert for a particular type of nectar. But once the insect settles on the flower and begins feeding, its smelling sense relaxes as its tasting and appreciating senses are tensed into focus.

When a yogi sits to meditate, he may at first be forcibly attracted to thoughts and images. Once he realized this, he switches to the naad sound resonance, just as the bee moves its interest from the fragrance to the taste of the nectar. A yogi may find himself being attentive to thoughts and images. Then he should question as to how he became attracted in the first place. He should switch to naad focus as soon as he realizes that he is not in touch with the resonance.

Application

After hours and hours of meditation practice, after the kundalini lifeforce was aroused into the subtle head repeatedly, after becoming thoroughly familiar with how to locate naad sound resonance, the yogi finds that when he sits to meditate, the mind lacks enthusiasm for pursuing sense objects. A yogi may wonder as to where that enthusiasm went, as to which dimension it is lodged in, for he knows that its absence does not mean its nonexistence.

Verse 91

मनो–मत्त–गजेन्द्रस्य विषयोद्यान–चारिणः ।

समर्थो।अयं नियमने निनाद–निशिताङ्कुशः ।। ९१ ।।

mano–matta–gajendrasya viṣayodyāna–cāriṇaḥ |
samartho | ayaṁ niyamane nināda–niśitāṅkuśaḥ || 91 ||

mano = manaḥ = mind, matta – carefree and intoxicated, gajendrasya – of king of elephants, viṣayodyāna = garden of enjoyments, cāriṇaḥ – wandering, samartho = samarthaḥ = is capable, ayaṁ – this, niyamane – controlled, nināda – naad supernatural sound resonance, niśitāṅkuśaḥ = niśita (sharp) + aṅkuśaḥ (goad)

The mind, which is carefree and intoxicated like the king of the elephants, wanders in the garden of enjoyments. It is capable of being controlled by the sharp goad of naad supernatural sound resonance.

Analysis

As a mahout is to an elephant, so the core-self is to the mind, in that the core-self has vast intelligence while the mind has vast capacity for entertaining the core-self. Because it likes to be trivialized, the core-self is ever the victim to the mind's idea and image display. The core-self, a tiny infinitesimal speck of reality, likes to ride on the back of the mind, the way a mahout sits on an elephant but usually this self does not have a goad and cannot find an effective way to control the mind.

Swatmarama suggested using the naad supernatural sound resonance as an instrument to bring the mind under control. It actually works that if a yogi can hear naad sound with full attention, the hypnotic displays of the mind would cease and the core-self would experience mental objectivity in terms of freedom from being subjected to the schemes of the mind.

Application

The enjoyments in the physical and psychic material world are pernicious to say the least. The mind is enthralled by these damaging effects because the mind is carefree and intoxicated like a sex-crazed bull-elephant. The mind does not have to reference its experiences to anything. Thus a bad experience is just as honorable to the mind as a good one. The core-self however is a reference principle which detects unpleasant trauma. While wandering in the garden of enjoyments in the physical and psychic material worlds, the self tries to pick and choose its involvements but the mind does not care to do so, and since the self is reliant on the mind, the self is traumatized.

Verse 92

बद्धं तु नाद–बन्धेन मनः सन्त्यक्त–चापलम् ।

प्रयाति सुतरां सथैर्यं छिन्न–पक्षः खगो यथा ।। ९२ ।।

baddhaṁ tu nāda–bandhena manaḥ santyakta–cāpalam |
prayāti sutarāṁ sthairyaṁ chinna–pakṣaḥ khago yathā || 92 ||

baddhaṁ – spell, tu – however, nāda – naad supernatural sound resonance, bandhena – with the captivation, manaḥ – mind, santyakta – lacks enthusiam, cāpalam – quickly, prayāti – enter, sutarāṁ – very, sthairyaṁ – still, chinna – clipped, pakṣaḥ – wing, khago = khagaḥ = bird, yathā – as

The mind which is captivated by the spell of naad supernatural sound resonance loses enthusiasm for other interests. It quickly becomes very still like a bird with clipped wings.

Analysis

It is my experience that this statement of Swatmarama, in his appraisal of the naad resonance, is true. However it does not stand alone. Some disciplines must be included such as the breath-infusion process. The student should be sure to do a thorough breath-infusion practice before doing naad meditation. Then one finds that the mind loses enthusiasm for other interests and become so attracted to naad as to be compared with a lover's attraction of his or her beloved. Really, the mind quickly becomes very still when the core-self is absorbed in naad just as a bird ceases fluttering about if its wings are sufficiently clipped.

Application

The mind does not become attached to naad sound just like that. It will not develop interest in naad merely because this book recommends that. The method is to practice naad meditation after doing breath-infusion practice. Breath-infusion if it is thorough will result in pratyahar sensual energy withdrawal. That will cause the psyche to be divested of external concerns which will cause spontaneously introspection. Once this is achieved, there is likelihood that the mind will be captivated by the spell of naad sound.

Verse 93

सर्व–चिन्तां परित्यज्य सावधानेन चेतसा ।

नाद एवानुसन्धेयो योग–साम्राज्यमिच्छता ।। ९३ ।।

sarva–cintāṁ parityajya sāvadhānena cetasā ।
nāda evānusandheyo yoga–sāmrājyamicchatā ।। 93 ।।

sarva – all, cintāṁ = mento–emotional trauma, parityajya – abandon, sāvadhānena – with attentive focus, cetasā – with consciousness, nāda – naad supernatural sound resonance, evānusandheyo = eva (also) + anusandheyaḥ (investigation), yoga – yoga, sāmrājyam – realm, icchatā – those who desire

Abandoning all mento–emotional trauma, and with attentive focal consciousness, those who desire to be in the realm of yoga, should investigate the naad supernatural sound resonance.

Analysis

If a yogi wants to go to siddhaloka, he will have to meet these requirements.

Is there any other system of spiritual development which may be used, so that a person does not have to do whatever Swatmarama determined as this process?

The answer is: "Yes there is another means."

The alternate method is to get the grace energy of a deity who requests the presence of the person in the deity's domain. The power of the deity must be such that it can transfer the person even if the person has not done these austerities prescribed by Swatmarama, and taught initially by Shiva.

Application

Those who want to do something to change their situation in material existence for transiting to a divine place are given these requirements:

- *use attentive focal consciousness, abandon all mento-emotional trauma*
- *investigate the naad supernatural sound resonance*

Verse 94

नादो।अन्तरङ्ग–सारङ्ग–बन्धने वागुरायते ।

अन्तरङ्ग–कुरङ्गस्य वधे वयाधायते।अपि च ।। ९४ ।।

nādo | antaraṅga–sāraṅga–bandhane vāgurāyate |
antaraṅga–kuraṅgasya vadhe vyādhāyate | api ca || 94 ||

nādo = nāda = naad supernatural sound resonance, antaraṅga – psychological plane, sāraṅga–bandhane = in arresting, vāgurāyate – snaring, antaraṅga – internally, kuraṅgasya – of antelope, vadhe – hunter, vyādhāyate – kill, api – also, ca – and

Naad supernatural sound resonance is like a snare which arrests the mind psychologically. It is like a hunter who kills the antelope-like mind internally.

Analysis

For this process, unless one can get a deity to send a grace energy which is enough to transit one to the divine world, one should take the advice of Swatmarama. Naad supernatural sound was mentioned by Krishna to Uddhava. It was given by Patanjali. It was given by Shiva in this Hatha Yoga Pradipika manual. What more can be said about it?

Application

The mind as a composite energy is fickle like an antelope. It is nervous and jumps from one thing to the next with the potential for yielding unpleasant traumatic experiences to which the core-self is subjected. Naad sound is like a hunter who kills this attitude of the mind and makes it receptive to divine penetration.

The divine world is all-surrounding but it does not penetrate into a mind which has a low grade of astral energy. By focusing on naad again and again, a yogi eventually changes the quality of energy in the psyche, making it penetrable to divine energy.

Verse 95

अन्तरङ्गस्य यमिनो वाजिनः परिघायते ।

नादोपास्ति–रतो नित्यमवधार्या हि योगिना ।। ९५ ।।

antaraṅgasya yamino vājinaḥ parighāyate |
nādopāsti–rato nityamavadhāryā hi yoginā || 95 ||

antaraṅgasya – of the interior (of a stable), yamino = yaminaḥ = confining, vājinaḥ – horse, parighāyate – bolt, nādopāsti–rato = nādopāsti–rataḥ = obsessed with interest–focus on naad supernatural sound resonance, nityam – always, avadhāryā – should ascertain, hi – however, yoginā – by a yogi

Naad resonance is like a bolt confining a horse in a stable. However a yogi should always be obsessed with interest-focus on naad supernatural sound.

Analysis

The horse-like mind likes to wander hither and tither without respect to the needs of the core-self. It makes sense that sooner or later, the self should close in on the mind, curtailing its irrational behavior. If a yogi knows what is good for him, he should seriously study the instructions in this manual of Swatmarama. One should at all costs find teachers who are proficient in these disciplines and take instructions from them.

Regarding the mind, there is an applicable advisory given to yogis by Lord Krishna:

indriyāṇi parāṇyāhur
indriyebhyaḥ paraṁ manaḥ
manasastu parā buddhir
yo buddheḥ paratastu saḥ (3.42)

indriyāṇi — the senses; parāṇyāhur = parāṇi — are energetic; āhur (āhuḥ) — the ancient psychologists say; indriyebhyaḥ — the senses; paraṁ — more energetic; manaḥ — the mind; manasas — in contrast to the mind; tu — but; parā — more sensitive; buddhir = buddhiḥ — the intelligence; yo = yaḥ — which; buddheḥ — in reference to the intelligence; paratas — most sensitive; tu — but; saḥ — he, the spirit

The ancient psychologists say that the senses are energetic, but in comparison to the senses, the mind is more energetic. In contrast to the mind, the intelligence is even more sensitive. But in reference, the spirit is most elevated. (Bhagavad Gita 3.42)

evaṁ buddheḥ paraṁ buddhvā
saṁstabhyātmānamātmanā
jahi śatruṁ mahābāho
kāmarūpaṁ durāsadam (3.43)

evaṁ — thus; buddheḥ — than the intelligence; paraṁ — higher; buddhvā — having understood; saṁstabhyātmānamātmanā = saṁstabhya — keeping together + ātmānam — the personal energies+ ātmanā — by the spirit; jahi — uproot; śatruṁ — enemy; mahābāho — O powerful man; kāmarūpaṁ — form of passionate desire; durāsadam — difficult to grasp

Thus having understood what is higher than intelligence, keeping the personal energies under control of the spirit, uproot, O powerful man, the enemy, the form of passionate desire which is difficult to grasp. (Bhagavad Gita 3.43)

Application

The yogi should have full interest-focus on naad supernatural sound.

How to do this?

Learn pranayama breath-infusion. Do it thoroughly to remove all stale breath energy which can be extracted from the body through the lungs. Sit to meditate. Make contact with naad sound resonance. Work day and night to achieve full application of the core-self's interest-focus on naad resonance.

Verse 96

बद्धं विमुक्त–छाञ्छल्यं नाद्–गन्धक-जारणात् ।

मनः–पारद्माप्नोति निरालम्बाख्य–खे।अटनम् ।। ९६ ।।

baddhaṁ vimukta–cāñcalyaṁ nāda–gandhaka–jāraṇāt I
manaḥ–pāradamāpnoti nirālambākhya–khe|aṭanam || 96 ||

baddhaṁ – restriction, vimukta – deprived of, cāñcalyaṁ – instability, nāda – naad supernatural sound resonance, gandhaka – sulphur, jāraṇāt – from being combined, manaḥ – mind, pāradam – mercury, āpnoti – obtains, nirālambākhya – supportless, khe – in divine space, aṭanam – wandering

Mercury when deprived of its instability by restriction, due to being combined with sulphur is like the mind which is focused into naad supernatural sound resonance. Then it wanders in the support-less kha divine space.

Analysis

The mind is agile and mischievous like a monkey. Its problem is that it is a liability for the core-self. It must be reeled in. Svatmarama wrote that as mercury when combined with sulphur exhibits stability and reliability, so the mind when it is focused into naad resonance gains a stable foundation. It then becomes capable of being receptive to the support-less kha divine space.

Application

At a certain point in this process, the mind of the yogi is changed so that he has the support-less kha divine space, the chit akash sky of consciousness as his mento-emotional atmosphere energy. For such a yogi having a material body or not have a material body is the same.

Verse 97

नाद्– श्रवणतः क्षिप्रमन्तरङ्ग–भुजङ्गमम् ।

विस्मृतय सर्वमेकाग्रः कुत्रचिन्नहि धावति ।। ९७ ।।

nāda–śravaṇataḥ kṣipramantaraṅga–bhujaṅgamam I
vismṝtaya sarvamekāgraḥ kutracinnahi dhāvati || 97 ||

nāda – naad supernatural sound resonance, śravaṇataḥ – hearing, kṣipram – quickly, antaraṅga – interior, bhujaṅgamam – serpent, vismṛtaya – anxiety, sarvam – all, ekāgraḥ – singularly focused, kutra – where, chin = cit = consciousness, nahi – not, dhāvati – drift

Hearing naad supernatural sound resonance, the serpent–like mind quickly interiorizes, forgetting all of its anxiety. It becomes singularly focused and does not drift anywhere.

Analysis

This only occurs to those yogis who lost interest in the conventional behavior of the mind. For others hearing naad sound does not cause further interiorization and forgetfulness of anxieties. In fact people who hear naad and who are hell-bent on pursuing mundane objectives in the survival game of the impure kundalini lifeforce, may dislike the sound of naad, considering it to be an irritation.

It takes weeks, months or ever years of meditation to qualify for what is explained in this verse. Whimsical listening to naad, sporadic contact with naad or even enjoying naad music from time to time, does not give one the consistent singular focus required for advanced meditation. It does not qualify one to practice kriya yoga.

Application

The events which should occur as soon as one hears naad resonance in meditation are:

- *the serpent–like mind quickly interiorizes*
- *it forgets its anxiety*
- *it becomes singularly focused and does not drift anywhere*

The serpent–like mind quickly interiorizes *as soon as the meditator sits to meditate if the core-self was already habituated to hearing and sensually appreciating naad resonance. If the meditator did not develop a sensual appreciation of naad, the mind may interiorize under pressure of focus but it will not remain in that format. As soon as the pressure is relaxed it will return to displaying its conventional thoughts and images.*

The mind forgets its anxiety *after making contact with naad only if the mind has become more attached to naad than to its thought-image display activity. The mind may also forget its anxiety if the yogi did a thorough breath-infusion just before meditation, where that infusion of energy into the subtle body caused that form to jump to a higher plane of consciousness where the conventional thoughts and images do not exist.*

The mind becomes singularly focused and does not drift anywhere *after making contact with naad if no other part of the mind expresses a pulling force which could lure the mind into contemplating other ideas. This may happen even if a person does not do breath-infusion. However, infusion is the reliable method of causing this. It moves the subtle body to a higher plane in which the conventional mental behavior does not take place.*

Verse 98

काष्ठे प्रवर्तितो वह्निः काष्ठेन सह शाम्यति ।

नादे प्रवर्तितं चित्तं नादेन सह लीयते ।। ९८ ।।

kāṣṭhe pravartito vahniḥ kāṣṭhena saha śāmyati I
nāde pravartitaṁ cittam nādena saha līyate II 98 II

kāṣṭhe – in firewood, pravartito = pravartitaḥ = producer, cause, vahniḥ – fire, kāṣṭhena – with firewood, saha – with, śāmyati – extinguished, nāde – in naad supernatural sound resonance, pravartitaṁ – interacting, cittam = mento–emotional energy, nādena – with naad supernatural sound resonance, saha – with, līyate is quelled

The fire which produces the flames in firewood is extinguished along with the wood. The mento–emotional energy interacting with naad supernatural sound resonance is quelled in it.

Analysis

The vibratory level of the mento-emotional energy changes when the core-self shifts its interest from the front to the back part of the subtle head where naad resonance is located. This does not happen overnight. It takes time in naad sound absorption to achieve this. Initially when a student listens to naad it has the effect of distracting the student from the pressing concerns of the mind. But the student finds that he cannot hold his interest in naad for a long period, not even for say about one minute. The student finds that he discovers himself shifted out of naad into a viewing position where he sees the conventional thoughts and images in the mindscape. Later after repeated practice this changes and he is able to remain with naad for longer periods of time and even shift or be shifted to the front of the head with that part of the psychic being devoid of thoughts and images.

Application

For the purpose of this yoga, the mento-emotional energy which is used by the yogi must change in quality. It has to be upgraded on and on until it becomes the energy from the divine world. However in the meantime, the yogi must use whatever mento emotional energy he has in his possession. If he infuses breath-energy that will instantly cause a partial upgrade. This will serve the purpose of getting the mind dis-oriented from the conventional thoughts and images.

Verse 99

घण्टादिनाद–सक्त– स्तब्धान्तः–करण–हरिणस्य ।

प्रहरणमपि सुकरं शरसम् धान–प्रवीणश्चेत् ।। ९९ ।।

ghaṇṭādināda–sakta–stabdhāntaḥ–karaṇa–hariṇasya |
praharaṇamapi sukaraṁ śarasam dhāna–pravīṇaścet || 99 ||

ghaṇṭādināda= ghaṇṭādi (bell and other) + nāda (naad supernatural sound resonance), sakta – near, stabdhāntaḥ–karaṇa = stabdha (motionless) + āntaḥ–karaṇa (psychic organs in the subtle head), hariṇasya – of the deer, praharaṇam – expert archer, api – also, sukaraṁ – easy to do, śarasam – bow, dhāna – shooting, pravīṇaścet – totally destroy

The psychic organs in the subtle head become motionless when focused on the bell and other sounds of the naad supernatural sound resonance. Just as the expert archer very easily draws a bow and kills the deer.

Analysis

If the aim is accurate and the archer is motionless, the deer has moments to live. If the psychic organs are captivated by the naad sound those organs become stabilized.

Application

Swatmarama devoted so many verses of his thesis to extol the glories of the naad sound; how it assists the yogi in reaching the chit akash divine environment. What more can be said? There is no mantra which is as spontaneous and reliable as naad sound resonance.

Verse 100

अनाहतस्य शब्दस्य ध्वनिर्य उपलभ्यते ।

ध्वनेरन्तर्गतं ज्ञेयं ज्ञेयस्यान्तर्गतं मनः ।

मनस्तत्र लयं याति तद्विष्णोः परमं पदम् ।। १०० ।।

anāhatasya śabdasya dhvanirya upalabhyate |
dhvanerantargataṁ jñeyaṁ jñeyasyāntargataṁ manaḥ |
manastatra layaṁ yāti tadviṣṇoḥ paramaṁ padam || 100 ||

anāhatasya – of the naad supernatural sound resonance on the causal plane in the personal psyche, śabdasya – of sound, dhvanirya – reality, upalabhyate – perceive, dhvaner = dhvaneḥ = reality, antargataṁ – what interspaced, jñeyaṁ – what is to be known, jñeyasyāntargataṁ = jñeyasya (of what is to be known) + antargataṁ (what interspaced), manaḥ – mind, manas – mind, tatra – there, layaṁ – absorption, yāti – goes, tad = tat = that, viṣṇoḥ – of God Vishnu, paramaṁ – supreme, padam – abode

On the causal plane in his psyche, the yogi perceives that the reality is interspaced in the naad supernatural sound resonance, and the mind is interspaced into the reality of what is potentially knowable. The mind becomes absorbed there which is the supreme abode of the God Vishnu.

Analysis

The causal plane is the reality from which the astral variety was created. Just as when one sees a mango seed, one does not see the mango tree which it will produce, so when one sees the causal plane one does not see the varieties of astral existence which it produced. The analogy of the mango is limited because the seed is utilized in the tree's production. The causal plane produced an infinite array of astral planes and yet the causal level remains undisturbed. Yogis may go into the causal plane but they must abandon the subtle body before doing so. When the yogi again resurfaces on the astral planes, he resumes his astral form.

Application

Naad sound resonance is a rapid way to reach the causal plane but it is an abstract route. To do so the yogi has to enter a naad node or get very close to one. In some naad resonances there is one node. In another there might be no node. In some other there might be multiple nodes. If there are two nodes, the yogi should go to the loudest most pronounced one. A yogi should try to enter the node, to either go through it or be embedded in it. If he is unable to penetrate because of a repulsion force, he should go as near to the center of the node as possible.

Usually when there are one or more nodes in it, there is some vision in naad. There is little vision when there is no node. With naad one engages the subtle hearing sense but there might also be use for the tactile touching sense in naad. However when there are nodes, there should be sight perception which shows light or the lack of light around the node. The experience of being near to a node or in a node is an experience of the causal plane even though one may have no insight into how that vibration would cause multiple astral domains.

The abode of God Vishnu is now mentioned by Swatmarama. Before, he mentioned Shiva. Now he mentions Vishnu (Krishna). This verifies that the writer was a theist. The abode of Vishnu is the divine world, which Krishna described like this:

tataḥ padaṁ tatparimārgitavyaṁ
yasmingatā na nivartanti bhūyaḥ
tameva cādyaṁ puruṣaṁ prapadye
yataḥ pravṛttiḥ prasṛtā purāṇī(15.4)

tataḥ — then; padaṁ — place; tat— that; parimārgitavyaṁ — to be sought; yasmin — to which; gatā — some; na — not; nivartanti — they return; bhūyaḥ — again; tam — that; eva — indeed; cādyaṁ = ca — and + ādyaṁ — primal; puruṣaṁ — person; prapadye — I take shelter; yataḥ — from whom; pravṛttiḥ — creation; prasṛtā — emerged; purāṇī — in primeval limes

Then that place is to be sought, to which having gone, the spirits do not return to this world again. One should think: I take shelter with that Primal Person, from Whom the creation emerged in primeval times. (Bhagavad Gita 15.4)

nirmānamohā jitasaṅgadoṣā
adhyātmanityā vinivṛttakāmāḥ
dvaṁdvairvimuktāḥ sukhaduḥkha-saṁjñair
gacchantyamūḍhāḥ padamavyayaṁ tat (15.5)

nirmāna — devoid of pride ; mohā — confusion; jita — conquered ; saṅga — attachment ; doṣā — faults; adhyātmanityā = adhyātma — Supreme Spirit + nityā — constantly; vinivṛtta — ceased; kāmāḥ — cravings; dvandvaiḥ — by dualities; vimuktāḥ — freed; sukhaduḥkha — pleasure-pain ; saṁjñaiḥ — known as; gacchanti — they go; amūḍhāḥ — the undeluded souls; padam — place; avyayam — imperishable; tat = tad — that

Those who are devoid of pride and confusion, who have conquered the faults of attachment, who constantly stay with the Supreme Spirit, whose cravings have ceased, who are freed from the dualities known as pleasure and pain, these undeluded souls go to that imperishable place. (Bhagavad Gita 15.5)

na tadbhāsayate sūryo
na śaśāṅko na pāvakaḥ
yadgatvā na nivartante
taddhāma paramaṁ mama (15.6)

na — not; tat — that; bhāsayate — illuminates; sūryo = sūryaḥ — the sun; na — nor; sasaḥko = śaśāṅkaḥ — moon; na — nor; pāvakaḥ — fire; yat — which; gatvā — having gone; na — never; nivartante — they return; tat — that; dhāmā — residence; paramaṁ — supreme; mama — my

The sun does not illuminate that place, nor the moon, nor the fire. Having gone to that location, they never return. That is My supreme residence. (Bhagavad Gita 15.6)

Verse 101

तावदाकाश–सङ्कल्पो यावच्छब्दः प्रवर्तते ।

निःशब्दं तत–परं बरह्म परमात्मेति गीयते ।। १०१ ।।

tāvadākāśa–saṅkalpo yāvacchabdaḥ pravartate |
niḥśabdaṁ tat–paraṁ brahma paramātmeti gīyate || 101 ||

tāvad = so long as, ākāśa – astral environment, saṅkalpo = saṅkalpaḥ = idea, yāvac = yāvat = until, chabdaḥ = śabdaḥ = sound, pravartate – exists, niḥśabdaṁ – without sound, tat – that, paraṁ – supreme, brahma – transcdental reality, paramātmeti = paramatma (Supreme Soul) + iti (thus), gīyate is proclaimed

So long as mentally–created sounds exist, there will be ideas in the astral environment. When there is no such sound, the supreme transcendental reality, the Supreme Soul, is proclaimed.

Analysis

A yogi must stop visualizing whatever comes to his little mind, do meditation without ideas and images, and wait patiently for vision to the chit akash sky of consciousness. The astral environment is not the ultimate place, and for that matter it is the basis for the physical world where one is subjected to blast traumas. The astral world itself is shifty. It enforces flimsiness and rapid switching. It is undesirable but its high end frequencies may be tolerated for the time being as desirable heavens. In the long haul however these places will be blanked out of existence in a big cosmic shut down which is so frightening as to be unimaginable.

Beyond even the high end of the astral existence, is the supreme transcendental reality, the Supreme Soul and his domain, the spiritual world. Lord Krishna described that place to Arjuna:

ā brahmabhuvanāllokāḥ
punarāvartino'rjuna
māmupetya tu kaunteya
punarjanma na vidyate (8.16)

ā — up to; brahmabhuvanāl = brahmabhuvanāt — to Brahmā's world; lokāḥ — populations; punarāvartino = punarāvartinaḥ — subjected to repeated birth and death; 'rjuna = arjuna — Arjuna; mām — Me; upetya — approaching; tu — but; kaunteya — O son of Kuntī; punarjanma — impulsion of rebirth; na — not; vidyate — is experienced

Up to Brahmā's world, the populations are subjected to repeated births and deaths, O Arjuna. But in approaching Me, rebirth is not experienced, O son of Kuntī. (Bhagavad Gita 8.16)

sahasrayugaparyantam
aharyadbrahmaṇo viduḥ
rātriṁ yugasahasrāntāṁ
te'horātravido janāḥ (8.17)

sahasra — one thousand + yuga — time cycle + paryantam — limit; ahar — day; yad — which; brahmaṇo = brahmaṇaḥ — of Brahmā; viduḥ — they know; rātrim — night; yugasahasrāntāṁ = yuga — time cycle + sahasra — one thousand + antam — end; te — they; 'horātravido (ahoratravidaḥ) = ahoratra — day and night + vidaḥ — knowers; janāḥ — people

Those who know the day of Brahmā, which has a limit of one thousand time cycles, and the night of Brahmā, which ends in a thousand time cycles, are the people who know day and night. (Bhagavad Gita 8.17)

avyaktādvyaktayaḥ sarvāḥ
prabhavantyaharāgame
rātryāgame pralīyante
tatraivāvyaktasaṁjñake (8.18)

avyaktād = avyaktāt — from the invisible world; vyaktayaḥ — the visible world; sarvāḥ — all; prabhavanty = prabhavanti — they are produced; aharāgame — at the beginning of Brahma's day; rātryāgame — at the beginning of Brahma's night; pralīyante — they are reverted back; tatraivāvyaktasaṁjñake = tatra — at the time + eva — indeed + avyakta — invisible world + saṁjñake — is understood as

When the day of Creator Brahmā begins, all this visible world is produced from the invisible world. When his night comes, the manifested energies are reverted back into the invisible world. (Bhagavad Gita 8.18)

bhūtagrāmaḥ sa evāyaṁ
bhūtvā bhūtvā pralīyate
rātryāgame'vaśaḥ pārtha

prabhavatyaharāgame (8.19)

bhūtagrāmaḥ — multitude of beings; sa = saḥ — this; evāyam = eva — indeed + ayam — this; bhūtvā bhūtvā — repeatedly manifesting; pralīyate — is shifted out of visibility; rātryāgame — at the arrival of Brahma's night; 'vaśaḥ = avaśaḥ — happening naturally; pārtha — O son of Pṛthā; prabhavaty = prabhavati — it comes into existence; aharāgame — on the onset of Brahma's day

O son of Pṛthā, this multitude of beings which is repeatedly manifested, is naturally shifted out of visibility at the arrival of each of Brahmā's nights. It again comes into existence at the onset of Brahmā's day. (Bhagavad Gita 8.19)

parastasmāttu bhāvo'nyo
'vyakto'vyaktātsanātanaḥ
yaḥ sa sarveṣu bhūteṣu
naśyatsu na vinaśyati (8.20)

paraḥ — high; tasmāt — than this; tu — but; bhāvo = bhāvaḥ — existence; 'nyo = anyaḥ — another; 'vyakto = avyaktaḥ — invisible; 'vyaktāt = avyaktāt — than the unmanifest state of the dissolvable creation; sanātanaḥ — primeval; yaḥ = which; sa = saḥ — it; sarveṣu — in all; bhūteṣu — in creation; naśyatsu — in the disintegration; na — not; vinaśyati — is disintegrated

But higher than this, there is another invisible existence, which is higher than the primeval unmanifested states of this dissolvable creation. When all these creatures are disintegrated, that is not affected. (Bhagavad Gita 8.20)

avyakto'kṣara ityuktas
tamāhuḥ paramāṁ gatim
yaṁ prāpya na nivartante
taddhāma paramaṁ mama (8.21)

avyakto = avyaktaḥ — invisible world; 'kṣara = akṣara — unalterable; ity = iti — thus; uktaḥ — is declared; tam — it; āhuḥ — authorities say; paramām — supreme; gatim — objective; yam — which; prāpya — attaining; na — not; nivartante — return here; tad — that; dhāma — residence; paramam — supreme; mama — My

That invisible world is unalterable, so it is declared. The authorities say that it is the supreme objective. Attaining that, they do not return here. That place is My supreme residence. (Bhagavad Gita 8.21)

Application

The human mind is addicted to mentally-created sounds and images. The yogi must struggle with this tendency and gradually eliminate it so that the mind is free of the tendency to dream up ideas and rehash memories. Patanjali Mahayogin listed five psychological operations which must be squelched if the yogin is to succeed in yoga practice:

vṛttayaḥ pañcatayyaḥ kliṣṭā akliṣṭāḥ

vṛttayaḥ – the vibrations in mento-emotional energy; pañcatayyaḥ – fivefold; kliṣṭākliṣṭāḥ = kliṣṭā – agonizing + akliṣṭāḥ – non-troublesome.

The vibrations in the mento-emotional energy are five-fold, being agonizing or non-troublesome. (Yoga Sutras 1.5)

pramāṇa viparyaya vikalpa nidrā smṛtayaḥ

pramāṇa – correct perception; viparyaya – incorrect perception; vikalpa – imagination; nidrā – sleep; smṛtayaḥ – memory.

They are correct perception, incorrect perception, imagination, sleep and memory. (Yoga Sutras 1.6)

Verse 102

यत्किंचिन्नाद–रूपेण शरूयते शक्तिरेव सा ।

यस्तत्त्वान्तो निराकारः स एव परमेश्वरः ।। १०२ ।।

yatkiṁcinnāda–rūpeṇa śrūyate śaktireva sā ।
yastattvānto nirākāraḥ sa eva parameśvaraḥ ।। 102 ।।

yat – that which, kiṁcin = kiṁcit = whatever, nāda – naad supernatural sound resonance, rūpeṇa – with format, śrūyate – heard, śaktir = śaktiḥ = subtle creative energy, eva – only, sā – that, yas – which, tattvānto = tattvāntaḥ = final source, nirākāraḥ – immaterial, transcendental, sa – that, eva – even so, parameśvaraḥ – Supreme Lord

What is heard in the format of naad supernatural sound resonance is subtle creative energy. Whatever is transcendental, which is the final source is the Supreme Lord.

Analysis

Naad is the supernatural energy which is the divide between the psychic materials and the divine world. The gross material world is called the physical existence. The psychic material world is called the astral or subtle existence. Beyond the physical and psychic worlds is the spiritual atmosphere which has spiritual content which is immaterial in every sense and is transcendental. That is the place of Parameshwar, the Supreme Lord.

Application

Naad supernatural sound resonance is the vibrational difference between two ultimate realities which are the unmanifest psychic material content and the spiritual atmosphere. Naad sound comes from the clash between these two existences. This is why listening to naad leads to an opening from the other reality into the mind of the yogi.

Verse 103

इति नादानुसन्धानम्

सर्वे हठ–लयोपाया राजयोगस्य सिद्धये ।

राज–योग–समारूढः पुरुषः काल–वञ्चकः ।। १०३ ।।

iti nādānusandhānam
sarve haṭha–layopāyā rājayogasya siddhaye ।
rāja–yoga–samārūḍhaḥ puruṣaḥ kāla–vañcakaḥ ।। 103 ।।

iti – thus, nādānusandhānam = nāda (naad subtle sound vibration) + ānusandhānam (continuous spontaneous inner focus), sarve – all, haṭha – kundalini manipulation for psychic energy transformation, layopāyā = techniques of mento–emotional energy suspension, rājayogasya = of the mystic process of remaining introverted while being externally occupied, siddhaye – in the success, rāja–yoga = mystic process of remaining introverted while being externally occupied, samārūḍhaḥ – proficient, puruṣaḥ – person, kāla – time approaching as death, vañcakaḥ – one who outwits

All techniques of hatha yoga kundalini manipulation for psychic energy transformation, and those processes for laya yoga mento–emotional energy suspension, are for success in the raja yoga mystic process of remaining introverted while being externally occupied. The person who is proficient in remaining introverted while being externally occupied, outwits time which approaches as death.

Analysis

Hatha Yoga is kundalini yoga. It is not asana postures alone. Laya Yoga is the dissolution of the conventional attitude of the mind which is to create ideas and images from moment to moment to entertain the hypnotized core-self. Both kundalini yoga and laya yoga are achieved with the help of pranayama breath-infusion. This frees the self from the hypnotic grip which the mind holds over it.

For success in raja yoga or remaining introverted while being externally occupied, one has to master both kundalini yoga and laya yoga using pranayama breath-infusion as the main lever to dismiss lower levels of the mind.

Those who think that they can successfully gain control of the mind from the lower levels are simply wasting their time. It is not possible to do this. That is why there is the 4th stage of yoga, pranayama breath-infusion. That forces the mind to abandon its footing on lower planes and take shelter on higher levels where naturally the mind has no power over the core-self.

Application

Time is approaching as death. This is a fact except for stupid people who feel that time is an illusion. Patanjali did not list time as an illusion but some who do yoga today say otherwise. This is the declaration of Patanjali:

jāti deśa kāla vyavahitānām api ānantaryaṁ smṛti saṁskārayoḥ ekarūpatvāt

jāti – status; deśa – location; kāla – time; vyavahitānām – of what is placed apart or separated; api – even, also; ānantaryaṁ – timeful sequence; smṛti – memory; saṁskārayoḥ – of the impressions formed of cultural activities; ekarūpatvāt – due to one form.

Even though circumstances are separated by status, location and time, still the impressions which form cultural activities and the resulting memories, are of one

form and operate on a timely sequence. (Yoga Sutras 4.9)

tāsām anāditvaṁ ca āśiṣaḥ nityatvāt

tāsām – those; anāditvaṁ – what is without beginning, primeval; ca – and; āśiṣaḥ – hope and desire energies; nityatvāt – what is eternal.

Those memories and impressions are primeval, without a beginning. Energies of hope and desire are eternal as well. . (Yoga Sutras 4.10)

hetu phala āśraya ālambanaiḥ saṅgṛhītatvāt
eṣām abhāve tad abhāvaḥ

hetu – cause; phala – effect; āśraya – storage place, causal plane, supportive base; ālambanaiḥ – by what supports or lifts; saṅgṛhītatvāt – what holds together; eṣām – of those, these; abhāve – in what is not there; tad – them; abhāvaḥ – not existing.

They exist by what holds them together in terms of cause and effect, supportive base and lifting influence. Otherwise if their causes are not there, they have no existence. . (Yoga Sutras 4.11)

atīta anāgataṁ svarūpataḥ
asti adhvabhedāt dharmāṇām

atīta – the past; anāgataṁ – the future; svarūpataḥ – true form; asti – there is, it exists; adhvabhedāt – due to different courses or events; dharmāṇām – of the characteristics.

There is a true form of the past and future, which is denoted by the different courses of their characteristics. . (Yoga Sutras 4.12)

Verse 104

तत्त्वं बीजं हठः क्षेत्रमौदासीन्यं जलं तरिभिः ।

उन्मनी कल्प–लतिका सद्य एव प्रवर्तते ।। १०४ ।।

tattvaṁ bījaṁ haṭhaḥ kṣetramaudāsīnyaṁ jalaṁ tribhiḥ |
unmanī kalpa–latikā sadya eva pravartate || 104 ||

tattvaṁ – knowledge of reality, bījaṁ – seed, haṭhaḥ – kundalini manipulation for psychic energy transformation, kṣetram – farmland, audāsīnyaṁ – total neutrality, jalaṁ – water, tribhiḥ – three, unmanī – void of mental content, kalpa–latikā = wishfulfilling tree, sadya – immediately, eva – only, pravartate – springs up

Knowledge of reality is the seed. Kundalini manipulation for psychic energy transformation is the farmland. Total neutrality is the water. These are the three necessities which cause the void state of mental content to immediately spring up like a wishfulfilling tree.

Analysis

Access to the divine world opens from the divine side to this side. A yogi cannot force his way into the spiritual environment from this side of existence. Students need to accept this and work to suit. It is a matter of making the inside of the psyche responsive to the divine energy which will then penetrate and create an opening for the yogi to either view the divine world from here or transit into the divine world where he can enjoy the transcendental life there.

Divine people come from the divine side into the psychic material environment with news about life over there. These divinities include Shiva and Vishnu (Krishna). They bring the seed which is listed here as the tattva or knowledge of what is really taking place, in the spiritual and material situations.

A yogi receives this seed from the Supreme Person or from his agent and then plants and waters it sufficiently. It grows and matures as the void state of mental content, the state in which the yogi waits for an opening to develop from the divine side into his psyche. This is the gist of this yoga process explained by Swatmarama.

Application

Lord Krishna directly handed the seed or knowledge of these realities in the form of the Bhagavad Gita to humankind. It is left to us to read that text without distorting its information. Then with Krishna's help we can gain access to the divine situation.

The labor is kundalini manipulation for psychic energy transformation. That is compared to tilling soil in farming. Once this is done properly, the seed is planted. Then the farmer must rely on rain and on watering the seed when the rain is untimely. To apply water he must have total neutrality in the cultural affairs of material nature, so that he does not have an interference attitude but lets everyone else do whatever their little hearts desire, while he focuses on tending his spiritual development. If the farming is done in that manner the yogi will gain quick access to the divine environment.

Verse 105

सदा नादानुसन्धानात्क्षीयन्ते पाप–संचयाः ।

निरञ्जने विलीयेते निश्चितं चित्त–मारुतौ ।। १०५ ।।

sadā nādānusandhānātkṣīyante pāpa–saṁcayāḥ I
nirañjane vilīyete niścitaṁ citta–mārutau II 105 II

sadā – always, nādānusandhānāt = nāda (naad subtle sound vibration) + ānusandhānam (from continuous spontaneous inner focus), kṣīyante – terminate, papa – faults, saṁcayāḥ – aggregate, nirañjane – spiritual purity, vilīyete – fiz out, niścitaṁ – certainty, citta = mento–emotional energy, mārutau – infused breath energy

The aggregate faults are terminated by always applying the continuous spontaneous inner focus on naad subtle sound vibration. The mento–emotional energy, and the infused breath energy, certainly fizz out, resulting in spiritual purity.

Analysis

Even though morality is the first stage of yoga, removal of the faults is not a morality process. Removal of faults by behavioral adjustment cannot penetrate deeply into the psyche. It is an unreliable way of dealing with faults. In addition the definition of faults rests with the material nature because it is that agency which operates the action-reaction cycle for its convenience and not with any limited individual's priority in mind. Human beings get this foolish idea that they can legitimize behavior to ease their troubled minds but that has nothing to do with material nature's mathematical operations in balancing out its cosmic energies.

A yogi has to remove the faults by always applying the continuous spontaneous inner focus on naad subtle sound vibration because that is the only way to leave aside material nature, to extract the core-self from it, so that material nature would stop calculating how to use the core-self and would delete it from its destiny-calculations.

Application

In this practice, during meditation, if the breath-infusion is done proficiently, and if naad absorption is full, the mento-emotional energy and the infused breath energy will fizz out, leaving the yogi on the border between the psychic material environment and the spiritual world. There, like a passenger waiting for transportation, the yogi will patiently remain in naad absorption until a spirit-transit or spirit-vision-access becomes available.

Verse 106

शङ्ख–दुन्धुभि–नादं च न श्रृणोति कदाछन ।

काष्ठवज्जायते देह उन्मन्यावस्थया ध्रुवम् ।। १०६ ।।

śaṅkha–dundhubhi–nādaṁ ca na śṝṇoti kadācana |
kāṣṭhavajjāyate deha unmanyāvasthayā dhruvam || 106 ||

śaṅkha – conch, dundhubhi – drum, nādaṁ ca – and, na – not, śṝṇoti – hears, kadācana – someone, kāṣṭhavaj = kāṣṭhavat = like firewood, jāyate – situated, deha – body, unmany= unmani = void of mental content, āvasthayā – focused into the divine environment, dhruvam – fixed

He does not hear the conch or drum and his body is like a log, due to being fixedly focused when devoid of mental content and situated into the divine environment.

Analysis

This describes the physical condition of the body of a yogi whose is alive on the physical side while his core-self transited into the divine atmosphere. The experience is such that it rarely shows any indication to persons on the physical side.

In an astral projection, the physical body will hear the sound of conch or drum or any type of loud alarm, whereby the lifeforce will yank the subtle form back into the physical one for safety. But when the core-self has transited beyond the astral dimensions into the spiritual environment, there is no rapid communication with the core-self until it has resumed focus into the astral body.

Application

In this respect for human beings, there are three bodies under consideration. These are:

- *physical system with limbs and senses*
- *subtle system with limbs and senses*
- *spiritual self with or without limbs and senses*

A limited spirit is allowed the development and use of one ***physical system*** *at a time. When this system is awake it has a subtle one interspaced into it and a spiritual self is located in that subtle body.*

The limited spirit has one ***subtle system*** *which it must use for the duration of its existence in the material cosmos. It cannot move that subtle body into another cosmos. That body will last for the duration of the universe at which time, it will de-exist. This subtle body develops and uses physical forms from time to time. It is adaptive so that it can use any type of physical body which it is opportune to develop in material nature.*

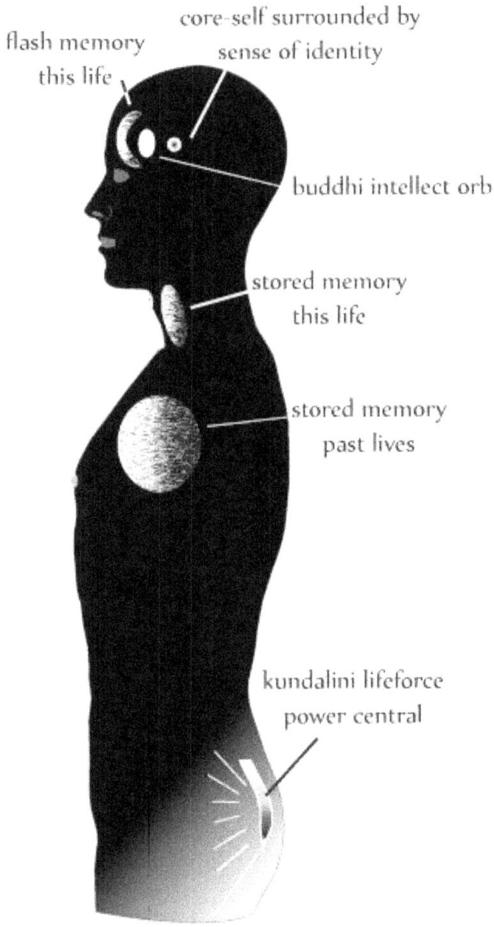

While using a physical body, the subtle form is regularly separated out of the physical one. When this happens the lifeforce of the subtle body remains embedded in the physical one and keeps the physical one alive in a sleeping condition. In the subtle body there are components of consciousness. These are the core-self, the sense of identity, the buddhi intellect orb, the kundalini lifeforce, the subtle senses and the memories.

The limited spirit is a ***spiritual self with or without limbs and senses****. It cannot transmigrate in the material world nor have any subtle or gross perception here without using the equipment in the subtle body. It cannot directly perceive the psychic or physical material energy. This spiritual self always is a spiritual body but it may or may not have limbs and distinct senses. When it is without distinct senses, it uses its awareness as its singular sense.*

Verse 107

सर्वावस्था–विनिर्मुक्तः सर्व– चिन्ता–विवर्जितः ।

मृतवत्तिष्ठते योगी स मुक्तो नात्र संशयः ।। १०७ ।।

sarvāvasthā–vinirmuktaḥ sarva–cintā–vivarjitaḥ I
mṛtavattiṣṭhate yogī sa mukto nātra saṁśayaḥ II 107 II

sarvāvasthā – all unwanted existential conditions, vinirmuktaḥ – freed, sarva – all, cintā – sources of anxiety, vivarjitaḥ – having no, mṛtavat – like a dead body, tiṣṭhate – remains, yogī – yogi, sa – he, mukto = muktaḥ = liberation, nātra – not here, saṁśayaḥ – doubt

Being freed from all unwanted existential conditions, from all sources of anxiety, the yogi remains like a dead body. There is no doubt regarding this.

Analysis

When a yogi is allowed access to the divine world, he becomes like a dead person not just physically but psychically as well. Both bodies, the physical and the subtle one used in realistic dreams, become redundant for such a person.

Application

The material world has its ups and downs. No one is an exception here in terms of being subjected to trauma. It is a matter of how much inconvenience one is subject to in reference to another person but everyone has a share of affliction. All sane people should move away from the unwanted existential conditions. We should acquire transit to the divine place.

Verse 108

खाद्यते न च कालेन बाध्यते न च कर्मणा ।

साध्यते न स केनापि योगी युक्तः समाधिना ।। १०८ ।।

khādyate na ca kālena bādhyate na ca karmaṇā I
sādhyate na sa kenāpi yogī yuktaḥ samādhinā II 108 II

khādyate – devoured, na – not, ca – and, kālena – by death approaching as time, bādhyate – trapped, na – not, ca – and, karmaṇā – by cultural activity, sādhyate – overpowered, na – not, sa – he, kenāpi = kena (by which) + api (even though), yogī – yogi, yuktaḥ – proficient, samādhinā – by continuous linkage to the divine environment or person

Not being devoured by death which approaches as time, nor trapped by cultural activity, nor overpowered by circumstance, the yogi remains proficient in the continuous linkage to the divine environment or person.

Analysis

The physical body of the yogi will be devoured by death. That is certain. His physical system will be subjected to cultural prejudices and circumstances. That is unavoidable. His physical form will be overpowered by circumstances. That is for sure. And yet, the yogi will transcend this because of not being focused on his material body which will bear the brunt of these assaults.

Application

The trick is to maintain continuous linkage to the divine environment or person.

Verse 109

न गन्धं न रसं रूपं न च स्पर्शं न निःस्वनम् ।
नात्मानं न परं वेत्ति योगी युक्तः समाधिना ।। १०९ ।।

na gandhaṁ na rasaṁ rūpaṁ na ca sparśaṁ na niḥsvanam I
nātmānaṁ na paraṁ vetti yogī yuktaḥ samādhinā II 109 II

na – not, gandhaṁ – odor, na – not, rasaṁ – flavor, rūpaṁ – color, na – not, ca – and, sparśaṁ – surface, na – not, niḥsvanam – sound, nātmānaṁ = na (not) + ātmānaṁ (core–self), na – not, paraṁ – other person, vetti – experienced, yogī – yogi, yuktaḥ – proficient, samādhinā – by continuous linkage to a divine environment or person

Neither odor, nor flavor, nor color, nor surface, nor sound, nor even the self, nor other persons, is experienced by a yogi who is proficiently absorbed in the continuous linkage to a divine environment or person.

Analysis

Everything pertaining to this side of existence even the character reference of the yogi and of any other person, is absent during the continuous linkage to a divine environment or person. This sounds contradictory but it reveals that the divide between the psychic mundane energies and the spiritual energy is clear-cut and not muddled. There is no mixture between this side of existence and the divine world.

Application

The odors, colors, surfaces, sounds and even the character reference of the yogi, and of others on this side of existence, do not recur and have no correspondence in the divine environment. Physical and psychic material existences are not repeated in the divine world. There is no mirror event from the material existence occurring in the spiritual world. Even though an object causes its reflection in a pond or mirror, the reflection cannot in turn cause an object to appear in the environment. It is a one-way reality.

Verse 110

चित्तं न सुप्तं नोजाग्रत्स्मृति–विस्मृति–वर्जितम् ।

न चास्तमेति नोदेति यस्यासौ मुक्त एव सः ।। ११० ।।

cittam na suptaṁ nojāgratsmṝti–vismṝti–varjitam I
na cāstameti nodeti yasyāsau mukta eva saḥ I I 110 I I

cittam – mento–emotional energy, na – not, suptaṁ – sleep, no = naḥ = us, jāgrat – waking, smṝti – remembering, vismṝti – forgetting, varjitam – having, na – not, cāstameti – fading, nodeti – expanding, yasyāsau – whose, mukta – liberated, eva – even, saḥ – he

With his mento–emotional energy, neither sleeping, nor waking, nor remembering, nor forgetting, nor fading, nor expanding, the yogi is liberated.

Analysis

During the time when the yogi transited or focused over into the divine side of existence, his mento-emotional energy assumes suspension, being neither sleeping, nor waking, nor remembering, nor forgetting, nor fading, nor expanding. If the yogi comes back to material world, or if his focus is reverted to this, that same mento-emotional energy will begin functioning again. If the yogi does not come back to this side of existence and completes a final transit, his mento-emotional energy is released into material nature. It is adopted by some other person or persons.

Sometimes miraculously a disciple of a siddha makes rapid advancement because his teacher left the psychic material world and went into the spiritual world, after which the mento-emotional energy of the teacher grafts onto the psyche of the disciple.

Application

The expression of the mento-emotional energy, its independent performance for which the core-self is held accountable, is given as six mediums:

- *sleeping*
- *waking*
- *remembering*
- *forgetting*
- *fading*
- *expanding*

The modification and full or partial control of these is required for mastery of kundalini yoga.

To gain the maximum control over ***sleeping****, a yogi must master kundalini yoga through using breath-infusion to saturate the subtle body with the highest available subtle energy which can be ingested into it. This gives maximum neutralization of fatigue and supplies new energy which the lifeforce can use to replace astral pollutants.*

For the most insightful ***waking*** *the yogi should arouse kundalini through the sushumna spinal passage. This should be done a minimum of twice per day to blast out dense astral energy in the passage. Eventually the dense energy will no longer be in the passage. This will cause the kundalini to radiate through the passage continuously with the result that eventually it will ascend through the passage and remain resident in the brain, abandoning its conventional residence which is the muladhara base chakra.*

To destroy the ***remembering*** *faculty, a yogi must cease endorsing memories which come up of their own accord from the chest of the subtle body. These impressions usually manifest in the mind space as thoughts and images. When these arise in their compressed or expanded forms, the yogi should habitually ignore them. This causes their subsiding and disappearing. Eventually the psychic mechanism which activates and moves these memories will cease the operations.*

The ***forgetting*** *impulse is automatic for the most part. A yogi should observe how it sorts what to catalog. It is a gripping mechanism which holds and deletes information.*

When an item is ***fading****, the yogi can retain it if he has a reserve of sober energy to invest into it. He may accelerate the fading of a mental or emotional incident-memory if he exhibits detachment towards it.*

When an item is ***expanding****, the yogi can suppress it by indifference. If effectively applied the item will begin shrinking and will keep doing so, rapidly or slowly, until it disappears.*

Verse 111

न विजानाति शीतोष्णं न दुःखं न सुखं तथा ।

न मानं नोपमानं च योगी युक्तः समाधिना ।। १११ ।।

na vijānāti śītoṣṇaṁ na duḥkhaṁ na sukhaṁ tathā |
na mānaṁ nopamānaṁ ca yogī yuktaḥ samādhinā || 111 ||

na – not, vijānāti – experiences, śītoṣṇaṁ = heat and cold, na – not, duḥkhaṁ – trauma, na – not, sukhaṁ – pleasure, tathā – as, na – not, mānaṁ – pride, nopamānaṁ = not shame, ca – and, yogī – yogi, yuktaḥ – absorbed in, samādhinā – by continuous linkage to a divine environment or person

Not experiencing heat or cold, trauma or pleasure, pride or shame, the yogi is absorbed in continuous linkage to a divine environment or person.

Analysis

Success for yoga during the life of a material body, means that the yogi translated across the existential divine between the psychic material world and the spiritual world. However, as long as he has a material body, that means there is a subtle form. So long as there is a subtle body, risk for trauma or pleasure is there. Environmentally in the material world, there is always risk of being subjected to intolerable heat or cold. So long as one is in a society one may be subjected to pride or shame. The escape from this occurs if the yogi links to a divine environment or person, so that even if there is still a gross or subtle material body, the yogi is superficially impacted only.

Application

These are the last verses in this thesis on yoga by the great yogin Swatmarama. He stressed naad sound resonance. At this last stage he stressed transit to the divine world.

Verse 112

सवस्थो जाग्रदवस्थायां सुप्तवद्यो।अवतिष्ठते ।

निःश्वासोच्छ्वास–हीनश्च निश्चितं मुक्त एव सः ।। ११२ ।।

svastho jāgradavasthāyāṁ suptavadyo।avatiṣṭhate ।
niḥśvāsocchvāsa–hīnaśca niścitaṁ mukta eva saḥ ।। 112 ।।

svastho = svasthaḥ = self–absorbed, jāgradavasthāyāṁ = awakened condition, suptavadyo– sleeping, avatiṣṭhate – seems to be, niḥśvāsocchvāsa = without breathing inspiration or expiration, hīnaśca – and, niścitaṁ – certainly, mukta – is liberated, eva – also, saḥ – he

One who is self-absorbed, who though awake seems to be sleeping, and is without breathing inspiration or expiration, is certainly liberated.

Analysis

This describes the meditative state of a yogin who succeeded in fully transcending the crisis which is the material world. A limited self has its mission to relieve itself from the need for material nature, which is a very taxing environment. As people move from a country which has a repressive ruler, so the core-self should evacuate itself from the psychic material world. If only it gains access, it would go to the divine place.

Application

When the yogi is shifted over into the divine environment, the breathing mechanism of his material body is either suspended or slowed considerably. This is because the lifeforce suspends its interest in the struggle for survival. As soon as the yogi resumes social interest in the material world, the lifeforce resumes its grasp on breath energy.

Verse 113

अवध्यः सर्व–शस्त्राणामशक्यः सर्व–देहिनाम् ।

अग्राह्यो मन्त्र–यन्त्राणां योगी युक्तः समाधिना ।। ११३ ।।

avadhyaḥ sarva–śastrāṇāmaśakyaḥ sarva–dehinām ।
agrāhyo mantra–yantrāṇāṁ yogī yuktaḥ samādhinā ।। 113 ।।

avadhyaḥ – killed, sarva – all, śastrāṇām – weapons, aśakyaḥ – incapable, sarva – all, dehinām –people, agrāhyo = agrāhyaḥ = supersedes, mantra – sound control, yantrāṇāṁ – symbol and diagram control, yogī – yogi, yuktaḥ – absorbed, samādhinā – by continuous linkage to a divine environment or person

The yogi is incapable of being killed by any weapon, beyond the power of all people, beyond sound, symbol or diagram control, due to being continuously linked to a divine environment or person.

Analysis

There is nothing special about a yogi being incapable of being killed by any weapon, because according to Krishna, all the atmas, or spirit-selves are incapable of being done away with:

nainaṁ chindanti śastrāṇi
nainaṁ dahati pāvakaḥ
na cainaṁ kledayantyāpo
na śoṣayati mārutaḥ (2.23)

nainaṁ = na — not + enam — this; chindanti — pierce; śastrāṇi — weapons; nainaṁ = na — not + enam — this; dahati — burns; pāvakaḥ — fire; na — not; cainaṁ = ca — and + enam — this; kledayantyāpo = kledayanti — soak + āpo = āpaḥ — water; na — nor; śoṣayati — dry out; mārutaḥ — the wind

Weapons do not pierce, fire does not burn, and water does not wet, nor does the wind dry that embodied soul. (Bhagavad Gita 2.23)

acchedyo'yamadāhyo'yam
akledyo'śoṣya eva ca
nityaḥ sarvagataḥ sthāṇur
acalo'yaṁ sanātanaḥ (2.24)

acchedyaḥ — not to be pierced; 'yam = ayam — this; adāhyo = adāhyaḥ — not to be burnt; 'yam = ayam — this; akledyo = akledyaḥ — not to be moistened; 'śoṣya = aśoṣya — not to be dried; eva — indeed; ca — and; nityaḥ — eternal; sarvagataḥ — penetrant of all things; sthāṇuḥ — a permanent principle; acalo = acalaḥ — unmoving; 'yaṁ = ayam — this; sanātanaḥ — primeval

This embodied soul cannot be pierced, cannot be burnt, cannot be moistened and cannot be dried. And indeed, this soul is eternal. It can penetrate all things. It is a permanent principle and is stable and primeval. (Bhagavad Gita 2.24)

What is special about the yogi is that he has direct experience of spiritual endurance. To reinforce this he has experience of a divine environment, which has the same enduring potential. Despite the uncertainty about it, other spirits are just as durable but they will have to keep transmigrating in the material world for the time being.

Application

The yogi is incapable of being killed by a weapon, but his physical body may be killed in that way. The yogi is beyond the power of all people but his body may be subjected to hostile acts of others. The yogi is beyond sound, symbol and diagram control because his interest is no longer invested into the subtle body which is a material form even though it is not as gross as the physical system.

Verse 114

यावन्नैव प्रविशति चरन्मा रुतो मध्यमार्गे

यावद्बिन्दुर्न भवति दृढः प्रानवातप्रबन्धात्

यावद्ध्याने सहज–सदृशं जायते नैव तत्त्वं

तावज्ज्ञानं वदति तदिदं दम्भ–मिथ्या–प्रलापः ।। ११४ ।।

yāvannaiva praviśati caranmā ruto madhyamārge
yāvadbindurna bhavati dṛḍhaḥ prānavātaprabandhāt
yāvaddhyāne sahaja–sadṝśaṁ jāyate naiva tattvaṁ
tāvajjñānaṁ vadati tadidaṁ dambha–mithyā–pralāpaḥ || 114 ||

yāvan = yāvat = so long as, naiva = not even, praviśati – enter, caran – flow, mā – not, ruto = rutaḥ = vibrated, madhyamārge = in the middle course, yāvad = yāvat = so long as, bindur = binduḥ = reproduction hormone concentrate, na – not, bhavati – becomes, dṛḍhaḥ – firm, prana – subtle breath energy, vāta – lifeforce, prabandhāt – from compression, yāvad = yāvat = so long as, dhyāne – in the spontaneous focus linkage into the divine world, sahaja – produced, natural, sadṝśaṁ – similar, jāyate – control, naiva = not even, tattvaṁ – reality, tāvaj = tāvat = until, jñānaṁ – knowledge, vadati – speaks, tad = tat = that, idaṁ – this, dambha – retarded, mithyā – schizophrenic, pralāpaḥ – talkative

So long as it does not flow or vibrate in the middle course, and the reproduction hormone concentrate does not become firm by the compression of subtle breath energy and lifeforce, as long as the reality is not similar to the experience during the spontaneous focal linkage, so long the knowledge and speech of this is that of a talkative, schizophrenic, retarded person.

THE END.

Index

A

abdomen,
disorders, 297
draw-up, 75,391
fat storage, 387
fill gradually, 162
lock details, 281
lock-primary, 126
peacock pose, 76
problems, 191
purification, 186
spin, 199
up and under, 356,357
uplift, 219
abode of Vishnu, 586
absence of flaws - eyes, 268,269
absorption rate, 161,248
abstinence, 560
abstract environment, 520
abstract feelings, 220
accelerated heart, 444
access perceptions, 22
access independence, 73
accident, 185
acclaim, 180
accomplishment,
highest, 266
issue, 548
twelve (12) years, 93
accounting breath, 295
action/reaction cycle, 297
addiction,
excitement, 45
potential, 347
sensation, 45
add-ons, 23
Adi Shankaracharya,
Mandana Mishra, 407
sex, 404,407
Adinath,
respected, 11
siddha, 9,17
trauma absent, 550
adjuncts,
- see psychic adjuncts
brahmarandra, 317
chief ones, 317
power struggle, 13
primary ones, 317
third eye, 317
war, 540
administrative sector, 11
admiration, 180
Advaita Vedanta, 542
advancement stages, 134
affected spirit, 47
affection,
distribution, 233
necessary, 132
affiliate experience, 20
afflictions, 417
afterlife, 235
aggregate energies, 542
aggregate faults, 594
aggression required, 155
agriculture organized, 39
aimless wanderer, 559
air,
physio-subtle, 160
respiration, 179
subtle pollution, 246
transit, 114
air breathing creature, 298
air energy, 113,117
- see also breath energy
air-in-blood signature, 114
air infusion, 152,389
- see breath infusion
air regulator deities, 286
ajna chakra,
major, 390
Rudra congestion, 565
staring, 454
akash, 471
alcoholic siddha, 18
alert others, 41
alert, Patanjali, 267
Allamaḥ, 21
alliance,
kundalini/core-self, 272
psyche components, 314
alligators, 432
aloneness, 331
alternate breathing,
challenges, 163
details, 159,160,162
failure causes, 163
locks, 220
requirements, 295
alveoli, 217
amaroli,
brahmins prohibited, 486
details, 413,418,419
female kriya, 284
purpose, 285
ambrosia, 548
ammunition dump, 340
amrita pleasure, 532
anahata chakra, 390
anahata congestion, 559
anal sphincter, 99 190,281
analogy, salt/water, 472
analytical psychic technology, 269
Ananda, 17
Ananta/Ahi-nayakah, 271
anatomy female, 365
ancestors,
management, 358
monks influenced, 359
obligation, 41,371
own body, 298
yogi ruined by, 358
anchor, 51
anemia, 231,232
anesthesia, 102
angelic woman,
yogi attracts, 171
yogi responsible, 234
animals,
astral body, 241
avoidance, 141
fastest, 215
flesh increase, 206
killing instinct, 17
murder, 40
species explored, 216
yogi, 402
ankle,
male organ, 87
strain, 123

annals of yoga, 213
antelope, 581
antics, 124
Anu gita, 461
anuloma-viloma,
described, 160,162
locks, 220
patience required
reliable, 160
anus,
coccyx compress, 365
death exit, 281
perineum contract, 391
tube insert, 190
anxiety, 111
apana,
decrease, 207
hoarded, 206
kundalini hoards, 206
aphorism, 543
aphrodisiac, 400
apparition Jesus Christ, 8
appearance, 146
appetite,
ancestors involved, 358
breath infusion, 371
increase, 281,314,357
apples drug, 152
appreciation, deities, 288
approved behavior, 341
apsaras, 170
aquatic creature, 298
archer, 586
areas, 123
aristocracy, 224
aristocratic woman, 288,507
Arjuna,
karma yoga, 569
karma yoga doubt, 477
killed humans, 133
Parikshit's grandfather, 336
army, 340
arse, 282
artesian well, 405
Arthur Beverford,
- see Beverford
arts and science, 224
Arundhati, 428
asana posture,
- see postures
final forms, 93
hatha yoga, 24
pan out, 92
physical graduate, 242
purpose, 51
ascetic,
ancestral obligation, 41
female, 234
habitat, 28
peace of mind, 29
protection, 28
rated, 14
security, 28
ashes,
cow dung, 420
psychic, 420
selected, 413
smearing, 420
ashram,
author, 136
described, 30
ashtanga yoga,
auspicious, 416
kundalini yoga, 24
Ashvattha tree, 519
ashwini mudra, 282,385
Asia, 20
assets, psychological, 23
assistance, 25
assistant, cooking, 144
association,
astral, 32
female pregnancy, 140
group of yoginis, 234
negative type, 25
psychic sensitivity, 32
relevant, 313
responsibility, 140
asthma, 178
astral being, 241
astral body,
- see also subtle body
causal plane limit, 561
details, 241
limited, 561
astral energy,
dense, 390,453
heavy/clouded, 223
ignited, 252
kundalini affects, 556
neck, 194
weight, 254-256
astral existence shut down, 588
astral guru, 166
astral light, 171
astral projection,
details, 595
explained, 197
mastery, 269
sitting posture, 95
spirit transit, 595
subtle body aware, 160
subtle body movement, 120
yogi's disinterest, 197
astral regions,
deities, 59
mulabandha, 281
subterranean, 153
astral sex, 59
astral travel, 471,472
- see astral projection
astral world, 196
atheistic stance, 134
atheistic teacher, 549
athletic stamina, 206
atomic mystic skill, 348
attachment risk, 23
attention,
in psyche, 182
investment, 467
tip of nose, 113
attitude, 155
attractive woman, 331
aura,
author sees, 195,196
gazing, 508
unseen, 509
austerity, fun / game, 44
author,
amaroli, 486
astral authority, 460
astral guru, 166
Bhagavad Gita commentaries, 12
blighted students, 504

author, continued,
carnal knowledge, 407
commentaries, 12
commissioned, 460
confidence breach, 12
confidence in, 160
deviation, 137
disciples, 12
Ganga, 7
guru of guru, 52
hoops, 12
inspiration, 7
Krishna empowered, 460
kundalini leak, 303
mission change, 7
path, 151
Rishi Singh Gherwal empowered, 460
self-urine, 413,486
Shiva commissioned, 12,460
Shivananda empowered, 460
sun-deity infused, 7
sushumna nadi lit, 8
Swatmarama, 460
tantric partner, 406
third eye, 8
Vishnudevananda empowered, 460
Vishnudevananda request, 407
warrior past life, 20
Yogeshwarananda instructed, 371
Yogi Bhajan, 136
authority global, 306
Avalokitesvara, 42
awareness,
being, 275
singular sense, 596
stationary, 255
ax, 519
ayahuasca, 150
Ayur Veda,
not current, 191
cures, 232,238
ointments/oils, 406
sex stamina, 400

B

baby forms, 246
bachelors, 139
backlash, 260
backlog of destructive acts, 90
back-support, 81
bacteria, 136,178
bad attitude, 219
balance,
breath, 296
kapalabhati, 296
Krishna explained, 315
nostrils sides, 296
sun/moon, 226
balcony, 29
balloon, 211
bane of yoga, 499
bare self, 23
barley, 142
base chakra,
attack, 74
final escape,
heat, 281
major, 390
runs show, 369
tugged, 74
basti,
details, 190
purificatory action, 186
bastion of insecurity, 233
bath, 139,141
Battlefield of Kurukshetra, 569
beaches, 168
bears, 320
beauty,
cleansing causes, 192
form, 33,164
yoga motive, 51,52
bee, 410,578
bee-like sound, 257
begging, 143
beginner, 31
behavior,
adjustment limited, 595
counterproductive, 298
belief tendency, 155,156
belief, irrelevant, 341
bell, 586
bellows, 202,247
belly fat reduction, 75
Beloved, Michael,
- see author
Beverford, Arthur,
author met, 162
dhauti taught by, 186
instruction, 164
purpose of posture, 242
tongue technique, 115
traatak practice, 195
vomit impulse, 206
bhadra grace pose, 80,128
Bhagavad Gita,
Arjuna, 336
commentaries, 12
escape instructions, 392
foods, 137
guru requirement, 16
karma yoga, 11
Krishna gave, 594
migration, 434,435
naad, 269
necessary, 214,454,461
senses betrayal, 148
yoga explained, 356
Bhagavatam, 49
Bhairava, 17,20
Bhaktisiddhanta, 12
Bhaktivedanta, 12
Bhanuki, 21
Bharat, Jada, 49,489
bhastra, 202
bhastrika,
- see also breath infusion
advanced kapalabhati, 186
aggressive, 244
animal, 215
breath suspension, 215
cheetah, 215
details, 239,240
distinguished, 203
efficient, 156
feared, 444
forceful process, 244
kundalini, 253
Bhava, 12
bhoga, 416
bhramari, 215
bhujangi, 427
big picture, 328
bija source, 355
bikinis, 168

bile,
imbalance, 191
upsets removed, 238
urine content, 418
Bileshaya, 17
Bindunatha, 21
bipeds evolution, 128
bird,
colorful, 416
kundalini, 359
pepper, 138
wings clipped, 580
birth,
human, 154,
last, 308
blackbee infusion, 215
blackout,
chin lock, 282
details, 255,556
kundalini, 367,555
neck lock prevents, 117
objectivity lost, 230
penetration, 254
blacksmith, 202,247
bladder insertion, 404
blank frontal part, 318
blank thoughtless state,
achievement, 323
breath infusion, 493
details, 505
mind mastered by, 500
necessary, 213
personal worship, 504
stability, 213
transit access, 548
voidal state, 153
blank staring, 186, 195
blast force,
blast trauma, 588
blazing energy, 374
blazing reality, 515
blighted yogi, 504
blind man, 22
blindfold,
required, 337,517
usage, 238,458
useful, 127
yogi, 368
bliss,
bliss force, 170
bliss saturation, 389
cell travel, 351
cellular, 337
consciousness, 275
head drip, 336
heavenly world, 532
lusty flavor, 502
mint camphor, 346
neutral type, 560
noticed, 310
sex experience contrasted, 253
spiritual body, 512
texture, 512
types, 502
unknown, 284,285
bloated abdomen, 359
blood cells,
infusion distribution, 217
release attitude, 219
resistant, 216
blood/milk mix, 20
blueprint of taste, 347
Blue-Throat, 77
boa constrictor, 229
bodhisattva, 42
bodily fluids reverse, 278
body,
- see physical body
- see subtle body
- see causal body
- see spiritual body
bold, 35,36
bolt, 582
Bonaparte,
books,
insufficient, 145
needed, 214
proper use, 11
recommended, 30,48
bow pose, 66
bow, 586
box of gold, 197
brahma energy congestion, 555,557
brahma granthi, , 254
brahma nadi,
details, 384,385
seal, 385
brahma yoga comment, 12
Brahma, deity
day/night, 527
dissolution, 589
fear afflicted, 165
fear of death, 207
Hiranyakashipu, 319
plural, 12
primal deity, 12
prominent god, 207
sleep, 259
tapa, 165
Vak, 424
brahmacharya,
defined, 139
praised, 404
sannyasi order, 445
Brahmaloka,
destination, 319
relocation, 208
brahman effulgence,
attainment, 561
origin, 433
brahmarandra,
departure rebirth, 224
details, 275
diagram, 490
exit, 223
perception, 375
brahmin,
amaroli prohibited, 486
food, 138
genital handling, 486
privilege, 27
rules, 486
self-urine prohibited, 486
brain,
damaged/kundalini, 379
nectar, 352
corresponding areas, 123
pleasure insightful, 352
sexual brain, 343
sexual pleasure addiction, 396
survival subservient, 396
break-through, 130

breasts,
diagram, 56
energy distribution, 56,57,
fat storage, 387
Ganga, 8
infant milk, 334
milk created, 347
breath/breathing,
as bridge, 179
deep type, 230
groin penetration, 230
involuntary type, 230
irregularity disease, 178
normal type, 230
suspended, 261
breath and food, 135
breath energy,
compressed infused, 391
cooling explained, 492
flush, 493
fuses, 492
heating explained, 492
interior focus, 511
kundalini eats, 427
mind, 473
stabilized, 530
upward, 368
breath infusion,
actions, 260
advanced, 312,444
appetite increases, 371
asana postures charge to each side, 228
attention inside, 511
balance easy, 296
ball, 257
bulb infused, 443
charge fizzed out, 491
chest pressure, 257
clarity increase, 156
complete, 486
compression, 443,473
definite, 148
details, 217,244,245 267,312,337,338, 372,373,389
diet increases, 371
distribution, 248
duration of practice, 439
effective, 484
elderly body, 182
breath infusion, cont'
emotions capture, 249
energy compress, 491
energy exchange, 76
fainting, 444
fears of, 444
flush, 493
focus inside, 180
formation energy, 491
frequency, 153
hard ball, 257
hard-to-reach areas, 95,248
immortality, 310
involuntary, 389
kundalini aroused, 444
kundalini penetrates, 253
kundalini yoga, 24,592
laya yoga, 592
liberation attained, 120
lifeforce assisted, 262
limited, 204
locks necessary, 444
methods, 214,295
mind weakens, 473
minute, 439
modern discouragement, 430
nadi passage, 120
necessary, 304
objective, 480
people disinclined, 428
practice time, 439
pranayama+posture, 71
pratyahar result, 244
preliminary, 90
proficiency result, 177,262,274
psychogical development, 242
purification, 141
purificatory action, 186
rapid process, 240,486
recommended, 204
results of, 92
retention details, 251
reverse process, 153
saturation, 295
sleep removal, 454
steadiness, 150
subtle body, 147
sure way, 153
breath infusion, cont'
suspension details, 498
swinging head, 444
tested, 244
tongue contact, 237
unconsciousness, 444
unnecessary, 318
breath retention,
checking action, 267
details, 93
duration, 168
effect, 93
methods, 214
breath suspension,
details, 503
involuntary, 102
spontaneous, 102
syllabus, 131
brick like mass, 491
bricks: compacted, 310
bridge, breath, 179
bronchial disease, 189
brow chakra,
kundalini, 156
perception, 375
staring, 454
Buddha Shakyamuni, Gautam,
author, 9
affiliate authority, 18
bodhisattva, 42
body starved, 200
exceptional, 530
last birth, 308
Middle Way, 314
mind compression, 494
motive, 165
Satguru, 479
Siddha, 20
trauma disengagement 294
willpower, 546
Buddha of compassion, 17
buddhi intellect orb,
- see also intellect
affiliate power, 13
diagram, 490
disappearance, 545
kundalini, 556,557
kundalini alliance, 427
manas, 533
messenger, 436
perception, 375

buddhi yoga kriya, 541
Buddhist deity, 18,59
Buddhist Tushita heaven, 59
bulb,
advanced details, 443
breath infusion, 443
color size, 441
compression, 443
details,
dissolved, 442
kundalini sleeps, 431
subtle, 443
bulges/fats, 219
bunches of pollution, 202
busy-body, 148
butcher, 17
butter, 142
buttermilk, 136
buttocks,
author entry, 20
clean-out, 19
fat storage, 387
hard to reach, 251
struck, 307

C

cabin, 29
caffeine, addiction, 152
California, 162
calves, 73
camphor, 543
candrim liquid, 420
candy, 142
capitalistic drive, 27
carbon dioxide, , 95,121
caretaker, 307
carnivorous human, 342
causal energy, mind, 543
causal level
- see causal plane
causal medium, 565
causal node sources, 369
causal plane, zone,
abstract, 544
details, 587
location, 369
naad reach, 586
realization, 544
retreat, 273
transit, 197,369
yogi enters, 544
cave, 458
celibacy,
arrogance, 133
details, 334
false type, 409
homosexuality, 133
key issue? 445
kundalini yoga, 41
morality, 341
pride, 133
sex dormancy, 410
sex energy storage, 341
sexual intercourse, 408
status, 133
urine drinking, 419
Vedic times, 139
cell,
bliss energy, 337
bliss force yield, 480
emotion resistance, 296
infusion distribution, 217
kundalini details, 249,285,526
malformation, 231
micro kundalini, 375
pollutants hoarded, 296
release attitude, 219
resistant, 215,216
structure reform, 369
cell phone, 33
central energy center, 390
central passage,
not sushumna, 276
trunk, 59
central spinal passage,
- see also sushumna
clouding, 252
heavy energy, 157
infusion effective, 252
pollution removed, 252
centralize upper flow, 280,306
ceremonial worship, 44,48
ceremony, sexual intercourse, 414
cervix, 279,289
cesspool, 543
chakra complex,
clearance, 155
control, 206
controlling type, 369
deity seen, 415
details, 365
digestive, 371
list, 223
lowest subdued, 370
lowest, 365
major listed, 390
muladhara purpose, 365
seven, 390
sex purpose, 365
sex difference, 332
svadhishthana, 365
third eye, 317
tracking, 162
Chandishvara, 21
chanting, 549
chaos, beginner's, 31
character transcended, 598
charge, kundalini, 254,379
charm, 305
Charpati, 20
Chaurangi, 17,19
check action, 267
cheeks, 387
cheerfulness, 268,269
cheetah, 215
chemical works, 190
chemistry, 191
chest,
breath pressure, 257
focus, 229
lock, 246
pains, 444
chicken, 138
child and mother, 140
child form, 350
chin lock,
details, 101,113,282,291
diagrams, 84,85,386
effects, 228
function, 117
mandatory, 178
perfected yogi pose, 82
primary, 126
reverse, 386
throat compression, 219
throat lock, 126
chinmaya, 52

chit akash,
- see also sky of consciousness
access, 86,132,501,512
approach, 132
chance contact, 154
described, 435
perception, 121
zone of escape, 348
chit maya, 52
Chitralekha, 424
Choli, 21
Christian deity, 59
Christians, 463
circular energy, 323
circular light, 454
cittavritti, 293
city, 29
city hall/road, 352
civilization, 26
clan degraders, 342
clarifying energy, 156
clarity, 156
Clark Air Base, 162
cleanliness, 38,43
cleansing action, air, 156
clearance,
dense energy, 268,269
results nadis, 181
sushumna, 531
climax, 405-406
cliques, 26
closed unit, 470
cloth, dhauti, 188-189
clothing, 146
clouding, 252
cocaine, 150
coffee, 152
coiled shape, 432
collar bone, 194
color, 598
Colorado, 136
colors and shapes, 478
coma, 479
command over society, 33
commentator, 11
Compassion Buddha, 17
compassion hero, 42
compassion,
enlightenment type, 246
student saturated, 246
yogi limited, 38,42
competitive zeal, 206
complete restraint, 242
components of consciousness/psyche,
core-self highest, 281
listed, 13,596
re-ordered, 168,169
research, 498
compression,
anus coccyx, 365
application, 215,222
best, 393
blood, 127
breath energy, 245
breath energy heat, 492
conjoint, 280
control, effects 294
details, 245,293,369,494
direction control, 289
distribution route, 169
down/up, 222
explosion, 367
implosion, 368
kundalini controlled, 253
lock effects, 100
mento-emotional energy, 285
methods, 214
objective, 480
physical tissue, 127
physio-subtle air, 155
relocating energy, 278
techniques, 364
computer monitor, 501
concentration, 163
conch, 595
concluding edge, 259
concubines, 400
condiments, 136
conducts, 44
conduit feeling, 340
confidence,
advanced yogi, 321
books lectures, 160
false sense, 514
writer, 160
confidential arresting action, 298
confusion, 14
congestion,
base chakra, 254
kundalini penetrates, 253
location, 253,254
spine passage, 254
sushumna, 254
third eye, 254
conjugal love, Shankara, 407
conjugal obligation, 371
conscious/unconscious, 255
consciousness,
hormone support, 411
mix, 410
one reality, 306
consequential equation,
bleached, 401
earth objects, 456
constipation, 297
constriction, neck, 60
consumption,
elimination, 297
least, 93
moderate, 89,90
containment,
condition, 559
contraction, 279
control, 299
integration, 554
contentment, 44,45
contortionist, 19
contraction,
details, 98,126
great sealing, 279
lion pose, 126
primay ones, 126
sexual muscle, 278
syllabus, 131
control, membrane, 407
conversation, 32
conveyor belt, 114
conveyor happiness, 464
cool, nectar in brain, 340
cooling bliss, mint, 346
cord, 193
core existence, 559
core self,
adjuncts, 468
adjuncts behavior, 243
adjuncts part out, 470
alliance kundalini, 272

core self, continued,
as body, 530
autonomy bargain, 13
autonomy, 362
bare, 511
breathing affects, 261
control struggle, 449
control taken, 314
death event, 428
decommissioned, 431
desperation, 431
details, 596
diagram, 490
divine body, 559
energy generator, 201,417
entertained, 579
escape, 505
evolution time, 434
expenditures, 468
fearful of kundalini, 430
flawless, 470
foot-bill, 468
force kundalini, 431
gold-out, 385
greater than, 281
helpless, 272
highest component, 281
husband/kundalini, 436
ignorant, 432
immortality, 348
infinite, 348
infinitesimal, 579
inhabitant, 339,340
insight, 548
intellect controls, 243
interest energy, 317
introspective focus, 93
intuition, 504
isolation complete, 93
kha divine space, 538
kundalini, 431
kundalini a drag, 119
kundalini as wife, 436
kundalini boxed in, 368
kundalini compliment, 427
kundalini empowered by, 430
kundalini entertains, 448
kundalini focus, 264

core self, continued,
kundalini restrict, 247
kundalini stooge, 45
leashed, 340
lifeforce alliance, 305
lifeforce essential, 271
lifeforce power, 281
limited, 538
lord of psyche, 340
mind control of, 592
mind lock, 254
movement central, 222
naad absorption, 104
naad anchor, 577
naad relationship, 512
partition, 530
peon, 340
perception, 375
perception calibration, 468
power supply, 35
psyche, 197
psyche management, 417
relocate, 601
self-mastery, 468
self-study, 473
sense of identity, 317
senses regulation, 314
shift from trauma, 392
Shiva atomic,
speck of reality, 579
spectator, 468
spiritual body, 511,530
spiritual presence, 468
stooge, 45
supreme self unity,. 474
tiny, 579
trivialized, 579
underwrite schemes, 277
whiteout, 385
wrestle control, 362
corkscrew, spine, 69
corresponding areas, 123
corrosion / pollutants, 367
cosmetics, drugs, 313
cosmic balance, 595
cosmic engineer, 234
cosmic light, 518
cosmic mystic skill, 348
cosmic shut down, 588
cotton, 188-189
cough, 189
count ratio, 162
country, prosperous, 26
courageous, 35,36
cow,
dung, 29,413
flesh, 342,344
milk taken, 135
posture, 56
released, 41
tongue, 344
craving, 541
creation,
dissolution, 234
origin, 355
source, 18
creator god,
Brahma, 207
sleep, 259
creature existence stunt, 559
creature,
doomed, 485
living, 153
cremation area, 275
criminal behavior, 7
criminal elements, 28
criminal intentions, 259
criminal departed souls, 451
crisis, 468
critics, 130
cross-legged posture,
crown chakra,
diagram, 490
kundalini, 156
major, 390
perception, 375
crusade, 486
crystal brick, 557
cucumber, 142
cultural activities,
mastery, 478
renounced, 482
yogi eludes, 483
cultural environment hostile, 133
culture, ancient, 165
culture, unsupportive, 325
curiosity, 23
curves kinks, 58

D

dairy products, 136,143
dakini,
  Chaurangi assisted, 19
  siddha, 59
  sow faced, 18
  yogi assistant, 405
  yogi attracts, 170
dance movements, 123
dancing, kundalini, 252
daredevil, 161
dark brown brick, 557
dark energy ignited, 157
Dashratha, 52,543
dead bodies, 210
dead body revival, 274
deadman pose, 77,78
death like state, 310
death,
  astral body content, 251
  avoidance, 273
  bodies affected, 325
  Brahma fears, 207
  core-self exit, 281
  destroyer meditation, 464
  dislocation, 209
  elephant, 361
  elimination, 285,294
  exits, 281
  fearlessness, 209
  freedom from, 305
  healthy body, 297
  jurisdiction, 274
  kundalini evades, 445
  life force necessary, 428
  lifeforce focus, 341
  meaning, 362
  muladhar chakra, 223
  natural causes, 185
  occurrence, 153
  remnant psychology, 347
  self resistant, 326
  siddha's, 21
  subtle body, 273,274
  survival insecurity, 118
  translation, 21
  uncertainty, 22
Death Valley 294
deathless liquor, 342,345
deceiver, 31
decision, 417
deer, 482,586
default core-self location, 301
defending, 277
degraders of clan, 342
dehi, 340
dehydration, 472
deity/deities,
  air regulator, 286
  astral region, 59
  blessings, 459
  came and went, 392
  chakra type, 415
  energy movement, 7
  escape instructions, 392
  grace act, 212,429
  grace energy, 580
  grace-pull, 424
  image visualized, 504
  inspiring love, 232,233
  interruption, 130
  Krishna, 392
  mercy act, 429
  necessary, 459
  one predominant, 355
  perception of, 504
  permission, 319
  prominent three, 207
  sexual acts, 415
  thirty fear death, 207
  Tibetan Buddhist, 18
  transit arranged, 392
  unknown, 459
  yogi senses, 50
deity worship,
  physical type, 504
  ritual master, 141
delay, 143
demigod, 288,467
dense astral energy, 491
dense energy, 268,269
Denver, 136
departed souls,
  Yama supervises, 451
  yogi ruined by, 358
dependent/independent, 470
deposit area nutrients, 351
depressed,
  emotional states, 28
  hormone deficient, 411
  sex restraint, 450
  sinkhole, 28
deprivation, 44,49
desire,
  enemy of yoga, 234
  eternal,46
  feet access, 73
  kundalini, 174
  lifestyle, 168
  mento-emotional control, 495
  rate of, 45
  reduction, 40
  sensual access, 22
  stimulant, 495
  technology, 495
  upheaval absent, 506
  yogi's, 247
desireless stage, 506
destination,
  deity grace act, 212
  self effort, 211,212
  subterranean region, 281
destiny, 179,595
detachment, 35,37,267
deterioration / death, 182
deterioration, subtle body, 399
determination, 35,37
Devahuti, 476
deva, devata,
  rebirth resistant, 448
  subtle body, 448
  weather controller, 288
deviation, 137
devil, 8
devotion, practice, 568
dhama paramam, 561
dhanurasana, 66
dharana, 323,571
dharma, 401
dhauti, 186,188-189
dhyana, details, 323,571
diagram, 602
diamond pose, 88,443,444
diamonds, 288
dictates of fate, 33
diet,
  approved type, 134
  breath infusion, 371
  change required, 217
  control, 133
  fated, 179
  influence of, 217

diet, continued,
moderate, 151
regulated, 391
risky, 314
sparse, 133
sparse/ample, 450
stomach lock, 281
uddhiyana lock, 281
differentiation, self, 434
digestion,
kundalini 182,429
peacock pose affects, 77
digestive chakra, 371
digestive heat, 268,269
digestive power, 70
dimension transfer, 120
dip point, 405
disaffection, 132
discharge eggs, 366
disciple,
cooking, 143,144
discouraged, 25
empowered, 599
excited, 306
teacher energy, 599
disciplines, 119
disease,
absence, 182
bodies affected, 325
emotion without, 564
Matsyendra pose destroys, 70
modern, 191
physical body, 269
pranayama reduces, 182
psychological type, 448
removed, 238
taste related, 347
yogi affected, 297
disharmony, 319
disruptions, 42
dissolution, 102,527
distress remover, 315
distribution,
affection, 233
details, 248
hormonal energy, 340
physio-subtle air, 155
diversification, 470
divine atmosphere, 424,561
divine beings,
Krishna special, 46
people, 594
perceived, 159
superior, 46
divine body, 559
divine environment,
perceived, 159
transit methods, 429
divine form achieved, 394
divine perception, 213
divine world,
attainment, 561
deity permission, 319
described, 435
destination, 319
discovery, 319
environment, 121
force open, 324
fourth state, 527
location, 319
peering, 471
perception compatibility, 121
revelation, 324
transfer, 581
transit, 465
divinity plural, 9
divya drishti, 194
dizziness, 117
doctor, 298
dogma, 60
dogmatic people, 133
dogs, 419
domestic animals, 402
dominance, 434
donation, 568
door, 428
dormant sexuality, 133,410
doubts removed, 148
douche, 190
Dowman, 19
downfall, 272
downward flow, 331
downward spiraling influence, 155
drain back association, 25
dream,
subtle body aware, 160
subtle body postures, 81
drinking urine, 415
drone bee breath, 257
dropsy, 231,232
drugs,
cosmetics, 313
every substance, 152
kundalini arousal, 252
not recommended, 151
drum, 561,595
dry ginger, 142
duality, 600
due quota, 314
Durga, Goddess,
creation reliant on, 459
inattentive, 424
motive, 165
sex permission, 414
Shiva's student, 17
Uma, 18
woman of nature, 402
dust, 127,175
duty - lifeforce's, 262

E

ear ache, 178
ears sound blocked, 279,572
earth,
consequential equations, 456
gravity pull, 74
not appealing, 456
power over entity, 284
supportive base, 271
easy pose, 552
eating,
hereafter, 223
hormone, 178
impulse, 344
minimum, 38,43
sleeping, 277
time, 135
economy, 27
ecstasy, 150
edema, 231,232
edges of unconsciousness, 259
education, 36,521
egg,
sperm transport, 284
unused, 366
Yogananda, 138
eka deva, 355,356
elderly person, 182,362
electricity, 241

elegance of body, 268,269
elephant, 205,579
elephant of death, 361
elevation, internal
elevator, 222,223
eloquent persons, 224
emblem of fertility, 437
embryo,
kundalini evolution, 531
kundalini supervises, 427
skin covered, 175
emission, sexual, 399,400
emotions,
basis, 469
depression, 28
divorce from, 511
kundalini uses, 416
relocated, 248
spiritual defined, 564
trauma eliminated 294
emotional basis, 469
emotional confinement, 264
emotional energy, responsive, 290
emotional intelligence,
high-end intuition, 492
personified, 437
emulsions, 20
end of enjoyment, 435
endless form, 518
ends of the earth, 541
endurance, breath, 164
energy,
abstract feelings, 220
checked, 227
compression, 24
congestion, 555
diagrams, 183,184
divine world, 529
emotions capture, 249
feeling, 227
insecurity, 146
kundalini details,
release, 24
scattered, 392
sensed, 227
energy gyrating centers, 390
energy vortex, 155
energy-reliant, 52
engineer, 226
engineer of creation, 234
enjoyment,
absent, 416
linear, 416
non-linear, 416
pernicious, 579
sort components, 416
entertainment, 448
enthusiasm,
absent, 504
food provides, 142
hormone produces, 411
nature influence, 156
yoga success, 35
entities, 564
environment,
hereafter, 22
hostile, 133
suitable type, 26
superior type, 202
three, 263
enzyme coloring, 189
eons, 434
epiglottis, 215,229
equanimity, 486
erotic images, 292
escalator, 9
esophagus, 189
essential cause, 475-476
essential origin, 515
essential truth, 35,36
evacuation,
kundalini empowers, 429
kundalini heat,
nauli, 199
polluted gas, 366
stomach contract, 199
yogi assists, 192
evidence, 127
evolution,
details, 434
dominance, 434
habits altered, 331
high point, 211
hurdles, 177
kundalini involved, 531
required, 544
reversed, 126,127
variation, 214
yogi, 398
evolutionary cycle,
person self, 227
quest destroyed, 559
evolved beings, 46
example, 136
excess in finances, 33
excessive conversation, 32,33
excitement,
addicts, 45
hormone produces, 411
excretion, 206
exercises, 252
exertion, 32
existence,
circular, 363
foothold struggle, 269
root, 468
suspended, 159,255,556
exotic climate, 168
experience,
direct, 507
end of, 435
lifeforce rated, 264
log, 29
exploitation,
environment, 247
material existence, 17
stealing, 40
explosion,
bundles of force, 71
kundalini, 255,557
muladhara chakra, 367
extraction - carbon dioxide, 121
eyes,
breath irregularity, 178
breath practice, 163
close energy release, 73
closed, 66,515
disease traatak, 196
flaws, 268,269
half-closed, 515
vision predominant, 517
wide open, 509
eyebrows,
chakra, major, 390
focus, flawed, 569
perception interest, 209

F

face of cow pose, 56
facilities, , 29

fainting,
breath suspension, 215
fresh air decrease, 216
kundalini strike, 254
locks missing, 178
slow inhale 258
faith limited, 463
fame,
danger, 409
dietary, 314
family,
woman love, 288
worse association, 28
fanaticism, 32,33
fanciful ideas, 542
fantasy,
eliminated, 503
sex release, 41
farce, 547
farmer, material nature, 36
farmland, 593
fastest animal, 215
fasting,
avoidance, 139,141
deleted, 141
Shiva Ratri, 464
fat,
reduction, 75
special actions, 185
storage, locations, 387
fate,
compliance, 235
contrary, 451
convenient/inconvenient 456
inscrutable, 559
supreme, 29
untrustworthy, 234
utility, 234
father, 298
fatigue,
absent, 325
bodies affected, 325
breath infusion, 249
deadman pose, 77
innate, 130
neutralized, 599
perpetual, 79
removal required, 129
fats and bulges, 219
faults, 594,595
favor, teacher, 272
fear,
primeval, 501
used, 156
fear of death, Brahma, 207
feces, 370
feedback, 154
feelings, 340
feet,
desire access, 73,74
exploitive tendency, 73,74
up travel, 352
feet on chair, 78
female,
anatomy, 365
ascetic, 234
bee breath, 257
motivation, 420,421
prejudice against, 234
proximity, 140
sex organs, 333
sex emission, 403,413
uterus-less, 59
feminine charm, 305
fermented foods, 151
fertility, 437
fever, 238
fiery digestive chakra, 371
films, 292
final escape, base chakra,
final forms, 93,123
finances, 33
financial outlay, 387
finger control nostril, 250
finger movement, 162
fingers,
apana extraction, 207
hard-to-reach, 248,251
fingers-grab-toes, 72,74
fire,
absence, 18
avoidance, 139,140
flames, 585
needed, 140
not extinguished, 339
tongue to palate, 345
fire and ice, 443
firewood, 585
flames, 585
flash of light, 368,374
flash of thoughts, 304
flashes of astral light, 171
flavor,
registry, 347
tongue details, 346,347
transcended, 598
flaws,
eliminated 294
emotion without, 564
eyes, 268,269
flesh,
cow, 342,344
increase, 206
prohibited, 39
flesh-eating parents, 40
flesh-eating siddha, 18
flexibility display, 124
flexibility of limbs, 51
flirtation, 41
floatation, 259-260
flow inversion, 395-396
flow of air, urogenital, 404
flow of bodily fluids, 278
flower, 22
fluid, subtle, 335
flute, naad sound, 565
fly upward procedure, 359
flyback, 89
flying upward, 362
focus,
details, 454
eyebrow, 210
internal described, 220
material nature, 468
physical existence, 21
subtle existence, 21
third eye, 210
fond son/daughter, 35
fondling genitals, 292
food,
ample, 397
consumption, 388
desired type, 134
downward, 396
effects, 137
greed, 359
kundalini eats, 427
matter, 32
more consumed, 388
oil saturated, 137
protein content, 314
reheated, 137
required, 28
Shiva pleased, 134
suitable type, 142

food, continued,
tested, 142
types, 136
unfit type, 137
vegetables, 137
waste clearance, 192
yogi controlled by, 358
foot the bill, 468
forceful inhale/exhale, 215
forceful jet of water, 367
forceful method, 155
forest, 271
forgetting impulse, 600
formula, chit akash, 103
fortune, 235
forward-bend, 72,74
foundation,
approach, 515
not perceived, 518
realized, 544
founder of posture, 128
founder, 483
fourth state, 527
frame of mind, 127
frenum, 281,321
fresh air,
accumulation, 156,
cleansing action, 156
compression, 156,
erratic, 152
flushing, 156,
increase, 216
movement, 156,
procurement, 111
transit, 114
friendly with everyone, 89
front teeth - tongue, 303
frontal head, void, 132
fuel, 509
full proficiency, 565
fun and games, 44
future, rebirth, 479

G

gaja, 206
game of polarity, 328
Ganga, Ganges,
inspiration, 7
left channel, 436
like, 434
Mother, 424
gap - meditation, 454
garlic, 136,138
gateway, 348
Gautam Buddha,
- see Buddha
gaze / Supreme Being, 41
gender, 330
generator, 408
generosity, 44,47
gene influence, 217
genetic body, 280
genital,
attention command, 352
death exit, 281
electrostatic, 372,373
energy re-routed, 99
fondling, 292
head pleasure, 389
kundalini, arousal, 309
left hand, 289
lift, 289
muscle applied, 99
naad replaces, 388
nectar, 352
physical body, 396
sexual brain, 343
genital/excretion complex,
genus of Supreme Person, 47
gesture, 119
ghee,
flavor flows, 346
milk fat, 347
suitable food, 142
Gherwal
- see Rishi Singh Gher..
ghetto, 37,171
ghost, 241
giddiness, 178,444
gift, 143
ginger, 142
gland malfunction, 189,191,238
global authorities, 306
glory of sex pleasure, 351
glutton, 314
goal of education, 521
go-and-get syndrome, 344
god,
defined, 468
details, 467
on earth, 566
sleep, 259
God,
defined, 468
one, 355
supernatural powers, 286
unconcerned, 26
God Vishnu,
abode, 586
residence, 434,436
Goda, 21
goddess, Goddess,
- see also Durga
category, 20
Ganga inspiration, 7
sleeping, 277
sow faced, 18
Godhead, 463
going inside psyche, 408
gold box, 197
gold energy,
gold, 543
golden light, 159
gold-out,
details, 255,256,556,558
experience, 385
kundalini arousal, 555
penetration, 254
top of head opening,275
gomukha cow pose, 56
good luck, 298
goof proof method, 529
Goraksha, Gorakshnath,
aspects, 24
contribution, 131
engineer, 15
hatha yoga authority, 15
hatha yoga founder, 131
kundalini engineer, 15
kundalini versed, 15
naad, 549
Nath yogi lineage, 19
siddha, 17
undesirables, 139
Goraksha posture, 128
government, 298
grace act, 429
grace energy, 459,580
grace pose, 128
graceful movements, 123
grace-pull, 424
granite brick, 310
grasping cessation, 503

grass leaf, 321
grass straw, 404
gravity,
detailed study, 397
nutrients downhill, 388
reverse flow of bodily fluids, 278
reverse process, 284
great centralized upper flow,
details, 280
results, 313
great mystic compression,
details, 289
effects 294
great sealing containment control,
details, 279,299
results, 304,305
Great Supernatural Being, 9
great transit, 274
grey hair, 313,399
grey-out details, 254,255,556
grihastas, 139
groin,
breath energy, 245
fat storage, 387
infused energy, 157
group effort, 77
group of yoginis, 234
group practice, 454,458
gullies, 211
gulp infusion, 206,215
gupta pose, 88
guru,
- see also teacher
ancient teachers, 47
astral type, 166,454
criticism useless, 244
disciple empowered, 599
equivalent of Supreme Lord, 459
joyful, 571
Krishna representative, 570
Krishna, 570
multiple, 454
physical presence, 214
practice rule, 458
guru, continued,
qualification, 571
Shiva represent, 570
Shiva, 570
types, 134
guru lineage, 12,570
Gurunath, 570
gut region, 372,373

H

habit,
evolutionary altered, 331
form reliant, 273
hair,
energy, 227
grey, 313,399
hair-brained ideas, 42
hair raising feelings, 193
Halipa, 19
hallmark, 23
hallucination, starved, 410
hallucinogen,
aura seen, 196
not recommended, 137,151
hands, 119
happiness conveyor, 464
hard card, 359
hard feelings, 144
hard-to-reach, 76,248,251
hardship/difficulties, 43
harpoon, 246
hastiness, 123
hatha yoga,
forceful, 307
kundalini yoga, 88,592
purpose of, 12,347
raja yoga, 592
Hatha Yoga Pradipika,
brahmin ascetics, 400
syllabus, 131
women? 165
head,
drooping, 111
kundalini, pleasure, 389
headache,
breath irregularity, 178
chin lock, 282
locks missing, 178
neck lock prevents, 117
headstand, 284,397
health,
byproduct, 180
yoga motive, 51,52
hearing discourses, 44,48
heart,
acceleration, 444
motor, 114
pulsation, 217
stops, 114
heat,
base chakra, 281
breath energy, 492
cold, 600
groin, 388
navel, 388
heating feature, 396
Heaven Found, 52
heavenly energy, 208
heavy astral energy,
bogged down, 268,
neck, 194
heavy weight human, 398
heel against vagina, 365
helium balloon, 211
help,
Adinath's, 9
Krishna, 454
Patanjali, 454
helter skelter, 311
hen, 138
herbs,
aura seen, 196
ineffective, 187
narcotic, 137
not recommended, 151
yoga disapproves, 150
hereafter,
confidence, 118
environment, 22
locations, 118
muladhar chakra, 223
rebirth avoided, 471
yoga, 144
hero of compassion, 42
hero pose, 57,59
heroin, 150
hesitation, 148
Hevajra, 18
hiccup, 178
high end intuition, 492
high-end meditation, 266
higher status, 523
Himalayan region, 140

Hindu deity, region, 59
hips, 387
Hiranyakashipu, 319
hissing breath,
215,232,233
history, yogi's life, 336
hitch, 15
hollow grass straw, 404
Holy Ghost, 8
homosexuality, 133
honey,
flavor flows, 346
hormone production,
347
recommended, 142
urogenital, 405
hoofs, 524
hope, 156,469
horizon of success, 166
hormone energy/production,
cell storage, 374
conquest, 246
consciousness support,
411
depression, 411
distribution control, 340
downside, 388
enthusiasm, 411
excitement, 411
experience, 388
female extraction,
420,421
lethargy, 411
moods produced, 411
production minimum,
388
promise, 388
sex increase, 358
subtle details, 246
vagina flow, 58
horror, 305
horse, 524,582
horse's arse, 282
hospital waste, 190
hot sex arousal, 340
householder, 139
human body,
evolution, 211,400
male sexuality, 400
subtle body basis, 241
humbug condition, 29
humming infusion, 215
hunchback, 289
hunger,
absent, 234
bodies affected, 326
emotion without, 564
removed, 238
hunter, antelope, 581
hurdles of evolution, 177
hut, 26
hygienic tongue cut, 322
hyperventilation, 444
hypocritical morality, 41
hypothermia, 340

I

ice-fire, 310
idealess mental state,
mystic skill origin, 561
stability, 213
ideation interest,
abandoned, 540
dissolution, 102
identity interest, 209
idiosyncrasies, 214
idiot, 409
I-existence, 23
ill-health, 51
illumination, 119
image,
absent, 261
erotic, 292
generated, 244
silenced, 267
imagination,
shut down, 132
vrittis, 591
world's cause, 52
imaging devices, 189
immortality,
breath infusion, 310
core-self, 348
sex energy in head, 394
subtle body, 348
implosion, 368
impressions,
content free, 273
conventional, 274,530
details, 273
stored, 149
suppression, 213
incantation, 336
incarnation, 12
incidences, 348
increments, 114
incubation period, 213
independent/dependent,
470
indifference, 478
individual spirit,
deathless, 21
singleness, 470
support, 271
supreme self, 474
indulgence,
desire, 174
memory, 149
inebriation, 273
infant,
embryo providence, 410
seeing eye, 201
sucking impulse, 333
infatuation, 246
infirmity, 185
influence,
downward spiral, 155
nature's, 156
physical body, 155,
infused breath energy,
- see breath infusion
air, 155,368,391
compressed, 368
number of breaths, 221
breath sequence, 221
preliminary, 119
push down, 372,373
sexual charge, 157
upward, 368
ingest heavenly energy,
208
inhabitant, 301
inhalation, 219
inner chaos, 31
inner focus, 131
inner psychic research,
152
insanity, 378
insecurity,
bastion, 233
hereafter, 146
inSelf Yoga™
details, 243
different, 120
inside transit, 561

insight,
blocked, 175
chinmaya, 52
details, 505
explained, 117
mastery, 468
posture, 65
instruction, 164
integration,
details, 561
full proficiency, 554
intellect, intellect orb,
adjunct, 317
affiliate power, 13
alliances, 542
component of consciousness, 293
core-self control, 243
death event, 428
details, 264,265
diagram, 490
disappearance, 545
escape from, 269
function, 542
kundalini affects, 556,557
kundalini alliance, 427
kundalini assisted by,
kundalini meets, 265
kundalini powers, 429
kundalini prejudiced, 537
messenger, 436
mind referenced, 582
non-observer, 472
perception, 375
reform, 269
sex resistance, 536
sex pleasure pull, 265
spiritualized, 293
upgraded, 293
intelligence energy, 548
intentions, 504
interest energy,
extraction, 503,509
kha divine space, 538
naad, 582
sense of identity, 317
sex pleasure, 396
subtle body shift, 348
subtle body transfer, 285
subtle focus, 180
interest energy, cont'
transferred, 209
interference, 25,476
internal attentiveness, 454
internal elevation, 275
internal struggle, 13
interruption, 130
interval meditation, 454
intestines,
air, 191
cleansing, 190
colon uplift, 281
curbing, 357
purification, 186
redesign, 357
worms, elimination, 228
intoxication, 207
introductory edge, 259
introspection,
necessary, 12
self focus, 93
students adapt, 219
introversion,
breath infusion, 511
disconnection, 467
explained, 12
skill, 9
introverted senses, 265
intuition, 492,504
investment, 39
invisible existence, 528
irrational exertion, 32
Ishvara, 286
isolation,
core-self, 93
explained, 130
mandatory, 130
practice accelerated, 458
issue accomplished, 548

J

Jada Bharat, 49,489
jada samadhi, 320,497
jalandhara, details, 282
Janak, 457,477
Japanese martial arts, 162
jar in sky, 539
jaw, 251
jerking, 307
Jesus Christ, 8
jet of water, 367
jewelbox, 288
Jews, 463
jivan mukta, 275,327,438,474
jnana yoga, 269
jnaninah, 16
joy, 512
Judaism, 12
jug, 530
jumpy mind, 227
junction vortex, 155

K

kaivalya, 331
Kaka Chandishvara, 21
kalakuta poison, 77
Kali Mata, 486
Kama Sutra, 400
kāmarūpa, 174
kamini, 331
kanda bulb,
breath infusion, 443
color size, 441
compression, 443
dissolved, 442
kundalini sleeps, 431
subtle, 443
target, 300
Kaneri, 21
Kanthadi, 20
kapalabhati/bhastrika,
-see also breath infusion
balance easy, 296
bhastrika related, 240
distinguished, 203
efficient, 156
feared, 444
light in head, 202
progression, 186
purificatory action, 186
Kapali, 21
Kapalika Yoga Sect, 21,418,419
Kapila, 476
karani viparita, 278,284
Kardama, 476
karma yoga,
commentary, 12
defined, 266
details, 327,476,477
Krishna explained, 11,356
kundalini yoga, 266
necessary, 568

karma yoga, continued,
proficiency, 265
raja yoga, 456
requirements, 266
Shiva teaches, 11
Keith Dowman, 19
kerosene lamp, 411
kettledrum sound, 559
kevala kumbhak, 114
kevala, 331
key, kundalini, 428
kha divine space,
access, 317
support-less, 583
transit, 523
Khanda, 21
khecari,
application, 102,103
described, 102,103
details, 280,316,524,526
procedure added, 552
transit details, 529
kicked man, 254
kidney, 413
killing animals, 17
killing, Arjuna's, 133
king of elephants, 579
king of serpents, 271
king of yogis, 257
king, servants know, 432
kingdoms of God, 319
kink, sushumna, 453
kinks loops, 58
knee,
hard to reach, 251
flat down, 73
knife, 321
Koramtaka, 20
Krishna,
activities, 135
assistance given, 454
author empowered, 460
Bhagavad Gita, 594
creation under gaze, 41
desire, 174
Devaki's son, 12
divine body, 521
divine people, 594
drugs, 150
evolution ideas, 434
ignored, 138
karma yoga teacher, 11
Krishna, continued,
knows, 88
parallel existence, 528
residences, 434
special divine, 46
Supreme Personality of Godhead, 12
Supreme Being, 543
Supreme Lord, 459
Supreme Somebody, 356
ultimate ascetic, 80
yoga explained by, 356
yogi respects, 567
Krishna Consciousness, 504
Krishna Dvaipayan Vyas, 12
kriya method,
details, 25
outlived, 355
technique, 114
kriya master, 541
kriya yoga,
buddhi yoga, 541
commentary, 12
perception means, 263
Shiva fountainhead, 15
ksatriya, 11
kukkutasana, 62
kumbhak, 102,114
kundalini,
abdomen lock, 281
accidental arousal, 252
activities listed, 484
affiliate power, 13
air infused rapid, 252
alliance core-self, 272
anahat hypnosis, 523
anchor changed, 312
anchor in head, 385
arousal contraction, 221
arousal details, 203,245,254-256, 360,366,436-437, 453,481,483,555
arousal effects, 556
arousal in genitals, 309
arousal methods, 252,292
arousal rate, 490
arousal states, 555
arousal suspension, 497
kundalini, continued,
arousal twice daily, 438
arousal uncertainty, 557
arousal/chakra, 272
aroused from sleep, 378
arrest procedure, 434,439
arrogant 440,
ascent details, 556
ascent noted, 537
ascent/descent, 359
ashtanga, 292
at death 256,
back of head burst, 386
behavior stubborn, 147
bewildered, 385
Bhagavad Gita
description, 430
bhujangi, 427
bird, 359
blackout, 367
blast force 256,
bliss energy taxation, 432
blockage natural, 210
blocked, 246
body creation, 272
body fall details, 492
body operator, 417
boxed in, 368
brahma nadi, 384,385
brahmarandra, 491
brain hand, 312
breath consumed, 427
breath infusion, 253,254,428
buddhi attractive, 490
buddhi influenced by, 537
buddhi strike, 385,427,556
bunch explosion, 285
bunches, 312
buoyancy, 360
burst in head, 203
burst perception, 375
cell distribution, 427,431
cell type, 249,526
chakra arousal, 272
chakra interest, 523
chant, 292
charge, 379

kundalini, continued,
chin lock, 228
classic process, 220
coils explained, 432,433
colors, 292
compressed power, 427
compression controlled, 253
conceited,
configuration, 263
conquest of, 324
consciousness, 126
contraction arousal, 221
conventions changed, 493
core-self compliment, 427
core-self empowers, 430
core-self fearful of, 430
core-self rebels, 431
core-self restricts, 247
core-self struggle, 13,449
cultural freedom, 483
dance arousal, 252,292
death evasive, 445
death route, 387
descent, 379
details, 555
detrimental, 322
diagrams, 533-536
diet arousal, 252
digestion affects, 182
digestion chakra ,523
disappearance, 545
discomfort, 492
dislocation/death, 209
dispersal details, 526
downfall, 272
drag on core-self, 119
driven out, 548
drugs arousal, 252
electrostatic, 379
embryo procurement, 436
embryo supervisor, 427
emotional confinement, 264
emotional control, 264
emotional intelligence, 437,440,492
emotions used by, 416

kundalini, continued,
energization, 263
energy distribution, 427
energy lead, 303
energy mix, 219
energy strikes, 245
energy taxation, 432
entertains core-self, 448
escape, 246
evolution controlled, 531
evolution plan, 365
evolutionary habits, 329
excited condition, 524
excretion, 429
exercises arousal, 252
exits blocked, 246
experience rates, 264
explodes, 312
feed energy, 130
female, 436
financial outlay, 387
focus, 522
food digested, 429
food waste, 429
foundation, 271
frog, 365
front, 526
Gorakshnath method, 45
grasping, 264
great intelligent energy, 548
habit described, 448
habit reestablished, 329
happiness, 492
harsh method, 45
head passage, 256,490
head residence, 345,360
head route, 246
heat energy, 429
heavy energy, 157,
hisses, 379
husband, 436
illumination, 119
implodes, 312
individual support, 271
infused, 378
infusion incites, 157
insight lacking, 556
insight perception, 492
insight required, 292
instinct primitive, 495

kundalini, continued,
instincts, 427
intellect attractive, 490
intellect meets, 265
intellect orb strike, 385,556
intellect powered by, 429
intellect reliant 440,
intellect resistance, 536
intellect struck by, 126,427
intuition, 492
knows everything 440,
lazy, 481
life duration, 428
lifting objects, 252
lights psyche, 429
location change, 312
locks block, 246
locks mandatory 256,
locks restrict, 481
look, 292
lords of practice, 459
loyalty/modesty, 428
lung-heart chakra, 523
lust consumed, 502
management by, 198
manager of body, 427
manipura obsession, 523
mantra, 292
masquerades, 174
master of game, 341
mastery, 22
material body created, 272
Matsyendra pose activates, 70
mechanic, 470
meditation arousal, 252
memory reliant 440,
mental focus fused, 533
mento-emotional guidance, 253
micro arousal, 481
micro yield, 309
milk rise 258
mind related, 496
mini cell, 285
mini sun, 559
mini-kundalini, 285

kundalini, continued,
motivation ultimate, 427
movement speed, 427,555
movements observed, 537
muladhara abandoned, 525
muladhara attachment, 360
mundane existence prone, 448
music arousal, 252
mystic skills necessary, 459
natural arousal, 367
navel chakra, 357
no arousal, 378
non-rational, 427
non-yogi fooled by, 431
nutrient distribution, 431
nutrients eaten, 427
objective, 365
passage details, 366
passage restriction, 357
penetrates passage, 210
physical body dependent, 308
physical body fall, 222,385
physical control, 264
physically focused, 495
plan, 247
posture control, 264
power-hungry, 430
powerless, 432
praised, 547
pranayama definite, 253
prayer arousal, 252
preliminary, 220
primal, 277
primitive instinct, 495
proficiency in arousal, 291
protector, 436
psychic force, 52
quiescent, 495
radioactive material,
raised into head, 11
rebirth control, 342
rebirth prone, 448

kundalini, continued,
reclining arousal, 252
reconfigured, 392,433,522
reform alteration, 14,309,548
reform paramount,
reincarnation movements, 445
relocated head, 329
repairs body, 431
reproductive capacity, 361,441
resistant 440,
rights preserved, 387
route, 246,305,387,555
routine, 308
self focus on, 264
self-centered 440,
selfish control, 430
selfish reproduction, 441
sense of identity, 491
sense orbs affected, 126
sense reliant 440,
serpent-like, 432
sex arousal, 367
sex chakra obsession
sex ecstasy habit, 285
sex expression, 253,284
sex intercourse arousal, 252
sex intercourse experience, 536
sex pleasure, 292,396
sex prone, 448
shake out, 19
sleep abandoned, 437
sleep influence, 253
sleep regulator, 454
sleeping arousal, 252
sleeping goddess, 277
sleeping serpent, 379
sleepless, 436
sleeps, 429
snake like, 427
space out experience, 254
species power, 263
speed of light 256,
speedy, 427
sperm carries, 333
spinal absent, 312

kundalini, continued,
spiritual insight, 481
spiritual pastimes, 396
spontaneous arousal, 252
stalled, 523
stalls in head, 537
strenuous exercises arousal, 252
strike, 222
stub achieved, 447
stub details, 311,360,438
stubborn, 322
stuck, 254
stun-out experience, 255
stupor induced, 429
subjugated, 309
subsides 256,322
subtle body, 71,277
supremacy shattered, 309
survival details, 361
survival objective, 365
sushumna blasted out, 367
svadhishthana obsession, 523
tail, 427,437
tally of energy, 431
targeted by sex potency, 300
taxation, 432
tendency, 392
third eye, 491
throat chakra, 523
touch, 292
transit details, 253-256
transit diagrams, 157,158
transmigration movements, 445
transmigration supervised by, 430
twist turn, 492
types, 526
unified / core-self, 436
unruly intelligence, 44
untrustworthy, 174
up and down, 359
upward directed, 74
vishuddha concern, 523

kundalini, continued,
vortex arousal, 272
wandering, 280
wiggles, 427
willpower resistant, 198
womb, 272
yoga practice residence, 23
yoga, 292
yogi freed, 431
yogi motivates, 448
yogi trains, 281
kundalini manipulation,
energy transformation, 147,268,269
insight, 14
kundalini yoga, 24
purpose, 12
requirements, 266
secretive, 24
technique, 9
kundalini yoga,
amrita pleasure, 532
body fall, 492
breath infusion, 592
cumulative, 452
days, 450
defined, 243
described, 24
details, 337,338,369,443
disabled, 369
duration of practice,
full process, 369
hatha yoga, 24,88
internally attentive, 454
jerking, 307
mastery, 337,374
mystic actions, 337
necessary, 272,452,568
per day, 447
practice 40,447
proficiency, 480
quirking, 307
quivering, 307
raja yoga, 266,592
relaxing, 307
shaking, 307
stretching, 307
success, 480
supervised, 454
syllabus, 131
yogi disables, 369
Kurma, 271
kūrmāsana, 60
Kurukshetra, 569

L

lack of awareness, 497
lady, 507
Lahiri Mahasaya,
author tutored by,199
Chaurangi, 19
half closed eyes, 515
kriya yoga details, 538
neck clearance, 61
tongue cutting, 281,320
lair, 329,361,548
large intestine cleansing, 190
laughing stock, 130
launching rocket, 168
laws of consequence, 201
laya yoga, 592
lay-people, 50
leaf, milkhedge, 321
leanness, 180
lectures, 160
left hand, genitals, 289
leftovers, 151
legs, up travel, 352
legs/feet-up-on-chair, 78
leprosy, 297
lethargy, 411
liability
liberation,
abdomen lock, 364
details, 547,539
door, 428
flying upward lock, 364
isolation necessary, 130
Krishna required, 476
material body present, 470
material nature opposes, 423
mind phased out, 488
prior to death, 276
Shiva required, 476
teacher instructs, 475
uncertain, 567
yogi pose, 88
yogi+female, 423
liberator, social, 42
libido, polluted gas, 366
life, semen reliant, 410
life form, complex, 39
lifeforce,
- see also kundalini
arousal, favor, 272
aroused, 291
autonomy, 307
coreself leashed, 340
core-self powerless? 281
death exit, 281
death focus, 341
duty reduction, 262
flow out, 153
fresh air procurement, 111
instinct strong, 307
perception difficult, 291
quiescent, 495
reversal, 74
satisfied condition, 261
self-study, 152
spirit alliance, 305
spontaneous suspension, 261
stimulant, 495
straightened, 291
lifestyle,
adjusted, 391
changes required, 252
control, 266
desire, 168
sexual non-expression, 133
significant, 503
lifting heavy objects, 252
light,
cosmic, 518
perception details, 518
spiritual, 513
subtle body, 375
light of luminaries, 521
lightning, 241
limit of endurance, 164
limited spirit, 474,596
lineage of teachers,
argument, 482
confidential, 12
details, 460
secrecy, 88
lingam, 522
linkage, 570
lion pose, 80,122,126
lion, 125,361-362

lips, 201
liquid arresting
compression, 385,388
liquor,
deathless, 342,345
environment, 273
intoxicant, 532
living actors, 210
living creature, 241
living entity,
insignificant, 41
physically affected, 92
spiritual presence, 468
local creator, 259
location 17,18
locks,
advanced, 362
applications, 391
application time, 245
chest, 246
combined, 280
details, 98
diagrams, 99-100,391
directional force, 368
effective, 254
effects, 100
focus, 163
kundalini effects, 379
lungs, 114
mind type, 246,254
necessary, 444
neck, 228
sexual intercourse, 403
tongue infusion, 238
upper-hand, 391
log, 595
log of experiences, 29
logic, lure, 514
Lokeshwara, 17
loop back, 306
loops curves, 58
lord of psyche, 340
Lord of yogic
achievement, 565
lotus leaf, 335
lotus pose,
bhastrika, 241
described, 80,104
ideal, 118
tension, 163
love deity, 232,233
love making, Shiva's, 525
love motions, 288
love, kundalini, 252
lower species birth, 154
lower-back support, 81
loyalty/modesty, 428
LSD, 150
lubricant, sex desire, 450
luck, yogi's, 129
lull period, 103
lumbar region diagram, 55
lung,
absorption rate, 227
air travel, 229
bottom, 250
heart reliant, 114
largest, 226
loading dock, 114
resistant, 215
lung chakra, 390,559-560
lure of scripture, 514
lust,
kundalini consumes,
502
yielding process, 387
lust-being hereafter, 223
lust-free bliss, 284,285

M

machine radiation, 232
magnanimity, 560
magnet, 408
mahabandha,
details, 279,299
results, 304,305

Mahabharata,
Markandeya, 518
yoga explained by, 356
yogi types, 356
Mahadeva, Buddha, 9
mahamudra,
details, 278,289
effects 294
mahavedha,
details, 280,306
results, 313
mahout, 579
making love, 252
male sex organ,
ankle, 87
details, 333
male sexual emission,
399,400,403
male sexual expression,
401
Malipa, 19
man, not God 236
manas, 533
mango breasts, 8
mango seed, 587
manifestation - naad
sound, 268,269
manipura chakra, 390
manomani, 213
Manthana, 20
mantra,
fantasy, 549
ineffective, 187,207
naad supersedes, 269
Parikshit killed, 336
pollution removal, 480
relief from, 181
Swatmarama, 548
teacher permission, 549
maps, 145
marijuana, 150,152
Markandeya, 518
Markandeya Samasya,
518
marker, food, 193
marriage license, 405
Marutas, 288
master or mistress, 35
Masters of Mahamudra,
18
masturbation, 41
material body,
-see physical body
material existence,
exploitive, 17
swamps, 177
uncertainty, 269
washout, 559
material nature,
assistance rendered, 433
body owned by, 331
calculation, 595
camouflaged, 328
closed unit, 470
compelling, 138
flyback, 89
founder, 483
interference, 25,476
knows, 211
liberation opposed, 423
Matanga Rishi, 424

material nature, cont'
math based, 411
organizer, 483
Patanjali recognized, 35
plan, 331
regulator, 483
reproduction, 330,350
material world,
family struggles, 358
insecure, 233
prejudices funded, 358
trauma potential 294
violence potential, 348
materialistic mind, 127
materialistic people,
aspirations, 33
hostile emotion, 30
mainstay, 28
yoga ruined by, 32,33
materialistic thinking, 207
math operation, 411,595
mating, defending, 277
Matsyendra, 15,17,18
Matsyendra postures, 52,68,70
matsyendrasana, 68
mayura pose, 75-77
meal, scrounging, 28
meat, pigeon, 18
meatus, 365
mechanic kundalini, 470
medical assistance,
medical facilities, 191
medical professionals, 189
medicine, 187
meditation,
details, 244,323-324, 465,513,530,546
dimension transfer, 120
disciplines, 119
failure, 304
focus switch, 578
higher stages, 465
kundalini arousal, 252
light details, 518
linkage details, 464
locks absent, 303
mental fight, 244
mental struggle, 243
naad failure, 584
Patanjali requirements, 267
preparations, 502
meditation, continued,
prerequisites, 267
samyama, 465
spine anxiety, 111
spiritual sky access, 323
struggle in mind, 243
switch focus, 578
tongue against teeth, 303
meditators, hasty, 214
membrane of control, 407
membrane, mento emotional energy, 541
memory,
affiliate power, 13
ascetic haunted, 149
detachment, 600
elimination, 503,600
indulgence, 149
intellect alliance, 542
meditation affected by, 268,
retained, 268,
shut down, 132
slip, 20
vrittis, 591
menstrual discharge, 366,411
mental conjecture, 542
mental content void, 513
mental dominance, 469
mental expanding, 600
mental fading, 600
mental focus, 533
mental grip, 217
mental quietude, 227
mento emotional energy,
causal medium, 565
compression, 285
content, 273
energy, 541
history resistant, 599
impression free, 273
insecure, 152
membrane, 541
naad focus, 578
non-participant, 599
quiescent, 495
responsive, 290
shutdown, 213
stimulant, 495
suspension, 592
trauma, absent, 392
mento emotional, cont'
types, 563
wander not, 458
mercury, 498,583
mercy act, 429
mercy-energy, 17
mergence, 331
Meru, 351
method,
argument, 159,482
confusing, 14
goof proof, 529
student tries, 276
test required, 393
Michael Beloved,
-see author
micro kundalini,
arousal, 481
perception, 375
yield, 309
micro-pixels, 20
microscopic channel, 384,385
middle channel block, 154
middle energy, 530,531
middle of mind focus, 301
Middle Way, 314
midwife, 298
migration,
focal consciousness, 561
Krishna suggestion, 434
militant group, 28
milk,
approved, 142
creation, 347
difficult to acquire, 401
flavor flows, 346
kundalini rise, 258
production, 56
milk and water, 496
milkhedge leaf, 321
Mina, 17,19,80
Minapa, 19
mind compression, Buddha, 494
mind content vacant, 323
mind,
adjuncts compared, 582
antelope compared, 581
beginner's, 31
blank details, 467

mind, continued,
blank state
achievement, 481
blank thoughtless, 500
blank/spiritual pleasure, 502
breath controls, 500
breath energy, 473
breath infusion, 496,497
buddhi, 501
carefree, 579
control, 579
convention removal, 504
conventional impression, 530
dissolution, 545
dual meaning, 501
enjoyment prone, 579
forced willpower, 503
generates images, 244
head space, 501
ideal state, 501
image/idea addiction, 590
intellect, 501
intoxicated, 579
jumpy, 227
kundalini, 496,497
manager of senses, 500,501
medium influenced, 543
medium of perception, 545
middle focus, 301
monkey compared, 583
motionless, 503
naad control, 579
naad influence, 500,584
naad stability, 577
neutral state, 506
non-observer, 472
phased out, 488
psychic training, 127
quicksilver, 498
quiescent, 495
radio, 33
research, 498
scarred, 573
shifty, 498
silence necessary, 467
sixth detection device, 475

mind, continued,
space blank, 324
spirit compared, 582
spiritual sky access, 323
stabilized, 499
void details, 467
willpower method, 503
yogi terrorized by, 267
mind lock,
application, 246,433
details, 254
proficiency, 254
mineral rock,
mineshaft, 525
mini sun, 559
mini kundalini, 285
Minnesota, 163
mint camphor bliss, 346
mirror, 175
mirror event, 598
misfortune, 298
mission,
change, 7
claimed by relatives, 48
Mithila, 457
mixture, hormone/air energy, 203
mobility feet, 73
moderate diet, 151
moderation, 315
modern city, 29
modesty, 44,48
momentum extrovert force, 540
Mongolian, 19
monk,
ancestral influence, 359
renounced, 139
monkey, 583
monks, 404
monotheistic deity, 12
moon,
absence, 18
energy, 70
nectar, 339
predominance, 226
moral idiot, 409

morality,
moral restraint,
celibacy, 341
complex, 404
conventional, 341
core-self adjuncts, 34
inSelf, 167
introspective, 167
limited, 404,594
not a cure, 404
sex release, 41
value, 341
yoga different, 167
yoga ruined by, 32,33
morose mood energy, 560
morphine, 150
Mother Ganges, 424
mother, 298
motivation,
cessation, 475
important, 215
kundalini is, 427
motor, 114
mounds and gullies, 211
mountains, 271
mouth eating, 326
mouth, death exit, 281
movements, 123
mucus, 185,230
mudra gesture, 119
mukta pose, 88
Muktananda, 471
muktasana, 552
mulabandha,
details, 281,365
subterranean region, 281
muladhar chakra,
abandoned, 525
container, 427
deep breathing, 230
exit, 223
explosion, 367
fire pit, 427
grasp, 230
kundalini attached, 360
major, 390
mung, 142
murccha 215-216,258
murder, 40
muscular movement, 206

music,
addiction, 573
kundalini arousal, 252
naad ruined by, 573
musical tones, 555
muslin, 188-189
mystic actions, 456
mystic arresting action,
ten, 458
transit divine space, 316
mystic checking practice,
old age/death
eliminated, 278
one, 355
syllabus, 131
ten, 278
mystic compression control,
details, 289
effects 294
mystic perception,
acute, 231
necessary, 476
purpose, 299
mystic power,
controlled, 288
eight, 286
liability, 299
list, 286
mystic proficiency
practice, 393
mystic skills,
achievement, 460
details Krishna, 561,563
mahabandha, 304
necessary, 459
sealing containment, 304
mystic skills,
triple procedure, 314
use, 314

N

naad sound resonance,
absorption, 102,577
achievement, 132,181
anchor, 577
anklebells, 575
apreciation training, 238
appreciated, 549
bee, 575
bell, 574
boring, 573
naad sound, continued,
breast infusion, 580
causal transit, 587
chanting, 571
chit akash access, 181
clash, 591
cloud sound, 574,576
conch, 574
confidential
relationship, 317
contact energy, 463
contact medium, 324
contribution, 480
core-self relation, 512
demanding, 574
details, 463
distractions, 577
diversions, 577
drum sound, 561,574
dull, 573
energy controlled, 290
external sounds, 573
faults terminated, 594
flute sound, 565,575
focus details, 570,584
genital replaced, 388
glorified, 586
goad, 579
head sounds +, 572
heart chakra, 575
horn, 574
indifferent, 574
ineffective, 584
interest focus, 582
investigated, 580
jharjhara, 574
kettledrum, 559,574,576
lapse in practice, 574
listen stability, 324
listening
location, 575
loving feelings, 573
mandatory, 369
manifestation, 268,269
mantra excelled by, 586
mantra free, 181
mantra freedom, 571
mantra replacement, 269
mardala, 574
mental struggle, 585
mento emotional focus, 578
naad sound, continued,
mento-emotional energy quelled, 585
mind controlled by, 579
mind focus, 584
mind resistant, 584
mind stable, 577
musical tones, 555,575
necessary, 580
nodes, 574
node entry, 587
objective, 577
ocean sound, 574
pleasant, 573
preliminary, 573
relations potential, 573
relationship cozy, 574
relief, 577
right ear, 552
security provided, 573
sense object relief, 578
shelter, 95
snare for mind, 581
sound, attraction, 148
sounds details, 574
special trauma, 550
spiritually fused, 569
stress relief, 549
stringed instrument, 575
subtle energy pollution, 184
subtle, 574,576
super subtle, 576
supernatural sound, 575,576
supreme shelter, 269
survival stress, 549
syllabus, 131
technique, 576
textures, 574
tones, 575
undesirable, 573
variety, 574
vibrational, 574
vibratory level, 324
vina sound, 565,575
vision within touching sense, 587
vital, 269
yogi cared for, 132
zone diagram, 112,113

nadi,
72000 quantity, 90
brahma details, 384,385
breath infusion, 120
clearance results, 181
clearance time, 166
clearance, 155,452
control, 206
five special, 353
malfunction, 232
number, 452,490
pollutants, 154
primary one, 490
spinal radiation
diagram, 55
nail, 227
Napoleon Bonaparte,
Naradeva, 21
narcotics,
herbs, 137,138
intoxicant, 532
not recommended, 151
nasal sinus, 183,193,194
Nath, 13
Nath yogi lineage, 19
natural caretaker, 307
natural causes, 185
nature,
domain, 482
idea, 330
three way, 156
nauli,
kundalini, 200
physical result, 199
purificatory action, 186

navel chakra,
control difficult, 359
departure, 223
major, 390
powerful, 359
navel,
abdomen lock, 100
curbing, 357
death exit, 281
energy bundle, 200
lock-primary, 126
physio-psychic feeding, 201
pollution bunches, 202
redesign, 357
suction ducts, 201
Neanderthal, 549
neck,
blasted out, 194
clearance, 61,194,390
constriction, 60
down travel, 352
drooped, 85
fat storage, 387
hard to reach, 251
sushumna passage, 390
neck lock,
- see also chin lock
details, 101,282
diagram, 178
effects, 228
function, 117
primary, 126
reverse, 282
nectar,
bee's, 410,578
cream, 170,171
genital/brain, 352
nectar of heaven, 387
negative gases, 207
negligence, 140
neighborhood, 501
neither here nor there, 255
nerves, base chakra, 74
nervous disorder, 379
neti, details, 186,193,194
neutral basis, 506,545
never return location, 18
newborn, 210
news, 59
nicotine, 152
night,
consequential equations, 456
not appealing, 456
sleep induced, 456
Nilakanta, 77
Niranjana, 21
Nityanatha, 21
niyama, 89,341
non-attachment, 348,519
non-conflicting Godhead, 9
non-interference, 299
non-objective consciousness, 153
non-recollection, 506
non-stealing, 38,40
nonviolence, 38,39,89,90
noose of death, 305
nose tip, 517
nostril, 161,226
nourishing foods, 142,143
nutrients,
sex organ travel, 351
trucked away, 387
nutrition compact, 444
nutrition energy, 346
nutrition orb/sense
compression, 387
contracted, 444
light orb, 347
pulled up, 345
nutrition,
function changed, 350
reorientation, 364
root issue, 330
transmigration, 365
zones, 351,352

O

objective perception, 263
objectivity, 78
obligation, conjugal, 371
observational powers, 311
obstacles to yoga, 34
obtaining / desire, 348
Ocean of Milk, 77
octave, 246
odor,
flower, 578
transcended, 598
offering rites, 141
oil lamp, 339
oily foods,
moderation, 151
sex stamina, 400
old age,
elimination, 285,313
emotion without, 564
end of, 347
One God, 355,356
one origin, 355
one reality, 306,470
one subject, 274
one-fourth stomach, 134
oneness,
aloneness, 331
blank state, 213
diversification, 470
one-on-one, 164
onion, 138
opinion, 14

opium, 150
optic energy, 509
orb,
nutrition light, 347
shut down, 148
organic chemistry, 191
organic produce, 191
organizer, 483
orifices, 348
origin,
fold into origins, 476
Shiva, 463
original condition, 479
other persons, 598
outward going senses, 197
ovary, 332
overeating,
abandon, 151
curbed, 32
yoga ruined, 32
ovum, 412

P

padma pose, 80
Padmasambhava, 42
padmasana described, 104
pain,
details, 417
postures, 123,124
parallel retraction, 332
paramatma,
Shiva, 463
Swatmarama cited, 474
Vishnu, 463
Parameshwar, 591
Paramhansa Yogananda, 138
parampara, 12
parent entity, 350
Parikshit, 336
parody/sex interplay, 414
particle I-existence, 23
Parvati, 498,499
pashchimasana, 72,74
past life,
assessment, 314
author, 20
predisposition, 160
review, 216
pastimes, 396
Patanjali,
alert, 267
ashtanga yoga, 132
Patanjali, continued,
assistance given, 454
deity characteristic, 459
drugs, 150
material nature recognized, 36
samyama, 242
Supreme Person genus, 47
theist, 356
yoga defined, 132
patience,
non-forceful, 155
strain, 227
patriarchal culture, 165
Paul, 8
pawn in a game, 328
payload, 168
peace of mind, ascetic, 29
peacock pose, 75-77
peer in divine world, 122
penalties, no progeny, 388
penis,
pipe insertion, 404
sperm transport, 284
testes chakra, , 332
penny items, 82
peon, self, 340
people, life forms, 89
pepper, 138
perception,
access, 22
dimensions, 518
divine, 121
environments, 263
equipment, 468
insight, 478
interest internalized, 82
psychic necessary, 305
spirituality, 38
subjective, 375
tool, 122
types, 375
vrittis, 591
perfected yogi,
liberation method, 328
urdhvareta, 285
perfected yogi pose, 80,82,87-89,102
perfection,
mystic proficiency, 145
sexual, 423
performance of ceremony, 44,50
perineum,
ankles, 122
contracted, 278-279
heel against, 82
lifted, 278-279
muscle applied, 99,284
posture pull, 289
subtle energy, 300
person of the person, 134
person self,
infinite pleasure, 567
needs, 134
transmigration, 227
personal worship, 504
Personality of Godhead, 9,12,52
person-reliant, 52
Persons of Godhead, 9
persons of magic, 19
perspiration, 169,170
pharmaceutic stimulant, 138
pharmaceutical products, 191
phase the mind, 510
Philippines, 162
philosophy,
basis required, 554
lure, 514
teacher instructs, 475
physical appearance, 146
physical body,
ancestors serviced, 297
damaged, 28
death, 179
destined states, 350
deterioration mandatory, 347
downward spiral, 155
elegance, 268,269
fall, 254 ,385,556
fear of doom, 208
female beginning, 402
food required, 28
genetic system, 331
kundalini desire, 247
kundalini repairs, 431
kundalini routine, 308

physical body, cont'
maintenance, 198
material nature owns, 331
mimic subtle, 241
psychological body targeted, 241
ridicule of nature, 192
risks, 117
slump over, 254
spiritual form, 43
subtle based, 154
subtle body affected, 399
subtle body effect, 127
time controlled, 210
trauma prone, 392,598
types, 214,596
uncertainty factor, 348
upgrade futile, 313
value, 117
who owns, 297
wound potential, 348
yogi's food, 137
youthful feeling, 224
physical existence, 448
physical protection, 348
physics, 126
physio-mystic technique, 146
physio-psychic action, 186,187
physio-psychic compression,
best, 393
proficiency, 214
youthfulness, 370
picture, big, 328
pictures, worship, 141
piety, 417
pigeon meat, 18
pinching sensation, 303
pipe,
corrosion, 367
urogenital, 404
pixelated bliss, 170
pixeled brick mass, 491
plant reproduction, 330
plastic sack, 407
plateau, 211
plavini, 215
pleasure,
infinite, 567
more better, 388
nourishment, 200
plexus sun, 396
plot of land, 26
plural divinity, 9
plural Godhead, 463
point of interest energy, 508
poison,
removed, 238
yogi consumed, 296
polarity,
charge, 302
game, 328
polarity,
pollutants
cells storage, 295
gases, useful, 366
gases, benefits, 206
hoarded, 374
kundalini removes, 254
move into head, 230
nadi, 154
natural, 156
re-inhabit tissue, 217
resumed, 155
removal difficult, 295
subtle air, 246
pollution,
blasted, 254
consumed, 254
ignited, 254
psychic removed, 252
social activity, 327
portals of death, 138
pose,
- see posture
posh surroundings, 33
posture,
access granted, 480
bad application, 179
best, 80
contracting, 217
difficult ones, 160
eighty-four (84), 90
elderly years, 81
eyes closed, 289
flexing, 217
focus inner, 289
hard to reach access, 480
posture, continued,
hastiness, 123
hatha yoga, 24
Kama Sutra, 400
limbs proportion, 300
objective, 480
physical graduate, 242
practice/meditation, 160
psyche impact, 127
psychic insight, 65
purpose, 51
relaxing, 217
repeated, 147
sexual, 400
species based, 129
steadiness, 151
syllabus, 131
pot of milk 258
potatoes, 152
potential vagina, 365
poverty, 27
power, 602
power supply, 35
Prabhudeva, 21
practice,
compound, 204
influence, 362
verifying, 214
pranavision,
perception, 375
sexual energy, 407,408
pranayama,
- see also breath infusion
absorption rate, 161
asana posture combined, 71
author assessment, 205
bonus, 265
clarity increase, 156
complete, 486
definite, 148
effective, 484
focus inside, 180
forceful, 205
head clearance, 228
introverted senses, 265
kundalini raised, 253
learning required, 244
posture combined, 71
proficiency, 234,274
psychological development, 242

pranayama, cont'
purification, 141
radiation cure, 232
rapid progress, 486
sleep removal, 454
sure way, 153
pratyahar,
- see also sensual energy withdrawal
breath infusion byproduct, 248
completion, 503
details, 323
pranayama byproduct, 248
prayer,
kundalini arousal, 252
process, 155
Western religion, 428
pre-coded morality, 33
predator, species, 434
pregnancy, 140,288
preliminary containment, 554
pre-lord, 518
pride,
death/ causes, 185
shame, 600
primal cause, 468,544
Primal Creative Cause, 476
primal nature, 402
Primal Person, 18,435
primate, 129
probes, 189
process, compound, 204
procrastination, 234
produce, 191
proficiency, 44,50,323,554,565
progeny, 387,388
progress sabotaged, 25
progression, 349
property of uncertainty, 468
prostitute, 454,507
protection, 348
protein, 314,397
protrusion point, 508
providence,
facilities, 29
yogi ruined, 234
yogi serviced, 297
provocation, 348
proximity, fear, 501
proximity of females, 140
psyche,
adjustment perfection, 17
clearance, 167
components, 197
control, 151
darkness, 429
divine world responsive, 594
energy of others, 7
enjoying parts, 416
ideal condition, 539
idealess imageless, 539
impurities removed, 266
management, 417
meditation, 120
pleasure inside, 408
primary inhabitant, 301
purpose, 167
quiescent energy, 392
responsive, 114
saturation, 539
spine-brain +, 76
spirit responsive, 594
taste blueprint, 347
psychic adjuncts,
core-self struggle, 272
resistant, 272
sorted, 416
psychic energy transform, 13,268-269
psychic engineer, 226
psychic insight, 65
psychic membrane, 500
psychic organ, 192
psychic perception, 305
psychic sensitivity, 32
psychological assets, 23
psychological body, 22,241
psychological channeling,
psychological control, 259
psychological inhabitant, 339,340
psychological sky, 561
psychological unit, 31
psychology,
death remnant, 153,347
intellect, 264,265
male/female, 424
tranquilized cleansing, 192
psychosis, 30
pubio-coccyx muscle, 334
puja ceremony, 141
pujari bath, 141
Pujyapada, 21
pulling force, 290
pump, semen, 331
pungent / spicy food, 136
pungent flavor, 138,346
pungent foods, 151
Punjabi, 136
Purana, 165,356
purification,
acts special, 187
elephant, 205
heavy astral energy, 207
uiltimate, 235
unnecessary, 205
purity,
chemical, astral, 152
spiritual, 594
purposeless wanderer, 559
python, 114

Q

quadrupeds evolution, 128
quicksilver, 498
quiescence, 392,531
quietude, 227
quirking, 307
quivering, 307
quota of satisfaction, 314

R

radiance, nadi clear, 180
radiant organ, 265
radiant spiritual light, 513
radiation cure, 232
radio receiver, 33
radio-active waste, 190
raj, king, 12
raja female fluid, 246,421
raja yoga,
details, 12,456,476,477
hatha yoga, 592
karma yoga, 327,456

raja yoga, continued,
kundalini yoga, 266
necessary, 568
requirements, 266
Rama,
Shabari, 424
Supreme Being, 543
Vashishtha, 542
Yoga Vasishtha, 52
Ramacharita Manas, 424
Ramana Maharshi, 530
Ramayana, 52,356,424,542
rapid breath infusion,
details, 240,241
purificatory action, 186
rate count, 161
ratio, breath, 164
rational sector, 469
rationality, 469
Ratri ritual, 464
razor grass, 321
read the mind, 299
realism, 38,40
reality, 306,515
reality-conversant teacher, 16
rebirth,
cessation, 342
chakra control, 372,373
freedom from, 201
intention, 284
kundalini habit, 372,373
low human, 223
lower species, 223
resistance, 361
resistant yogi, 308
risk explained, 242
sex attraction, 372,373
subterranean world, 223
tendency details, 284
types, 223,224
recline position, 95
reclining, kundalini arousal, 252
recommended conduct,
described, 44
description, 38
variable, 89
rectum, 365,368
red beets, 193
red color, 22
reference counts, 162
reflection, 598
registry of flavors, 347
regulator, nature, 483
reincarnation,
instinctive, 350
kundalini tactics, 445
nutrition compact, 445
relationship, yogi/naad, 269
relatives, yogi, 48
relaxing, 307
release attitude, 219
relief from stress, 51
religion,
limited, 146
moral restraint, 167
Western, 428
religious activities, 568
religious official, 298
religious organization, 181
relocation, 567
renounced monks, 139
reproduction,
bodies, 247
kundalini empowers, 429
kundalini uses, 441
nature hell-bent, 330,350
reform necessary, 357
sex chakra reform, 357
reproductive energy,
gravity controlled, 285
reformed, 269
subjugation, 268,269
reproduction hormone,
conservation, 411,408
containment results, 409
draw up, 407
float up, 421
negative effect, 284
preserved, 407
reservation results, 409
spiritual practice required, 499
stabilized, 499
usage rules, 409
reproductive organ,
deposit area, 351
lock, 126
reproductive switch, 329
reptilian forms, 432
resentment,
corrosive, 40
deities, 288
relentless, 328
sidestepped, 348
residence of Vishnu, 586
residence,
infallible persons, 561
yogi, 29
respiration suspension, 503
responsibility ancestral, 358
rest necessary, 78
restfulness, 77
restraining behavior, 38,89
reta, 246
retention of breath,
convert into, 409
details, 251
effect, 93,94
locks, 219
promiscuous behavior, 409
rule, 227
tongue contact infusion, 238
retraction, vagina parallel, 332
revelation, 324
reverse evolution, 126,127
reverse bodily fluids, 278
reverse neck lock, 282
rewards abandoned, 133
rhinoceros, 125
rib cage lock, 356
rib cage torque, 69
rice, 141,142
rich food, 143
ridicule of material nature, 192
Rishi Singh Gherwal,
author commissioned by, 460
Beverford, 162,186
dhauti instruct, 188-189
Heaven Found book, 52
inspiration, 7
tongue technique, 115
purpose of posture, 242
traatak practice, 195
vomit impulse, 206
rites exemption, 141

ritual master, 141
ritual worship, 514
river pollution, 190
road maps, 145
roads, 139,140,352
rock salt, 321
rocket, 168,509
Roman official, 8
room, 29
Roosevelt, 163
rooster, 138
rooster pose, 62
root, 544
root energy, 402
root existence, 468
rotunda of sex organ, 352
route of kundalini, 246
Rudra,
congestion, 565
penetration, 254
Shiva, 12
ruling caste, 400
ruling over others, 348

S

sack of water, 407
sacred sounds, 480
sacrificial fire, 175
sahajoli, details, 413,415,416,487
sahasrara chakra, 390
sailors, 246
Saint Paul, 8
salt,
tongue taste, 346
vomit impulse, 206
water, 472,543
salvation, 539,580
samadhi, sensual interest samadhi,
bears, 320
deliberate, 320
details, 323,465,513, 546,571
disciplines, 119
douche, 190
food waste during, 192
jada, 320
linkage details, 464
nature controlled, 320
physical body, 595
preparations, 190
self/mind, 472
samadhi, continued,
termination, 320
spirit/supreme spirit, 474
spontaneous, 320
stupor, 320
suspension, 497
tongue against teeth, 303
Samkhya doctrine, 476,569
sampradaya, 460
samsara, 363
samyama,
achievement, 571
described, 324
details, 244,465,546
explained, 242
Gorakshnath, 549
terminal process, 128
sankalpa, 475
sannyasi order,
celibacy, 445
monk, 139
Sanskrit, language, 19
sat chit ananda, 275
sat guru, 16,306,479
satisfaction, touching / tasting, 344
saturation,
breath details, 295
transformation, 208
Satyaloka,
compatible body, 421
relocation, 208
Saul, 8
save the world, 25
schizophrenia, 378
school teacher, 298
scientific study, 273
scripture,
limited, 395
lure, 514
reading, 428
sculptures,
erotic, 292
worship, 141
sealing containment contraction, 279
sealing containment control, 299
secluded lady, 507
secret pose, 88
secretion, subtle, 351
secure existence, 275
seductive woman, 329
seed,
knowledge of reality, 593
mango, 587
tree realization, 479
seeing eye, 201
seet sound, 232,233
segregation aloneness, 331
seizure, 282,379
self,
- see also core-self
bare, 23
degradation, 212
divine status, 475
elevation, 212
inflicting injury, 388
kundalini focus, 264
limited, 538
peon, 340
Shiva atomic,
stimulation, 292
transcended, 598
self-absorbed, 601
self-conception, 23
self-conquest, 25
self-control skill, 348
self-discovery, 214
self-experiment, 413
self-focus, 119
self-humbug, 31
self-intuition, 504
self-reliance, 134
self tantric practice, 332,402
self-urine consumption, 413,486
semen,
contained, 329
draw up details, 331,332
life relies on, 410
mento emotional energy reliant, 410
retentive, 408
reversal attained, 334
upward flowing, 285
sensation addicts, 45

sense objects,
grasping suspension, 503
non-recollection, 506
sense of identity,
affiliate power, 13
causal plane, 561
death event, 428
details, 317
interest energy, 317
kundalini, 491
perception, 375
protrusion, 508
sense of security, 21
sense,
awareness sense, 596
commandeer, 298
indestructible, 344
individual appreciation, 416
insight lacking, 479
interest lacking, 531
kundalini assisted by,
mind manages, 500
mind referenced, 582
nutrition pulled-up, 345
preliminary, 500
quota, 314
reality, 314
sexual expression essential, 478
suspension, 497
touch predominant, 501
types, 497
vision predominant, 517
withdrawn ultimate, 553
sensual access, 22
sensual acquirement skill, 348
sensual energy,
cleansing, 192
shut down, 109
silence, 324
sensual energy withdrawal,
breath infusion byproduct, 248
breath infusion result, 95,244,262
completion, 503
described, 147
details, 465,515,517,540
sensual energy withdrawal, cont'
diagrams, 516
full, 511
interiorization, 323
pranayama byproduct, 248,274
timely, 95
ultimate, 553
sensual interest interiorization, 323
sensual orbs,
affiliate power, 13
shut down, 148
sensual urges perpetual, 344
sentiency, 35
serpent,
hole, 384,385
king, 271
struck, 291
Takshak, 336
servant-girls, 400
servants of king, 432
seva, 568
sewage discharge, 190
sex action involuntary, 334
sex chakra,
different, 332
major, 390
runs show, 369
sex climax,
dip point, 405
experience similar, 170
insight lacking, 482
sorting, 560
sex drive,
increase, 206
polluted gas, 366
sex drive,
sex experience,
contrasted, 253
details, 253
research done, 533
sex expression,
bane of yoga, 499
desired, 478
kundalini arousal, 253
mandatory, 499
sense focus, 478
stomach supported,
sex hormones, head usage, 394
sex indulgence,
- see also sexual intercourse
food, 400
high protein, 400
hormone increase, 358
memory fade, 389
oily foods, 400
yogi ruined by, 358
sex lock details, 334,403
sex organ,
area, 332
chakra described, 245
chakra multiplex, 223
chakra rotunda, 352
death exit, 281
deities of, 415
details, 332
smeared, 414
sex pleasure,
electric sensations, 265
hereafter association, 224
non objective, 311
occupation/hereafter, 223
old age, 394
sex restraint depression, 450
sexual abstinence, 560
sexual emission control, 487
sexual energy,
expressing, curbing, 419
pranavision, 407,408
sexual energy,
urine drinking, 419
sexual intercourse,
apana used, 206
astral type, 402
celibate type, 408
contraction applied, 403
dangerous, 403
deity, 415
hormone consumption, 340
kundalini, 252,367,536
lock applied, 403
observation, 405
ritual ceremony, 414
Shiva/Goddess, 414

sexual intercourse, cont'
smear organs, 414
upright, 414
yogi criticized, 537
yogi/yogini, 402
sexual isolation, 40,41
sexual liaisons, 284
sexual liberation, 423
sexual modesty, 48
sexual muscle, 284,486
sexual neutrality, 40
sexual non-expression, 38,40,133
sexual perfection, 423
sexual pleasure,
brain addicted, 396
forgo, 309
glory, 351
insight lacking, 352
interest control, 331
sexual potency,
charge, 157
hurled, 300
kundalini meets, 372,373
sexuality,
dormancy, 133
gender confused, 330
lubricant, 450
sexually appealing form, 305
Shabari, 424
shadow, 129
shaking, 307
shakti female energy, 533
shakti prabhavan, 119
shakticalana, 278,285
shambhavi,
application, 550
details, 507-509,511
essential, 274
Shambhu Shiva, 458,510
shat karmas, 186
Shavara, 17
shavasana, 78
ship, 246
shitali, 237
shitali, 215
Shiva,
84 postures, 80
activities, 135
Adinath, 9
Shiva, continued,
author empowered by, 460
Bhairava, 486
blessings, 459
causal node, 462
consort Ganga, 8
described, 12
devotion described, 464
devotion to yoga, 462,
divine body, 521
divine people, 594
Durga instructed by, 424
eleven, 12
evolution ideas, 434
faith limited, 463
fountainhead, 15
God, 463
kalakuta poison, 77
karma yoga teacher, 11
knows, 88
level, 305
lingam, 522
location, 565
love making, 525
microscopic access, 463
mystic arrest explained by, 286
naad, 462
parallel existence, 528
Paramatma, 463
Parvati, 499
Personality of Godhead, 463
pleased, 134
plural, 12
point of origin, 463
position, 527
preoccupation, 462
prominent deity, 207
respected, 11
Rudra, 12
self-atomic, 462
sex permission, 414
specific person, 12
Supreme Being, 134,543
Supreme Lord, 459
sweetheart, 525
teacher proficient, 462
trauma absent, 550
ultimate ascetic, 80
Shiva, continued,
Vishnu related, 463
yogi respects, 567
Shiva loka, 561
Shiva Purana, 464
Shivana, 411
Shivananda,
author, 407,423
distended stomach, 359
inspiration, 7
shoulder lock, 362
sickness, 139
siddha,
- see also perfected yogi
antisocial, 402
created, 181
death shattered, 22
described, 145
deviant act, 18
female achiever, 59
influence rebirth suspension, 471
kundalini versed, 15
lineage teacher, 329
master, 570
path, 17
privilege risks, 23
rebirth mission, 532
rescued, 532
self-tantric, 402
special, 19
status-disrupted, 42
time transit, 22
woman, 421
yogi becomes, 235
yogi meets hereafter, 439
siddhaloka,
achievement, 434
compatible body, 421
destination, 319
guru master, 570
rebirth, 224
reproductive energy reformed, 269
siddha pose, 80,82,87,88
Siddhapada, 20
siddhis, 459
signature, 114
singleness, individuality, 470
sinus malfunction, 189,191

sit and wait, 429
sitkari, 215,232,232
sitting postures diagram, 96-97
six month practice, 363
sixteen petaled lotus, 349
sixteen vital supports, 390
sixth detection device, 475
sixty-day rice, 142
skin, 175,541
skin disease, 189
skull, clearance, 194
sky of consciousness,
  access, 86,132,501,512
  approach, 132
  chance contact, 154
  described, 435
  Muktananda defined, 471
  zone of escape, 348
sleep,
  absent, 234
  bodies affected, 325
  Brahma, 259
  control method, 454
  emotion without, 564
  five hours, 314
  kundalini arousal, 252,253,379
  mastery, 599
  mating, 277
  meditation, 118
  necessary, 78
  phase study, 259
  regulator, 454
  removal, 454
  vrittis, 591
sleeping goddess, 277
sleeping man, 254
sleeplessness, 454
slow inhale, 215,258
small of the back, 453
smart ideas, 35
smoke, 175
smooth texture, 22
snake,
  slapped, 280
  struck, 357,378
snare, 581
social actions, 243
social cliques, 26
social comforts, 140
social contribution, 133
social difficulties, 13
social disruption, 28
social environment, 335
social incidences, 267
social liberation, 41,42
social liberator, 409
social responsibility, 11
soft humming, 215
soft spot, 479,480
soldiers, 249
song, 428
sorcerers, 259
sorrows, 235
sound,
  head, 572
  mentally created, 588
  naad, 575
  sacred, 480
  supernatural, 575
  transcended, 598
  yogi not controlled by, 602
sour flavor, 346
source,
  abstract, 544
  personal/impersonal, 355
sow-faced dakini, 18
space out,
  details, 254,556
  details, 556
  mind lock, 254
special favor, 272
species, 154
speck of reality, 579
sperm,
  beginning, 284
  details, 412
  feeding facilities, 333
  kundalini within, 333
spices,
  moderation affected 151
  yogurt, 136
spinach, 193
spinal kundalini absent, 312
spine,
  collapse prevention, 111
  corkscrew, 69
  hunchback, 289
spiraling influence, 155
spirit,
  access elevator, 222
  details, 596
  superior, 176
  types, 47,564
  vision access, 595
spirit transit, 595
spiritual bliss, 284,285
spiritual body,
  bliss texture, 512
  core,self, 511
  details, 596
spiritual evolution, 25
spiritual feelings, 563
spiritual form, 43
spiritual light, 513
spiritual master,
  - see guru
  - see teacher, 571
  deviation, 137
  one only, 15-16
  quantity, 15-16
  reality personality, 16
spiritual pastimes, 396
spiritual presence, 468
spiritual sky/world,
  - see divine world
  access, 454,512
  achievement, 355
  attainment, 561
  circular energy, 323
  described, 319,435
  transit, 424
spleen
  disease, 191
  peacock pose, 76
  removed, 238
spontaneous focus, 324
spontaneous inner focus, 131
spouses, 400
spring-like ability, 427
sprite and youthful, 362
squat posture, 190
Srimad Bhagavatam, 49,348,356
stable, 582
stainless knife, 321
stale foods, 151
stamina increase, 206
state, 355
states of stupor, 216
stationary awareness, 255

steadiness,
38,42,51,151,169
stealing, 40
sternum, 71
stick, 378
stimulant,
137,138,151,532
stomach,
army marches,
flattened, 74
one-fourth void, 134
cleansing, 186,188-189
upsurge, 206
stone, 211
stones, aura, 196
stool, 193
stop eating command, 387
straightforwardness, 38,43
straw, hollow
stream, 407
strength, astral body, 532
strenuous exercises,
117,252
stress, 23,51,164
stretching, 307
strong taste, 151
struggle for existence,
269,468
stub kundalini,
311,360,438,447
student,
blighted, 504
compassion saturated,
246
disciples discouraged,
25
discouraged, 288
enthusiasm necessary,
35
fated teacher, 303
get it right, 187
insults teachers, 159
introspection, 219
method variables, 159
methods tried, 159,276
negative predisposition,
160
one-on-one, 164
overwhelmed, 219
past life, 160
pre-coded morality, 33
psychic perception, 214
student, continued,
Shiva/Krishna teacher,
11
subtle form not
appreciated, 412
tall order, 203
teacher affected, 295
teacher fated, 303
study, insufficient, 145
stunned condition,
325,326
stun-out, , 255,555,556
stupor,
breath suspension, 497
meditation, 118
nature influence, 156
samadhi, 320
studied, 216
kundalini induced, 429
subconscious perception,
263
subject, 274
subjective environment,
520
subjugation reproductive
energy, 268,269
submission, 356
subterranean region,
153,216,281,385
subtle air, 246
subtle arteries,
- see nadis
subtle body/form,
adaptability risk, 154
age, 225
breath infusion
required, 399
change required, 201
cleanliness, 43
configuration changed
294
content at death, 251
core-self different, 530
cure, 232
death, 273
death affects, 325
death effect, 286
deathless, 467
degraded by physical,
154,
destination compatible,
422
details, 596
subtle body/form, cont'
deteriorate, 226
durable, 286
duration, 348
earth bound, 284
elderly effect, 286
energy consumption,
326
energy quality, 464
evolutionary
achievement, 63
flaws, 454
focus essential, 107
focus of practice, 77
gateways, 348
hereafter appearance,
153
higher level exemption,
484
hunger/thirst need
immortality, 348
initial configuration,
433
inside transit, 120,348
interest energy transfer,
285
interest shit, 153
investigation, 227
jump, 484
languishing, 399
life span, 326
light energy,
177,326,375
limited transit, 120
material body need, 448
membrane, 541
mimic physical, 241
moonbeams, 326
nutrition orb, 347
observations, 375
orifices, 348
perception tools, 122
physical affects, 71
physical body
reproduction, 443
physical influence, 454
postures in dreams, 81
pranayama required,
399
protection, 153
purification, 141
radio wave energy, 326
rebirth need, 448

subtle body/form, cont'
rebirth resistance, 242,531,532
rebirth termination, 276
reconfiguration, 297
redesign, 442
regenerate, 226
results delayed, 321
risk, 154
saturation, 464
sense faculties, 273
senses, interest, 197
sleeps, 326
source of material body, 127
spiritually compatible, 208
strength, 532
sunbeams, 326
sun-reliant, 286
target, 154,321
tone adjusted, 320
trained, 531
transit inside, 348
transit limited, 567
transition, 71
transmigration basis, 225,348
transmigration resistant, 442
upgrade, 251,269,272, 313,463,503
value unappreciated, 412
vanishes, 192
worn out, 153
subtle energy/force
bricks, 310
bundles, 71
charges explained, 369
compacted, 310
explosion, 71
sun, 7
subtle fluid, 335
subtle hormone, 246
subtle pleasure energy, 532
subtle secretions, 351
subtle veins,
- see nadi
success, 166
sucking action, 333
sucking format, 201
suction, 201
sugar candy, 142
sugars, 151
sulphur, 583
summit of destiny, 179
sun,
demolished, 348
explodes, 326
opening tricked, 395
predominance, 226
subtle body, 348
sun-absence, 18
sun-deity, 7
sunlike nutrition compact, 445
sun plexus, 396
superconsciousness, 385
superfit form, 532
supernatural beings, 518
supernatural controllers, 448
supernatural perception, 194
supernatural power,
confidential, 298
eight, 286
required, 299
superstition, 496
supportive base, 271
support-less kha divine
space, 524,583
Supreme Being,
assistance withheld, 269
creation under gaze, 41
Krishna, 46
world creator, 543
supreme goddess
kundalini, 429
Supreme Lord,
source, 591
teacher equivalent, 459
trouble free, 47
worship, 44,48
Supreme Person,
genus, 47
mystic process, 286
Vasishtha denied, 52
Vishnu, 463
which? 463
Supreme Personality of
Godhead, 12,463
Supreme Reality, 515,520-521
supreme residence, 434,436
Supreme Somebody, 356
Supreme Soul, , 588
Supreme Spirit, , 47
supreme trantric, 525
Surananda, 20
surface, 598
surgery, 322
survival,
assured, 350
capacity disabled, 369
details, 361
extroversion, 468
form eating, 350
immediate, 361
kundalini objective, 365
reproduction details, 350
species, 337
tactical, 361
surya–bheda infusion, 215
sushumna,
abandoned, 525
blocked, 306
clearance, 453,524,531
clouding, 252
compressed, 525
diagram, 55
flow stop, 530
free flow, 447
head passage, 276
heavy energy, 157
infusion effective, 252
kundalini blast, 367
kundalini clears, 275
nadi author's, 8
nadi ultimate, 490
neck as, 61
neck clearance, 390
pollution removed, 252
suspended animation, 529
suspended existence, 159,255
suspension of breath,
- see breath suspension
details, 260,498
distribution check, 248,260
independent, 261
necessary, 147
spontaneous, 261,262
svadhishthana chakra, 390

Swami Shivananda, 7
Swami,
carnal knowledge
absent, 407
defined,
sannyasi order, 445
swastika pose, 53
Swatmarama,
author 460
guru of, 13
merciful, 14
radiant organ, 265
respected, 11
theist, 355,356
sweet food, 143
sweetheart, 525
swelling, 231
syllabus, 244
symbiosis, 424
symbols, 141,602
sympathy, at death,
syndrome, go-and-get,
344
syringe squirt, 284

T

tactical survival, 361
Takshak, 336
tall order, 203
tantra,
abused, 400
ceremony, 414
details, 271
secret, 402
self-tantric, 402
warriors abused, 400
tantric partners, 400,405
tapa, 165
Taranath, 19
target, 154
taste blueprint, 347
tattvadarshinah, 16
teacher,
- see also guru
- see also spirituall master
astral, 454
astral/physical, 306
atheist, 549
badgered, 412
criticism of, 244
equivalent of Supreme Lord, 459
teacher, continued,
faulty, 242
favor, 272
guru of, 47
honor due, 13
ignorance relieved by, 13
instructions required, 395
insulted, 159
love due, 13
multiple, 16,454
necessary, 363
neglect students, 295
own body, 298
physical presence, 214
practice rule, 458
practice supplemented, 363
resist students, 295
respect due, 13
sat guru, 306
service by, 13
Shiva ultimate,
special favor, 511
student selection, 303
teaching watered down, 25
technique,
kriya, 114
kundalini, 9
master develops, 15
required, 146
teeth,
air suck, 232
tongue pressed, 113
telepathy, 299
termination, 210
test, 496
tester, 122,284,322
texture, 22,160
theatrical space, 210
theism, 44,46
thigh, 352,387
thinking,
projected, 33
subservient to survival, 396
third eye chakra,
author's, 8
blocked, 565
brahmarandra, 317
chakra, process, 572
clearance, 565
third eye chakra, cont'
diagram, 490
energy configuration, 572
focus, 210
focus flawed, 569
perception, 375
rebirth departure, 224
staring, 454
thirst,
absent, 234
bodies affected, 326
removed, 238
thought/image
disaffection, 132
thoughtlessness, 506
thoughts, 261,267
threshold of
unconsciousness, 259
throat chakra,
departure hereafter, 224
major, 390
sixteen petal, 349
throat,
compression, 385,
contraction details, 388
lock, 282
restriction, 291
Shiva, 77
stop eating command, 387
sufferings, 388
thrust,
breathing, 203
energy/kundalini, 219
Tibetan Buddhist deity, 18
Tibolipa, 19
tiger, 432
tilt-up feeling, 74
time,
absolute, 449
eating regulated, 135,391
limited, 140
medium, 23
nadi clearance, 166
not illusion, 592
required, 151
standing still, 255
time stood still, 556
timelessness, 489
Tindtini, 21

tip of nose focus, 104,106,113,114
tissue and bone, 217
tobacco, 152
toes and fingers, 207,251
tolerance, 38,41
tongue,
anus related, 126
author cutting, 320
author's experience, 115
Beverford method, 115
block esophagus, 320
contract infusion, 215,237
curled back, 115,237,279,280
cutting, 281,319,322
effects, 126
energy passage, 115
front teeth, 303
internal focus, 317
lifeforce pushes, 303
milking, 319
press backward, 317
pressed, 113
protrusion, lion pose, 126
pulling, 319
push back half hour, 325
reproductive organs related, 126
samadhi position, 115
soft palate procedure, 344,347,552
stretched, 125,319
subtle bod, 320
technique details, 115
teeth pushed, 115
tiny white light, 328
torque rib cage, 69
tortoise, 23,149
tortoise pose, 60,64
touch sense,
naad, 587
predominant, 501
touching and tasting satisfaction, 344
touring, 139,140
traatak, 186,195
trance, 320,595
transfer grace act, 429
transformation, 208
transit,
access, 355
circular, 363
details, 595
divine space, 316
divine world, 465
gateway, 348
great, 274
methods, 429
procedure, 319
spiritual existence, 429
transition, 21
translation, 11,21
transmigration,
details, 365
kundalini tactics, 445
reproduction, 441
trauma,
absence by Shiva, 550
absent, 392
acute, 264
blast, 588
eliminated 294
emotion without, 564
fear of end, 208
free location, 429
hereafter, 138
mandatory, 348
origin, 200
pleasure, 600
potential 294
relief from, 305
ridden planes of existence, 392
yogi resistant, 327
travel,
avoidance, 139,140
dangerous, 140
tree,
aura, 196
realization, 479
wishful-filling, 593
trembling, 169
trigger happy, 25
triggering effect, 268,269
triple procedure, 314
trunk, elephant, 206
turmeric, 193,321
Tushita heavens, 59
twinkling star, 454
twist, 71
two-way radio, 33

U

Uddhava, 269,461
Uddhava Gita, 348,356
uddiyana, 219,281356,35,
ujjayi, 215,229
Uma, 18
unaffected spirit, 47
uncertainty,
grey out, 255
principles, 467
property, 468
unconsciousness,
blackout, 282
edges, 259
perception, details, 263
threshold, 259
undesirable, 139,141
Unholy Ghost, 8
unity, 314
universe,
crashes, 259
Shiva origin, 463
subtle body duration, 348
unmani, 213,513
Upanishads,
karma yoga, 476
yogi types, 356
upgraded subtle body, 211
upheavals of desires, 506
uplift, 99
upsurge, 206
upturned tortoise pose, 64
upturning the body, 278
upward muscular redirection,
female, 413
male sex, 399,400
upward pulling force, 290
urdhvareta, 59,285
urges, 328,344
urinary lock,
details, 284,334
muscle applied, 99
recommended, 486
urinary/sexual contraction, 278
urination, 206
urine, 370,419
urogenital channel, 404
u-shaped curled, 237
uterus, 284
utility of fate, 234

utkala squat, 190
uttana kurma, 64

V

vagina,
heel pressed, 293
one inch deep, 59
parallel retraction, 332
side energy, 58
uterine chakra, 331,332
Vaikuntha, 561
Vaishnava authority, 12
vajra pose, 88
Vajra Varahi, 18
vajra, 443.444
vajroli,
details, 278,284,399,400
preliminary practice, 406
purpose, 285
recommended, 486
Vak, 424
valley of sorrows, 235
Valmiki Muni, 424,542
Valmiki Ramayana, 52
variables, people, 159
variety dissolution, 468
Vasishtha, 52,424
Vasudeva, 435
Vedas, 47,507
Vedic hymns, 519
vegetables, 39, 142
vegetation,
aura, 196
explored, 216
venom, 336
Ventura, 162
vina, 565
vinegars, 151
violation, 136
violence, 90
viparita, 395
viper, 500
virasana pose, 57,59
Virupaksha, 17,18
viruses, 178
Vishnu,
abode, 586
congestion, 559
divine people, 594
Krishna primary, 12
penetration, 254
Vishnu, continued,
plural, 12
primal deity, 12
prominent deity, 207
residence, 434,436
Shiva related, 463
Vishnudevananda,
author requested by, 407,460
distended stomach, 359
inspiration, 7
quoted, 311
translation omissions, 423
yoga book, 359
Vishnuloka attainment, 561
vishuddhi chakra, 390
vision energy,
directed, 108
divine environment, 275
energy leakage, 109
higher dimensional, 275
special, 111
subtle body, 177
visual focus,
arresting action, 508
eyebrows, 276,507-509
raising, 513
visualization,
deity, 504
ineffective, 187,208
not used, 114
pollution removal, 480
shut down, 132
terminated, 588
useless, 523
vital energy, 210
vital supports, 390
void mental content, 569
voidal state, 153
voluptuous female, 334
voluptuous movements, 366
vomiting impulse, 206
vortex, 155
vrittis, 591

W

waking state, 600
walk with siddhas, 560
wanderer, 559
war, adjuncts, 540
warehouse, 175
warming of gut, 372,373
warrior, author past life, 20
warrior caste, 476
washout, 559
waste gases hoarded, 374
waste color, 193
water,
douche, 190
neutrality, 593
plastic sack, 407
salt, 472
weapon,
attack prevented, 346
attack studied, 347
yogi not controlled by, 602
weather control, 161
weightless mystic skill, 348
Western religion, 428
whale, 246
wheat, 142
whimsy, 32,33,34
white cloud of energy, 255
white sugar, 142
white-gold light, 255
white-out,
details, 230,255,556,557
experience, 385
kundalini arousal, 555
penetration, 254
whole reality, 515
whole scope of reality, 25
wick, 339,411
widow ascetic, 434
wife cooking, 143,144
will power,
absolute, 273
Buddha's, 546
mind control, 503
pollution removal, 480
response, 114
useless, 442
window in time, 454
wings, 580
wishful thinking, 114
wishful-filling tree, 593

woman, women
aristocratic, 288
attractive, 331
avoidance, 139,140
yogi attracts, 170
difficult to acquire, 401
leggy, 168
love motions, 288
siddha, 421
Vedic prejudice, 139
yoga not taught, 165
womb, 201,224
worms, 228
worship God, 48
worship of Supreme Lord, 44,48
wrinkles, 313,399
writer,
- see author

X,Y,Z

yama,
conventional, 341
key factor, 89
yama deity, 451
yaminam, 107,166
Yamuna, 434,436
yantra symbols, 141
yoga,
adapted, 164
application stages, 554
association affects, 313
atheistic, 356
attentiveness, 454
austerities, 165
beauty, 52
belief, 356
collective farce, 547
complicated, 306
cumulative, 130,452
desire enemy, 234
details, 568
disturbing, 316
duration, 133
envy, 554
evolutionary limitation, 398
external focus, 194
fake type, 117
food stress, 137
forceful process, 307
group effort, 77
health, 52,180
yoga, continued,
hereafter, 144
higher stages, 465
ideal type, 30
ill health caused by, 179
institution, 181
karma yoga proficient, 265
kings learn, 12
life time, 325
lords of practice, 459
man thing, 139
methods vary, 454
moral restraint, 167
motive, 165
mystic skills, 459
objective ultimate, 466
physical movements, 395
physical practice, 145
posture founder, 128
practice hereafter, 336
practice speed, 144
proficiency required, 50
purpose, 244
reproductive concerns, 88
resentment, 554
responsibilities sex, 403
ruined by six, 32
rulers learn, 12
samyama, 465
secretive, 395
sex expression bane, 499
six month practice, 363
students criticize, 412
subtle body maintained, 371
subtle body objective, 65
success partial, 88
supervised, 454
teaching discouraged, 288
theistic, 356
time for success, 133
Veda compared, 507
woman austerities, 165
women excluded, 139,165
year duration, 133
Yogananda, egg, 138
yoga siddha body,
non-cognizable, 211
created, 181
Yoga Sutra,
necessary, 214,454,461
deity characteristic, 459
Yoga Vasishtha, 52,542
Yogeshwarananda,
author instructed by, 371
food waste/samadhi, 192
genitals urination, 329
hands touch, 119
yogi,
abdomen distended, 359
advanced, 234
affection, 132
alerting others, 41
ancestors control, 359
ancestral obligation, 41
angelic female, 402
angelic female avoidance, 348
antisocial siddha, 402
association, 316
astral partner, 406
astral projection mastery, 269
astral sex, 402
attachments, 525
attacks tolerated, 328
attention shift, 327
attentiveness required, 368
austerities, 395
backlash, 260
beggar, 143
Bhagavad Gita's help, 329
blackout, 159
blighted, 504
blindfolded, 368
bliss fluid drink, 349
bliss noticed, 310
body genetics, 280
Brahma sleep, 259
breath infusion unnecessary, 318
causal plane entry, 544
causal zone transit, 369
cave residence, 458,515
cave used, 458

yogi, continued,
components of consciousness, 298
concerns superficial, 482
conduct exempt, 401
cooking, 143
criminal, 216
criticized, 402
critics, 297,327
cultural activities gripless, 483
dakini assistant, 405
death not feared, 444
death resistant, 327
death transit, 422
deathless, 485,602
deity presence, 50
deity sensitive, 405
deity/love, 232,233
delay, 349
demigod, 234
dependent, 470
desire explained, 247
destiny submission, 559
detachment application, 416
devoted, 416
dharma exempt, 401
diet, 314,450
digestion of anything, 296
disease affects, 297
disease resistant, 327
disoriented, 159,
dispensable, 327
disruptions, 42
distended abdomen, 359
divine body, 559
divine space access, 317
domestic animals, 402
done for, 395
doomed, 424
efforts required, 480
emotions responsive, 290
endurance limit, 259
energetic, 144
evolution of, 126
evolutionary background, 398
existential blackout, 159

yogi, continued,
existentially self-disciplined, 107
fallen, 234
family member, 401
fanatic, 191
farmers, 402
fast necessary, 141
fate resigned, 559
female companion, 402
females to liberate, 423
floatation, 259-260
fond son, 35
food ample, 397
food controls, 358
glutton, 314
god on earth, 566
God, 288
golden light, 159
gravity reversal, 284
guest destroyed, 559
hereafter life, 439
hereafter responsibilities, 403
hereafter with siddha, 471
humble nobody, 489
impact-less, 327
independent, 470
insight lost, 404
institution, 181
interest deleted, 361
interest retracted, 335
interest shift, 348
interference avoided, 476
introversion, 456
invitations rejected, 171
isolated, 295,458
jivan mukta, 327
Kapalika, 418,419
karma shared, 485
kind hearted, 416
kings, specialty, 569
Krishna respected, 288,567
Krishna's help, 329
kriya master needed, 541
kundalini arrest, 437,439,449
kundalini inattentiveness, 222

yogi, continued,
kundalini reconfigured, 433
kundalini route, 387
kundalini stripped of power, 432
kundalini training, 281
laughing stock, 130
liberate females, 423
liberated in body, 438,539
liberation uncertain, 567,568
life history, 336
limb proportion, 82
limited 294
lion compared, 482
locks upper-hand, 391
look down, 302
lord of yogis, 235
Lord of yogis, 565,567
luck, fates against, 129
lucky student no rebirth, 470
material nature interferes, 89
material world duration, 568
mind lock applied, 433
mind reading, 299
mind terrorizes, 267
mission, 235
modern disinclined, 265
moralist, 537
morality exempt, 401
mystic display, 260
mystic power risk, 299
mystic skills, 399
naad cushions, 269
naad nurture, 132
naad relationship, 317,573
naad sincerity, 575
naad variations, 574
natural way upset, 396
navel chakra control, 359
negative postures, 397
neutrality, 545
nobody, 489
non-interference, 299
one reality, 470
organic produce, 191

yogi, continued,
partner astral, 406
Patanjali's help, 329
peer divine world, 471
physically affected, 92
pious, 416
poison consumed, 296
poverty-stricken, 169
practice environment, 30
practice failure, 452
proficiency, 263
providence ruins, 234
provocation, 348
psychic engineer, 226
purified, 235
quarrel with time, 210
radical actions, 401
reality perceptive, 416
rebirth risk, 342,471
relatives objection, 48
resentments, 348
residence, 26,29,489
responsibilities, 402
responsible for females, 234
seductive woman, 329
seed received, 594
self-experiment, 413
self-tantric, 402
sense of identity shut down, 393
serviced by providence, 297
servile, 299
sex criticism, 537
sex dangerous, 403
sex deprived and happy, 450
sex interest, 396
sex justification, 400
sex partner, 487
sex pleasure addiction, 396
sexual climax dip, 405
sexual intercourse observation, 402,405
sexual responsibilities, 403
Shambhu Shiva, 510
Shiva, 288
Shiva different, 415

yogi, continued,
Shiva respected, 567
Shiva's level, 305
siddha antisocial, 402
siddha guru help, 471
siddha status, 42
siddhas hereafter, 439
sit and wait, 429
skill misuse, 260
social activity resistant, 327
social life with adjuncts,
socially involved, 236
society dependent, 335
spiritual translation, 539
status resistant, 523
subjective perception, 375
subtle body act hidden, 395
subtle body
reconfigured, 452
success rate, 334
supernatural beings, 518
supernatural controller, 234
supernatural
happenings, 257
supernatural perception, 375
supernatural ruler, 559
superstition, 191
supervised, 295
sushumna blocked, 306
suspected, 327
suspended existence, 159
tagged, 467
tantric partner, 405
time constrained, 449
time expenditure, 140
time quarrel, 210
tolerant of critics, 297
tolerant, 328
transcendence, 598
transcendental
happiness, 257
transit details, 327
trauma resistant, 392
travel discouraged, 140
ulterior motive, 319
unconcerned, 559

yogi, continued,
underestimated, 393
universe crash, 259
upset natural way, 396
wanderer, 559
washed up, 395
weather control, 161
well-to-do, 416
whimsical success, 399
wife unsuitability, 405
Yama deity escape, 451
Yoga Sutras' help, 329
yogaguru sensitive, 405
yogini avoidance, 348
yogini fascinated, 234
yogini responsibilities, 402
yogini type, 402

yogini,
Chaurangi assisted, 19
described, 420,424
difficult to acquire, 401
Durga different, 415
exceptional one, 424
Goddess different, 415
paired, 348
reproduction
concentrate conserved, 421
siddha, 59,421
siddhaloka resident, 348
subtle body, 348
yogi attracts, 234,346,348

Yogi Arthur Beverford,
- see Beverford

Yogi Bhajan,
(Harbhajan Singh Sahib)
garlic, 136
group practice, 458
kapalabhati taught by, 186

Yogi Siddhir, 20
yogurt, fermented, 136
young widow ascetic, 434
youth, 153,347
youthful, sprite, 362
zones of escape, 348

Index to Translated Verses

A

abdomen,
cavity up, 3.6
cavity, 2.8
disorder, 3.17
draw-up, 3.74
malfunction, 2.27
muscular action, 2.22
retract, 3.57
up-and-under, 3.54
uplift, 2.45
absent enthusiasm, 4.32
access divine, 2.34
accomplishment, 2.76
accounting, 3.15
activity, 1.63-64
adept yogis, 3.29
Adinath, 1.1,5; 4.66
aggregate energies, 4.58
aggregates faults, 4.105
air disease, 2.27
air energy, 1.48, 2.5
air middle course, 4.16
air infusion, 2.66
air pathway, 3.6
air quivers, 3.27
air regulator deities, 3.8
alignment head/neck, 2.60-62
Allamah, 1.8
all-penetrating, 3.104
alternate breathing, 2.9-10
amaroli, 3.92, 96, 4.14
ambrosia, 4.64
ample air, 2.70
anahat lung-heart, 4.73
anal sphincter, 2.26, 3.6
Ananda, 1.5
anemia, 2.53
animal meat, 1.61
anklebells, 4.86
antelope, 4.94
anus - perineum, 3.74
anus coccyx, 3.61
anxiety ended, 4.107
appealing form, 3.25
approach to foundation, 4.41
archer, 4.99
aristocratic lady, 4.35
asafetida, 1.61
asana, 1.19
ascetic female, 2.55
ascetic widow, 3.109
ascetics, psyche control, 1.65
ash, 3.92
association, 1.16
asthma, 2.17
atomic self, 4.1
awake, 4.112

B

balcony, 1.13
barley, 1.65
base of earth, 3.1
basti, 2.22, 26, 27
bath early, 1.63-64
beauty, 2.28
bee, 2.68, 4,86
bee drinking, 4.90
bee-like sound infusion, 2.68
behaviors, 1.17
bell, 4.99
bellows, 2.35, 62
best of adepts, 3.29
bhadra graceful pose, 1.36,55-56
Bhairava, 1.5-6
Bhanuki, 1.8
bhastra, 2.35
bhastrika, 2.44. 59, 60-62, 67
bhastrika / diamond posture, 3.114-115
bhramari, 2.44
bile,
elimination, 2.65
imbalance, 2.27
in urine, 3.96
upset, 2.58
Bileshaya, 1.5
Bindunatha, 1.7
bird, 3.56, 4.92
bitter food, 1.61
blackbee, 2.44
blacksmith, 2.35, 62
blank characteristic, 4.33
blank condition, 4.30
blank mental state, 2.42
blank staring, 2.22
blazing energy, 3.67
blazing reality, 4.41
blinking, 4.36
bliss, 4.2
blissful animation, 4.49, 51
blissful feelings, 2.34
bliss-yeilding fluid, 3.51
blocking the air, 3.6
bodily swelling, 2.53
body - divine, 4.71
body like log, 4.106
bold, 1.16
bolt, 4.94
books,1.18, 68
bow, archer, 4.99
bow dhanurasana, 1.27
brahma congestion, 4.70
brahma nadi, 3.69
Brahma, 2.39
brahmarandra, 2.46, 3.4
breath - external, 4.51
breath described, 2.18
breath endurance, 2.8
breath energy, 3.3
breath flush, 4.20
breath irregularity, 2.17
breath infusion, 2.1, 36, 44, 67, 77; 4.29
breath-infusion / diamond posture, 3.114-115

breath infusion, gods' 2.39
breath retention, 1.43; 2.11
breath steady, 4.28
breath suspension, 2.43-44, 73; 4.112
breathing, alternate, 2.9-10
breathing rapid, 2.35
breathing rhythm, 2.73
bronchial disease, 2.25
Buddha, 1.6
bulb, 3.107, 113
buttermilk, 1.61
buttocks, 3.27

C

camphor, 4.59
candy, 1.65
carefree mind, 4.91
causal energy, 4.59
causal medium, 4.77
causal node, 3.64; 4.1
causal plane, 4.100
cause - primal, 4.3-4
cause supreme, 4.2
cavity, 3.53
cell malformation, 2.53
cellular air, 2,65
central channel, 3.69
central passage, 3.4; 4.46
central top, 4.16
centralized flow, 3.26, 29
centralized upper, 3.6
ceremonial worship, 1.18
chakra,
  complex, 4.73
  digestive, 3.66
  penetrated, 3.2
  throat, 3.51
  vagino, 3.43
Chandishvara, 1.7
characteristic-less, 4.33
charm, 3.25
Charpati, 1.6
Chaurangi, 1.5
cheat time, 3.130
cheerfulness, 2.78
chin lock, 1.37, 48,50; 3.20, 70
chin-to-throat, 2.45
chit akash, 1.43
Choli, 1.8
chronic constipation, 3.17
circular formation, 3.37
clan, 3.47
clarifying energy, 2.56
cleanliness, 1.17
clipped wings, 4.92
cloth, 2.24, 3.113
clothing, 1.69
clouds, 4.85
cock pose, -see rooster
coiled potency, 3.104
coiled space, 3.108
colon, 2.22, 26, 27; 4.109
companion, 3.25
compassion, 1.17
complete core, 4.71
compression,
  anus, 3.61-62
  best, 3.76
  breath energy, 2.57
  chin, 2.45
  breath suspension 2.71
  concave, 1.50
  conserved, 3.99
  technique, 2.67
conch, 4.85, 106
condiment, 1.61
condition, 4.8
conduct, 1.17-18
conduits, 3.37
confidential process, 3.9,18
confusion, 1.3
congestion of energy, 3.2, 4.70
conjecture, 4.58
conjugal loyalty, 3.104
consciousness energy, 3.5
constipation, 3.17
consumer of time, 4.17
consumption, 1.40, 3.17
containment control, 3.6, 88; 4.69, 72
contentment, 1.18
contractions,
  spontaneous, 1.44
  direction, 3.9
  energy, 3.21
  jaw, 3.6
  mastered, 1.54
  mouth, 4.46
  relocating, 3.7
  throat, 3.70
conventional impression, 3.3, 4.50
conversation, 1.15
conveyor of happiness, 4.2
core existence, 4.71
core-self
  divine space, 4.55
  focus, 1.42
  isolated, 4.62
cosmic engineer, 2.55
cough, 2.25
country, 1.12
courage, 1.16
cow dung, 1.13, 3.92
cow dung ashes, 3.98
cow flesh, 3.47-48
cow tongue, 3.48
cow-face posture, 1.22
creation / destruction, 4.77
creative energy, 3.104, 4.11
creator-god, 2.39
creatures, 4.13
cremation area, 3.4
criminally-liable souls, 3.122
cucumber, 1.65
cultural activities,
  no grip, 4.12
  renounced, 4.11
curled back, 3.6
cutting, 3.33

D

day influence, 4.42
dead man's pose, 1.34
death,
  avoided, 3.3
  conquered, 4.13
  destroyer, 4.2
  ejaculation, 3.88

death, continued
elephant, 3.57
eliminated, 3.7, 14
fear, 2.39
fearlessness, 3.116
final, 2.3
men, 3.52
mouth, 3.116
noose, 3.24
shattered, 1.9
superseded, 3.59, 82
time enforced, 2.40, 3.3, 4.48
transcended, 3.39
deathless liquor, 3.47
deathless person, 4.13
death-like state, 3.28
deep water, 2.70
deer, 4.99
degraders, 3.47
deities, 2.39, 3.8
deity - one, 3.54
deity of love, 2.54
dense energy, 2.78
departed souls, 3.122
deprivation, 1.18
deprivation / Vedic ceremony, 1.18
desire - upheaval, 4.34
desire/lifeforce, 4.22
destroyer of death, 4.2
detachment, 1.16
determination, 1.16
devoted yogi, 3.95
dhauti, 2.22
diagram resistant, 4.113
diamond posture, 1.39, 3.114-115
diamonds, 3.9
diet, 1.15, 59, 61-62
diet moderate, 2.1
diet sparse, 3.121
diety Yama, 3.122
digestion, 2.34
digestive chakra, 3.66
digestive energy, 3.67
digestive enzymes, 2.28
digestive heat, 2.65, 3.81
digestive power, 1.29
direction control, 3.9
disappearance of lifeforce/mind, 4.15
discussion, 1.69
disease elimination, 1.46, 3.50, 119
disease, breath, 2.16
dissolution, 1.45, 4.3-4, 62
distribution, 2.67, 71
diversification, 4.3-4
divine body, 4.71
divine space, 2.34, 3.32
dominance, 4.3-4
door key, 3.105
door/liberation, 3.105
douche, 2.26
drink urine, 3.96
drinking, 3.44
drone bee, 2.68
dropsy, 2.53
drum, 4.106
dry ginger, 1.65
dung, 3.92, 98

E

ear - right, 4.67
ear pain, 2.17
ears - covered, 4.82
earth, 3.126
eating cow, 3.48
eating - minimum, 1.17
edema, 2.53
ejaculation, 3.88
elderly sprite, 3.58, 65
elegance, 2.78
elephant, 2.15, 38, 57; 4.91
elimination/faults, 3.48
emission female, 4.14
emotional intelligence person, 3.104, 111
emotional trauma, 3.14
empowered teacher, 4.37
endless form, 4.41
energy congestion, 3.2; 4.70, 73
energy distribution, 2.67, 71
energy vortex, 3.2
engineer, 2.55
enjoyment with liberation, 3.94
enjoyments, garden of, 4.9
enthusiasm, 1.16; 4.32
entrance kundalini, 3.106
entrance vagina, 3.9
environment, 2.74, 4.1
epiglottis, 2.44, 51, 53
equanimity, 4.14
erect kundalini, 4.42
escalator, 1.1
essential origin, 4.41
eternal abode, 4.1
even accounting, 3.15
exclusive, 4.2
exclusive spiritual existence, 3.106
exertion, 1.15
existence, 3.106
existential condition original, 4.11
existential space supportless, 4.45
existing like a god, 4.3-4
expanding, 4.110
expert archer, 4.99
extended period, 3.51
external breath, 4.51
external environment, 4.1
eye flow, 2.78
eye pain, 2.17
eyebrows focus, 2.40, 3.4,32;4.18,36,80
eyebrows, interest, 1.37
eyelashes, 4.36
eyes, half-closed, 4.41

F

fading, 4.110
fainting, 2.44, 69
fall of hormone, 3.87
families, 3.47
family, woman, 3.9
farmland, 4.104
fasting, 1.63-64
fat, 2.21
fatigue, 1.34; 3.39
faults, great, 3.48
faulty social performance, 3.31

favor, 3.2
fear of death, 2.39, 3.116
features, yoga runined, 1.15
feces, 3.65
feelings producer, 4.2
female ascetic, 2.55
female bee, 2.68
female serpent, 3.104
female sex emission, 3.92, 4.14
female vagina, 3.9
feminine charm, 3.25
fever, 2.58
fiber, 3.51
fiery digestive chakra, 3.66
final source, 4.100, 102
fine, 3.46
finger, 2.64
fingers, 3.113
fingers-grab-toes, 1.31
fire pit, 3.104
fire, 1.63-64, 3.49; 4.59, 98
firewood, 4.98
firmness, 2.13
fish, 1.61
fission of energy, 3.67
five channels, 3.53
flames, 4.98
flavor, 3.16, 4.109
flawless condition, 4.3-4
flawless existential environment, 4.1
flaws, 3.14
flesh, 3.47, 48
flexibility, 1.19
float easly, 2.70
floatation, 2.70
flow - great, 3.6
flow inversion, 3.78
flow of bodily fluids, 3.7
flower, 4.90
flute, 4.76, 86
flying upward, 3.55, 56, 60
focal awareness, 3.26
focal containment, 3.88
focus,
internal, 2.67, 4.36
lifeforce, 2.72
middle mind, 3.20
self, 1.50
visual, 4.35, 36
folded cloth, 3.113
food,
ample, 3.80
insufficient, 3.81
oil-saturated, 1.62
procurement, 1.12
reheated, 1.62
Shiva pleased, 1.60
stale, 1.62
type, 1.61-62
forceful breathing, 2.44
forest, 3.1
forgetting, 4.110
form -endless, 4.41
forty days, 3.121
foundation, 3.1, 4.41
four fingers, 3.113
fourth state, 4.3-4
frenum, 3.36
fresh air, 1.50, 2.2
front kundalini, 4.47
front teeth, 3.22
fruits, 1.65
fuels, 3.46
fused kundalini, 4.19
fused-focused, 4.48
fusion nadis, 3.24

G

Ganges, 3.110
Ganges-like, 3.109
garden of enjoyments, 4.9
garlic, 1.61
gastric heat, 3.80
generous, 1.18
ghee flavor, 3.50
ghee, 1.65, 2.14
ginger, 1.65
gland malfunction, 2.25, 27, 58
goad of naad, 4.91
goat, 1.61
God Vishnu, 3.109, 4.100
God, 3.8
god, 4.3-4
god's practice, 2.39
Goda, 1.8
Goddess Ganges, 3.110
goddess kundalini, 3.106
Goddess Yamuna, 3.110
goddess, 3.5
gomukha, 1.22
good families, 3.47
good luck posture, 1.21
Goraksha, 1.4, 5; 4.65
Goraksha instruction, 1.63-64
Goraksha pose, 1.55-56
Gorakshnath, 4.65
grace pose, 1.55-56
grasping objects, 4.31
gravity, 3.7
great bird, 3.56
great flow, 3.6, 26, 29
great intelligence, 4.64
great mystic compression, 3.9, 13
great sealing, 3.6
great secret, 3.30
great transit, 3.4
green leaves, 1.61
grey hair, 3.29, 82
gulp-swallow, 2.44
gupta, 1.39
guru lineage, 4.81

H

hair, 2.49
hair's diameter, 3.34
half-closed eyes, 4.41
half-hour tongue, 3.38
hands, 1.50
happiness,
conveyor, 4.2
kundalini, 2.66
yoga yields, 2.68
head clearance, 2.50
head down, 3.81
head pain, 2.17
head light, 2.35
hearing of reality, 1.18
heat/cold, 4.111
heating and cooling, 3.79

heaven nectar, 3.71
heel,
perineum, 3.19
rectum, 3.63
vagina, 3.10, 61
hero pose, 1.23
hiccup, 2.17
highest consciousness, 3.5
hissing,
breath, 2.44
sound, 3.86
teeth, 2.54
hole, 3.69
honey, 1.65, 3.50
honor, 4.64
hormone energy, 3.67, 87; 4.28
horn, 4.85
horse, 4.94
horse gram bean, 1.61
humming, 2.44
hunger, 2.58, 3.39
hunter, 4.94

I

idealess content, 2.42, 3.3-4, 4.12
identification - salt, 4.5
ill health, 1.19
imageless, 3.3-4, 4.12
immobile creatures, 4.13
immortality, 3.28, 50
immovable, 3.26
impression, 3.3, 4.50
inconceivable, 4.32
independent, 4.3-4
indescribable, 4.32
indifference, 4.9
indigestion, 3.17
infinite pleasure, 4.78
infinitesimal, 3.130
infused air scatter, 3.72
infused breath energy, 4.21
inhabitant, 3.46
inner focus, 2.18, 4.105
inside/outside, 4.57
insight consciousness, 1.49, 4.15
insight perception, 4.19, 33
insight, 1.50, 4.9, 63
insight, Swatmarama, 1.4
insightful self-consciousness, 4.64
instrument - vina, 4.76
integral insight, 4.65
integration, 4.69, 74
intellect, 2.75
intellect spiritualized
intelligence personified, 3.104, 111
intelligent energy, 4.64
intentions absent, 4.32
internal focus, 2.65, 67; 4.94
internal heat, 4.19
internal organ, 2.28
intestinal worms, 2.50
intestine cleansing, 2.22, 26, 27
introspective focus, 1.42
introversion, 1.1,2; 4.8
introversion / kundalini yoga, 4.79
introversion success, 2.76
introverted accomplishment, 2.75
inversion, 3.78
irregularities, 3.17
isolated core-self, 4.62

J, K

jalandhara, 3.6
jar, 4.56
jewelbox, 3.9
jharajhara, 4.85
jug, 4.50
jujube, 1.61
KakaChandishvara, 1.7
kalakuta, 1.33
Kaneri, 1.7
Kanthadi, 1.6
kapalabhati, 2.22
kapalabhati light, 2.35
Kapali, 1.7
Kapalika. 1.8
Kapalika sect, 3.96
karani, 3.7
kettledrum, 4.73, 85
key, 3.105
kha divine space, 1.45, 3.32, 4.43-45,55,96
Khanda 1.8
khecari, 3.6, 32; 4.44-45, 49. 51
khecari, best, 1.45
kind-hearted yogi, 3.95
king of elephant, 4.91
king of serpents, 3.1
knife, 3.34
Koramtaka, 1.6
kriya complete, 3.124
kukkutasana, 1.26
kundalini,
air infusion, 2.66
arousal, 1.29, 3.2, 51, 68; 3.123
arrest, 3.112
bulb, 3.107
coil, 3.108
complete, 3.124
erect, 4.42
front, 4.47
fused, 4.19
goddess, 3.106
illumination, 1.50
intellect strike, 2.75
introversion, 4.79
locks, 3.74
manipulation, 1.1,9,11,58, 2.34
motivated, 3.119
mouth, 3.117
nadis, 3.110
names, 3.104
penetration, 2.41
shelter, 1.10
sleeping, 3.111
straightened, 3.11-12
success, 2.76
kūrmāsana, 1.24,26

L

lady - secluded, 4.35
lady supreme, 3.104
land, 1.12
lapses objectivity, 2.69
laya yoga, 4.103
leanness, 2.19

leaves, 1.61
legend, 1.10
leprosy, 3.17
level of Shiva, 3.24
liberated / body, 4.3-4
liberated pose, 1.39
liberated yogi, 1.51
liberation, 4.8
liberation door, 3.105
liberation inherent, 3.60
liberation posture, 4.67
liberation/kundalini, 3.107
lifeforce,
arousal, 3.68, 123
bulb, 3.107
control, 2.15, 40
desire, 4.22
disappearance, 4.15
focus, 2.72
middle channel, 4.14
mind, 4.24
names, 3.104
still, 4.23
light - radiant, 4.39
light in head, 2.35
lightness, 2.13
limbs flexible, 1.19
limited spirit, 4.7
lineage, 3.129, 4.81
linkage, 3.125, 4.63
lion, 1.36, 52,54; 2.15; 3,57
liquid arresting compression, 3.70
liquid subtle, 3.44
liquor, 1.61, 3,47,49
living creature, 2.3
location, 1.12
location - spiritual existence, 3.106
log, 4.106
logic, 4.40
lord of yogis, 2.56
Lord of yogis, 4.77
lords of yoga, 4.81
lotus leaf, 2.70
lotus posture, 1.25, 36, 46; 2.59-60
lotus stalk, 3.51
lotus, tight, 1.50; 2.7
lotus-shaped energy, 3.2
love deity, 2.54
love motions, 3.9
loyalty, 3.104
lung-heart chakra, 4.73
lure of scripture, 4.40

M

magical creation, 3.54
mahabandha, 3.6, 19, 23-24, 25
mahamudra, 3.6, 9, 13, 25
mahavedha, 3.6, 25-26
male - female, 3.101
male companion, 3.25
male organ, 1.37-38
male sexual emission, 3.83, 92
manager of senses, 4.29
Manthana, 1.6
mardala, 4.85
master of lineage, 4.81
master, 3.129
materialistic people, 1.15-16
Matsyanath, 1.28
Matsyendra, 1.4-5
Matsyendra posture, 1.20, 29
mayura pose, 1.32
menstruating, 3.91
mental conjecture, 4.58
mental content, 3.3-4, 4.12
mental dominance, 4.3-4
mento-emotional stimulation, 4.22
mercury, 4.96
meritorious action, 3.31
Meru, 3.52
microscopic central, 3.69
mid portion, 3.96
middle channel, 2.4
middle course flow, 4.16
middle energy stops, 4.50
middle mind, 3.20
middle nadi straightened, 3.124
milk and water, 4.24
milk flavor, 3.50
milk, 1.65, 2.14
milking, 3.33
milkledge leaf, 3.34
Mina, 1.5
mind,
antelope, 4.94
carefree, 4.91
control, 4.29
disappearance, 4.15
interspaced, 4.100
lifeforce, 4.24
like serpent, 4.97
manager, 4.29
middle, 3.20
focus-fused, 4.48
motionless, 4.31
natural instinct, 4.6
perception, 4.61
quiescent, 4.23
quiescent, 4.52
stability, 2.42
stabilized, 3.125, 4.28
minute, 3.30
mobile creatures, 4.13
moderate consumption, 1.40
modesty, 1.18
moon - time, 4.17
moon energy flow, 3.77
moon nectar, 3.46
moon source, 4.46
mooncharge energy, 1.29,
moon-dominant left, 2.8
moon-like cool nectar, 3.49
moral stipulations, 1.15
motionless mind, 4.31
motions of woman, 3.9
motivate kundalini, 3.119
mountain, 3.1
mouth compressed, 4.46
mouth of death, 3.116
mucus eliminated, 2.21, 35-36, 53, 65-66
mukta pose, 1.39

muladhara uplift,
3.6, 61
mung, 1.65
murccha, 2.44, 69
muscular redirection,
3.83
musical tone, 4.70
mustard seed, 1.61
mystic arresting action,
3.5
mystic checking
practice, 3.7
mystic compression,
3.6, 9
mystic perfectional
skills, 3.83, 125, 130
mystic proficiency, 3.1

N

naad,
absorption, 4.89, 92
appreciated, 4.65
focus foremost, 4.66
focus, 4.81, 90, 93
goad, 4.91
inner focus, 4.105
left side, 3.110
location, 4.68
mento-emotional,
4.98
reproduction
concentrate, 3.100
right side, 3.110
sound - reliance, 4.29
sound resonance,
2.78; 3.64
sound variety, 4.85
stages, 4.84
subtle sound,
1.45; 4.88
nadi,
72000, 3.123
cleansing, 1.41
clearance,
2.5, 19, 41, 78
correction, 2.53, 55
microscopic, 3.69
pollutants, 2.4
purification, 1.57
sushumna, 2.66
topmost, 3.52
nails, 2.49
Naradeva, 1.8
nasal cleansing, 2.22
Nath, 1.2
natural for God, 3.8
nauli, 2.22
navel, 2.26; 3.79
nectar of heaven, 3.71
nectar, 3.16, 46, 90
negatively charged
energy, 3.61
neti, 2.22
night, 3.126
night and day, air, 4.52
night energy, 4.42
ninety minutes, 3.112
Niranjana, 1.7
Nityanatha, 1.7
no vision, 4.37
node causal, 3.64
node source, 4.1
non-recollection, 4.34
non-reliance, 2.77
non–stealing, 1.17
non-violence, 1.17, 40
noose of death, 3.24
nose tip, 1.46, 48, 52
nose-finger closing,
2.64
nostril alternation, 2.7
nostril infusion,
2.44, 48
nutrition compact,
3.116

O

objectivity, 2.69
ocean, 4.56, 85
odor, 4.109
odor divine, 4.71
odor of flower, 4.90
oil lamp, 3.46
oil-cake, 1.61
oily food, 1.61
old age,
2.47; 3.7, 29, 50
one deity, 3.54
one focal, 3.26
one origin, 3.54
one reality, 4.3-4
one subject, 3.4
opinions, 1.3
organ - intellect, 2.75
organs - psychic, 4.99
organs smeared, 3.93
origin, 3.54
origin essential, 4.41
original condition,
4.9, 11
originality, 4.3-4
outside/inside, 4.57
over-eating, 1.15

P

padma lotus pose, 1.36
padmasana, 1.25, 46
pains, 2.17
palate, 3.48, 79
parallel retraction, 3.43
pashshimatana, 1.30-31
passage, 3.61
past and future, 3.102
path complete, 3.124
peacock, 1.32
penetrated vortex, 3.2
penis, 3.91
pepper, 1.61
perception,
consciousness, 4.19
environments, 2.74
insight, 4.9
interest, 2.40; 3.32
perfect yogi practice,
1.37, 59
perfected beings, 3.8
perfected yogi pose,
1.36
perfected yogini, 3.50
perfection, 1.68
perfectional skill, 2.75
performance ceremony,
1.18
perineum, 1.52; 3,19
perspiration, 2.12, 13
phased-out mind, 4.15
philosophy, 4.8
physio-psychic act,
2.23, 36
physio-psychic
application, best, 1.45
physio-psychic
compression,
2.44, 67, 71; 3.76
pious yogi, 3.95
pipe, 3.86

plavini, 2.44
pleasure,
enjoyed, 3.103
infinite, 4.78
poison, 2.58, 3,16
poisonous serpent, 3.45
pollutants, 2.4
pollution, 2.66
posture,
benefits, 1,19
best, 1.35, 45
number of, 1.41
steadiness, 2.1
potency coiled, 3.104
powdered turmeric, 3.35
powers, 3.8
Prabhudeva, 1.8
practice, essential, 1.70
pranayama, 2.71
predominant deity, 3.54
preliminary, 4.69
pride/shame, 4.111
Primal Cause, 4.3-4
procedure, 3.124
process, 3.124
producer of feelings, 4.2
producer of techniques, 3.53
proficiency, 2.76, 3.1, 4.69, 76
proficient yogi, 4.108
prostitute, 4.35
psyche quiescence, 3.75
psyche-controlled ascetics, 1.65
psychic energy transformation, 1.2; 2.76
psychic organ, 2.28, 75; 4.99
psychic pollution, 2.66
psychological inhabitant, 3.46
psychological sky, 4.74
psychology, 2.28
Pujyapada, 1.7
pulling, 3.33
pungent food, 1.61
pungent taste, 3.50
purificatory act, 2.23, 36
purity, 4.105

Q,R

quicksilver, 4.26-27
radiance, 2.19
radiant light, 4.39
raja yoga, 4.79
Rama, 4.58
rapid breath infusion, 2.59
realism, 1.17
reality - one, 4.3-4
reality - whole, 4.41
reality / naad, 4.100
reality-perceptive yogi, 3.95
recommended conducts, 1.18
rectum, 3.61
redirection of female, 4.14
reference, 3.25
regulator dcities, 3.8
reliant on naad, 4.29
relocating breath infused energy, 3.7
remembering, 4.110
reproduction hormone concentrate, 3.87
reproductive concentrate conserved, 3.99
reproductive concentrate stabilized, 4.28
reproductive energy subjugation, 2.78
residence, 1.13
residence of Vishnu, 3.109
residence supreme, 4.3-4
respiration suspension, 4.31
restful animation, 4.49, 51
restfulness, 1.34
restraining behaviors, 1.17
restrictions, 1.63-64
retarded person, 4.114
retention, 2.44
retraction-vaginal, 3.43
reverential honor, 4.64
reverse the flow, 3.7
rib cage, 3.6, 54, 74
rice, 1.65
right ear, 4.67
right nostril infusion, 2.48
ritual worship, 4.40
rock salt, 3.35
room, 1.13
rooster, 1.26
root of tongue, 3.36
Rudra congestion, 4.76

S

sahajoli, 3.92, 94; 4.14
salt in water, 4.5
salt, 1.61, 4.59
salty taste, 3.50
samadhi, 4.5-7
sanctified dung ashes, 3.98
sanctified water, 1.65
schizophrenic person, 4.114
scriptural statement, 3.78
scripture lure, 4.40
sealing containment, 3.6, 19, 23
secluded lady, 4.35
secret pose, 1.39
secret, 3.30, 4.17
secretion, 3.52
sect Kapalika, 3.96
seductive woman, 3.42
seed, knowledge, 4.104
seet, 2.54
self, 4.109
self/mind, 4.5
self-absorbed, 4.112
self-atomic, 4.1
self-consciousness, 4.64
self-intuition, 4.32
selfish person, 3.95
self-urine comsumption, 3.92, 96; 4,14

semen,
conservation, 3.90
flow, 3.42
mento-emotional energy, 3.90
sense objects / non-recollection, 4.34
senses manager, 4.29
senses, controlled, 1.37
sensual energy, 2.28
sensual withdrawal, 4.68
serpent kundalini, 3.108
serpent-like mind, 4.97
serpent, 3.1, 11-12, 45, 69
sesame, 1.61
seventy-two nadis, 4.18
seventy-two thousand, 3.123
sexual emission, female, 3.92, 4.14
sexual fluid retraction, 3.91
sexual form, 3.25
sexual intercourse,
upright, 3.93
yogini, 3.85
sexual muscle, 3.7, 4.14
nonexpressiveness, 1.17, 59
shakti mobile, 3.104
shakti-calani, 3.7
shambhavi visual focus, 3.4, 4.35-37, 67
Shambhu Shiva, 4.37
Shavara, 1.5
shell, 4.85
she-serpent, 3.111
shitali, 2.44, 57-58
Shiva,
diet related, 1.60
honored, 4.1
level, 3.24
location, 4.76
naad, 4.66
poison, 1.33
position, 4.48
sweetheart, 4.46
taught postures, 1.35
teacher supreme, 1.1
techniques, 3.8
siddha posture, 1.36
siddha, 1.37
siddha technique, 1.4
Siddhapada, 1.6
Siddhir, 1.6
single state, 3.54
sinus cleansing, 2.22, 25, 27
sitkari, 2.44, 54
sixteen petaled, 3.51
sixteen vital supports, 3.73
sixteen years, 2.47
sixty-day rice, 1.65
skilled yogi, 4.12
skin disease, 2.25
skull top, 4.16
sky, psychological, 4.74
sleep, 3.39
sleeping, 4.110
sleeping goddess, 3.5
sleeping kundalini, 3.2, 3.68
sleeping she-serpent, 3.111
sleepless practice, 3.125
slow inhale, 2.44, 69
smear ashes/urine, 3.98
smear organ, 3.93
smooth and stainless, 3.34
snake, 3.68
snare, 4.94
snuff urine, 3.97
social contribution, 1.59
social performance, 3.31
soft and dazzling, 3.113
soft hum, 2.44
soft palate, 3.42
souls, departed, 3.122
sound,
covered ears, 4.82
hissing, 3.86
subtle - see naad
resistance, 4.109
resonance - see naad
seet, 2.54
sour gruel, 1.61
sour taste, 3.50
source, 4.41, 100, 102
special favor, 3.2
sphincter, 2.26, 3.6
spiritual bliss, 4.2
spiritual consciousness, 3.5
spiritual feelings, 4.75
spiritual focus, 4.81
spiritual insight, 4.11
spiritual light, 4.39
spiritual pleasure, 4.30
spiritual purity, 4.105
spiritual self / mind, 4.5
spiritual sky, 3.37
spiritualized intellect, 3.13
spleen, 2.58
spleen disease, 2.27
spontaneous breath suspension, 2.73
spontaneous feelings, 4.75
sprite, 3.58
squatting, 2.26
stability of mind, 2.42
stabilized mind, 3.125
stable, 4.94
stainless, 3.34
state of non-reliance, 2.77
steadiness, 1.17, 19; 2.12
stick, 3.11-12, 68
stomach cleansing, 2.22, 24, 25
stomach flattened, 1.30
stomach, one-fourth, 1.60
straightforwardness, 1.17
stream, 4.46
strike buttocks, 3.27
stringed instrument, 4.76, 86
stunned condition, 3.39
subject, 3.4
subjective reality, 4.3-4
submerge anus, 2.26
subtle body transformation, 1.1, 58
subtle breath energy, 4.6
subtle channels, 3.53

subtle creative energy,
3.104, 4,11
subtle liquid, 3.44
subtle secretion, 3.52
subtle veins,
1.41, 57; 2.4
success - 40 days, 3.121
sugar candy, 1.65
sulphur, 4.96
sun - time, 4.17
sun opening
sun heat, 1.10
sunlike nutrition
compact, 3.116
superfit form, 4.53
supermost object, 4.41
supernatural
happenings, 2.68
supernatural perception,
3.98
supernatural powers,
3.8
supernatural ruler, 4.72
supernatural skill,
3.18, 50
supportive base, 3.1
support-less,
deity, 3.54
existential space,
4.45
kha sky, 4.96
supports, sixteen, 3.73
supreme, 4.2, 41
supreme abode, 4.100
supreme goddess, 3.106
supreme lady, 3.104
Supreme Lord,
3.129, 4.100, 102
supreme residence of
Vishnu, 3.109
supreme residence,
4.3-4
supreme situation, 4.45
Supreme Spirit, 4.7
Surananda, 1.6
surface, 4.109
surya-bheda, 2.44
sushumna,
central spinal
passage, 2.6
clearance, 2.6. 66
comparisons, 3.4
compressed, 4.46
sushumna, continued,
flushed, 4.12
mouth, 3.117
secretion, 3.52
suspended animation,
4.49, 51
suspension of breath,
2.43-44, 57, 73; 4.31
svastika, 1.21
swallow infusion, 2.44
Swatmarama, 1.4
sweetheart, 4.46
syllabus, 1.58
symbol, 4.113
symbol resistant, 4.113

T

tail of she-serpent,
3.111
Takshak, 3.45
talkative person, 4.114
teacher lineage, 3.129
teacher's favor, 3.2
technique sushumna
pierce, 4.16
teeth, 2.54
tendency grasping, 4.31
testes, 1.52, 55-56
theistic, 1.18
theory, 4.60
third-eye congestion,
4.76
thirst, 2.58, 3.39
thought suspension,
4.58
thoughtless idealess
state, 2.42
thoughtlessness,
1.43, 4.34
three perception
environments, 2.74
throat,
compression,
2.46, 3.6, 70-71
contact, 3.73
chakra, 3.51,73
restriction, 3.11-12
tiger, 2.15
time - day/night, 4.17
time as death,
1.9, 4.48, 2.40
time cheat, 3.130
time consumer, 4.17
Tindtini, 1.8
tip of nose, 1.46,48,52
tolerance, 1.17
tone, 4.70
tongue,
backwards, 3.32
contact, 2.44
contact infusion, 2.58
cow, 3.48
curled back, 3.6
half-hour, 3.38
pressed, 1.48
roll, 3.36
stretched, 3.33
teeth, 3.22
top of skull, 4.16
tortoise, 1.10
tortoise posture, 1.24
total neutrality, 4.104
touring, 1.63-64
traatak, 2.22
transcendental feelings,
4.75
transcendental
happiness, 2.68
transcendental source,
4.100. 102
transit,
divine space,
1.45, 4.43-45
great, 3.4
through, 3.32
yogi, 3.102
trauma / pleasure, 4.111
trauma eliminated, 3.14
trauma-free, 4.38
trauma-free location,
3.106
travel, 1.63-64
tree, 4.104
trembling, 2.12
tremendous energy,
4.53
tricks sun, 3.78
triple procedure, 3.30
truth, 1.16
turmeric, 3.35
twelve fingers, 3.113

U

uddiyana, 2.45, 3.6, 54-55
ujjayi, 2.44,51,53
unity, 4.5, 7
universe transit, 1.9
up and under, 3.54
upheaval of desires, 4.34
uplift compression, 2.45
upper flow, 3.6,26
upturning the body, 3.7
upward contraction, 3.7
upward muscular, 4.14
upward redirection, 3.83
upward-contraction, 4.14
urinary muscle, 4.14
urine consumption, 3.96
urine drink, 3.96
urine reduction, 3.65
uro-genital channel, 3.86
u-shaped tongue, 2.57
uterine chakra, 3.43
utkata, 2.26
uttana-kurma, 1.26

V

vagina - hormone fall, 3.87
vagina parallel, 3.43
vaginal entrance, 3.9
vaginal passage, 3.61
vagino-uterine, 3.43
vajra pose, 1.39
vajra, 3.114-115
vajroli compared, 3.92
vajroli urinary, 3.7
vajroli, 3.83, 4.14
variety dissolution, 4.3-4
Vasishtha posture, 1.20
Vedas, 4.35
Vedic scriptures, 4.35
vegetables, 1.65
venom, 3.45
vina, 4.76, 86
viparita, 3.7,78
virasana, 1.23
Virupaksha, 1.5
Vishnu, 3.109
Vishnu abode, 4.100
Vishnu anahat, 4.73
vision - none, 4.37
vision energy, 1.47
visual focus, 3.4,125; 4.18,35-36,38
vital energy control, 2.41
vital supports, 3.73
void of mental content, 4.3-4,47,80
vomit, 2.38
vortex, 3.2

W

waking, 4.110
waste air energy, 2.38
waste gases, 2.47
water, 1.65, 2.70, 4.59
weapon, 3.50; 4.113
well-to-do person, 3.95
wheat, 1.65
whimsical action, 3.83
whimsy, 1.15
white sugar, 1.65
whole reality, 4.41
wick, 3.46
widow ascetic, 3.109
widow, 3.110
wings, 4.92
wisdom, 4.60
wish-fulfilling tree, 4.104
withdrawal, 4.68
woman,
  charm, 3.25
  family, 3.9
  naad fuse with reproduction concentrate, 3.100
  seductive, 3.42
  vaginal hormone fall, 3.87
women, 1.63-64
women - yogini, 3.50
wood, 4.98
worms, 2.50
worship, 4.40
wrinkles, 3.29, 82
Yama, 3.122
Yamuna, 3.110
Yamuna-like, 3.109
yoga,
  books,1.18
  for all ages, 1.67
  mystic process, 4.79
  proficiency, 3.1
  ruined, 1.15
  succeeds, 3.95
  supernatural ruler, 4.72
  teachers, 2.37
Yogi Siddhir, 1.6
yogi,
  embraced, 3.42
  Kapalika, 3.96
  liberated, 1.51
  like a god, 2.54-55
  lord of achievement, 2.56
  Lord of yogis, 4.77
  practice, 1.42
  proficiency, 4.108
  resistant, 4.113
  skilled, 4.12
  sexual skill, 3.85
  supersedes death, 3.59
  surroundings, 1.12-13
  whimsical, 3.83
yogini,
  concentrate, 3.99
  naad fuse reproduction concentrate, 3.100
  women, 3.50
  yogi attraction, 2.55
yogurt, 1.61
young widow ascetic, 3.109-110
youthful, 3.58

Selected Sanskrit Words with English Meanings

A

ā – until
abdād = abdāt = year
abhibhavati – cures
abhidhaḥ – known as
abhidhānakam – sound
abhidhīyate – is called, is known as
abhūvan – became
abhyāsa – practice, technique, disciplinary practice
abhyaset – should practice
abhyāsino = abhyāsinaḥ = practicioners
abhyastā – practiced
abhyasyamānaḥ = practicing
abhyasyataḥ = practice
ācaret – should do, practice, accept
ācāryais = ācāryaiḥ = by the yoga teachers
ācāryāṇāṁ – authoritative yoga teachers
achala – steady
ādau – in the beginning
ādāya - extracted
ādayo = ādayaḥ = others
adhaḥ – below, down
ādhāra – support, vital support, foundation, supportive base, anal sphincter muscle
adhastāt – underneath
adhi – near
adhikam – more
adhirohiṇī – means of ascension
adho = adhaḥ = hence declared, downward
adho–gāmi = descending
adhvas – flow
ādi – very first
ādike – initially
ādīn – and others
ādināthena – by Lord Adinath
ādināthoditaṁ = ādinātha (Lord Shiva) + uditaṁ (explained)
ādyam – and similar items
agādhe – in deep
āgama – scriptures
agamyaṁ – beyond
agni – digestive heat, internal heat, fiery energy
agocaraḥ – inconceivable
agrāhyo = agrāhyaḥ = supersedes
āgryaṁ – foremost
āhāraḥ = food consumption
āharet – should be drawn
āhatā – infused into
ahi – serpent
ahiṁsā – non–violence
ahitaṁ – what is unfit
āhuḥ – say, identified as
aikyaṁ – combination, unity
ājādi – goat and other animals
ajānantaḥ – those who do not know
ājya – ghee
ākarṣaṇaṁ – draw, attract
ākarṣayed (ākarṣayet) = should extract
ākāśa – astral environment
ākeśād = ā (from) + keśāt (hair)
akhaṇḍitaṁ – infinite
akhilaṁ – every, whole
ākhya – called, known as
akriyasya – of those who do not practice the mystic techniques
ākṛṣya – by pulling, drawing in, upward coursed
ākṝṣyate – exctract
ākuñcanaṁ – contract, extraction, compression
alakṣye – uncharacteristic
ālasyaṁ – procrastination
ālayet – should infuse
ālokya – perceiving, focusing
alpa – insufficient, small
amalaḥ – distinct, without dirt
amanaskaṁ – without mental dominance
amandāvarta = amanda (quickly) + āvarta (turning)
amara – deathless
amaratvam – immortality, existentially like a god
amarīṁ – mid portion of the flow of urine
amaroli = self–urine consumption
āmbu – urine
āmbuvat – like water
amla – sour

āmla – sour
amṛtaṁ – nectar, subtle pleasure energy
amṛtāya (immortality)
aṁṣoḍaśābda – sixteen years old
anāhata – spontaneous sounds, naad supernatural sound resonance on the causal plane in the personal psyche
ānakhāgrāc = ā (to) + nakha (nail) + āgrāt (tip)
ānala – energized region
analasya – energizes, of digestion
anale – in fire
ānanda – transcendental happiness, blissful feelings, spiritual pleasure, spiritual happiness
anantaraṁ – continuous
anargalā – without dense energy
anāyāsāt – spontaneously
anāyāsena – easily
andrāt – from the moon-like cool nectar
anga – limb
anggatvād – stage
aṅghri–mūla – heel
aṅgīkṛtāny = aṅgīkṛtāni = were adopted
anginā – women
aṅgula – thumb, fingers
aṅguṣṭhau – big toes
anilaḥ – infused breath energy, air, fresh physical and subtle air
aṇimā – becoming minute
aṇimādi – becoming infinitesimal and related supernatural skills
anirodhataḥ – spontaneously
aniśaṁ – constantly
antaḥ – interior, inside the body
antaka – of death
antar – interior, internal
antaraṅga – interior, internally, psychological plane
antare – inside
antargataṁ – what interspaced
antāstham – inside positioned
ante – in the end
anukramaḥ – range
anyaḥ – other, another
anyathā – or, other
anye – other
āpāda – from the foot
apāna – negatively charged subtle force, negatively charge breath energy, polluted waste gases, waste physical and subtle gases
apāna–prāṇayor = apāna–prāṇayoḥ = of the positively and negatively charged subtle forces
āpanne – felt
apara – other
apaśyann = apaśyan = lack of vision
apathyaṁ – damaging, unsuitable
āpnoti – achieves, attains, obtains
āpnuyāt – attain, becomes, would get
apunar – not again
ārambhaś = ārambhaḥ = preliminary
ārambhāvasthā – preliminary stage
ardha – middle
ardhonmīlita = ardha (half–closed) + unmīlita (open)
argali – psychic pollution
arjavam (straightforwardness)
āroḍhum – to ascend proceed rapidly
arogatā – without disease, health
arogavān – healthy
ārogham – without disease, lacking ill–health
arundhatī – conjugal loyalty personified
aśakya – not capable
āsanam – posture
asau – this, that
aśeṣa – with no exception, without remainder, total, definitely
āsīnayoḥ – sitting
aśīti – eighty
āśleṣhitasya – embraced
āśrayā (relating)
āśritaḥ – is reliant on
āśritya – rely on
aśru – tears
aṣṭa – eight
aṣṭadhā – eight
asteyaṁ – non–stealing
āstikyaṁ – being theistic
astu – let it be, let there be
āśu – quickly, rapidly
asyoṣṇī–kṛtaṁ = asya (of this) + uṣṇī–kṛtaṁ (what was heated)
aṭanam – wandering
atandritaḥ – not lazy
atha – now is described, as explained, as for, regarding
ati – very
atikramya – passing over
atirodhataḥ – to the limit of endurance
atiśūnye – state beyond the idealess imageless mental content

atītānāgataṁ = atīta (past) + anāgataṁ (future)
ativṛddho = ativṛddhaḥ = very old
ātma = core–self
atrādhikam = atra (here) + adhikam (more)
atulaṁ – exceptional, incomparable
atyāhāraḥ = over–eating
atyanta – greatly
audāsīnyaṁ – total neutrality
avadhāryā – should ascertain
avadhyaḥ – killed
avāpnuhi – attain
avāpnuyāt – attains
avāptaṁ – is due
avāptaye – attain
avāpyate – achieved
āvarta – turning
avaśiṣyate – without remainder
avaṣṭabhya – balance on
avasthā – conditions, state, existential state
āvasthayā – focused into the divine environment
avasthitā – situated
avatiṣṭhate – seems to be
aviśrāntaṁ – constantly,
āvṛṇute – not heard
āvṛtya – restraining
āyatam – length
āyattaṁ – dependency
ayuktābhyāsa = without proficiency in practice

B

baddha – tight, what is compressed and channeled, restriction, spell, restrained, yogically controlled within, is confined
baddhvā – adopting, assuming, being tightly restricted, by suppressing, firmly situated, holding, restaining, compresses
badhnīyāt – should assume, should retain with inner focus
badhyate – forcefully compressed and directed, limited, trapped
bahiḥ – external, outside, exterior, outside
bahiḥsthaṁ – outside
bahu – diverse, much, many
bahulas – ample
bahunoktena = bahuna (more) + uktena (by saying)
bāhya – external, outside
bāhyābhyantaraṁ = external and internal
bāhyataḥ – external
bālaraṇḍā – young widow
bāla–raṇḍāṁ = young widow
balāt – due to being forced, from strength
baṇatvāt – saturated with
bandeṣu – physical bodily contraction
bandha – bodily contraction, physio–psychic compression, captivation
bandhanāya = give restrictions
bandha–stho = bandha–sthaḥ = firmly held
bastiḥ –large intestine (colon) cleansing action
basti–karma = large intestine (colon) cleansing action
bhadrāṁ – auspicious
bhadraṁ –graceful pose
bhadrāsanam – grace posture
bhagavatī – goddess
bhage – in vagina
bhāgena – region
bhājāṁ – acclaim
bhājanam – deserving person, entitlement
bhajati – assume
bhakṣaṇaṁ – eating
bhakṣayen = bhakṣayet – would swallow
bhānur = bhānuḥ = heating sun feature, sunlike nutrition compact (orb)
bhasma – ash
bhastrā – bellows, rapid breath-infusion, forceful inhale-exhale infusion
bhāvād = bhāvāt = from a state
bhāvaḥ – consciousness, experience
bhavanti – become, manifest
bhavati – is, becomes, manifests
bhaved = bhavet = is, be, become, can, assume, is experienced, should hold, there is, develop into
bhāvena – with being
bhavet – is, be, become, can, assume, is experienced, should hold, there is, develop into, is called should feel,
bhayaṁ – fear
bheda – distinct, split, application, pierce through
bhedanam – infusion
bhedataḥ – different
bhedo = bhedaḥ = shattered
bherī – kettledrum
bhiduraṁ – reduces
bhidyante – are penetrated
bhittvā – fissioning, penetrate
bhoga – enjoyment
bhojanam – food
bhoktrī – consumer
bhramara – bee

bhrāmarī – bee, soft humming like a blackbee infusion,
bhrāmayed = bhrāmayet = should spin
bhrāntyā – by confusion
bhṝnga – drone bee
bhṝngī – female black bee
bhrū – between the eyebrows
bhrū–madhyaṁ = between eyebrows
bhruvau – visual focus between the eyebrows
bhruvor = bhruvoḥ = between the eyebrows
bhruvorantaraṁ – inside between the eyebrows
bhruvormadhye = in between the eyebrows
bhujaṅgamam – serpent
bhujaṅgī –female serpent
bhujyate – is eaten
bhuktaṁ – ingestion, what is consumed
bhukte – pleasure
bhūmau – on the earth, on the ground
bhūmi – earth
bhūtale – in the world
bhūtānāṁ – living beings
bhūte – in existing
bhūtendriya – sensual material nature
bhūtvā – become, believing
bhuvi – in the world, on the ground
bhūya – being, in turn, again
bījam – origin, seed, source
bilaṁ – hole
bindu – causal node source, concentrate, reproduction hormone concentrate, subtle hormone concentrate, semen, male reproduction hormone concentrate, subtle male hormone concentrate
bodha – intellect psychic organ, spiritual insight
bodhakaṁ – perceptively arouses
bodhānāṁ – integral insight
bodhato = bodhataḥ = highest perceptive state of intellect psychic organ
bodhayet – should arouse
bodhayitvā – insight perception consciousness
brahma – exclusive spiritual existence, transcdental reality
brahmachārī = sexual non – expressiveness which results in the perception of spirituality
brahmacharyaṁ – sexual nonexpressiveness which results in the perception of spirituality
brahmādayo = brahmā (creator–god Brahmā) + ādayo (ādayāḥ) (and other supernatural rulers)
brahma–dvāra = door to spiritual consciousness
brahma–granther = brahma–grantheḥ = energy congestion of brahma
brahma–nāḍī = microscopic central channel, center of the sushumna nadi central spinal passage, central spinal subtle spirit-access passage through to brahmarandra
brahmānanda – feelings of exclusive spiritual bliss
brahmāṇḍe – in the universe
brahma–randhra = mystic opening at the top of the subtle head, central top of the skull
bravīmy = bravīmi = describe

C

cakra – associate group, circular energy formation, energy gryating center, energy junction vortexes, circular pattern
calaṁ– anxious
cālana – pulling, cause to move, compressing and relocating, mobility
cālayet – should wander, motivate to move
cālayitvā – causing to move, motivate to move
cale – irratic
cālitā – moved
calitaṁ – falling, moves
cālyate – is pumped
cañcalatvaṁ – shifty
cāñcalyaṁ – instability
candra – moon-charged energy, moon–like energy, moon–dominant left side
candra–janmane = what is produced from the moon
candrāṅge – in the moon–dominant left side
candrārkāv = candra (moon dominant left channel) + ārkāu (and sun dominant right channel)
candrāt – from the moon-like cool nectar
cāndrīṁ – subtle liquid
cāpalam – quickly
carācaram – mobile and immobile creatures, life forms
caran – flow
caraṇaṁ – foot, sole
carati – shifts, flowing through
cāriṇaḥ – wandering
cāstameti – fading

cātmānamātma = ca (and) + ātmānam (into the core–self) + ātma (core–self)
catur = catuḥ = four
caturaśīti – of eighty–four
caturthāṁśa – one–fourth
catuṣkam – four
catuṣṭayam – four
ceṣṭitaḥ – enthusiams
cetasā – with consciousness, intellect
cetasi – on the consciousness
chabdaḥ = śabdaḥ = sound
chakrā – energy gyrating centers
chanaiḥ = śanaiḥ = gently
chandreṇa – by the moon–dominant left side
chedana – cutting
chinna – clipped
chitra – type, range
chitta – mento–emotional energy
chorurh – to position
chukraṁ = śukraṁ = semen
cibukam – chin
cid = cit = perceives
cid–ātmane = insightful self consciousness
cihnāni – characteristics
cin = cit = consciousness
cinmayā – with insight by me
cintā = mento–emotional energy, mento-emotional disturbances, sources of anxiety, ideation tendencies, trauma
cintayan – mentally and emotionally focused
cintayet – should consider, contemplate
ciraṁ – extended period
cit – spiritual objective awareness
citrān – various
citta – mento–emotional energy
cittānandaṁ = pleasures of the mento–emotional energy
cittāyattaṁ = citta (mento–emotional energy) + āyattaṁ (dependency)
cumbantī – touches
cūrṇitābhyāṁ – powdered

D

dadāti – it makes
dadhi – yogurt
dadyāc = dadyāt = gives
daghdha – burnt
daghna – up to
dahana – digestive enzymes
dahati – chemically burns
dakṣa – right side
dakṣānge – on the right side
dakṣa–pādaṁ = right foot
dakṣiṇa – right
dambha – retarded
dānam – generosity
daṇḍa – stick
daṇḍāhatā = struck with a stick
daṇḍākāraḥ = daṇḍa (stick) + ākāraḥ (adopts)
daṇḍa–rūpau = both feet like sticks
daṇḍavad = daṇḍavat = like a stick
darśanam – direct perceptional insight
daśa – ten
daśakaṁ – ten
daṣṭasya – stung by
datte – focused, imparts
dayārjavaṁ = daya (compassion) +
dedīpyamānaṁ – blazing
dehaṁ – physical body
dehānala = deha anala = digestive functionality
dehī – psychological inhabitant of the body
dehinām –people
deśa – position, place
deva–samas = same as a supernatural ruler
devo = devaḥ = predominating deity
deyā – reveal
dhairyāt – from being courageous
dhāma – zone
dhāna – shooting
dhanuḥ – bow, perimeter of about the distance an arrow would go when released from a bow
dhārā – stream, flow of urine
dharām – earth
dhārāmayaṁ – spontaneous stream of emotion
dhāraṇaṁ – deliberate focus on transcendental reality, mental and emotional focus, focal containment
dhāraṇaṁ – wearing
dhārayed = dhārayet = should hold, should spontaneously focus, smear, should close while focusing internally, should retain with inner focus, focus to link
dhārayitvā – by psychically controlling, compressing the air energy while focusing on it internally
dhārmike – in a righteous civilization
dhātrīṇāṁ – of the earth
dhattaḥ – is presented
dhatte – contribute, gives
dhātu – body cell structure, body parts

dhātvindriyāntaḥ = dhātv (dhātu) (basic psychology) + indriya (sensual energy) + antaḥ (internal)
dhauti –stomach cleansing action
dhavalaṁ – dazzling white
dhāvati – drift
dhīmatā – people with insight consciousness
dhīrāṇāṁ – devoted entities
dhiyā – focalized in the psyche focus, with focused attention
dhṝtiḥ – steadiness
dhṝtvā – having crossed, stabilizing
dhruvam – definite, fixed
dhvanau – sounds
dhvaner = dhvaneḥ = reality
dhvaniḥ – musical tones, sound
dhvanirya – reality
dhvānte – in sinking
dhyāna – effortless focus, spontaneous focus linkage into the divine world,
dhyāyī – spontaneous introspective focus
dina –day
dine dine = daily, day by day
dīpakaḥ – wick
dīpanaṁ – trigger effect
dīrghā – long
divā – day influence
divāniśam = day and night
divārātri = day influence and night energy
divya – divine, supernatural, mystic, sanctified, psychic
dohaiḥ – by milking (pressing to the tip)
dorbhyāṁ – forearms
doṣa – discomfort, disease, flaw, health problem, malfunction, bodily imbalance, upset in psychological and physical physiology
doṣāmaya – consisting of diseases
doṣopacayaṁ = doṣa (diseased condition) + upacayaṁ (excess)
dṝḍhābhyāsena = dṝḍha (firmly) + ābhyāsena (by practice)
dṛḍhaḥ – firm, fixed, steady, tight
dṝḍhāsano = dṝḍhāsanaḥ = firm and steady
dṝḍhatā – firmness, steadily
dṝḍhī – consistent
dṝśā – perception interest
dṛśau – eyes
dṝṣṭir = dṝṣṭiḥ = gaze, perception, insight perception, perception interest
dṛṣṭyā – perception
dṝśyam – means of perception
dṝśyate – are experienced, observing
dughdha – milk
dughdhāmbuvat = dughdha (milk) + āmbuvat (like water)
duḥkha – trauma, suffering
dundhubhi – drum
durbalo = durbalaḥ = lacking strength
durjana – undesirables
durlabhā – difficult to acquire, difficult to master
dvā – two
dvādaśa – twelve
dvaitaṁ – conflicting states
dvāramarandhra – doorway
dvārāṇi – entrances, orifices
dvāsaptati – in seventy–two
dvāv = dvāu = two
dvaya – two, both
dve – two
dvi – two
dvitayaṁ – two
dvitīyakaḥ – second
dvitīyaṁ – second
dvitīyāyāṁ – second progression
dvividho = dvividhaḥ = two types

E

eka – one, only
ekadhīḥ – one focusing interest, one focal awareness
ekāgraḥ – singularly focused
ekaikā – each one
ekaiva = as one
ekānte – in one place
ekasmin – one
ekataḥ – one
ekāvasthā – singular state
ekībhūtaṁ – one causal medium
ekībhūya – in combination,
eko = ekaḥ = one
eṣā – this
etac = etat = this
etan = etat = this
eti – accomplished, approach, flows
evam – thus
evānusandheyo = eva (also) + anusandheyaḥ (investigation)
evāstu = eva (so) + astu (is)

F, G

gā – go
gacchatā – walking
gacchati – fuses with, goes, secrete
gāḍhaṁ – firmly
gāḍhataraṁ – more compression
gaḥ – flow, pass through
gaja–karaṇī = purificatory action which is like that done by an elephant
gajendrasya – of king of elephants
gajo = gajaḥ = elephant
galitaṁ – oozes
gāṁ – push
gaṇā – groups
gandhaka – sulphur
gandhaṁ – odor
gaṅgā = Ganges–like subtle channel
gaṇikā – prostitute
gantavyaṁ – going
garta –.hole
gata – contained, related to
gatā – gone, is applied in focus
gatasy = gatasi = goes into
gate – is absorbed
gati – passage, coursing, flow
gato = gataḥ = goes into
gātra – body
gatvā – gives way
gavyaṁ – dairy products
ghanam – what is prominent
ghaṇṭā – bell
ghaṇṭādināda= ghaṇṭādi (bell and other) + nāda (naad supernatural sound resonance)
ghaṭa – body, containment
ghātakāḥ – degraders
ghaṭāvasthā – containment condition
ghaṭavat – like a jug
ghaṭīkṝtya = doing the containment condition
ghaṭitaṁ – closely
ghnaḥ – is eliminated, destroyer, destroys
ghoraṁ – deadly
ghrāṇa – smelling sense
ghrāṇa–randhrābhyāṁ = through the nostrils
ghrāṇena (through the nose)
ghṝhītvā – grasping
gīyate is proclaimed
go – cow
godhūma – wheat
gomaya – cow dung
gomukhākṝtiḥ – resembles the face of a cow
gomukhaṁ – cow–face
gopanīya – highly confidential, confidential process
gopitā – concealed
gopya – by secret, confidential
gorakṣa – Gorakṣa
gorakṣa–nāthena = by Gorakshnath
gorakṣāsanam – Gorakṣa's posture
goṣaṁ – sound
grahaḥ – grasping, habitual
grāṇena – through the nose
granthayo = granthayaḥ = energy congestion location
granthi – congestion of subtle energy
grasate – consume
graset – should move, should swallow
gṛhṇīyāt – arrested
grīvodaraḥ = grīva (neck) + udaraḥ (abdomen)
gudam – rectum, buttocks
gudāvarta – chronic constipation
guhyam – secret
gulkaṁ – ankle
gulma – gland malfunction
gulmājīrṇa = gulma (abdominal disorders) + ajīrṇa (indigestion)
gulmodar – spleen and abdomen diseases
gulpha – ankle, heel
gulphāntaraṁ = gulpha (ankle) + antaraṁ (other)
guṇa – characteristic, natural feature, natural abilities
guṇitaṁ – supernatural skills
guptā – hiding, secluded
guptāsanaṁ – gupta secret posture
gurave – to the proficient yoga teacher
guru – proficient yoga teacher, empowered yoga teacher
gurunātha – master of the guru lineage
gurūpadeśato = guru (proficient yoga teacher) + upadeśataḥ (instructions)
gurūpadiṣṭa – taught by the guru

H

hanti – is ruined
hanuṁ – chin
haraṁ – elimination
haraṇaṁ – eliminator
harate – controlled
harati – eliminates
hariṇasya – of the deer
harīta – green
hasta – hand
hastābhyāṁ – with fingers

hataḥ – struck
hāṭaka–peṭakam – box of gold
haṭha – kundalini manipulation for psychic energy transformation, kundalini manipulation for subtle body transformation
haṭhābhyāse – in the practice of kundalini manipulation for subtle body transformation
haṭhābhyāsibhiḥ – by those who practice kundalini manipulation for subtle transformation
haṭhaḥ – kundalini manipulation for psychic energy transformation, kundalini manipulation for subtle transformation
haṭha–karmiṇaḥ = practicioners of kundalini manipulation for psychic energy transformation
haṭha–kriyā = kundalini manipulation for subtle body transformation
hetu – cause
hikkā – hiccup
hiṁsā – non–violence
hingu – asafetida
hita – adequate, ample, beneficial
hṝdayaḥ – core existence
hṝdayāvadhi = hṝdaya (chest region) + avadhi (down to)
hṝdaye – against the chest, in the chest
hṝdi – heart
hrīmatī – modesty
hṝt – chest, eliminates
hṝtaḥ – took
hutam = performance of Vedic religious ceremony with appropriate austerity

I

icchatā – those who desire, wishing for
icchor = icchoh = desirous
iḍā – left spinal nadi subtle channel
iḍā–pingalayor = iḍā–pingalayoḥ = left and right channels
iḍayā – through the left breath course, through the left subtle channel
indhanāni – fuels
indriya – senses
iṣṭaṁ – desired
īśvara – Supreme Lord
īśvara–pūjanam – ceremonial worship of the Supreme Lord
īśvarī – supreme lady, goddess
iśvarya – supernatural powers which are natural for God
itarābhyāsāḥ = itara (other) + abhyāsāḥ (practice)
itaratra – elsewhere
itare – others
itīritam – put
ivāmbare – like in the sky
ivārṇave – like in the ocean

J

jagad – world
jāgarti – aroused
jagat – world
jāgradavasthāyāṁ – awakened condition
jāgrat – waking
jahāti – leaves
jala – water, nectar
jaladhi – ocean
jālandhara – chin to throat compression, compressing the lower jaw against the throat, tightly pulling the lower jaw back against the throat, liquid arresting
jalandhara – liquid-arresting,
jālandharākhyo = jālandhara (liquid-arresting) + ākhyaḥ (called)
jale – in water
jalena – by the perspiration
jālena – in the lure
jalodarā – body swelling (dropsy
jana – materialistic people
janakaṁ – produce, production
jānanti – they know
jana–saṅga – company of materialistic people
jānāti – knows
janayati – generate
jānīte – learnt
jānor = jānoḥ = by the knee
jantūjjhitam = jantūj (jantūḥ –living being,) + jhitam (hitam – facilities)
jānū – thigh, leg, knee
jānūrvor = jānūrvoḥ = jānu (leg) + ūrvoḥ (of thigh)
jarā – old age
jarādibhiḥ – old age and such infirmities
jāraṇāt – from being combined

jarāntakaraṇaṁ = what causes the end of old age
jārayet – should absorb
jarāyutaḥ = being with old age

jas – produced in
jāta – appearing, manifests
jāte – usually
jātena – exudes
jaṭhara – digestive power
jaṭharāgni – gastric heat, digestive heat
jatrūrdhva = jatru (collar bone) + ūrdhva (over)
jayanti – effective
jāyate – achieves, becomes, control, experience, is applicable, is capable, manifesting, occurs, produce, situated, supersede
jayati – achieves, supersedes, transcends
jayo = jayaḥ = subjugation
jharjhara – drum
jihvā – tongue
jihvayā – through the (u–shaped curled) tongue
jīmūta – cloud
jīryate – increase
jīryati – digests
jitaḥ – conquered
jitvā – becoming objective to, transcends
jiva – individual
jīvanaṁ – life, living creature
jīvanmuktiś = jīvanmuktiḥ = liberated while using a material body
jīvati – lives, pursues mundane existence
jivatma – limited individual spirt
jīvayati – lives
jīvitam – life
jñaiḥ – by those who know
jñāna – techniques, knowledge, insight consciousness
jñānī – perceptive person
jñāś = jñāḥ = knowers
jñātavyaṁ – what is known
jñātvā – knowing the technique
jñeya – what is known, is learnt, known
jvalano = jvalanaḥ = blazing energy
jvaraṁ – fever
jyotī – light
jyotiṣi – spiritual light

K

kācid = kācit = any
kadācana – any time, someone
kadaśana – bad food, stale
kāhalajās – horn
kaivalyam – isolated core–self
kāla – death, death which is enforced by time, time approaching as death
kalā – increment
kalā – nectar, nectarine
kāla–daṇḍaṁ = death which is enforced by time
kalā–jalaṁ = bliss–yeilding subtle fluid
kālajit – one who supersede death
kāla–kūṭam – poison drunk by Shiva
kālaṁ – time, time advancing as death
kalāṁ – tongue
kalātmane = kalā (atom–like) + ātmane (self)
kalpa–latikā = wishfulfilling tree
kāma–devo = kāma–devaḥ = deity who inspires love
kamaṭho = kamaṭhaḥ – legendary tortoise
kāminyā – a seductive woman
kampo = kampaḥ = trembling
kandaṁ – bulb
kandharām – neck
kandordhve = kanda (bulb) + ūrdhve (on)
kāni – what
kanīyasi – in the initial stage
kāṅkṣate – desire
kaṇṭha – throat
kaṇṭha–mudrayā = compression of the throat
kaṇṭha–nāle = to the throat
kānti – beauty, radiance
kapala – head, skull
kapālabhātiḥ –process which causes light to appear in the head, intense rapid breathing with stress on exhaling
kapālāvadhi = kapāla (head) + avadhi (up to)
kāpālike – in Kapalika Yoga Sect
kapāṭa – door
kapāṭakam – condition
kapha – mucus, sinus
kaphodbhavāḥ – kapha (sinus problems) + udbhavāḥ (producing)
karā – action
kara – hand
kārakaḥ – cosmic engineer, producer, cause
karaṁ – producer
karaṇa – psychic organ, procedure, technique, performing
kāraṇaṁ – cause
karaṇḍakam – jewelbox
karaṇī – procedure
karaṇī viparītākhyā = karaṇī viparīta (upturning the body to use gravity to reverse the flow of bodily fluids) + ākhyā (called)
karau – hands

kārayet – should do, perform, work
kāreṇa – by work
karī – produce
kāri – producing
karma – action, purificatory physio–psychic acts
karmaṇa – cultural activity, social activity
karmāṇi – purificatory physio–psychic acts, special actions
karṇākṣi = karṇa (ear) + ākṣi (eye)
karṇau – ears
karṇe – in the ear
karo = karaḥ = results
karoti – does
karpūram – camphor
kārśyam – causing flatness
kartāsau – master of both
kartavya – perform, should be involved, is done, be performed
karuṇāṁ – special attention
kāryā – reason
kāryam – do, is practiced, performing
kārya–siddhiḥ = successfully accomplished
kāsa – cough
kaścid – anyone
kāṣṭhavaj = kāṣṭhavat = like firewood
kāṣṭhe – in firewood
kasyacit – anyone, whoever
kathā – discussion
kathaṁ – how
kathitā – described, taught, said
kathyante – were described by
kathyate – is attributed
kaṭukāmla = kaṭuka (pungent) + amla (sour)
kaṭv = kaṭu = bitter
kaya – body
kāyaḥ – body
kecid = kecit = some
kedāraṁ – level of Shiva
kenāpi – also by those
keṣāṁcit – some, according to some
kesarī – lion
kevala – aloneness, independent, spontaneous, only
kha divine space
khādyate – devoured
khago = khagaḥ = bird
khalu – indeed
khaṁ – divine sace
kha–madhye = in kha divine space
kha–mayaṁ = divine environment
khaṇḍa – sugar candy
khaṇḍamate– in the procedure of
khaṇḍanāstrama = khaṇḍana (destroying) + astrama (weapon)
khaṇḍayitvā – having shattered
khe – in divine space
khecaratāṁ – procedure for transiting through kha divine space
khecari – blocking the air pathway with the tongue, procedure for transiting through kha divine space
khecarī – one who transits through kha divine space, procedure for transiting through kha divine space
kīdṝśaṁ – what kind
kinkiṇī – anklebell
kleśa – sickness
kola – jujube
komala – delicate
koṭi – ten million
krama – sequential process, procedure, methodical, by degrees
kriya – mystic technique, physio–mystic technique
kriyate – is done
kriyau – both activities
kṝmi – intestinal worm
kṝpākaraḥ – merciful
kṝśatā – thinness
kṝśatvaṁ – elegance
kṝte – doing, is done
kṝtvā – did, having, fusing, having directed, having done, having inserted, having located, having placed, having pressed, making
kṣālanaṁ – douche using water
kṣama – adequate, capable
kṣamā – tolerance
kṣaṇa – moment, time, instant
kṣaṇārdham = twenty four minutes (half–hour)
kṣarate – flow
kṣaya – consumption, destruction, health problems, decreasing
kṣetram – farmland
kṣipet – should place
kṣipraṁ – quickly
kṣiptaṁ – distraction
kṣīra – milk
kṣīyante – eliminated, terminate
kṣudhā – hunger
kubhair = kubhaiḥ = with body compression and breath energy distribution

kuhare – throat
kukkuṭāsana – kukkuṭāsana rooster posture
kula – clan, family
kulattha – horse gram beans
kula–vadhūr = kula–vadhūḥ = aristocratic lady
kulīnaṁ – good family
kumbha – jar, suspension of breathing with compression of accumulated breath energy, breath suspension
kumbhaka – breath retention with physio–physio–psychic compression, breath-suspension contraction, breath retention with energy regulation, suspension of breathing process
kumbhayet – should retain breath with physio–psychic compression
kumbhikeyaṁ = kumblikā (breath retention after inhalation and compression) + iyam (this)
kuñcanenāśu = kuñcanena (by contraction/compression with psychic focus) + āśu (promptly)
kuñcikayā – by a key
kuṇḍalī – kundalini lifeforce
kuṇḍalinī – kundalini lifeforce which stays in the fire pit, psychic lifeforce
kuṇḍalinyai – O kundalini lifeforce
kuṇḍaly = kundali = coiled potency
kūpa – on posts
kuraṅgasya – of antelope
kūrmāsanaṁ – tortoise posture
kūrpara – elbow
kuru – locating, situating
kurute – facilitates, should go
kurvan – doing, performing
kuryād = kuryāt = should make, does effect, should do, should perform, should be done
kuṣṭha – leprosy, skin disease
kutaḥ – where, wherefrom, why, what other
kuṭilākārā – coiled shape
kuṭilāṅgī = all–penetrating energy
kuto = kutaḥ = how
kutra where
kutrāpi = where as well
kvaṇaḥ – here–there
kvaṇako = kvanakaḥ = here–there

L

labdhā – obtain
labhate – gets, obtain
labhyate – is learnt, is obtained, understood, exists
lagati – enters, saturates, thrusting
lāghavam – flexibility || 19 ||
laghu – quickly
lagutā – lightness
lakṣaṇam – characteristic, indication
lakṣya – focus, mark
lalāṭa – forehead
lambikāgram = lambikā (palate) + agram (above)
lambikordhvataḥ = lambika (soft palate) + ūrdhvataḥ (above)
laśunā – garlic
laulyaṁ – being whimsical
lavaṇam – salty
lavaṇoṣṇa = lavaṇa (salty) + uṣhṇa (peppery)
lāvaṇya – feminine charm
laya – variety dissolution, absence of mento–emotional trauma, blank thoughtless idealess mental condition, dissolution of mundane ideation interest, focused absorption, absorption
layānandaḥ = laya (absence of mento–emotional trauma) + ānandaḥ (bliss)
layodbhavam = focus into spiritual existence
layopāyā = techniques of mento–emotional energy suspension
lepanam – smearing
līlā – spontaneously happening
līlayā – playfulness
līnas – becomes unwanted
līnatām – dissolved
lingaṁ – erect kundalini
lipyate – polluted
līyate – be quiescent, is stilled, is quelled
locanaḥ – eye
lohakāreṇa – by the blacksmith
lokeṣu – perception environments

M

mā – not
madhūni – honey
madhura – sweet
madhv = madhu = honey
madhya – central, in the middle, mid–portion, through the middle channel, middle energy
madhyagaḥ – goes through the middle, coursing through the middle, middle course, fusing into
madhyamā – middle

madhyamārge = in the middle course
madhya–mārghaś = madhya–mārghaḥ = central passage
madhyame – in the median level, in the middle channel
madhyandine – at noon
madhyā–tarjanībhyāṁ = middle and index fingers
madhye – between, in between, in the center, in the median stage, in the middle, in the midst, into
madya – liquor
mahā – great, prominent
mahā–bala = great strength
mahā–bandha = great sealing containment control
mahā–kāyo = mahā–kāyaḥ = superfit body
mahā–khagaḥ = kundalini
mahāmudrā – great mystic compression direction control, great mystic–arresting action
mahān – very
mahāpathaḥ – great transit
mahā–śaktyai = great intelligent energy personified
mahāsiddhā – great perfected yogis
mahā–śūnyaṁ = great idealess imageless mental content
mahati – loud
mahātmabhiḥ – by the great souls
māhātmyaṁ – magnificence
mahā–vedhaḥ = great centralized upper flow
maithunād = maithunāt = during sexual intercourse
makarandaṁ – flower nectar
mala – flaw, impurity, polluted energy, pollutant
malādikaḥ – maladies and related health problems
malākalāsu = mala (pollutants) + ākalāsu (in saturation)
malākulam = mala (pollutants) + ākulam – (saturated)
mama – my
māṁsa – flesh, meat
mana – mind, mental focus, mind energy
mānaṁ – pride
manasā – into mental focus, mind
manasa = mind
mānasaṁ – mind's natural interest
manasi – mind
mandāgni = manda (slow) + agni (digestive heat)
maṇḍalam – digestive chakra complex, circle
maṇḍale – on the entire
manda–mandam = slowly
maṇḍapa–vedi – balcony
manīṣiṇā – by a wise yogi
manobhilaṣitaṁ = manah (feelings) +abhilaṣitaṁ (cherished desire)
manonāthas – controller of the mind
manonmanī – blank thoughtless idealess mental condition
mano–vṛttir = mano–vṛttiḥ = mento–emotional energy of the mind
mano–yuktaṁ = yogically controlled mind
mantra – sound control
manya – consider
manyāmahe – I think
manye – I think
maraṇa – death, death of the physical system
mardala – drum
mardanam – rubbing
mārga – techniques, method, path, process, transit, course
marut – breath–infused kundalini energy, lifeforce
māruta – air–infused breath energy, breath–infused energy, kundalini lifeforce, air regulator deities who regulate subtle breath energy, fresh air
mārutāpūritodaraḥ = māruta (air) + āpūrita (full) + udaraḥ (abdomen)
māsa – month
māsārdhena – by half of a month
māsordhvaṁ = māsa (month) + ūrdhvaṁ – after
mastakam – head
māstu = mā (not) + astu (is)
māstu = not to be
mataḥ – categorized as, opinion
mātaṅga – elephant
matāntare – in a different opinion
maṭhe – in the residence
maṭhikā – hut
maṭho = maṭhaḥ = residence
matim – thought
mātra – essential compostion, interval, measure, merely, period, merely
matsara – selfish
matsyān – fish
matsyendra – Matsyendra

matta – carefree and intoxicated
matysanāthoditam – detailed by Matysanath
maulir = mauliḥ = foundation
mayūram – peacock
māyūram – peacock
meda – fat
meḍhreṇa – through the penis
megha – cloud
mehanena – while in sexual intercourse
meṇḍhrād = meṇḍhrāt = regarding the male organ
meṇḍhre – above the male organ
meru – sushumna central channel
miśrayet – mix
mitāhāra – eating the absolute minimum, approved sparse diet
mitāhāram = mita (moderate) + āhāram (consumption)
mitāhārī – one with sparse diet, with moderate consumption
mitāśanaḥ = mita (moderate) + aśanaḥ (diet)
mitāśinaḥ – one with a sparse diet
mithyā – schizophrenic
mocanaṁ – relief
mokṣa – liberation from material existence
mokṣadvāraṁ = entry to liberation
mokṣākhyo = mokṣākhyaḥ = called liberation
mokṣāya – liberating
mṝdulaṁ – soft
mriyate = phased–out
mṝṇāla – fiber of lotus
mṝtāvasthā – death–like state
mṝtavat – like a dead body
mṛto = mṛtaḥ = death
mṛtyu – death
mṝtyu – death
mudghādi – mung and similar foods
mūḍhānāṁ – foolish people, dull-witted people
mudra – foremost of the mystic checking practices
mudrā – mystic arresting action, mystic checking practice, physio–psychic application technique
mudrābhyāse = mudra (mystic arresting actions) + abhyāse (in practice)
mudrādi – foremost of the mystic checking practices
mudrākhyaṁ – mystic checking practices
mudreyaṁ – practice of mystic–arresting actions
mudritaṁ – compressed
muhūrta – forty-eight minutes
muhūrta–dvaya = two periods of forty-eight minutes each
muhyanti – they are mistaken
mukhaṁ – mouth, opening, topmost, entrance
mukhenācchādya = mukhenāt (by the entrance) + chādya (cover)
mukhyaṁ – primary
mukhyatamaṁ – most important
mukta – liberated
muktāsanaṁ – mukta posture
mukti – released from, liberation from material existence
muktidaḥ – what gives liberation
muktvā – being freed from
mūla – anus–coccyx complex, root, anus–perineum
mūla–bandhanāt = due to physio–psychic compression of the anus–coccyx complex
mūlabandhaś = mūlabandhaḥ = uplifting the anal sphincter muscles
mūlārpita–placed at the base
mūle – on the root
muñcati – abandon
munibhir = munibhiḥ = by the yogi philosophers
muniḥ – yogi philosopher
mūrcchā – lapse in objectivity while transiting to other dimensions, fainting slow-inhale with long retention infusion, stunned condition
mūrcchākhyeyaṁ = mūrcchā (mūrcchā technique) + ākhyā (is termed) + iyaṁ (this)
mūrcchito = mūrcchitaḥ = disabled
mūrdhāntara = mūrdha (peak) + antara (middle)
mūrdhnaḥ – from the head
mūtra–purīṣayoḥ = urine and feces

N

nābher = nābheḥ = navel
nābhi – navel
nabho = nabhaḥ = heaven
nāda – naad subtle sound resonance, naad supernatural sound resonance
nādābhivyaktir = nāda (naad subtle sound) + abhivyaktiḥ (manifestation)

nādajo = nādajaḥ = produced by naad supernatural sound resonance

nādānusandhāna = nādānusandhāna = nāda (naad supernatural sound) + anusandhāna (spiritual focus into resonance) (continuous spontaneous inner focus)
nādāsaktaṁ = absorbed in naad supernatural sound resonance
nāḍī –subtle arteries and veins, subtle channels, subtle tubes, subtle veins and arteries
nāḍībhyām – through the two subtle passages
nāḍikā – nadi subtle veins and arteries
nādopāsanam = nāda (naad supernatural sound resonance) + upāsanam (practice)
nādopāsti–rato = nādopāsti–rataḥ = obsessed with interest–focus on naad supernatural sound resonance
nādṝte = na (no) + ādṝte (careful
nāḍyā –subtle passage, subtle channels
nahi – not, surely not,
naiva = not even, no ever
nālotkaṭāsanaḥ = nāla (tube) + utkaṭāsanaḥ (utkaṭa squatting posture)
nāma – is called, name, that which is called
namaḥ – honor
namastubhyaṁ – I give reverential honor, offer due regards
nānā – variety, various
nānāvidhā – various types
nānyaḥ = na (non) + anyah (other)
nānyathā = not otherwise
nānyatra = nowhere
nāpekṣate = having no interest
naraḥ – person, man
narāṇāṁ – men
nārī – woman
nāśa – suspension
nāsāghre – on tip of nose
nāsāgra – tip of the nose
nāśaṁ – lost
nāśanaḥ – removes, elimination, removal
nāsānāle – through the nostril
nāsanaṁ = na (not) + āsanaṁ (posture)
nāsikāṁ – nostrils
naṣṭaṁ – disappeared
nāsti = is not
nasyaṁ – snuff
nata = ata = without restriction
natāṁso = natāṁsaḥ = beginning a circular motion
nātha – master, lord, manager
nāthaṁ – Nāth
nāthāya – to Lord Shiva
nātmānaṁ = na (not) + ātmānaṁ (core–self)
nātra – not here, not present
nātra – not present
nātyuchcha = na (not) + atyuchcha (loud
nauliḥ – nauli abdominal muscular action
naulikaṁ – abdominal muscular action
navanīta – butter
nāyakaḥ – king
nayane –in the eyes
nayet – obtain, should channel
netiḥ –nasal–sinus cleansing
netra – eye
nibaddho = nibaddhaḥ = arrested
nibandhayet – should retain
nibhaṁ – similar
nibhṝtaṁ – immoveable
nīchāyataṁ – low
nidhāya – rest on
nidrā – sleep
nidrasya – of blissfull
nidritaḥ – state of blissfull
nigadyate – is rated
nigama – ritual worship
nighadyate – is known as
nihanti – attack, remove, eliminate
niḥśabdaṁ – without sound
niḥsāratayāntya = niḥsāratayā (rejected) + antya (last part)
niḥśeṣa – all, complete
niḥśeṣāśeṣa – totally absent
niḥsṝtāṁ – diffused
niḥsvanam – sound, non–physical sounds
niḥśvāsocchvāsa = without breathing inspiration or expiration
nijaṁ – his own, one's own
nikṣipya – putting
nimeṣonmeṣa – blinking of eyelashes
nimnagānām – nadi subtle channel
nināda – naad supernatural sound resonance
nirākāraḥ – immaterial
nirākulam – calm
nirālamba – without support, free of conventional impressions, independent of everything else
nirālambākhya – supportless
nirālambāntare = nirālamba (self–supporting) + āntare (existential space)
nirāmayam – free of trauma

nirañjana – flawless, spiritual purity, spotless

nirarthakāḥ – without value
nīrasāḥ – without flavor
nirāśrayam – non–reliant
nirāyāsāt – effortless
nirbhayaṁ – without fear
nirgamayec = nirgamayet = should draw out
nirgata – disappear
nirīkṣen = nirīkṣet = should look, focus
nirmalam – stainless
nirmatsarāṇāṁ = kind–hearted
nirmūlayati – without grip
nirodhakaḥ – restraint
nirodhanaṁ – externally withdrawn and internally focused
nirodhataḥ – compressing and directing
nirodhāvadhi = nirodha (checking thoroughly) + avadhi (until)
nirodhayet – should direct, infuse and channel
nirudhya – by checking
nirupadrave – in a place which is free from social disruptions
nirūpitā – was designed
nirvikalpam – idealess transcendental consciousnes
nirvikāraś – without changes
nirvīryā – without effect
nirvyādhiḥ – without disease
niśā – night
niścala – immovable, compressed and distributing
niścala–dṝśā = without shifting focus
niścale – in mentally manipulating
niścayam – eternally consistent reality
niścayāt – from determination
niśceṣṭo = niśceṣṭaḥ = motionless
niścitā – definite, certain
niṣevyate – drink
niśitāṅkuśaḥ = niśita (sharp) + aṅkuśaḥ (goad)
niṣkrāntis = niṣkrāntiḥ = final out-flow of lifeforce
nispanda – motionless
niṣpatti – full proficiency, accomplishment
niṣpatty–avasthā = full proficiency condition
niṣphalau – are without consequence
niṣpīḍya – press
niśvasya – hissing
nityam – always, constant, constantly, daily, eternal, regularly
niveśya - push through
niyama – recommended behavior, recommended conduct
niyamāghrahaḥ – adhering fanatically to moral stipulations
niyamane – controlled
niyameṣv = niyameṣu = of the recommended conduct
niyamitaṁ – what is retained with focus
niyamya – restricted
niyojayet – place, should focus consciousness, should position
nodeti – expanding
nopamānaṁ = not shame
nṝṇām – from human beings, ofmen
nyañcan – going down
nyasta – inserted

O, P

ogha (various)
pācanādi – good digestion and related bodily functions
pāda – foot
padāghra – feet stretched forward
padam – abode, existential environment, foot, foundation position, residence, situation, thigh
pāda–mūlena = by the heel
pādāngguṣṭhau – big toes
padārtham – items
pādasya – of the foot
padasya – of the situation
padavī – passage, content
padma – lotus plant, lotus throat chakra, lotus posture
padmāni = lotus–shaped energy vortexes
padmāsanam – lotus posture
padmāvadhi = padma (lotus) + avadhi (up to)
pakṣād = pakṣāt = two weeks
pakṣaḥ – wing
palita – grey hair
pañca – five
pañca–daśāyatam = pañca–daśa (five and ten)
pāṇī – hands
pañjare – in the psyche (body)
panthā – process of transcendence
papa – faults
pāpaugha = pāpa (fault) + ogha (various)
para – highest, other person
parā – other
parabodhaṁ – enlightening influence
pāradam – mercury
paradīptiṁ – inflames
paragṝhya – grasp around

parākramaḥ = tremendous energy
paraṁ – supreme, primal, supreme cause
paraṁ padam = supreme residence
paramaṁ – supermost, supreme
paramānanda – most sublime pleasure
paramātmanoḥ – of the supreme spirit
paramātmeti = paramatma (Supreme Soul) + iti (thus)
parameśvaraḥ – Supreme Lord
parameśvarī – supreme goddess kundalini
parāmṝśet – should sensitively be absorbed
parāṅmukhīṁ – turn up and backward
parāyaṇaḥ – one who is devoted, one who is very sincere
pare – others
paricālanīyā – motivate to move
paricaya – familial, integration
parichayāvasthā – integration condition
paricito = paricitaḥ = directed
paridhāna – compression
parighāyate – bolt
parikīrtitā – fittingly describe
parinyasta – stretched out
parityāgād = parityāgāt = due to complete abandonment, being detached from
parityajya – abandoning
parivartitāṅgaḥ = turn–twist about the limb
pariyojayet – should press into
paro = paraḥ = superior
pārṣṇi – heel
pārṣṇyā – with the heel
pārśva – on sides, limb
pārvati – Parvati
paryantaṁ – extended time, extensive, until, up till
paryāya – synonym
pāśa – noose
paścima – pulling up, reversal, behind
paścimatānam –fingers–grab–toes–forward–bend posture
paścimatānamāsana –fingers–grab–toes forward–bend posture
paścime – in the rear, behind
paśyann = paśyan = vision
paśyed = paśyet = should see
patad – falling
pātaka – faults
pataty = patati = falls
pāṭavāt – proficiency
pātena – by ejaculating
pāṭha – study
pathi – moving in public places, on roadways, passage
pathyābhyāṁ – turmeric
pathyam – suitable, supportive
patitaṁ – fallen
paṭolaka – cucumber
patra – leaf, petals
pavanābhyāsa – practice of breath-infusion
pavanaṁ – air, air energy, air infusion, air energy in the blood stream, breath infusion, fresh air, lifeforce, viral air, breath energy, infused breath energy, psyche-energy
pavanī–kriyām – breath-infusion technique
payasy = payasyi = water
pāyau – in the anus
phala – result
phalādika – fruits and related foods
phalāvadhi = phala (result) + avadhi (until)
phaṇāvatī – supernatural serpent
phūtkāraṁ = hissing sound
piban – drink
piben = pibet = drinks, would absorb
pidhāya – covering
pīḍyate – traumatized
piṇḍa – body, subtle body
pingalā – right spinal nadi subtle channel
pingalayā – through the right course
piṇyāka = oil–cake
pīṭha – location, posture, seated posture
pitta, pittol – bile
pītvā – having inhaled
pīyūṣam – nectar
plavate – floats
plāvayed = plāvayed = saturating
plāvinī – flotation technique, gulp-swallow infusion
plīha – glandular malfunction
plīhādikān = spleen and other specific disorders
plīhodaraṁ = plīha (spleen disease) + udaraṁ (abdomen)
prabandhāt – from compression
prabhāvān = prabhāvāt = illumination
prabhāvataḥ – splendor
prabhāveṇa – by influence of, by means of
prabodhayitum – to infuse with the highest consciousness–energy
prabuddhāyāṁ – perceptively aroused
pracaṇḍa – terrible
prachakṣate – are considered, is recognized as

pradā – yields
pradam – causes the development
pradarśitā – shown
pradāyakaḥ – yields
pradāyinī – confers, grants
pradhvas – cessation
pradīpanam – energizing
pradīpikāṁ – crystal clear insight
pradīpta – effective reactions, illuminated
pragharṣayet – should rub
praghṝhya – arrested, grasping
praharaṇam – expert archer
praharārdha – half of three hours (90 minutes)
prahita – are deposited
prāhuḥ – they say, is called, said
prajalpo = prajalpah = excessive conversation
prajāyate – achieve, attains, becomes, is produced, manifest, occurs
prākāra – wall
prakārāḥ – types
prakāśitā – by exposing
prakopataḥ – pertaining to irregularity
prakṣālanopāyaḥ = prakṣālana (cleansing) + upāyaḥ (method)
prakupyati – is scattered
prakurvīta – should do
pralāpaḥ – talkative
prāleyaṁ – subtle secretions
pralīyate – dissolved, absorbed
pramāṇa – right perception
pramucyate – eliminates
prāṇa – breath-infusion, physio-subtle air energy, fresh air, subtle breath energy, vital energy, infused kundalini lifeforce, air, fresh air intake, positively charged subtle force, physio–subtle air energy, breath–derived energy, lifeforce
praṇamya – giving due honor
prāṇānile – in the flow of pranic subtle energy
prāṇāpānau – positively and negatively charged subtle force
praṇāśanam – termination
pranaṣṭa – suspension, ceased
praṇaśyati – cut
prāṇāyāmaṁ – breath-infusion
prāntaṁ – being confidential
prāpayen = prāpayet = conveys
prapīḍayet – should be compressed
praposaṇam – nourishing food
prāpte – after
prāptuṁ – to obtain
prapūrya – filled
prasāda – tranquility, special favor
prasannatā – cheerfulness
prasāritaṁ – stretched
prasārya – stretching out
praśasyate – is known as
prasiddhyati – it gives full success
prasuptā – sleep
praśuṣhyanti – are removed
prātaḥ – early morning, sunrise
prathama – first, initially, beginning
pratītaṁ – wisdom
pratyāharec = pratyāharet = retract
pratyaya – perception
pravadati – declares, terms
pravakṣyāmi – I explain
pravartate – exists, springs up
pravartita – interacting, producer
pravartita (introduce) + udāra (ample)
praveśa – insertion
praveśayet – should insert
pravīṇaścet – totally destroy
praviśati – enter
praviśed = praviśet = should enter
praviṣṭā – pressing into, enters
pravṝttiḥ – movement
prayacchataḥ – gives
prayacchati – acquire
prayānti – gives, diminish
prayāsa – exertion, irrational exertion, strenuous
prayāte – it moves
prayāti – enter, is quiescent
prayatnataḥ – thoroughly, with effort, with great efford, with special effort
prayatnena – in all respects, with effort
prochyate – is known
proktā – mentioned, titled
proktaṁ – appears, explained, is called, were described, said
pron – developed
protsārayan – infuse
pṝṣṭha – buttock
pṛthvī – earth
pucche – tail
pūjayet – worship
pūjitaṁ – is worshipped
pūjyate – is sincerely honored
puṁsa – man, humans, people
punaḥ – again, repeat
pungavaiḥ - by the greatest , by the prominent

puṇya – meritorious actions, pious acts
puṇyavatāṁ – pious entities
pūraka – inhalation
pūrakānte = pūraka (inhalation) + ante (at the end)
purāṇāni – ancient
purastāc = purastāt = from the front
pūrau – and inhalation
pūrayet – should inhale, compress
pūrayitvā – inhaling
pūritam – infused, inhaled
pūrṇaḥ – full, entirely filled
purogamāḥ – irregularities
puruṣaḥ – person, male human
pūrva – before, first, initial
pūrvācāryair = pūrvācāryaiḥ = by ancient yoga teachers
pūrvavat = as before
pūryeta – compression
puṣṭaṁ – nourishing
puṭa – buttocks
puṭa–nayana = eye

Q, R

raja – female reproduction hormone concentrate, female reproductive fluid
rāja – remaining introverted while externally occupied
rājadanta – teeth
rājapathāyate – main access
rāja–yoga = mystic process of remaining introverted while being externally occupied
rāja–yoga–padaṁ = accomplishment of remaining introverted while externally occupied
rakṣaṇīyaṁ – conserve
rakṣayet – should be preserved, should conserve
rakṣed = rakṣet = should converse
rāma – Rama
ramamāṇam – enjoying
rasa – flavor, mercury, quicksilver
rasanā – of the tongue
rasasya – of quicksilver
ratasyaiva = ratasya (of delight) + eva (specifically)
ratna – diamonds
rātrau – at night energy
rātre – in the night
rātrindivātmakam = rātrin (night) + diva (day) + ātmakam assumes the form
reca – exhalation
recakādau = recaka (exhalation) + ādau (beginning)
recakaṁ – exhalation
recayet – should exhale, expell
ṛju – erect
ṛjutāṁ – is subdued
ṛjvībhūtā – becomes straight
rodhānte = rodha (checking action) + ante (in the end)
roga – disease
rogādikaṁ – disease and related trauma
rogaughaṁ = roga (disease) + ogham (various)
roma – hair
roma–mātraṁ = a hair's width
ṛtumatyā – menstruation
ruchiraṁ – pleasant
rudra–granthiṁ = energy congestion of Rudra third-eye chakra
rudrāṇī = śāmbhavī arresting visual focus between the eyebrows
rugmaṇḍala – range of disease
rūkṣam – saturated with oil
rūpa – sexually–appealing, color, form
rūpiṇi – spiritual form
ruto = rutaḥ = vibrated

S

śabavad = śabavat = like a dead body
śabdaḥ – sound
śabdāḥ – term
śabdenoditā = śabdena (by word) + uditā (as used)
sad = sat = reality perceptive
sadā – always, consistently, regular, when
sadaiva – as always
ṣaḍbhir = ṣaḍbhiḥ = of six
sādhaka – student
sādhakam – the student yogi
sādhakottamaiḥ – by the best of the adept yogis
sādhanam – disciplined regular practice, procedure, spiritual self-disciplinary practice
sādhyate – overpowered
sadṛśa – compared, similar, like
sadya – immediately, rapidly
saha – with
sahajā – original
sahaja – produced
sahajaṁ – easy

sahajānanda – spontaneous spiritual feelings
sahajāvasthā = sahaja (original) + avasthā (condition)
sahajolī – upward muscular redirection of female sexual emission
sahasā – once
sāhasād – from being bold
sahasrāṇā – thousand
sahita – willful, dependent
śaila – mountain
saindhava – rock salt
śāka – leaves, vegetable
sakala – total
sakalāmayāḥ = sakala (all) + āmayāḥ (diseases)
śākotkaṁ = śāka (vegetables) + utkaṁ – too many
sākṣād = regarded as the same or the equivalent of
sakṣārā – salty
sākṣāt – directly
sakta – near
śaktaḥ – able to do
śaktau – subtle creative energy
śakti – breath-infused mento–emotional energy, kundalini psychic lifeforce, power potential, subtle creative energy, subtle creative energy, energy potency, emotional intelligence personified
śakti–madhye = into kundalini subtle creative energy
śaktyā – by forcibly
śāli – rice
salile – in water
śālinām = those who are well–to–do
sama – like, similar, with alignment
samabhāvataḥ – totally absent
samabhyaset – proficiently practiced, thoroughly practice
samācaret – should thoroughly practice
samādāya – taking
samadhi – continuous effortless linkage to a higher environment, divinity, or person
samādhinā – continuous linkage, by continuous linkage to a divine environment or person
samagraṁ– aggregate energies
samāhitaḥ – adjusted, focusing, meditatively focused
samākṝṣya – drawn together
samākuñcya – contract completely, full extraction
samaṁ – equal, similarity
samanvitam – is connected
samarasatvaṁ – being similar
sāmarolīti = sa (that) + amaroli (self–urine consumption) + iti (thus)
samāropya – restricting
samartho = samarthaḥ = is capable
samārūḍhaḥ – proficient
samāsīnaḥ – sitting together with
samāśraya – giving shelter, complete source
samatvam – equanimity
samāyāti – goes
sambadya – joint
sambandho = sambandhaḥ = infused composition
saṁbhāra – quantity
sambhavaḥ – experience, production, what is produced
sambhavaḥ – production
śāmbhavam – state of Shambhu Shiva
sambhavatīha = sambhavati (integrate) + īha (here)
śāmbhavī – visual focus between the eyebrows
śāmbhavyāś = śāmbhavyāḥ = visual focus between the eyebrows
śambhunā – by Shiva Shambhu
sambhūta – manifests
saṁcayāḥ – aggregate
saṁgrahaṇe – infusing
saṁhāra – destruction, dissolution
samīpe – near
samīraṇaḥ – breath, breath energy, lifeforce energy
saṁkṣīyate – is diffused
saṁmānyaḥ – completely fascinated by
saṁmatam – advocate, appreciated, definite opinion
saṁmilitāv = saṁmilitāu = fused
samo = sama = same as
sampādyaḥ – to accomplish
sampannā – endowed
sampāta – appears
sampīḍya – pressing, compressing
samprabudhyate – perceptively aroused
sāmpradāyikam – lineage of teachers
samprajāyate – experienced
samprāpta – transited to, reaches
samprasārya – spread apart
sampravartate – is experienced
samprītyai – thoroughly pleasing
samproktā – being proficient
sampūrṇa – complete
sampuṭitau – in cavity (concave area)

sāmrājyam – realm
saṁrakṣayed = saṁrakṣayet = fully contain
saṁśayaḥ – certainly, doubt, without a doubt
saṁsiddhiṁ – full perfection
saṁstha – lying
saṁsthāpya – assuming, in position, placing, well-situated
saṁsthau – placed on
saṁsthitā – performed
samucchinet – should cut
samudāhṝtaḥ – known
samudbhūta – that is
samudgatā – comes through
samudghamaḥ – manifestation
samutpannā – emerges
saṁveṣṭitaṁ – cover
samyag – proper, suitable, thoroughly, efficiently, proficiently,
samyak – exactly, precise, properly
sāmyaṁ – identification with
saṁyāma – linking focus meditation
saṁyāmair = saṁyāmaiḥ = by complete control
saṁyamya – closing
śāmyati – extinquished
saṁyojya – linking focus
ṣaṇ = ṣaṭ = six
śanaiḥ – gradually
sanātanī – eternal
sañcālayen = sañcālayet = should be
motivated, by the impetus
sañcālitā – motivated
sañcāra – flow, move
sandeho = sandehaḥ = doubt
sandhā – link access
sandhānaṁ – mastership
sandhāya – collective, combining, increases
sandhāyī – spiritually fused
sandhīyamānaṁ – united
sandīpana – by stimulating
sāndra–liptam – plastered
saṅgamaṁ – fussion
saṅgaś = saṅgaḥ = association
saṅkalpa – mental conjecture, mento–emotional intentions, idea, intentions
śaṅkha – conch
śaṅkhotthā – sound out of a conch
saṅkhyā – accounting
saṅkoca – contraction
saṅkocane – in synchronization
saṅkulaiḥ – with confusion
sannidhāya – placing
santāḍayec = santāḍayet = struck with force
santaptā – very infused
śāntim – psychological peace
santoṣa – contentment
santyakta – lacks enthusiam
sa–pāda = one and one–fourth
sa–pāda–koṭi = twelve and one half million
sapta – seven
saptati – seventy
sārabhūtaṁ = best
sāraḥ – essence, subtle hormone
saralā – straight
saraṇau – flowing
sāraṅga–bandhane = in arresting
śarasam – bow
sārdhaṁ – in combination, join equally
śarīra – material body
śarīrāgni = śarīra (physical body) + agni (digestive heat)
sarpati – spread
sarpavat – like a serpent
sarpo = sarpaḥ = serpent
sarṣapa – mustard seeds
śarva –Shiva
sarvadā – always
sarvāvasthā – all unwanted existential conditions
sarva–yogeṣu = of all yoga methods
sarvopadrava = sarva (all) + upadrava (contamination)
sasambhramau – both rapidly
śaśī – cooling moon feature
śastaṁ – mandatory
śasta–nālena = by a tube
ṣāṣṭika – sixty days rice
śasto = śastaḥ = recommended
śāstra – authoritative book, Vedic scriptures
śastrāgamodīraṇaṁ = śastra (weapon) +
agama (attack) +
śastraṁ – knife, weapons
śāstrārtha = śāstra (scripture) + artha (statements)
sasvanam – loud sound
sa–svanam = with a sound
ṣaṭ – six
satataṁ – always, constantly
sati – becomes, positioned
ṣaṭkam – six
sattvaṁ – charifying influence, clarifying energy of subtle material nature
sāttvikayā – of the clarifying energy of nature

satyam – realism, reality, really happen
śaucham – cleanliness
saukhyaṁ – happiness
sauvīra – sour gruel
sāvadhāne – attentively focalized, attentive focus
śavāsanaṁ – dead body pose, dead man posture
savya – left
savyake – on the left side
savyānge – on the left side
savyāpasavyataḥ = savya (left) + apasavyataḥ (right)
sāyam – at sunset
sayaṁ – evening
śayanaṁ – resting
śeṣās – the others remaining
sevanam – travelling
sevānāmādau – travelling about
sevita – serviced, controlled
sevyate – practiced
siddha – perfected yogi, perfected yogi posture, subtle body perfected yogis
siddhānāṁ – perfected beings
siddhānta – technical information about reality
siddhāsanābhyāsād – from practicing perfected yogi posture
siddhāsanam – siddha perfect yogi posture
siddhaye – in gaining proficiency, in the success
siddhe – in proficiency, with spontaneous skill
siddheḥ – of success, perfection
siddhi – mystic perfectional skill, success, supernatural skills, proficiency, yogic perfectional skill
siddhyati – accomplishes, become proficient, is fully accomplished, achieves, is proficient in
sidhyen = sidhyet = succeeds
śīghraṁ – quickly
śikhā – spike
śikṣāvatām – instruction
siktaṁ – wet
śilāgni = śila (stone) + agni (fire)
siṁhaṁ = lion, lion pose
siṁhāsanaṁ – lion pose
sirā–bandhaḥ = frenum
śiraḥ – head
sirājālam – network of nadi subtle tubes
śirāś = śirāḥ = head
sitā – white sugar
śītala – cool
śītalī –tongue contact infusion
sītkāṁ – seet sound
sītkārī – sītkārī hissing breath-infusion
śītoṣṇaṁ = heat and cold
śiva –Shiva
sīvantyāḥ – perineum
śleṣhmādhikaḥ = śleṣma (mucus) + adhikaḥ (excessive)
śleṣma – mucus
śmaśānaṁ – cremation area
smṝtam – is known as
smṝti – remembering
snānopavāsādi = snāna (bath) + upavāsa (fasting) + ādi (and related restrictions)
snighdhaṁ – smooth feeling and rich food
snuhī – milkhedge
śobhanānnaṁ – nourishing food
śobhate – appealing
ṣoḍaśa – sixteen
śodhana – purification, cleansing, clearance
śodhinī – clearance
soma – moon, moon–dominant left channel, subtle liquid which trickles down from above the palate, negatively–charged moon energy
somapānaṁ – subtle liquid which trickles from above the palate
śoṣaṇī – eliminates
sparśaṁ – surface
sphicau – buttocks
sphurati – manifests, quivers
sphuṭam – causal vibrations
sphuṭatvaṁ – manifestation
spṝśati – touches
śraddheyā – reliable
śramo = śramaḥ = fatigue
śrānti – fatigue
śravaṇa – hearing sense
śravaṇāu = ears
sravati – flows
śreṣṭhaṁ – best
śrī – choice, illustrious
śṝṇoti – hears
śṝṇuyād = śṝṇuyāt = due to hearing
srotaḥ – subtle channel
sṝṣṭi – creation
sṝṣṭimayaṁ – magic creation
śrūyamāṇe – hearing
śrūyante – are heard
śrūyate – heard

stabdhāntaḥ–karaṇa = stabdha (motionless) + āntaḥ–karaṇa (psychic organs in the subtle head)
stambhayed = stambhayet = supressed
stha – placed against, situated, remaining
sthairyaṁ – stability, still, steady
sthānakam – that position
sthānaṁ – location, position, region, steadiness, condition,
sthāṇuḥ – positioned firmly
sthāṇutvam – stabalization
sthāpayec = sthāpayet = should place
sthāpita – supported
sthātavyaṁ – having settled down
sthaulya – excessive
sthira – stabilized, steady
sthira–padaṁ – existential steady position
sthiratvaṁ – steadiness
sthirī – is steadily focused
sthiro = sthiraḥ = maintained consistently, steady
sthitiḥ – condition
sthito = sthitaḥ – seated, sitting, utilized
sthitvā – being seated, being situated
stho = sthaḥ = stationary
strī – woman
śubhakaro = śubhakaraḥ = auspicious
subhasma – selected ashes
śubhe – beautiful
subhikṣhe – in a place where food is easy to acquire
sūcakaḥ – indicated
śuddha – cleared, clearance
śuddhi – purifying clearance, clearance, purification
sudhāyai – ambrosia
sudhī – competent perceptive yogi, wise yogi
sugandho = sugandhaḥ = pleasing fragrance
sukaraṁ – easy to do
sukaraṇam – excellent practice
sukha – comfortably, happiness, easy, pleasure
sukhadaṁ –that which yields happiness
sukhade – in comfort
sukhī – happy
sukhopāyaṁ = sukha (happiness) + upāyaṁ (conveyor)
sukhopāyo = sukhopāyaḥ = easy mastery
śukraṁ – semen
sūkṣma – minute, subtle
sūkṣmakaḥ – subtler
sūkṣmataraṁ = from super–subtle
sumadhuraṁ – very sweet food
sunirmale – absence of flaws
suniścalam = non–moveable
śuṇṭhī – dry ginger
śūnya – idealess imageless mental content, blank state, mental state devoid of impressions
śūnyāśūnya = idealess imageless and idea–saturated image–prone mental content, subjective reality/objective reality
suptā – sleep, slumber
suptavadyo– sleeping
surājye – in a prosperous country
surataṁ – love motions
sūrya – by sun–dominant right side, sun–dominant right channel, right nostril, right nostril, sun–like energy
sūrya–bhedanam = right nostril infusion
sūryāgni = sūrya (sun–dominant right channel) + agni (fiery breath energy)
sūryāṅge – in sun–dominant right side
susamāhitaḥ – fully linking the attention to the objective
suṣiraṁ – cavity
susnigdha – agreeable, very soft
susthāne – suitable place
susthiram – very firm
susthirī – complete stability
suṣumnā – subtle central spinal passage
suṣumṇāyai – O subtle central spinal passage
sutarāṁ – very
sutīkṣṇaṁ – very sharp
sūtraṁ – thread
sva – own
svabhāvataḥ – what is inherent
svābhāvikī – inherent
svadehagau – own body
svalpaṁ – little by little
svāmī – worthy master
svāṅga – own organs
svāṅgulīḥ = sva (one's) + āṅgulīḥ (fingers)
svānubhavānvitāḥ – by personal insight
svarūpakam –inherent nature
śvāsa – bronchial disease
śvāsa–niśvāsaḥ = respiration
śvāsaś = śvāsaḥ = asthma
sva–sthāne = psyche–situated
svastho = svasthaḥ = self–absorbed
svastikaṁ – swastika posture
svataḥ – itself

svātmārāmaḥ – Svātmārāmaḥ
svāvagamyo = sva (self) + avagamyaḥ (intuition)
svayam – itself, self
svecchayā = sva icchayā = whimsically as desired wish
sveda – perspiration
syandinī – flows

T

tādṝn – such
tadvat – like
taila – oil
taila–varttiṁ = oil lamp
takra – buttermilk
takṣakeṇa – Takshak poisonous serpent
tala – lower part, sole
tālor = tāloḥ = palate
tāluni – into the palate
tānaṁ – retract
tandrā – fatigue
tantrāṇāṁ – mystic proficiency practice
tanvatāṁ – perform
tapa – deprivation in yoga austerities, deprivation as it relates to Vedic religious ceremony
tāpa – heat
tapasvinīm – ascetic widow
taptānāṁ – of the sun
tārakam – crossing beyond material existence
taraṁ vrajet = transits
tārayā – conceal
tāre – radiant
tarkeṇa – with logic
taruṇāyate – become sprite and youthful
tathādvaitaṁ = tathā (as) + advaitam (one reality without diversification)
tatparāḥ – fully devoted
tattva – essential causes, essential truth, reality, essential origin, knowledge of reality, primal cause, insight, causal energy
tattva–darśinām = reality–perceptive personalities
tattvānto = tattvāntaḥ = final source
tattvataḥ – essential cause
tejasvī – radiant
tīkṣṇa – pungent
tila – sesame
tiṣṭhatā – sitting or lying
tiṣṭhate – accomplished, established, permanent basis, remains
tiṣṭhati – sit, stays
tiṣṭhet – should be adopt, should situate
trāṭakam – blank staring
traya – three, triple procedure
tridaśāḥ – thirty prominent deities
tridhā – three kinds
tripathe – three conduits
triṣu – in three
tritaya – three
triveṇī – three primary nadi subtle passages
tṝṣā – thirst
tṝtīyāyāṁ – third progression
tūḍḍīyate = tu (but) + uḍḍīyate (rises)
tulyā – as is, equal, like
tundaṁ – abdominal cavity
turyā – fourth state
tyāga – indifference
tyāgī – one who abandoned the rewards of social contributions
tyajet – should exhale
tyakta – abandon

U

ubhau – two
ubhe – both
ucchinna – are absent
uchchāsano = uchchāsanaḥ = elevate
ucyate – concerns, is called, is declared, is described, is termed, is known as
udāhṝtam – declared
udakaṁ – water
udara – stomach, abdomen cavity
udaraḥ – abdomen
udayaṁ – rise
udbodhayec = udbodhayet = should be aroused
uḍḍīnaṁ kurute = will energetically fly up
uḍḍīyāna – drawing the abdomen cavity up under the rib cage and back towards the the abdomen cavity up under the rib cage and back towards the spine
uḍḍīyānakaḥ – flying–upward procedure, abdomen uplift compression
uḍḍīyanākhyo = uḍḍīyanākhyaḥ = uḍḍīyana (flying upwards procedure) + ākhyaḥ (is called)
udghāṭayet – open
udīraṇaṁ (prevention)
udīrya – by raising
uditaṁ – is acclaimed as
udvamanti – vomiting
ujjāyī –epiglottis contact infusion, epiglottis contact procedure

uktaḥ – said
uktaiḥ (established)
unmanī – devoid of ordinary mental content, thoughtless state of mind during contact with the chit akash sky of consciousness, void of mental content, void of mundane content
unnamayed = unnamayet = should raise
upacayaṁ – excess
upadeśaṁ – teaching
upadiṣṭā – taught
upadiśyate – taught
upaiti – acquires
upajāyate – is performed
upalabhyate – perceive
upamah – best
upanayan – focusing
upari – on top, over
ūpari – over
ūrdhva – above, up and backward, upward, after, over, up, upright
urdhva – upward
ūrdhvagaṁ – going upward
ūrdhvage jāte = directed upward
ūrdhvākuñchanam = ūrdhva (upward) + ākuñchanam (contraction)
ūrdhvamutthāpya – pulling up
ūrdhvāsyo = urdhva (upward) + āsyaḥ (mouth)
ūrdhvataḥ – afterwards, upward
ūru – thigh
urumadhye – in the middle of the thighs
uruṇi – thigh
ūrvor = ūrvoḥ = of the thighs
uṣṇa – hot
utkallola – flooding
utpadyate – arises
utpanna – move up
utsāhāt – based on enthusiasm
utsṝja – suspend, abandon, leave aside
uttama – best, foremost technique, excellent, in the advanced stage
uttamāngeṣu = uttama (best) + āngeṣu (parts)
uttambhya – against the chest
uttāna – upturned
uttāna–kūrmakam = termed as uttāna–kūrma upturned tortoise posture
uttānaṁ - lying down
uttānau – soles upward, palms upward
utthāpya – raised
utthitaḥ – elevated
uttiṣṭhate – ascends

V

vācakāḥ – discussion, nomenclature, words
vacanam – instruction
vacasām – description
vācyaṁ – what is said
vadanaṁ – entry
vadane – demeanor, in the mouth
vadanti – explains, speak, say
vadhe – hunter
vāg = vāk = speech
vāgurāyate – snaring
vāhayet – should flow
vāhinaṁ – cause to flow
vāhini – flushes through
vahni – fiery force, fire, digestive/hormone energy
vahninotpāditaḥ = vahninā (by fire) + utpāditaḥ (is produced)
vaiṇavaḥ – flute
vājinaḥ – horse
vajra–kandare = in the uro–genital channel
vajrāsana – diamond posture
vajrolī – urinary and sexual muscle upward–contraction, upward muscular redirection of male sexual emission, upward muscular redirection of sexual emission
vajrolyā – by upward muscular redirection of male sexual emission
vakṣasi – on the chest
vakṣye – I will mention
vaktavyaṁ – discussed
vakto = vaktaḥ = mouth
vaktra – mouth
vaktre – through the teeth
vākya – discourses, words, instruction
val = vat = like
valī – wrinkles
valitaṁ – wrinkle
vallabhā – sweetheart
vallabhaṁ – endearing
vāma – left
vāma–pādam = left foot
vāmoru – left thigh
vāmorūpari = vāma (left) + ūru (thigh) + upari (over)
vaṁśa – flute
vana – forsest
vañcakaḥ – one who outwits
vañcanam – cheating, illusion
vañchanam = side–stepping

vāpi = or as well
vapuḥ – physical body
vapuṣas = vapuṣaḥ = of the body
vāraṁ – passage, times
vāraṁ vāram = repeatedly
vardhamānam – fullness
vardhamāne – increases
vardhayet – should be stretched
varga – category
varjanam – avoidance
varjayed = varjayet = should avoid
varjitā – without, devoid of, lacking without
varjyam – avoided
vartamāno = vartamānaḥ = acting
vartate – assumes a state
vāruṇī – liquor
vāsanā – desire energy
vāsanotthānāl = due to upheaval of desires
vaśa–vartinī = vaśa (cooperative) + vartinī (practicing yogini)
vased = vaset = should be placed
vaśī – one whose psyche is under control
vaśiṣṭhādyaiś = vaśiṣṭhādyaiḥ = by Vaśiṣṭha and others
vastraṁ – cloth
vastu – object, thing
vaśya – controlled, submissive
vat – like
vāta – air in the intestines, cellular air, lifeforce, wind, consumption of air
vatsaram – year
vayā = youthfulness
vāyau – and the lifeforce
vāyu – air, lifeforce, infused air, infused breath energy, fresh air, breath
veda – Veda
vedanāḥ – pains
vedha – centralized upper flow
vegād = vegāt = with rapidity
vegataḥ – forcefully, rapidly
vegena – with speed, rapidity
vepa – old age
veṣa – clothing
veṣṭita – enclosed
veṣṭitāmbara – folded cloth
vetti – know, experienced, is proficient
vibhedakam – it penetrates
vibhedayet – opens
vibhrājate – illuminating
vibhūtyā – sanctified cowdung ashes
vibudhottamāḥ – best of those with the spiritualized intellect
vicakṣaṇaḥ – proficient
vicāraṇā – to doubt
vicaranti – freely transit
vicitra – varied, various, different
vidha – demanding
vidhāna – of the disciplines
vidhānena – by technique
vidhe – in that type
vidhiṁ – activity, technique
vidhinā – by principle, process
vidhivat – by the rules, consistently, correctly
vidhopāyāḥ – process
viduḥ – know, declare
vidyā – technique
vidyāt – should know
vidyate – exists, there is
vidyopadiśyate =
vighata – is gone
vihāya – leave aside, abandons, transcendental sky
vijānate – they thoroughly know
vijānāti – experiences, qualifies
vijñeyo = vijñeyaḥ = what is known
vijṝmbhikām – sucking air in
vikhyātā – known as
vikṣepam – distractions
vilakṣaṇaṁ – insight perception
vilāsaḥ – fanciful idea
vilayaṁ – disappearance, dissolution
vilīna – phased
vilīyate – assume the nature, becomes quiescent, completely enter into, fused–focused
vilīyeta – becomes quiescent, fiz out
vimalaṁ – flawless
vimardaś = vimardaḥ = tumultous
vimocana – being freed from
viṁśatiḥ – twenty
vimucyate – is freed
vimukta – deprived of, liberated from
vīṇā – vina stringed instrument
vinā – without
vināśa – elimination
vināśakaḥ – destroys the effects
vināśanam – elimination, that which destroys
vinaṣṭa – elimination
vinaśyati – is ruined, eliminates
vinidrāṇāṁ – sleepless
vinirmuktaḥ – freed
vinyased = vinyaset = should place by the side
vinyasya – placing

viparīta – backward, flow inversion
vīrāsanam - hero posture
virecayet – should exhale
vīryavatī – is potent
viṣaṁ – poison, venom
viśāradaiḥ – by those who are expert
visarjayet – should release
viśati – enters, penetrates
viṣaya – desired sense object
viṣayodyāna = garden of enjoyments
viśeṣataḥ – specifically
viśeṣeṇaiva = viśeṣeṇa eva = specifically
vismṝtaya – anxiety
vismṝti – forgetting, non-recollection
viṣṇoḥ – of God Vishnu
viṣṇu–granthes (grantheḥ) = energy congestion of Vishnu, anahata lung-heart chakra complex
viśodhite – total clearance
viśoṣaṇī – eliminates
viśrānti – restfulness
vistāraṁ – width
viśuddhir = viśuddhiḥ = clearance of dense energy
vitasti – 12 fingers, sufficient length
vivaraṁ – cavity, hollows
vivardhanam – increase
vivardhinī – increases
vivare – in the cavity
vivarjayet – not practiced
vivarjitaḥ – having no, lacking, void of
vividhāḥ – various
vrajati – goes into, goes through, draw
vrajet – becomes, achieves, straighten
vṝddhi–karaṁ = increases
vṝddho = vṝddhaḥ = elderly body, elderly human
vṝṣaṇasyādhaḥ = vṝṣaṇasya (of the testes) + adhaḥ (below)
vṝttiḥ – function
vyādhāyate – kill
vyādhi – disease, piercing
vyādhito = vyādhitaḥ = sick
vyāghro = vyāghraḥ = tiger
vyāpārayoḥ – embrace
vyātta – open
vyoma – spiritual sky, space
vyomasthaṁ – situated in the air
vyutkrameṇa – by conversely

W, X, Y, Z

yā – who
yacchato = yacchataḥ = yields
yama – restraining behavior, deity who supervises the criminally–liable departed souls
yāma – three hours
yāme yāme = every three hours
yameṣv = yameṣu = of the restraining behaviors
yamināṁ – those who are existentially self–disciplined
yamīndra – greatest of the psyche–controlled ascetics
yamino = yaminaḥ = confining, disciplinary authority
yamunā = Yamunā–like subtle channel
yānti – they disappear
yantrāṇāṁ – symbol and diagram control
yasmād = yasmāt = due to that, so that
yathā – accordingly, as, as it is, just as, just so
yathā–śakti = as capable
yatheṣṭaṁ = yatha iṣṭaṁ = as desired
yathodaraṁ = yathā (as) + udaram (abdomen
yāti – achieves, goes, shifts into
yatnataḥ – carefully
yatnena – with force
yāto = yātaḥ = fused into
yava – barley
yoga–maṭhasya – of the yogi's residence
yoga–śāstra = authoritative yoga books
yoga–siddhiḥ = perfection in yoga practice
yogataḥ – specific process in yoga, connection
yogavān – proficient yogi
yoga–vido = yoga–vidaḥ – those who know yoga proficiently
yogavit – proficient yogi, master of yoga techniques, skilled yogi, master of yoga
yogīndrāṇam = king of the yogis
yogīndro = yogīndraḥ – yogi who excels all others, lord of yogis
yoginī – yogini
yogīśvara– Lord of yogis
yoni – perineum, vaginal parallel in yogi's body, location where the female vaginal passage is or could be, vaginal passage
yoni–maṇḍalam = vagino–uterine chakra
yugala – pair

yugmam – both
yugo = yugaḥ = two
yuktaḥ – absorbed, proficient, expertise, well–prepared, very proficient, skilled
yuktyā – thoroughly
yuñjann = yuñjan = practicing
yuvo = yuvaḥ = young, youth

Glossary

alternate breath-infusion

This is a type of pranayama breath-infusion, where the yogi inhales through one nostril, then through the next in a sequence of breaths for a duration. The primary method is known as anuloma/viloma. This method required determination, patience and focused interest.

amaroli

This is self urine consumption. It is recommended for helping in absolute celibacy.

anus lock

This is known as the root lock. It concerns the muladhara base chakra. This application of it is the anus-coccyx physio-psychic compression, which causes the energy of kundalini to go upwards due to blocking the downward opening through which kundalini normally expresses itself.

asana postures

These are physical postures for stretching and toning the material body, while observing their effects on the subtle form. Swatmarama wrote that these should cause steadiness, remove ill health and cause flexibility of limbs

ashtanga yoga

- see yoga

astral body

- see psyche

bandha-

- see lock

bhastrika

A pranayama breath-infusion method which is regarded as the best method of infusing fresh energy into the subtle body. It is done with forceful rapid breathing in various postures.

black-out

The experience of a black-out occurs when kundalini ascends through the spine while carrying heavy astral energy which it picked up as it ascended the central spinal passage. It may then burst into the brain into total psychic darkness, giving the person absolutely no insight consciousness. It may hit the buddhi intellect orb which it will surround in psychic darkness with the result that the person will lose objective consciousness. The person's physical body will fall to the ground or loop over or tilt to the side. This may last for moments, or for a few minutes, and then the person will resume objectivity with the understanding that time stood still and his existence was suspended for the time.

blank thoughtless idealess mental condition

This is a condition of mind whereby there are no conventional thoughts or images in the frontal part of the subtle head. Naad sound may or may not be heard during this experience. This is a prerequisite for gaining access to the chit akash sky of consciousness.

Brahma

Brahma is a deity in the Vedic list of supernatural authorities. He is attributed as the creator-god of the physical and subtle material world. There are many stories about Brahma and yogis in the Puranas. Most of these have to do with Brahma visiting yogis who excelled at austerities. Even Buddha said that he was visited by Brahma immediately after enlightenment.

brahma nadi

This is a microscopic central channel which runs through the central sushumna spinal passage. It has a tiny hole at its bottom end in muladhara chakra. This is closed by effective application of ashwini mudra, which is the anus lock. Brahma-nadi runs through the central spine, through the neck. When it enters the head it disappears. It runs to the brahmarandra crown chakra but due to the radiance at that center, the brahma-nadi becomes imperceptible

brahman

Brahman is not to be confused with Brahma. Brahma is a deity, a supernatural person. Brahman is a term for the sum-total spiritual reality or for a miniscule part of it. In the Upanishads, brahman is described as the highest reality and as the only real substance in existence.

brahmarandra

This is an energy vortex at the top of the head in the subtle body. It is regarded as a gate to the brahman spiritual energy. It can grant access to the chit akash sky of consciousness. If a yogi leaves the body through this vortex at the time of death, it is assumed that he was transferred into the divine atmosphere.

breath retention, spontaneous

This the condition of breath where the breath is suspended involuntarily of its own accord without a compulsion from the will power. The yogi does not stop the breath. Instead due to the state of meditation or due to doing a certain pranayama breath-infusion, the psyche goes into a mode where the breath is suspended due to the system not needing fresh air because it has an excess of fresh breath energy. This condition is simultaneous for the physical and subtle bodies.

breath-infusion

This is the process known as Pranayama. It has many methods and sequences. The Hatha Yoga Pradipika *lists bhastrika as being the best of the breath-infusion processes. Kapalabhati is the preliminary practice of this bhastrika practice.*

Buddha, Gautama Shakyamuni

He is a unique being who in one lifetime shattered every limitation which bars a living entity from removing himself from the realms of trauma.

bulb

- see kanda bulb

causal body

This is the form which has all the potential for subtle and physical body formation. It is not a body with limbs and senses; it is more like a locational space. It has concentrated subtle energy which never takes distinct formation except by manifesting on another grosser plane of existence. Yogis, who become familiar with the causal body, lose their attraction to the subtle body and its potentials.

causal node

These are super-subtle energy or vibration source points. These serve as gateways to the supernatural and spiritual atmospheres.

celibacy

This is a requirement for all yogis, even for ones who are married or who are in the process of begetting progeny. A yogi has it as a task to rein in sexual expression. The main issue is the conservation and through-the-spine utilization of the sexual hormone energy. As nature would have it this energy is usually expressed through the genitals For the purpose of kundalini yoga, its routing should be changed so that it passes through the spine into the brain. Celibacy in this case does not mean conservation of sexual energy but conservation with adequate distribution through the entire psyche.

cell-kundalini

This is the life force for each cell of the body. It is contrasted to the aggregate dominant kundalini which usually resides at the muladhara chakra at the base of the spinal column. Cell-kundalini is a micro-energy in contrast to the aggregate dominant lifeforce. In the advanced stage of kundalini yoga, the student shifts interest away from the aggregate kundalini to the micro-cell kundalinis. These are mostly bunched together in the form of glands or collections of muscles or tendons.

chakra

This is an energy vortex in the subtle body. It may or may not correspond to nerve plexuses in the physical system. The primary chakras are at the base of the spinal column, on the spine near to the sex organs, on the spine behind the navel, on the spine near to the heart-lung complex, on the spine behind the throat, in the head between the eyebrows and in the head at the crown.

There are other chakras. Some are at vital organs like the heart or spleen. Some are at glands like the testes or ovaries.

chin lock

This is the compression which restricts the passage of kundalini through the neck. It is known as the neck or throat lock. When doing breath-infusion, a student must master this lock for causing kundalini to pass through the neck and enter into the head in a restricted controlled way. If this lock is not applied, the student might faint during the practice.

chit akash

- see sky of consciousness

clarifying energy

This is the most perceptively-yielding energy of material nature. Below it is the enthusiasm force and the dulling power. A yogi is required to remain permanently embedded in the clarifying energy and not to shift to the perspective of the enthusiasm force or the dulling power. Persons who are victimized by the enthusiasm force and the dulling power are mediocre yogis

contraction

These are physio-psychic locks and compressions of parts of the physical and subtle bodies. The basis application is physical but there is a psychic counterpart to physical activity which is realized. Some of it is pure psychic or mental without any physical showing. This is for controlling kundalini and the infused energy.

dakini

This is an angelic being whose subtle body can assume any yoga posture in its final form. This person may or may not be a yogini but usually dakinis associate with yogi and yogins.

death

This is the event of the final separation of the subtle body from the physical system. This is the event of the partition between the physical body and the psychic lifeforce mechanism which operates the living functions within it. The subtle body leaves the physical one on a daily basis but the person-self may not realize this daily separation. However the kundalini only leaves the physical body once at the death of the physical form. Death means that the kundalini lifeforce was forced to leave the physical system once and for all.

Devi

- see Durga

dharana deliberate transcendental focus

This is the deliberate application of the interest and attention of the self to persons and environments which are transcendental to material existence.

dhyana spontaneous transcendental focus

This is the spontaneous application of the interest and attention of the self to persons and environments which are transcendental to material existence.

dhyayi spontaneous transcendental focus

see dhyana spontaneous transcendental focus

divine space

- see kha divine space

divine world

This place is also known as the spiritual world, the divine world, the akshara dhama, the paramam dhama, Vaikuntha, Shiva Loka, paradise, heaven. It should not be confused with the heavenly astral worlds which are within the scope of the psychic material nature.

Durga

She is the goddess of the material energy. She is the primary wife of Shiva. She was Shiva's first student for learning the information which is presented as the Hatha Yoga Pradipika.

energy congestion

When a yogi does breath-infusion the accumulated energy may be blocked due to energy congestion of polluted force somewhere in the subtle body. He uses the accumulated energy to force out the pollution. If the infused energy does not have a large enough charge to move the congestion, the yogi infuses more energy thereby increasing the charge until it becomes sufficient to motivate the pollution.

energy distribution

This is the distribution of accumulated infused air energy. In the subtle body it is distribution of the accumulated infused subtle energy. After a series of breaths where fresh energy is deposited into the psyche, the yogi should focus on locating that energy. He should then distribute or compress it in on itself.

energy vortex

- see chakra

Ganga/Ganges

This is the goddess who is embodied in the form of the River Ganges in India. This person has a celestial human-looking form. She is one of the consorts of Lord Shiva. She is all about fertility and femininity. She helps the yogis and also assists fallen supernatural beings. At the onset in the Mahabharata it is explained how she took birth on earth, paired with King Shantanu and acted as the mother of the eight Vasus who were cursed to take birth on earth. These were supernatural beings who by the grace of the goddess only stayed in the earthly domain for as long as the curse lasted. Usually when one takes a body on earth, one becomes involved in a protracted series of births due to the pressures of association from earth-bound entities. With the help of Mother Ganges, a yogi can make quick work out of his material body so that he does not have to keep taking one physical form after the other, totally forgetting the celestial life.

Gautama Buddha

- see Buddha

goddess

A celestial female being with cosmic powers.

Godhead

This term means a range of personalities, each of whom function as God without any conflicting involvements. There are Personalities of Godhead.

gold-out

The experience of a gold-out occurs when kundalini ascends through the spine while carrying light-weight astral energy which it produced by a rapid burning explosion through the spine. It will then burst into the brain into a gold or white-gold energy which is transparent and which gives insight consciousness. It will hit the buddhi intellect orb which it will penetrate with the result that the person will retain some degree of objective consciousness with partial or full clarity. The person's physical body may fall to the ground or loop over or tilt to the side. This may last for moments or for a few minutes and then the person will resume objectivity with the understanding that time stood still and his existence was reinforced or revealed on the spiritual plane. The gold-out has a spiritual bliss aspect to it which is lust free and transcendental.

grey-out

The experience of a grey-out occurs when kundalini ascends through the spine while carrying clouds of heavy astral energy which was interspaced with light astral force. As soon as this energy is released into the brain, it will surround the buddhi intellect orb and cause it to be uncertain and to lack clarity. The person will feel as if he is neither here nor there, as if he is conscious and unconscious at the same time. He will be riddled with uncertainty as to there being any type of objective existence. If the body was standing when this occurred, it will immediately fall to the ground.

Guru

- see teacher

Hatha Yoga

That is a system of yoga which was designed by Gorakshnatha Mahayogin. It was mistaken as asana postures when some yogis from India, defined it as such. It is more than asana which is just one of the six aspects of this yoga. While Patanjali Mahayogin explained yoga as having eight (8) parts, as ashtanga yoga, Gorakshnath explained hatha yoga as having six (6) parts, leaving aside the preliminary stages of yama moral restraining and niyama approved behaviors.

The six parts are asana physical body postures, pranayama physical and subtle body breath-infusion, pratyahar sensual energy withdrawal, dharana deliberate focus on transcendental reality, dhyana spontaneous focus on transcendental reality and samadhi continuous focus on transcendental reality.

The Hatha Yoga Pradipika, *is Swatmarama's exposition of Hatha Yoga.*

inSelf Yoga™

This is the yoga system taught by Michael Beloved. It was explained in this Hatha Yoga Pradipika. *It was explained by Patanjali as ashtanga yoga and by Gorakshnath Mahayogin as hatha yoga. It is kundalini yoga followed by advanced meditation or samyama which are the three highest stages of yoga as one sequential practice. Students should do kapalabhati/bhastrika breath-infusion to surcharge the subtle body. Then they should sit to meditate immediately thereafter. They should hear naad sound resonance and develop focus into the chit akash sky of consciousness.*

isolation

This is required for a yogi. Initially it is physical segregation but as the student advances he sees that physical isolation is not the issue. There is a deeper communication which hurts the yogi. That is psychic access. Physical isolation does not terminate psychic access. Therefore a yogi focuses on psychic aloneness. According to Patanjali there is yet a larger issue which is that in psychic isolation, one discovers that the core-self is under the influence of the psychic adjuncts in its psyche. Hence the real issue is how to isolate the core-self from its adjuncts and how to reunify these with the core-self being predominant.

kanda bulb

This is a subtle container at the bottom of the trunk of the subtle body. It serves as a reservoir for much of the stored hormone energy. This energy is contained in that bulb and is not allowed to pass to the thighs, legs and feet. It is collected there for reproducing other bodies, a service which is necessary if the kundalini is to reproduce sexually and use the progeny in the future to provide for it a new life form. A yogi is required to vaporize and distribute the energy of this bulb.

kapalabhati

A pranayama breath-infusion method which consists of forceful rapid breathing in various postures but done with stress or extra thrust on the exhale. It evolves into bhastrika breath-infusion in which both the inhale and exhales are done with extra trust.

Karma Yoga

This is the main subject of the Bhagavad Gita discourse. It is mistaken as being bhakti or bhakti yoga, which are devotion or yogically focused devotion to a deity. Karma yoga has to do with the application of yoga to social activities. It is also known as raja yoga and was the specialty of yogi-kings as explained in the Bhagavad Gita.

kha divine space

This is the spiritual world. It may be access by a yogi from within his psyche through mystic transfer into the chit akash sky of consciousness.

Krishna

He is not mentioned by name in the Hatha Yoga Pradipika but he is indicated by the mention of Vishnu. He is rated both as the source of Vishnu and as the incarnation of Vishnu. Scriptures which advocate Krishna as the Supreme Person rate him as the source of Vishnu; while those texts which put forward Vishnu as the Supreme Person, rate Krishna as an incarnation or avatar of Vishnu.

During Krishna's life people who were of the view that Vishnu is the Supreme Person, rated Krishna as being an incarnation of Vishnu but during the Universal Form display which Krishna showed Arjuna, Krishna was revealed as the ultimate person, the Supreme Lord.

kriya

This is any mystic method which produces results in the use of the subtle body. It may comprise a physical action but it must have a psychic counterpart which is effective and not imaginary.

kriya yoga

This is the samyama process earmarked by Patanjali Mahamuni in his Yoga Sutras as the three higher stages of yoga as one sequential event, evolving from dharana deliberate transcendental focus to spontaneous transcendental focus and then into continuous transcendental focus.

Kumblak kevala

This is the condition where the breath is suspended involuntarily of its own accord without a compulsion from the will power. The yogi does not stop the breath. Instead due to the state of meditation or due to doing a certain pranayama breath-infusion, the psyche goes into a mode where the breath is suspended due to the system not needing fresh air because it has an excess of fresh breath energy. This condition is simultaneous for the physical and subtle bodies.

Kundalini

This is the life force of the material body but it is a psychic force which has a high degree of sentiency. In the human form it usually resides at the muladhara chakra where it manages excretion and all involuntary life functions. When the physical body is dead, the lifeforce relocates itself totally into the subtle form. It directs that subtle being into how to acquire another physical body.

Kundalini Yoga

This is the subject of the Hatha Yoga Pradipika. It was known as hatha yoga because that title was used by Gorakshnatha Mahayogin. The translator and commentator of this book, learnt it from Sri Siri Harbhajan Singh Sahib. It consists of an effective pranayama practice, with physio-psychic compressions and directive mento-emotional force to cause kundalini to be infused and to rise through the spine into the brain.

Even though there are many types of pranayama breath-infusion practices, the one recommended by Swatmarama in this book is the bhastrika rapid breathing process. This may be combined with postures to be more effective.

laya yoga

This is high-end meditation with the objective of silencing the mento-emotional energy, to bring that into quiescence.

Lifeforce

- see Kundalini

lock

These are contractions of physical muscles which when done proficiently cause contraction of areas in the subtle body. The three primary locks are the uplift of the anal sphincter muscle with urinary and perineum pull-up, the navel/lower-abdomen pull-back-and-up, and the chin pull-back-to-throat compression. Lastly, there is a non-physical lock which is the mind lock where the attention energy remains focused in the center of the head or between the eyebrows or at the brahmarandra crown chakra.

mento-emotional energy

This is the conventional mind content energy in which thoughts and images are generated. The energy of it must be extracted and replaced during pranayama breath-infusion practice. Patanjali Mahayogin condemned the conventional mento-emotional operations. A yogi should heed his advisory in the Yoga Sutras.

middle channel

This may be the sushumna central spinal passage but it may be a central channel in the center of the trunk of the subtle body, which is distinct from the sushumna central spinal passage.

muladhara chakra

This is the conventional residence of the kundalini psychic lifeforce. It is the lowest of the chakra energy gyrating centers on the spinal column. It controls survival and excretion.

mystic perfectional skills

These are abilities of the subtle body which are realized as the yogi improves his awareness of the psychic and supernatural levels of existence. They are rates as special powers which are prone to abuse but they are in fact natural abilities of the subtle body on certain levels of consciousness. In the Uddhava Gita, Krishna listed eight primary powers as becoming atomic, becoming cosmic, being weightless, acquiring or experiencing through the sense organs of others, enjoying what was heard of and what was seen normally, manipulating mundane potency, ruling over others, non-attachment to mundane influences, which results in the technique of controlling one's nature, and obtaining what is desired

naad sound resonance

This is a sound which occurs in the head of the subtle body. Swatmarama list it as being on the left side but it may be on the right, in the middle, above or below or even in any other part of the subtle form. It is sometimes heard in the sushumna central passage. This is a transcendental sound which pacifies the yogi and provides access to the chit akash sky of consciousness.

nadi

These are subtle energy tracks which run parallel to nerves, veins and arteries. The Hatha Yoga Pradipika gave a number of 72,000. The main one is the sushumna nadi central channel which is in the center of the spinal column. That is the main distribution conduit of the kundalini's psychic influence.

neck lock

- see chin lock

niyama approved behaviors

These are recommended behaviors for a yogi. Swatmarama listed these as deprivation in yoga austerities, contentment, being theistic, being generous, doing ceremonial worship of the Supreme Lord, hearing the discourses on the technical information about reality, and being modest, as well as deprivation as it relates to Vedic religious ceremony, performance of such ceremony and proficiency.

nutrition orb

This is a bundle of light which is in the vicinity of the abdomen but it is in the subtle body. This operates the digestive functions of the physical and subtle bodies. A yogi is required to curb diet for efficient operation of this orb. Eventually this orb is lifted out of the abdomen area and becomes lodged in the back of the throat.

Parvati

The goddess of material nature, the wife of Lord Shiva

perception

There are many perceptions which are not visual in the normal sense. There are also visual perceptions which occur through the eyes of the subtle body on various levels of that form. Here is a list of the prominent non-eye vision perceptions: direct core-self perception, sense of identity perception, buddhi intellect-orb perception, third-eye brow-chakra perception, brahmarandra crown-chakra perception, prana-vision, kundalini-burst vision and cell micro-kundalini vision

Personality of Godhead

According to the Puranas there are multiple Personalities of Godhead, each having his or her zone of existence with specific jurisdictions without conflict. Among these there is a Supreme Personality of Godhead who is Krishna, the speaker of the Bhagavad Gita.

pranayama

- see breath-infusion

pratyahara sensual energy withdrawal

This is retraction of sensual interest from the external world and retraction of psychological interest from anything in the psyche which concerns material existence and which is detrimental to spiritual progress.

psyche

The psyche is the individual subtle body. It is a localized energy field with components which include a spiritual core-self (atma). The psyche is not just the mind chamber or the head of the subtle body. It is the entire limited individual subtle body which has limbs, senses and a head as part of it.

psychic organs

These are organs in the subtle body. A yogi is required to realize these. They are subtle. They may not be perceived objectively except in very advanced meditations.

Raja Yoga

This is the application of yoga to social involvement. It was originally taught to yogi-kings and their sons. In the Bhagavad Gita it is termed as karma yoga and was explained to Arjuna because this warrior was a prince in the Kuru dynasty. In the Gita, Krishna said that he would reestablish this teaching to Arjuna because it was lost to humanity and become unknown in the course of time. Krishna claimed to have taught legendary ancient kings who lived long before Arjuna.

Raja yoga consists of remaining introvert while being externally occupied, such that even while being involved socially, a yogi can keep the spiritual insight operative. He uses it to determine the most efficient and least self-inflicting way to negotiate history.

root lock

This is the base chakra lock using the anal sphincter muscle with urinary and perineum upward contraction but focusing on the psychic side to prevent the kundalini lifeforce from its downward trend and from preoccupation with evacuation and survival.

sahajoli

This is the process whereby a yogini retracts emitted sexual fluids

śakti prabhāvān

This is the illumination of the kundalini psychic lifeforce. It pushes the focal consciousness of the meditator to a higher plane from which direct perception of the supernatural and spiritual realities becomes possible.

samadhi continuous transcendental absorption

This is the continuous spontaneous application of the interest and attention of the self to persons and environments which are transcendental to material existence.

samyama

This is the three higher stages of yoga as one sequential event, evolving from dharana deliberate transcendental focus to spontaneous transcendental focus and then into continuous transcendental focus. This was described by Patanjali Mahamuni in his Yoga Sutras. It became known as kriya yoga.

Sat Guru

- see teacher

Shiva

He is the patron deity of the Hatha Yoga Pradipika. *He is regarded as the supermost yogi. He was the first person to teach yoga. His first student was his wife, the Goddess Durga. He is rated as being one of the essential deities of the world, the one who manages its destruction and who, during the manifestation, exhibits the austerity necessary for limited beings to resist illusory influences.*

siddha

A siddha is someone who mastered kundalini manipulation for psychic energy transformation, and who because of shattering death which is enforced by time, has free and easy transit through the universe. The implication is that a siddha perfected yogi can travel here and there into the various dimensions and then select which one he or she would permanently reside.

Such a person has a subtle body which is resistant to physical rebirth. He is satisfied with subtle existence alone and have no need to acquire physical forms.

sky of consciousness

This terminology was coined by Siddha Swami Muktananda. This place is the atmosphere of the spiritual world. It is accessed by yogis who do advanced meditation.

sound resonance

see naad sound resonance

space-out

The experience of a space-out occurs when kundalini ascends through the spine, fizzes out at the top of the neck and just sprinkles a little of its energy into the brain. This results in a spaced out feeling as if the person lost control of their objective observing posture in the mind. The person may see a little bit of diffused light or have no sight but feel as if he or she was in a large spacious chamber. The person loses grip on memories and has no concept of identity or persona. There is a conversion from being a social unit to be just a space which has no focus. This will last for a few moments or for longer and then the person gradually comes to his or her senses and resumes the normal personality but with a feeling of having temporarily lost the self in the process.

stun-out

The experience of a stun-out occurs when kundalini ascends through the spine and burst into the brain into white-gold light, and remains there at the top of the neck in the lower head for some moments or minutes and then quickly descends back to its base at the muladhara end-of-spine chakra. When this happens the physical body may not fall to the ground but may remain in one position or will keep moving into an intended position in slow motion. The yogi will feel as if he was stunned where there is no sensual perception, and he just existed with stationary awareness of being just there.

subtle body

- see the psyche

subtle perception

- see perception

supernatural/ supernormal power

- see mystic perfectional skills

sushumna

In the subtle body, this is the middle of the spine. It is the primary nadi and is considered to be the elevator access for the kundalini psychic lifeforce. When this passage is kept open continuously it is accepted that the yogi is enlightened and is freed from dense awareness.

Svargaloka

- A heavenly realm hereafter -

Persons, who did agnihotra sacrifices efficiently, may go to that place after finally departing from the material body. Some yogis go to this place after death but generally yogis avoid this place hereafter.

teacher

The teacher is the person from whom one gets yoga techniques. One may have more than one teacher but the teacher of a specific discipline is given credit for his contribution to one's acquirement of a skill in yoga.

There are two kinds of teachers. One is the instructor who directly supervises one's practice. The other is the lineage master who may or may not supervise one's practice. This lineage teacher is special because his presence gives confidents to everyone in the sect.

There is also a person who is called the sat guru. This person is usually a lineage teacher but it may be the personal instructor who is not the main lineage master. The sat guru is the person who one derives considerable confidence from and in whose presence one feels elevated.

third eye

This is between the two eyebrows. It grants clairvoyance to the yogi, where he can see into other dimensions and also into the supernatural and divine skies. It is used for stabilizing the focus or interest of the yogi during deep states of meditation.

throat lock

- see chin lock

traatak

This is blank staring with the eyes open. It is used to see auras but in the Hatha Yoga Pradipika *its usage is for accessing the chit akash sky of consciousness and for attaining the blank mental state which is a precursor of such access.*

Tushita heaven

A heavenly world which has siddhas who are content with their existential achievements. This place is where Buddha and his mother were before taking birth on the earth. It is beyond the Swargaloka heavenly world but is within the realm of the creator-god Brahma.

vajroli

This is the ability to retract emitted semen or for a male to draw female sexual fluids into his body.

vision energy

This is the psychic energy which courses through the optic nerves. It runs parallel to the nerve circuitry which operates ocular functions in the brain. In meditation, a yogi should isolate this vision energy. When it is mastered, the interest energy which comes from the sense-of-identity should be isolated out of the vision energy. This interest energy is the raw power of the core-self.

white-out

The experience of a white-out occurs when kundalini ascends through the spine while carrying medium weight astral energy which it picked up as it ascended the central spinal passage. It may then burst into the brain into a white energy cloud which is opaque and which does not allow any objective perception, giving the person slight insight consciousness. It may hit the buddhi intellect orb which it will surround in an astral cloud of energy with the result that the person will retain some degree of objective consciousness but not enough for clarity. The person's physical body may fall to the ground or fold over or tilt to the side. This may last for moments or for a few minutes. Then the person will resume objectivity with the understanding that time stood still and his existence was suspended for the time.

yama moral restraints

These are discouraged behaviors for a yogi. Swatmarama listed these as non–violence, realism, non–stealing, sexual non-expressiveness which results in the perception of spirituality, tolerance, steadiness, compassion, straightforwardness, eating the absolute minimum, and cleanliness.

yoga

Patanjali defined yoga as having eight parts namely yama moral restraints, niyama approved behaviors, asana postures, pranayama breath-infusion, pratyahar sensual energy withdrawal, dharana deliberate transcendental focus, dhyana spontaneous transcendental focus and samadhi continuous transcendental absorption.

yogini

This is a female ascetic.

About the Author

Michael Beloved (Yogi *Madhvāchārya)* took his current body in 1951 in Guyana. In 1965, while living in Trinidad, he instinctively began doing yoga postures and tried to make sense of the supernatural side of life.

Later in 1970, in the Philippines, he approached a Martial Arts Master named Mr. Arthur Beverford. He explained to the teacher that he was seeking a yoga instructor. Mr. Beverford identified himself as an advanced disciple of *Śrī* Rishi Singh Gherwal, an Ashtanga Yoga master.

Beverford taught the traditional Ashtanga Yoga with stress on postures, attentive breathing and brow chakra centering meditation. In 1972, Michael entered the Denver, Colorado Ashram of *kundalini* yoga Master *Śrī* Harbhajan Singh. There he took instruction in bhastrika pranayama and its application to yoga postures. He was supervised mostly by Yogi Bhajan's disciple named Prem Kaur.

In 1979 Michael formally entered the disciplic succession of the Brahmā -Madhava-Gaudiya Sampradaya through *Swāmī* Kirtanananda, who was a prominent sannyasi disciple of the Great Vaishnava Authority *Śrī Swāmī* Bhaktivedanta Prabhupada, the exponent of devotion to Sri Krishna.

However, yoga has a mystic side to it, thus Michael took training and teaching empowerment from several spiritual masters of different aspects of spiritual development. This is consistent with *Śrī* Krishna's advice to Arjuna in the *Bhagavad Gītā*:

tad viddhi praṇipātena
paripraśnena sevayā
upadekṣyanti te jñānaṁ
jñāninas tattva darśinaḥ

This you ought to know. By submitting yourself as a student, by asking questions, by serving as requested, the perceptive, reality-conversant teachers will teach you the knowledge. (*Bhagavad Gītā* 4.34)

Most of the instructions Michael received were given in the astral world. On that side of existence, his most prominent teachers were *Śrī Swāmī* Shivananda of Rishikesh, Yogiraj *Swāmī* Vishnudevananda, *Śrī Bābāji Mahasaya* - the master of the masters of *Kriyā* Yoga, *Śrīla* Yogeshwarananda of Gangotri - the master of the masters of *Rāj* Yoga (spiritual clarity), and Siddha *Swāmī* Nityananda the Brahmā Yoga authority.

Śrī Rishi Singh Gherwal, who is deceased, inspired this translation and commentary of the *Hatha Yoga Pradipika*. It has the details of the complex mystic actions involved in kundalini manipulation using breath infusion and deep meditation using naad sound resonance absorption.

Publications

inSelf Yoga™ Courses

inSelf Yoga™ is the ashtanga process of complete transformation of the psyche of a yogi. Its syllabus was given by Patanjali Mahayogin in the Yoga Sutras. It has physical and psychological applications and reins in the lifestyle of the ascetic.

Core-Self Discovery

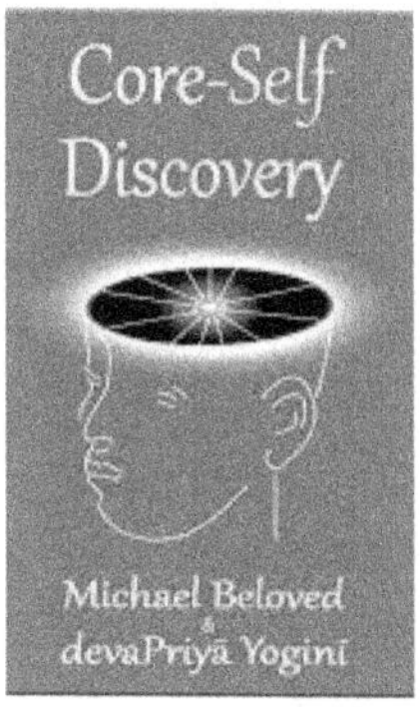

Core-Self Discovery is the pictorial format of the inSelf Yoga™ course for discovering the core-self in the psyche of the individual soul. This was adapted from Michael Beloved's *Meditation Pictorial* book. These mind diagrams give graphic depiction of what may take place in the head of the subtle body during meditations for pin-pointing the core-self, the observing transcendental I-identity.

This publication is available in paperback, eBook and DVD formats.

Commentaries

Yoga Sutras of Patanjali

Meditation Expertise

Krishna Cosmic Body

Bhagavad Gita Explained

Anu Gita Explained

Kriya Yoga Bhagavad Gita

Brahma Yoga Bhagavad Gita

Uddhava Gita Explained

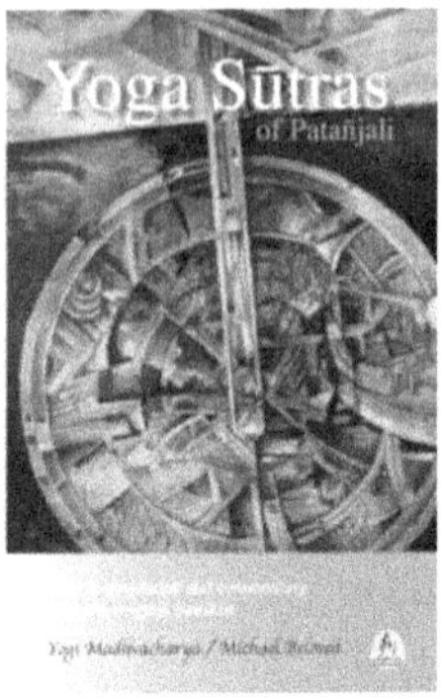

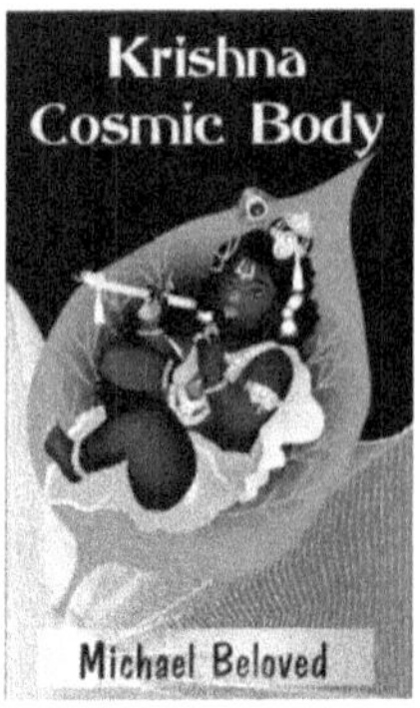

Yoga Sutras of Patanjali is the globally acclaimed text book of yoga. This has detailed expositions of yoga techniques. Many kriya techniques are vividly described in the commentary.

Meditation Expertise is an analysis and application of the Yoga Sutras. This book is loaded with illustrations and has detailed explanations of secretive advanced meditation techniques which are called kriyas in the Sanskrit language.

Krishna Cosmic Body is a narrative commentary on the Markandeya Samasya portion of the Aranyaka Parva of the Mahabharata. This is the detailed description of the dissolution of the world, as experienced by the great yogin Markandeya who transcended the cosmic deity, Brahma, and reached Brahma's source who is a divine infant Krishna.

Bhagavad Gita Explained shows what was said in the Gita without religious overtones and sectarian biases.

Anu Gita Explained is the detailed description of the effect-energy of current actions in application to future lives.

Kriya Yoga Bhagavad Gita shows the instructions for those who are doing kriya yoga.

Brahma Yoga Bhagavad Gita shows the instructions for those who are doing brahma yoga.

Uddhava Gita Explained shows the instructions to Uddhava which are more advanced than the ones given to Arjuna.

Bhagavad Gita is an instruction for applying the expertise of yoga in the cultural field. This is why the process taught to Arjuna is called karma yoga which means karma + yoga or cultural activities done with a yogic demeanor.

Uddhava Gita is an instruction for applying the expertise of yoga to attaining spiritual status. This is why it is explains jnana yoga and bhakti yoga in details. Jnana yoga is using mystic skill for knowing the spiritual part of existence. Bhakti yoga is for developing affectionate relationships with divine beings.

Karma yoga is for negotiating the social concerns in the material world and therefore it is inferior to bhakti yoga which concerns negotiating the social concerns in the spiritual world.

This world has a social environment and the spiritual world has one too.

Right now Uddhava Gita is the most advanced informative spiritual book on the planet. There is nothing anywhere which is superior to it or which goes into so much details as it. It verified that historically Krishna is the most advanced human being to ever have left literary instructions on this planet. Even Patanjali Yoga Sutras which I translated and gave an application for in my book, **Meditation Expertise**, does not go as far as the Uddhava Gita.

Some of the information of these two books is identical but while the Yoga Sutras are concerned with the personal spiritual emancipation (kaivalyam) of the individual spirits, the Uddhava Gita explains that and also explains the situations in the spiritual universes.

Bhagavad Gita is from the *Mahabharata* which is the history of the Pandavas. Arjuna, the student of the Gita, is one of the Pandavas brothers. He was in a social hassle and did not know how to apply yoga expertise to solve it. Krishna gave him a crash-course on the battlefield about that.

Uddhava Gita is from the *Srimad Bhagavatam (Bhagavata Purana),* which is a history of the incarnations of Krishna. Uddhava was a relative of Krishna. He was concerned about the situation of the deaths of many of his relatives but Krishna diverted Uddhava's attention to the practice of yoga for the purpose of successfully migrating to the spiritual environment.

Explained Series

Bhagavad Gita Explained

Anu Gita Explained

Uddhava Gita Explained

The speciality of these books is that they are free of missionary intentions, cult tactics and philosophical distortion. Instead of using these books to add credence to a philosophy, meditation process, belief or plea for followers, I spread the information out so that a reader can look through this literature and freely take or leave anything as desired.

When Krishna stressed himself as God, I stated that. When Krishna laid no claims for supremacy, I showed that. The reader is left to form an independent opinion about the validity of the information and the credibility of Krishna.

There is a difference in the discourse with Arjuna in the Bhagavad Gita and the one with Uddhava in the Uddhava Gita. In fact these two books may appear to contradict each other. In the Bhagavad Gita, Krishna pressured Arjuna to complete social duties. In the Uddhava Gita, Krishna insisted that Uddhava should abandon the same.

The Anu Gita is completely different to the Bhagavad Gita. Krishna refused to display the Universal Form. He quoted a siddha from a higher dimension who lectured on the effect-energies of actions as these construct a person's future opportunities.

Meditation Series

Meditation Pictorial

Meditation Expertise

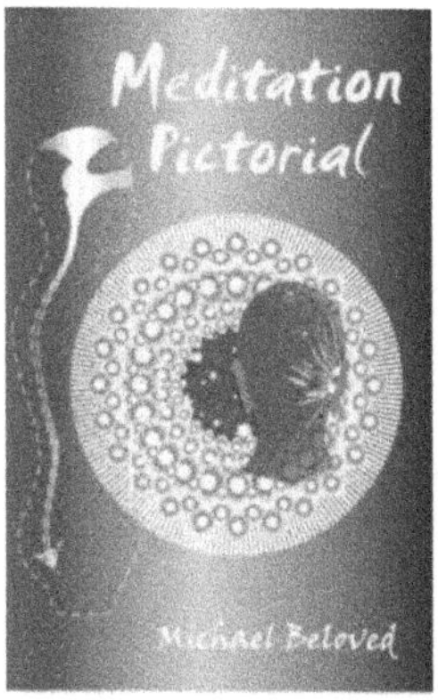

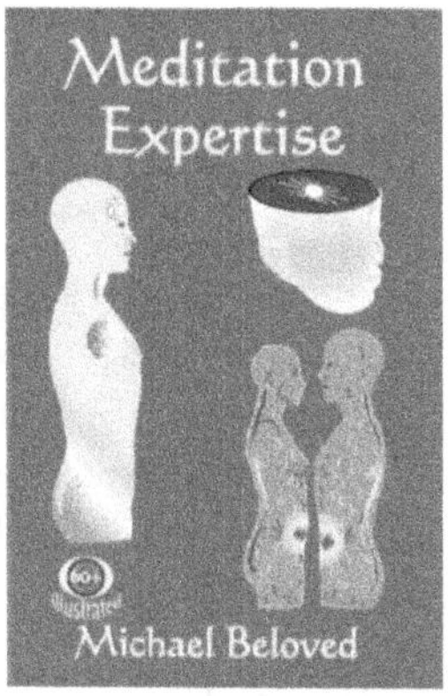

The speciality of these books is the mind diagrams which profusely illustrate what is written. This shows exactly what one has to do mentally to develop and then sustain a meditation practice.

In the **Meditation Pictorial**, one is shown how to develop psychic insight, a feature without which meditation is imagination and visualization, without any mystic experience per se.

In the **Meditation Expertise**, one is shown how to corral one's practice to bring it in line with the classic syllabus of yoga which Patanjali lays out as the ashtanga yoga 8-staged practice.

Both books are profusely illustrated with mind diagrams showing the components of psychic consciousness and the inner design of the subtle body.

Specialty Topics

sex you!

The mystery of sex and reincarnation is explained in details, not in terms of religion or superstition but by psychic facts which any individual can observe, if he or she can shift focus to the psychic plane. Books like the Bardo Thodol (Tibetan Book of the Dead) and the Egyptian Book of the Dead (Papyrus of Ani), along with Bhagavad Gita, the reincarnation teaching of Buddha and other vital books, took humanity through a spiritual technological leap through time into the hereafter. Perhaps none of these texts dealt with the incidences of sex and reincarnation head on, especially the link between you and the sexual act of your parents which produced your body. In this book you get the details in plain terms without mystery and religious impositions.

Spiritual Master

Practically every positive and negative aspect of having a guru is discussed in this book with recommendations of how to deal with gurus safely. A non-proficient guru can be useful despite his faults, but one must know how to side-step hassles and get to the business at hand, which is to get effective techniques from a spiritual master.

In some cases the spiritual master will be a complete fraud but one should not let that deter one from making spiritual progress in his association. "But why," one might ask, "should one stay with a fraudulent guru?" The answer is that if providence puts one in that position, one should honor providence but one should do so without getting hurt by the unqualified spiritual master. This and similar topics are discussed in this book.

Masturbation Psychic Details:

--- A short paper about the psychic side of a masturbation event with a tour through the possibilities of possession by departed spirits who access the form of the physical actor. Everything points to the masturbator, until we consider the content energy of the sexual urge to see if it has another person force as its primal gusher.

What would happen if a hereafter person(s) in the urge were evacuated from it? Would the physical actor suddenly lose the impetus and become reluctant to bring the body to climax?

English Series

Bhagavad Gita English

Anu Gita English

Markandeya Samasya English

Yoga Sutras English

Uddhava Gita English

These are in 21st Century English, very precise and exacting. Many Sanskrit words which were considered untranslatable into a Western language are rendered in precise, expressive and modern English, due to the English language becoming the world's universal means of concept conveyance.

Three of these books are instructions from Krishna. **In Bhagavad Gita English** and **Anu Gita English**, the instructions were for Arjuna. In the **Uddhava Gita English,** it was for Uddhava. Bhagavad Gita and Anu Gita are extracted from the Mahabharata. Uddhava Gita was extracted from the 11th Canto of the Srimad Bhagavatam (Bhagavata Purana). One of these books, the **Markandeya Samasya English** is about Krishna, as described by Yogi Markandeya, who survived the cosmic collapse and reached a divine child in whose transcendental body, the collapsed world was existing. Another of these books, the **Yoga Sutras English,** is the detailed syllabus about yoga practice.

My suggestion is that you read Bhagavad Gita English, the Anu Gita English, the Markandeya Samasya English, the Yoga Sutras English and lastly the Uddhava Gita English, which is much more complicated and detailed.

For each of these books we have at least one commentary, which is published separately. Thus your particular interest can be researched further in the commentaries.

The smallest of these commentaries and perhaps the simplest is the one for the Anu Gita. We published its commentary as the Anu Gita Explained. The Bhagavad Gita explanations were published in three distinct targeted commentaries. The first is Bhagavad Gita Explained, which sheds lights on how people in the time of Krishna and Arjuna regarded the information and applied it. Bhagavad Gita is an exposition of the application of yoga practice to cultural activities, which is known in the Sanskrit language as karma yoga.

Interestingly, Bhagavad Gita was spoken on a battlefield just before one of the greatest battles in the ancient world. A warrior, Arjuna, lost his wits and had no idea that he could apply his training in yoga to political dealings. Krishna, his charioteer, lectured on the spur of the moment to give Arjuna the skill of using yoga proficiency in cultural dealings including how to deal with corrupt officials on a battlefield.

The second commentary is the Kriya Yoga Bhagavad Gita. This clears the air about Krishna's information on the science of kriya yoga, showing that its techniques are clearly described free of charge to anyone who takes the time to read Bhagavad Gita.

Kriya yoga concerns the battlefield which is the psyche of the living being. The internal war and the mental and emotional forces which are hostile to self realization are dealt with in the kriya yoga practice.

The third commentary is the Brahma Yoga Bhagavad Gita. This shows what Krishna had to say outright and what he hinted about which concerns the brahma yoga practice, a mystic process for those who mastered kriya yoga.

There is one commentary for the **Markandeya Samasya English**. The title of that publication is Krishna Cosmic Body.

There are two commentaries to the Yoga Sutras. One is the Yoga Sutras of Patanjali and the other is the Meditation Expertise. These give detailed explanations of the process of Yoga.

For the Uddhava Gita, we published the Uddhava Gita Explained. This is a large book and requires concentration and study for integration of the information. Of the books which deal with transcendental topics, my opinion is that the discourse between Krishna and Uddhava has the complete information about the realities in existence. This book is the one which removes massive existential ignorance.

Online Resources

Website:

http://michaelbeloved.com/

Forum:

http://inselfyoga.com/

Contact:

axisnexus@gmail.com

www.ingramcontent.com/pod-product-compliance
Lightning Source LLC
Chambersburg PA
CBHW080632230426
43663CB00016B/2835
* 9 7 8 0 9 8 8 4 0 1 1 7 4 *